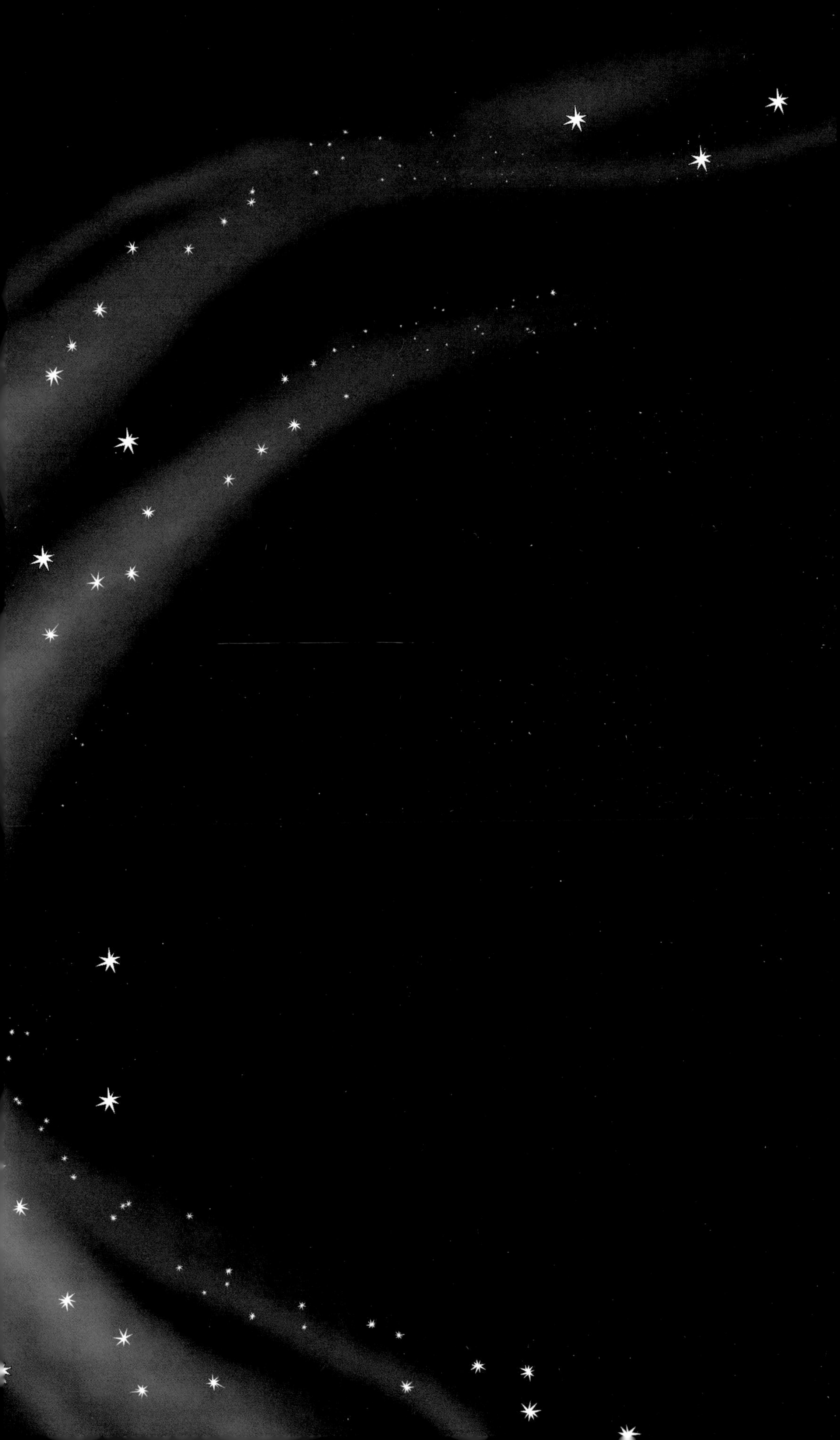

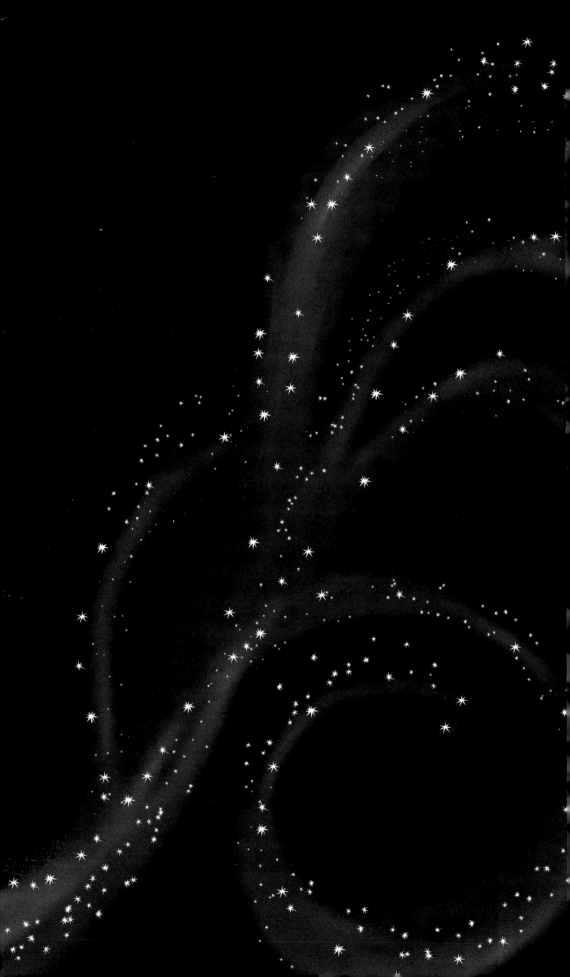

Teri S. Wood's

Wandering Star

Foreword by
Maggie Thompson

Afterword by
Carla Speed McNeil

Dover Publications, Inc.
Mineola, New York

Proofreading by

Preston A. Sweet and T. Hamben

Bibliographical Note

Wandering Star, first published by Dover Publications, Inc., in 2016, is a slightly revised republication in one volume of *Wandering Star*, a comics series of twenty-one issues published between 1993 and 1997. The first eleven issues were self-published by Teri S. Wood under the imprint Pen & Ink Comics. The remaining ten were published by Sirius Entertainment Inc., Dover, New Jersey. The author has provided a new Introduction and a new thirty-two-page color section. Maggie Thompson has provided a new Foreword, and Carla S. McNeil has provided a new Afterword specially prepared for this Dover edition.

International Standard Book Number
ISBN-13: 978-0-486-80162-9
ISBN-10: 0-486-80162-4

Manufactured in China by RR Donnelley
80162401   2016
www.doverpublications.com

FOREWORD

More than two decades? Can it really be more than two decades since a simple star field with title lettering formed the cover image for the black-and-white interior of that issue from Pen & Ink Comics?

Wandering Star Book One of Twelve: That was the cover text itself—simple and stark. But the verve with which the story began quickly brought the tale to life.

Beginning as a self-published graphic novel with a twelve-issue arc, *Wandering Star* evolved, moving from that self-published Pen & Ink imprint to Sirius Entertainment. (*"Reason Number One:* I, Teri S. Wood, am one heck of a lousy businesswoman. Trust me when I tell ya that.") Orders on her first print run of 3,000 had been only 1,100. Nevertheless, she received a boost via Dave Sim's *Cerebus* #173, the word spread, and more and more people wanted to see more. The story arc? It ran 21 issues, although, in an inside joke on the next-to-last story page, interviewer Aldar tells Casandra he is going to write the story in twelve parts. ("Do you think it'll fit into twelve?" "I think so.")

So long ago—yet so fresh in my memory. My late husband, Don, and I were attracted by Wood's power of narration and confidence in storytelling, the enticing nature of the story itself, and the thoughtfulness of her concept. We were editing *Comics Buyer's Guide* and delighted to go behind the scenes, when Jeff Mason offered us an in-depth interview with this little-known creator. It was the last article Don laid out before his death in 1994, and I know he'd have been as delighted as I was to see that Wood would so elegantly complete her story of the personal costs of intergalactic conflict.

Her tale wrapped up in 1997. It was the sort of beginning, middle, and end that was so often lacking from the work of other creators in the world of self-published comics of 1993, when she began. And it was an honor to have been a part of spreading the word of the accomplishment that could be achieved by a skilled dynamo dedicated to telling a powerful story.

—Maggie Thompson, December 2015

INTRODUCTION

Wandering Star was born in 1988, in a bedroom of my parent's house in El Centro, California. I was just a kid, a few years out of high school, but I loved comics, and I dreamed about making my own. So I sat down, and wrote a story, and drew the pages on plain, poster board. Then printed it all out on a Xerox machine, and folded, and stapled the books together on our dining room table.

That very first incarnation *of Wandering Star* was ... pretty rough. I still had a lot to learn about drawing and story-telling. But ya know what? Ya gotta start somewhere.

Even so, I am still a little surprised to see what it grew into. 400 pages, and one heck of ride! The book you are holding has about double the pages I'd originally planned for when I re-launched *Wandering Star*, as a professional *Wandering Star* was supposed to be only twelve issues. I made sure everybody knew it. I even put it on the covers of the first three issues, so nobody would forget. And then ... there was a thirteenth issue. And a fourteenth issue. Until, I finally wrapped up with twenty-one books.

It become a bit of a joke. I got teased all the time by fans and other creators in the field. Nobody told me to stop ... but that didn't mean they weren't gonna tease me about it. It still makes me laugh.

And it taught me a very valuable lesson. Stories can grow.

The 1990s was a wonderful time for American comics. There were so many talented creators pushing the limits on what a comic could be. And so many fancy, cover gimmicks to entice you to buy. But I was a very small publisher, still working out of the back of my parent's house, with no advertising budget at all, so I had to be creative or I'd never get noticed.

The first thing I did was print out 500 limited edition postcards. I signed them, and mailed them off to every store I found listed in the back of the *Comics Buyers Guide* newspaper. Next, I knew I could not compete with the holograms and gold-leaf covers of the time, so I went in the opposite direction. I did starscapes. My thought was, it would stand out. And people would say, "what the heck is that?" and pick it up. And zing, I had their attention.

I even wrote an editorial, in one of my first books, asking readers to take Kit Kat candy bars (my favorite) into their local comic shop, and use them to bribe the store owners into ordering a copy of *Wandering Star*.

And then, one night, while staring up at the ceiling, wondering what else I could do to push *Wandering Star*, I remembered the *Comic Buyer's Guide*. The *CBG* gave out one free classified ad to all of their subscribers.

And pretty much everyone bought the *CBG*. So I thought, "ya know? I still have about a hundred of those old, small press *Wandering Stars* from 1988. I wonder what would happen, if I told people I'd give one free copy to everyone who used that free ad to say they loved *Wandering Star*?"

What followed was months of free ads! There was a time when you could not open a copy of the *Comics Buyer's Guide* newspaper without seeing somebody saying, "Hi, my name is __, and I love Wandering Star!" My sales took off!

And, here we are, over 22 years later, and *Wandering Star* still exists. Then recently, while on Facebook, looking at pictures of cats, comics, cars and *Star Trek*, Drew Ford sent me a message, and pitched me the idea of doing a *Wandering Star Omnibus* for Dover Publications.

And boom, we had a great, big, beautiful book. Isn't it pretty?

But best of all, are the memories. Creating *Wandering Star* wasn't just sitting behind an art desk for hours and hours, even though there was lots of that. It was also phone calls from the friends I'd collected in the comic industry, hanging out at comic conventions, and after con antics. Friends, you ain't had a comicon dinner till you've had it with a bunch of tired, yet happy, comic book creators. Good times!

There was this little Mexican place across the street from the San Diego Convention that decided just to keep the darn place mats us artists kept drawing on, and hang them on the walls. I think it was a good idea, because left unattended, no blank surface is truly safe from a cartoonist's pen.

Heck, even writers are not immune. Nope, and thank goodness. For on my wall I have these cute little, hand-drawn postcards from writer Neil Gaiman, mailed to me from England, doodled sometime in the late 80s, when he was still writing DC's Sandman. Tell me that's not awesome!

And therein lies a little secret I'd like to share with you all. If you create something, and put it out there, you are no longer alone. You are now part of the magical world of creation. Put love in it, buff it till it shines, and you will draw other people who create to you. It's practically inevitable.

It might start at a desk, alone, in the back of your parent's house. But like my twelve issue, limited series, it grows.

May your own story grow.

All my best wishes,
Teresa Challender
Forks, WA

teriwood@teriwood.com
http://www.teriwood.com

Teri S. Wood's

Wandering Star

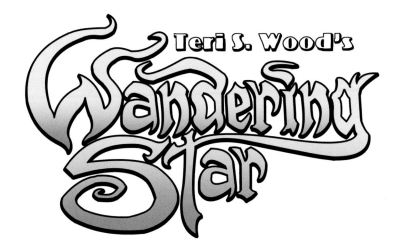

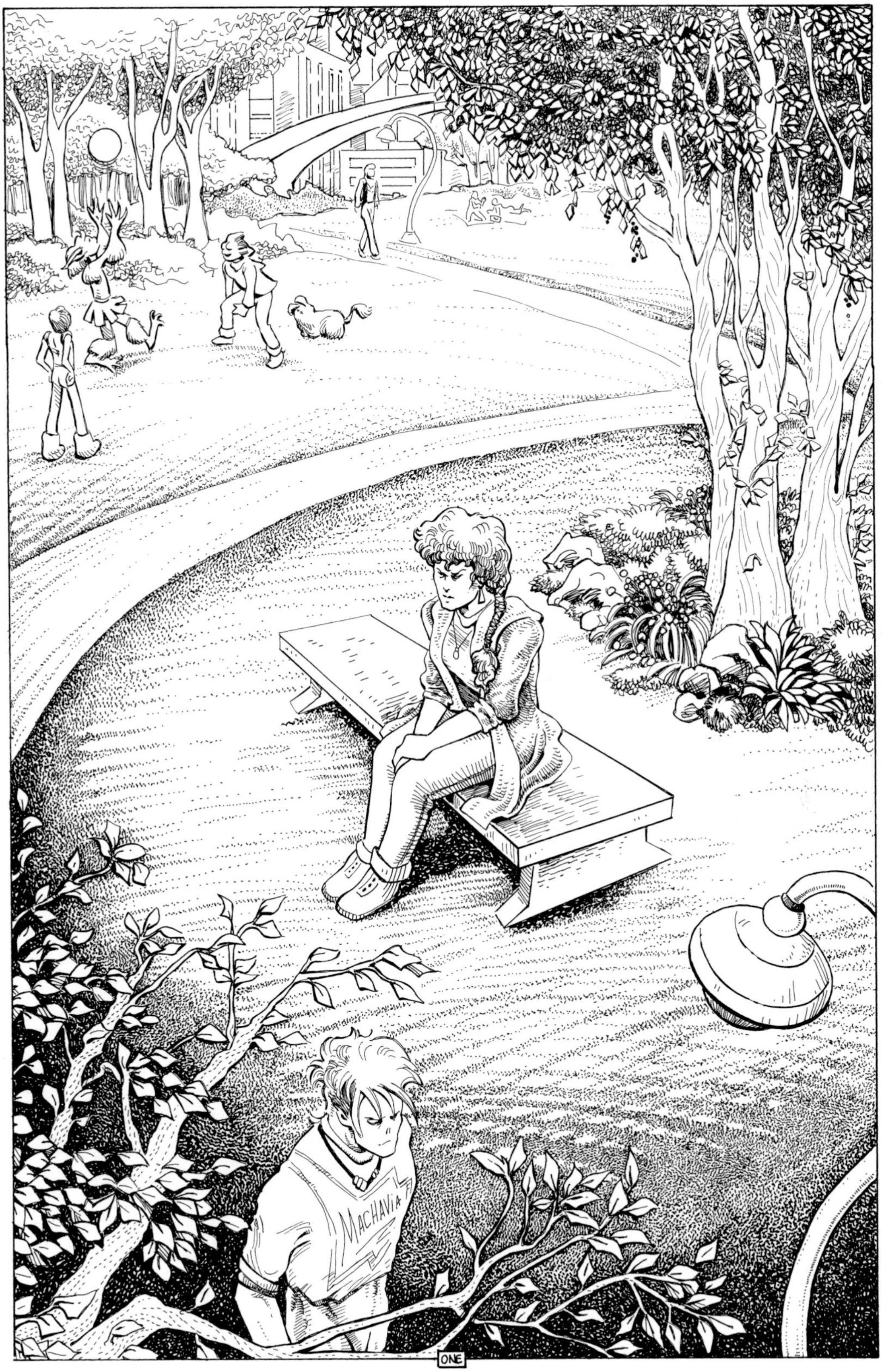
MACHAVIA

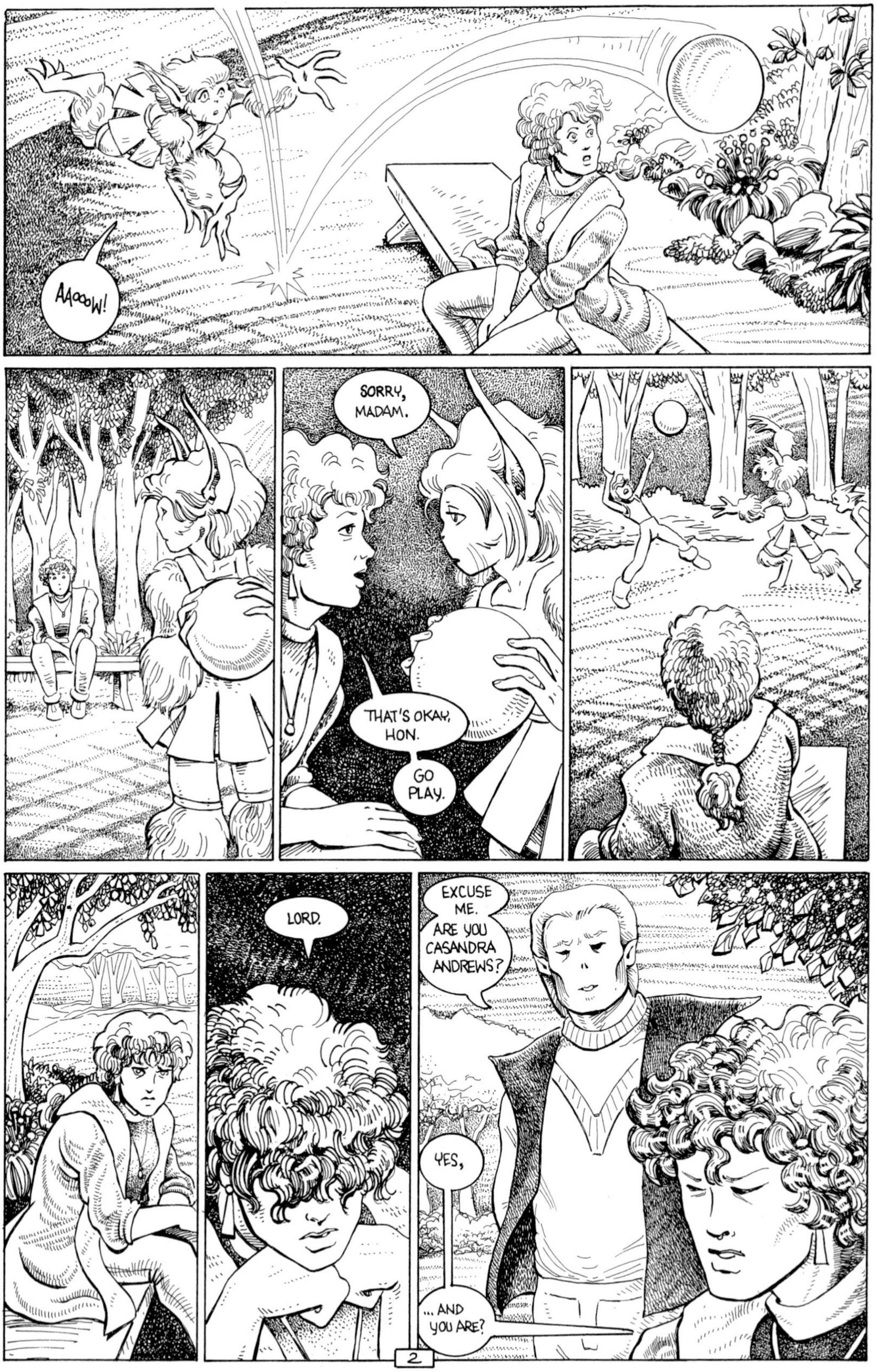
AAooooW!
SORRY, MADAM.
THAT'S OKAY, HON.
GO PLAY.
LORD.
EXCUSE ME. ARE YOU CASANDRA ANDREWS?
YES,
...AND YOU ARE?

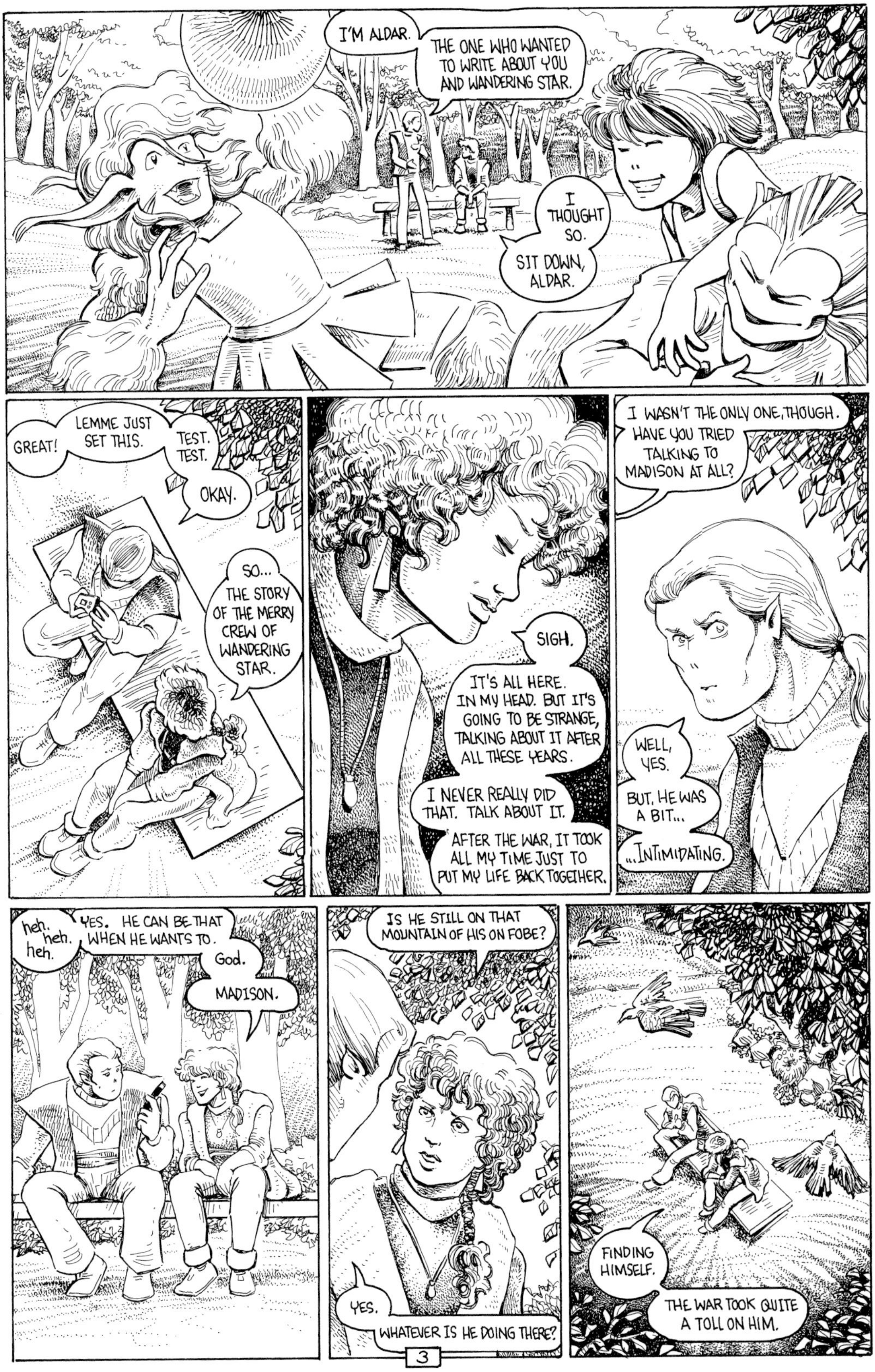
I'M ALDAR.
THE ONE WHO WANTED TO WRITE ABOUT YOU AND WANDERING STAR.
I THOUGHT SO.
SIT DOWN, ALDAR.
GREAT!
LEMME JUST SET THIS.
TEST. TEST.
OKAY.
SO... THE STORY OF THE MERRY CREW OF WANDERING STAR.
SIGH.
IT'S ALL HERE. IN MY HEAD. BUT IT'S GOING TO BE STRANGE, TALKING ABOUT IT AFTER ALL THESE YEARS.
I NEVER REALLY DID THAT. TALK ABOUT IT.
AFTER THE WAR, IT TOOK ALL MY TIME JUST TO PUT MY LIFE BACK TOGETHER.
I WASN'T THE ONLY ONE, THOUGH. HAVE YOU TRIED TALKING TO MADISON AT ALL?
WELL, YES.
BUT, HE WAS A BIT...
...INTIMIDATING.
heh. heh. heh.
YES. HE CAN BE THAT WHEN HE WANTS TO.
God.
MADISON.
IS HE STILL ON THAT MOUNTAIN OF HIS ON FOBE?
YES.
WHATEVER IS HE DOING THERE?
FINDING HIMSELF.
THE WAR TOOK QUITE A TOLL ON HIM.

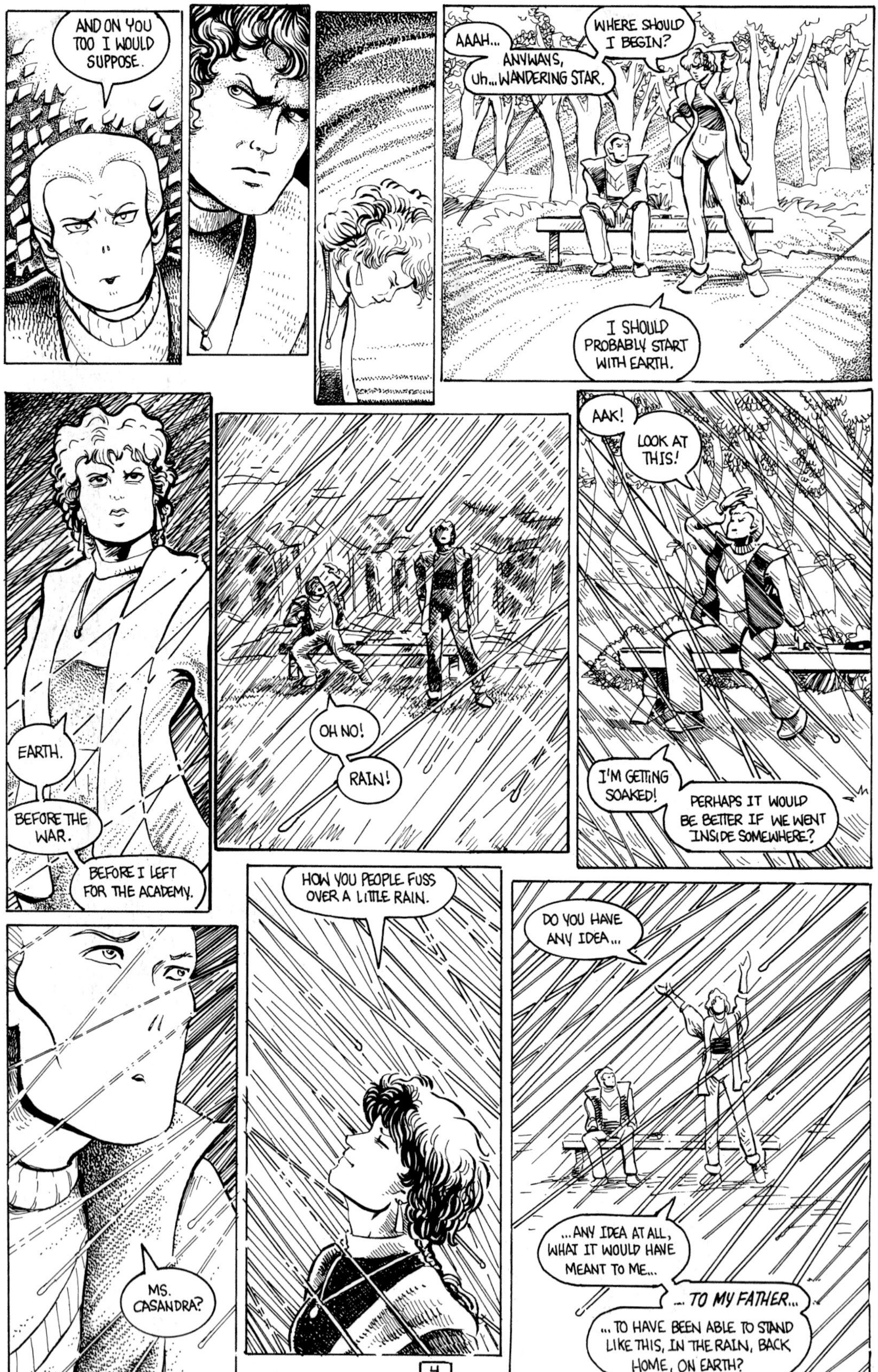
AND ON YOU TOO I WOULD SUPPOSE.
AAAH...
ANYWAYS, Uh... WANDERING STAR.
WHERE SHOULD I BEGIN?
I SHOULD PROBABLY START WITH EARTH.
EARTH.
BEFORE THE WAR.
BEFORE I LEFT FOR THE ACADEMY.
OH NO!
RAIN!
AAK!
LOOK AT THIS!
I'M GETTING SOAKED!
PERHAPS IT WOULD BE BETTER IF WE WENT INSIDE SOMEWHERE?
MS. CASANDRA?
HOW YOU PEOPLE FUSS OVER A LITTLE RAIN.
DO YOU HAVE ANY IDEA...
...ANY IDEA AT ALL, WHAT IT WOULD HAVE MEANT TO ME...
... TO MY FATHER...
... TO HAVE BEEN ABLE TO STAND LIKE THIS, IN THE RAIN, BACK HOME, ON EARTH?

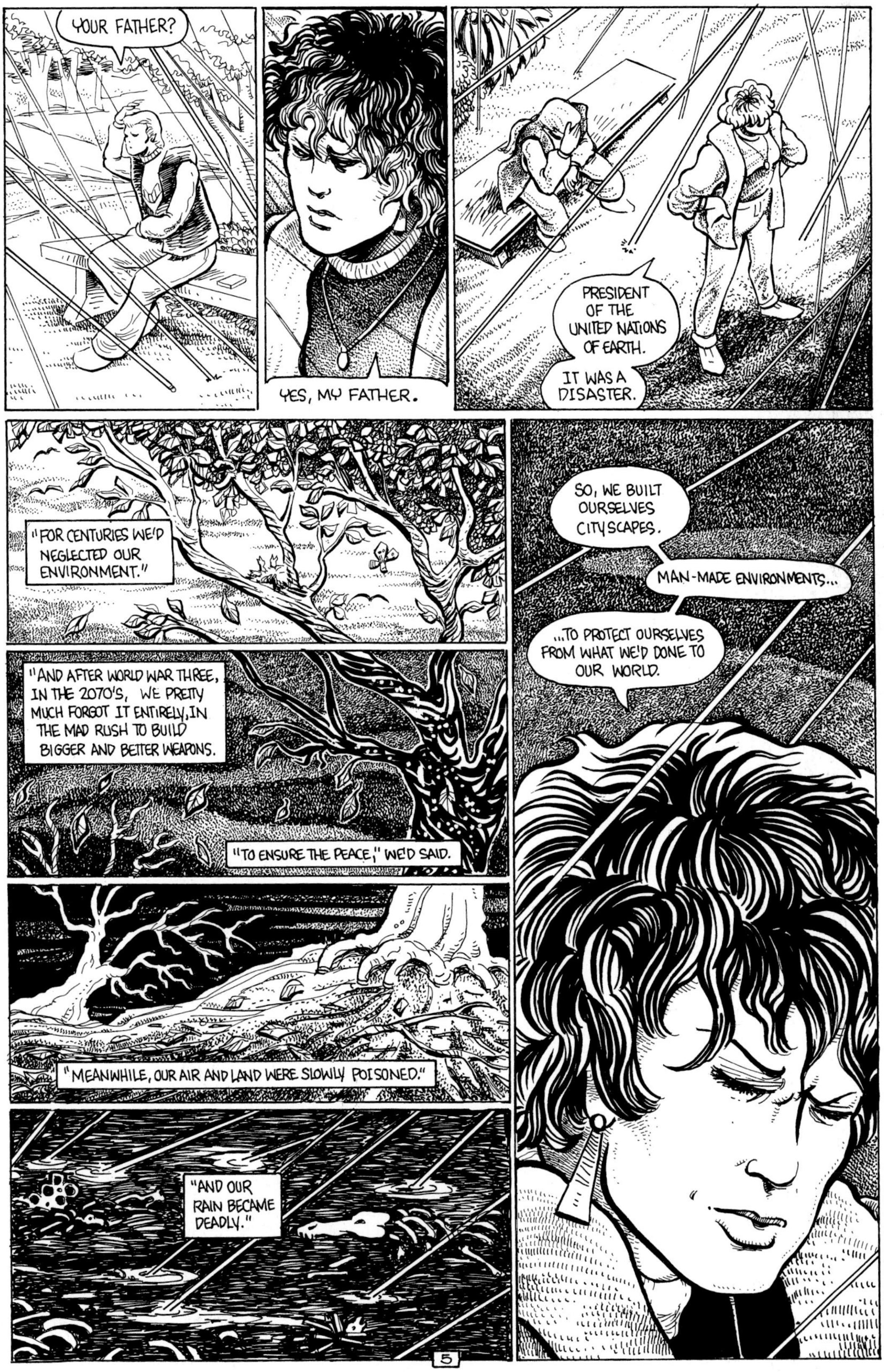
YOUR FATHER?
YES, MY FATHER.
PRESIDENT OF THE UNITED NATIONS OF EARTH.
IT WAS A DISASTER.
"FOR CENTURIES WE'D NEGLECTED OUR ENVIRONMENT."
"AND AFTER WORLD WAR THREE, IN THE 2070'S, WE PRETTY MUCH FORGOT IT ENTIRELY, IN THE MAD RUSH TO BUILD BIGGER AND BETTER WEAPONS.
"TO ENSURE THE PEACE," WE'D SAID.
"MEANWHILE, OUR AIR AND LAND WERE SLOWLY POISONED."
"AND OUR RAIN BECAME DEADLY."
SO, WE BUILT OURSELVES CITYSCAPES.
MAN-MADE ENVIRONMENTS...
...TO PROTECT OURSELVES FROM WHAT WE'D DONE TO OUR WORLD.

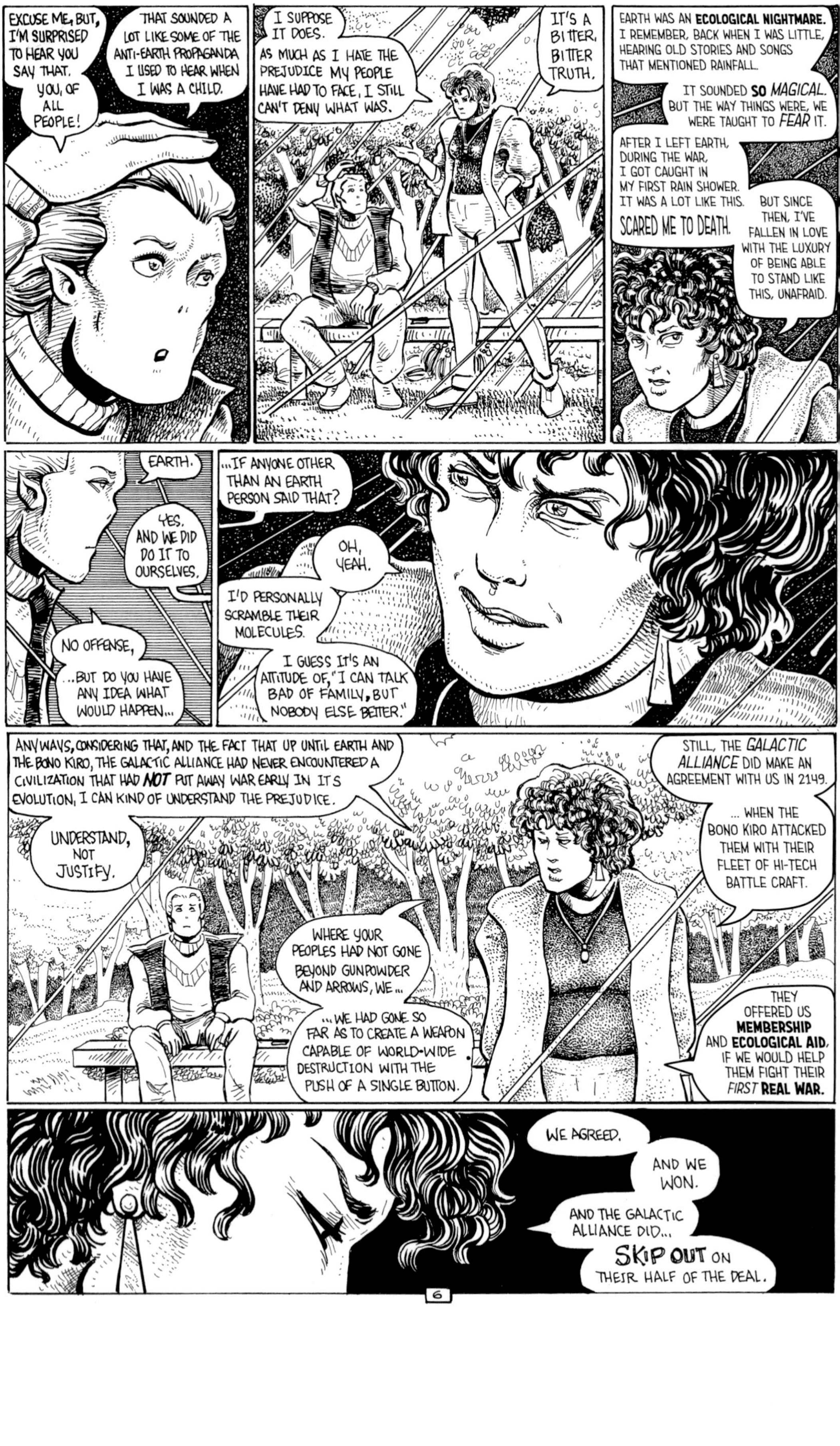
EXCUSE ME, BUT, I'M SURPRISED TO HEAR YOU SAY THAT. YOU, OF ALL PEOPLE!
THAT SOUNDED A LOT LIKE SOME OF THE ANTI-EARTH PROPAGANDA I USED TO HEAR WHEN I WAS A CHILD.
I SUPPOSE IT DOES.
AS MUCH AS I HATE THE PREJUDICE MY PEOPLE HAVE HAD TO FACE, I STILL CAN'T DENY WHAT WAS.
IT'S A BITTER, BITTER TRUTH.
EARTH WAS AN ECOLOGICAL NIGHTMARE. I REMEMBER, BACK WHEN I WAS LITTLE, HEARING OLD STORIES AND SONGS THAT MENTIONED RAINFALL.
IT SOUNDED SO MAGICAL. BUT THE WAY THINGS WERE, WE WERE TAUGHT TO FEAR IT.
AFTER I LEFT EARTH, DURING THE WAR, I GOT CAUGHT IN MY FIRST RAIN SHOWER. IT WAS A LOT LIKE THIS. SCARED ME TO DEATH.
BUT SINCE THEN, I'VE FALLEN IN LOVE WITH THE LUXURY OF BEING ABLE TO STAND LIKE THIS, UNAFRAID.
EARTH.
YES. AND WE DID DO IT TO OURSELVES.
NO OFFENSE,
...BUT DO YOU HAVE ANY IDEA WHAT WOULD HAPPEN...
...IF ANYONE OTHER THAN AN EARTH PERSON SAID THAT?
OH, YEAH.
I'D PERSONALLY SCRAMBLE THEIR MOLECULES.
I GUESS IT'S AN ATTITUDE OF, "I CAN TALK BAD OF FAMILY, BUT NOBODY ELSE BETTER."
ANYWAYS, CONSIDERING THAT, AND THE FACT THAT UP UNTIL EARTH AND THE BONO KIRO, THE GALACTIC ALLIANCE HAD NEVER ENCOUNTERED A CIVILIZATION THAT HAD NOT PUT AWAY WAR EARLY IN ITS EVOLUTION, I CAN KIND OF UNDERSTAND THE PREJUDICE.
UNDERSTAND, NOT JUSTIFY.
STILL, THE GALACTIC ALLIANCE DID MAKE AN AGREEMENT WITH US IN 2149.
... WHEN THE BONO KIRO ATTACKED THEM WITH THEIR FLEET OF HI-TECH BATTLE CRAFT.
WHERE YOUR PEOPLES HAD NOT GONE BEYOND GUNPOWDER AND ARROWS, WE...
...WE HAD GONE SO FAR AS TO CREATE A WEAPON CAPABLE OF WORLD-WIDE DESTRUCTION WITH THE PUSH OF A SINGLE BUTTON.
THEY OFFERED US MEMBERSHIP AND ECOLOGICAL AID, IF WE WOULD HELP THEM FIGHT THEIR FIRST REAL WAR.
WE AGREED.
AND WE WON.
AND THE GALACTIC ALLIANCE DID... SKIP OUT ON THEIR HALF OF THE DEAL.

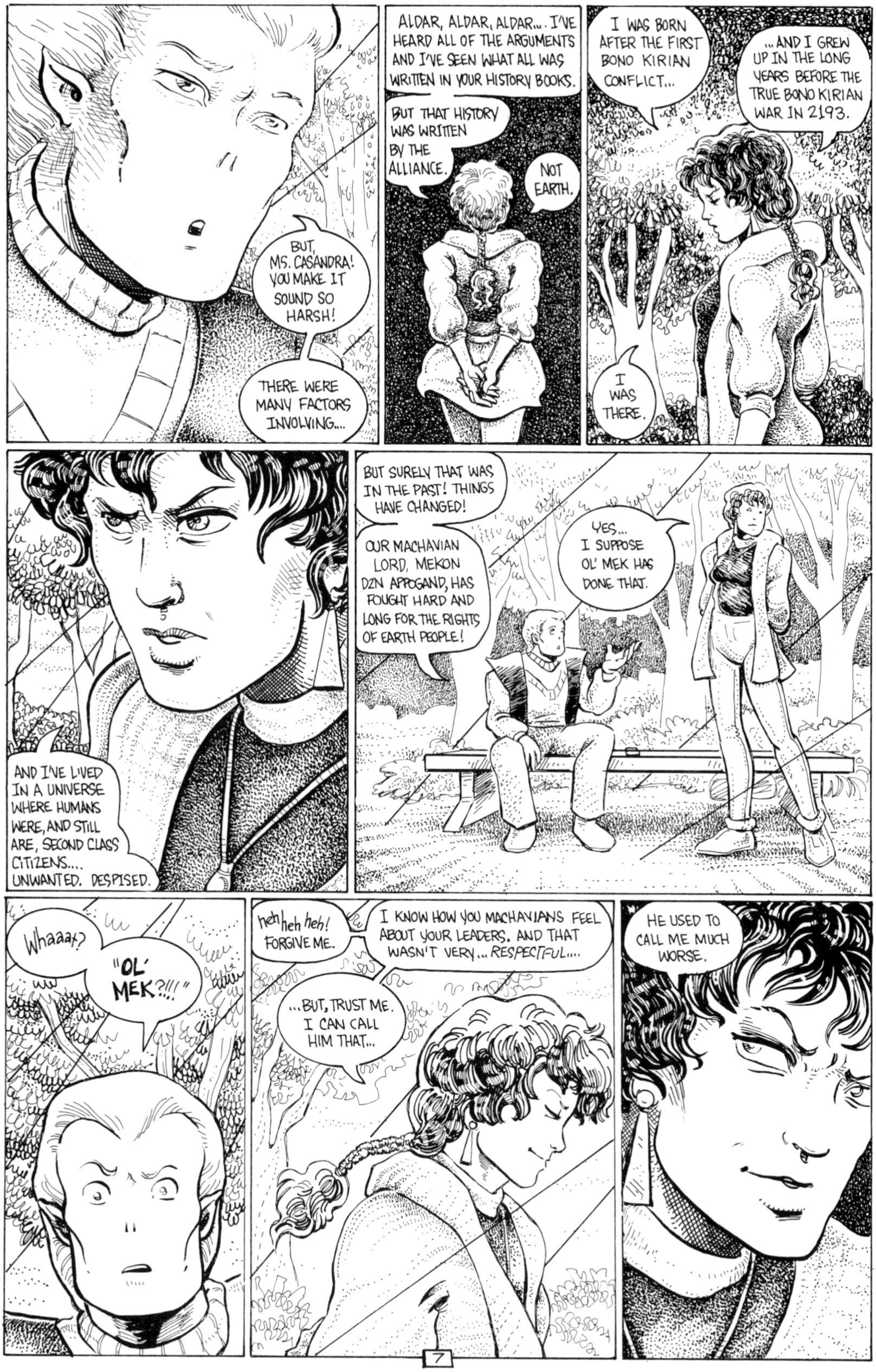
BUT, MS. CASANDRA! YOU MAKE IT SOUND SO HARSH!
THERE WERE MANY FACTORS INVOLVING...
ALDAR, ALDAR, ALDAR... I'VE HEARD ALL OF THE ARGUMENTS AND I'VE SEEN WHAT ALL WAS WRITTEN IN YOUR HISTORY BOOKS.
BUT THAT HISTORY WAS WRITTEN BY THE ALLIANCE.
NOT EARTH.
I WAS BORN AFTER THE FIRST BONO KIRIAN CONFLICT...
...AND I GREW UP IN THE LONG YEARS BEFORE THE TRUE BONO KIRIAN WAR IN 2193.
I WAS THERE.
AND I'VE LIVED IN A UNIVERSE WHERE HUMANS WERE, AND STILL ARE, SECOND CLASS CITIZENS.... UNWANTED. DESPISED.
BUT SURELY THAT WAS IN THE PAST! THINGS HAVE CHANGED!
OUR MACHAVIAN LORD, MEKON DZN APPOGAND, HAS FOUGHT HARD AND LONG FOR THE RIGHTS OF EARTH PEOPLE!
YES... I SUPPOSE OL' MEK HAS DONE THAT.
Whaaat?
"OL' MEK?!!!"
heh heh heh! FORGIVE ME.
I KNOW HOW YOU MACHAVIANS FEEL ABOUT YOUR LEADERS. AND THAT WASN'T VERY... RESPECTFUL....
...BUT, TRUST ME. I CAN CALL HIM THAT...
HE USED TO CALL ME MUCH WORSE.

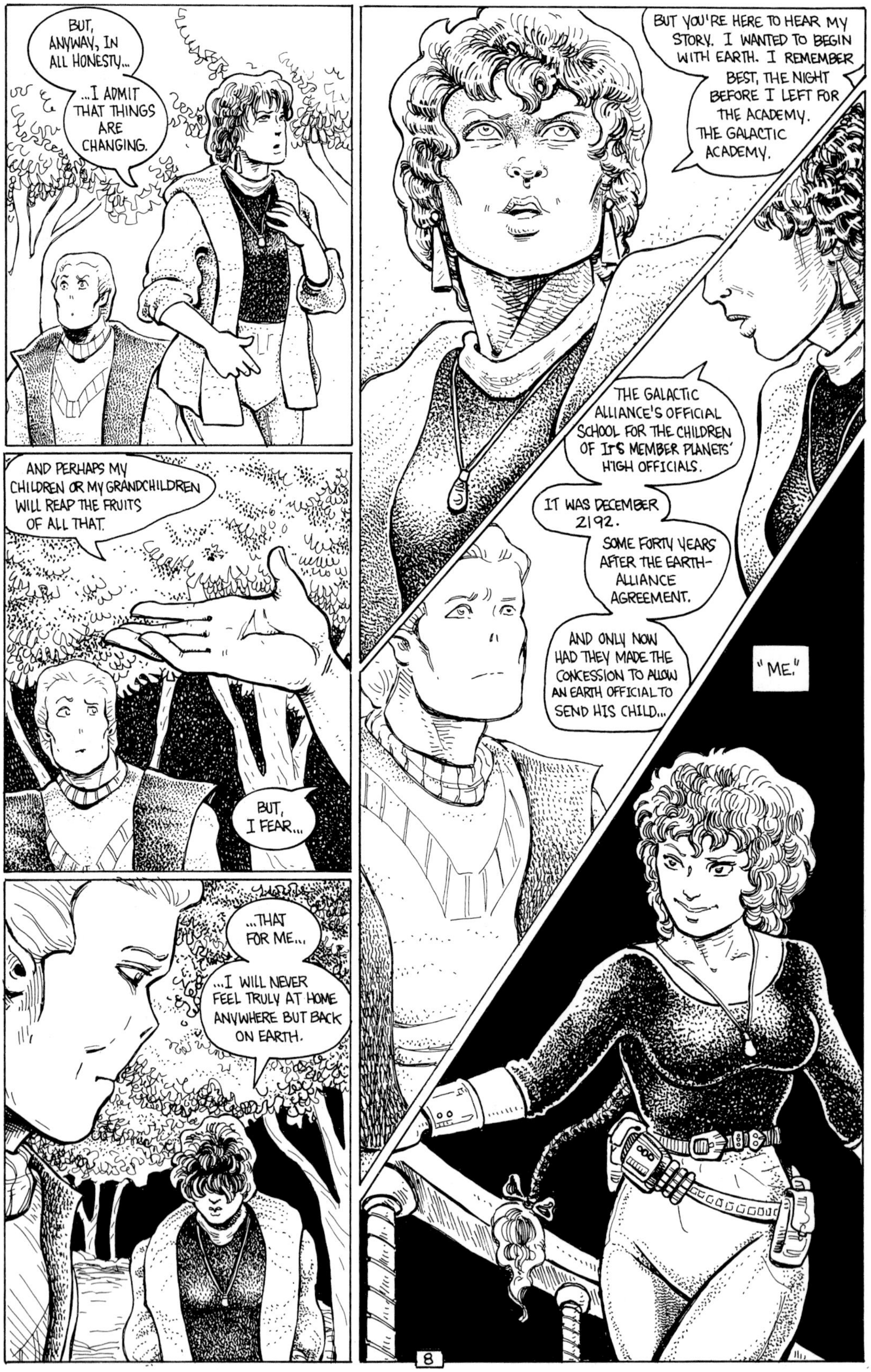

BUT, ANYWAY, IN ALL HONESTY...
...I ADMIT THAT THINGS ARE CHANGING.
AND PERHAPS MY CHILDREN OR MY GRANDCHILDREN WILL REAP THE FRUITS OF ALL THAT.
BUT, I FEAR...
...THAT FOR ME...
...I WILL NEVER FEEL TRULY AT HOME ANYWHERE BUT BACK ON EARTH.
BUT YOU'RE HERE TO HEAR MY STORY. I WANTED TO BEGIN WITH EARTH. I REMEMBER BEST, THE NIGHT BEFORE I LEFT FOR THE ACADEMY. THE GALACTIC ACADEMY.
THE GALACTIC ALLIANCE'S OFFICIAL SCHOOL FOR THE CHILDREN OF IT'S MEMBER PLANETS' HIGH OFFICIALS.
IT WAS DECEMBER 2192.
SOME FORTY YEARS AFTER THE EARTH-ALLIANCE AGREEMENT.
AND ONLY NOW HAD THEY MADE THE CONCESSION TO ALLOW AN EARTH OFFICIAL TO SEND HIS CHILD...
"ME."

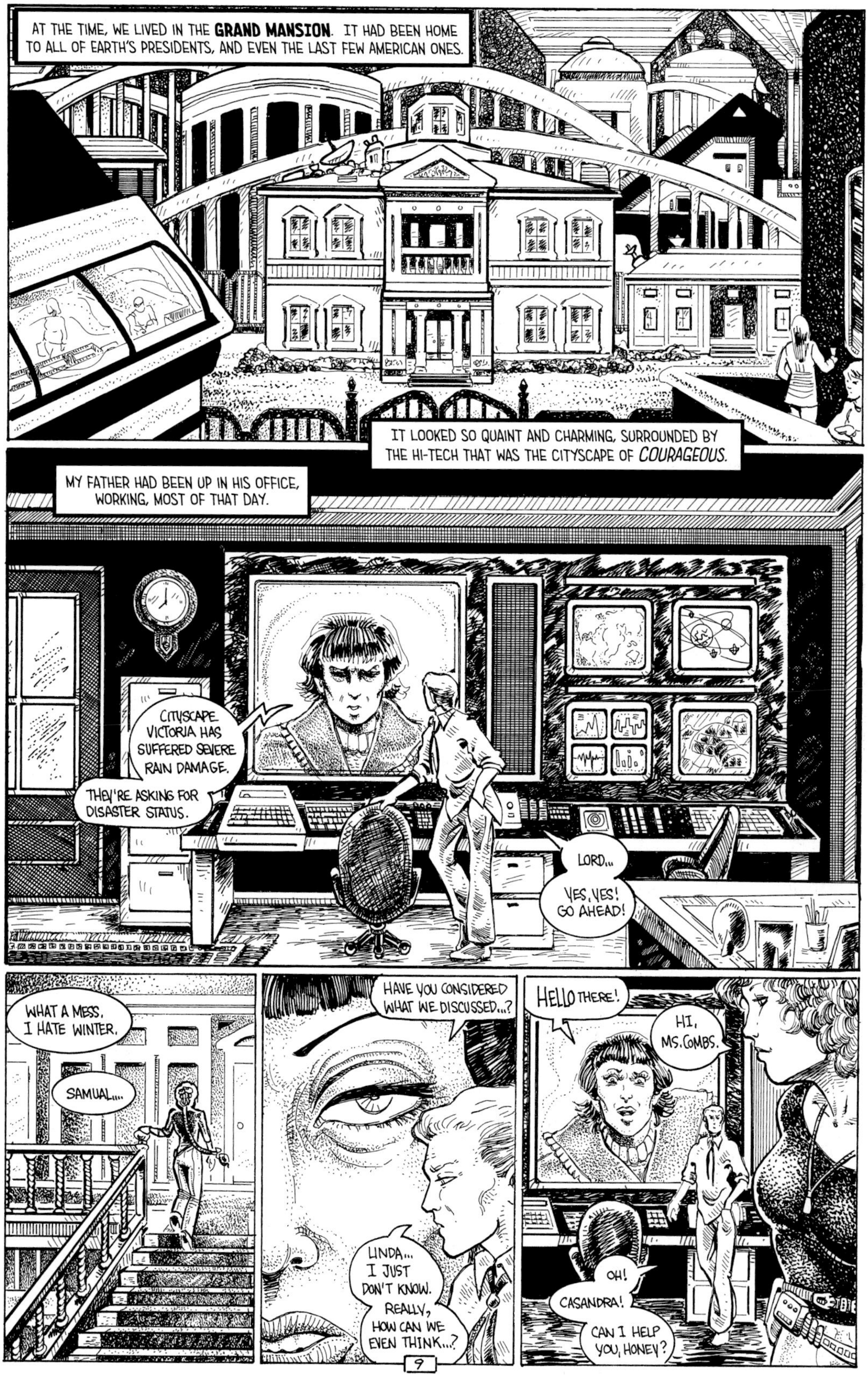
AT THE TIME, WE LIVED IN THE **GRAND MANSION**. IT HAD BEEN HOME TO ALL OF EARTH'S PRESIDENTS, AND EVEN THE LAST FEW AMERICAN ONES.
IT LOOKED SO QUAINT AND CHARMING, SURROUNDED BY THE HI-TECH THAT WAS THE CITYSCAPE OF *COURAGEOUS*.
MY FATHER HAD BEEN UP IN HIS OFFICE, WORKING, MOST OF THAT DAY.
CITYSCAPE VICTORIA HAS SUFFERED SEVERE RAIN DAMAGE.
THEY'RE ASKING FOR DISASTER STATUS.
LORD...
YES, YES! GO AHEAD!
WHAT A MESS. I HATE WINTER.
SAMUAL...
HAVE YOU CONSIDERED WHAT WE DISCUSSED...?
LINDA... I JUST DON'T KNOW.
REALLY, HOW CAN WE EVEN THINK...?
HELLO THERE!
HI, MS. COMBS.
OH!
CASANDRA!
CAN I HELP YOU, HONEY?

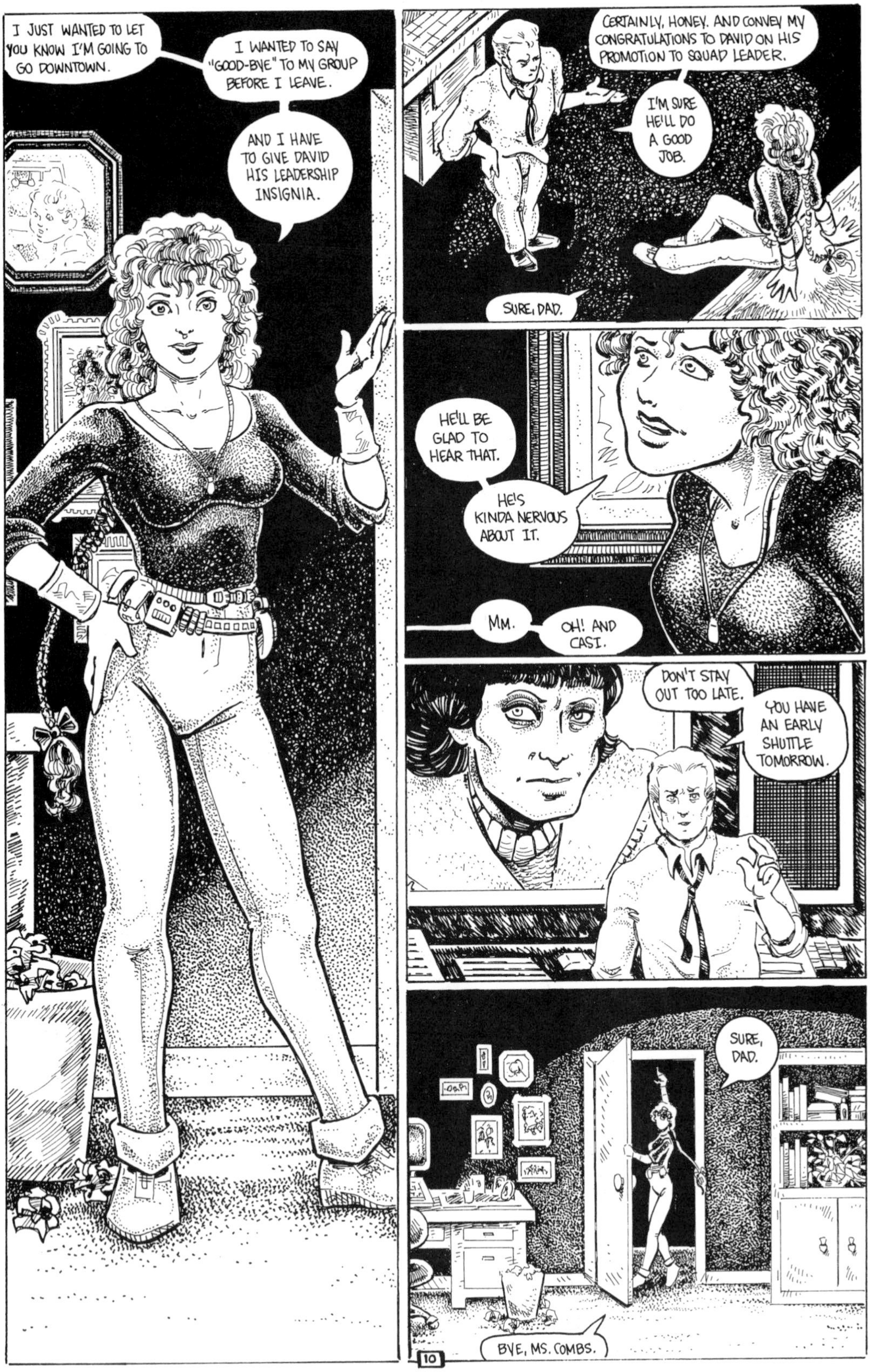
I JUST WANTED TO LET YOU KNOW I'M GOING TO GO DOWNTOWN.
I WANTED TO SAY "GOOD-BYE" TO MY GROUP BEFORE I LEAVE.
AND I HAVE TO GIVE DAVID HIS LEADERSHIP INSIGNIA.
CERTAINLY, HONEY. AND CONVEY MY CONGRATULATIONS TO DAVID ON HIS PROMOTION TO SQUAD LEADER.
I'M SURE HE'LL DO A GOOD JOB.
SURE, DAD.
HE'LL BE GLAD TO HEAR THAT.
HE'S KINDA NERVOUS ABOUT IT.
MM.
OH! AND CASI.
DON'T STAY OUT TOO LATE.
YOU HAVE AN EARLY SHUTTLE TOMORROW.
SURE, DAD.
BYE, MS. COMBS.

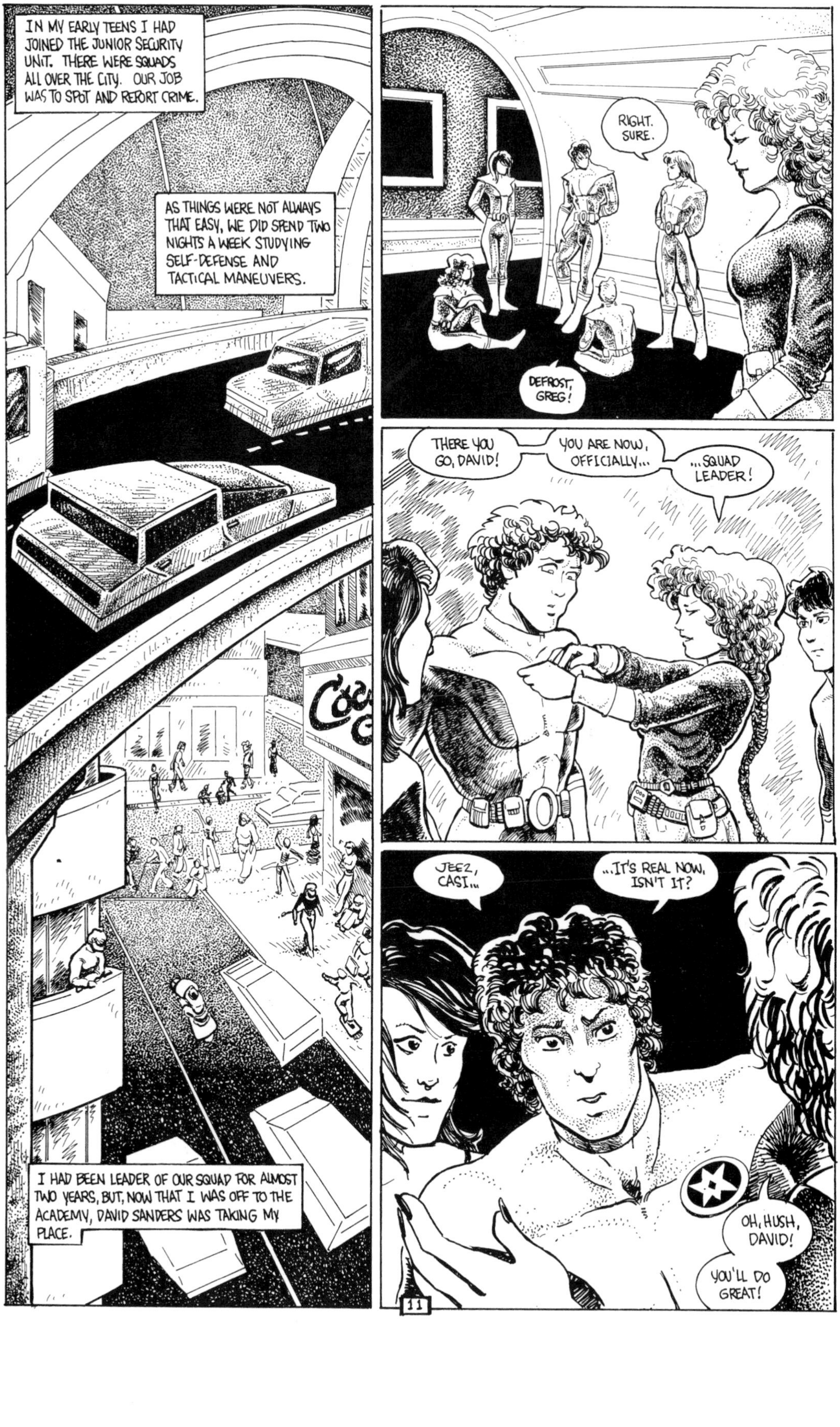
IN MY EARLY TEENS I HAD JOINED THE JUNIOR SECURITY UNIT. THERE WERE SQUADS ALL OVER THE CITY. OUR JOB WAS TO SPOT AND REPORT CRIME.
AS THINGS WERE NOT ALWAYS THAT EASY, WE DID SPEND TWO NIGHTS A WEEK STUDYING SELF-DEFENSE AND TACTICAL MANEUVERS.
I HAD BEEN LEADER OF OUR SQUAD FOR ALMOST TWO YEARS, BUT, NOW THAT I WAS OFF TO THE ACADEMY, DAVID SANDERS WAS TAKING MY PLACE.
RIGHT. SURE.
DEFROST, GREG!
THERE YOU GO, DAVID!
YOU ARE NOW, OFFICIALLY...
...SQUAD LEADER!
JEEZ, CASI...
...IT'S REAL NOW, ISN'T IT?
OH, HUSH, DAVID!
YOU'LL DO GREAT!

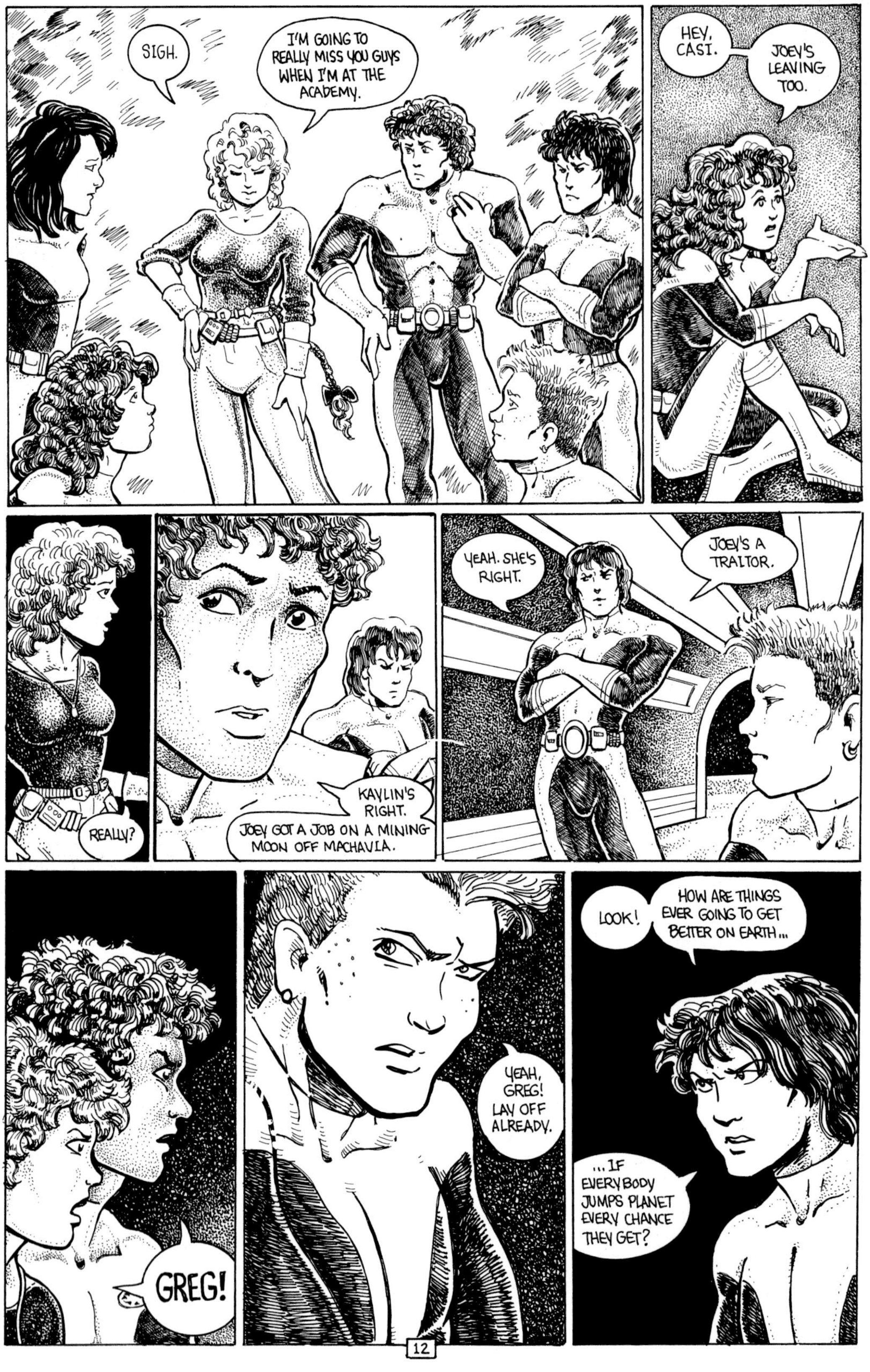
SIGH.
I'M GOING TO REALLY MISS YOU GUYS WHEN I'M AT THE ACADEMY.
HEY, CASI.
JOEY'S LEAVING TOO.
REALLY?
KAYLIN'S RIGHT.
JOEY GOT A JOB ON A MINING MOON OFF MACHAVIA.
YEAH. SHE'S RIGHT.
JOEY'S A TRAITOR.
GREG!
YEAH, GREG! LAY OFF ALREADY.
LOOK!
HOW ARE THINGS EVER GOING TO GET BETTER ON EARTH...
...IF EVERYBODY JUMPS PLANET EVERY CHANCE THEY GET?

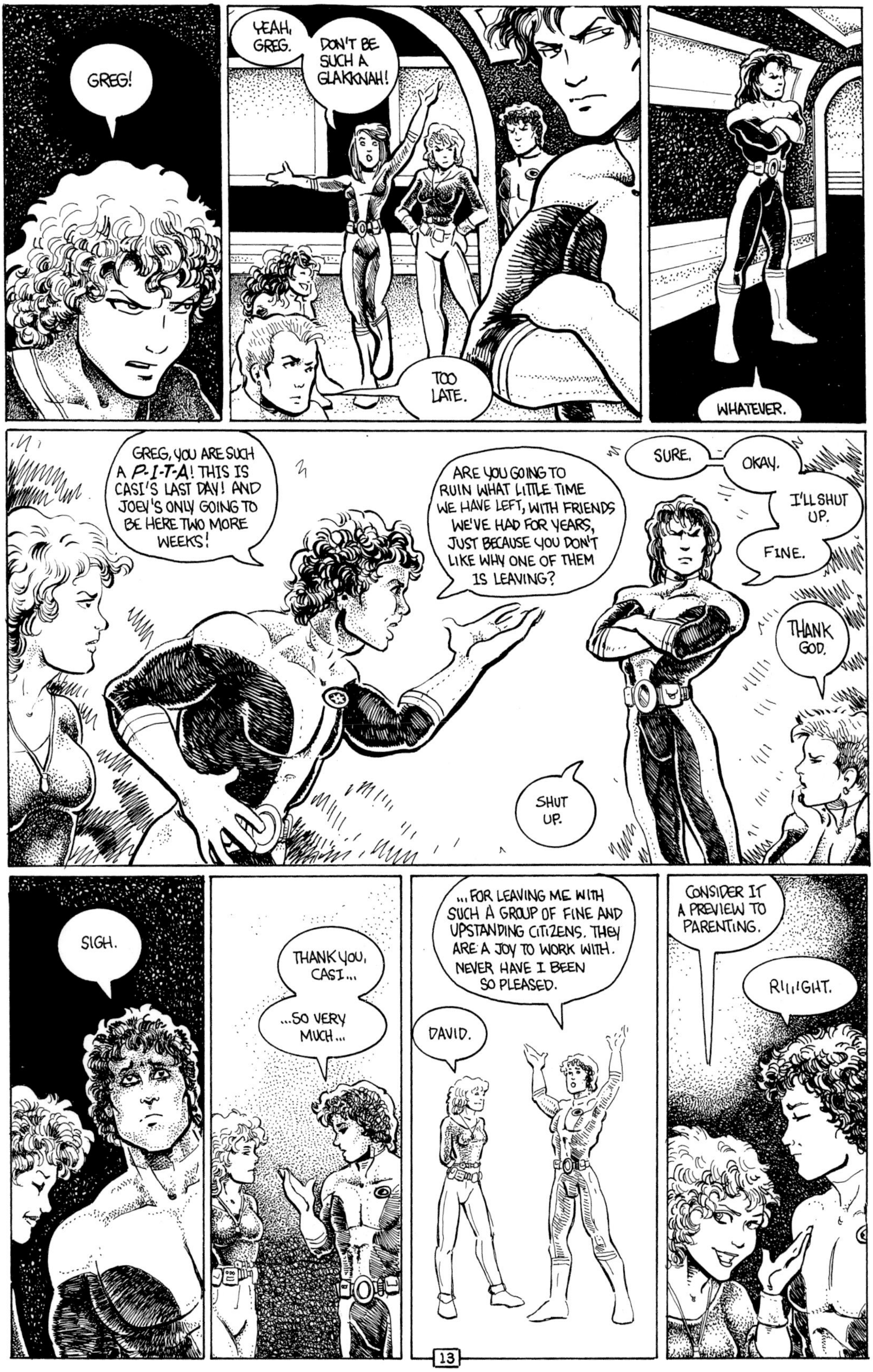
GREG!
YEAH, GREG.
DON'T BE SUCH A GLAKKNAH!
TOO LATE.
WHATEVER.
GREG, YOU ARE SUCH A P-I-T-A! THIS IS CASI'S LAST DAY! AND JOEY'S ONLY GOING TO BE HERE TWO MORE WEEKS!
ARE YOU GOING TO RUIN WHAT LITTLE TIME WE HAVE LEFT, WITH FRIENDS WE'VE HAD FOR YEARS, JUST BECAUSE YOU DON'T LIKE WHY ONE OF THEM IS LEAVING?
SURE.
OKAY.
I'LL SHUT UP.
FINE.
THANK GOD.
SHUT UP.
SIGH.
THANK YOU, CASI...
...SO VERY MUCH...
...FOR LEAVING ME WITH SUCH A GROUP OF FINE AND UPSTANDING CITIZENS. THEY ARE A JOY TO WORK WITH. NEVER HAVE I BEEN SO PLEASED.
DAVID.
CONSIDER IT A PREVIEW TO PARENTING.
RIIIIGHT.

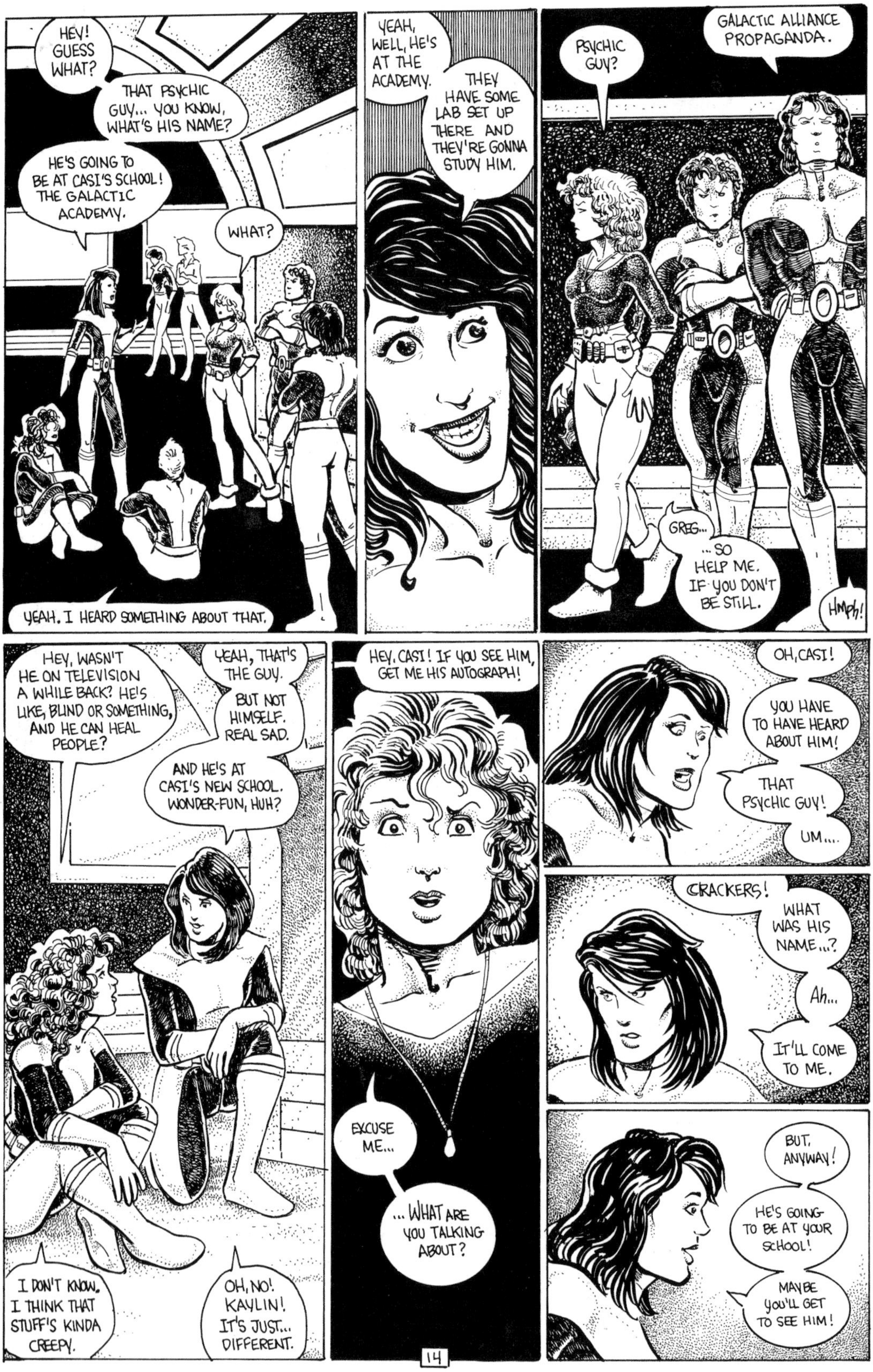
HEY! GUESS WHAT?
THAT PSYCHIC GUY... YOU KNOW, WHAT'S HIS NAME?
HE'S GOING TO BE AT CASI'S SCHOOL! THE GALACTIC ACADEMY.
WHAT?
YEAH. I HEARD SOMETHING ABOUT THAT.
YEAH, WELL, HE'S AT THE ACADEMY.
THEY HAVE SOME LAB SET UP THERE AND THEY'RE GONNA STUDY HIM.
PSYCHIC GUY?
GALACTIC ALLIANCE PROPAGANDA.
GREG...
...SO HELP ME. IF YOU DON'T BE STILL.
HMPH!
HEY, WASN'T HE ON TELEVISION A WHILE BACK? HE'S LIKE, BLIND OR SOMETHING, AND HE CAN HEAL PEOPLE?
YEAH, THAT'S THE GUY.
BUT NOT HIMSELF. REAL SAD.
AND HE'S AT CASI'S NEW SCHOOL. WONDER-FUN, HUH?
I DON'T KNOW. I THINK THAT STUFF'S KINDA CREEPY.
OH, NO! KAYLIN! IT'S JUST... DIFFERENT.
HEY, CASI! IF YOU SEE HIM, GET ME HIS AUTOGRAPH!
EXCUSE ME...
...WHAT ARE YOU TALKING ABOUT?
OH, CASI!
YOU HAVE TO HAVE HEARD ABOUT HIM!
THAT PSYCHIC GUY!
UM....
CRACKERS!
WHAT WAS HIS NAME...?
Ah...
IT'LL COME TO ME.
BUT, ANYWAY!
HE'S GOING TO BE AT YOUR SCHOOL!
MAYBE YOU'LL GET TO SEE HIM!

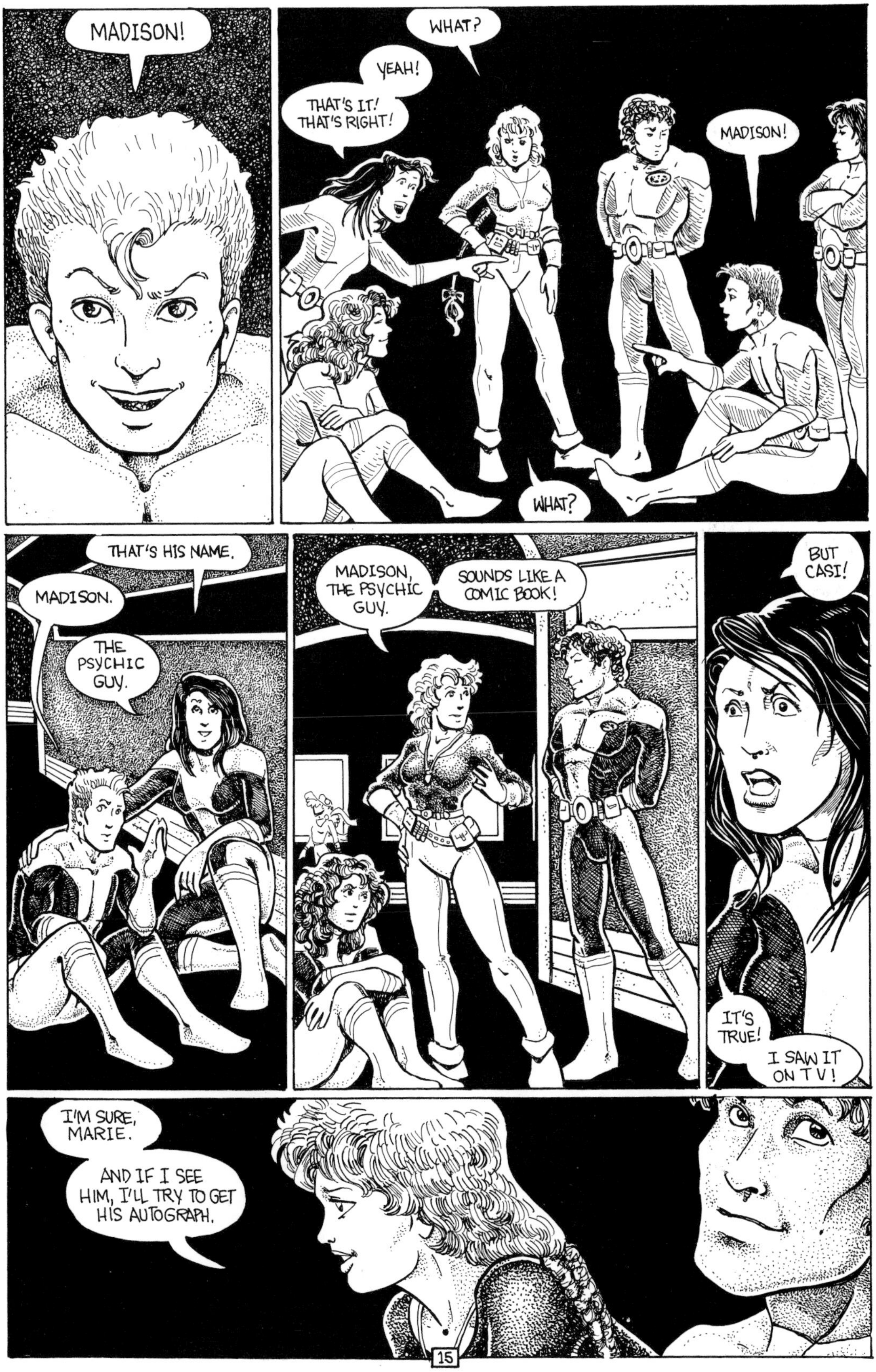
MADISON!
WHAT?
YEAH!
THAT'S IT! THAT'S RIGHT!
MADISON!
WHAT?
THAT'S HIS NAME.
MADISON.
THE PSYCHIC GUY.
MADISON, THE PSYCHIC GUY.
SOUNDS LIKE A COMIC BOOK!
BUT CASI!
IT'S TRUE!
I SAW IT ON TV!
I'M SURE, MARIE.
AND IF I SEE HIM, I'LL TRY TO GET HIS AUTOGRAPH.

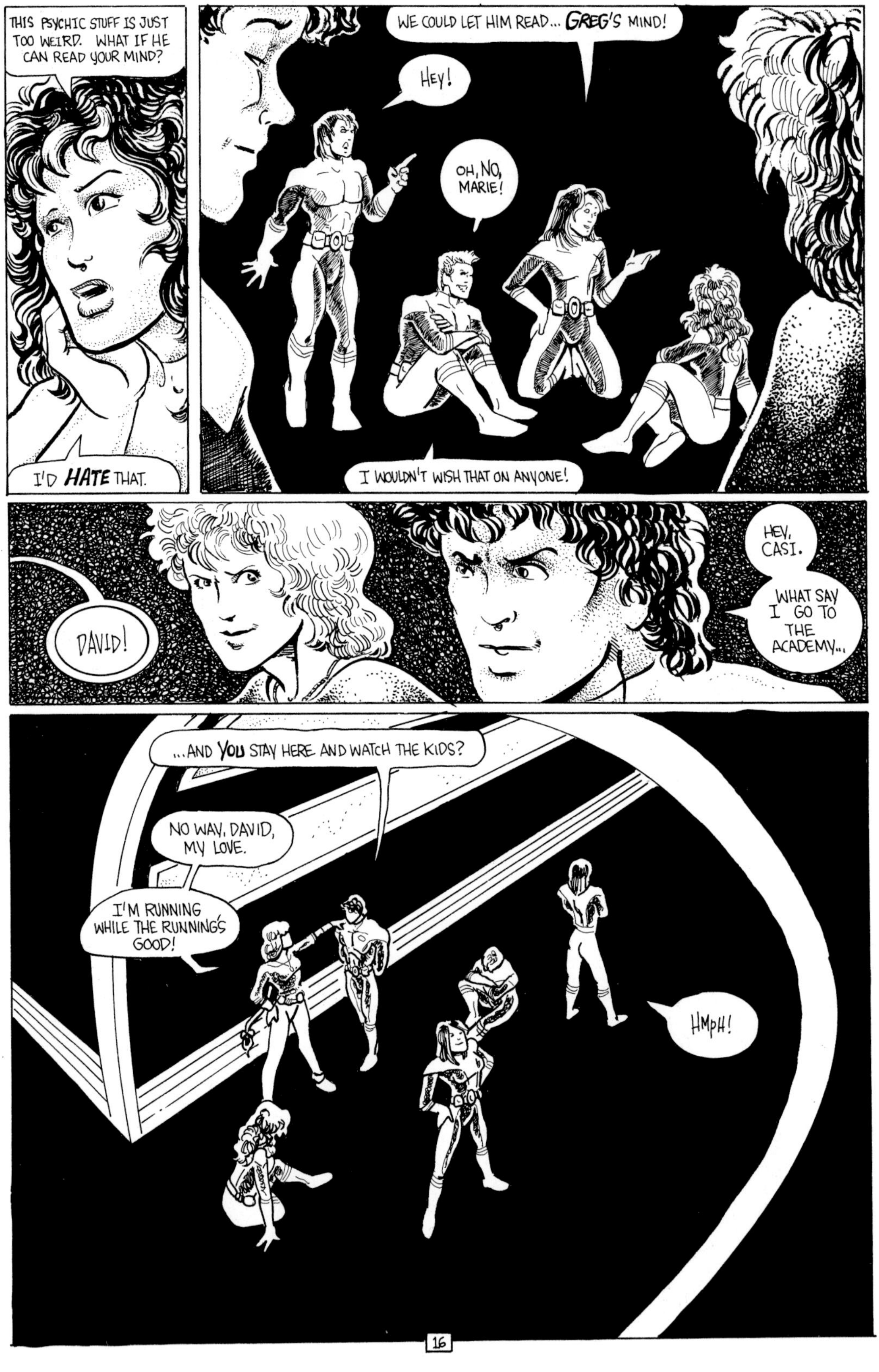
THIS PSYCHIC STUFF IS JUST TOO WEIRD. WHAT IF HE CAN READ YOUR MIND?
I'D HATE THAT.
WE COULD LET HIM READ... GREG'S MIND!
HEY!
OH, NO, MARIE!
I WOULDN'T WISH THAT ON ANYONE!
DAVID!
HEY, CASI.
WHAT SAY I GO TO THE ACADEMY...
...AND YOU STAY HERE AND WATCH THE KIDS?
NO WAY, DAVID, MY LOVE.
I'M RUNNING WHILE THE RUNNING'S GOOD!
HMPH!

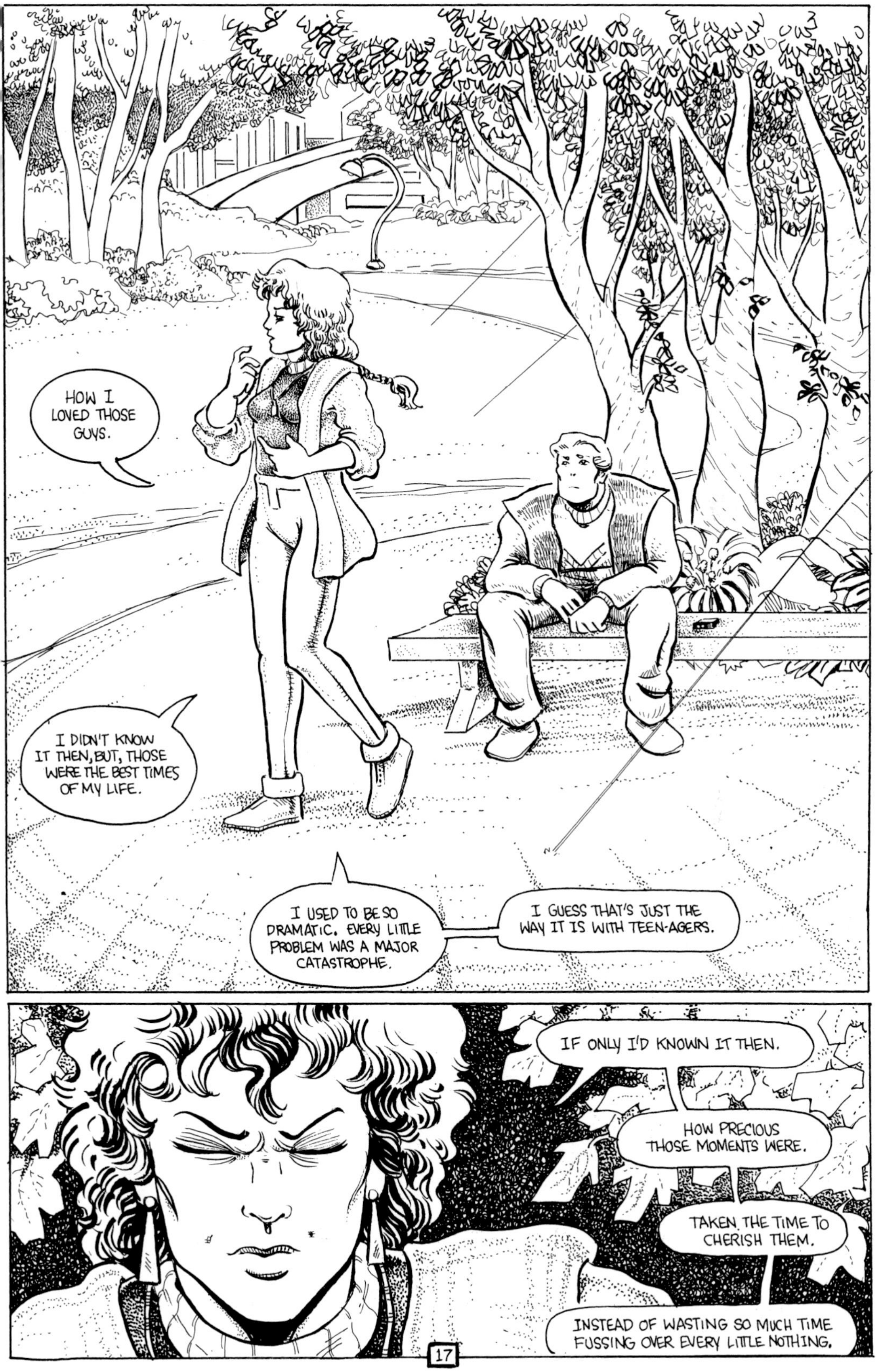

HOW I LOVED THOSE GUYS.
I DIDN'T KNOW IT THEN, BUT, THOSE WERE THE BEST TIMES OF MY LIFE.
I USED TO BE SO DRAMATIC. EVERY LITTLE PROBLEM WAS A MAJOR CATASTROPHE.
I GUESS THAT'S JUST THE WAY IT IS WITH TEEN-AGERS.
IF ONLY I'D KNOWN IT THEN.
HOW PRECIOUS THOSE MOMENTS WERE.
TAKEN THE TIME TO CHERISH THEM.
INSTEAD OF WASTING SO MUCH TIME FUSSING OVER EVERY LITTLE NOTHING.

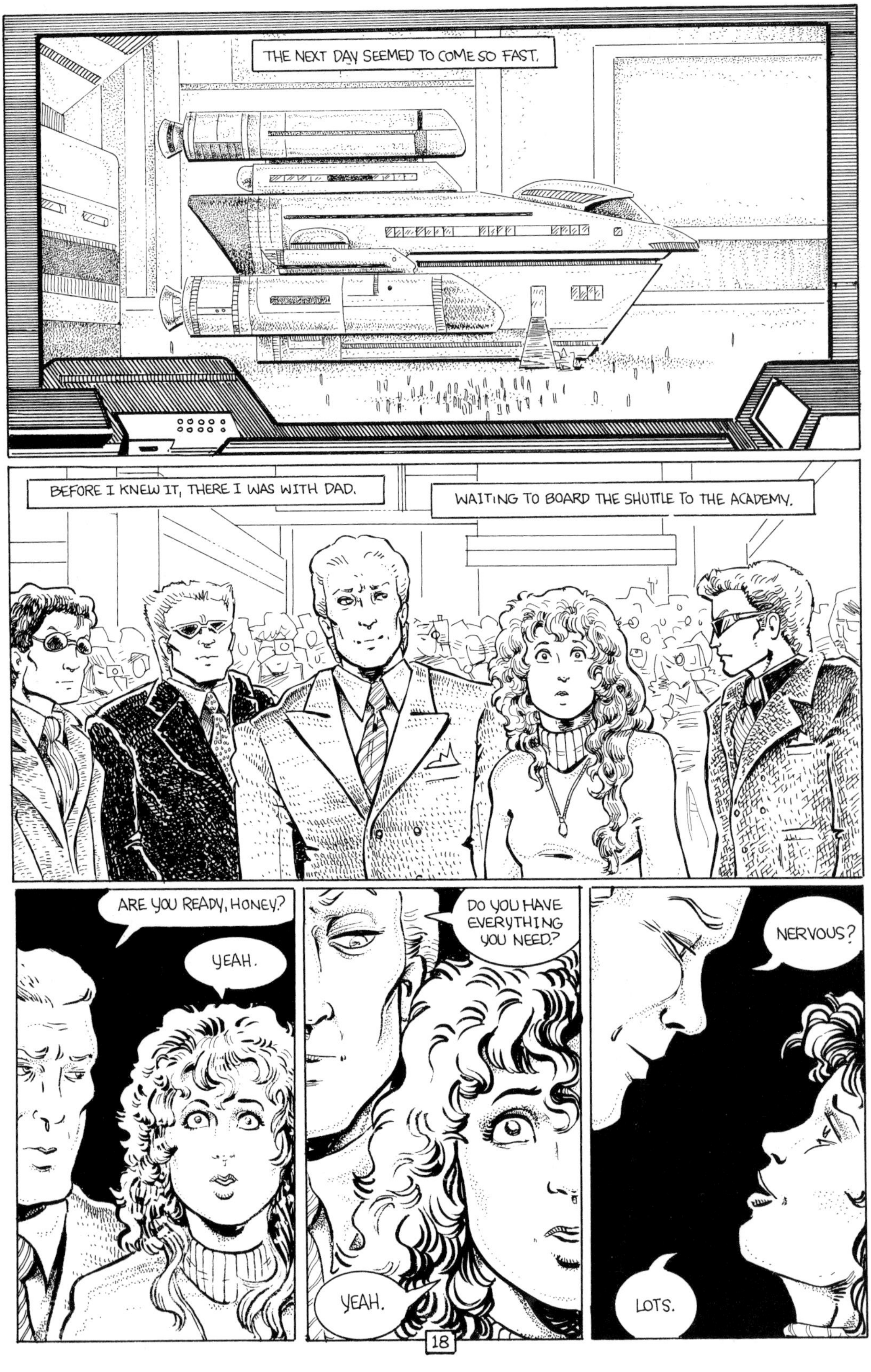
THE NEXT DAY SEEMED TO COME SO FAST.
BEFORE I KNEW IT, THERE I WAS WITH DAD.
WAITING TO BOARD THE SHUTTLE TO THE ACADEMY.
ARE YOU READY, HONEY?
YEAH.
DO YOU HAVE EVERYTHING YOU NEED?
YEAH.
NERVOUS?
LOTS.

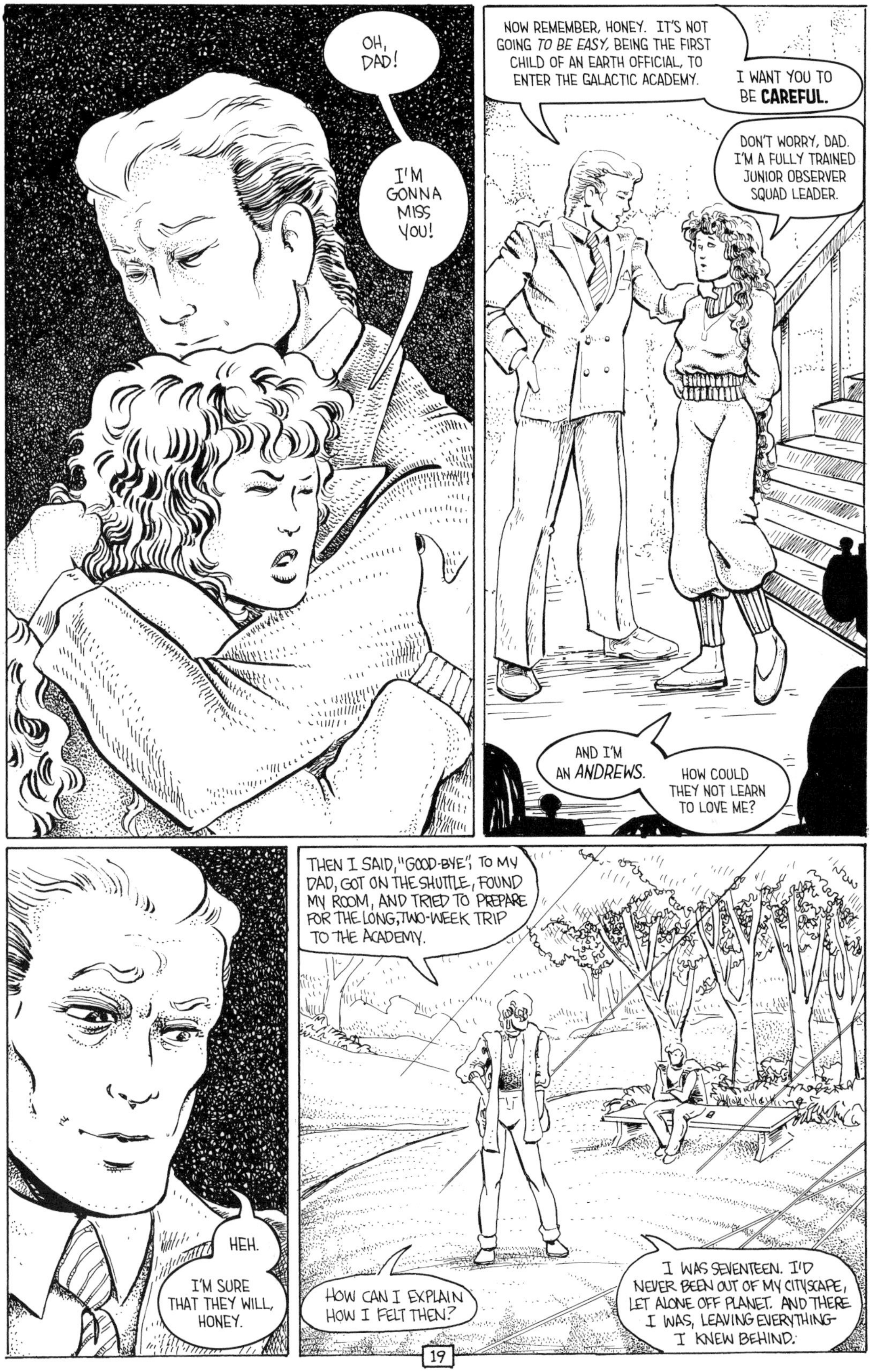
OH, DAD!
I'M GONNA MISS YOU!
NOW REMEMBER, HONEY. IT'S NOT GOING *TO BE EASY,* BEING THE FIRST CHILD OF AN EARTH OFFICIAL, TO ENTER THE GALACTIC ACADEMY.
I WANT YOU TO BE **CAREFUL.**
DON'T WORRY, DAD. I'M A FULLY TRAINED JUNIOR OBSERVER SQUAD LEADER.
AND I'M AN *ANDREWS.*
HOW COULD THEY NOT LEARN TO LOVE ME?
HEH.
I'M SURE THAT THEY WILL, HONEY.
THEN I SAID, "GOOD-BYE", TO MY DAD, GOT ON THE SHUTTLE, FOUND MY ROOM, AND TRIED TO PREPARE FOR THE LONG, TWO-WEEK TRIP TO THE ACADEMY.
HOW CAN I EXPLAIN HOW I FELT THEN?
I WAS SEVENTEEN. I'D NEVER BEEN OUT OF MY CITYSCAPE, LET ALONE OFF PLANET. AND THERE I WAS, LEAVING EVERYTHING-I KNEW BEHIND.

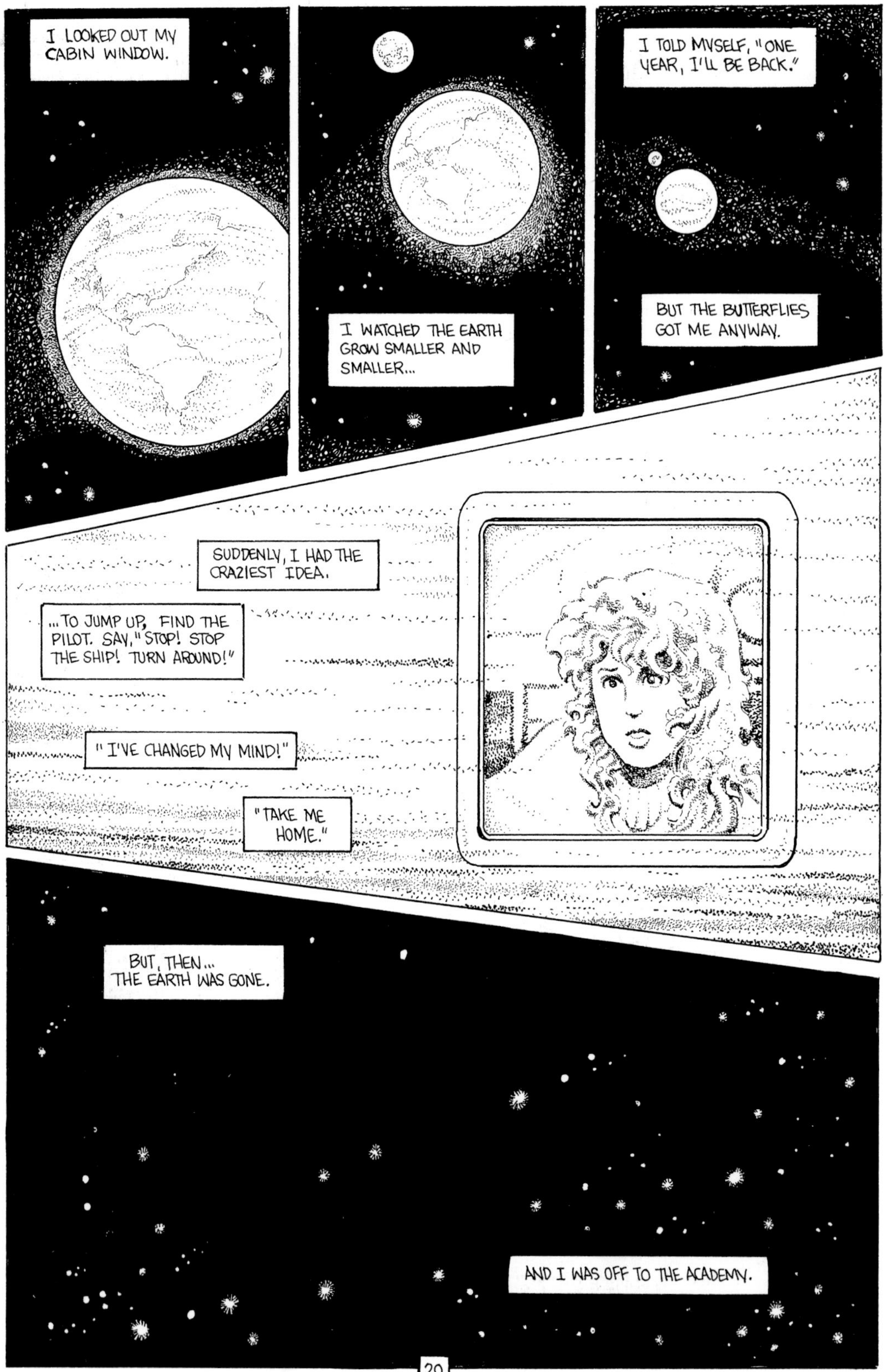
I LOOKED OUT MY CABIN WINDOW.
I WATCHED THE EARTH GROW SMALLER AND SMALLER...
I TOLD MYSELF, "ONE YEAR, I'LL BE BACK."
BUT THE BUTTERFLIES GOT ME ANYWAY.
SUDDENLY, I HAD THE CRAZIEST IDEA.
...TO JUMP UP, FIND THE PILOT. SAY, "STOP! STOP THE SHIP! TURN AROUND!"
"I'VE CHANGED MY MIND!"
"TAKE ME HOME."
BUT, THEN... THE EARTH WAS GONE.
AND I WAS OFF TO THE ACADEMY.

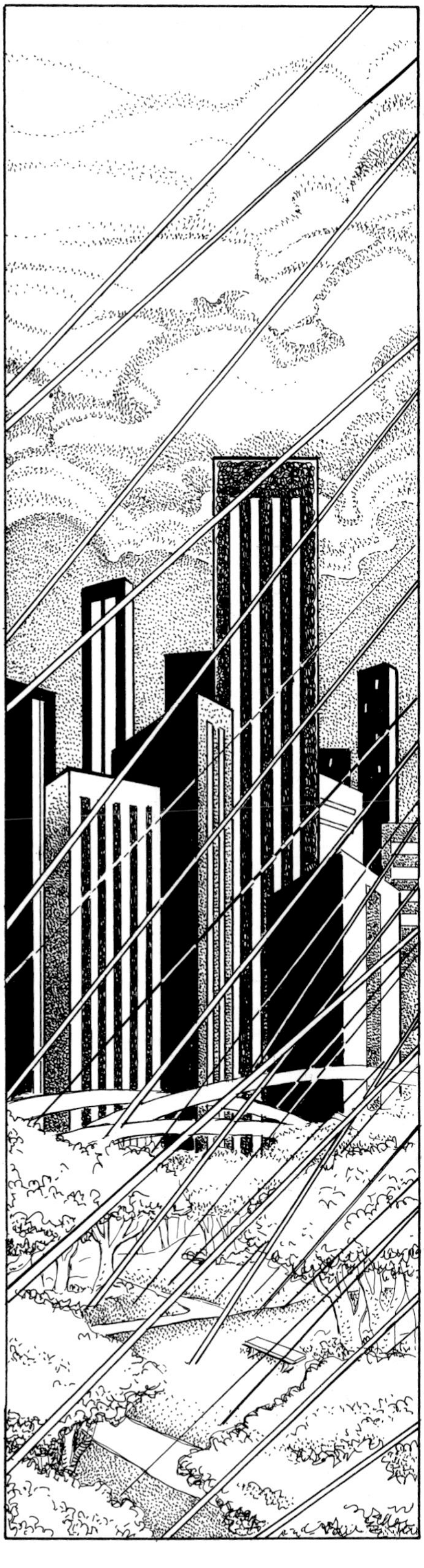

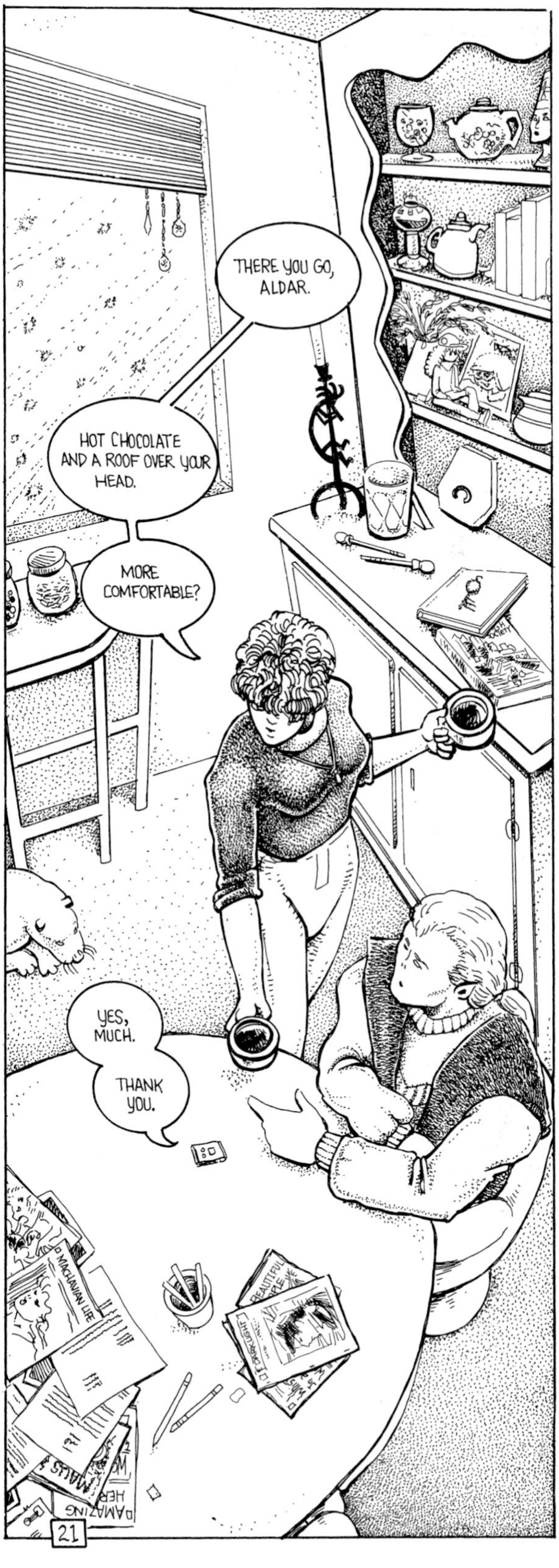
THERE YOU GO, ALDAR.
HOT CHOCOLATE AND A ROOF OVER YOUR HEAD.
MORE COMFORTABLE?
YES, MUCH.
THANK YOU.

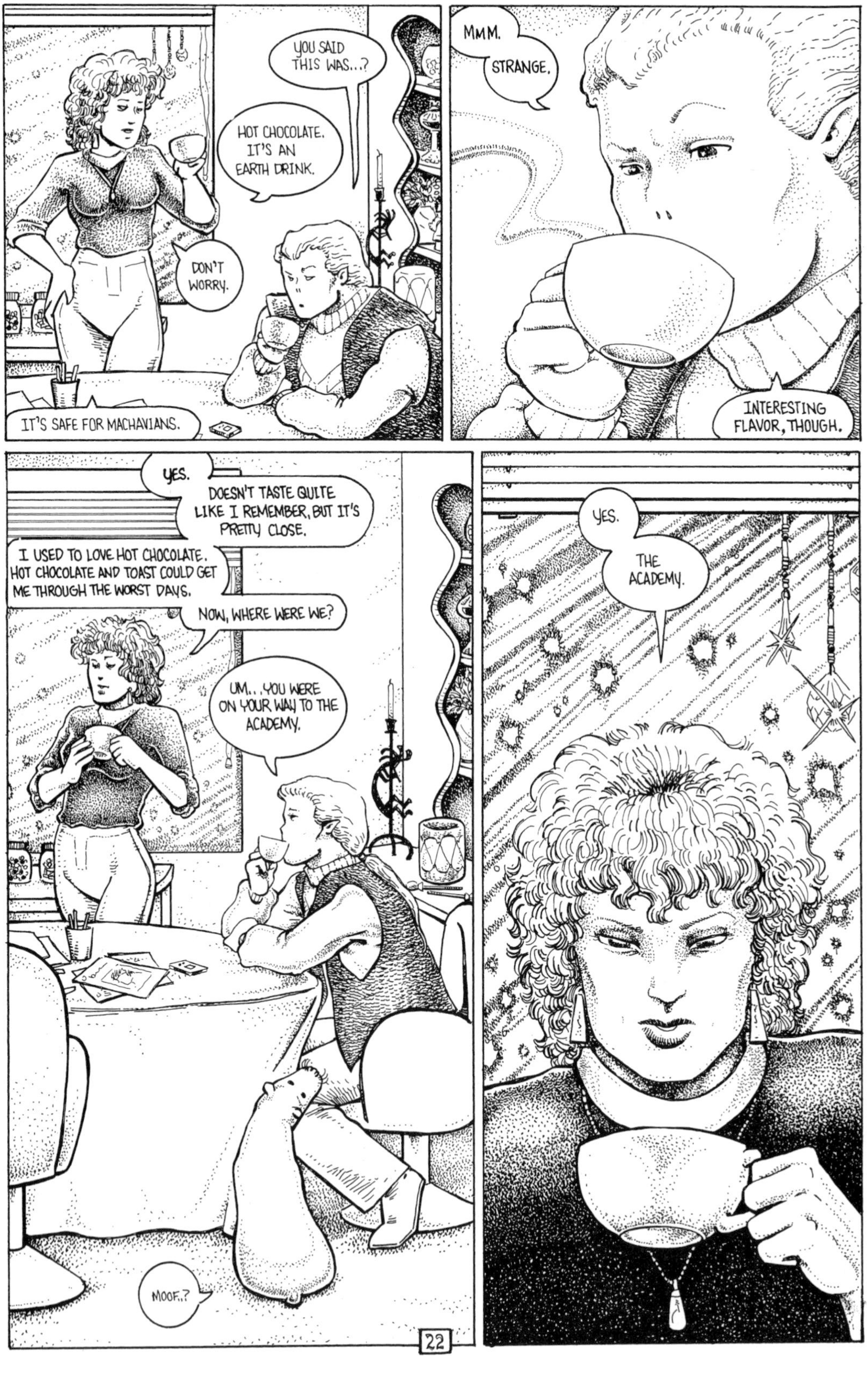
YOU SAID THIS WAS...?
HOT CHOCOLATE. IT'S AN EARTH DRINK.
DON'T WORRY.
IT'S SAFE FOR MACHAVIANS.
MMM.
STRANGE.
INTERESTING FLAVOR, THOUGH.
YES.
DOESN'T TASTE QUITE LIKE I REMEMBER, BUT IT'S PRETTY CLOSE.
I USED TO LOVE HOT CHOCOLATE. HOT CHOCOLATE AND TOAST COULD GET ME THROUGH THE WORST DAYS.
NOW, WHERE WERE WE?
UM...YOU WERE ON YOUR WAY TO THE ACADEMY.
MOOF..?
YES.
THE ACADEMY.

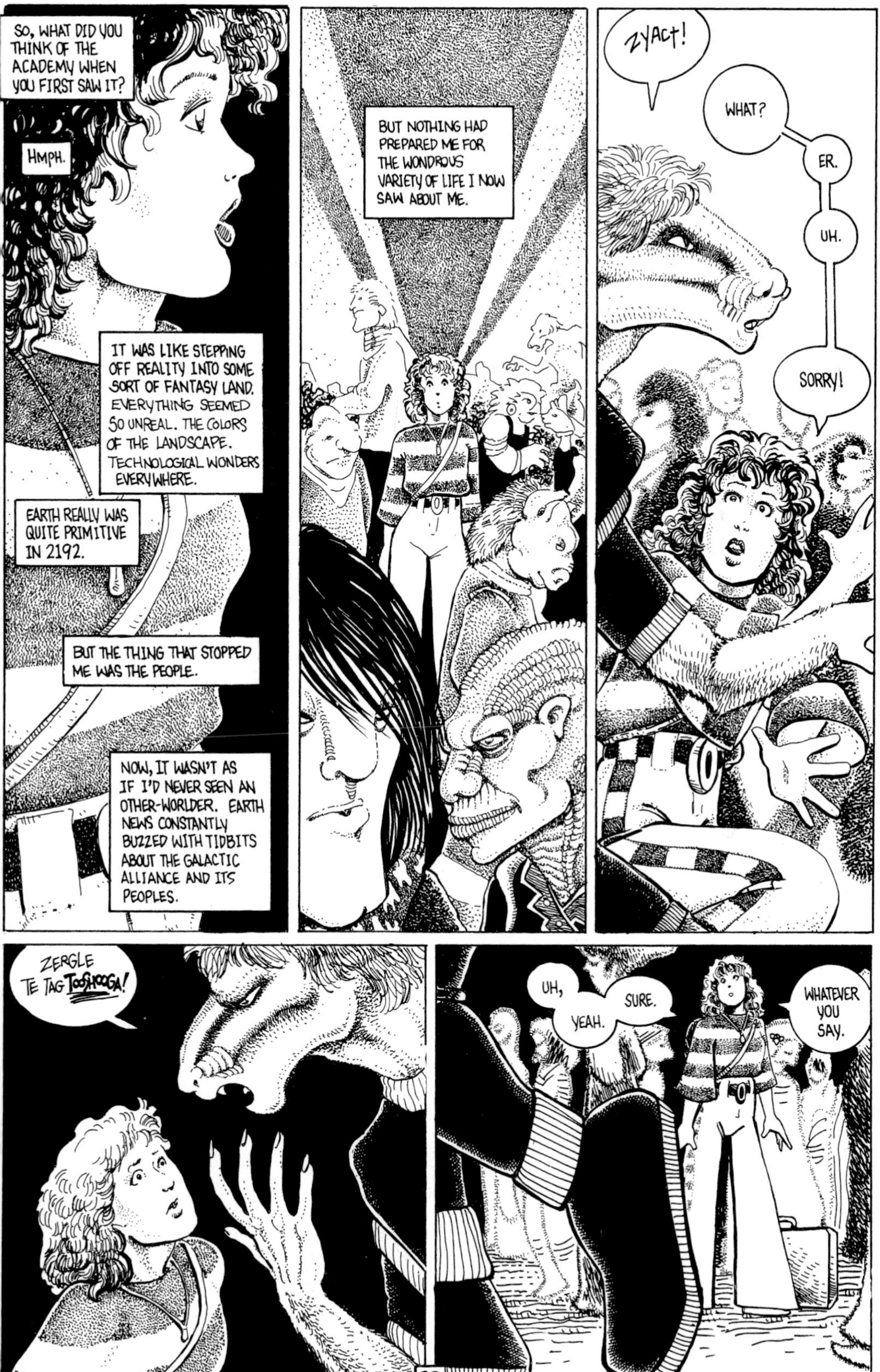

SO, WHAT DID YOU THINK OF THE ACADEMY WHEN YOU FIRST SAW IT?
HMPH.
IT WAS LIKE STEPPING OFF REALITY INTO SOME SORT OF FANTASY LAND. EVERYTHING SEEMED SO UNREAL. THE COLORS OF THE LANDSCAPE. TECHNOLOGICAL WONDERS EVERYWHERE.
EARTH REALLY WAS QUITE PRIMITIVE IN 2192.
BUT THE THING THAT STOPPED ME WAS THE PEOPLE.
NOW, IT WASN'T AS IF I'D NEVER SEEN AN OTHER-WORLDER. EARTH NEWS CONSTANTLY BUZZED WITH TIDBITS ABOUT THE GALACTIC ALLIANCE AND ITS PEOPLES.
BUT NOTHING HAD PREPARED ME FOR THE WONDROUS VARIETY OF LIFE I NOW SAW ABOUT ME.
ZYACT!
WHAT?
ER.
UH.
SORRY!
ZERGLE TE TAG TOOSHOOGA!
UH,
YEAH.
SURE.
WHATEVER YOU SAY.

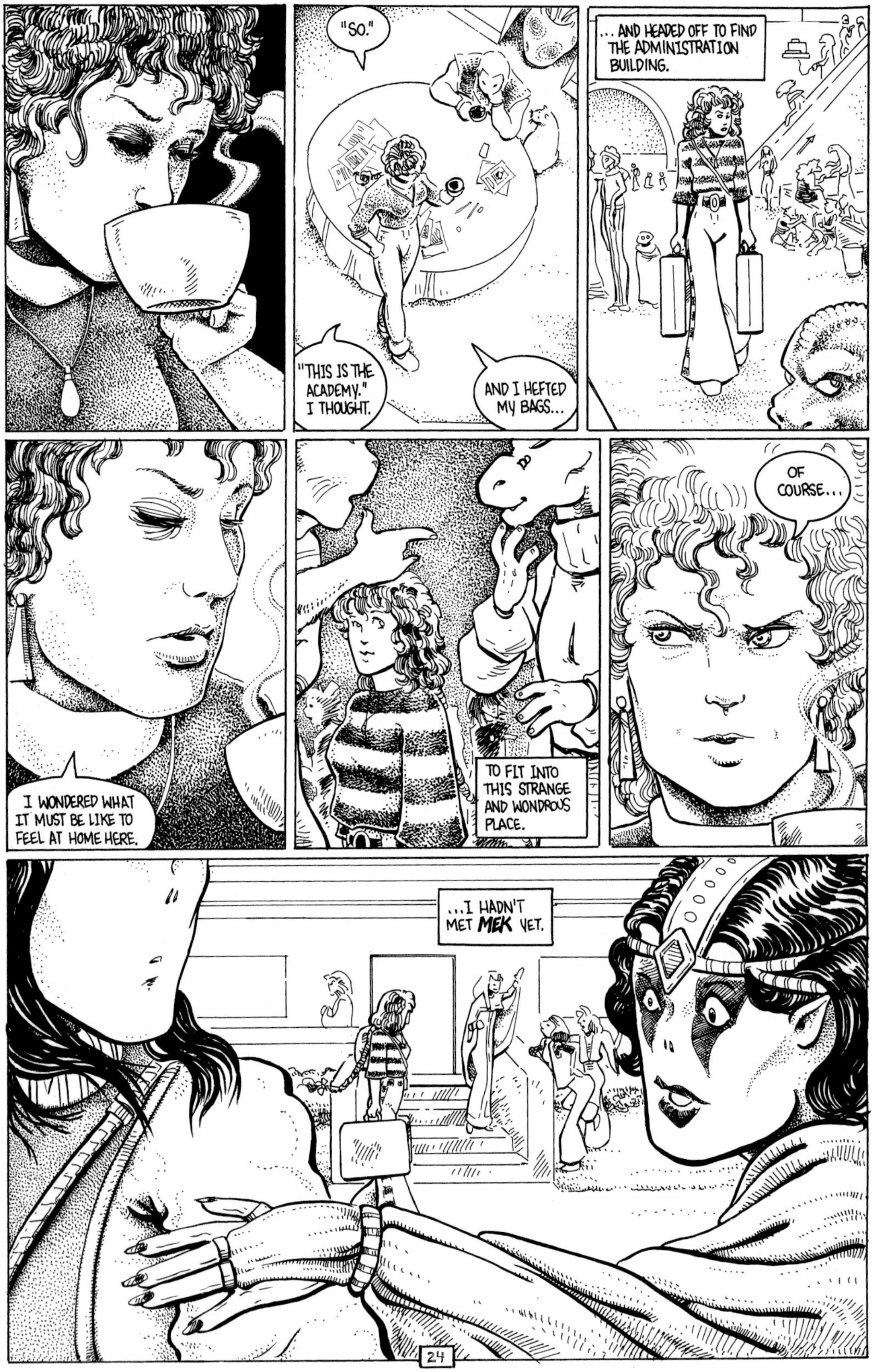
"SO."
"THIS IS THE ACADEMY." I THOUGHT.
AND I HEFTED MY BAGS...
...AND HEADED OFF TO FIND THE ADMINISTRATION BUILDING.
I WONDERED WHAT IT MUST BE LIKE TO FEEL AT HOME HERE.
TO FIT INTO THIS STRANGE AND WONDROUS PLACE.
OF COURSE...
...I HADN'T MET **MEK** YET.

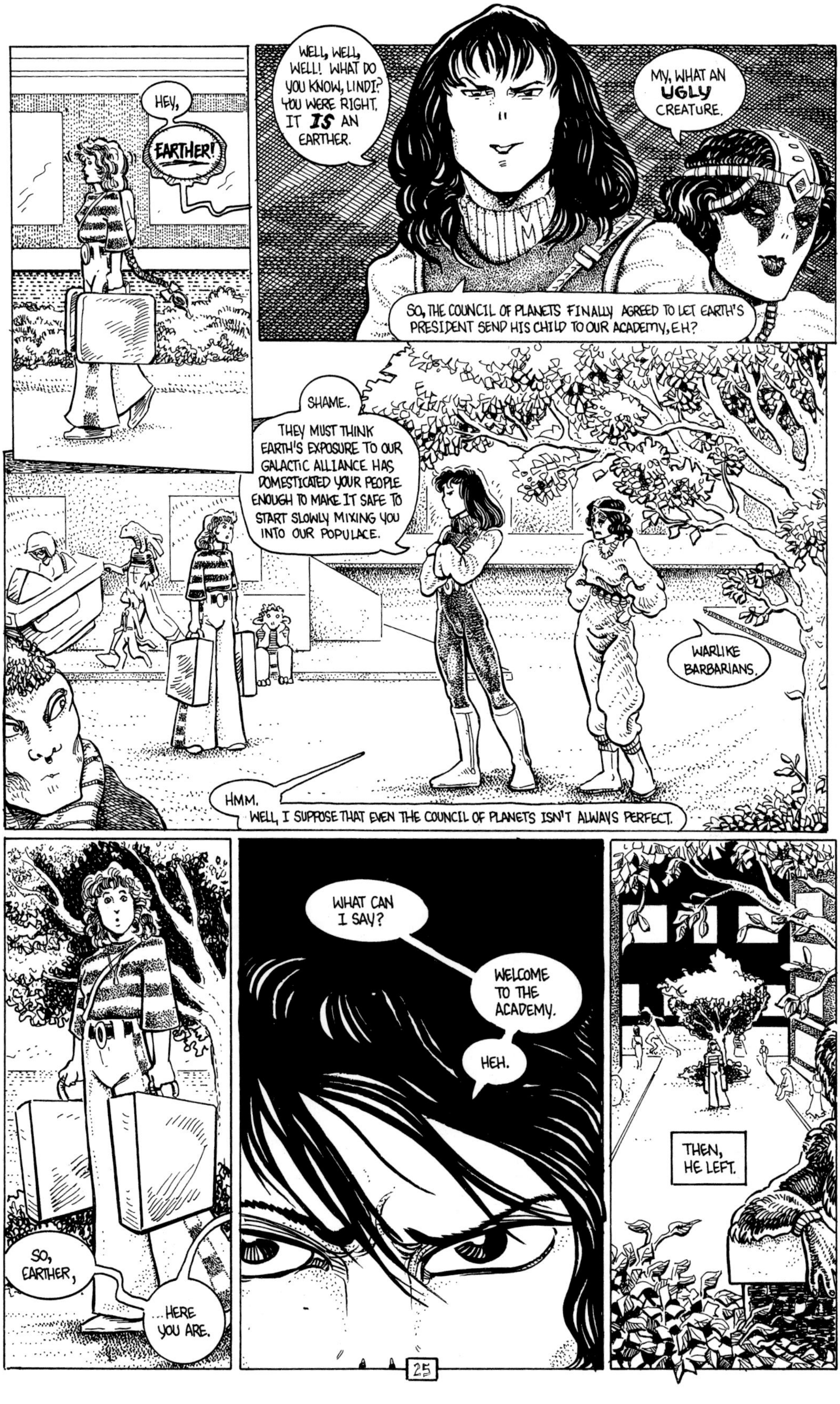
HEY,
EARTHER!
WELL, WELL, WELL! WHAT DO YOU KNOW, LINDI? YOU WERE RIGHT, IT IS AN EARTHER.
MY, WHAT AN UGLY CREATURE.
SO, THE COUNCIL OF PLANETS FINALLY AGREED TO LET EARTH'S PRESIDENT SEND HIS CHILD TO OUR ACADEMY, EH?
SHAME.
THEY MUST THINK EARTH'S EXPOSURE TO OUR GALACTIC ALLIANCE HAS DOMESTICATED YOUR PEOPLE ENOUGH TO MAKE IT SAFE TO START SLOWLY MIXING YOU INTO OUR POPULACE.
WARLIKE BARBARIANS.
HMM.
WELL, I SUPPOSE THAT EVEN THE COUNCIL OF PLANETS ISN'T ALWAYS PERFECT.
SO, EARTHER,
...HERE YOU ARE.
WHAT CAN I SAY?
WELCOME TO THE ACADEMY.
HEH.
THEN, HE LEFT.

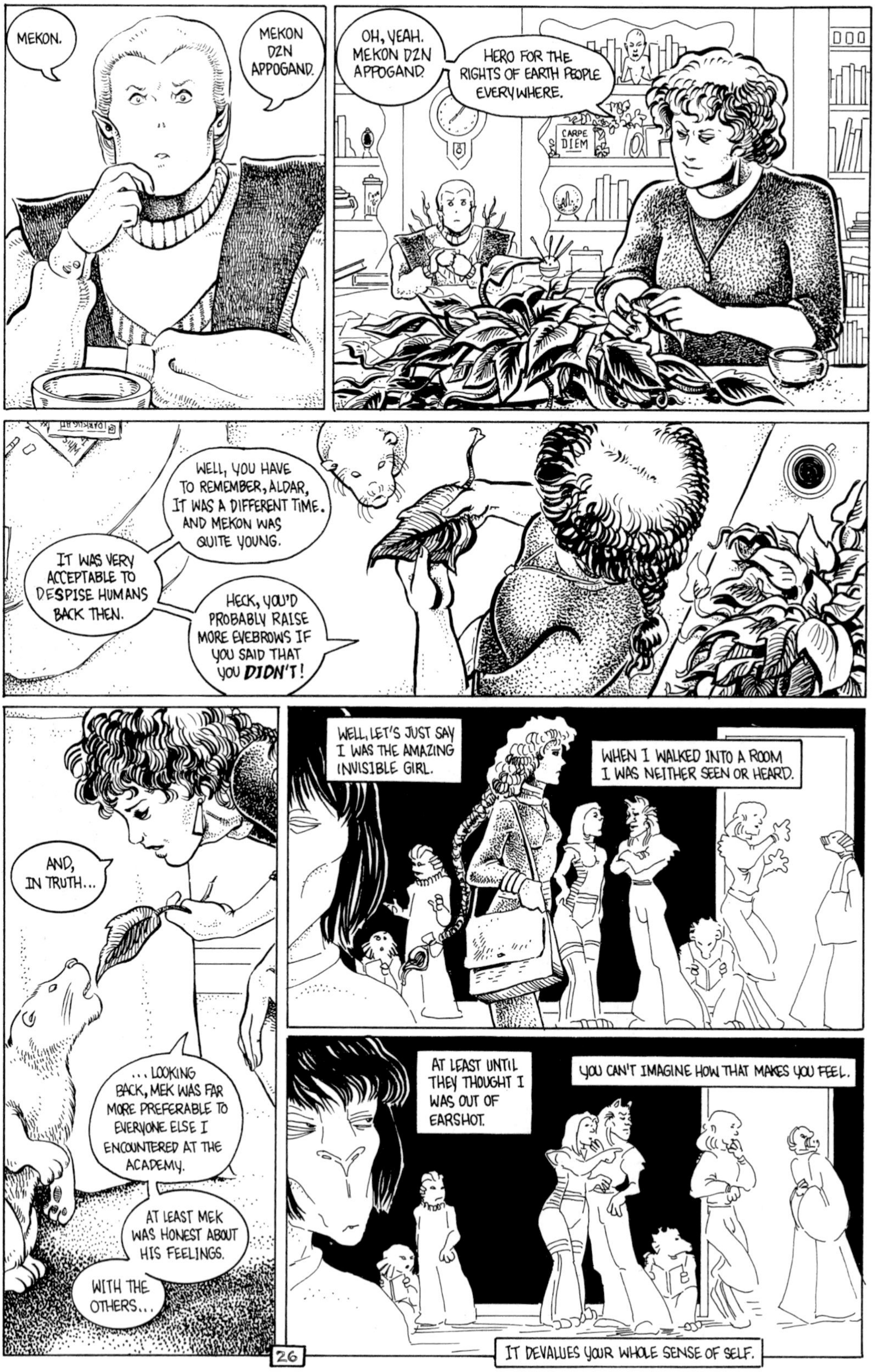

MEKON.
MEKON DZN APPOGAND.
OH, YEAH. MEKON DZN APPOGAND.
HERO FOR THE RIGHTS OF EARTH PEOPLE EVERYWHERE.
CARPE DIEM
WELL, YOU HAVE TO REMEMBER, ALDAR, IT WAS A DIFFERENT TIME. AND MEKON WAS QUITE YOUNG.
IT WAS VERY ACCEPTABLE TO DESPISE HUMANS BACK THEN.
HECK, YOU'D PROBABLY RAISE MORE EYEBROWS IF YOU SAID THAT YOU **DIDN'T**!
AND, IN TRUTH...
...LOOKING BACK, MEK WAS FAR MORE PREFERABLE TO EVERYONE ELSE I ENCOUNTERED AT THE ACADEMY.
AT LEAST MEK WAS HONEST ABOUT HIS FEELINGS.
WITH THE OTHERS...
WELL, LET'S JUST SAY I WAS THE AMAZING INVISIBLE GIRL.
WHEN I WALKED INTO A ROOM I WAS NEITHER SEEN OR HEARD.
AT LEAST UNTIL THEY THOUGHT I WAS OUT OF EARSHOT.
YOU CAN'T IMAGINE HOW THAT MAKES YOU FEEL.
IT DEVALUES YOUR WHOLE SENSE OF SELF.

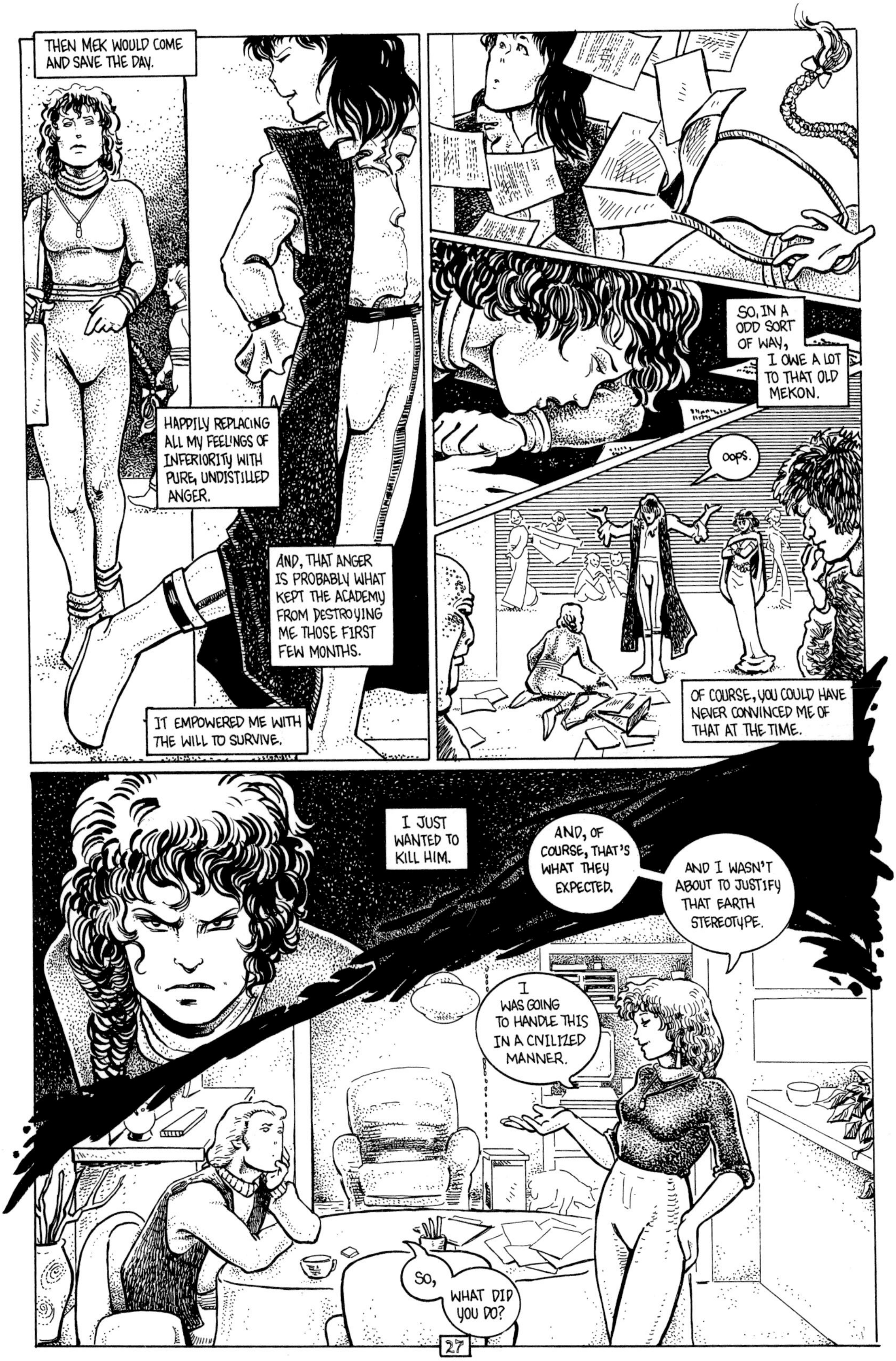
THEN MEK WOULD COME AND SAVE THE DAY.
HAPPILY REPLACING ALL MY FEELINGS OF INFERIORITY WITH PURE, UNDISTILLED ANGER.
AND, THAT ANGER IS PROBABLY WHAT KEPT THE ACADEMY FROM DESTROYING ME THOSE FIRST FEW MONTHS.
IT EMPOWERED ME WITH THE WILL TO SURVIVE.
SO, IN A ODD SORT OF WAY, I OWE A LOT TO THAT OLD MEKON.
OOPS.
OF COURSE, YOU COULD HAVE NEVER CONVINCED ME OF THAT AT THE TIME.
I JUST WANTED TO KILL HIM.
AND, OF COURSE, THAT'S WHAT THEY EXPECTED.
AND I WASN'T ABOUT TO JUSTIFY THAT EARTH STEREOTYPE.
I WAS GOING TO HANDLE THIS IN A CIVILIZED MANNER.
SO, WHAT DID YOU DO?

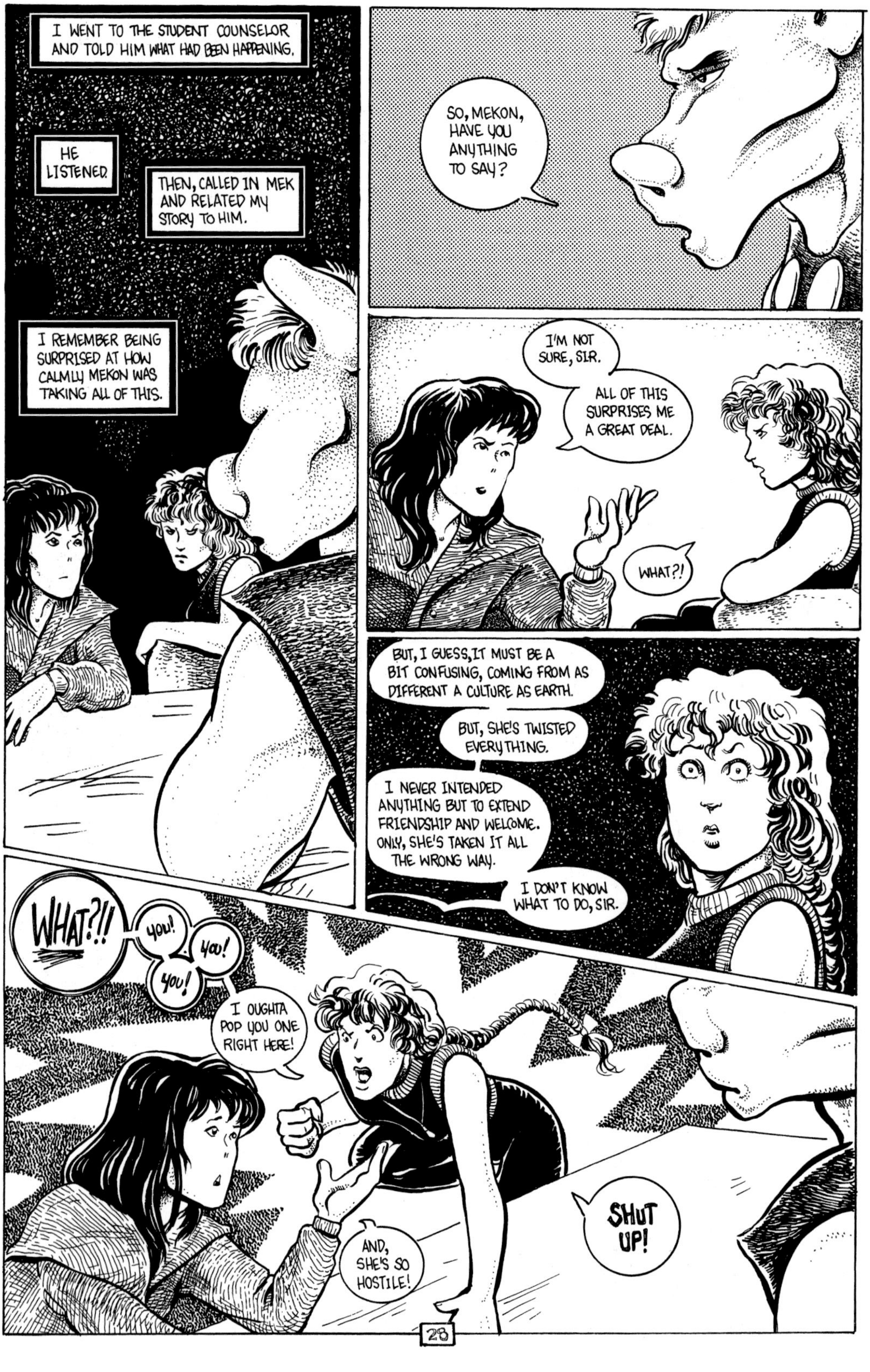

I WENT TO THE STUDENT COUNSELOR AND TOLD HIM WHAT HAD BEEN HAPPENING.
HE LISTENED.
THEN, CALLED IN MEK AND RELATED MY STORY TO HIM.
I REMEMBER BEING SURPRISED AT HOW CALMLY MEKON WAS TAKING ALL OF THIS.
SO, MEKON, HAVE YOU ANYTHING TO SAY?
I'M NOT SURE, SIR.
ALL OF THIS SURPRISES ME A GREAT DEAL.
WHAT?!
BUT, I GUESS, IT MUST BE A BIT CONFUSING, COMING FROM AS DIFFERENT A CULTURE AS EARTH.
BUT, SHE'S TWISTED EVERYTHING.
I NEVER INTENDED ANYTHING BUT TO EXTEND FRIENDSHIP AND WELCOME. ONLY, SHE'S TAKEN IT ALL THE WRONG WAY.
I DON'T KNOW WHAT TO DO, SIR.
WHAT?!!
YOU! YOU! YOU!
I OUGHTA POP YOU ONE RIGHT HERE!
AND, SHE'S SO HOSTILE!
SHUT UP!

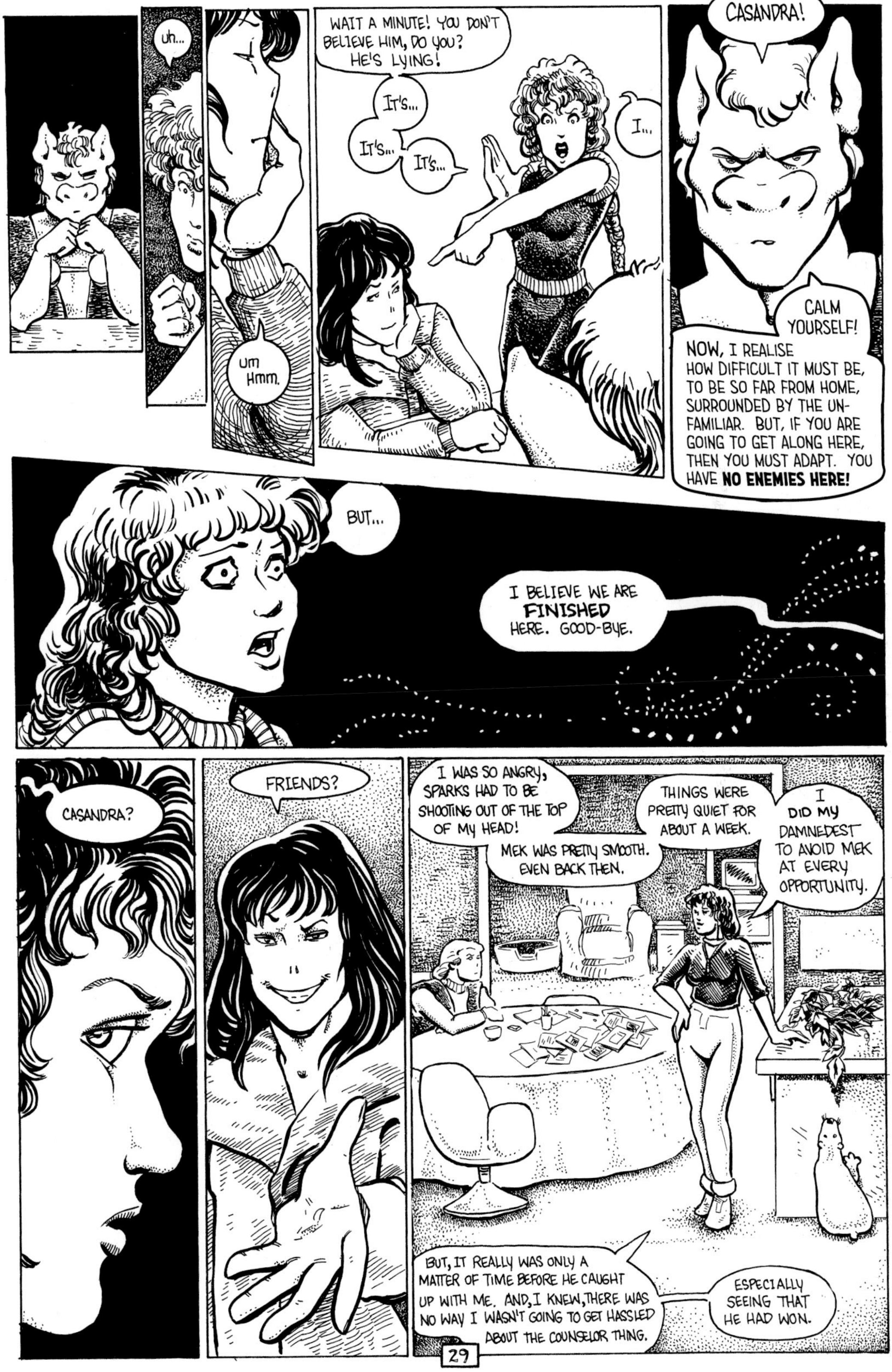
uh...
Um Hmm.
WAIT A MINUTE! YOU DON'T BELIEVE HIM, DO YOU? HE'S LYING!
IT'S...
IT'S...
IT'S...
I...
CASANDRA!
CALM YOURSELF!
NOW, I REALISE HOW DIFFICULT IT MUST BE, TO BE SO FAR FROM HOME, SURROUNDED BY THE UN-FAMILIAR. BUT, IF YOU ARE GOING TO GET ALONG HERE, THEN YOU MUST ADAPT. YOU HAVE **NO ENEMIES HERE!**
BUT...
I BELIEVE WE ARE **FINISHED** HERE. GOOD-BYE.
CASANDRA?
FRIENDS?
I WAS SO ANGRY, SPARKS HAD TO BE SHOOTING OUT OF THE TOP OF MY HEAD!
MEK WAS PRETTY SMOOTH. EVEN BACK THEN.
THINGS WERE PRETTY QUIET FOR ABOUT A WEEK.
I DID MY DAMNEDEST TO AVOID MEK AT EVERY OPPORTUNITY.
BUT, IT REALLY WAS ONLY A MATTER OF TIME BEFORE HE CAUGHT UP WITH ME. AND, I KNEW, THERE WAS NO WAY I WASN'T GOING TO GET HASSLED ABOUT THE COUNSELOR THING.
ESPECIALLY SEEING THAT HE HAD WON.

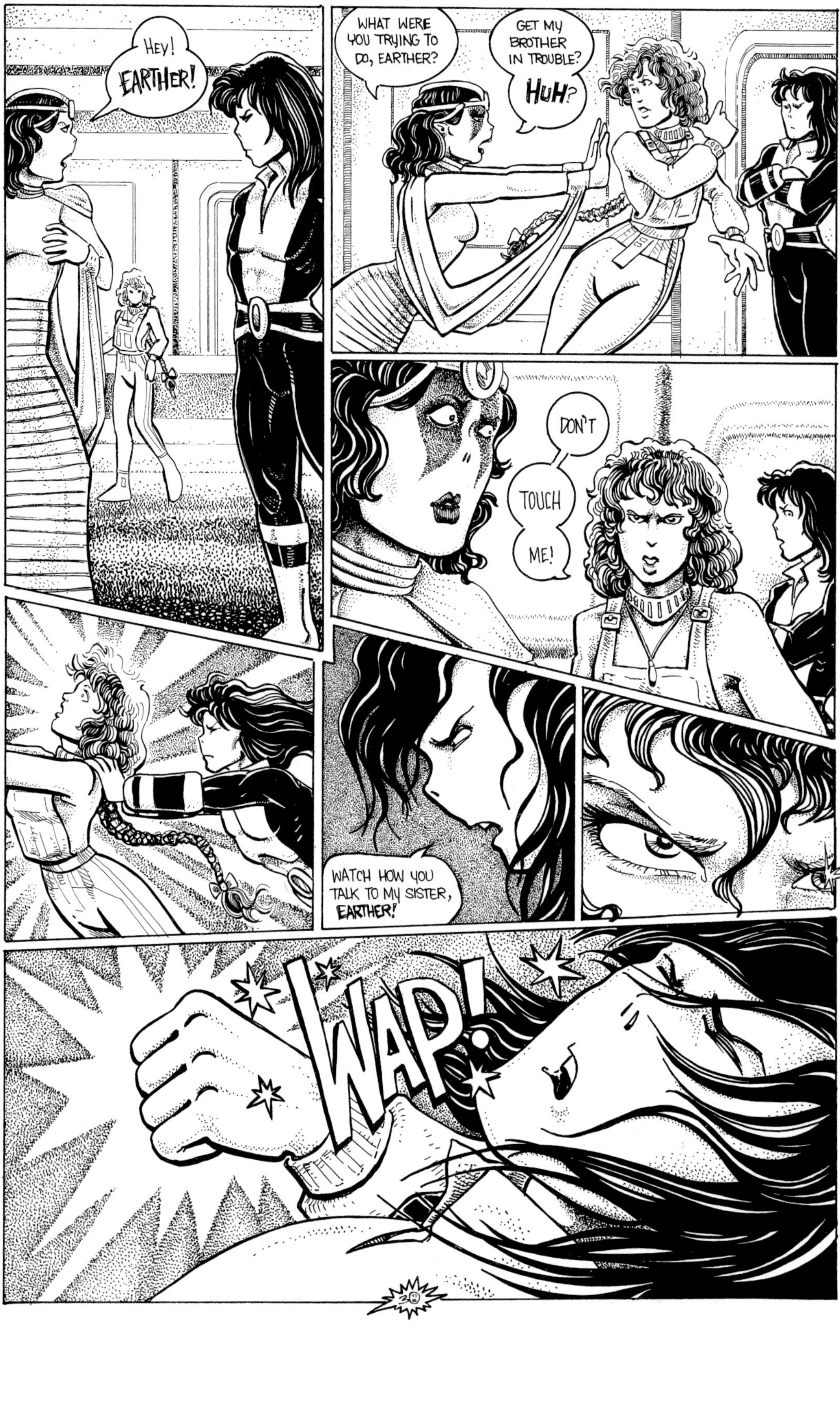
Hey! EARTHER!
WHAT WERE YOU TRYING TO DO, EARTHER?
GET MY BROTHER IN TROUBLE? HUH?
DON'T TOUCH ME!
WATCH HOW YOU TALK TO MY SISTER, EARTHER!
WAP!

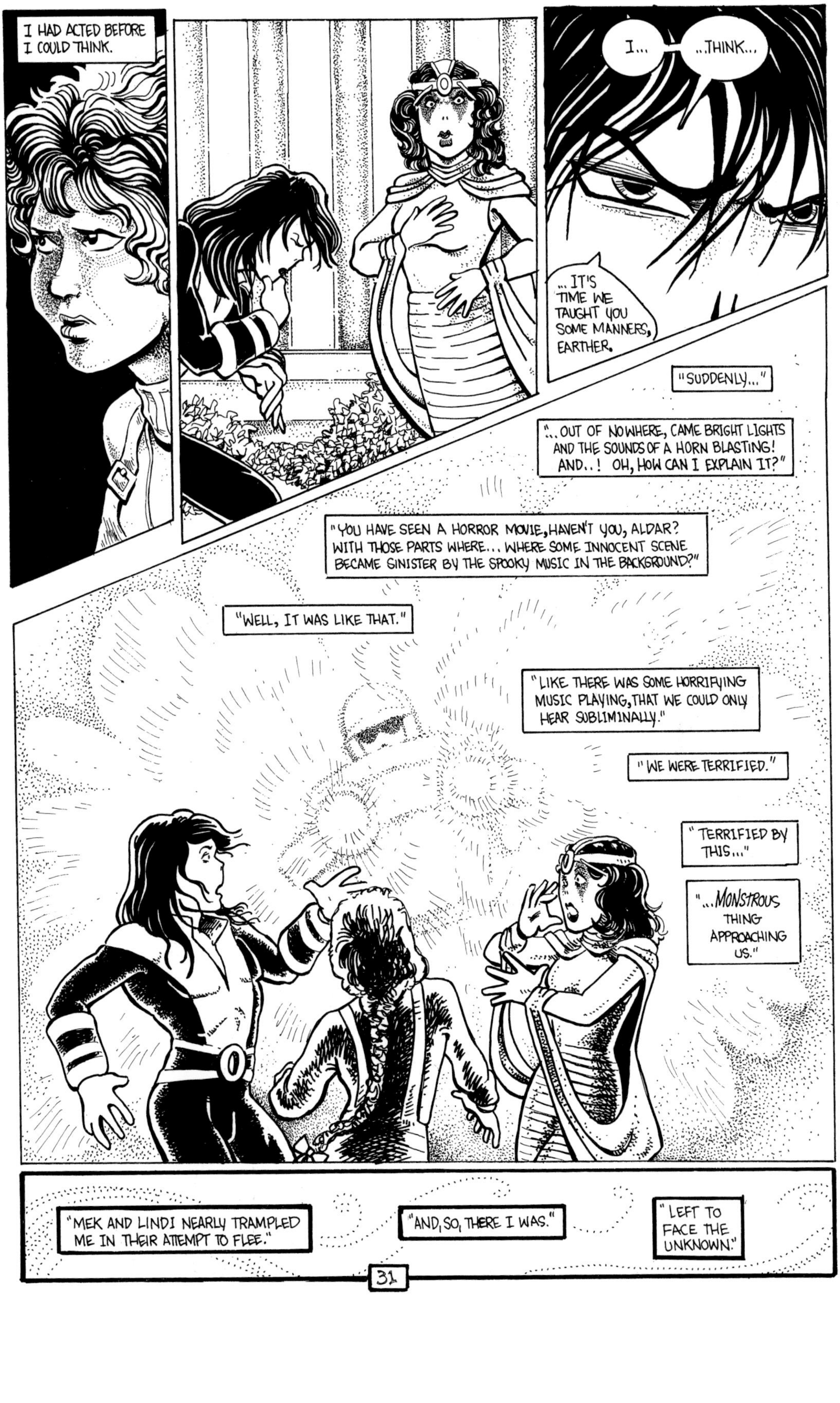
I HAD ACTED BEFORE I COULD THINK.
I...
...THINK...
...IT'S TIME WE TAUGHT YOU SOME MANNERS, EARTHER.
"SUDDENLY..."
"...OUT OF NOWHERE, CAME BRIGHT LIGHTS AND THE SOUNDS OF A HORN BLASTING! AND..! OH, HOW CAN I EXPLAIN IT?"
"YOU HAVE SEEN A HORROR MOVIE, HAVEN'T YOU, ALDAR? WITH THOSE PARTS WHERE... WHERE SOME INNOCENT SCENE BECAME SINISTER BY THE SPOOKY MUSIC IN THE BACKGROUND?"
"WELL, IT WAS LIKE THAT."
"LIKE THERE WAS SOME HORRIFYING MUSIC PLAYING, THAT WE COULD ONLY HEAR SUBLIMINALLY."
"WE WERE TERRIFIED."
"TERRIFIED BY THIS..."
"...*MONSTROUS* THING APPROACHING US."
"MEK AND LINDI NEARLY TRAMPLED ME IN THEIR ATTEMPT TO FLEE."
"AND, SO, THERE I WAS."
"LEFT TO FACE THE UNKNOWN."

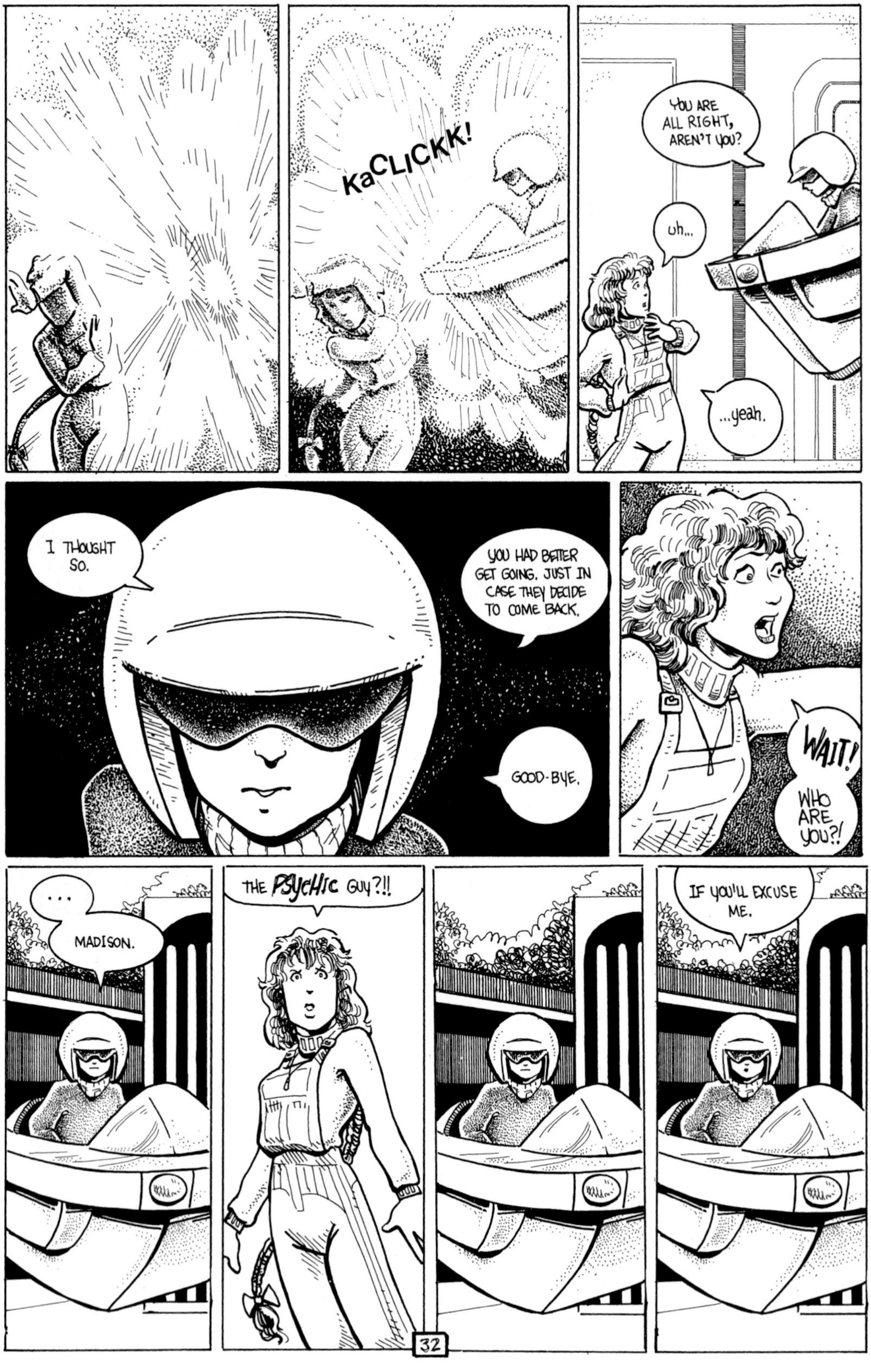
KaCLICKK!
YOU ARE ALL RIGHT, AREN'T YOU?
uh...
...yeah.
I THOUGHT SO.
YOU HAD BETTER GET GOING, JUST IN CASE THEY DECIDE TO COME BACK.
GOOD-BYE.
WAIT!
WHO ARE YOU?!
...
MADISON.
THE PSYCHIC GUY?!!
IF YOU'LL EXCUSE ME.

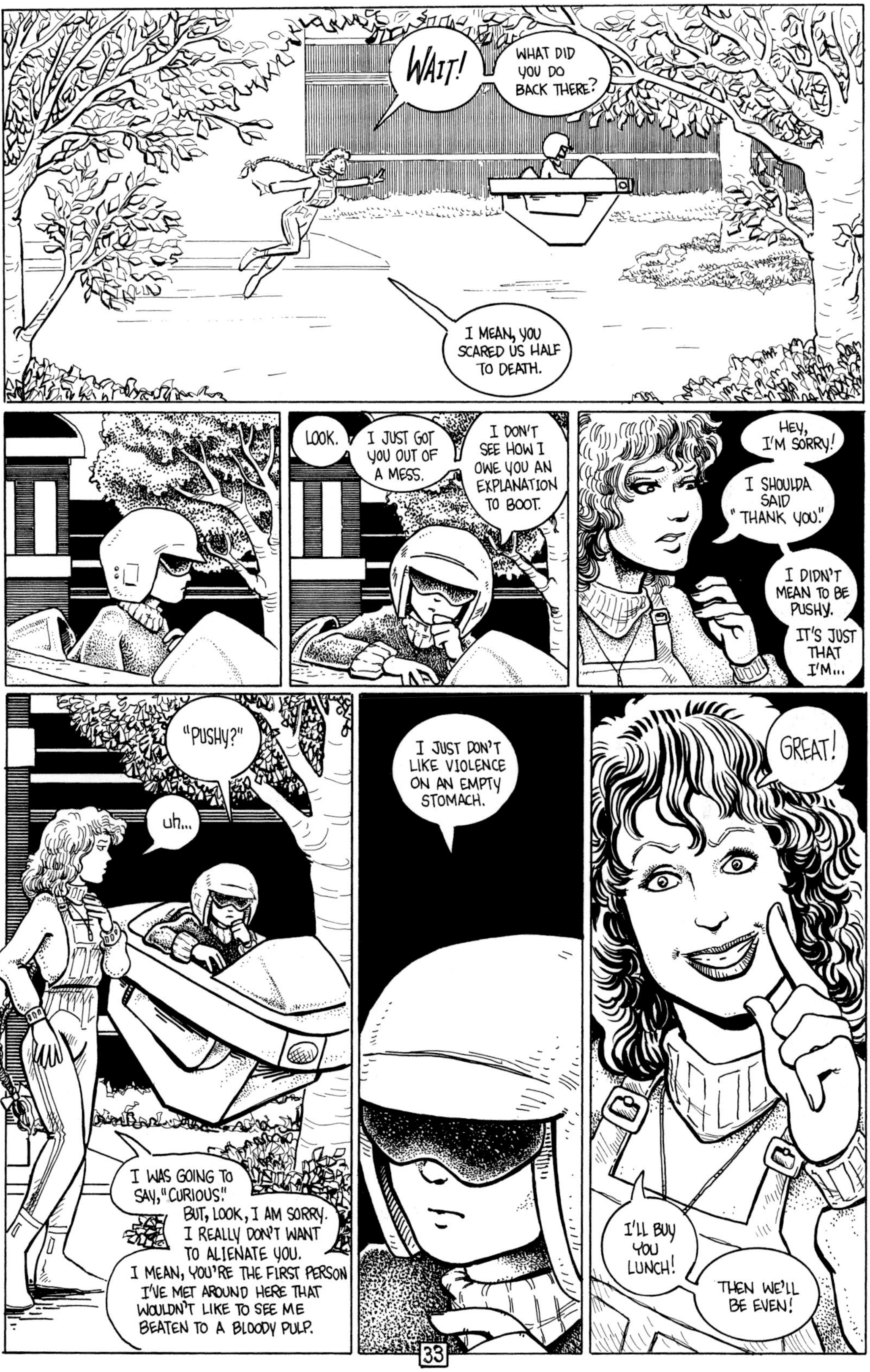
WAIT!
WHAT DID YOU DO BACK THERE?
I MEAN, YOU SCARED US HALF TO DEATH.
LOOK.
I JUST GOT YOU OUT OF A MESS.
I DON'T SEE HOW I OWE YOU AN EXPLANATION TO BOOT.
HEY, I'M SORRY!
I SHOULDA SAID "THANK YOU."
I DIDN'T MEAN TO BE PUSHY.
IT'S JUST THAT I'M...
"PUSHY?"
uh...
I WAS GOING TO SAY, "CURIOUS."
BUT, LOOK, I AM SORRY. I REALLY DON'T WANT TO ALIENATE YOU.
I MEAN, YOU'RE THE FIRST PERSON I'VE MET AROUND HERE THAT WOULDN'T LIKE TO SEE ME BEATEN TO A BLOODY PULP.
I JUST DON'T LIKE VIOLENCE ON AN EMPTY STOMACH.
GREAT!
I'LL BUY YOU LUNCH!
THEN WE'LL BE EVEN!

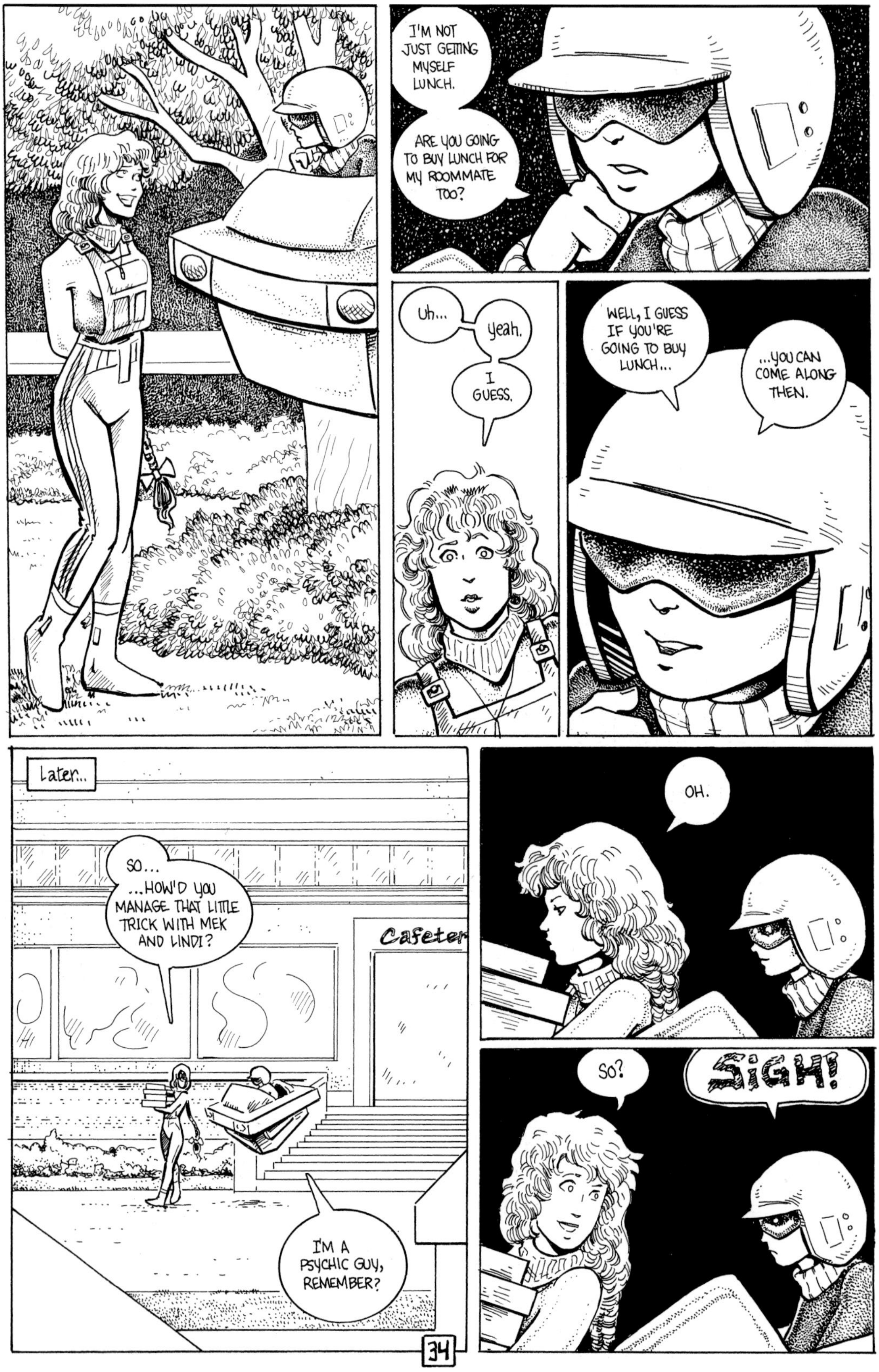
I'M NOT JUST GETTING MYSELF LUNCH.
ARE YOU GOING TO BUY LUNCH FOR MY ROOMMATE TOO?
Uh... yeah. I GUESS.
WELL, I GUESS IF YOU'RE GOING TO BUY LUNCH...
...YOU CAN COME ALONG THEN.
Later..
SO... ...HOW'D YOU MANAGE THAT LITTLE TRICK WITH MEK AND LINDI?
Cafeter
I'M A PSYCHIC GUY, REMEMBER?
OH.
SO?
SIGH!

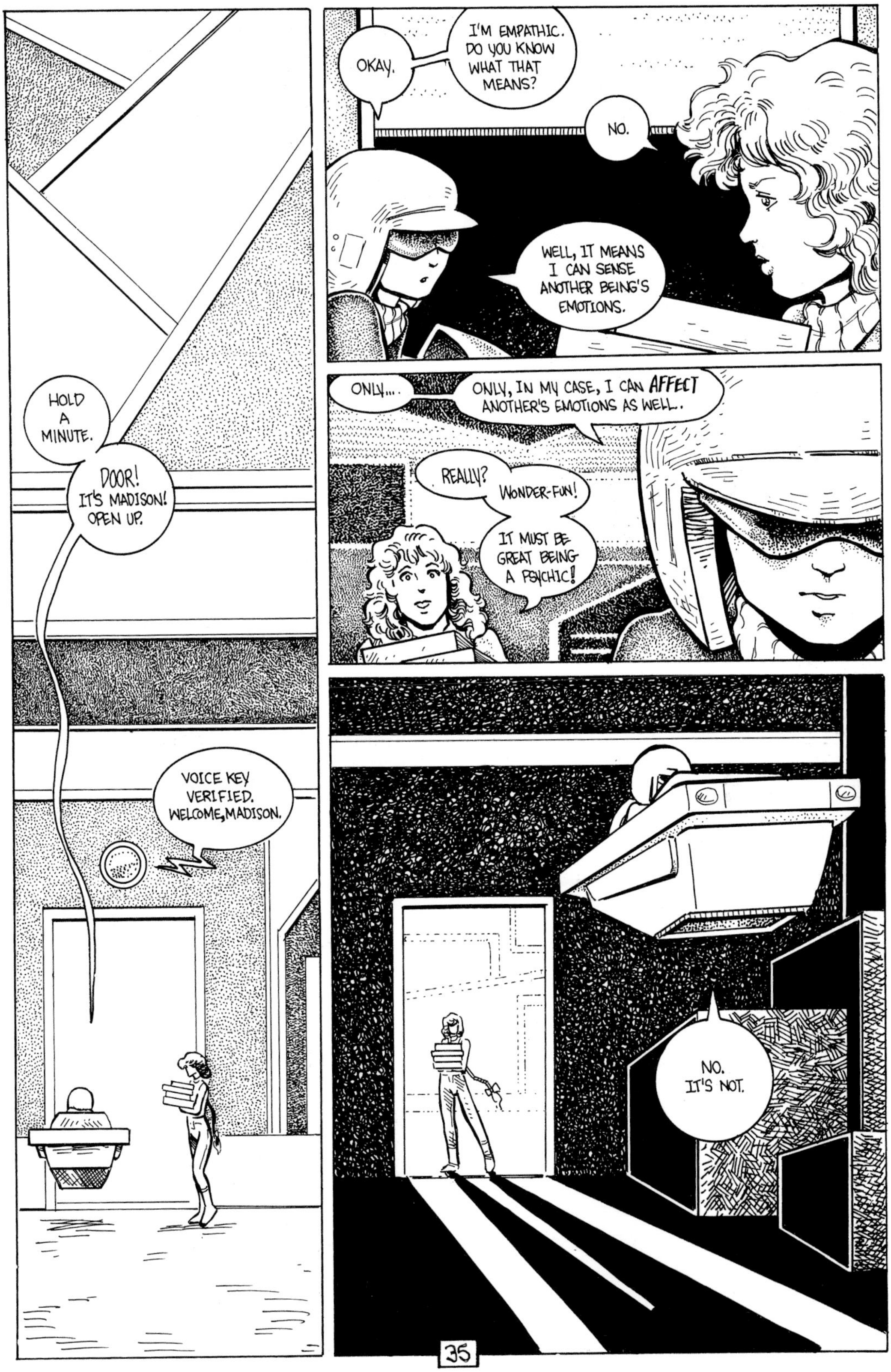
HOLD A MINUTE.
DOOR! IT'S MADISON! OPEN UP.
VOICE KEY VERIFIED. WELCOME, MADISON.
OKAY.
I'M EMPATHIC. DO YOU KNOW WHAT THAT MEANS?
NO.
WELL, IT MEANS I CAN SENSE ANOTHER BEING'S EMOTIONS.
ONLY....
ONLY, IN MY CASE, I CAN AFFECT ANOTHER'S EMOTIONS AS WELL.
REALLY? WONDER-FUN!
IT MUST BE GREAT BEING A PSYCHIC!
NO. IT'S NOT.

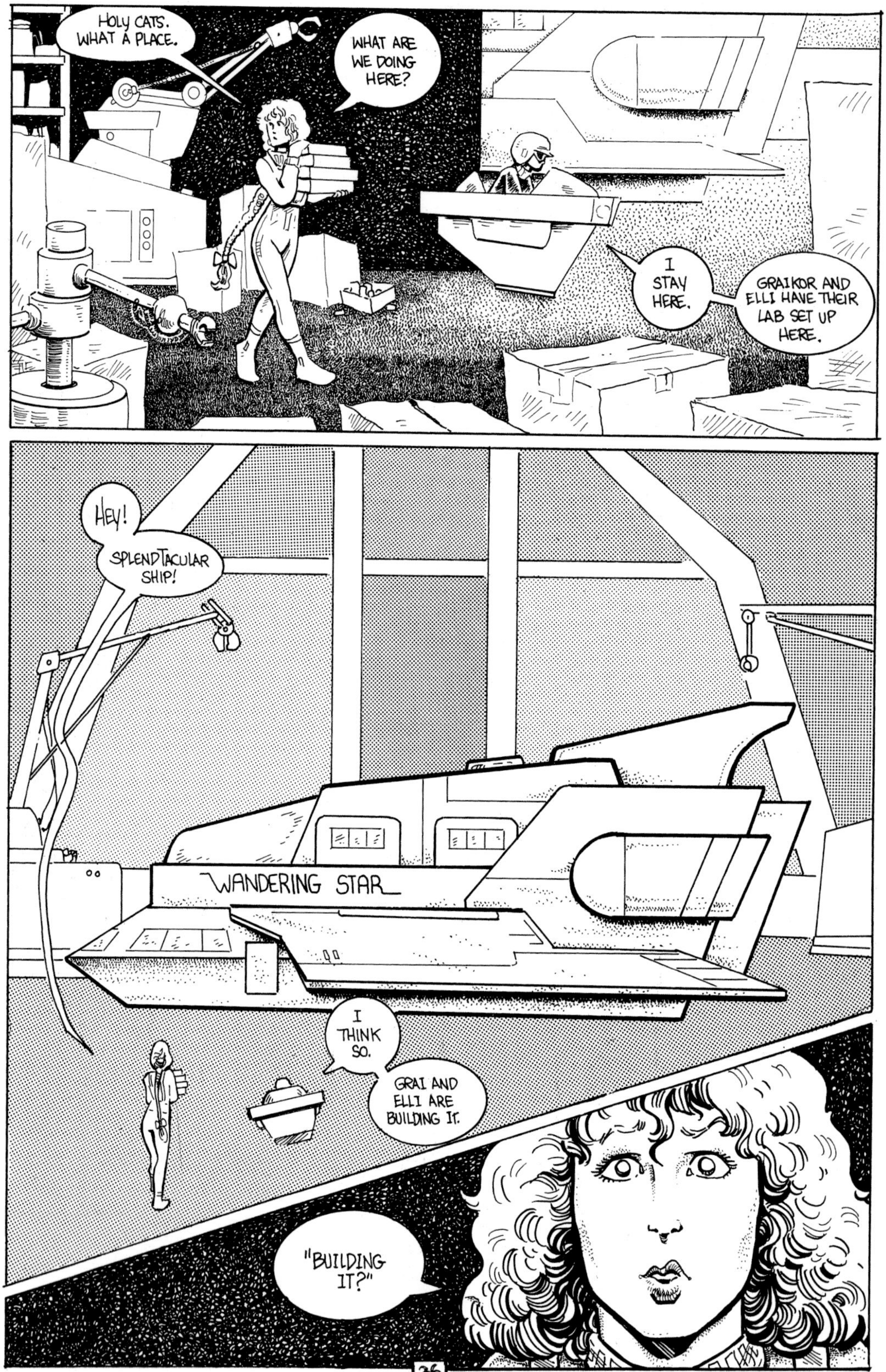
HOLY CATS. WHAT A PLACE.
WHAT ARE WE DOING HERE?
I STAY HERE.
GRAIKOR AND ELLI HAVE THEIR LAB SET UP HERE.
HEY!
SPLENDTACULAR SHIP!
WANDERING STAR
I THINK SO.
GRAI AND ELLI ARE BUILDING IT.
"BUILDING IT?"

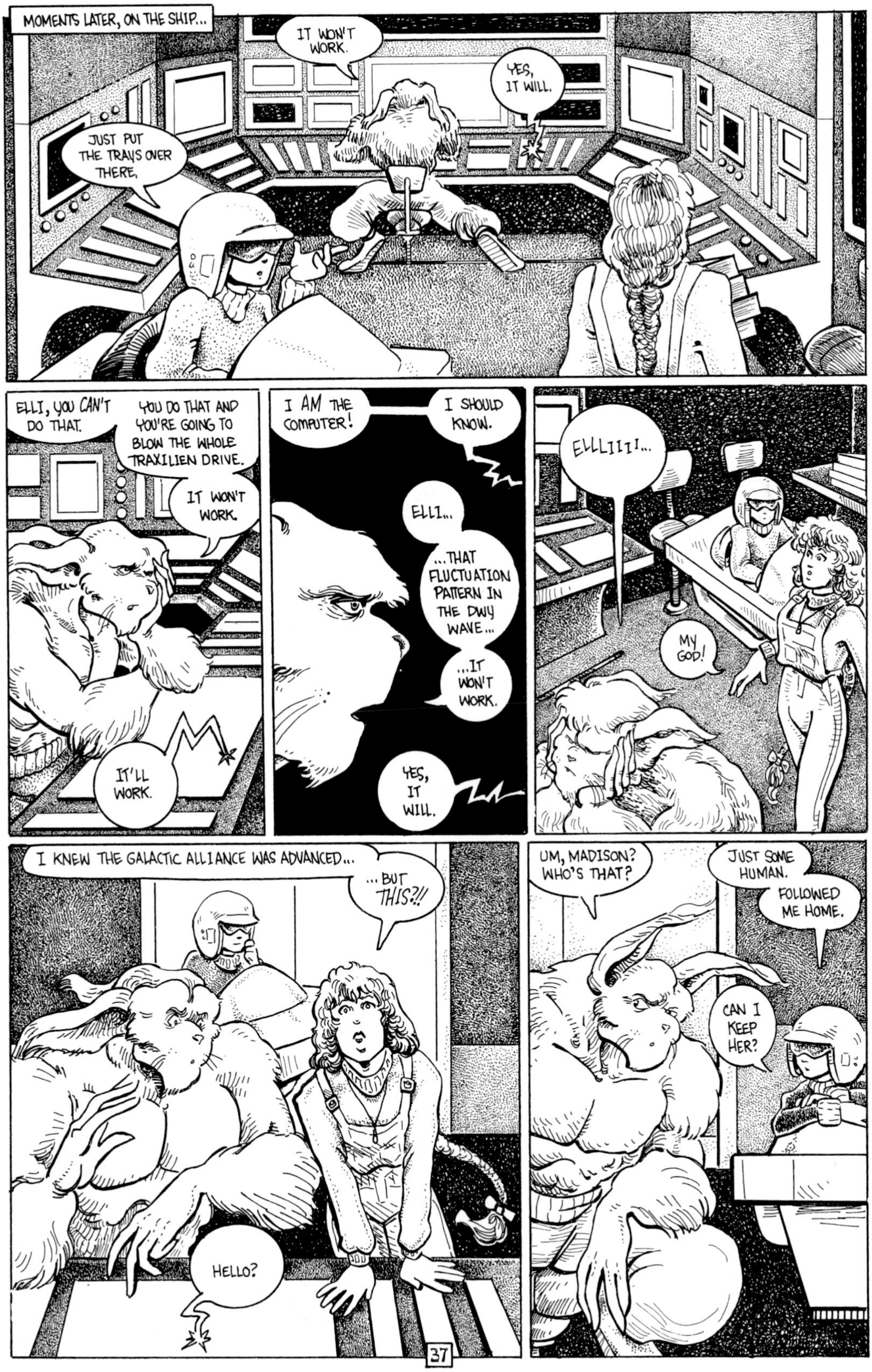
MOMENTS LATER, ON THE SHIP...
IT WON'T WORK.
YES, IT WILL.
JUST PUT THE TRAYS OVER THERE.
ELLI, YOU CAN'T DO THAT.
YOU DO THAT AND YOU'RE GOING TO BLOW THE WHOLE TRAXILIEN DRIVE.
IT WON'T WORK.
IT'LL WORK.
I AM THE COMPUTER!
I SHOULD KNOW.
ELLI...
...THAT FLUCTUATION PATTERN IN THE DWY WAVE...
...IT WON'T WORK.
YES, IT WILL.
ELLIIII...
MY GOD!
I KNEW THE GALACTIC ALLIANCE WAS ADVANCED...
...BUT THIS?!!
HELLO?
UM, MADISON? WHO'S THAT?
JUST SOME HUMAN.
FOLLOWED ME HOME.
CAN I KEEP HER?

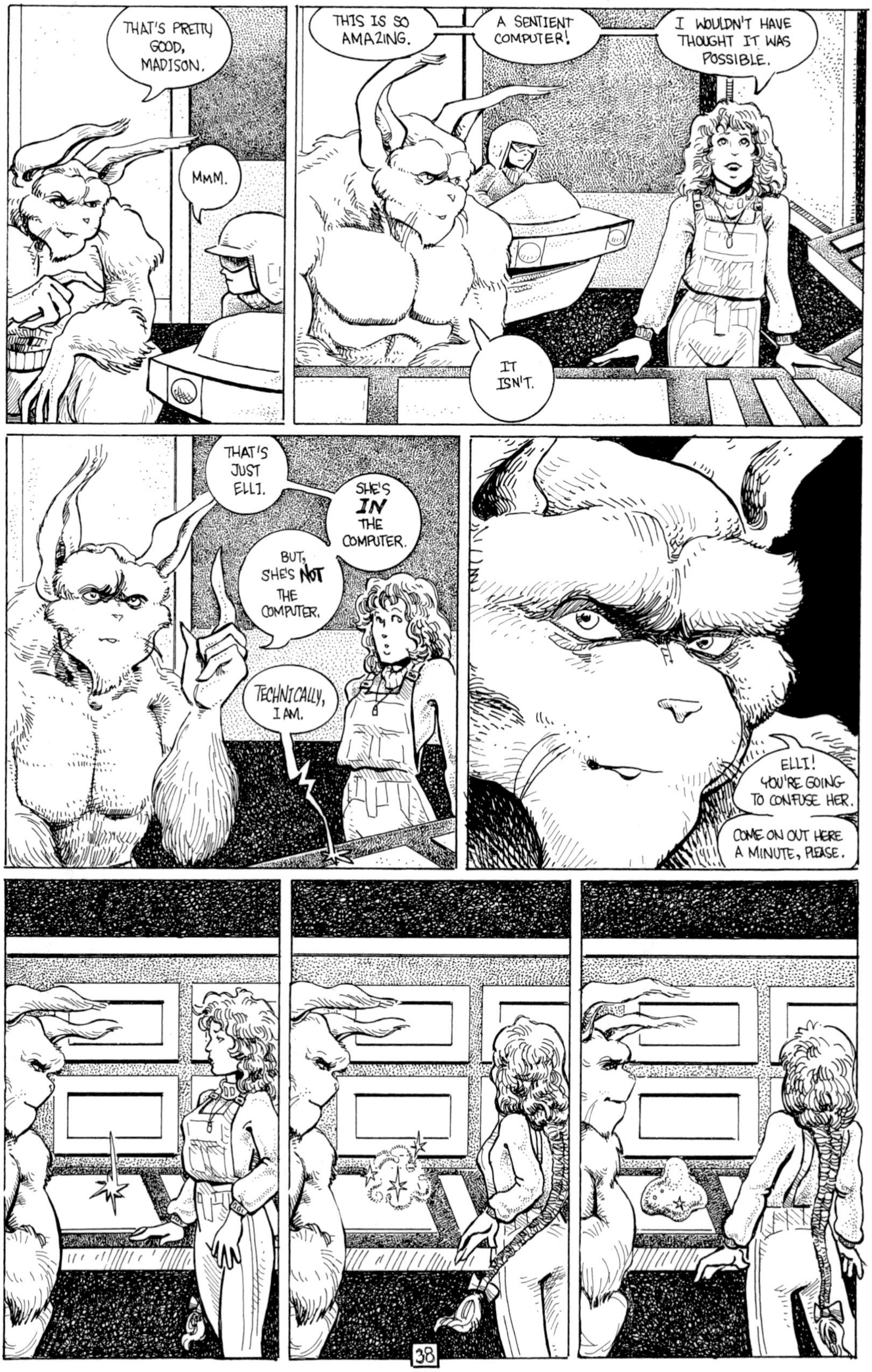
THAT'S PRETTY GOOD, MADISON.
MMM.
THIS IS SO AMAZING.
A SENTIENT COMPUTER!
I WOULDN'T HAVE THOUGHT IT WAS POSSIBLE.
IT ISN'T.
THAT'S JUST ELLI.
SHE'S IN THE COMPUTER.
BUT, SHE'S NOT THE COMPUTER.
TECHNICALLY, I AM.
ELLI! YOU'RE GOING TO CONFUSE HER.
COME ON OUT HERE A MINUTE, PLEASE.

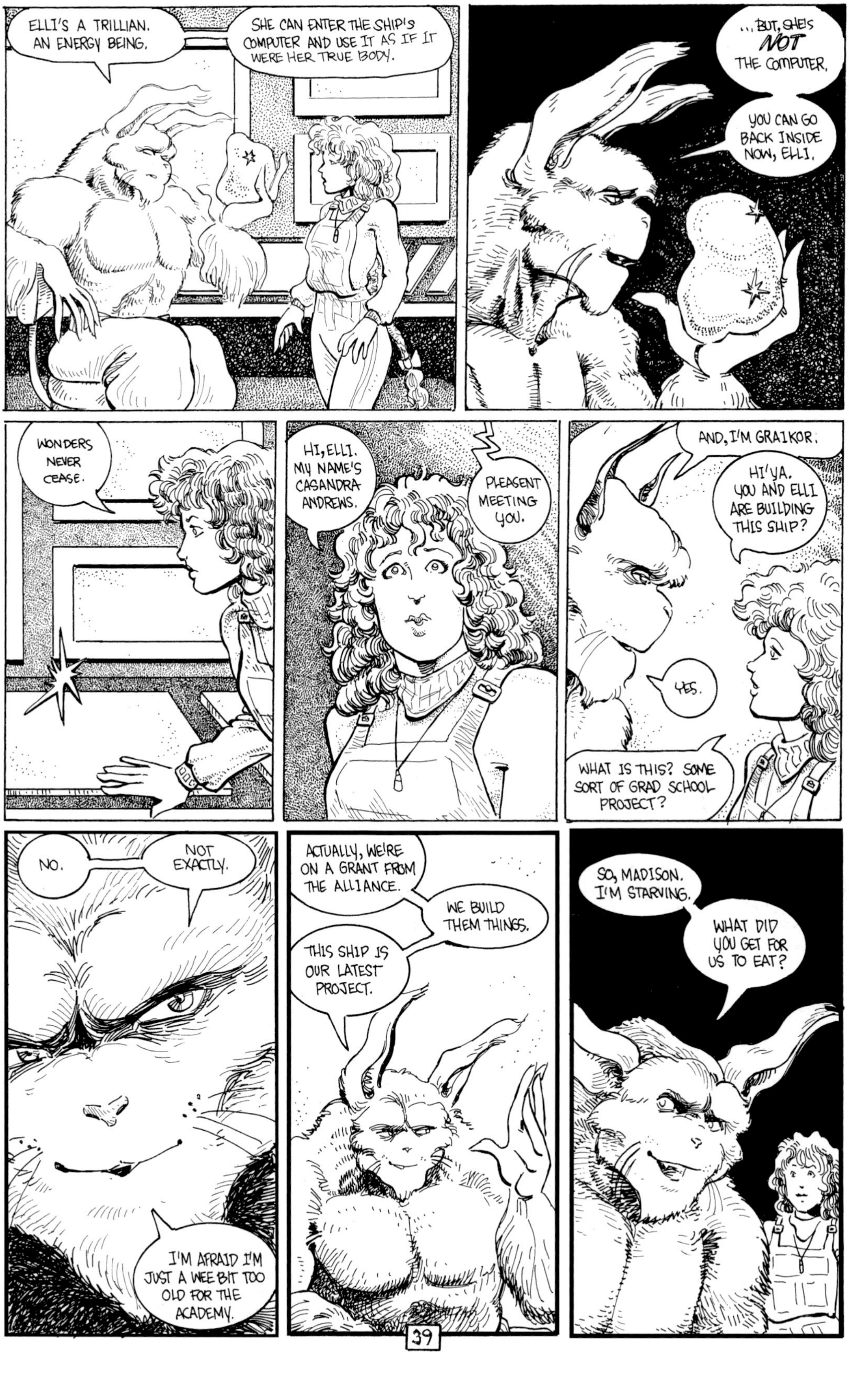
ELLI'S A TRILLIAN. AN ENERGY BEING.
SHE CAN ENTER THE SHIP'S COMPUTER AND USE IT AS IF IT WERE HER TRUE BODY.
...BUT, SHE'S NOT THE COMPUTER.
YOU CAN GO BACK INSIDE NOW, ELLI.
WONDERS NEVER CEASE.
HI, ELLI. MY NAME'S CASANDRA ANDREWS.
PLEASENT MEETING YOU.
AND, I'M GRAIKOR.
HI'YA. YOU AND ELLI ARE BUILDING THIS SHIP?
YES.
WHAT IS THIS? SOME SORT OF GRAD SCHOOL PROJECT?
NO.
NOT EXACTLY.
I'M AFRAID I'M JUST A WEE BIT TOO OLD FOR THE ACADEMY.
ACTUALLY, WE'RE ON A GRANT FROM THE ALLIANCE.
WE BUILD THEM THINGS.
THIS SHIP IS OUR LATEST PROJECT.
SO, MADISON. I'M STARVING.
WHAT DID YOU GET FOR US TO EAT?

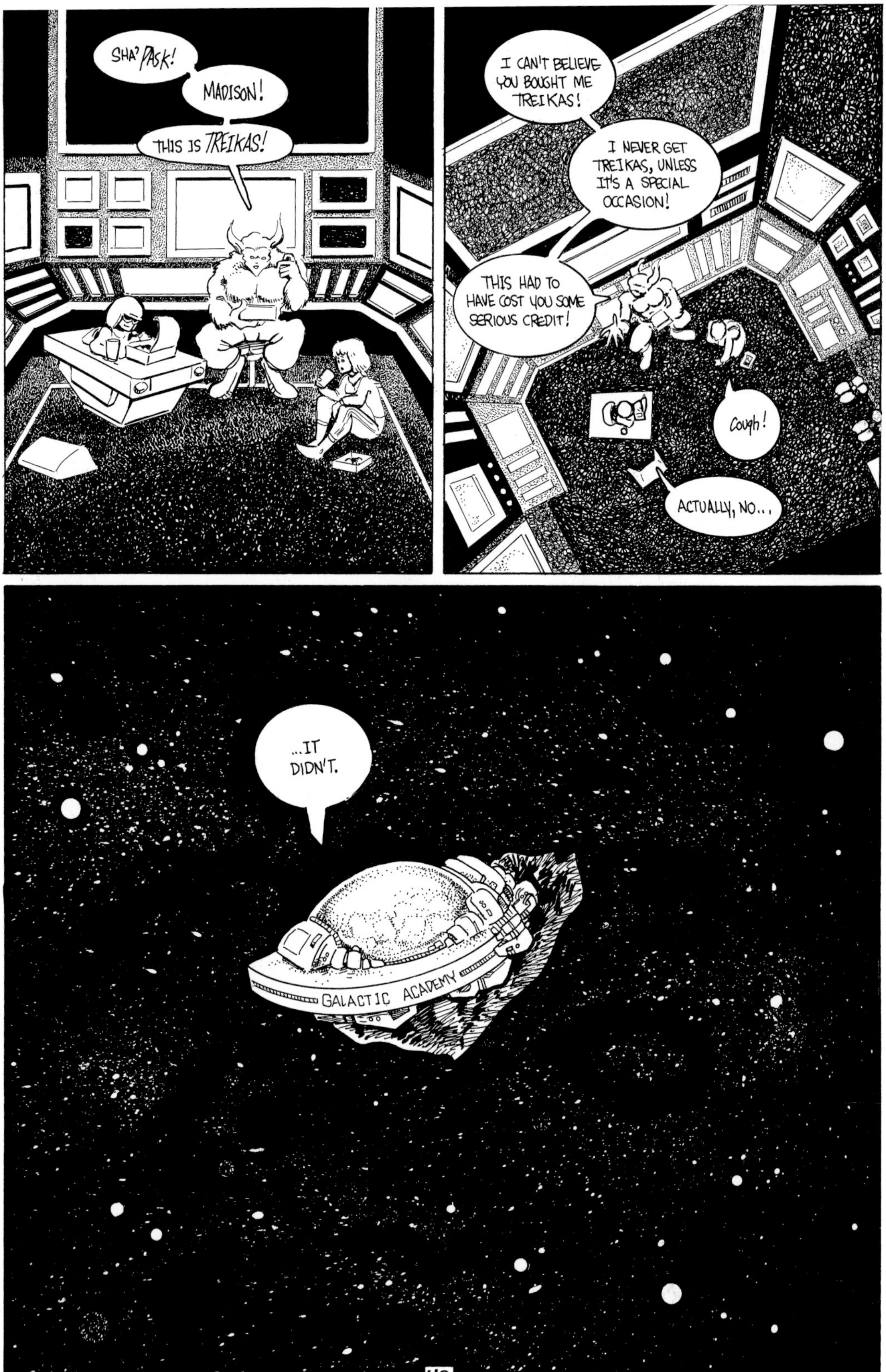
SHA'PASK!
MADISON!
THIS IS TREIKAS!
I CAN'T BELIEVE YOU BOUGHT ME TREIKAS!
I NEVER GET TREIKAS, UNLESS IT'S A SPECIAL OCCASION!
THIS HAD TO HAVE COST YOU SOME SERIOUS CREDIT!
Cough!
ACTUALLY, NO...
...IT DIDN'T.
GALACTIC ACADEMY

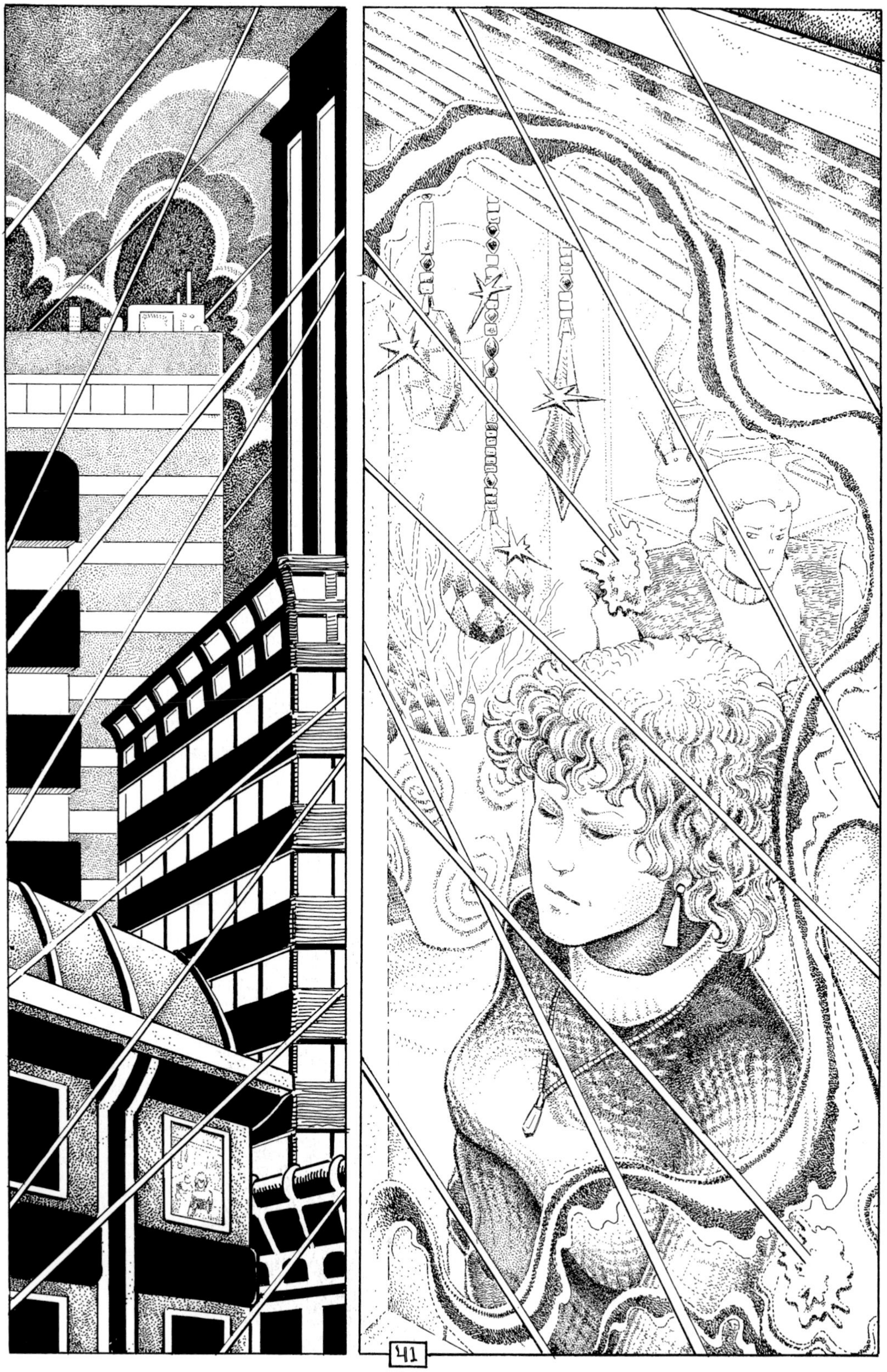

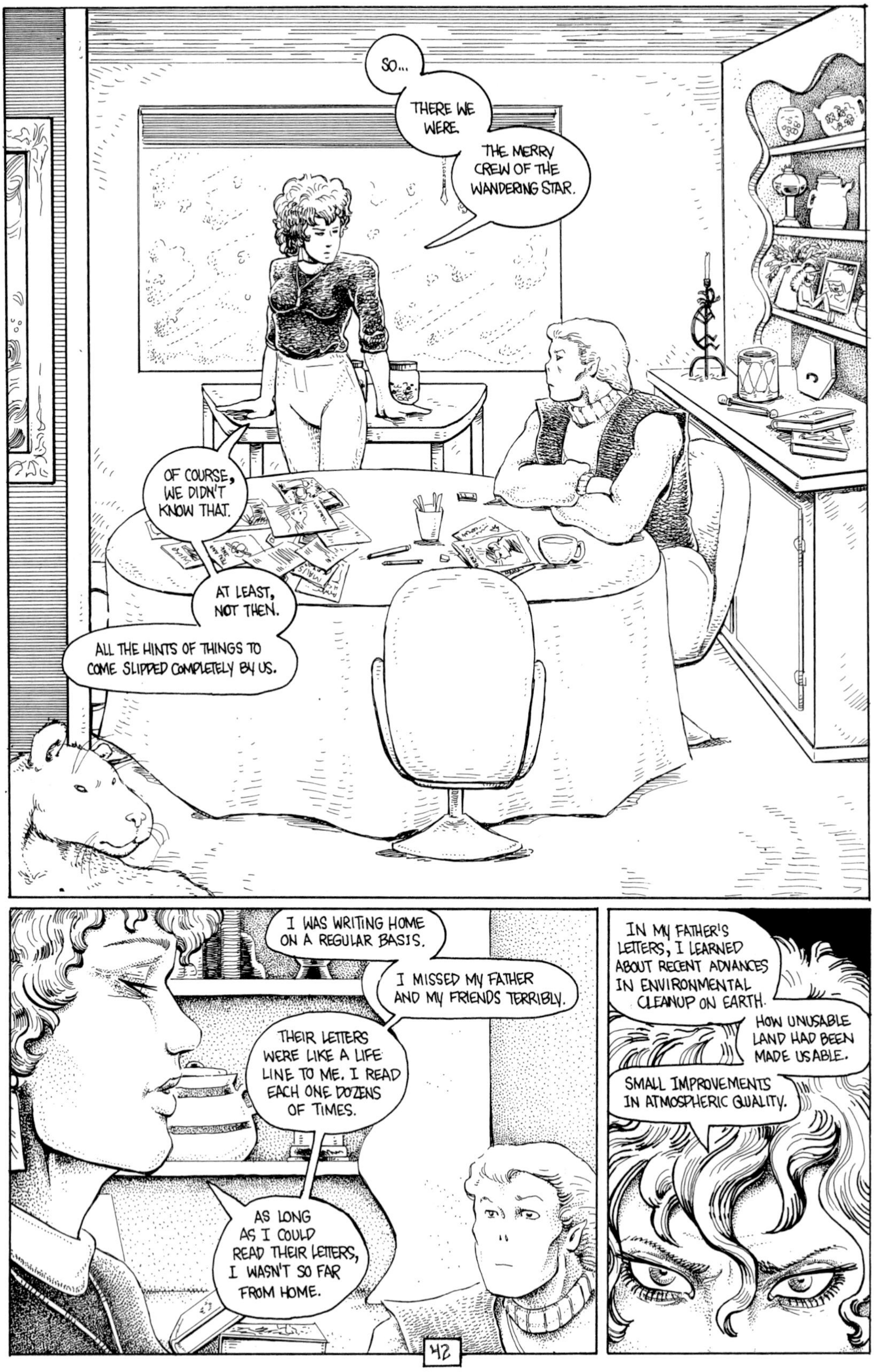
SO...
THERE WE WERE.
THE MERRY CREW OF THE WANDERING STAR.
OF COURSE, WE DIDN'T KNOW THAT.
AT LEAST, NOT THEN.
ALL THE HINTS OF THINGS TO COME SLIPPED COMPLETELY BY US.
I WAS WRITING HOME ON A REGULAR BASIS.
I MISSED MY FATHER AND MY FRIENDS TERRIBLY.
THEIR LETTERS WERE LIKE A LIFE LINE TO ME. I READ EACH ONE DOZENS OF TIMES.
AS LONG AS I COULD READ THEIR LETTERS, I WASN'T SO FAR FROM HOME.
IN MY FATHER'S LETTERS, I LEARNED ABOUT RECENT ADVANCES IN ENVIRONMENTAL CLEANUP ON EARTH.
HOW UNUSABLE LAND HAD BEEN MADE USABLE.
SMALL IMPROVEMENTS IN ATMOSPHERIC QUALITY.

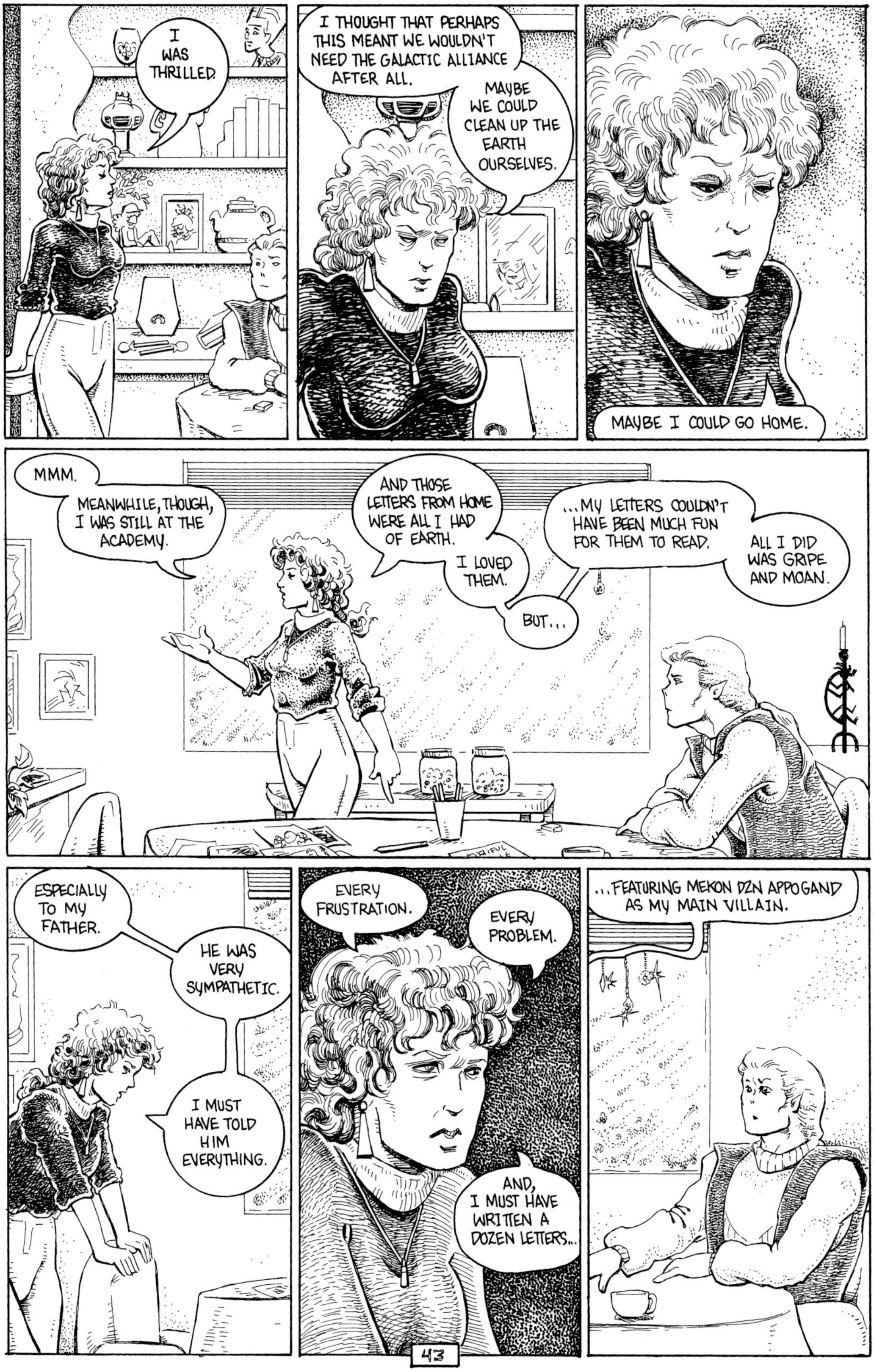
I WAS THRILLED.
I THOUGHT THAT PERHAPS THIS MEANT WE WOULDN'T NEED THE GALACTIC ALLIANCE AFTER ALL.
MAYBE WE COULD CLEAN UP THE EARTH OURSELVES.
MAYBE I COULD GO HOME.
MMM.
MEANWHILE, THOUGH, I WAS STILL AT THE ACADEMY.
AND THOSE LETTERS FROM HOME WERE ALL I HAD OF EARTH.
I LOVED THEM.
BUT...
...MY LETTERS COULDN'T HAVE BEEN MUCH FUN FOR THEM TO READ.
ALL I DID WAS GRIPE AND MOAN.
ESPECIALLY TO MY FATHER.
HE WAS VERY SYMPATHETIC.
I MUST HAVE TOLD HIM EVERYTHING.
EVERY FRUSTRATION.
EVERY PROBLEM.
AND, I MUST HAVE WRITTEN A DOZEN LETTERS...
...FEATURING MEKON DZN APPOGAND AS MY MAIN VILLAIN.

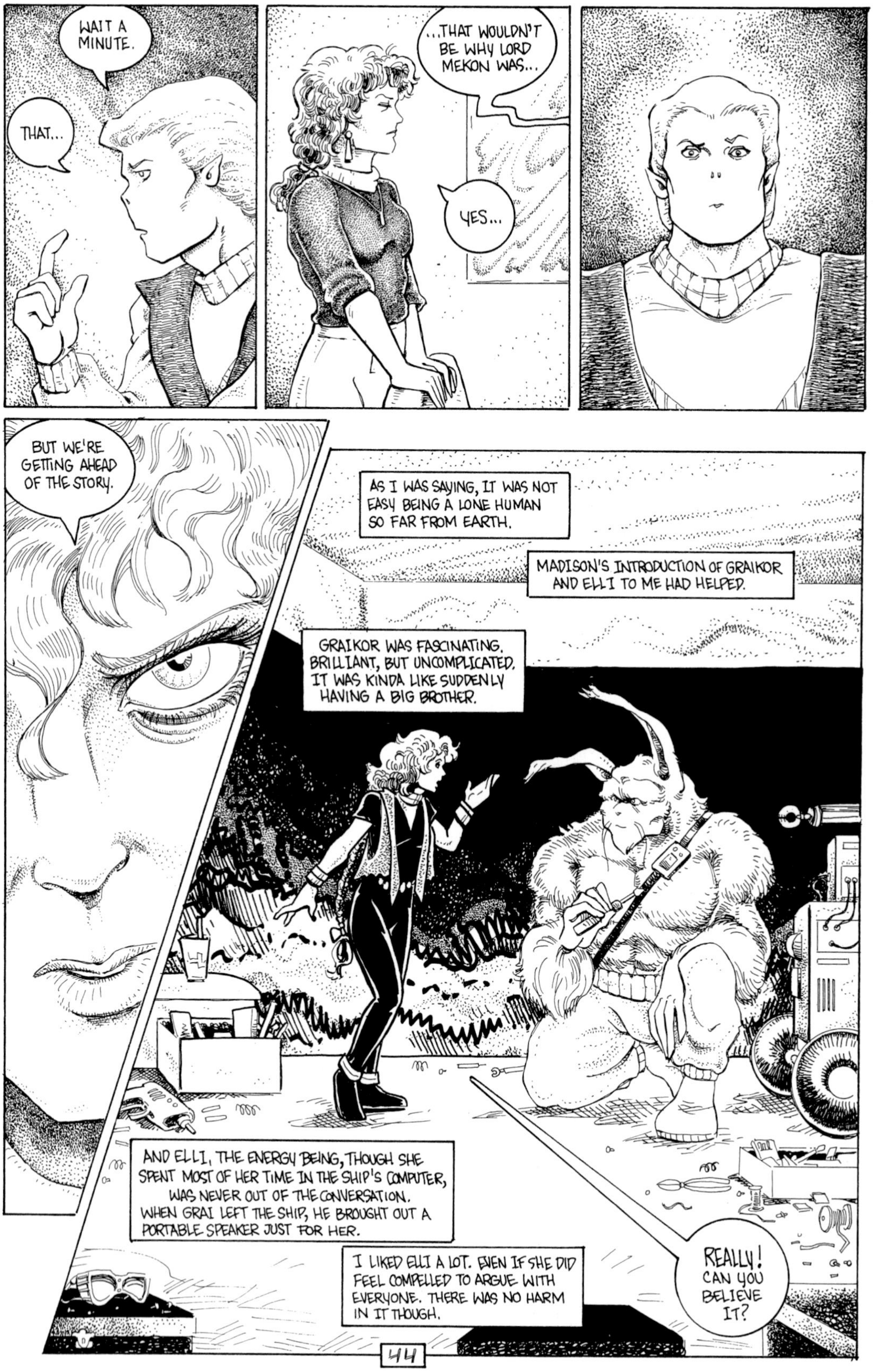
WAIT A MINUTE.
THAT...
...THAT WOULDN'T BE WHY LORD MEKON WAS...
YES...
BUT WE'RE GETTING AHEAD OF THE STORY.
AS I WAS SAYING, IT WAS NOT EASY BEING A LONE HUMAN SO FAR FROM EARTH.
MADISON'S INTRODUCTION OF GRAIKOR AND ELLI TO ME HAD HELPED.
GRAIKOR WAS FASCINATING. BRILLIANT, BUT UNCOMPLICATED. IT WAS KINDA LIKE SUDDENLY HAVING A BIG BROTHER.
AND ELLI, THE ENERGY BEING, THOUGH SHE SPENT MOST OF HER TIME IN THE SHIP'S COMPUTER, WAS NEVER OUT OF THE CONVERSATION. WHEN GRAI LEFT THE SHIP, HE BROUGHT OUT A PORTABLE SPEAKER JUST FOR HER.
I LIKED ELLI A LOT. EVEN IF SHE DID FEEL COMPELLED TO ARGUE WITH EVERYONE. THERE WAS NO HARM IN IT THOUGH.
REALLY! CAN YOU BELIEVE IT?

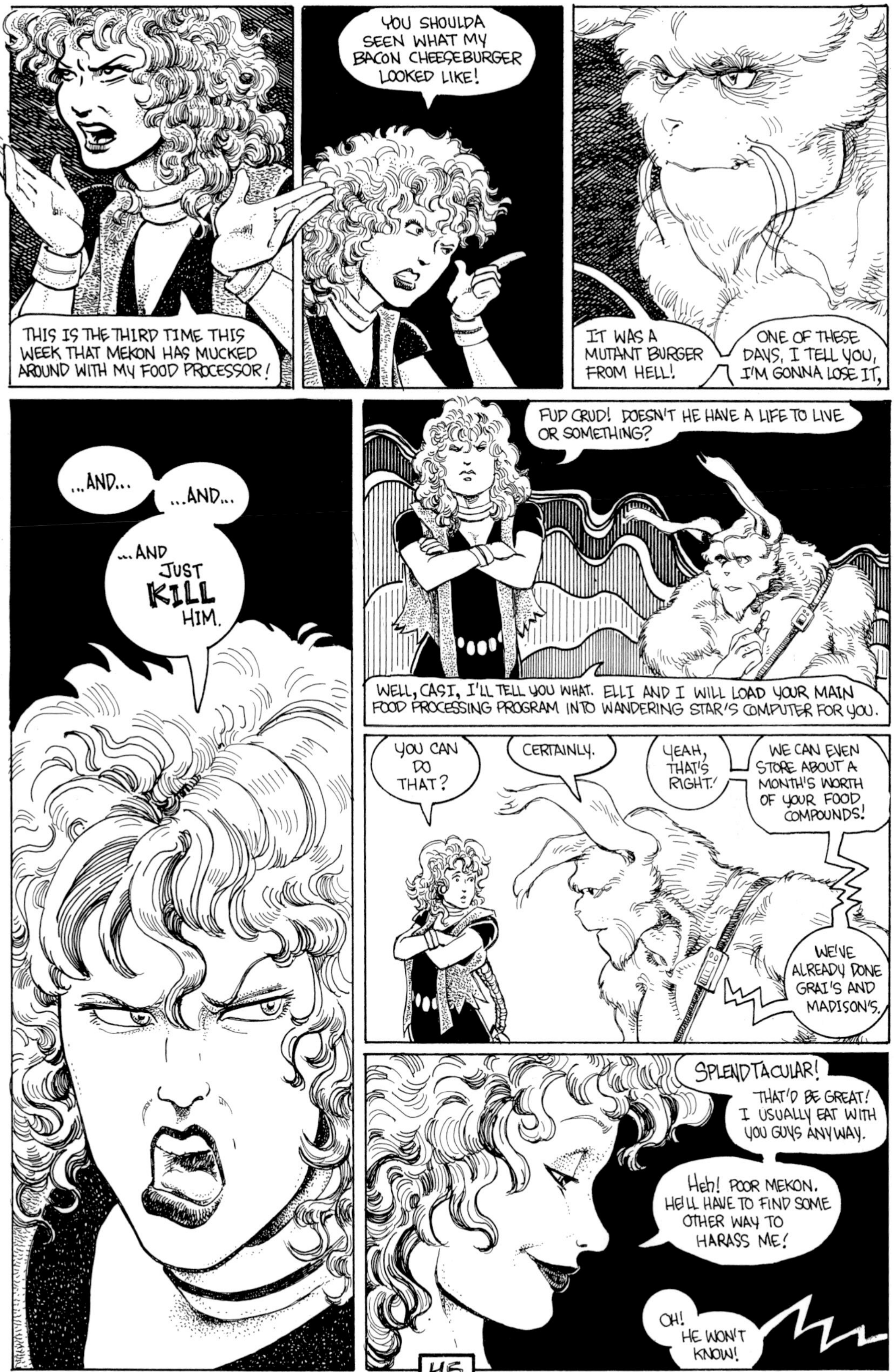
THIS IS THE THIRD TIME THIS WEEK THAT MEKON HAS MUCKED AROUND WITH MY FOOD PROCESSOR!
YOU SHOULDA SEEN WHAT MY BACON CHEESEBURGER LOOKED LIKE!
IT WAS A MUTANT BURGER FROM HELL!
ONE OF THESE DAYS, I TELL YOU, I'M GONNA LOSE IT,
...AND...
...AND...
...AND JUST KILL HIM.
FUD CRUD! DOESN'T HE HAVE A LIFE TO LIVE OR SOMETHING?
WELL, CASI, I'LL TELL YOU WHAT. ELLI AND I WILL LOAD YOUR MAIN FOOD PROCESSING PROGRAM INTO WANDERING STAR'S COMPUTER FOR YOU.
YOU CAN DO THAT?
CERTAINLY.
YEAH, THAT'S RIGHT!
WE CAN EVEN STORE ABOUT A MONTH'S WORTH OF YOUR FOOD COMPOUNDS!
WE'VE ALREADY DONE GRAI'S AND MADISON'S.
SPLENDTACULAR!
THAT'D BE GREAT! I USUALLY EAT WITH YOU GUYS ANYWAY.
Heh! POOR MEKON. HE'LL HAVE TO FIND SOME OTHER WAY TO HARASS ME!
OH! HE WON'T KNOW!

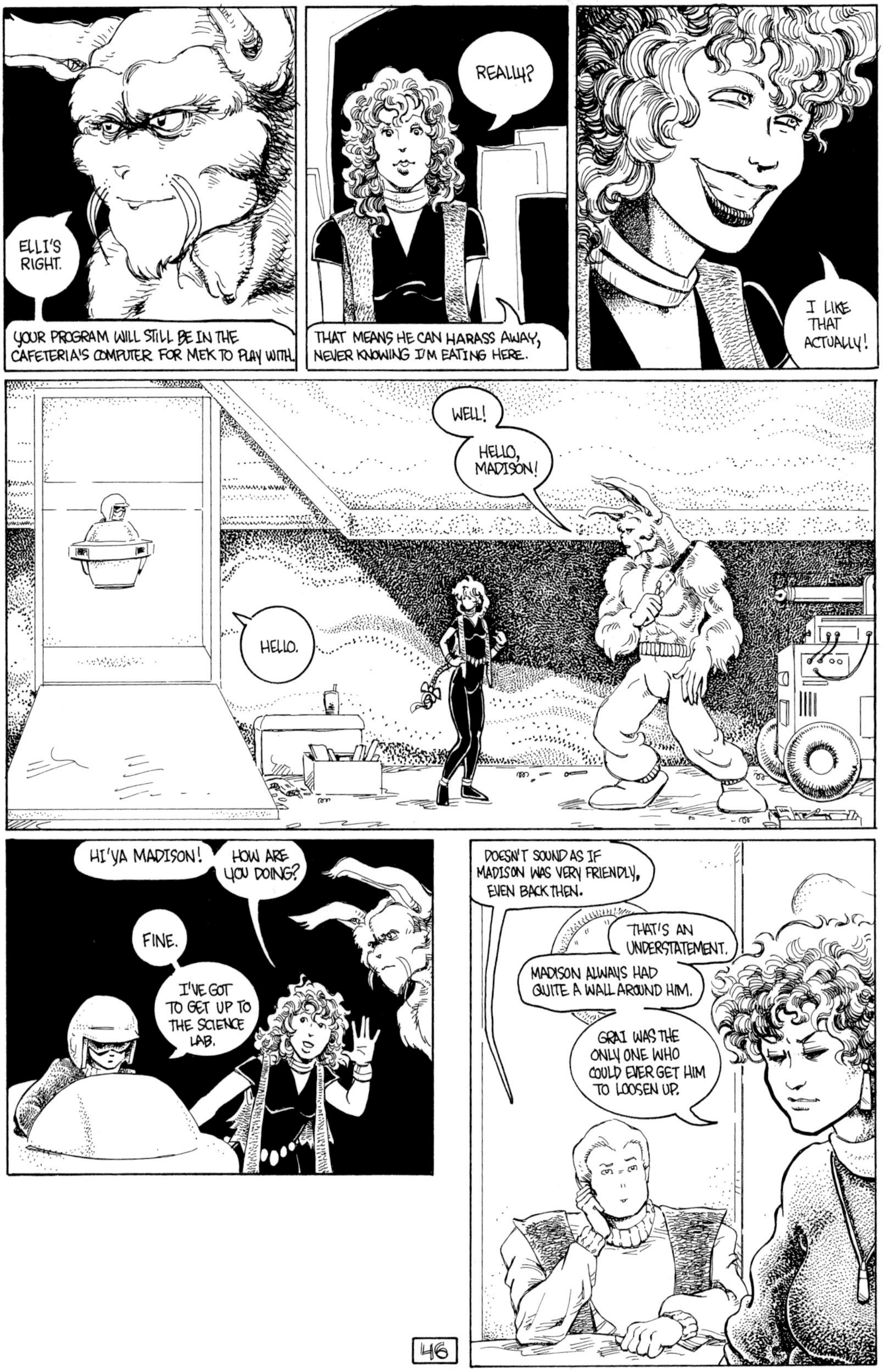
ELLI'S RIGHT.
YOUR PROGRAM WILL STILL BE IN THE CAFETERIA'S COMPUTER FOR MEK TO PLAY WITH.
REALLY?
THAT MEANS HE CAN HARASS AWAY, NEVER KNOWING I'M EATING HERE.
I LIKE THAT ACTUALLY!
WELL!
HELLO, MADISON!
HELLO.
HI'YA MADISON!
HOW ARE YOU DOING?
FINE.
I'VE GOT TO GET UP TO THE SCIENCE LAB.
DOESN'T SOUND AS IF MADISON WAS VERY FRIENDLY, EVEN BACK THEN.
THAT'S AN UNDERSTATEMENT.
MADISON ALWAYS HAD QUITE A WALL AROUND HIM.
GRAI WAS THE ONLY ONE WHO COULD EVER GET HIM TO LOOSEN UP.

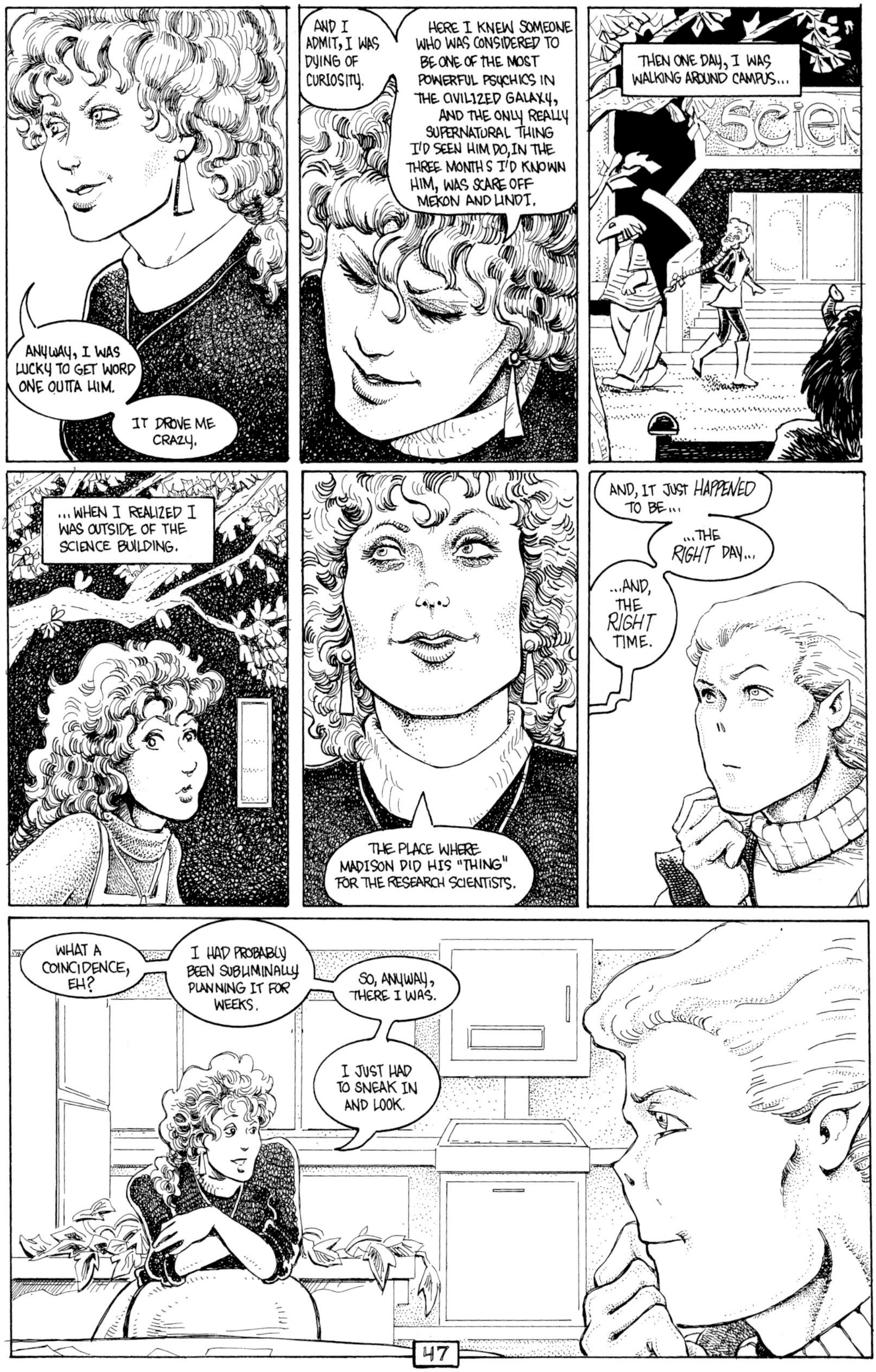
ANYWAY, I WAS LUCKY TO GET WORD ONE OUTTA HIM.
IT DROVE ME CRAZY.
AND I ADMIT, I WAS DYING OF CURIOSITY.
HERE I KNEW SOMEONE WHO WAS CONSIDERED TO BE ONE OF THE MOST POWERFUL PSYCHICS IN THE CIVILIZED GALAXY, AND THE ONLY REALLY SUPERNATURAL THING I'D SEEN HIM DO, IN THE THREE MONTHS I'D KNOWN HIM, WAS SCARE OFF MEKON AND LINDT.
THEN ONE DAY, I WAS WALKING AROUND CAMPUS...
...WHEN I REALIZED I WAS OUTSIDE OF THE SCIENCE BUILDING.
THE PLACE WHERE MADISON DID HIS "THING" FOR THE RESEARCH SCIENTISTS.
AND, IT JUST HAPPENED TO BE...
...THE RIGHT DAY...
...AND, THE RIGHT TIME.
WHAT A COINCIDENCE, EH?
I HAD PROBABLY BEEN SUBLIMINALLY PLANNING IT FOR WEEKS.
SO, ANYWAY, THERE I WAS.
I JUST HAD TO SNEAK IN AND LOOK.

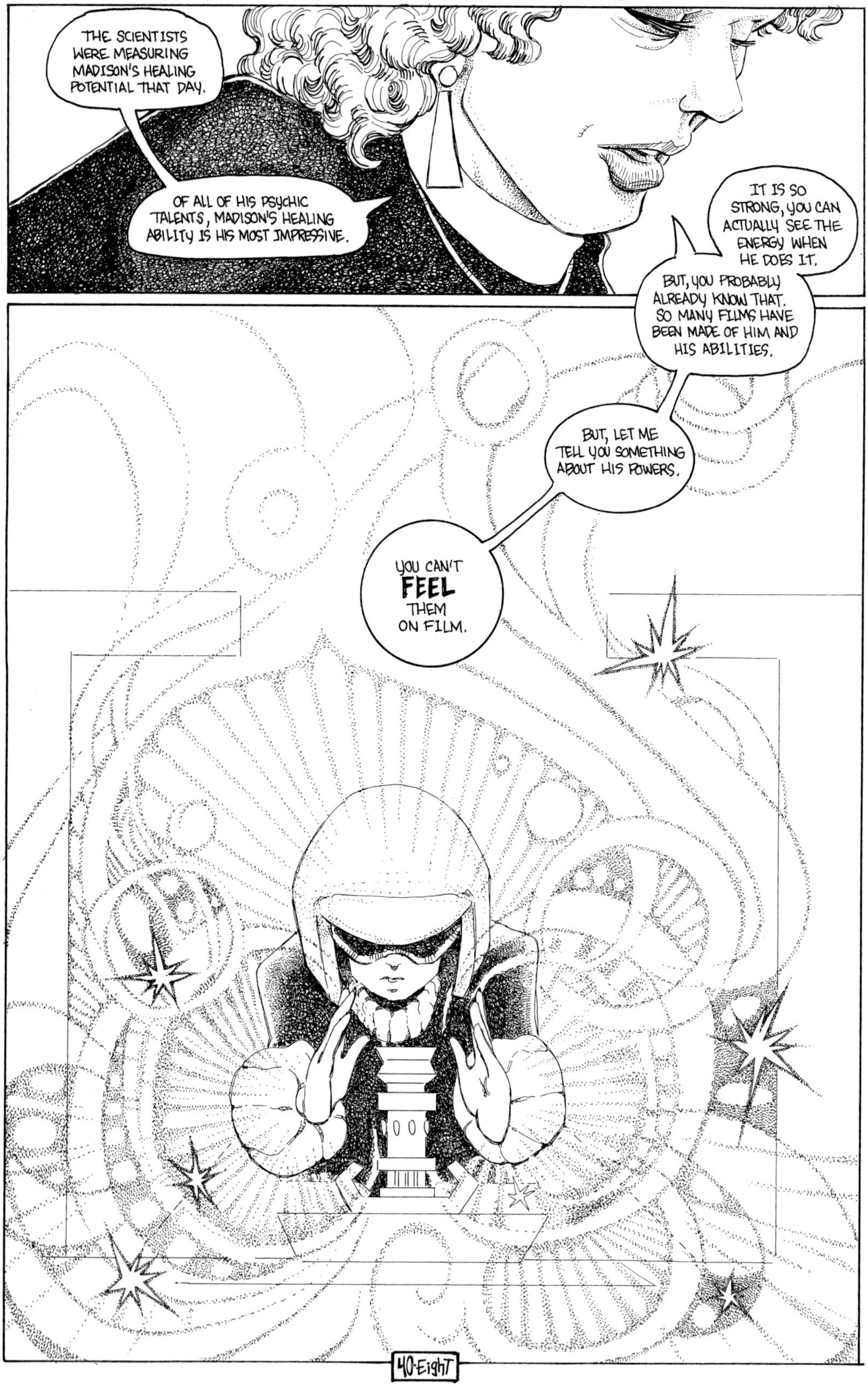
THE SCIENTISTS WERE MEASURING MADISON'S HEALING POTENTIAL THAT DAY.
OF ALL OF HIS PSYCHIC TALENTS, MADISON'S HEALING ABILITY IS HIS MOST IMPRESSIVE.
IT IS SO STRONG, YOU CAN ACTUALLY SEE THE ENERGY WHEN HE DOES IT.
BUT, YOU PROBABLY ALREADY KNOW THAT. SO MANY FILMS HAVE BEEN MADE OF HIM AND HIS ABILITIES.
BUT, LET ME TELL YOU SOMETHING ABOUT HIS POWERS.
YOU CAN'T **FEEL** THEM ON FILM.

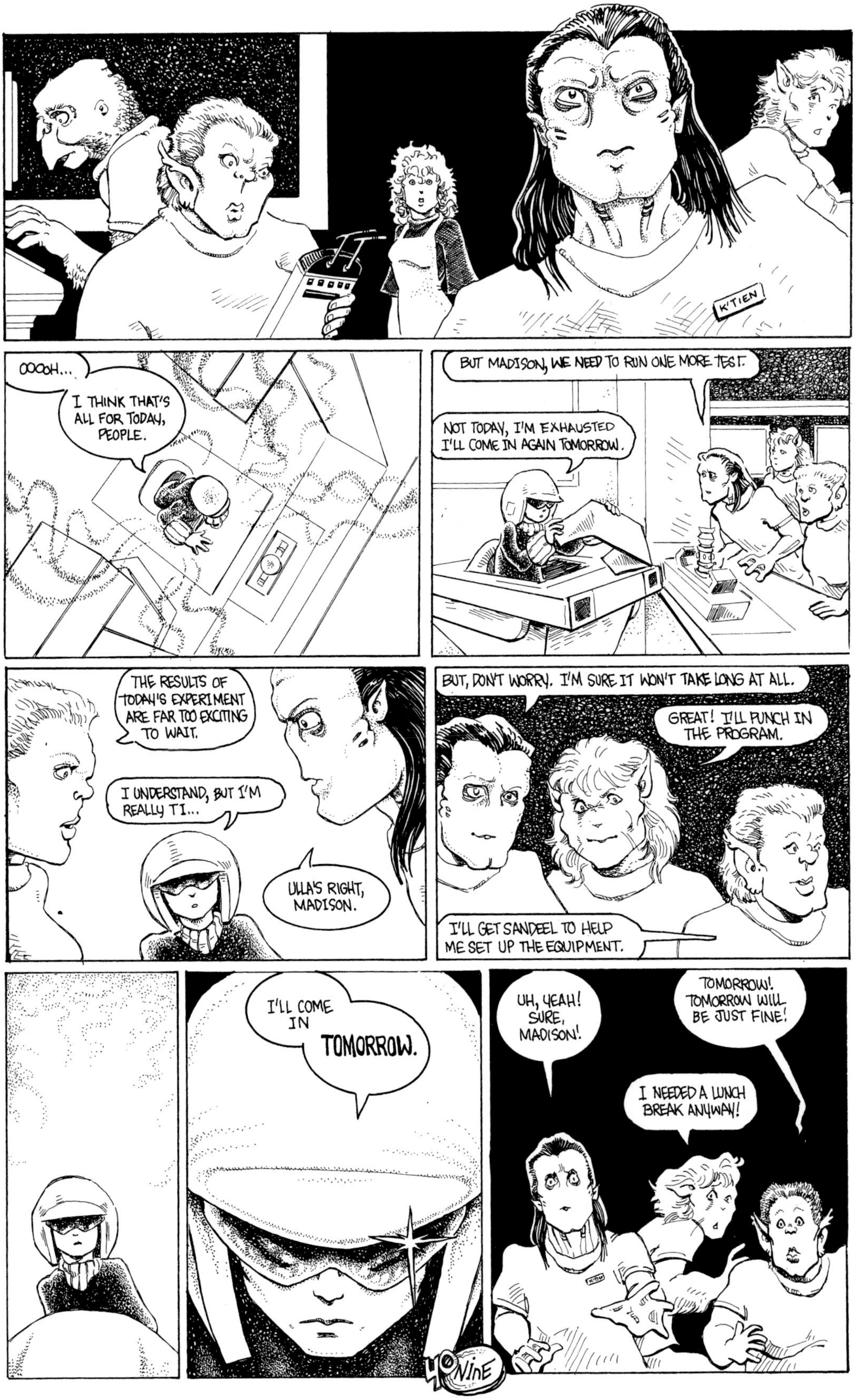
K'TIEN
OOOOH...
I THINK THAT'S ALL FOR TODAY, PEOPLE.
BUT MADISON, WE NEED TO RUN ONE MORE TEST.
NOT TODAY, I'M EXHAUSTED I'LL COME IN AGAIN TOMORROW.
THE RESULTS OF TODAY'S EXPERIMENT ARE FAR TOO EXCITING TO WAIT.
I UNDERSTAND, BUT I'M REALLY TI...
ULLA'S RIGHT, MADISON.
BUT, DON'T WORRY. I'M SURE IT WON'T TAKE LONG AT ALL.
GREAT! I'LL PUNCH IN THE PROGRAM.
I'LL GET SANDEEL TO HELP ME SET UP THE EQUIPMENT.
I'LL COME IN TOMORROW.
UH, YEAH! SURE, MADISON!
TOMORROW! TOMORROW WILL BE JUST FINE!
I NEEDED A LUNCH BREAK ANYWAY!
40 NINE

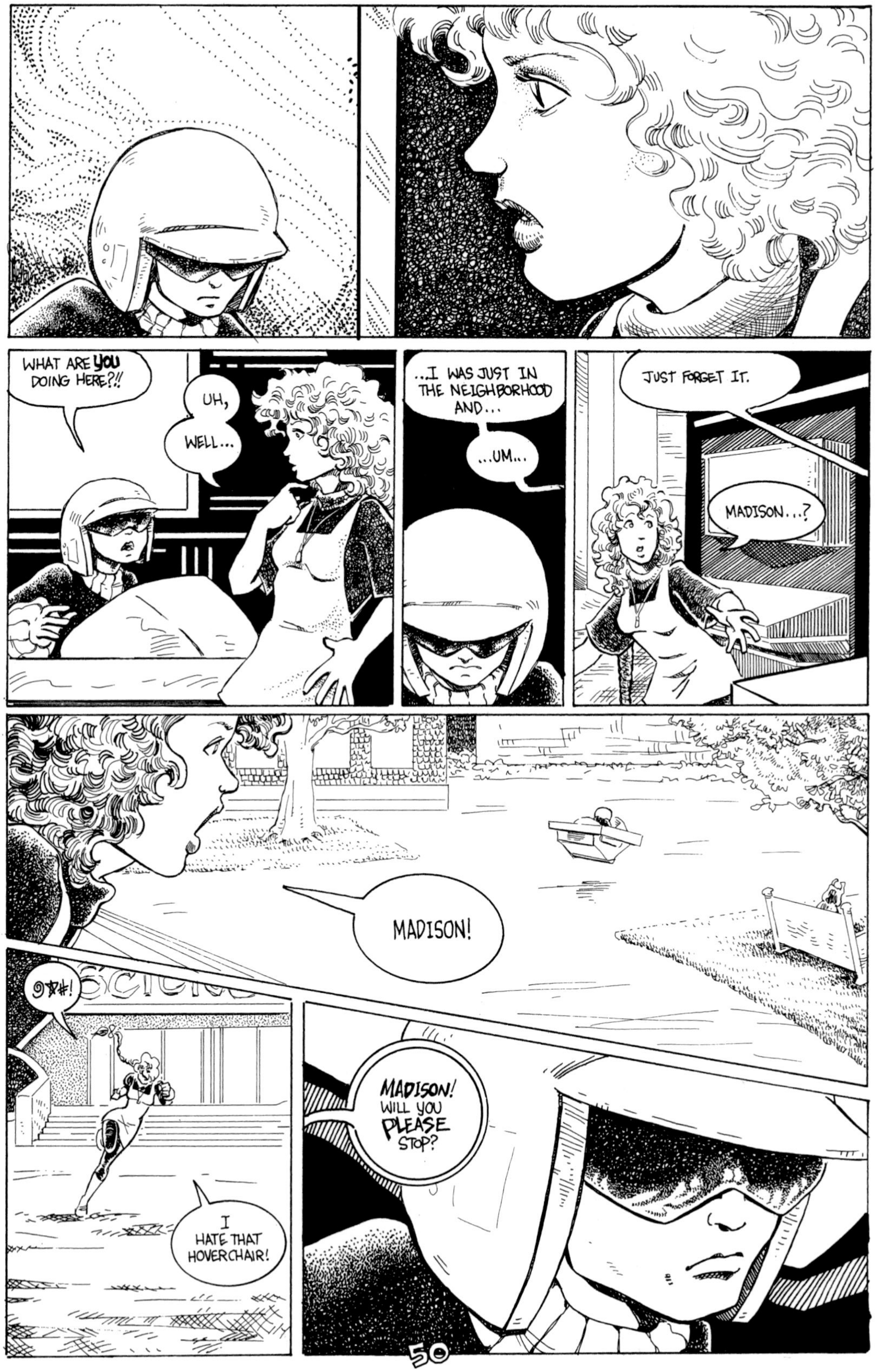
WHAT ARE YOU DOING HERE?!!
UH,
WELL...
...I WAS JUST IN THE NEIGHBORHOOD AND...
...UM...
JUST FORGET IT.
MADISON...?
MADISON!
I HATE THAT HOVERCHAIR!
MADISON! WILL YOU PLEASE STOP?

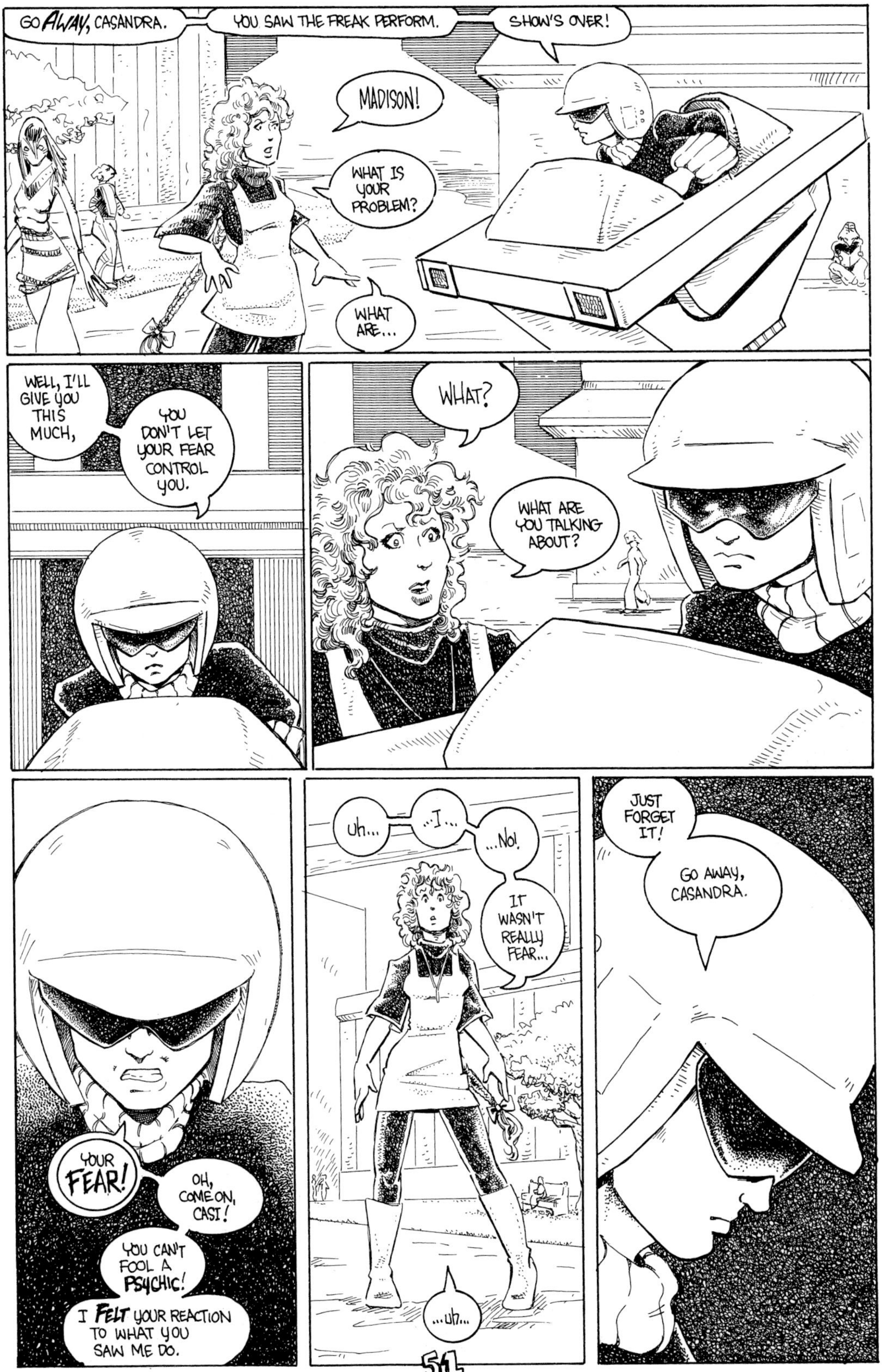
GO AWAY, CASANDRA.
YOU SAW THE FREAK PERFORM.
SHOW'S OVER!
MADISON!
WHAT IS YOUR PROBLEM?
WHAT ARE...
WELL, I'LL GIVE YOU THIS MUCH,
YOU DON'T LET YOUR FEAR CONTROL YOU.
WHAT?
WHAT ARE YOU TALKING ABOUT?
YOUR FEAR!
OH, COME ON, CASI!
YOU CAN'T FOOL A PSYCHIC!
I FELT YOUR REACTION TO WHAT YOU SAW ME DO.
uh...
...I...
...No!
IT WASN'T REALLY FEAR...
...uh...
JUST FORGET IT!
GO AWAY, CASANDRA.

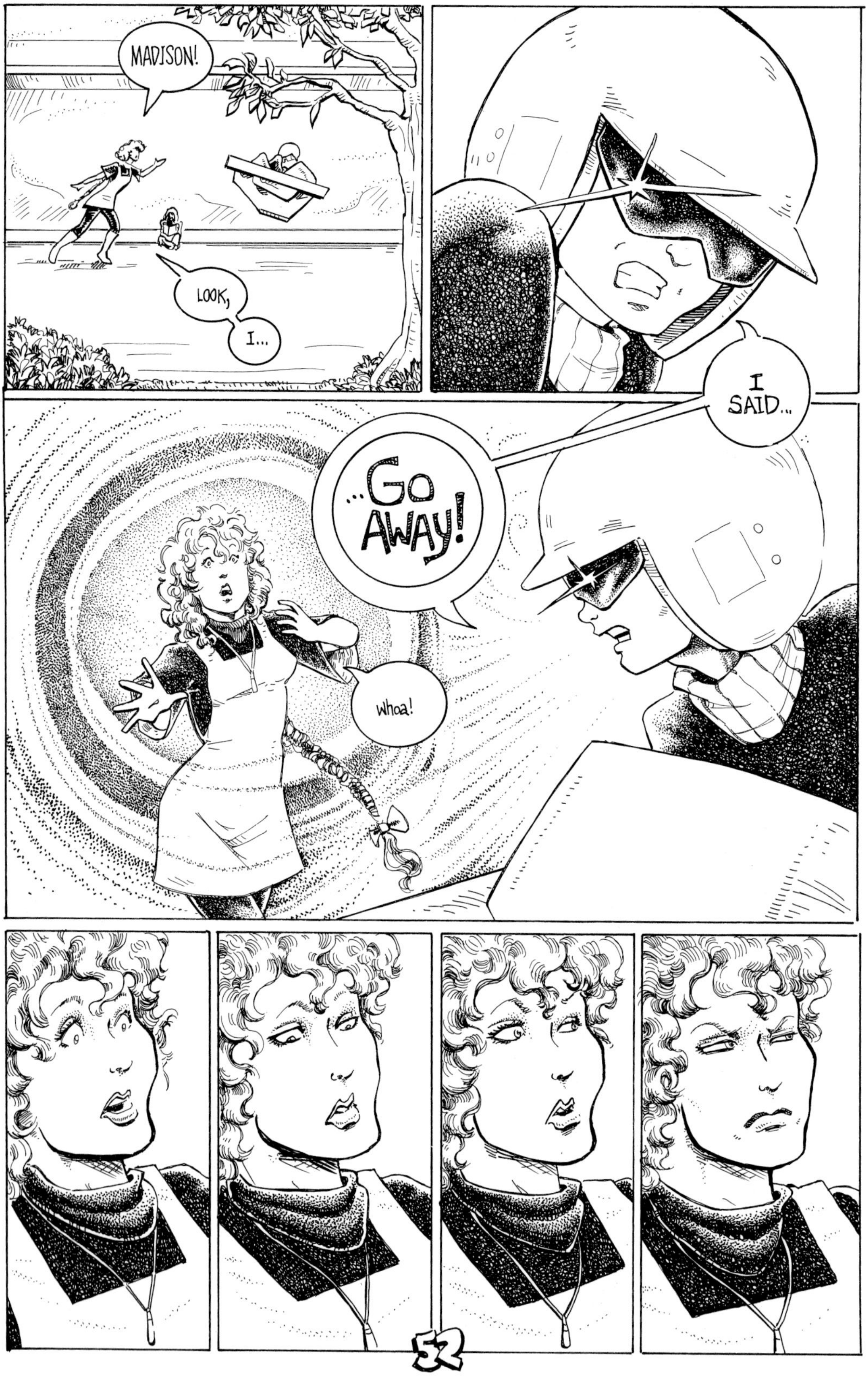
MADISON!
LOOK,
I...
I SAID...
...GO AWAY!
Whoa!

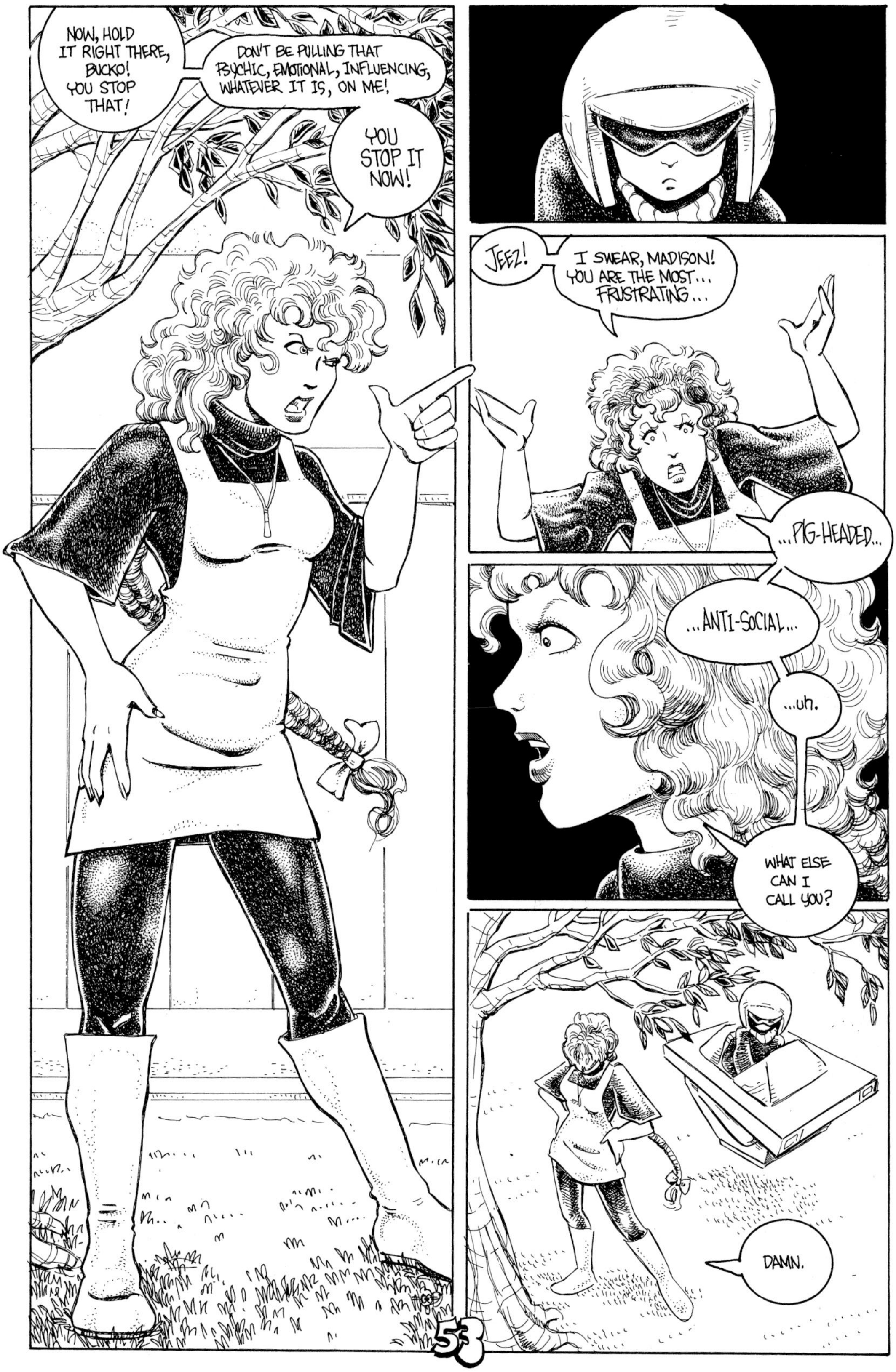
NOW, HOLD IT RIGHT THERE, BUCKO! YOU STOP THAT!
DON'T BE PULLING THAT PSYCHIC, EMOTIONAL, INFLUENCING, WHATEVER IT IS, ON ME!
YOU STOP IT NOW!
JEEZ!
I SWEAR, MADISON! YOU ARE THE MOST... FRUSTRATING...
...PIG-HEADED...
...ANTI-SOCIAL...
...uh.
WHAT ELSE CAN I CALL YOU?
DAMN.

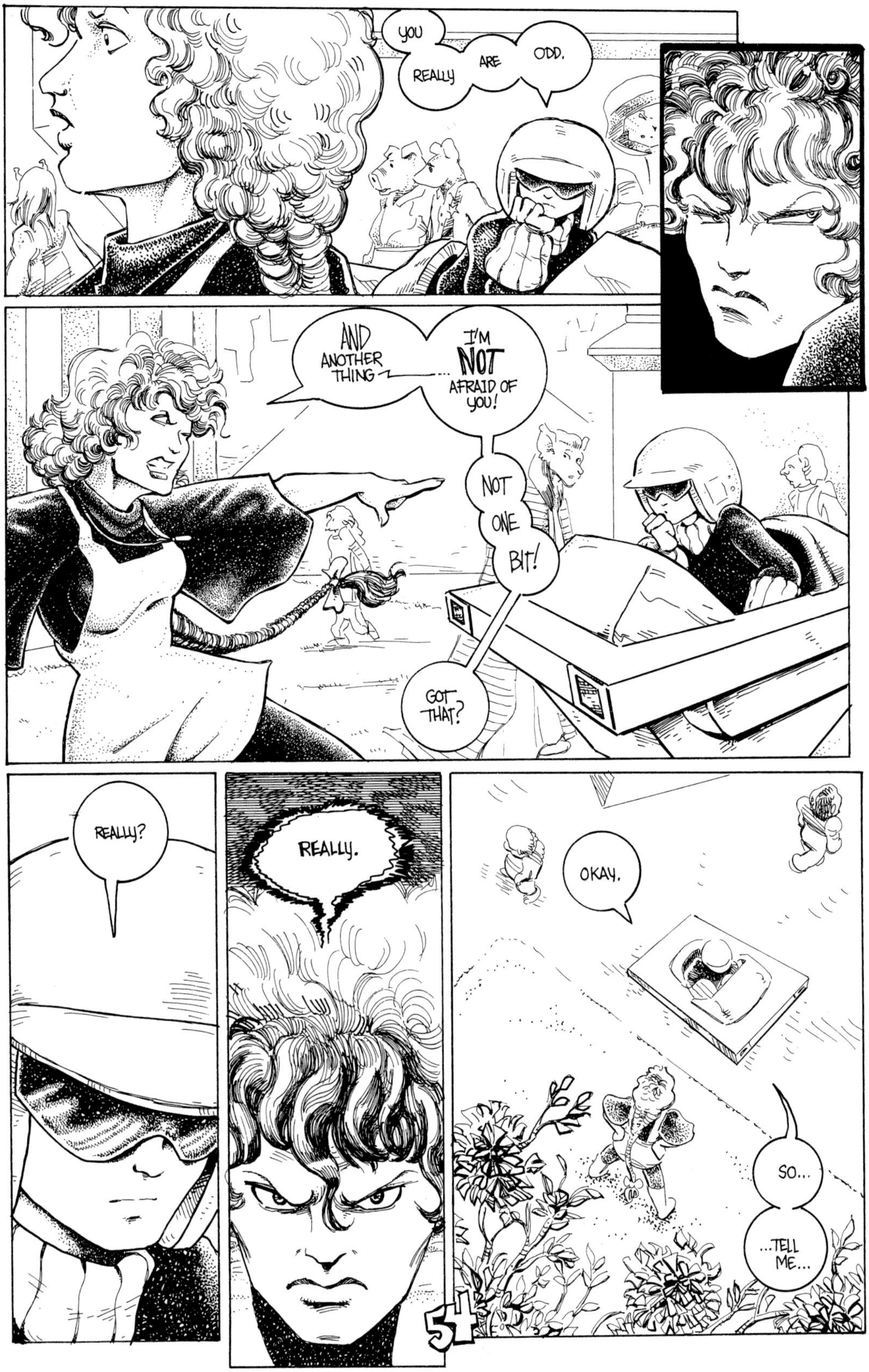
YOU REALLY ARE ODD.
AND ANOTHER THING— ...I'M NOT AFRAID OF YOU!
NOT ONE BIT!
GOT THAT?
REALLY?
REALLY.
OKAY.
SO...
...TELL ME...

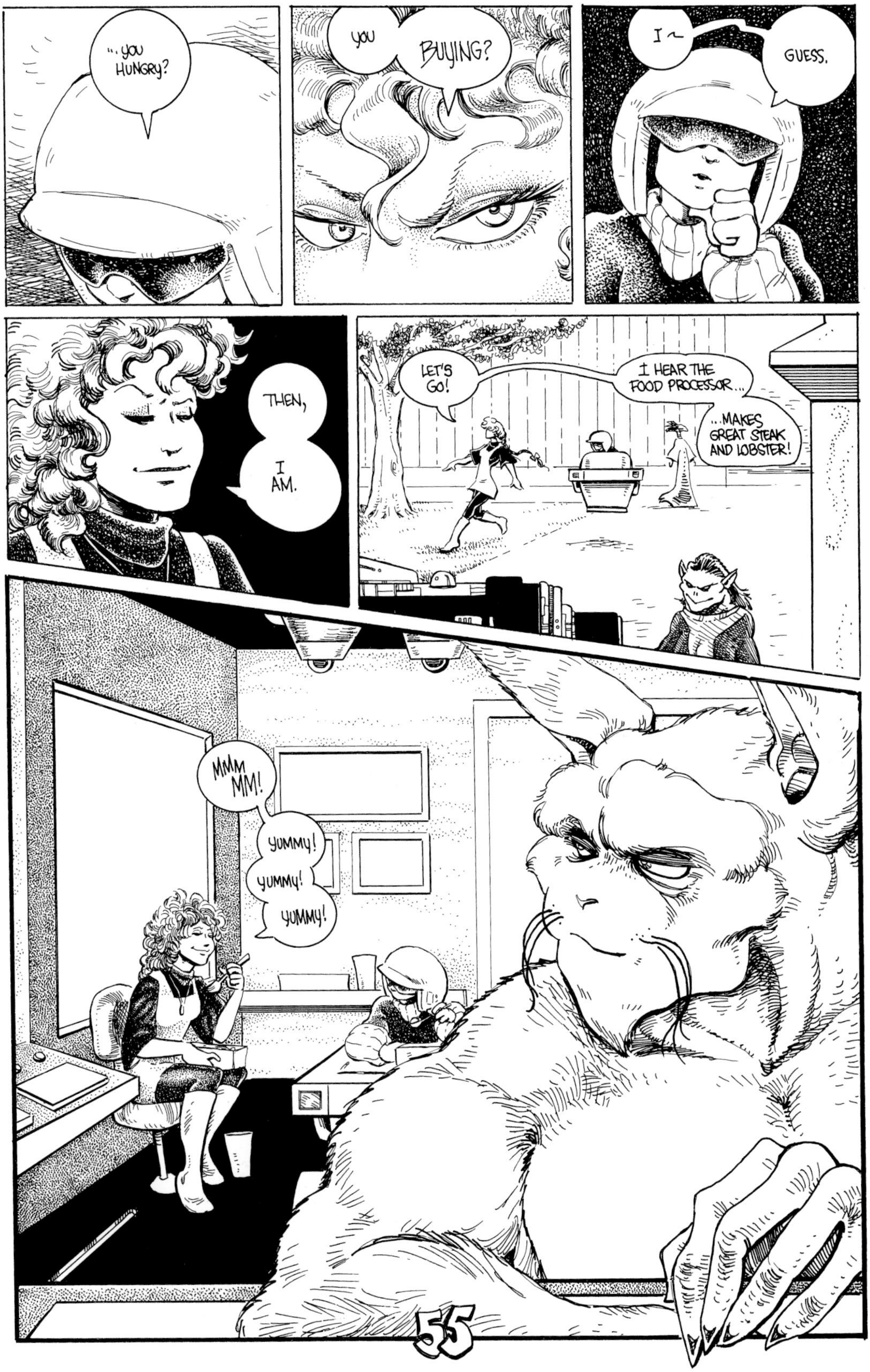
..you HUNGRY?
YOU
BUYING?
I ~
GUESS.
THEN,
I AM.
LET'S GO!
I HEAR THE FOOD PROCESSOR...
...MAKES GREAT STEAK AND LOBSTER!
MMM MM!
YUMMY!
YUMMY!
YUMMY!

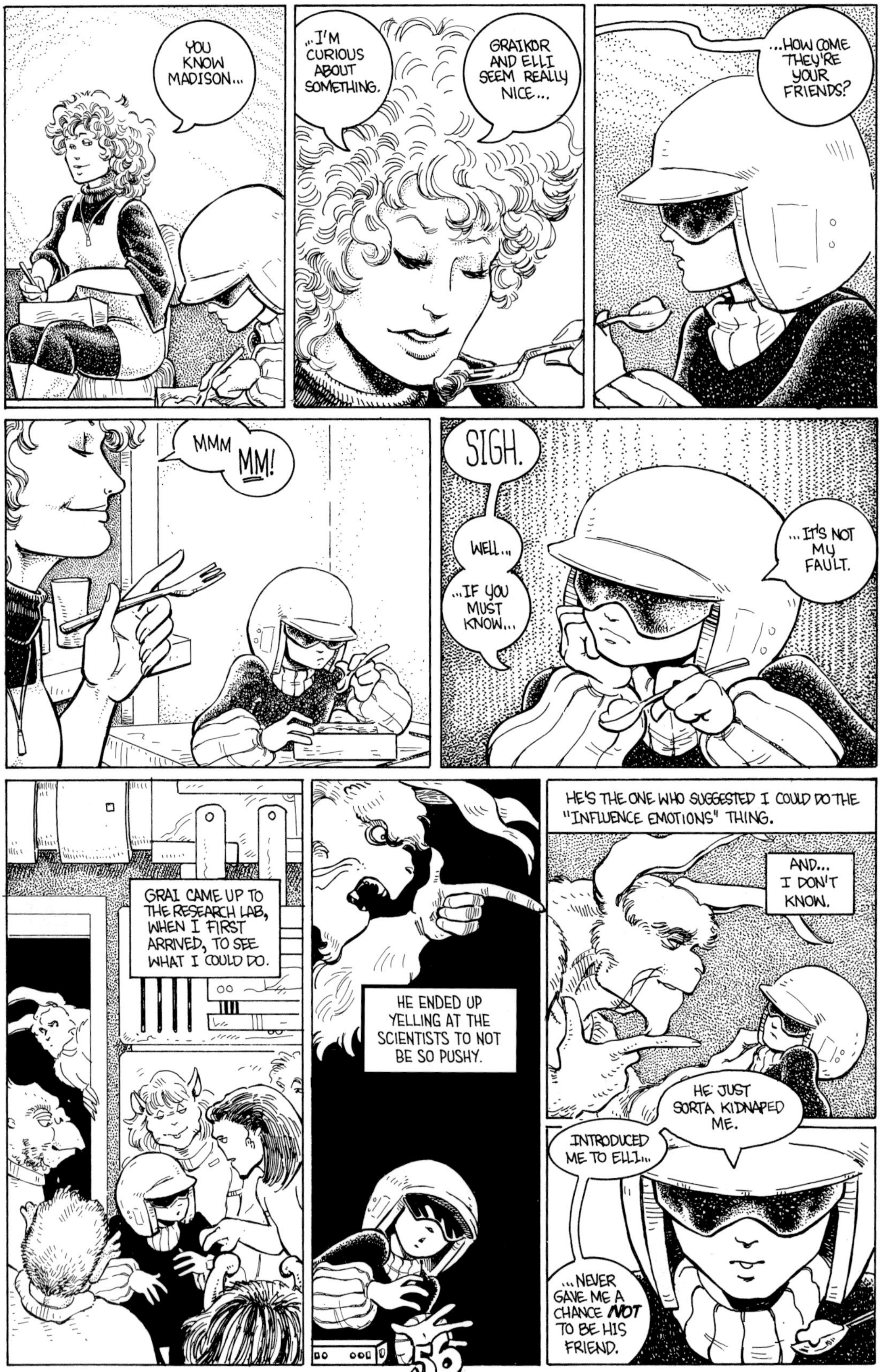
YOU KNOW MADISON...
...I'M CURIOUS ABOUT SOMETHING.
GRAIKOR AND ELLI SEEM REALLY NICE...
...HOW COME THEY'RE YOUR FRIENDS?
MMM MM!
SIGH.
WELL...
...IF YOU MUST KNOW...
...IT'S NOT MY FAULT.
GRAI CAME UP TO THE RESEARCH LAB, WHEN I FIRST ARRIVED, TO SEE WHAT I COULD DO.
HE ENDED UP YELLING AT THE SCIENTISTS TO NOT BE SO PUSHY.
HE'S THE ONE WHO SUGGESTED I COULD DO THE "INFLUENCE EMOTIONS" THING.
AND... I DON'T KNOW.
HE JUST SORTA KIDNAPED ME.
INTRODUCED ME TO ELLI...
...NEVER GAVE ME A CHANCE NOT TO BE HIS FRIEND.

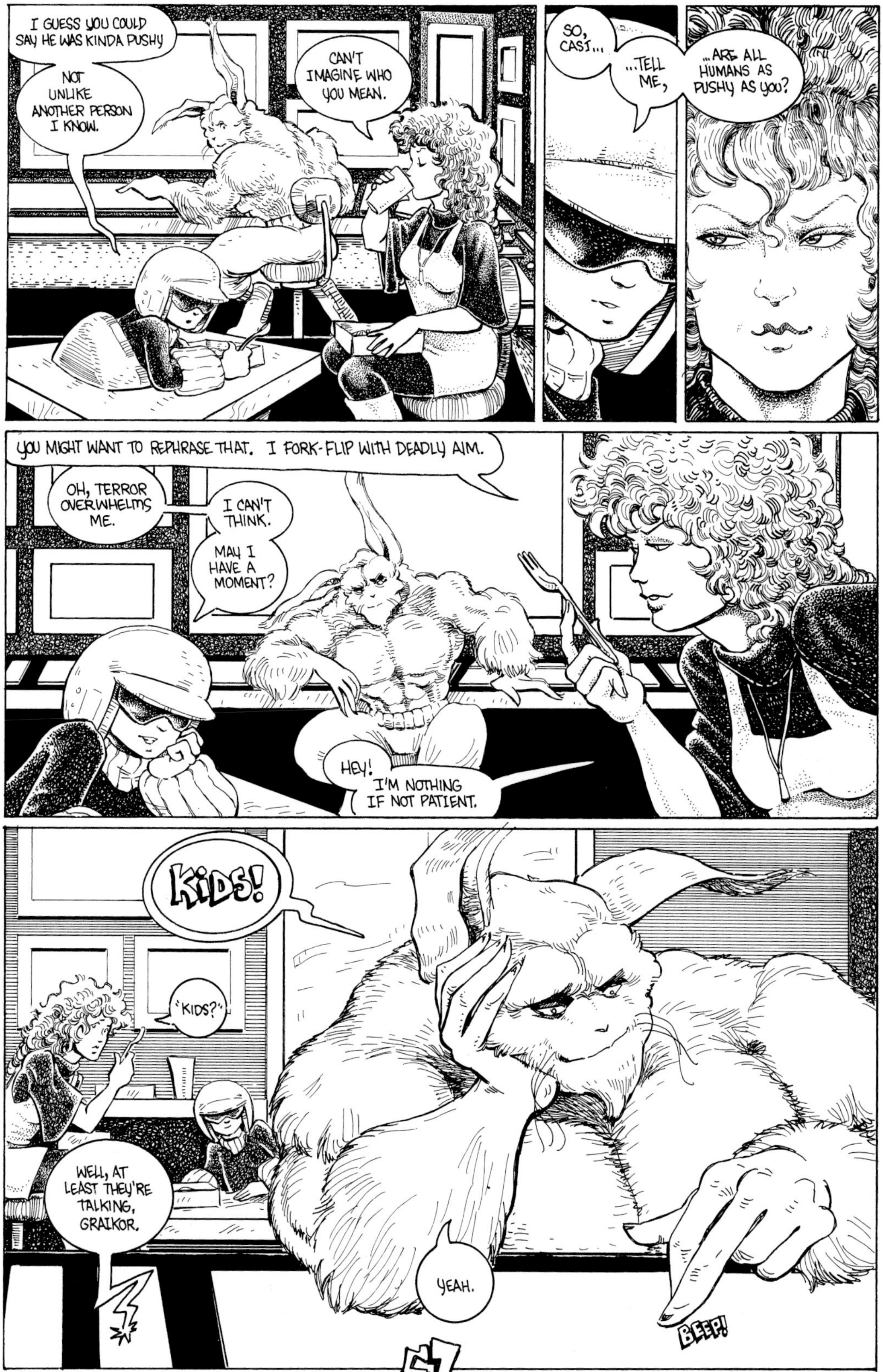
I GUESS YOU COULD SAY HE WAS KINDA PUSHY
NOT UNLIKE ANOTHER PERSON I KNOW.
CAN'T IMAGINE WHO YOU MEAN.
SO, CASI...
...TELL ME,
...ARE ALL HUMANS AS PUSHY AS YOU?
YOU MIGHT WANT TO REPHRASE THAT. I FORK-FLIP WITH DEADLY AIM.
OH, TERROR OVERWHELMS ME.
I CAN'T THINK.
MAY I HAVE A MOMENT?
HEY! I'M NOTHING IF NOT PATIENT.
KIDS!
"KIDS?"
WELL, AT LEAST THEY'RE TALKING, GRAIKOR.
YEAH.
BEEP!

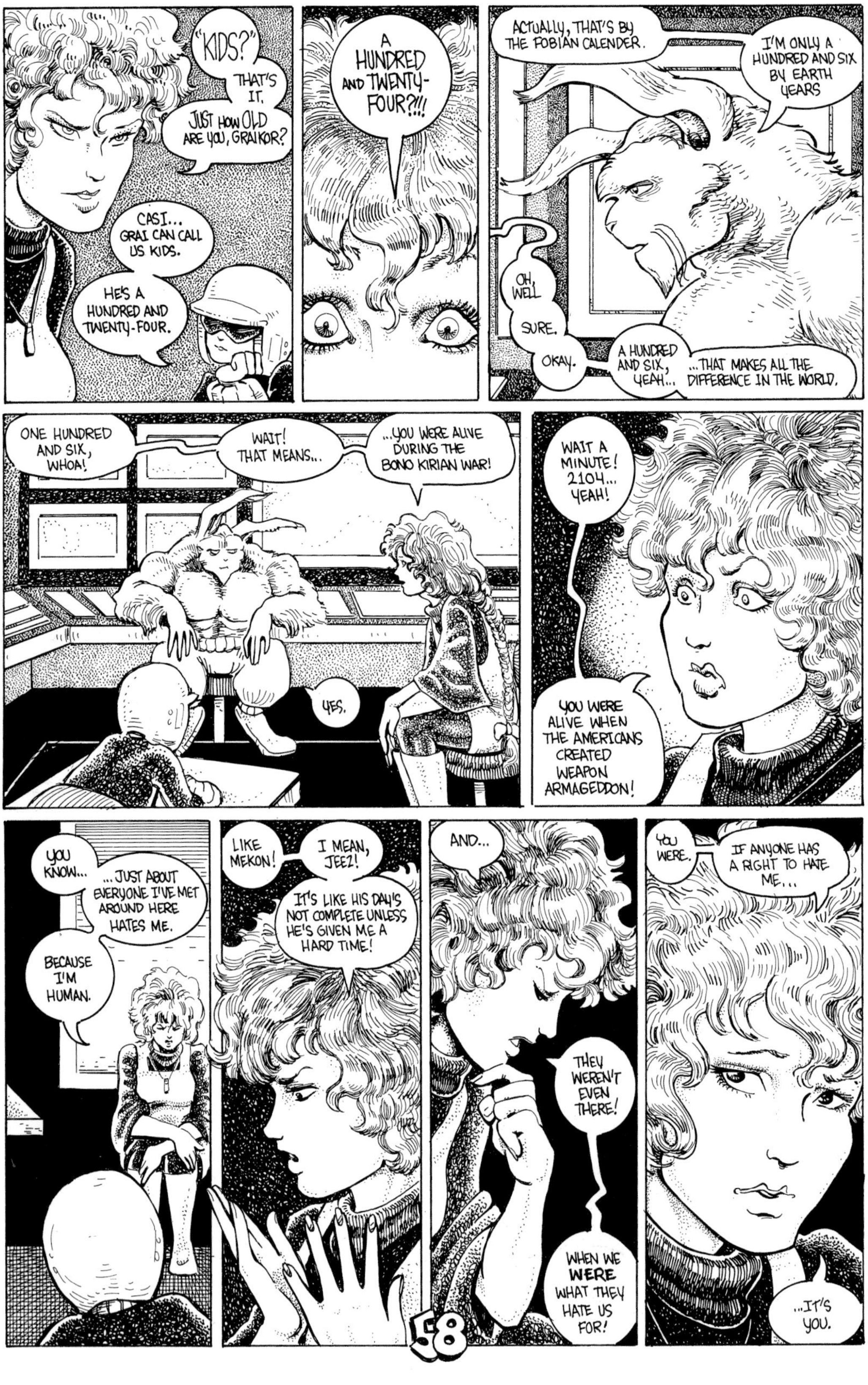
"KIDS?"
THAT'S IT. JUST HOW OLD ARE YOU, GRAIKOR?
CASI... GRAI CAN CALL US KIDS.
HE'S A HUNDRED AND TWENTY-FOUR.
A HUNDRED AND TWENTY-FOUR?!!!
ACTUALLY, THAT'S BY THE FOBIAN CALENDER.
I'M ONLY A HUNDRED AND SIX BY EARTH YEARS
OH, WELL
SURE.
OKAY.
A HUNDRED AND SIX, YEAH...
...THAT MAKES ALL THE DIFFERENCE IN THE WORLD.
ONE HUNDRED AND SIX, WHOA!
WAIT! THAT MEANS..
...YOU WERE ALIVE DURING THE BONO KIRIAN WAR!
YES.
WAIT A MINUTE! 2104... YEAH!
YOU WERE ALIVE WHEN THE AMERICANS CREATED WEAPON ARMAGEDDON!
YOU KNOW...
...JUST ABOUT EVERYONE I'VE MET AROUND HERE HATES ME.
BECAUSE I'M HUMAN.
LIKE MEKON!
I MEAN, JEEZ!
IT'S LIKE HIS DAY'S NOT COMPLETE UNLESS HE'S GIVEN ME A HARD TIME!
AND...
THEY WEREN'T EVEN THERE!
WHEN WE **WERE** WHAT THEY HATE US FOR!
YOU WERE.
IF ANYONE HAS A RIGHT TO HATE ME...
...IT'S YOU.

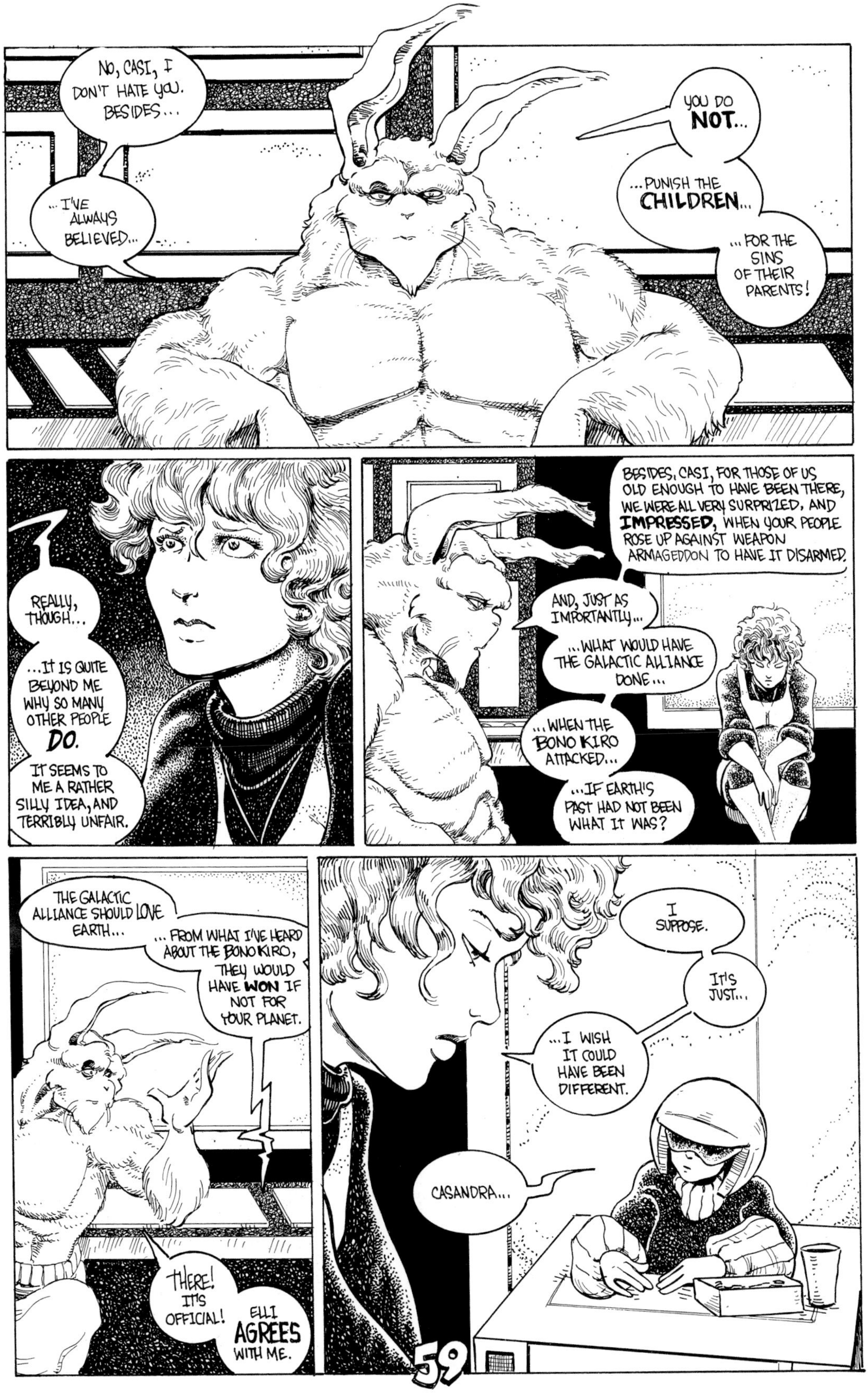

NO, CASI, I DON'T HATE YOU. BESIDES...
...I'VE ALWAYS BELIEVED...
YOU DO NOT...
...PUNISH THE CHILDREN...
...FOR THE SINS OF THEIR PARENTS!
REALLY, THOUGH...
...IT IS QUITE BEYOND ME WHY SO MANY OTHER PEOPLE DO.
IT SEEMS TO ME A RATHER SILLY IDEA, AND TERRIBLY UNFAIR.
BESIDES, CASI, FOR THOSE OF US OLD ENOUGH TO HAVE BEEN THERE, WE WERE ALL VERY SURPRIZED, AND IMPRESSED, WHEN YOUR PEOPLE ROSE UP AGAINST WEAPON ARMAGEDDON TO HAVE IT DISARMED.
AND, JUST AS IMPORTANTLY...
...WHAT WOULD HAVE THE GALACTIC ALLIANCE DONE...
...WHEN THE BONO KIRO ATTACKED...
...IF EARTH'S PAST HAD NOT BEEN WHAT IT WAS?
THE GALACTIC ALLIANCE SHOULD LOVE EARTH...
...FROM WHAT I'VE HEARD ABOUT THE BONO KIRO, THEY WOULD HAVE WON IF NOT FOR YOUR PLANET.
THERE! IT'S OFFICIAL!
ELLI AGREES WITH ME.
I SUPPOSE.
IT'S JUST...
...I WISH IT COULD HAVE BEEN DIFFERENT.
CASANDRA...

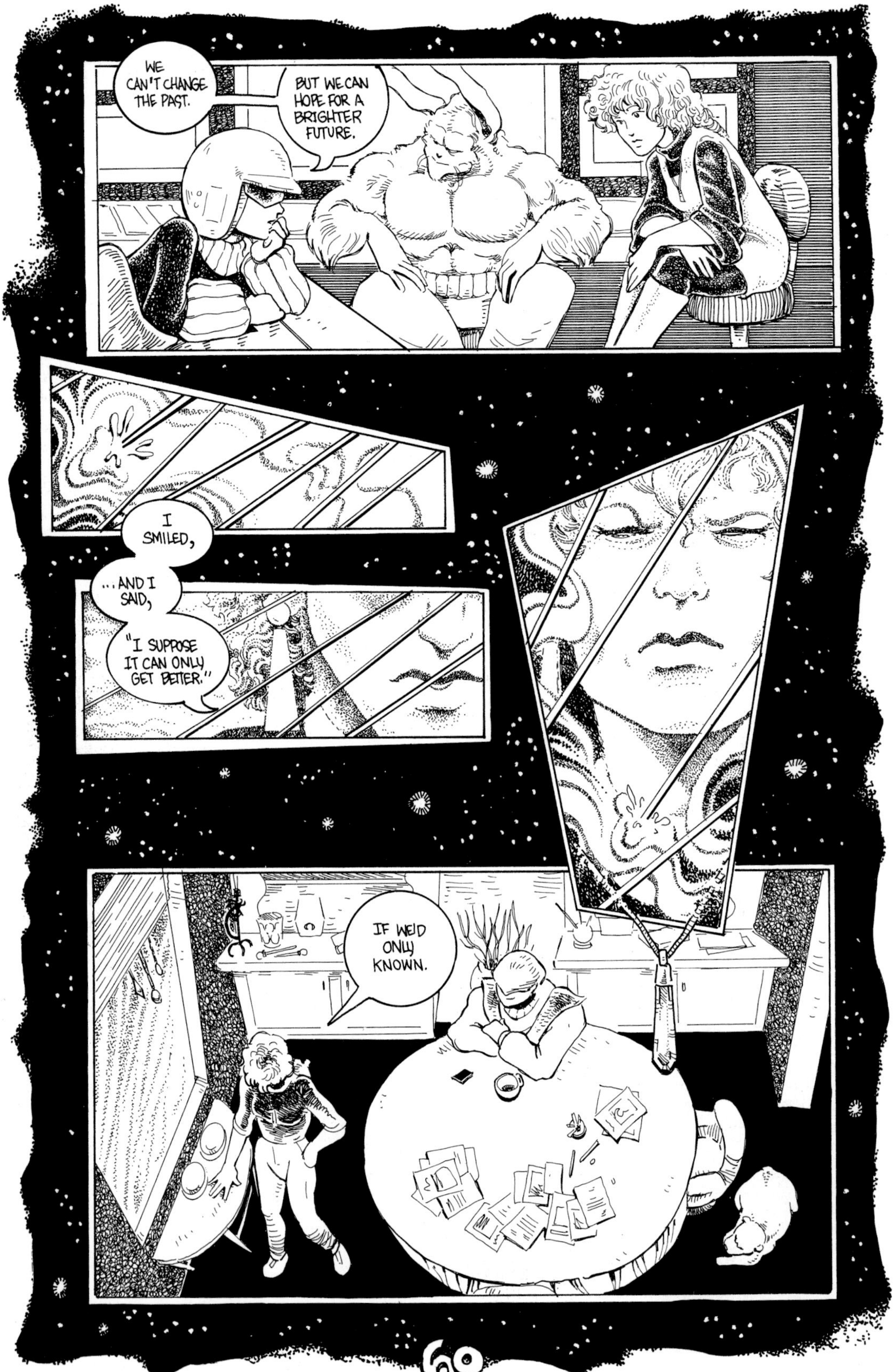
WE CAN'T CHANGE THE PAST.
BUT WE CAN HOPE FOR A BRIGHTER FUTURE.
I SMILED,
...AND I SAID,
"I SUPPOSE IT CAN ONLY GET BETTER."
IF WE'D ONLY KNOWN.

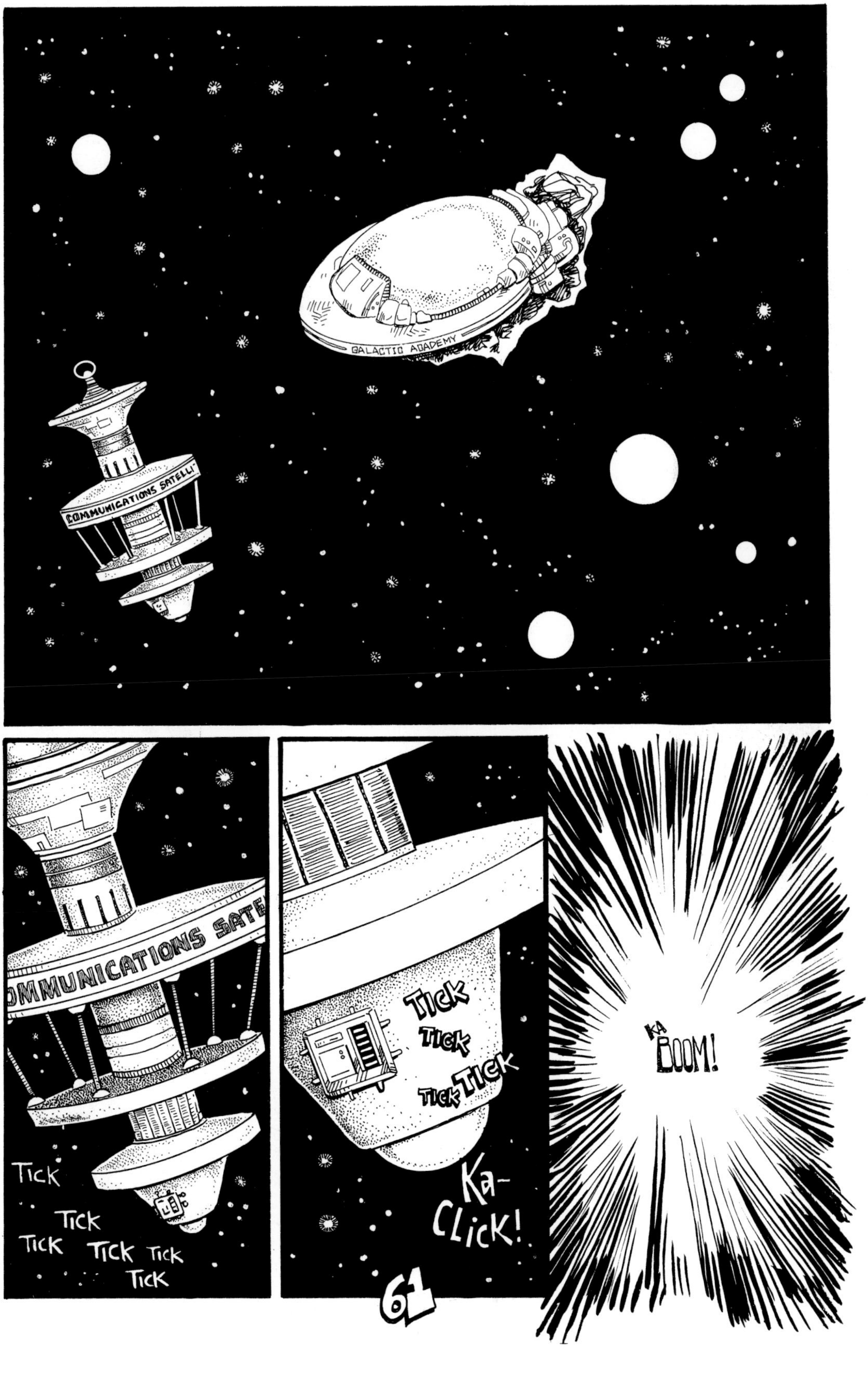
GALACTIC ACADEMY
COMMUNICATIONS SATELLI
COMMUNICATIONS SATE
TICK
TICK
TICK TICK TICK
TICK
TICK
TICK
TICK TICK
KA-CLICK!
KA BOOM!

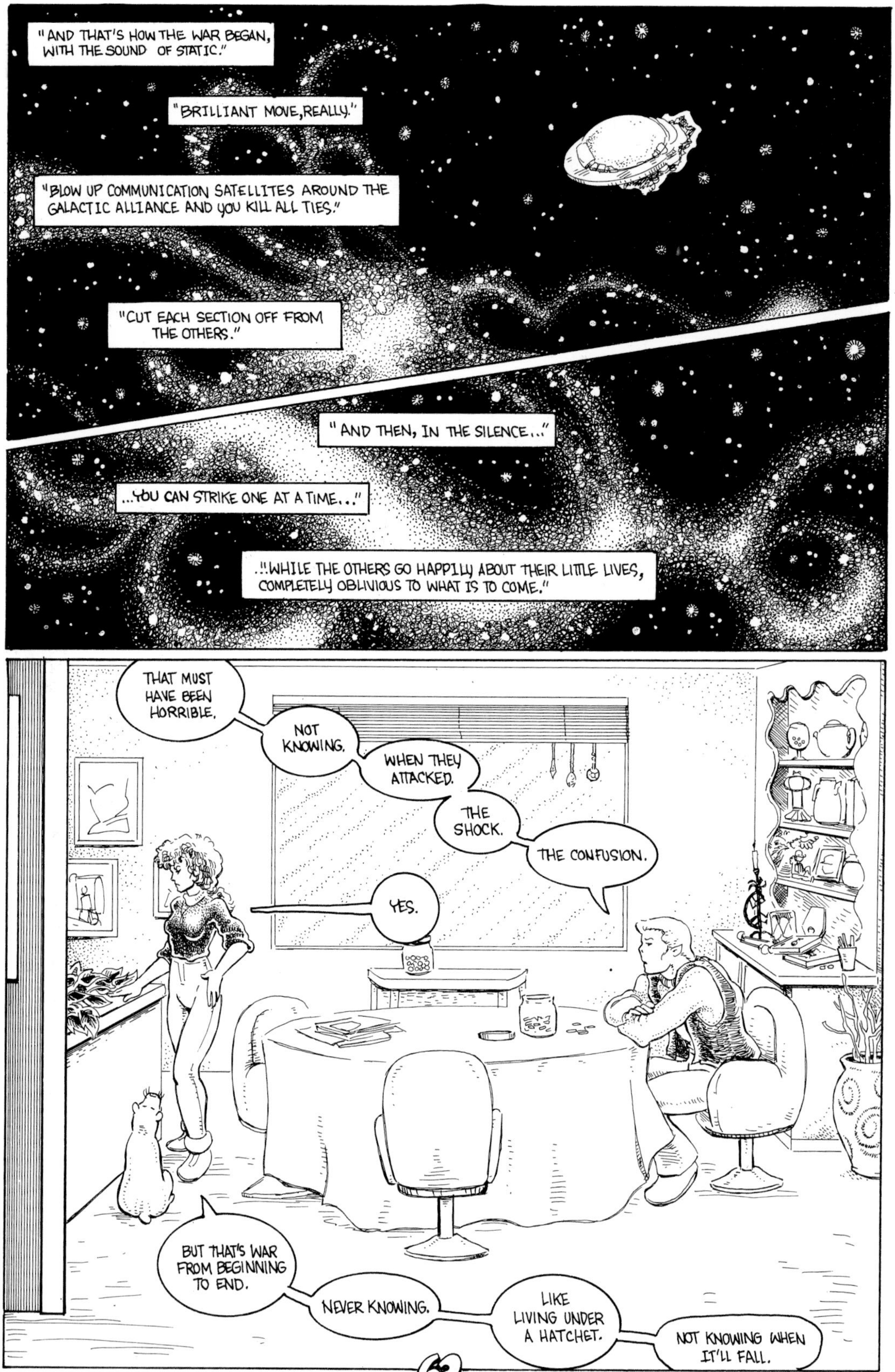
"AND THAT'S HOW THE WAR BEGAN, WITH THE SOUND OF STATIC."
"BRILLIANT MOVE, REALLY."
"BLOW UP COMMUNICATION SATELLITES AROUND THE GALACTIC ALLIANCE AND YOU KILL ALL TIES."
"CUT EACH SECTION OFF FROM THE OTHERS."
"AND THEN, IN THE SILENCE..."
...YOU CAN STRIKE ONE AT A TIME..."
..!!WHILE THE OTHERS GO HAPPILY ABOUT THEIR LITTLE LIVES, COMPLETELY OBLIVIOUS TO WHAT IS TO COME."
THAT MUST HAVE BEEN HORRIBLE.
NOT KNOWING.
WHEN THEY ATTACKED.
THE SHOCK.
THE CONFUSION.
YES.
BUT THAT'S WAR FROM BEGINNING TO END.
NEVER KNOWING.
LIKE LIVING UNDER A HATCHET.
NOT KNOWING WHEN IT'LL FALL.

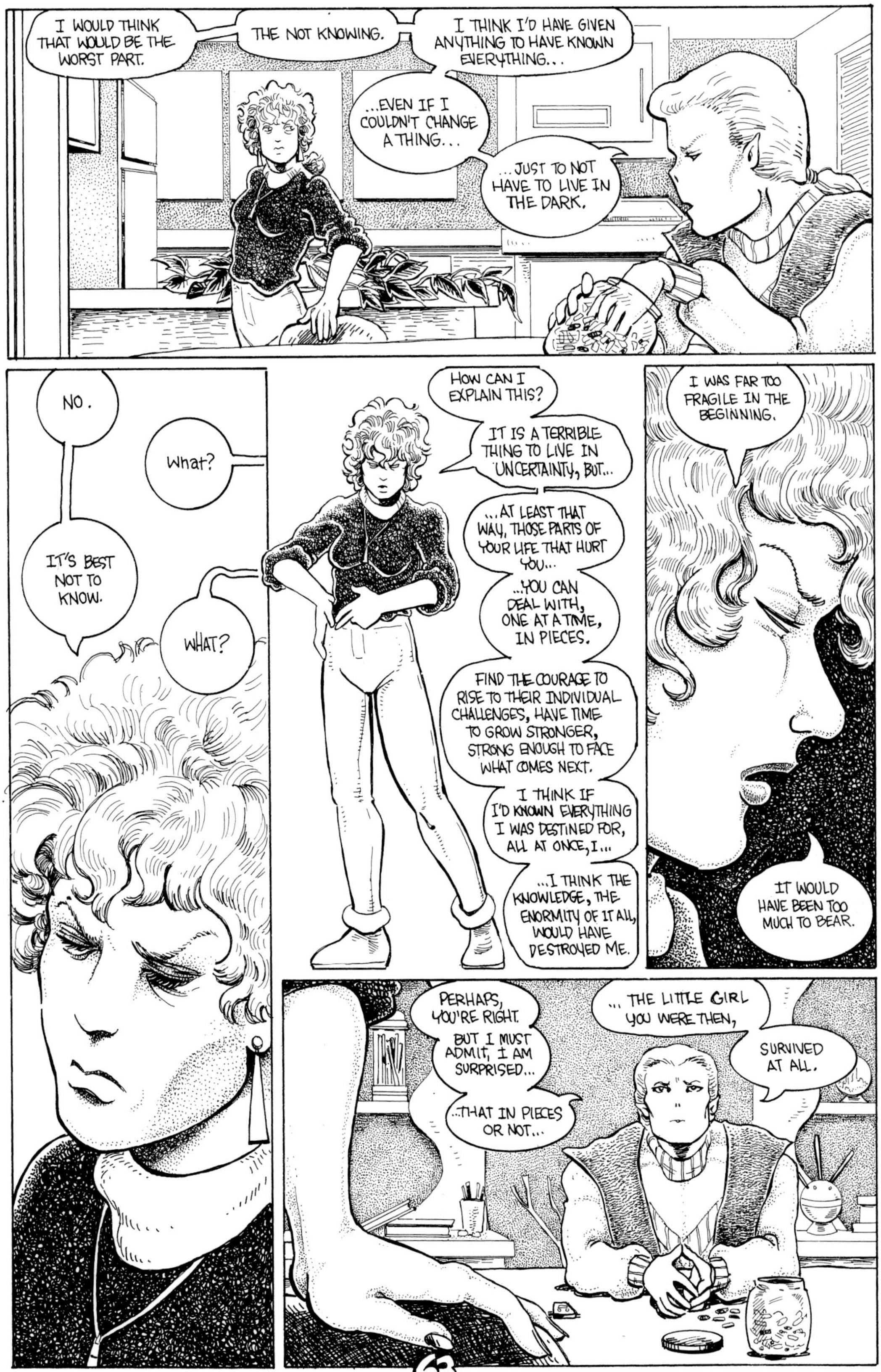
I WOULD THINK THAT WOULD BE THE WORST PART.
THE NOT KNOWING.
I THINK I'D HAVE GIVEN ANYTHING TO HAVE KNOWN EVERYTHING...
...EVEN IF I COULDN'T CHANGE A THING...
...JUST TO NOT HAVE TO LIVE IN THE DARK.
NO.
What?
IT'S BEST NOT TO KNOW.
WHAT?
HOW CAN I EXPLAIN THIS?
IT IS A TERRIBLE THING TO LIVE IN UNCERTAINTY, BUT...
...AT LEAST THAT WAY, THOSE PARTS OF YOUR LIFE THAT HURT YOU...
...YOU CAN DEAL WITH, ONE AT A TIME, IN PIECES.
FIND THE COURAGE TO RISE TO THEIR INDIVIDUAL CHALLENGES, HAVE TIME TO GROW STRONGER, STRONG ENOUGH TO FACE WHAT COMES NEXT.
I THINK IF I'D KNOWN EVERYTHING I WAS DESTINED FOR, ALL AT ONCE, I...
...I THINK THE KNOWLEDGE, THE ENORMITY OF IT ALL, WOULD HAVE DESTROYED ME.
I WAS FAR TOO FRAGILE IN THE BEGINNING.
IT WOULD HAVE BEEN TOO MUCH TO BEAR.
PERHAPS, YOU'RE RIGHT.
BUT I MUST ADMIT, I AM SURPRISED...
...THAT IN PIECES OR NOT...
...THE LITTLE GIRL YOU WERE THEN,
SURVIVED AT ALL.

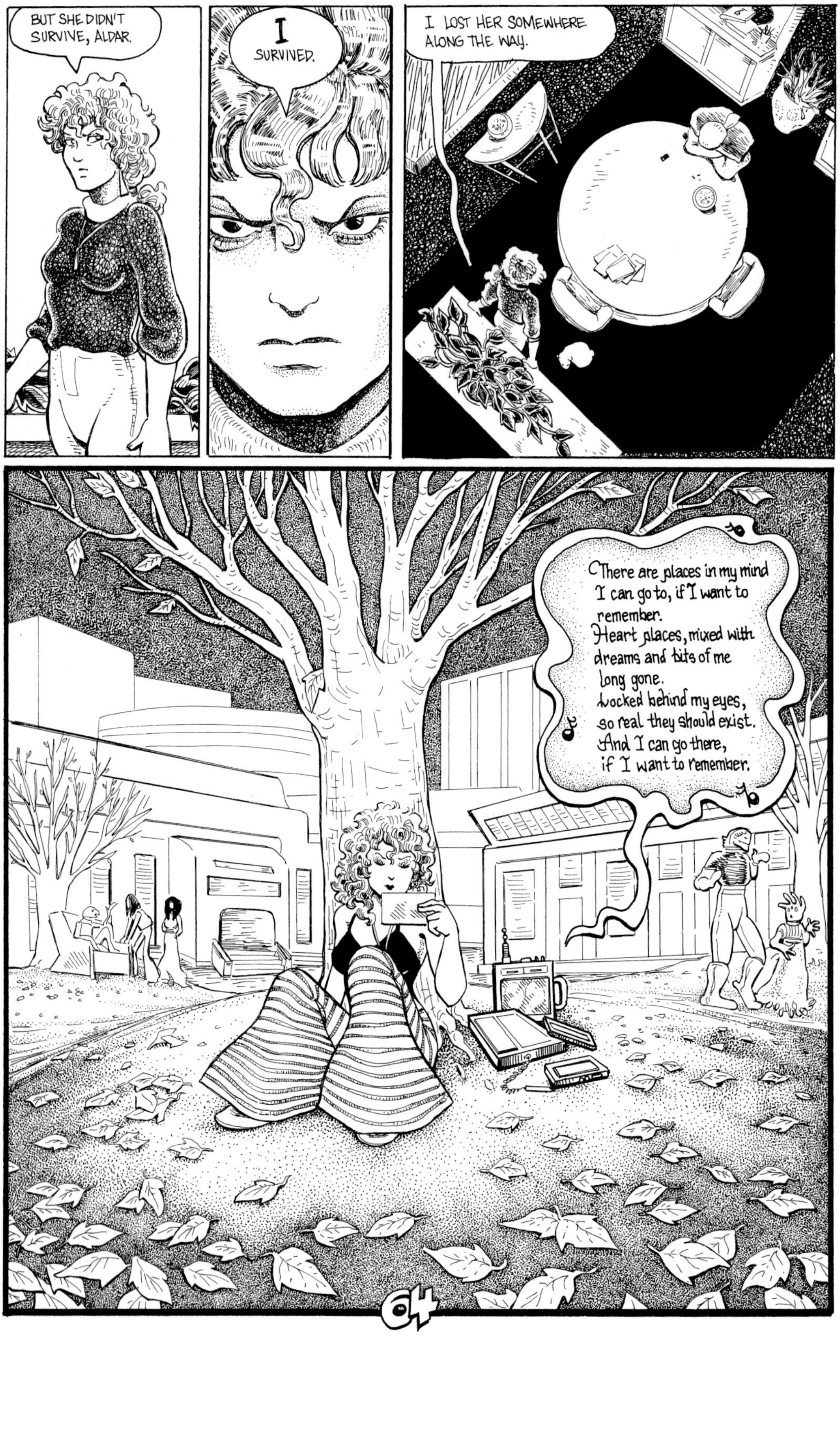
BUT SHE DIDN'T SURVIVE, ALDAR.
I SURVIVED.
I LOST HER SOMEWHERE ALONG THE WAY.
There are places in my mind
I can go to, if I want to
remember.
Heart places, mixed with
dreams and bits of me
long gone.
Locked behind my eyes,
so real they should exist.
And I can go there,
if I want to remember.

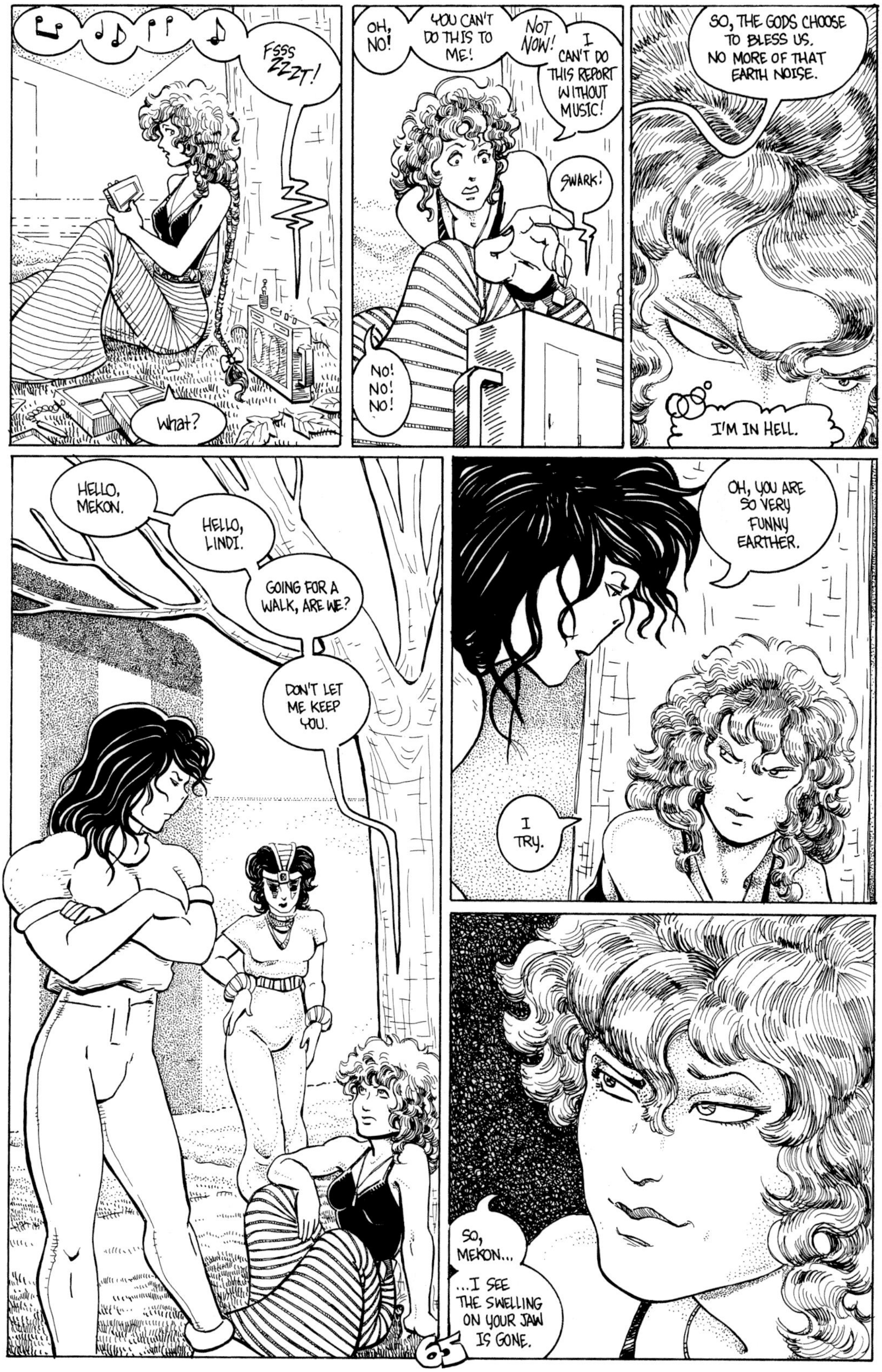
FSSS ZZZT!
What?
OH, NO!
YOU CAN'T DO THIS TO ME!
NOT NOW!
I CAN'T DO THIS REPORT WITHOUT MUSIC!
SWARK!
NO! NO! NO!
SO, THE GODS CHOOSE TO BLESS US. NO MORE OF THAT EARTH NOISE.
I'M IN HELL.
HELLO, MEKON.
HELLO, LINDI.
GOING FOR A WALK, ARE WE?
DON'T LET ME KEEP YOU.
OH, YOU ARE SO VERY FUNNY EARTHER.
I TRY.
SO, MEKON...
...I SEE THE SWELLING ON YOUR JAW IS GONE.

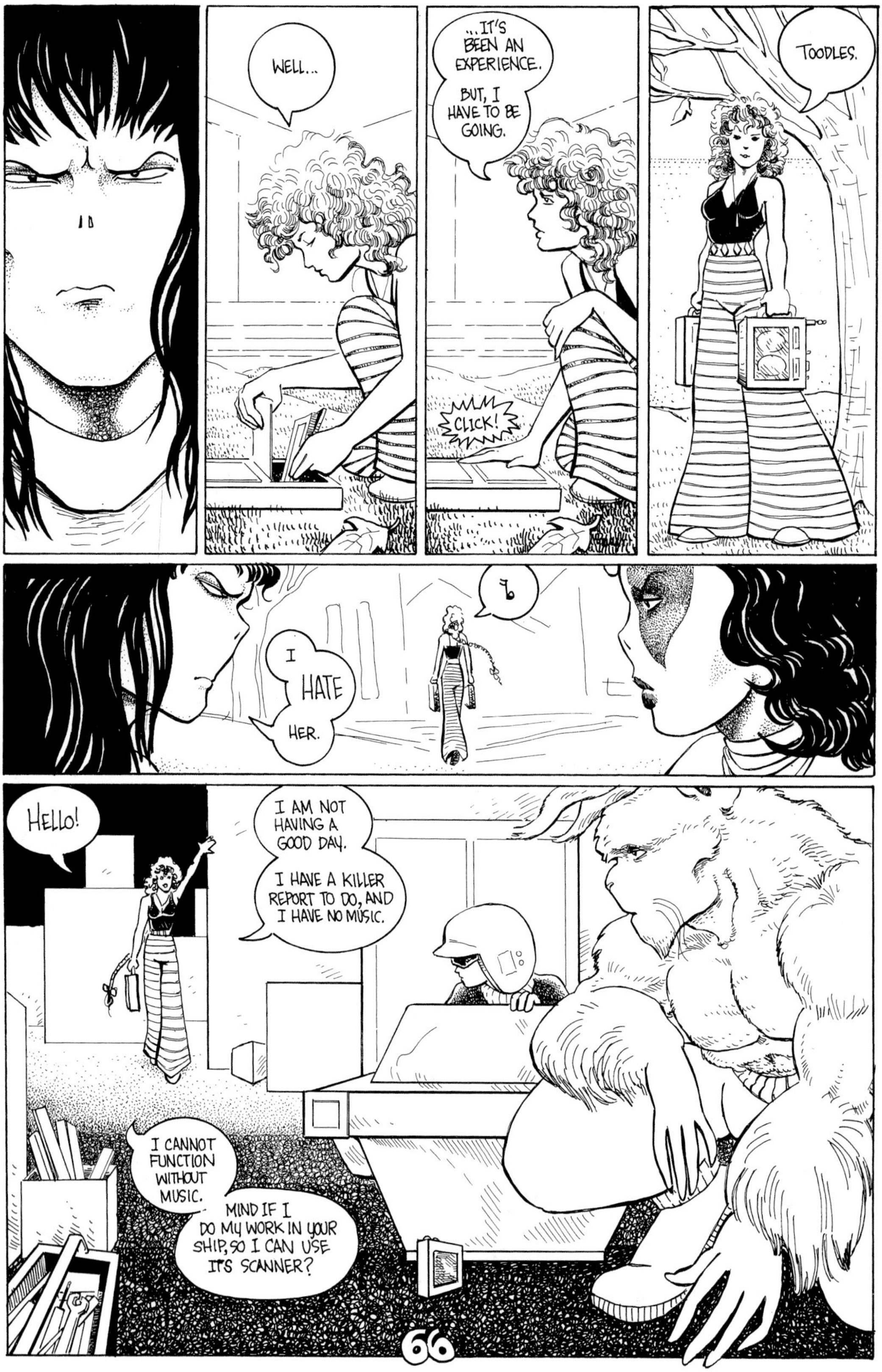
WELL...
...IT'S BEEN AN EXPERIENCE.
BUT, I HAVE TO BE GOING.
CLICK!
TOODLES.
I HATE HER.
HELLO!
I AM NOT HAVING A GOOD DAY.
I HAVE A KILLER REPORT TO DO, AND I HAVE NO MUSIC.
I CANNOT FUNCTION WITHOUT MUSIC.
MIND IF I DO MY WORK IN YOUR SHIP, SO I CAN USE IT'S SCANNER?

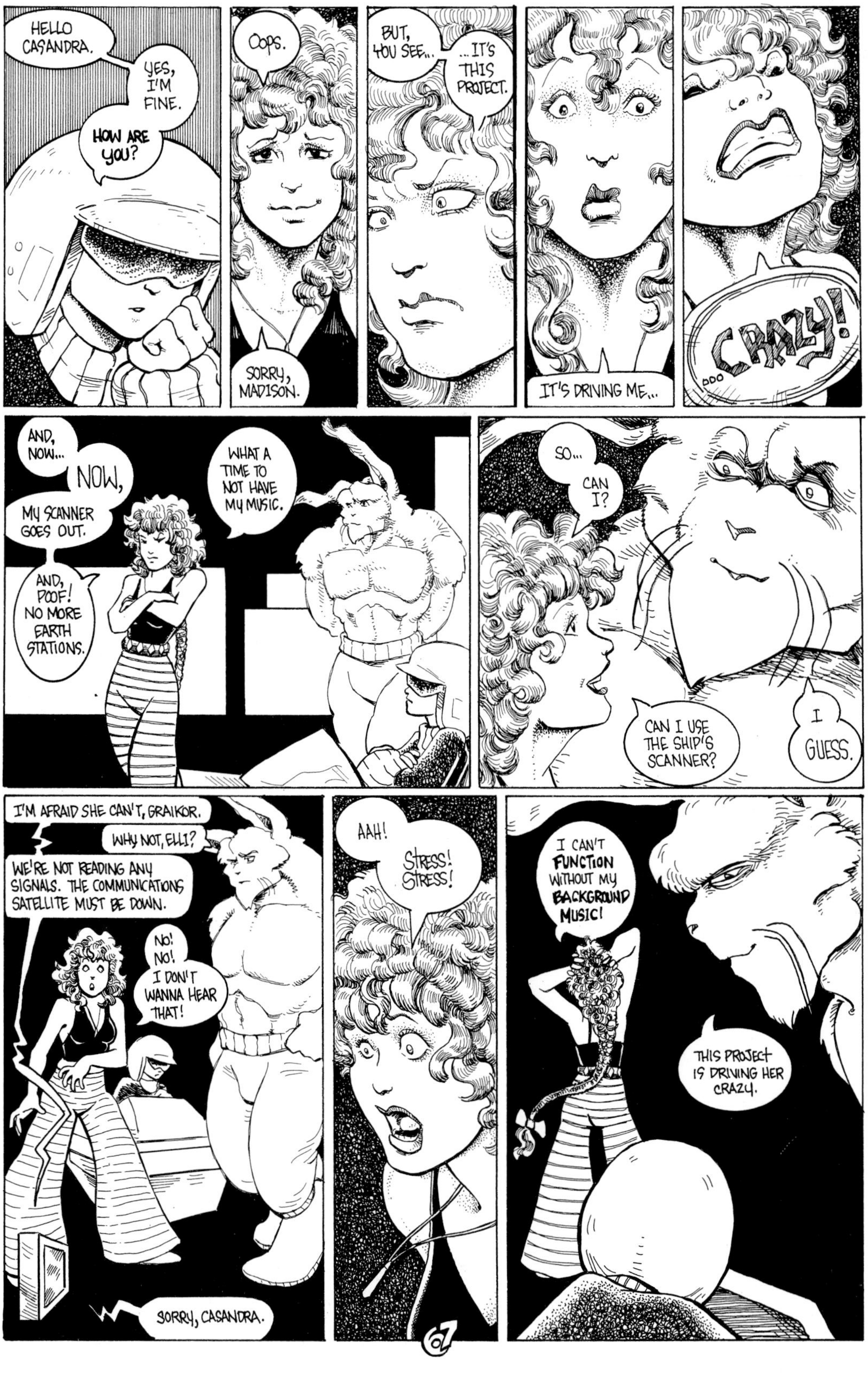
HELLO CASANDRA.
YES, I'M FINE.
HOW ARE YOU?
Oops.
SORRY, MADISON.
BUT, YOU SEE...
...IT'S THIS PROJECT.
IT'S DRIVING ME...
...CRAZY!
AND, NOW...
NOW,
MY SCANNER GOES OUT.
AND, POOF! NO MORE EARTH STATIONS.
WHAT A TIME TO NOT HAVE MY MUSIC.
SO...
CAN I?
CAN I USE THE SHIP'S SCANNER?
I GUESS.
I'M AFRAID SHE CAN'T, GRAIKOR.
WHY NOT, ELLI?
WE'RE NOT READING ANY SIGNALS. THE COMMUNICATIONS SATELLITE MUST BE DOWN.
NO! NO! I DON'T WANNA HEAR THAT!
SORRY, CASANDRA.
AAH!
STRESS! STRESS!
I CAN'T FUNCTION WITHOUT MY BACKGROUND MUSIC!
THIS PROJECT IS DRIVING HER CRAZY.

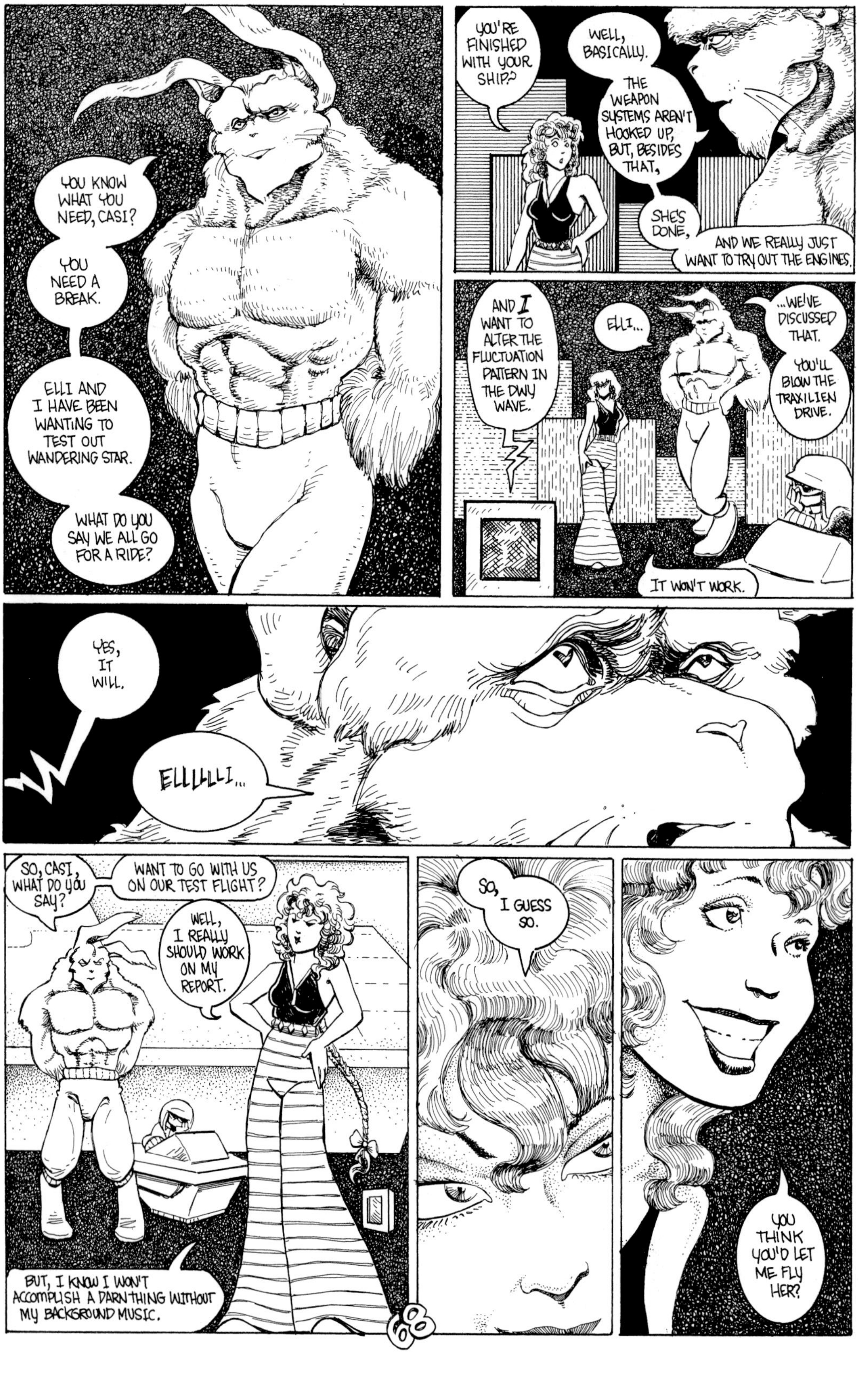
YOU KNOW WHAT YOU NEED, CASI?
YOU NEED A BREAK.
ELLI AND I HAVE BEEN WANTING TO TEST OUT WANDERING STAR.
WHAT DO YOU SAY WE ALL GO FOR A RIDE?
YOU'RE FINISHED WITH YOUR SHIP??
WELL, BASICALLY.
THE WEAPON SYSTEMS AREN'T HOOKED UP, BUT, BESIDES THAT,
SHE'S DONE,
AND WE REALLY JUST WANT TO TRY OUT THE ENGINES.
AND I WANT TO ALTER THE FLUCTUATION PATTERN IN THE DWY WAVE.
ELLI...
...WE'VE DISCUSSED THAT.
YOU'LL BLOW THE TRAXILIEN DRIVE.
IT WON'T WORK.
YES, IT WILL.
ELLLLLLI...
SO, CASI, WHAT DO YOU SAY?
WANT TO GO WITH US ON OUR TEST FLIGHT?
WELL, I REALLY SHOULD WORK ON MY REPORT.
BUT, I KNOW I WON'T ACCOMPLISH A DARN THING WITHOUT MY BACKGROUND MUSIC.
SO, I GUESS SO.
YOU THINK YOU'D LET ME FLY HER?

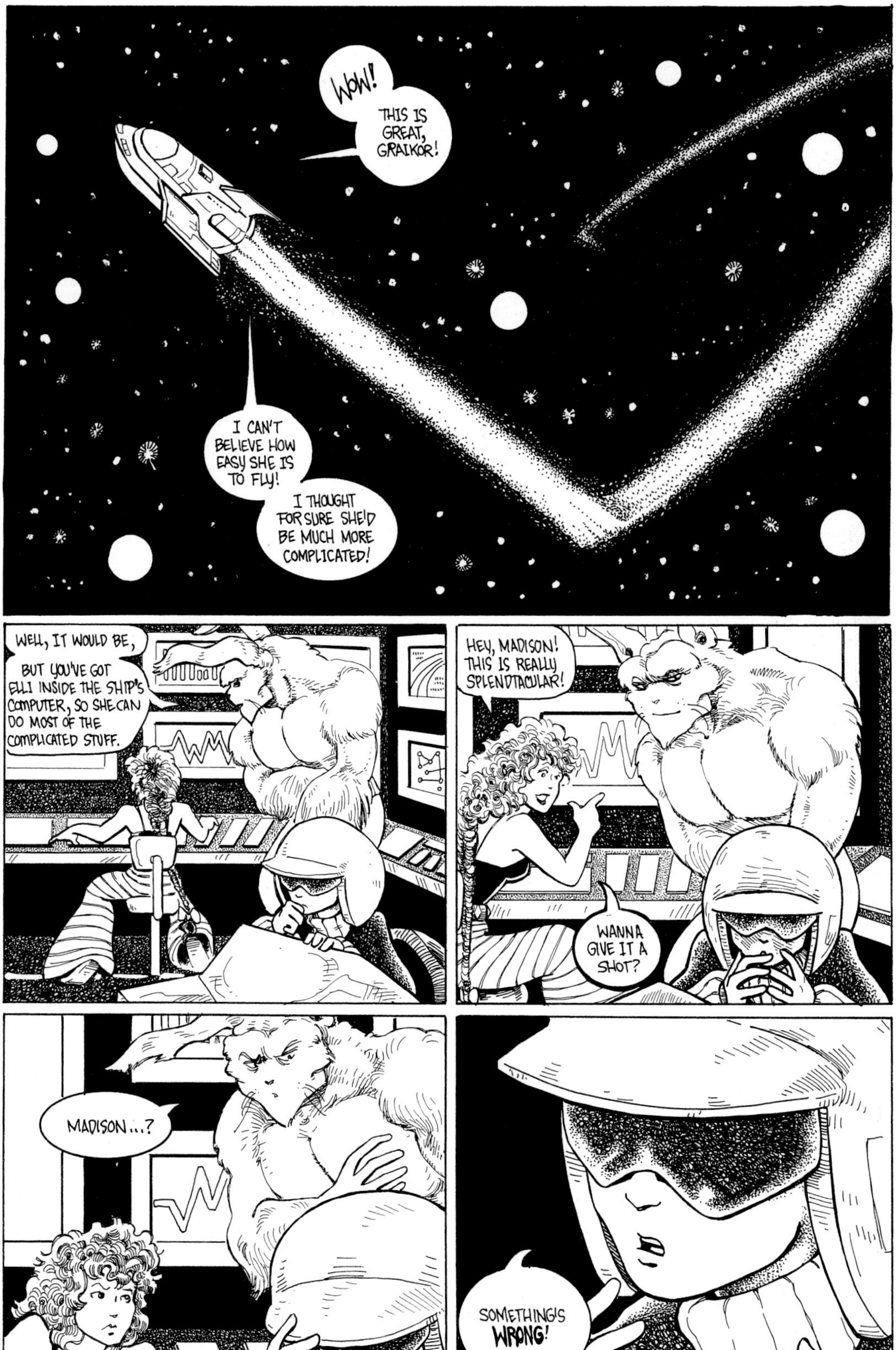
WOW!
THIS IS GREAT, GRAIKOR!
I CAN'T BELIEVE HOW EASY SHE IS TO FLY!
I THOUGHT FOR SURE SHE'D BE MUCH MORE COMPLICATED!
WELL, IT WOULD BE,
BUT YOU'VE GOT ELLI INSIDE THE SHIP'S COMPUTER, SO SHE CAN DO MOST OF THE COMPLICATED STUFF.
HEY, MADISON! THIS IS REALLY SPLENDTACULAR!
WANNA GIVE IT A SHOT?
MADISON...?
SOMETHING'S WRONG!

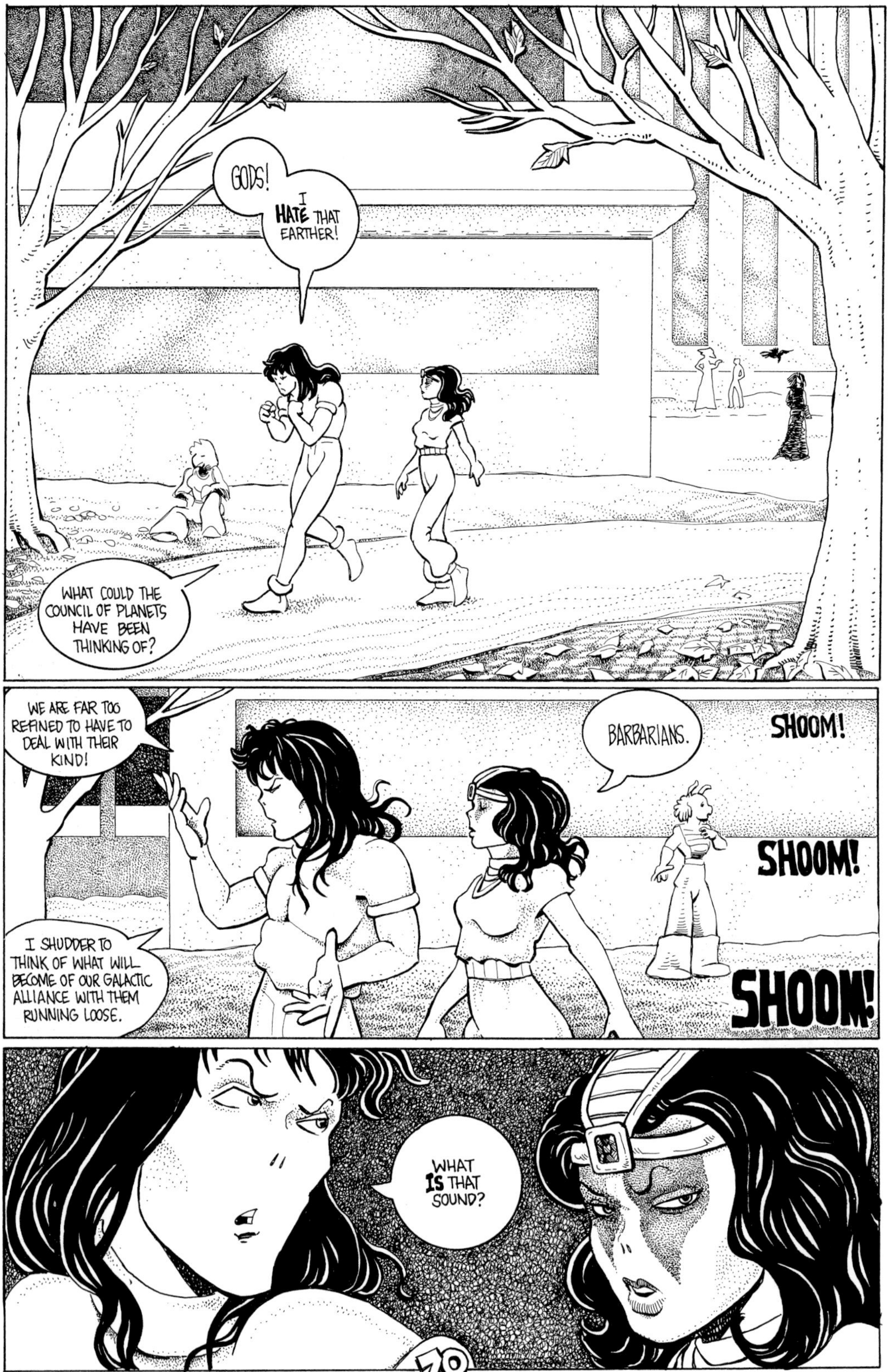
GODS!
I HATE THAT EARTHER!
WHAT COULD THE COUNCIL OF PLANETS HAVE BEEN THINKING OF?
WE ARE FAR TOO REFINED TO HAVE TO DEAL WITH THEIR KIND!
I SHUDDER TO THINK OF WHAT WILL BECOME OF OUR GALACTIC ALLIANCE WITH THEM RUNNING LOOSE.
BARBARIANS.
SHOOM!
SHOOM!
SHOOM!
WHAT IS THAT SOUND?

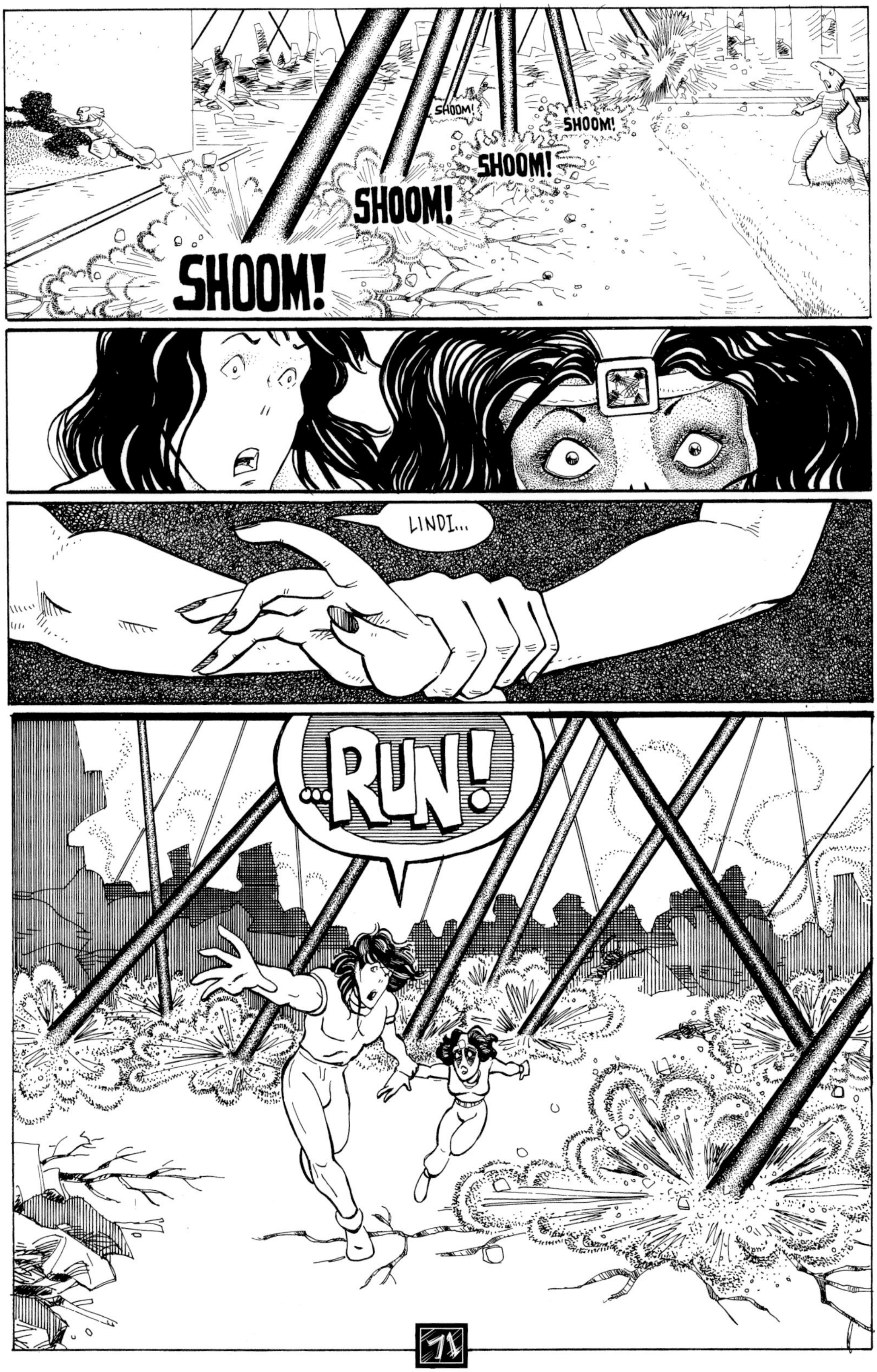
SHOOM!
SHOOM!
SHOOM!
SHOOM!
SHOOM!
LINDI...
...RUN!

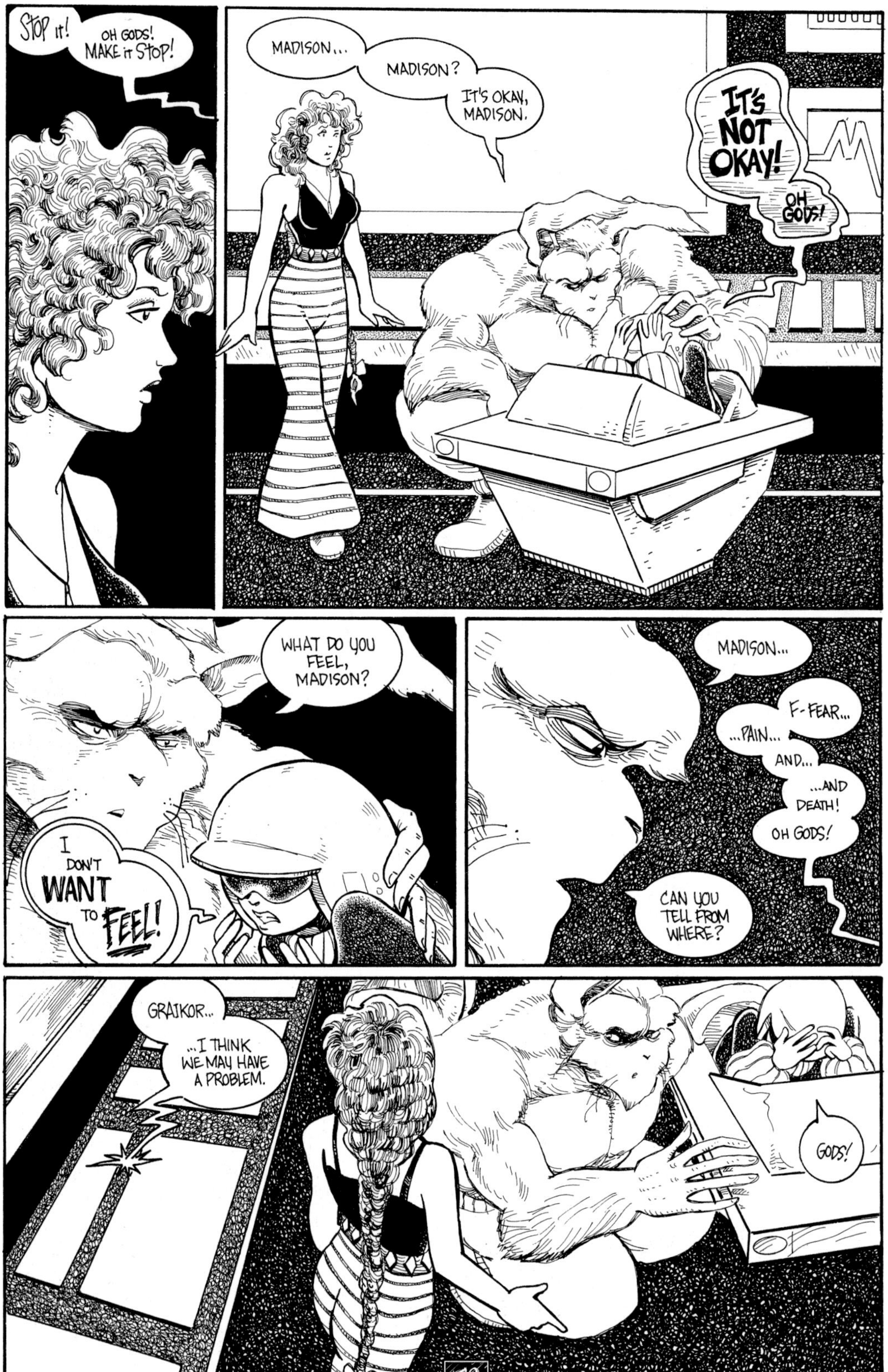
STOP IT!
OH GODS! MAKE IT STOP!
MADISON...
MADISON?
IT'S OKAY, MADISON.
IT'S NOT OKAY!
OH GODS!
WHAT DO YOU FEEL, MADISON?
I DON'T WANT TO FEEL!
MADISON...
F-FEAR...
...PAIN...
AND...
...AND DEATH!
OH GODS!
CAN YOU TELL FROM WHERE?
GRAIKOR...
...I THINK WE MAY HAVE A PROBLEM.
GODS!

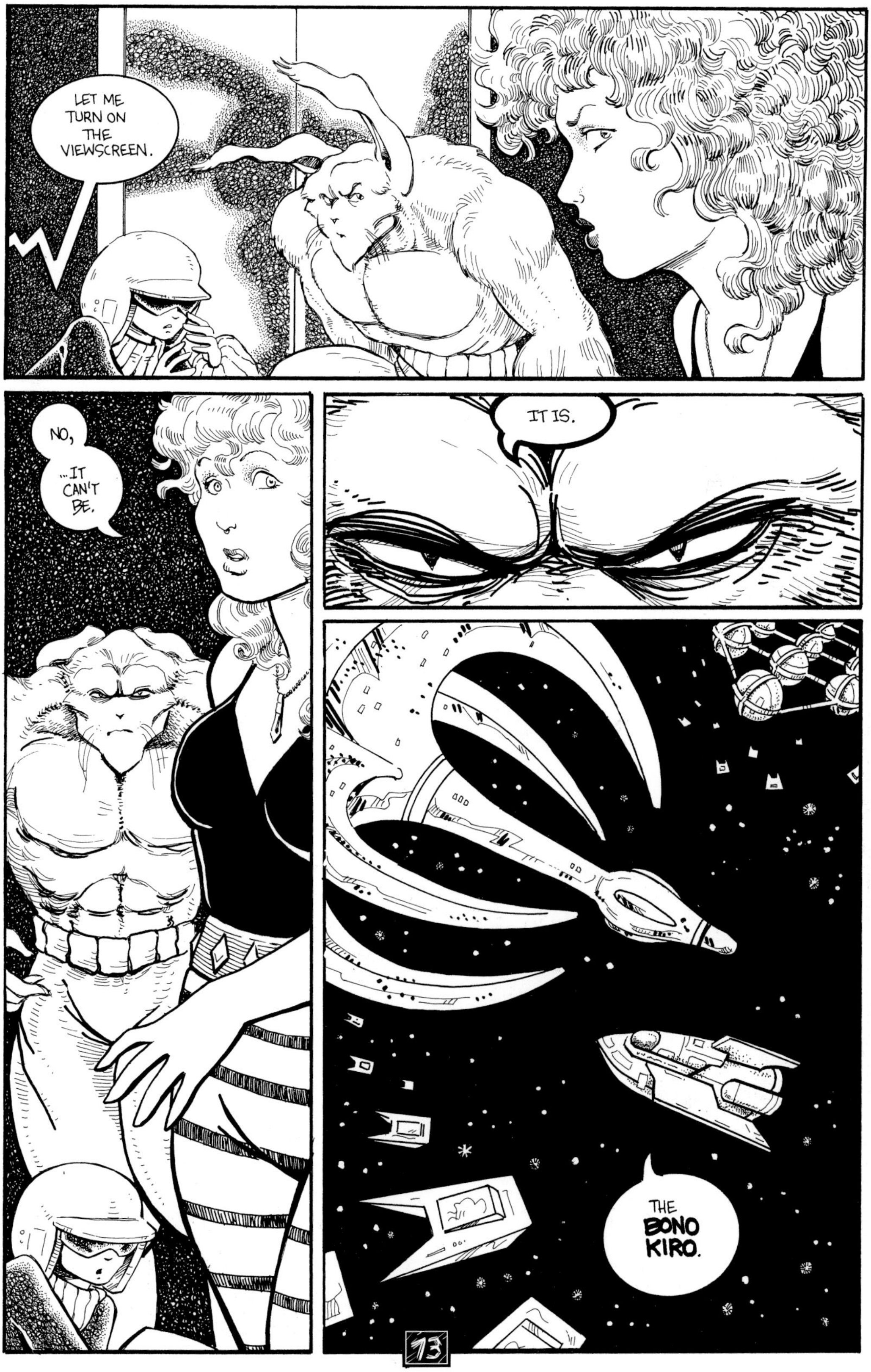
LET ME TURN ON THE VIEWSCREEN.
NO,
...IT CAN'T BE.
IT IS.
THE BONO KIRO.

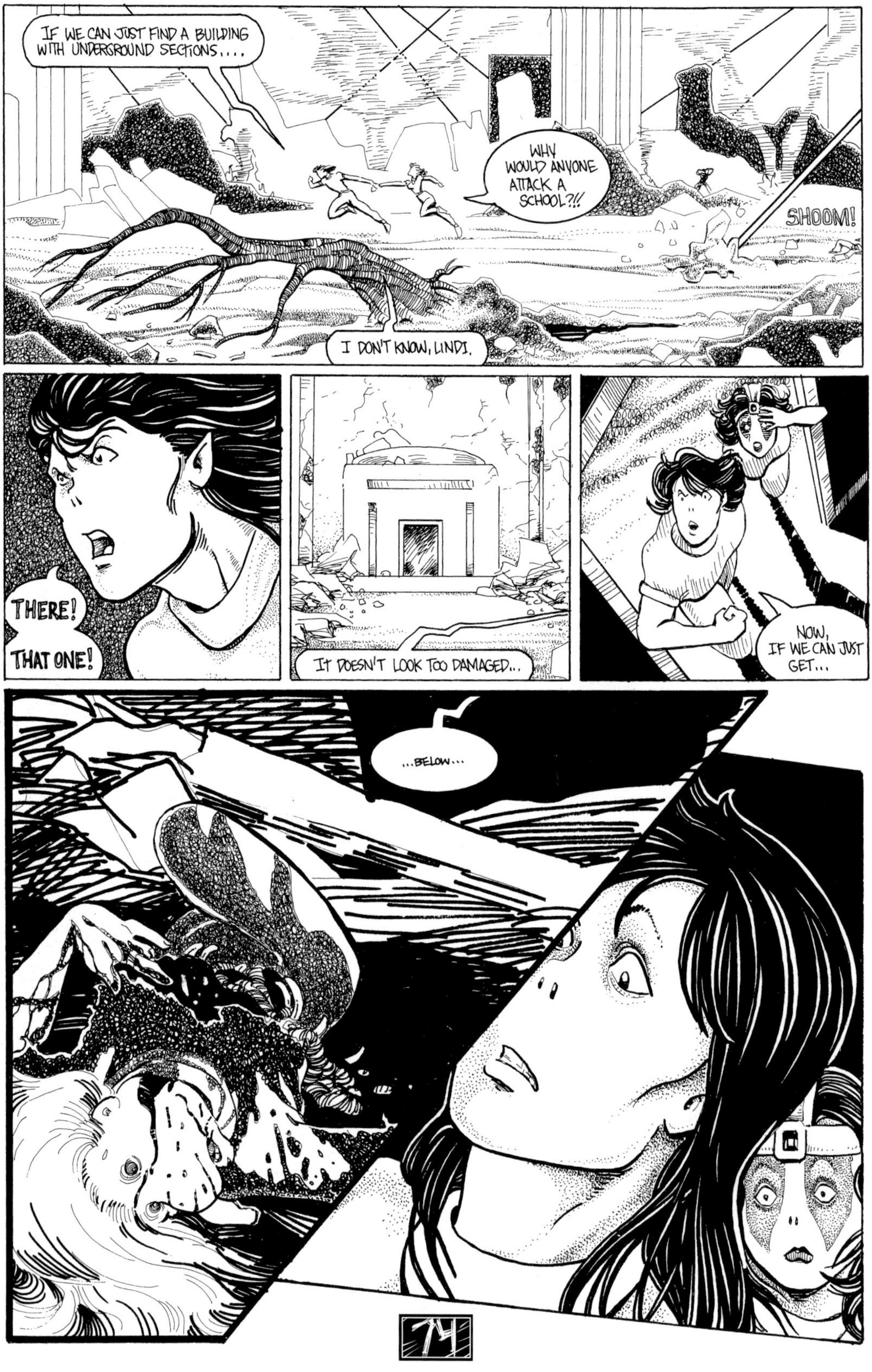
IF WE CAN JUST FIND A BUILDING WITH UNDERGROUND SECTIONS....
WHY WOULD ANYONE ATTACK A SCHOOL?!!
SHOOM!
I DON'T KNOW, LINDI.
THERE!
THAT ONE!
IT DOESN'T LOOK TOO DAMAGED...
NOW, IF WE CAN JUST GET...
...BELOW...

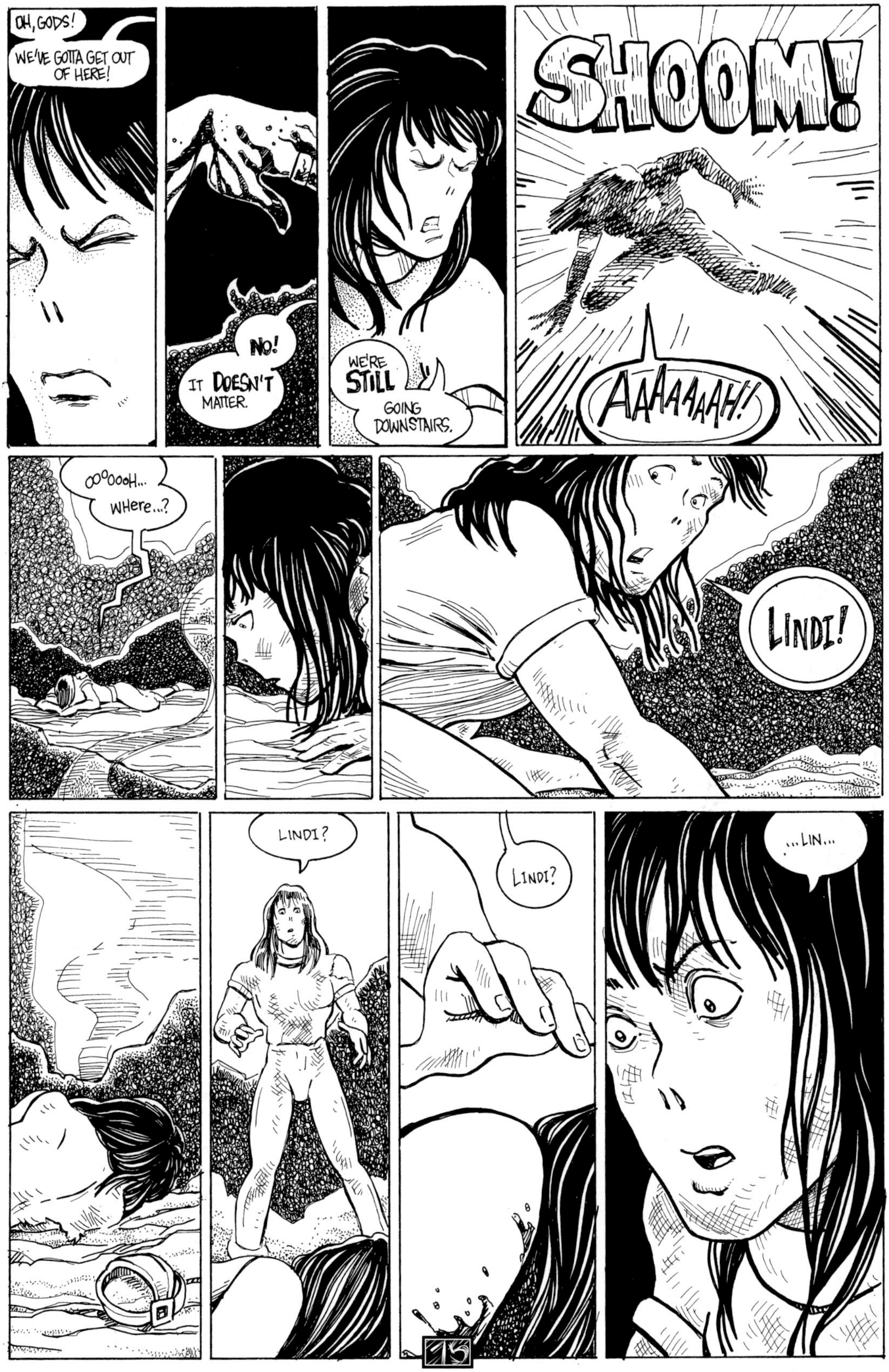
OH, GODS!
WE'VE GOTTA GET OUT OF HERE!
NO! IT DOESN'T MATTER.
WE'RE STILL GOING DOWNSTAIRS.
SHOOM!
AAAAAAAH!
OOOoooH... WHere...?
LINDI!
LINDI?
LINDI?
...LIN...

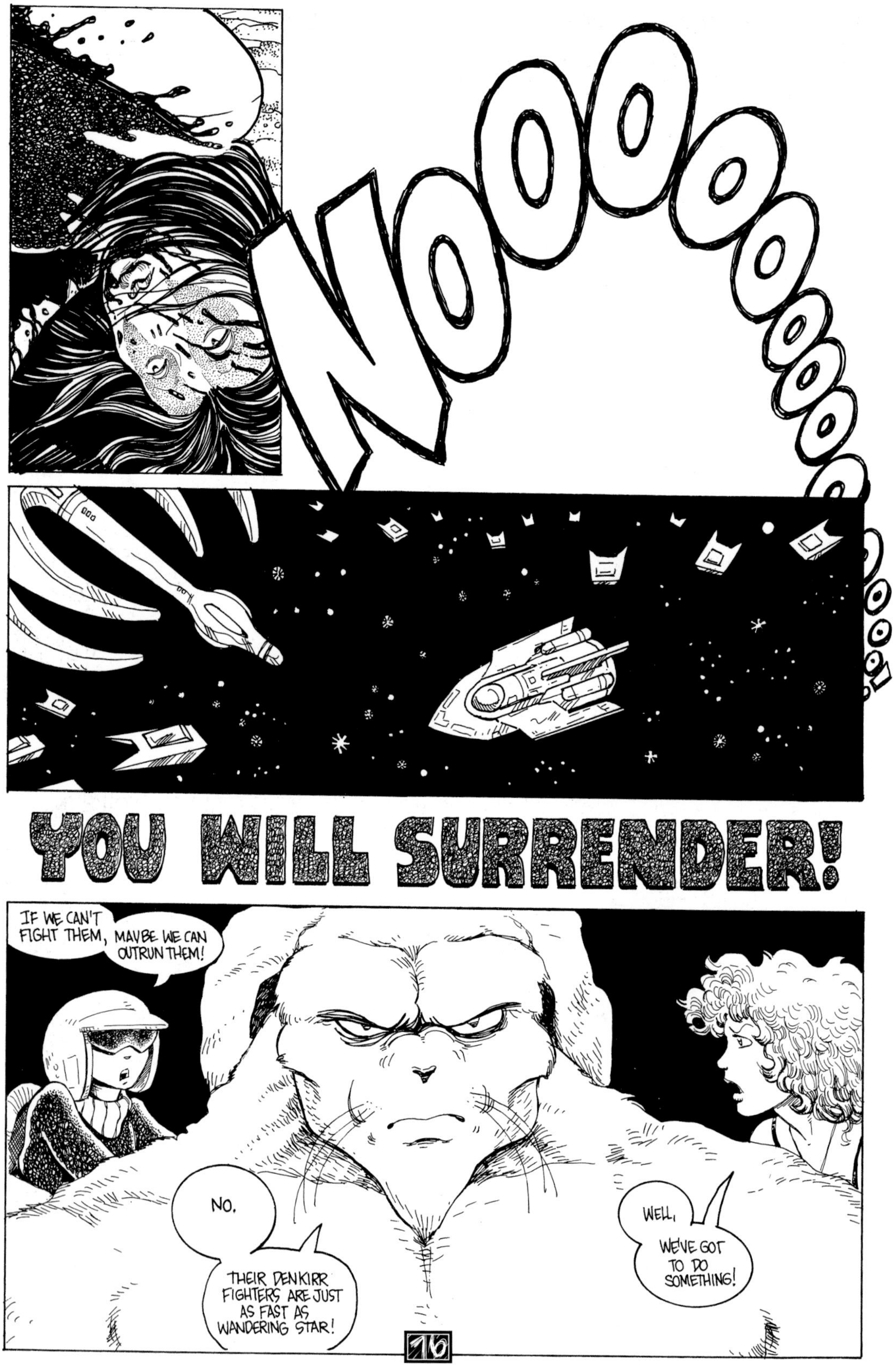

NOOOOOOOOOOOOO!
YOU WILL SURRENDER!
IF WE CAN'T FIGHT THEM,
MAYBE WE CAN OUTRUN THEM!
NO.
THEIR DENKIRR FIGHTERS ARE JUST AS FAST AS WANDERING STAR!
WELL,
WE'VE GOT TO DO SOMETHING!

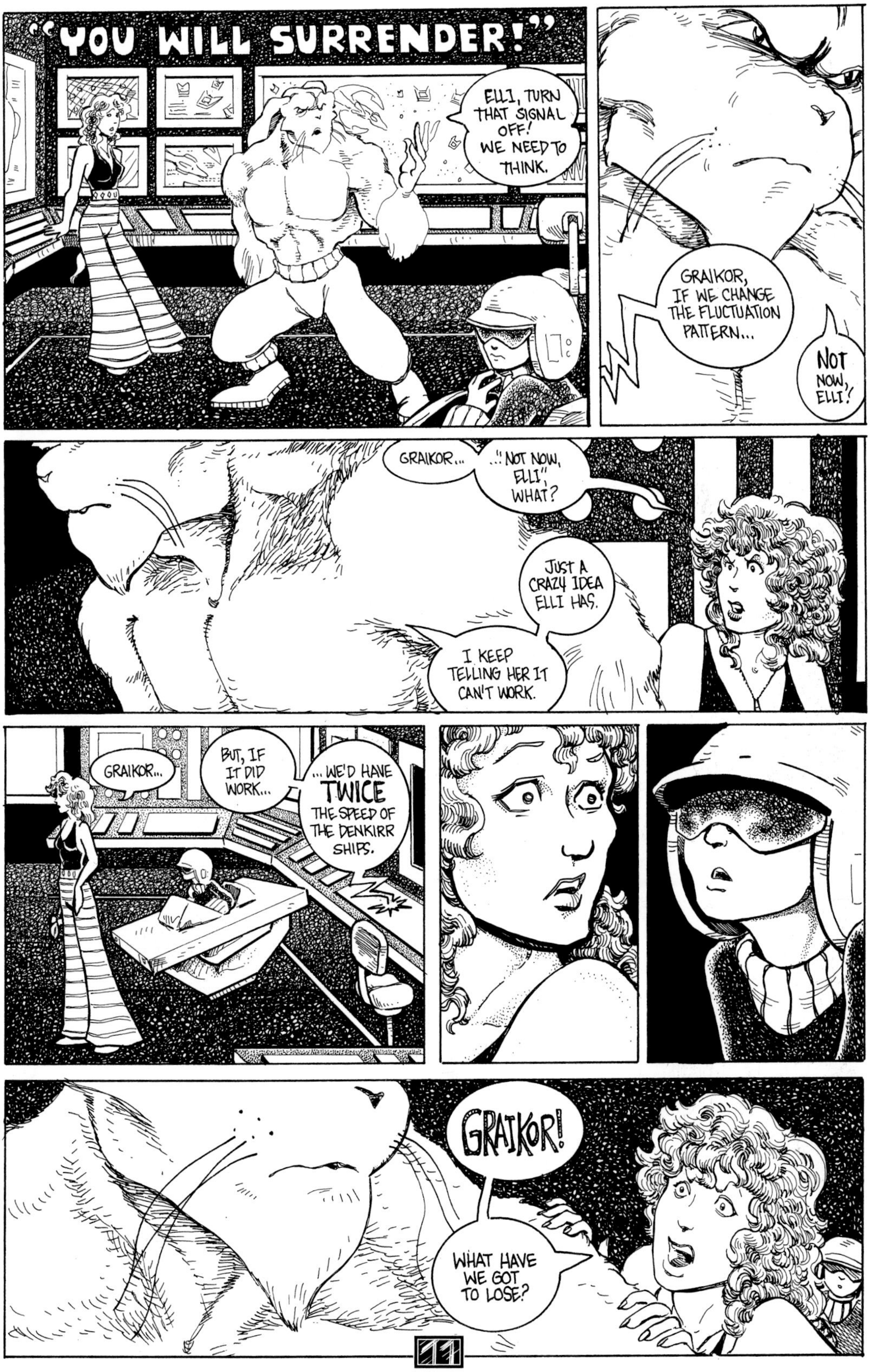
"YOU WILL SURRENDER!"
ELLI, TURN THAT SIGNAL OFF! WE NEED TO THINK.
GRAIKOR, IF WE CHANGE THE FLUCTUATION PATTERN...
NOT NOW, ELLI!
GRAIKOR...
..."NOT NOW, ELLI," WHAT?
JUST A CRAZY IDEA ELLI HAS.
I KEEP TELLING HER IT CAN'T WORK.
GRAIKOR...
BUT, IF IT DID WORK...
...WE'D HAVE TWICE THE SPEED OF THE DENKIRR SHIPS.
GRAIKOR!
WHAT HAVE WE GOT TO LOSE?

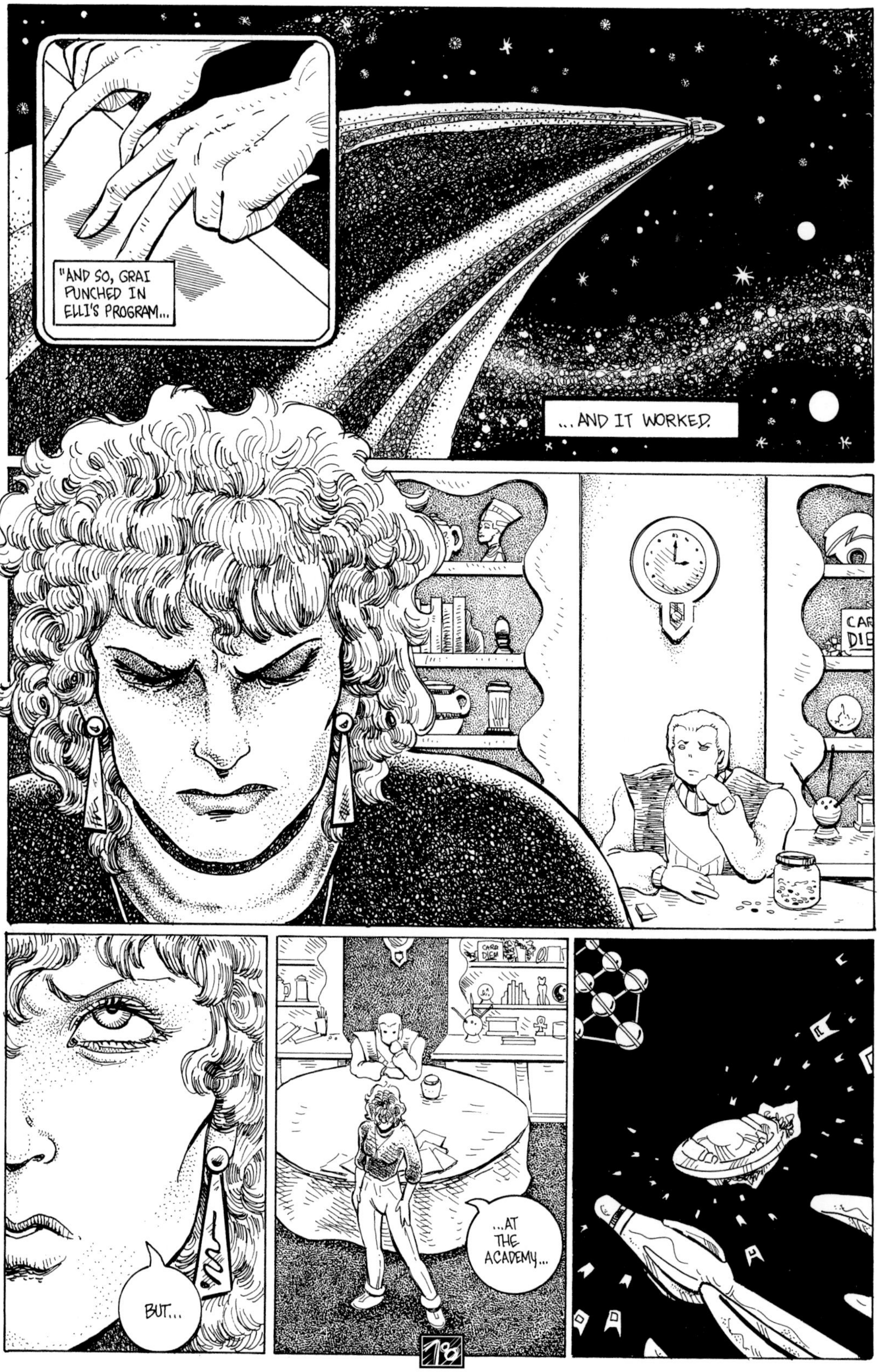
"AND SO, GRAI PUNCHED IN ELLI'S PROGRAM...
...AND IT WORKED.
BUT...
...AT THE ACADEMY...

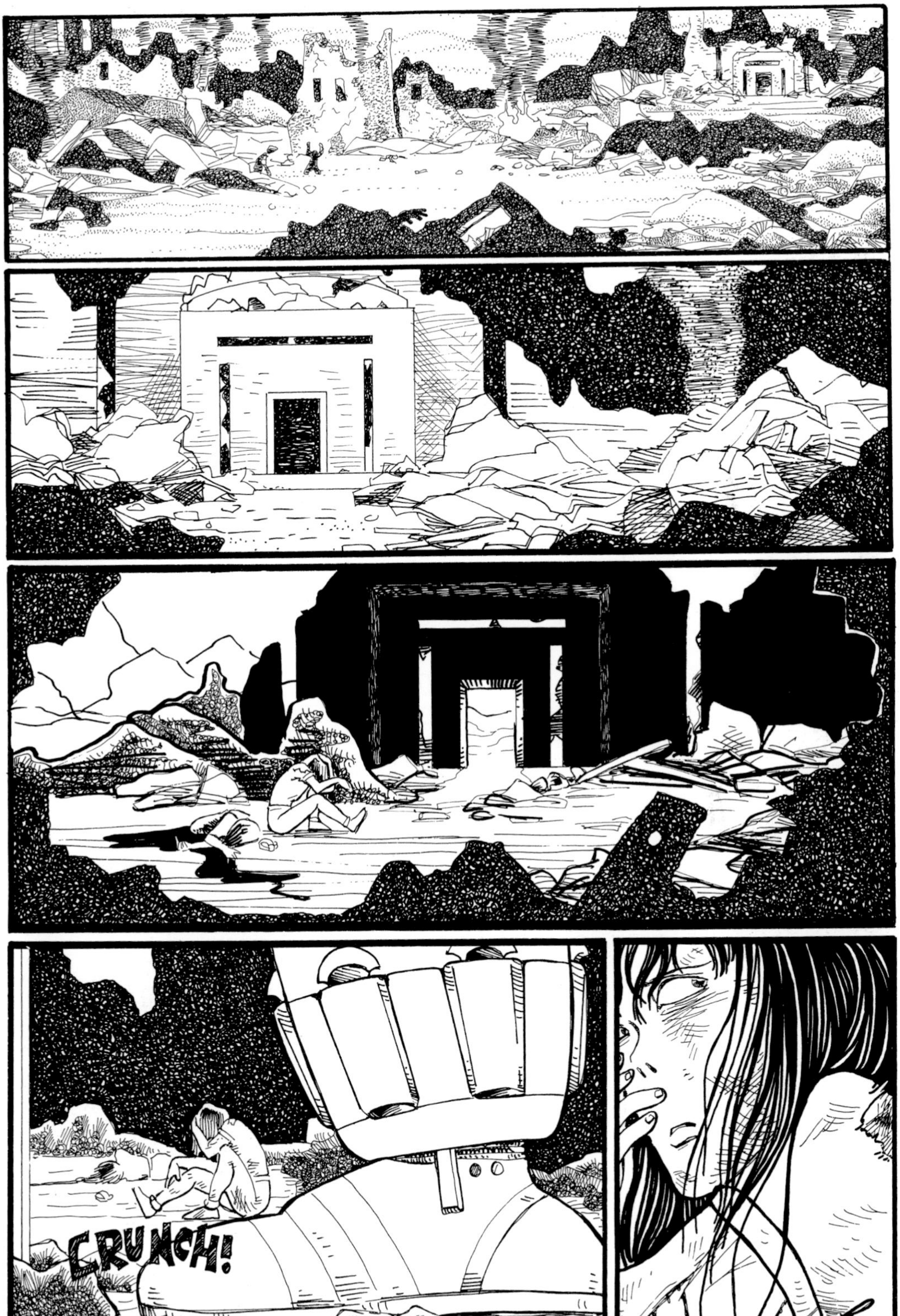
CRUNCH!

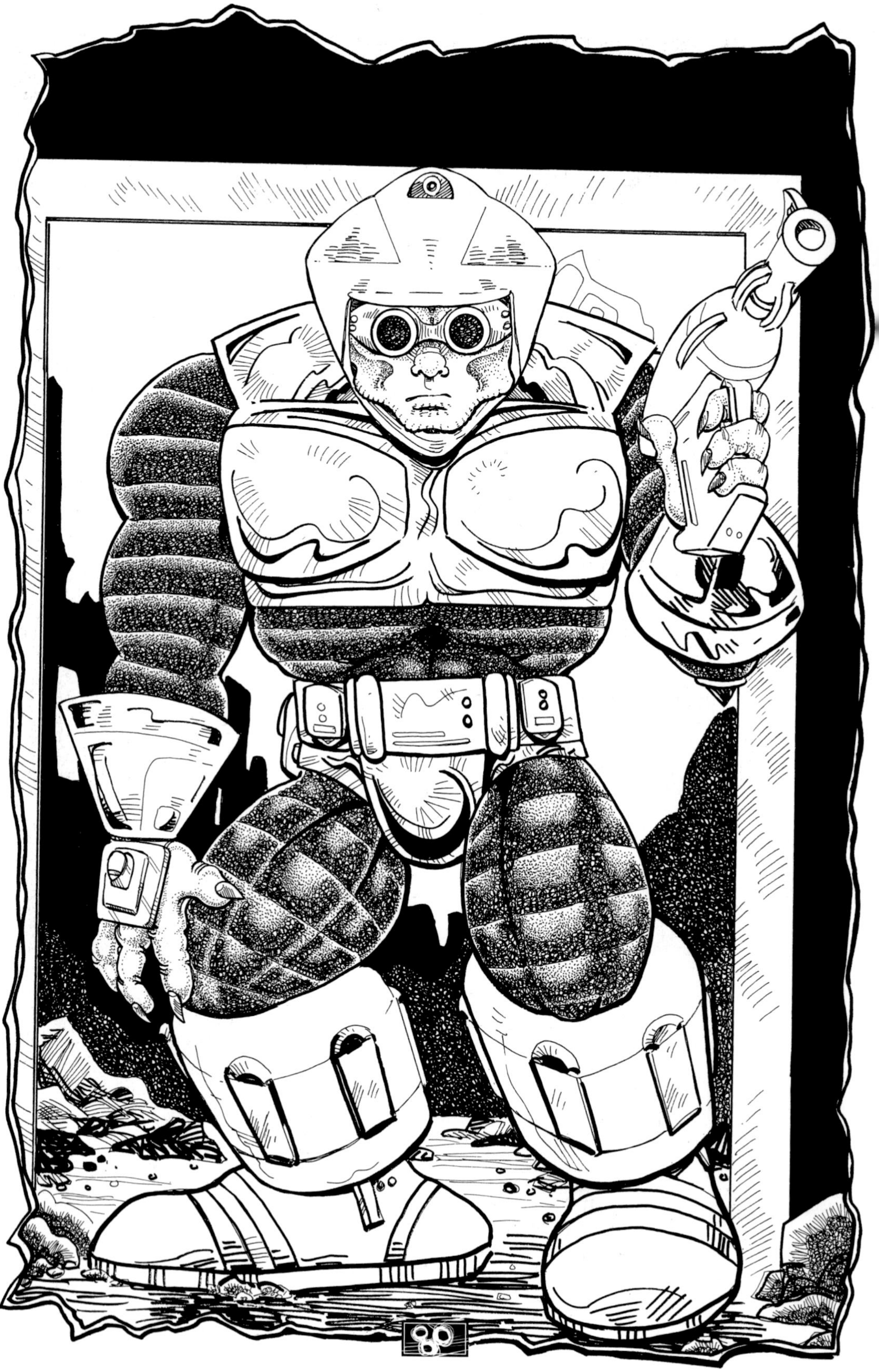

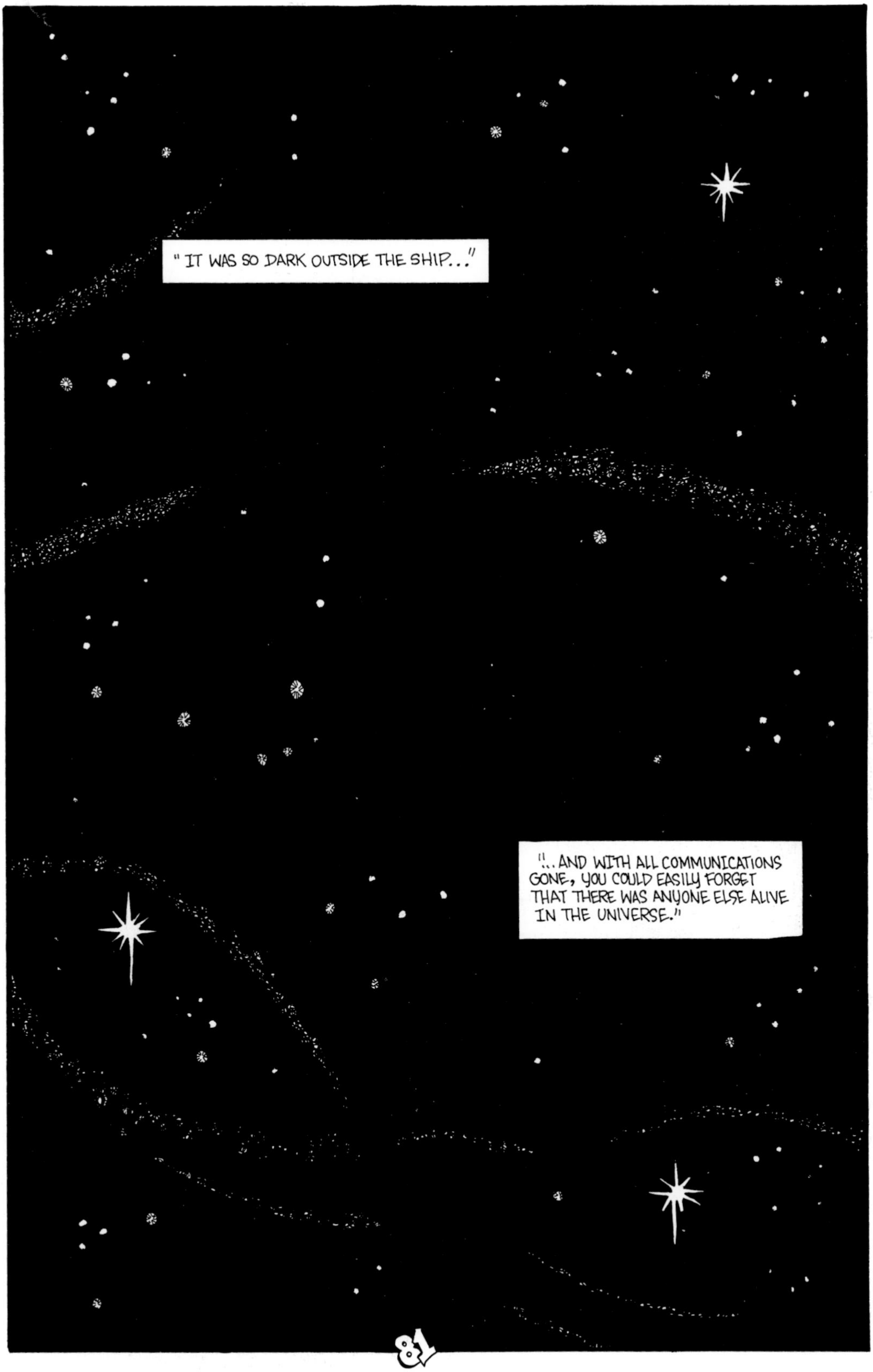
"IT WAS SO DARK OUTSIDE THE SHIP..."
"...AND WITH ALL COMMUNICATIONS GONE, YOU COULD EASILY FORGET THAT THERE WAS ANYONE ELSE ALIVE IN THE UNIVERSE."

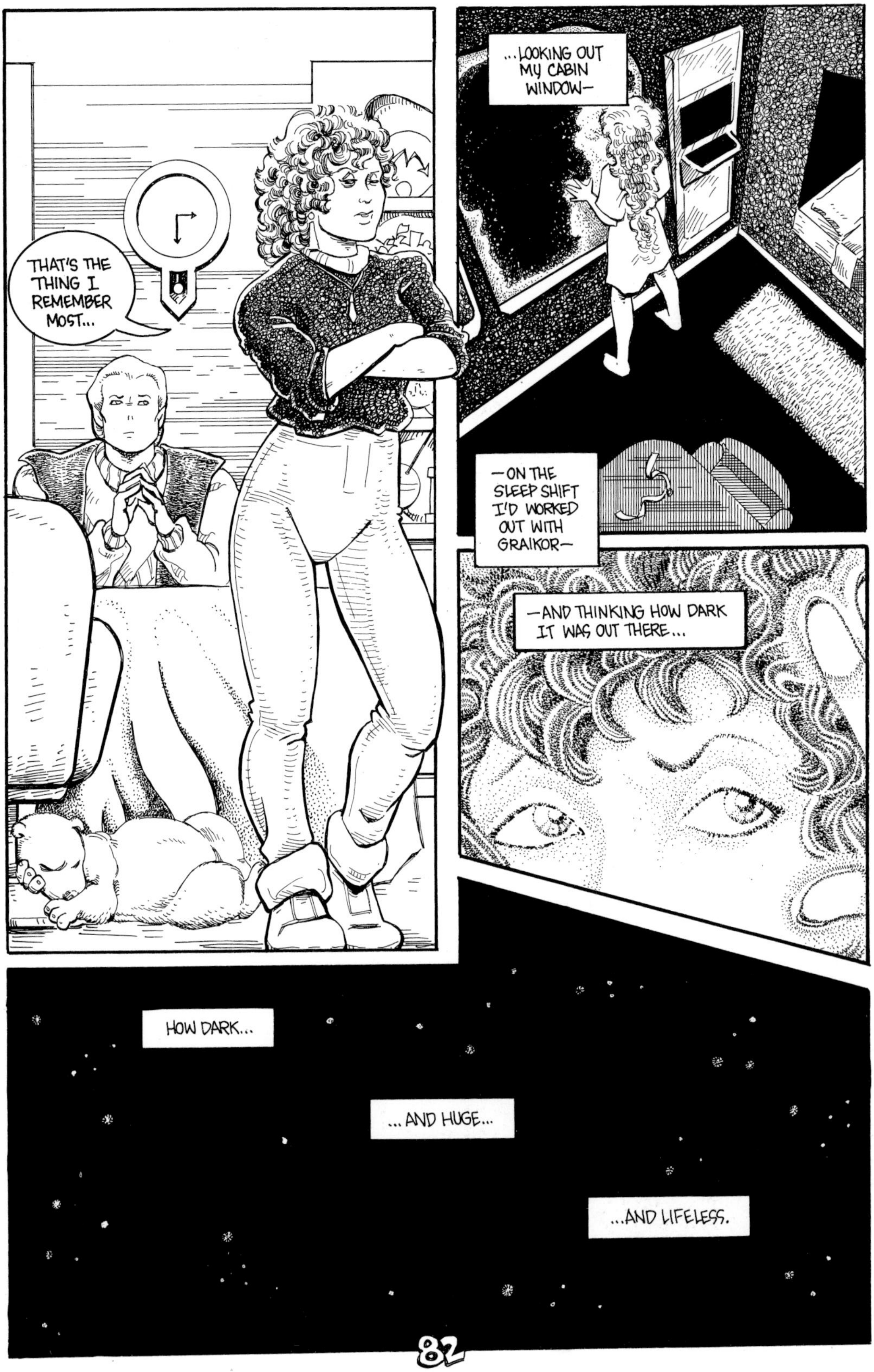
THAT'S THE THING I REMEMBER MOST...
...LOOKING OUT MY CABIN WINDOW—
—ON THE SLEEP SHIFT I'D WORKED OUT WITH GRAIKOR—
—AND THINKING HOW DARK IT WAS OUT THERE...
HOW DARK...
...AND HUGE...
...AND LIFELESS.

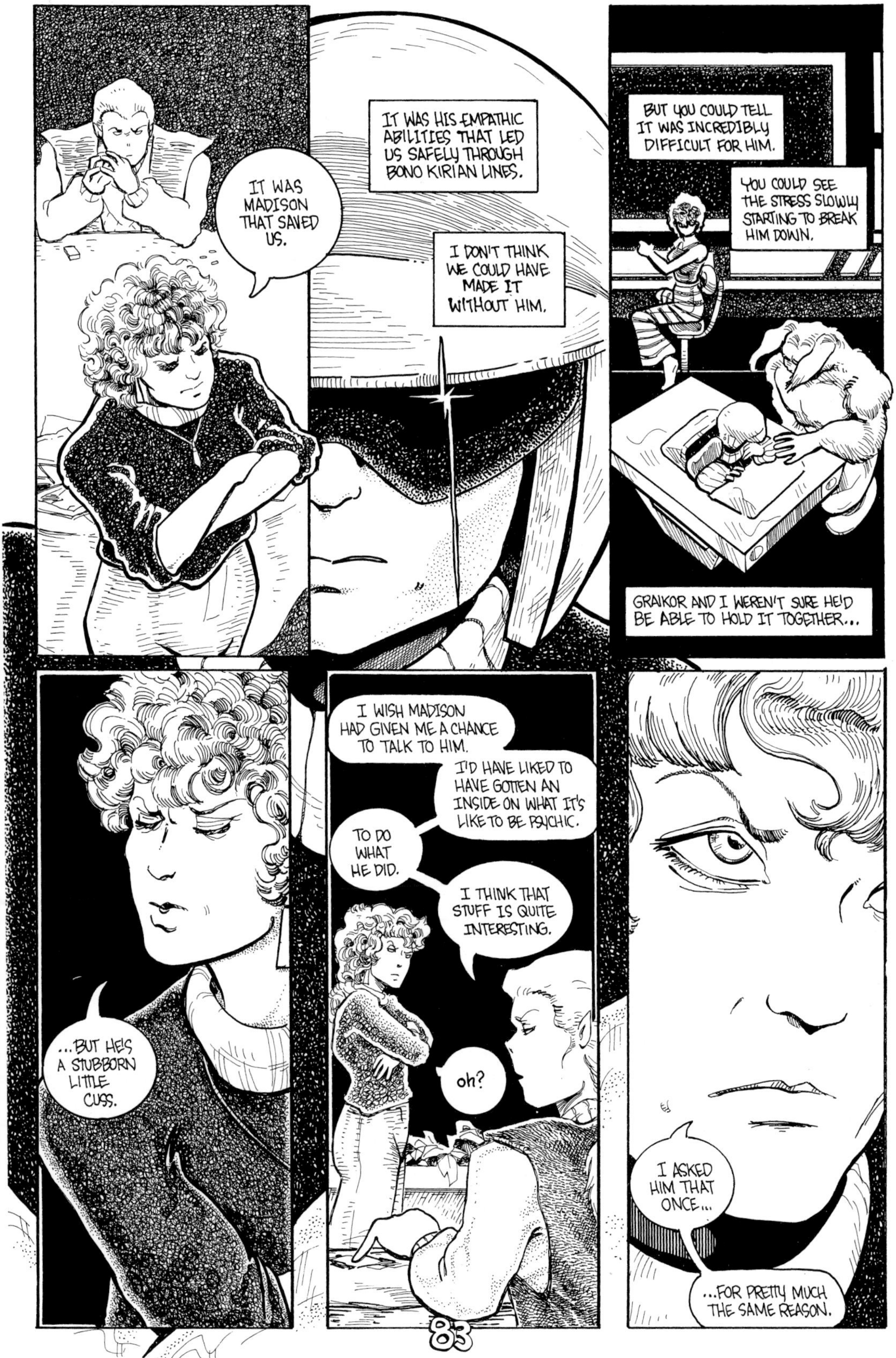
IT WAS MADISON THAT SAVED US.
IT WAS HIS EMPATHIC ABILITIES THAT LED US SAFELY THROUGH BONO KIRIAN LINES.
I DON'T THINK WE COULD HAVE MADE IT WITHOUT HIM.
BUT YOU COULD TELL IT WAS INCREDIBLY DIFFICULT FOR HIM.
YOU COULD SEE THE STRESS SLOWLY STARTING TO BREAK HIM DOWN.
GRAIKOR AND I WEREN'T SURE HE'D BE ABLE TO HOLD IT TOGETHER...
...BUT HE'S A STUBBORN LITTLE CUSS.
I WISH MADISON HAD GIVEN ME A CHANCE TO TALK TO HIM.
I'D HAVE LIKED TO HAVE GOTTEN AN INSIDE ON WHAT IT'S LIKE TO BE PSYCHIC.
TO DO WHAT HE DID.
I THINK THAT STUFF IS QUITE INTERESTING.
oh?
I ASKED HIM THAT ONCE...
...FOR PRETTY MUCH THE SAME REASON.

HE LOOKED AT ME A LONG TIME.

I STARTED TO THINK HE WASN'T GOING TO ANSWER ME...

...AND THEN HE SAID...

"...IT'S LIKE BEING LOCKED ALONE IN A ROOM."

"NEXT DOOR THEY BEGIN TO **KILL** SOMEONE."

"YOU CAN HEAR EVERYTHING."

"THE SCREAMS."

"THE SOBS."

"THE PLEADING."

"AND YOU CAN'T DO A THING."

"ALL YOU CAN DO IS **LISTEN**."

THAT'S WHAT IT'S LIKE, ALDAR.

THAT'S WHAT MADISON DID FOR US OUT THERE ON THE SHIP.

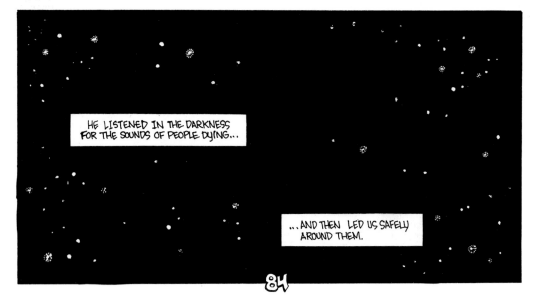

HE LISTENED IN THE DARKNESS FOR THE SOUNDS OF PEOPLE DYING...

...AND THEN LED US SAFELY AROUND THEM.

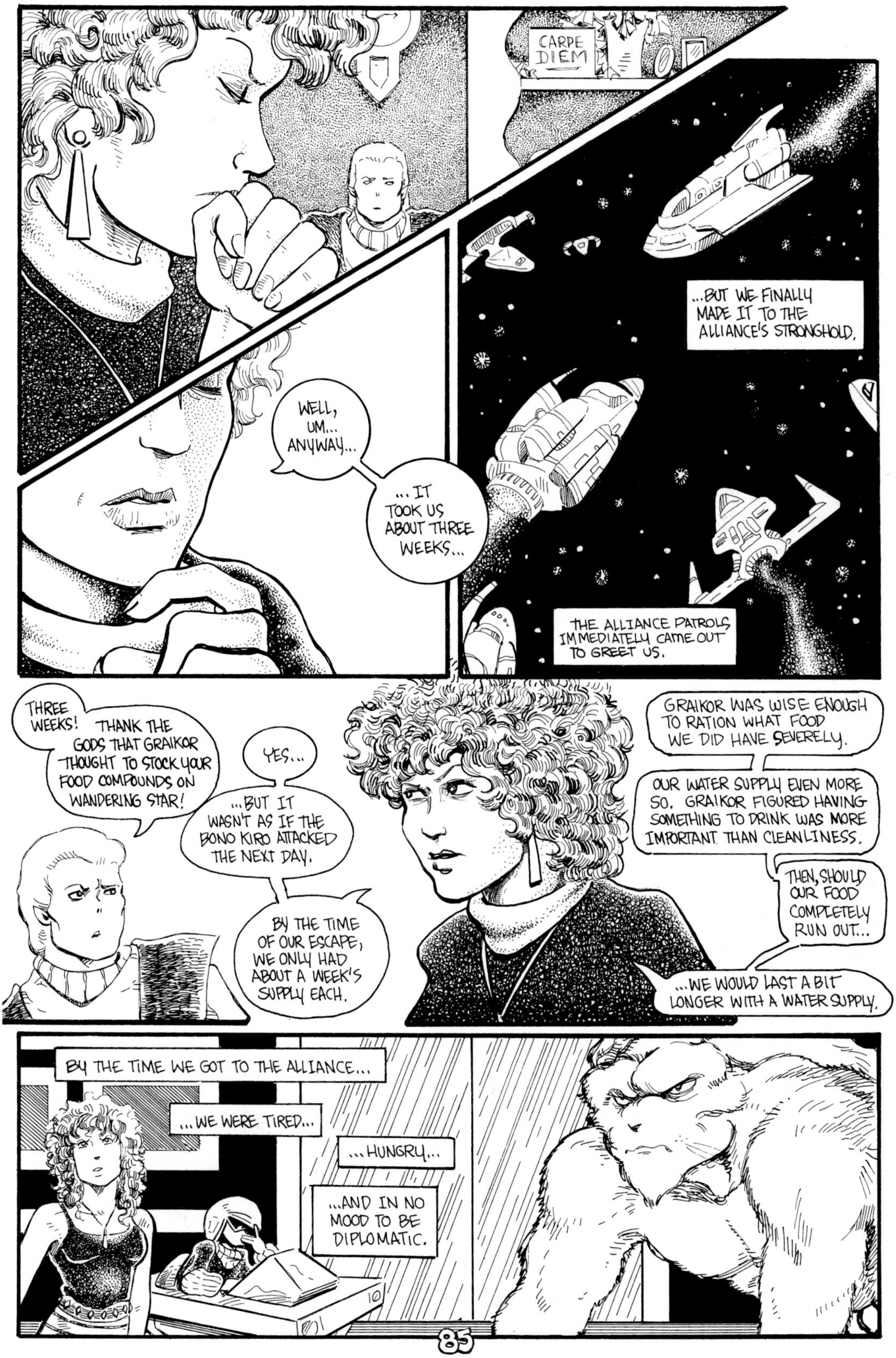
CARPE DIEM
WELL, UM... ANYWAY...
...IT TOOK US ABOUT THREE WEEKS...
...BUT WE FINALLY MADE IT TO THE ALLIANCE'S STRONGHOLD.
THE ALLIANCE PATROLS IMMEDIATELY CAME OUT TO GREET US.
THREE WEEKS! THANK THE GODS THAT GRAIKOR THOUGHT TO STOCK YOUR FOOD COMPOUNDS ON WANDERING STAR!
YES...
...BUT IT WASN'T AS IF THE BONO KIRO ATTACKED THE NEXT DAY.
BY THE TIME OF OUR ESCAPE, WE ONLY HAD ABOUT A WEEK'S SUPPLY EACH.
GRAIKOR WAS WISE ENOUGH TO RATION WHAT FOOD WE DID HAVE SEVERELY.
OUR WATER SUPPLY EVEN MORE SO. GRAIKOR FIGURED HAVING SOMETHING TO DRINK WAS MORE IMPORTANT THAN CLEANLINESS.
THEN, SHOULD OUR FOOD COMPLETELY RUN OUT...
...WE WOULD LAST A BIT LONGER WITH A WATER SUPPLY.
BY THE TIME WE GOT TO THE ALLIANCE...
...WE WERE TIRED...
...HUNGRY...
...AND IN NO MOOD TO BE DIPLOMATIC.

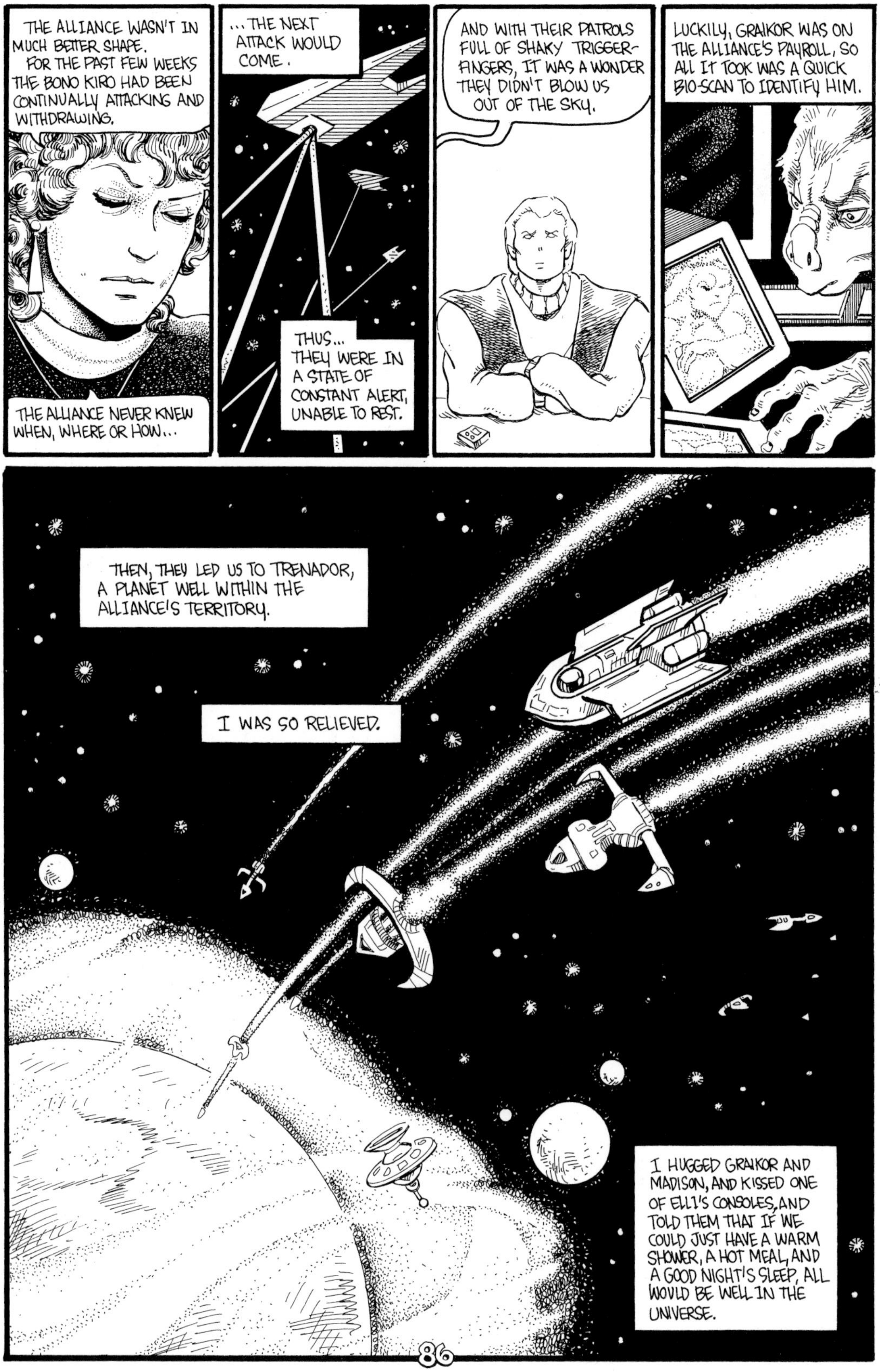
THE ALLIANCE WASN'T IN MUCH BETTER SHAPE.
FOR THE PAST FEW WEEKS THE BONO KIRO HAD BEEN CONTINUALLY ATTACKING AND WITHDRAWING.
THE ALLIANCE NEVER KNEW WHEN, WHERE OR HOW...
...THE NEXT ATTACK WOULD COME.
THUS... THEY WERE IN A STATE OF CONSTANT ALERT, UNABLE TO REST.
AND WITH THEIR PATROLS FULL OF SHAKY TRIGGER-FINGERS, IT WAS A WONDER THEY DIDN'T BLOW US OUT OF THE SKY.
LUCKILY, GRAIKOR WAS ON THE ALLIANCE'S PAYROLL, SO ALL IT TOOK WAS A QUICK BIO-SCAN TO IDENTIFY HIM.
THEN, THEY LED US TO TRENADOR, A PLANET WELL WITHIN THE ALLIANCE'S TERRITORY.
I WAS SO RELIEVED.
I HUGGED GRAIKOR AND MADISON, AND KISSED ONE OF ELLI'S CONSOLES, AND TOLD THEM THAT IF WE COULD JUST HAVE A WARM SHOWER, A HOT MEAL, AND A GOOD NIGHT'S SLEEP, ALL WOULD BE WELL IN THE UNIVERSE.

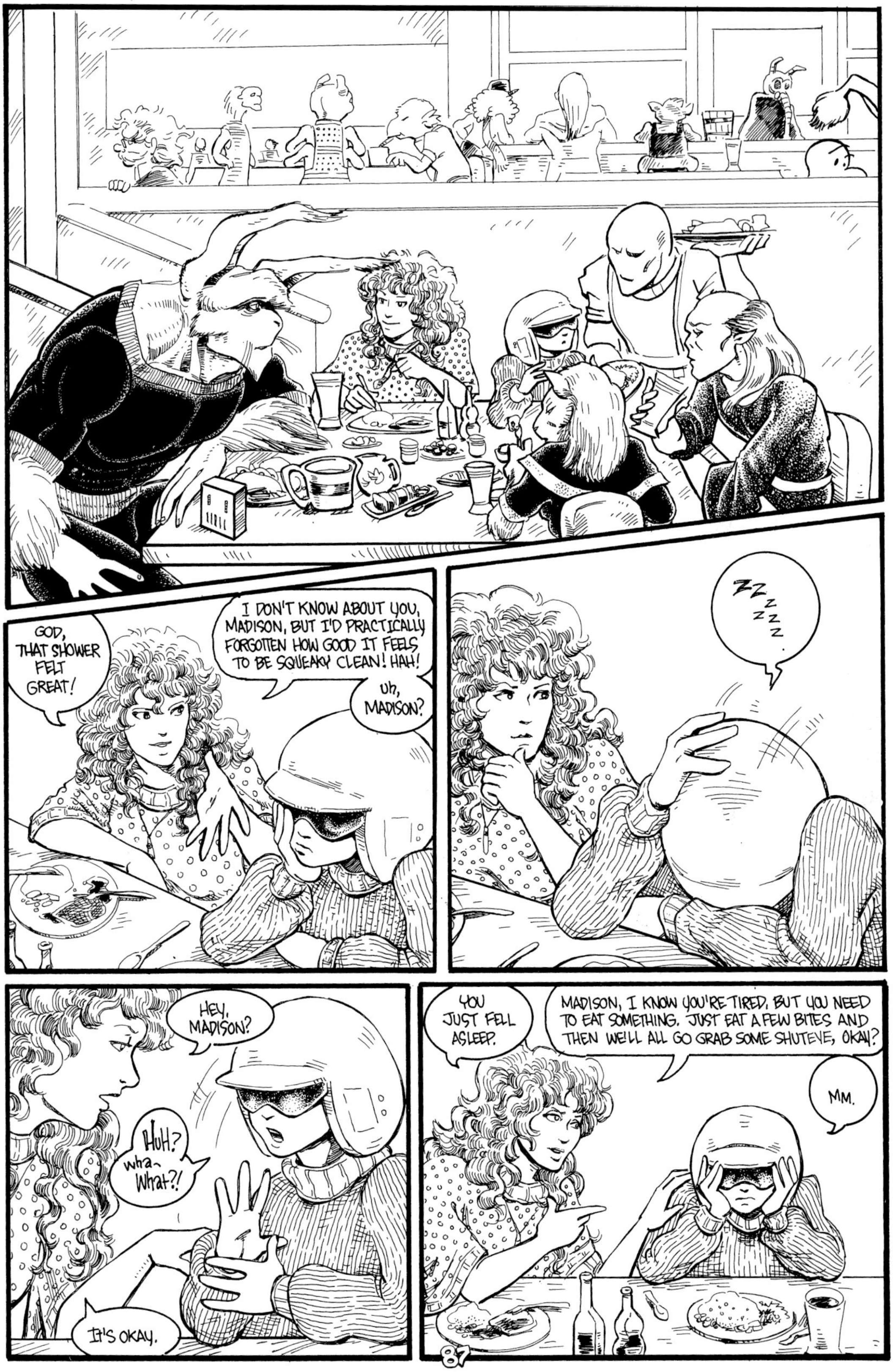
GOD, THAT SHOWER FELT GREAT!
I DON'T KNOW ABOUT YOU, MADISON, BUT I'D PRACTICALLY FORGOTTEN HOW GOOD IT FEELS TO BE SQUEAKY CLEAN! HAH!
uh, MADISON?
ZZZZZ
HEY, MADISON?
HUH? wha- What?!
IT'S OKAY.
YOU JUST FELL ASLEEP.
MADISON, I KNOW YOU'RE TIRED, BUT YOU NEED TO EAT SOMETHING. JUST EAT A FEW BITES AND THEN WE'LL ALL GO GRAB SOME SHUTEYE, OKAY?
MM.

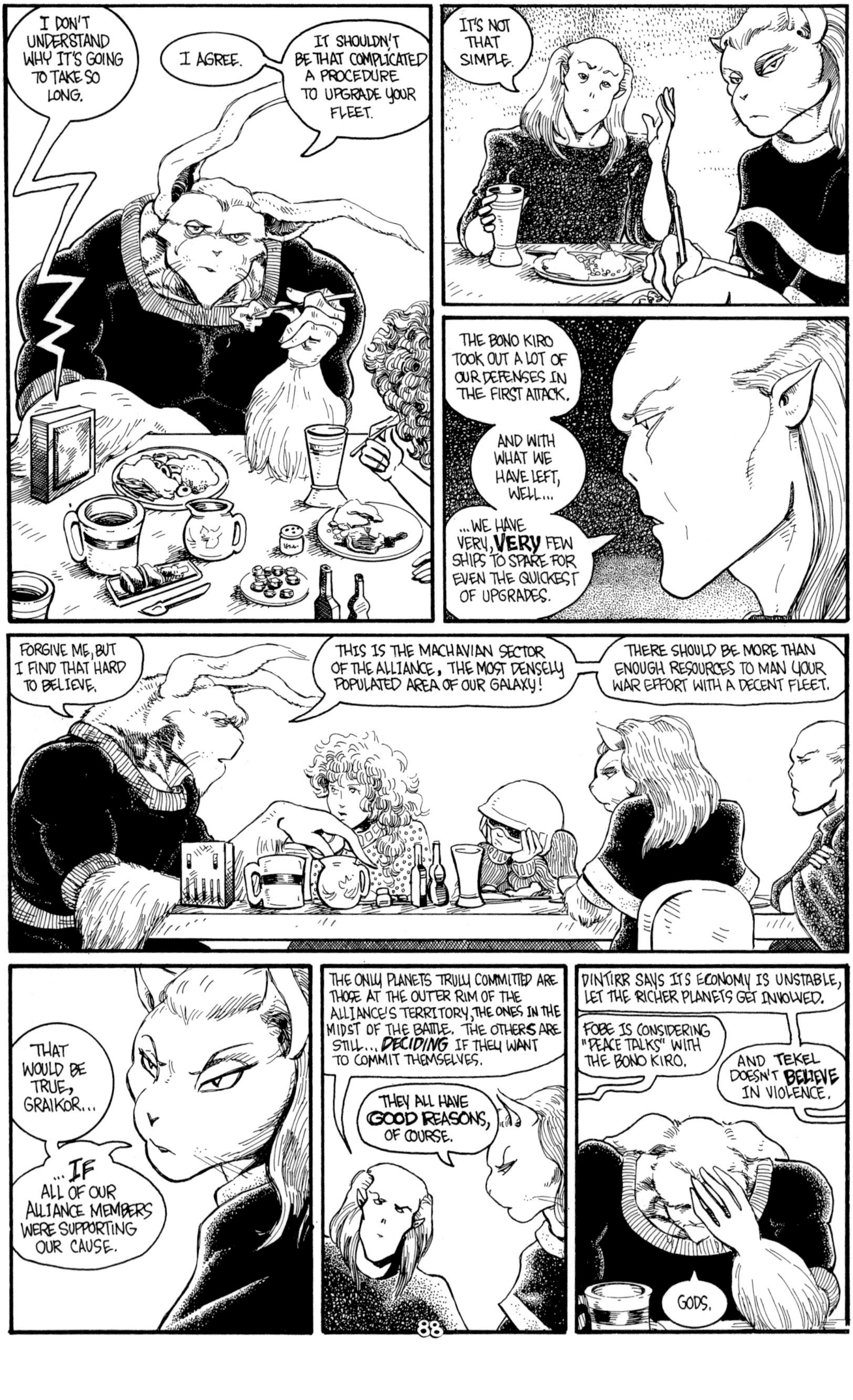
I DON'T UNDERSTAND WHY IT'S GOING TO TAKE SO LONG.
I AGREE.
IT SHOULDN'T BE THAT COMPLICATED A PROCEDURE TO UPGRADE YOUR FLEET.
IT'S NOT THAT SIMPLE.
THE BONO KIRO TOOK OUT A LOT OF OUR DEFENSES IN THE FIRST ATTACK.
AND WITH WHAT WE HAVE LEFT, WELL...
...WE HAVE VERY, **VERY** FEW SHIPS TO SPARE FOR EVEN THE QUICKEST OF UPGRADES.
FORGIVE ME, BUT I FIND THAT HARD TO BELIEVE.
THIS IS THE MACHAVIAN SECTOR OF THE ALLIANCE, THE MOST DENSELY POPULATED AREA OF OUR GALAXY!
THERE SHOULD BE MORE THAN ENOUGH RESOURCES TO MAN YOUR WAR EFFORT WITH A DECENT FLEET.
THAT WOULD BE TRUE, GRAIKOR...
...**IF** ALL OF OUR ALLIANCE MEMBERS WERE SUPPORTING OUR CAUSE.
THE ONLY PLANETS TRULY COMMITTED ARE THOSE AT THE OUTER RIM OF THE ALLIANCE'S TERRITORY, THE ONES IN THE MIDST OF THE BATTLE. THE OTHERS ARE STILL... ***DECIDING*** IF THEY WANT TO COMMIT THEMSELVES.
THEY ALL HAVE **GOOD REASONS**, OF COURSE.
DINTIRR SAYS ITS ECONOMY IS UNSTABLE, LET THE RICHER PLANETS GET INVOLVED.
FOBE IS CONSIDERING "PEACE TALKS" WITH THE BONO KIRO.
AND **TEKEL** DOESN'T **BELIEVE** IN VIOLENCE.
GODS.

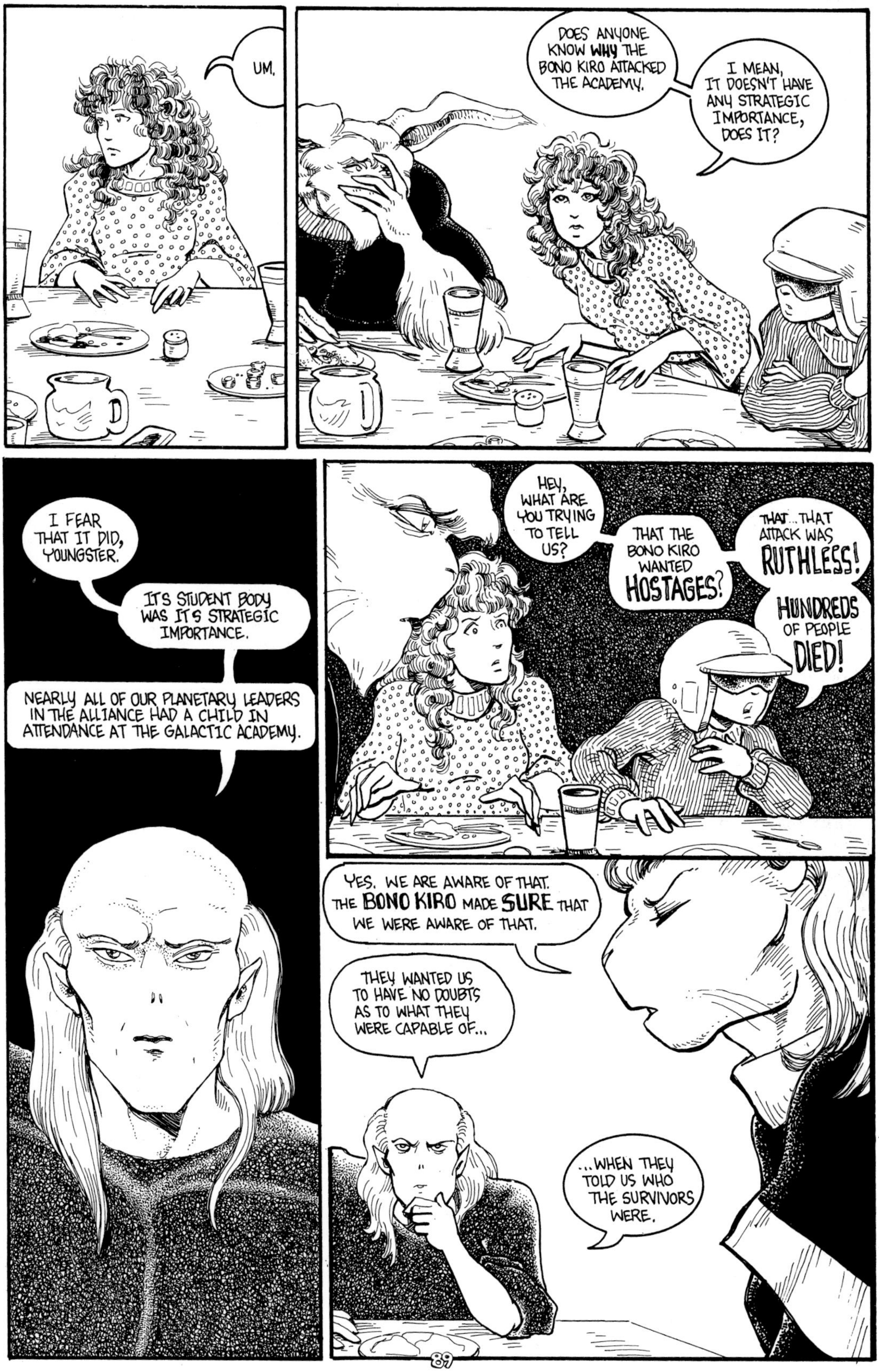
UM.
DOES ANYONE KNOW WHY THE BONO KIRO ATTACKED THE ACADEMY.
I MEAN, IT DOESN'T HAVE ANY STRATEGIC IMPORTANCE, DOES IT?
I FEAR THAT IT DID, YOUNGSTER.
IT'S STUDENT BODY WAS IT'S STRATEGIC IMPORTANCE.
NEARLY ALL OF OUR PLANETARY LEADERS IN THE ALLIANCE HAD A CHILD IN ATTENDANCE AT THE GALACTIC ACADEMY.
HEY, WHAT ARE YOU TRYING TO TELL US?
THAT THE BONO KIRO WANTED HOSTAGES?
THAT... THAT ATTACK WAS RUTHLESS!
HUNDREDS OF PEOPLE DIED!
YES. WE ARE AWARE OF THAT. THE BONO KIRO MADE SURE THAT WE WERE AWARE OF THAT.
THEY WANTED US TO HAVE NO DOUBTS AS TO WHAT THEY WERE CAPABLE OF...
...WHEN THEY TOLD US WHO THE SURVIVORS WERE.

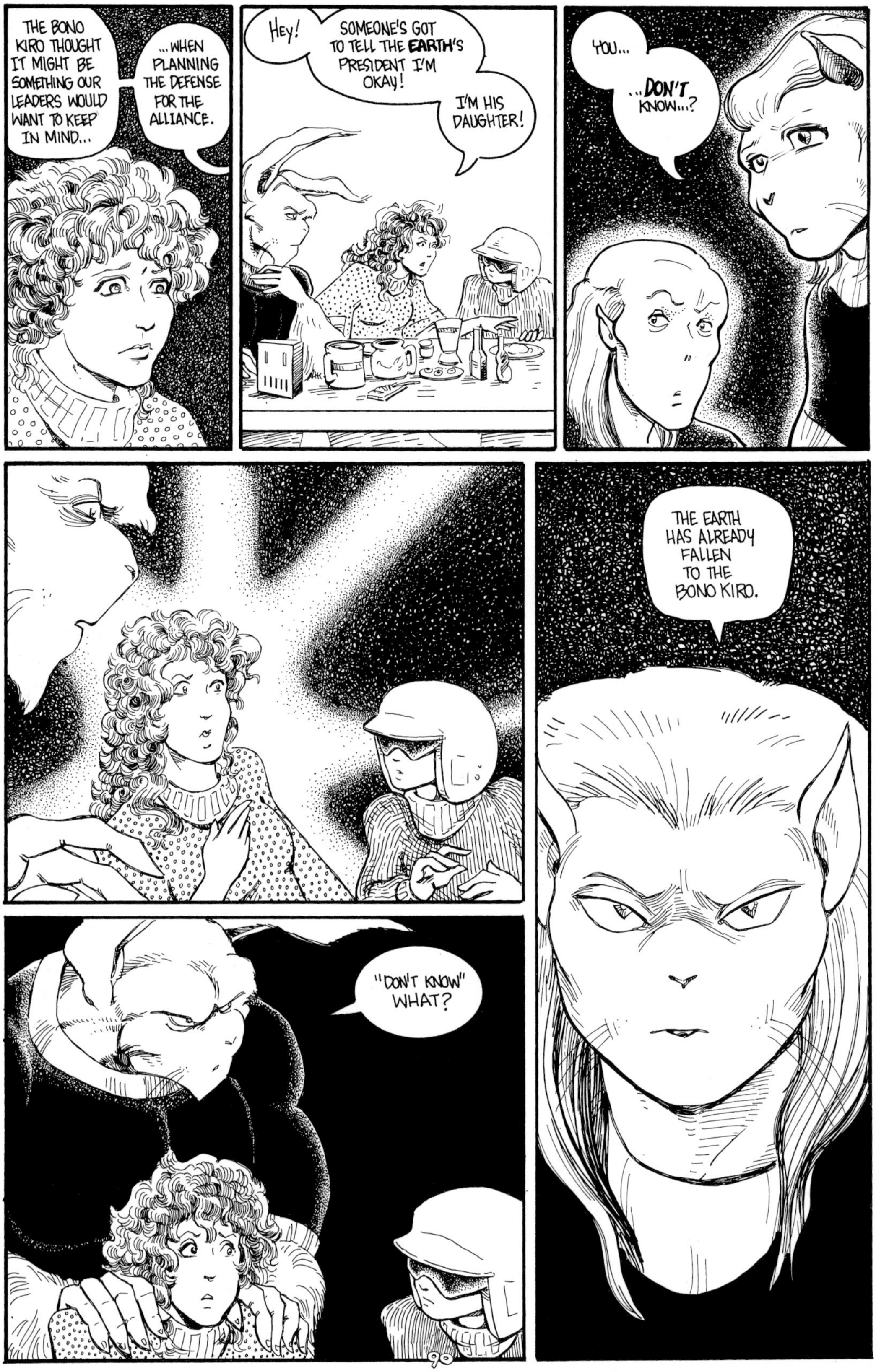
THE BONO KIRO THOUGHT IT MIGHT BE SOMETHING OUR LEADERS WOULD WANT TO KEEP IN MIND...
...WHEN PLANNING THE DEFENSE FOR THE ALLIANCE.
Hey!
SOMEONE'S GOT TO TELL THE EARTH'S PRESIDENT I'M OKAY!
I'M HIS DAUGHTER!
YOU...
...DON'T KNOW...?
THE EARTH HAS ALREADY FALLEN TO THE BONO KIRO.
"DON'T KNOW" WHAT?

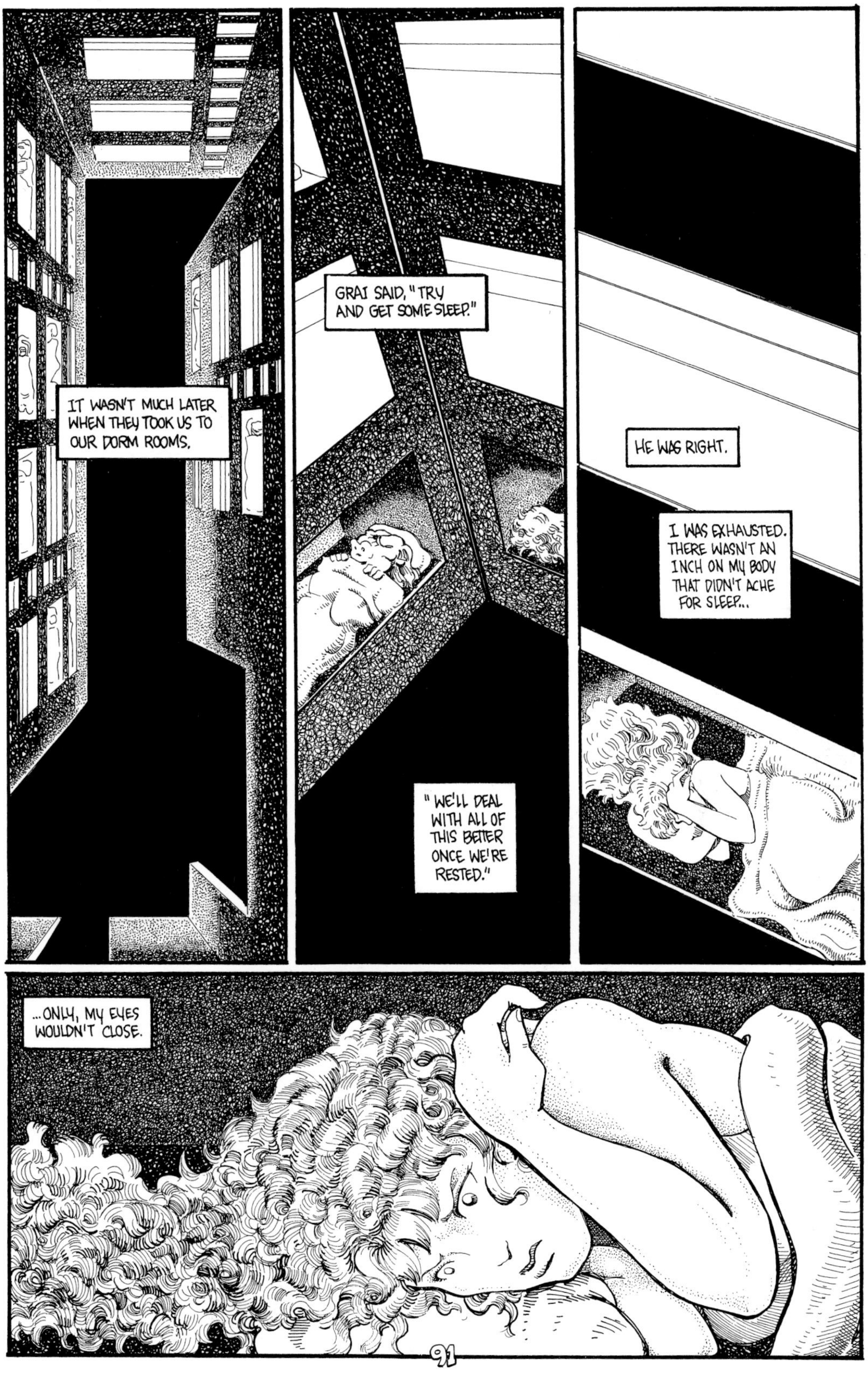
IT WASN'T MUCH LATER WHEN THEY TOOK US TO OUR DORM ROOMS.
GRAI SAID, "TRY AND GET SOME SLEEP."
"WE'LL DEAL WITH ALL OF THIS BETTER ONCE WE'RE RESTED."
HE WAS RIGHT.
I WAS EXHAUSTED. THERE WASN'T AN INCH ON MY BODY THAT DIDN'T ACHE FOR SLEEP...
...ONLY, MY EYES WOULDN'T CLOSE.

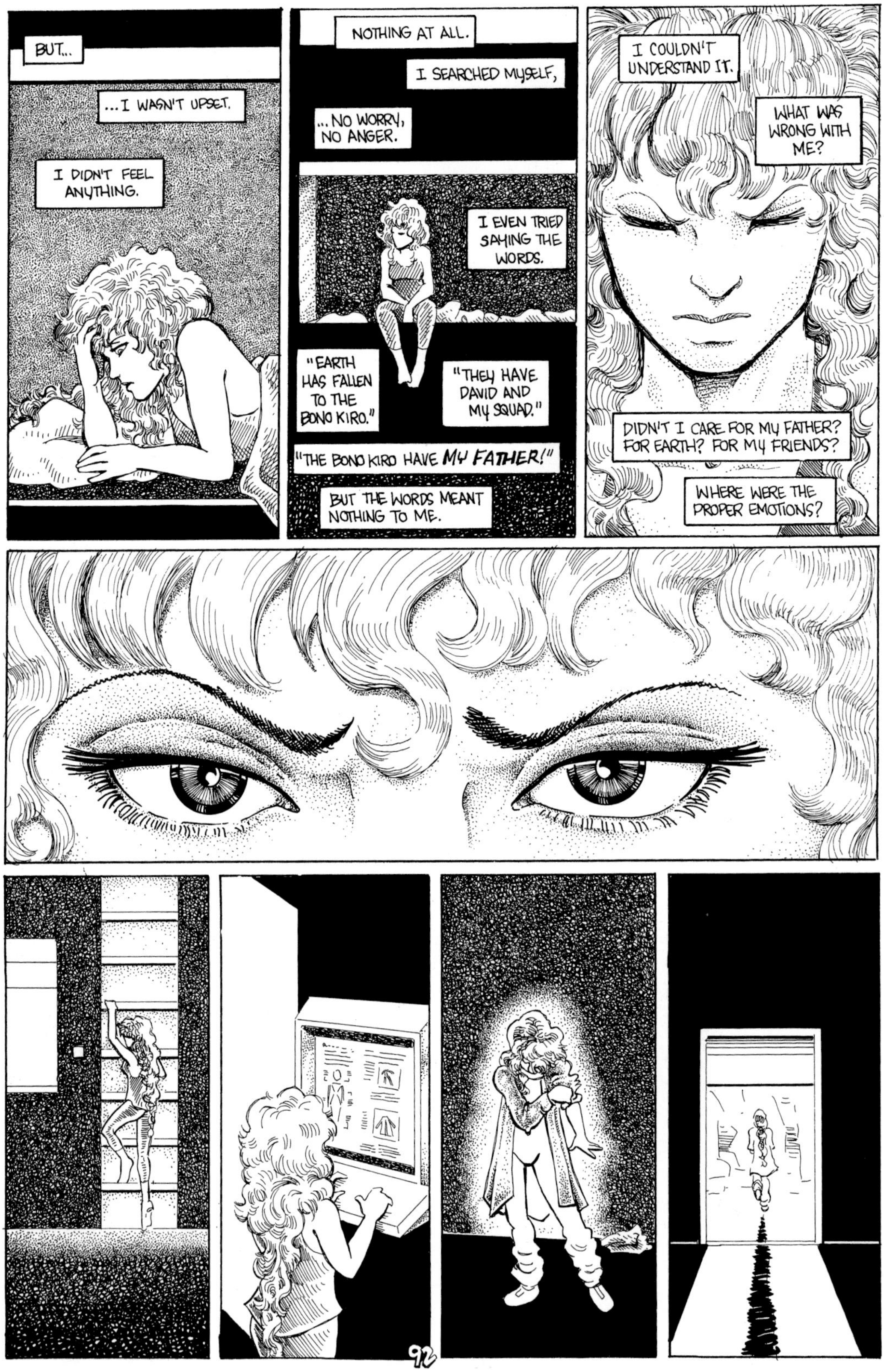
BUT...
...I WASN'T UPSET.
I DIDN'T FEEL ANYTHING.
NOTHING AT ALL.
I SEARCHED MYSELF,
...NO WORRY, NO ANGER.
I EVEN TRIED SAYING THE WORDS.
"EARTH HAS FALLEN TO THE BONO KIRO."
"THEY HAVE DAVID AND MY SQUAD."
"THE BONO KIRO HAVE MY FATHER!"
BUT THE WORDS MEANT NOTHING TO ME.
I COULDN'T UNDERSTAND IT.
WHAT WAS WRONG WITH ME?
DIDN'T I CARE FOR MY FATHER? FOR EARTH? FOR MY FRIENDS?
WHERE WERE THE PROPER EMOTIONS?

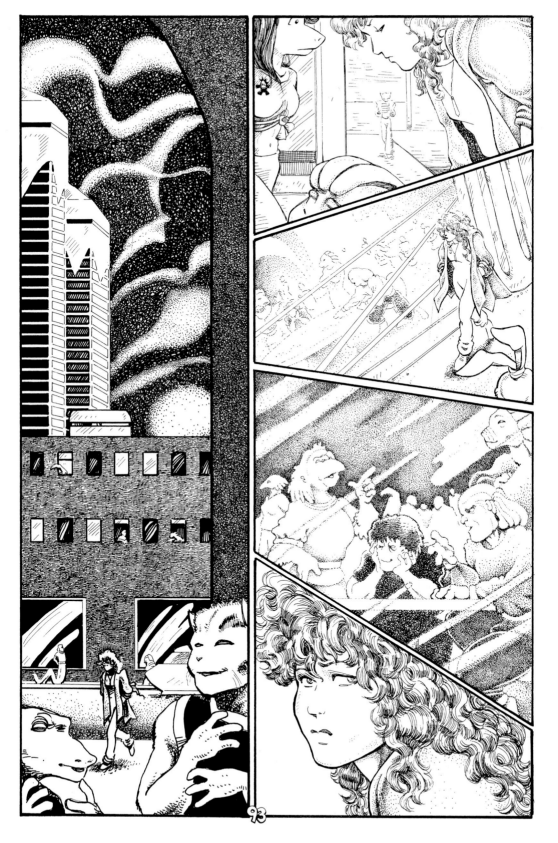

93

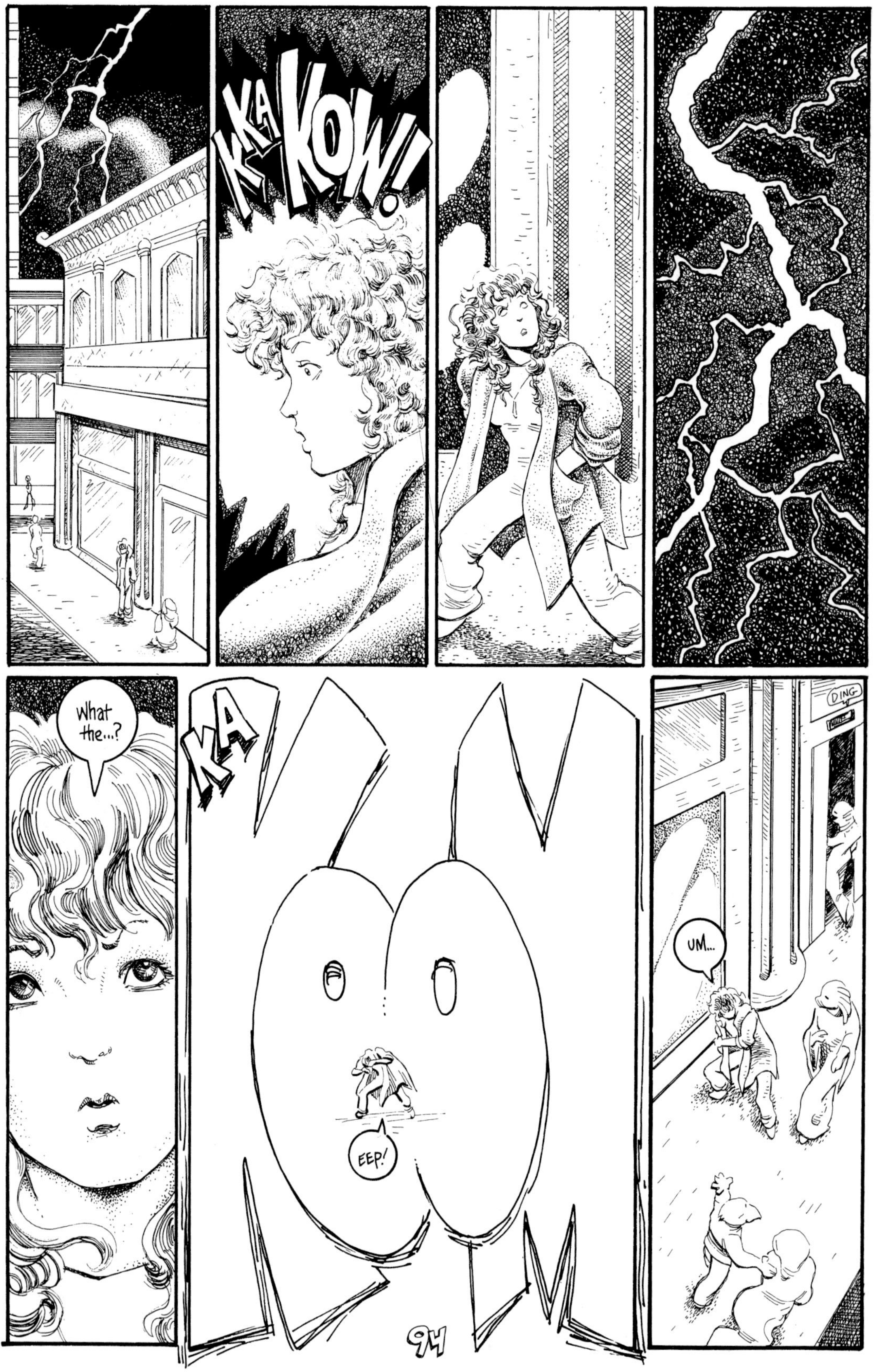

KKA KOW!
What the...?
KA
EEP!
DING
UM...

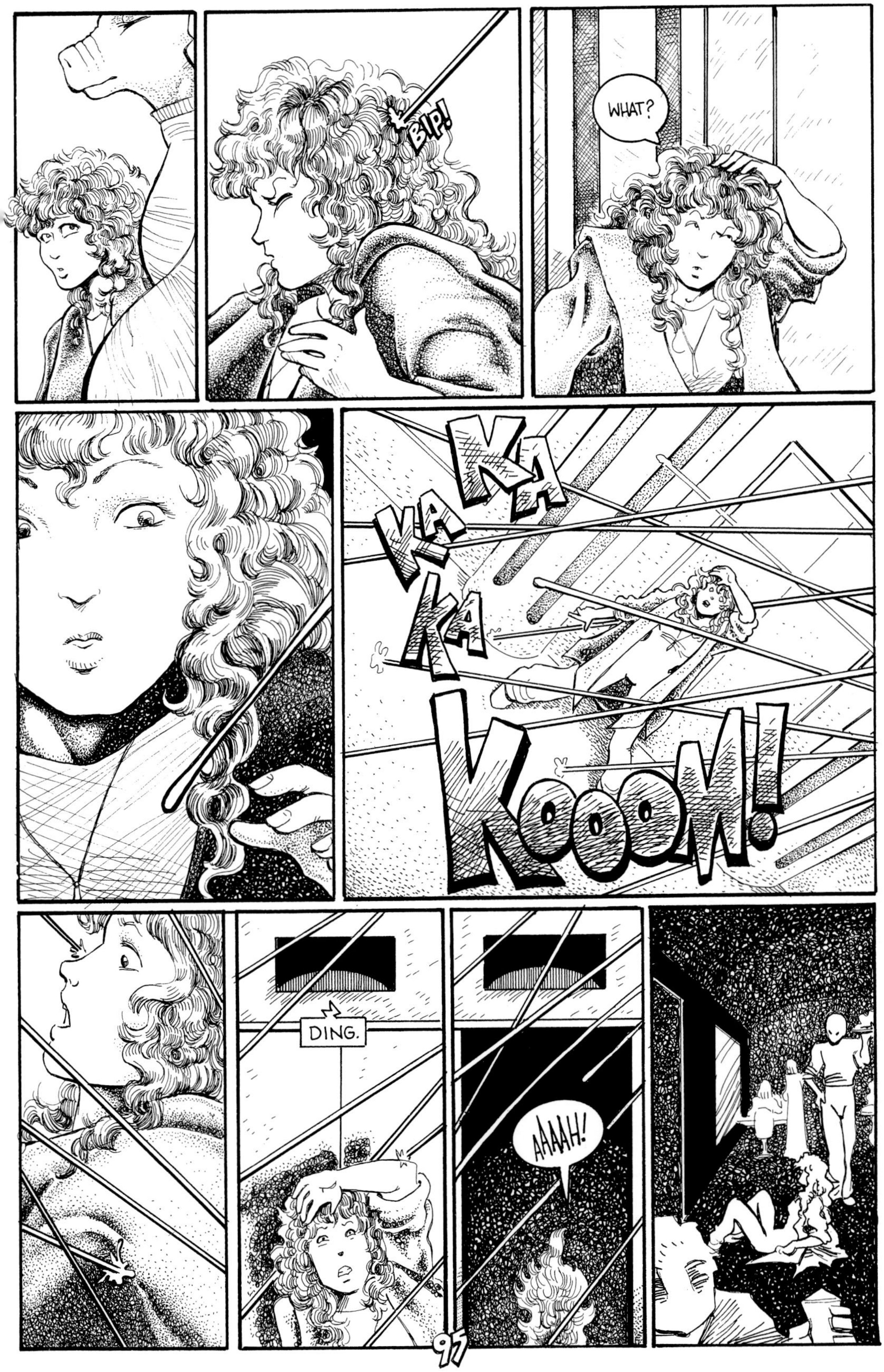
BIP!
WHAT?
KA
KA
KA
KA
KOOOM!
DING.
AAAAH!

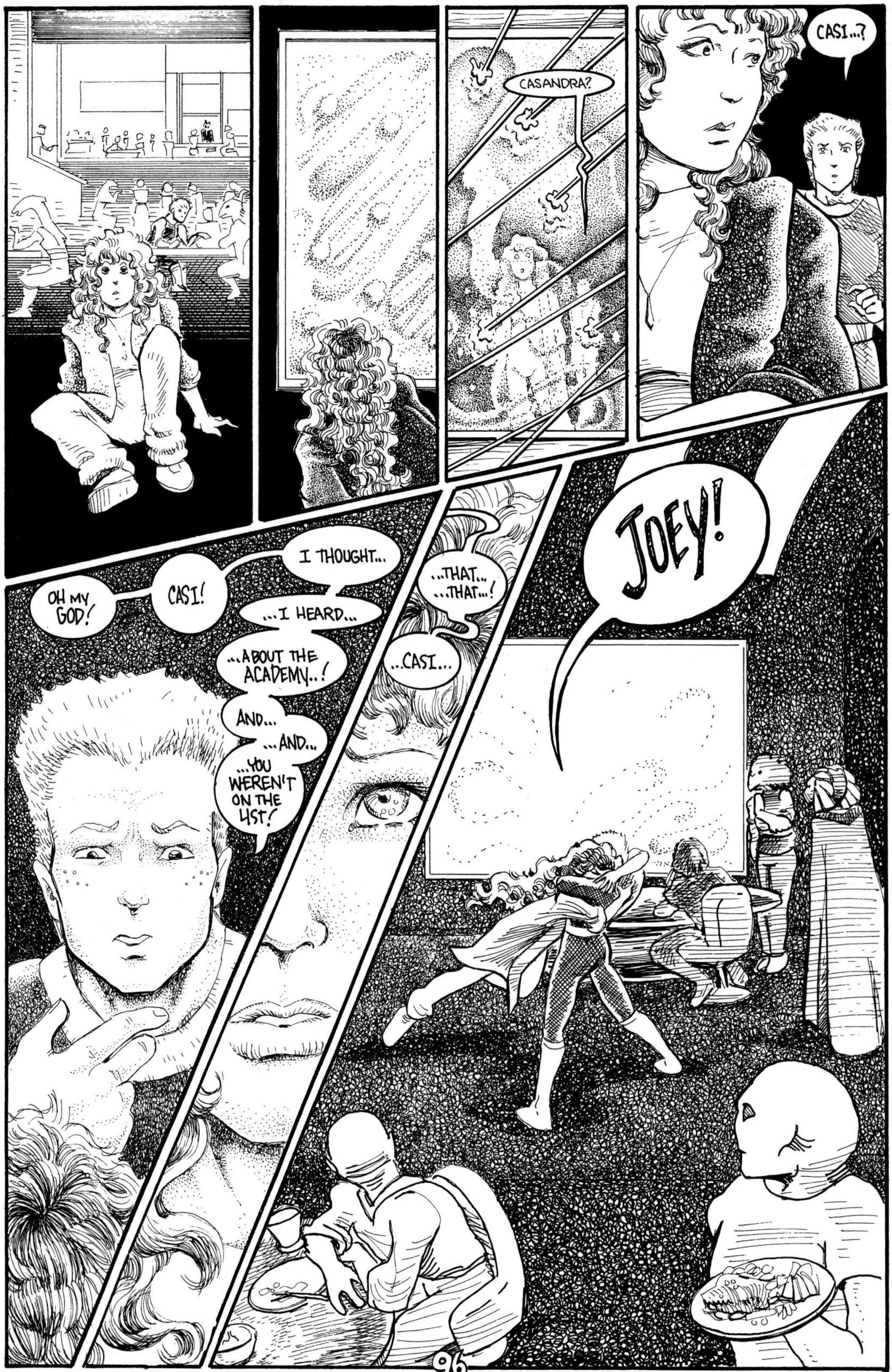
CASANDRA?
CASI...?
JOEY!
OH MY GOD!
CASI!
I THOUGHT...
...I HEARD...
...ABOUT THE ACADEMY...!
AND...
...AND...
...YOU WEREN'T ON THE LIST!
...THAT...
...THAT...!
...CASI...

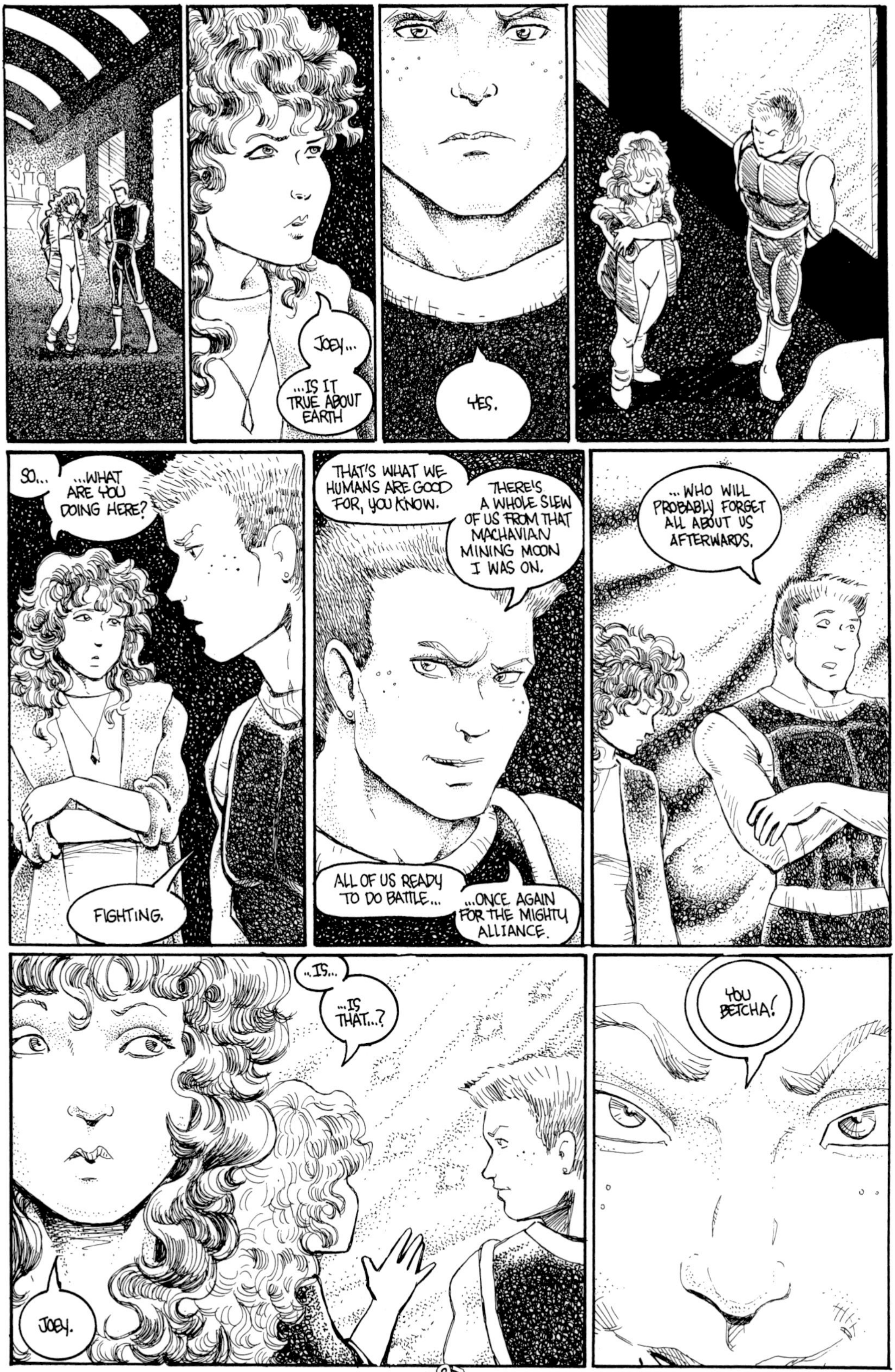
JOEY...
...IS IT TRUE ABOUT EARTH
YES.
SO...
...WHAT ARE YOU DOING HERE?
FIGHTING.
THAT'S WHAT WE HUMANS ARE GOOD FOR, YOU KNOW.
THERE'S A WHOLE SLEW OF US FROM THAT MACHAVIAN MINING MOON I WAS ON.
ALL OF US READY TO DO BATTLE...
...ONCE AGAIN FOR THE MIGHTY ALLIANCE.
...WHO WILL PROBABLY FORGET ALL ABOUT US AFTERWARDS.
...IS...
...IS THAT...?
JOEY.
YOU BETCHA!

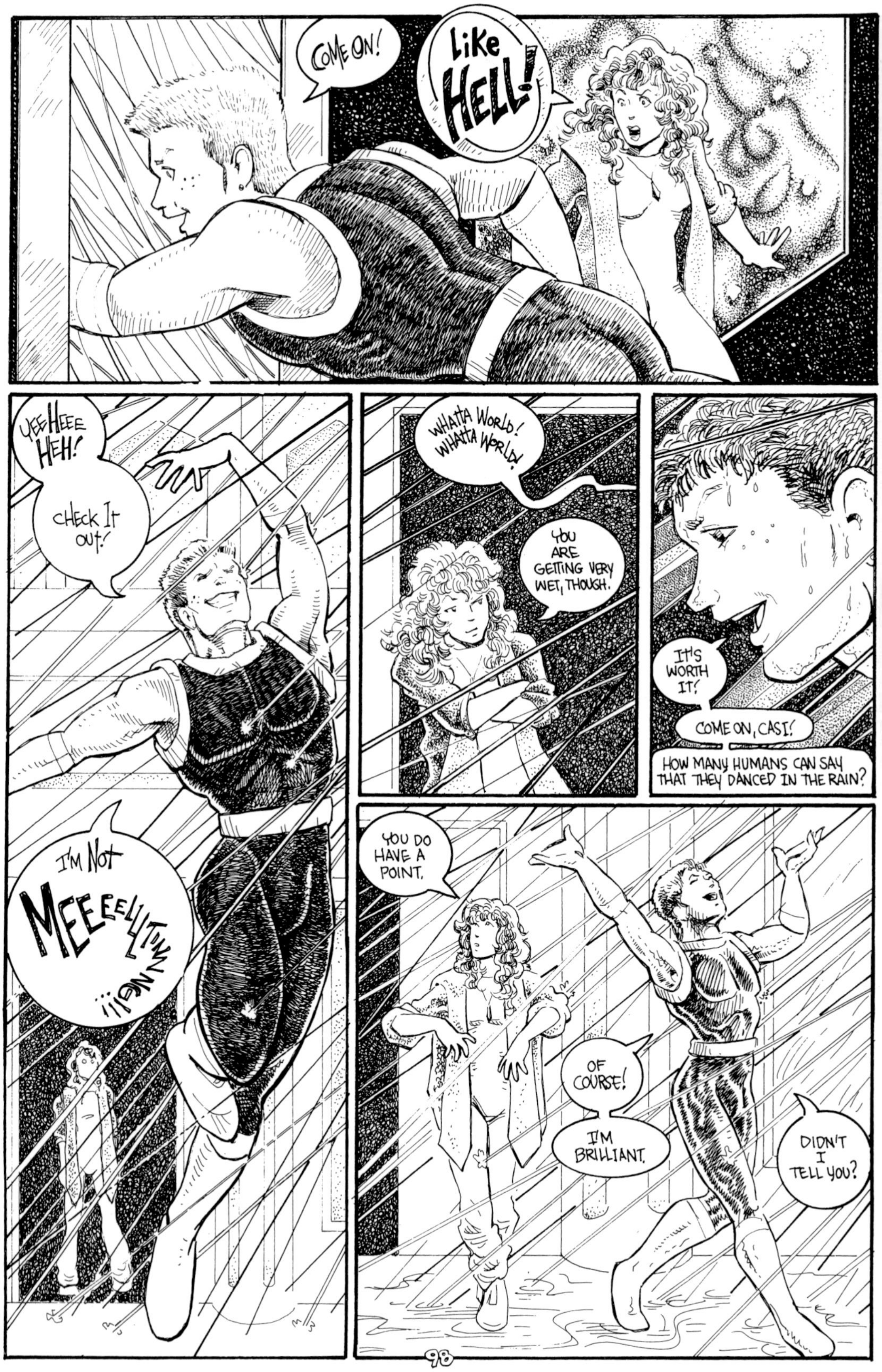
COME ON!
Like HELL!
YEE HEEE HEH!
CHECK IT OUT!
I'M NOT MEEEEELLLTINNNG!!!
WHATTA WORLD! WHATTA WORLD!
YOU ARE GETTING VERY WET, THOUGH.
IT'S WORTH IT!
COME ON, CASI!
HOW MANY HUMANS CAN SAY THAT THEY DANCED IN THE RAIN?
YOU DO HAVE A POINT.
OF COURSE!
I'M BRILLIANT.
DIDN'T I TELL YOU?

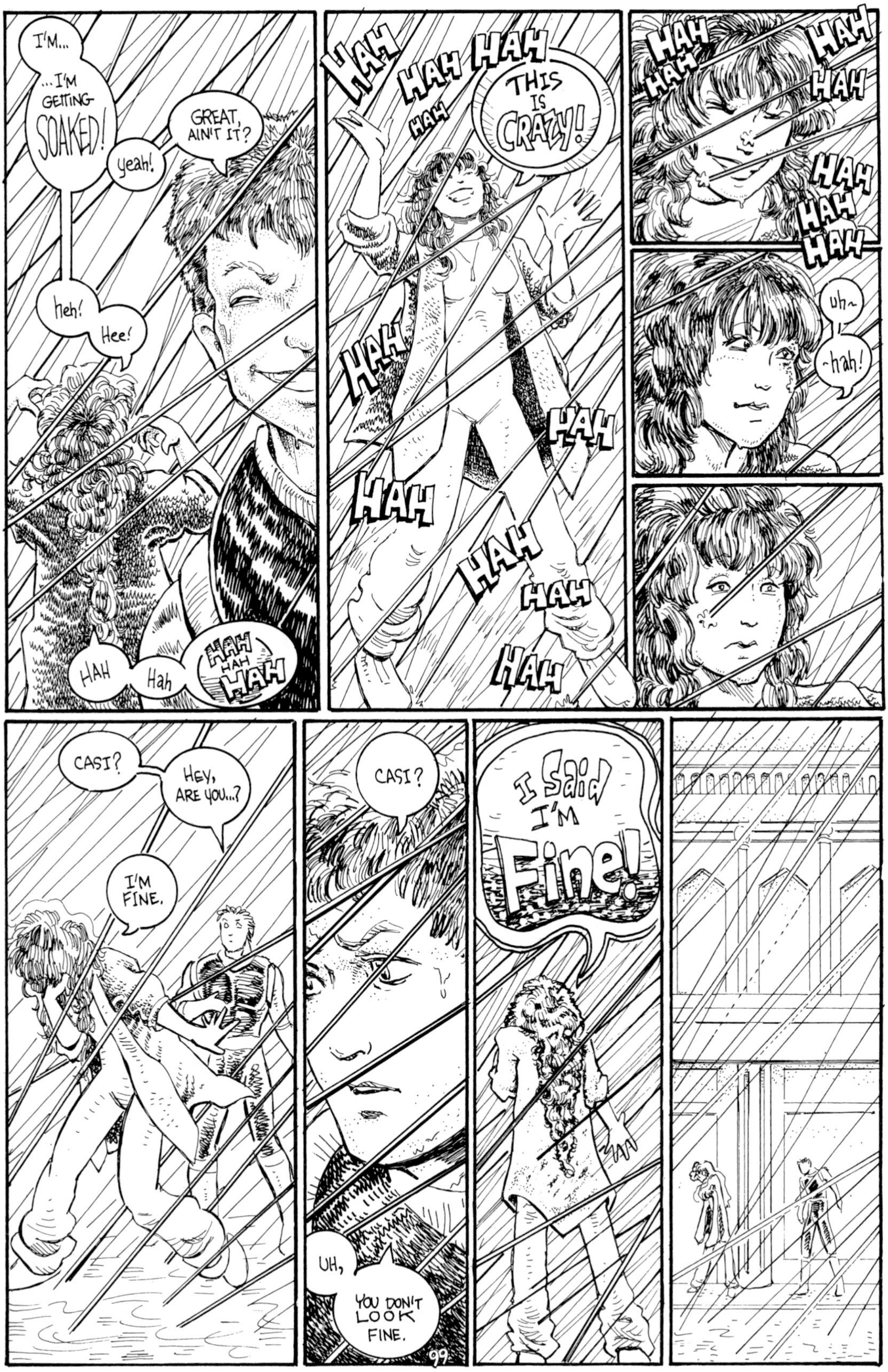

I'M...
...I'M GETTING SOAKED!
yeah!
GREAT, AIN'T IT?
heh!
Hee!
HAH
Hah
HAH HAH HAH
HAH
HAH
HAH HAH
THIS IS CRAZY!
HAH
HAH
HAH
HAH
HAH
HAH
HAH
HAH HAH
HAH
HAH
HAH
HAH
HAH
uh~
~hah!
CASI?
HEY, ARE YOU...?
I'M FINE.
CASI?
UH,
YOU DON'T LOOK FINE.
I Said I'M Fine!

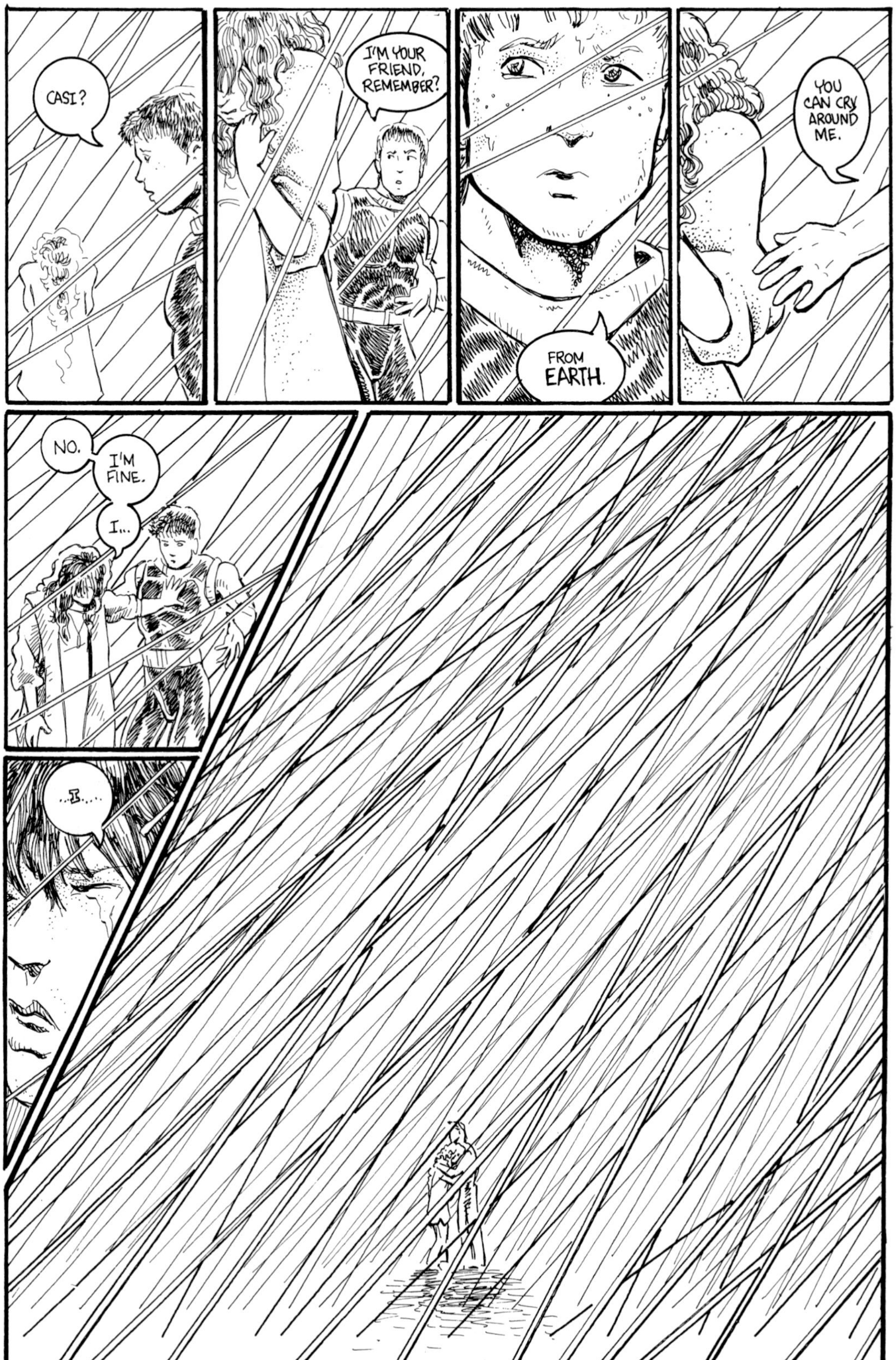
CASI?
I'M YOUR FRIEND, REMEMBER?
FROM EARTH.
YOU CAN CRY AROUND ME.
NO.
I'M FINE.
I...
...I...

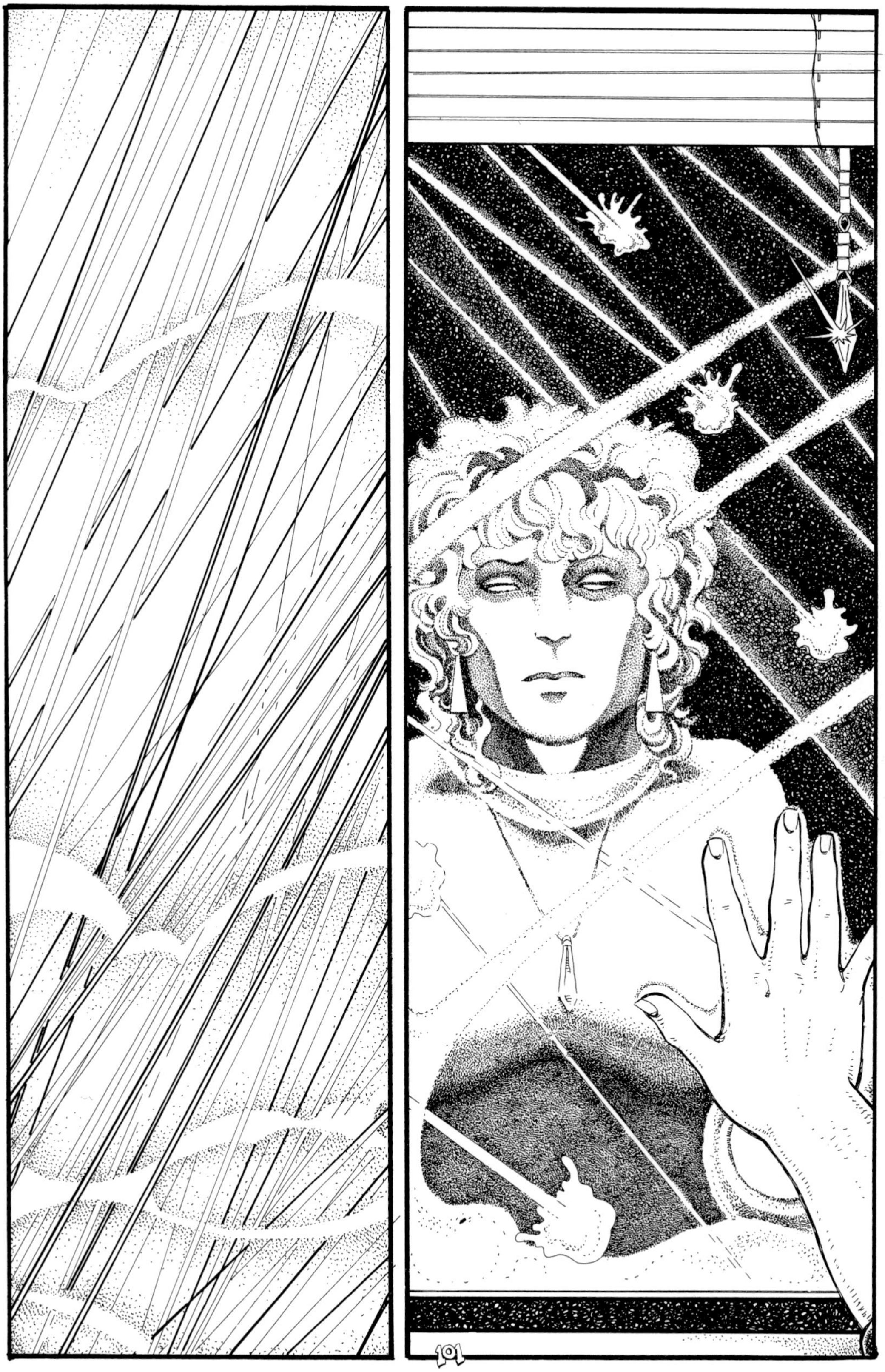

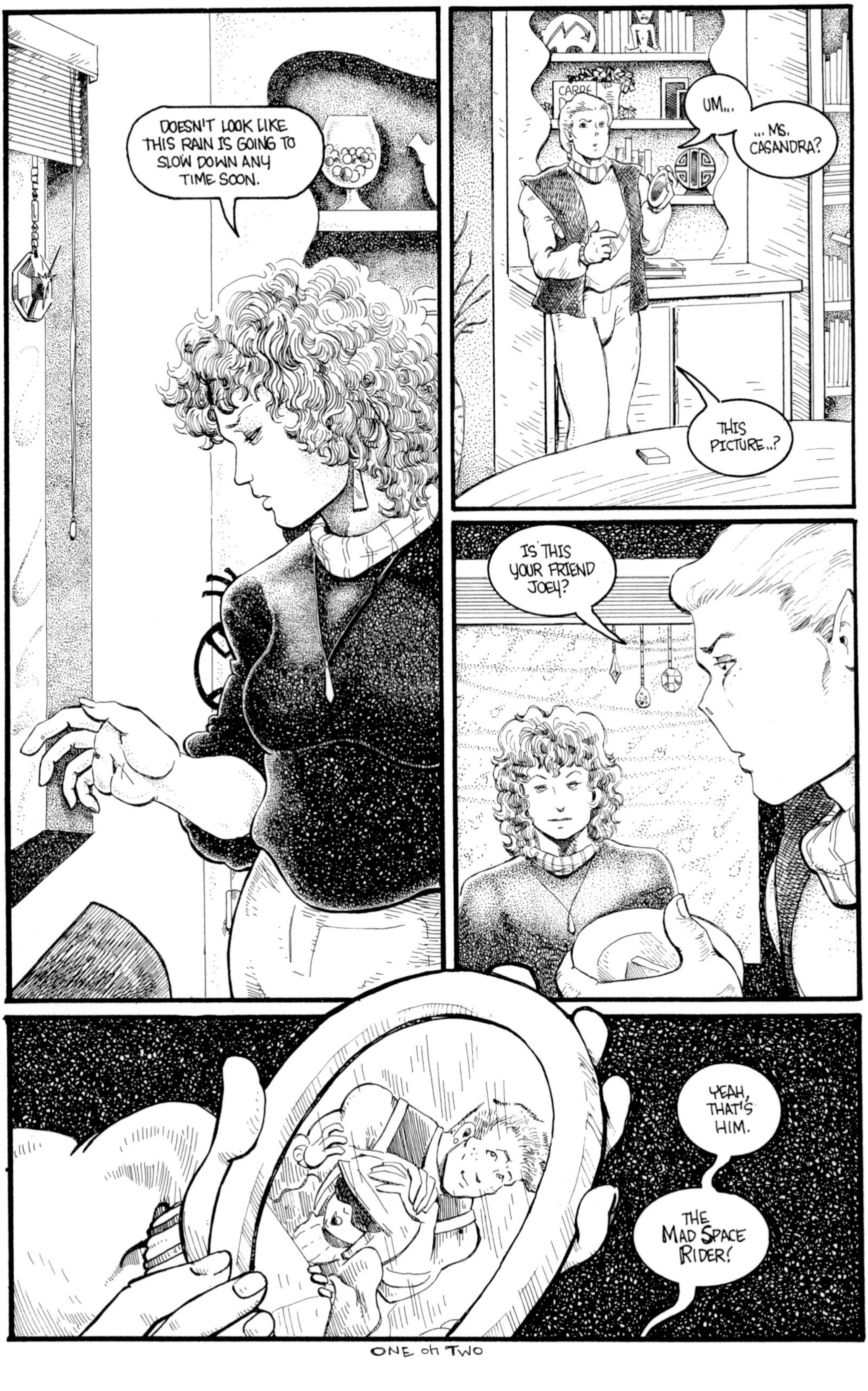
DOESN'T LOOK LIKE THIS RAIN IS GOING TO SLOW DOWN ANY TIME SOON.
UM...
... MS. CASANDRA?
THIS PICTURE...?
IS THIS YOUR FRIEND JOEY?
YEAH, THAT'S HIM.
THE MAD SPACE RIDER!

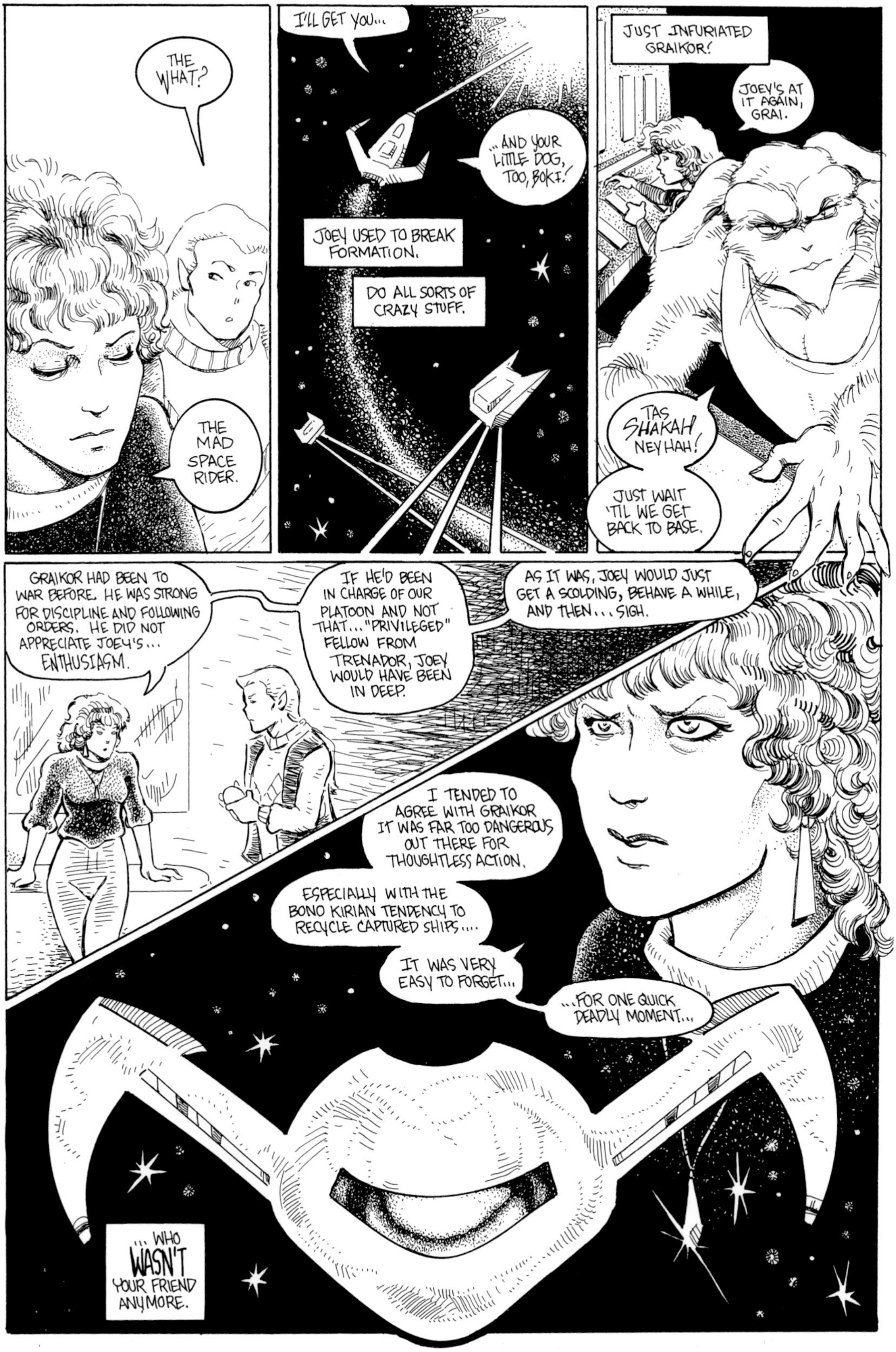
THE WHAT?
THE MAD SPACE RIDER.
I'LL GET YOU...
...AND YOUR LITTLE DOG, TOO, BOKI!
JOEY USED TO BREAK FORMATION.
DO ALL SORTS OF CRAZY STUFF.
JUST INFURIATED GRAIKOR!
JOEY'S AT IT AGAIN, GRAI.
TAS SHAKAH NEY HAH!
JUST WAIT 'TIL WE GET BACK TO BASE.
GRAIKOR HAD BEEN TO WAR BEFORE. HE WAS STRONG FOR DISCIPLINE AND FOLLOWING ORDERS. HE DID NOT APPRECIATE JOEY'S... ENTHUSIASM.
IF HE'D BEEN IN CHARGE OF OUR PLATOON AND NOT THAT..."PRIVILEGED" FELLOW FROM TRENADOR, JOEY WOULD HAVE BEEN IN DEEP.
AS IT WAS, JOEY WOULD JUST GET A SCOLDING, BEHAVE A WHILE, AND THEN... SIGH.
I TENDED TO AGREE WITH GRAIKOR. IT WAS FAR TOO DANGEROUS OUT THERE FOR THOUGHTLESS ACTION.
ESPECIALLY WITH THE BONO KIRIAN TENDENCY TO RECYCLE CAPTURED SHIPS....
IT WAS VERY EASY TO FORGET...
...FOR ONE QUICK DEADLY MOMENT...
...WHO WASN'T YOUR FRIEND ANYMORE.

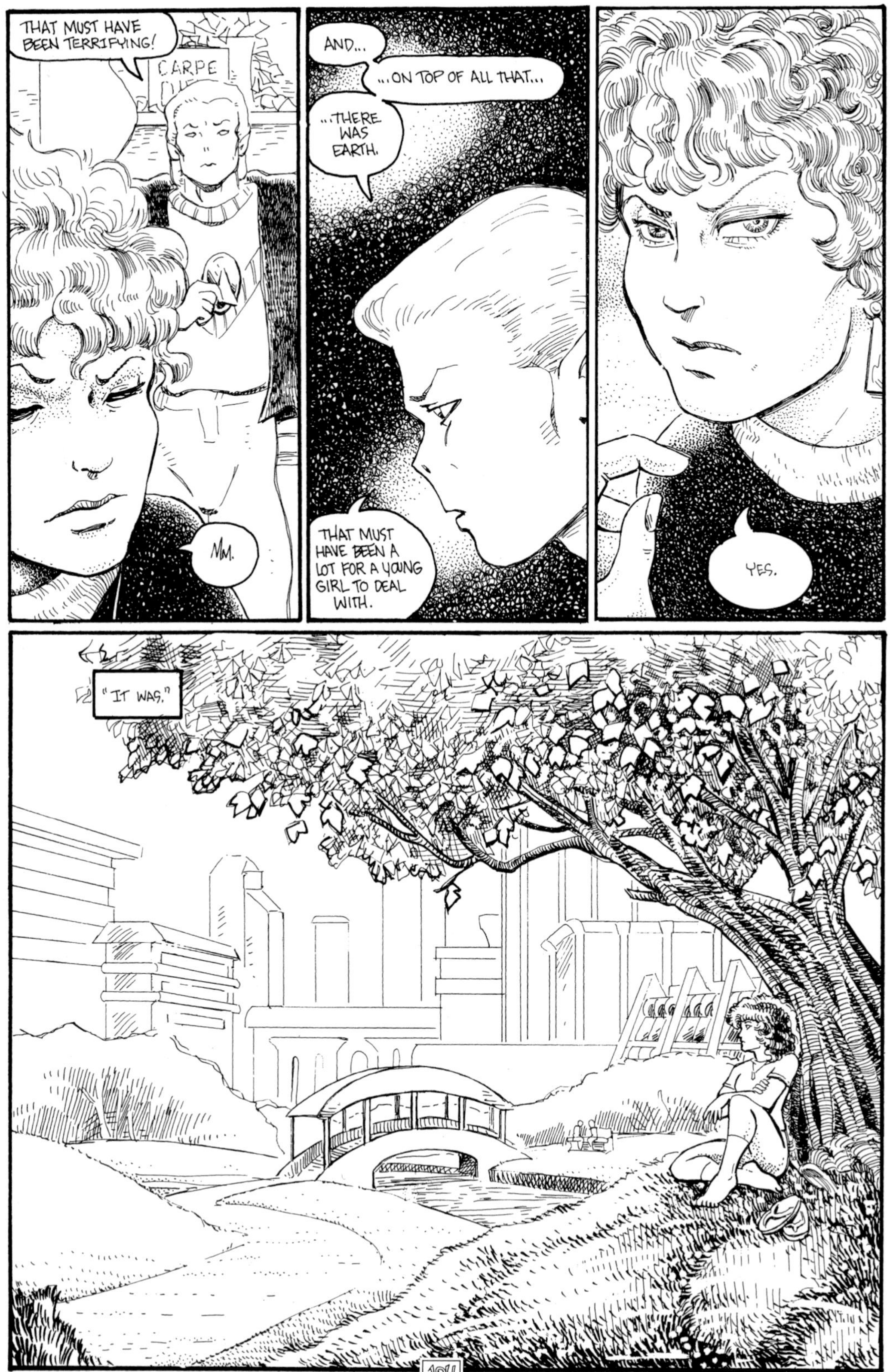
THAT MUST HAVE BEEN TERRIFYING!
CARPE
MM.
AND...
...ON TOP OF ALL THAT...
...THERE WAS EARTH.
THAT MUST HAVE BEEN A LOT FOR A YOUNG GIRL TO DEAL WITH.
YES.
"IT WAS."

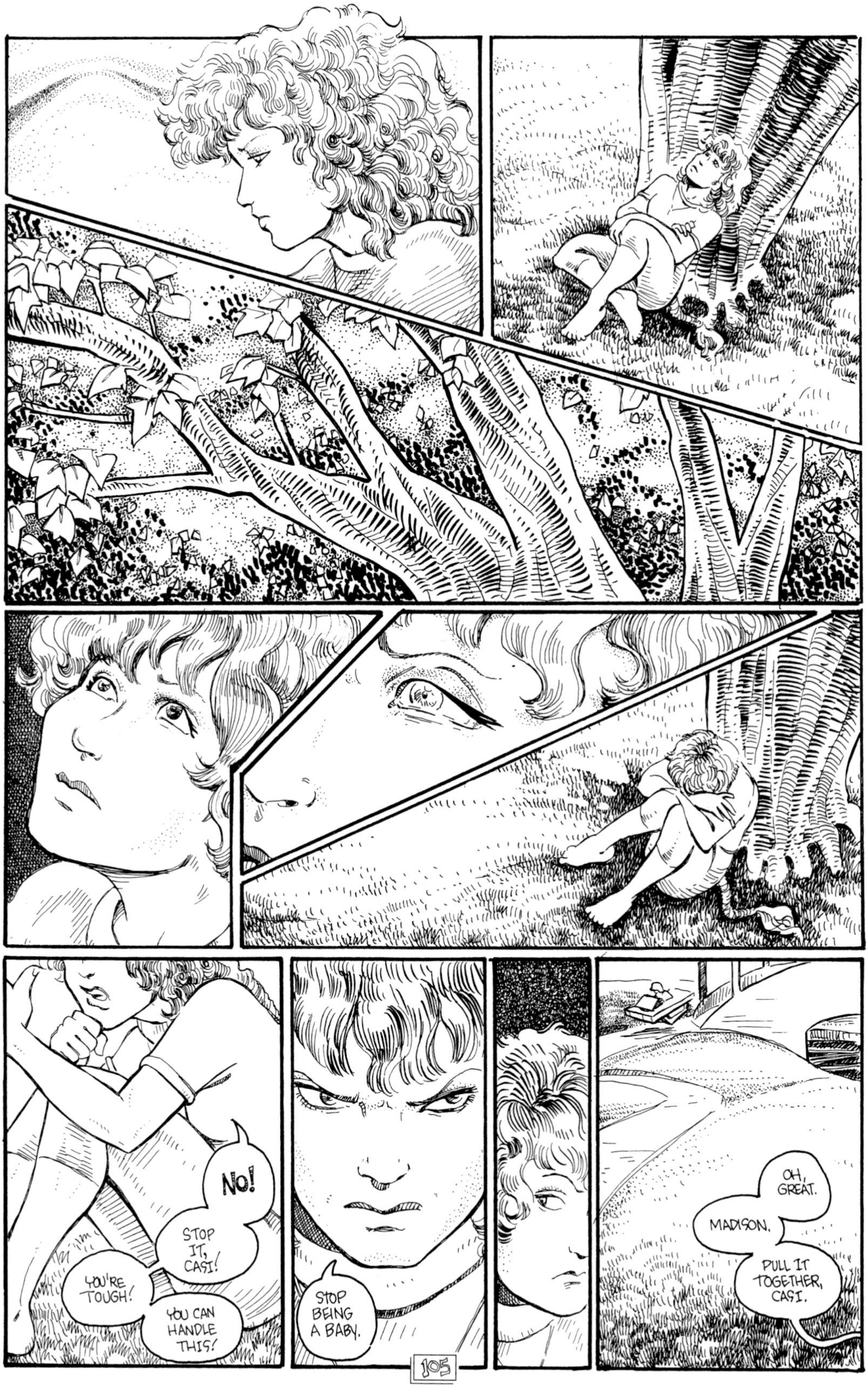
No!
STOP IT, CASI!
YOU'RE TOUGH!
YOU CAN HANDLE THIS!
STOP BEING A BABY.
OH, GREAT.
MADISON.
PULL IT TOGETHER, CASI.

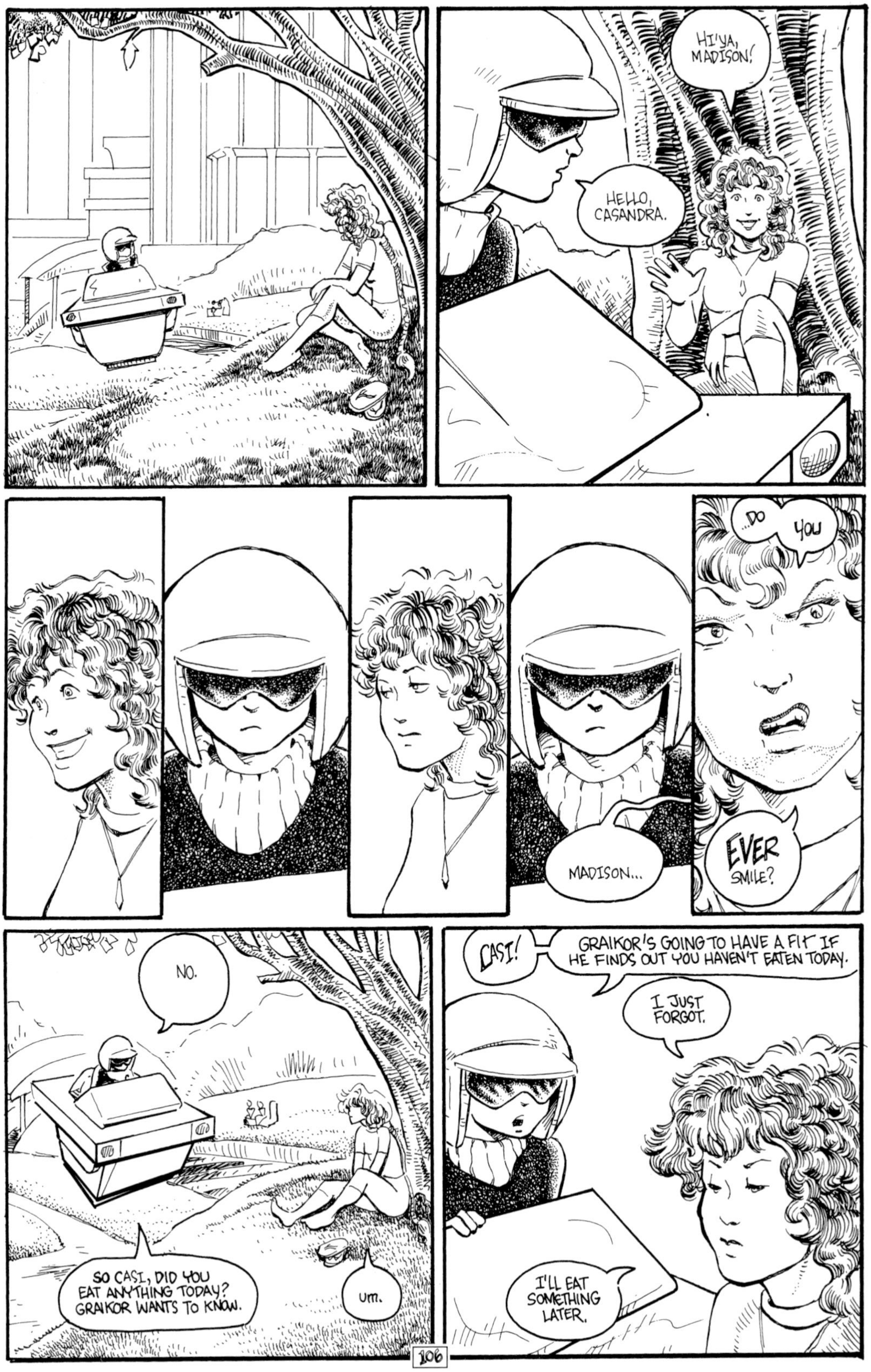
HI'YA, MADISON!
HELLO, CASANDRA.
...DO YOU
MADISON...
EVER SMILE?
NO.
SO CASI, DID YOU EAT ANYTHING TODAY? GRAIKOR WANTS TO KNOW.
Um.
CASI!
GRAIKOR'S GOING TO HAVE A FIT IF HE FINDS OUT YOU HAVEN'T EATEN TODAY.
I JUST FORGOT.
I'LL EAT SOMETHING LATER.

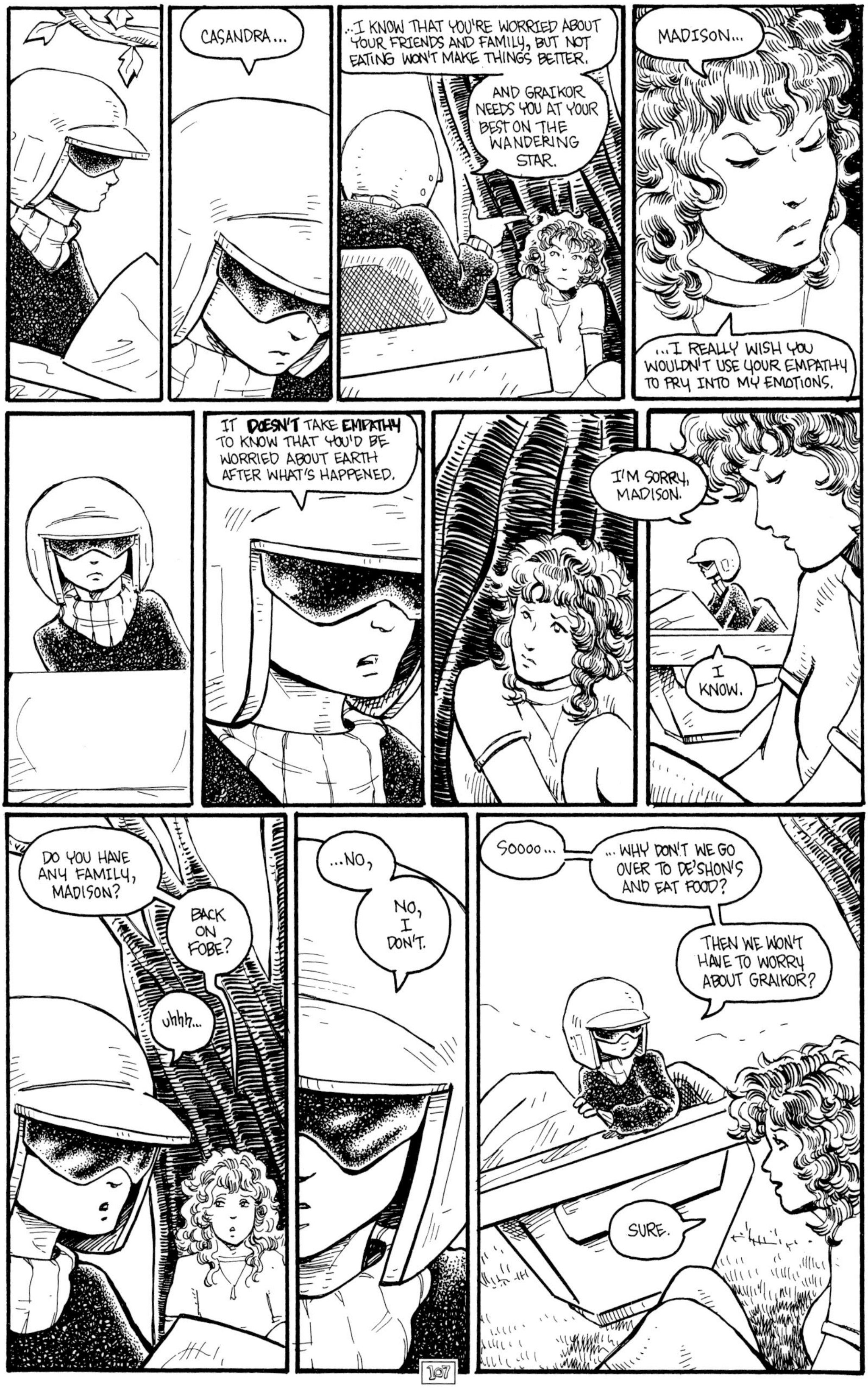
CASANDRA...
...I KNOW THAT YOU'RE WORRIED ABOUT YOUR FRIENDS AND FAMILY, BUT NOT EATING WON'T MAKE THINGS BETTER.
AND GRAIKOR NEEDS YOU AT YOUR BEST ON THE WANDERING STAR.
MADISON...
...I REALLY WISH YOU WOULDN'T USE YOUR EMPATHY TO PRY INTO MY EMOTIONS.
IT DOESN'T TAKE EMPATHY TO KNOW THAT YOU'D BE WORRIED ABOUT EARTH AFTER WHAT'S HAPPENED.
I'M SORRY, MADISON.
I KNOW.
DO YOU HAVE ANY FAMILY, MADISON?
BACK ON FOBE?
uhhh...
...NO,
NO, I DON'T.
Soooo...
...WHY DON'T WE GO OVER TO DE'SHON'S AND EAT FOOD?
THEN WE WON'T HAVE TO WORRY ABOUT GRAIKOR?
SURE.

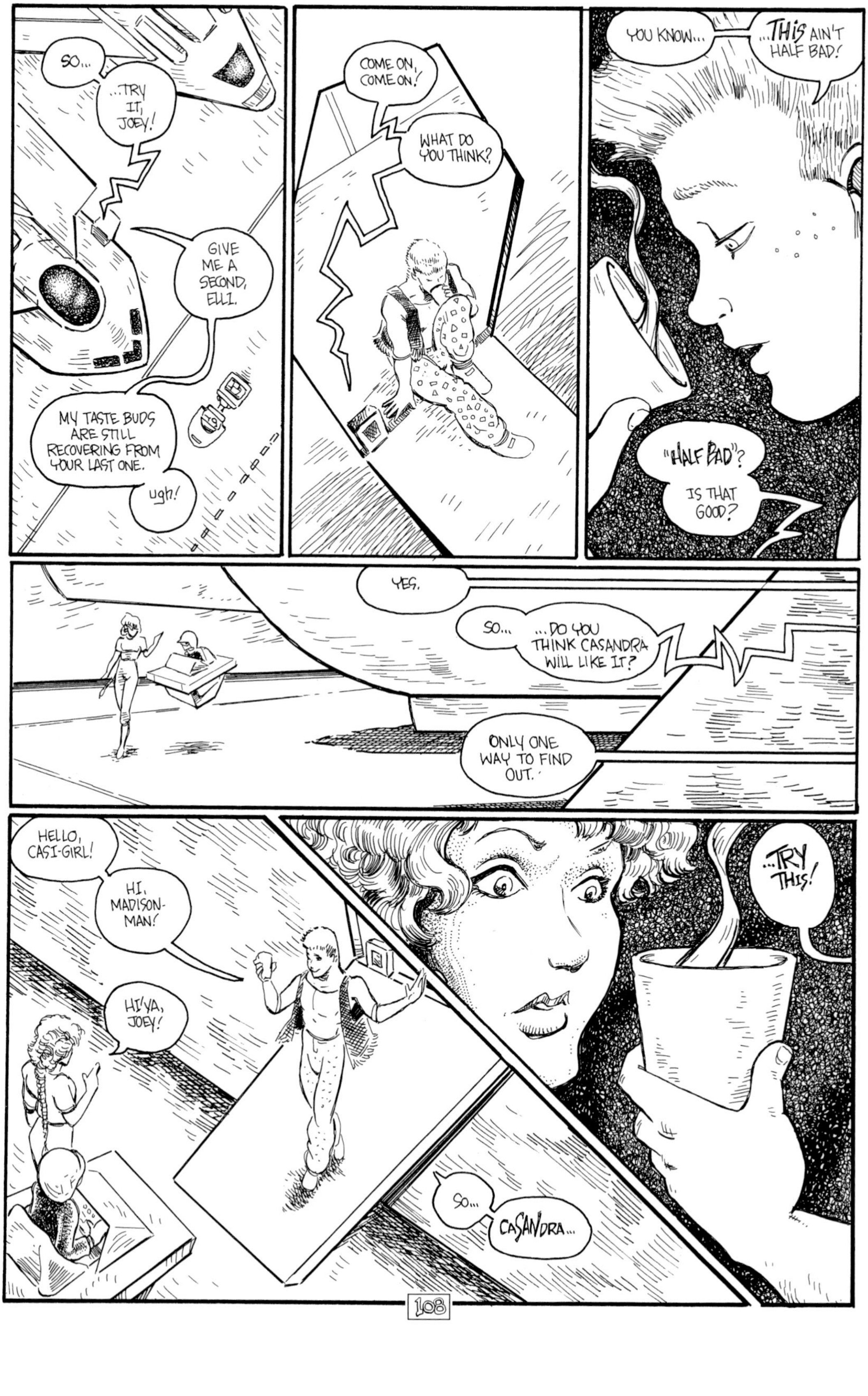
SO...
...TRY IT, JOEY!
GIVE ME A SECOND, ELLI.
MY TASTE BUDS ARE STILL RECOVERING FROM YOUR LAST ONE.
ugh!
COME ON, COME ON!
WHAT DO YOU THINK?
YOU KNOW...
...THIS AIN'T HALF BAD!
"HALF BAD"?
IS THAT GOOD?
YES.
SO...
...DO YOU THINK CASANDRA WILL LIKE IT?
ONLY ONE WAY TO FIND OUT.
HELLO, CASI-GIRL!
HI, MADISON-MAN!
HI'YA, JOEY!
...TRY THIS!
SO...
CASANDRA...

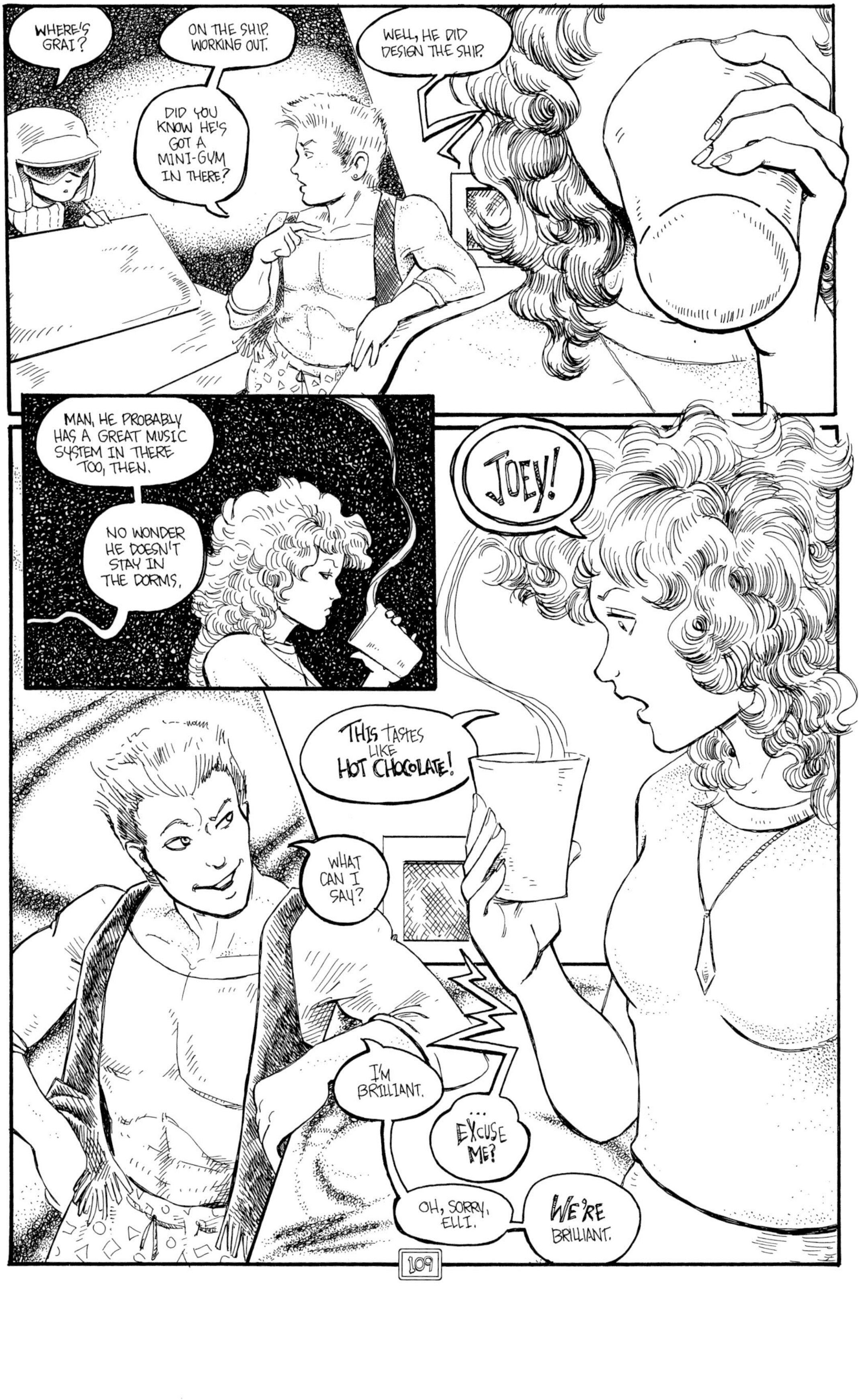
WHERE'S GRAI?
ON THE SHIP. WORKING OUT.
DID YOU KNOW HE'S GOT A MINI-GYM IN THERE?
WELL, HE DID DESIGN THE SHIP.
MAN, HE PROBABLY HAS A GREAT MUSIC SYSTEM IN THERE TOO, THEN.
NO WONDER HE DOESN'T STAY IN THE DORMS.
JOEY!
THIS TASTES LIKE HOT CHOCOLATE!
WHAT CAN I SAY?
I'M BRILLIANT.
... EXCUSE ME?
OH, SORRY, ELLI.
WE'RE BRILLIANT.

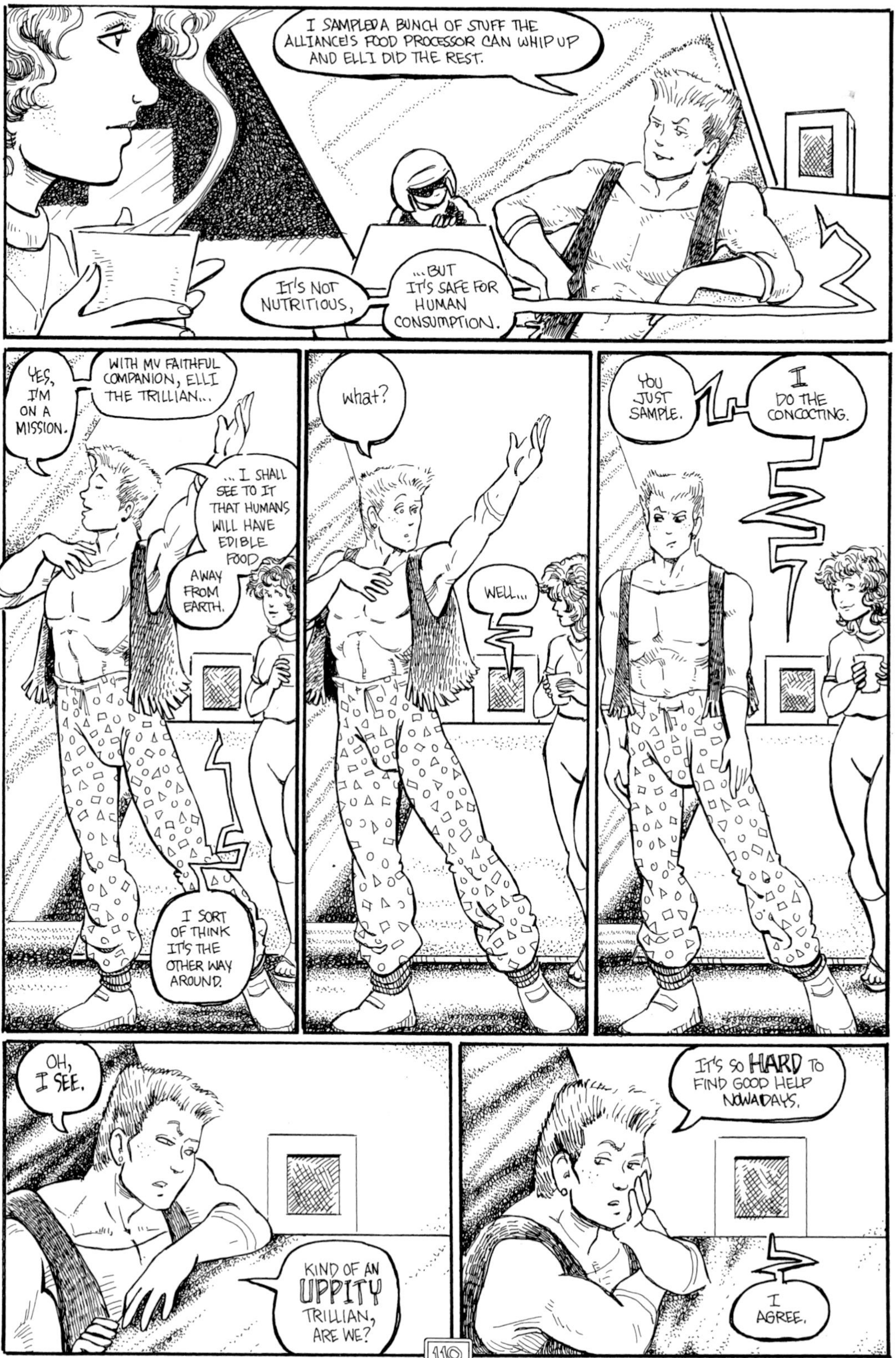

I SAMPLED A BUNCH OF STUFF THE ALLIANCE'S FOOD PROCESSOR CAN WHIP UP AND ELLI DID THE REST.
IT'S NOT NUTRITIOUS,
...BUT IT'S SAFE FOR HUMAN CONSUMPTION.
YES, I'M ON A MISSION.
WITH MY FAITHFUL COMPANION, ELLI THE TRILLIAN...
...I SHALL SEE TO IT THAT HUMANS WILL HAVE EDIBLE FOOD
AWAY FROM EARTH.
I SORT OF THINK IT'S THE OTHER WAY AROUND.
what?
WELL...
YOU JUST SAMPLE.
I DO THE CONCOCTING.
OH, I SEE.
KIND OF AN UPPITY TRILLIAN, ARE WE?
IT'S SO HARD TO FIND GOOD HELP NOWADAYS.
I AGREE.

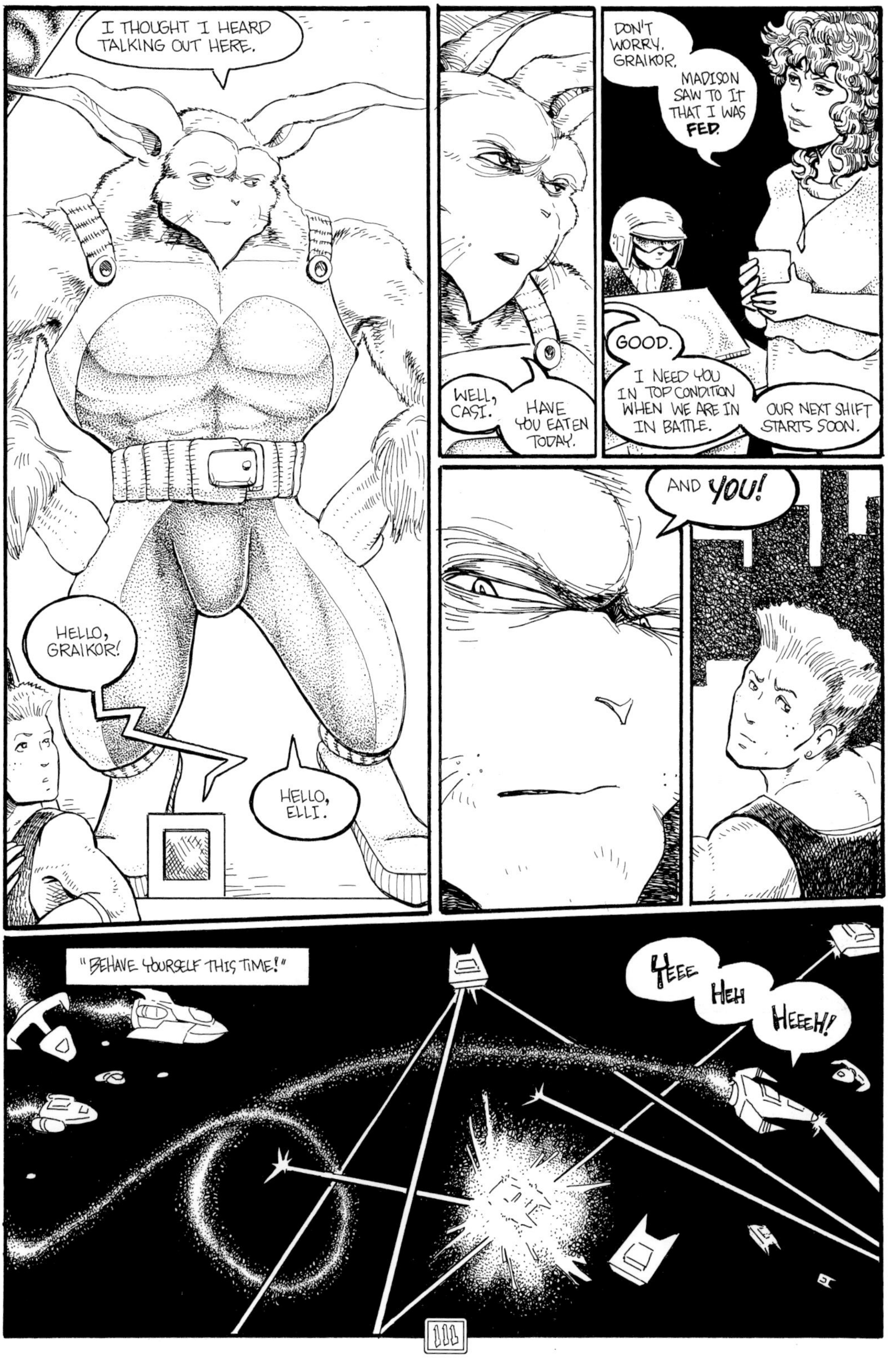
I THOUGHT I HEARD TALKING OUT HERE.
HELLO, GRAIKOR!
HELLO, ELLI.
WELL, CASI.
HAVE YOU EATEN TODAY.
DON'T WORRY, GRAIKOR,
MADISON SAW TO IT THAT I WAS FED.
GOOD.
I NEED YOU IN TOP CONDITION WHEN WE ARE IN BATTLE.
OUR NEXT SHIFT STARTS SOON.
AND YOU!
"BEHAVE YOURSELF THIS TIME!"
YEEE HEH HEEEH!

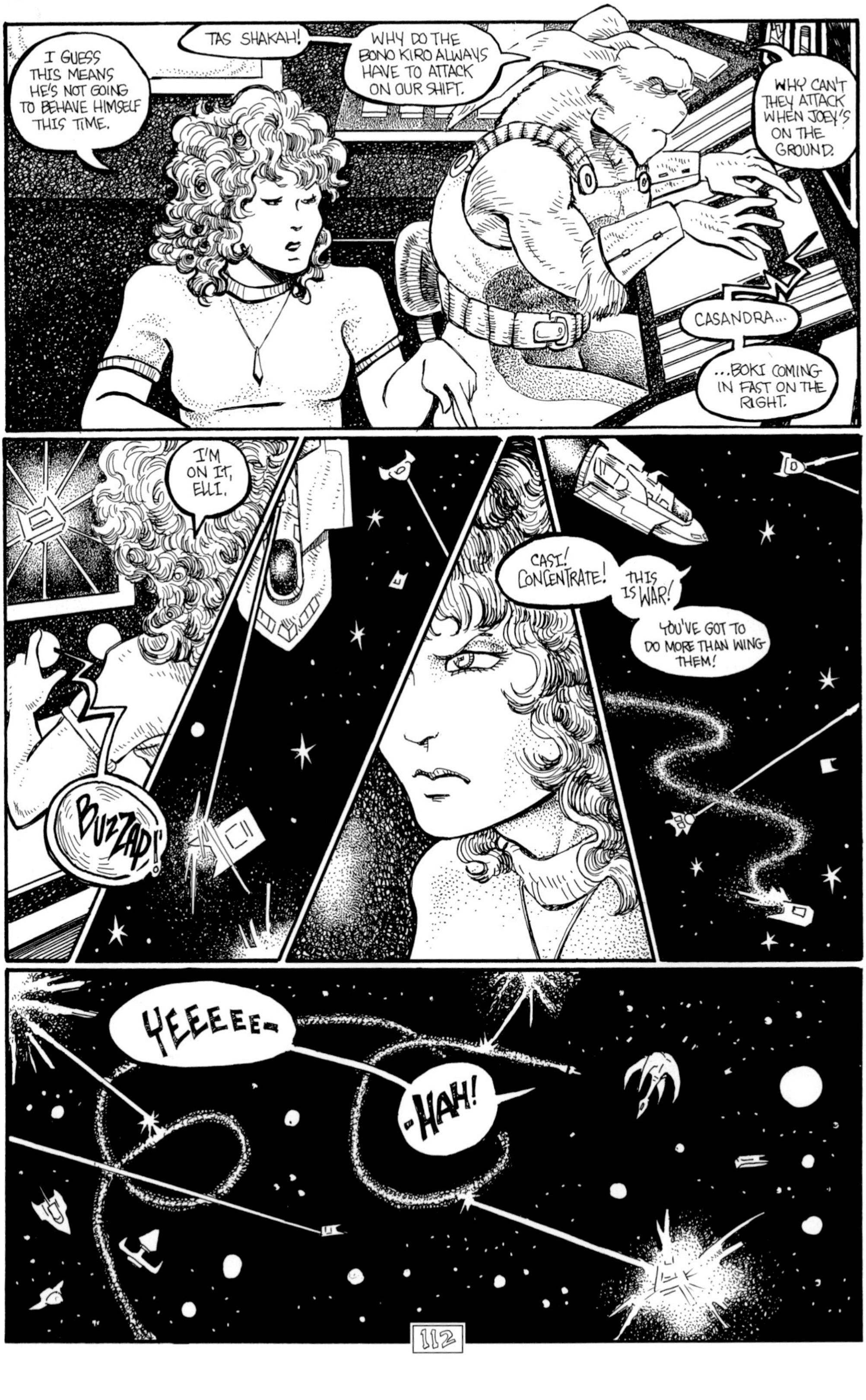

I GUESS THIS MEANS HE'S NOT GOING TO BEHAVE HIMSELF THIS TIME.
TAS SHAKAH!
WHY DO THE BONO KIRO ALWAYS HAVE TO ATTACK ON OUR SHIFT.
WHY CAN'T THEY ATTACK WHEN JOEY'S ON THE GROUND.
CASANDRA...
...BOKI COMING IN FAST ON THE RIGHT.
I'M ON IT, ELLI.
BUZZAP!
CASI! CONCENTRATE!
THIS IS WAR!
YOU'VE GOT TO DO MORE THAN WING THEM!
YEEEEE-
-HAH!

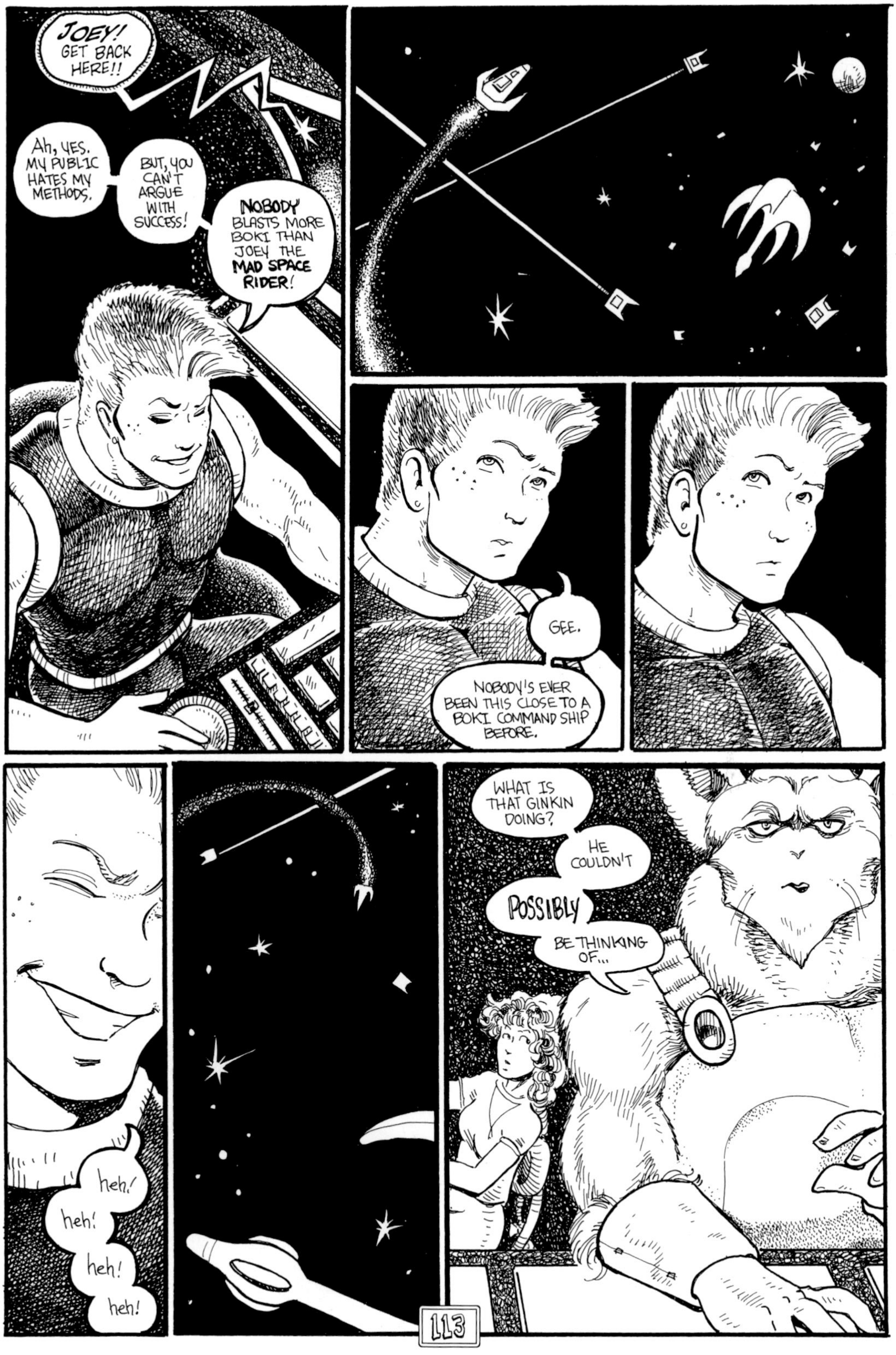
JOEY! GET BACK HERE!!
Ah, YES. MY PUBLIC HATES MY METHODS.
BUT, YOU CAN'T ARGUE WITH SUCCESS!
NOBODY BLASTS MORE BOKI THAN JOEY THE MAD SPACE RIDER!
GEE.
NOBODY'S EVER BEEN THIS CLOSE TO A BOKI COMMAND SHIP BEFORE.
heh! heh! heh! heh!
WHAT IS THAT GINKIN DOING?
HE COULDN'T POSSIBLY BE THINKING OF...

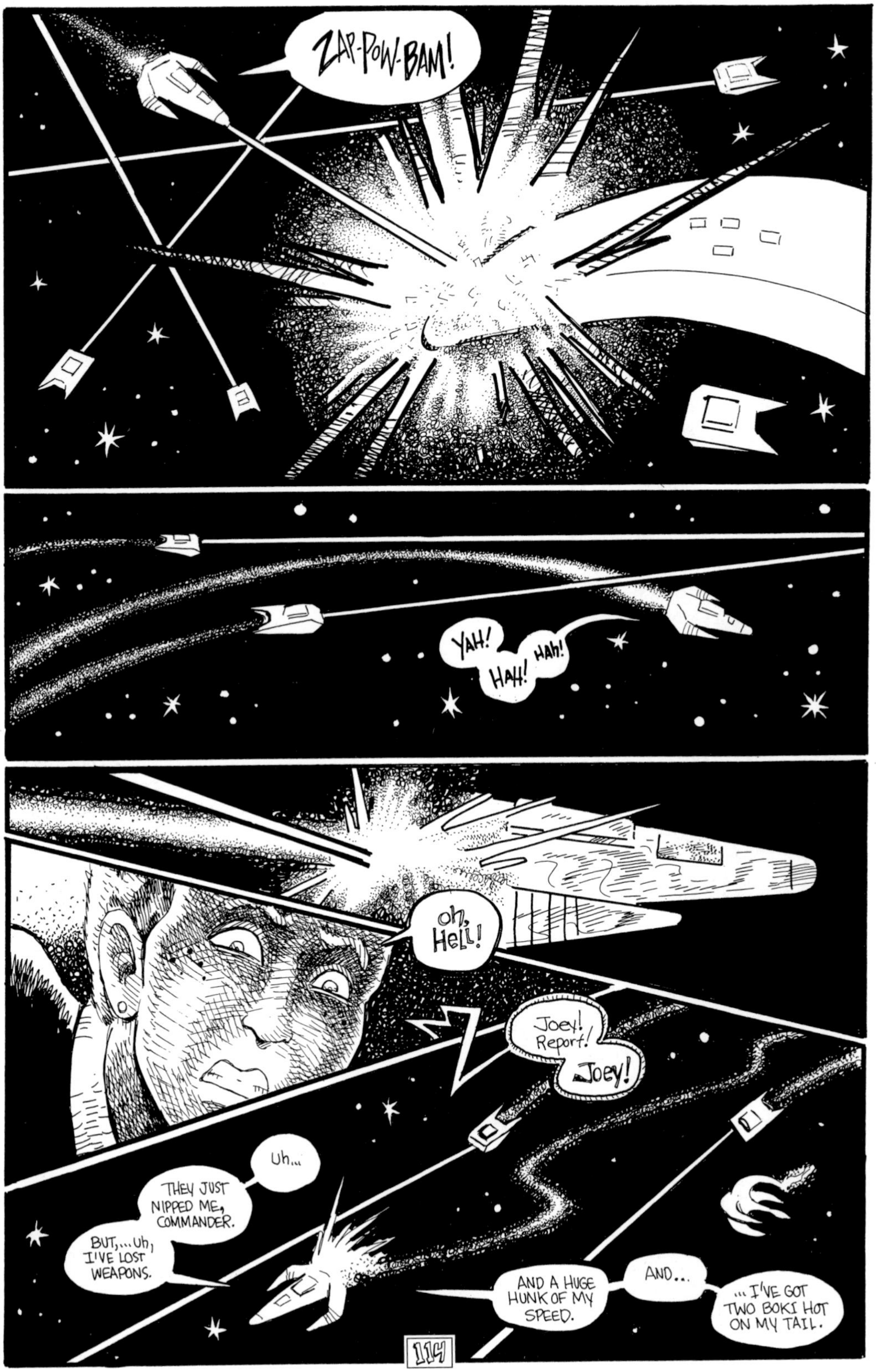
ZAP-POW-BAM!
YAH! HAH! HAH!
oh, Hell!
Joey! Report! Joey!
Uh...
THEY JUST NIPPED ME, COMMANDER.
BUT,...Uh, I'VE LOST WEAPONS.
AND A HUGE HUNK OF MY SPEED.
AND...
...I'VE GOT TWO BOKI HOT ON MY TAIL.

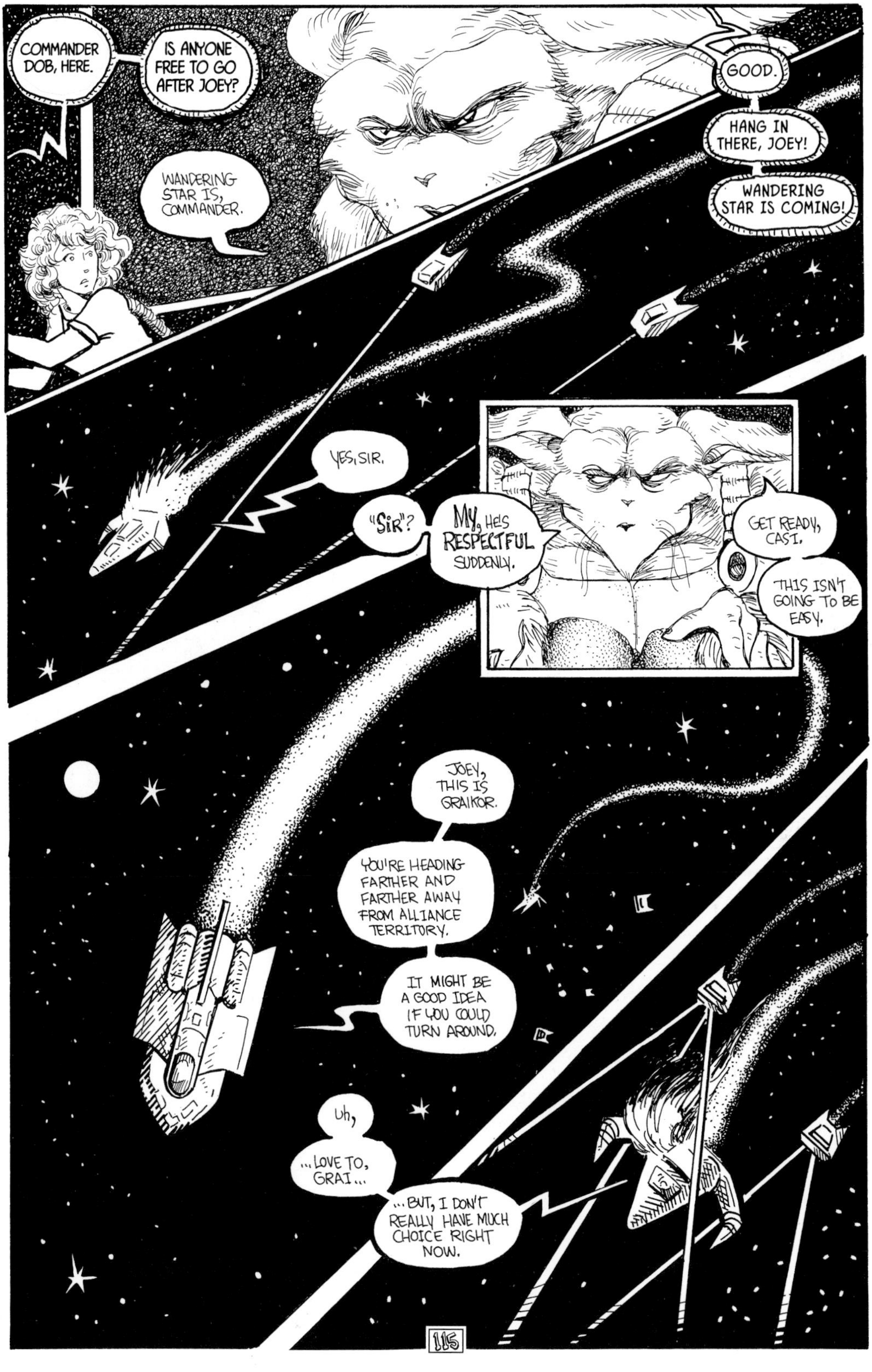
COMMANDER DOB, HERE.
IS ANYONE FREE TO GO AFTER JOEY?
WANDERING STAR IS, COMMANDER.
GOOD.
HANG IN THERE, JOEY!
WANDERING STAR IS COMING!
YES, SIR.
"SIR"?
MY, HE'S RESPECTFUL SUDDENLY.
GET READY, CAST.
THIS ISN'T GOING TO BE EASY.
JOEY, THIS IS GRAIKOR.
YOU'RE HEADING FARTHER AND FARTHER AWAY FROM ALLIANCE TERRITORY.
IT MIGHT BE A GOOD IDEA IF YOU COULD TURN AROUND.
Uh,
...LOVE TO, GRAI...
...BUT, I DON'T REALLY HAVE MUCH CHOICE RIGHT NOW.

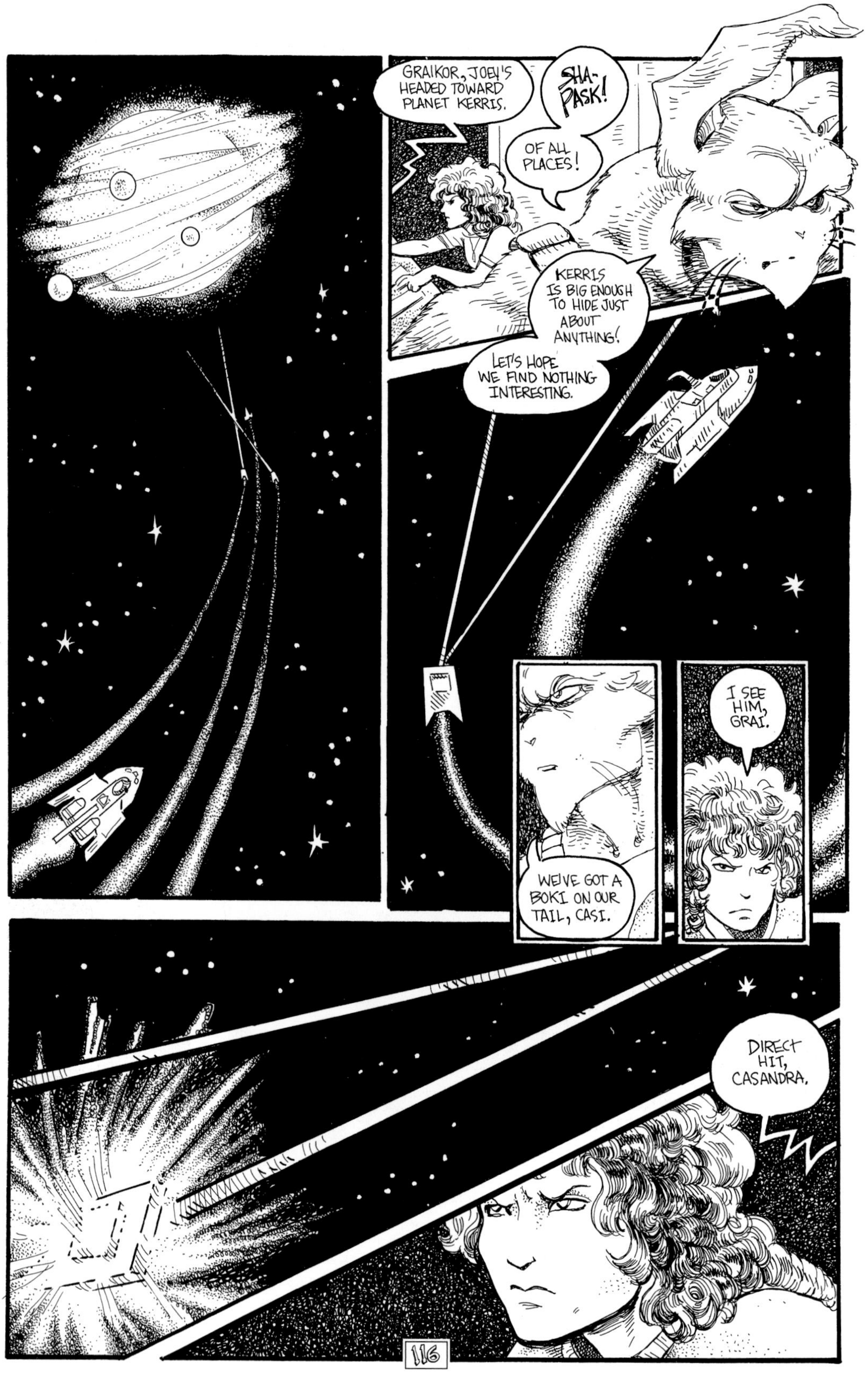
GRAIKOR, JOEY'S HEADED TOWARD PLANET KERRIS.
SHA-PASK!
OF ALL PLACES!
KERRIS IS BIG ENOUGH TO HIDE JUST ABOUT ANYTHING!
LET'S HOPE WE FIND NOTHING INTERESTING.
WE'VE GOT A BOKI ON OUR TAIL, CASI.
I SEE HIM, GRAI.
DIRECT HIT, CASANDRA.

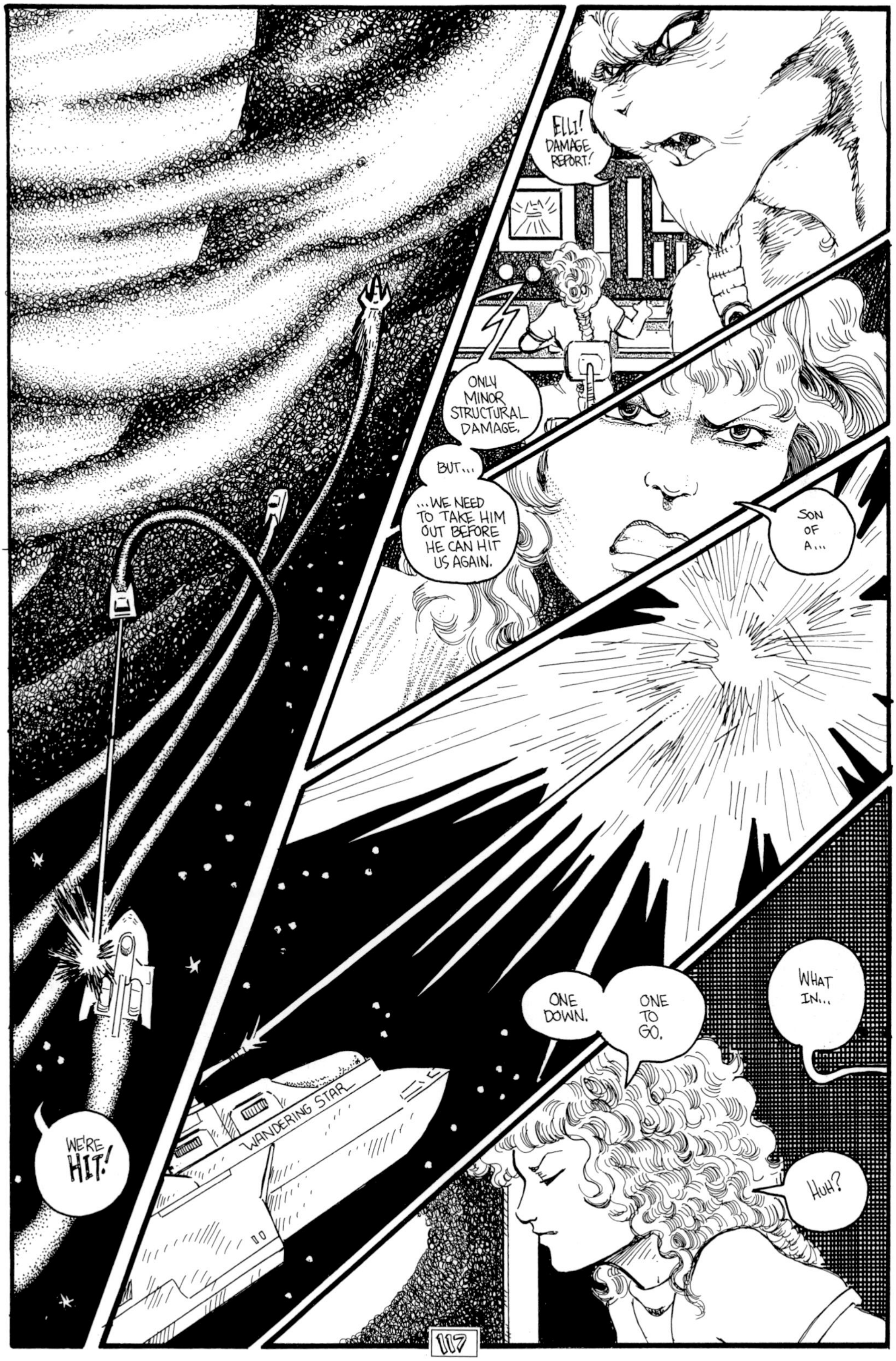

ELLI! DAMAGE REPORT!
ONLY MINOR STRUCTURAL DAMAGE,
BUT...
...WE NEED TO TAKE HIM OUT BEFORE HE CAN HIT US AGAIN.
SON OF A...
WE'RE HIT!
WANDERING STAR
ONE DOWN.
ONE TO GO.
WHAT IN...
HUH?

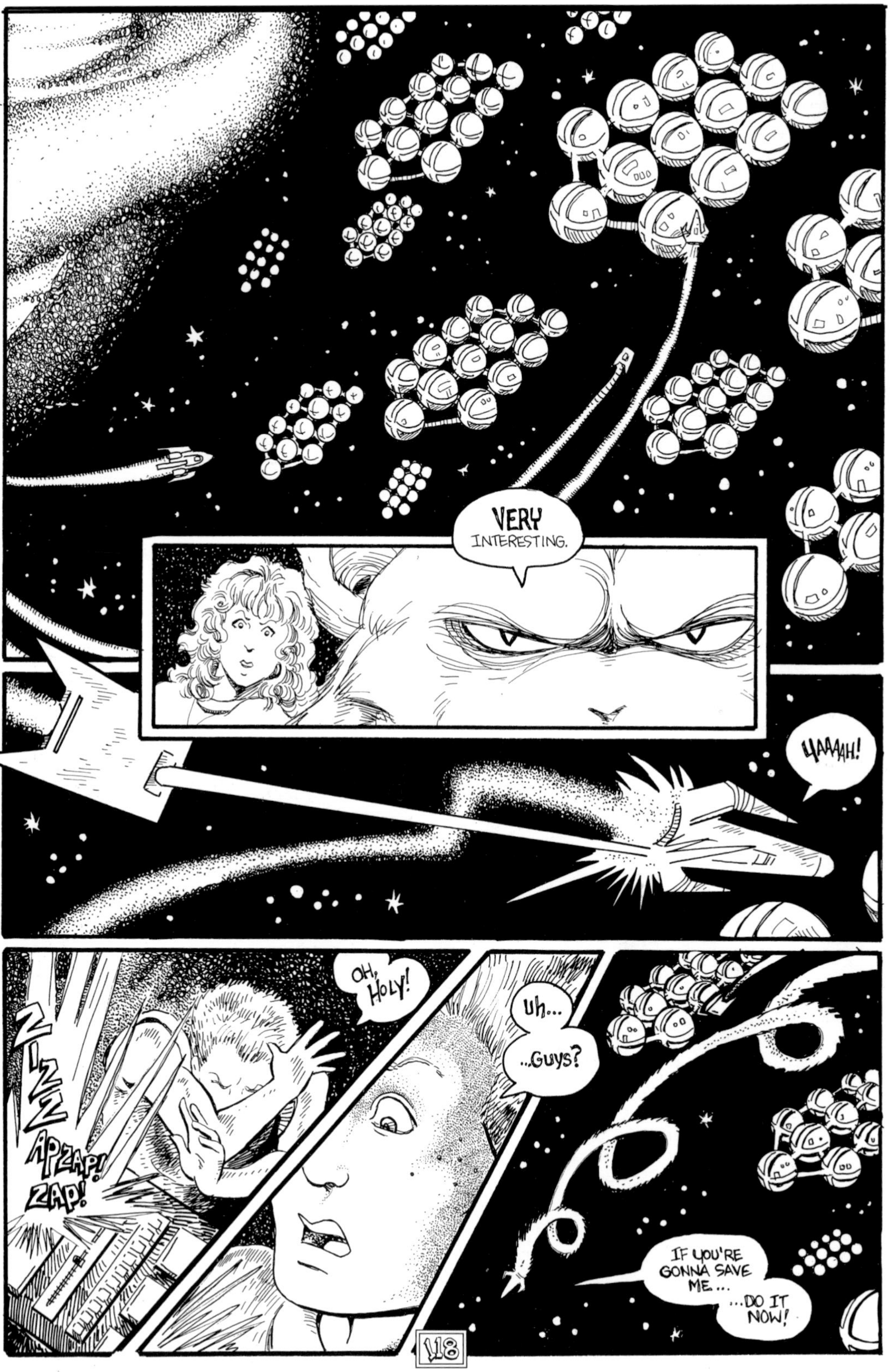
VERY INTERESTING.
YAAAAH!
ZIZZ
APZAP!
ZAP!
OH, HOLY!
Uh...
...Guys?
IF YOU'RE GONNA SAVE ME... ...DO IT NOW!

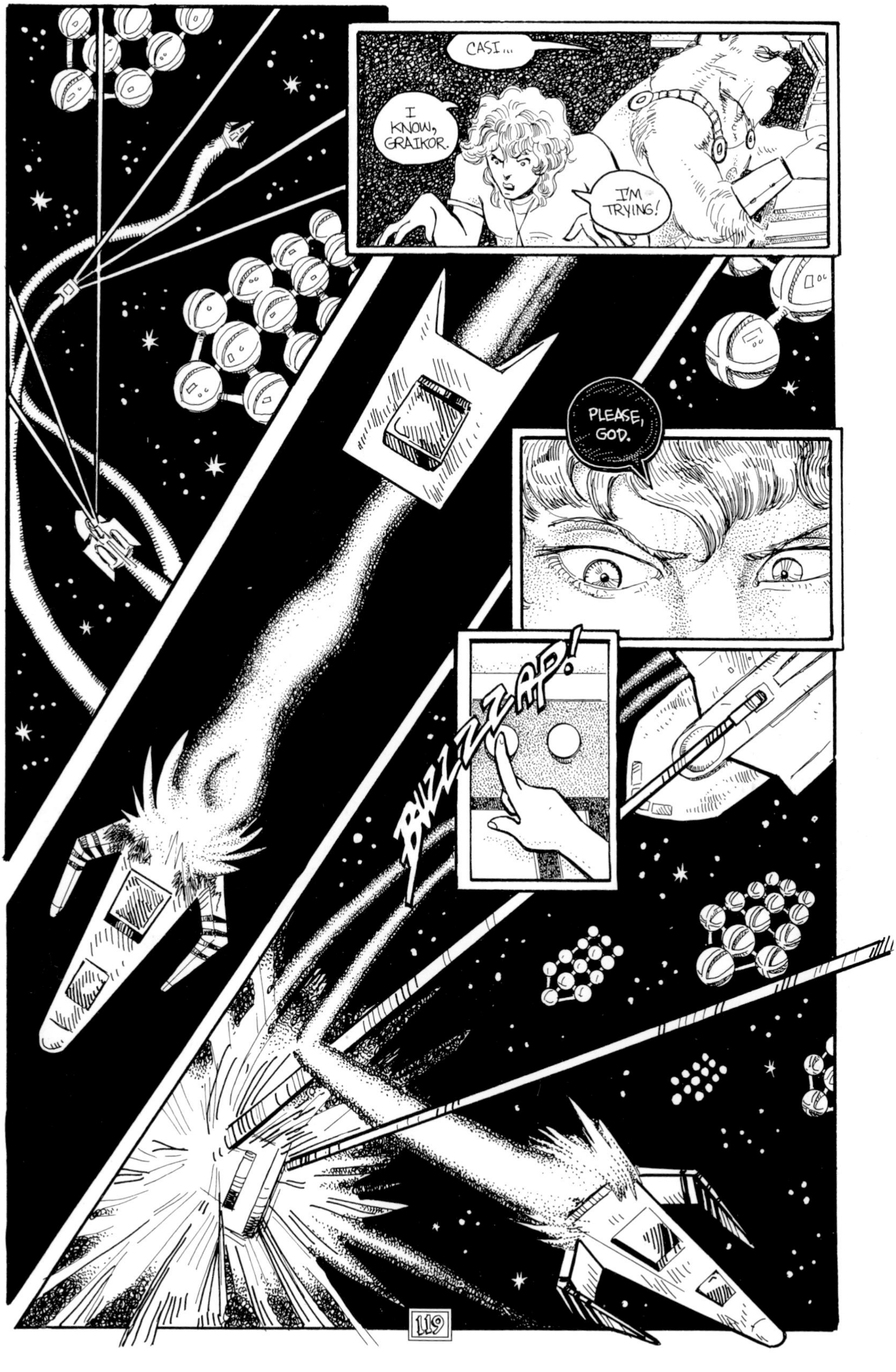
CASI...
I KNOW, GRAIKOR.
I'M TRYING!
PLEASE, GOD.
BUZZZZZAP!

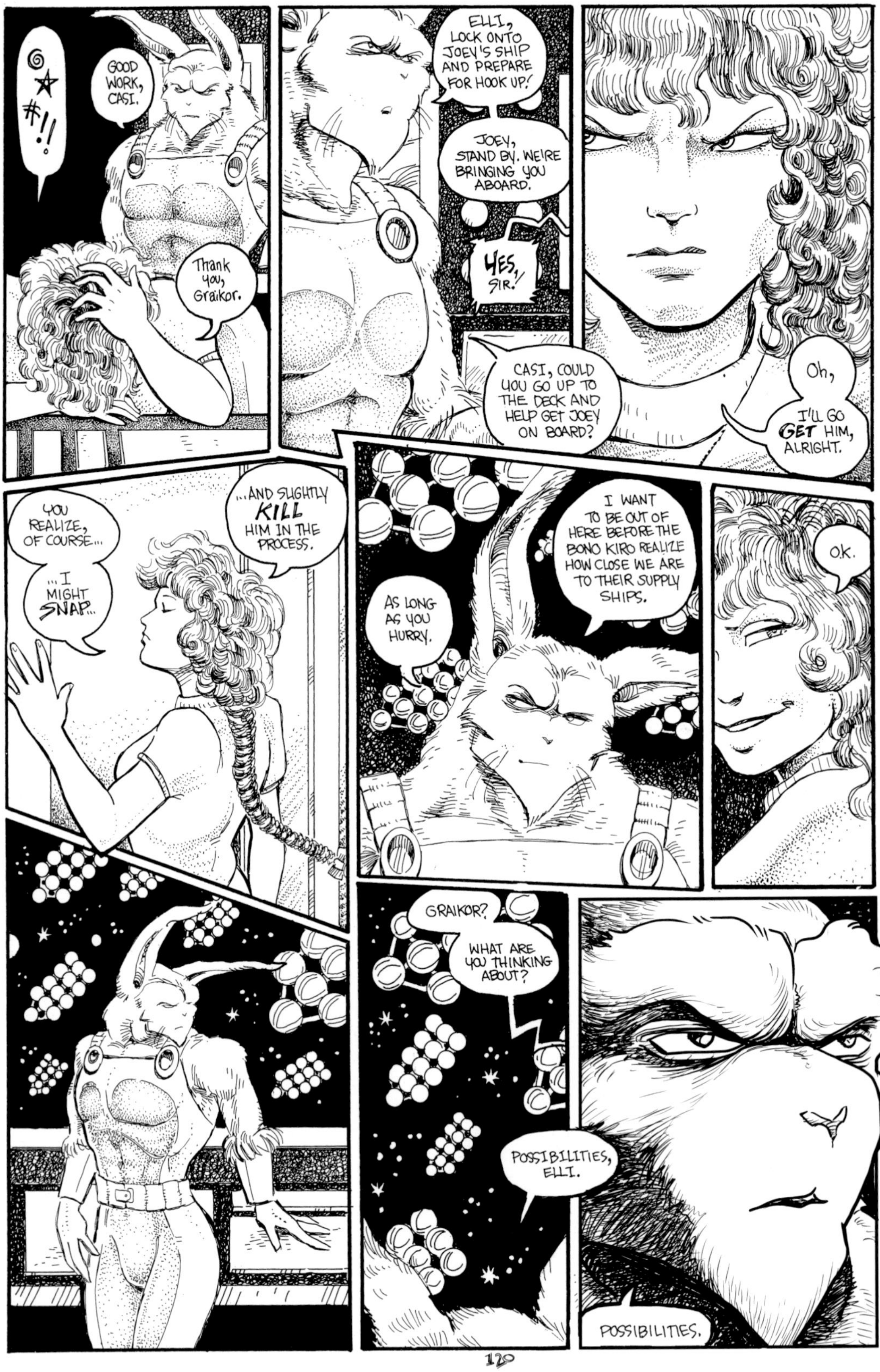
@☆#!!
GOOD WORK, CASI.
Thank you, Graikor.
ELLI, LOCK ONTO JOEY'S SHIP AND PREPARE FOR HOOK UP!
JOEY, STAND BY. WE'RE BRINGING YOU ABOARD.
YES, SIR!
CASI, COULD YOU GO UP TO THE DECK AND HELP GET JOEY ON BOARD?
Oh,
I'LL GO GET HIM, ALRIGHT.
YOU REALIZE, OF COURSE...
...I MIGHT SNAP...
...AND SLIGHTLY KILL HIM IN THE PROCESS.
I WANT TO BE OUT OF HERE BEFORE THE BONO KIRO REALIZE HOW CLOSE WE ARE TO THEIR SUPPLY SHIPS.
AS LONG AS YOU HURRY.
O.K.
GRAIKOR?
WHAT ARE YOU THINKING ABOUT?
POSSIBILITIES, ELLI.
POSSIBILITIES.

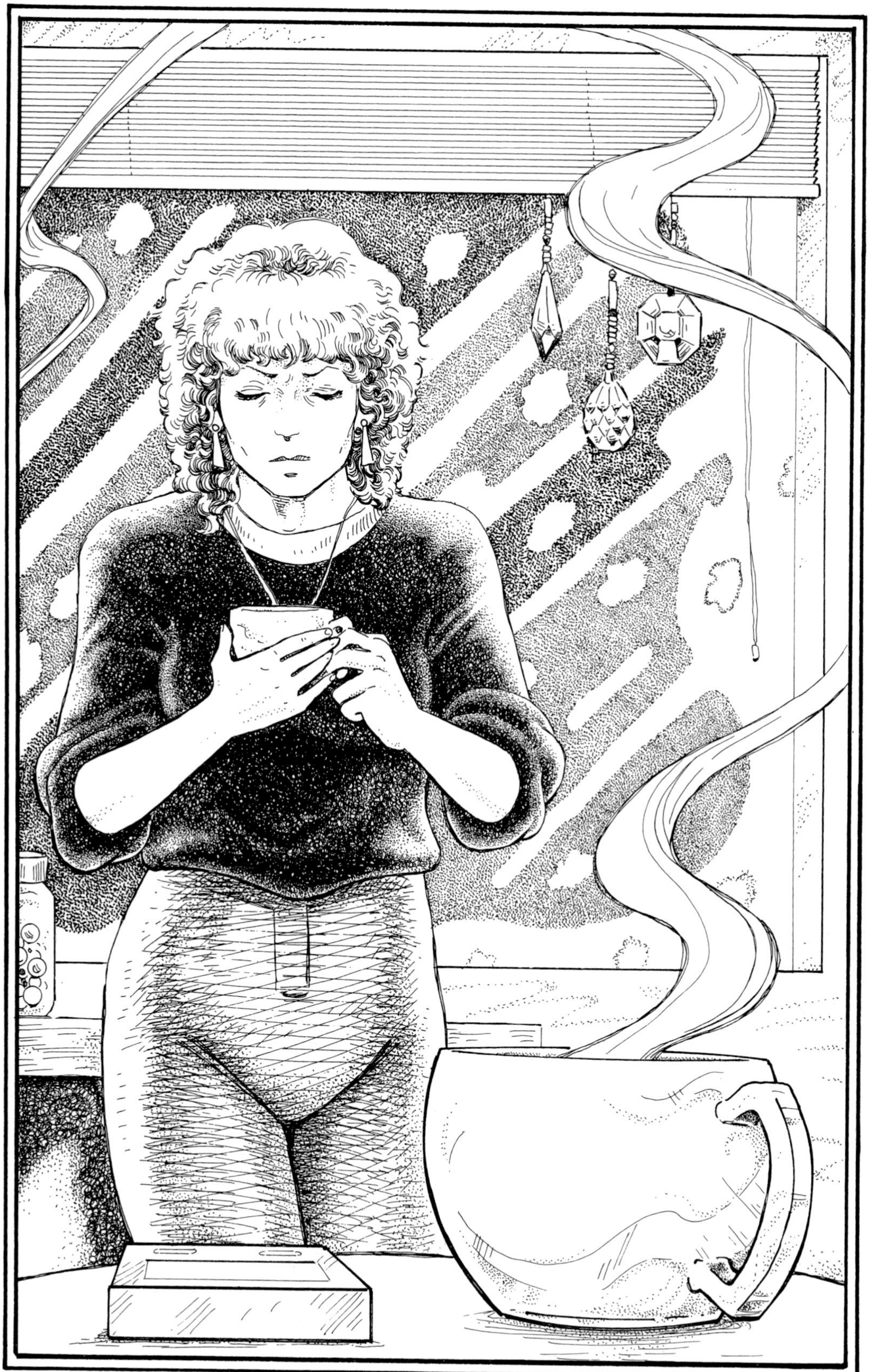

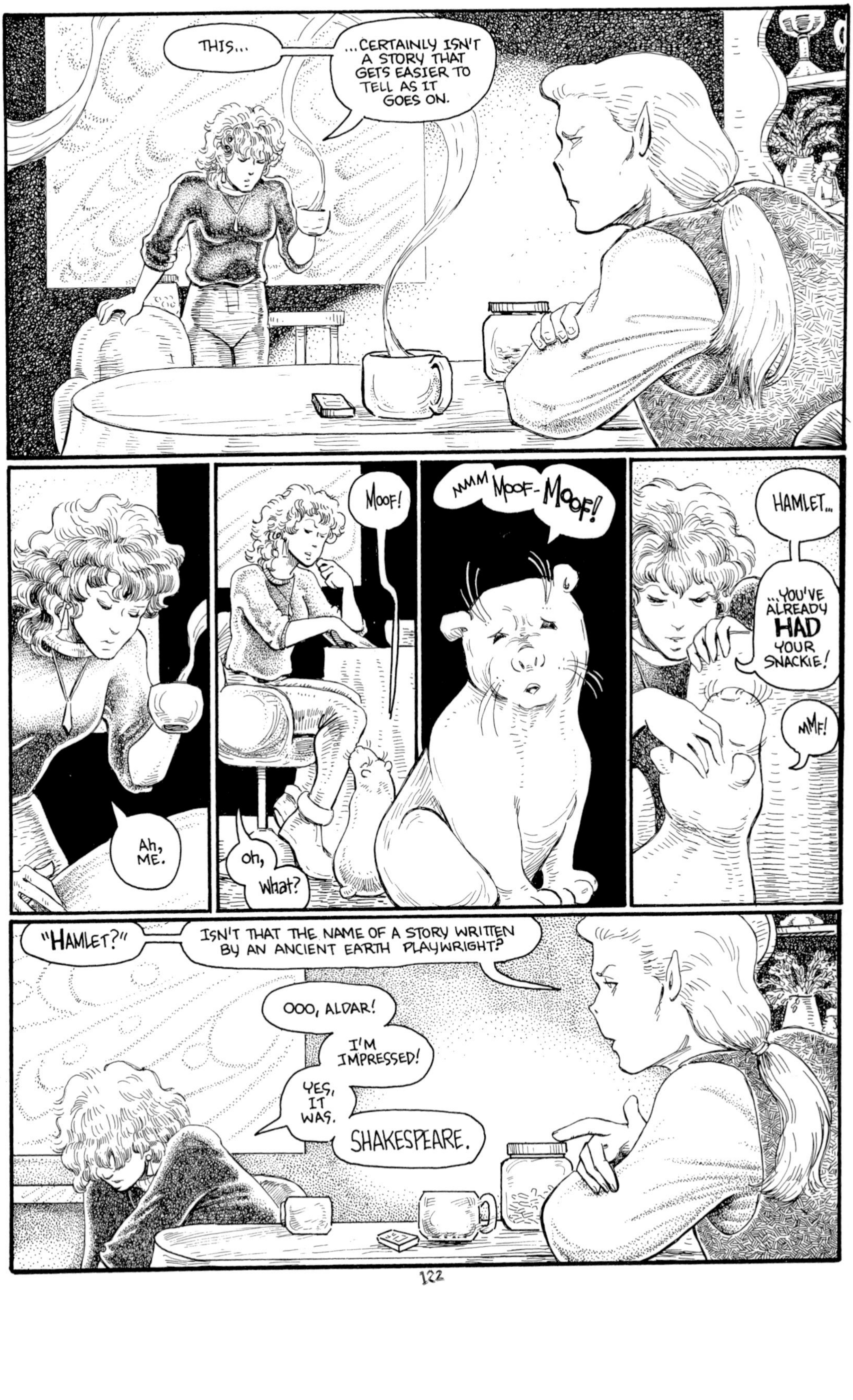
THIS...
...CERTAINLY ISN'T A STORY THAT GETS EASIER TO TELL AS IT GOES ON.
AH, ME.
MOOF!
OH, WHAT?
NMM MOOF-MOOF!
HAMLET...
...YOU'VE ALREADY HAD YOUR SNACKIE!
MMF!
"HAMLET?"
ISN'T THAT THE NAME OF A STORY WRITTEN BY AN ANCIENT EARTH PLAYWRIGHT?
OOO, ALDAR!
I'M IMPRESSED!
YES, IT WAS.
SHAKESPEARE.

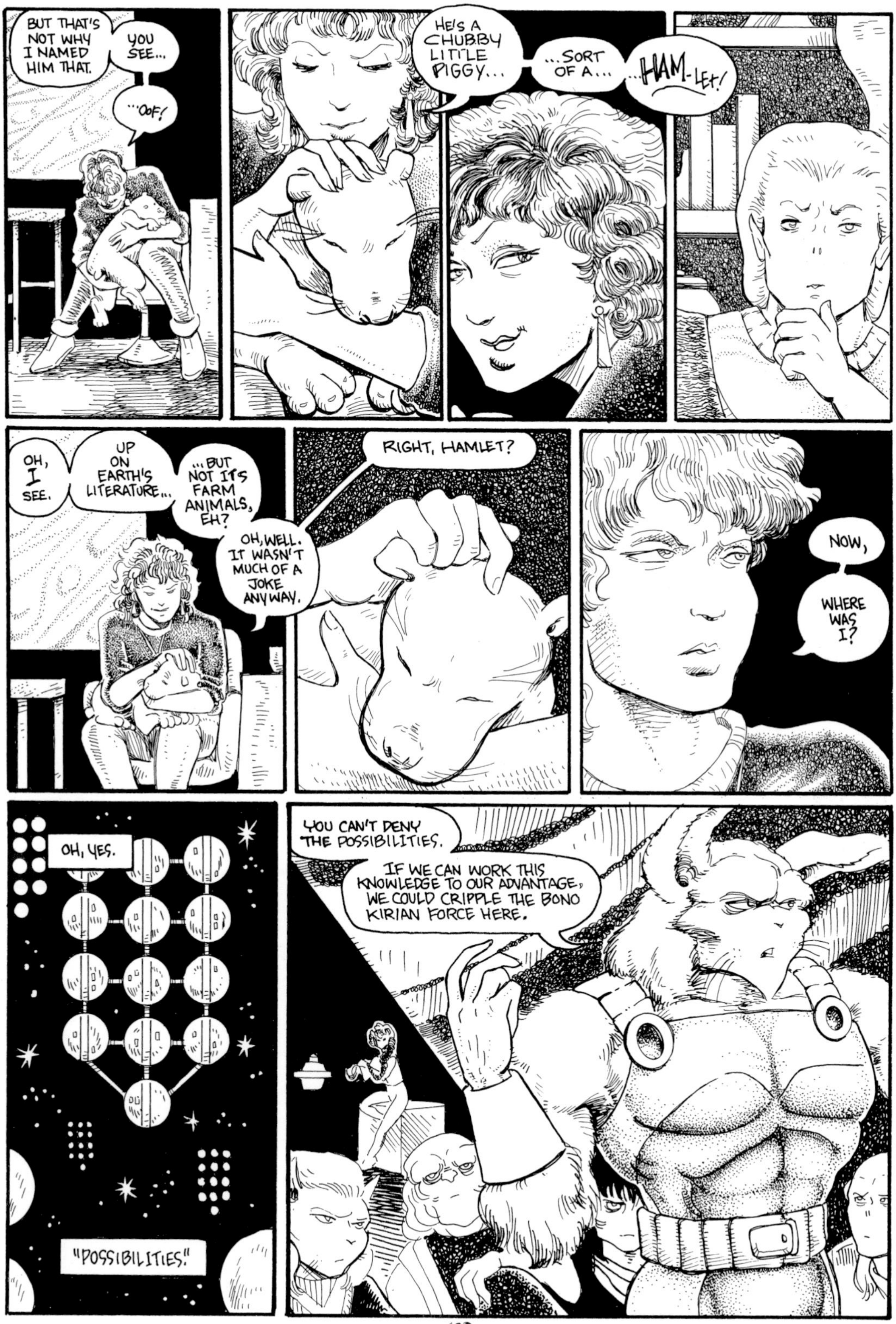
BUT THAT'S NOT WHY I NAMED HIM THAT.
YOU SEE...
...OOF!
HE'S A CHUBBY LITTLE PIGGY...
...SORT OF A...
...HAM-LET!
OH, I SEE.
UP ON EARTH'S LITERATURE...
...BUT NOT ITS FARM ANIMALS, EH?
OH, WELL. IT WASN'T MUCH OF A JOKE ANYWAY.
RIGHT, HAMLET?
NOW,
WHERE WAS I?
OH, YES.
"POSSIBILITIES."
YOU CAN'T DENY THE POSSIBILITIES.
IF WE CAN WORK THIS KNOWLEDGE TO OUR ADVANTAGE, WE COULD CRIPPLE THE BONO KIRIAN FORCE HERE.

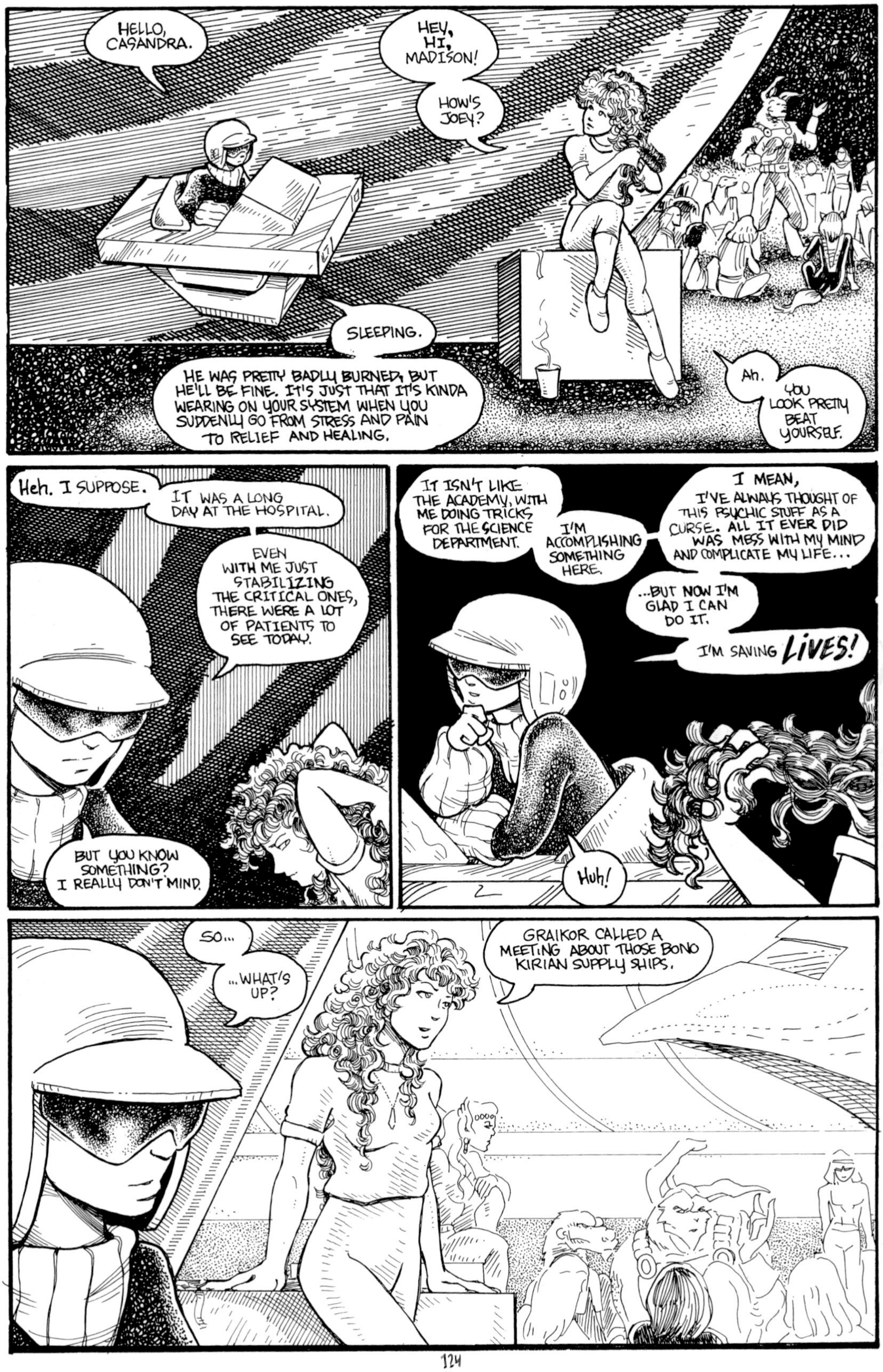

HELLO, CASANDRA.
HEY, HI, MADISON!
HOW'S JOEY?
SLEEPING.
HE WAS PRETTY BADLY BURNED, BUT HE'LL BE FINE. IT'S JUST THAT IT'S KINDA WEARING ON YOUR SYSTEM WHEN YOU SUDDENLY GO FROM STRESS AND PAIN TO RELIEF AND HEALING.
Ah.
YOU LOOK PRETTY BEAT YOURSELF.
Heh. I SUPPOSE.
IT WAS A LONG DAY AT THE HOSPITAL.
EVEN WITH ME JUST STABILIZING THE CRITICAL ONES, THERE WERE A LOT OF PATIENTS TO SEE TODAY.
BUT YOU KNOW SOMETHING? I REALLY DON'T MIND.
IT ISN'T LIKE THE ACADEMY, WITH ME DOING TRICKS FOR THE SCIENCE DEPARTMENT.
I'M ACCOMPLISHING SOMETHING HERE.
I MEAN, I'VE ALWAYS THOUGHT OF THIS PSYCHIC STUFF AS A CURSE. ALL IT EVER DID WAS MESS WITH MY MIND AND COMPLICATE MY LIFE...
...BUT NOW I'M GLAD I CAN DO IT.
I'M SAVING LIVES!
Huh!
SO...
...WHAT'S UP?
GRAIKOR CALLED A MEETING ABOUT THOSE BONO KIRIAN SUPPLY SHIPS.

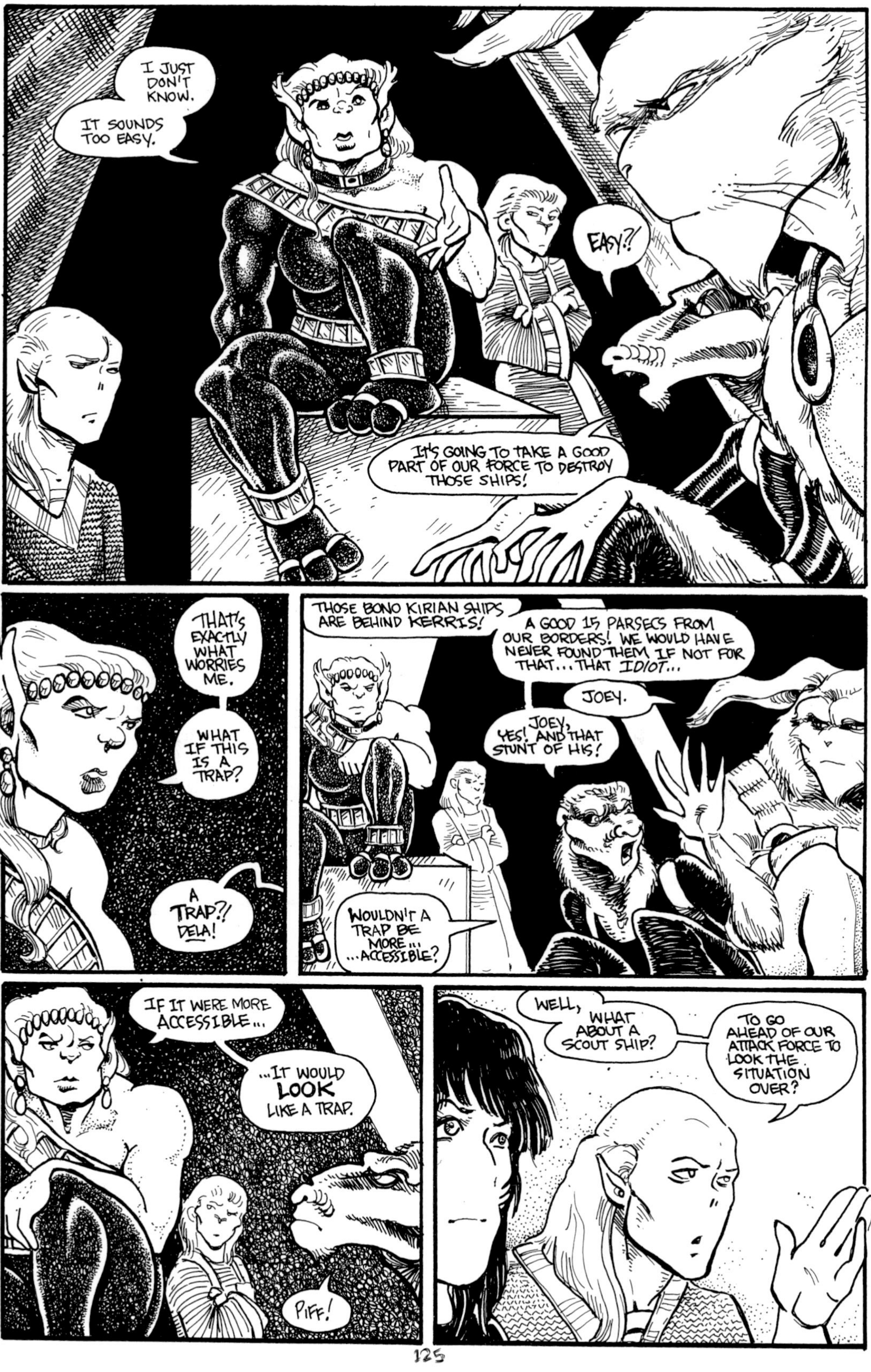
I JUST DON'T KNOW.
IT SOUNDS TOO EASY.
EASY?!
IT'S GOING TO TAKE A GOOD PART OF OUR FORCE TO DESTROY THOSE SHIPS!
THAT'S EXACTLY WHAT WORRIES ME.
WHAT IF THIS IS A TRAP?
A TRAP?! DELA!
THOSE BONO KIRIAN SHIPS ARE BEHIND KERRIS!
A GOOD 15 PARSECS FROM OUR BORDERS! WE WOULD HAVE NEVER FOUND THEM IF NOT FOR THAT... THAT IDIOT...
JOEY.
JOEY, YES! AND THAT STUNT OF HIS!
WOULDN'T A TRAP BE MORE... ...ACCESSIBLE?
IF IT WERE MORE ACCESSIBLE...
...IT WOULD LOOK LIKE A TRAP.
PIFF!
WELL, WHAT ABOUT A SCOUT SHIP?
TO GO AHEAD OF OUR ATTACK FORCE TO LOOK THE SITUATION OVER?

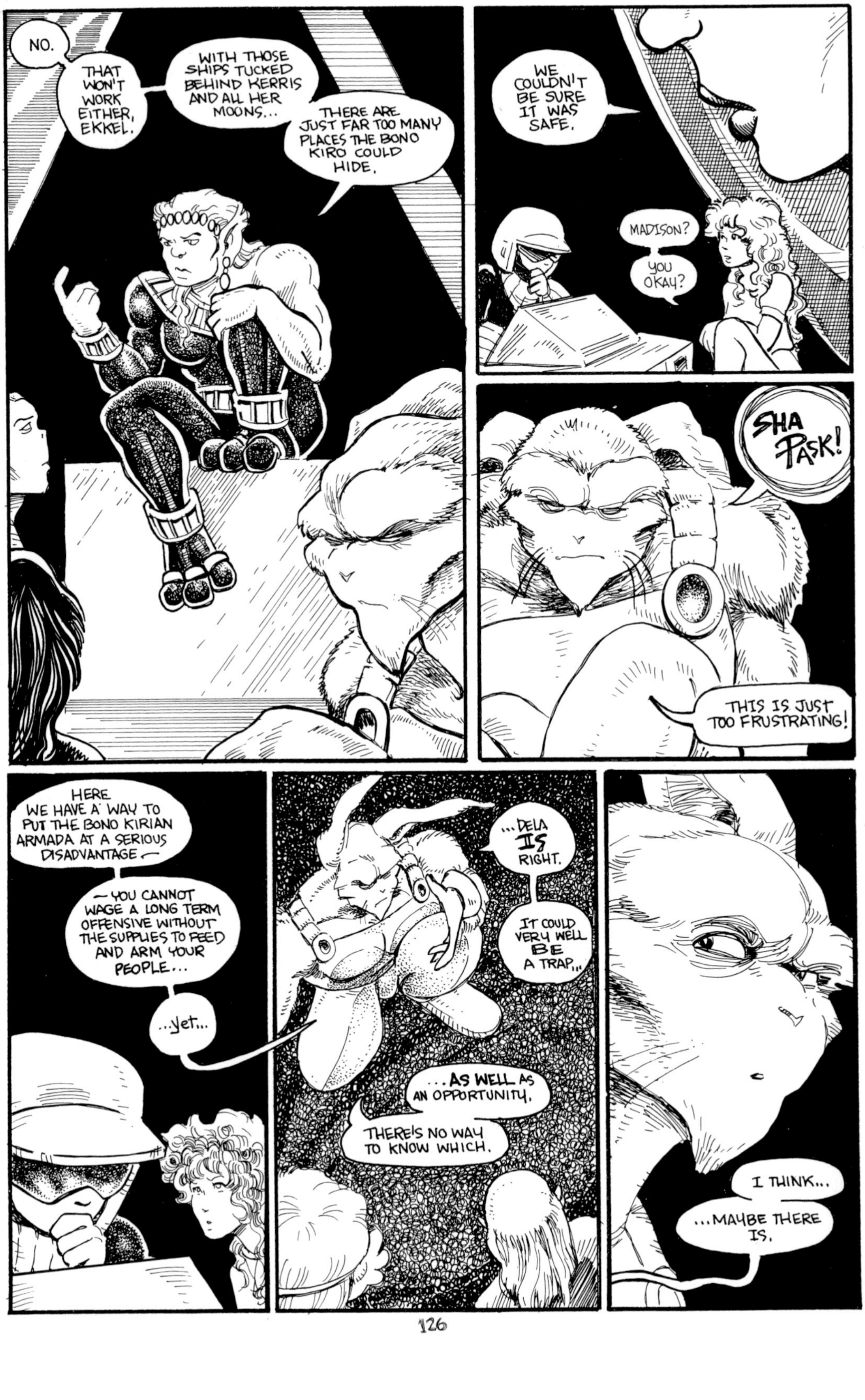
NO.
THAT WON'T WORK EITHER, EKKEL.
WITH THOSE SHIPS TUCKED BEHIND KERRIS AND ALL HER MOONS...
THERE ARE JUST FAR TOO MANY PLACES THE BONO KIRO COULD HIDE.
WE COULDN'T BE SURE IT WAS SAFE.
MADISON?
YOU OKAY?
SHA PASK!
THIS IS JUST TOO FRUSTRATING!
HERE WE HAVE A WAY TO PUT THE BONO KIRIAN ARMADA AT A SERIOUS DISADVANTAGE—
—YOU CANNOT WAGE A LONG TERM OFFENSIVE WITHOUT THE SUPPLIES TO FEED AND ARM YOUR PEOPLE...
...yet...
...DELA IS RIGHT.
IT COULD VERY WELL BE A TRAP...
...AS WELL AS AN OPPORTUNITY.
THERE'S NO WAY TO KNOW WHICH.
I THINK...
...MAYBE THERE IS.

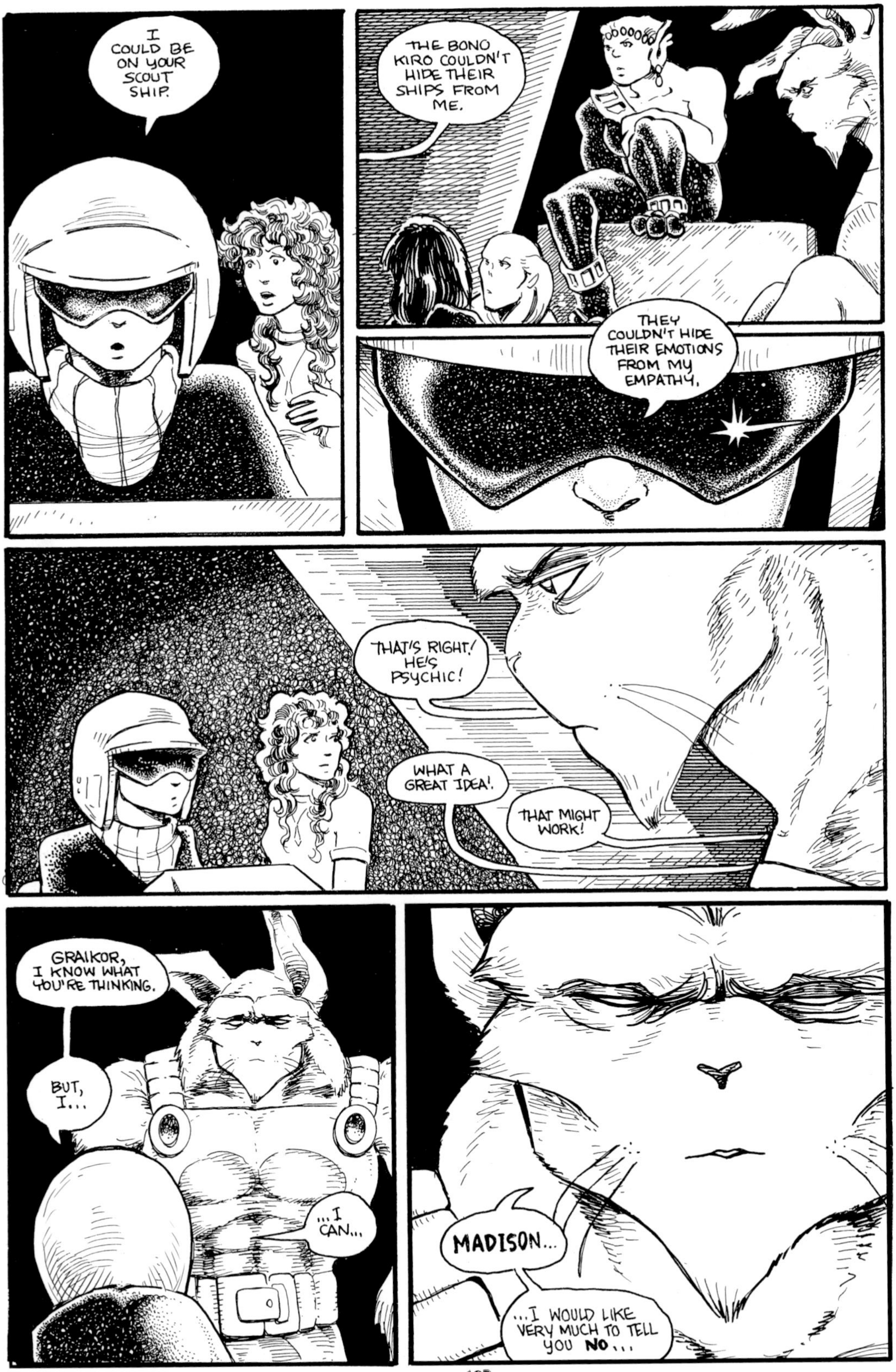
I COULD BE ON YOUR SCOUT SHIP.
THE BONO KIRO COULDN'T HIDE THEIR SHIPS FROM ME.
THEY COULDN'T HIDE THEIR EMOTIONS FROM MY EMPATHY.
THAT'S RIGHT! HE'S PSYCHIC!
WHAT A GREAT IDEA!
THAT MIGHT WORK!
GRAIKOR, I KNOW WHAT YOU'RE THINKING.
BUT, I...
...I CAN...
MADISON...
...I WOULD LIKE VERY MUCH TO TELL YOU **NO**...

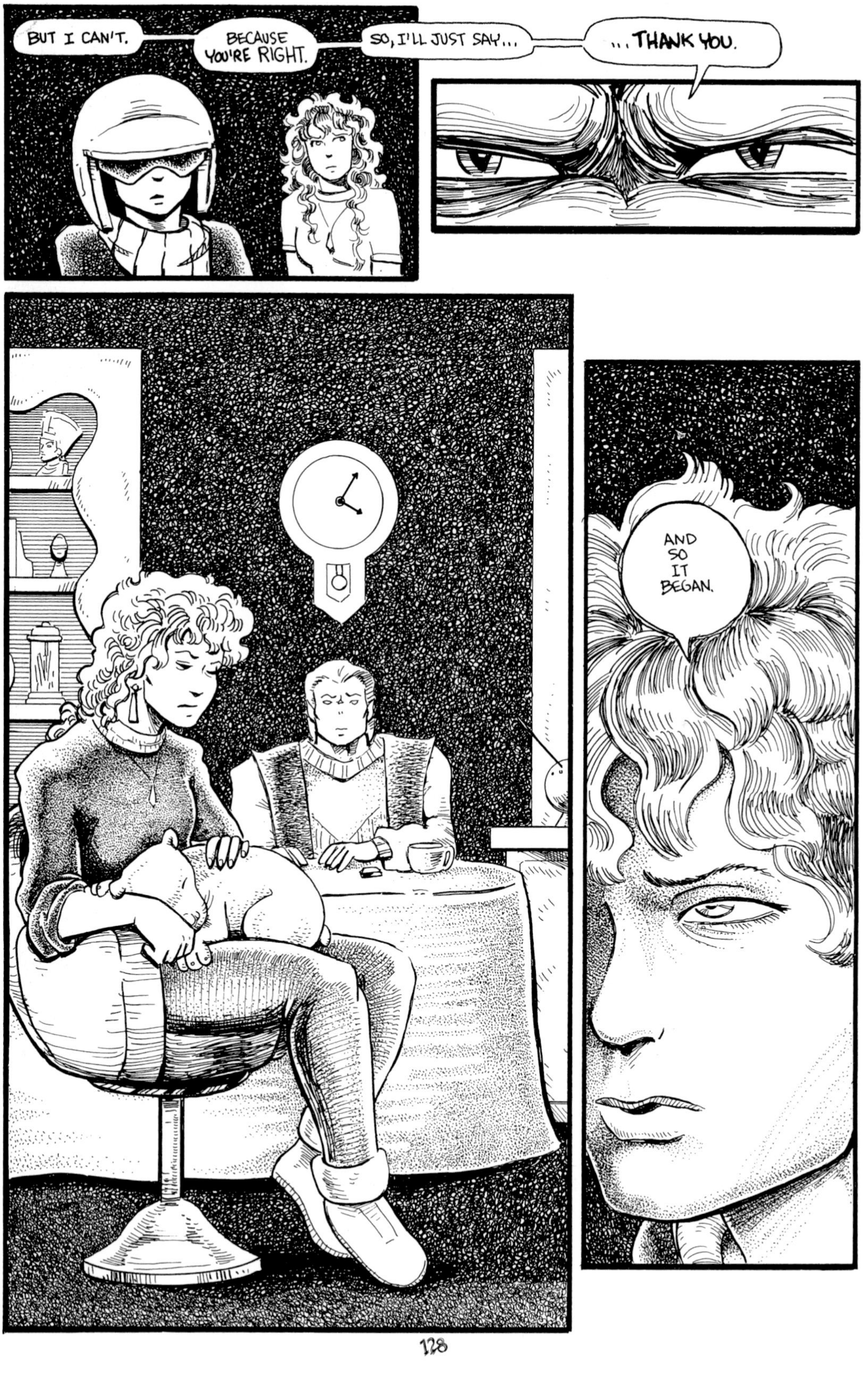

BUT I CAN'T.
BECAUSE YOU'RE RIGHT.
SO, I'LL JUST SAY...
...THANK YOU.
AND SO IT BEGAN.

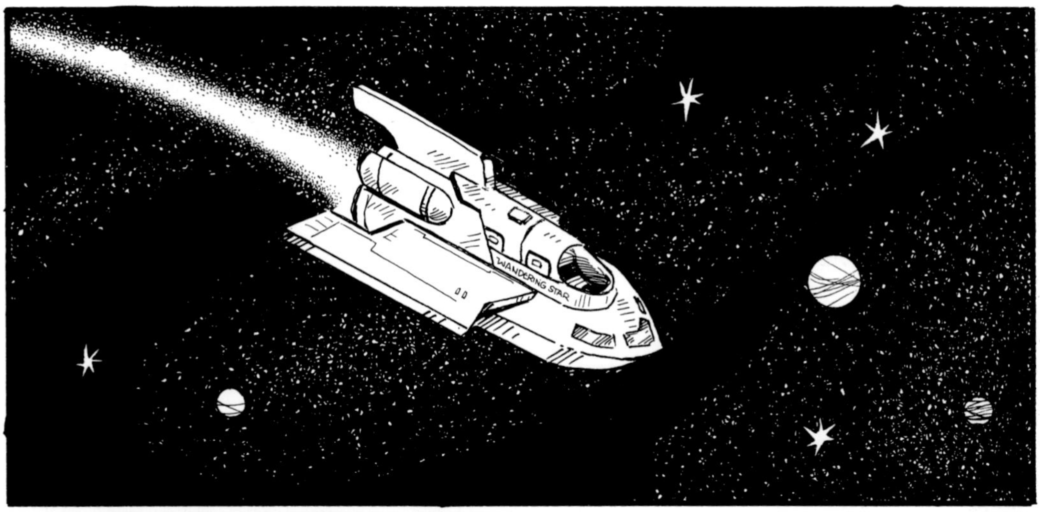
WANDERING STAR

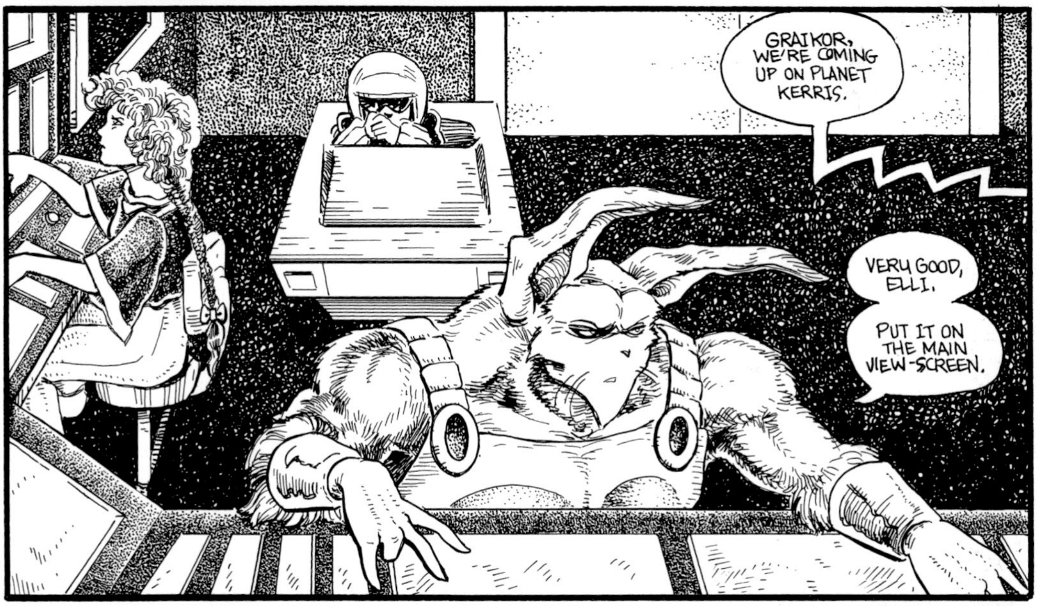
GRAIKOR, WE'RE COMING UP ON PLANET KERRIS.
VERY GOOD, ELLI.
PUT IT ON THE MAIN VIEW-SCREEN.

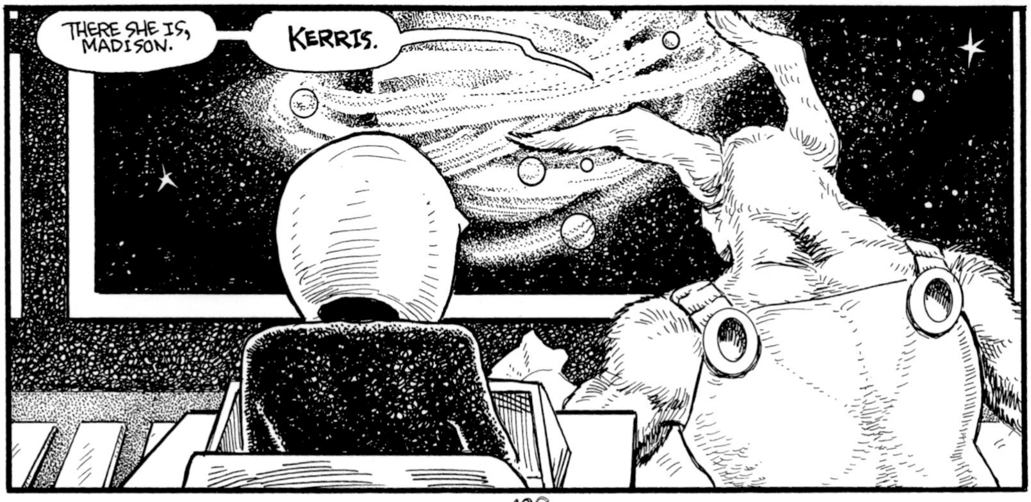
THERE SHE IS, MADISON.
KERRIS.

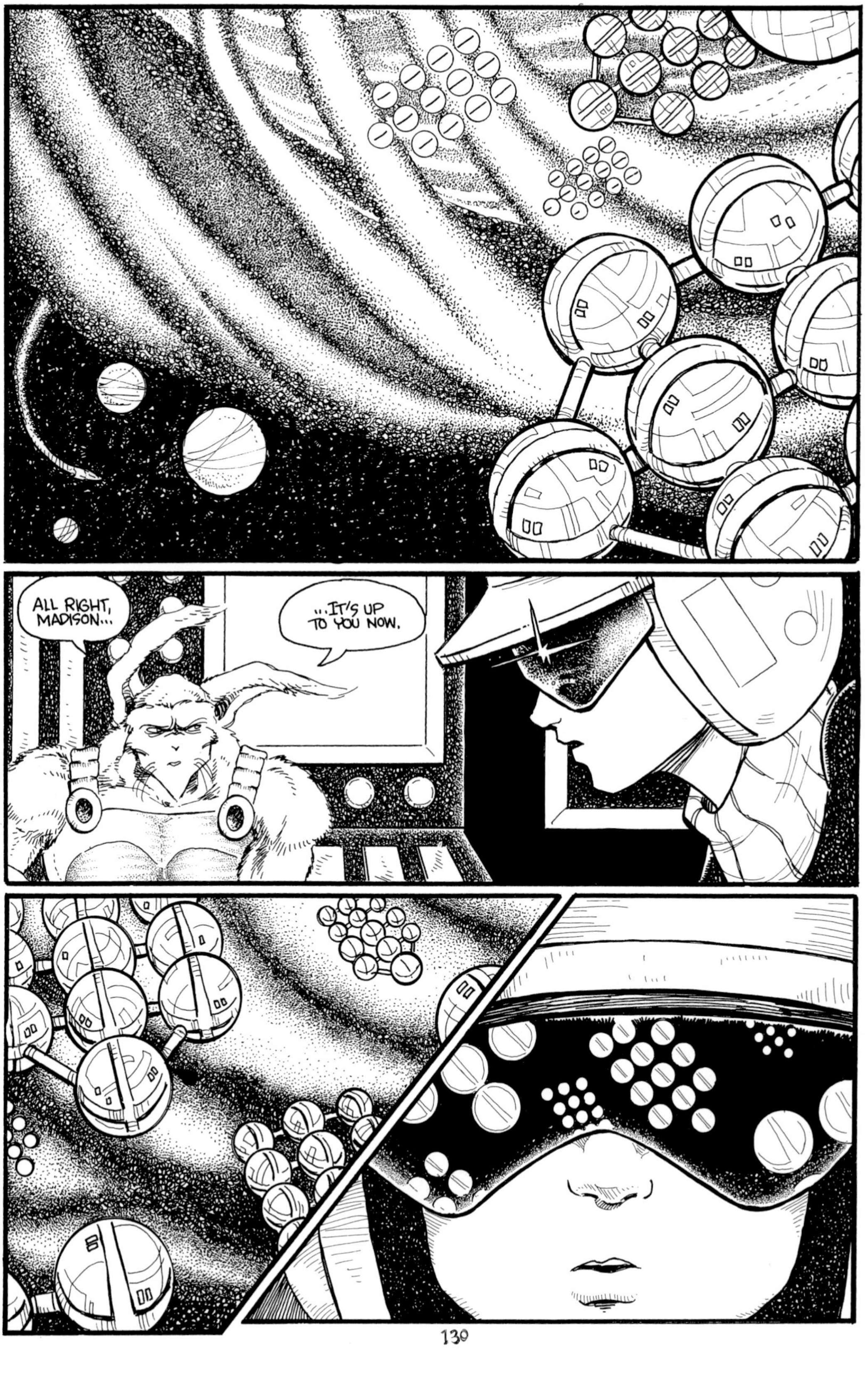
ALL RIGHT, MADISON...
...IT'S UP TO YOU NOW.

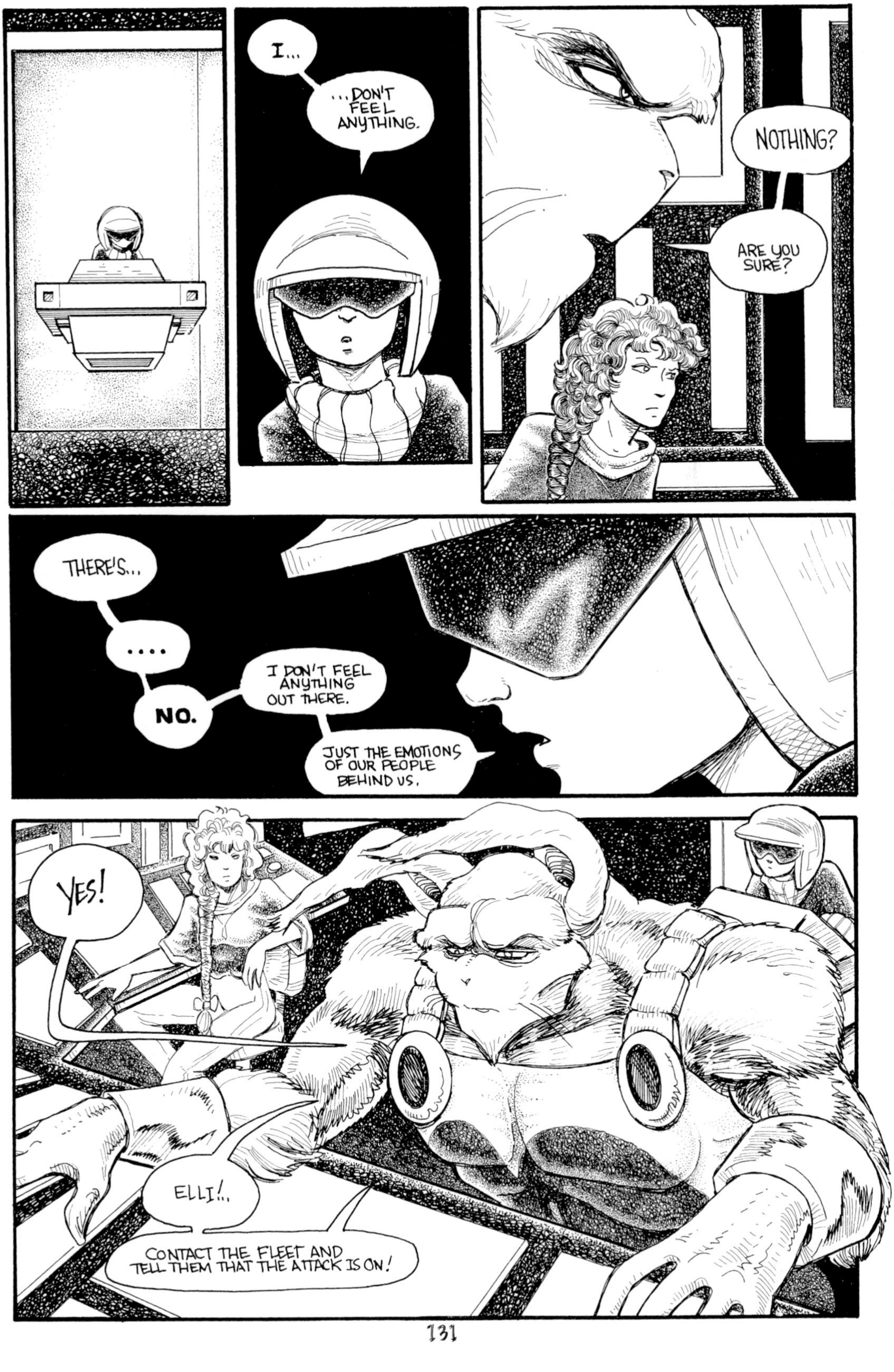
I...
...DON'T FEEL ANYTHING.
NOTHING?
ARE YOU SURE?
THERE'S...
.....
NO.
I DON'T FEEL ANYTHING OUT THERE.
JUST THE EMOTIONS OF OUR PEOPLE BEHIND US.
YES!
ELLI!..
CONTACT THE FLEET AND TELL THEM THAT THE ATTACK IS ON!

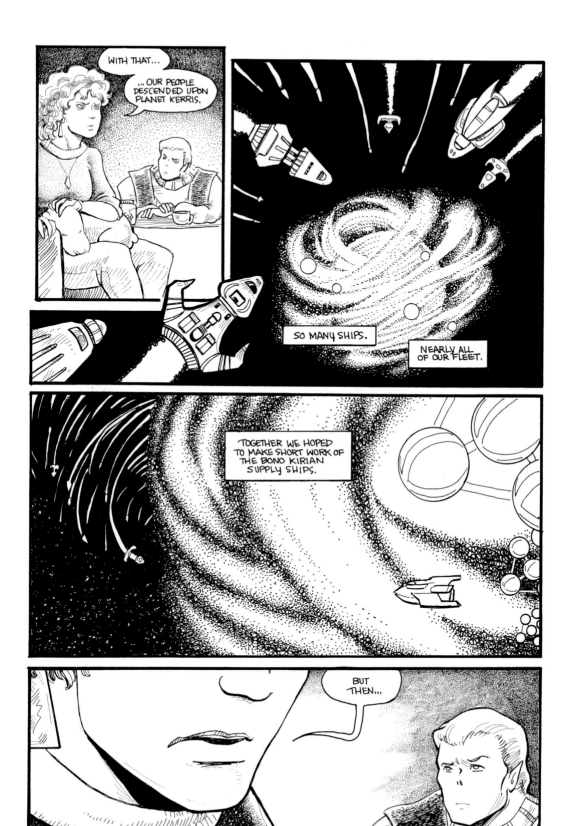

WITH THAT...

...OUR PEOPLE DESCENDED UPON PLANET KERRIS.

SO MANY SHIPS.

NEARLY ALL OF OUR FLEET.

TOGETHER WE HOPED TO MAKE SHORT WORK OF THE BONO KIRIAN SUPPLY SHIPS.

BUT THEN...

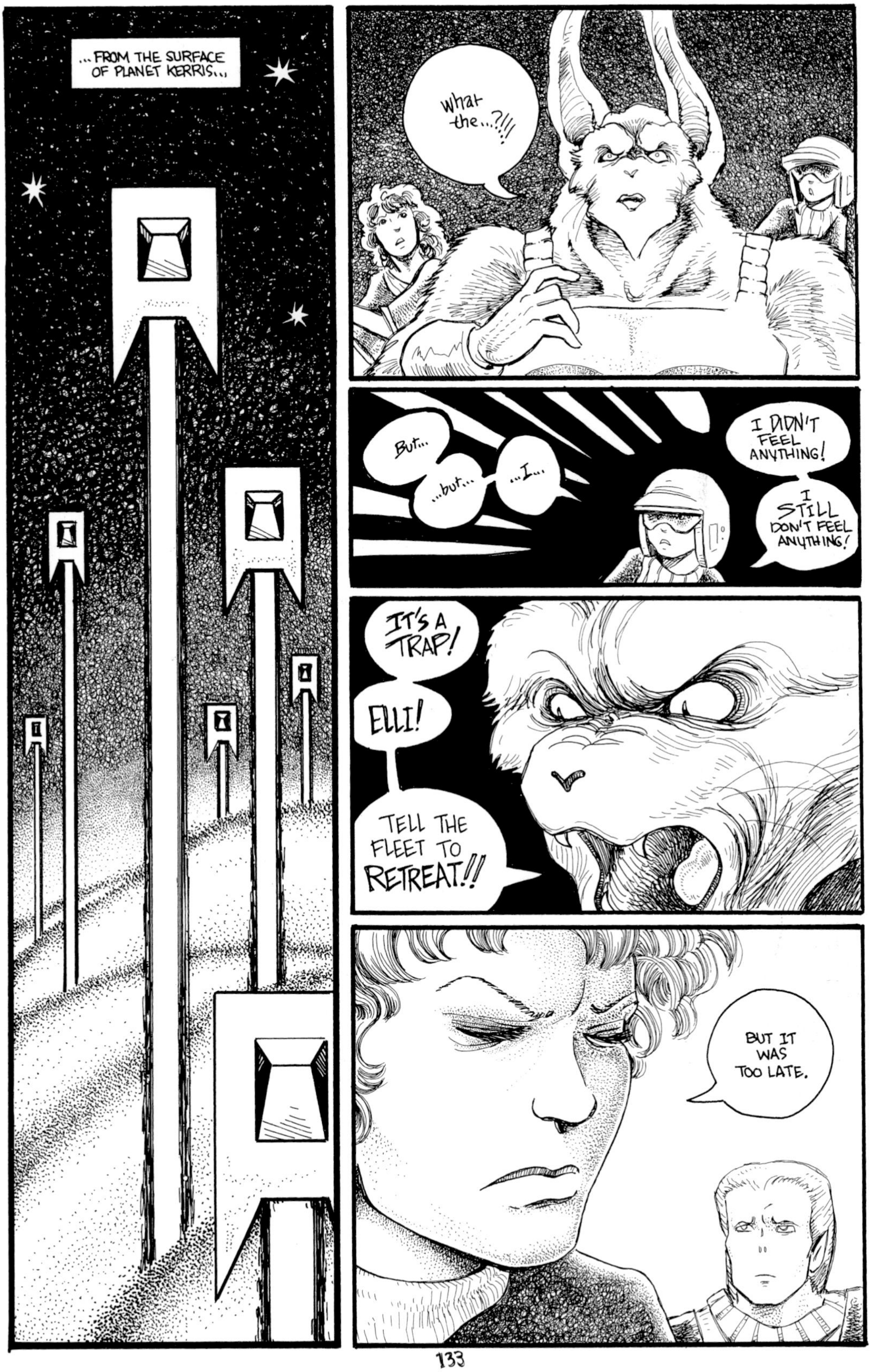
...FROM THE SURFACE OF PLANET KERRIS...
What the...?!!
But...
...but...
...I...
I DIDN'T FEEL ANYTHING!
I STILL DON'T FEEL ANYTHING!
IT'S A TRAP!
ELLI!
TELL THE FLEET TO RETREAT!!
BUT IT WAS TOO LATE.

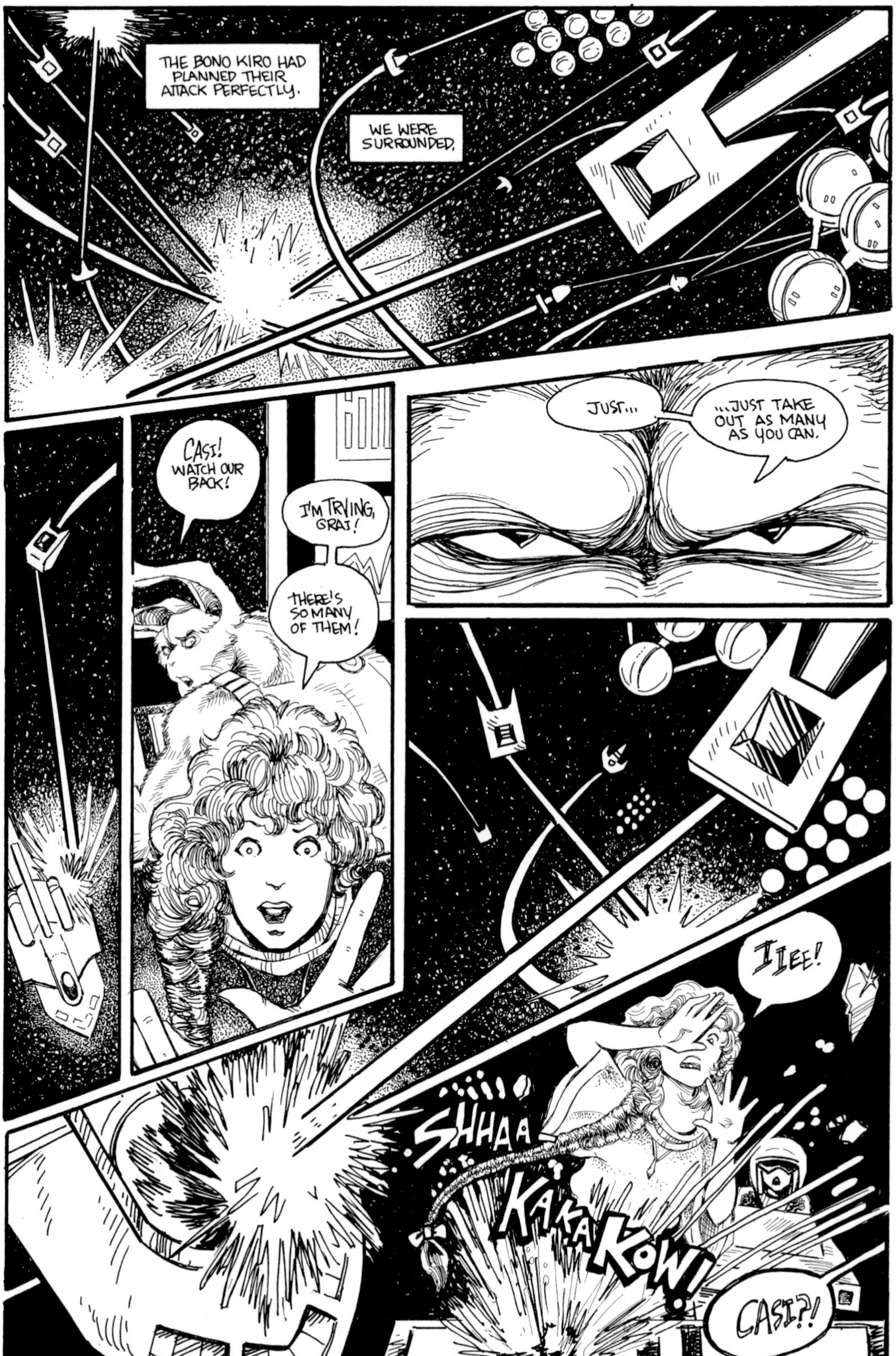
THE BONO KIRO HAD PLANNED THEIR ATTACK PERFECTLY.
WE WERE SURROUNDED.
JUST...
...JUST TAKE OUT AS MANY AS YOU CAN.
CASI! WATCH OUR BACK!
I'M TRYING, GRAJ!
THERE'S SO MANY OF THEM!
IIEE!
SHHAA
KAKAKOW!
CASI?!

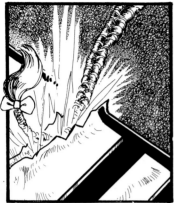

SHooo
PLIP PLIP PIT!

KRIKRT
SSSSSSSPOOM!

ELLI, TRANSFER WEAPONS TO...

...AAK?!!

MY HAIR'S STUCK!

I DON'T BELIEVE THIS!

ELLI— TRANSFER WEAPONS TO THE OPEN SECTION OF THE MAIN PANEL!

IT'S DONE, BUT GRAIKOR...

...CASANDRA'S GOT TO GET AWAY FROM THAT PANEL, IF WE'RE HIT AGAIN...

...IT'LL BLOW!

CASI!

I HEARD, GRAIKOR! BUT I...

...I'M STUCK!

135

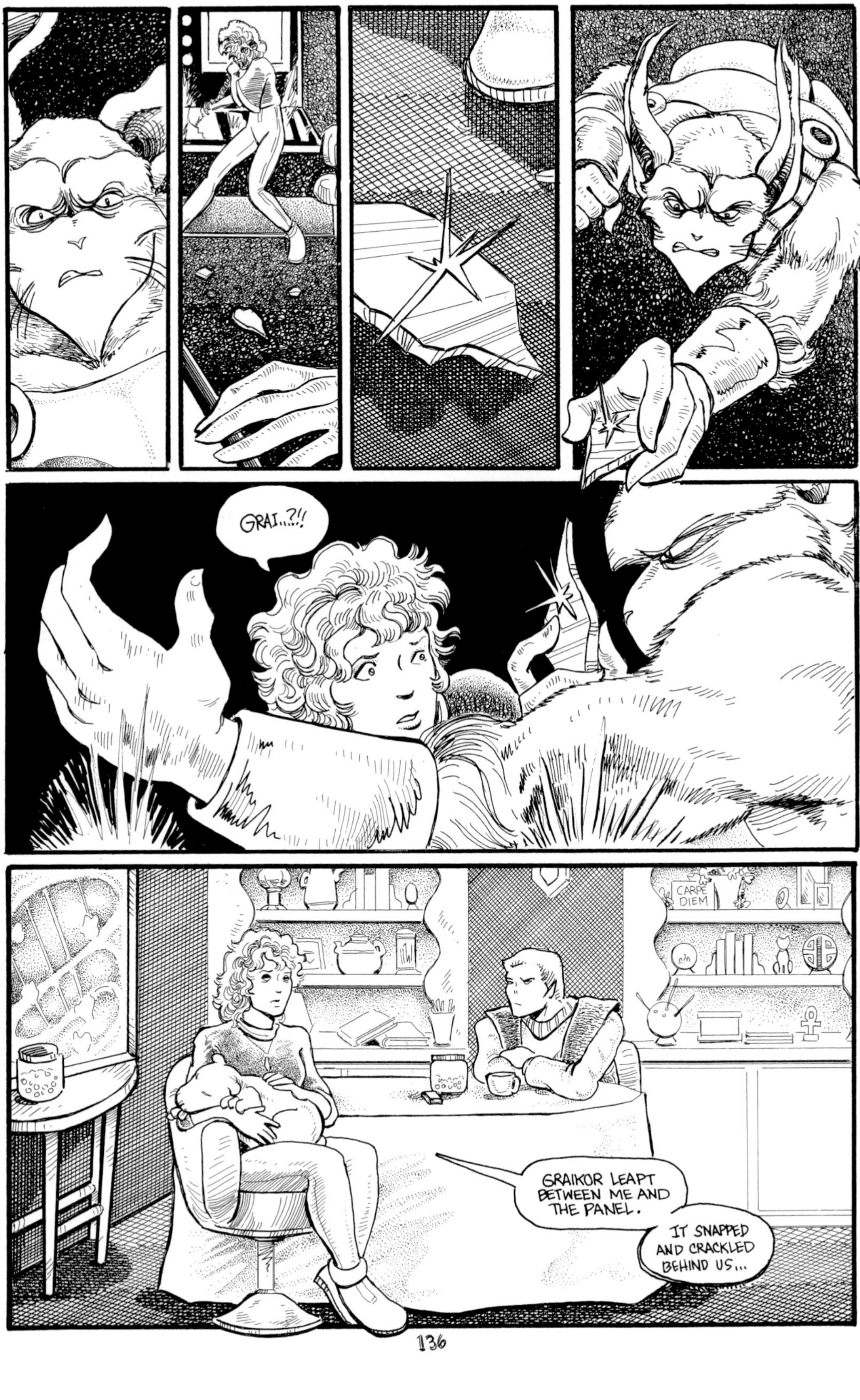
GRAI...?!!
GRAIKOR LEAPT BETWEEN ME AND THE PANEL.
IT SNAPPED AND CRACKLED BEHIND US...
CARPE DIEM

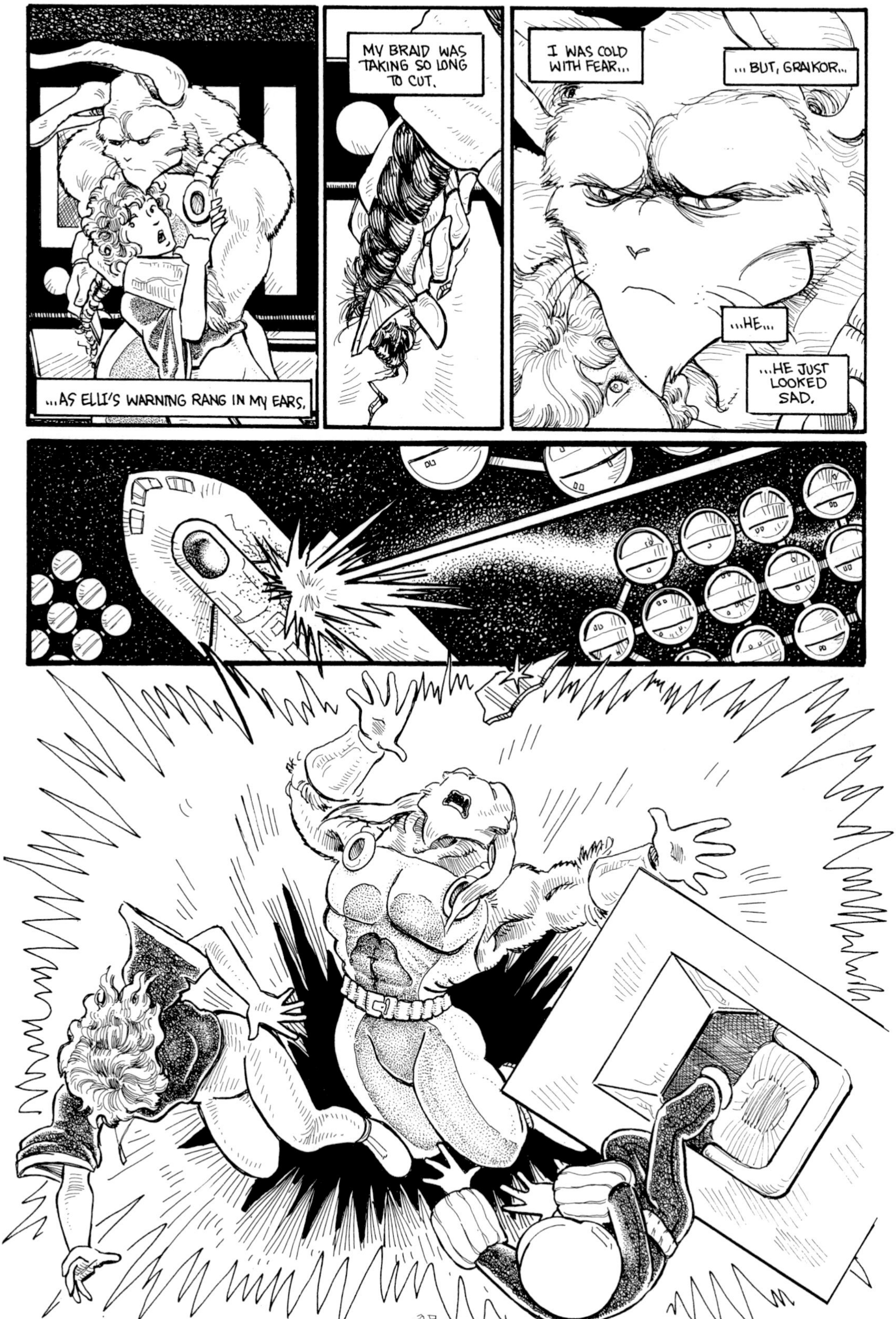
...AS ELLI'S WARNING RANG IN MY EARS.
MY BRAID WAS TAKING SO LONG TO CUT.
I WAS COLD WITH FEAR...
...BUT, GRAIKOR...
...HE...
...HE JUST LOOKED SAD.

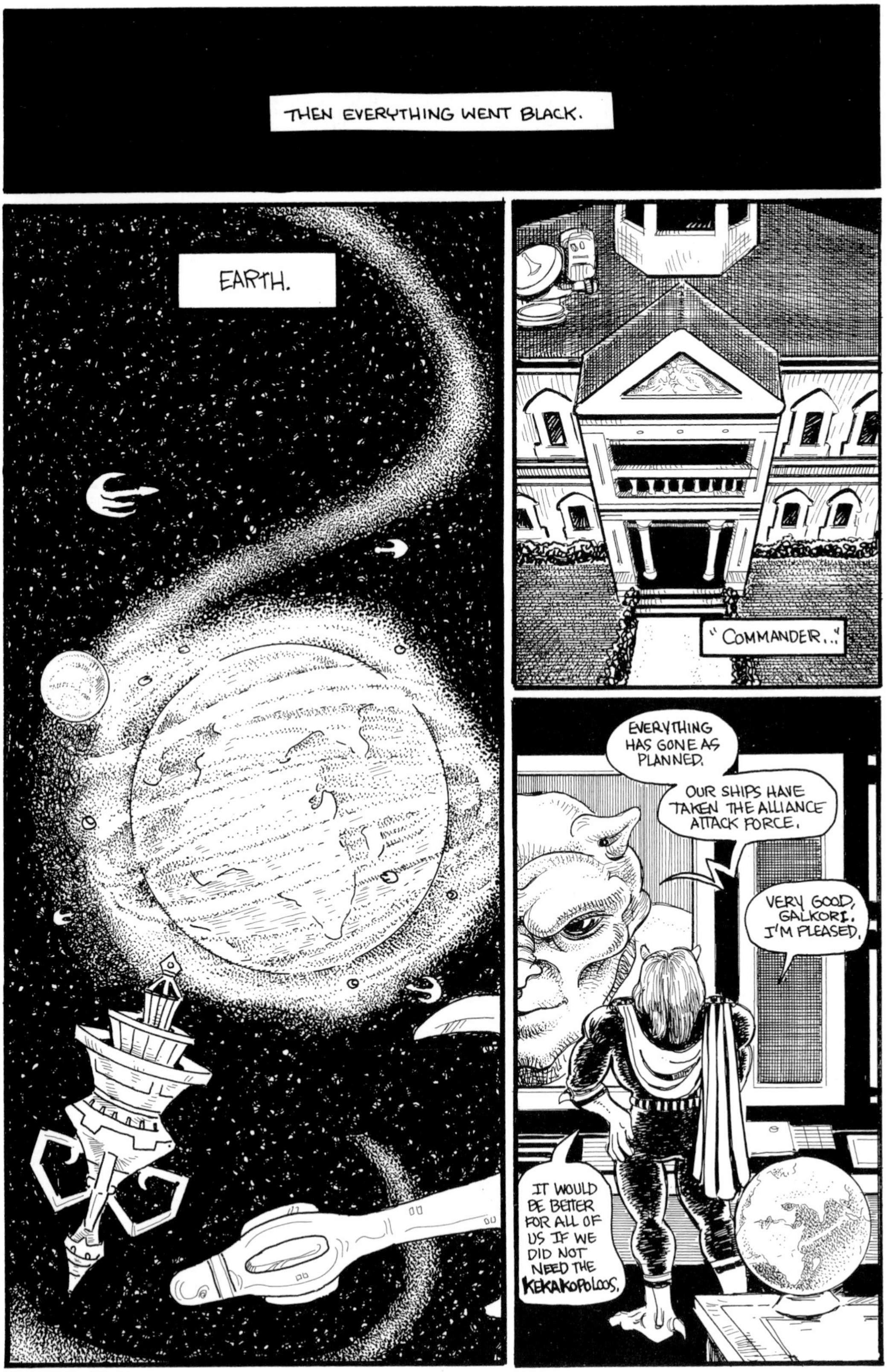
THEN EVERYTHING WENT BLACK.
EARTH.
"COMMANDER..."
EVERYTHING HAS GONE AS PLANNED.
OUR SHIPS HAVE TAKEN THE ALLIANCE ATTACK FORCE.
VERY GOOD, GALKORI. I'M PLEASED.
IT WOULD BE BETTER FOR ALL OF US IF WE DID NOT NEED THE KEKAKOPOLOOS.

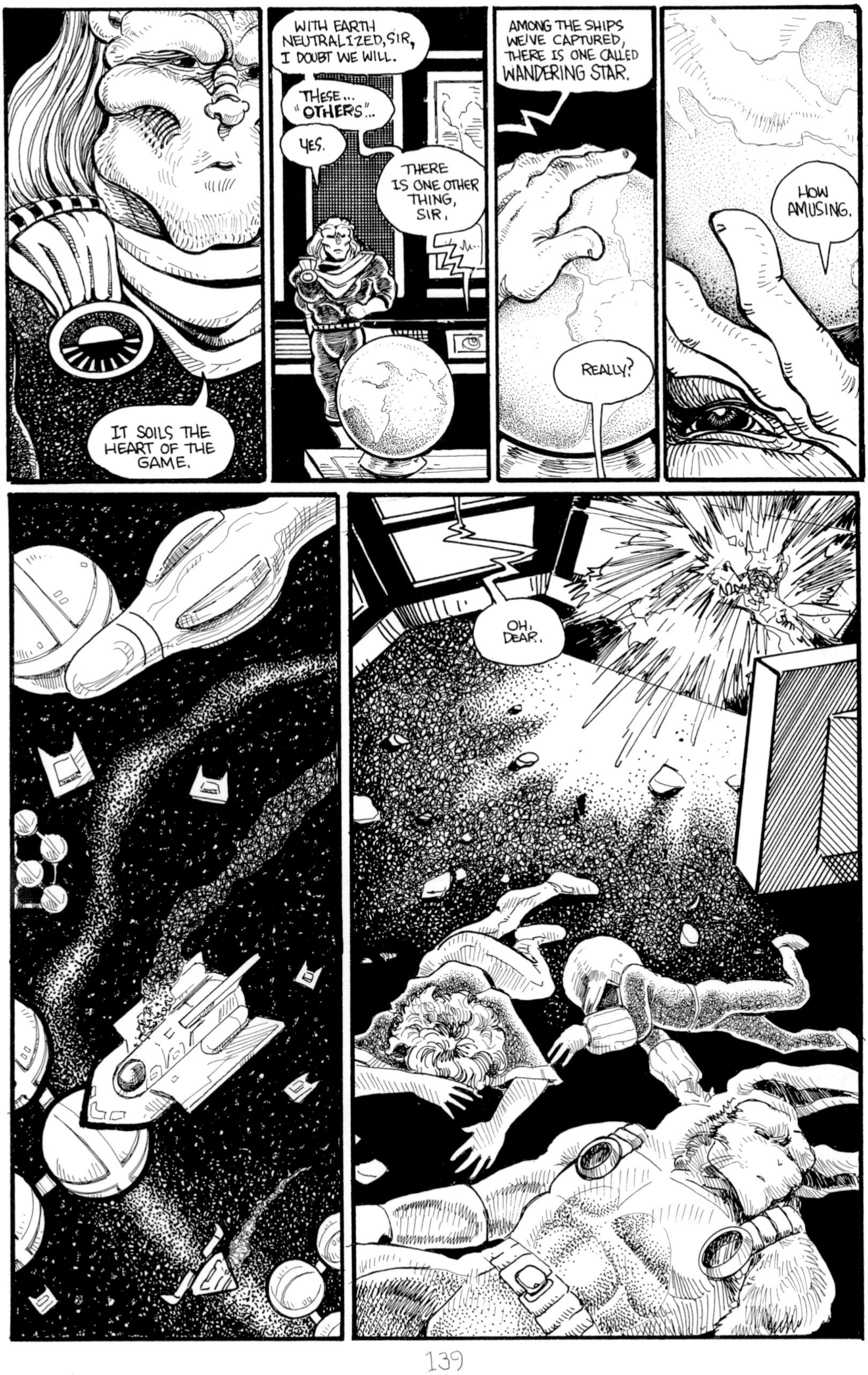
IT SOILS THE HEART OF THE GAME.
WITH EARTH NEUTRALIZED, SIR, I DOUBT WE WILL.
THESE... "OTHERS"...
YES.
THERE IS ONE OTHER THING, SIR.
AMONG THE SHIPS WE'VE CAPTURED, THERE IS ONE CALLED WANDERING STAR.
REALLY?
HOW AMUSING.
OH, DEAR.

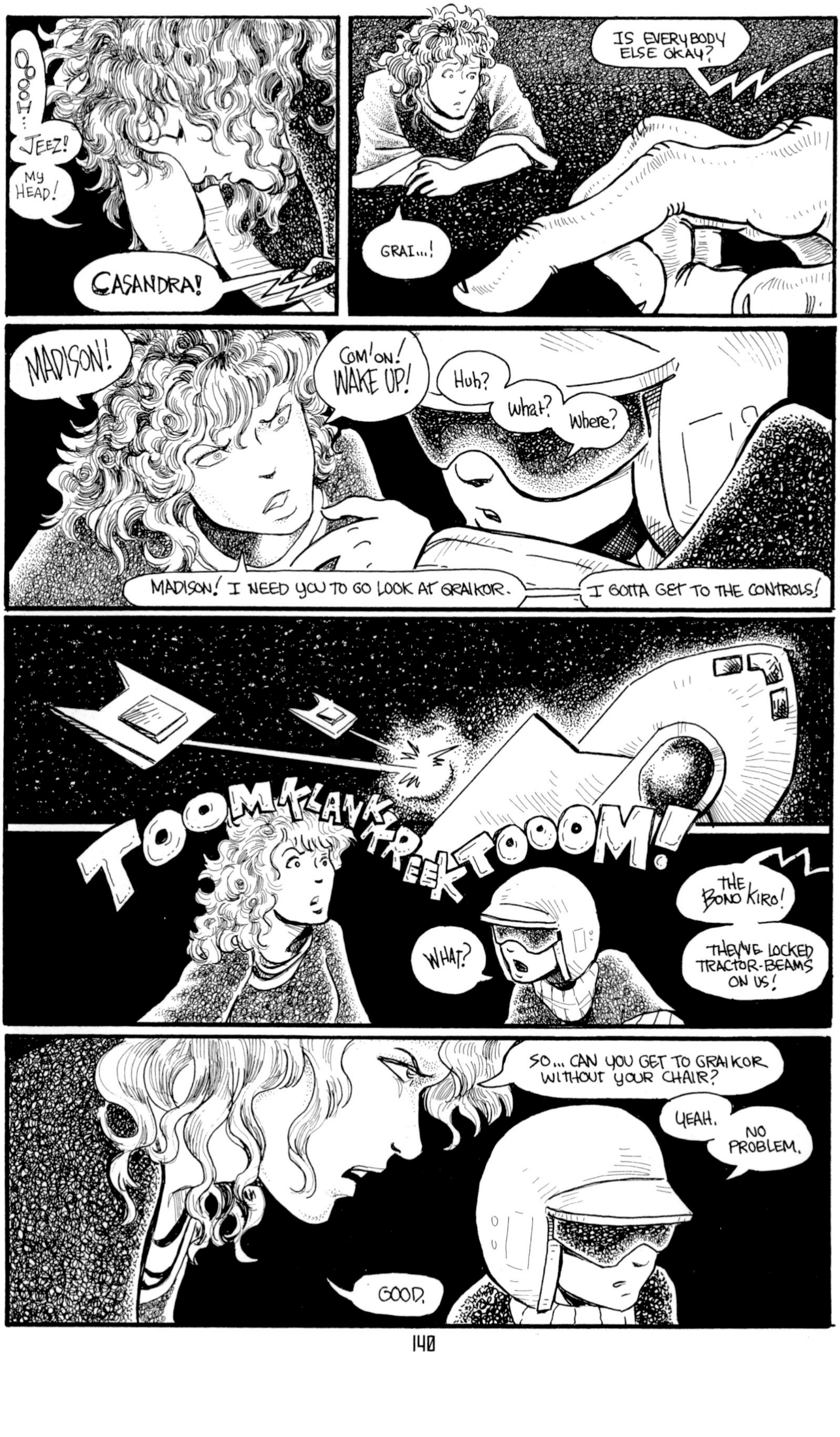
OOOOH... JEEZ!
MY HEAD!
CASANDRA!
IS EVERYBODY ELSE OKAY?
GRAI...!
MADISON!
COM'ON! WAKE UP!
Huh?
What?
Where?
MADISON! I NEED YOU TO GO LOOK AT GRAIKOR.
I GOTTA GET TO THE CONTROLS!
TOOMKLANKKREEKTOOOM!
THE BONO KIRO!
WHAT?
THEY'VE LOCKED TRACTOR-BEAMS ON US!
SO... CAN YOU GET TO GRAIKOR WITHOUT YOUR CHAIR?
YEAH.
NO PROBLEM.
GOOD.

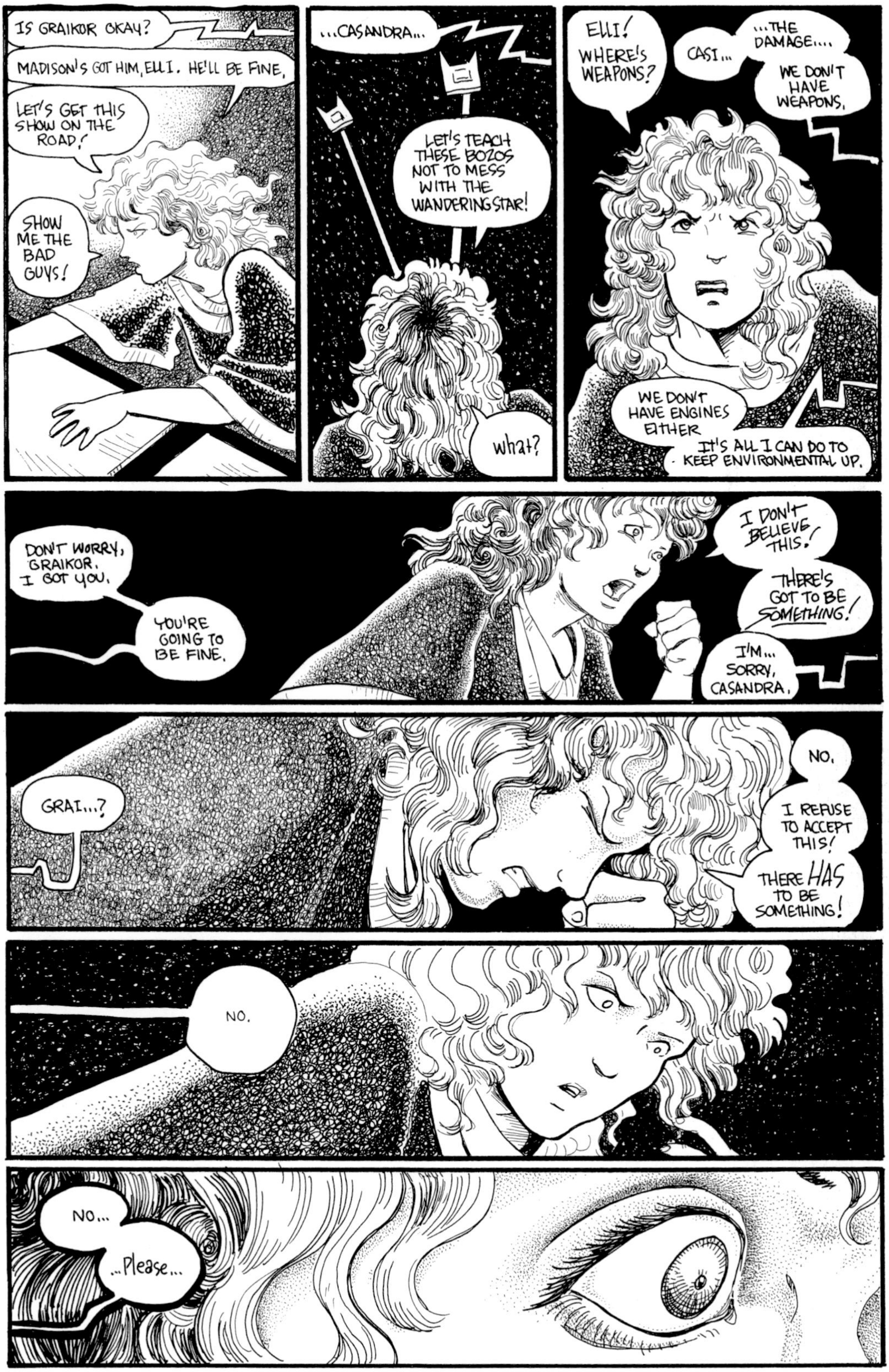
IS GRAIKOR OKAY?
MADISON'S GOT HIM, ELLI. HE'LL BE FINE.
LET'S GET THIS SHOW ON THE ROAD!
SHOW ME THE BAD GUYS!
...CASANDRA...
LET'S TEACH THESE BOZOS NOT TO MESS WITH THE WANDERING STAR!
what?
ELLI! WHERE'S WEAPONS?
CASI...
...THE DAMAGE....
WE DON'T HAVE WEAPONS.
WE DON'T HAVE ENGINES EITHER
IT'S ALL I CAN DO TO KEEP ENVIRONMENTAL UP.
DON'T WORRY, GRAIKOR. I GOT YOU.
YOU'RE GOING TO BE FINE.
I DON'T BELIEVE THIS!
THERE'S GOT TO BE SOMETHING!
I'M... SORRY, CASANDRA.
GRAI...?
NO.
I REFUSE TO ACCEPT THIS!
THERE HAS TO BE SOMETHING!
NO.
NO...
...Please...

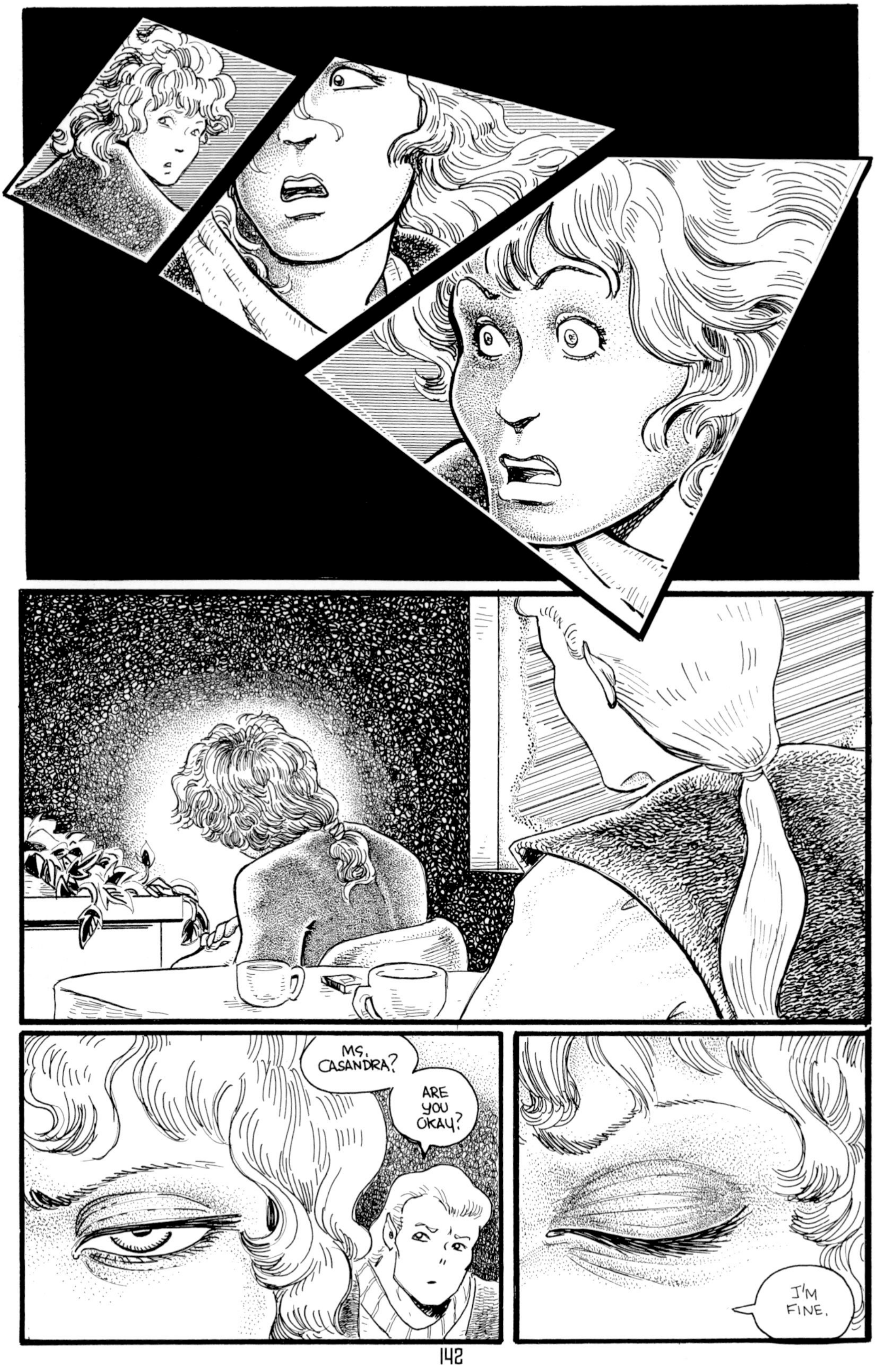
MS. CASANDRA?
ARE YOU OKAY?
I'M FINE.

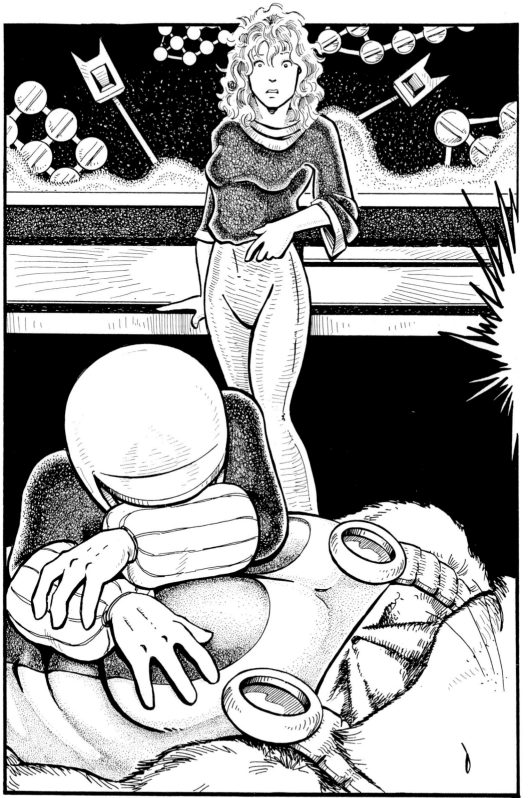

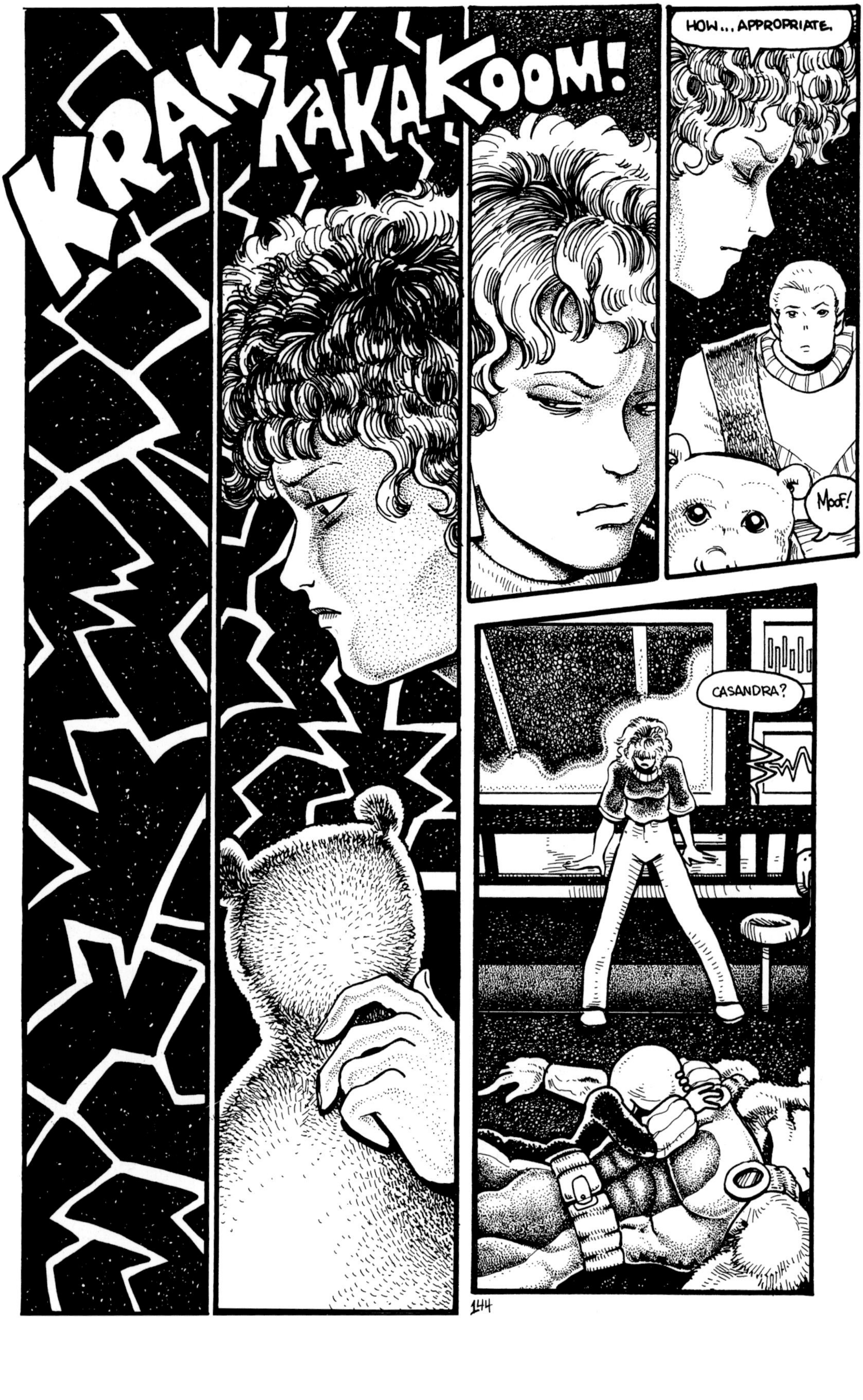
KRAKKAKAKAKOOM!
HOW... APPROPRIATE.
MOOF!
CASANDRA?

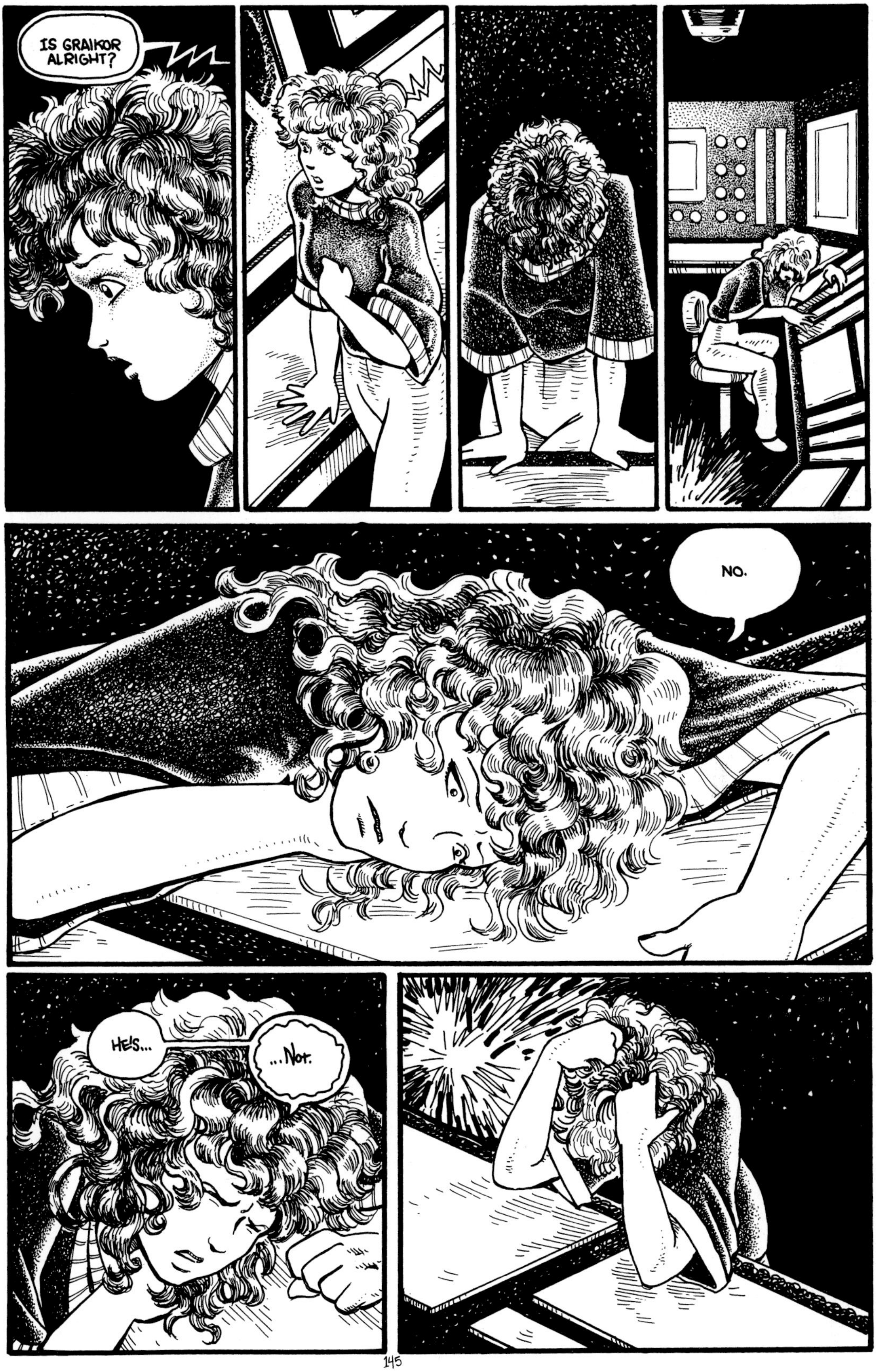
IS GRAIKOR ALRIGHT?
NO.
HE'S...
...Not.

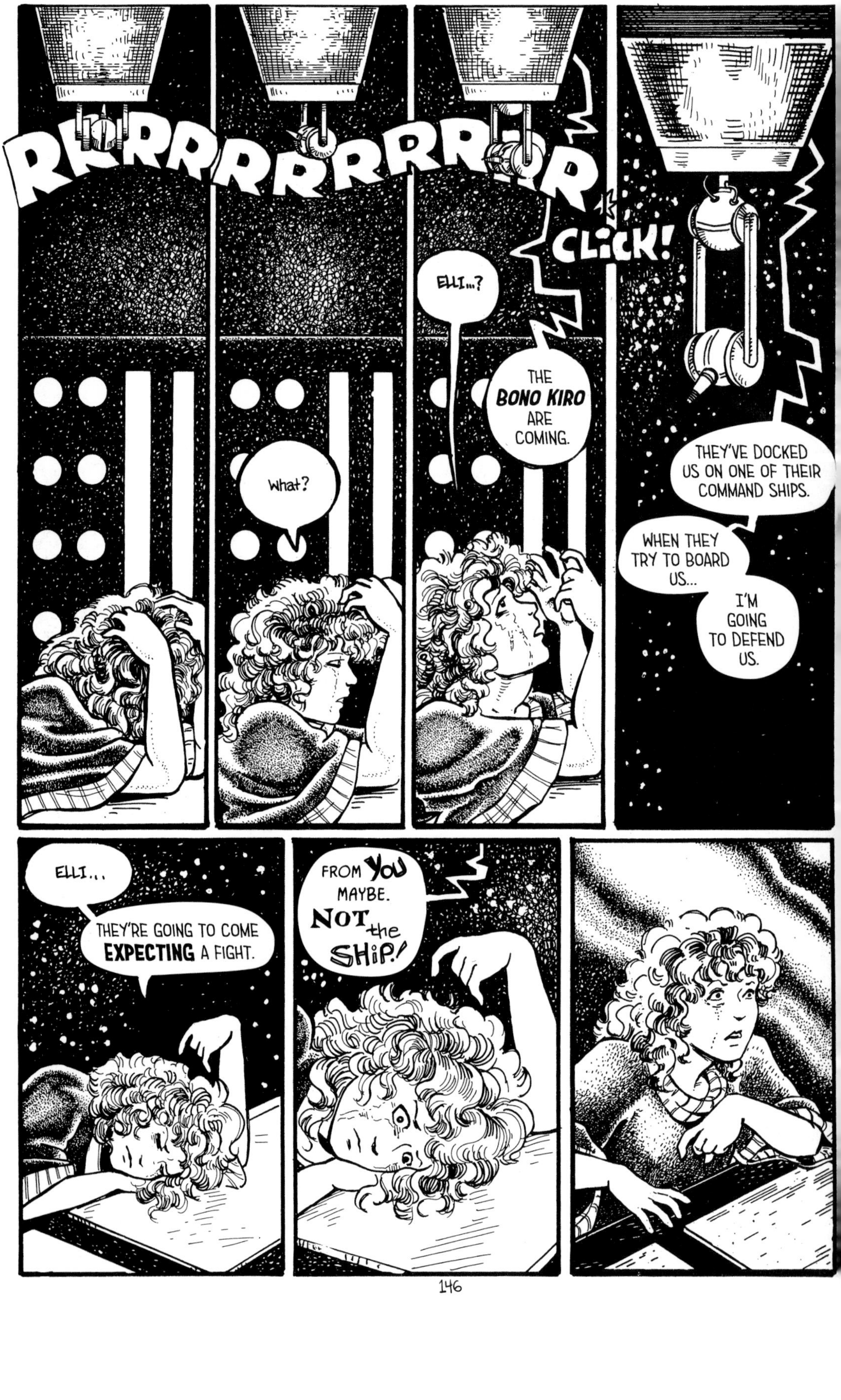
RRRRRRRRRRRR
CLICK!
What?
ELLI...?
THE BONO KIRO ARE COMING.
THEY'VE DOCKED US ON ONE OF THEIR COMMAND SHIPS.
WHEN THEY TRY TO BOARD US...
I'M GOING TO DEFEND US.
ELLI...
THEY'RE GOING TO COME EXPECTING A FIGHT.
FROM YOU MAYBE. NOT the SHIP!

THAT...

...THAT'S RIGHT.

THE BONO KIRO WOULDN'T KNOW ABOUT THE TRILLIANS, WOULD THEY?

I...

...THINK...

...I HAVE AN IDEA.

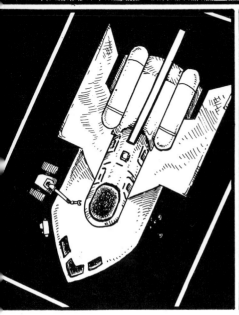

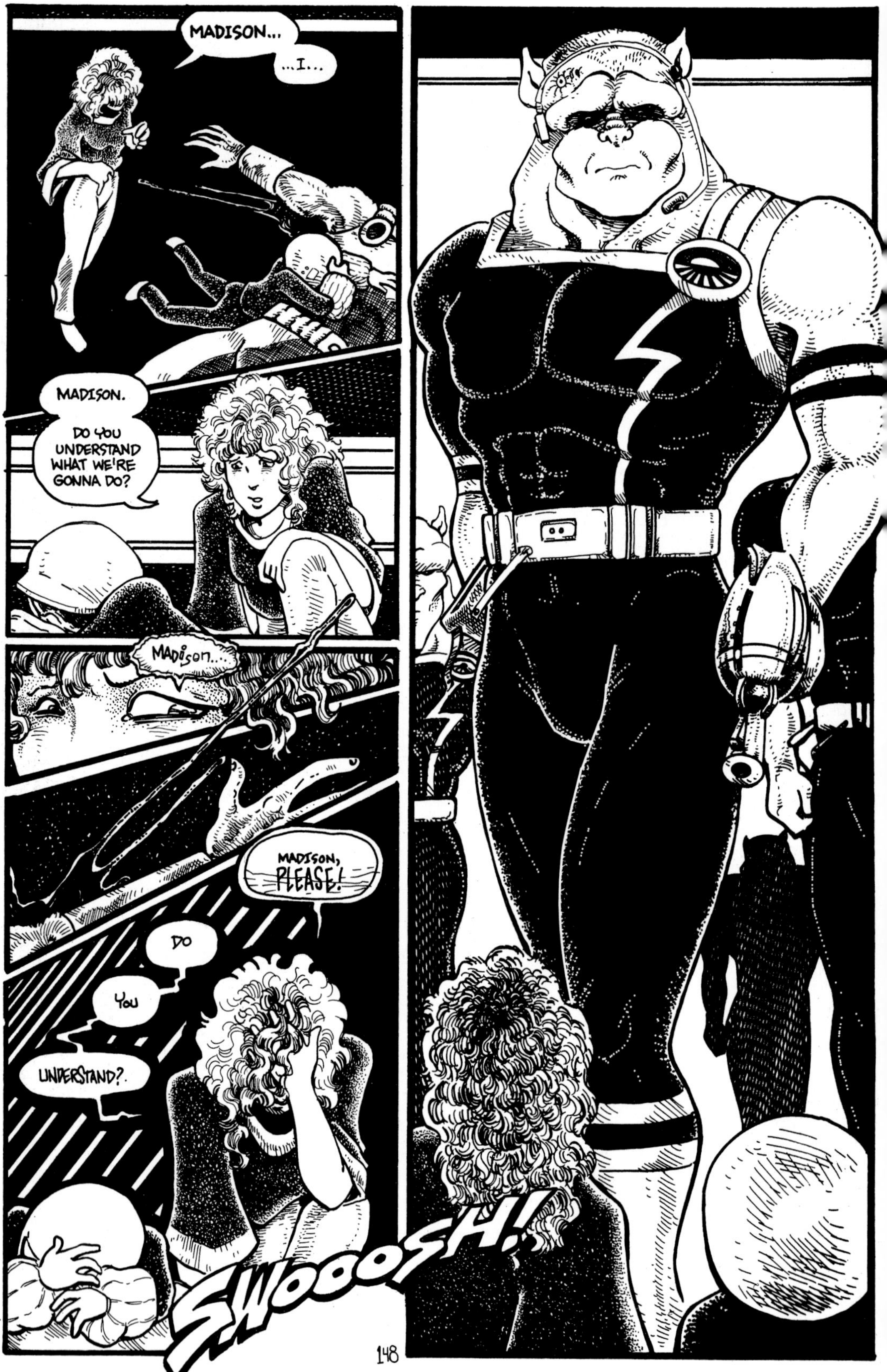
MADISON...
...I...
MADISON.
DO YOU UNDERSTAND WHAT WE'RE GONNA DO?
MADison...
MADISON, PLEASE!
DO
YOU
UNDERSTAND?.
SWOOOOSH!

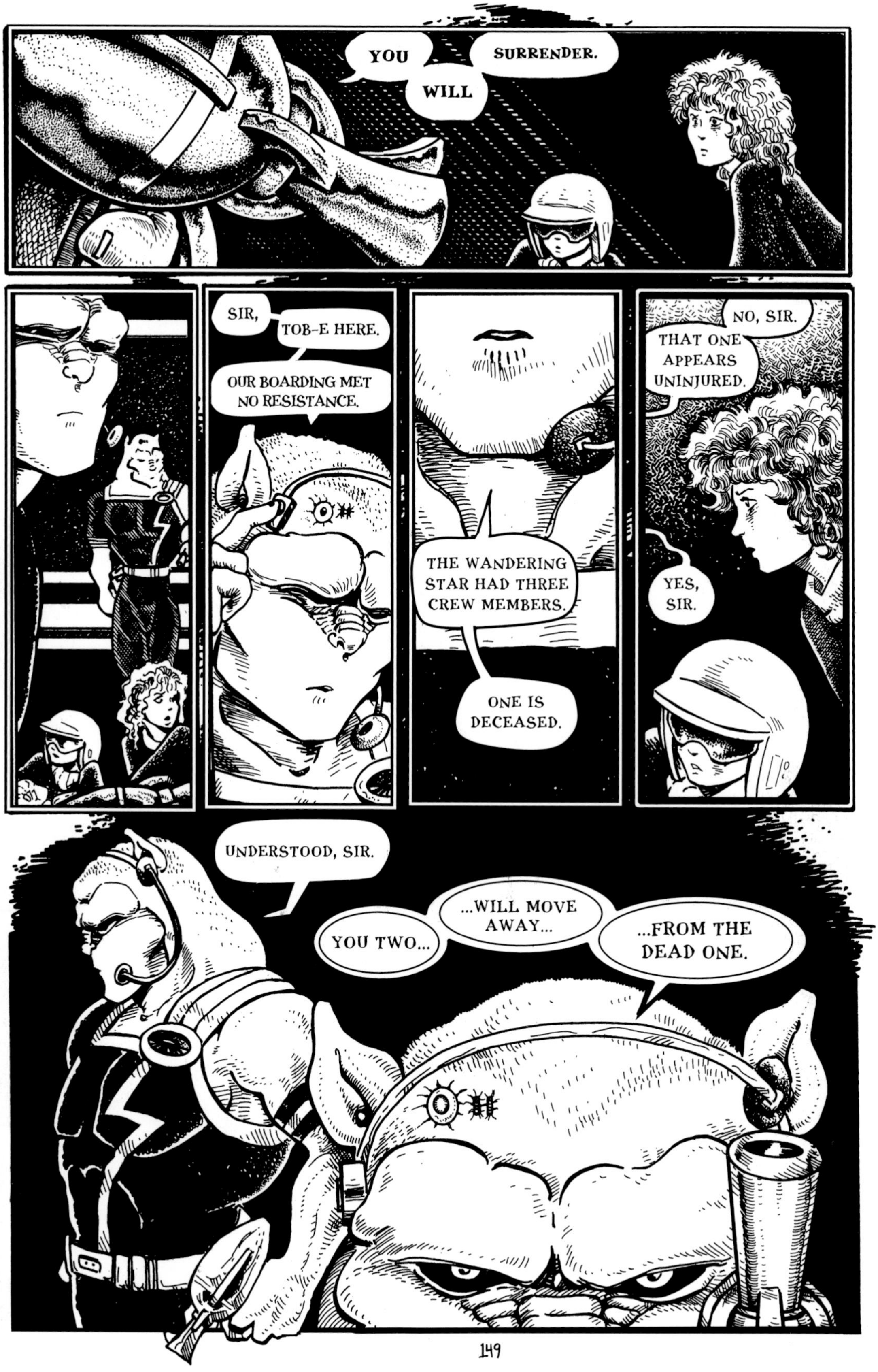
YOU
WILL
SURRENDER.
SIR,
TOB-E HERE.
OUR BOARDING MET NO RESISTANCE.
THE WANDERING STAR HAD THREE CREW MEMBERS.
ONE IS DECEASED.
NO, SIR.
THAT ONE APPEARS UNINJURED.
YES, SIR.
UNDERSTOOD, SIR.
YOU TWO...
...WILL MOVE AWAY...
...FROM THE DEAD ONE.

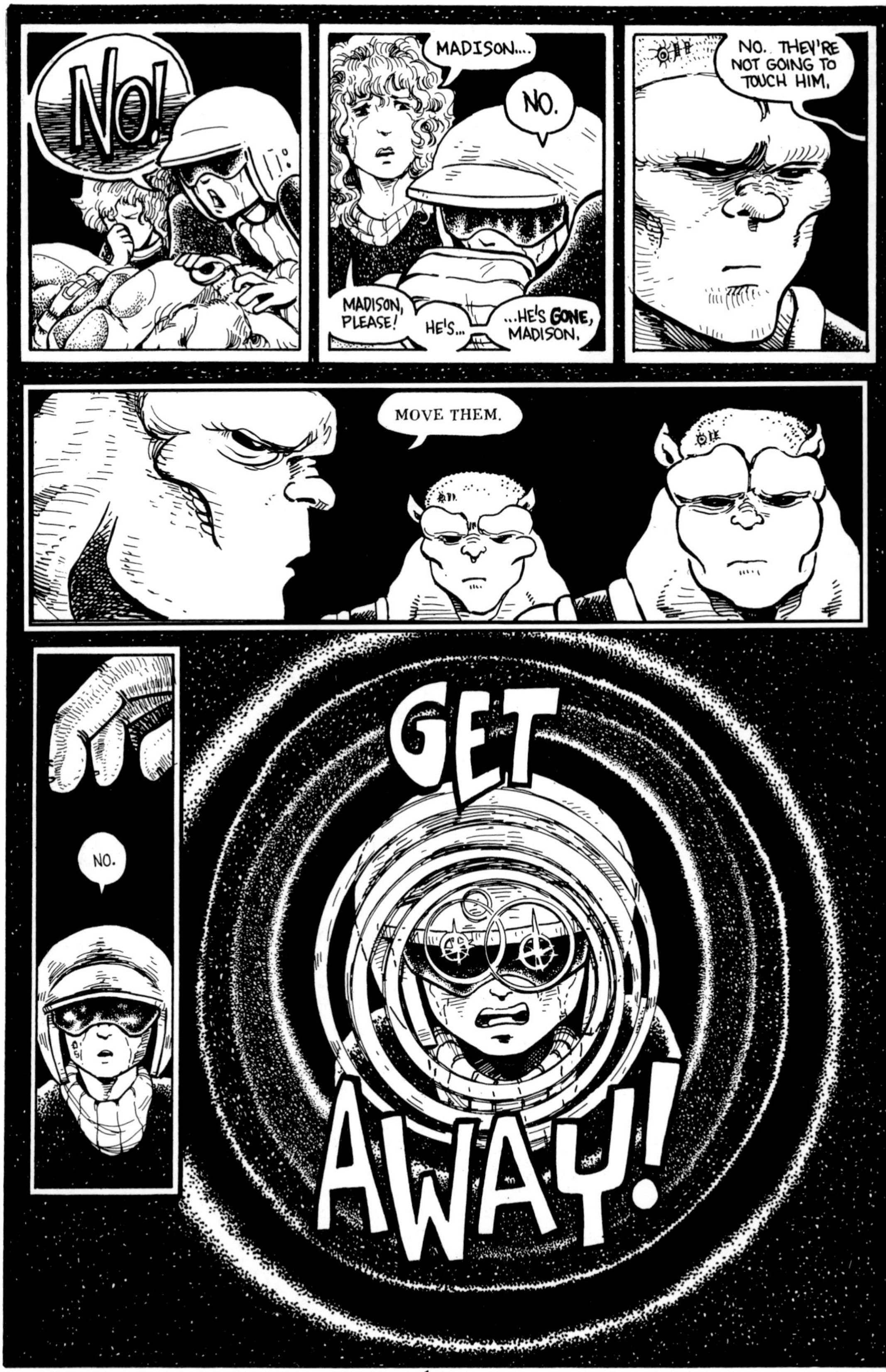
NO!
MADISON....
NO.
MADISON, PLEASE!
HE'S...
...HE'S GONE, MADISON.
NO. THEY'RE NOT GOING TO TOUCH HIM.
MOVE THEM.
NO.
GET AWAY!

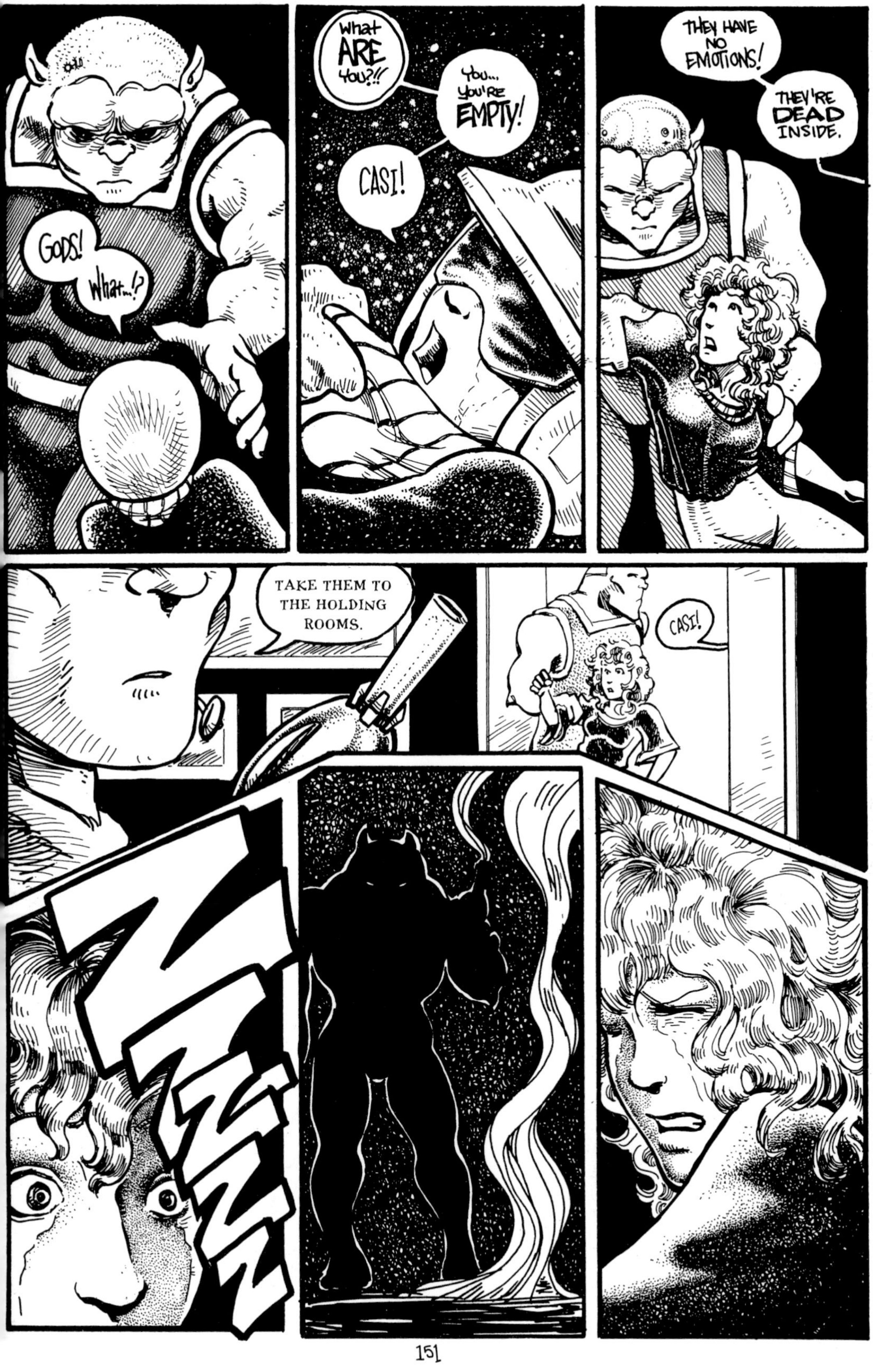
GODS!
What...!?
What ARE You?!!
You... You're EMPTY!
CASI!
THEY HAVE NO EMOTIONS!
THEY'RE DEAD INSIDE.
TAKE THEM TO THE HOLDING ROOMS.
CASI!
NNNNN

THEY SEPARATED US.

I WAS TAKEN TO A SMALL, DIMLY LIT ROOM.

Wait!

WHAT ABOUT MADISON?!

WAIT!

AND THERE I STAYED.

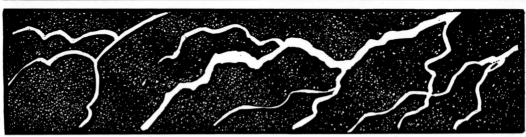

YOU CAN'T IMAGINE WHAT IT WAS LIKE.

NOT KNOWING WHAT WAS HAPPENING TO MADISON.

NOT KNOWING WHAT WOULD HAPPEN TO ME.

I STILL REMEMBER THAT ROOM...

...SO CLEARLY.

THE GUARDS WITH THEIR EMPTY EYES AND FACES OF STONE...

...COMING AND GOING WITH MY TRAYS OF FOOD.

THE "CLICK" OF THE DOOR.

AND...

THOSE DAMN, GRAY WALLS!

I
HATED
THOSE
WALLS!

aaah,
...damn.

you
see...

WHAT I
NEEDED...

...WAS
DISTRACTIONS.

SOMETHING
TO KEEP MY
MIND **OFF**
OF MY THOUGHTS.

WHAT I GOT...

...WERE
EMPTY
GRAY
WALLS.

...WHICH
SEEMED TO
COAX AT EVERY
DEMON IN
MY MIND.

IT WAS A
NIGHTMARE.

BUT ALL THINGS
COME TO AN END.

CLICK!

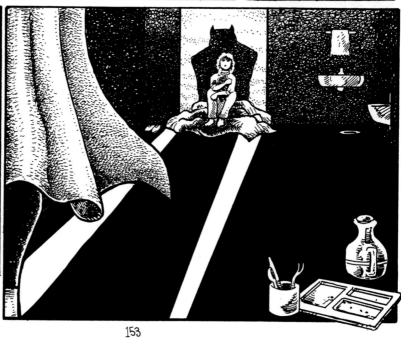

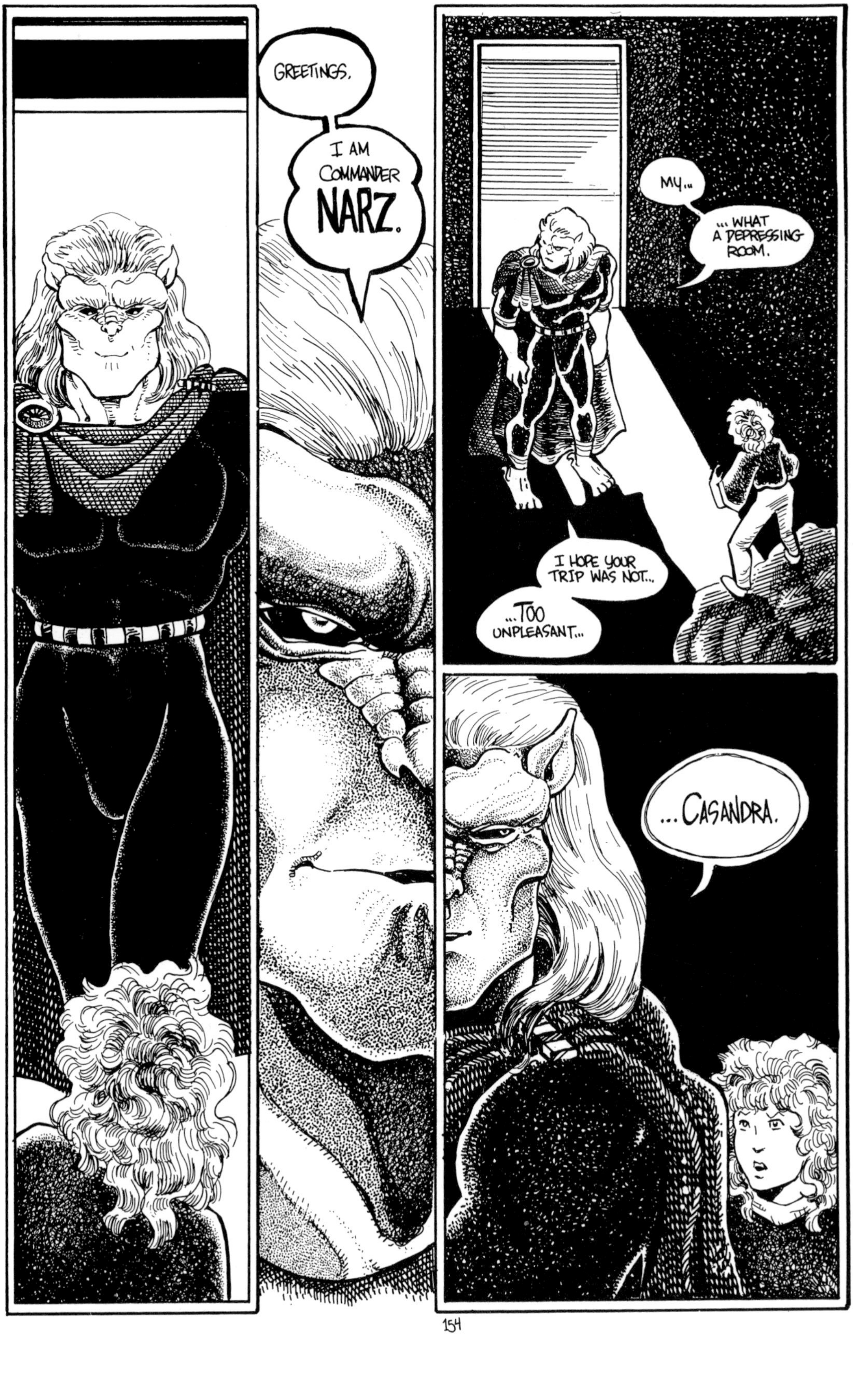
GREETINGS.
I AM COMMANDER NARZ.
MY...
...WHAT A DEPRESSING ROOM.
I HOPE YOUR TRIP WAS NOT...
...TOO UNPLEASANT...
...CASANDRA.

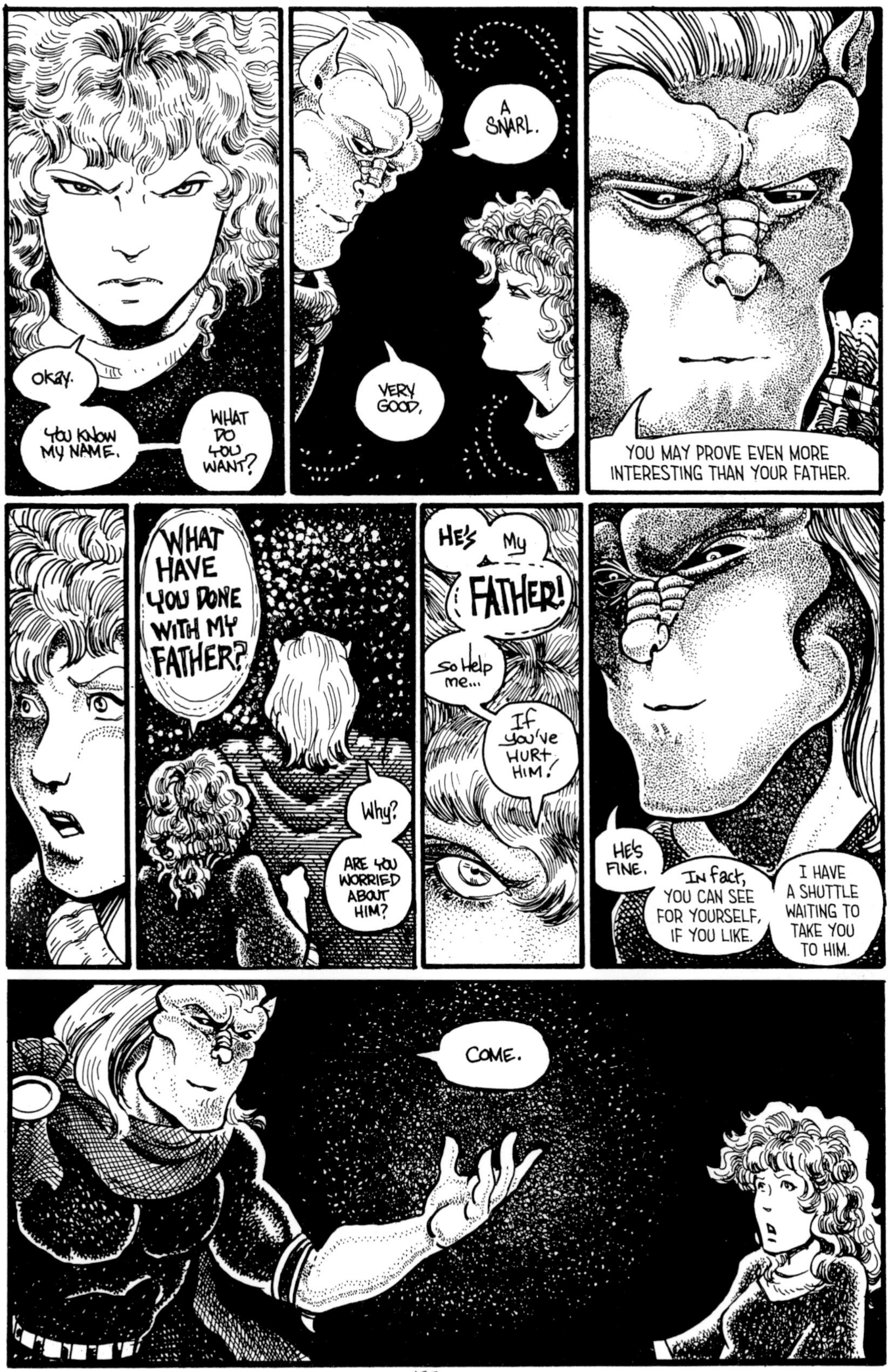
Okay.
You know my name.
What do you want?
A snarl.
Very good.
You may prove even more interesting than your father.
What have you done with my father?
Why?
Are you worried about him?
He's my father!
So help me...
If you've hurt him!
He's fine.
In fact, you can see for yourself, if you like.
I have a shuttle waiting to take you to him.
Come.

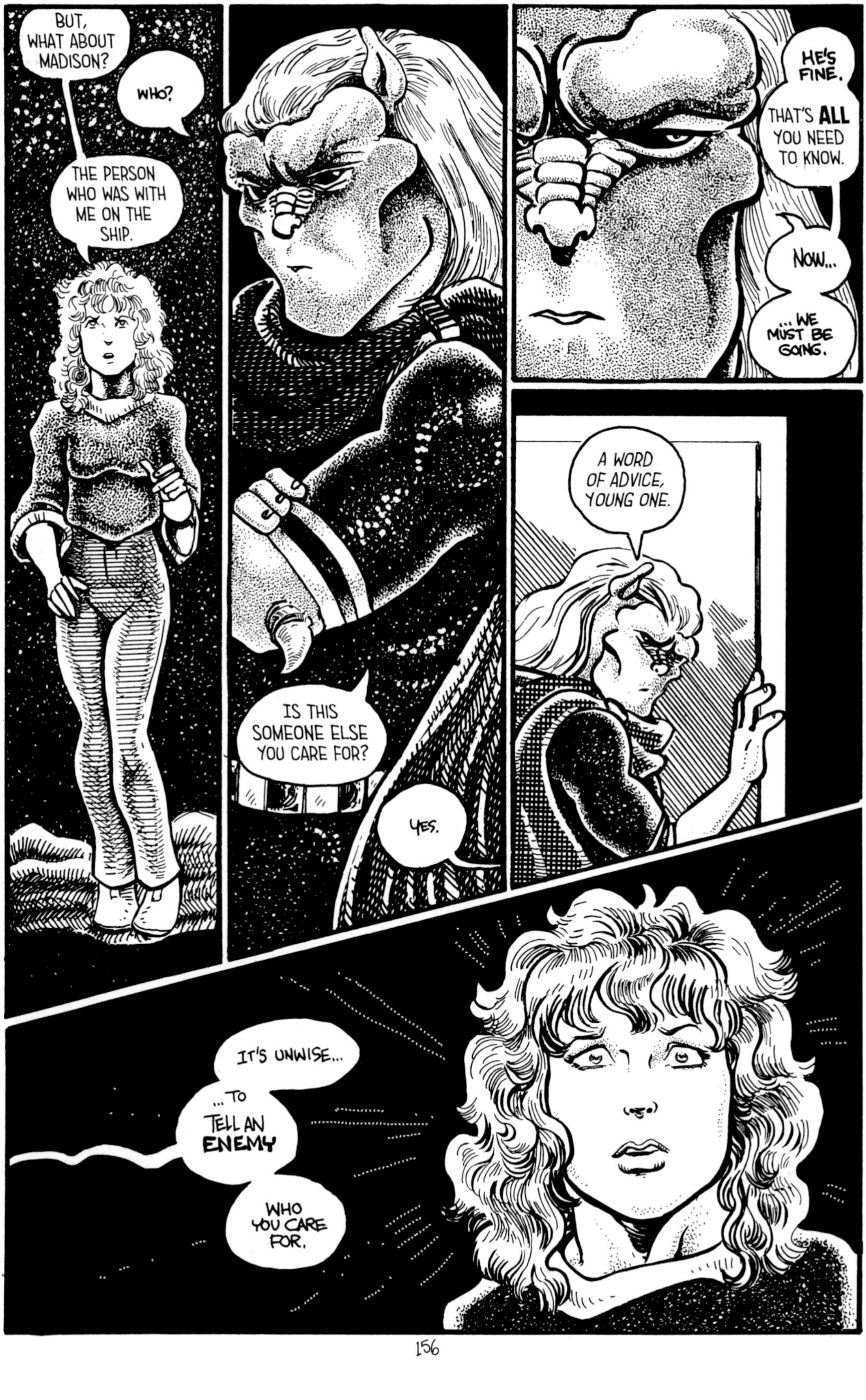
BUT, WHAT ABOUT MADISON?
WHO?
THE PERSON WHO WAS WITH ME ON THE SHIP.
IS THIS SOMEONE ELSE YOU CARE FOR?
YES.
HE'S FINE.
THAT'S **ALL** YOU NEED TO KNOW.
NOW...
...WE MUST BE GOING.
A WORD OF ADVICE, YOUNG ONE.
IT'S UNWISE...
...TO TELL AN **ENEMY**
WHO YOU CARE FOR.

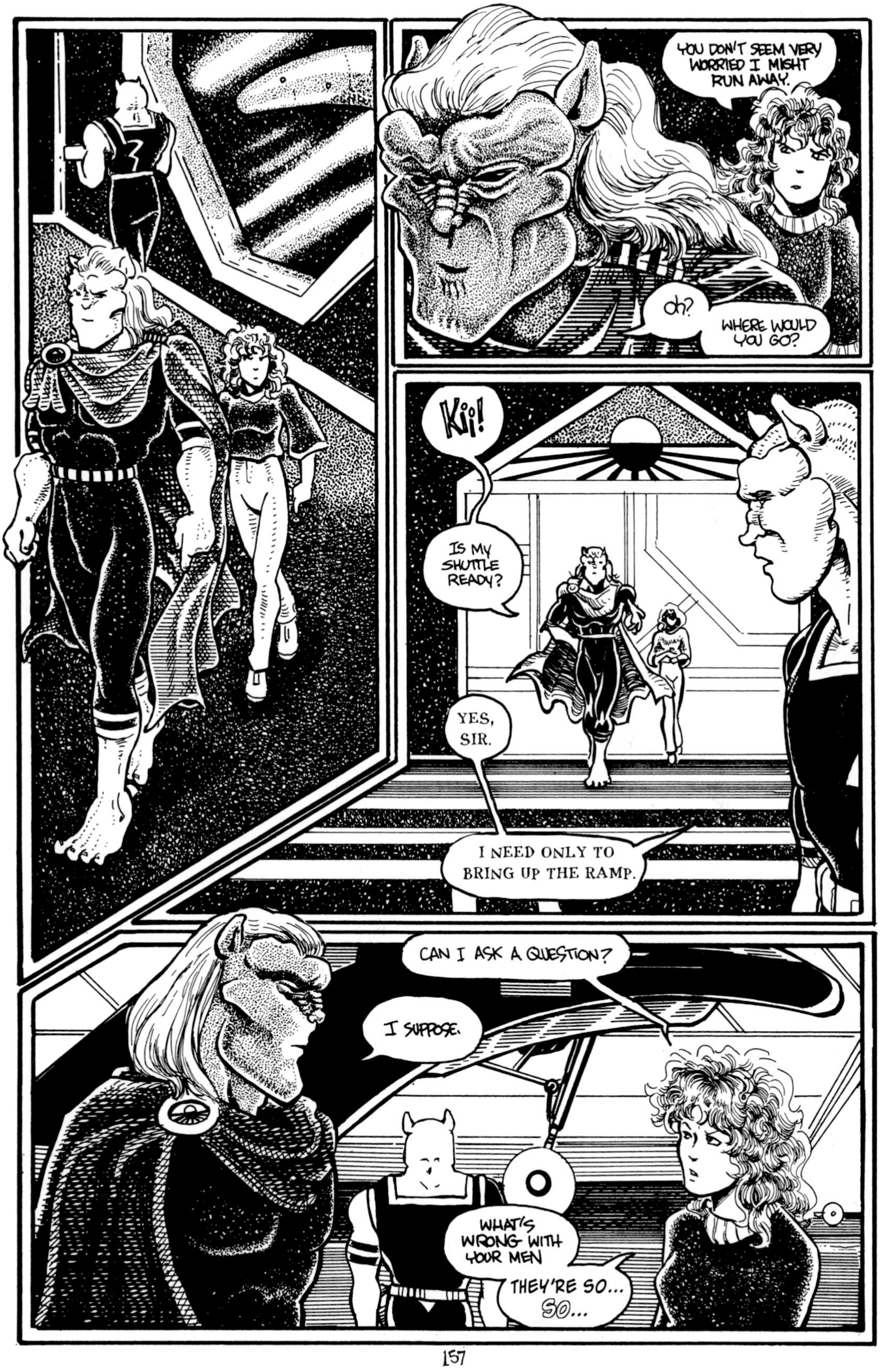
YOU DON'T SEEM VERY WORRIED I MIGHT RUN AWAY.
oh?
WHERE WOULD YOU GO?
Kii!
IS MY SHUTTLE READY?
YES, SIR.
I NEED ONLY TO BRING UP THE RAMP.
CAN I ASK A QUESTION?
I SUPPOSE.
WHAT'S WRONG WITH YOUR MEN
THEY'RE SO... SO...

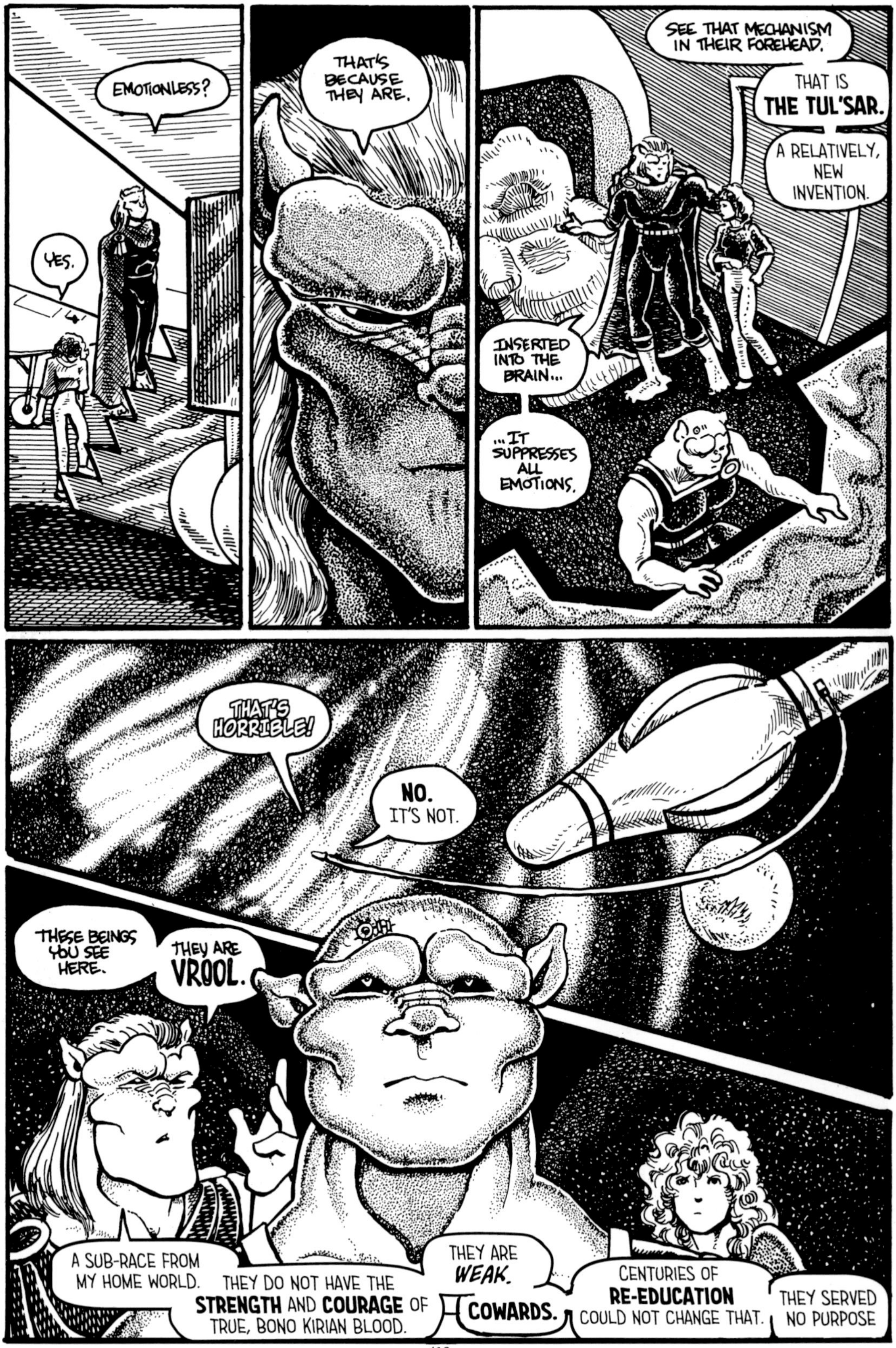
EMOTIONLESS?
YES.
THAT'S BECAUSE THEY ARE.
SEE THAT MECHANISM IN THEIR FOREHEAD.
THAT IS THE TUL'SAR.
A RELATIVELY, NEW INVENTION.
INSERTED INTO THE BRAIN...
...IT SUPPRESSES ALL EMOTIONS.
THAT'S HORRIBLE!
NO. IT'S NOT.
THESE BEINGS YOU SEE HERE.
THEY ARE VROOL.
A SUB-RACE FROM MY HOME WORLD.
THEY DO NOT HAVE THE STRENGTH AND COURAGE OF TRUE, BONO KIRIAN BLOOD.
THEY ARE WEAK.
COWARDS.
CENTURIES OF RE-EDUCATION COULD NOT CHANGE THAT.
THEY SERVED NO PURPOSE

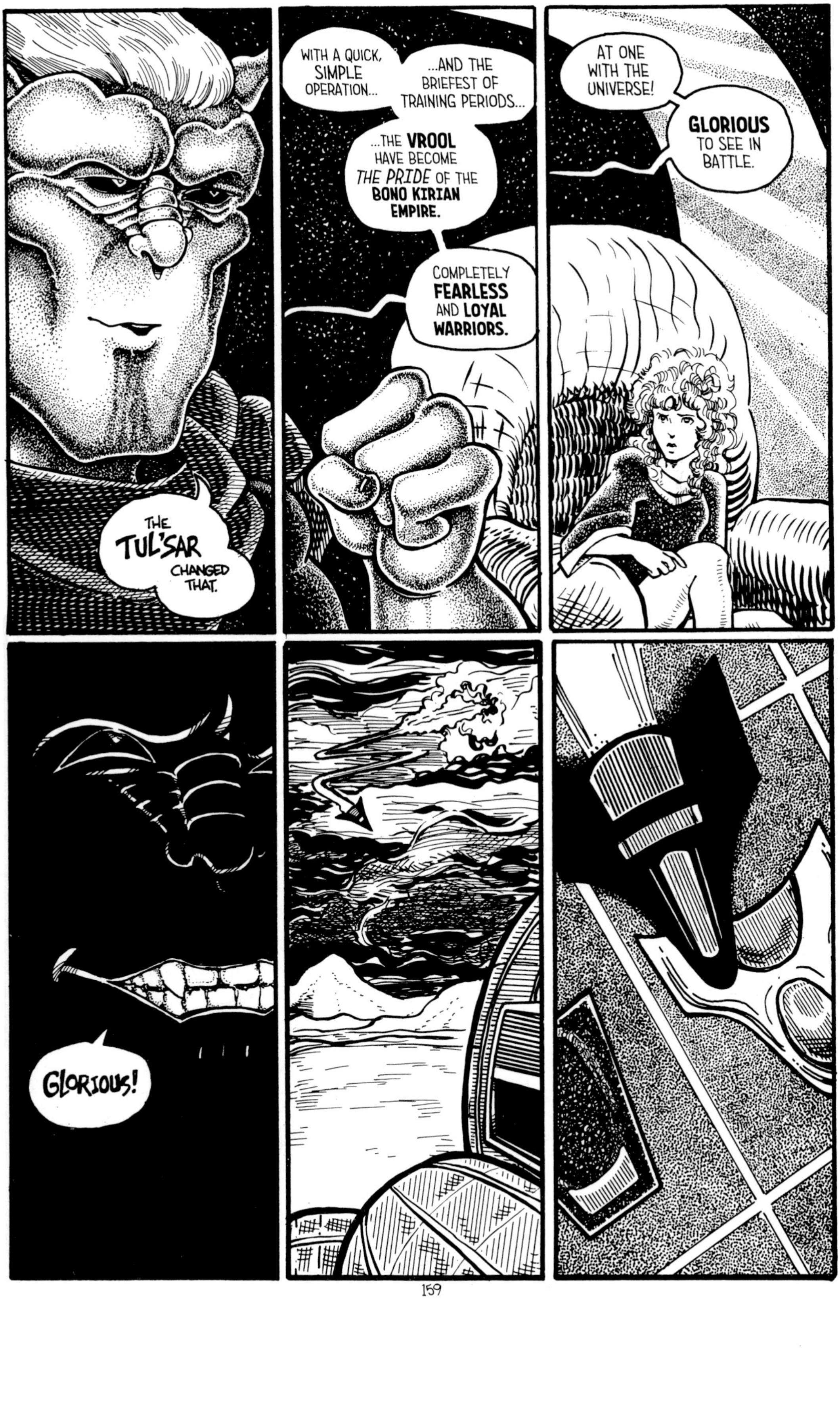
THE TUL'SAR CHANGED THAT.
WITH A QUICK, SIMPLE OPERATION...
...AND THE BRIEFEST OF TRAINING PERIODS...
...THE VROOL HAVE BECOME THE PRIDE OF THE BONO KIRIAN EMPIRE.
COMPLETELY FEARLESS AND LOYAL WARRIORS.
AT ONE WITH THE UNIVERSE!
GLORIOUS TO SEE IN BATTLE.
GLORIOUS!

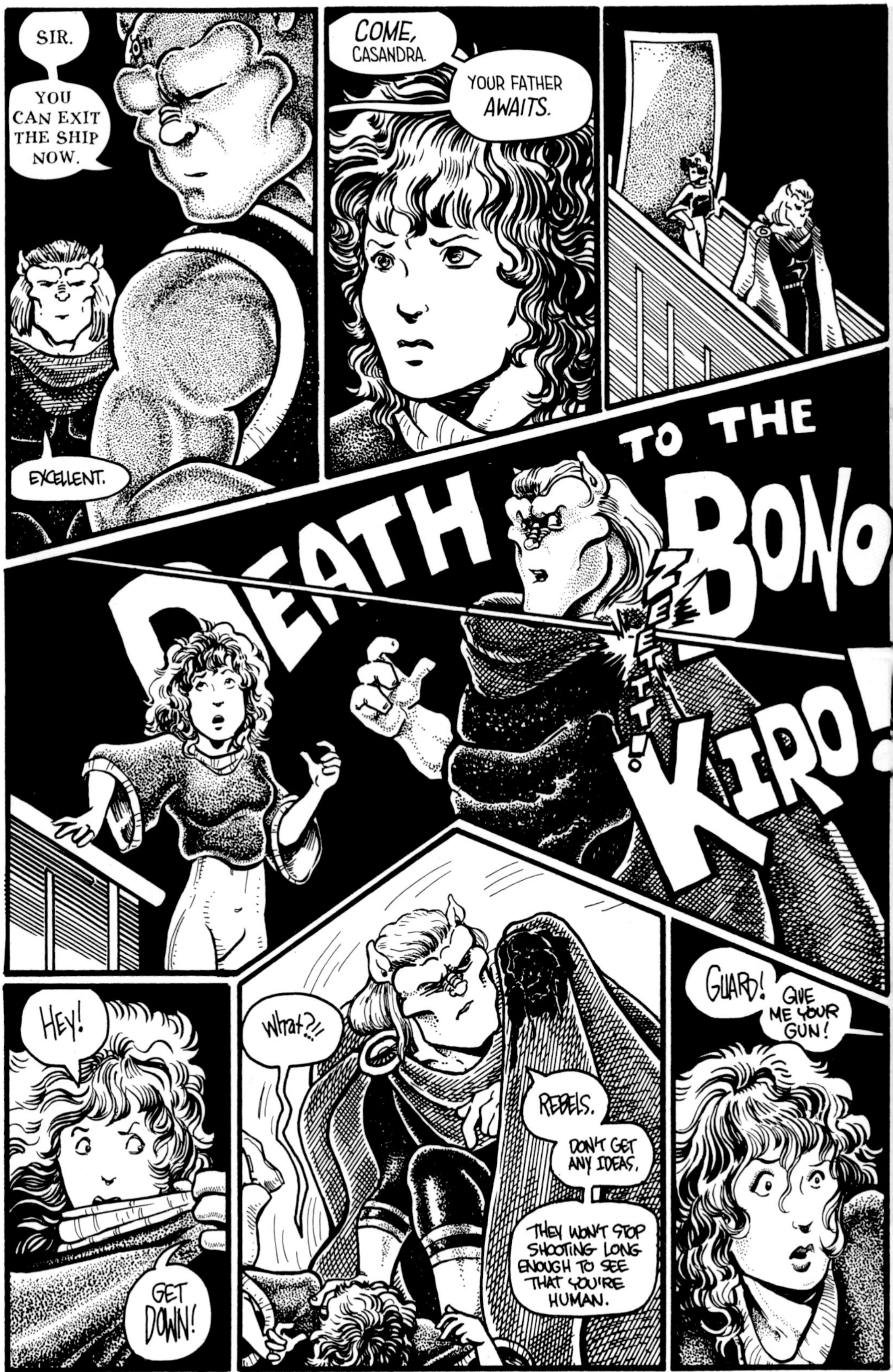
SIR.
YOU CAN EXIT THE SHIP NOW.
EXCELLENT.
COME, CASANDRA.
YOUR FATHER AWAITS.
DEATH TO THE BONO KIRO!
ZEETTT!
HEY!
GET DOWN!
What?!!
REBELS.
DON'T GET ANY IDEAS.
THEY WON'T STOP SHOOTING LONG ENOUGH TO SEE THAT YOU'RE HUMAN.
GUARD!
GIVE ME YOUR GUN!

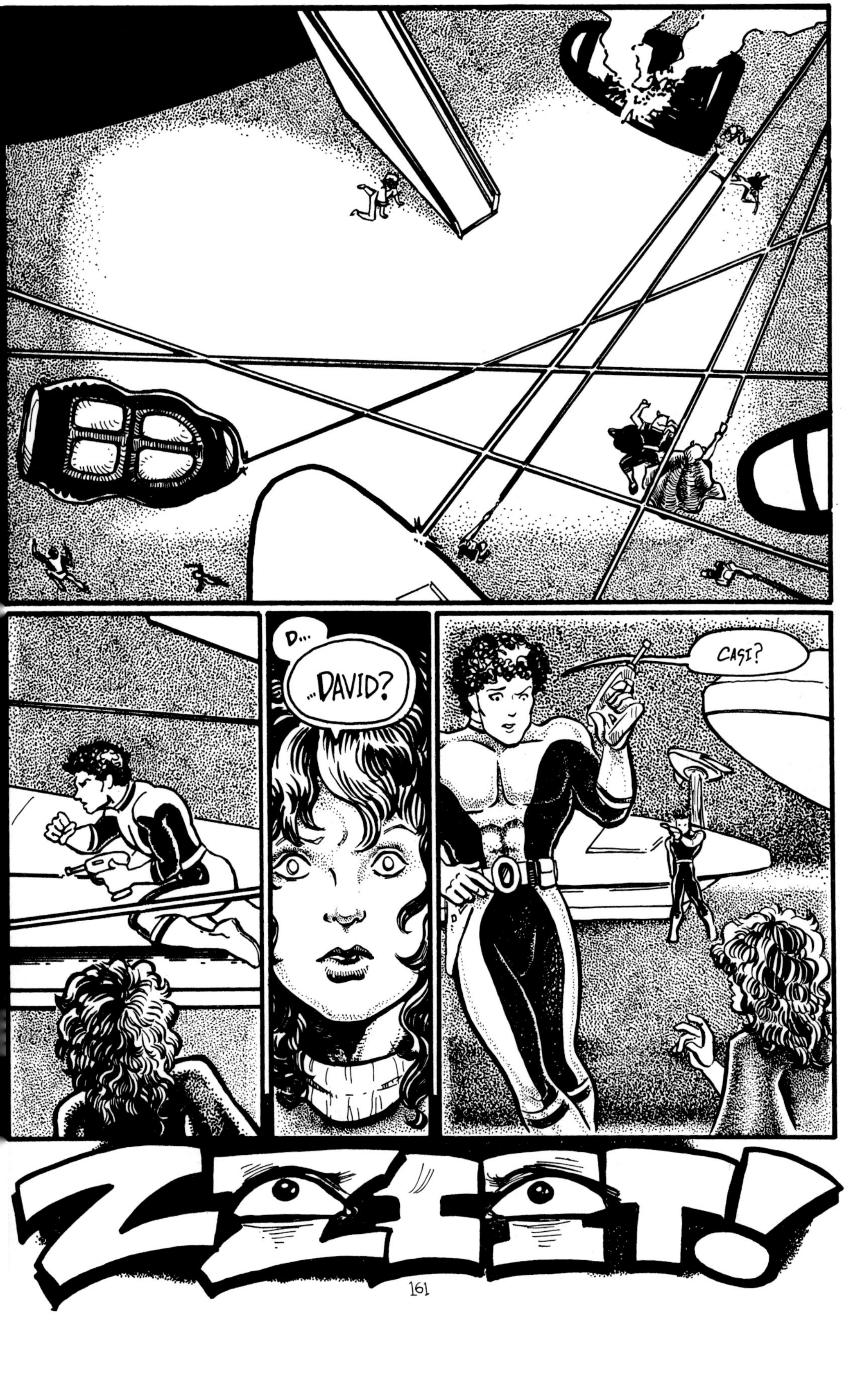
D...
..DAVID?
CASI?
ZZZT!

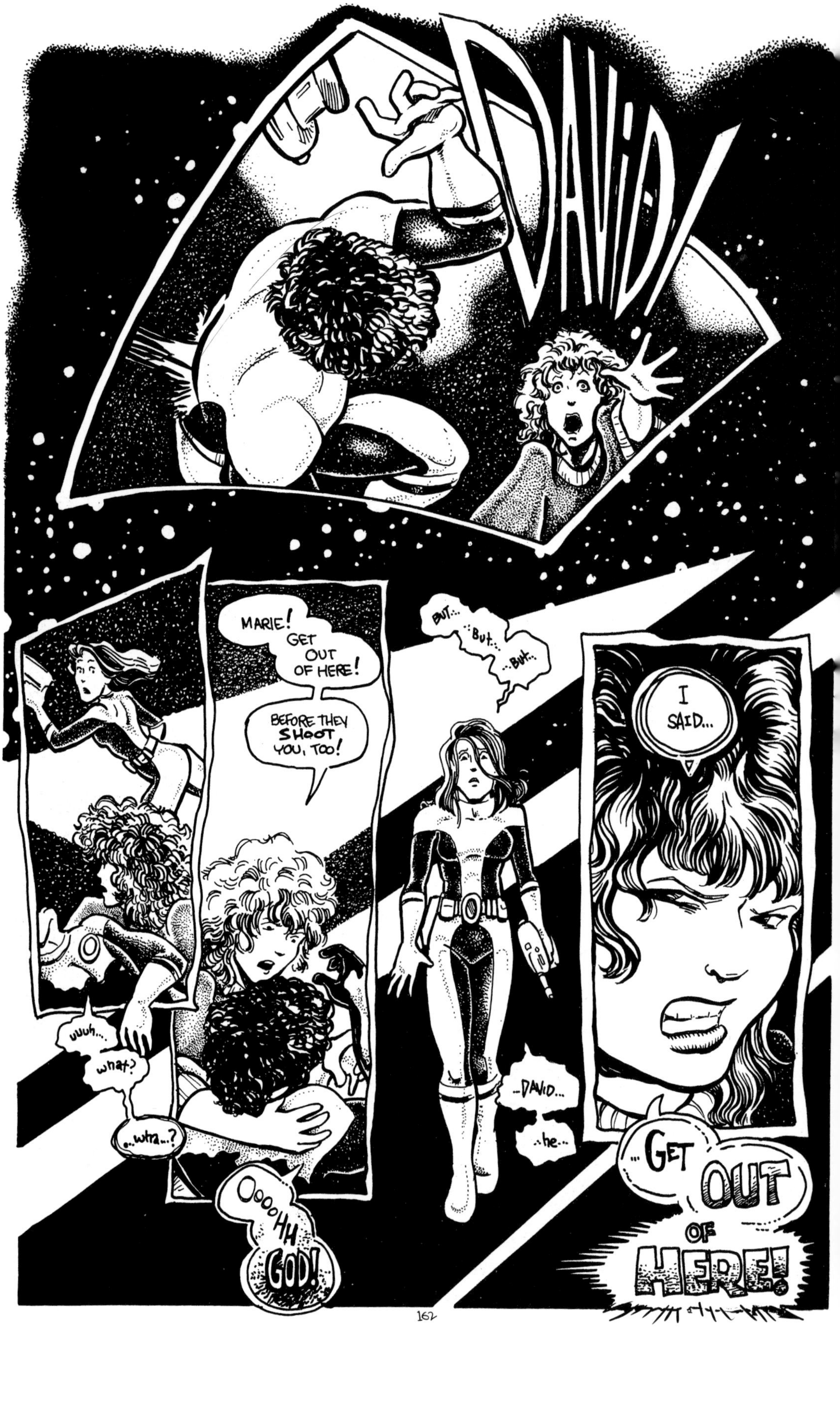
DAVID!
MARIE! GET OUT OF HERE!
BEFORE THEY SHOOT YOU, TOO!
uuuh...
what?
...wha...?
OooooHH GOD!
BUT... ...BUT... ...BUT...
...DAVID...
...he...
I SAID...
...GET OUT OF HERE!

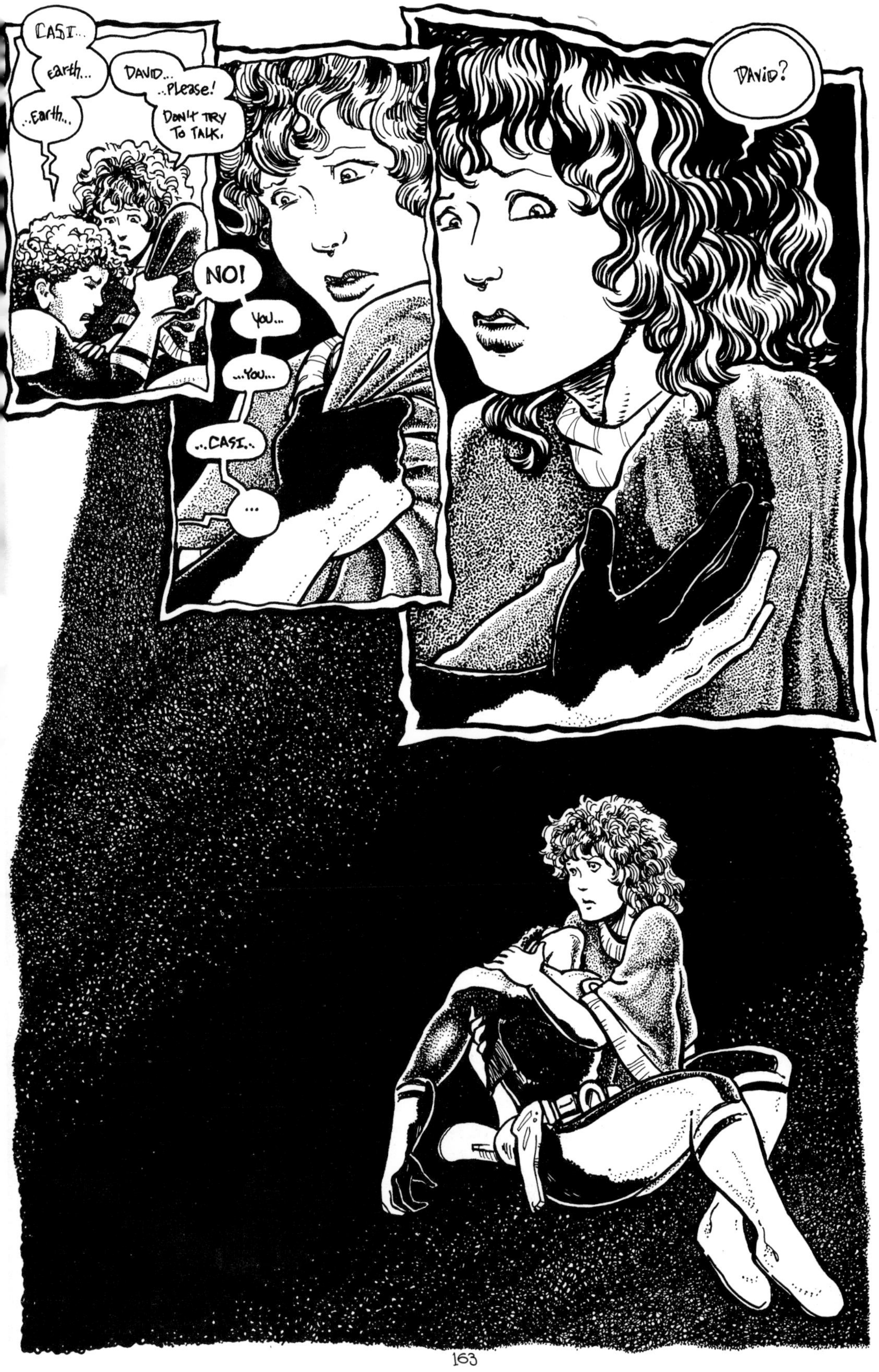
CASI...
earth...
...Earth...
DAVID...
...Please!
DON'T TRY TO TALK.
NO!
YOU...
...YOU...
...CASI...
...
DAVID?

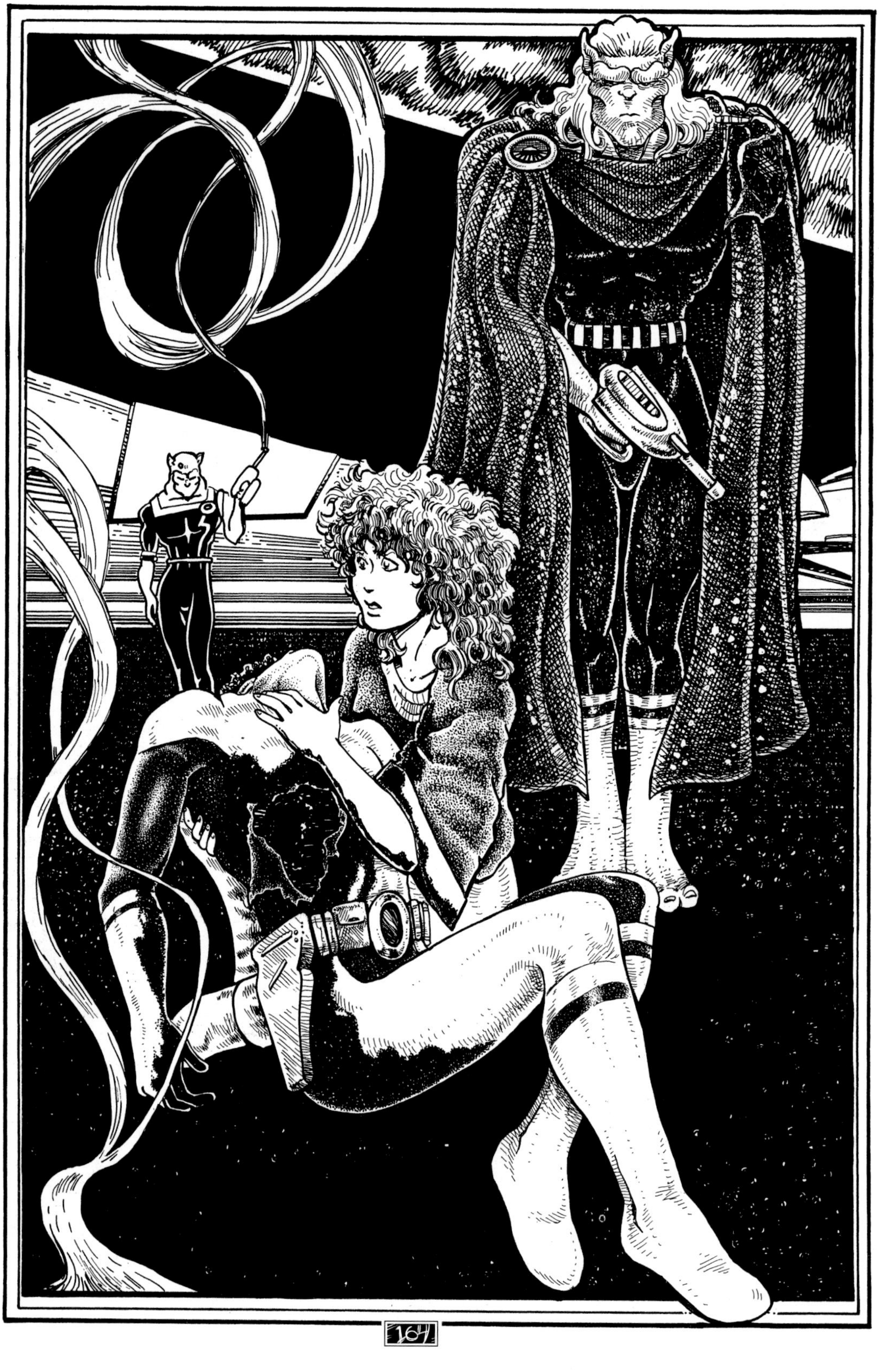

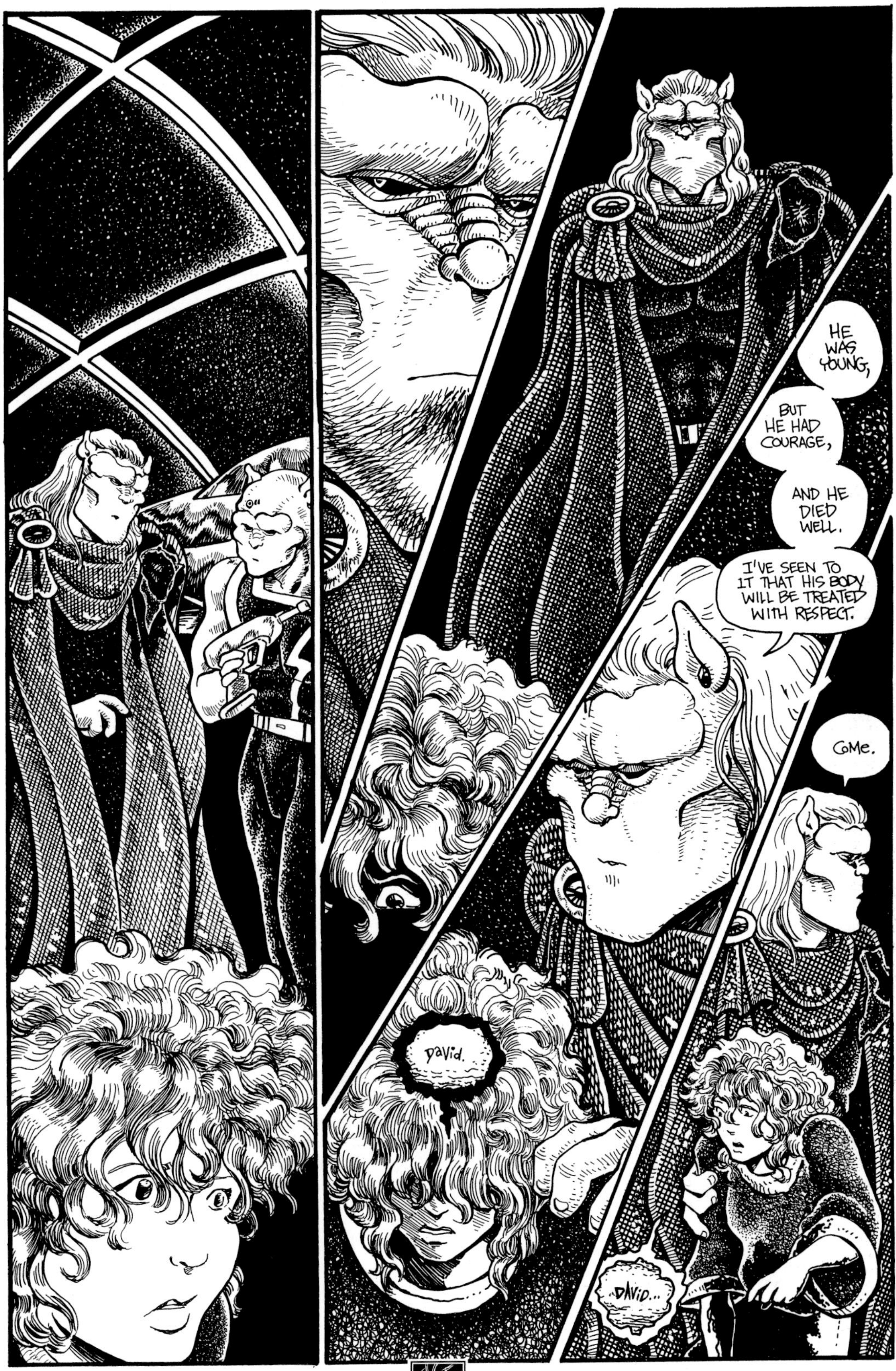
HE WAS YOUNG,
BUT HE HAD COURAGE,
AND HE DIED WELL.
I'VE SEEN TO IT THAT HIS BODY WILL BE TREATED WITH RESPECT.
David.
COME.
DAVID...

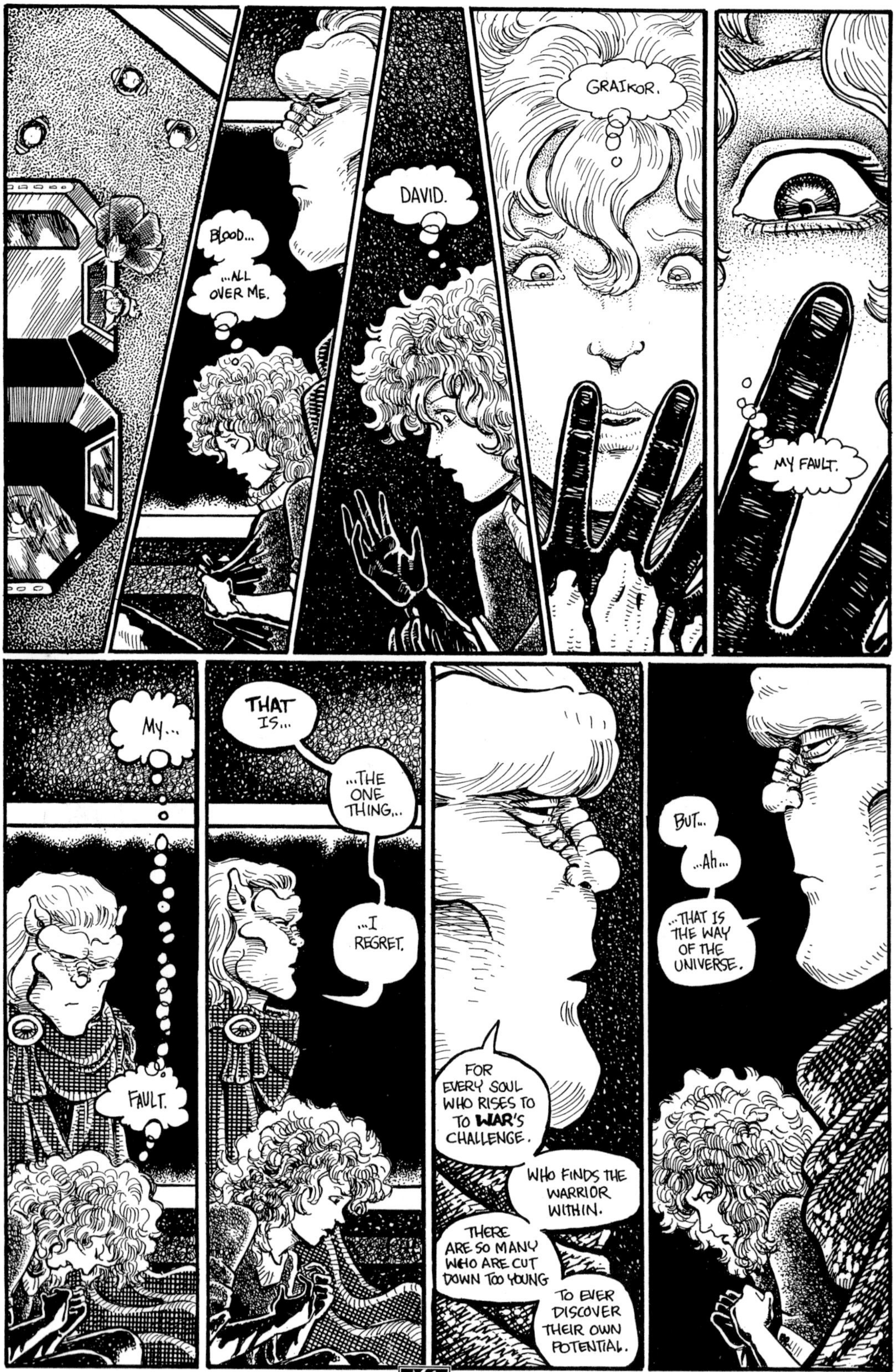
BLOOD...
...ALL OVER ME.
DAVID.
GRAIKOR.
MY FAULT.
MY...
FAULT.
THAT IS...
...THE ONE THING...
...I REGRET.
FOR EVERY SOUL WHO RISES TO TO WAR'S CHALLENGE.
WHO FINDS THE WARRIOR WITHIN.
THERE ARE SO MANY WHO ARE CUT DOWN TOO YOUNG
TO EVER DISCOVER THEIR OWN POTENTIAL.
BUT...
...AH...
...THAT IS THE WAY OF THE UNIVERSE.

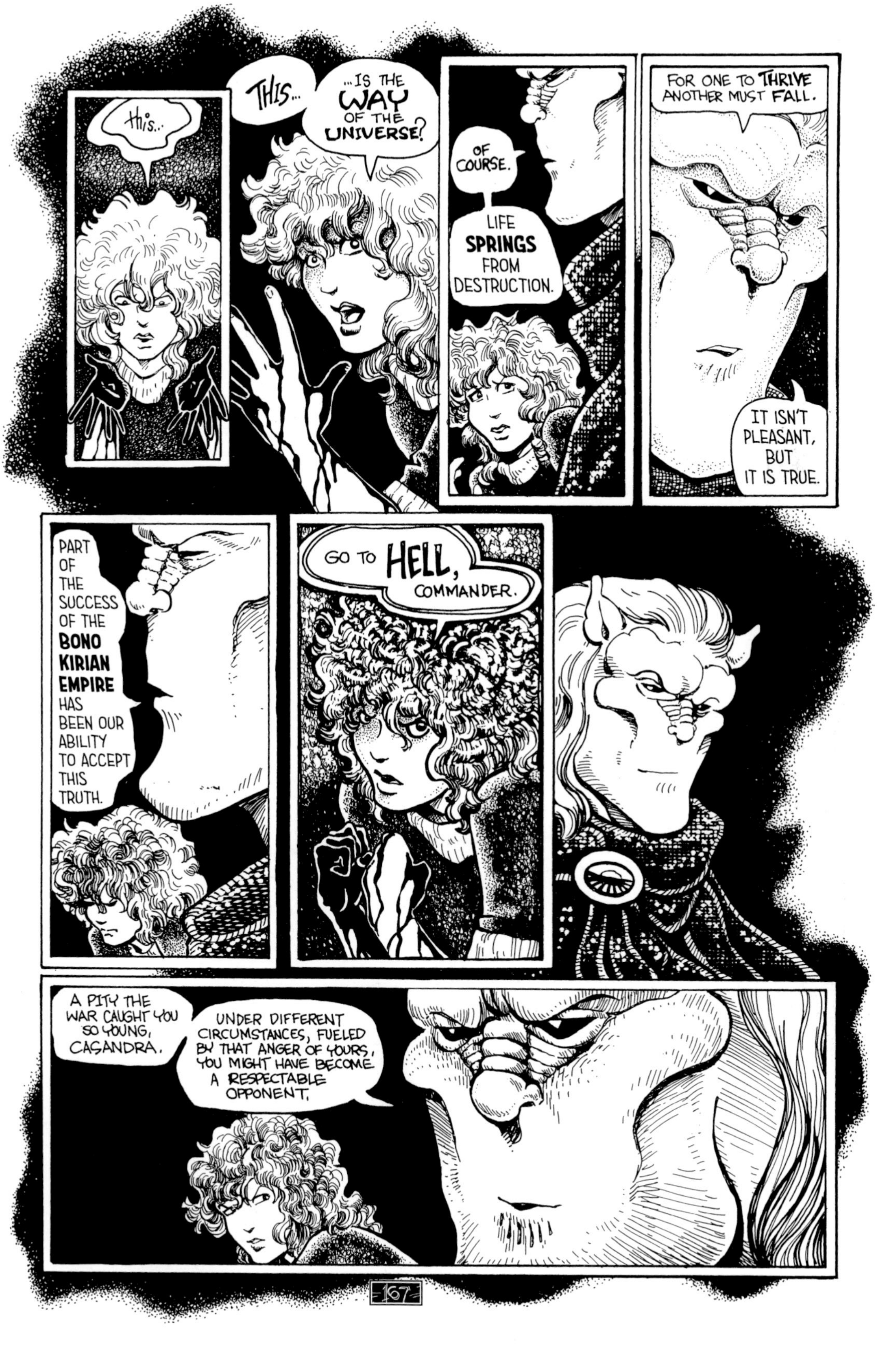
this...
THIS...
...IS THE WAY OF THE UNIVERSE?
OF COURSE.
LIFE SPRINGS FROM DESTRUCTION.
FOR ONE TO THRIVE ANOTHER MUST FALL.
IT ISN'T PLEASANT, BUT IT IS TRUE.
PART OF THE SUCCESS OF THE BONO KIRIAN EMPIRE HAS BEEN OUR ABILITY TO ACCEPT THIS TRUTH.
GO TO HELL, COMMANDER.
A PITY THE WAR CAUGHT YOU SO YOUNG, CASANDRA.
UNDER DIFFERENT CIRCUMSTANCES, FUELED BY THAT ANGER OF YOURS, YOU MIGHT HAVE BECOME A RESPECTABLE OPPONENT.

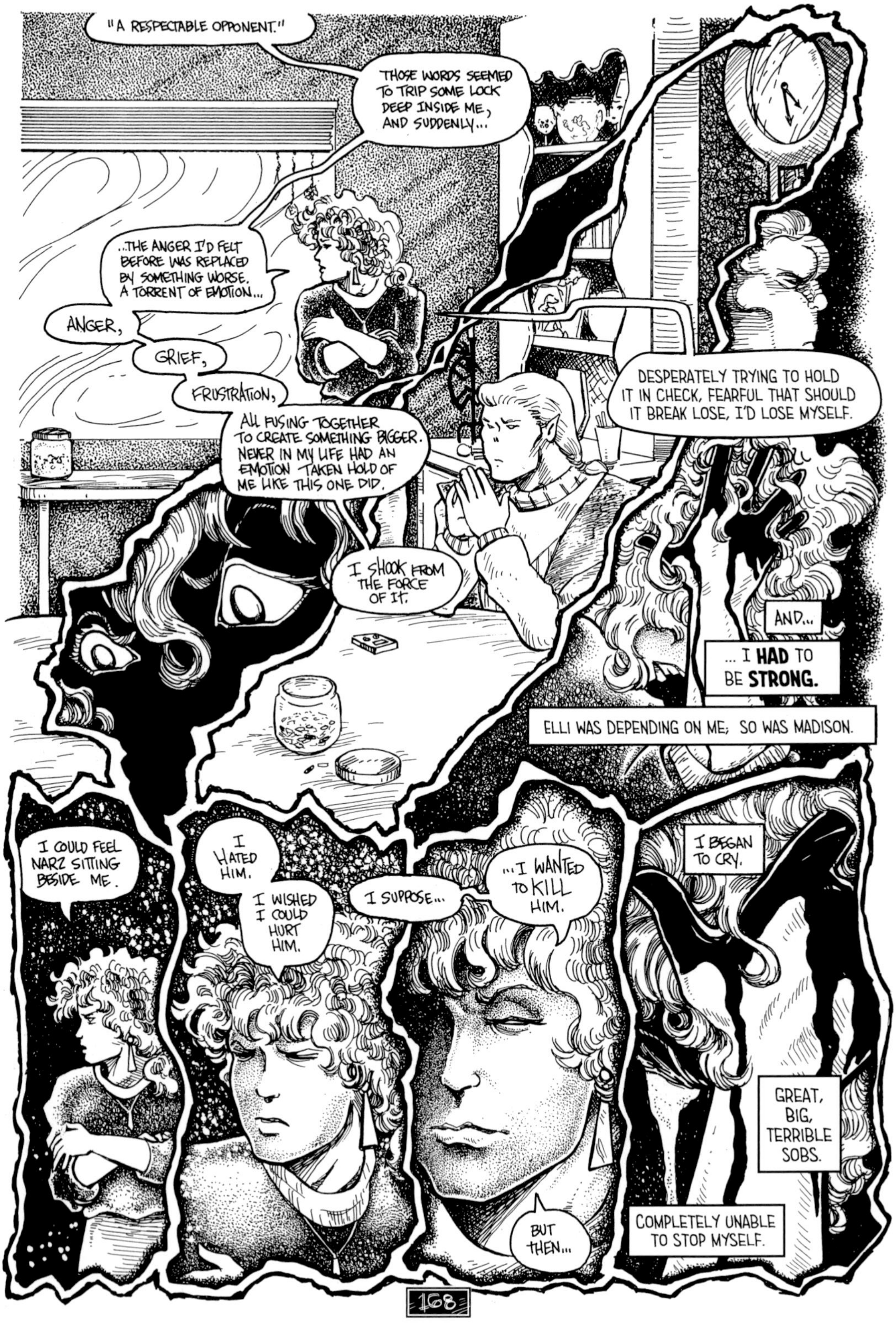
"A RESPECTABLE OPPONENT."
THOSE WORDS SEEMED TO TRIP SOME LOCK DEEP INSIDE ME, AND SUDDENLY...
...THE ANGER I'D FELT BEFORE WAS REPLACED BY SOMETHING WORSE. A TORRENT OF EMOTION...
ANGER,
GRIEF,
FRUSTRATION,
ALL FUSING TOGETHER TO CREATE SOMETHING BIGGER. NEVER IN MY LIFE HAD AN EMOTION TAKEN HOLD OF ME LIKE THIS ONE DID.
I SHOOK FROM THE FORCE OF IT.
DESPERATELY TRYING TO HOLD IT IN CHECK, FEARFUL THAT SHOULD IT BREAK LOSE, I'D LOSE MYSELF.
AND...
... I **HAD** TO BE **STRONG.**
ELLI WAS DEPENDING ON ME; SO WAS MADISON.
I COULD FEEL NARZ SITTING BESIDE ME.
I HATED HIM.
I WISHED I COULD HURT HIM.
I SUPPOSE...
...I WANTED TO KILL HIM.
BUT THEN...
I BEGAN TO CRY.
GREAT, BIG, TERRIBLE SOBS.
COMPLETELY UNABLE TO STOP MYSELF.

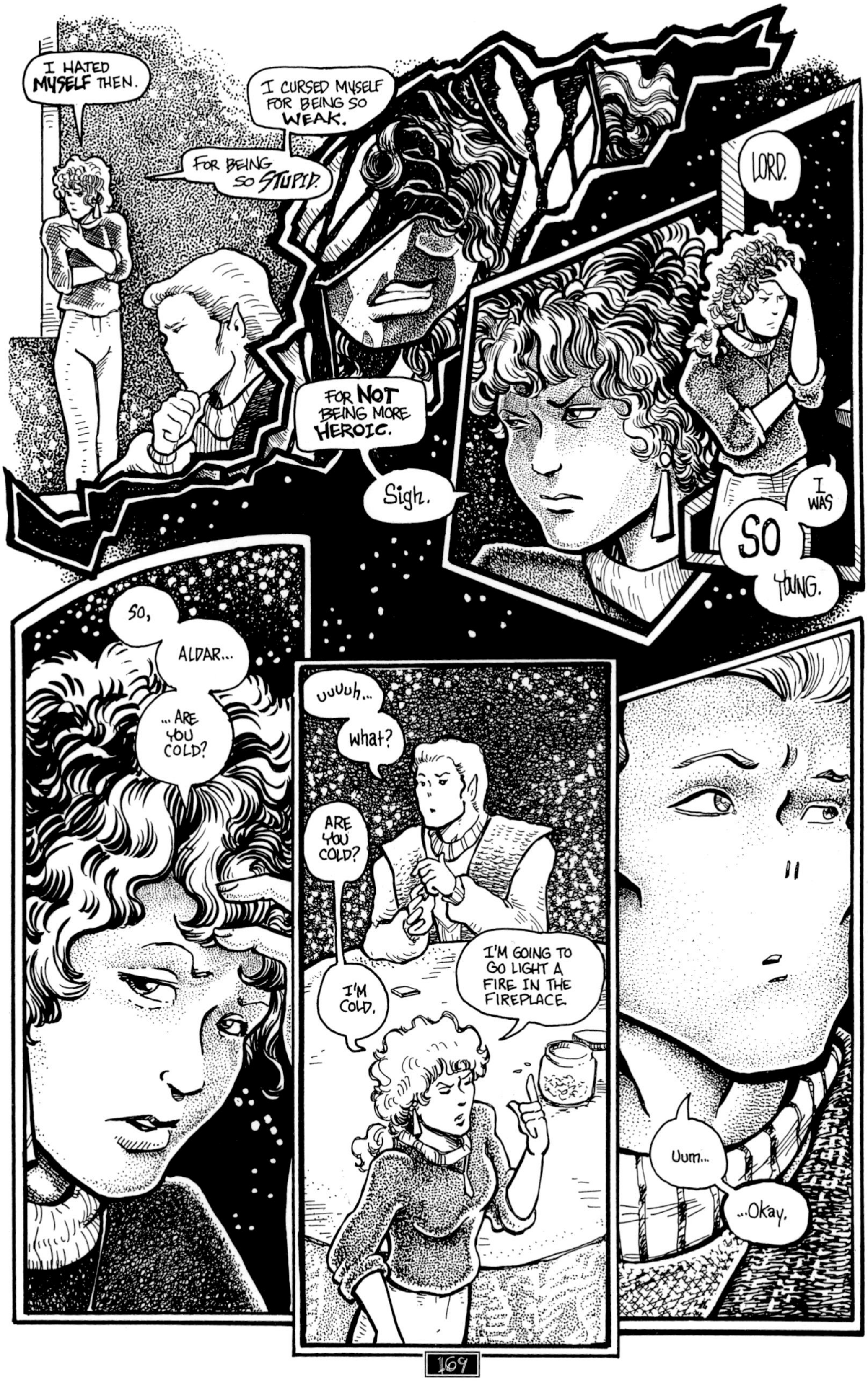
I HATED MYSELF THEN.
I CURSED MYSELF FOR BEING SO WEAK.
FOR BEING SO STUPID.
FOR NOT BEING MORE HEROIC.
Sigh.
LORD.
I WAS SO YOUNG.
SO,
ALDAR...
...ARE YOU COLD?
uuuuh...
what?
ARE YOU COLD?
I'M COLD.
I'M GOING TO GO LIGHT A FIRE IN THE FIREPLACE.
Uum...
...Okay.

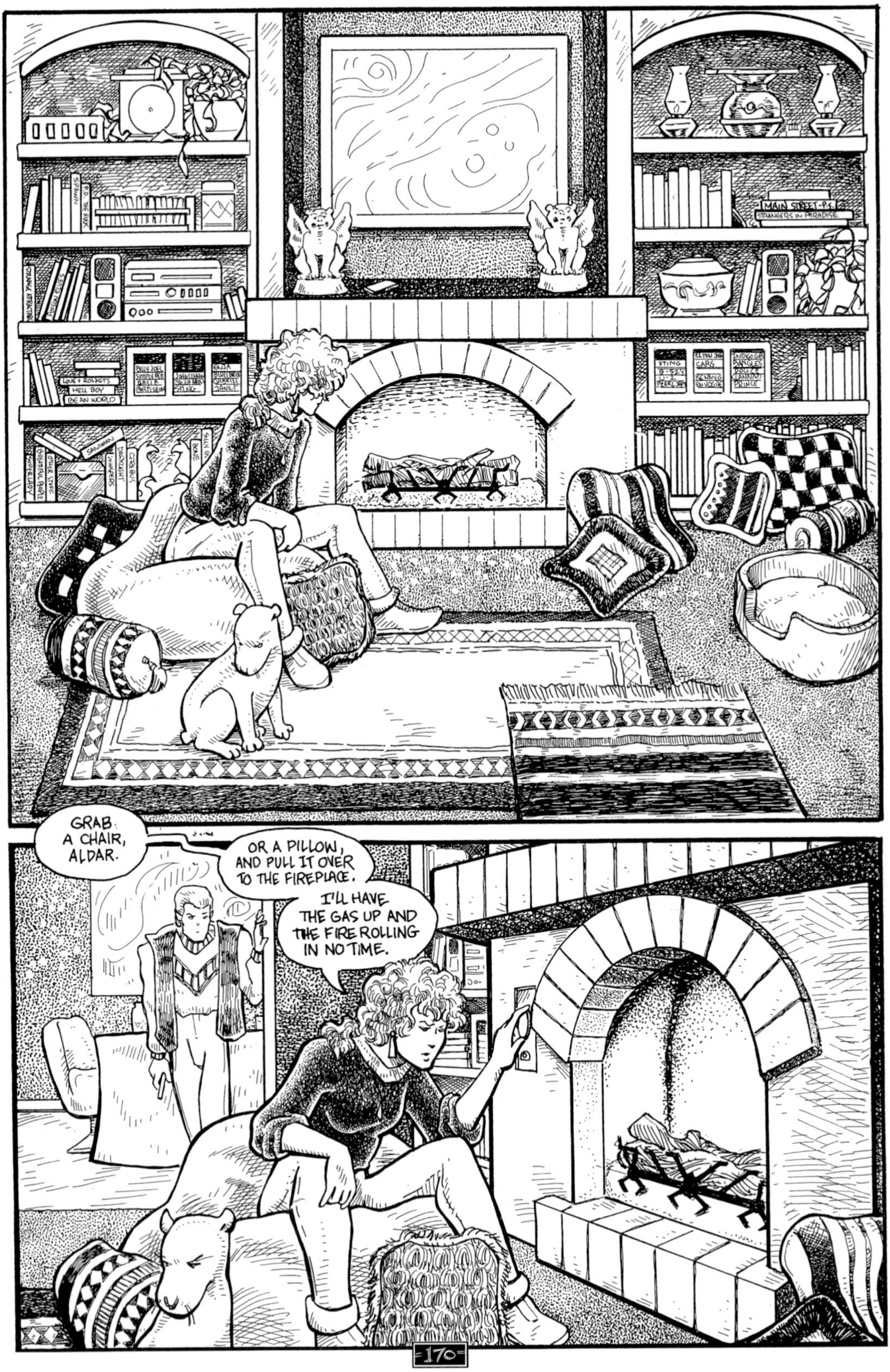
GRAB A CHAIR, ALDAR.
OR A PILLOW, AND PULL IT OVER TO THE FIREPLACE.
I'LL HAVE THE GAS UP AND THE FIRE ROLLING IN NO TIME.

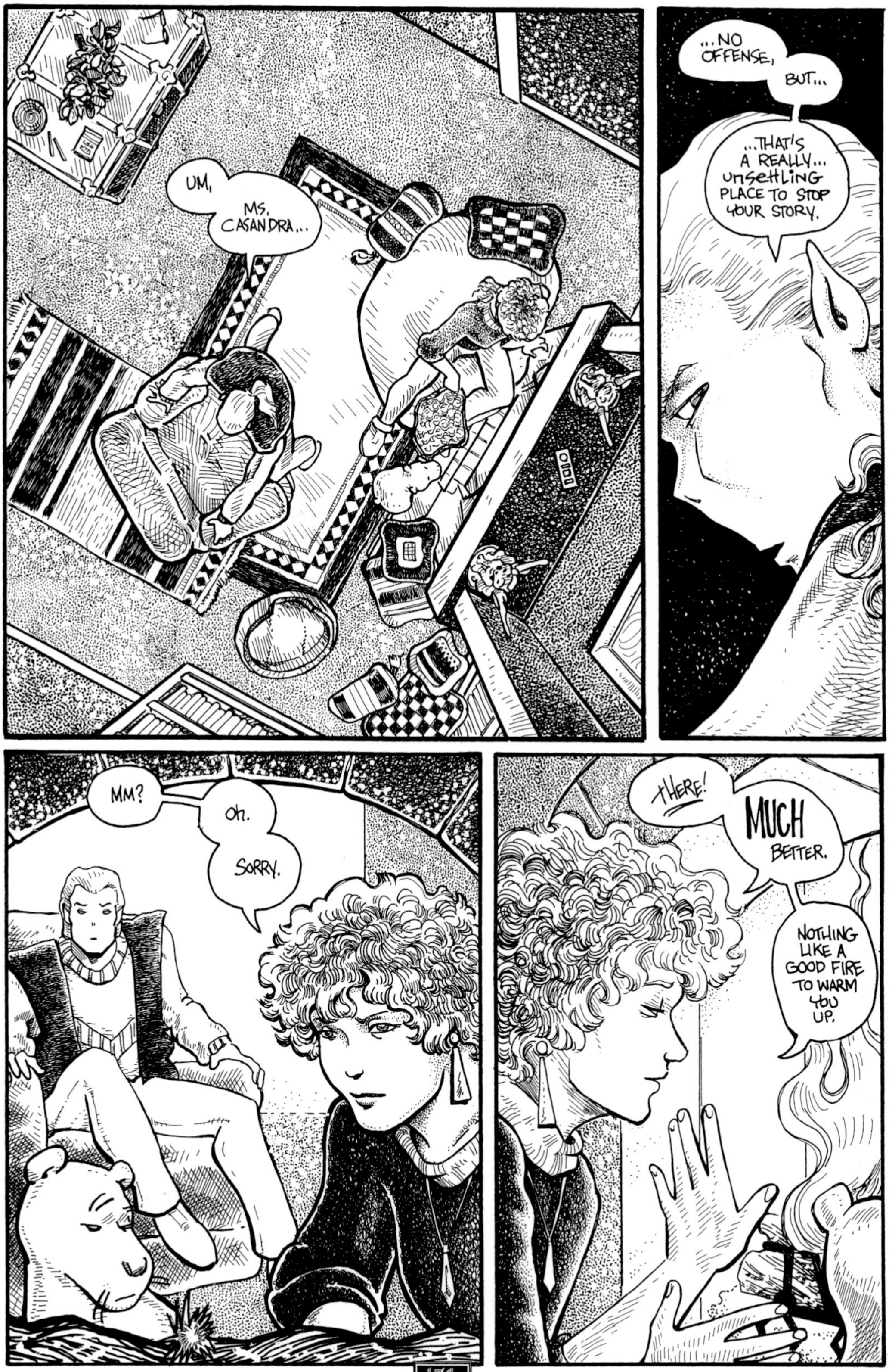
UM, MS. CASANDRA...
...NO OFFENSE,
BUT...
...THAT'S A REALLY... UNSETTLING PLACE TO STOP YOUR STORY.
MM?
Oh.
SORRY.
THERE!
MUCH BETTER.
NOTHING LIKE A GOOD FIRE TO WARM YOU UP.

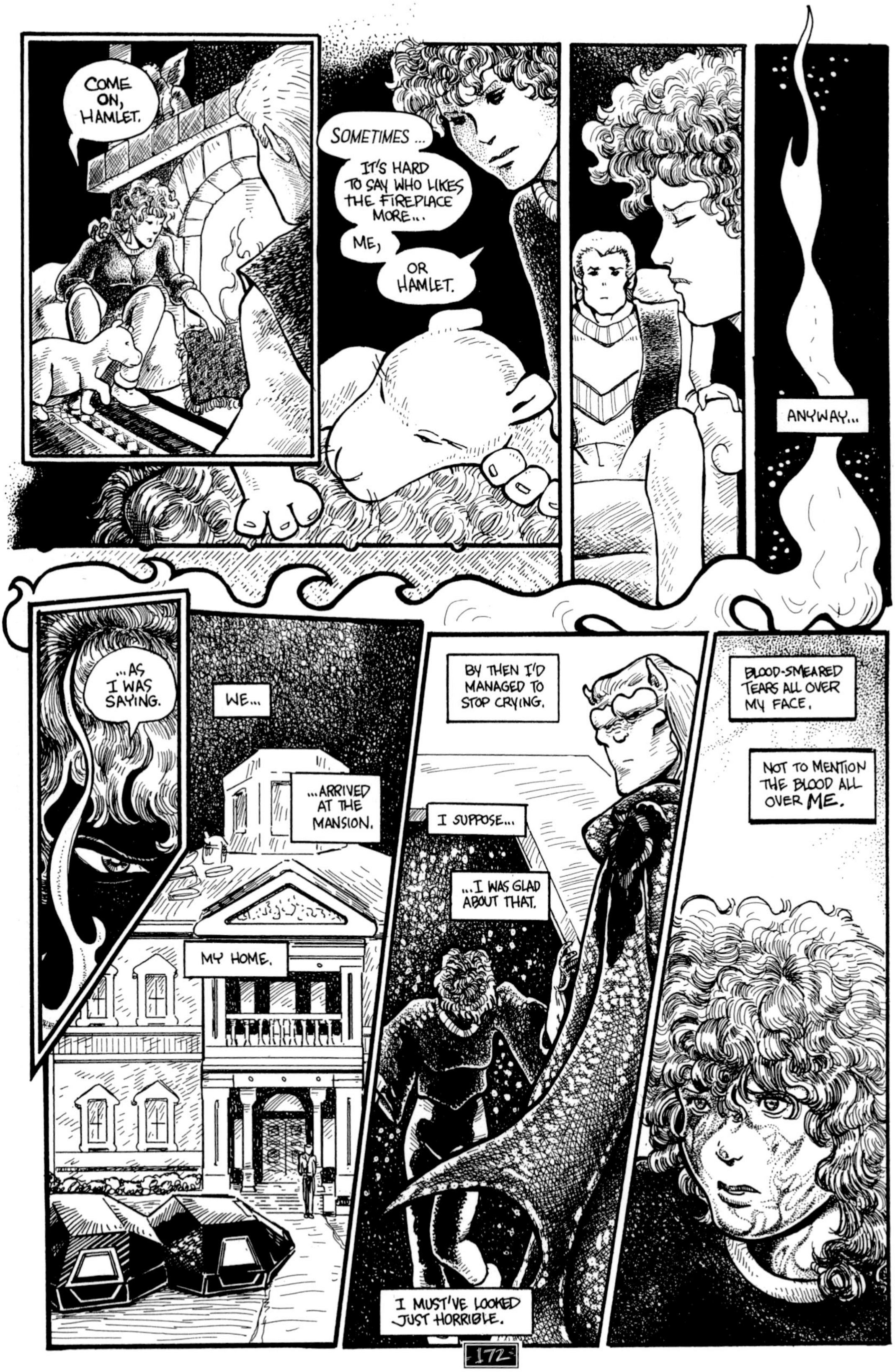
COME ON, HAMLET.
SOMETIMES ...
IT'S HARD TO SAY WHO LIKES THE FIREPLACE MORE...
ME,
OR HAMLET.
ANYWAY...
...AS I WAS SAYING.
WE...
...ARRIVED AT THE MANSION.
MY HOME.
BY THEN I'D MANAGED TO STOP CRYING.
I SUPPOSE...
...I WAS GLAD ABOUT THAT.
I MUST'VE LOOKED JUST HORRIBLE.
BLOOD-SMEARED TEARS ALL OVER MY FACE.
NOT TO MENTION THE BLOOD ALL OVER ME.

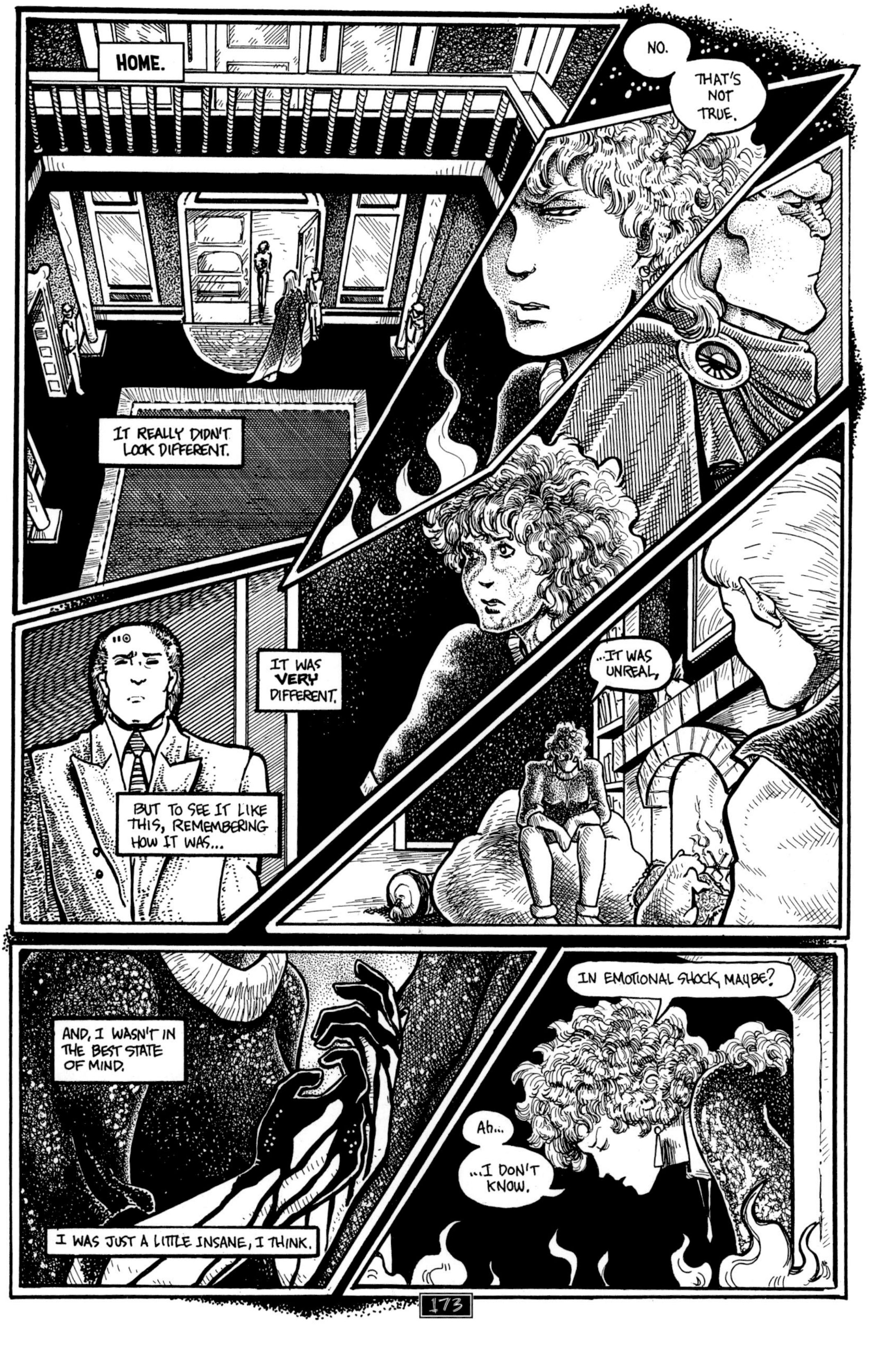
HOME.
IT REALLY DIDN'T LOOK DIFFERENT.
NO.
THAT'S NOT TRUE.
IT WAS VERY DIFFERENT.
BUT TO SEE IT LIKE THIS, REMEMBERING HOW IT WAS...
...IT WAS UNREAL,
AND, I WASN'T IN THE BEST STATE OF MIND.
I WAS JUST A LITTLE INSANE, I THINK.
IN EMOTIONAL SHOCK, MAYBE?
Ah...
...I DON'T KNOW.

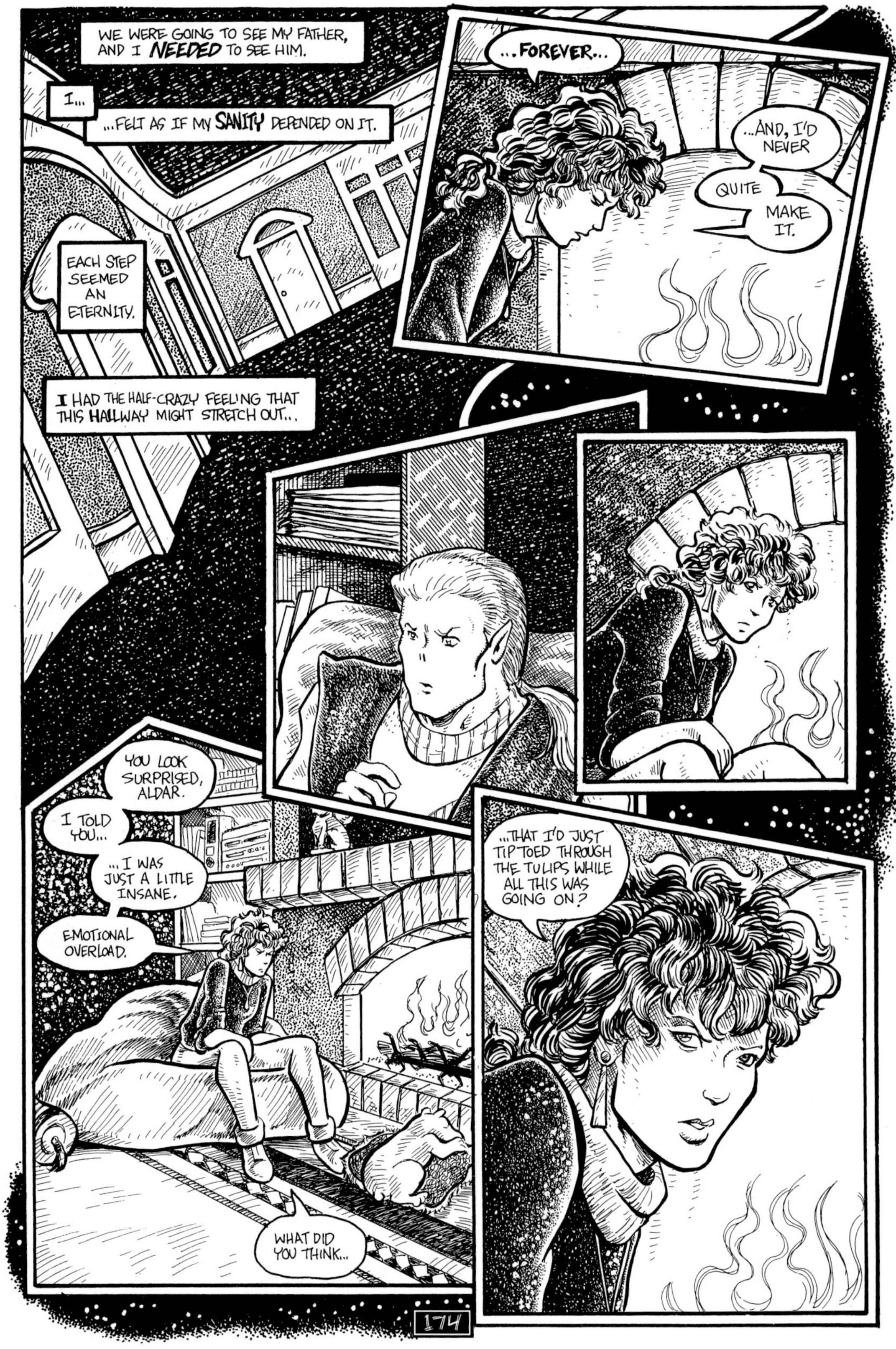
WE WERE GOING TO SEE MY FATHER, AND I NEEDED TO SEE HIM.
I...
...FELT AS IF MY SANITY DEPENDED ON IT.
EACH STEP SEEMED AN ETERNITY.
I HAD THE HALF-CRAZY FEELING THAT THIS HALLWAY MIGHT STRETCH OUT...
...FOREVER...
...AND, I'D NEVER
QUITE
MAKE IT.
YOU LOOK SURPRISED, ALDAR.
I TOLD YOU...
...I WAS JUST A LITTLE INSANE.
EMOTIONAL OVERLOAD.
WHAT DID YOU THINK...
...THAT I'D JUST TIPTOED THROUGH THE TULIPS WHILE ALL THIS WAS GOING ON?

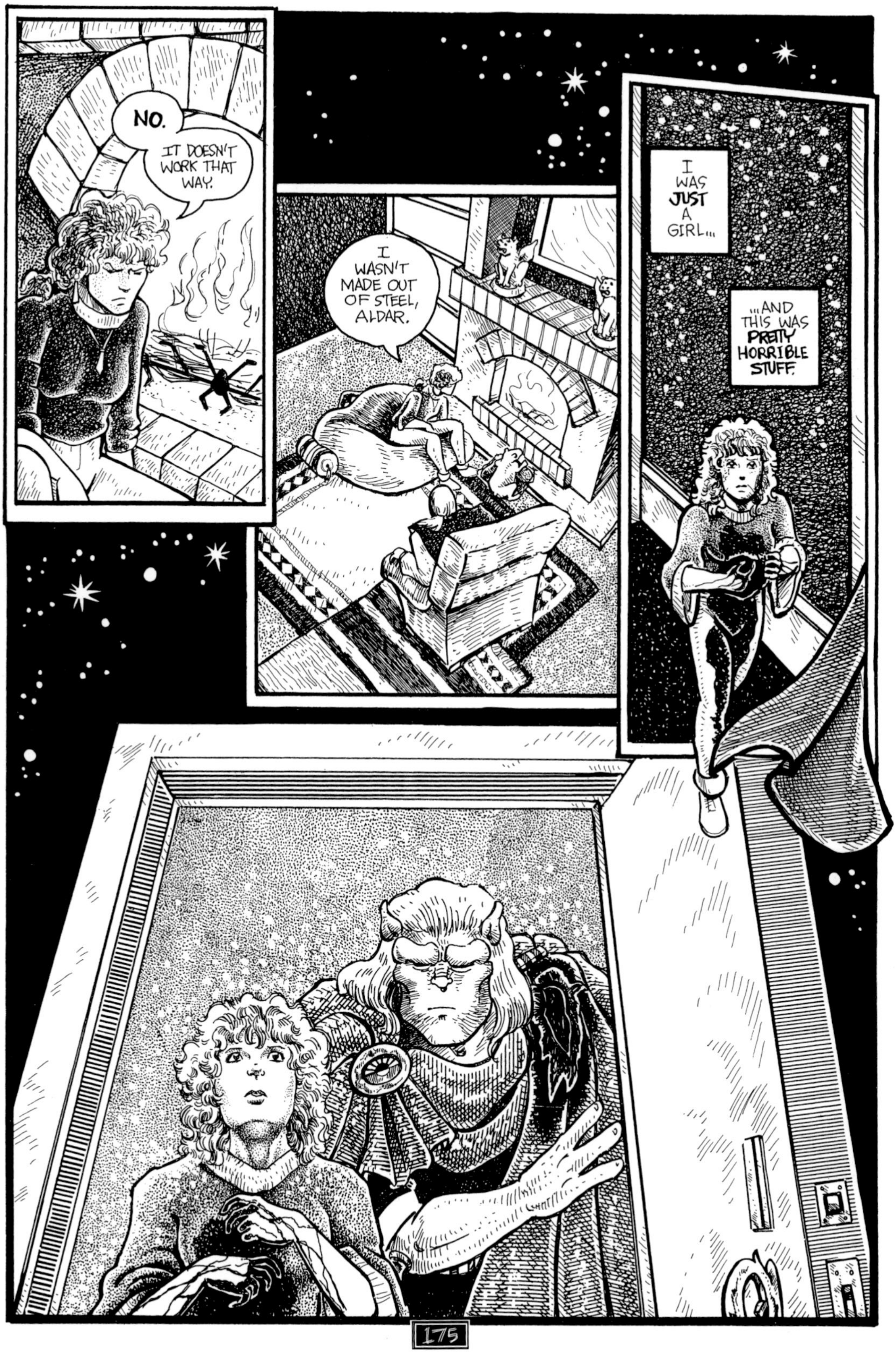
NO.
IT DOESN'T WORK THAT WAY.
I WASN'T MADE OUT OF STEEL, ALDAR.
I WAS JUST A GIRL...
...AND THIS WAS PRETTY HORRIBLE STUFF.

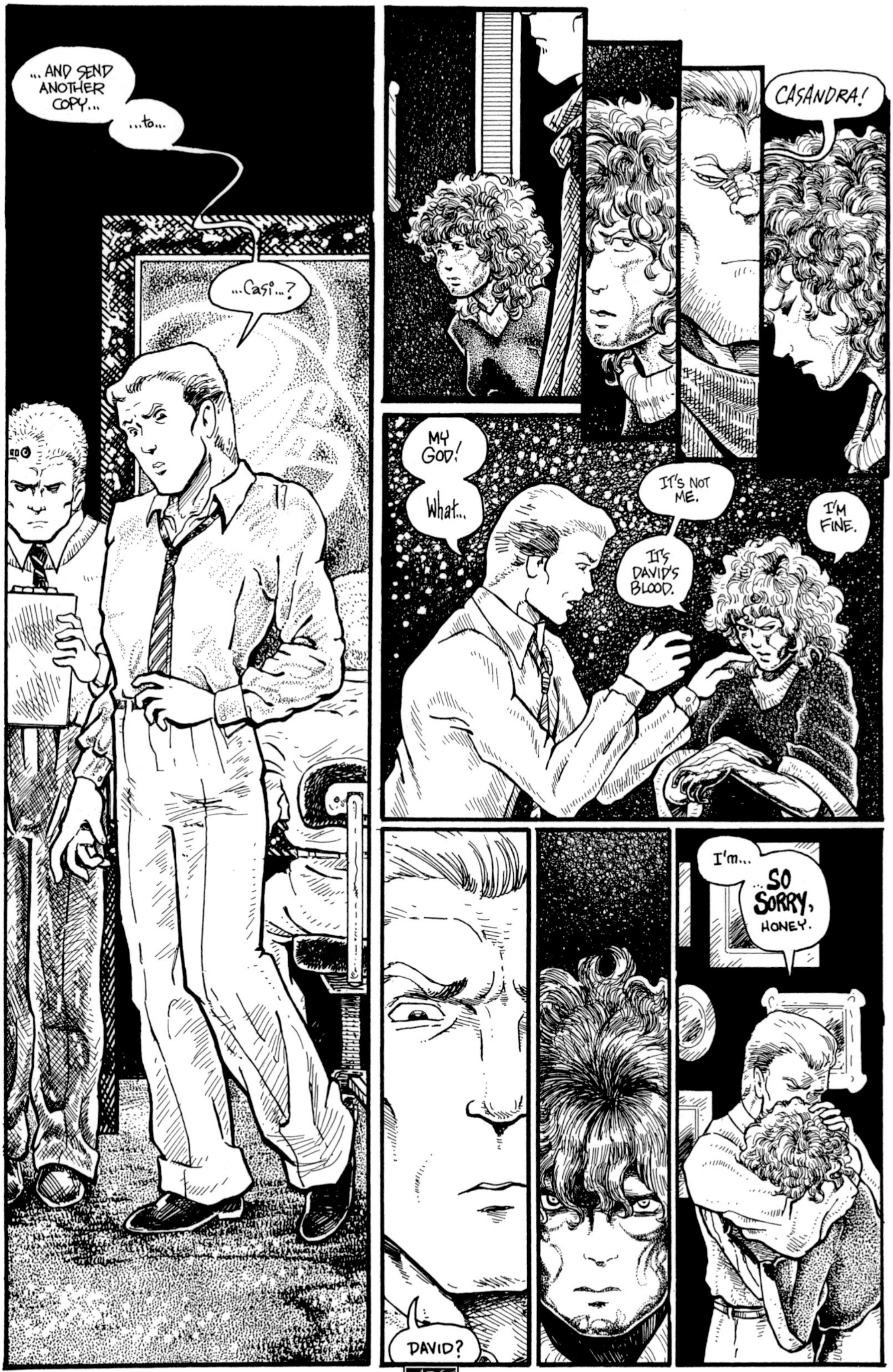
...AND SEND ANOTHER COPY...
...to...
...Casi...?
CASANDRA!
MY GOD!
What...
IT'S NOT ME.
IT'S DAVID'S BLOOD.
I'M FINE.
DAVID?
I'm...
...SO SORRY, HONEY.

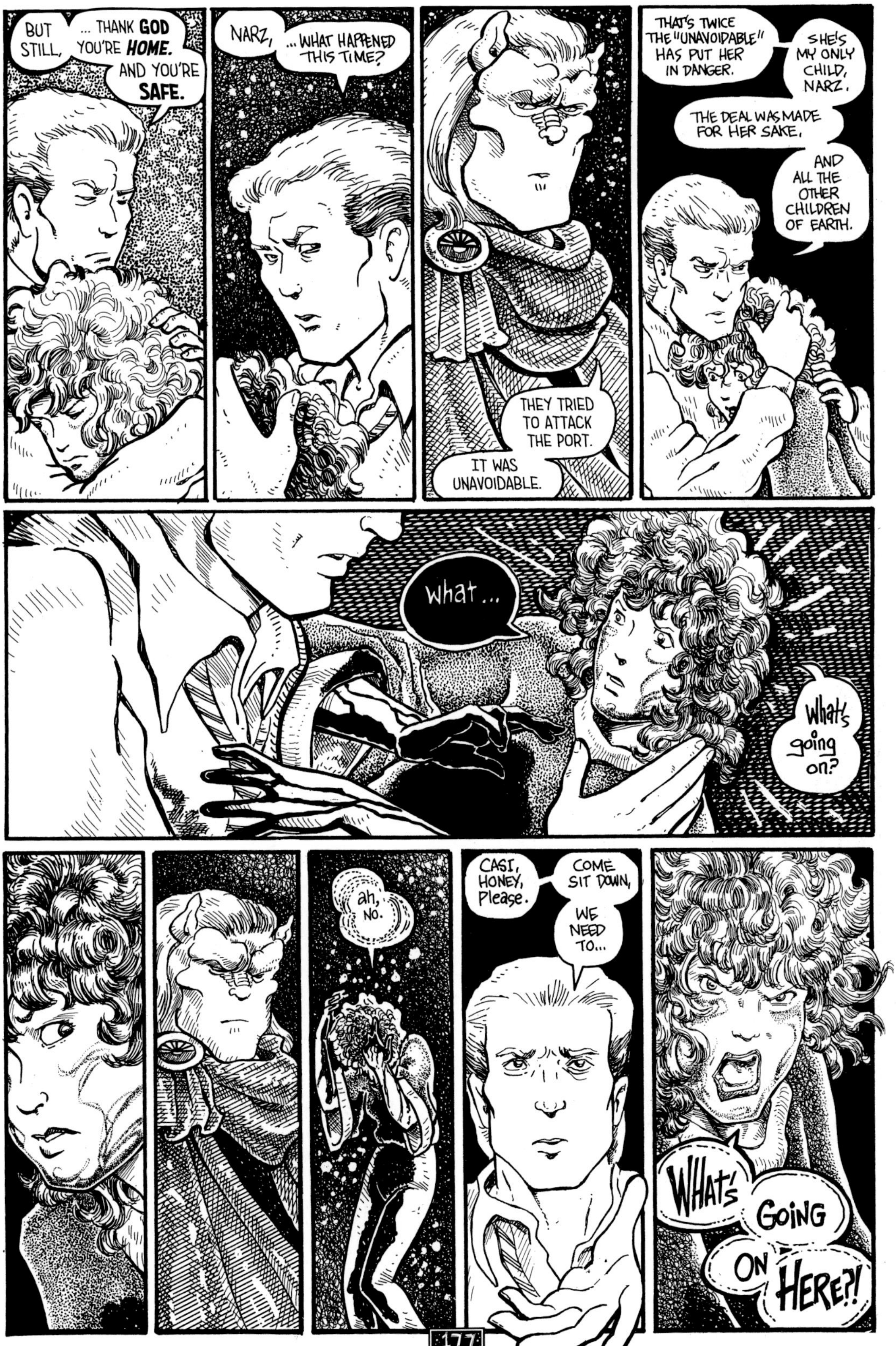

BUT STILL,
... THANK GOD YOU'RE HOME.
AND YOU'RE SAFE.
NARZ,
... WHAT HAPPENED THIS TIME?
THEY TRIED TO ATTACK THE PORT.
IT WAS UNAVOIDABLE.
THAT'S TWICE THE "UNAVOIDABLE" HAS PUT HER IN DANGER.
SHE'S MY ONLY CHILD, NARZ.
THE DEAL WAS MADE FOR HER SAKE,
AND ALL THE OTHER CHILDREN OF EARTH.
what...
What's going on?
ah, No.
CASI, HONEY, Please.
COME SIT DOWN,
WE NEED TO...
WHAT'S GOING ON HERE?!

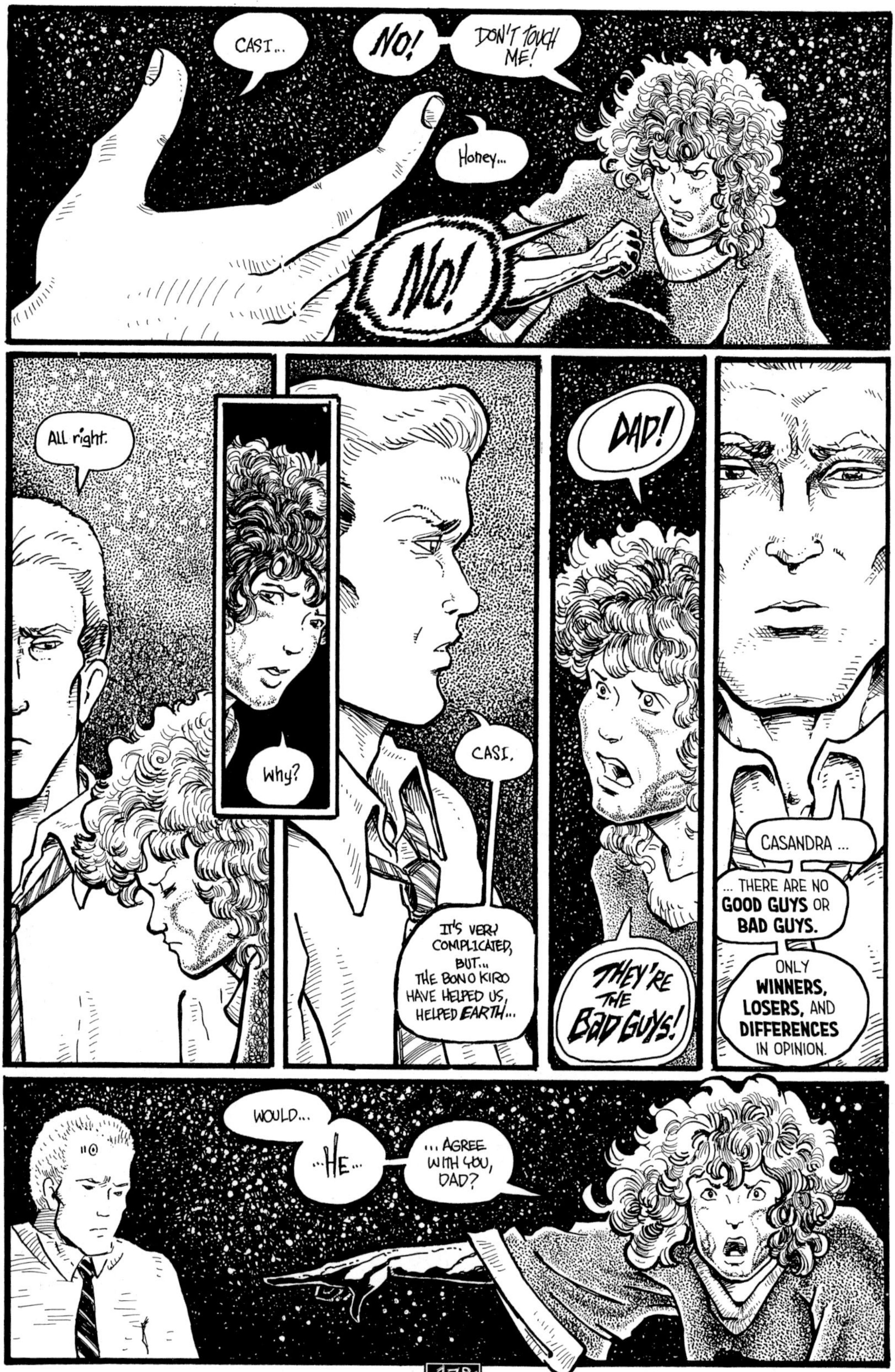

CASI...
NO!
DON'T TOUCH ME!
Honey...
NO!
All right.
Why?
CASI.
IT'S VERY COMPLICATED, BUT... THE BONO KIRO HAVE HELPED US, HELPED EARTH...
DAD!
THEY'RE THE BAD GUYS!
CASANDRA ...
... THERE ARE NO GOOD GUYS OR BAD GUYS.
ONLY WINNERS, LOSERS, AND DIFFERENCES IN OPINION.
WOULD...
...HE...
... AGREE WITH YOU, DAD?

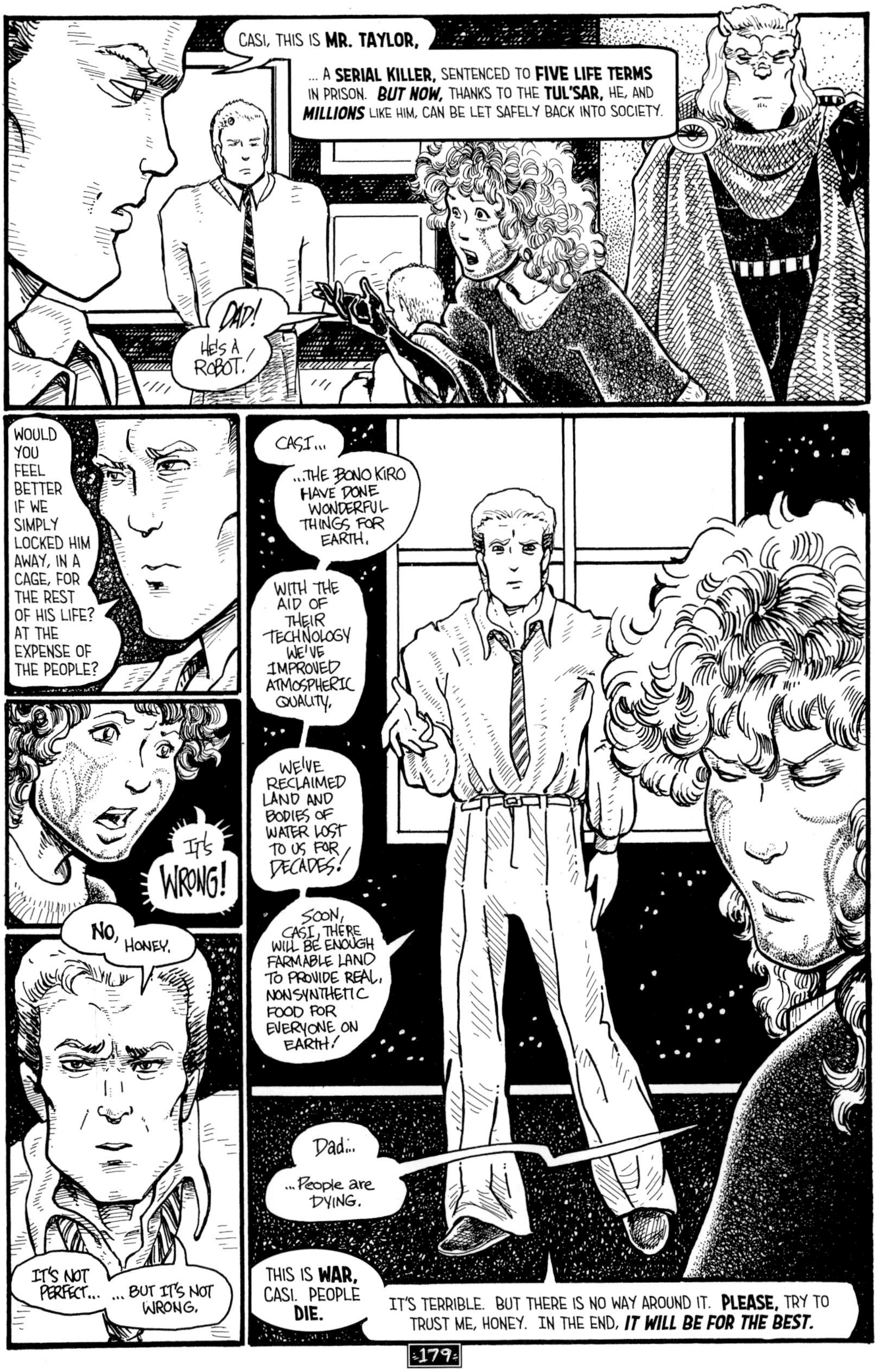
CASI, THIS IS **MR. TAYLOR,**
... A **SERIAL KILLER,** SENTENCED TO **FIVE LIFE TERMS** IN PRISON. ***BUT NOW,*** THANKS TO THE **TUL'SAR,** HE, AND ***MILLIONS*** LIKE HIM, CAN BE LET SAFELY BACK INTO SOCIETY.
DAD! HE'S A ROBOT!
WOULD YOU FEEL BETTER IF WE SIMPLY LOCKED HIM AWAY, IN A CAGE, FOR THE REST OF HIS LIFE? AT THE EXPENSE OF THE PEOPLE?
IT'S WRONG!
NO, HONEY.
IT'S NOT PERFECT...
... BUT IT'S NOT WRONG.
CASI...
...THE BONO KIRO HAVE DONE WONDERFUL THINGS FOR EARTH.
WITH THE AID OF THEIR TECHNOLOGY WE'VE IMPROVED ATMOSPHERIC QUALITY,
WE'VE RECLAIMED LAND AND BODIES OF WATER LOST TO US FOR DECADES!
SOON, CASI, THERE WILL BE ENOUGH FARMABLE LAND TO PROVIDE REAL, NONSYNTHETIC FOOD FOR EVERYONE ON EARTH!
Dad...
...People are DYING.
THIS IS **WAR,** CASI. PEOPLE **DIE.**
IT'S TERRIBLE. BUT THERE IS NO WAY AROUND IT. **PLEASE,** TRY TO TRUST ME, HONEY. IN THE END, ***IT WILL BE FOR THE BEST.***

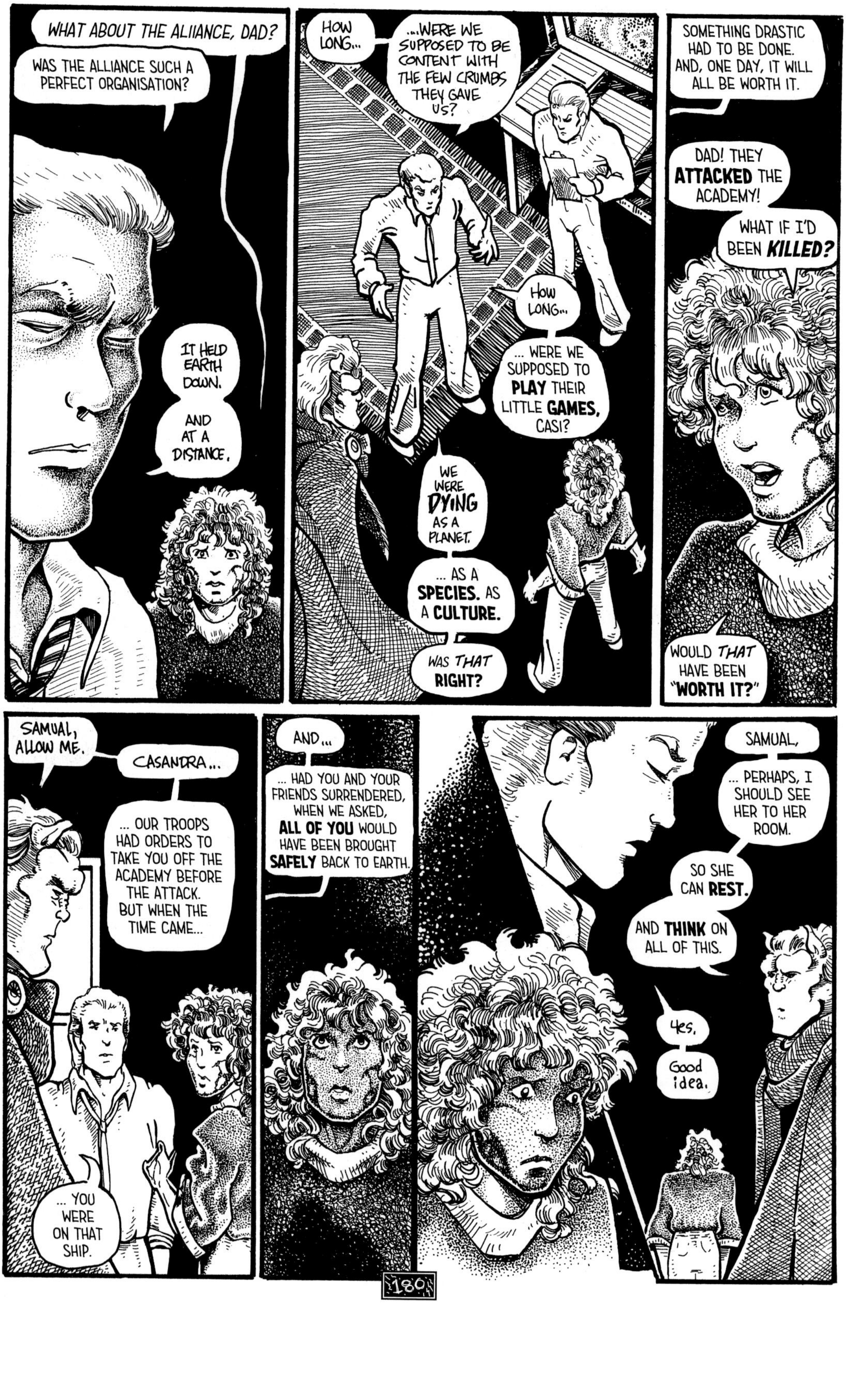
WHAT ABOUT THE ALIIANCE, DAD?
WAS THE ALLIANCE SUCH A PERFECT ORGANISATION?
IT HELD EARTH DOWN.
AND AT A DISTANCE.
HOW LONG...
...WERE WE SUPPOSED TO BE CONTENT WITH THE FEW CRUMBS THEY GAVE US?
HOW LONG...
... WERE WE SUPPOSED TO PLAY THEIR LITTLE GAMES, CASI?
WE WERE DYING AS A PLANET.
... AS A SPECIES. AS A CULTURE.
WAS THAT RIGHT?
SOMETHING DRASTIC HAD TO BE DONE. AND, ONE DAY, IT WILL ALL BE WORTH IT.
DAD! THEY ATTACKED THE ACADEMY!
WHAT IF I'D BEEN KILLED?
WOULD THAT HAVE BEEN "WORTH IT?"
SAMUAL, ALLOW ME.
CASANDRA...
... OUR TROOPS HAD ORDERS TO TAKE YOU OFF THE ACADEMY BEFORE THE ATTACK. BUT WHEN THE TIME CAME...
... YOU WERE ON THAT SHIP.
AND...
... HAD YOU AND YOUR FRIENDS SURRENDERED, WHEN WE ASKED, ALL OF YOU WOULD HAVE BEEN BROUGHT SAFELY BACK TO EARTH.
SAMUAL,
... PERHAPS, I SHOULD SEE HER TO HER ROOM.
SO SHE CAN REST.
AND THINK ON ALL OF THIS.
Yes.
Good idea.

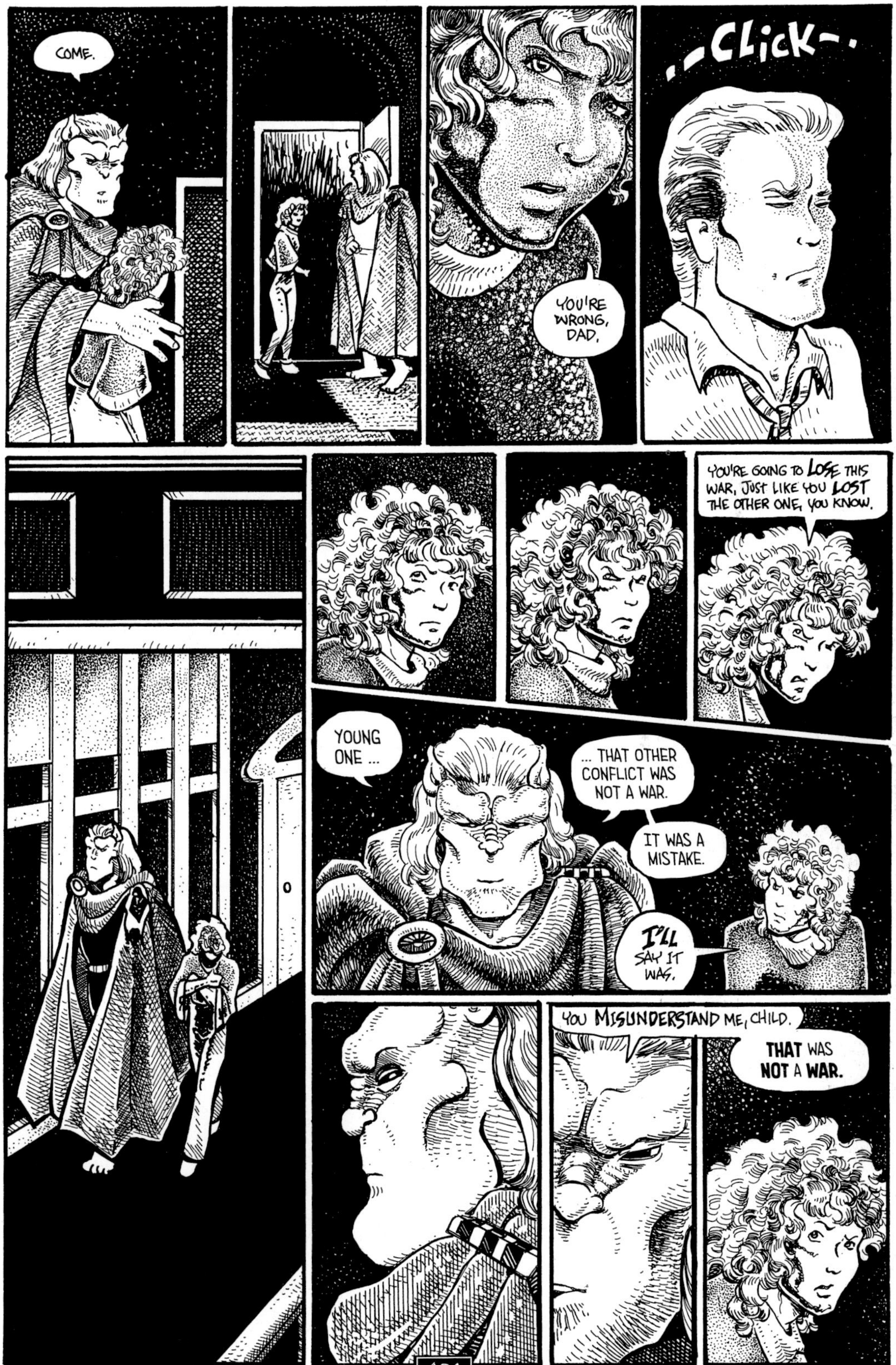
COME.
..CLICK..
YOU'RE WRONG, DAD.
YOU'RE GOING TO LOSE THIS WAR, JUST LIKE YOU LOST THE OTHER ONE, YOU KNOW.
YOUNG ONE ...
... THAT OTHER CONFLICT WAS NOT A WAR.
IT WAS A MISTAKE.
I'LL SAY IT WAS.
YOU MISUNDERSTAND ME, CHILD.
THAT WAS NOT A WAR.

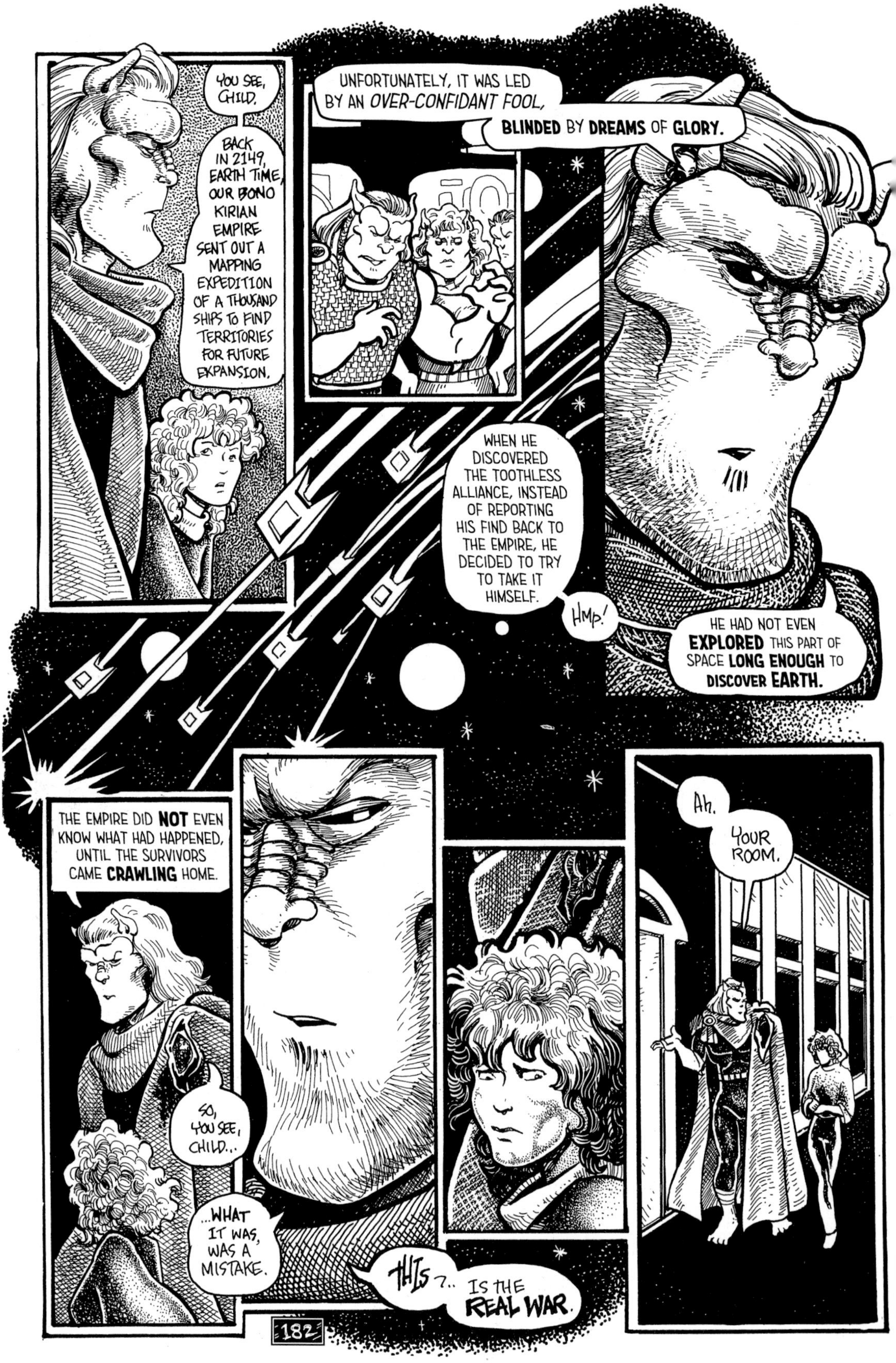

YOU SEE, CHILD.
BACK IN 2149, EARTH TIME, OUR BONO KIRIAN EMPIRE SENT OUT A MAPPING EXPEDITION OF A THOUSAND SHIPS TO FIND TERRITORIES FOR FUTURE EXPANSION.
UNFORTUNATELY, IT WAS LED BY AN OVER-CONFIDANT FOOL,
BLINDED BY DREAMS OF GLORY.
WHEN HE DISCOVERED THE TOOTHLESS ALLIANCE, INSTEAD OF REPORTING HIS FIND BACK TO THE EMPIRE, HE DECIDED TO TRY TO TAKE IT HIMSELF.
HMP!
HE HAD NOT EVEN EXPLORED THIS PART OF SPACE LONG ENOUGH TO DISCOVER EARTH.
THE EMPIRE DID NOT EVEN KNOW WHAT HAD HAPPENED, UNTIL THE SURVIVORS CAME CRAWLING HOME.
SO, YOU SEE, CHILD...
...WHAT IT WAS, WAS A MISTAKE.
THIS?..
IS THE REAL WAR.
AH.
YOUR ROOM.

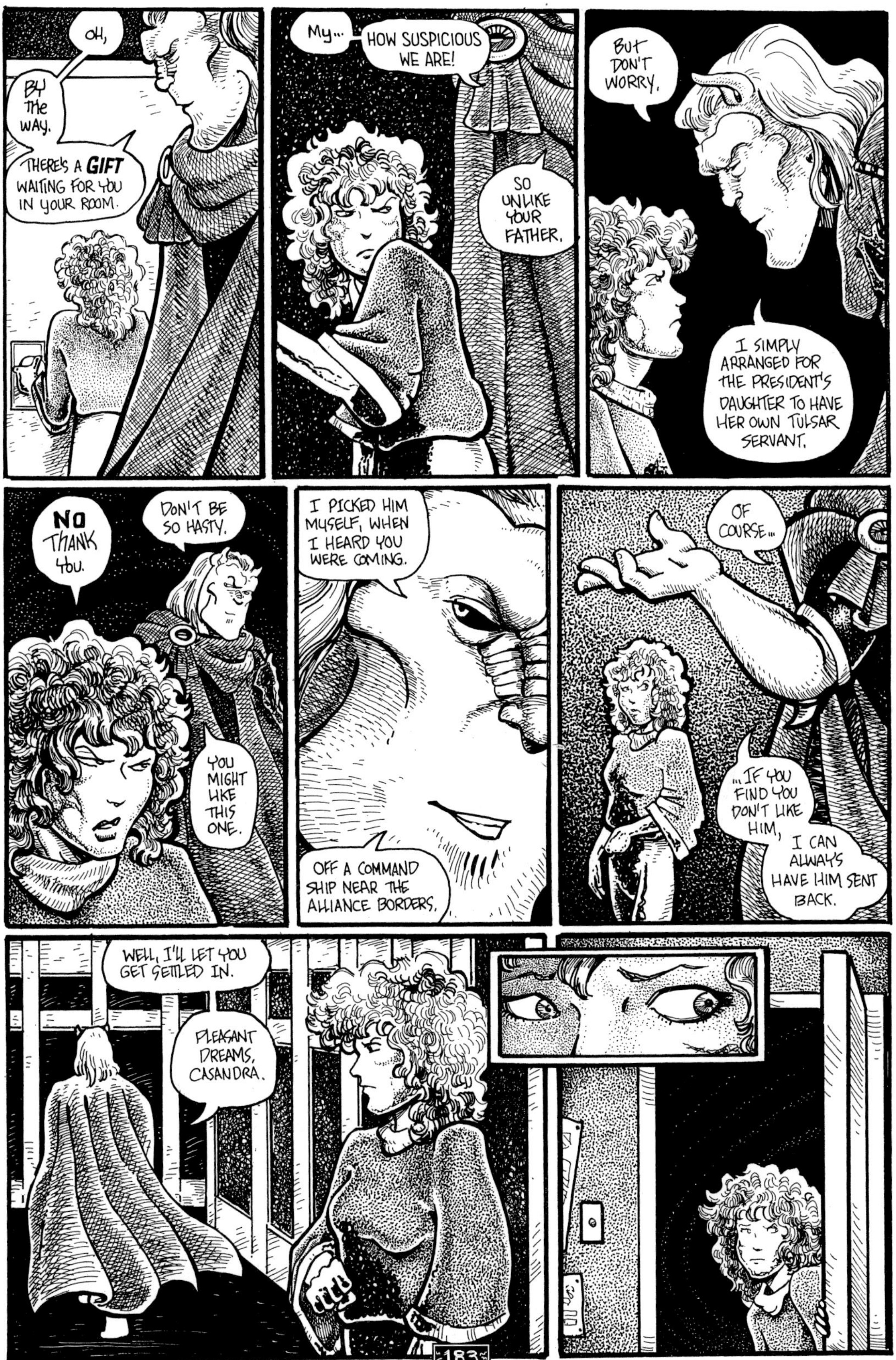
OH,
BY THE WAY,
THERE'S A GIFT WAITING FOR YOU IN YOUR ROOM.
My...
HOW SUSPICIOUS WE ARE!
SO UNLIKE YOUR FATHER.
BUT DON'T WORRY,
I SIMPLY ARRANGED FOR THE PRESIDENT'S DAUGHTER TO HAVE HER OWN TULSAR SERVANT.
NO THANK YOU.
DON'T BE SO HASTY.
YOU MIGHT LIKE THIS ONE.
I PICKED HIM MYSELF, WHEN I HEARD YOU WERE COMING.
OFF A COMMAND SHIP NEAR THE ALLIANCE BORDERS.
OF COURSE...
...IF YOU FIND YOU DON'T LIKE HIM,
I CAN ALWAYS HAVE HIM SENT BACK.
WELL, I'LL LET YOU GET SETTLED IN.
PLEASANT DREAMS, CASANDRA.

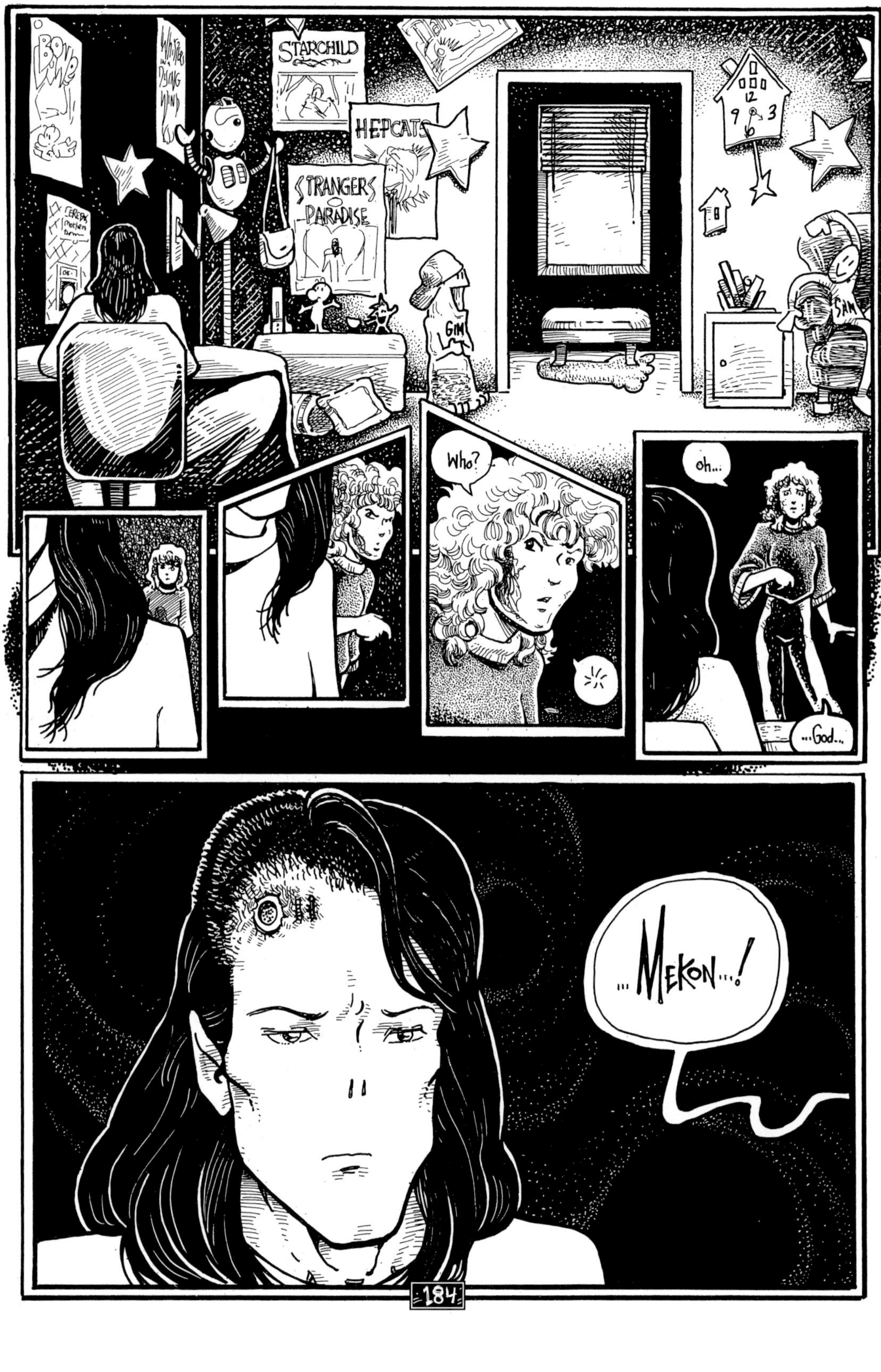
STARCHILD
HEPCATS
STRANGERS PARADISE
GIM
SAM
Who?
oh...
...God...
...MEKON...!

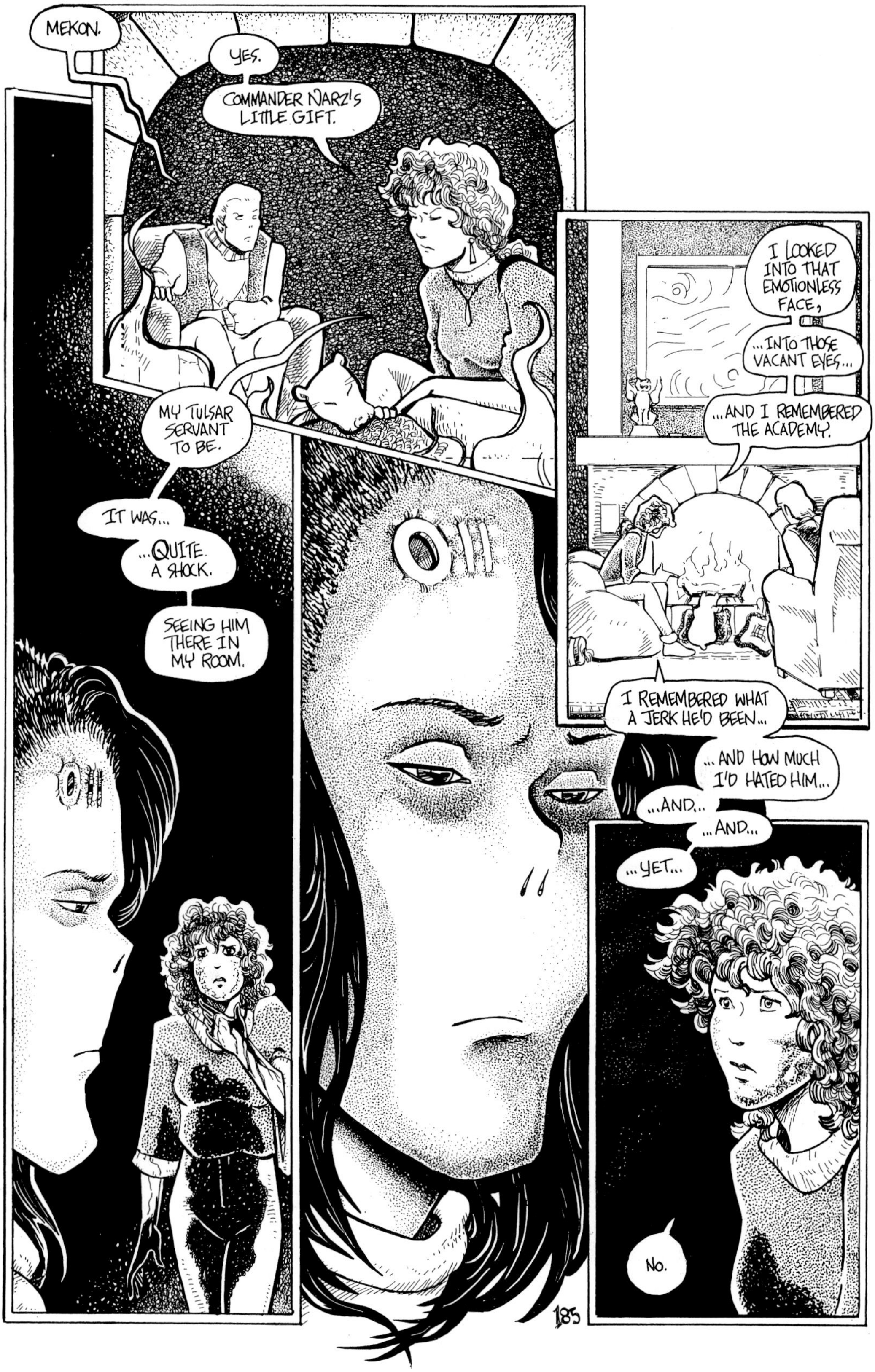
MEKON.
YES.
COMMANDER NARZ'S LITTLE GIFT.
MY TULSAR SERVANT TO BE.
IT WAS...
...QUITE A SHOCK.
SEEING HIM THERE IN MY ROOM.
I LOOKED INTO THAT EMOTIONLESS FACE,
...INTO THOSE VACANT EYES...
...AND I REMEMBERED THE ACADEMY.
I REMEMBERED WHAT A JERK HE'D BEEN...
...AND HOW MUCH I'D HATED HIM...
...AND...
...AND...
...YET...
No.

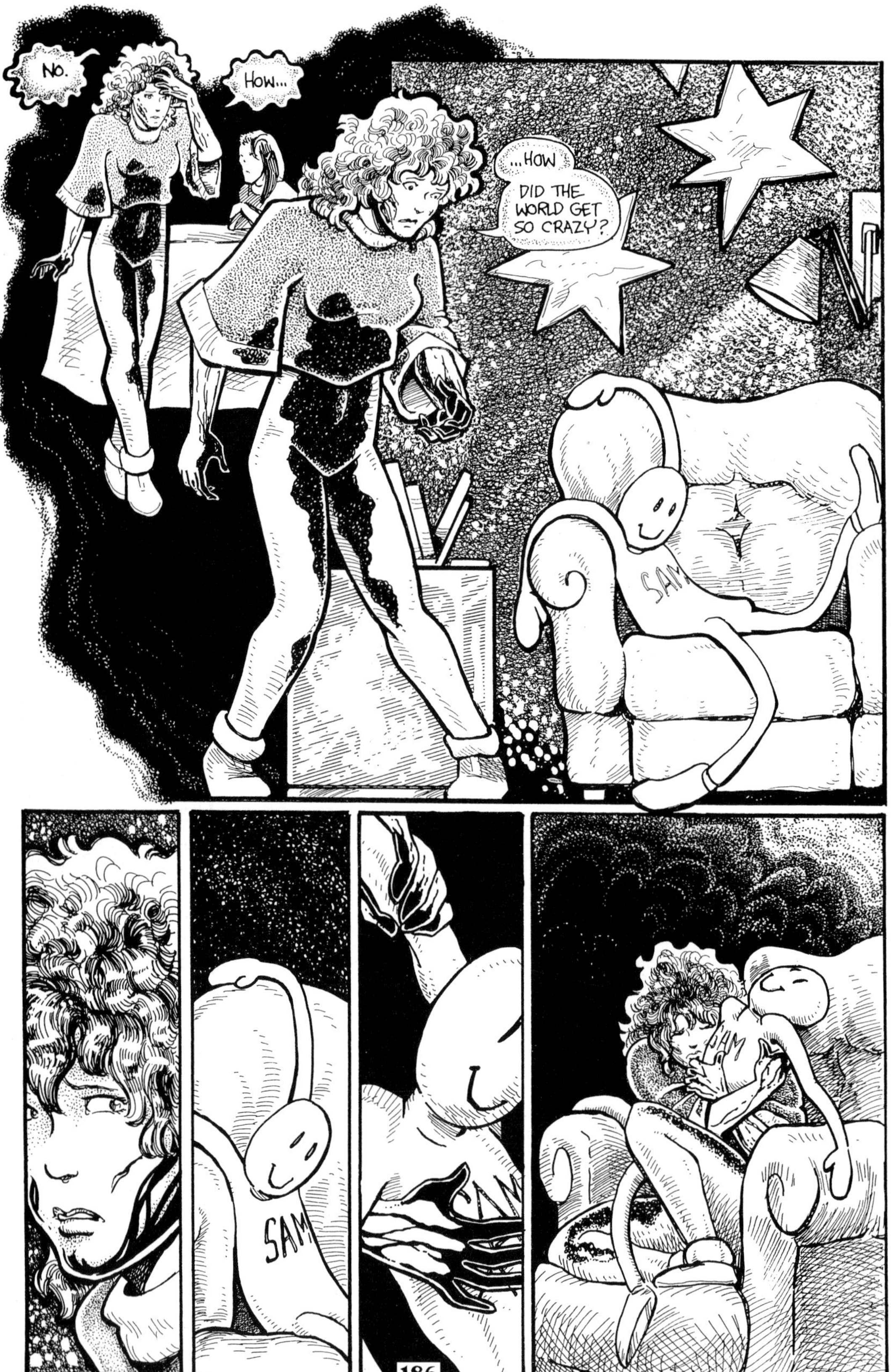
NO.
HOW...
...HOW
DID THE WORLD GET SO CRAZY?
SAM
SAM
SAM
SAM

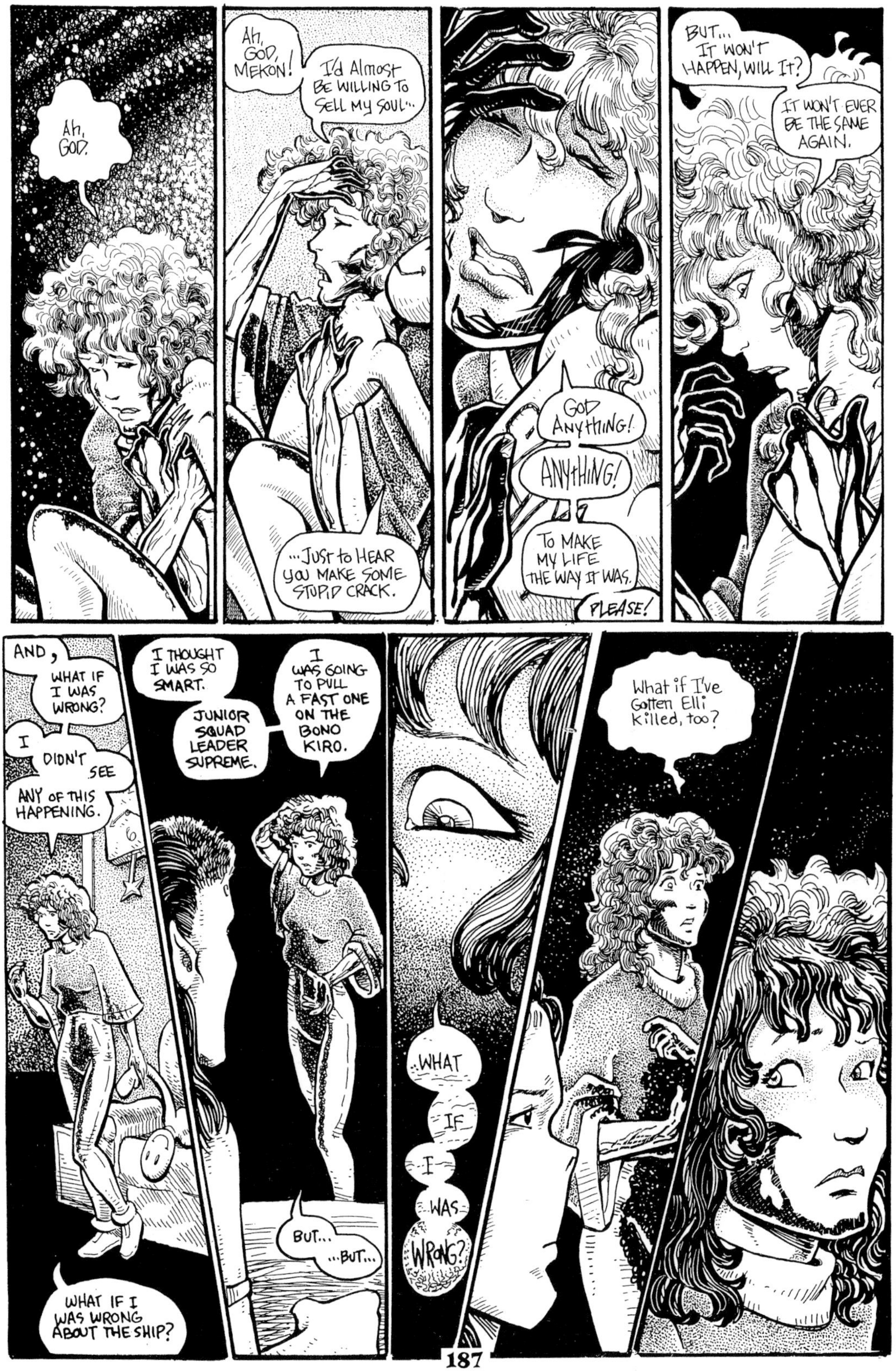
Ah, GOD.
Ah, GOD, MEKON!
I'd Almost BE WILLING TO SELL MY SOUL...
...JUST to HEAR YOU MAKE SOME STUPID CRACK.
GOD ANYTHING!
ANYTHING!
TO MAKE MY LIFE THE WAY IT WAS.
PLEASE!
BUT... IT WON'T HAPPEN, WILL IT?
IT WON'T EVER BE THE SAME AGAIN.
AND,
WHAT IF I WAS WRONG?
I DIDN'T SEE
ANY OF THIS HAPPENING.
WHAT IF I WAS WRONG ABOUT THE SHIP?
I THOUGHT I WAS SO SMART.
JUNIOR SQUAD LEADER SUPREME.
I WAS GOING TO PULL A FAST ONE ON THE BONO KIRO.
BUT...
...BUT...
WHAT
IF
I
WAS
WRONG?
What if I've Gotten Elli Killed, too?

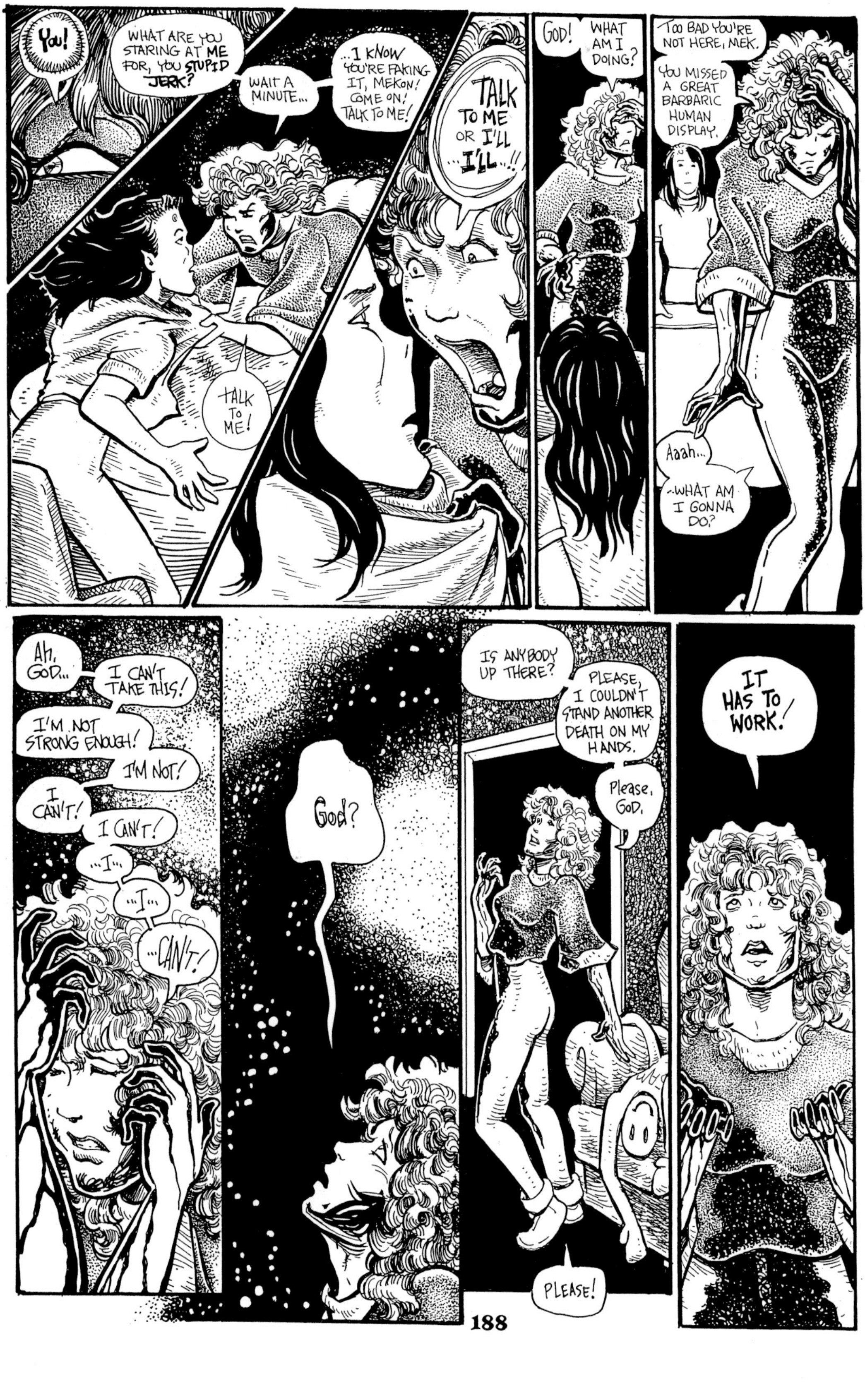
You!
WHAT ARE YOU STARING AT ME FOR, YOU STUPID JERK?
WAIT A MINUTE...
...I KNOW YOU'RE FAKING IT, MEKON! COME ON! TALK TO ME!
TALK TO ME!
TALK TO ME OR I'LL ...I'LL...!!
GOD!
WHAT AM I DOING?
TOO BAD YOU'RE NOT HERE, MEK.
YOU MISSED A GREAT BARBARIC HUMAN DISPLAY.
Aaah...
...WHAT AM I GONNA DO?
Ah, GOD...
I CAN'T TAKE THIS!
I'M NOT STRONG ENOUGH!
I'M NOT!
I CAN'T!
I CAN'T!
...I...
...I...
...CAN'T!
God?
IS ANYBODY UP THERE?
PLEASE, I COULDN'T STAND ANOTHER DEATH ON MY HANDS.
Please, GOD,
PLEASE!
IT HAS TO WORK!

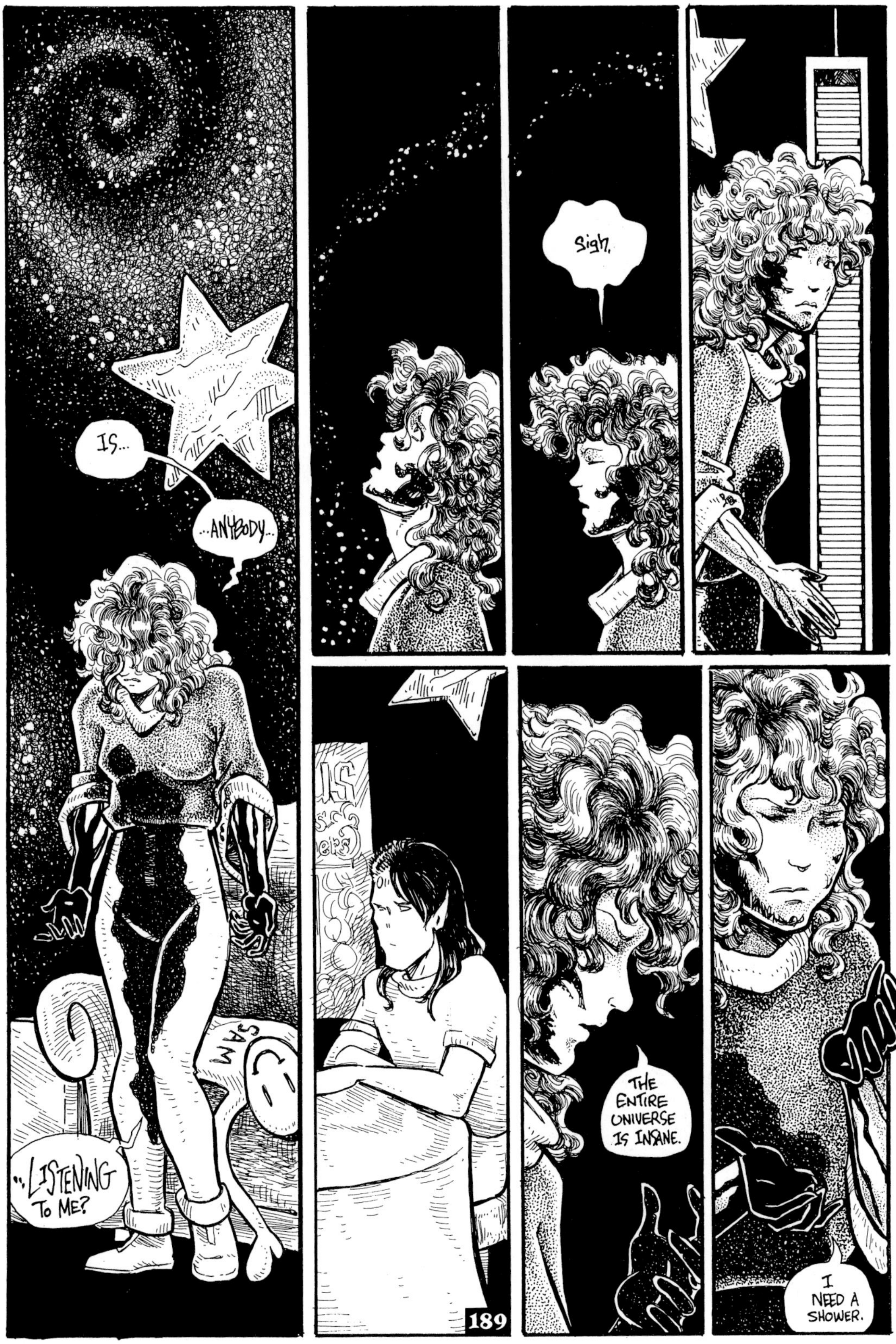
IS...
...ANYBODY...
...LISTENING TO ME?
SAM
SIGH.
THE ENTIRE UNIVERSE IS INSANE.
I NEED A SHOWER.

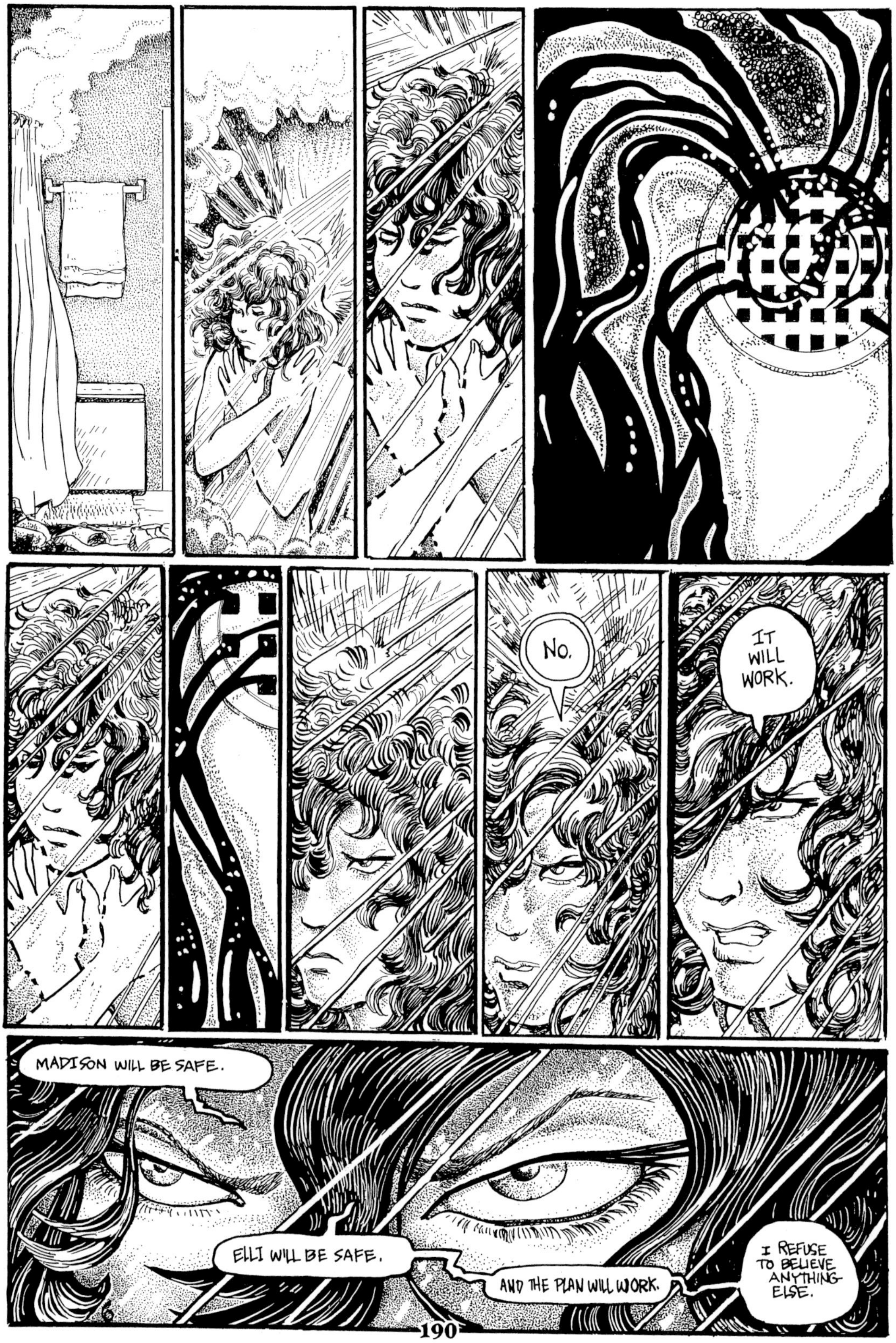
No.
IT WILL WORK.
MADISON WILL BE SAFE.
ELLI WILL BE SAFE.
AND THE PLAN WILL WORK.
I REFUSE TO BELIEVE ANYTHING ELSE.

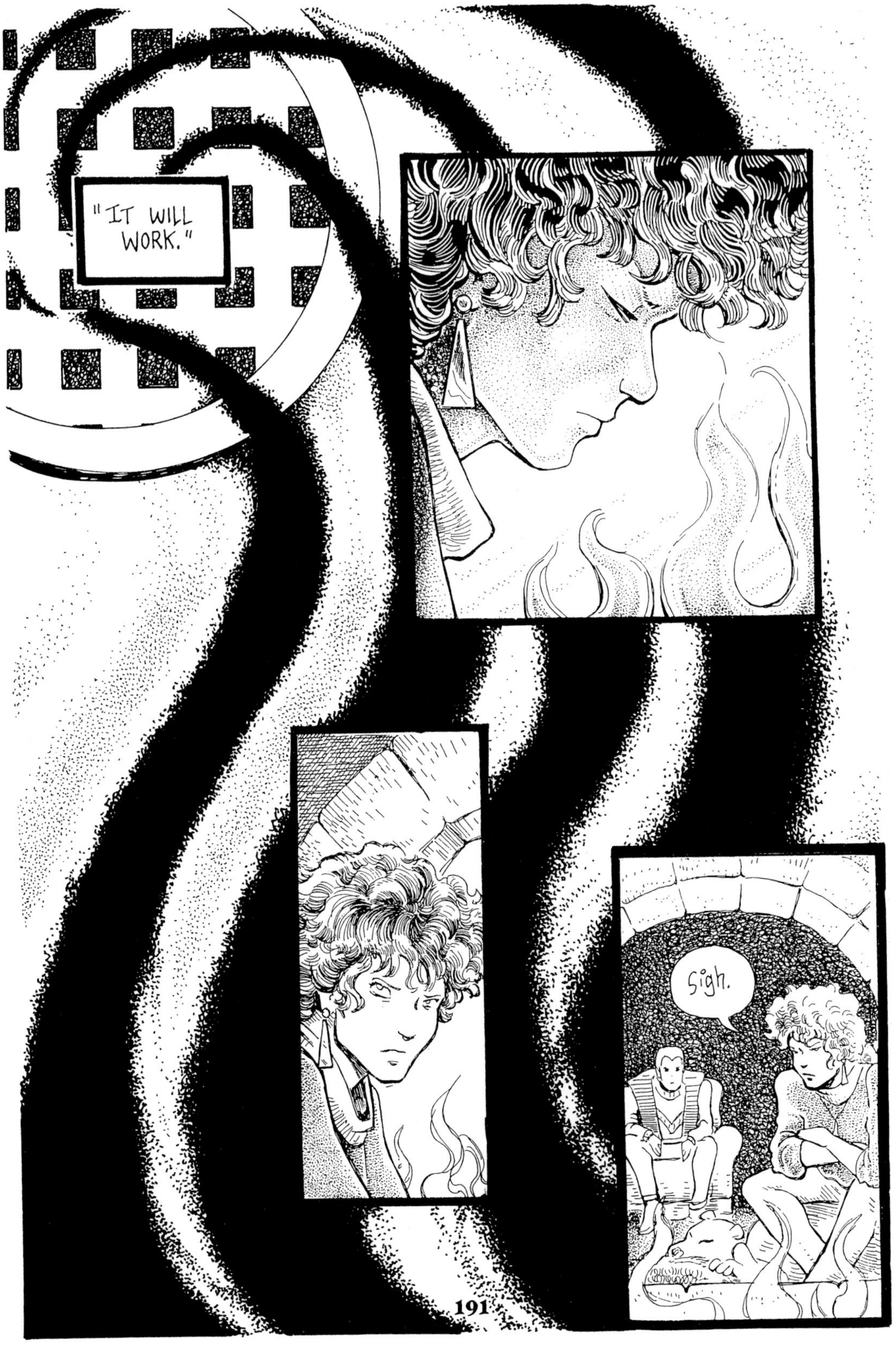
"IT WILL WORK."
Sigh.

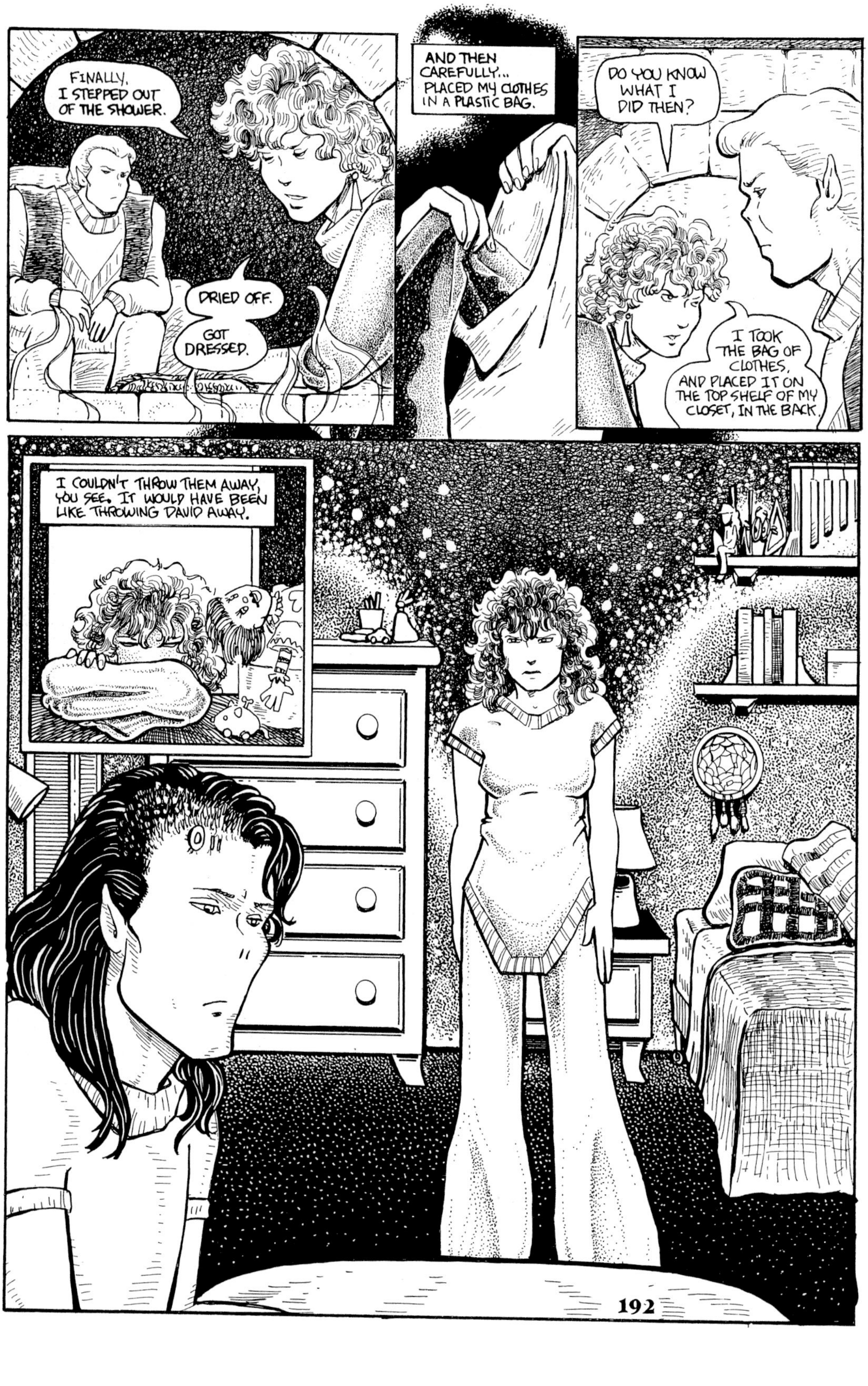
FINALLY, I STEPPED OUT OF THE SHOWER.
DRIED OFF.
GOT DRESSED.
AND THEN CAREFULLY... PLACED MY CLOTHES IN A PLASTIC BAG.
DO YOU KNOW WHAT I DID THEN?
I TOOK THE BAG OF CLOTHES, AND PLACED IT ON THE TOP SHELF OF MY CLOSET, IN THE BACK.
I COULDN'T THROW THEM AWAY, YOU SEE. IT WOULD HAVE BEEN LIKE THROWING DAVID AWAY.

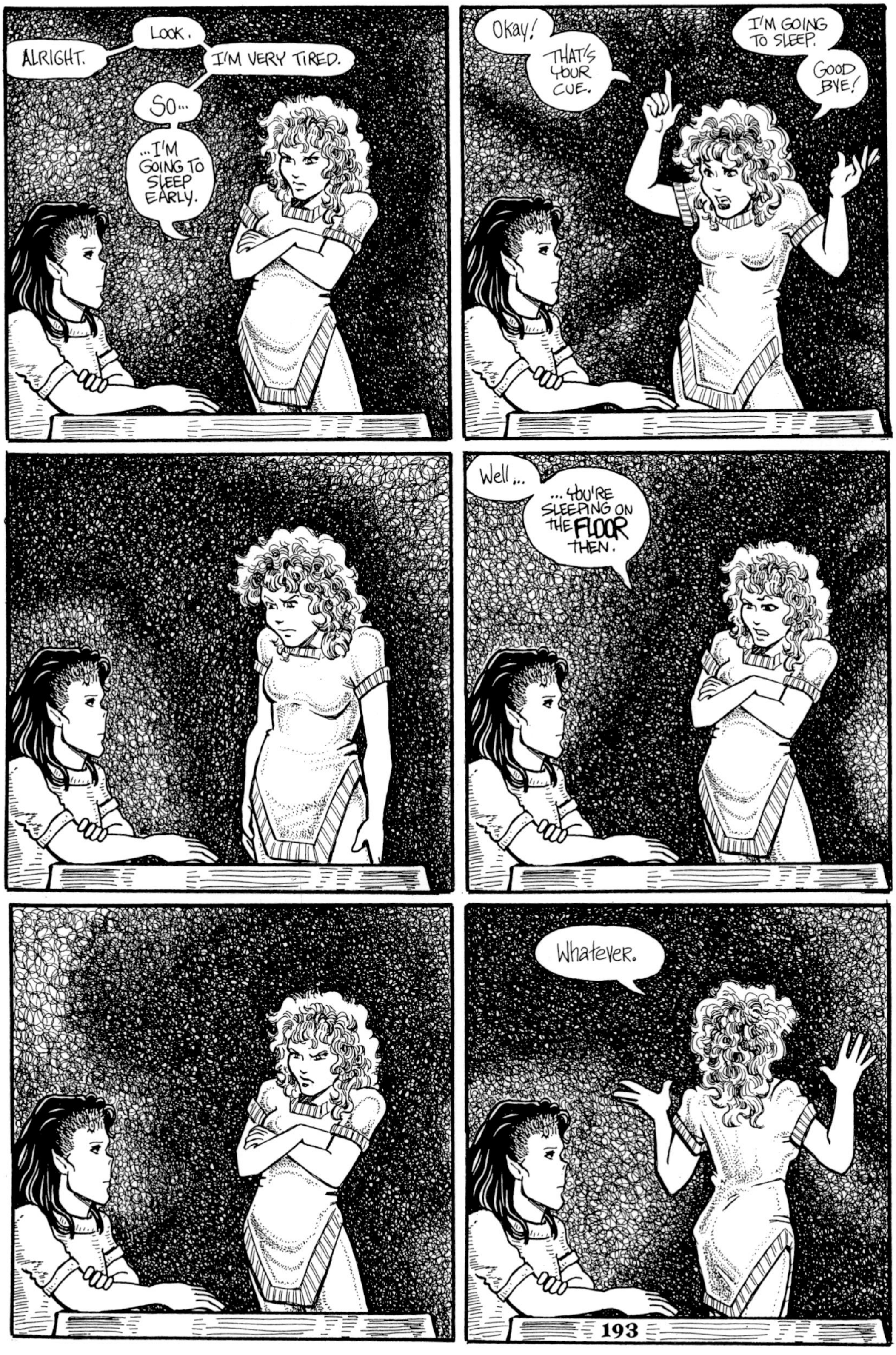
ALRIGHT.
LOOK.
I'M VERY TIRED.
SO...
...I'M GOING TO SLEEP EARLY.
Okay!
THAT'S YOUR CUE.
I'M GOING TO SLEEP.
GOOD BYE!
Well...
...YOU'RE SLEEPING ON THE FLOOR THEN.
Whatever.

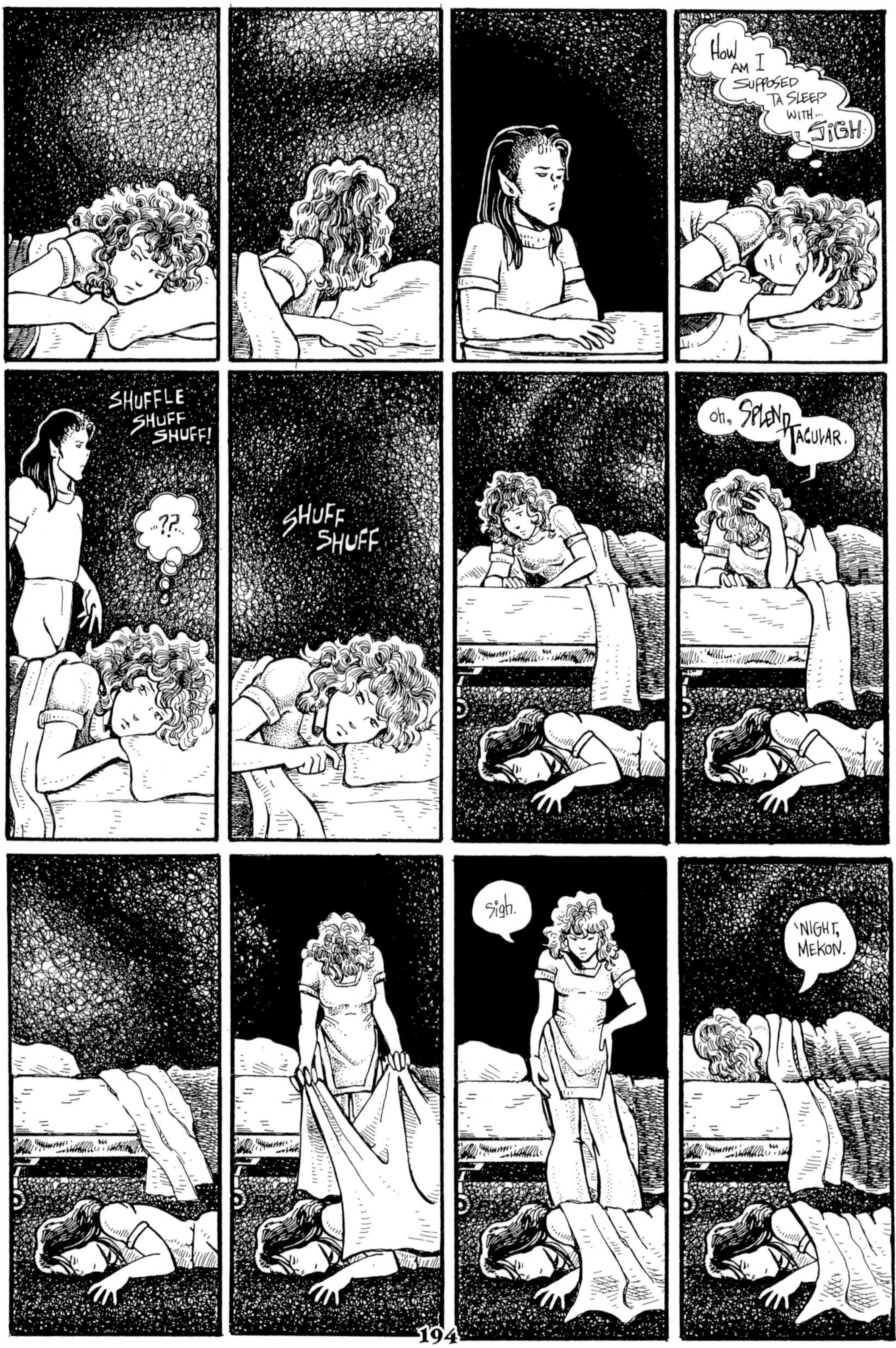
How am I supposed ta sleep with... Sigh.
SHUFFLE SHUFF SHUFF!
...??...
SHUFF SHUFF
oh, SPLENDTACULAR.
Sigh.
'NIGHT, MEKON.

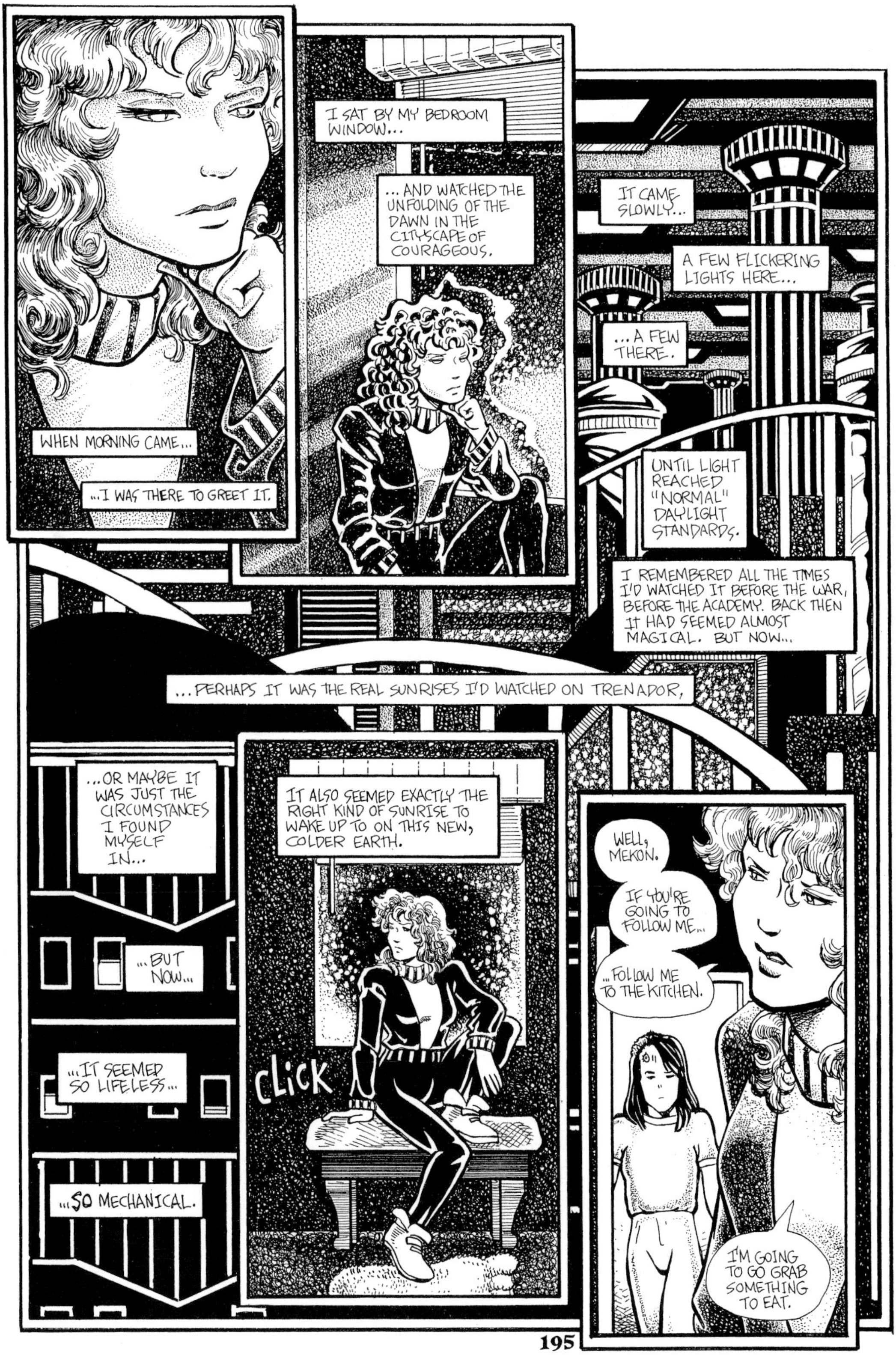
WHEN MORNING CAME...
...I WAS THERE TO GREET IT.
I SAT BY MY BEDROOM WINDOW...
...AND WATCHED THE UNFOLDING OF THE DAWN IN THE CITYSCAPE OF COURAGEOUS.
IT CAME SLOWLY...
A FEW FLICKERING LIGHTS HERE...
...A FEW THERE.
UNTIL LIGHT REACHED "NORMAL" DAYLIGHT STANDARDS.
I REMEMBERED ALL THE TIMES I'D WATCHED IT BEFORE THE WAR, BEFORE THE ACADEMY. BACK THEN IT HAD SEEMED ALMOST MAGICAL. BUT NOW...
...PERHAPS IT WAS THE REAL SUNRISES I'D WATCHED ON TRENADOR,
...OR MAYBE IT WAS JUST THE CIRCUMSTANCES I FOUND MYSELF IN...
...BUT NOW...
...IT SEEMED SO LIFELESS...
...SO MECHANICAL.
IT ALSO SEEMED EXACTLY THE RIGHT KIND OF SUNRISE TO WAKE UP TO ON THIS NEW, COLDER EARTH.
CLICK
WELL, MEKON.
IF YOU'RE GOING TO FOLLOW ME...
...FOLLOW ME TO THE KITCHEN.
I'M GOING TO GO GRAB SOMETHING TO EAT.

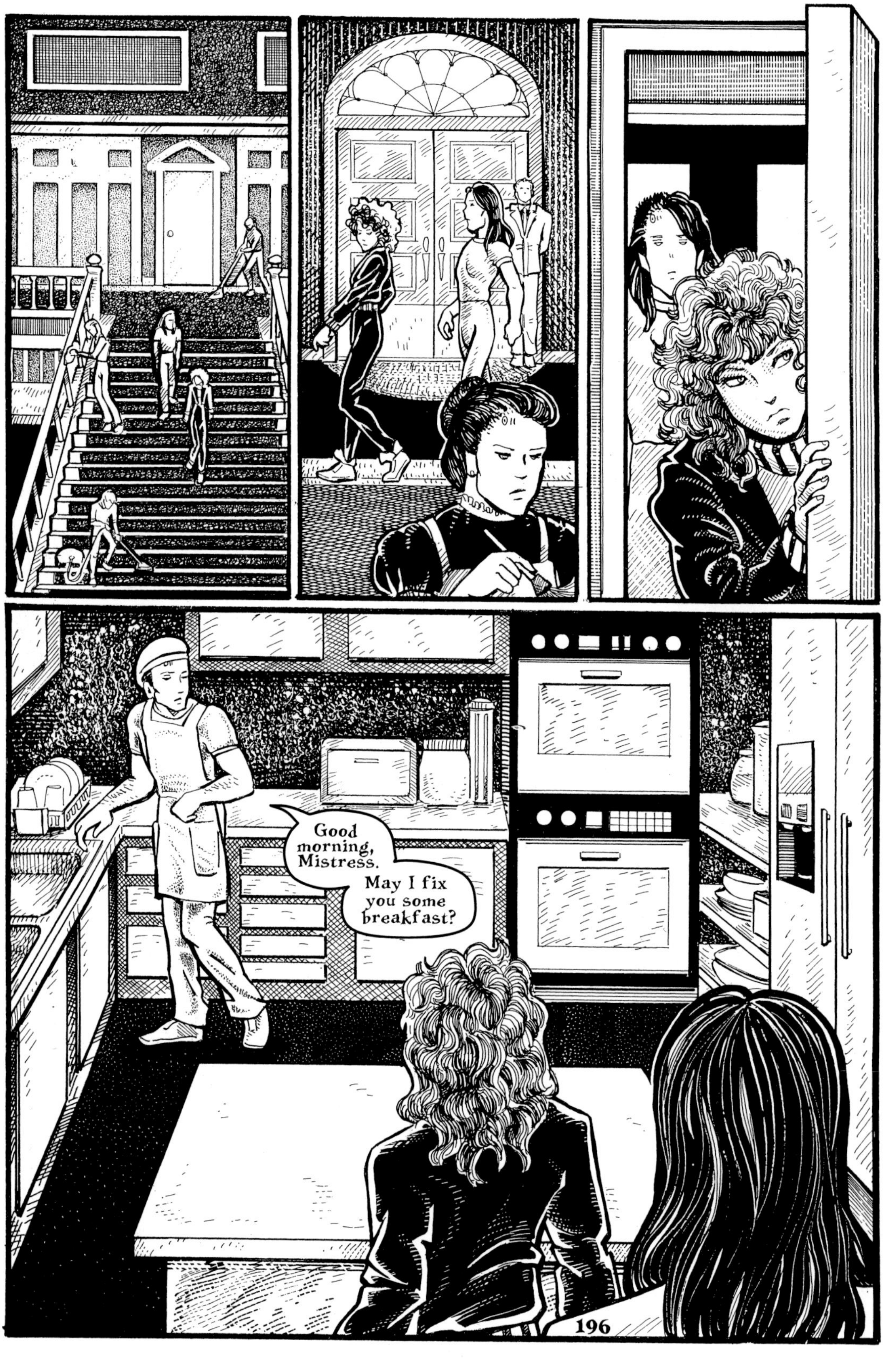
Good morning, Mistress.
May I fix you some breakfast?

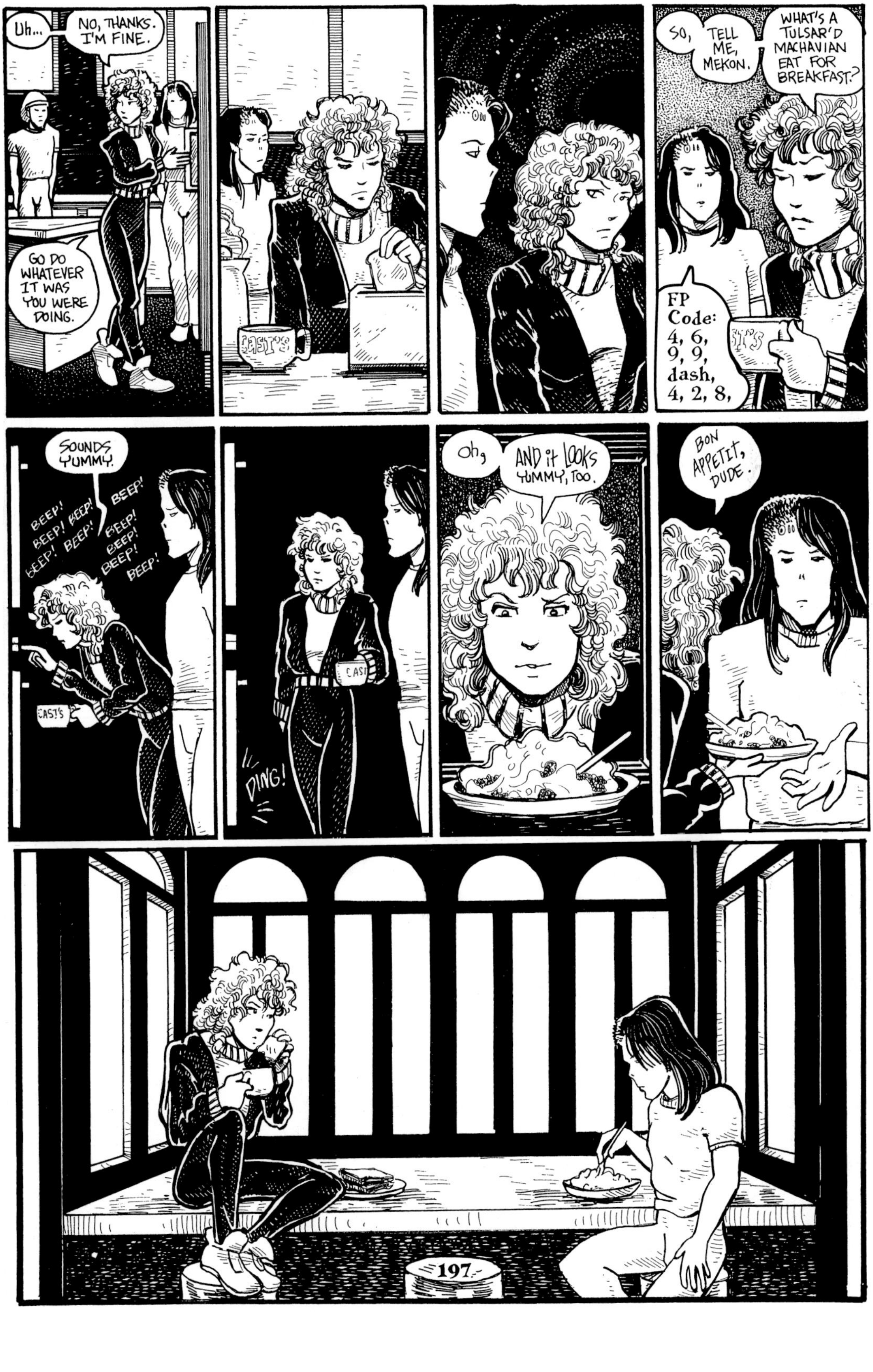

Uh...
NO, THANKS. I'M FINE.
GO DO WHATEVER IT WAS YOU WERE DOING.
SO,
TELL ME, MEKON.
WHAT'S A TULSAR'D MACHAVIAN EAT FOR BREAKFAST?
FP Code: 4, 6, 9, 9, dash, 4, 2, 8,
SOUNDS YUMMY.
BEEP! BEEP! BEEP! BEEP! BEEP! BEEP! BEEP! BEEP! BEEP! BEEP!
DING!
Oh,
AND it LOOKS YUMMY, TOO.
BON APPETIT, DUDE.

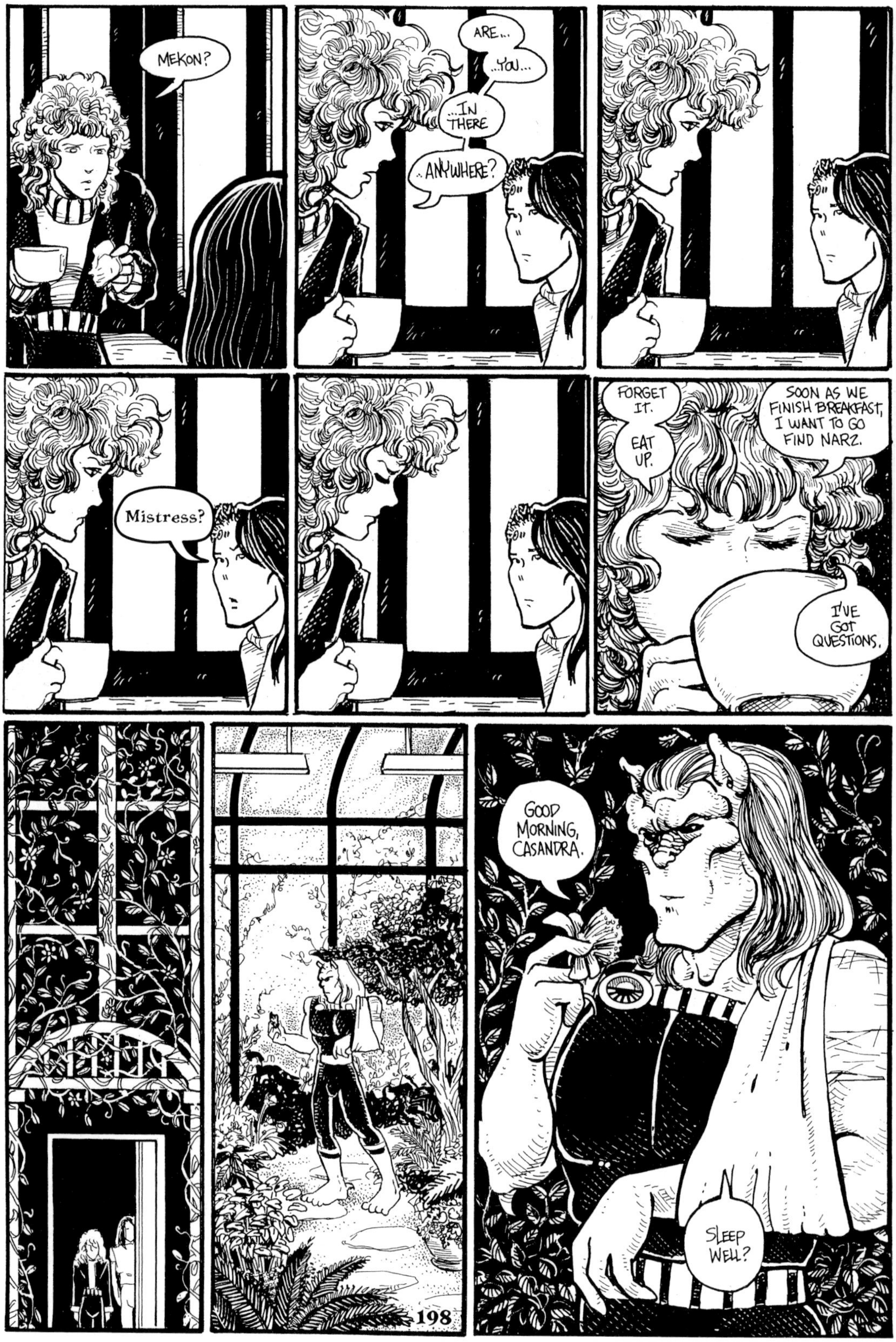

MEKON?
ARE...
...YOU...
...IN THERE
..ANYWHERE?
Mistress?
FORGET IT.
EAT UP.
SOON AS WE FINISH BREAKFAST, I WANT TO GO FIND NARZ.
I'VE GOT QUESTIONS.
GOOD MORNING, CASANDRA.
SLEEP WELL?

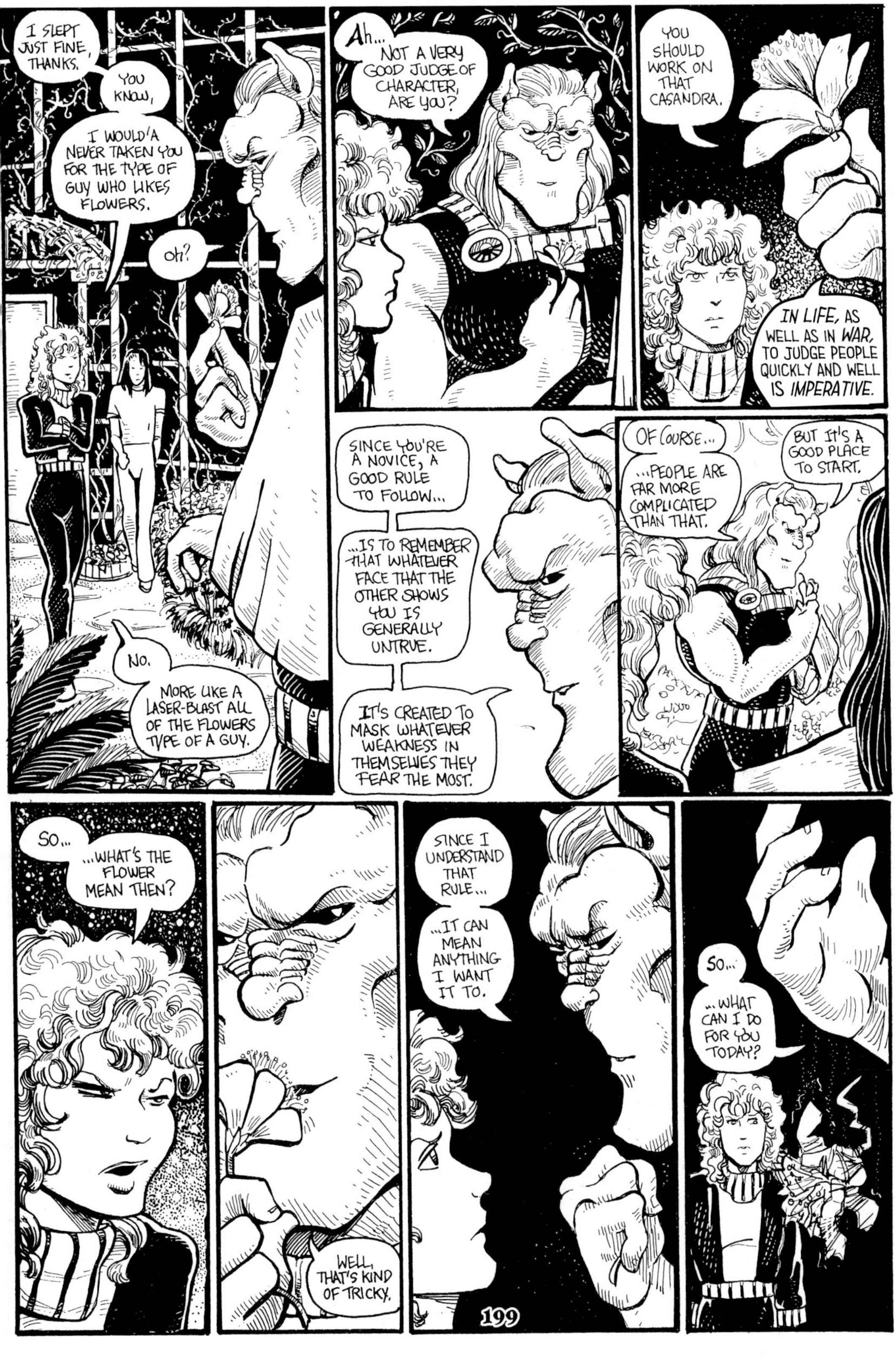
I SLEPT JUST FINE, THANKS.
YOU KNOW,
I WOULD'A NEVER TAKEN YOU FOR THE TYPE OF GUY WHO LIKES FLOWERS.
Oh?
NO.
MORE LIKE A LASER-BLAST ALL OF THE FLOWERS TYPE OF A GUY.
Ah... NOT A VERY GOOD JUDGE OF CHARACTER, ARE YOU?
YOU SHOULD WORK ON THAT CASANDRA.
IN LIFE, AS WELL AS IN WAR, TO JUDGE PEOPLE QUICKLY AND WELL IS IMPERATIVE.
SINCE YOU'RE A NOVICE, A GOOD RULE TO FOLLOW...
...IS TO REMEMBER THAT WHATEVER FACE THAT THE OTHER SHOWS YOU IS GENERALLY UNTRUE.
IT'S CREATED TO MASK WHATEVER WEAKNESS IN THEMSELVES THEY FEAR THE MOST.
OF COURSE...
...PEOPLE ARE FAR MORE COMPLICATED THAN THAT.
BUT IT'S A GOOD PLACE TO START.
SO...
...WHAT'S THE FLOWER MEAN THEN?
WELL, THAT'S KIND OF TRICKY.
SINCE I UNDERSTAND THAT RULE...
...IT CAN MEAN ANYTHING I WANT IT TO.
SO...
...WHAT CAN I DO FOR YOU TODAY?

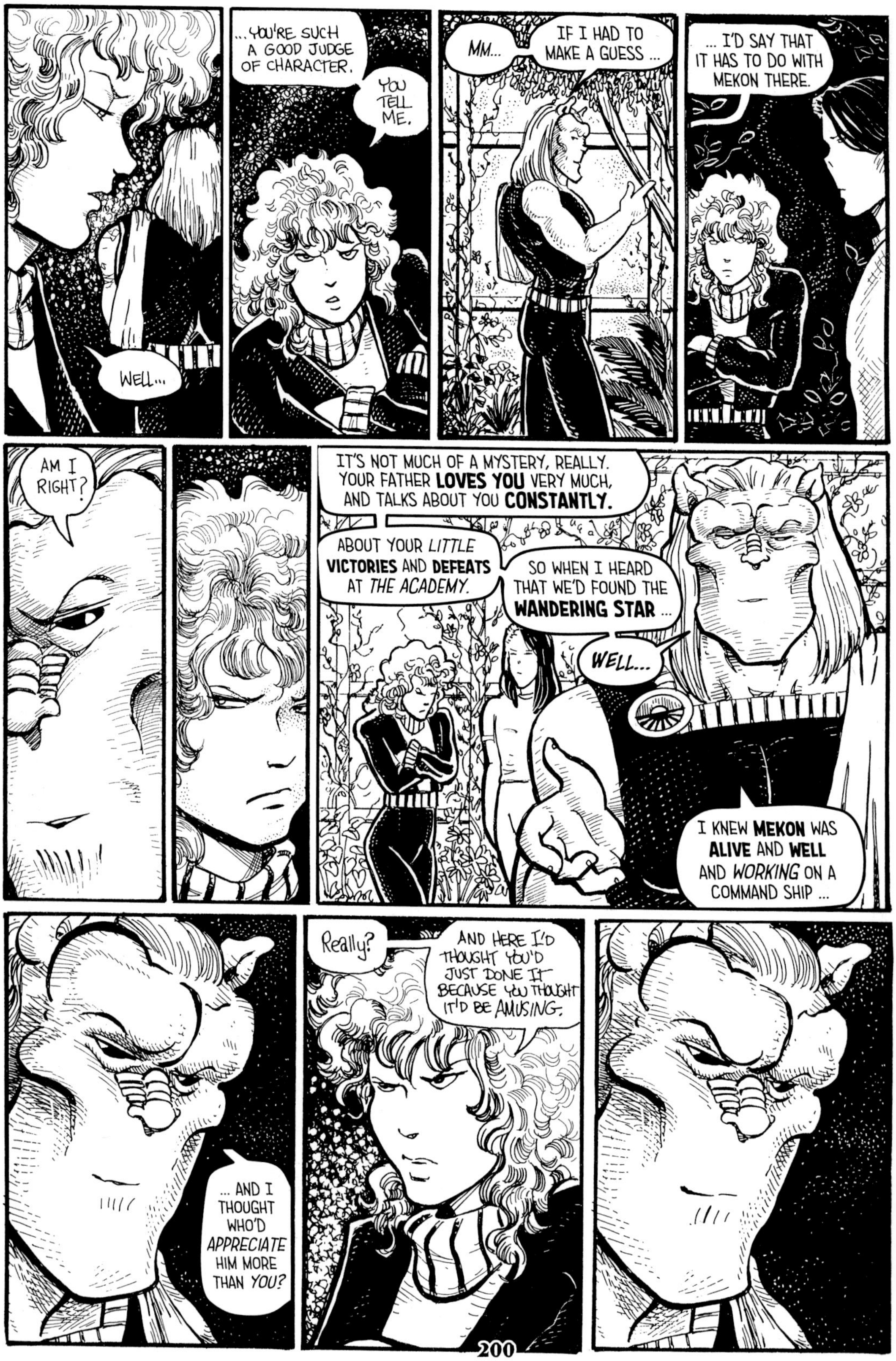

WELL...
... YOU'RE SUCH A GOOD JUDGE OF CHARACTER.
YOU TELL ME.
MM...
IF I HAD TO MAKE A GUESS ...
... I'D SAY THAT IT HAS TO DO WITH MEKON THERE.
AM I RIGHT?
IT'S NOT MUCH OF A MYSTERY, REALLY. YOUR FATHER LOVES YOU VERY MUCH, AND TALKS ABOUT YOU CONSTANTLY.
ABOUT YOUR LITTLE VICTORIES AND DEFEATS AT THE ACADEMY.
SO WHEN I HEARD THAT WE'D FOUND THE WANDERING STAR ...
WELL...
I KNEW MEKON WAS ALIVE AND WELL AND WORKING ON A COMMAND SHIP ...
... AND I THOUGHT WHO'D APPRECIATE HIM MORE THAN YOU?
Really?
AND HERE I'D THOUGHT YOU'D JUST DONE IT BECAUSE YOU THOUGHT IT'D BE AMUSING.

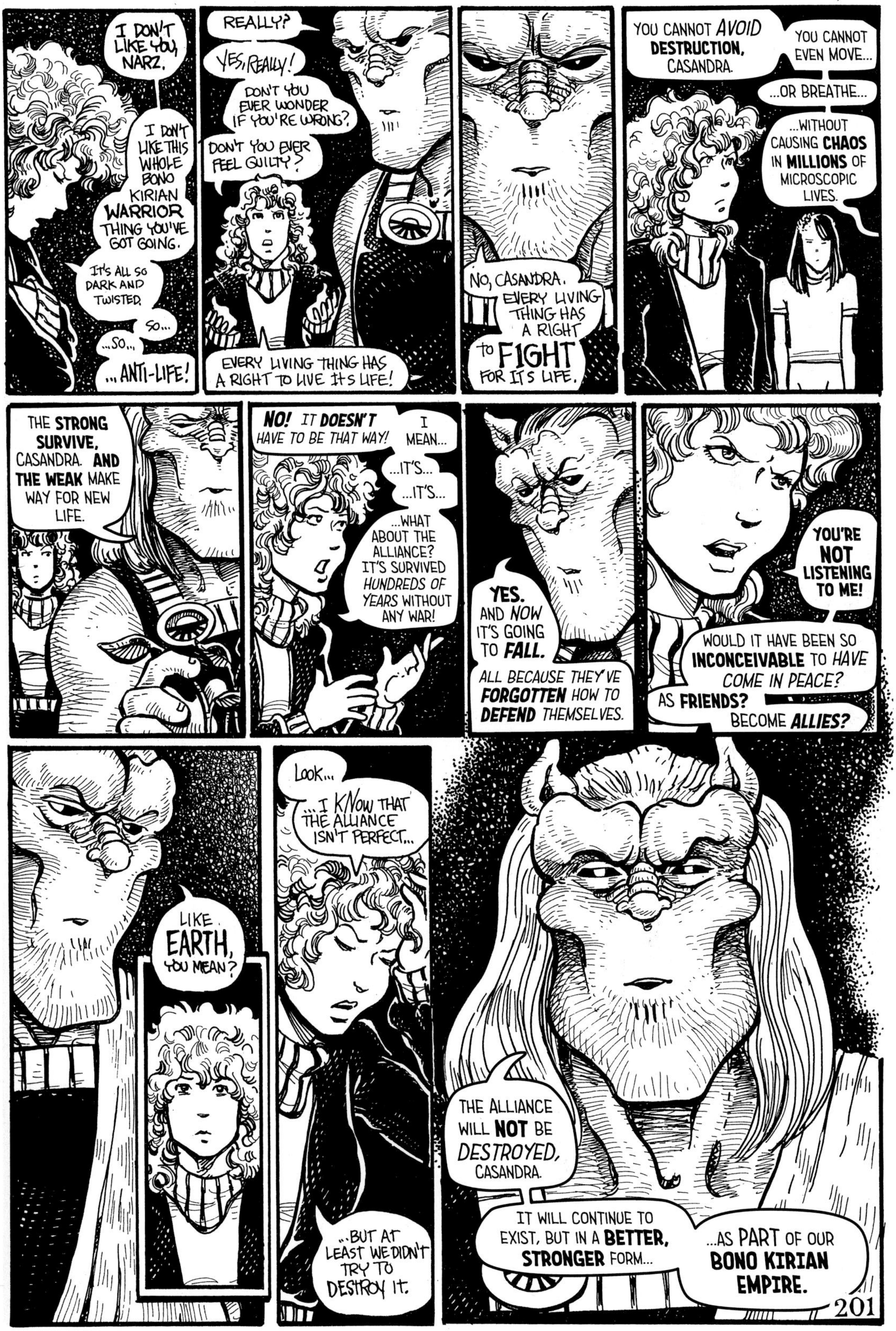
I DON'T LIKE YOU, NARZ.
I DON'T LIKE THIS WHOLE BONO KIRIAN WARRIOR THING YOU'VE GOT GOING.
IT'S ALL SO DARK AND TWISTED.
SO...
...SO...
... ANTI-LIFE!
REALLY?
YES, REALLY!
DON'T YOU EVER WONDER IF YOU'RE WRONG?
DON'T YOU EVER FEEL GUILTY?
EVERY LIVING THING HAS A RIGHT TO LIVE IT'S LIFE!
NO, CASANDRA.
EVERY LIVING THING HAS A RIGHT TO FIGHT FOR IT'S LIFE.
YOU CANNOT AVOID DESTRUCTION, CASANDRA.
YOU CANNOT EVEN MOVE...
...OR BREATHE...
...WITHOUT CAUSING CHAOS IN MILLIONS OF MICROSCOPIC LIVES.
THE STRONG SURVIVE, CASANDRA. AND THE WEAK MAKE WAY FOR NEW LIFE.
NO! IT DOESN'T HAVE TO BE THAT WAY!
I MEAN...
...IT'S...
...IT'S...
...WHAT ABOUT THE ALLIANCE? IT'S SURVIVED HUNDREDS OF YEARS WITHOUT ANY WAR!
YES. AND NOW IT'S GOING TO FALL.
ALL BECAUSE THEY'VE FORGOTTEN HOW TO DEFEND THEMSELVES.
YOU'RE NOT LISTENING TO ME!
WOULD IT HAVE BEEN SO INCONCEIVABLE TO HAVE COME IN PEACE?
AS FRIENDS?
BECOME ALLIES?
LIKE EARTH, YOU MEAN?
LOOK...
...I KNOW THAT THE ALLIANCE ISN'T PERFECT...
...BUT AT LEAST WE DIDN'T TRY TO DESTROY IT.
THE ALLIANCE WILL NOT BE DESTROYED, CASANDRA.
IT WILL CONTINUE TO EXIST, BUT IN A BETTER, STRONGER FORM...
...AS PART OF OUR BONO KIRIAN EMPIRE.

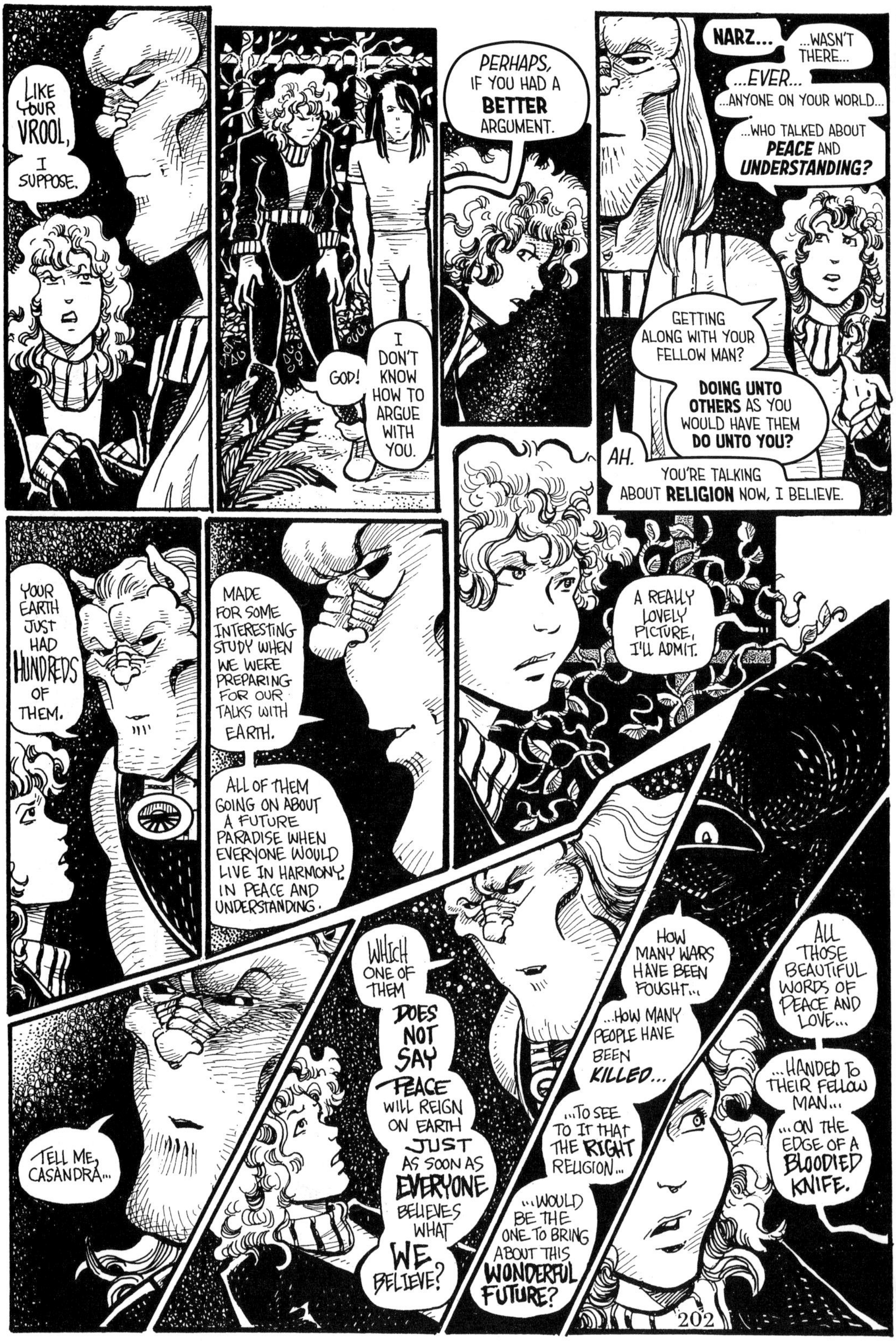
LIKE YOUR VROOL, I SUPPOSE.
GOD!
I DON'T KNOW HOW TO ARGUE WITH YOU.
PERHAPS, IF YOU HAD A BETTER ARGUMENT.
NARZ...
...WASN'T THERE...
...EVER...
...ANYONE ON YOUR WORLD...
...WHO TALKED ABOUT PEACE AND UNDERSTANDING?
GETTING ALONG WITH YOUR FELLOW MAN?
DOING UNTO OTHERS AS YOU WOULD HAVE THEM DO UNTO YOU?
AH.
YOU'RE TALKING ABOUT RELIGION NOW, I BELIEVE.
YOUR EARTH JUST HAD HUNDREDS OF THEM.
MADE FOR SOME INTERESTING STUDY WHEN WE WERE PREPARING FOR OUR TALKS WITH EARTH.
ALL OF THEM GOING ON ABOUT A FUTURE PARADISE WHEN EVERYONE WOULD LIVE IN HARMONY, IN PEACE AND UNDERSTANDING.
A REALLY LOVELY PICTURE, I'LL ADMIT.
TELL ME, CASANDRA...
WHICH ONE OF THEM DOES NOT SAY PEACE WILL REIGN ON EARTH JUST AS SOON AS EVERYONE BELIEVES WHAT WE BELIEVE?
HOW MANY WARS HAVE BEEN FOUGHT...
...HOW MANY PEOPLE HAVE BEEN KILLED...
...TO SEE TO IT THAT THE RIGHT RELIGION...
...WOULD BE THE ONE TO BRING ABOUT THIS WONDERFUL FUTURE?
ALL THOSE BEAUTIFUL WORDS OF PEACE AND LOVE...
...HANDED TO THEIR FELLOW MAN...
...ON THE EDGE OF A BLOODIED KNIFE.

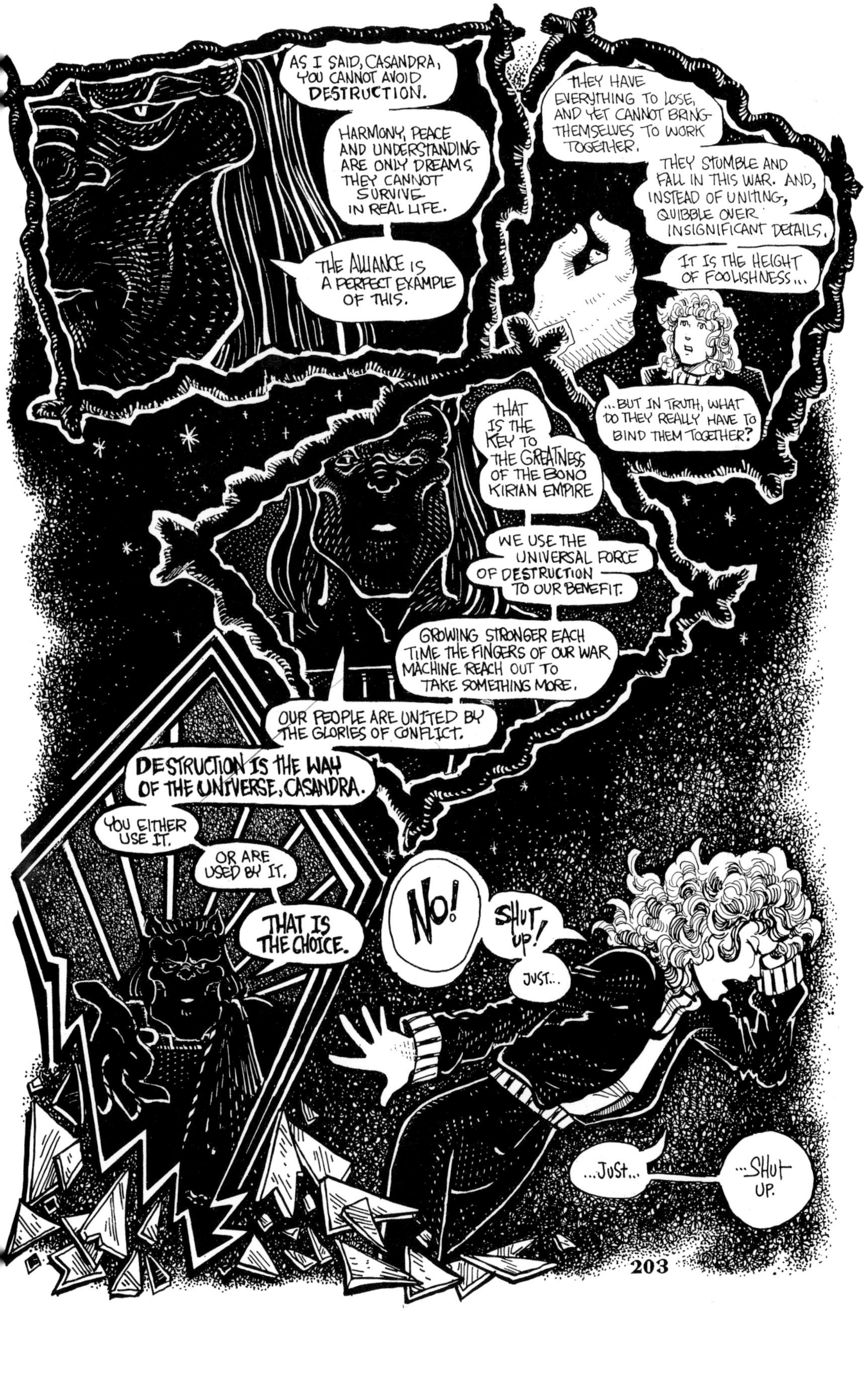
AS I SAID, CASANDRA, YOU CANNOT AVOID DESTRUCTION.
HARMONY, PEACE AND UNDERSTANDING ARE ONLY DREAMS. THEY CANNOT SURVIVE IN REAL LIFE.
THE ALLIANCE IS A PERFECT EXAMPLE OF THIS.
THEY HAVE EVERYTHING TO LOSE, AND YET CANNOT BRING THEMSELVES TO WORK TOGETHER.
THEY STUMBLE AND FALL IN THIS WAR. AND, INSTEAD OF UNITING, QUIBBLE OVER INSIGNIFICANT DETAILS.
IT IS THE HEIGHT OF FOOLISHNESS...
...BUT IN TRUTH, WHAT DO THEY REALLY HAVE TO BIND THEM TOGETHER?
THAT IS THE KEY TO THE GREATNESS OF THE BONO KIRIAN EMPIRE
WE USE THE UNIVERSAL FORCE OF DESTRUCTION TO OUR BENEFIT.
GROWING STRONGER EACH TIME THE FINGERS OF OUR WAR MACHINE REACH OUT TO TAKE SOMETHING MORE.
OUR PEOPLE ARE UNITED BY THE GLORIES OF CONFLICT.
DESTRUCTION IS THE WAY OF THE UNIVERSE, CASANDRA.
YOU EITHER USE IT.
OR ARE USED BY IT.
THAT IS THE CHOICE.
NO!
SHUT UP!
JUST...
...JUST...
...SHUT UP.

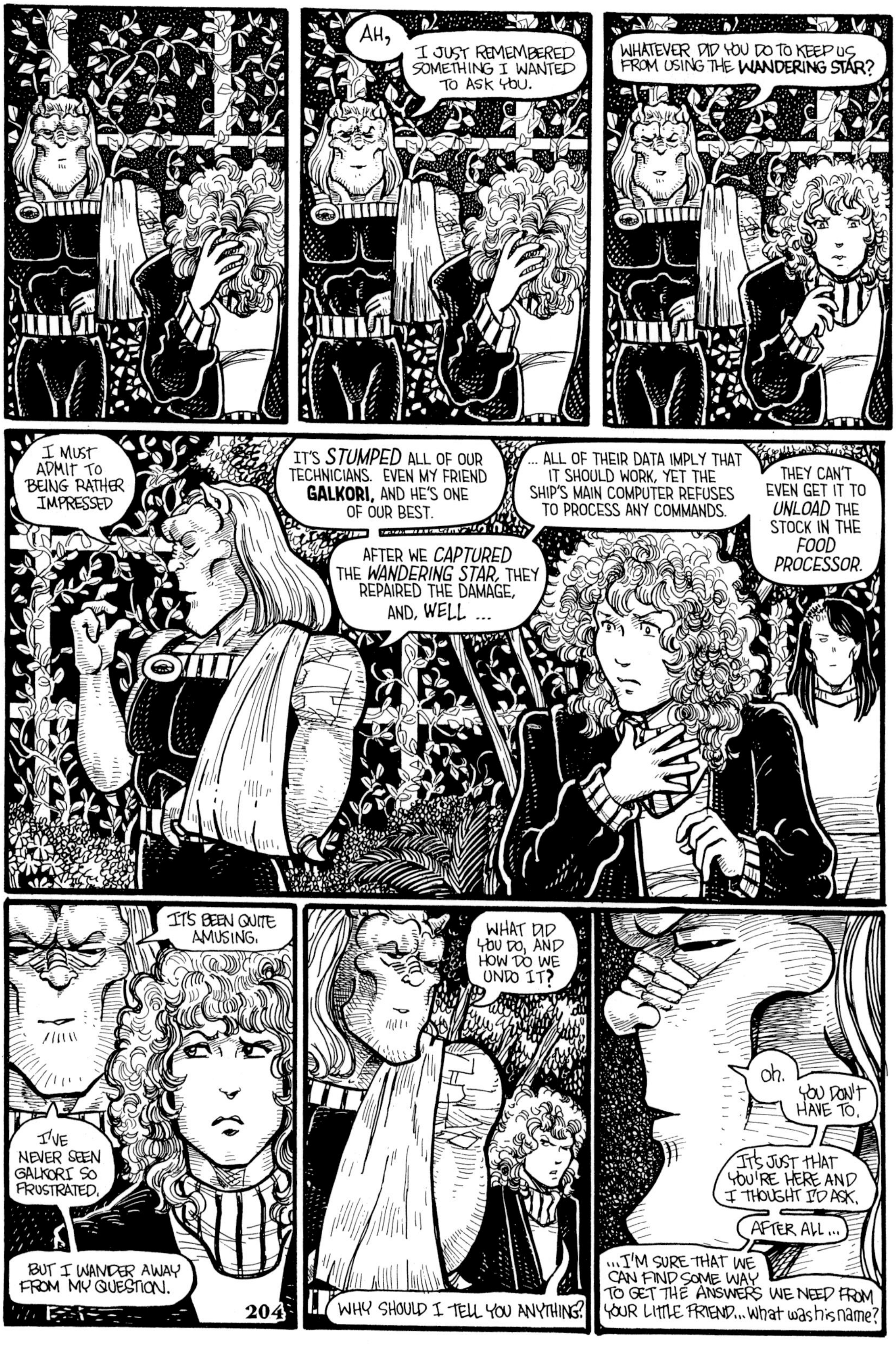
AH,
I JUST REMEMBERED SOMETHING I WANTED TO ASK YOU.
WHATEVER DID YOU DO TO KEEP US FROM USING THE WANDERING STAR?
I MUST ADMIT TO BEING RATHER IMPRESSED
IT'S STUMPED ALL OF OUR TECHNICIANS. EVEN MY FRIEND GALKORI, AND HE'S ONE OF OUR BEST.
AFTER WE CAPTURED THE WANDERING STAR, THEY REPAIRED THE DAMAGE, AND, WELL ...
... ALL OF THEIR DATA IMPLY THAT IT SHOULD WORK, YET THE SHIP'S MAIN COMPUTER REFUSES TO PROCESS ANY COMMANDS.
THEY CAN'T EVEN GET IT TO UNLOAD THE STOCK IN THE FOOD PROCESSOR.
IT'S BEEN QUITE AMUSING.
I'VE NEVER SEEN GALKORI SO FRUSTRATED.
BUT I WANDER AWAY FROM MY QUESTION.
WHAT DID YOU DO, AND HOW DO WE UNDO IT?
WHY SHOULD I TELL YOU ANYTHING?
oh.
YOU DON'T HAVE TO.
IT'S JUST THAT YOU'RE HERE AND I THOUGHT I'D ASK.
AFTER ALL ...
... I'M SURE THAT WE CAN FIND SOME WAY TO GET THE ANSWERS WE NEED FROM YOUR LITTLE FRIEND... what was his name?

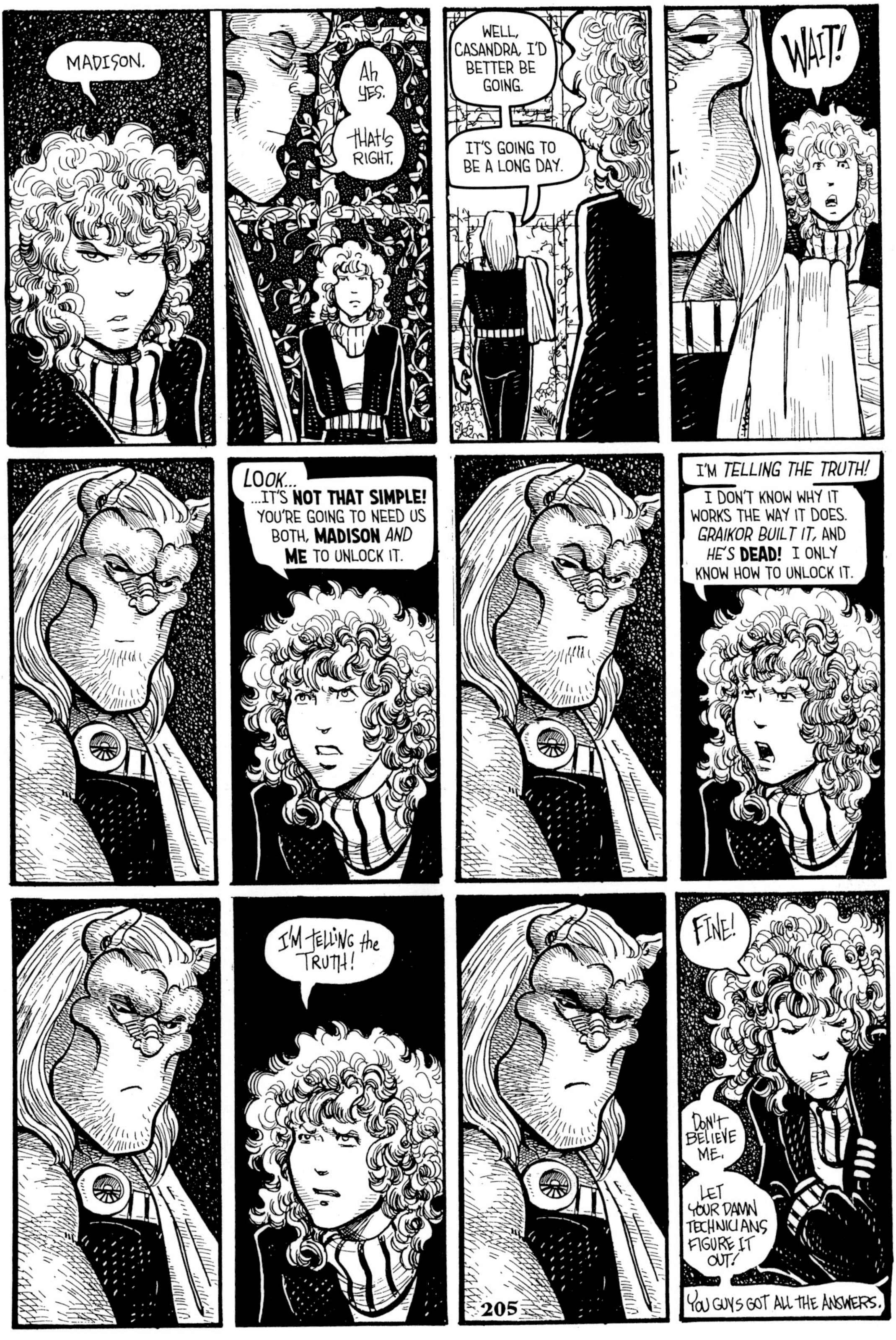
MADISON.
Ah yes.
That's right.
WELL, CASANDRA, I'D BETTER BE GOING.
IT'S GOING TO BE A LONG DAY.
WAIT!
LOOK... ...IT'S NOT THAT SIMPLE! YOU'RE GOING TO NEED US BOTH, MADISON AND ME TO UNLOCK IT.
I'M TELLING THE TRUTH!
I DON'T KNOW WHY IT WORKS THE WAY IT DOES. GRAIKOR BUILT IT, AND HE'S DEAD! I ONLY KNOW HOW TO UNLOCK IT.
I'M TELLING the TRUTH!
FINE!
DON'T BELIEVE ME.
LET YOUR DAMN TECHNICIANS FIGURE IT OUT!
YOU GUYS GOT ALL THE ANSWERS.

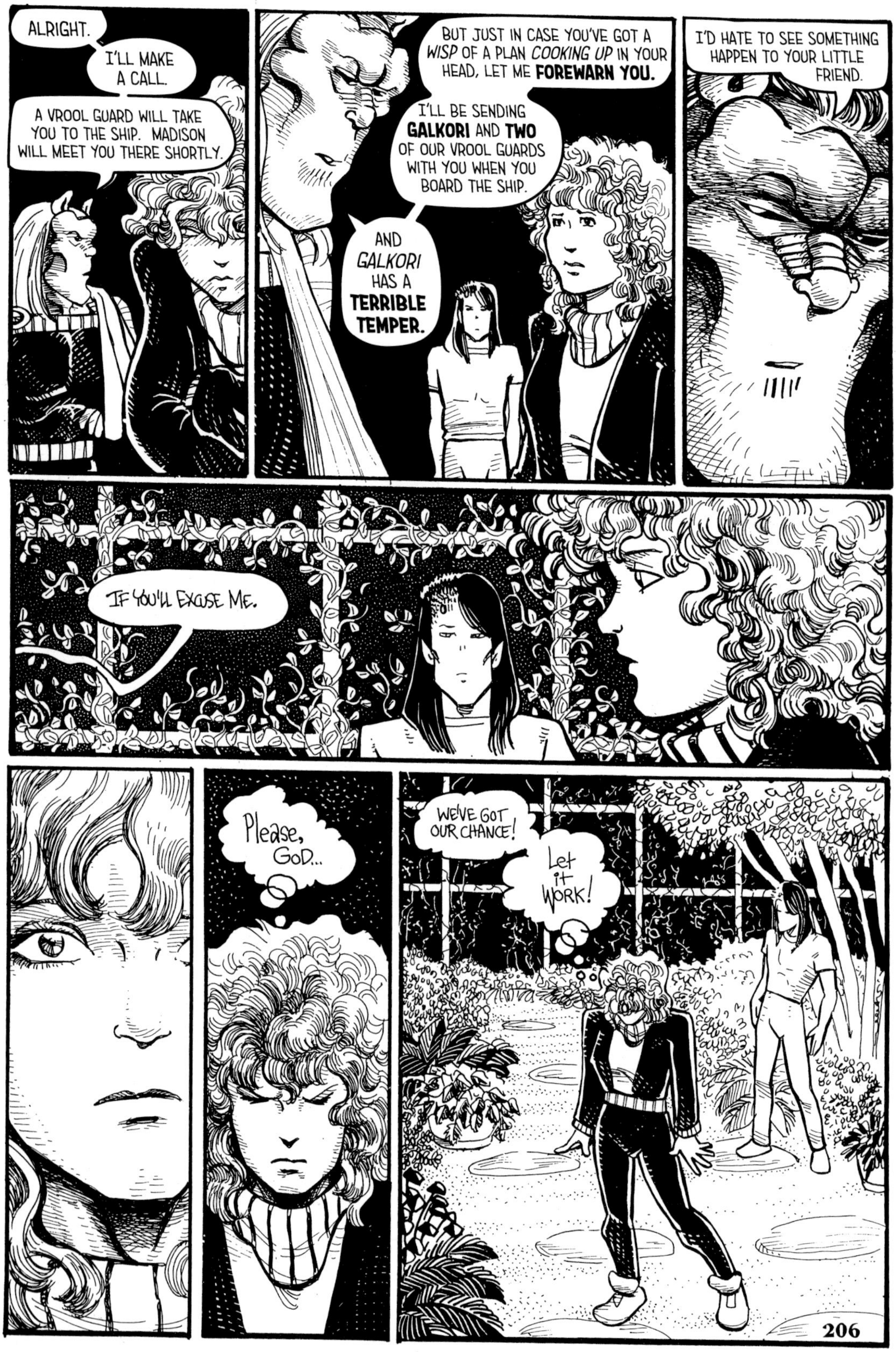

ALRIGHT.
I'LL MAKE A CALL.
A VROOL GUARD WILL TAKE YOU TO THE SHIP. MADISON WILL MEET YOU THERE SHORTLY.
BUT JUST IN CASE YOU'VE GOT A WISP OF A PLAN COOKING UP IN YOUR HEAD, LET ME FOREWARN YOU.
I'LL BE SENDING GALKORI AND TWO OF OUR VROOL GUARDS WITH YOU WHEN YOU BOARD THE SHIP.
AND GALKORI HAS A TERRIBLE TEMPER.
I'D HATE TO SEE SOMETHING HAPPEN TO YOUR LITTLE FRIEND.
IF YOU'LL EXCUSE ME.
Please, GOD...
WE'VE GOT OUR CHANCE!
Let it WORK!

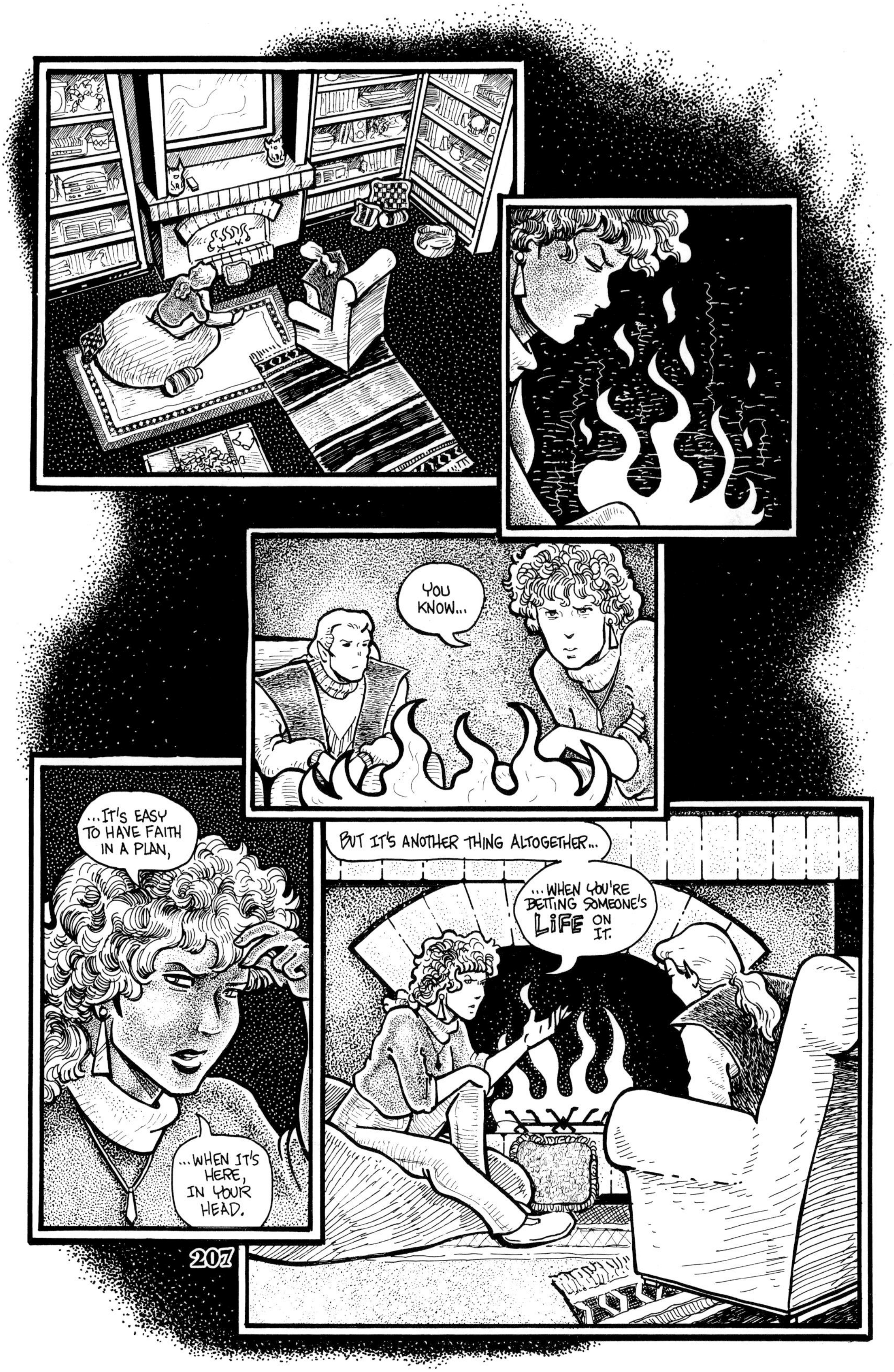
YOU KNOW...
...IT'S EASY TO HAVE FAITH IN A PLAN,
...WHEN IT'S HERE, IN YOUR HEAD.
BUT IT'S ANOTHER THING ALTOGETHER...
...WHEN YOU'RE BETTING SOMEONE'S LIFE ON IT.

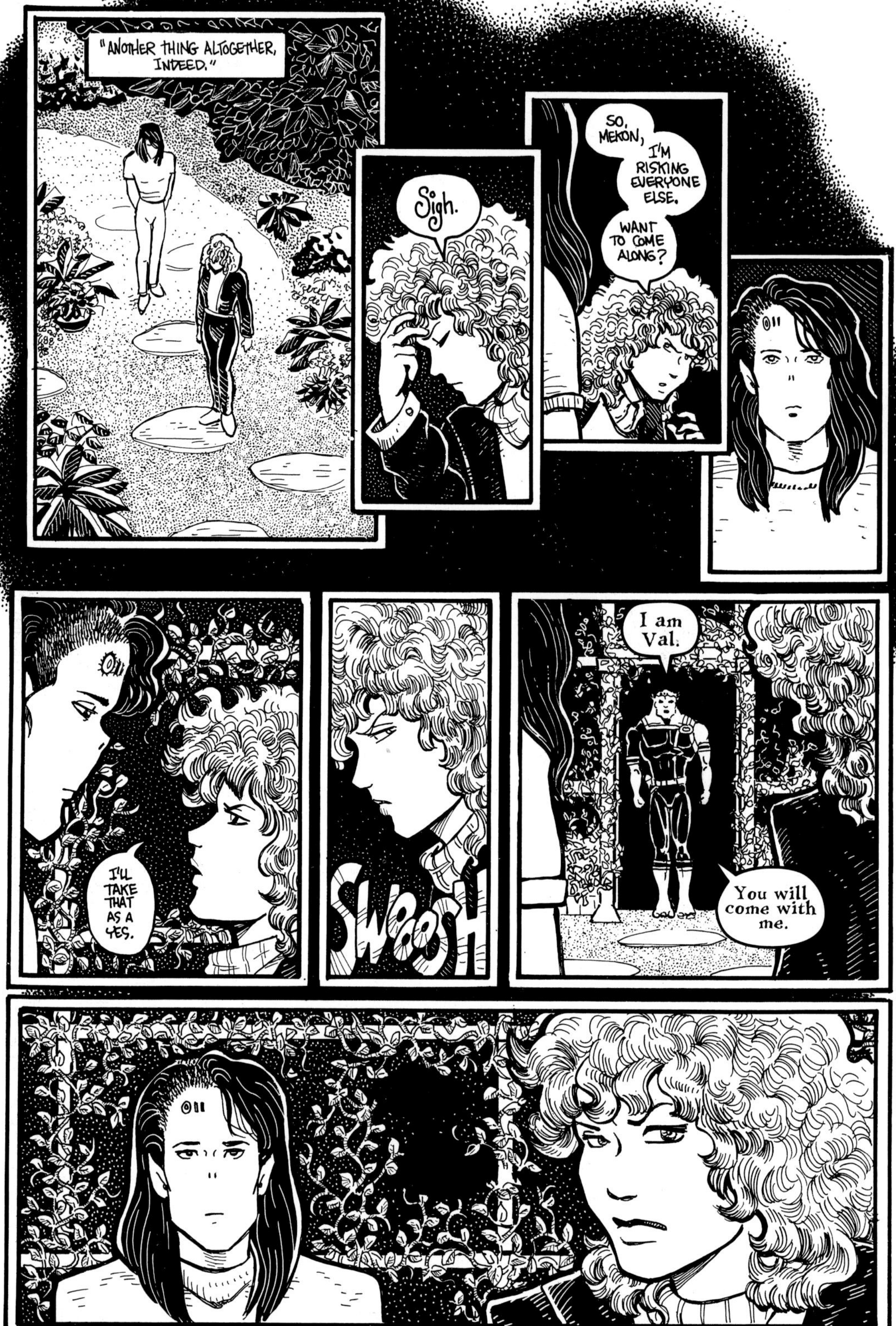
"ANOTHER THING ALTOGETHER, INDEED."
Sigh.
SO, MEKON, I'M RISKING EVERYONE ELSE.
WANT TO COME ALONG?
I'LL TAKE THAT AS A YES.
SWOOSH
I am Val.
You will come with me.

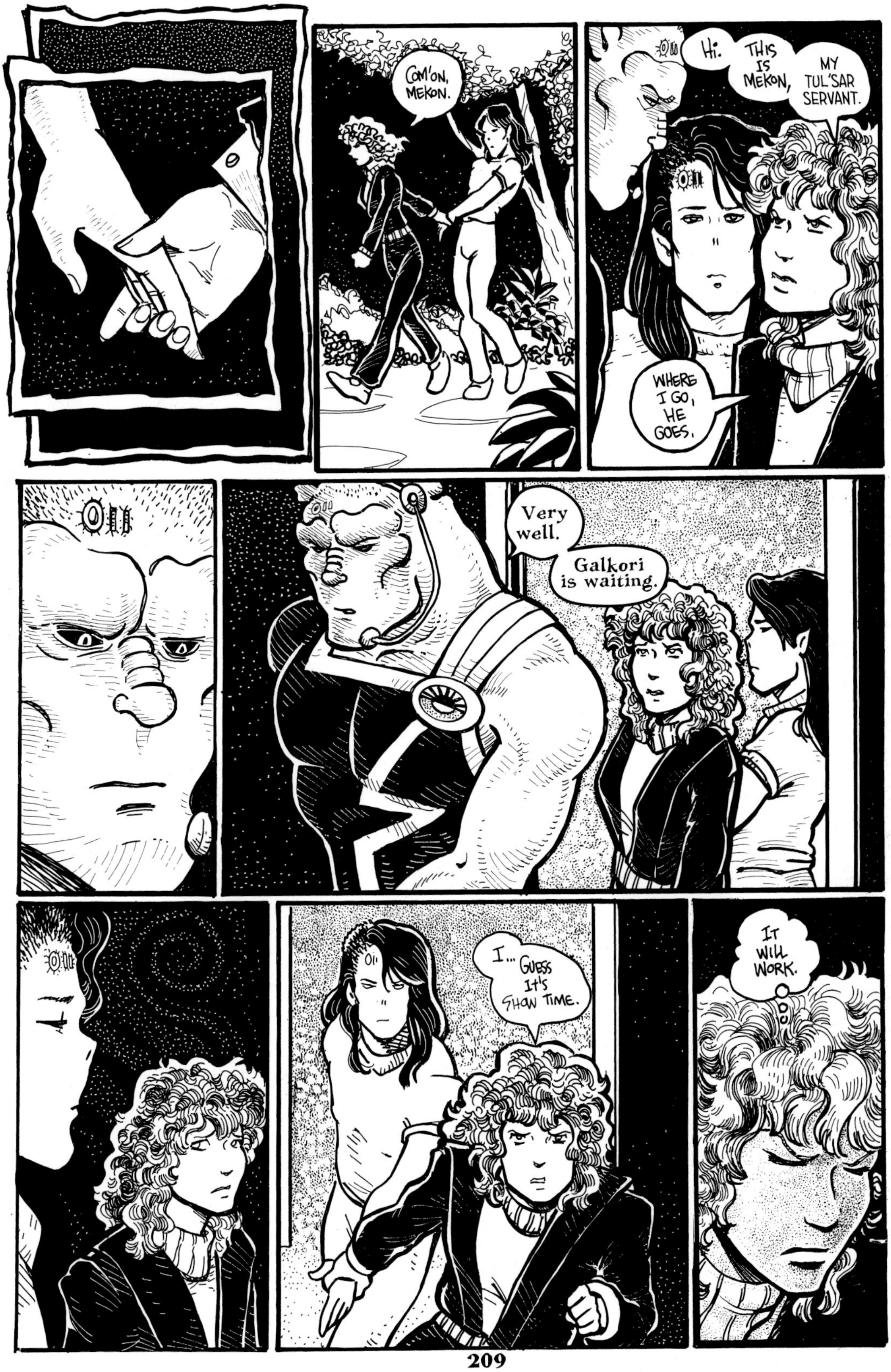
COM'ON, MEKON.
Hi.
THIS IS MEKON,
MY TUL'SAR SERVANT.
WHERE I GO, HE GOES.
Very well.
Galkori is waiting.
I... GUESS IT'S SHOW TIME.
IT WILL WORK.

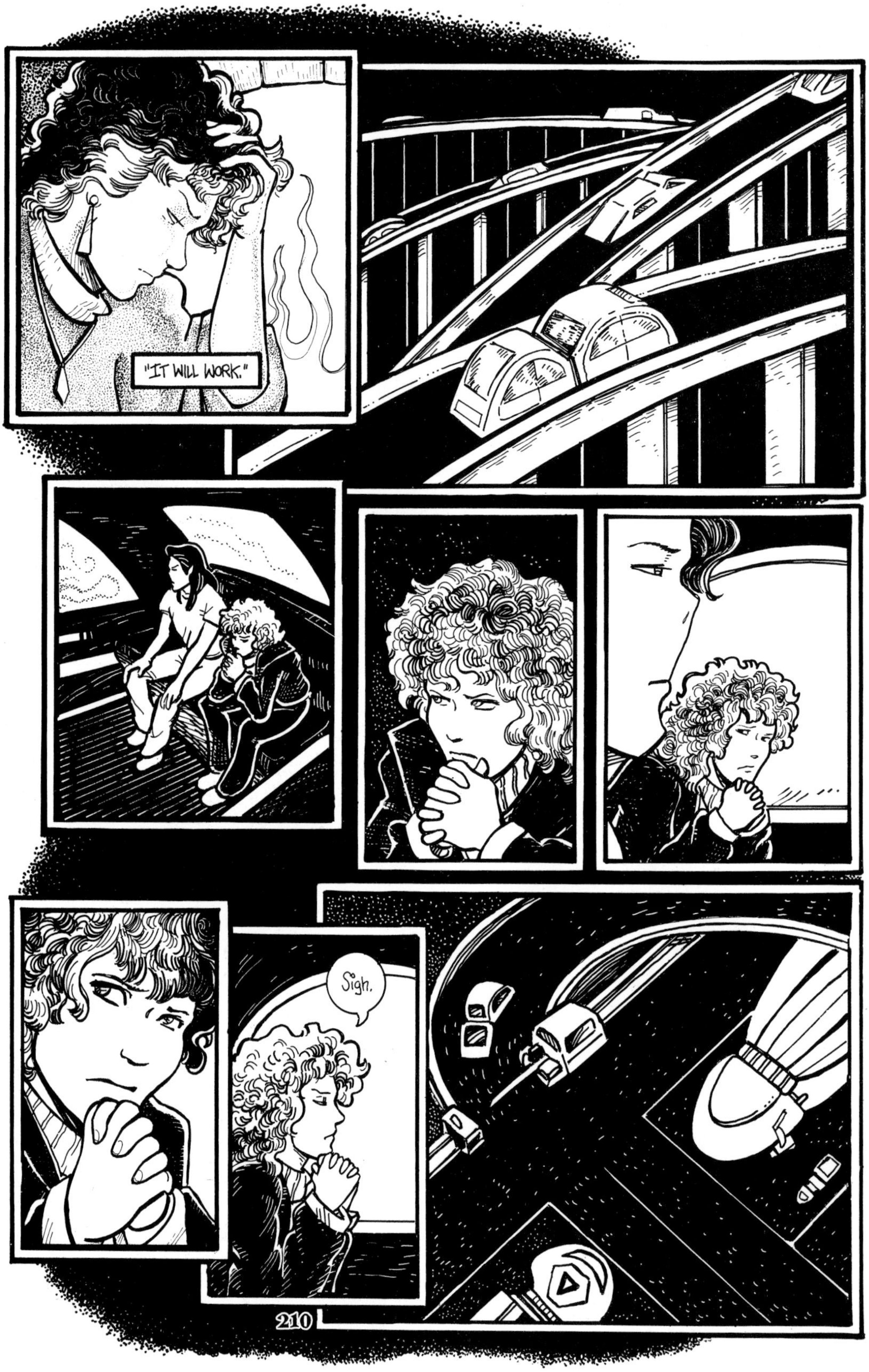
"IT WILL WORK."
Sigh.

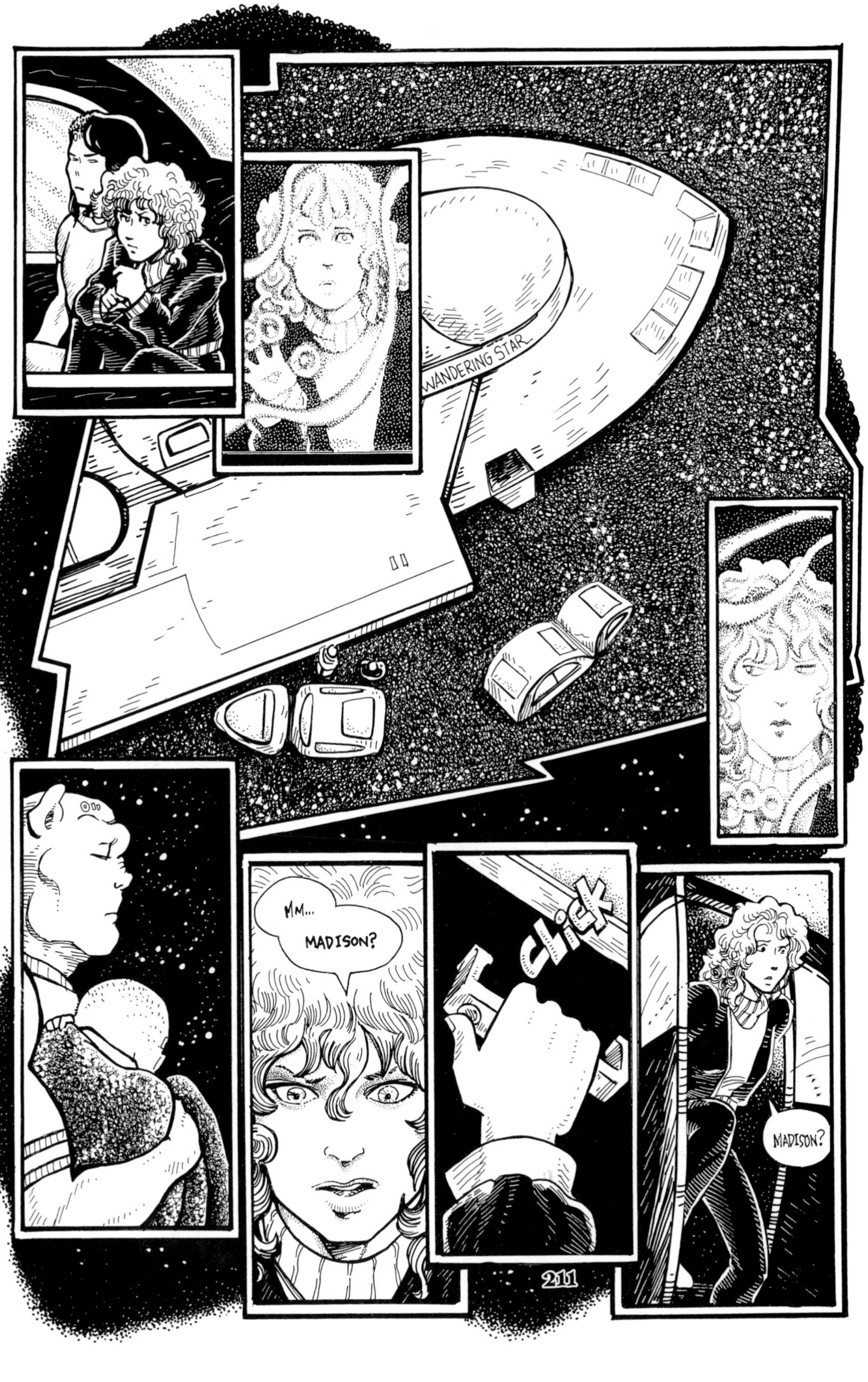
WANDERING STAR
MM... MADISON?
CLICK
MADISON?

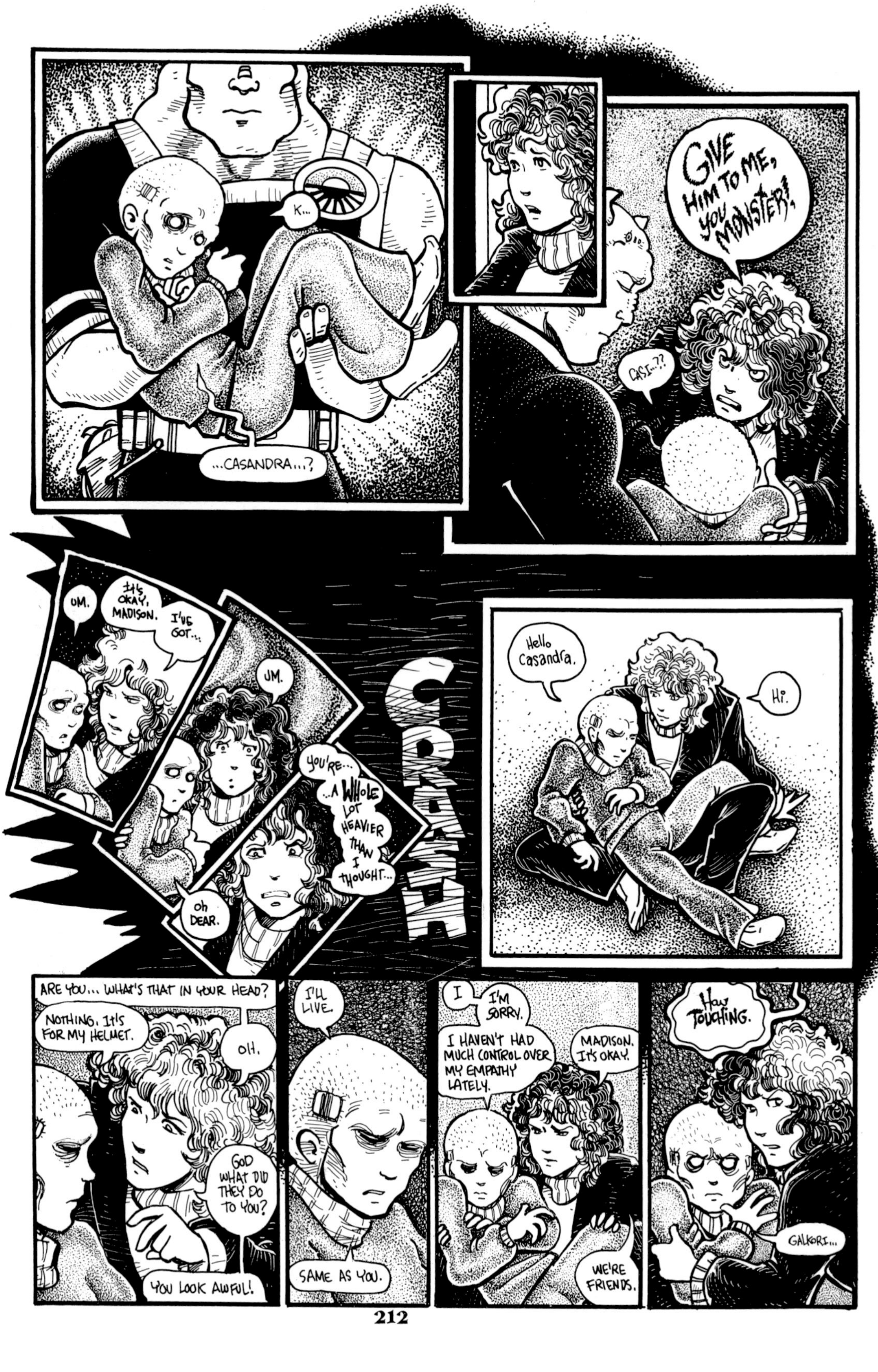
K...
...CASANDRA...?
GIVE HIM TO ME, YOU MONSTER!
CASI...??
UM.
It's OKAY, MADISON. I'VE GOT...
UM.
YOU'RE... ...A WHOLE LOT HEAVIER THAN I THOUGHT...
Oh DEAR.
CRASH
Hello Casandra.
Hi.
ARE YOU... WHAT'S THAT IN YOUR HEAD?
NOTHING. It's FOR MY HELMET.
OH.
GOD WHAT DID THEY DO TO YOU?
YOU LOOK AWFUL!
I'LL LIVE.
SAME AS YOU.
I
I'M SORRY.
I HAVEN'T HAD MUCH CONTROL OVER MY EMPATHY LATELY.
MADISON. It's OKAY.
WE'RE FRIENDS.
How TOUCHING.
GALKORI...

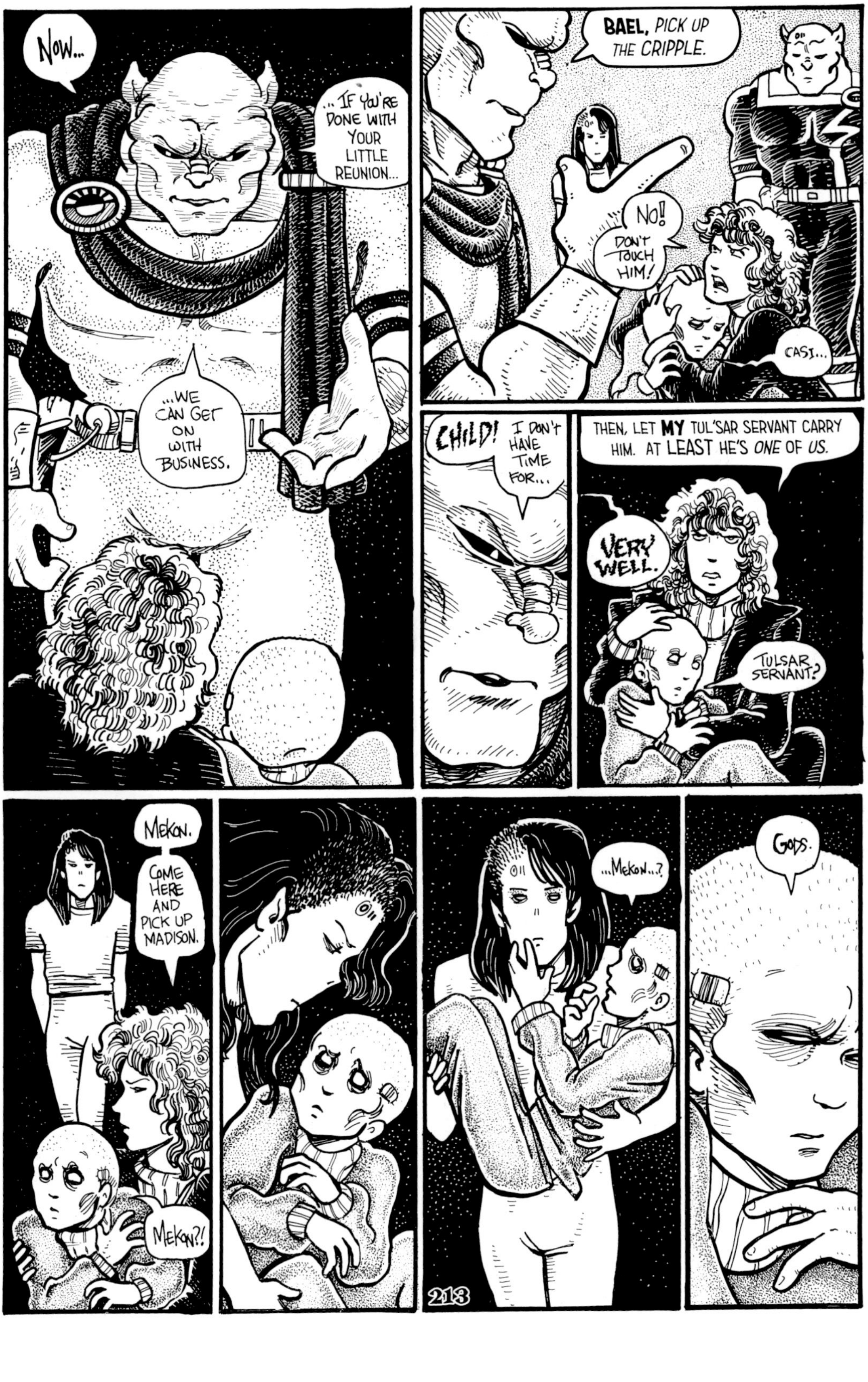
Now...
...If you're done with your little reunion...
...we can get on with business.
Bael, pick up the cripple.
No!! Don't touch him!
Casi...
Child! I don't have time for...
Then, let my Tul'sar servant carry him. At least he's one of us.
Very well.
Tulsar servant?
Mekon.
Come here and pick up Madison.
Mekon?!
...Mekon..?
Gods.

IT'S... A LONG STORY.

ENOUGH! WE HAVE **BUSINESS** TO ATTEND TO! *LET'S GO!*

OH, AND **PLEASE**... ...DO NOT FORGET WHO'S IN CHARGE.

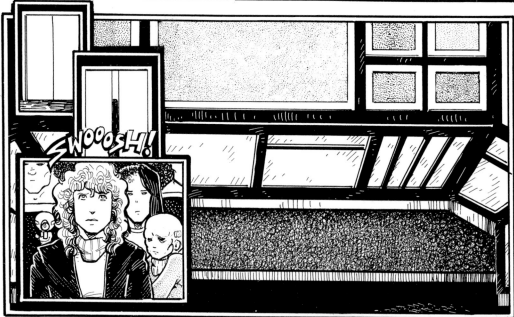

SWOOOSH!

CHILD, GET ON WITH IT!

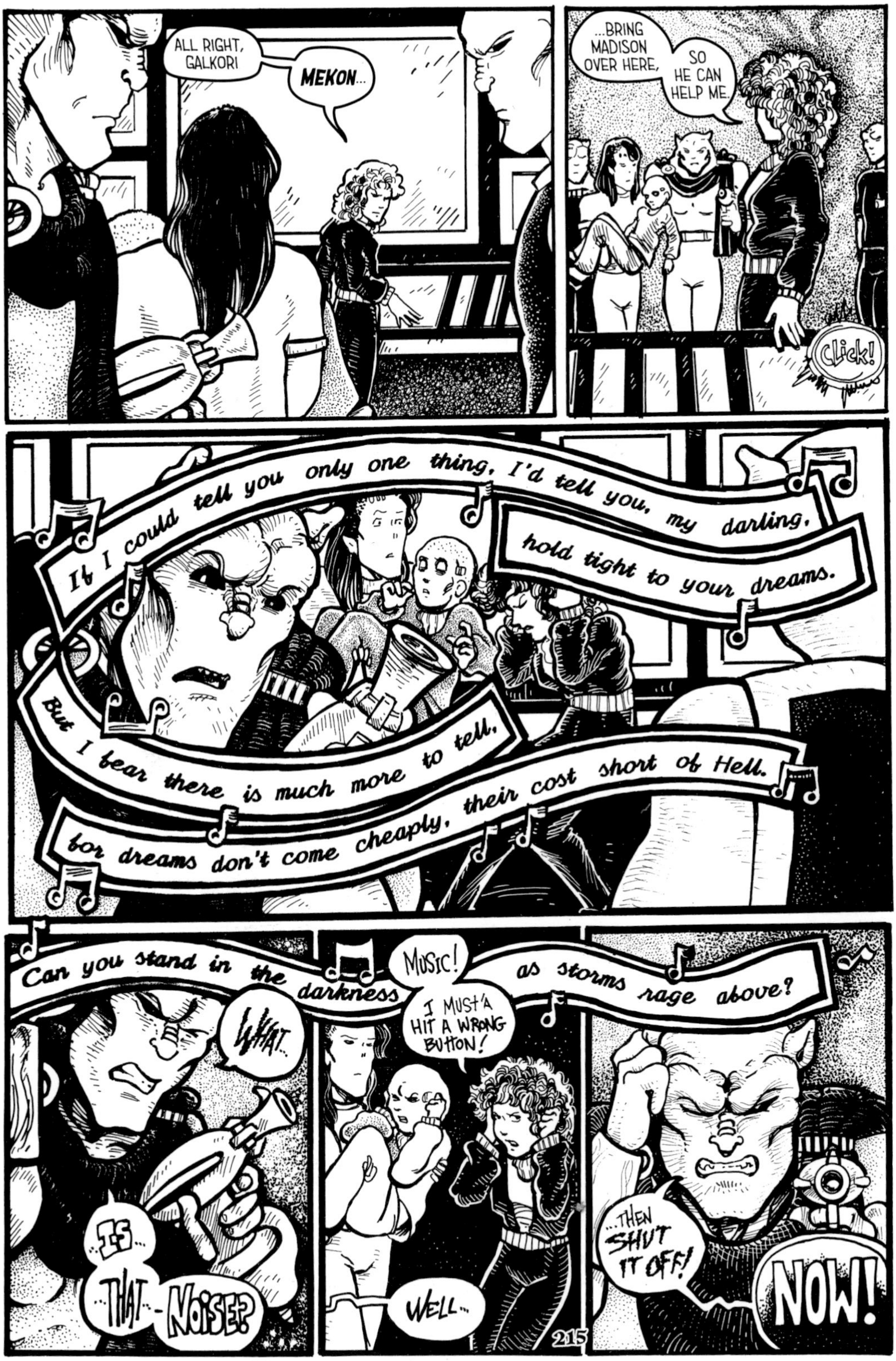
ALL RIGHT, GALKORI
MEKON...
...BRING MADISON OVER HERE,
SO HE CAN HELP ME.
Click!
If I could tell you only one thing, I'd tell you, my darling,
hold tight to your dreams.
But I fear there is much more to tell,
for dreams don't come cheaply, their cost short of Hell.
Can you stand in the darkness as storms rage above?
WHAT...
IS... THAT - NOISE?
MUSIC!
I MUST'A HIT A WRONG BUTTON!
WELL...
...THEN SHUT IT OFF!
NOW!

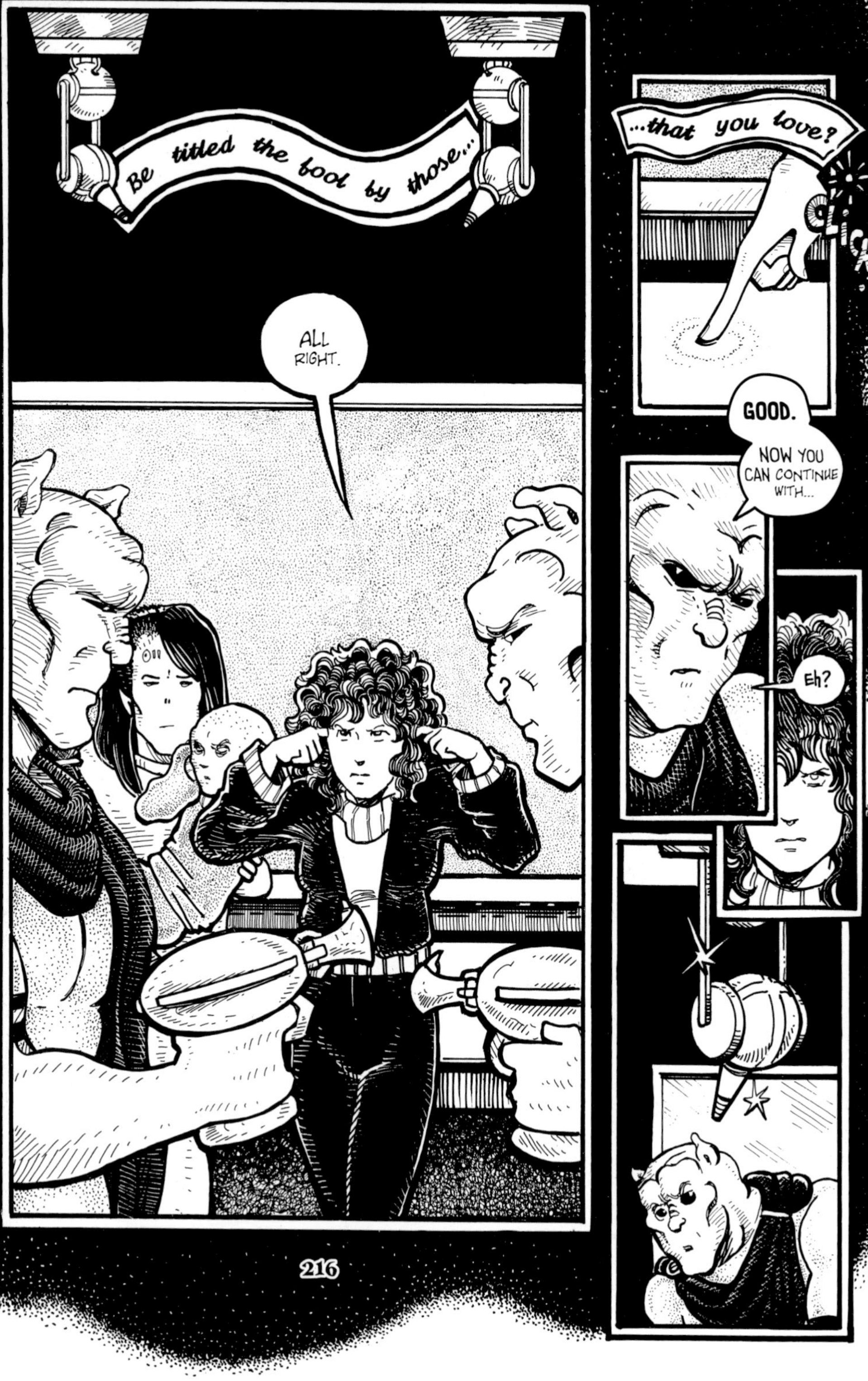
Be titled the fool by those...
ALL RIGHT.
...that you love?
CLICK!
GOOD.
NOW YOU CAN CONTINUE WITH...
Eh?

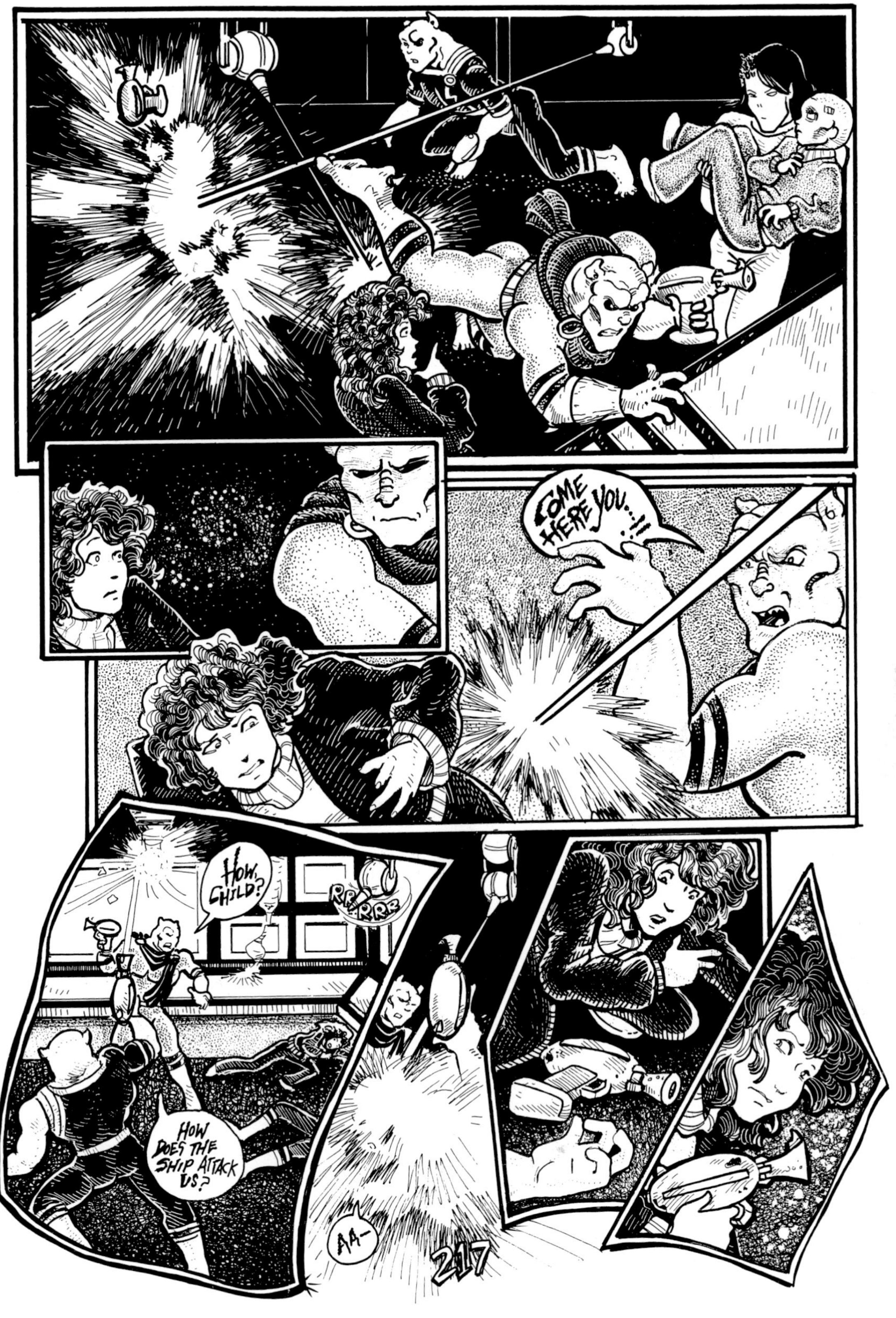
COME HERE YOU...!!
HOW, CHILD?
RRRRRR
HOW DOES THE SHIP ATTACK US?
AA-

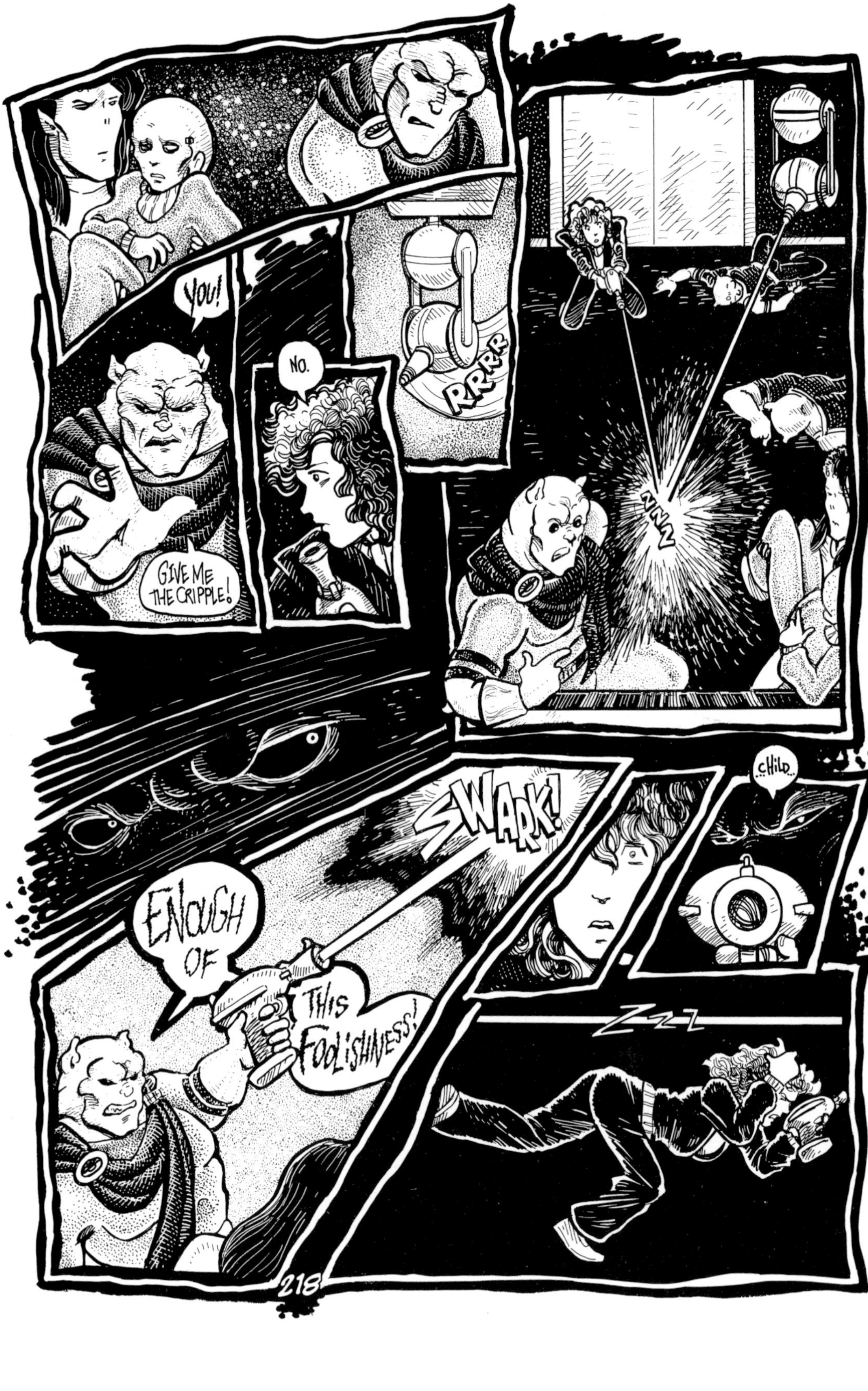
YOU!
NO.
RRRR
GIVE ME THE CRIPPLE!
ZZZZ
SWARK!
ENOUGH OF
THIS FOOLISHNESS!
..CHILD..
ZZZZ

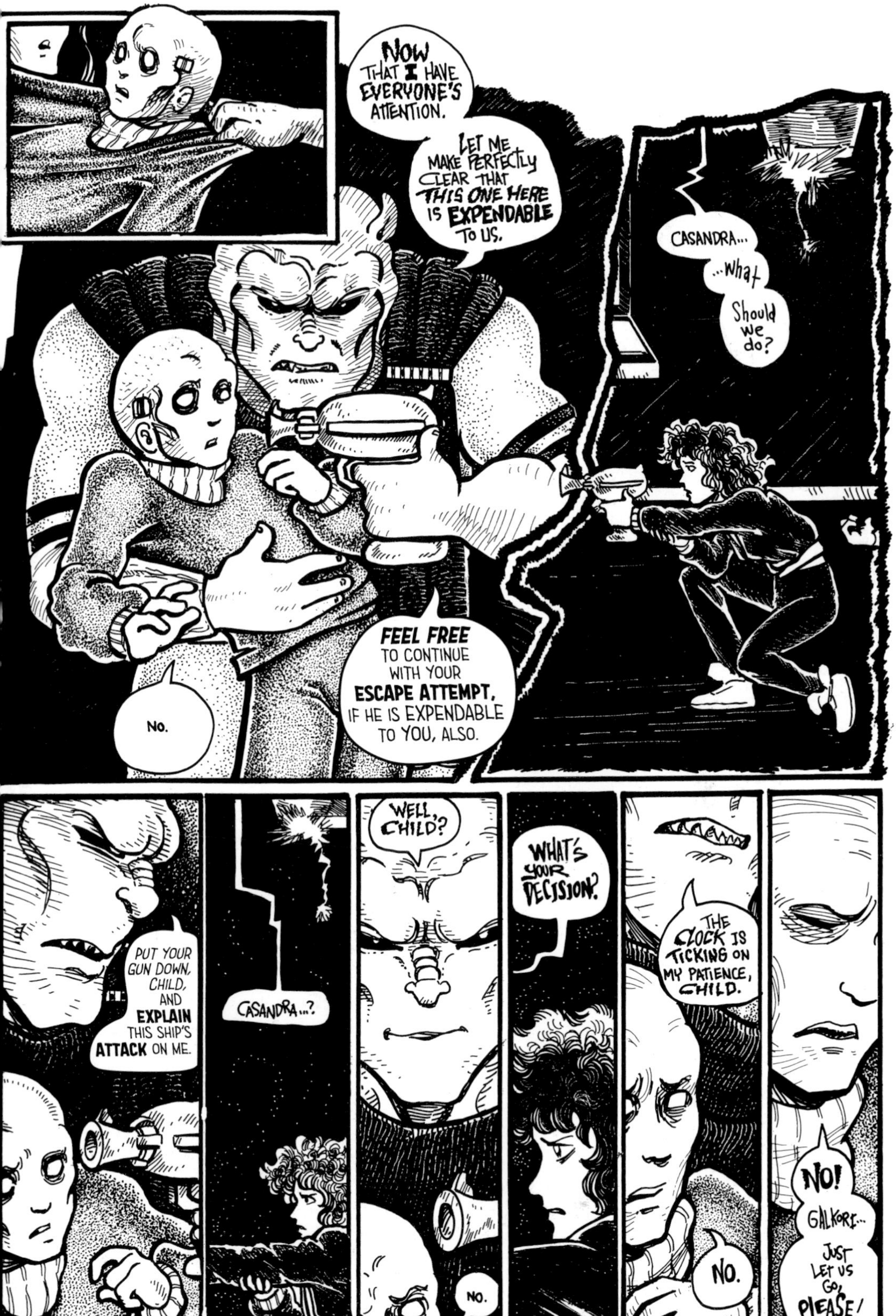
NOW THAT I HAVE EVERYONE'S ATTENTION.
LET ME MAKE PERFECTLY CLEAR THAT THIS ONE HERE IS EXPENDABLE TO US.
CASANDRA... ...what Should we do?
FEEL FREE TO CONTINUE WITH YOUR ESCAPE ATTEMPT, IF HE IS EXPENDABLE TO YOU, ALSO.
NO.
PUT YOUR GUN DOWN, CHILD, AND EXPLAIN THIS SHIP'S ATTACK ON ME.
CASANDRA...?
WELL, CHILD?
NO.
WHAT'S YOUR DECISION?
THE CLOCK IS TICKING ON MY PATIENCE, CHILD.
NO.
NO!
GALKORI...
JUST LET US GO, PLEASE!

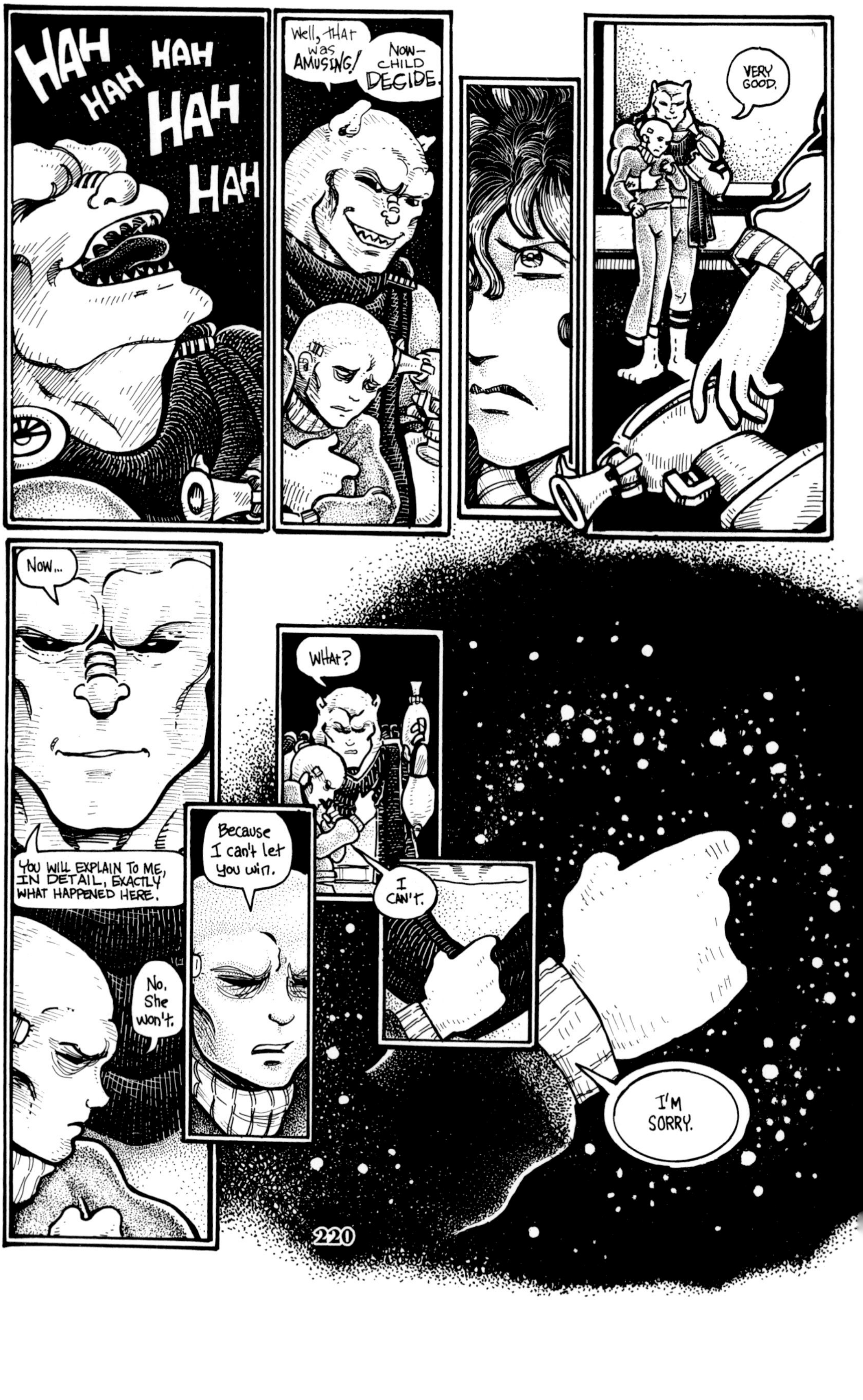
HAH HAH HAH HAH HAH HAH
Well, THAT was AMUSING!
NOW-CHILD DECIDE.
VERY GOOD.
Now...
YOU WILL EXPLAIN TO ME, IN DETAIL, EXACTLY WHAT HAPPENED HERE.
No, She won't.
Because I can't let you win.
WHAT?
I CAN'T.
I'M SORRY.

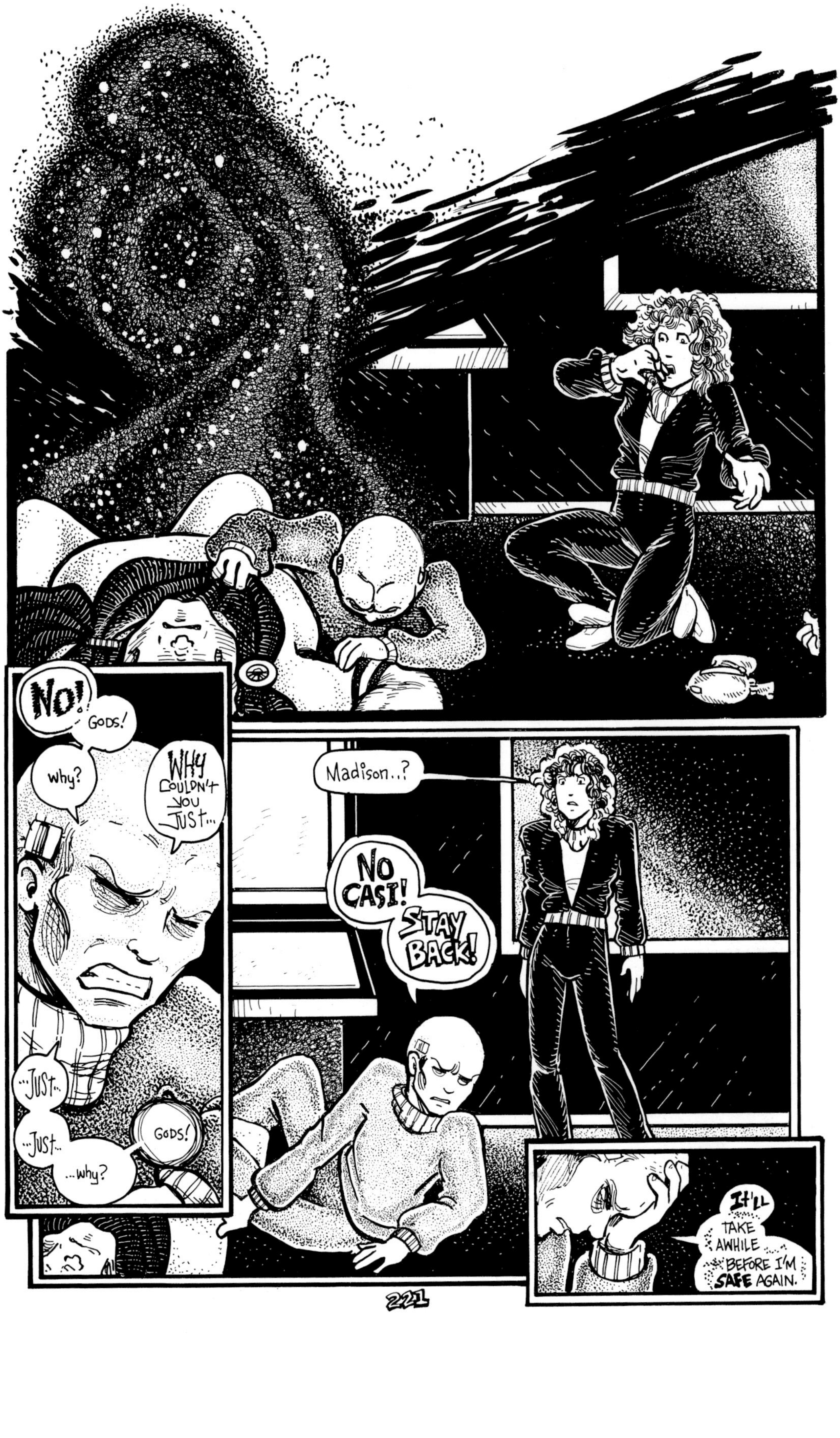
NO!
GODS!
why?
WHY COULDN'T YOU JUST...
...JUST...
...JUST...
GODS!
...why?
Madison..?
NO CASI! STAY BACK!
IT'LL TAKE AWHILE BEFORE I'M SAFE AGAIN.

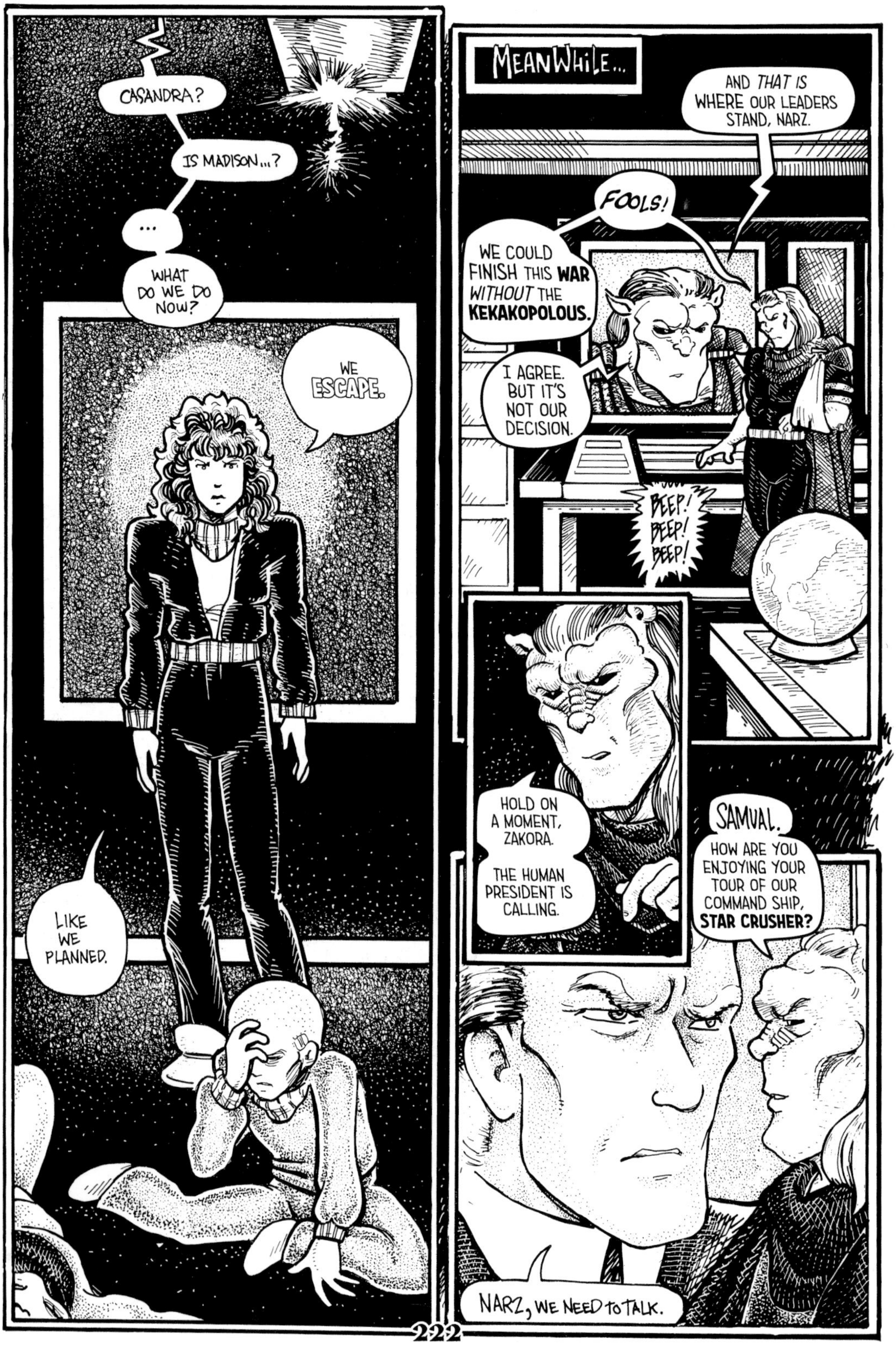
CASANDRA?
IS MADISON...?
...
WHAT DO WE DO NOW?
WE ESCAPE.
LIKE WE PLANNED.
MEANWHILE...
AND THAT IS WHERE OUR LEADERS STAND, NARZ.
FOOLS!
WE COULD FINISH THIS WAR WITHOUT THE KEKAKOPOLOUS.
I AGREE. BUT IT'S NOT OUR DECISION.
BEEP! BEEP! BEEP!
HOLD ON A MOMENT, ZAKORA.
THE HUMAN PRESIDENT IS CALLING.
SAMUAL.
HOW ARE YOU ENJOYING YOUR TOUR OF OUR COMMAND SHIP, STAR CRUSHER?
NARZ, WE NEED TO TALK.

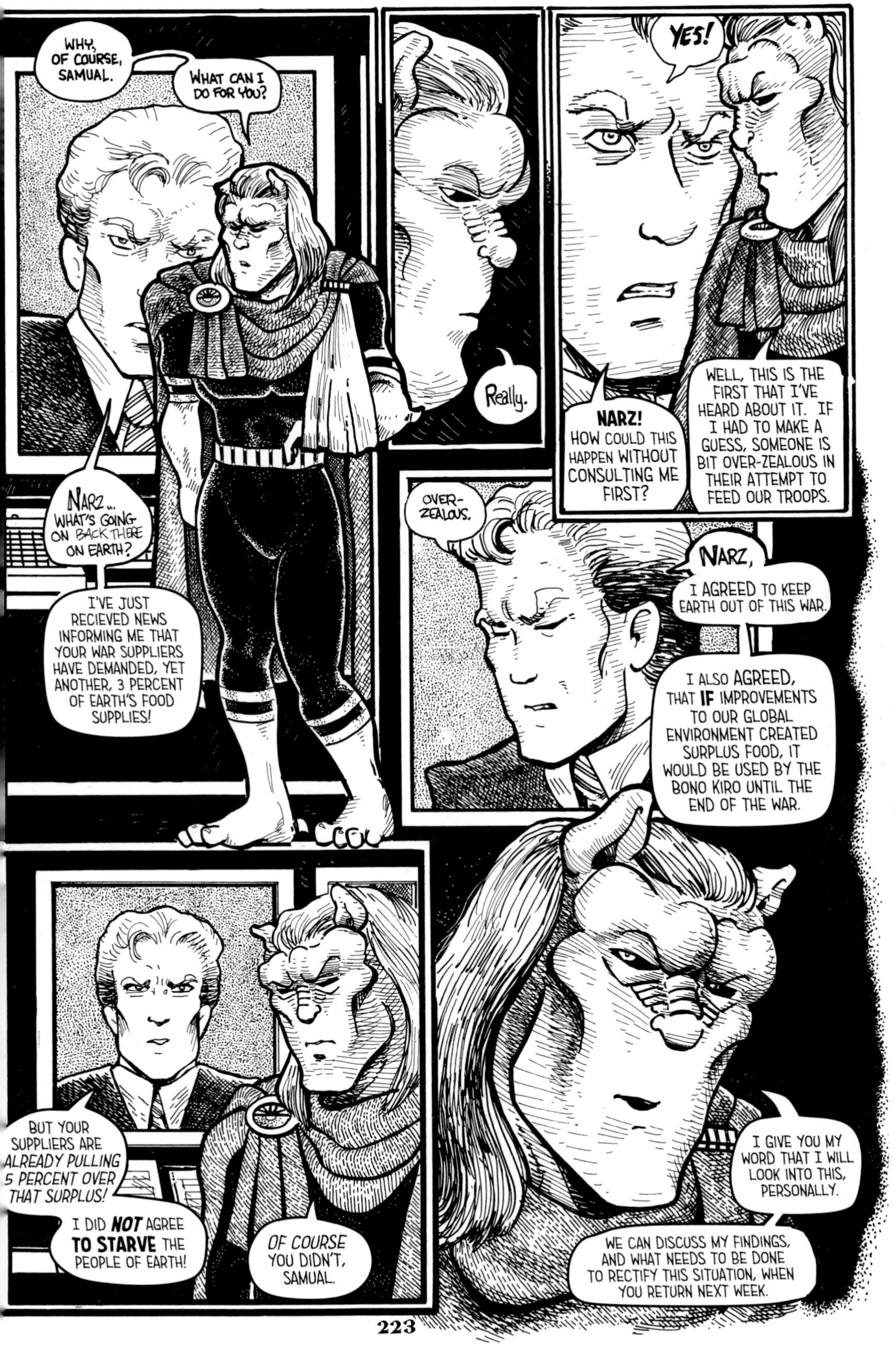
WHY, OF COURSE, SAMUAL.
WHAT CAN I DO FOR YOU?
NARZ... WHAT'S GOING ON BACK THERE ON EARTH?
I'VE JUST RECIEVED NEWS INFORMING ME THAT YOUR WAR SUPPLIERS HAVE DEMANDED, YET ANOTHER, 3 PERCENT OF EARTH'S FOOD SUPPLIES!
Really.
YES!
NARZ! HOW COULD THIS HAPPEN WITHOUT CONSULTING ME FIRST?
WELL, THIS IS THE FIRST THAT I'VE HEARD ABOUT IT. IF I HAD TO MAKE A GUESS, SOMEONE IS BIT OVER-ZEALOUS IN THEIR ATTEMPT TO FEED OUR TROOPS.
OVER-ZEALOUS.
NARZ,
I AGREED TO KEEP EARTH OUT OF THIS WAR.
I ALSO AGREED, THAT IF IMPROVEMENTS TO OUR GLOBAL ENVIRONMENT CREATED SURPLUS FOOD, IT WOULD BE USED BY THE BONO KIRO UNTIL THE END OF THE WAR.
BUT YOUR SUPPLIERS ARE ALREADY PULLING 5 PERCENT OVER THAT SURPLUS!
I DID NOT AGREE TO STARVE THE PEOPLE OF EARTH!
OF COURSE YOU DIDN'T, SAMUAL.
I GIVE YOU MY WORD THAT I WILL LOOK INTO THIS, PERSONALLY.
WE CAN DISCUSS MY FINDINGS, AND WHAT NEEDS TO BE DONE TO RECTIFY THIS SITUATION, WHEN YOU RETURN NEXT WEEK.

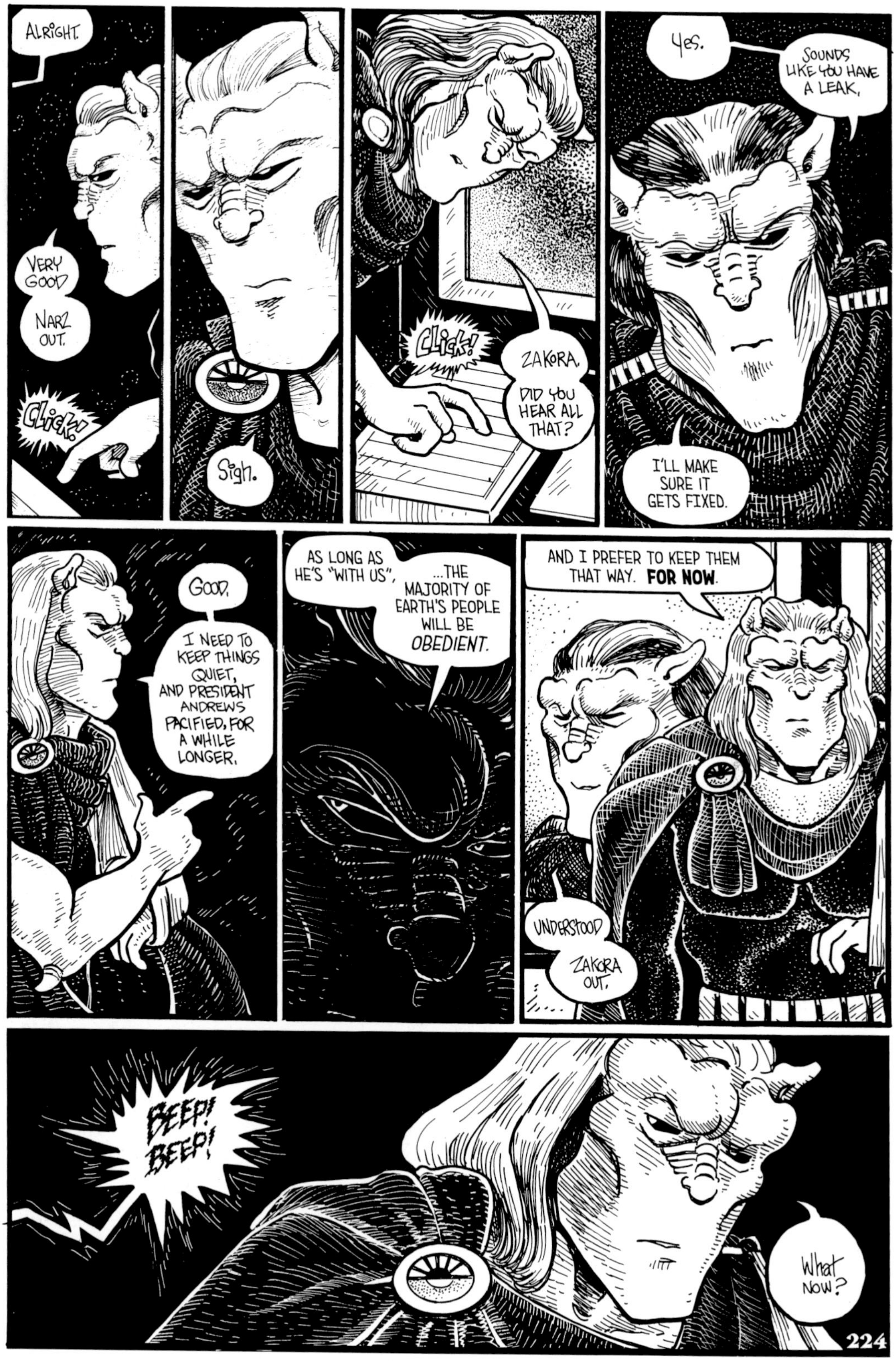
ALRIGHT.
VERY GOOD
NARZ OUT.
CLICK!
Sigh.
CLICK!
ZAKORA.
DID YOU HEAR ALL THAT?
Yes.
SOUNDS LIKE YOU HAVE A LEAK.
I'LL MAKE SURE IT GETS FIXED.
GOOD.
I NEED TO KEEP THINGS QUIET,
AND PRESIDENT ANDREWS PACIFIED, FOR A WHILE LONGER.
AS LONG AS HE'S "WITH US",
...THE MAJORITY OF EARTH'S PEOPLE WILL BE *OBEDIENT*.
AND I PREFER TO KEEP THEM THAT WAY. **FOR NOW**.
UNDERSTOOD
ZAKORA OUT.
BEEP! BEEP!
What now?

YES. WHAT IS IT?

SIR, WANDERING STAR HAS LEFT THE DOCKING BAY, AND IS NOT ANSWERING HAILS.

DID GALKORI PLAN TO TEST HER ENGINES ONCE THE COMPUTER...

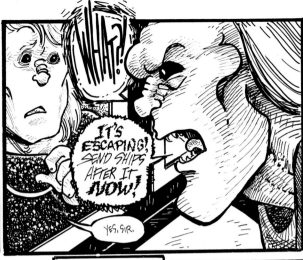

WHAT?!

IT'S ESCAPING! SEND SHIPS AFTER IT NOW!

YES, SIR.

FORGIVE ME, SIR!

IT'S JUST THAT, GALKORI...

...IF WE'D FIRED ON THAT SHIP...

...AND HE'D...

YOU WOULD HAVE BEEN WISER TO HAVE WORRIED ABOUT ME.

CLICK!

BY THE GODS!

SIGH.

ENJOY YOUR LITTLE VICTORY. FOR WHETHER YOU ESCAPE OR NOT,

OUR GAME HERE IS NEARLY OVER.

I'M SURROUNDED BY IDIOTS!

RRRRR!

VERY WELL, CHILD.

BE IT BY MY HAND OR BY THE KEKAKOPOLOUS.

225

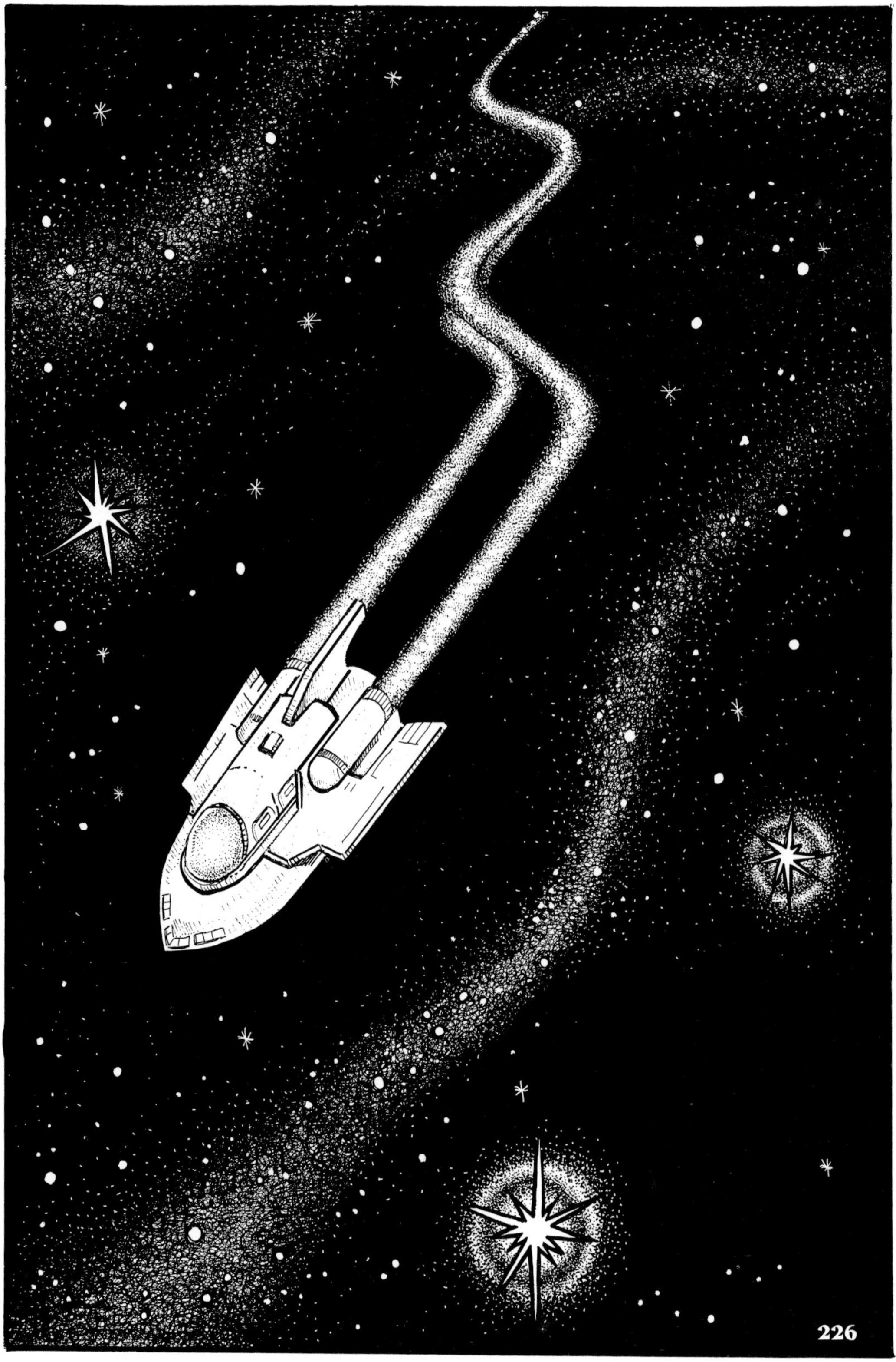

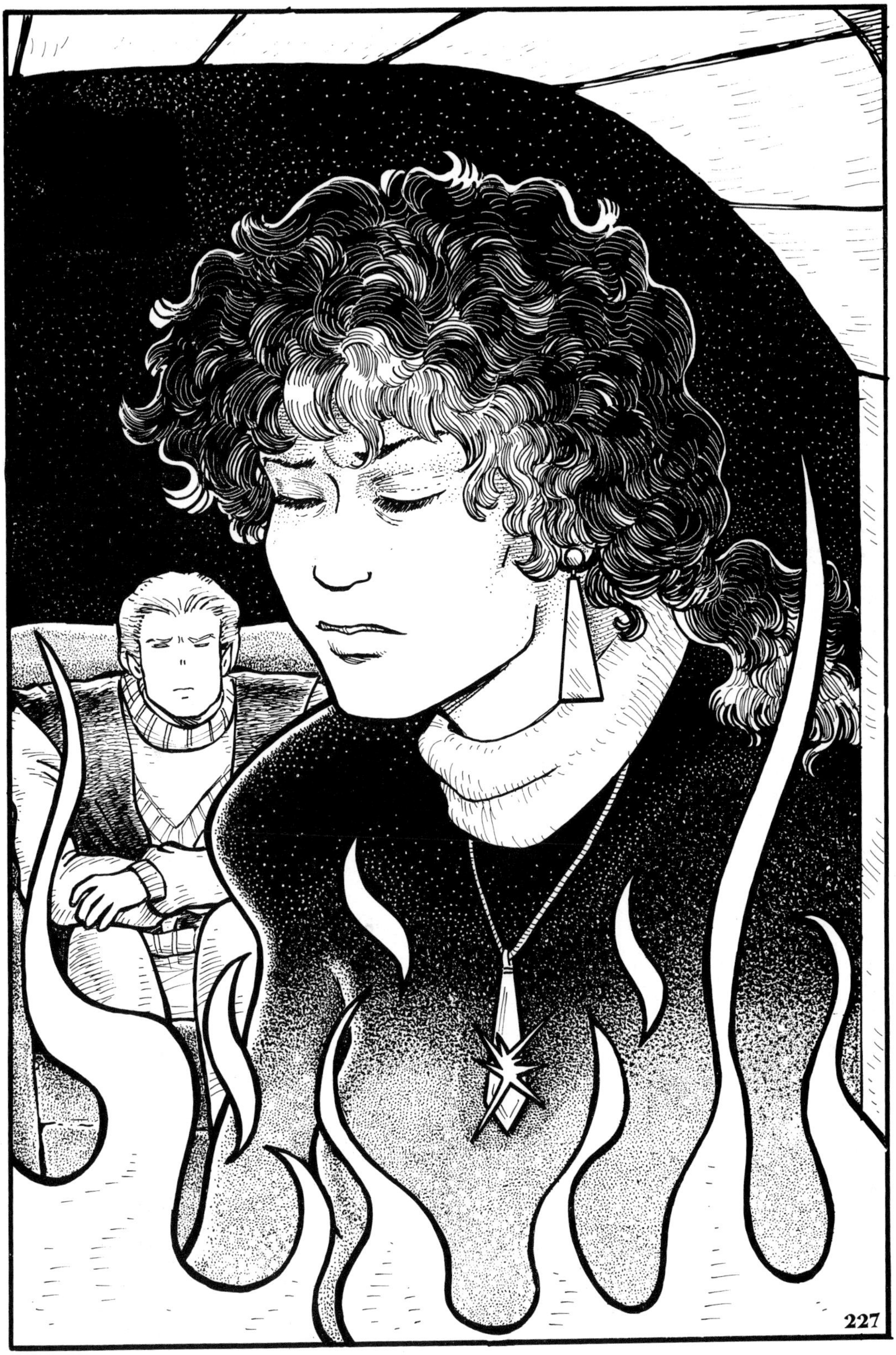

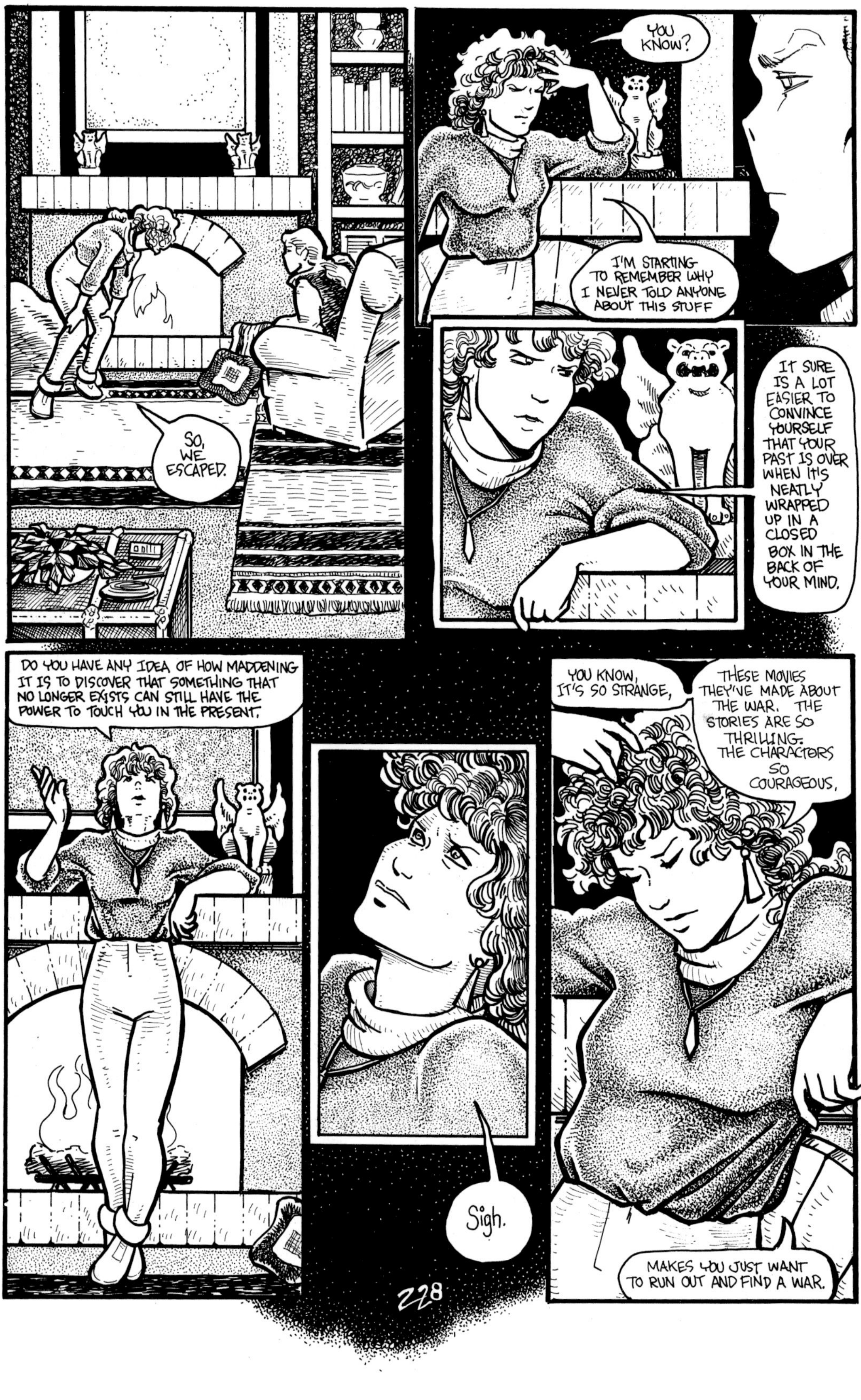

So, we escaped.
You know?
I'm starting to remember why I never told anyone about this stuff
It sure is a lot easier to convince yourself that your past is over when it's neatly wrapped up in a closed box in the back of your mind.
Do you have any idea of how maddening it is to discover that something that no longer exists can still have the power to touch you in the present.
Sigh.
You know, it's so strange,
These movies they've made about the war. The stories are so thrilling. The characters so courageous,
Makes you just want to run out and find a war.

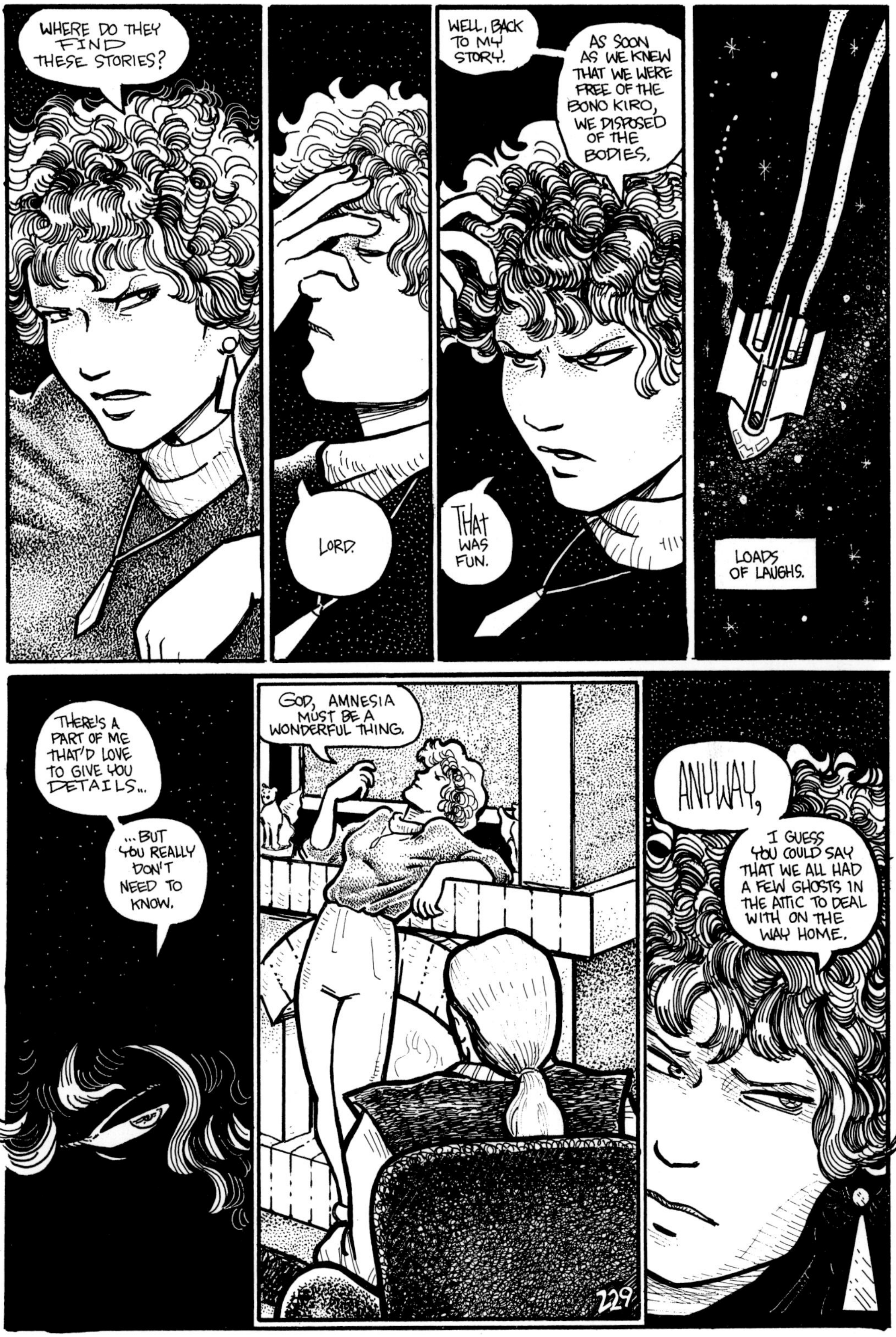
WHERE DO THEY FIND THESE STORIES?
LORD.
WELL, BACK TO MY STORY.
AS SOON AS WE KNEW THAT WE WERE FREE OF THE BONO KIRO, WE DISPOSED OF THE BODIES.
THAT WAS FUN.
LOADS OF LAUGHS.
THERE'S A PART OF ME THAT'D LOVE TO GIVE YOU DETAILS...
...BUT YOU REALLY DON'T NEED TO KNOW.
GOD, AMNESIA MUST BE A WONDERFUL THING.
ANYWAY,
I GUESS YOU COULD SAY THAT WE ALL HAD A FEW GHOSTS IN THE ATTIC TO DEAL WITH ON THE WAY HOME.
229

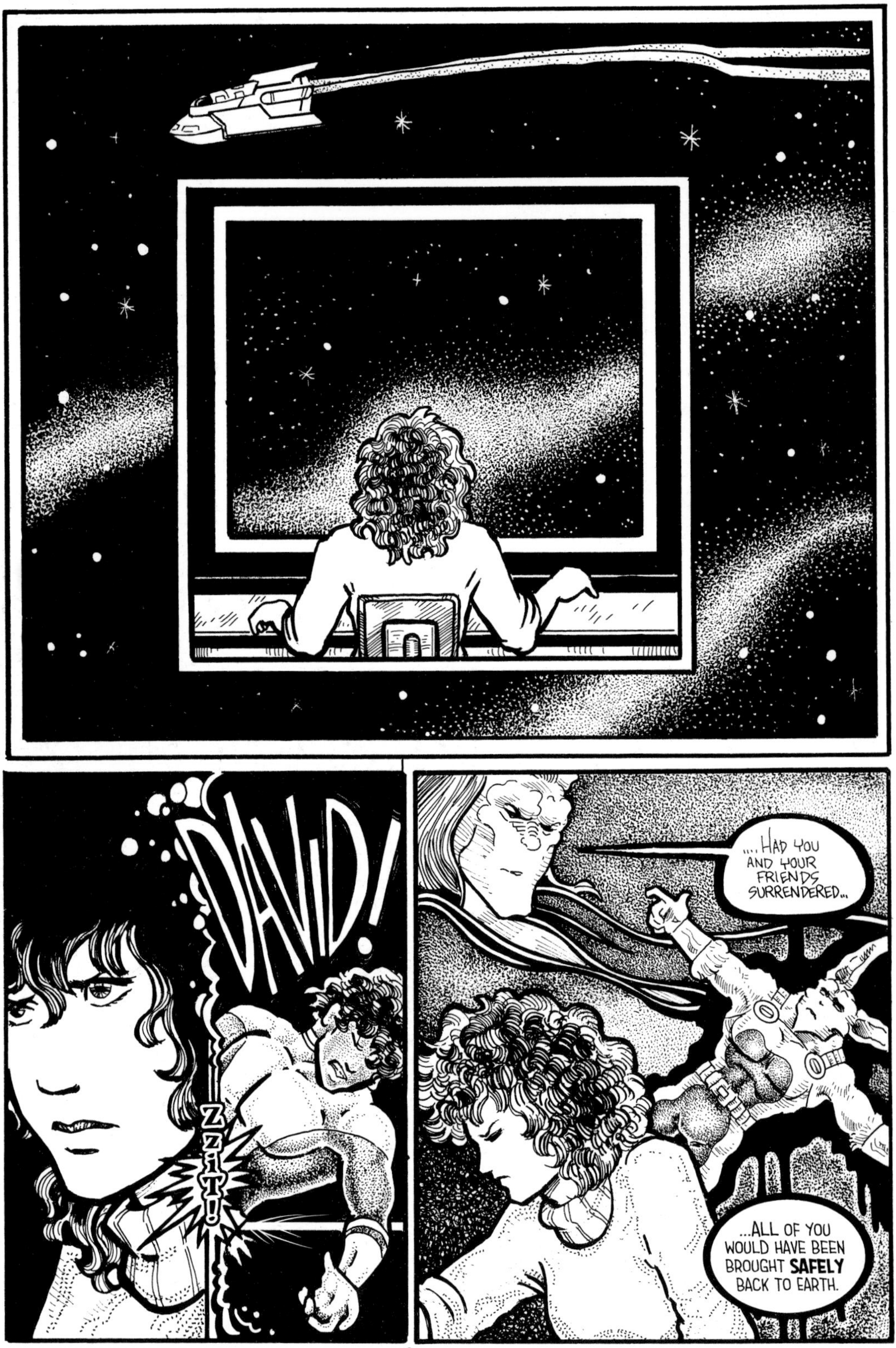
DAVID!
ZZiT!
...HAD YOU AND YOUR FRIENDS SURRENDERED...
...ALL OF YOU WOULD HAVE BEEN BROUGHT **SAFELY** BACK TO EARTH.

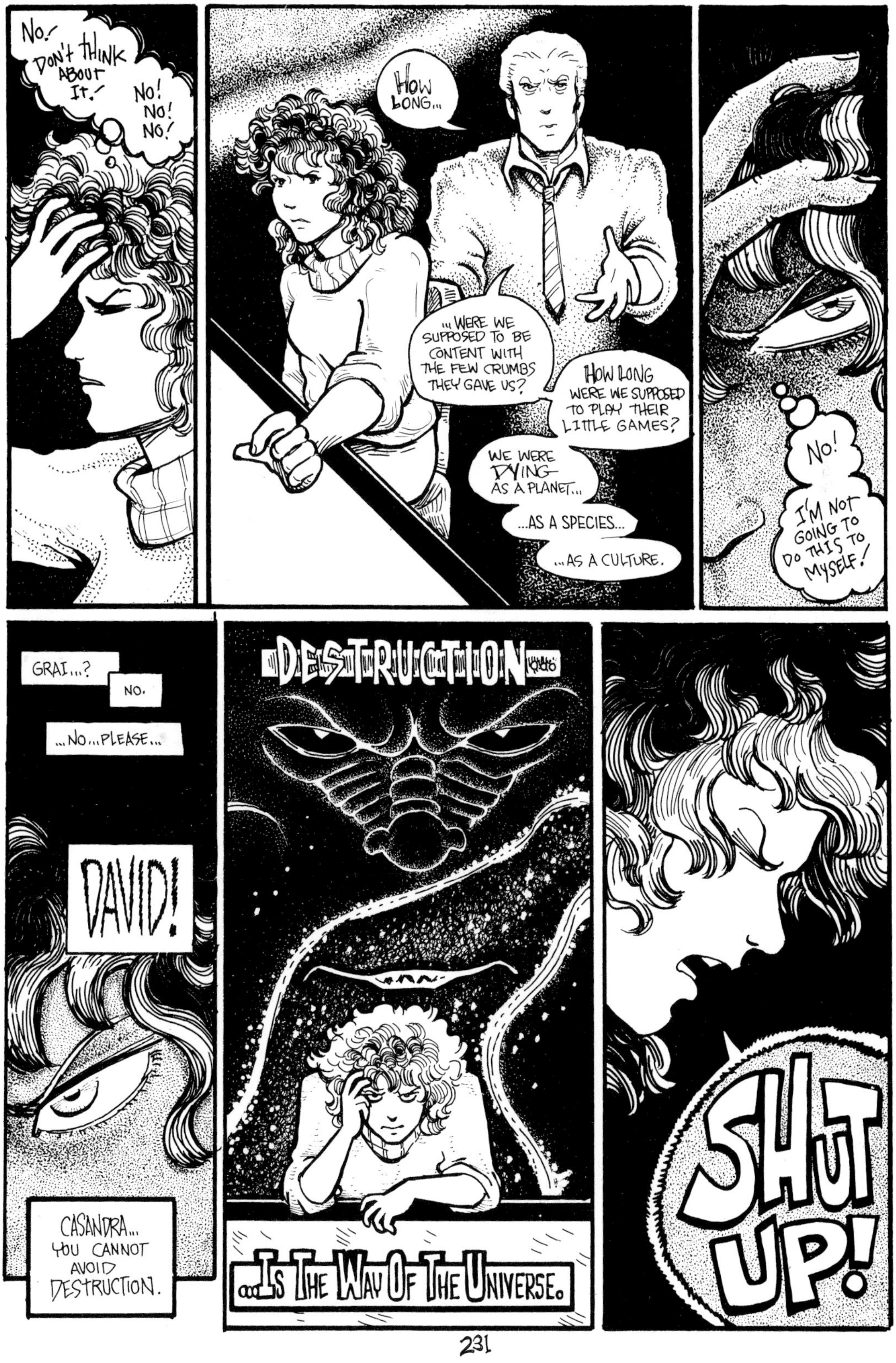
No! Don't think about it!
No! No! No!
How long...
...were we supposed to be content with the few crumbs they gave us?
How long were we supposed to play their little games?
We were dying as a planet...
...as a species...
...as a culture.
No!
I'm not going to do this to myself!
GRAI...?
NO.
...NO...PLEASE...
DAVID!
CASANDRA... YOU CANNOT AVOID DESTRUCTION.
DESTRUCTION
...IS THE WAY OF THE UNIVERSE.
SHUT UP!

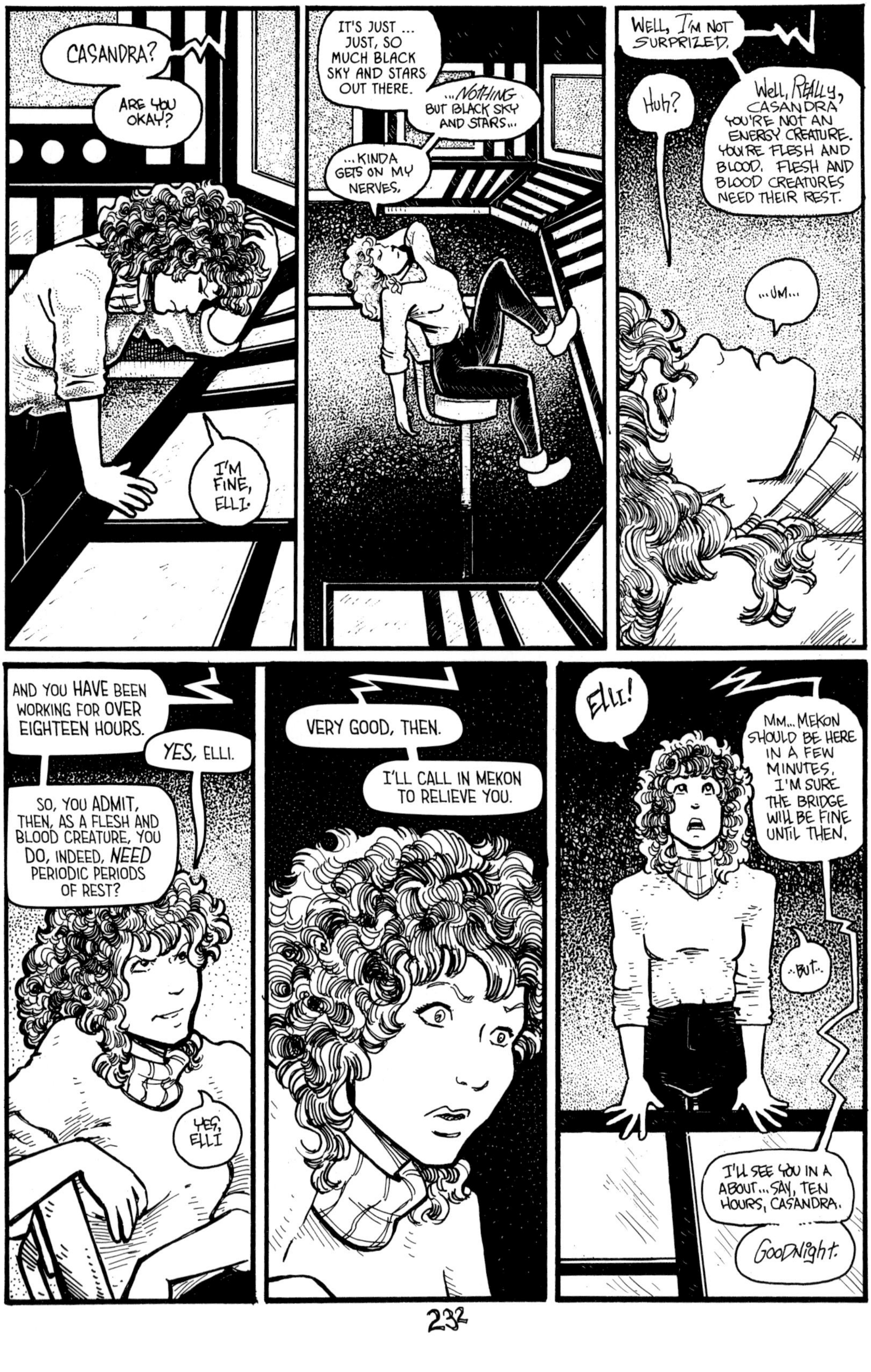
CASANDRA?
ARE YOU OKAY?
I'M FINE, ELLI.
IT'S JUST ... JUST, SO MUCH BLACK SKY AND STARS OUT THERE.
...NOTHING BUT BLACK SKY AND STARS...
...KINDA GETS ON MY NERVES.
WELL, I'M NOT SURPRIZED.
HUH?
WELL, REALLY, CASANDRA YOU'RE NOT AN ENERGY CREATURE. YOU'RE FLESH AND BLOOD. FLESH AND BLOOD CREATURES NEED THEIR REST.
...UM...
AND YOU HAVE BEEN WORKING FOR OVER EIGHTEEN HOURS.
YES, ELLI.
SO, YOU ADMIT, THEN, AS A FLESH AND BLOOD CREATURE, YOU DO, INDEED, NEED PERIODIC PERIODS OF REST?
YES, ELLI
VERY GOOD, THEN.
I'LL CALL IN MEKON TO RELIEVE YOU.
ELLI!
MM... MEKON SHOULD BE HERE IN A FEW MINUTES. I'M SURE THE BRIDGE WILL BE FINE UNTIL THEN.
..BUT..
I'LL SEE YOU IN A ABOUT... SAY, TEN HOURS, CASANDRA.
GOODNIGHT.

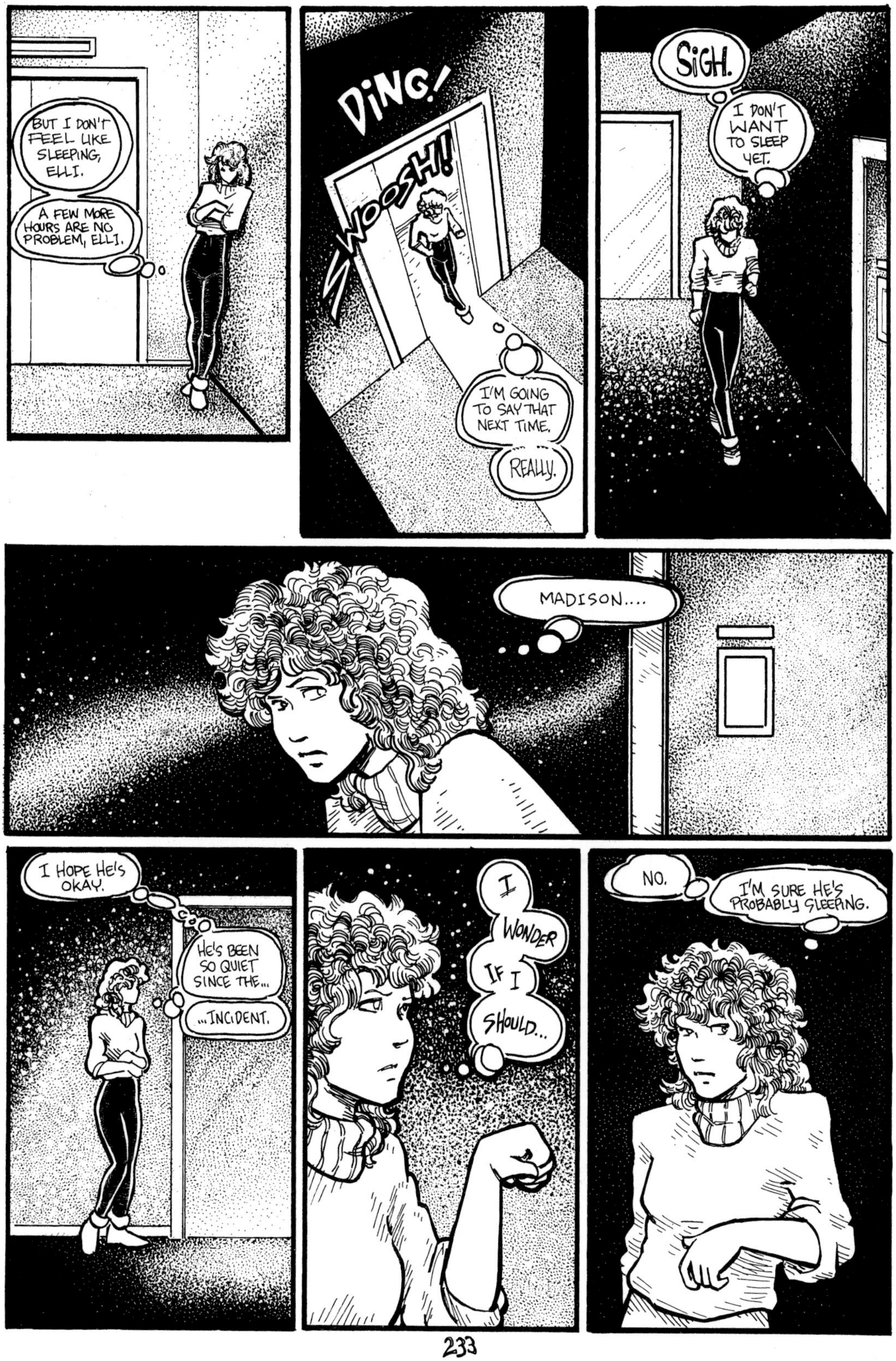
BUT I DON'T FEEL LIKE SLEEPING, ELLI.
A FEW MORE HOURS ARE NO PROBLEM, ELLI.
DiNG!
WOOSH!!
I'M GOING TO SAY THAT NEXT TIME.
REALLY.
SIGH.
I DON'T WANT TO SLEEP YET.
MADISON....
I HOPE HE'S OKAY.
HE'S BEEN SO QUIET SINCE THE...
...INCIDENT.
I WONDER IF I SHOULD...
NO.
I'M SURE HE'S PROBABLY SLEEPING.

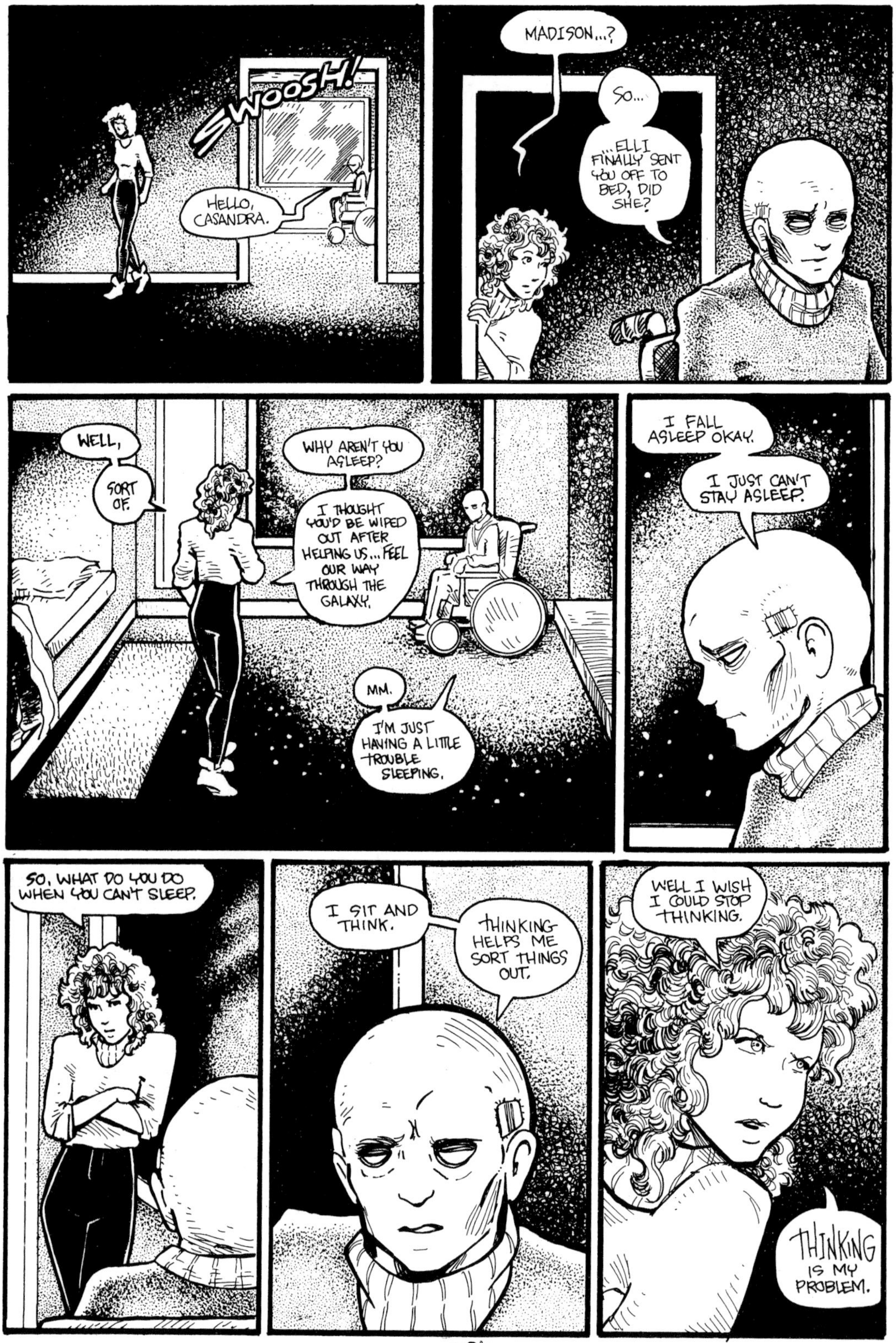
SWOOSH!
HELLO, CASANDRA.
MADISON...?
SO...
...ELLI FINALLY SENT YOU OFF TO BED, DID SHE?
WELL,
SORT OF.
WHY AREN'T YOU ASLEEP?
I THOUGHT YOU'D BE WIPED OUT AFTER HELPING US...FEEL OUR WAY THROUGH THE GALAXY.
MM.
I'M JUST HAVING A LITTLE TROUBLE SLEEPING.
I FALL ASLEEP OKAY.
I JUST CAN'T STAY ASLEEP.
SO, WHAT DO YOU DO WHEN YOU CAN'T SLEEP.
I SIT AND THINK.
THINKING HELPS ME SORT THINGS OUT.
WELL I WISH I COULD STOP THINKING.
THINKING IS MY PROBLEM.

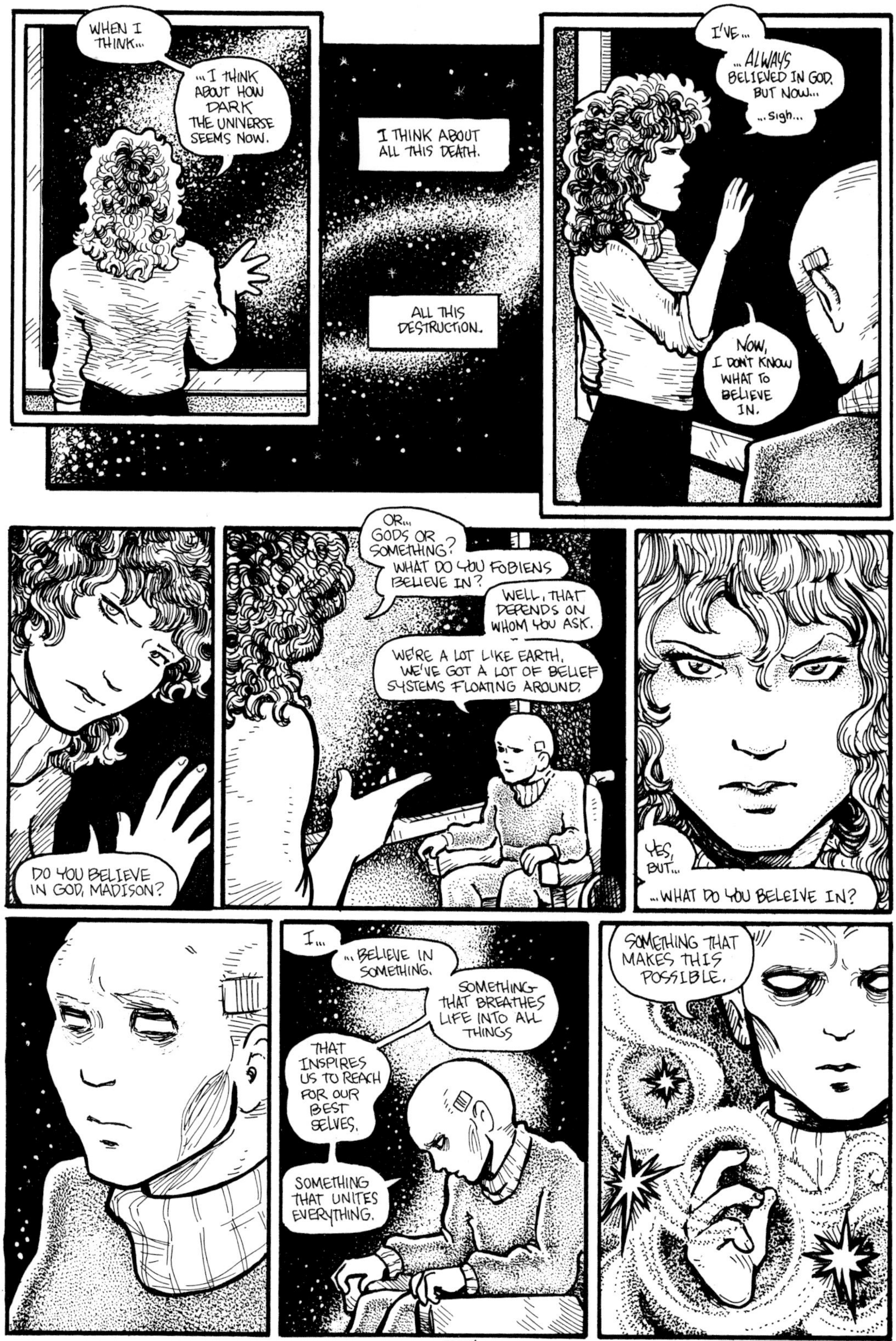
WHEN I THINK...
...I THINK ABOUT HOW DARK THE UNIVERSE SEEMS NOW.
I THINK ABOUT ALL THIS DEATH.
ALL THIS DESTRUCTION.
I'VE...
...ALWAYS BELIEVED IN GOD. BUT NOW...
...sigh...
NOW, I DON'T KNOW WHAT TO BELIEVE IN.
DO YOU BELIEVE IN GOD, MADISON?
OR... GODS OR SOMETHING?
WHAT DO YOU FOBIENS BELIEVE IN?
WELL, THAT DEPENDS ON WHOM YOU ASK.
WE'RE A LOT LIKE EARTH. WE'VE GOT A LOT OF BELIEF SYSTEMS FLOATING AROUND.
YES, BUT...
...WHAT DO YOU BELEIVE IN?
I...
...BELIEVE IN SOMETHING.
SOMETHING THAT BREATHES LIFE INTO ALL THINGS
THAT INSPIRES US TO REACH FOR OUR BEST SELVES.
SOMETHING THAT UNITES EVERYTHING.
SOMETHING THAT MAKES THIS POSSIBLE.

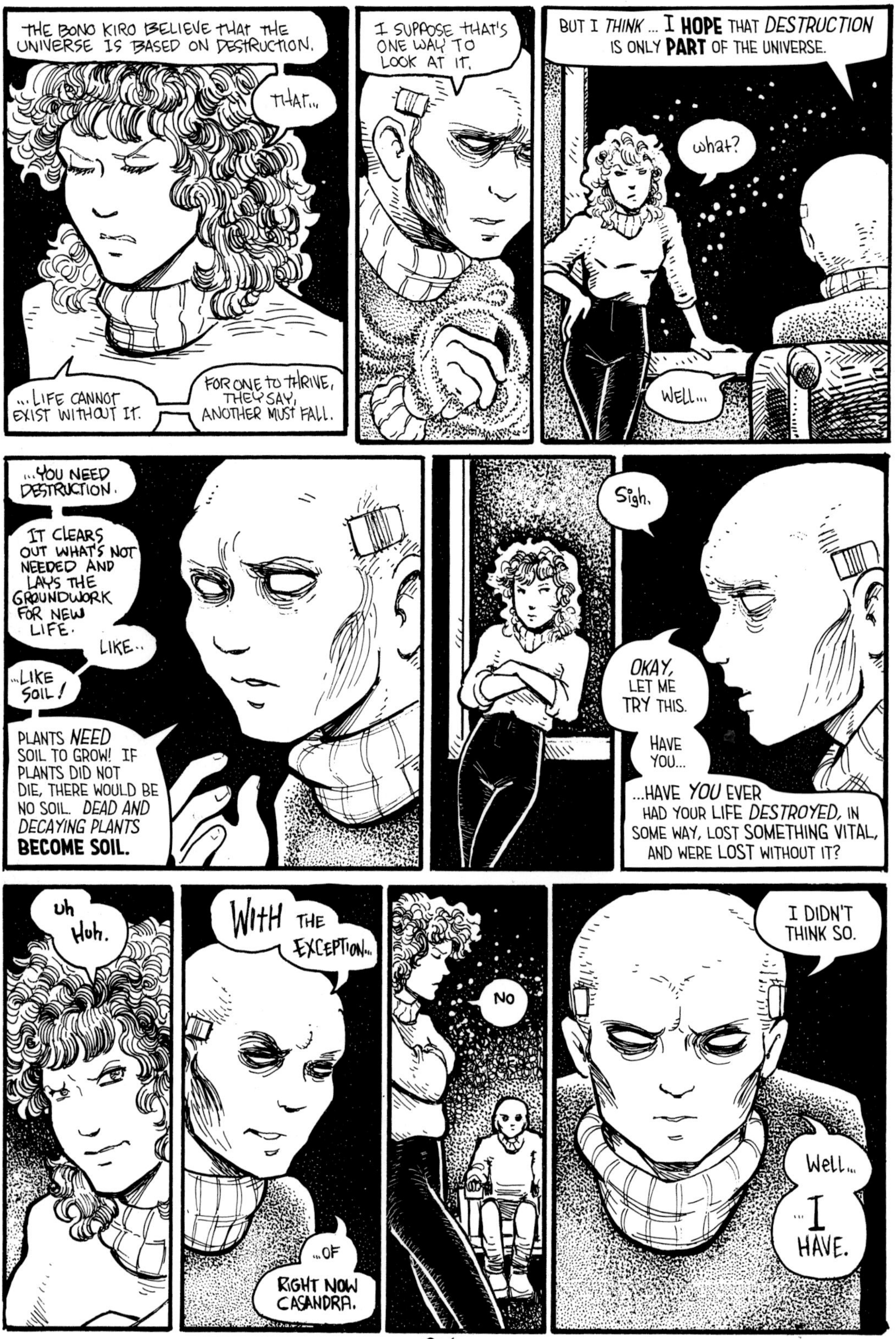
THE BONO KIRO BELIEVE THAT THE UNIVERSE IS BASED ON DESTRUCTION.
THAT...
...LIFE CANNOT EXIST WITHOUT IT.
FOR ONE TO THRIVE, THEY SAY, ANOTHER MUST FALL.
I SUPPOSE THAT'S ONE WAY TO LOOK AT IT.
BUT I THINK ... I HOPE THAT DESTRUCTION IS ONLY PART OF THE UNIVERSE.
what?
WELL...
...YOU NEED DESTRUCTION.
IT CLEARS OUT WHAT'S NOT NEEDED AND LAYS THE GROUNDWORK FOR NEW LIFE.
LIKE...
...LIKE SOIL!
PLANTS NEED SOIL TO GROW! IF PLANTS DID NOT DIE, THERE WOULD BE NO SOIL. DEAD AND DECAYING PLANTS BECOME SOIL.
Sigh.
OKAY, LET ME TRY THIS.
HAVE YOU...
...HAVE YOU EVER HAD YOUR LIFE DESTROYED, IN SOME WAY, LOST SOMETHING VITAL, AND WERE LOST WITHOUT IT?
uh Huh.
WITH THE EXCEPTION...
...OF
RIGHT NOW CASANDRA.
NO
I DIDN'T THINK SO.
Well...
...I HAVE.

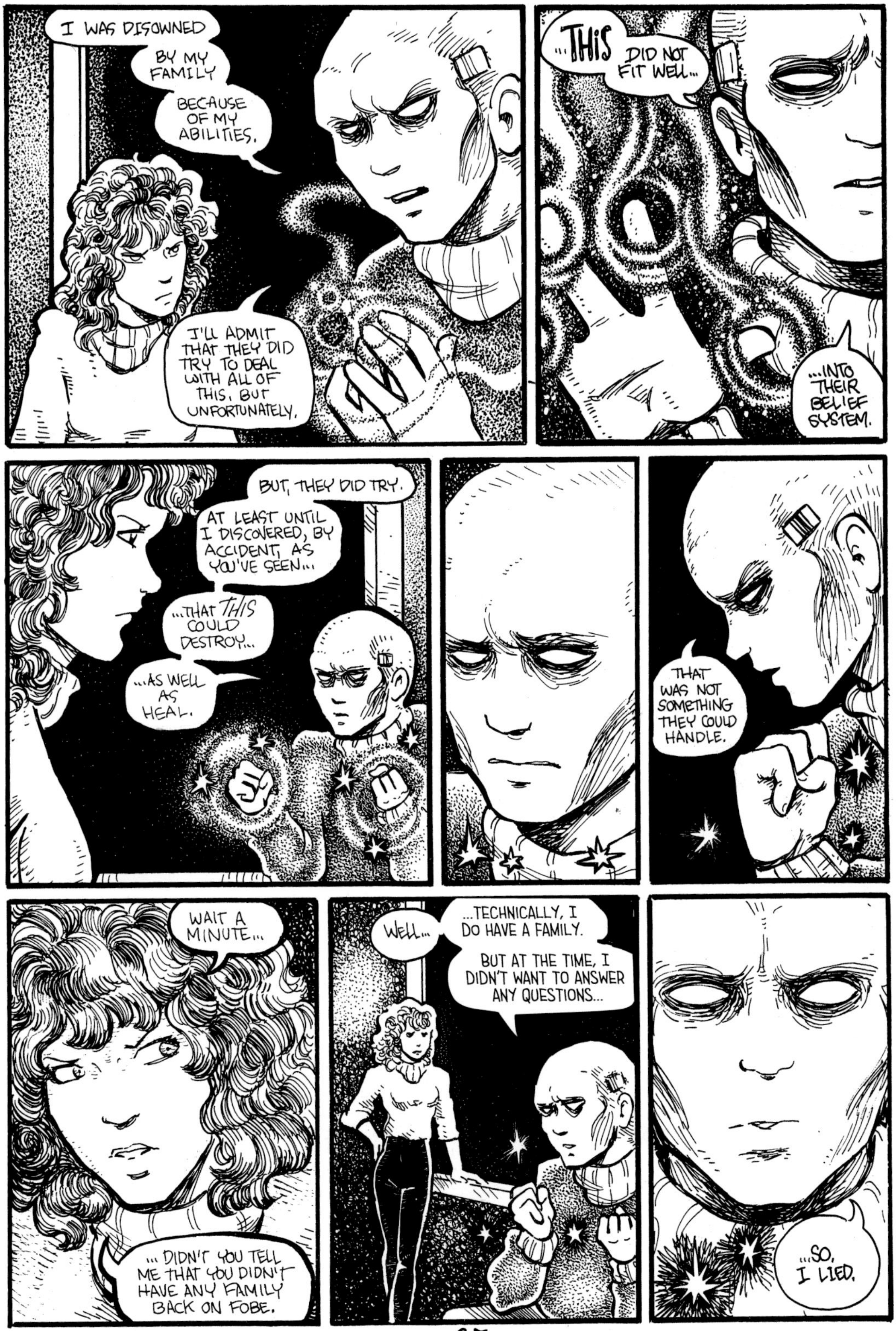
I WAS DISOWNED
BY MY FAMILY
BECAUSE OF MY ABILITIES.
I'LL ADMIT THAT THEY DID TRY TO DEAL WITH ALL OF THIS, BUT UNFORTUNATELY,
...THIS
DID NOT FIT WELL...
...INTO THEIR BELIEF SYSTEM.
BUT, THEY DID TRY.
AT LEAST UNTIL I DISCOVERED, BY ACCIDENT, AS YOU'VE SEEN...
...THAT THIS COULD DESTROY...
...AS WELL AS HEAL.
THAT WAS NOT SOMETHING THEY COULD HANDLE.
WAIT A MINUTE...
...DIDN'T YOU TELL ME THAT YOU DIDN'T HAVE ANY FAMILY BACK ON FOBE.
WELL...
...TECHNICALLY, I DO HAVE A FAMILY.
BUT AT THE TIME, I DIDN'T WANT TO ANSWER ANY QUESTIONS...
...SO, I LIED.

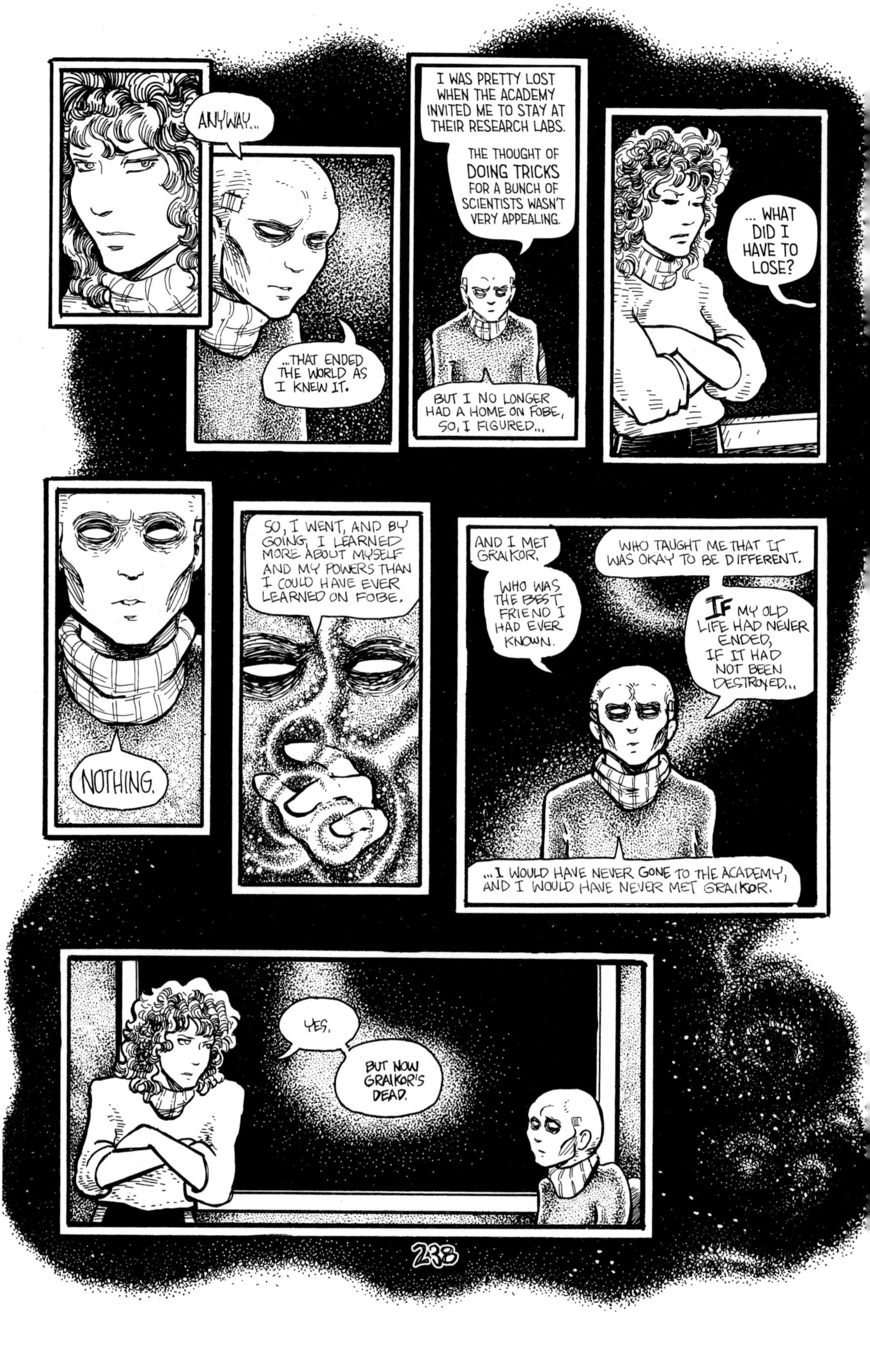
ANYWAY...
...THAT ENDED THE WORLD AS I KNEW IT.
I WAS PRETTY LOST WHEN THE ACADEMY INVITED ME TO STAY AT THEIR RESEARCH LABS.
THE THOUGHT OF DOING TRICKS FOR A BUNCH OF SCIENTISTS WASN'T VERY APPEALING.
BUT I NO LONGER HAD A HOME ON FOBE, SO, I FIGURED...
... WHAT DID I HAVE TO LOSE?
NOTHING.
SO, I WENT, AND BY GOING, I LEARNED MORE ABOUT MYSELF AND MY POWERS THAN I COULD HAVE EVER LEARNED ON FOBE.
AND I MET GRAIKOR,
WHO WAS THE BEST FRIEND I HAD EVER KNOWN.
WHO TAUGHT ME THAT IT WAS OKAY TO BE DIFFERENT.
IF MY OLD LIFE HAD NEVER ENDED, IF IT HAD NOT BEEN DESTROYED...
...I WOULD HAVE NEVER GONE TO THE ACADEMY, AND I WOULD HAVE NEVER MET GRAIKOR.
YES.
BUT NOW GRAIKOR'S DEAD.

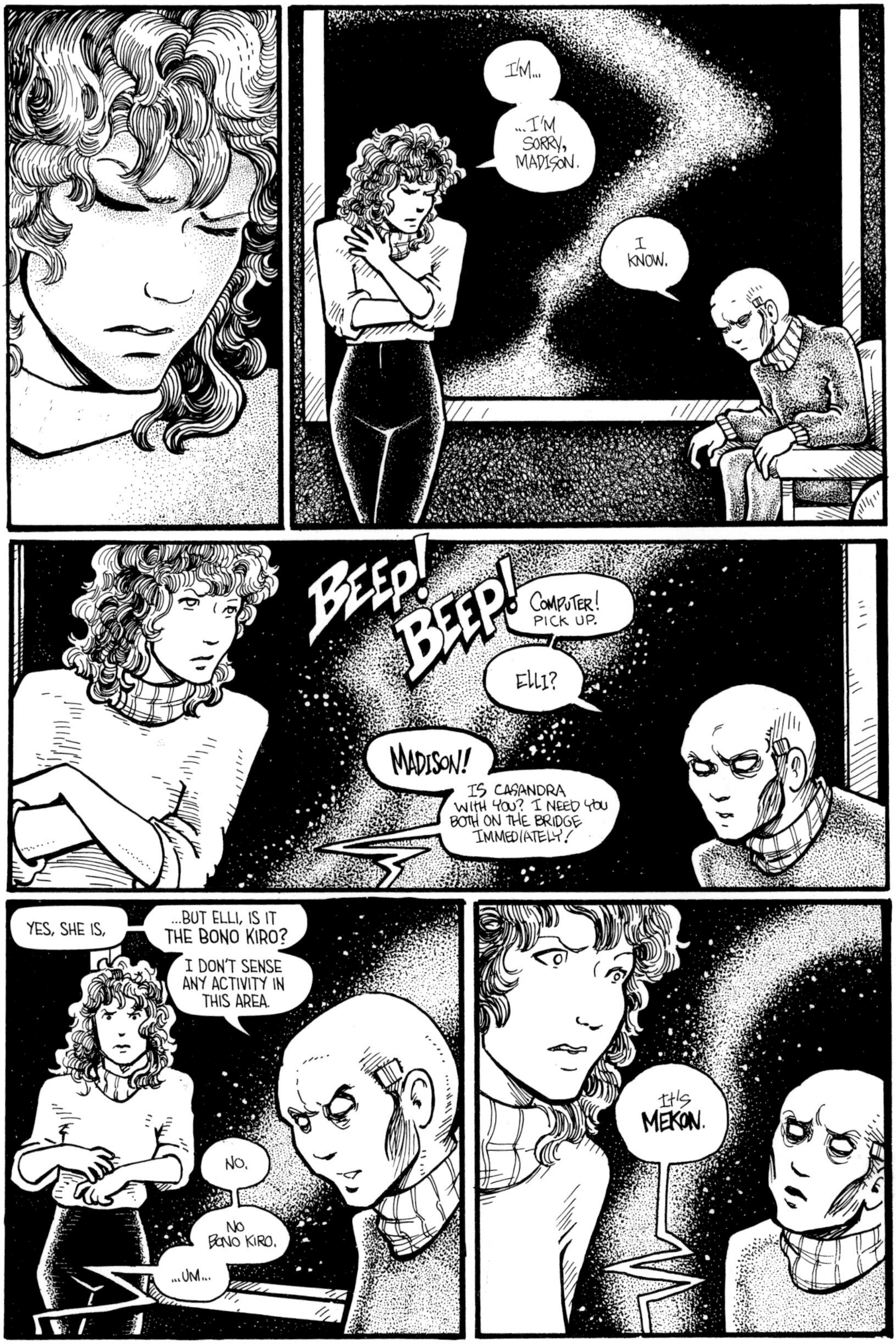
I'M...
...I'M SORRY, MADISON.
I KNOW.
BEEP! BEEP!
COMPUTER! PICK UP.
ELLI?
MADISON!
IS CASANDRA WITH YOU? I NEED YOU BOTH ON THE BRIDGE IMMEDIATELY!
YES, SHE IS,
...BUT ELLI, IS IT THE BONO KIRO?
I DON'T SENSE ANY ACTIVITY IN THIS AREA.
NO.
NO BONO KIRO.
...UM...
IT'S MEKON.

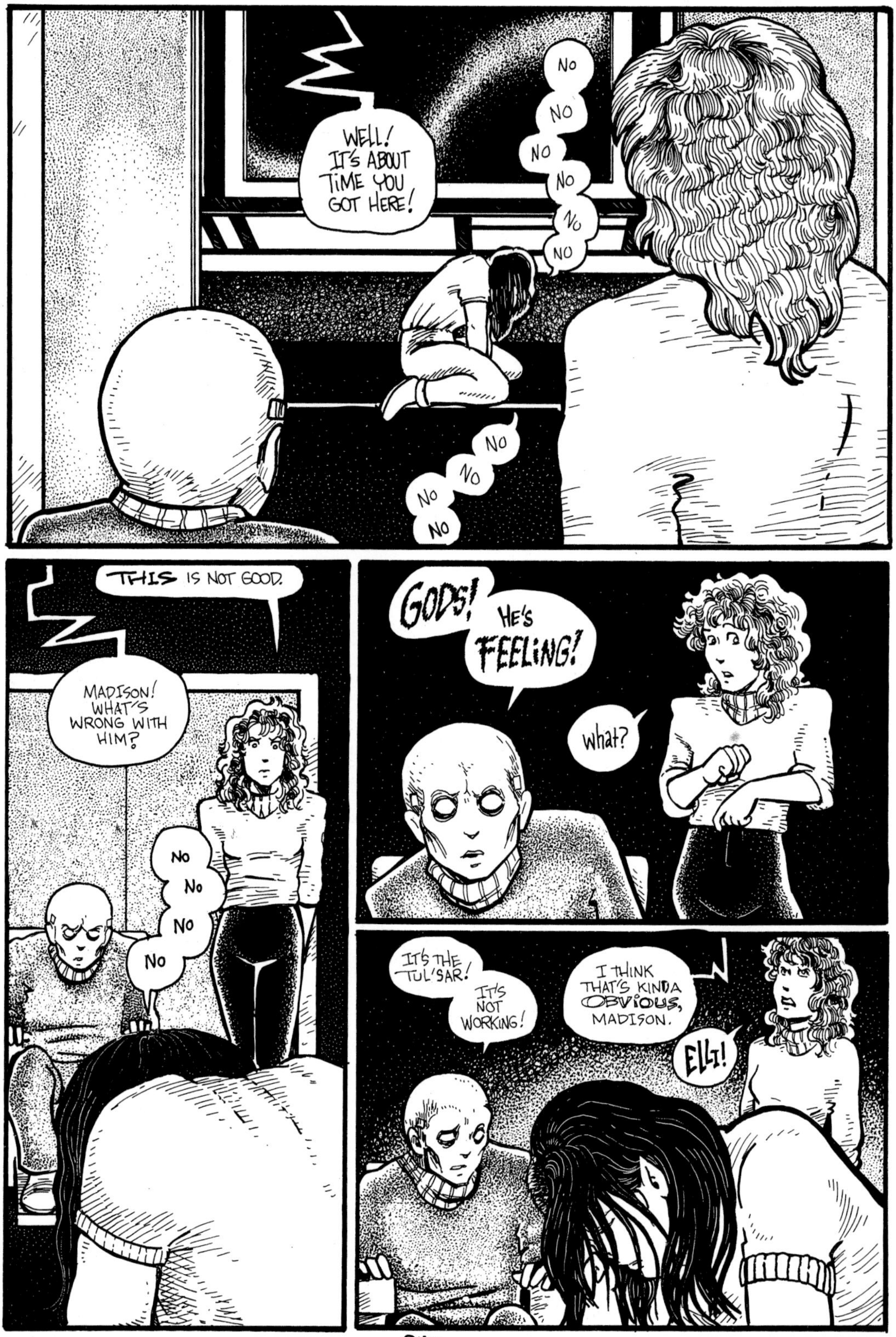
WELL! IT'S ABOUT TIME YOU GOT HERE!
NO NO NO NO NO NO
NO NO NO NO
THIS IS NOT GOOD.
MADISON! WHAT'S WRONG WITH HIM?
NO NO NO NO
GODS!
HE'S FEELING!
WHAT?
IT'S THE TUL'SAR!
IT'S NOT WORKING!
I THINK THAT'S KINDA OBVIOUS, MADISON.
ELLI!

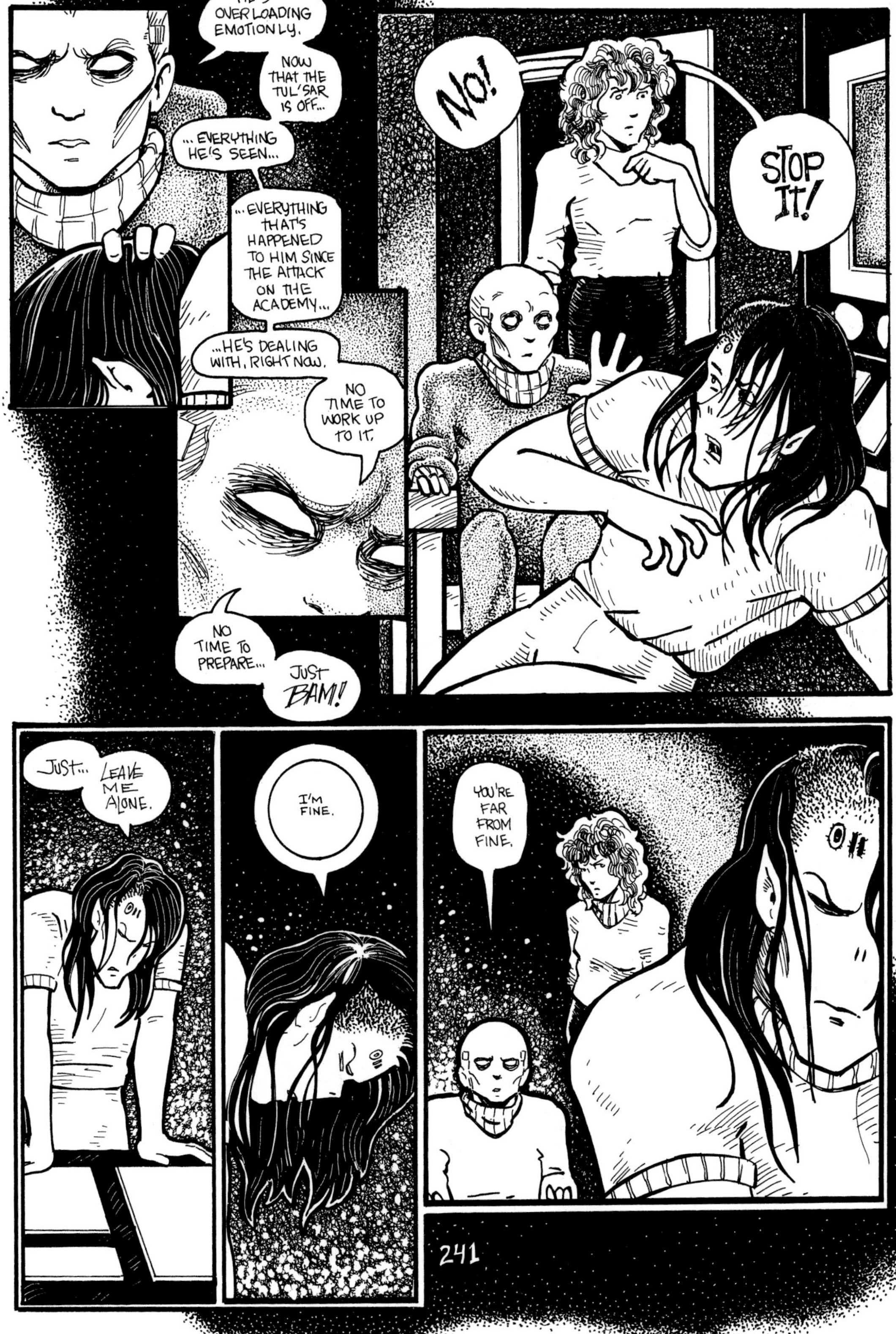
HE'S OVERLOADING EMOTIONLY.
NOW THAT THE TUL'SAR IS OFF...
...EVERYTHING HE'S SEEN...
...EVERYTHING THAT'S HAPPENED TO HIM SINCE THE ATTACK ON THE ACADEMY...
...HE'S DEALING WITH, RIGHT NOW.
NO TIME TO WORK UP TO IT.
NO TIME TO PREPARE...
JUST BAM!
NO!
STOP IT!
JUST... LEAVE ME ALONE.
I'M FINE.
YOU'RE FAR FROM FINE.

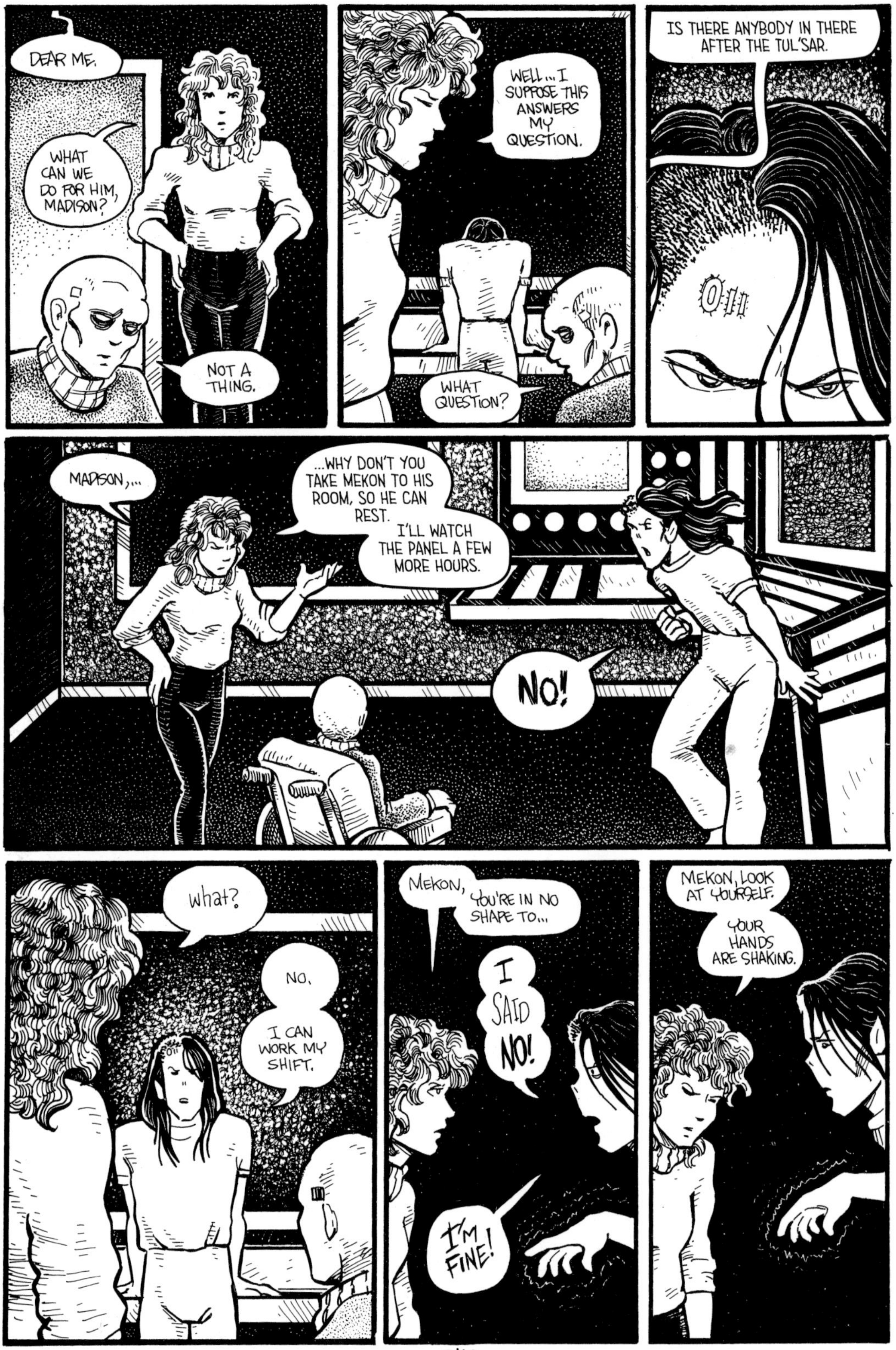
DEAR ME.
WHAT CAN WE DO FOR HIM, MADISON?
NOT A THING.
WELL... I SUPPOSE THIS ANSWERS MY QUESTION.
WHAT QUESTION?
IS THERE ANYBODY IN THERE AFTER THE TUL'SAR.
MADISON,...
...WHY DON'T YOU TAKE MEKON TO HIS ROOM, SO HE CAN REST.
I'LL WATCH THE PANEL A FEW MORE HOURS.
NO!
what?
NO,
I CAN WORK MY SHIFT.
MEKON,
YOU'RE IN NO SHAPE TO...
I SAID NO!
I'M FINE!
MEKON, LOOK AT YOURSELF.
YOUR HANDS ARE SHAKING.

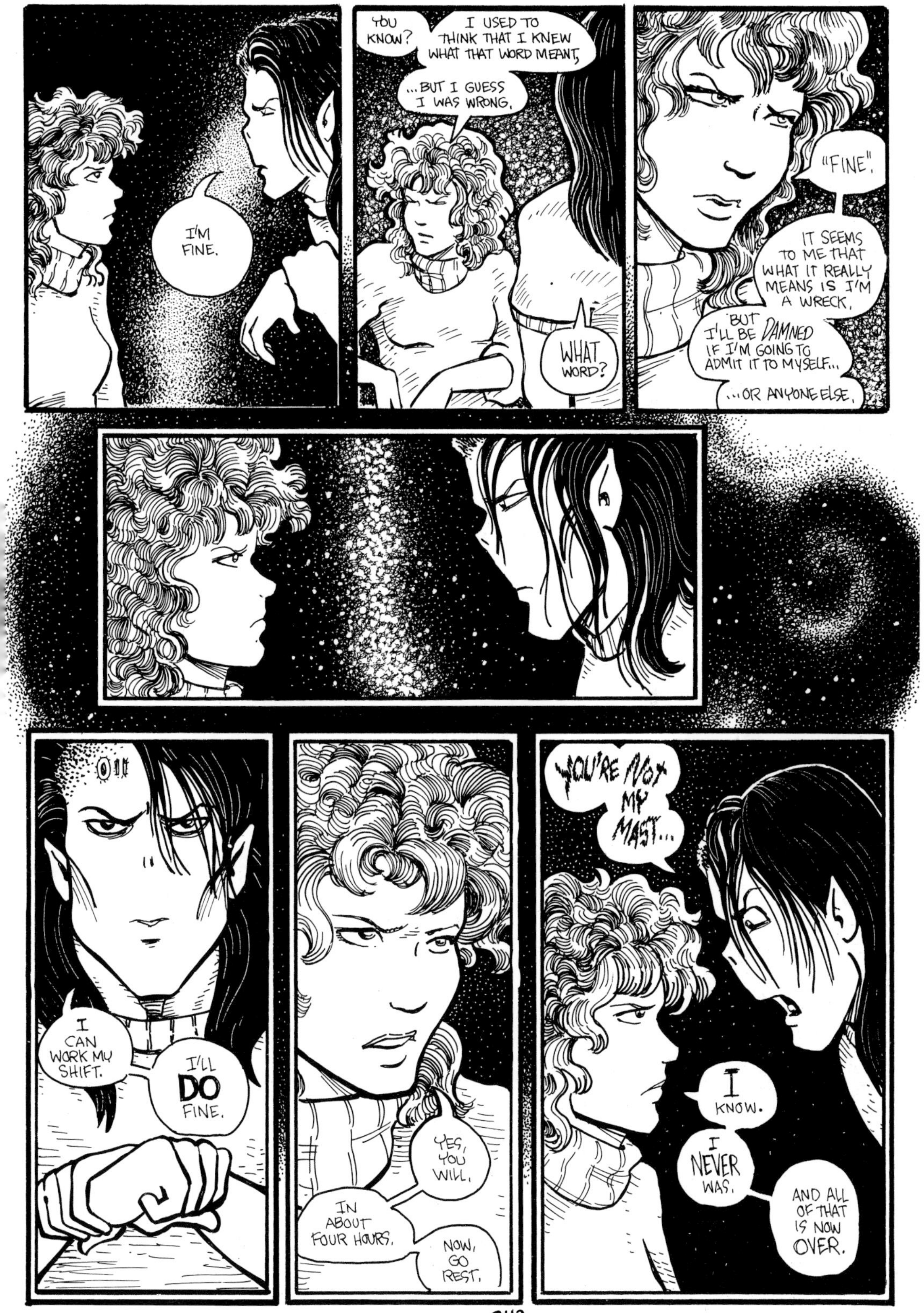
I'M FINE.
YOU KNOW?
I USED TO THINK THAT I KNEW WHAT THAT WORD MEANT,
...BUT I GUESS I WAS WRONG.
WHAT WORD?
"FINE".
IT SEEMS TO ME THAT WHAT IT REALLY MEANS IS I'M A WRECK,
BUT I'LL BE DAMNED IF I'M GOING TO ADMIT IT TO MYSELF...
...OR ANYONE ELSE.
I CAN WORK MY SHIFT.
I'LL DO FINE.
YES, YOU WILL.
IN ABOUT FOUR HOURS.
NOW, GO REST.
YOU'RE NOT MY MAST...
I KNOW.
I NEVER WAS.
AND ALL OF THAT IS NOW OVER.

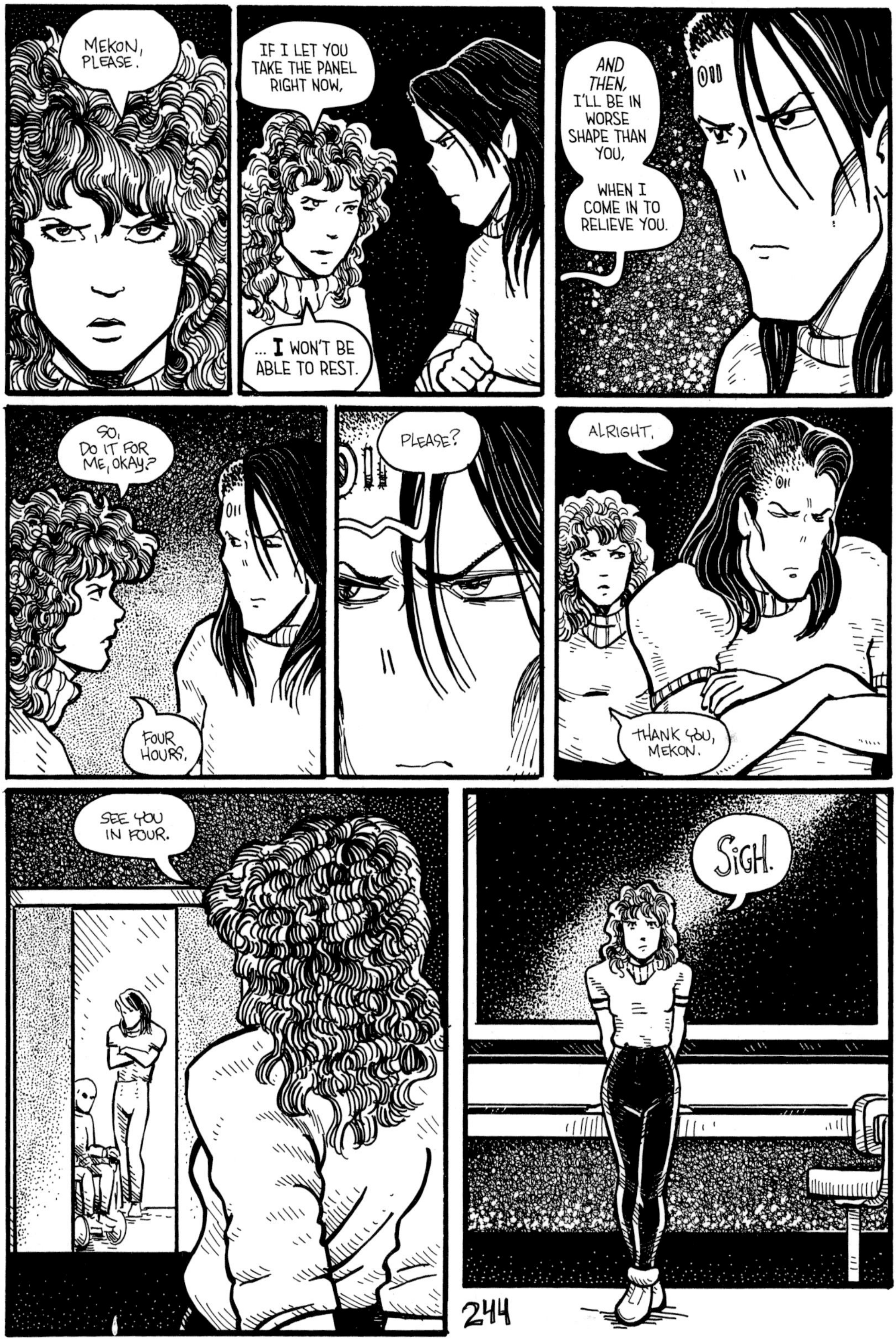
MEKON, PLEASE.
IF I LET YOU TAKE THE PANEL RIGHT NOW,
... I WON'T BE ABLE TO REST.
AND THEN, I'LL BE IN WORSE SHAPE THAN YOU,
WHEN I COME IN TO RELIEVE YOU.
SO, DO IT FOR ME, OKAY?
FOUR HOURS.
PLEASE?
ALRIGHT.
THANK YOU, MEKON.
SEE YOU IN FOUR.
SIGH.

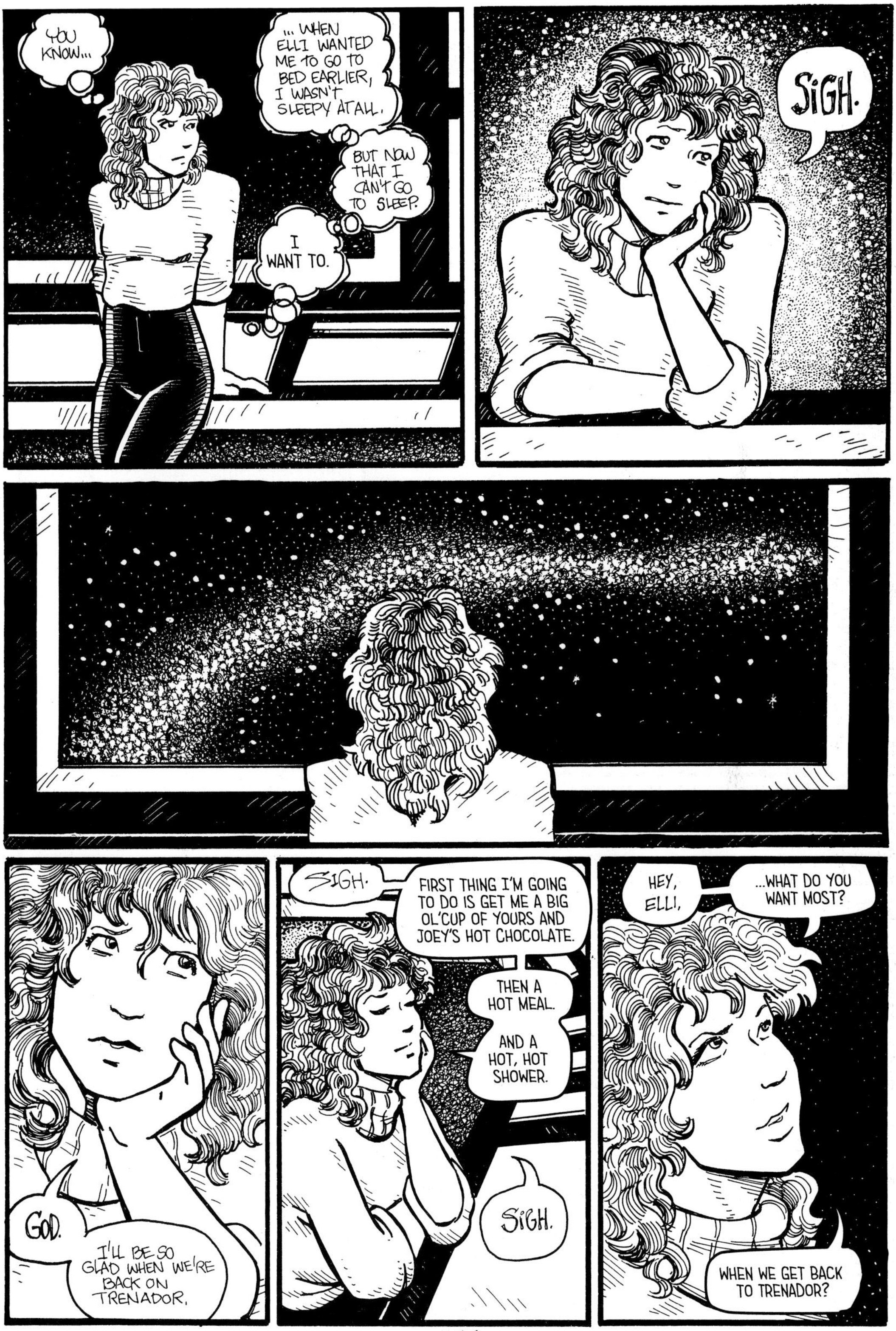
YOU KNOW...
... WHEN ELLI WANTED ME TO GO TO BED EARLIER, I WASN'T SLEEPY AT ALL.
BUT NOW THAT I CAN'T GO TO SLEEP,
I WANT TO.
SIGH.
GOD.
I'LL BE SO GLAD WHEN WE'RE BACK ON TRENADOR.
SIGH.
FIRST THING I'M GOING TO DO IS GET ME A BIG OL' CUP OF YOURS AND JOEY'S HOT CHOCOLATE.
THEN A HOT MEAL.
AND A HOT, HOT SHOWER.
SIGH.
HEY, ELLI,
...WHAT DO YOU WANT MOST?
WHEN WE GET BACK TO TRENADOR?

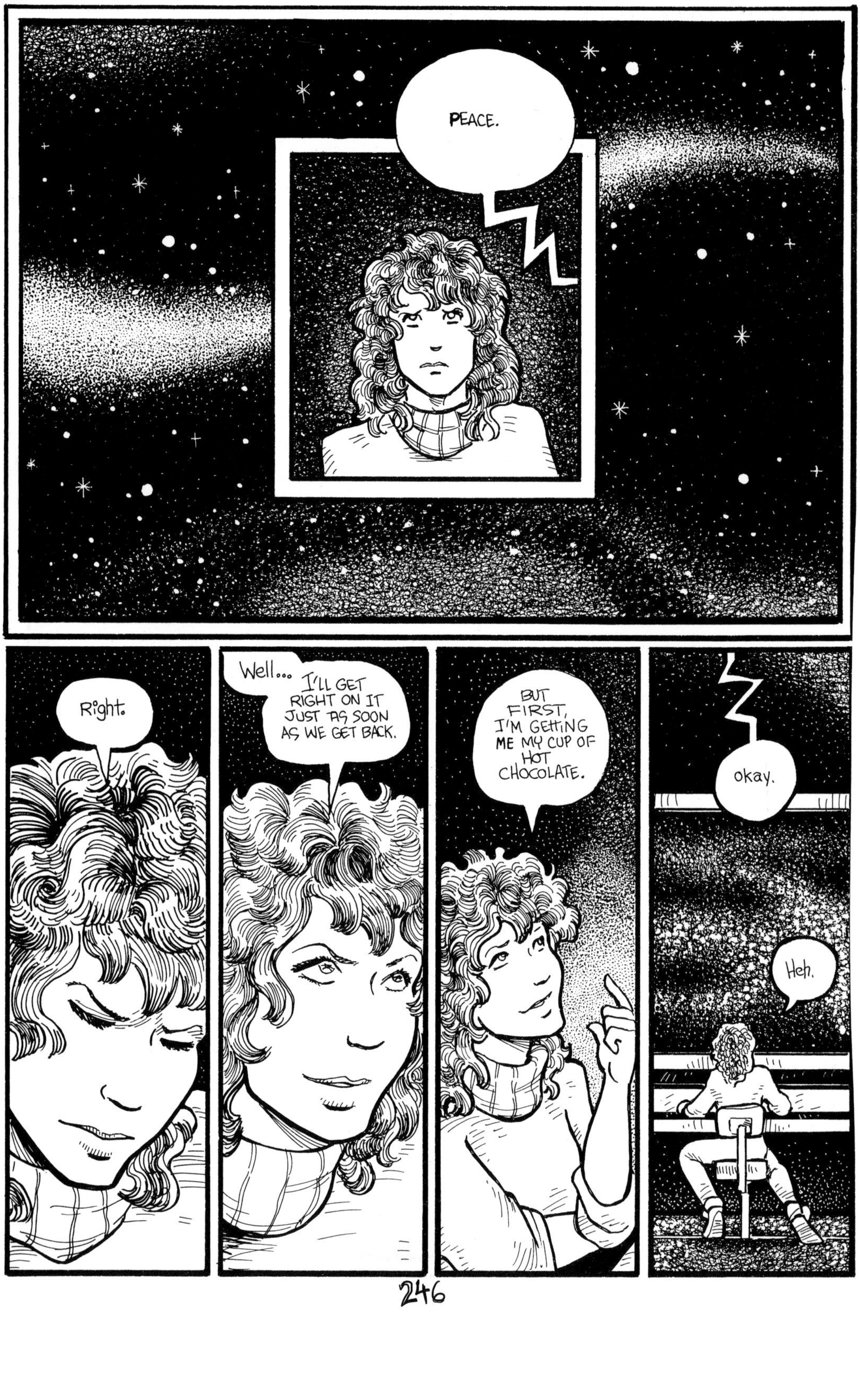
PEACE.
Right.
Well... I'LL GET RIGHT ON IT JUST AS SOON AS WE GET BACK.
BUT FIRST, I'M GETTING ME MY CUP OF HOT CHOCOLATE.
okay.
Heh.

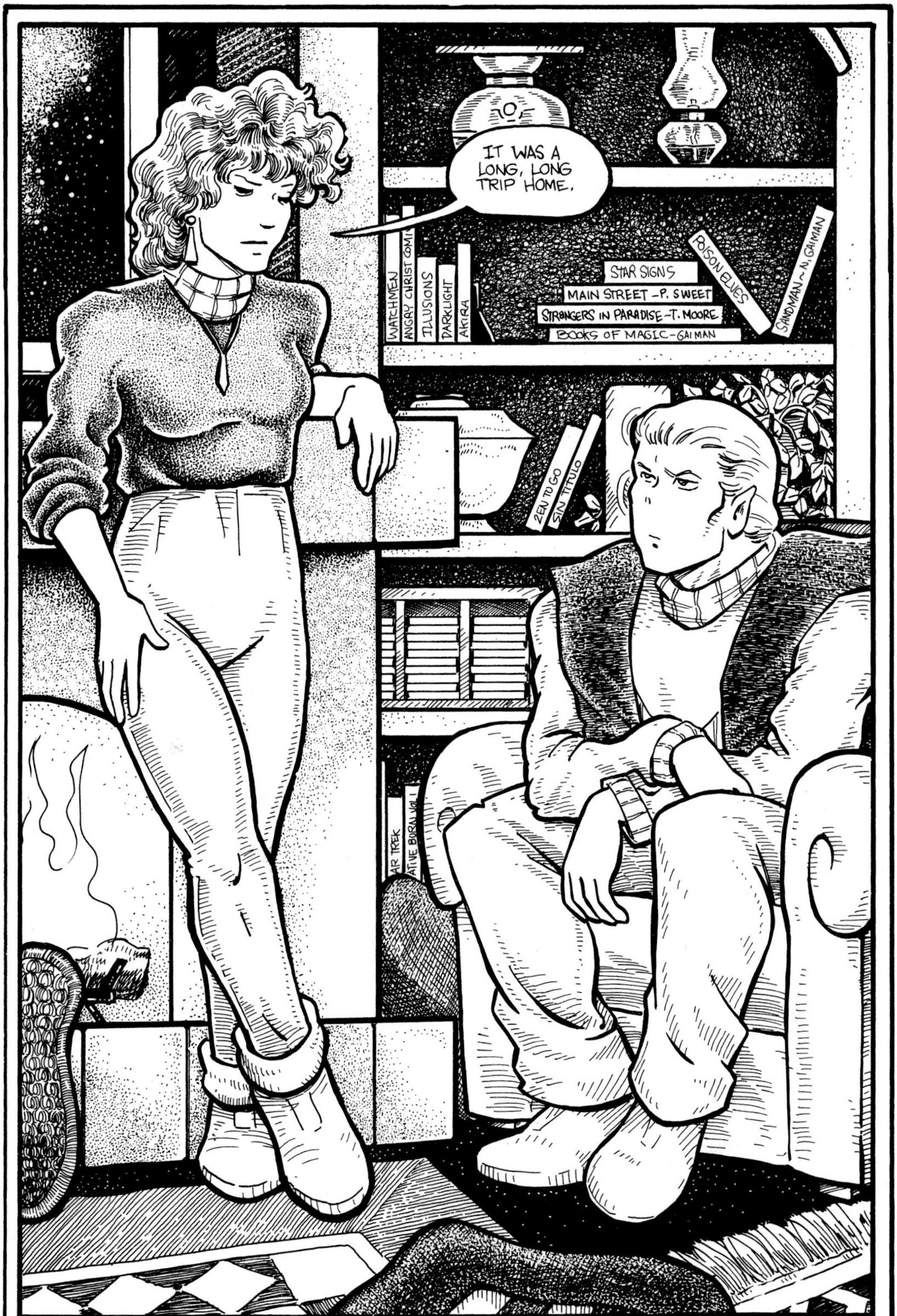
IT WAS A LONG, LONG TRIP HOME.
WATCHMEN
ANGRY CHRIST COMI
ILLUSIONS
DARKLIGHT
AKIRA
STAR SIGNS
MAIN STREET -P. SWEET
STRANGERS IN PARADISE -T. MOORE
BOOKS OF MAGIC -GAIMAN
POISON ELVES
SANDMAN ~N. GAIMAN
ZEN TO GO
SIN TITULO

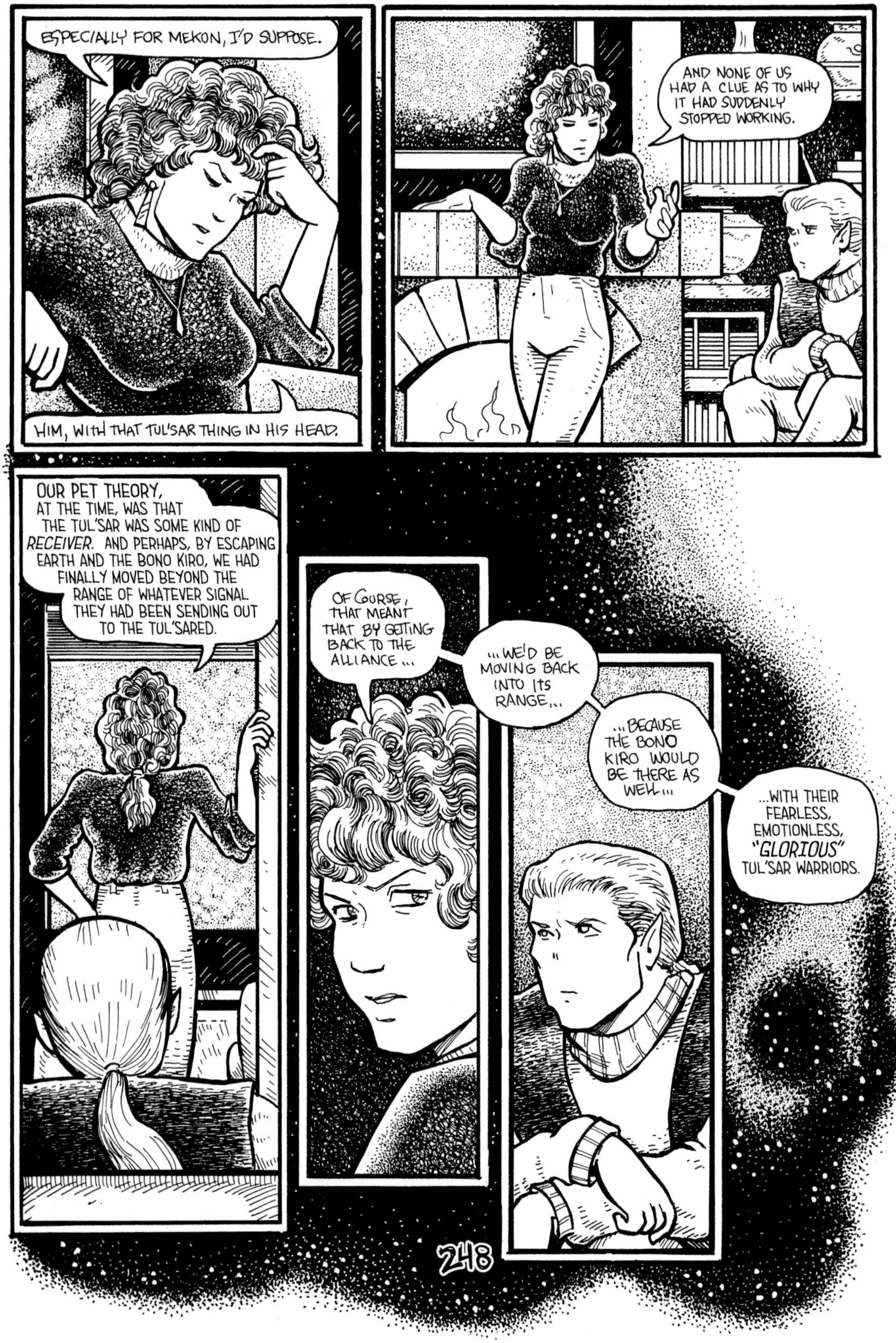
ESPECIALLY FOR MEKON, I'D SUPPOSE.
HIM, WITH THAT TUL'SAR THING IN HIS HEAD.
AND NONE OF US HAD A CLUE AS TO WHY IT HAD SUDDENLY STOPPED WORKING.
OUR PET THEORY, AT THE TIME, WAS THAT THE TUL'SAR WAS SOME KIND OF RECEIVER. AND PERHAPS, BY ESCAPING EARTH AND THE BONO KIRO, WE HAD FINALLY MOVED BEYOND THE RANGE OF WHATEVER SIGNAL THEY HAD BEEN SENDING OUT TO THE TUL'SARED.
OF COURSE, THAT MEANT THAT BY GETTING BACK TO THE ALLIANCE...
...WE'D BE MOVING BACK INTO ITS RANGE...
...BECAUSE THE BONO KIRO WOULD BE THERE AS WELL...
...WITH THEIR FEARLESS, EMOTIONLESS, "GLORIOUS" TUL'SAR WARRIORS.
248

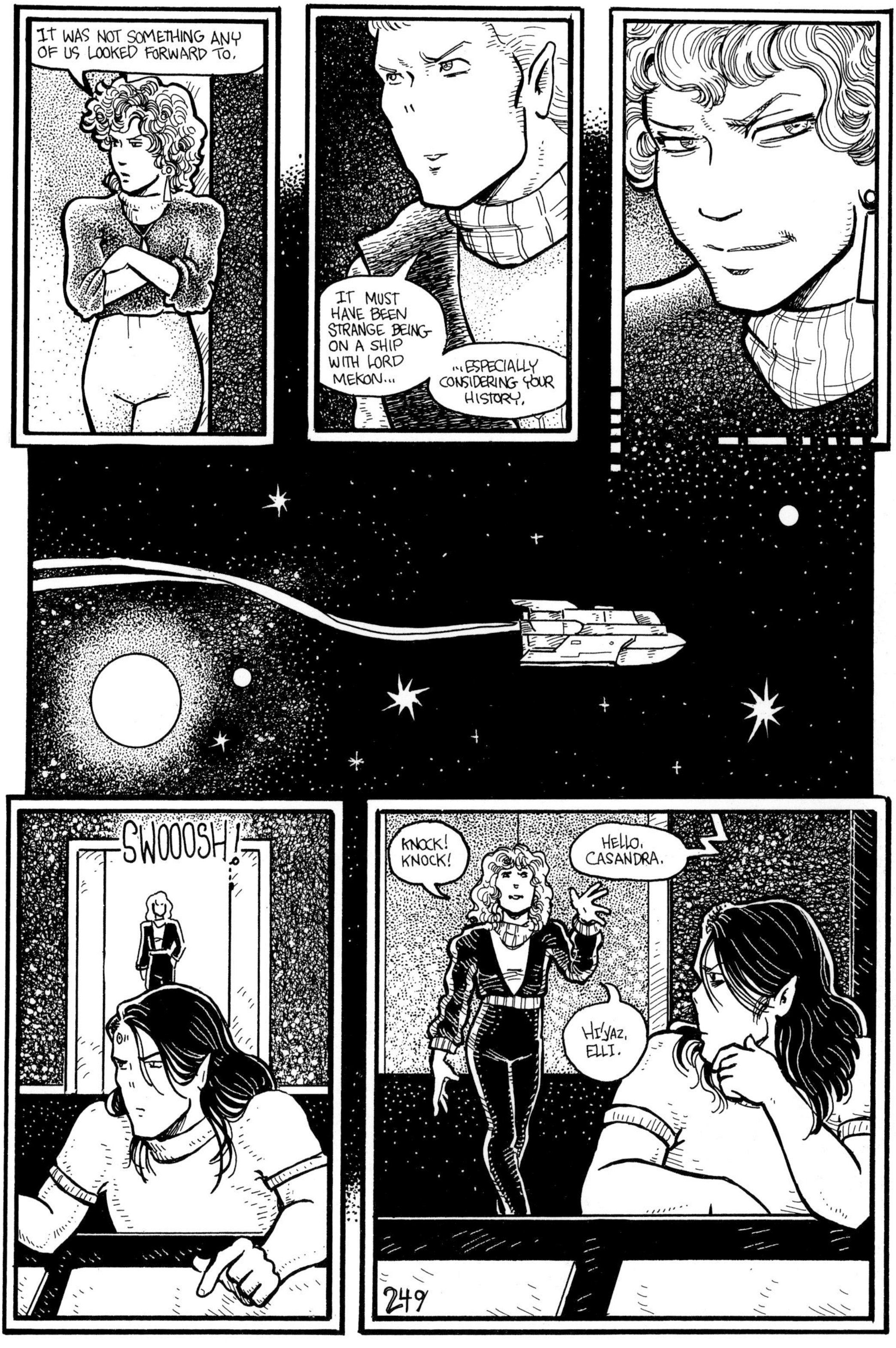
IT WAS NOT SOMETHING ANY OF US LOOKED FORWARD TO.
IT MUST HAVE BEEN STRANGE BEING ON A SHIP WITH LORD MEKON...
...ESPECIALLY CONSIDERING YOUR HISTORY.
SWOOOSH!
KNOCK! KNOCK!
HELLO, CASANDRA.
HI'YAZ, ELLI.
249

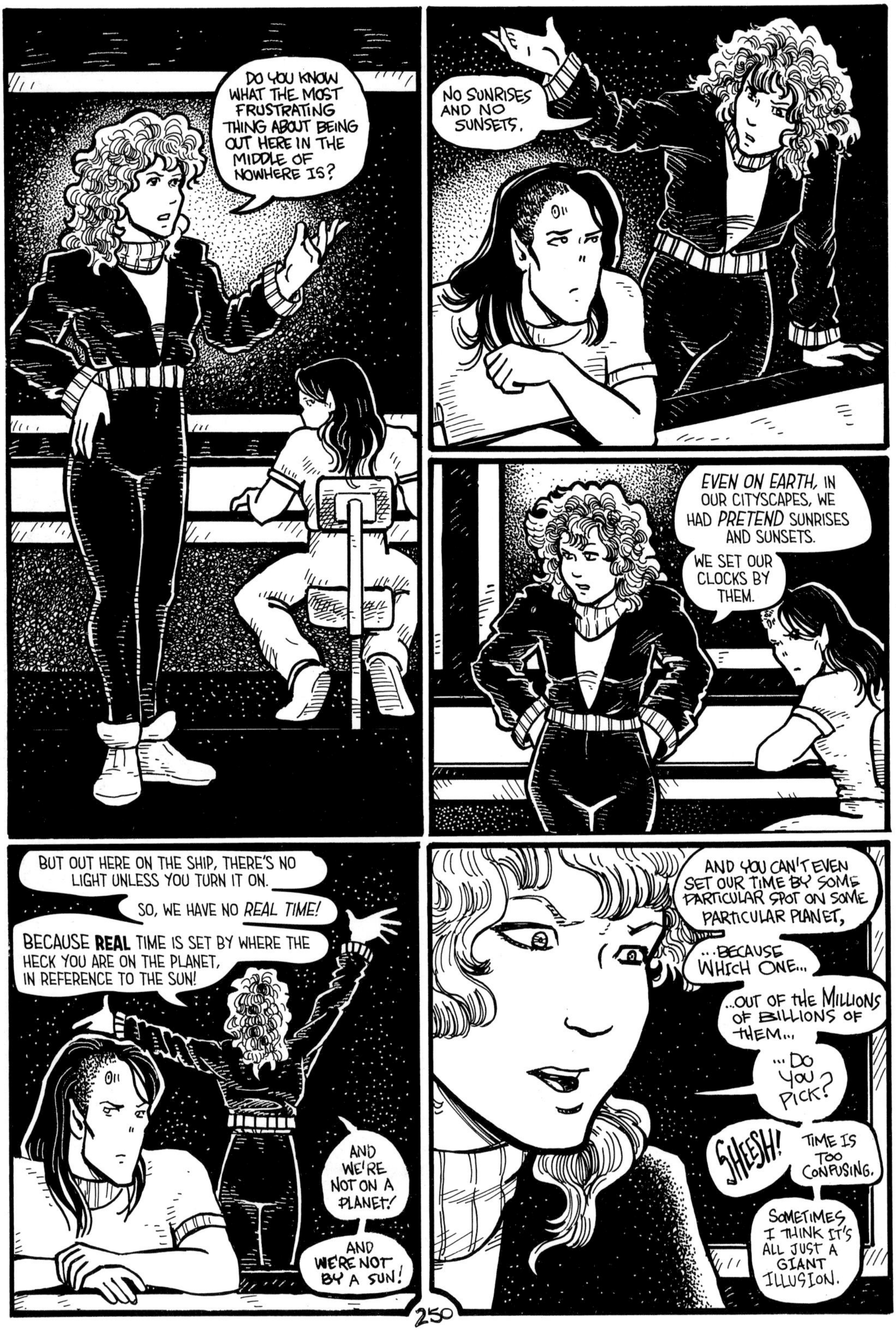
DO YOU KNOW WHAT THE MOST FRUSTRATING THING ABOUT BEING OUT HERE IN THE MIDDLE OF NOWHERE IS?
NO SUNRISES AND NO SUNSETS.
EVEN ON EARTH, IN OUR CITYSCAPES, WE HAD PRETEND SUNRISES AND SUNSETS.
WE SET OUR CLOCKS BY THEM.
BUT OUT HERE ON THE SHIP, THERE'S NO LIGHT UNLESS YOU TURN IT ON.
SO, WE HAVE NO REAL TIME!
BECAUSE REAL TIME IS SET BY WHERE THE HECK YOU ARE ON THE PLANET, IN REFERENCE TO THE SUN!
AND WE'RE NOT ON A PLANET!
AND WE'RE NOT BY A SUN!
AND YOU CAN'T EVEN SET OUR TIME BY SOME PARTICULAR SPOT ON SOME PARTICULAR PLANET,
...BECAUSE WHICH ONE...
...OUT OF THE MILLIONS OF BILLIONS OF THEM...
...DO YOU PICK?
SHEESH!
TIME IS TOO CONFUSING.
SOMETIMES I THINK IT'S ALL JUST A GIANT ILLUSION.

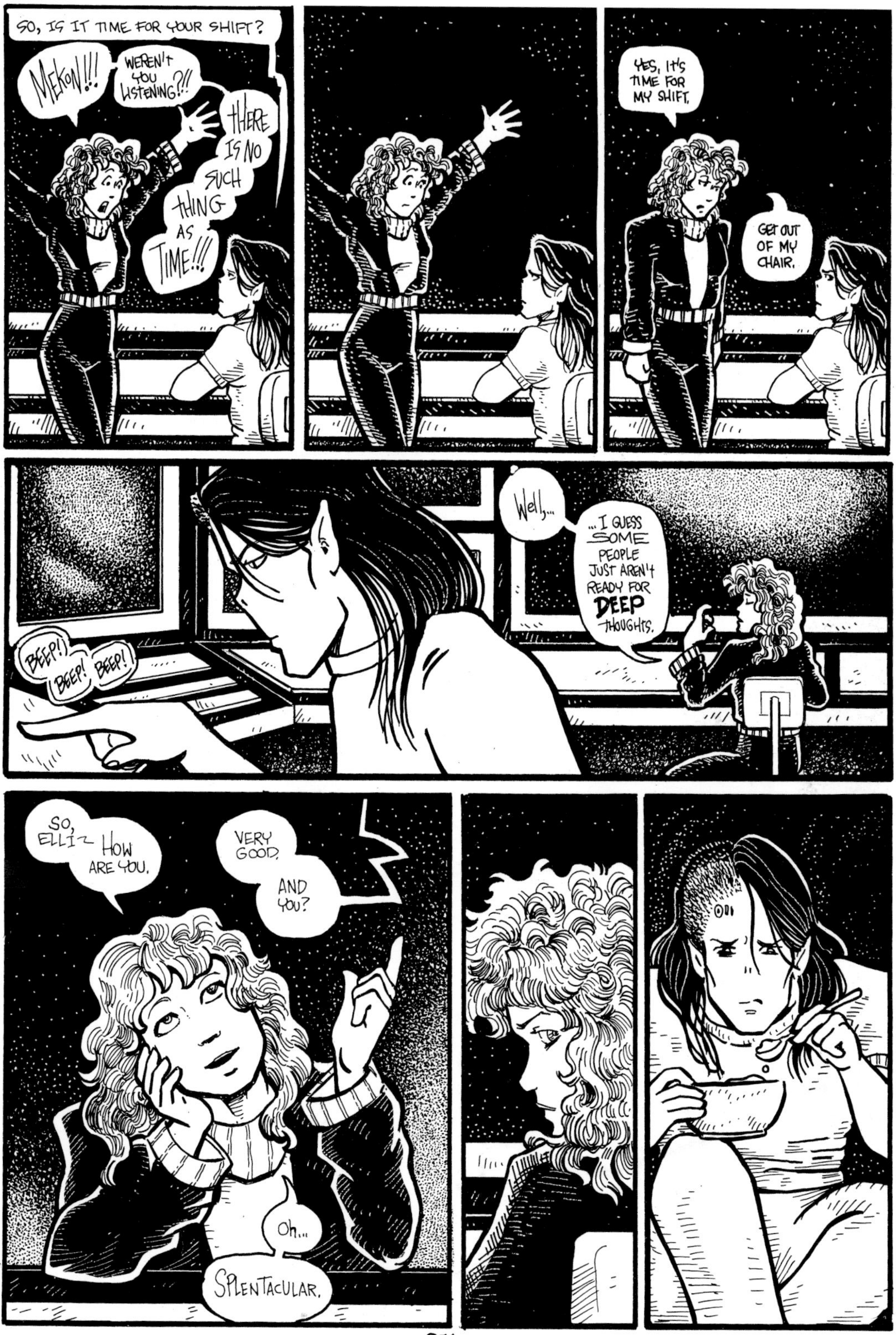

SO, IS IT TIME FOR YOUR SHIFT?
MEKON!!!
WEREN'T YOU LISTENING?!!
THERE IS NO SUCH THING AS TIME!!!
YES, IT'S TIME FOR MY SHIFT.
GET OUT OF MY CHAIR.
BEEP! BEEP! BEEP!
Well,...
...I GUESS SOME PEOPLE JUST AREN'T READY FOR DEEP THOUGHTS.
SO, ELLI~ HOW ARE YOU.
VERY GOOD.
AND YOU?
Oh...
SPLENTACULAR.

JOY AND A HALF, EH, MEKON?

What?

OH. YEAH.

IT DOESN'T TASTE VERY GOOD AT ALL,

...BUT I UNDERSTAND THE NEED TO RECOMBINE OUR FOOD COMPOUNDS INTO THE MOST NUTRITIOUS COMBINATION THAT WOULD LAST US THE LONGEST.

YEP.

TERRIBLE FOOD.

AND NOT ENOUGH TO FILL YOU UP EITHER.

WHAT A LIFE.

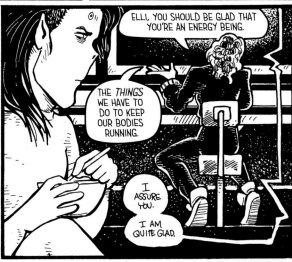

ELLI, YOU SHOULD BE GLAD THAT YOU'RE AN ENERGY BEING.

THE THINGS WE HAVE TO DO TO KEEP OUR BODIES RUNNING.

I ASSURE YOU.

I AM QUITE GLAD.

WELL, CASANDRA, IF ALL GOES WELL, WE WILL BE BACK INSIDE ALLIANCE TERRITORY SOON.

AND THEN, YOU CAN HAVE YOUR CUP OF HOT CHOCOLATE.

UMMM, YEAH.

AND I WANT A BIG BOWL OF MACARONI AND CHEESE.

AND A CHOCOLATE BAR!

AND PIZZA!

HEY, MEKON!

WHAT DO YOU WANT WHEN WE GET BACK TO THE ALLIANCE?

FOOD, YOU MEAN?

YEAH.

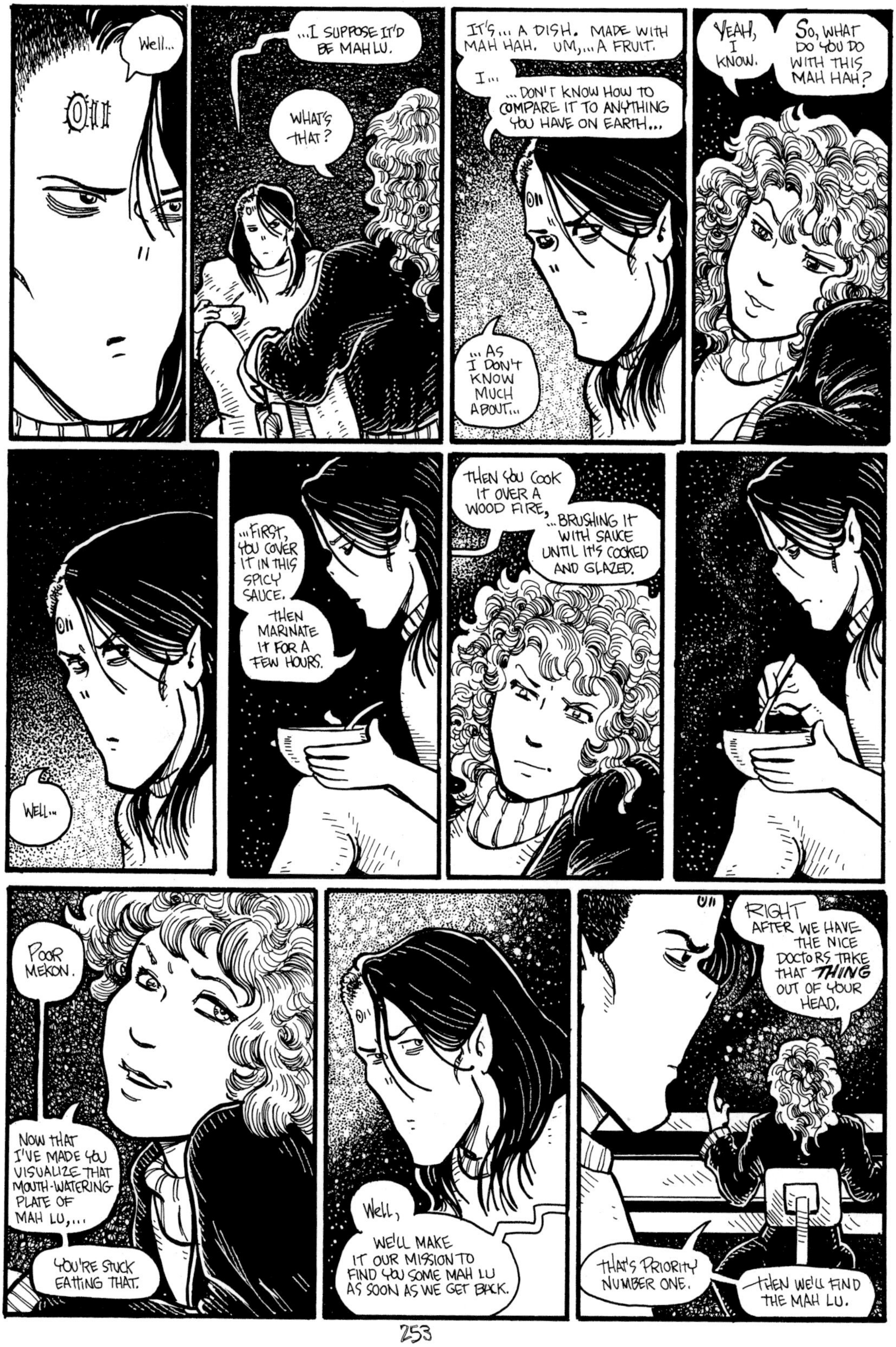

Well...
...I SUPPOSE IT'D BE MAH LU.
WHAT'S THAT?
IT'S... A DISH. MADE WITH MAH HAH. UM,...A FRUIT.
I...
...DON'T KNOW HOW TO COMPARE IT TO ANYTHING YOU HAVE ON EARTH...
...AS I DON'T KNOW MUCH ABOUT...
YEAH, I KNOW.
SO, WHAT DO YOU DO WITH THIS MAH HAH?
WELL...
...FIRST, YOU COVER IT IN THIS SPICY SAUCE.
THEN MARINATE IT FOR A FEW HOURS.
THEN YOU COOK IT OVER A WOOD FIRE,
...BRUSHING IT WITH SAUCE UNTIL IT'S COOKED AND GLAZED.
POOR MEKON.
NOW THAT I'VE MADE YOU VISUALIZE THAT MOUTH-WATERING PLATE OF MAH LU,...
YOU'RE STUCK EATING THAT.
Well,
WE'LL MAKE IT OUR MISSION TO FIND YOU SOME MAH LU AS SOON AS WE GET BACK.
RIGHT AFTER WE HAVE THE NICE DOCTORS TAKE THAT THING OUT OF YOUR HEAD.
THAT'S PRIORITY NUMBER ONE.
THEN WE'LL FIND THE MAH LU.

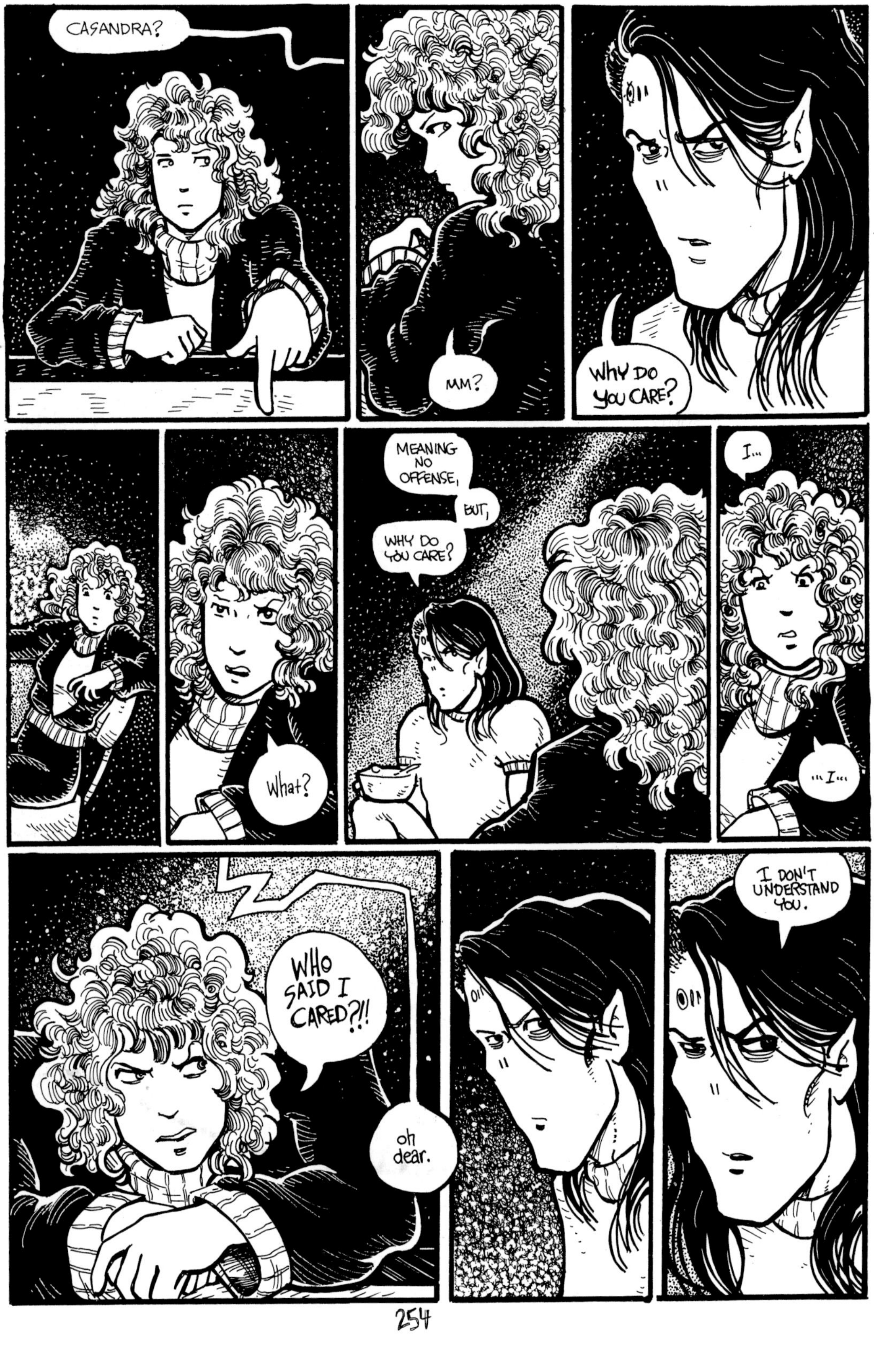
CASANDRA?
MM?
WHY DO YOU CARE?
What?
MEANING NO OFFENSE,
BUT,
WHY DO YOU CARE?
I...
...I...
WHO SAID I CARED?!!
oh dear.
I DON'T UNDERSTAND YOU.

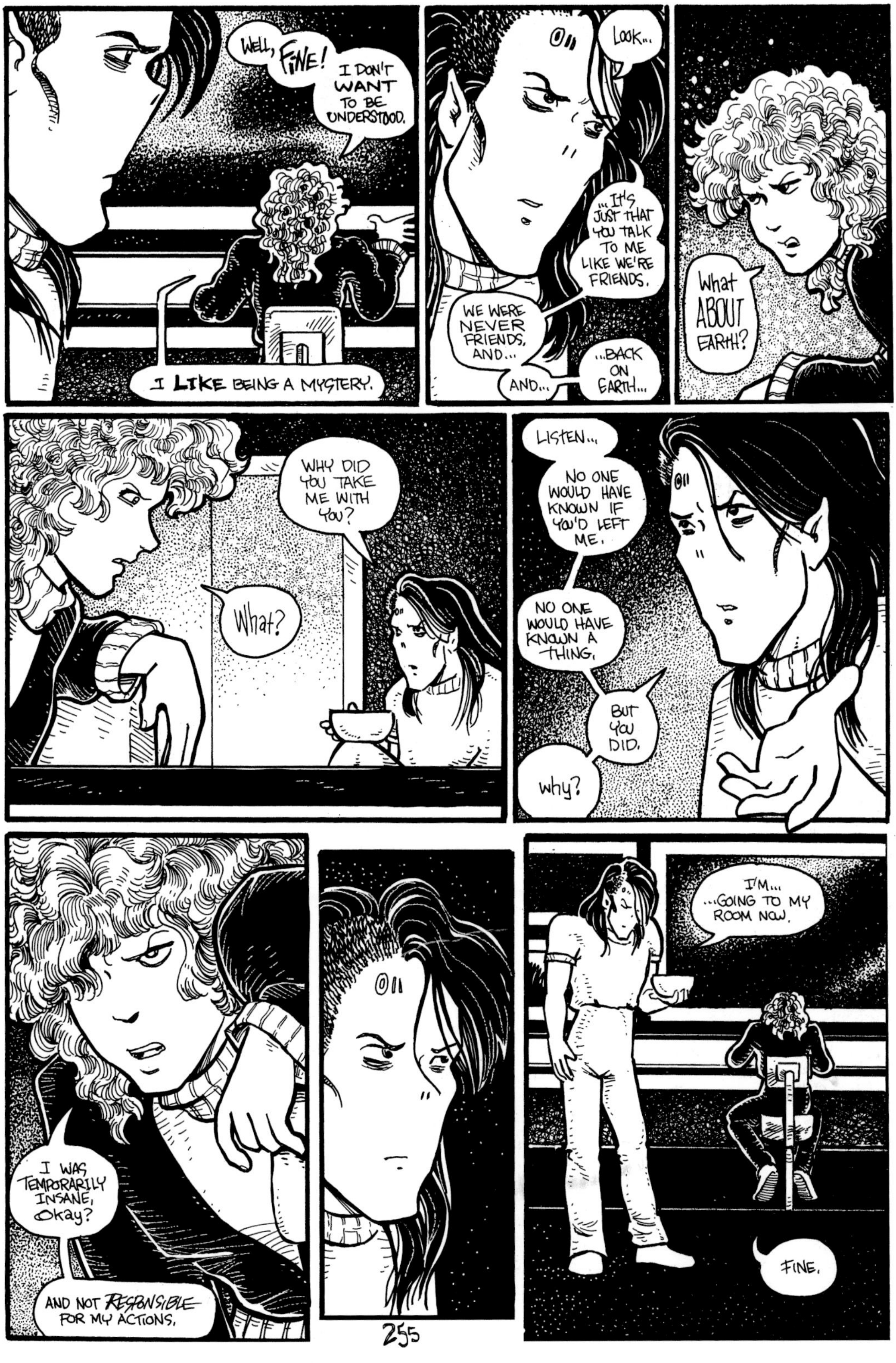
WELL, FINE!
I DON'T WANT TO BE UNDERSTOOD.
I LIKE BEING A MYSTERY.
LOOK...
...IT'S JUST THAT YOU TALK TO ME LIKE WE'RE FRIENDS.
WE WERE NEVER FRIENDS, AND...
AND...
...BACK ON EARTH...
What ABOUT EARTH?
WHY DID YOU TAKE ME WITH YOU?
What?
LISTEN...
NO ONE WOULD HAVE KNOWN IF YOU'D LEFT ME.
NO ONE WOULD HAVE KNOWN A THING.
BUT YOU DID.
why?
I WAS TEMPORARILY INSANE, Okay?
AND NOT RESPONSIBLE FOR MY ACTIONS.
I'M...
...GOING TO MY ROOM NOW.
FINE.

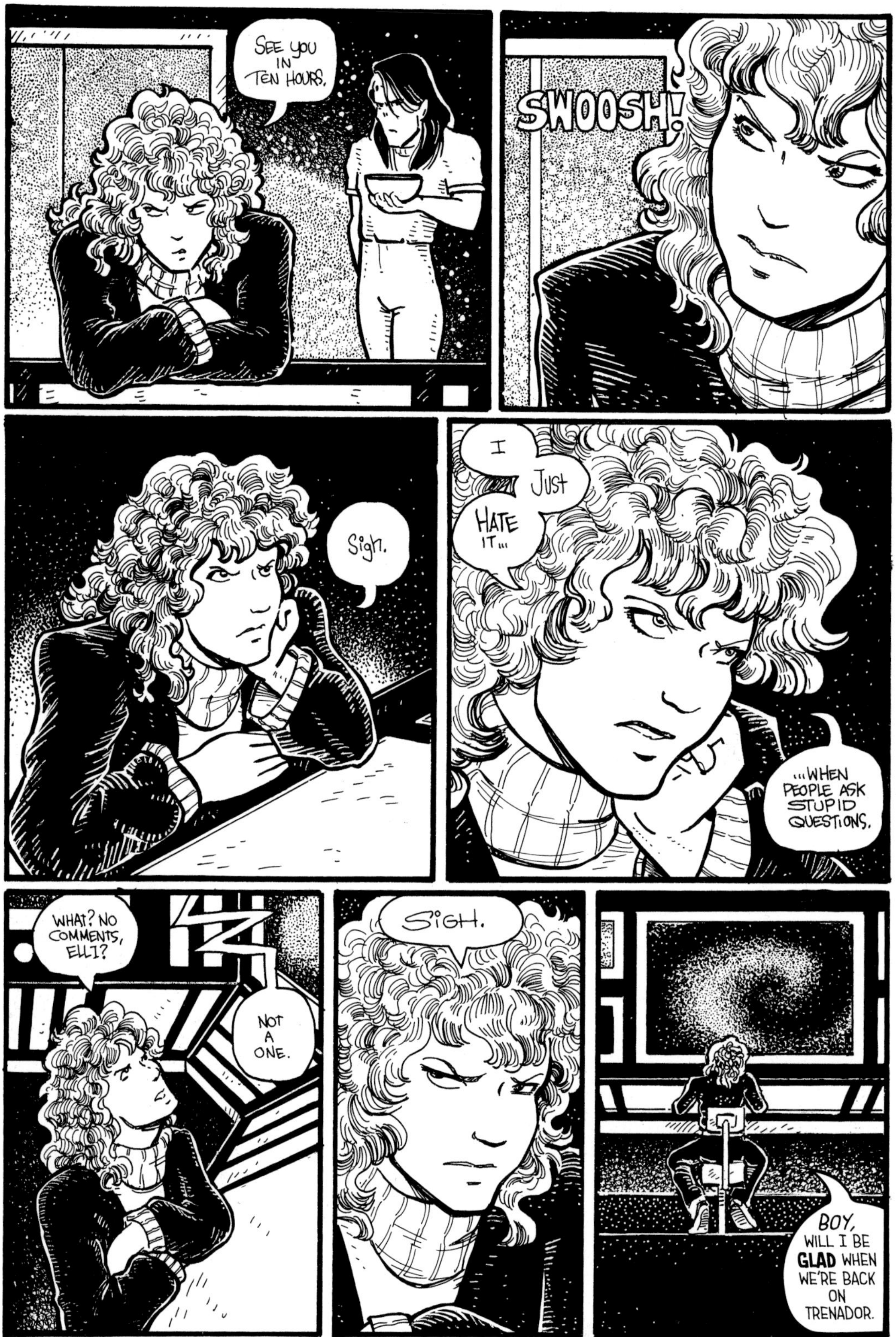
SEE YOU IN TEN HOURS.
SWOOSH!
Sigh.
I
JUST
HATE IT...
...WHEN PEOPLE ASK STUPID QUESTIONS.
WHAT? NO COMMENTS, ELLI?
NOT A ONE.
SIGH.
BOY, WILL I BE GLAD WHEN WE'RE BACK ON TRENADOR.

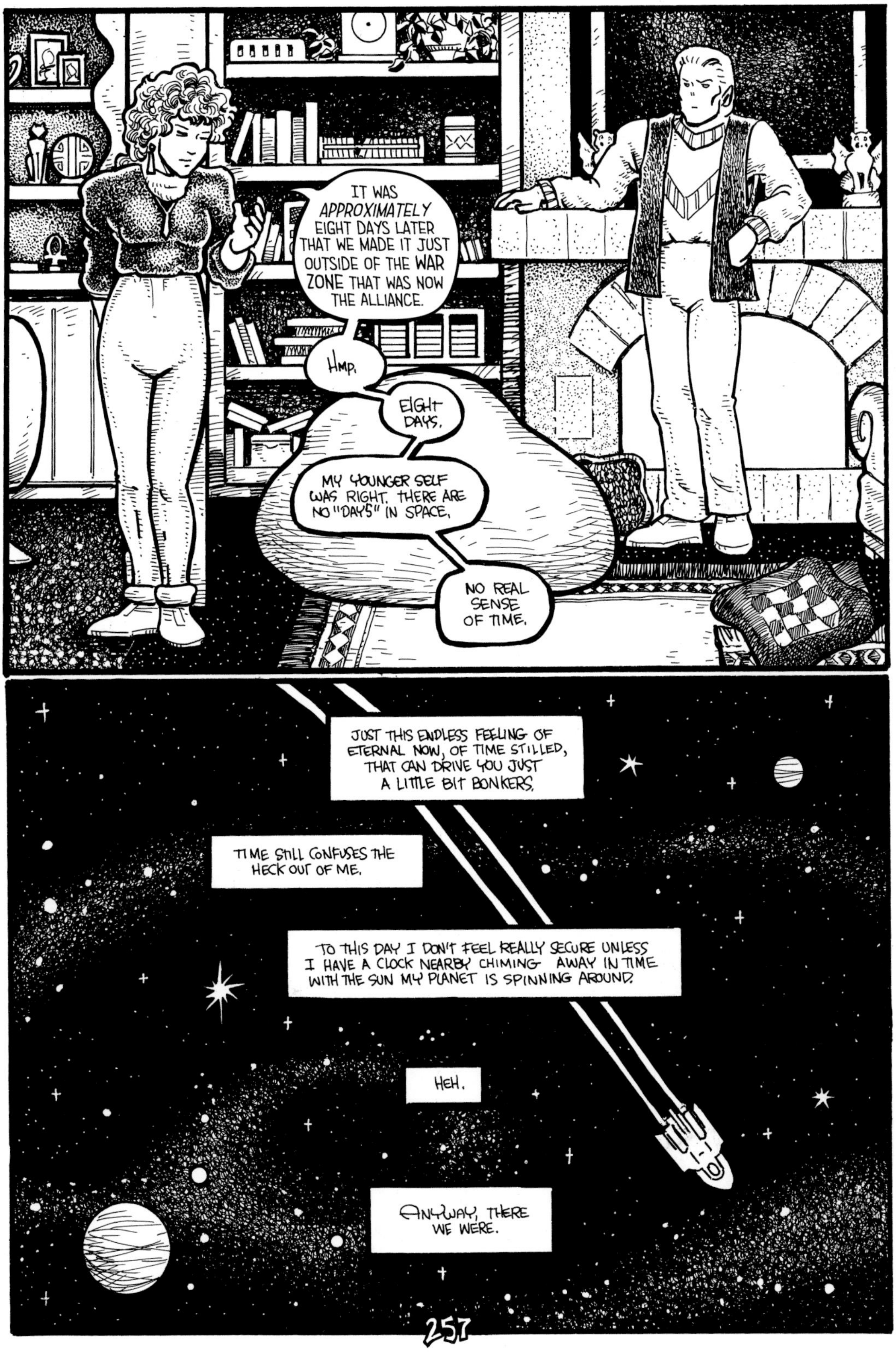
IT WAS APPROXIMATELY EIGHT DAYS LATER THAT WE MADE IT JUST OUTSIDE OF THE WAR ZONE THAT WAS NOW THE ALLIANCE.
Hmp.
EIGHT DAYS.
MY YOUNGER SELF WAS RIGHT. THERE ARE NO "DAYS" IN SPACE.
NO REAL SENSE OF TIME.
JUST THIS ENDLESS FEELING OF ETERNAL NOW, OF TIME STILLED, THAT CAN DRIVE YOU JUST A LITTLE BIT BONKERS.
TIME STILL CONFUSES THE HECK OUT OF ME.
TO THIS DAY I DON'T FEEL REALLY SECURE UNLESS I HAVE A CLOCK NEARBY CHIMING AWAY IN TIME WITH THE SUN MY PLANET IS SPINNING AROUND.
HEH.
ANYWAY, THERE WE WERE.

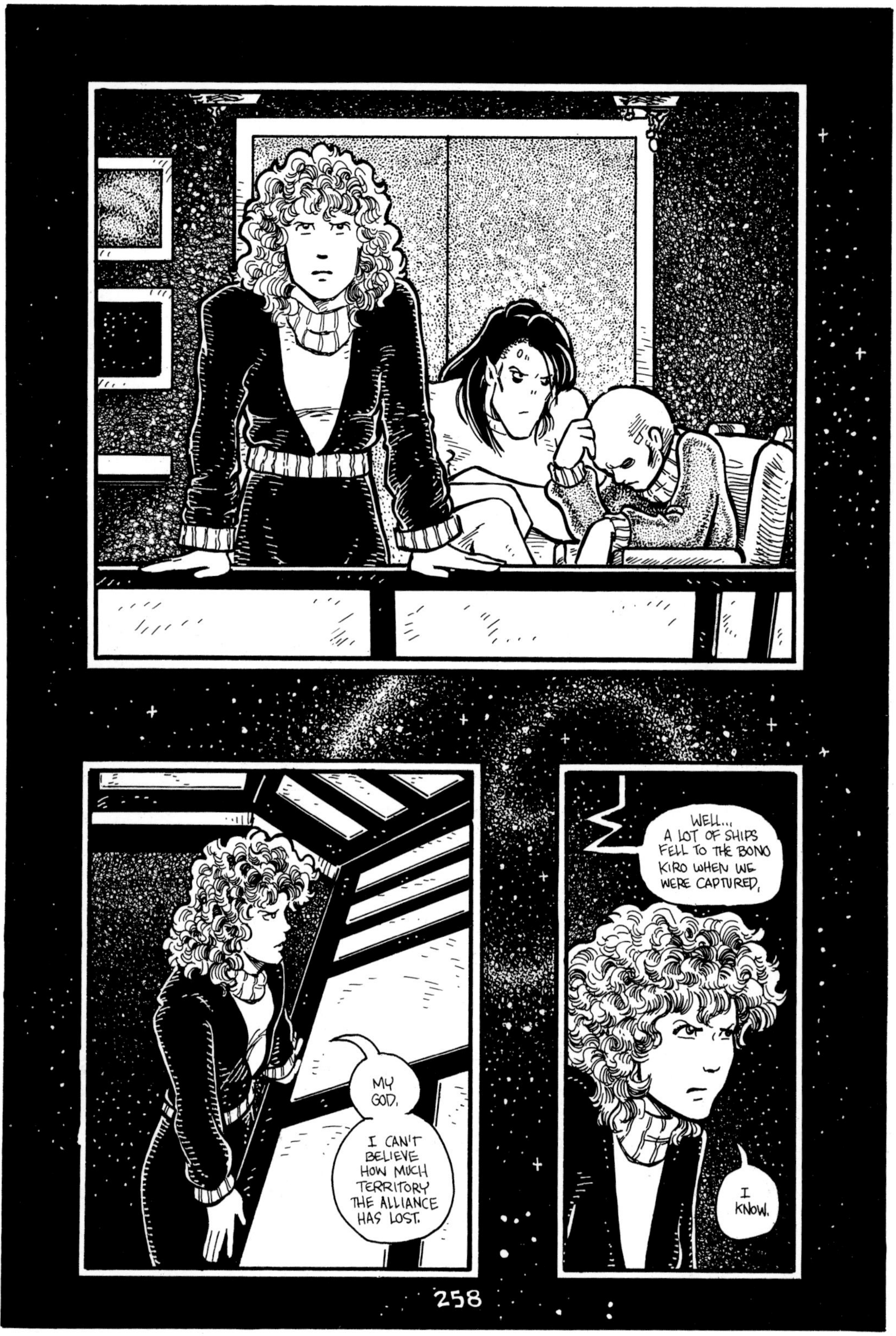
MY GOD.
I CAN'T BELIEVE HOW MUCH TERRITORY THE ALLIANCE HAS LOST.
WELL... A LOT OF SHIPS FELL TO THE BONO KIRO WHEN WE WERE CAPTURED.
I KNOW.

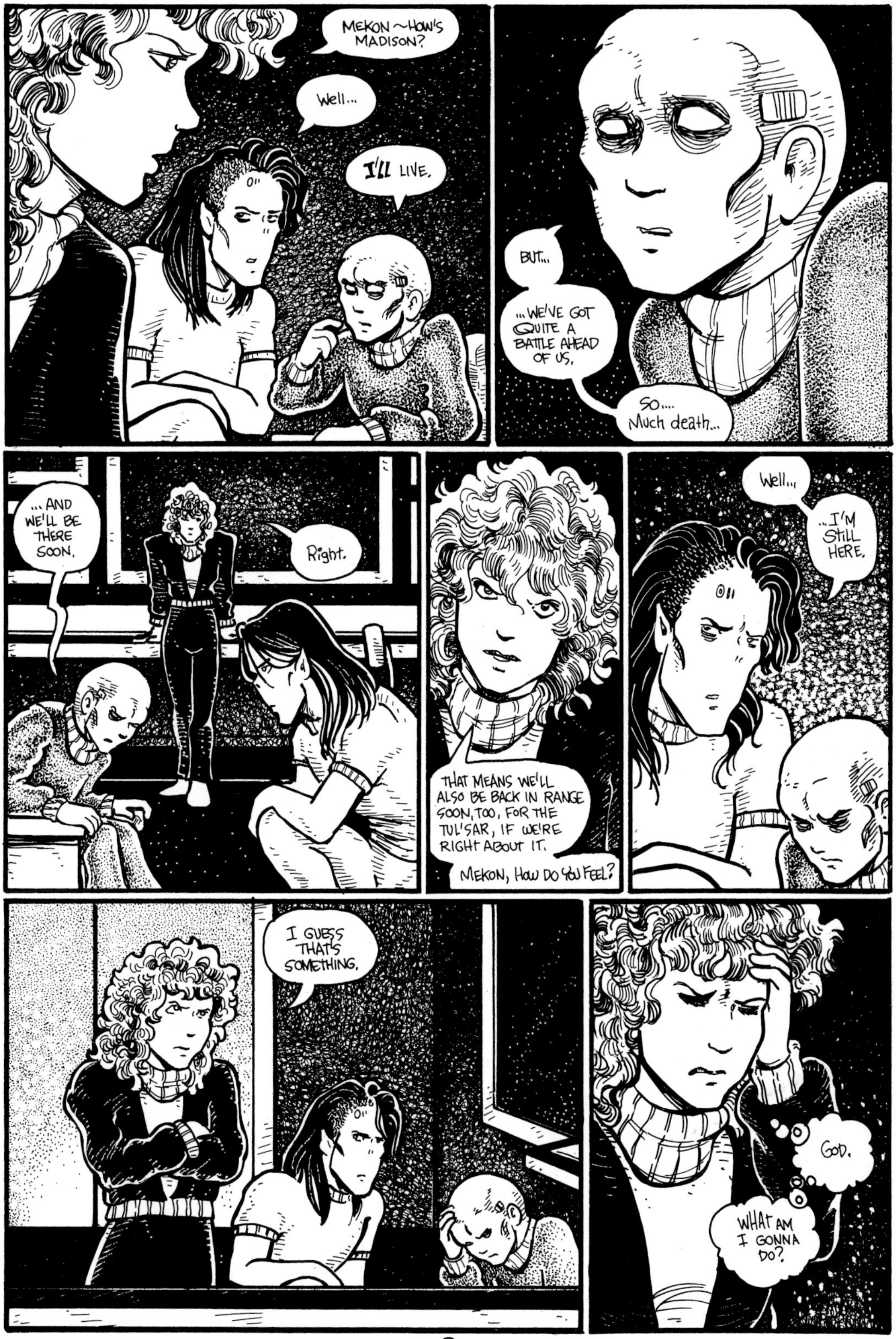
MEKON ~ HOW'S MADISON?
Well...
I'LL LIVE.
BUT...
...WE'VE GOT QUITE A BATTLE AHEAD OF US.
SO.... Much death...
...AND WE'LL BE THERE SOON.
Right.
THAT MEANS WE'LL ALSO BE BACK IN RANGE SOON, TOO, FOR THE TUL'SAR, IF WE'RE RIGHT ABOUT IT.
MEKON, HOW DO YOU FEEL?
Well...
...I'M STILL HERE.
I GUESS THAT'S SOMETHING.
GOD.
WHAT AM I GONNA DO?

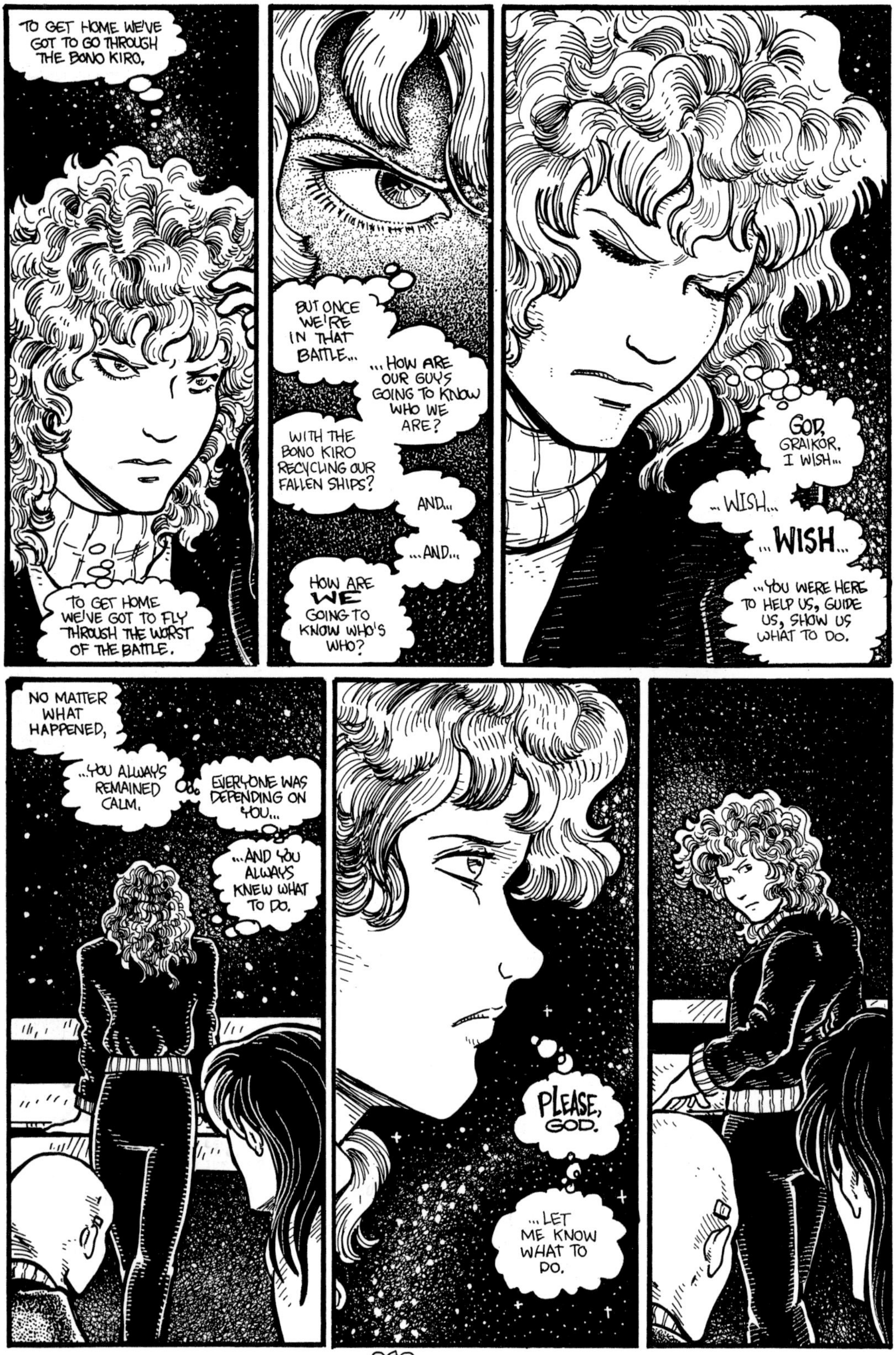
TO GET HOME WE'VE GOT TO GO THROUGH THE BONO KIRO,
TO GET HOME WE'VE GOT TO FLY THROUGH THE WORST OF THE BATTLE.
BUT ONCE WE'RE IN THAT BATTLE...
...HOW ARE OUR GUYS GOING TO KNOW WHO WE ARE?
WITH THE BONO KIRO RECYCLING OUR FALLEN SHIPS?
AND...
...AND...
HOW ARE WE GOING TO KNOW WHO'S WHO?
GOD, GRAIKOR, I WISH...
...WISH...
...WISH...
...YOU WERE HERE TO HELP US, GUIDE US, SHOW US WHAT TO DO.
NO MATTER WHAT HAPPENED,
...YOU ALWAYS REMAINED CALM.
EVERYONE WAS DEPENDING ON YOU...
...AND YOU ALWAYS KNEW WHAT TO DO.
PLEASE, GOD.
...LET ME KNOW WHAT TO DO.

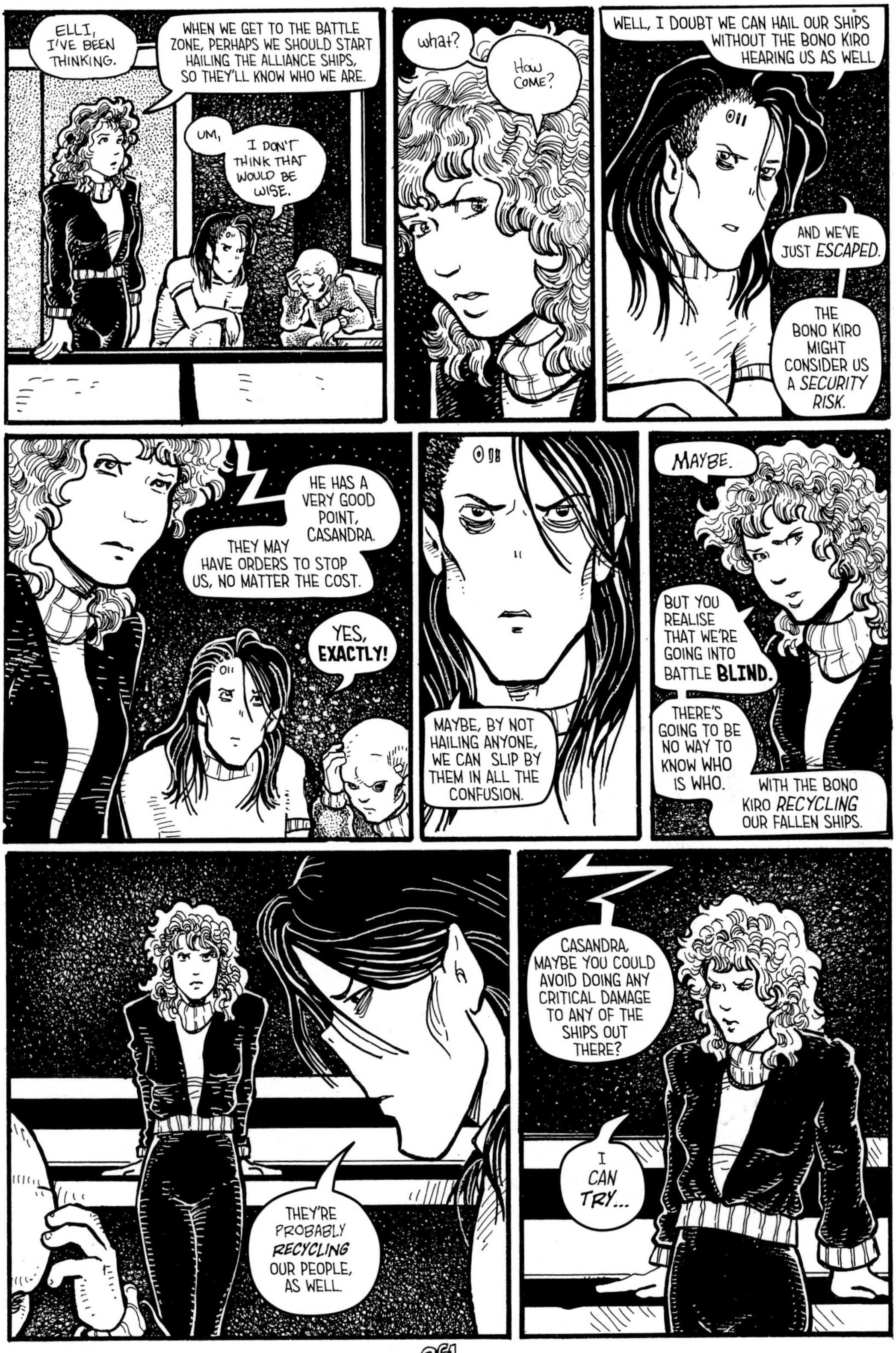
ELLI, I'VE BEEN THINKING.
WHEN WE GET TO THE BATTLE ZONE, PERHAPS WE SHOULD START HAILING THE ALLIANCE SHIPS, SO THEY'LL KNOW WHO WE ARE.
UM,
I DON'T THINK THAT WOULD BE WISE.
what?
How COME?
WELL, I DOUBT WE CAN HAIL OUR SHIPS WITHOUT THE BONO KIRO HEARING US AS WELL
AND WE'VE JUST ESCAPED.
THE BONO KIRO MIGHT CONSIDER US A SECURITY RISK.
HE HAS A VERY GOOD POINT, CASANDRA.
THEY MAY HAVE ORDERS TO STOP US, NO MATTER THE COST.
YES, EXACTLY!
MAYBE, BY NOT HAILING ANYONE, WE CAN SLIP BY THEM IN ALL THE CONFUSION.
MAYBE.
BUT YOU REALISE THAT WE'RE GOING INTO BATTLE BLIND.
THERE'S GOING TO BE NO WAY TO KNOW WHO IS WHO.
WITH THE BONO KIRO RECYCLING OUR FALLEN SHIPS.
THEY'RE PROBABLY RECYCLING OUR PEOPLE, AS WELL.
CASANDRA, MAYBE YOU COULD AVOID DOING ANY CRITICAL DAMAGE TO ANY OF THE SHIPS OUT THERE?
I CAN TRY...

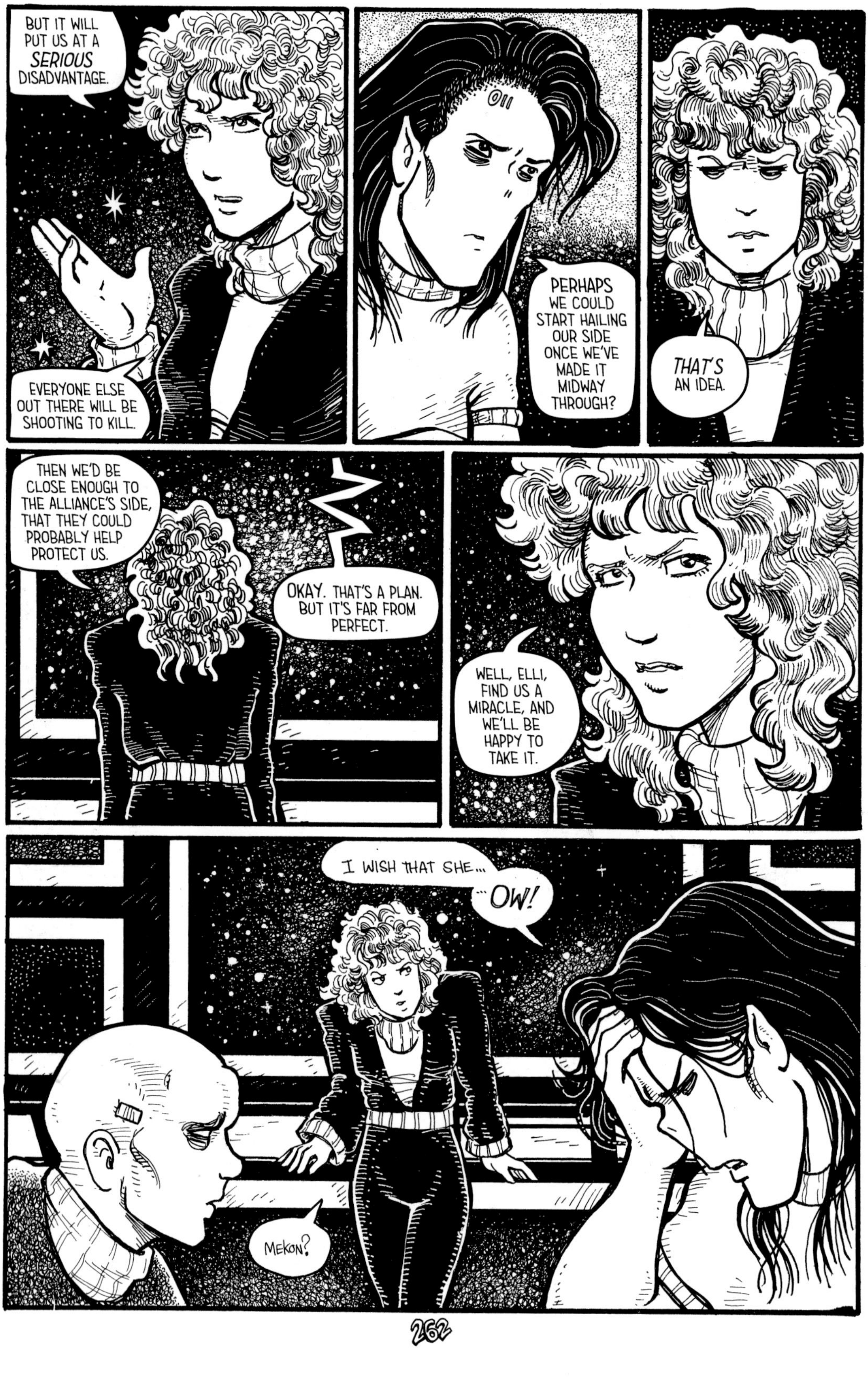
BUT IT WILL PUT US AT A SERIOUS DISADVANTAGE.
EVERYONE ELSE OUT THERE WILL BE SHOOTING TO KILL.
PERHAPS WE COULD START HAILING OUR SIDE ONCE WE'VE MADE IT MIDWAY THROUGH?
THAT'S AN IDEA.
THEN WE'D BE CLOSE ENOUGH TO THE ALLIANCE'S SIDE, THAT THEY COULD PROBABLY HELP PROTECT US.
OKAY. THAT'S A PLAN. BUT IT'S FAR FROM PERFECT.
WELL, ELLI, FIND US A MIRACLE, AND WE'LL BE HAPPY TO TAKE IT.
I WISH THAT SHE...
...OW!
MEKON?

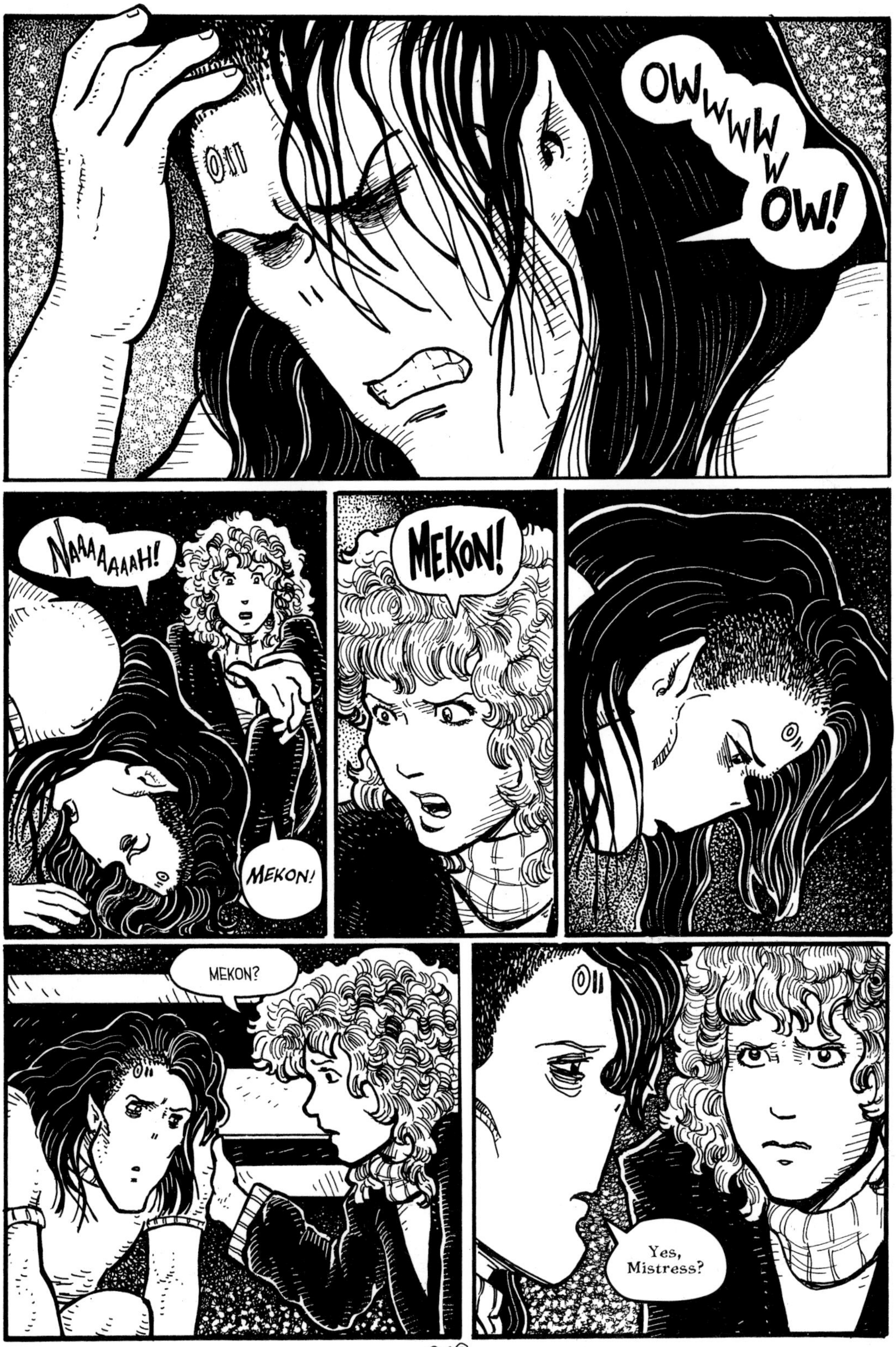
OWwwwwwOW!
NAAAAAAAH!
MEKON!
MEKON!
MEKON?
Yes, Mistress?

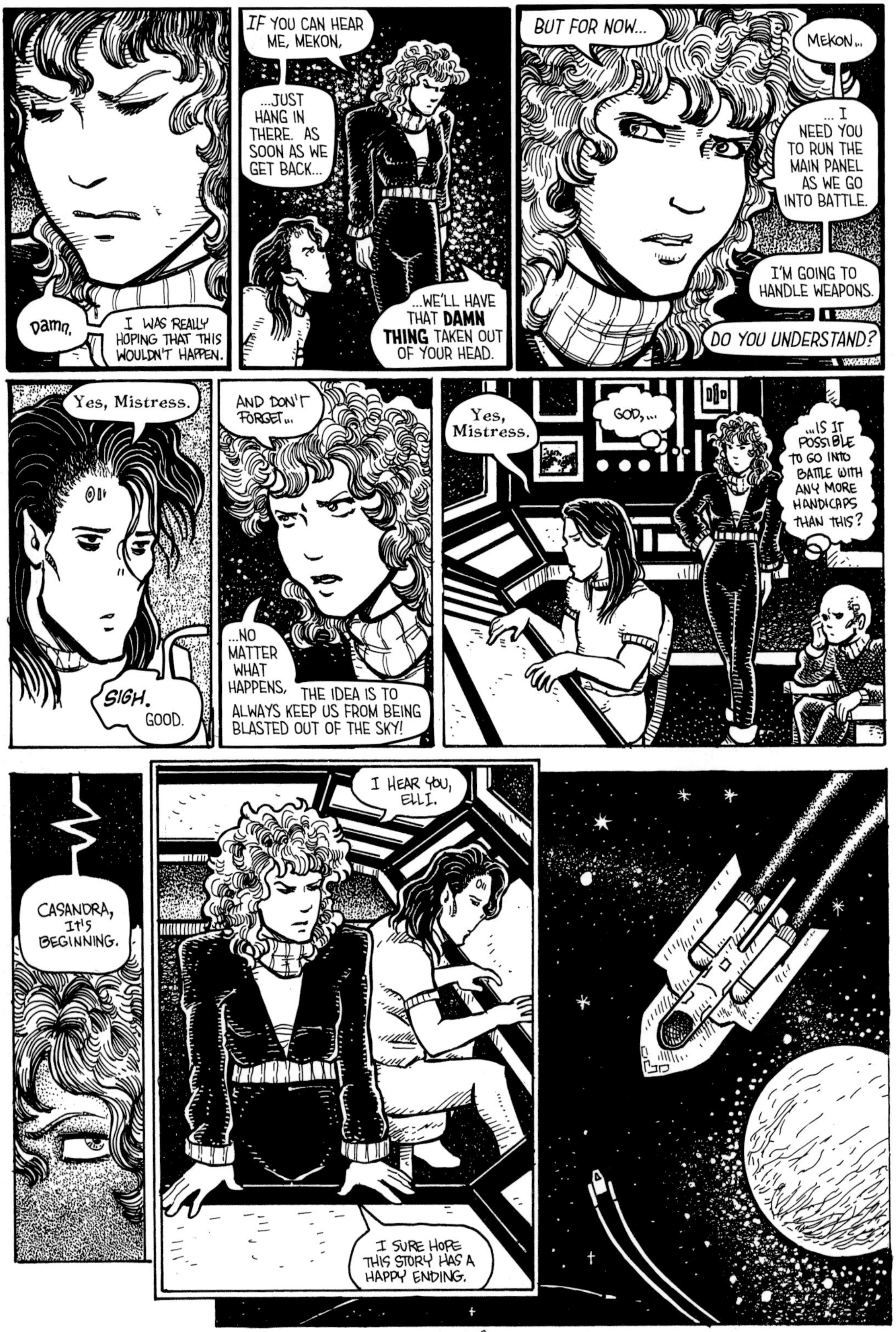
Damn.
I WAS REALLY HOPING THAT THIS WOULDN'T HAPPEN.
IF YOU CAN HEAR ME, MEKON,
...JUST HANG IN THERE. AS SOON AS WE GET BACK...
...WE'LL HAVE THAT DAMN THING TAKEN OUT OF YOUR HEAD.
BUT FOR NOW...
MEKON...
... I NEED YOU TO RUN THE MAIN PANEL AS WE GO INTO BATTLE.
I'M GOING TO HANDLE WEAPONS.
DO YOU UNDERSTAND?
Yes, Mistress.
SIGH. GOOD.
AND DON'T FORGET...
...NO MATTER WHAT HAPPENS, THE IDEA IS TO ALWAYS KEEP US FROM BEING BLASTED OUT OF THE SKY!
Yes, Mistress.
GOD,...
...IS IT POSSIBLE TO GO INTO BATTLE WITH ANY MORE HANDICAPS THAN THIS?
CASANDRA, IT'S BEGINNING.
I HEAR YOU, ELLI.
I SURE HOPE THIS STORY HAS A HAPPY ENDING.

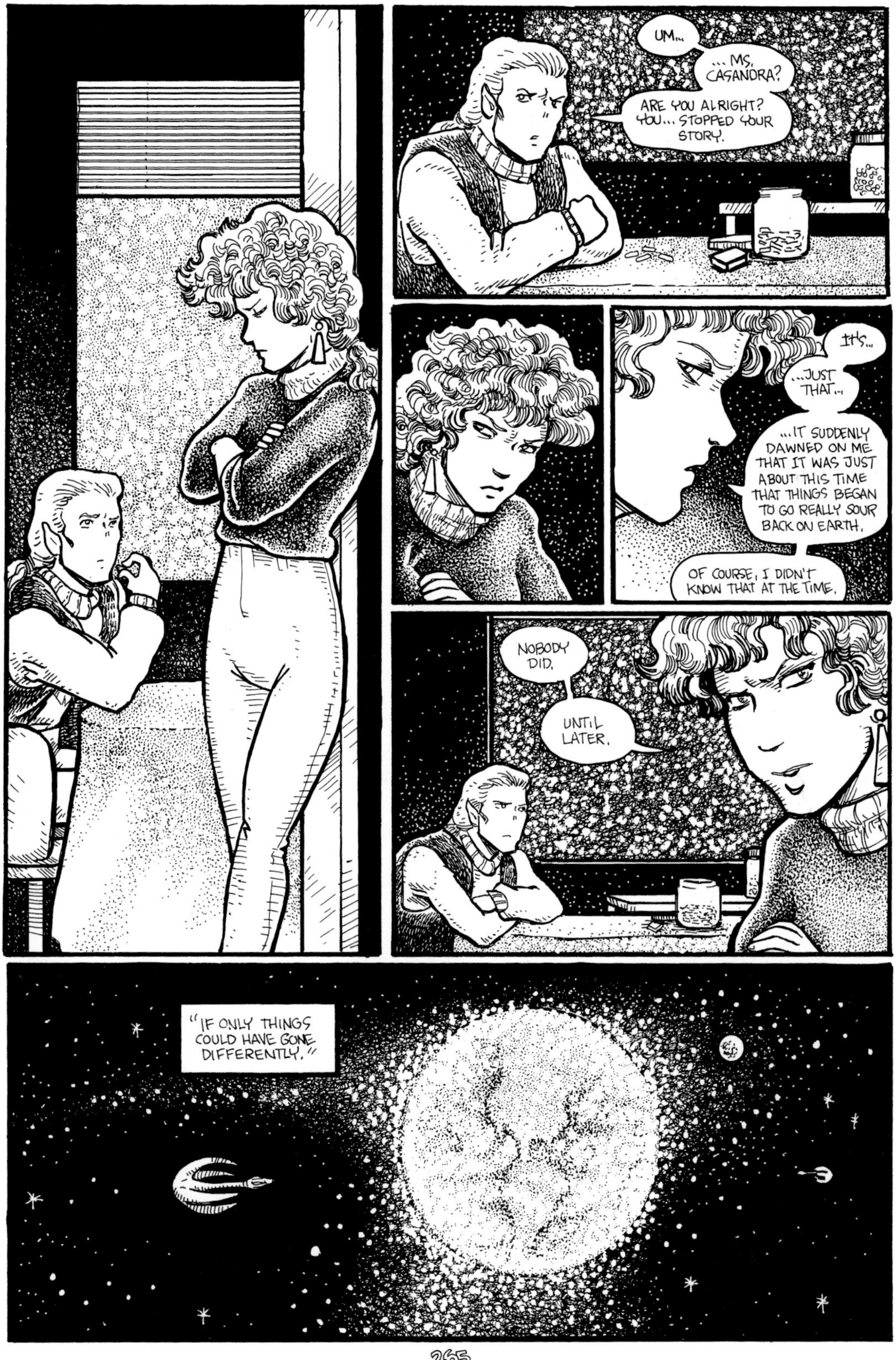
UM...
... MS. CASANDRA?
ARE YOU ALRIGHT? YOU... STOPPED YOUR STORY.
IT'S...
...JUST THAT...
...IT SUDDENLY DAWNED ON ME THAT IT WAS JUST ABOUT THIS TIME THAT THINGS BEGAN TO GO REALLY SOUR BACK ON EARTH.
OF COURSE, I DIDN'T KNOW THAT AT THE TIME.
NOBODY DID.
UNTIL LATER.
"IF ONLY THINGS COULD HAVE GONE DIFFERENTLY."

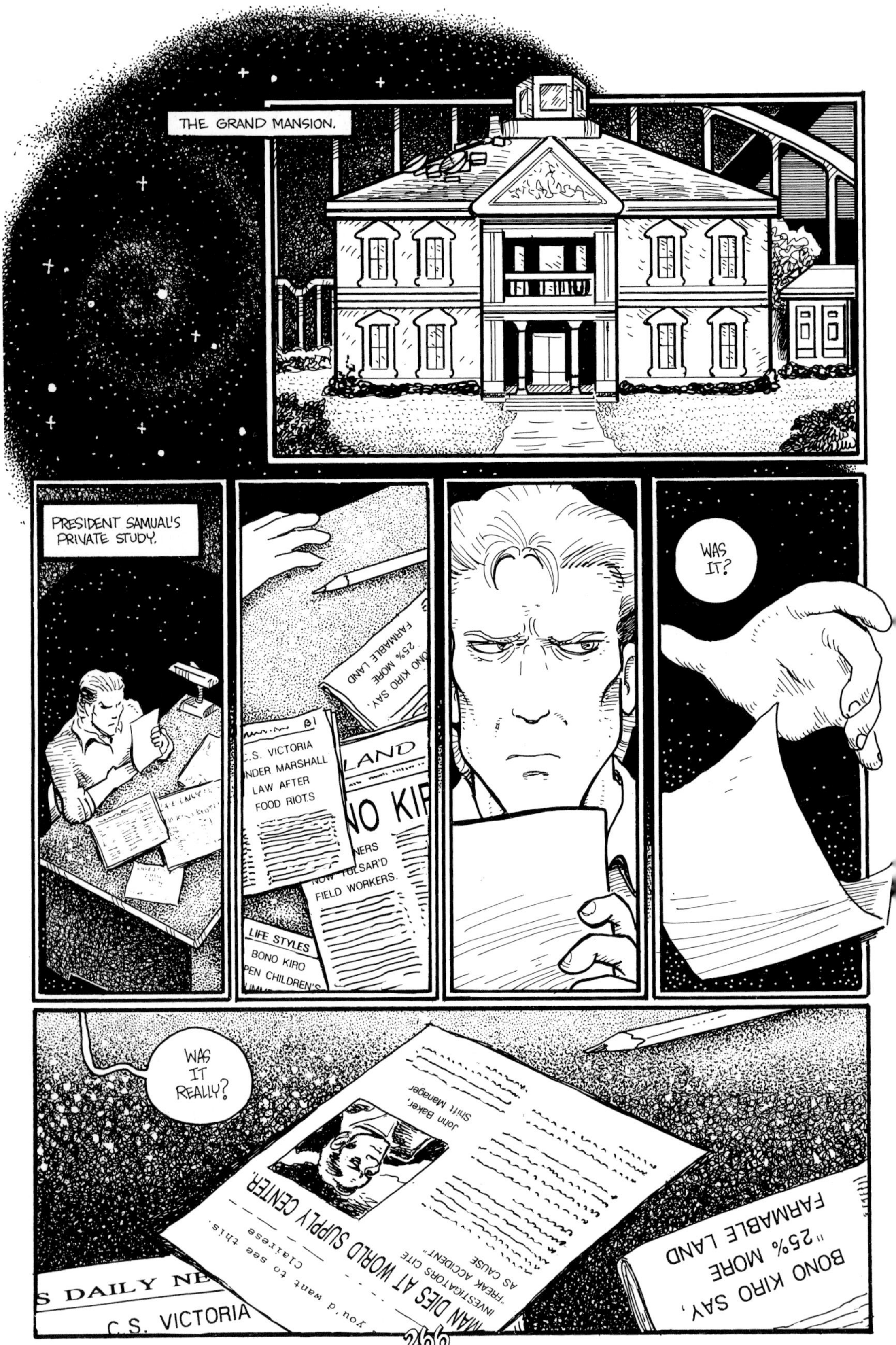
THE GRAND MANSION.
PRESIDENT SAMUAL'S PRIVATE STUDY.
C.S. VICTORIA UNDER MARSHALL LAW AFTER FOOD RIOTS
BONO KIRO SAY, "25% MORE FARMABLE LAND
FIELD WORKERS.
LIFE STYLES
BONO KIRO
WAS IT?
WAS IT REALLY?
John Baker, Shift Manager
INVESTIGATORS CITE "FREAK ACCIDENT" AS CAUSE
you'd want to see this.
Clairese
DAILY NE
C.S. VICTORIA
BONO KIRO SAY, "25% MORE FARMABLE LAND

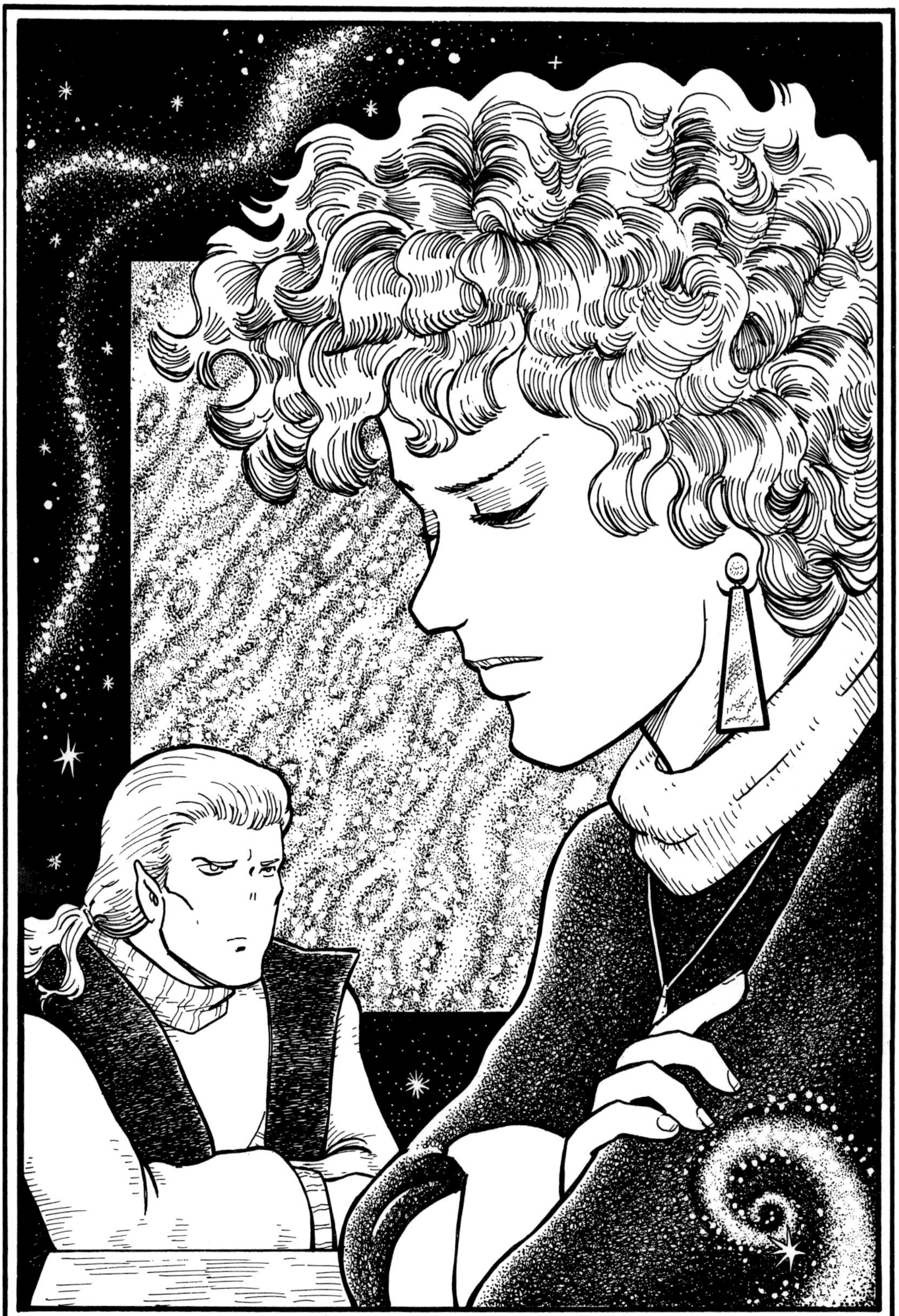

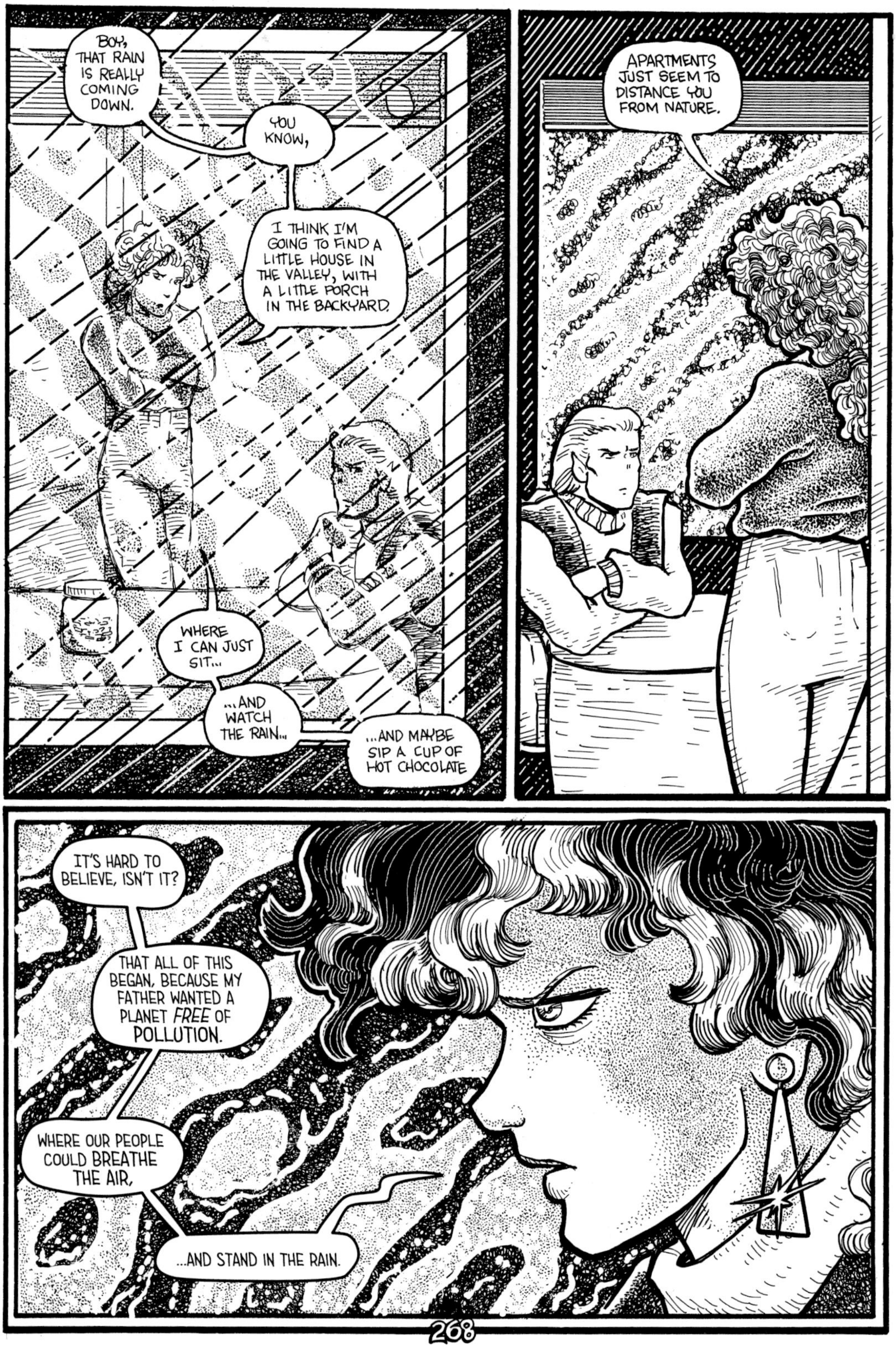
BOY, THAT RAIN IS REALLY COMING DOWN.
YOU KNOW,
I THINK I'M GOING TO FIND A LITTLE HOUSE IN THE VALLEY, WITH A LITTLE PORCH IN THE BACKYARD.
WHERE I CAN JUST SIT...
...AND WATCH THE RAIN...
...AND MAYBE SIP A CUP OF HOT CHOCOLATE
APARTMENTS JUST SEEM TO DISTANCE YOU FROM NATURE.
IT'S HARD TO BELIEVE, ISN'T IT?
THAT ALL OF THIS BEGAN, BECAUSE MY FATHER WANTED A PLANET *FREE* OF POLLUTION.
WHERE OUR PEOPLE COULD BREATHE THE AIR,
...AND STAND IN THE RAIN.

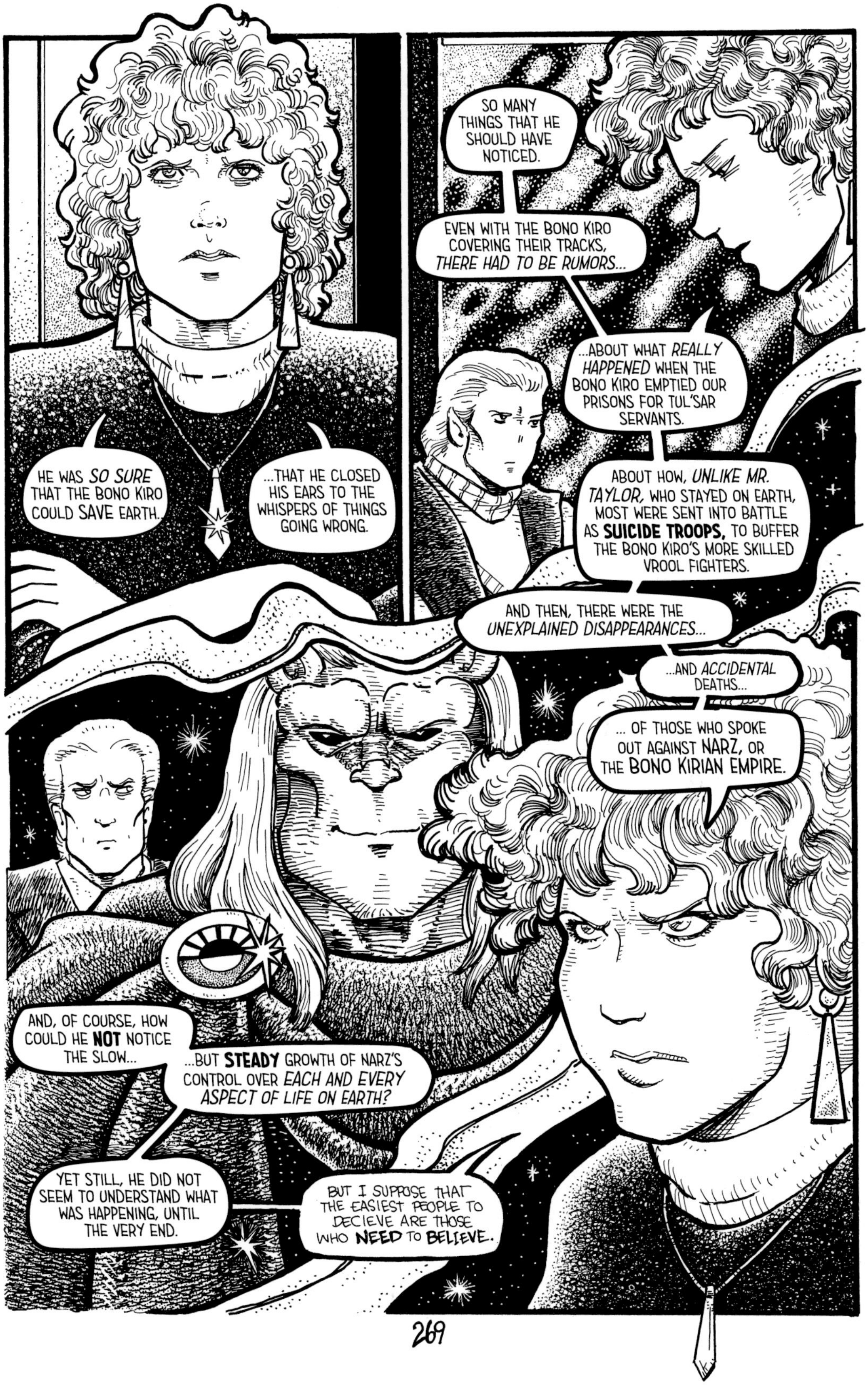
HE WAS SO SURE THAT THE BONO KIRO COULD SAVE EARTH...
...THAT HE CLOSED HIS EARS TO THE WHISPERS OF THINGS GOING WRONG.
SO MANY THINGS THAT HE SHOULD HAVE NOTICED.
EVEN WITH THE BONO KIRO COVERING THEIR TRACKS, THERE HAD TO BE RUMORS...
...ABOUT WHAT REALLY HAPPENED WHEN THE BONO KIRO EMPTIED OUR PRISONS FOR TUL'SAR SERVANTS.
ABOUT HOW, UNLIKE MR. TAYLOR, WHO STAYED ON EARTH, MOST WERE SENT INTO BATTLE AS SUICIDE TROOPS, TO BUFFER THE BONO KIRO'S MORE SKILLED VROOL FIGHTERS.
AND THEN, THERE WERE THE UNEXPLAINED DISAPPEARANCES...
...AND ACCIDENTAL DEATHS...
... OF THOSE WHO SPOKE OUT AGAINST NARZ, OR THE BONO KIRIAN EMPIRE.
AND, OF COURSE, HOW COULD HE NOT NOTICE THE SLOW...
...BUT STEADY GROWTH OF NARZ'S CONTROL OVER EACH AND EVERY ASPECT OF LIFE ON EARTH?
YET STILL, HE DID NOT SEEM TO UNDERSTAND WHAT WAS HAPPENING, UNTIL THE VERY END.
BUT I SUPPOSE THAT THE EASIEST PEOPLE TO DECIEVE ARE THOSE WHO NEED TO BELIEVE.

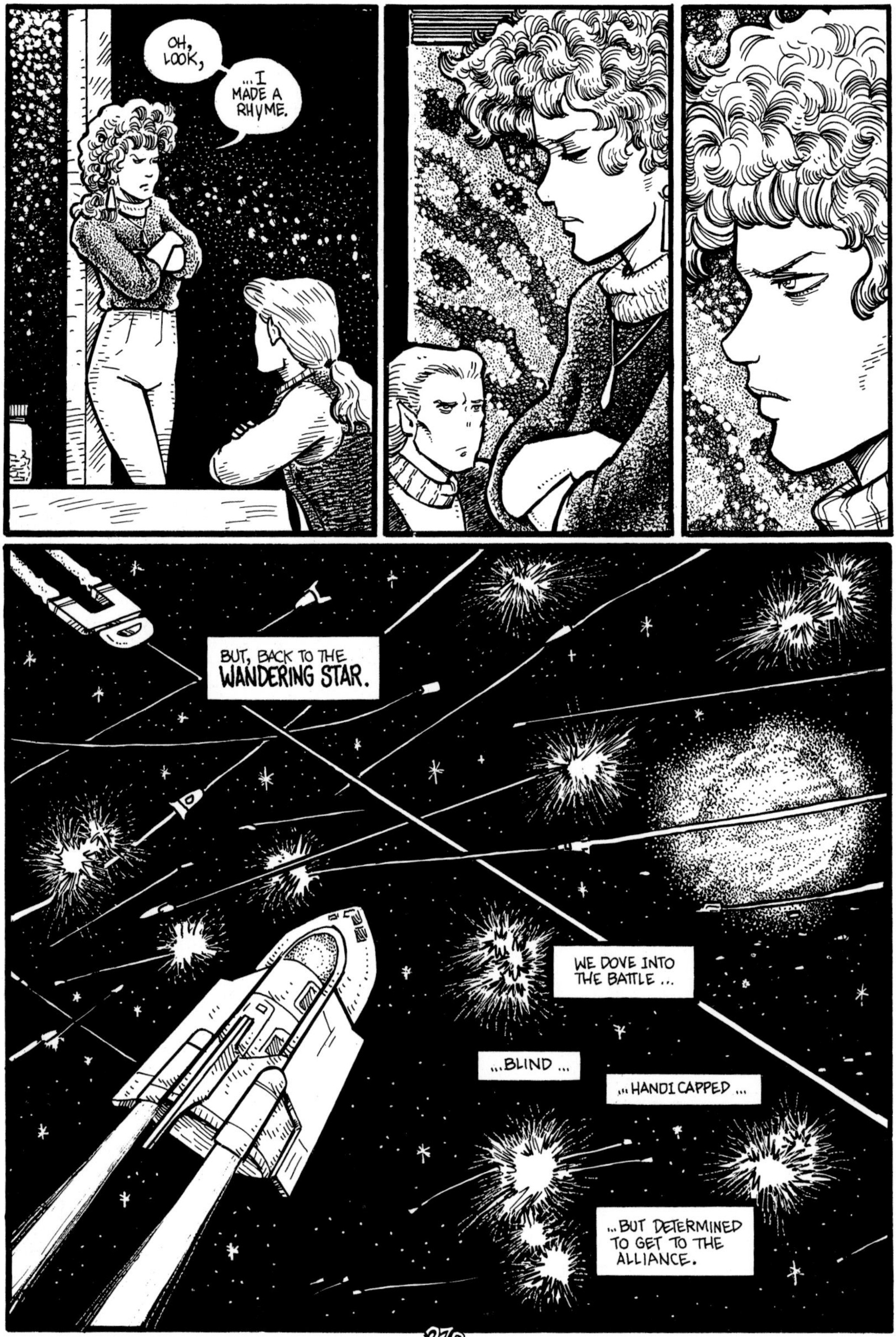
OH, LOOK,
...I MADE A RHYME.
BUT, BACK TO THE WANDERING STAR.
WE DOVE INTO THE BATTLE ...
...BLIND ...
...HANDICAPPED ...
...BUT DETERMINED TO GET TO THE ALLIANCE.

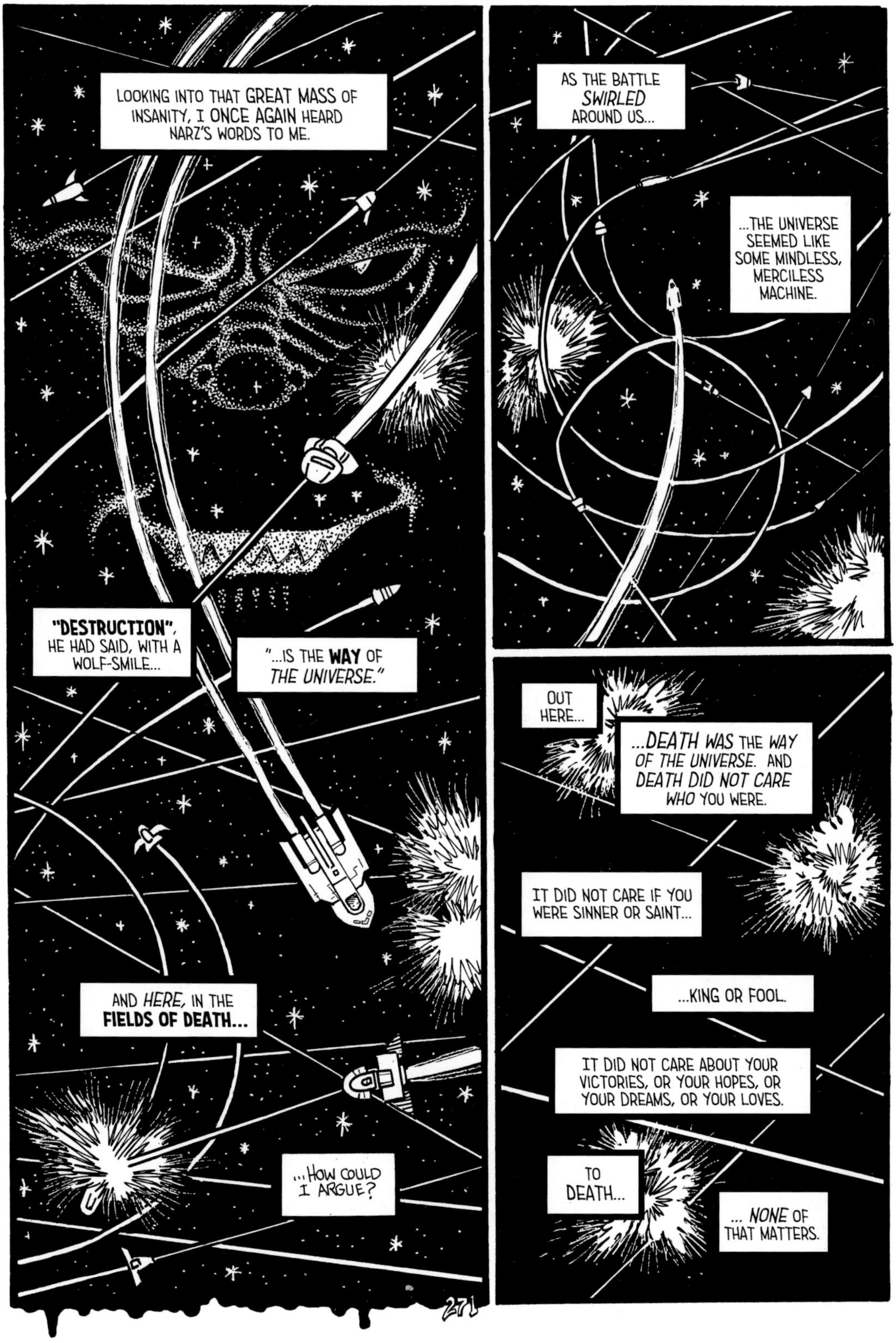
LOOKING INTO THAT GREAT MASS OF INSANITY, I ONCE AGAIN HEARD NARZ'S WORDS TO ME.
"DESTRUCTION", HE HAD SAID, WITH A WOLF-SMILE...
"...IS THE WAY OF THE UNIVERSE."
AND HERE, IN THE FIELDS OF DEATH...
...HOW COULD I ARGUE?
AS THE BATTLE SWIRLED AROUND US...
...THE UNIVERSE SEEMED LIKE SOME MINDLESS, MERCILESS MACHINE.
OUT HERE...
...DEATH WAS THE WAY OF THE UNIVERSE. AND DEATH DID NOT CARE WHO YOU WERE.
IT DID NOT CARE IF YOU WERE SINNER OR SAINT...
...KING OR FOOL.
IT DID NOT CARE ABOUT YOUR VICTORIES, OR YOUR HOPES, OR YOUR DREAMS, OR YOUR LOVES.
TO DEATH...
... NONE OF THAT MATTERS.

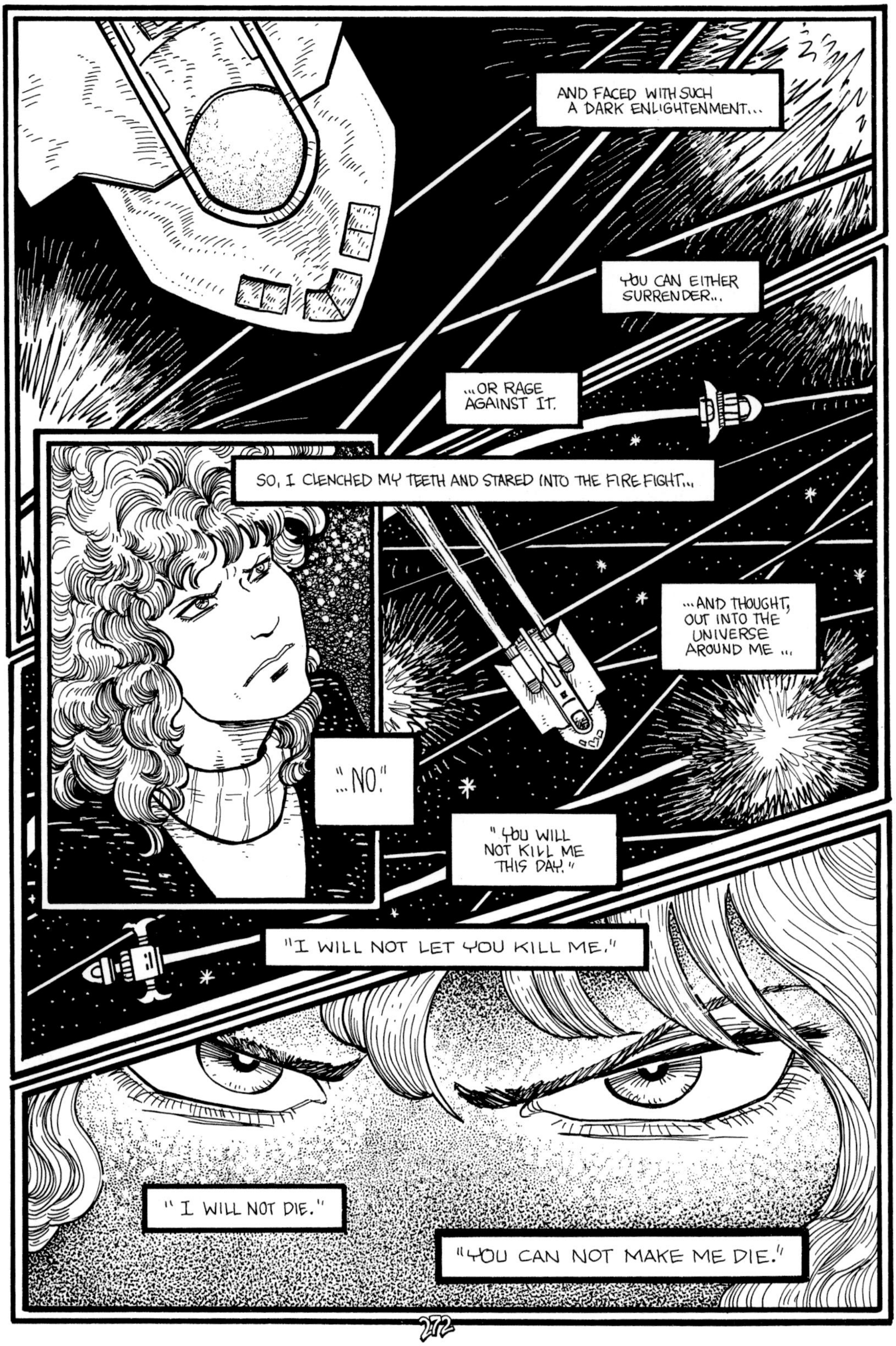
AND FACED WITH SUCH A DARK ENLIGHTENMENT...
YOU CAN EITHER SURRENDER...
...OR RAGE AGAINST IT.
SO, I CLENCHED MY TEETH AND STARED INTO THE FIRE FIGHT...
...AND THOUGHT, OUT INTO THE UNIVERSE AROUND ME ...
"...NO."
"YOU WILL NOT KILL ME THIS DAY."
"I WILL NOT LET YOU KILL ME."
"I WILL NOT DIE."
"YOU CAN NOT MAKE ME DIE."

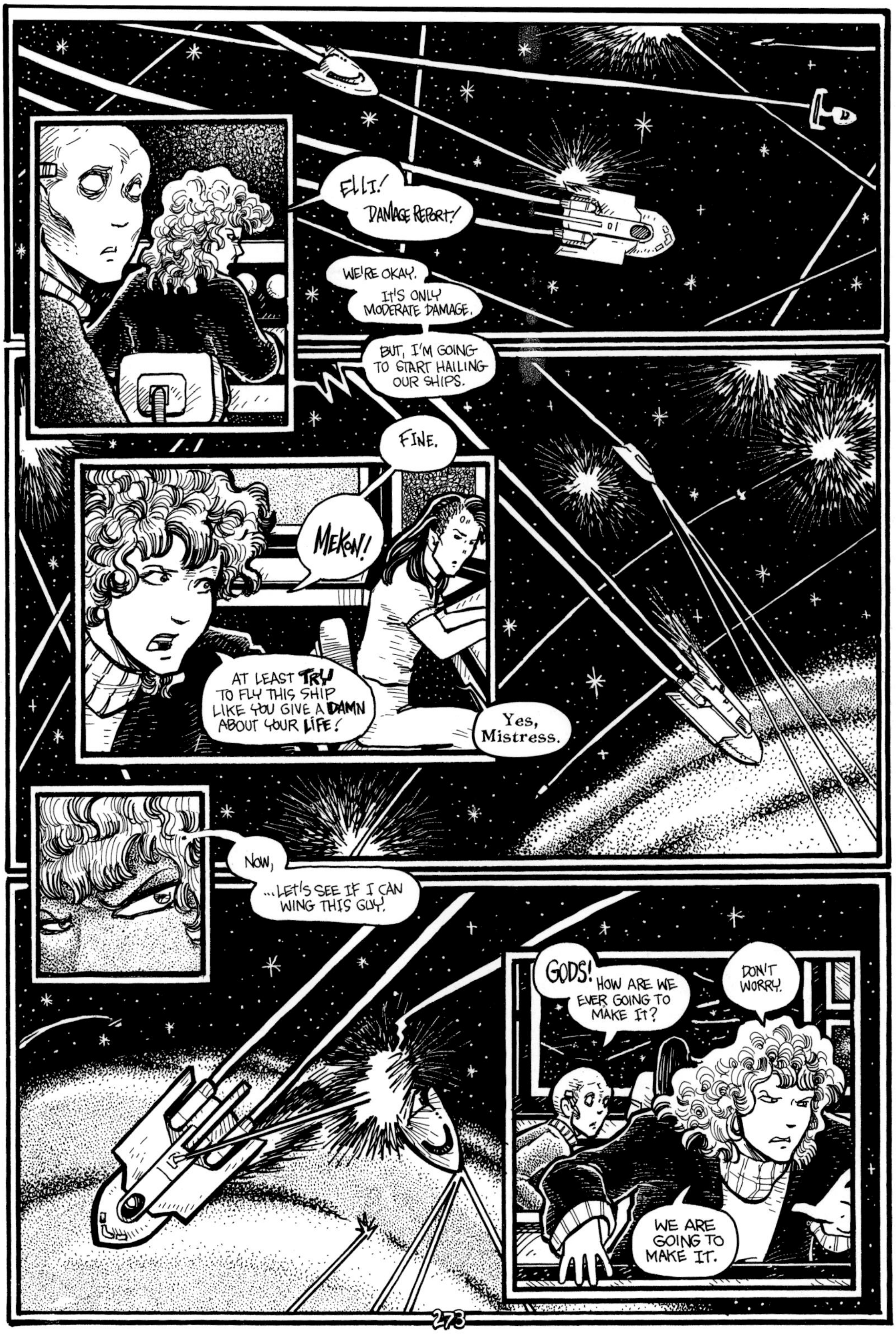
ELLI!
DAMAGE REPORT!
WE'RE OKAY.
IT'S ONLY MODERATE DAMAGE.
BUT, I'M GOING TO START HAILING OUR SHIPS.
FINE.
MEKON!
AT LEAST TRY TO FLY THIS SHIP LIKE YOU GIVE A DAMN ABOUT YOUR LIFE!
Yes, Mistress.
Now,
...LET'S SEE IF I CAN WING THIS GUY.
GODS!
HOW ARE WE EVER GOING TO MAKE IT?
DON'T WORRY.
WE ARE GOING TO MAKE IT.

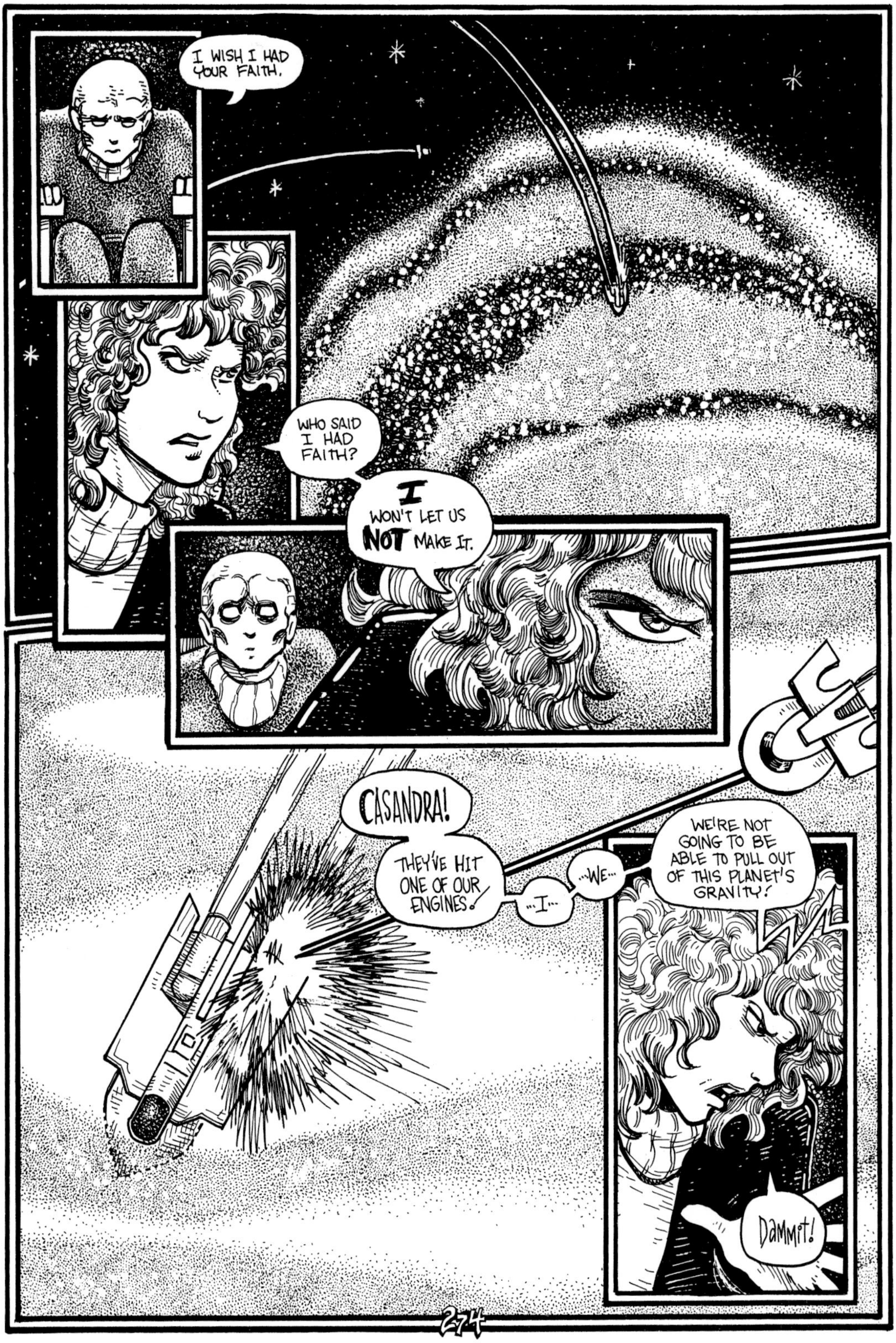
I WISH I HAD YOUR FAITH.
WHO SAID I HAD FAITH?
I WON'T LET US NOT MAKE IT.
CASANDRA!
THEY'VE HIT ONE OF OUR ENGINES!
...I...
...WE...
WE'RE NOT GOING TO BE ABLE TO PULL OUT OF THIS PLANET'S GRAVITY!
DAMMIT!

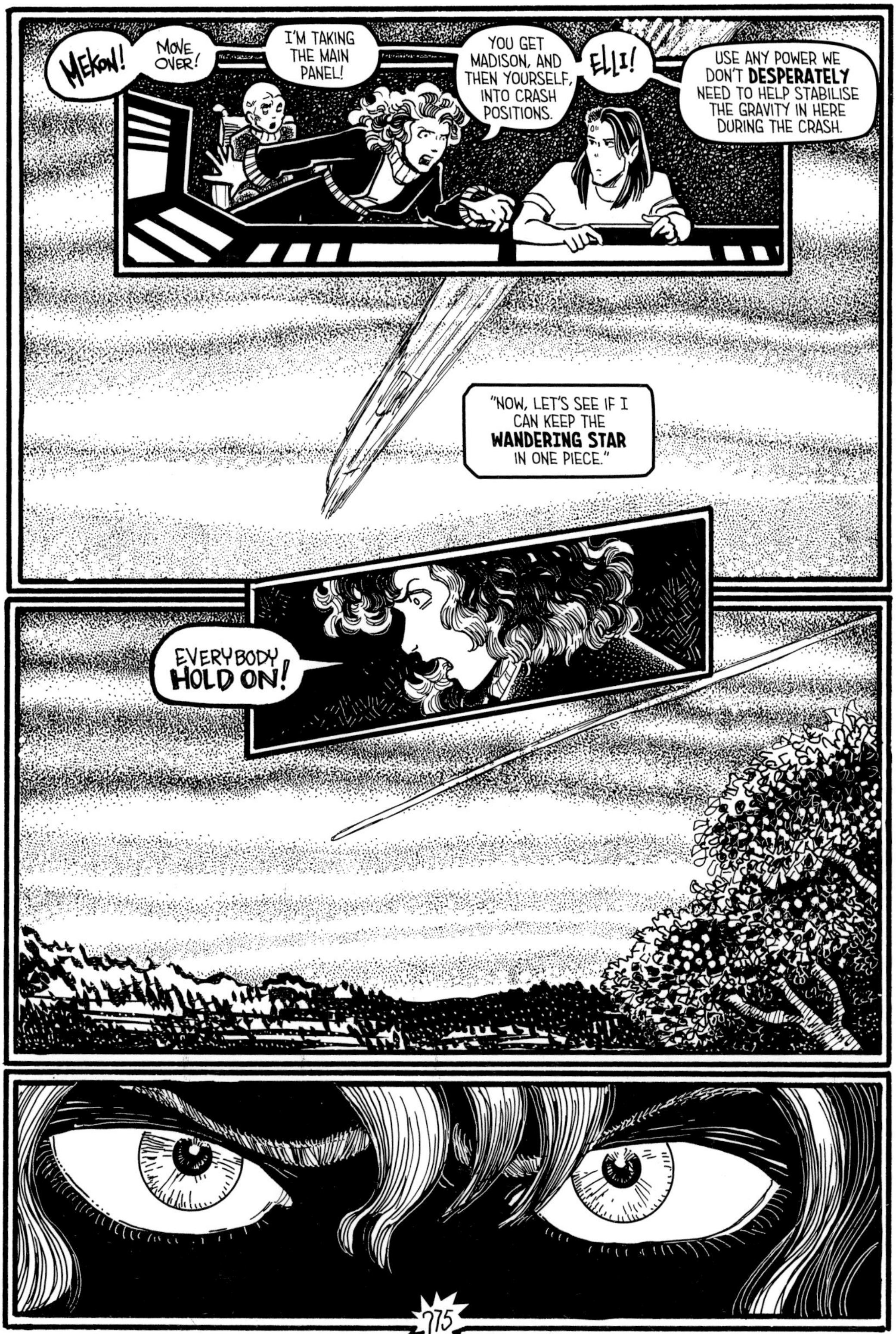
MEKON!
MOVE OVER!
I'M TAKING THE MAIN PANEL!
YOU GET MADISON, AND THEN YOURSELF, INTO CRASH POSITIONS.
ELLI!
USE ANY POWER WE DON'T **DESPERATELY** NEED TO HELP STABILISE THE GRAVITY IN HERE DURING THE CRASH.
"NOW, LET'S SEE IF I CAN KEEP THE **WANDERING STAR** IN ONE PIECE."
EVERYBODY **HOLD ON!**

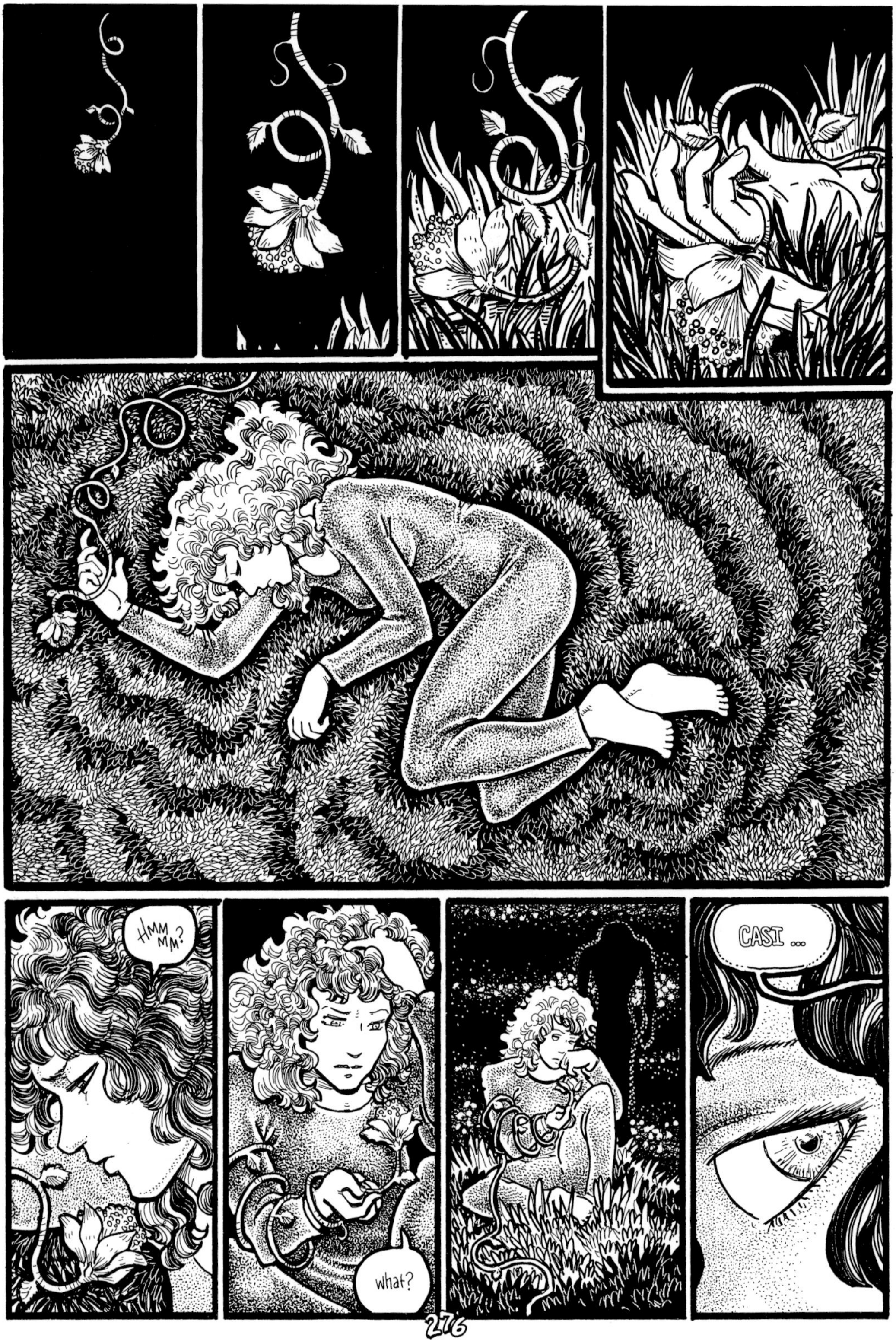
HMM MM?
what?
CASI ...

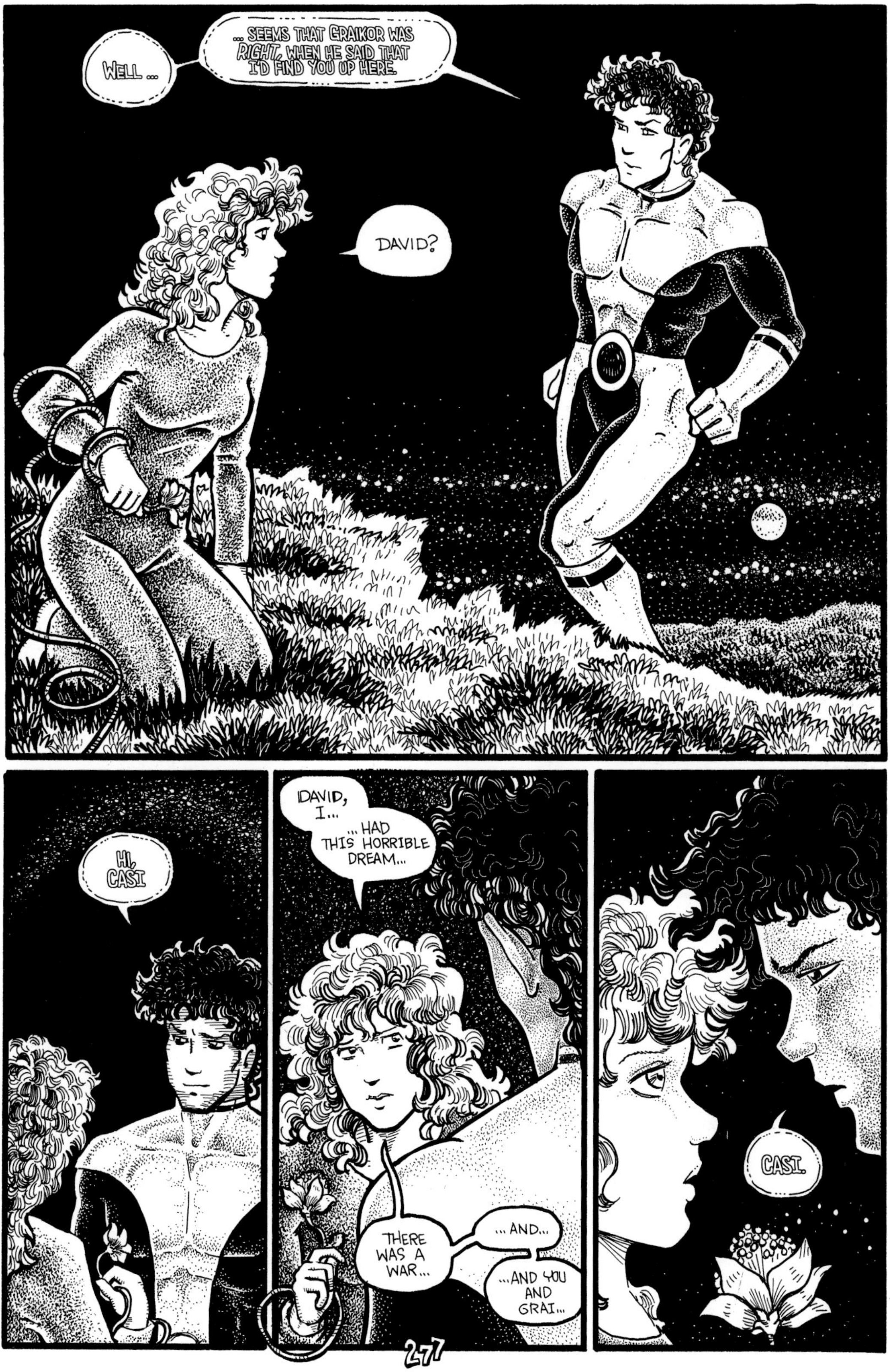
WELL ...
... SEEMS THAT GRAIKOR WAS RIGHT, WHEN HE SAID THAT I'D FIND YOU UP HERE.
DAVID?
HI, CASI
DAVID, I...
... HAD THIS HORRIBLE DREAM...
THERE WAS A WAR...
... AND...
... AND YOU AND GRAI...
CASI.

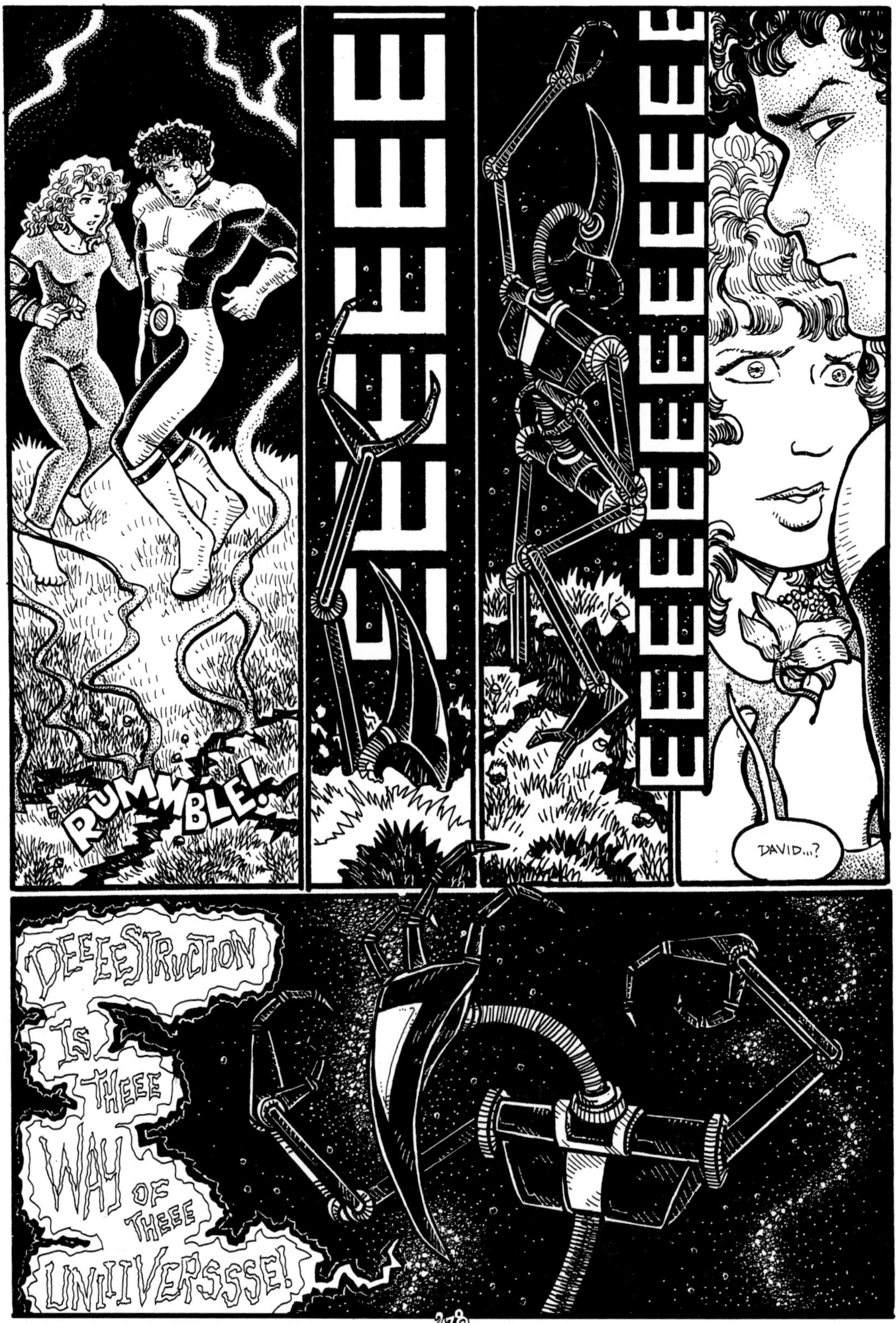
RUMMBLE!
EEEEEE
EEEEEEEEEEEE
DAVID...?
DEEEESTRUCTION IS THEEE WAY OF THEEE UNIIIVERSSSE!

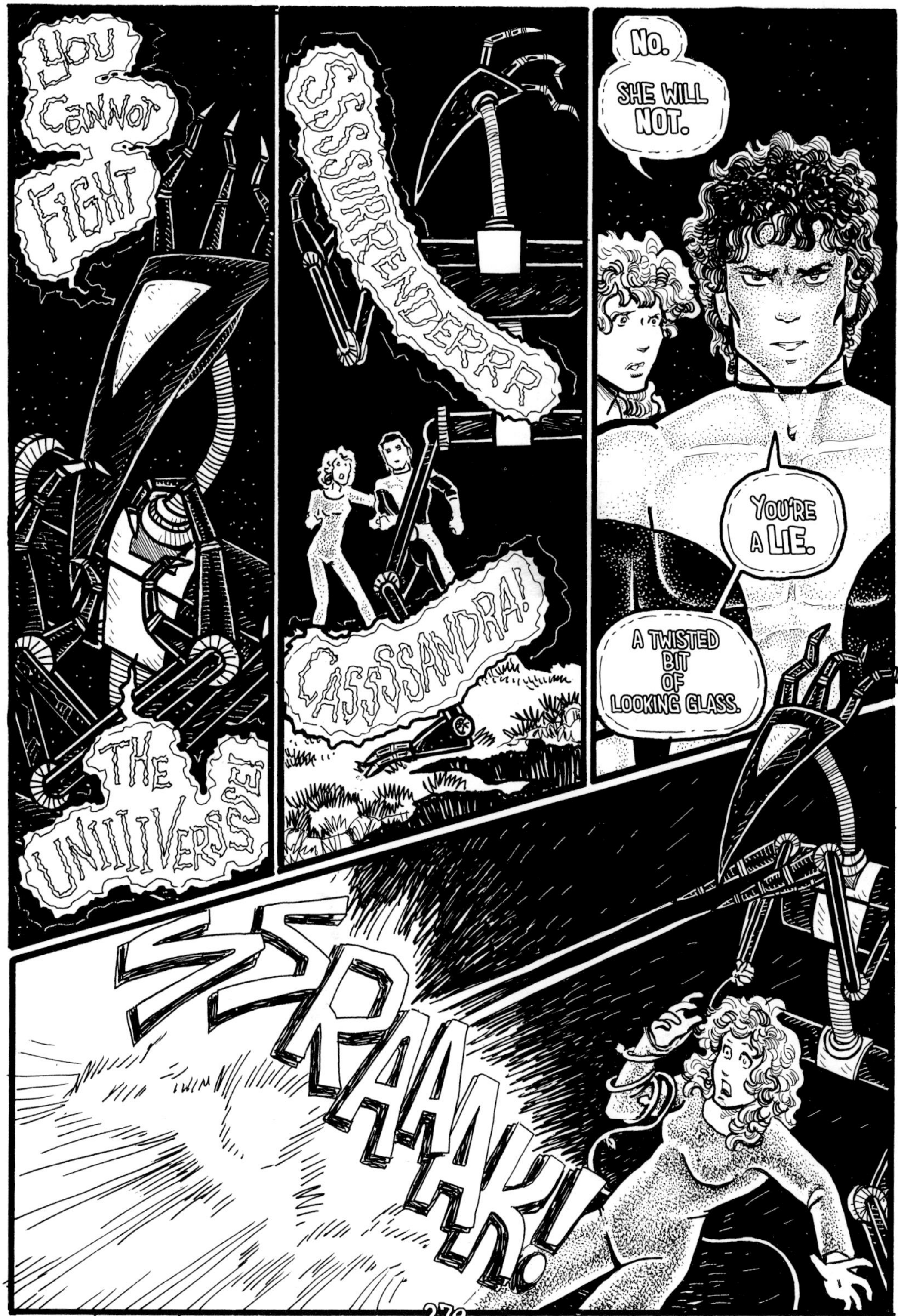
YOU CANNOT FIGHT
THE UNIIIVERSSSE!
SSSURRENDERRR
CASSSSANDRA!
NO.
SHE WILL NOT.
YOU'RE A LIE.
A TWISTED BIT OF LOOKING GLASS.
SSKRAAAKK!!

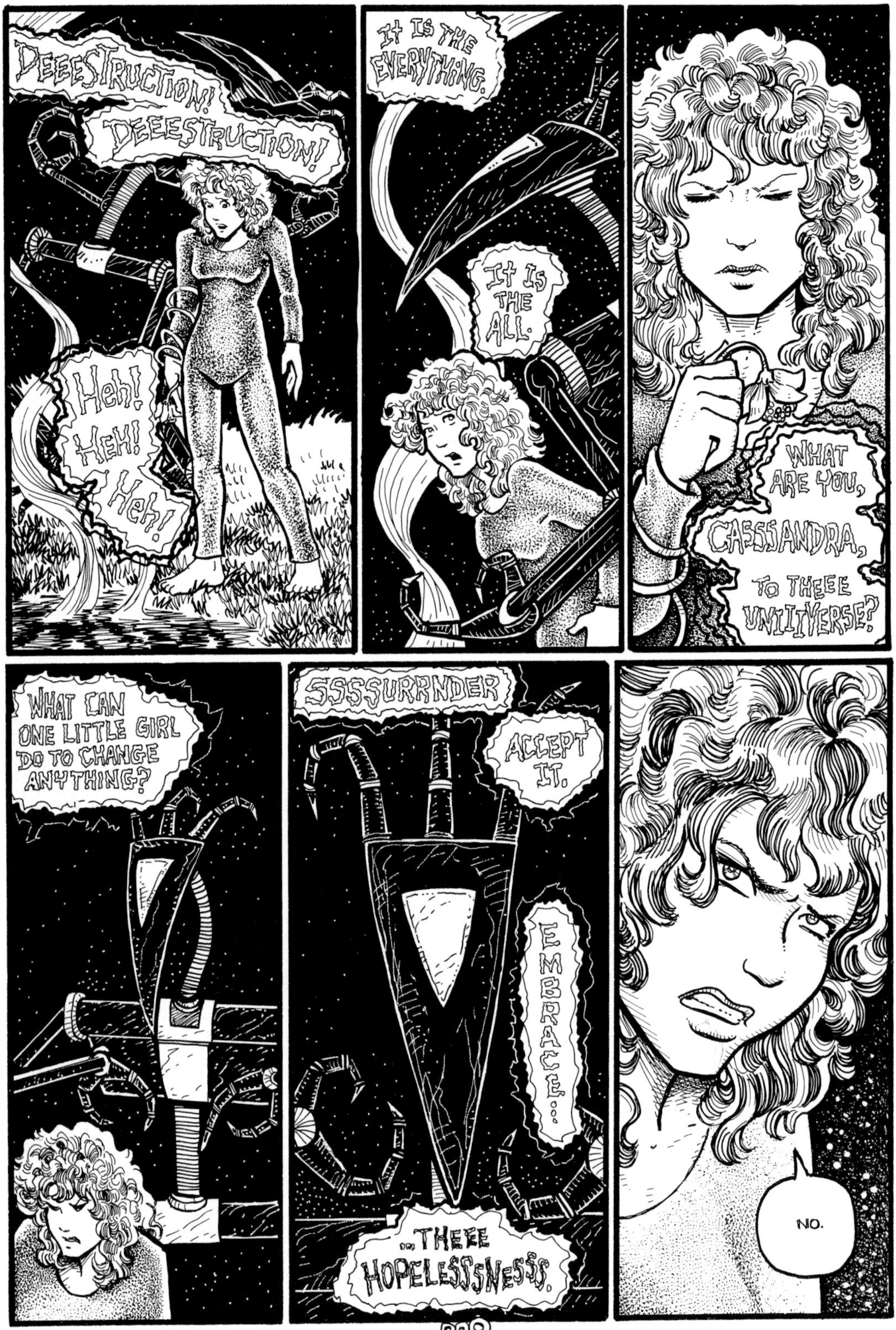
DEEESTRUCTION!
DEEESTRUCTION!
Heh! Heh! Heh!
IT IS THE EVERYTHING.
IT IS THE ALL.
WHAT ARE YOU, CASSSANDRA, TO THEEE UNIIIVERSE?
WHAT CAN ONE LITTLE GIRL DO TO CHANGE ANYTHING?
SSSSURRNDER
ACCEPT IT.
EMBRACE...
...THEEE HOPELESSSNESSS.
NO.

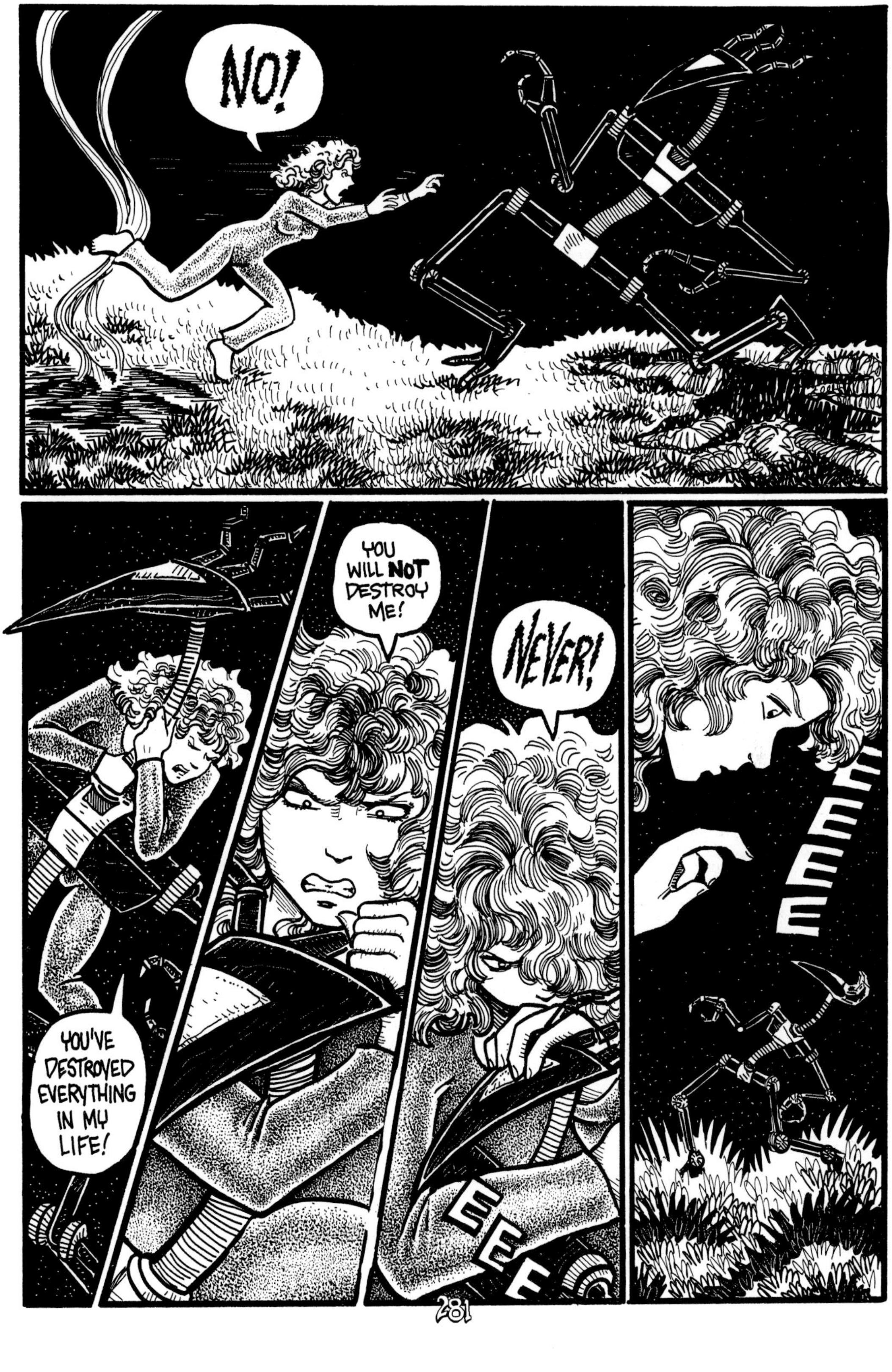
NO!
YOU'VE DESTROYED EVERYTHING IN MY LIFE!
YOU WILL NOT DESTROY ME!
NEVER!
EEE
EEEE

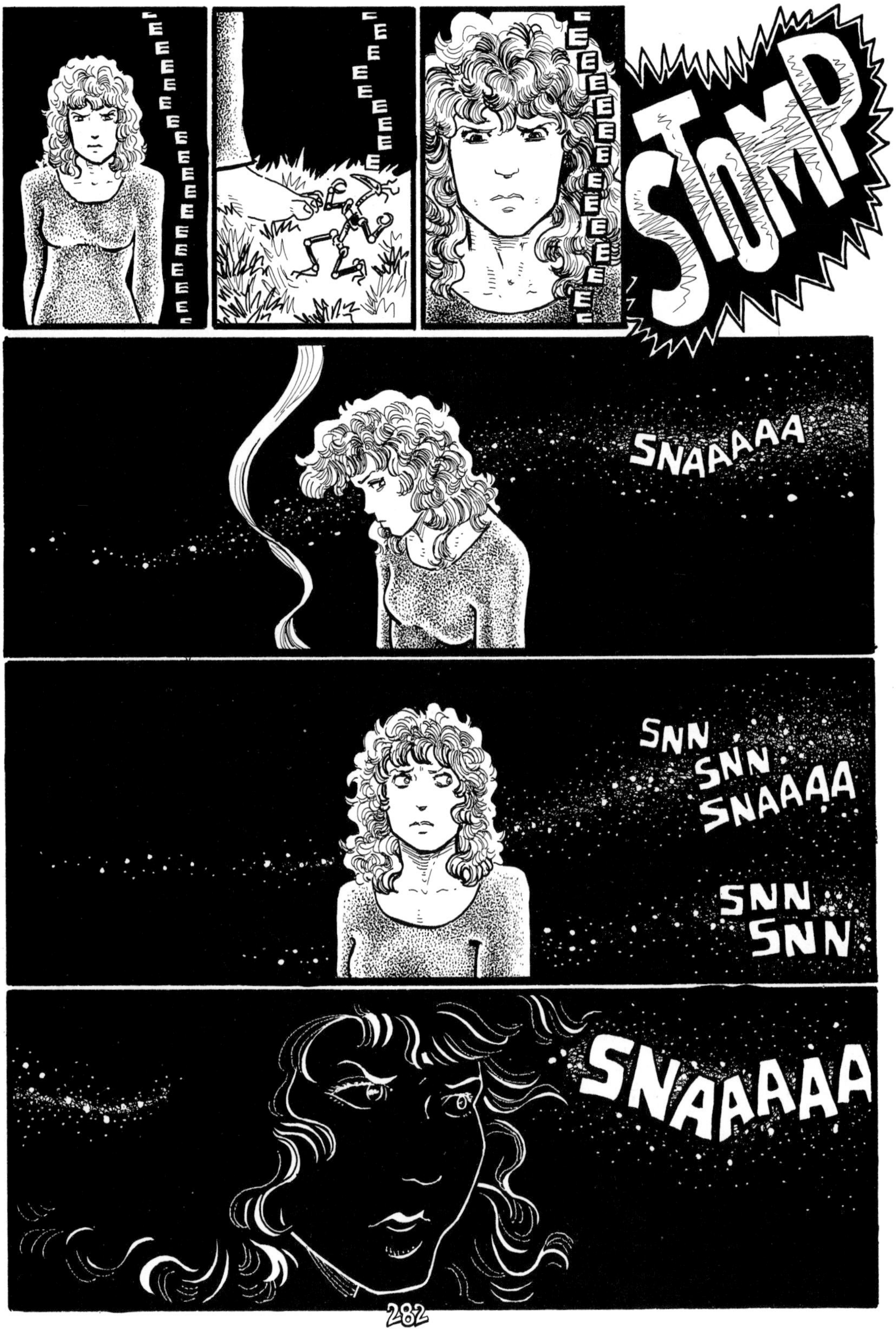
EEEEEEEEEEEEEEEE
EEEEEEEE
EEEEEEEEEEEEE
STOMP
SNAAAAA
SNN
SNN
SNAAAA
SNN
SNN
SNAAAAA

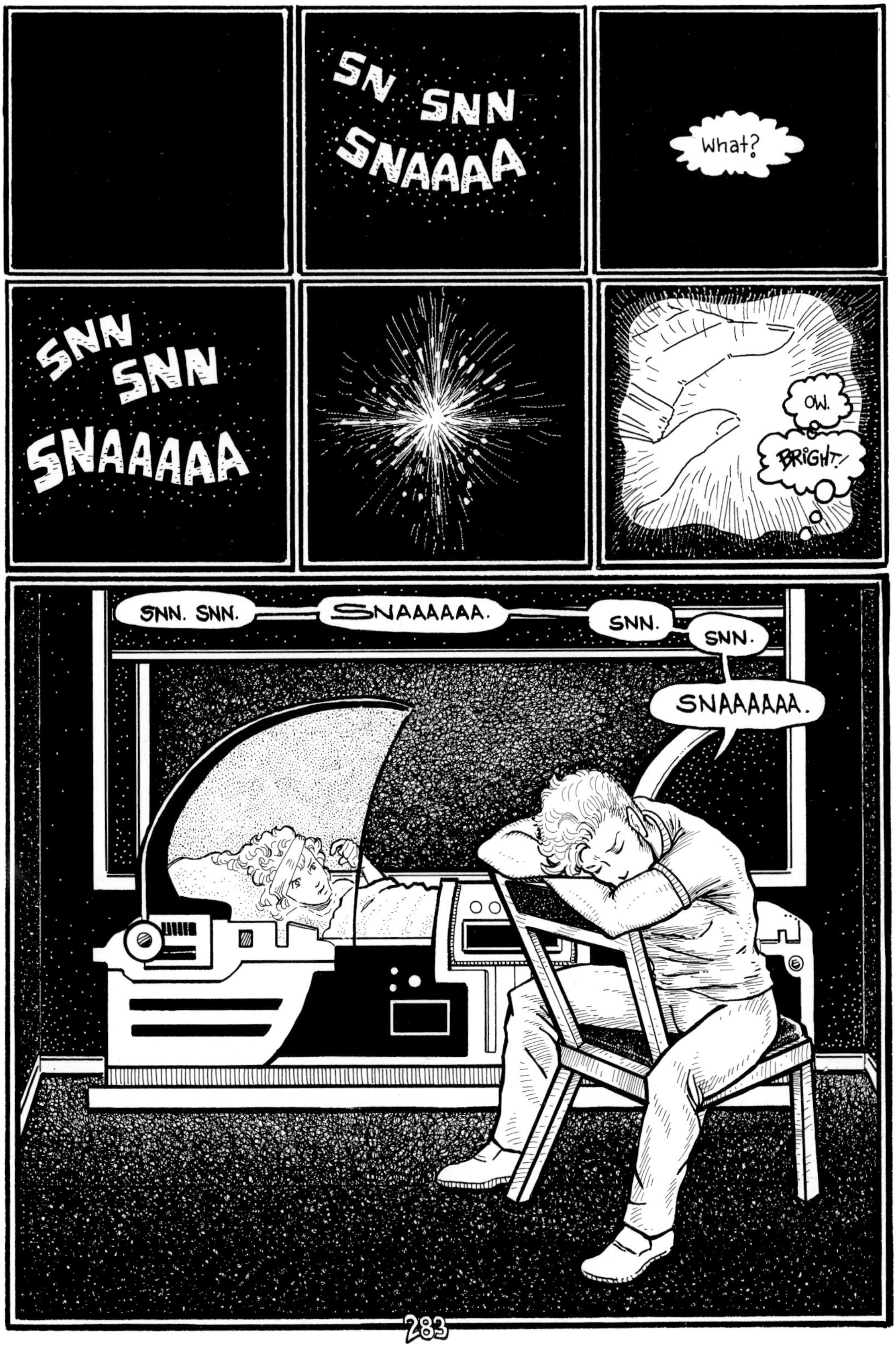
SN SNN
SNAAAA
What?
SNN
SNN
SNAAAAA
OW.
BRIGHT!
SNN. SNN.
SNAAAAAA.
SNN.
SNN.
SNAAAAAA.

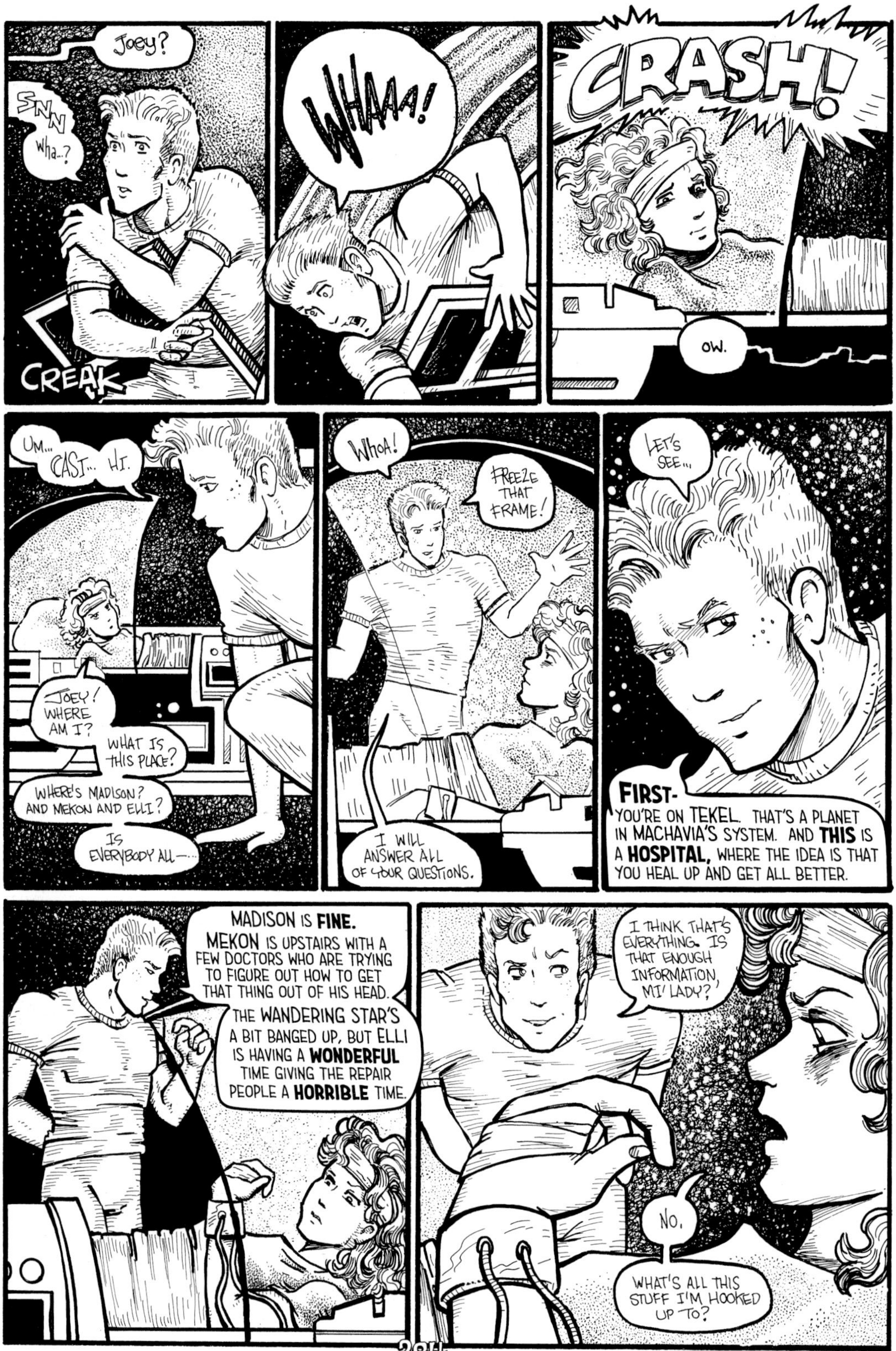
Joey?
SNN
Wha...?
CREAK
WHAAA!
CRASH!
OW.
UM... CAST... HI.
JOEY! WHERE AM I?
WHAT IS THIS PLACE?
WHERE'S MADISON? AND MEKON AND ELLI?
IS EVERYBODY ALL—
WHOA!
FREEZE THAT FRAME!
I WILL ANSWER ALL OF YOUR QUESTIONS.
LET'S SEE...
FIRST-
YOU'RE ON TEKEL. THAT'S A PLANET IN MACHAVIA'S SYSTEM. AND THIS IS A HOSPITAL, WHERE THE IDEA IS THAT YOU HEAL UP AND GET ALL BETTER.
MADISON IS FINE.
MEKON IS UPSTAIRS WITH A FEW DOCTORS WHO ARE TRYING TO FIGURE OUT HOW TO GET THAT THING OUT OF HIS HEAD.
THE WANDERING STAR'S A BIT BANGED UP, BUT ELLI IS HAVING A WONDERFUL TIME GIVING THE REPAIR PEOPLE A HORRIBLE TIME.
I THINK THAT'S EVERYTHING. IS THAT ENOUGH INFORMATION, MI' LADY?
NO.
WHAT'S ALL THIS STUFF I'M HOOKED UP TO?

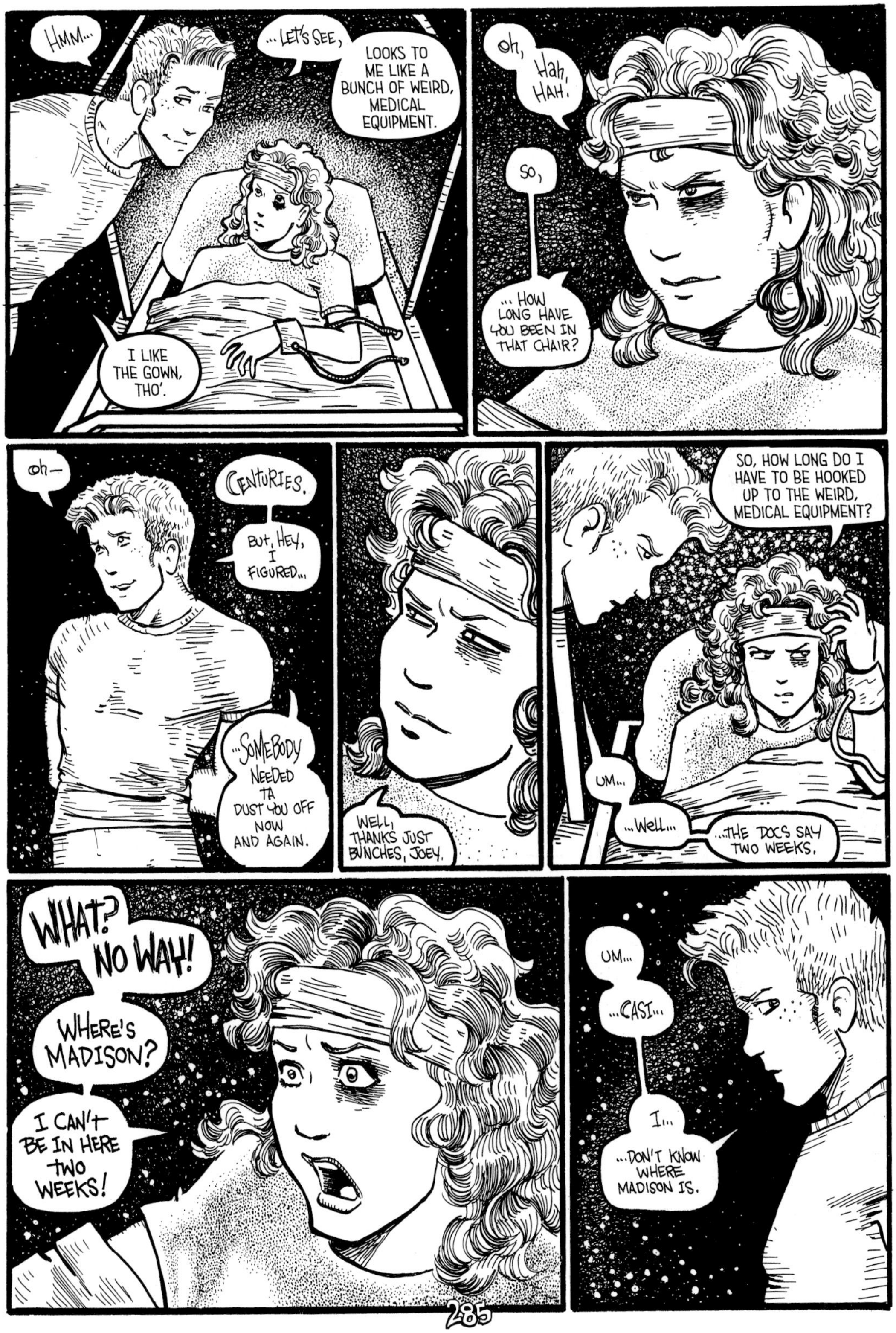
HMM...
...LET'S SEE,
LOOKS TO ME LIKE A BUNCH OF WEIRD, MEDICAL EQUIPMENT.
I LIKE THE GOWN, THO'.
oh, Hah, HAH.
So,
...HOW LONG HAVE YOU BEEN IN THAT CHAIR?
oh—
CENTURIES.
But, HEY, I FIGURED...
...SOMEBODY NEEDED TA DUST YOU OFF NOW AND AGAIN.
WELL, THANKS JUST BUNCHES, JOEY.
SO, HOW LONG DO I HAVE TO BE HOOKED UP TO THE WEIRD, MEDICAL EQUIPMENT?
UM...
...WELL...
...THE DOCS SAY TWO WEEKS.
WHAT? NO WAY!
WHERE'S MADISON?
I CAN'T BE IN HERE TWO WEEKS!
UM...
...CASI...
I...
...DON'T KNOW WHERE MADISON IS.

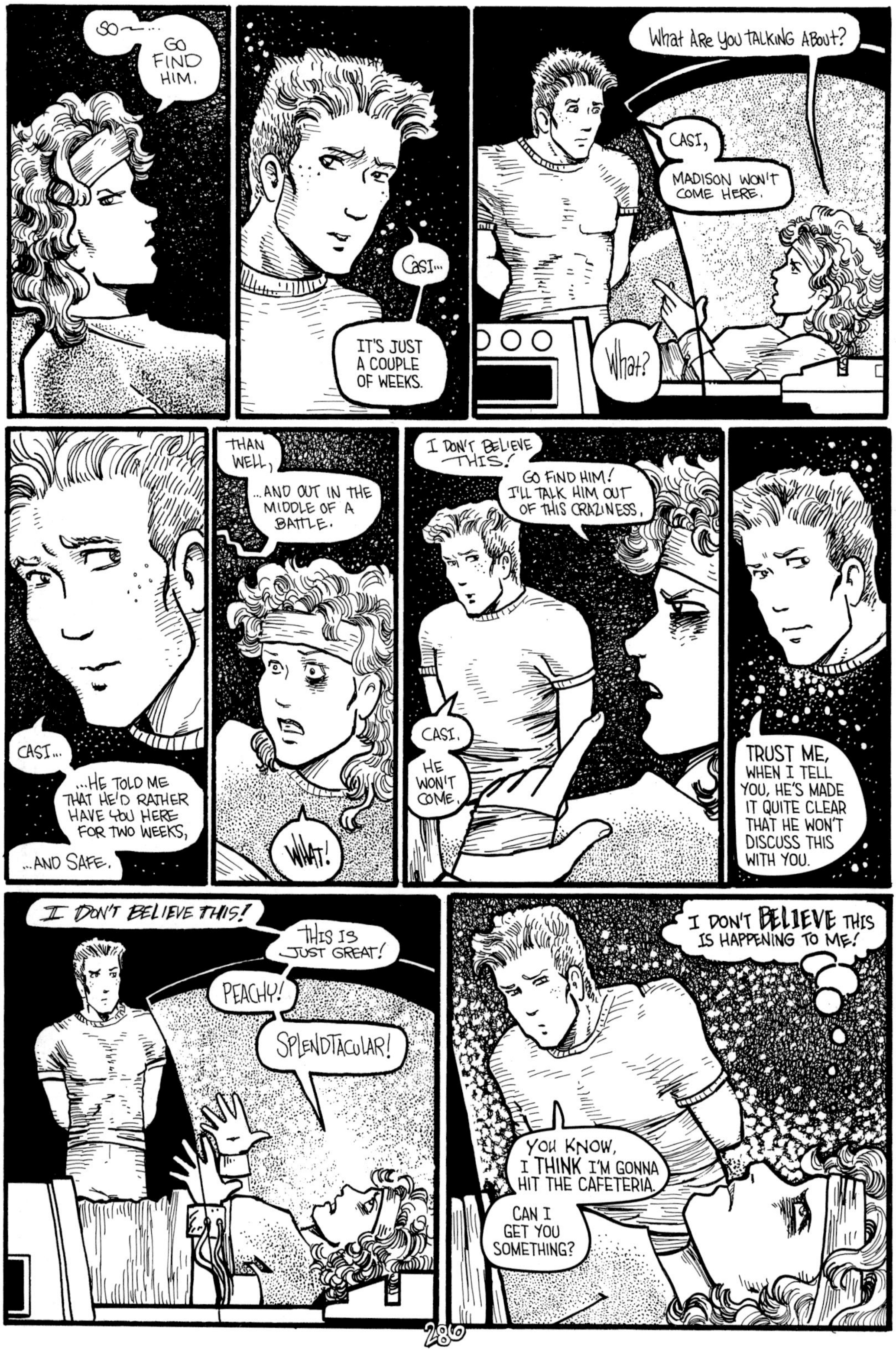
SO—...
GO FIND HIM.
CASI...
IT'S JUST A COUPLE OF WEEKS.
What Are You TALKING About?
CASI,
MADISON WON'T COME HERE.
What?
CASI...
...HE TOLD ME THAT HE'D RATHER HAVE YOU HERE FOR TWO WEEKS,
...AND SAFE.
THAN WELL,
...AND OUT IN THE MIDDLE OF A BATTLE.
WHAT!
I DON'T BELIEVE THIS!
GO FIND HIM! I'LL TALK HIM OUT OF THIS CRAZINESS.
CASI,
HE WON'T COME.
TRUST ME, WHEN I TELL YOU, HE'S MADE IT QUITE CLEAR THAT HE WON'T DISCUSS THIS WITH YOU.
I DON'T BELIEVE THIS!
THIS IS JUST GREAT!
PEACHY!
SPLENDTACULAR!
I DON'T BELIEVE THIS IS HAPPENING TO ME!
YOU KNOW, I THINK I'M GONNA HIT THE CAFETERIA.
CAN I GET YOU SOMETHING?

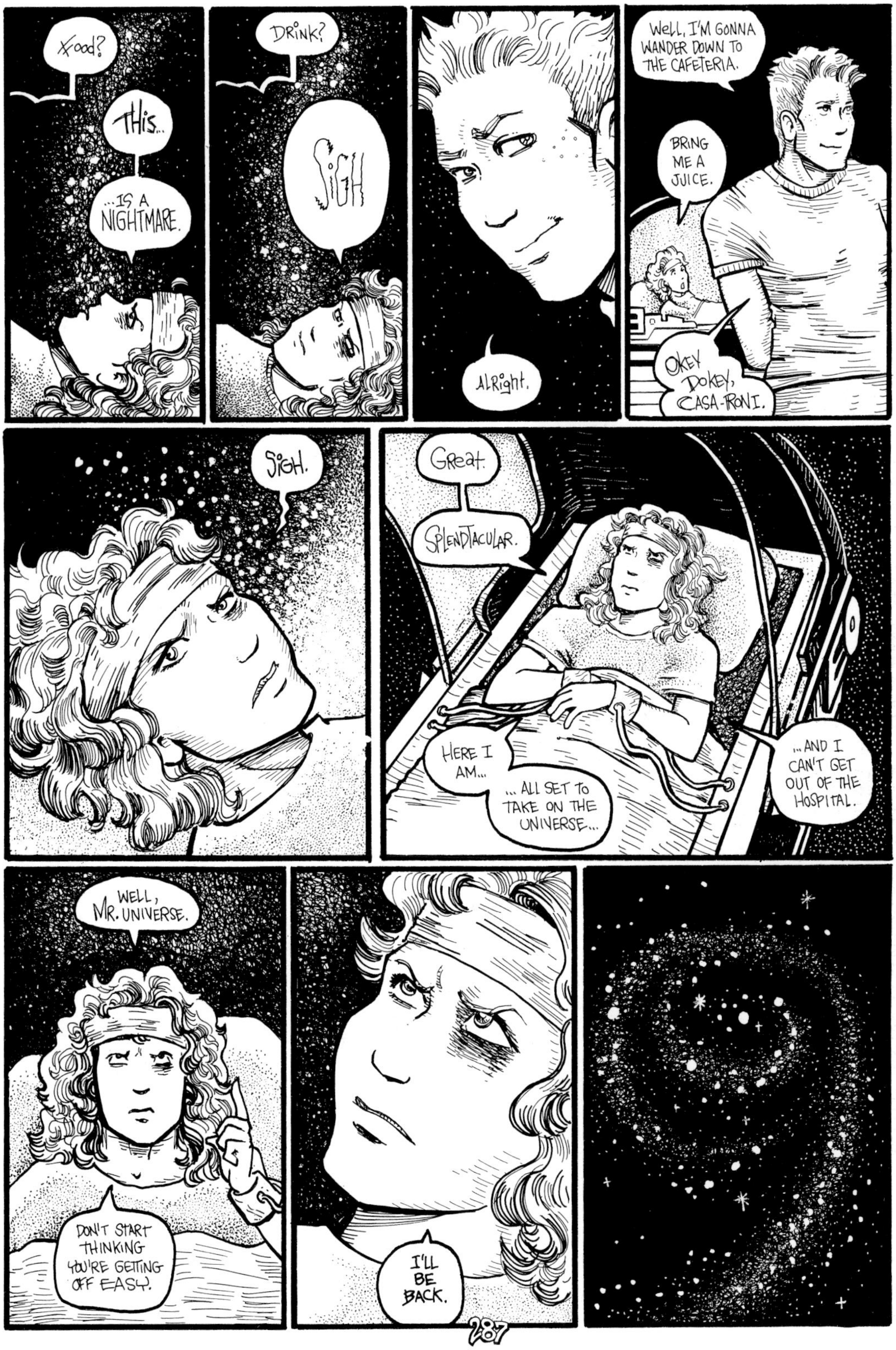
Food?
THIS...
...IS A NIGHTMARE.
DRINK?
SIGH
Alright.
WELL, I'M GONNA WANDER DOWN TO THE CAFETERIA.
BRING ME A JUICE.
OKEY DOKEY, CASA-RONI.
SIGH.
Great.
SPLENDTACULAR.
HERE I AM...
... ALL SET TO TAKE ON THE UNIVERSE...
...AND I CAN'T GET OUT OF THE HOSPITAL.
WELL, MR. UNIVERSE.
DON'T START THINKING YOU'RE GETTING OFF EASY.
I'LL BE BACK.

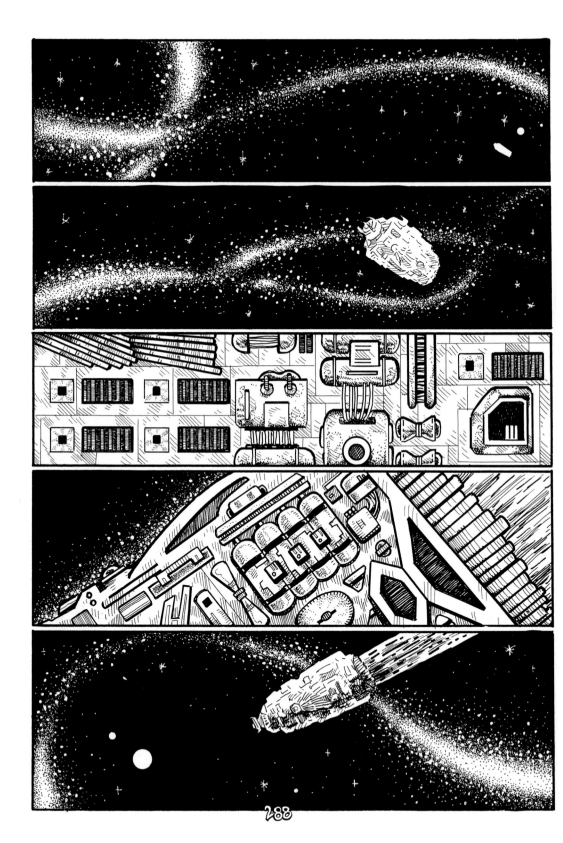

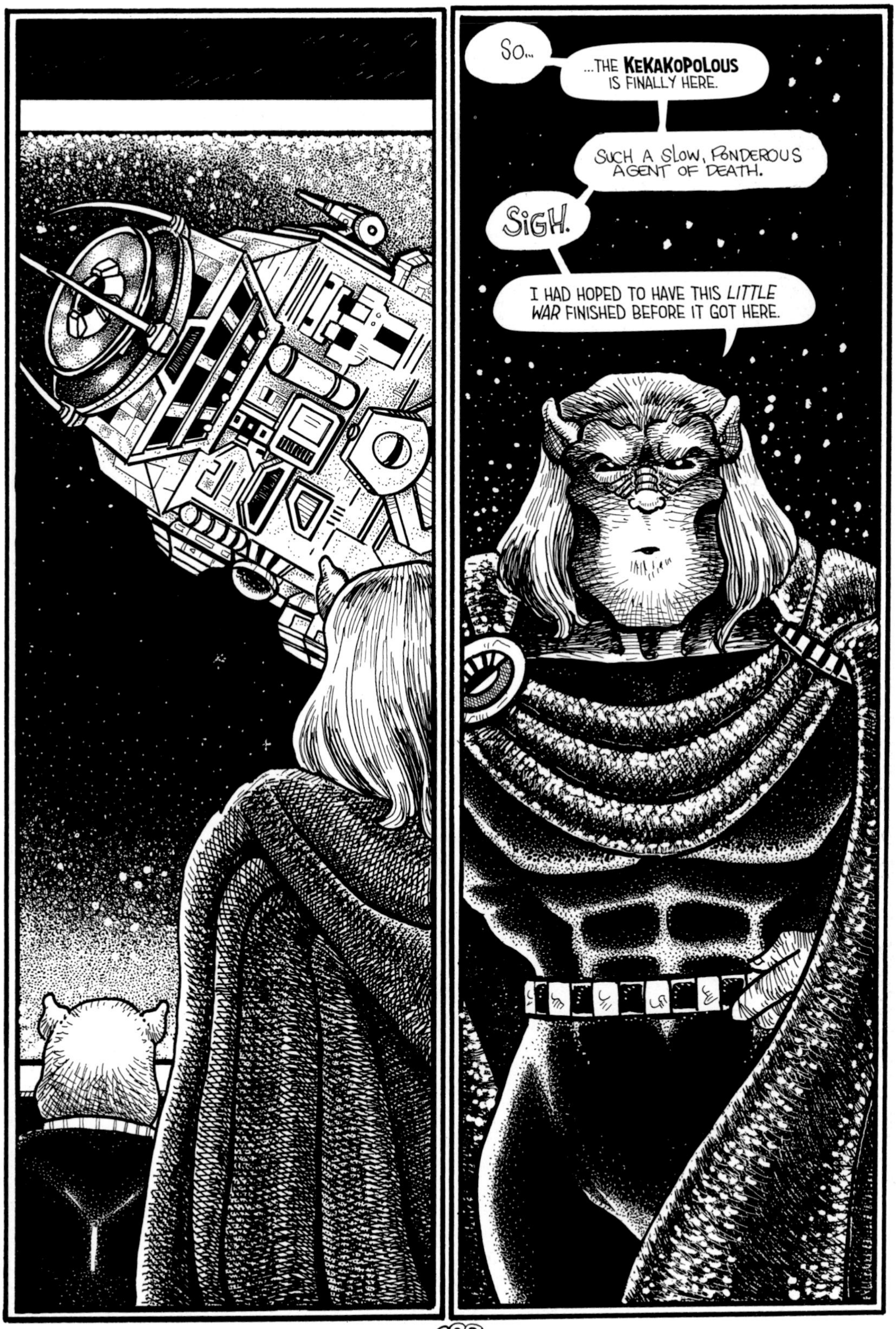
So...
...THE KEKAKOPOLOUS IS FINALLY HERE.
SUCH A SLOW, PONDEROUS AGENT OF DEATH.
SIGH.
I HAD HOPED TO HAVE THIS LITTLE WAR FINISHED BEFORE IT GOT HERE.

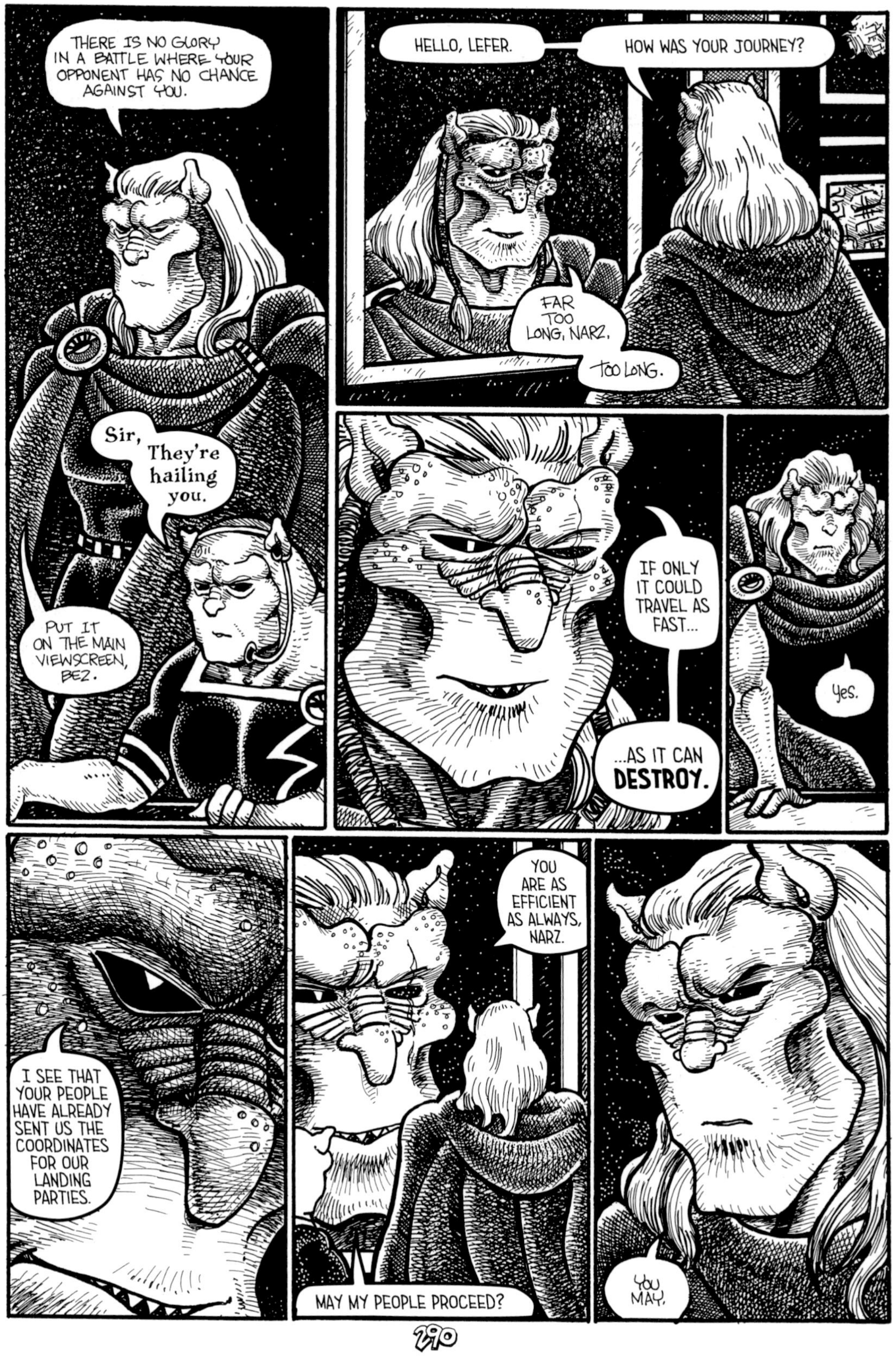
THERE IS NO GLORY IN A BATTLE WHERE YOUR OPPONENT HAS NO CHANCE AGAINST YOU.
Sir, They're hailing you.
PUT IT ON THE MAIN VIEWSCREEN, BEZ.
HELLO, LEFER.
HOW WAS YOUR JOURNEY?
FAR TOO LONG, NARZ.
TOO LONG.
IF ONLY IT COULD TRAVEL AS FAST...
...AS IT CAN DESTROY.
Yes.
I SEE THAT YOUR PEOPLE HAVE ALREADY SENT US THE COORDINATES FOR OUR LANDING PARTIES.
YOU ARE AS EFFICIENT AS ALWAYS, NARZ.
MAY MY PEOPLE PROCEED?
YOU MAY.

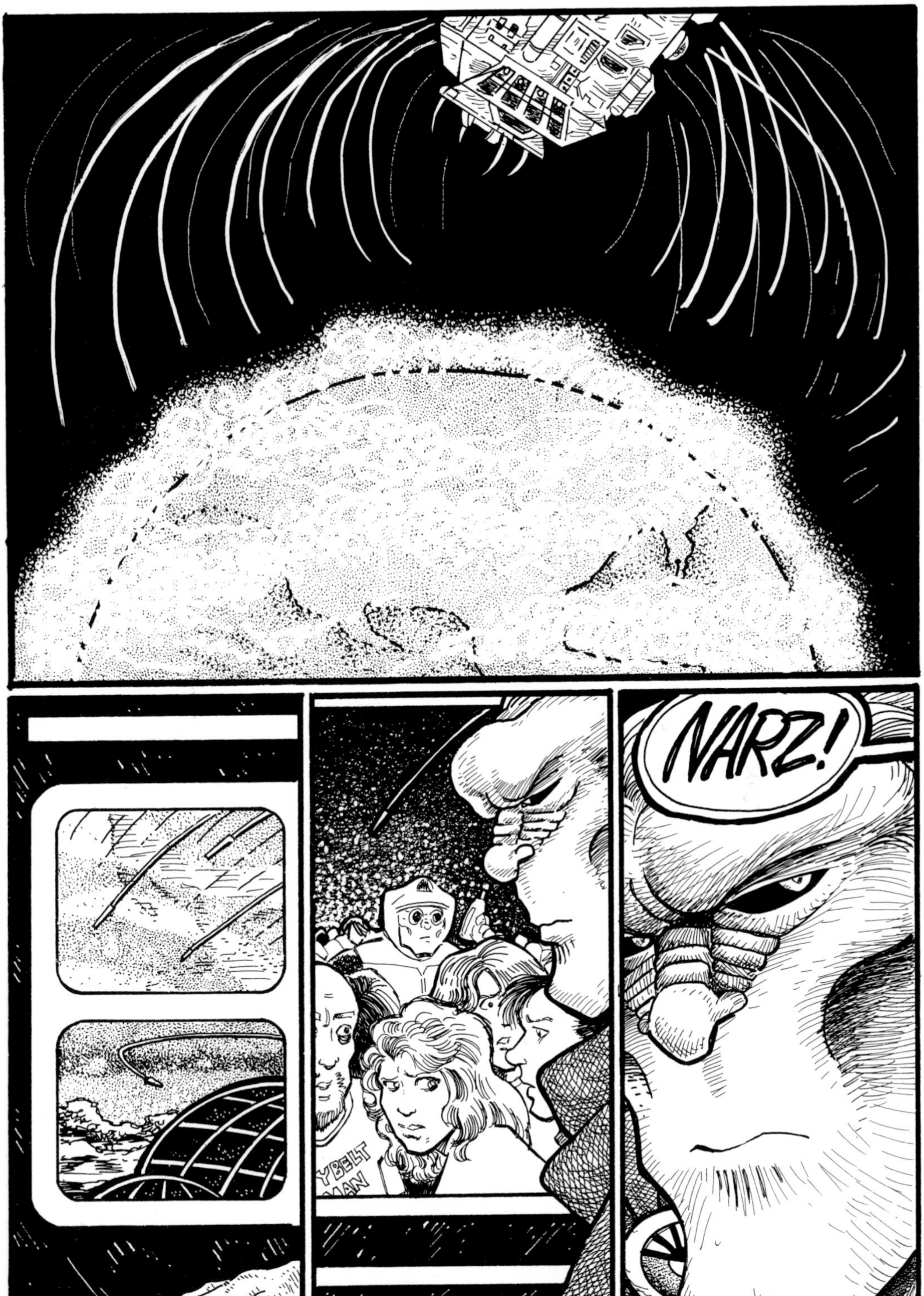
NARZ!

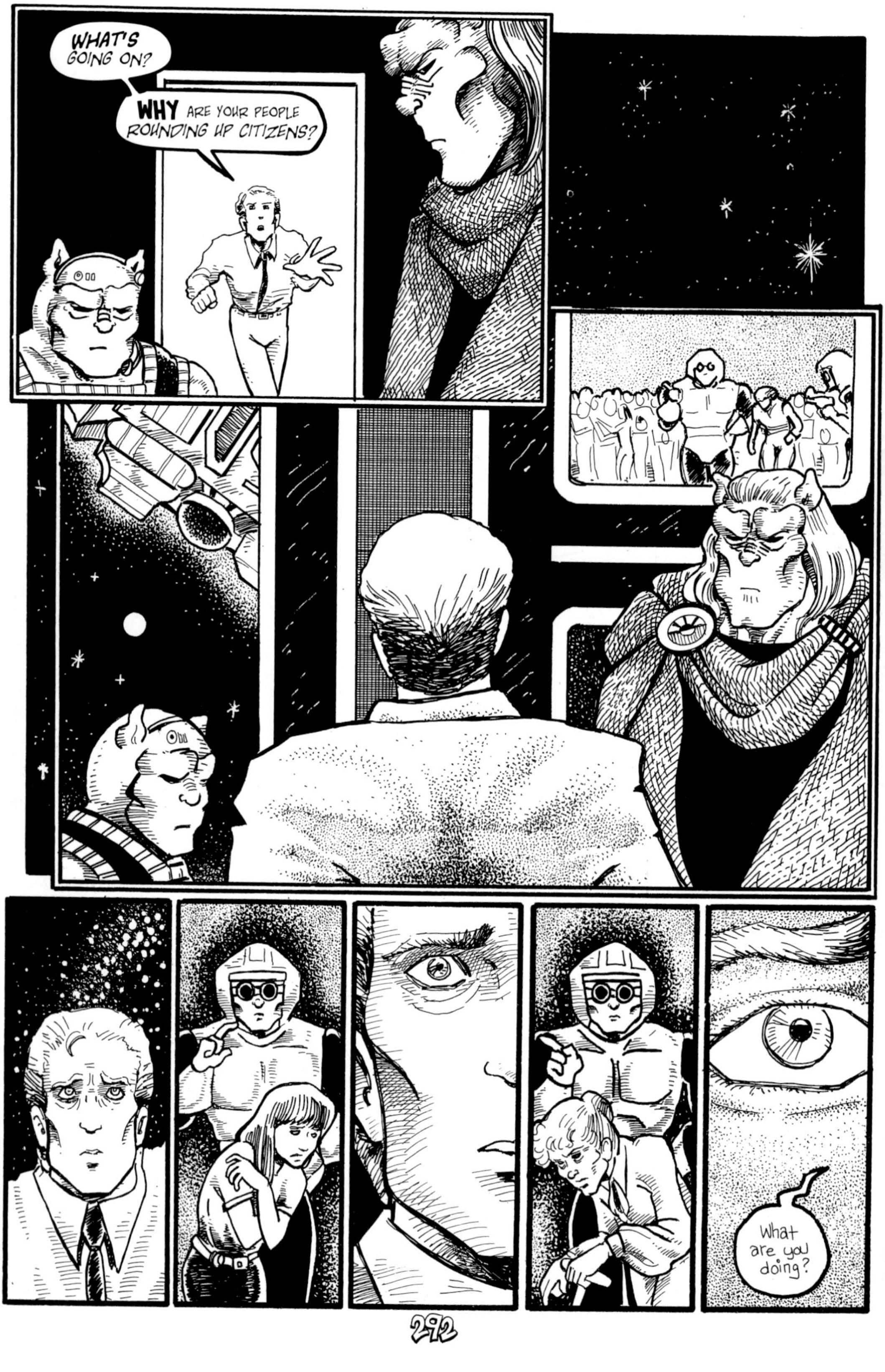

WHAT'S GOING ON?
WHY ARE YOUR PEOPLE ROUNDING UP CITIZENS?
What are you doing?

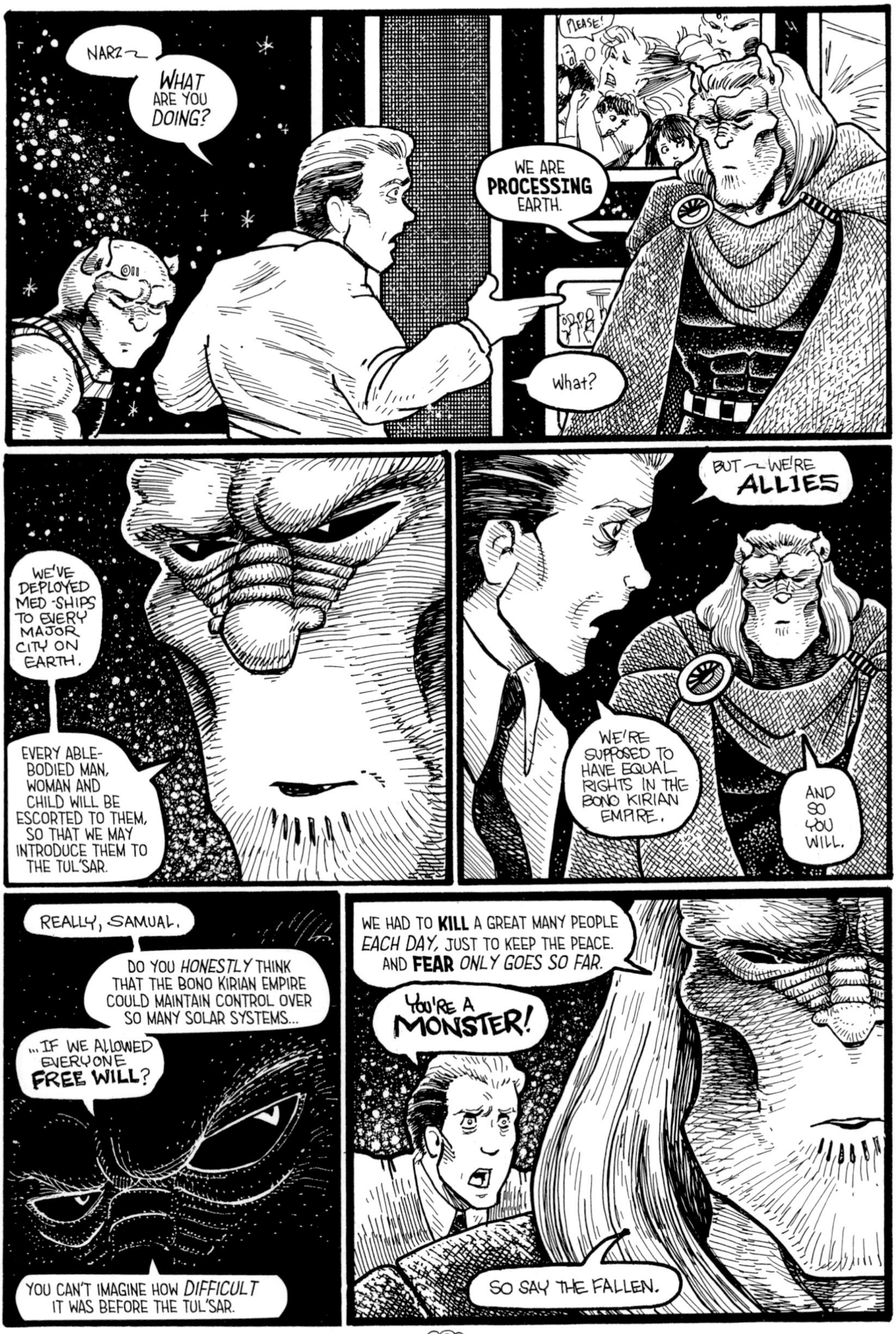
NARZ—
WHAT ARE YOU DOING?
PLEASE!
WE ARE PROCESSING EARTH.
What?
WE'VE DEPLOYED MED-SHIPS TO EVERY MAJOR CITY ON EARTH.
EVERY ABLE-BODIED MAN, WOMAN AND CHILD WILL BE ESCORTED TO THEM, SO THAT WE MAY INTRODUCE THEM TO THE TUL'SAR.
BUT—WE'RE ALLIES
WE'RE SUPPOSED TO HAVE EQUAL RIGHTS IN THE BONO KIRIAN EMPIRE.
AND SO YOU WILL.
REALLY, SAMUAL.
DO YOU HONESTLY THINK THAT THE BONO KIRIAN EMPIRE COULD MAINTAIN CONTROL OVER SO MANY SOLAR SYSTEMS...
...IF WE ALLOWED EVERYONE FREE WILL?
YOU CAN'T IMAGINE HOW DIFFICULT IT WAS BEFORE THE TUL'SAR.
WE HAD TO KILL A GREAT MANY PEOPLE EACH DAY, JUST TO KEEP THE PEACE. AND FEAR ONLY GOES SO FAR.
YOU'RE A MONSTER!
SO SAY THE FALLEN.

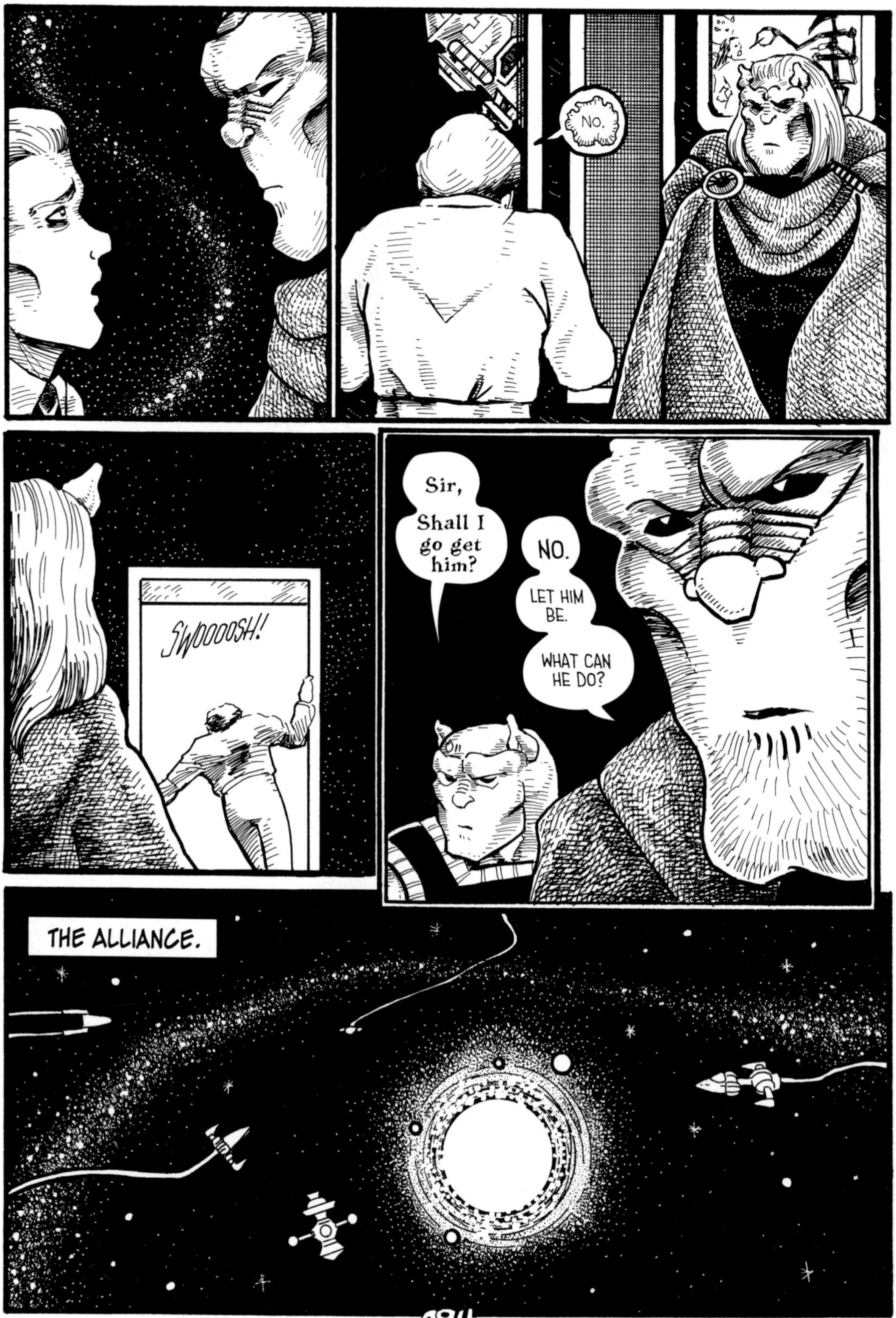

No.
SWOOOOSH!
Sir, Shall I go get him?
NO.
LET HIM BE.
WHAT CAN HE DO?
THE ALLIANCE.

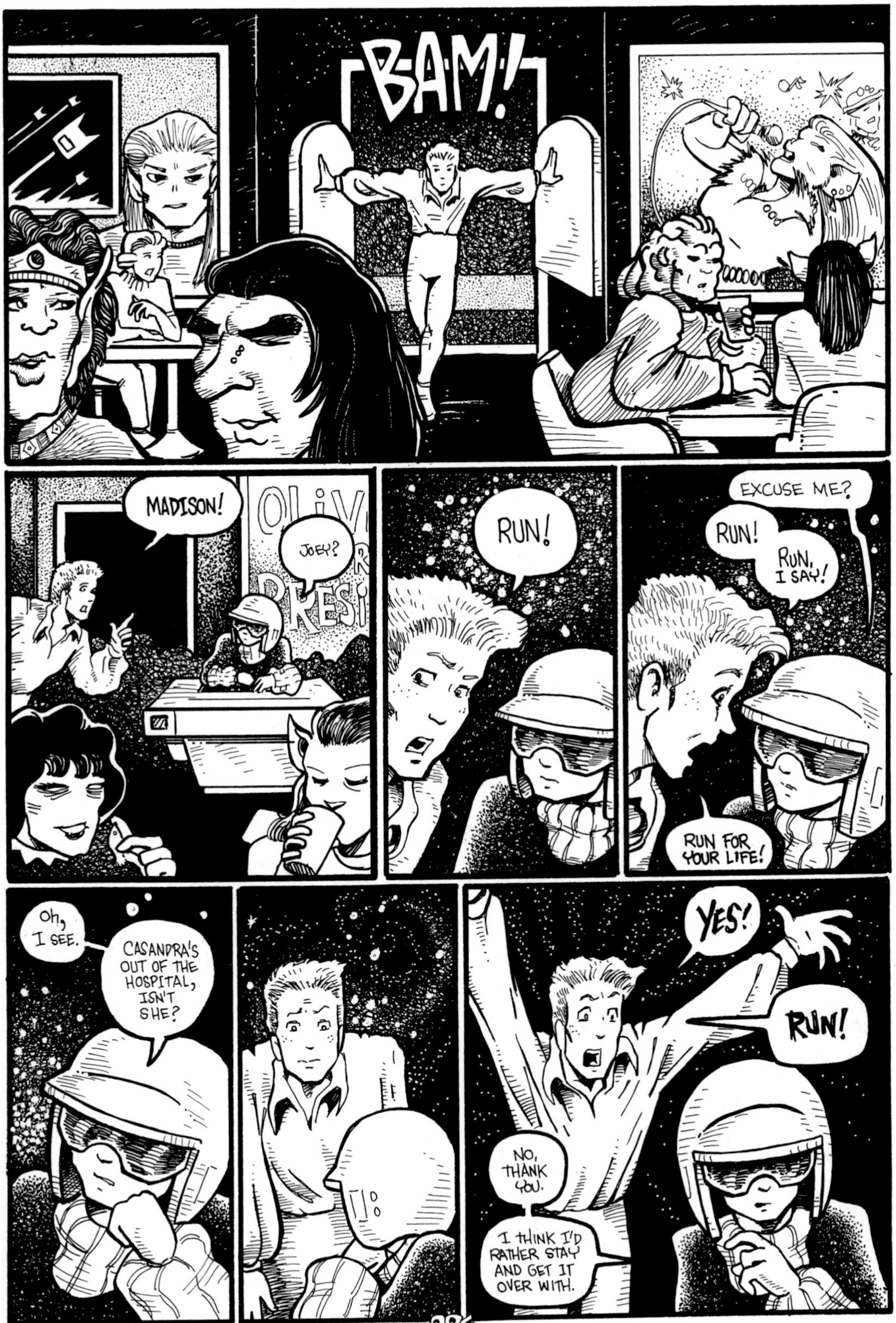
BAM!
MADISON!
JOEY?
OLIV
R
PRESI
RUN!
EXCUSE ME?
RUN!
RUN, I SAY!
RUN FOR YOUR LIFE!
Oh, I SEE.
CASANDRA'S OUT OF THE HOSPITAL, ISN'T SHE?
YES!
RUN!
NO, THANK YOU.
I THINK I'D RATHER STAY AND GET IT OVER WITH.

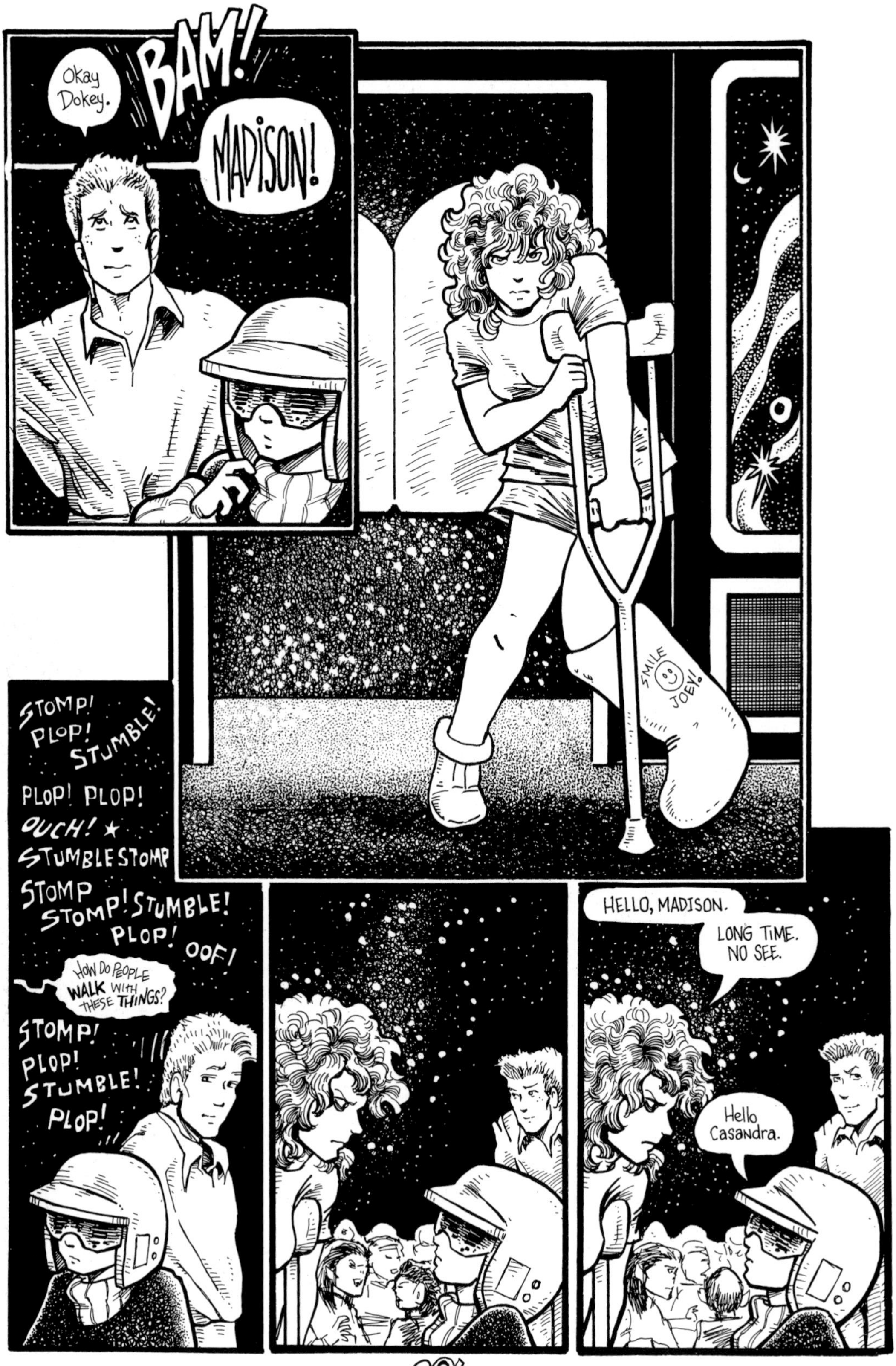
Okay Dokey.
BAM!
MADISON!
SMILE JOEY!
STOMP! PLOP! STUMBLE!
PLOP! PLOP!
OUCH! ★
STUMBLE STOMP
STOMP STOMP! STUMBLE! PLOP! OOF!
HOW DO PEOPLE WALK WITH THESE THINGS?
STOMP! PLOP! STUMBLE! PLOP!
HELLO, MADISON.
LONG TIME. NO SEE.
Hello Casandra.

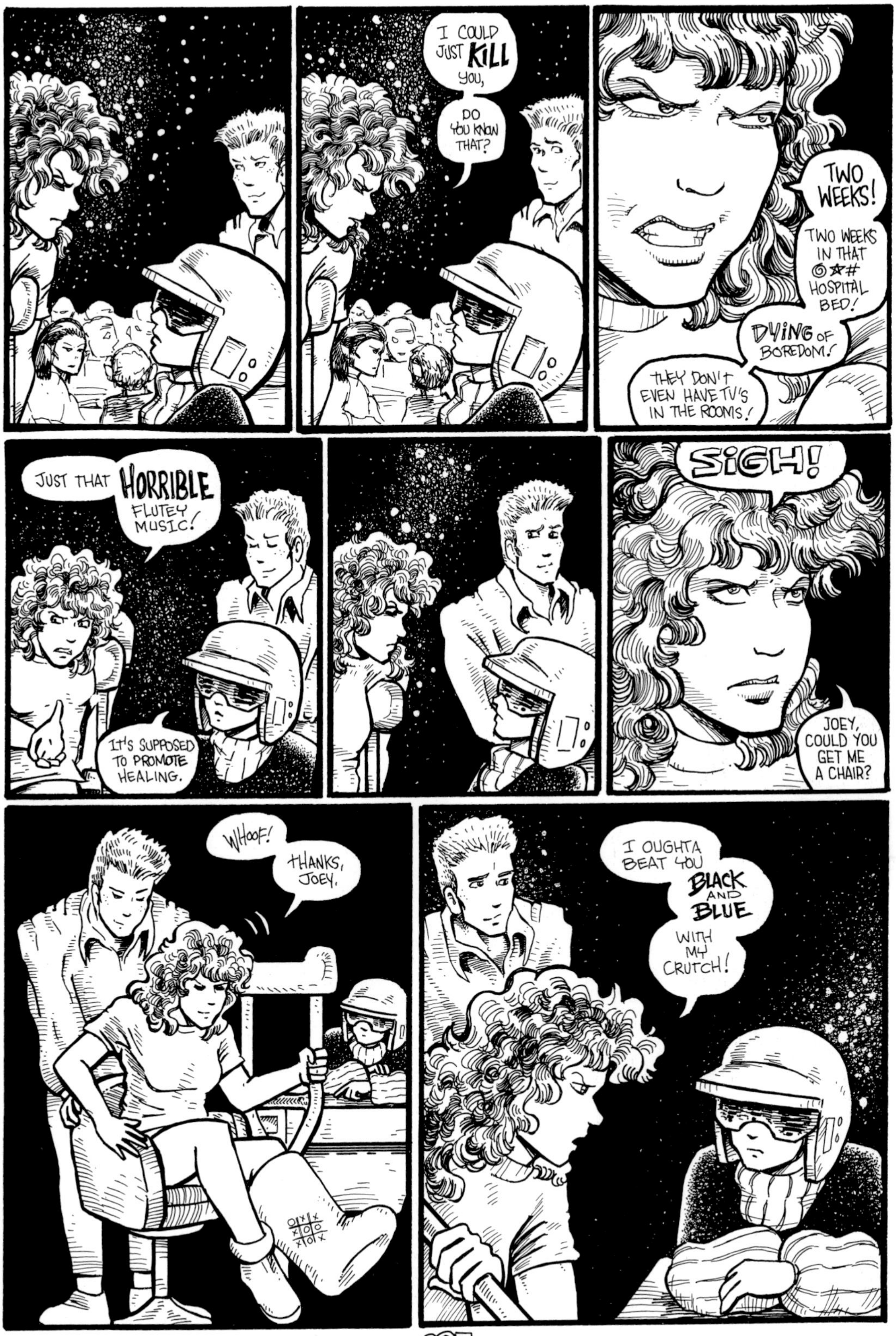
I COULD JUST KILL YOU,
DO YOU KNOW THAT?
TWO WEEKS!
TWO WEEKS IN THAT @☆# HOSPITAL BED!
DYING OF BOREDOM!
THEY DON'T EVEN HAVE TV'S IN THE ROOMS!
JUST THAT HORRIBLE FLUTEY MUSIC!
IT'S SUPPOSED TO PROMOTE HEALING.
SIGH!
JOEY, COULD YOU GET ME A CHAIR?
WHOOF!
THANKS, JOEY.
I OUGHTA BEAT YOU BLACK AND BLUE WITH MY CRUTCH!

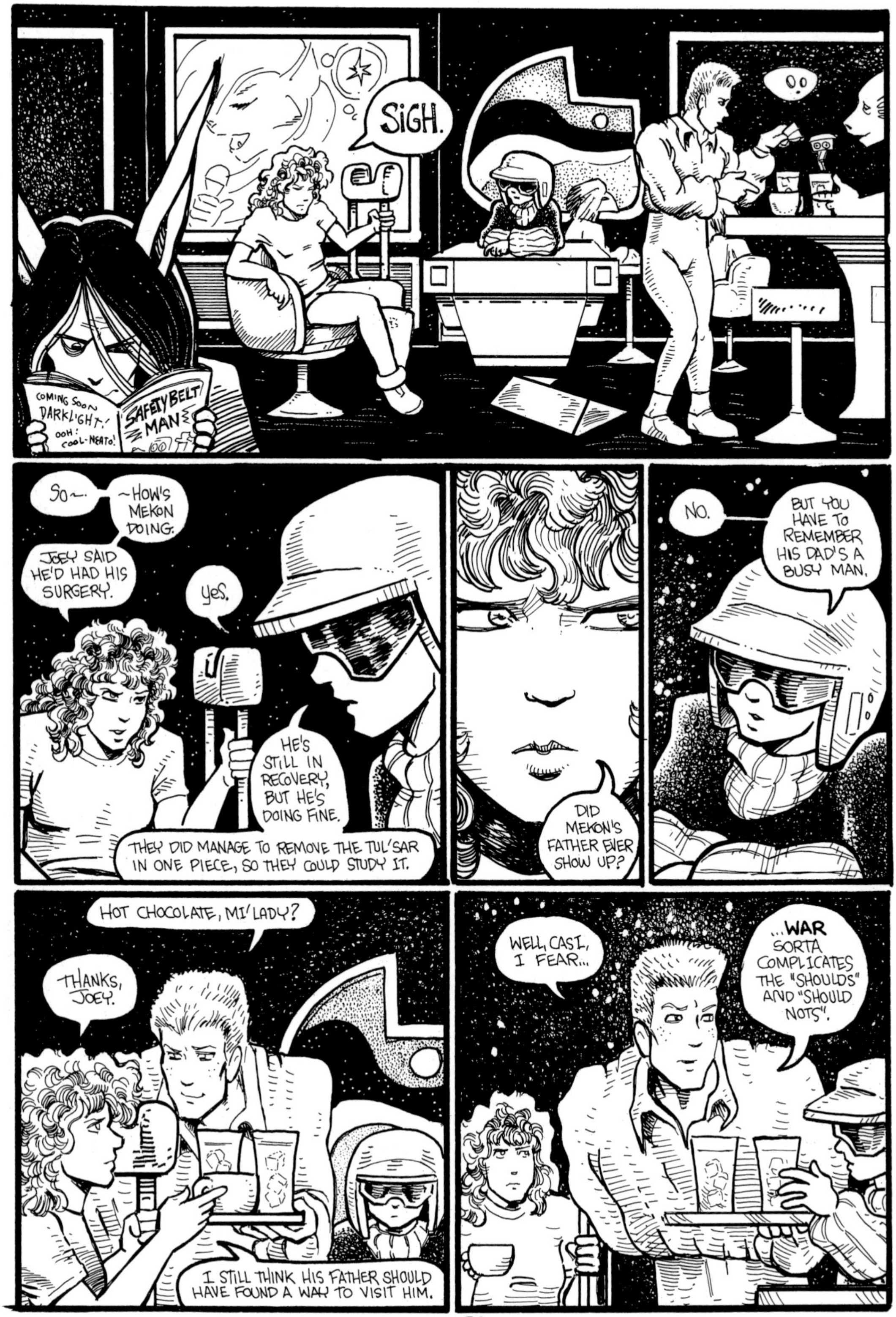
COMING SOON DARKLIGHT! OOH! COOL-NEATO!
SAFETY BELT MAN
SIGH.
So~.
~HOW'S MEKON DOING.
JOEY SAID HE'D HAD HIS SURGERY.
yes.
HE'S STILL IN RECOVERY, BUT HE'S DOING FINE.
THEY DID MANAGE TO REMOVE THE TUL'SAR IN ONE PIECE, SO THEY COULD STUDY IT.
DID MEKON'S FATHER EVER SHOW UP?
NO.
BUT YOU HAVE TO REMEMBER HIS DAD'S A BUSY MAN.
HOT CHOCOLATE, MI'LADY?
THANKS, JOEY.
I STILL THINK HIS FATHER SHOULD HAVE FOUND A WAY TO VISIT HIM.
WELL, CASI, I FEAR...
...WAR SORTA COMPLICATES THE "SHOULDS" AND "SHOULD NOTS".

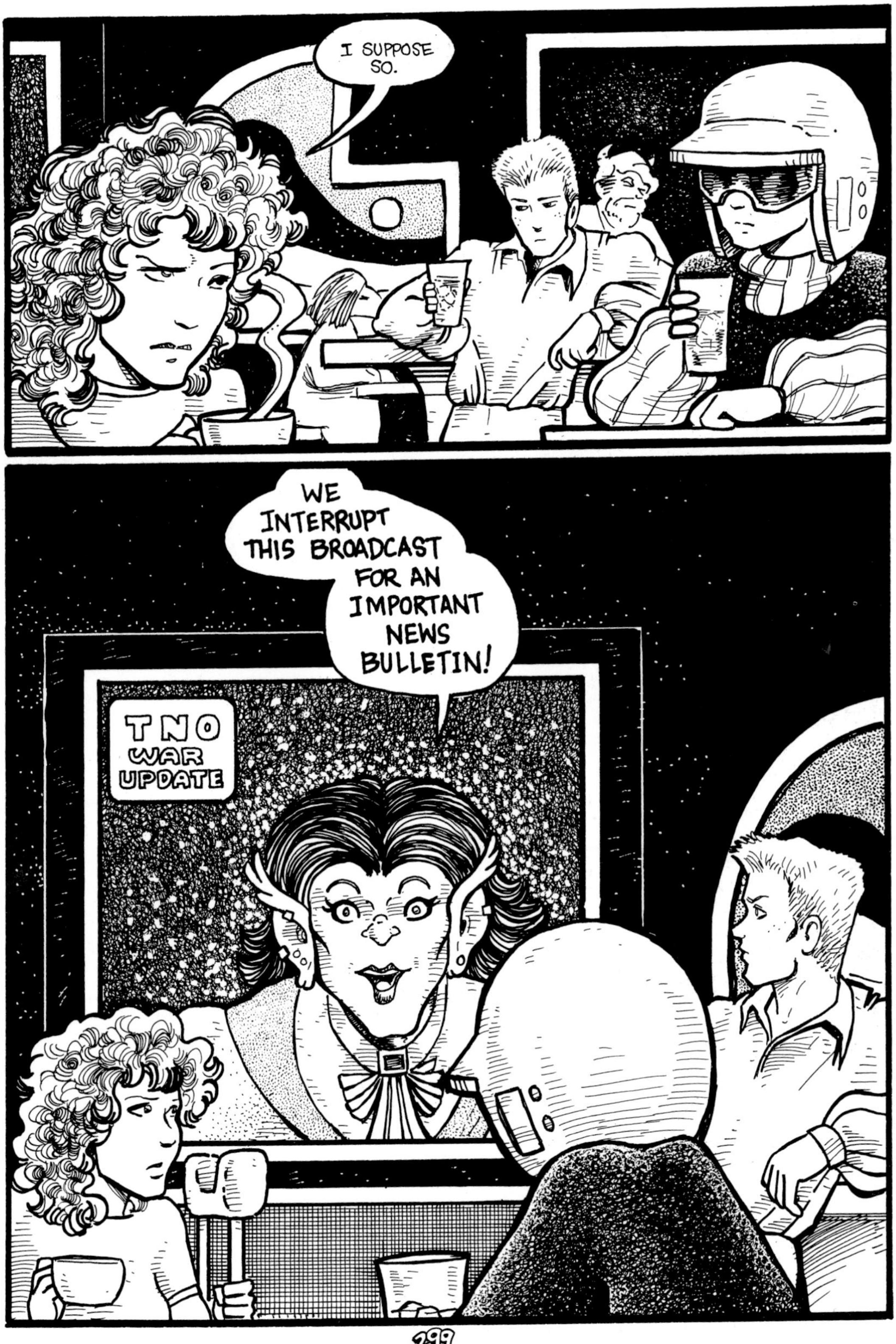
I SUPPOSE SO.
WE INTERRUPT THIS BROADCAST FOR AN IMPORTANT NEWS BULLETIN!
TNO WAR UPDATE

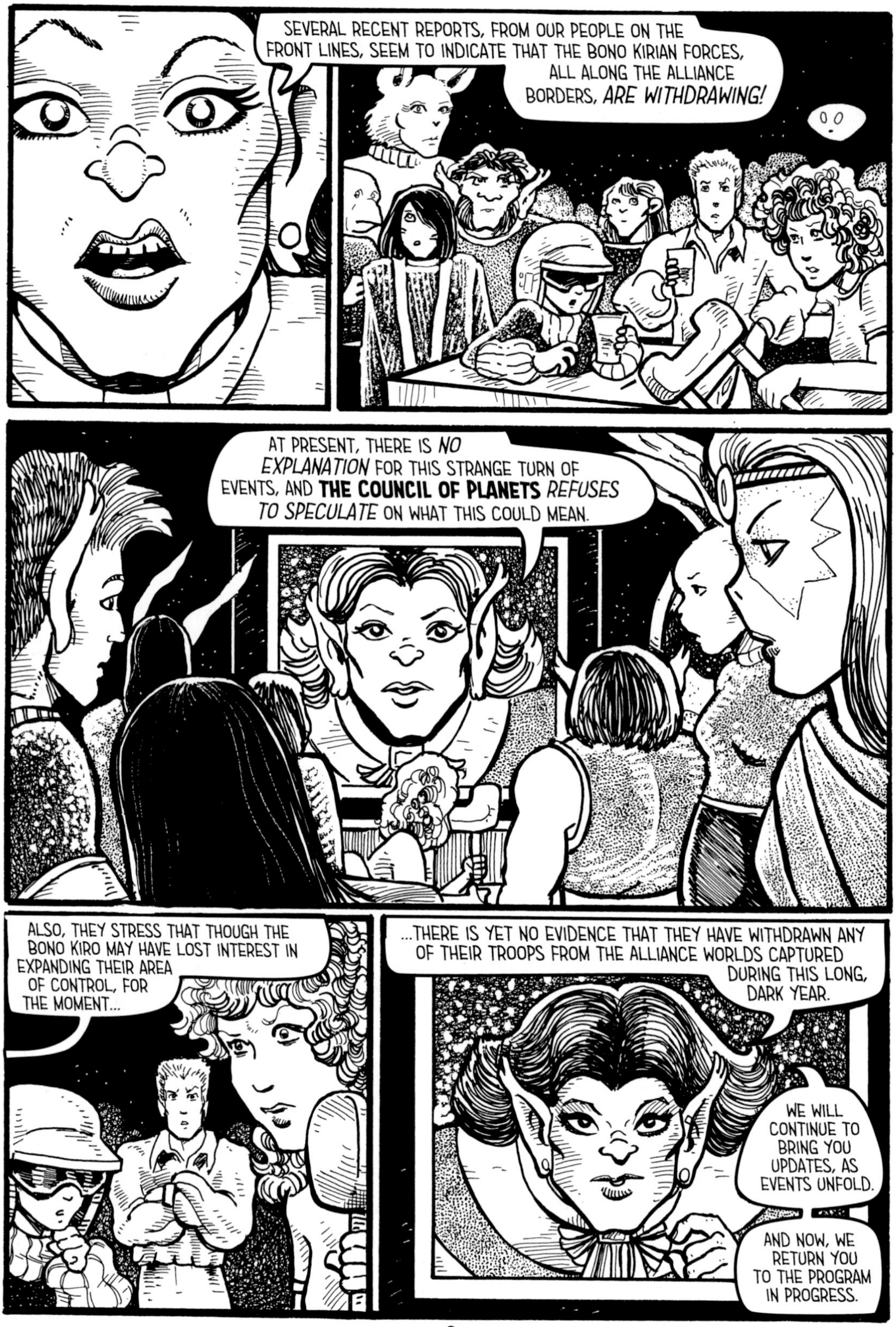

SEVERAL RECENT REPORTS, FROM OUR PEOPLE ON THE FRONT LINES, SEEM TO INDICATE THAT THE BONO KIRIAN FORCES, ALL ALONG THE ALLIANCE BORDERS, *ARE WITHDRAWING!*
AT PRESENT, THERE IS *NO EXPLANATION* FOR THIS STRANGE TURN OF EVENTS, AND **THE COUNCIL OF PLANETS** *REFUSES TO SPECULATE* ON WHAT THIS COULD MEAN.
ALSO, THEY STRESS THAT THOUGH THE BONO KIRO MAY HAVE LOST INTEREST IN EXPANDING THEIR AREA OF CONTROL, FOR THE MOMENT...
...THERE IS YET NO EVIDENCE THAT THEY HAVE WITHDRAWN ANY OF THEIR TROOPS FROM THE ALLIANCE WORLDS CAPTURED DURING THIS LONG, DARK YEAR.
WE WILL CONTINUE TO BRING YOU UPDATES, AS EVENTS UNFOLD.
AND NOW, WE RETURN YOU TO THE PROGRAM IN PROGRESS.

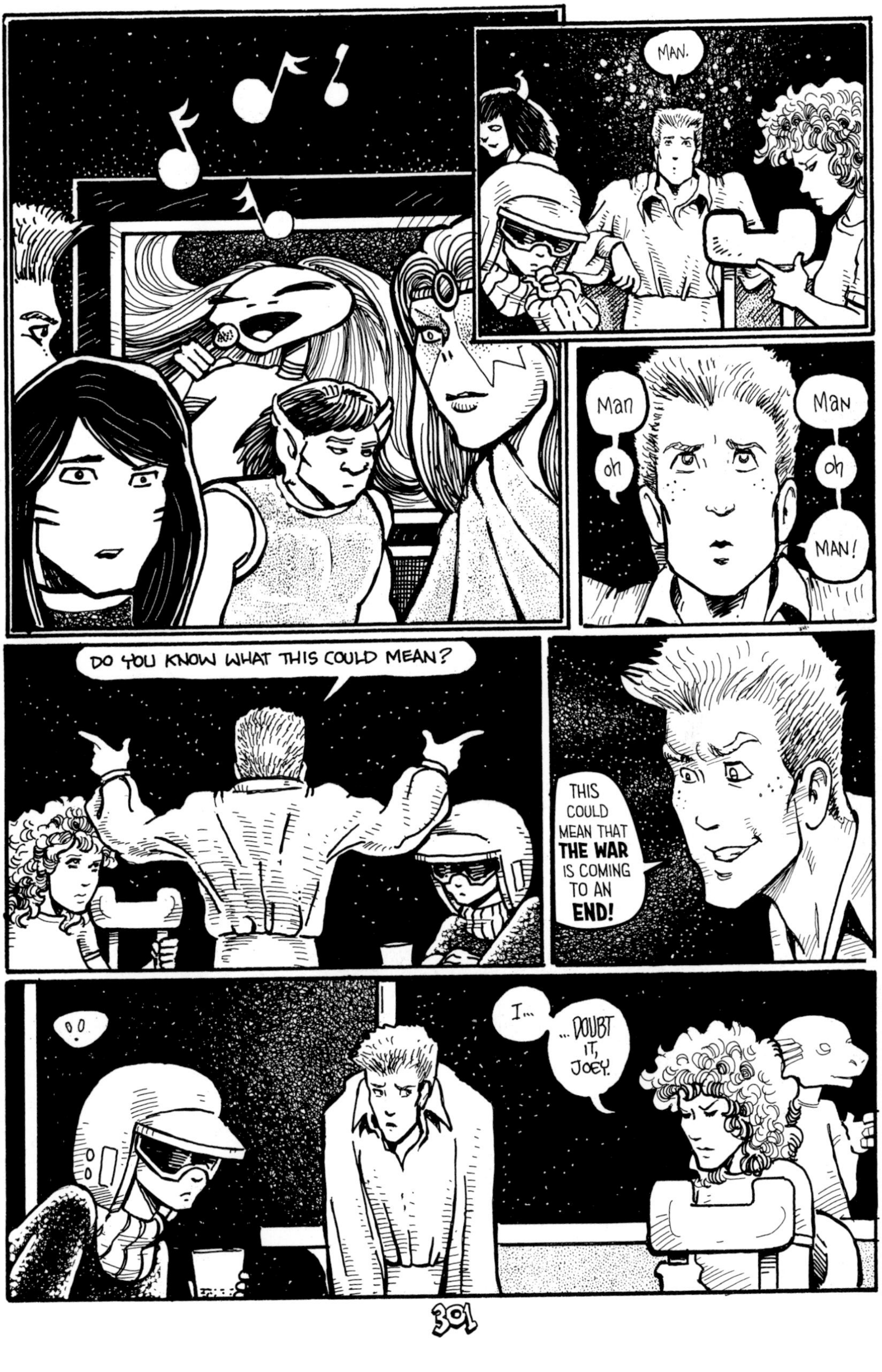

MAN.
Man
oh
Man
oh
MAN!
DO YOU KNOW WHAT THIS COULD MEAN?
THIS COULD MEAN THAT THE WAR IS COMING TO AN END!
I...
...DOUBT IT, JOEY.

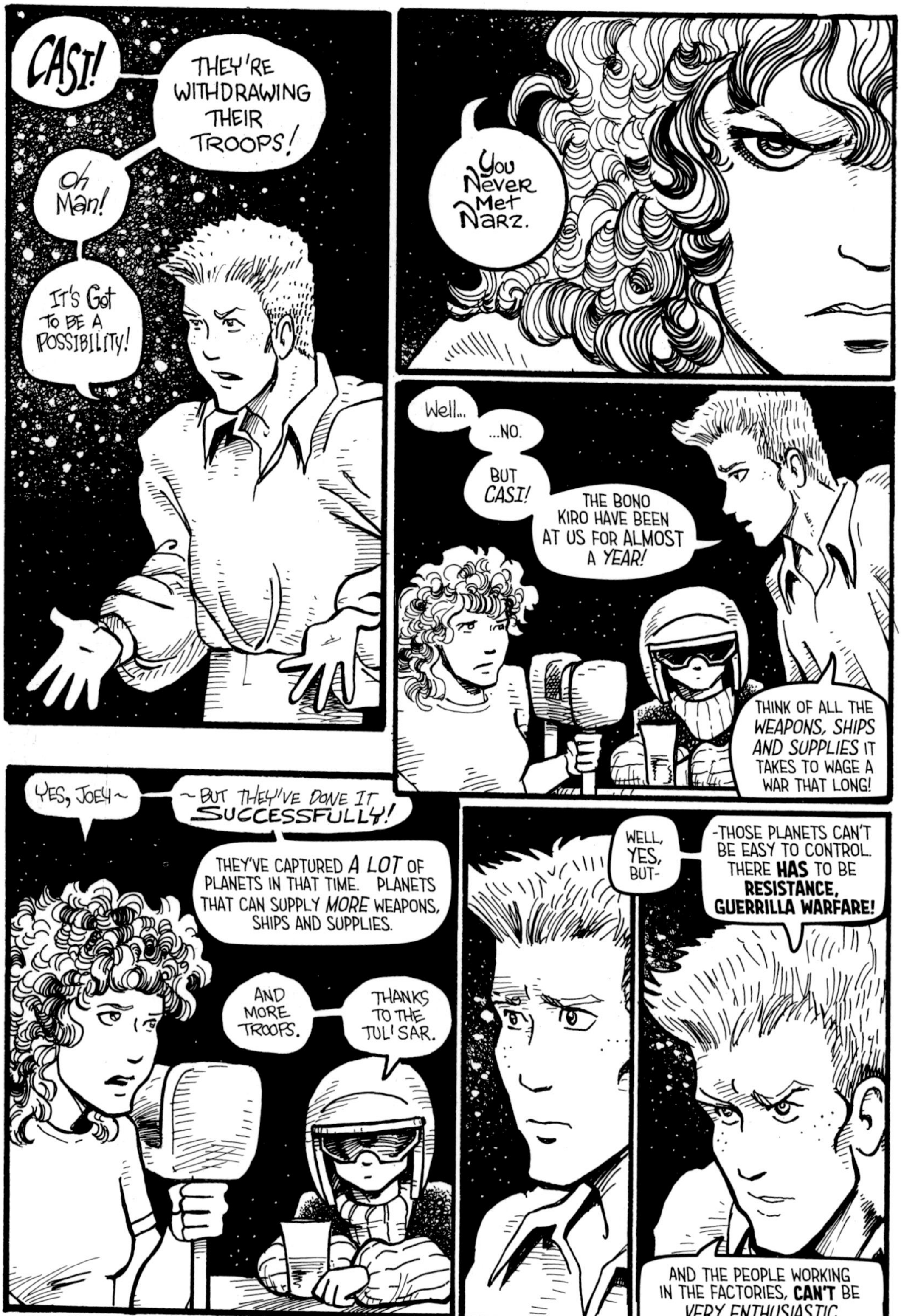
CASI!
THEY'RE WITHDRAWING THEIR TROOPS!
Oh Man!
IT'S Got TO BE A POSSIBILITY!
You Never Met Narz.
Well...
...NO.
BUT CASI!
THE BONO KIRO HAVE BEEN AT US FOR ALMOST A YEAR!
THINK OF ALL THE WEAPONS, SHIPS AND SUPPLIES IT TAKES TO WAGE A WAR THAT LONG!
YES, JOEY~
~BUT THEY'VE DONE IT SUCCESSFULLY!
THEY'VE CAPTURED A LOT OF PLANETS IN THAT TIME. PLANETS THAT CAN SUPPLY MORE WEAPONS, SHIPS AND SUPPLIES.
AND MORE TROOPS.
THANKS TO THE TUL'SAR.
WELL, YES, BUT-
-THOSE PLANETS CAN'T BE EASY TO CONTROL. THERE HAS TO BE RESISTANCE, GUERRILLA WARFARE!
AND THE PEOPLE WORKING IN THE FACTORIES, CAN'T BE VERY ENTHUSIASTIC.

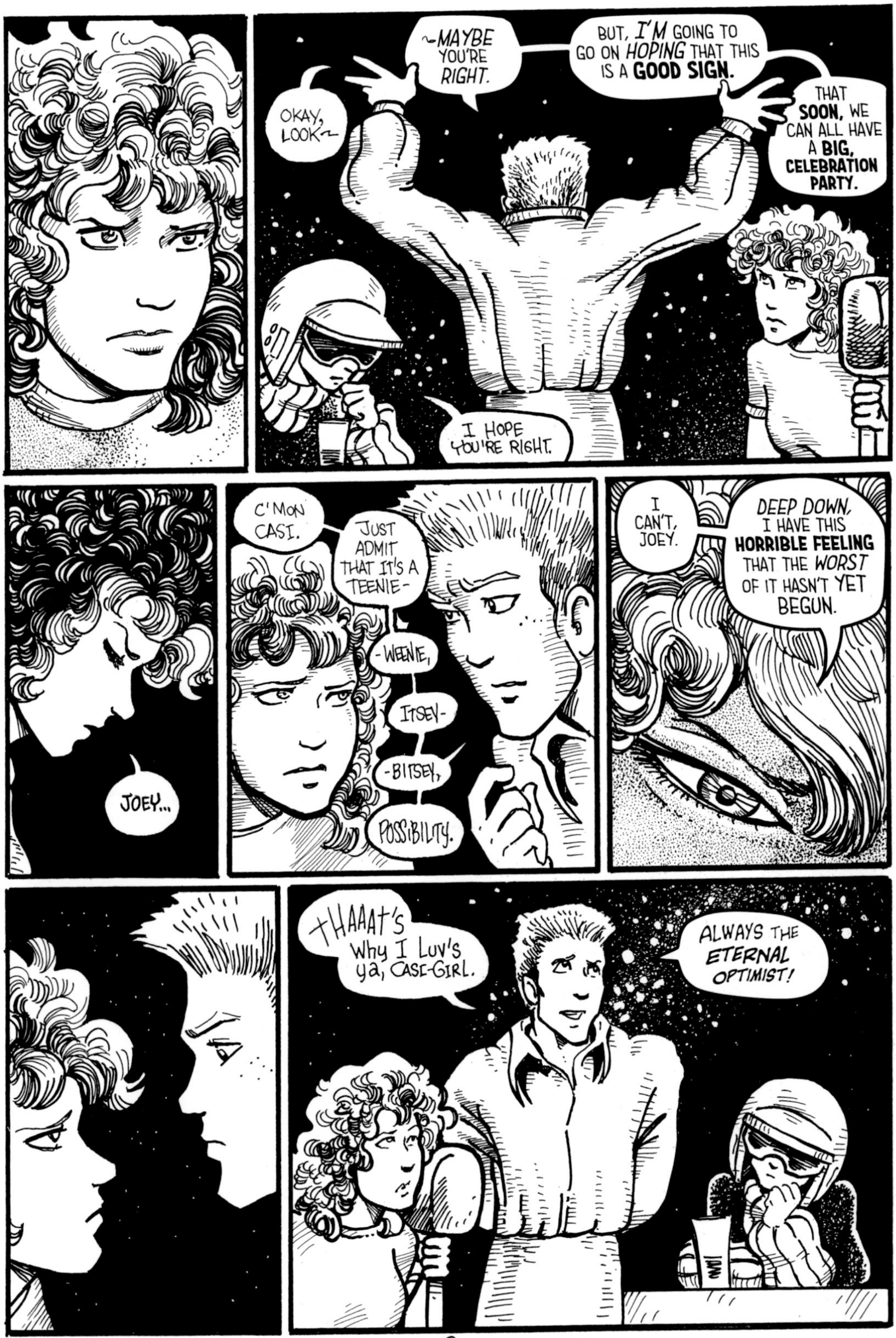
OKAY, LOOK~
~MAYBE YOU'RE RIGHT.
BUT, I'M GOING TO GO ON HOPING THAT THIS IS A GOOD SIGN.
THAT SOON, WE CAN ALL HAVE A BIG, CELEBRATION PARTY.
I HOPE YOU'RE RIGHT.
JOEY...
C'MON CASI.
JUST ADMIT THAT IT'S A TEENIE-
-WEENIE,
ITSEY-
-BITSEY,
POSSIBILITY.
I CAN'T, JOEY.
DEEP DOWN, I HAVE THIS HORRIBLE FEELING THAT THE WORST OF IT HASN'T YET BEGUN.
THAAAT'S Why I Luv's ya, CASI-GIRL.
ALWAYS THE ETERNAL OPTIMIST!

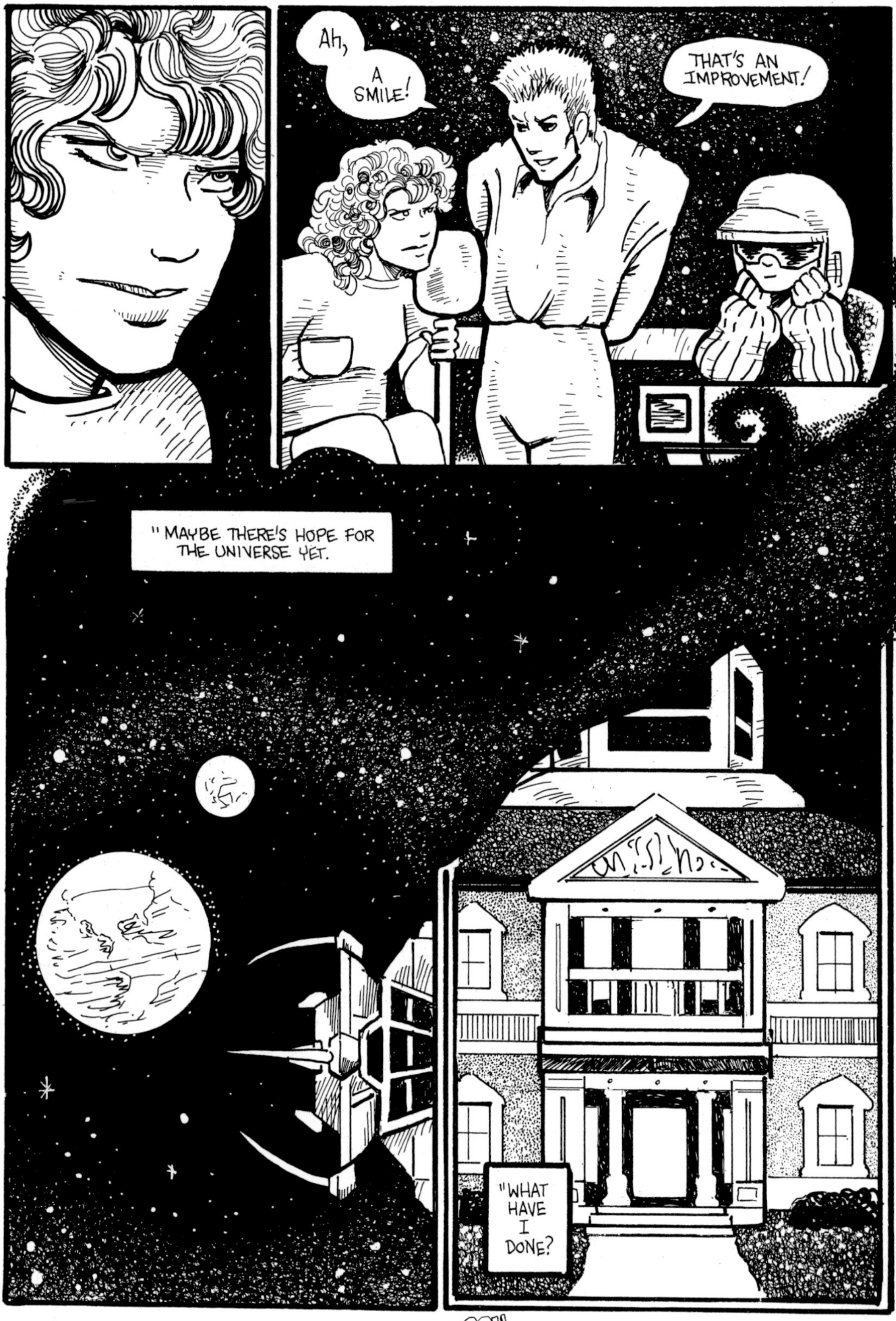
Ah, A SMILE!
THAT'S AN IMPROVEMENT!
"MAYBE THERE'S HOPE FOR THE UNIVERSE YET.
"WHAT HAVE I DONE?

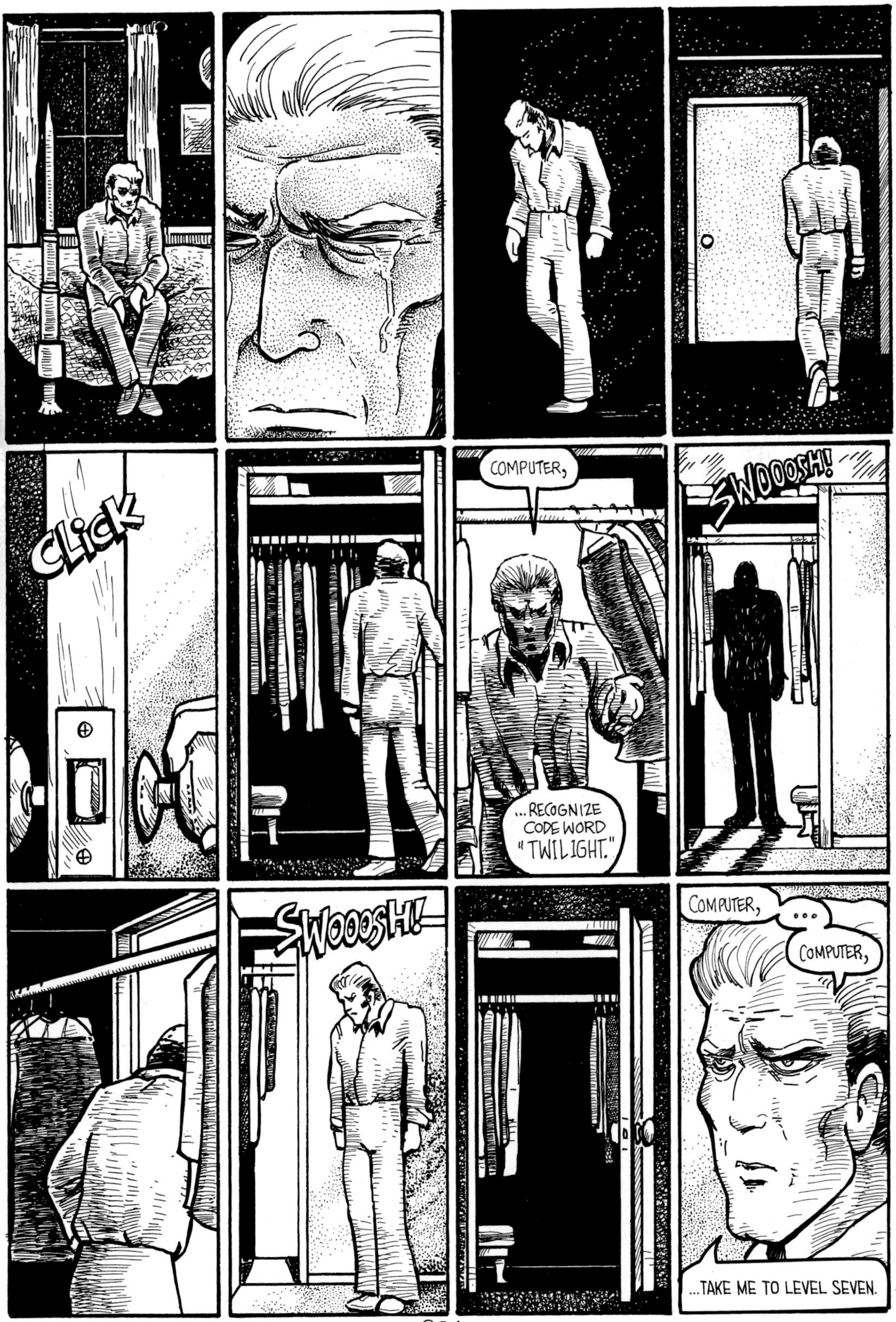
CLICK
COMPUTER,
...RECOGNIZE CODE WORD "TWILIGHT."
SWOOOSH!
SWOOOSH!
COMPUTER,
...
COMPUTER,
...TAKE ME TO LEVEL SEVEN.

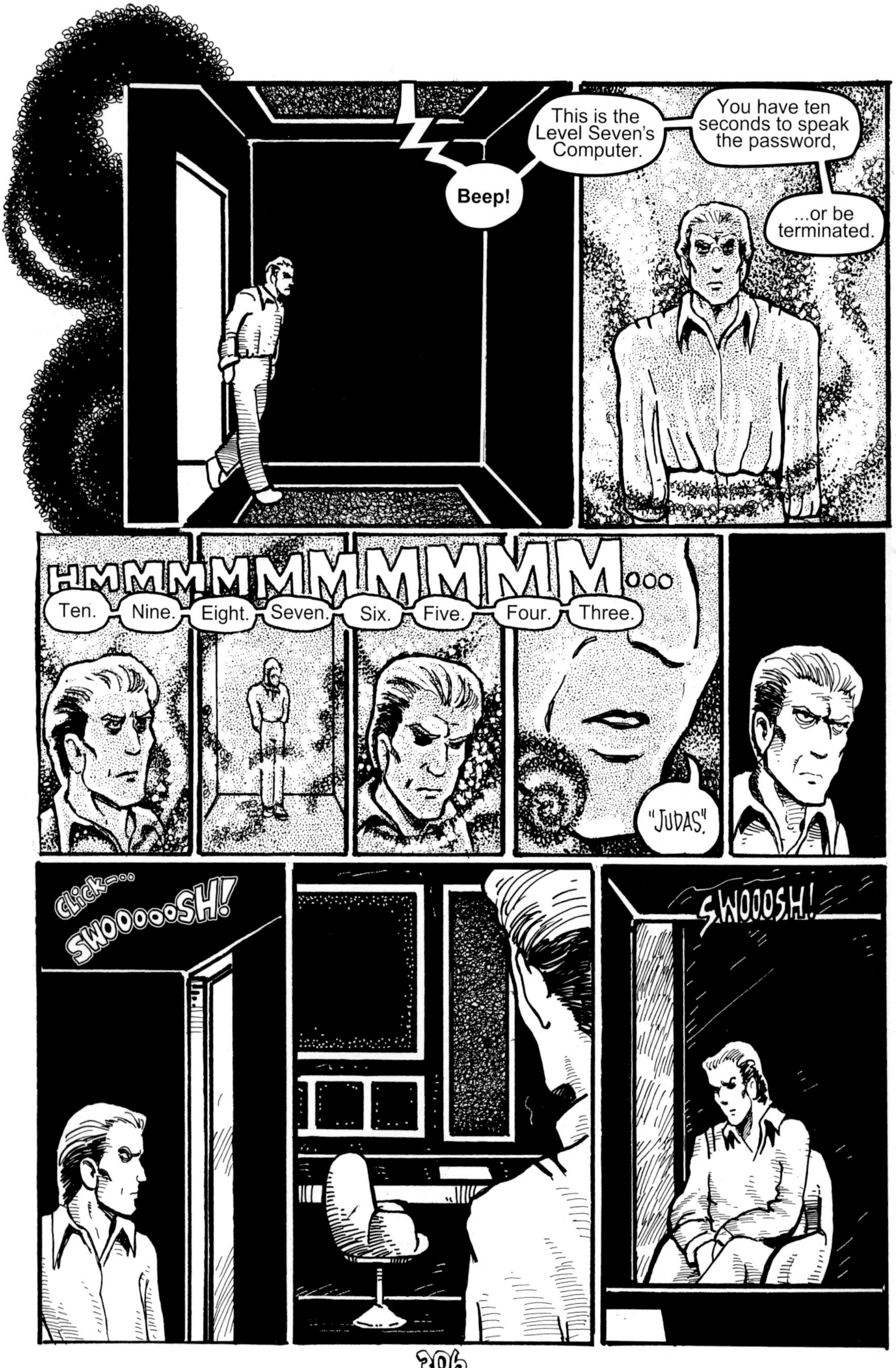

Beep!
This is the Level Seven's Computer.
You have ten seconds to speak the password,
...or be terminated.
HMMMMMMMMMMM...
Ten.
Nine.
Eight.
Seven.
Six.
Five.
Four.
Three.
"JUDAS."
CLICK—..
SWOOOOOSH!
SWOOOSH!

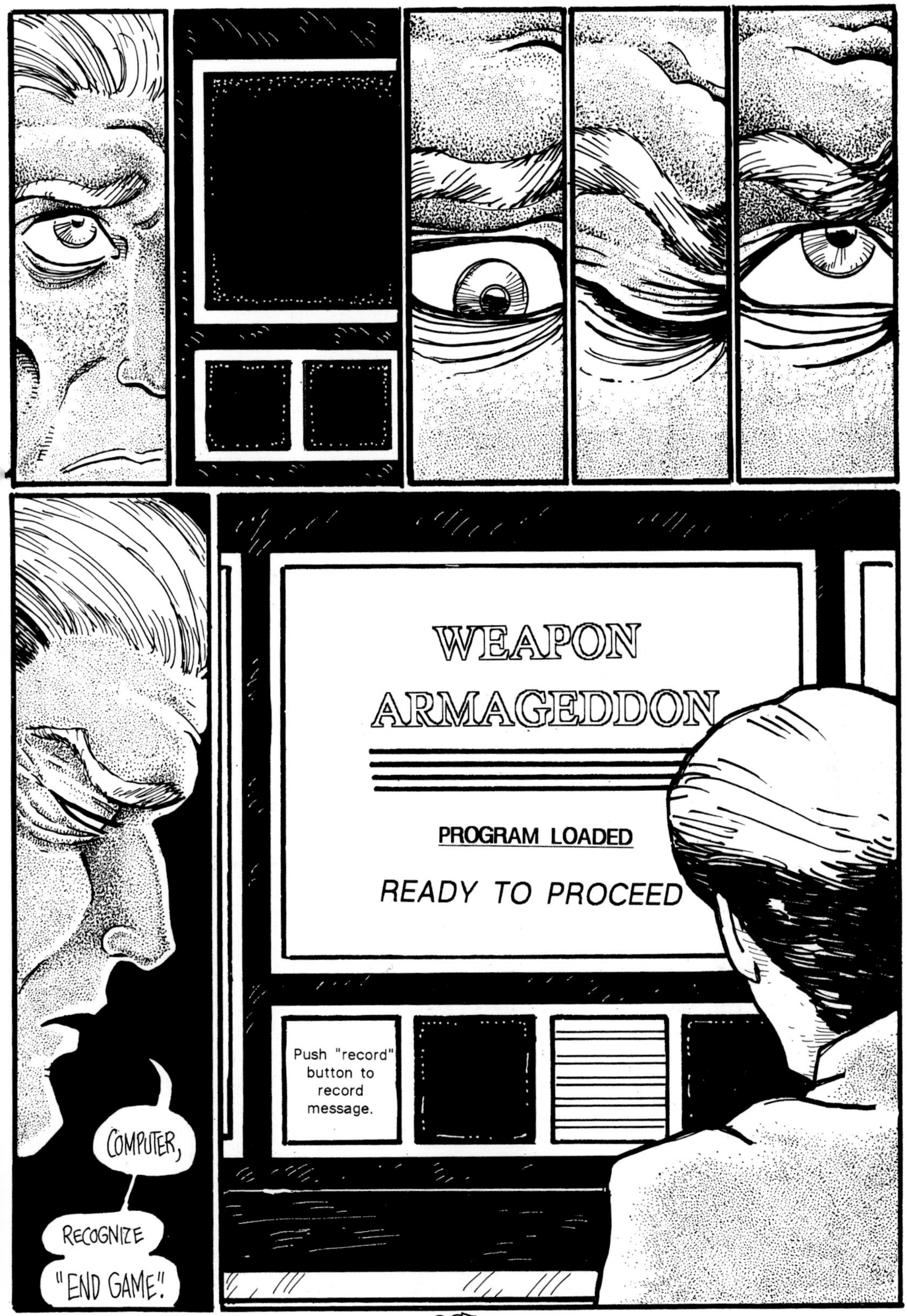
WEAPON
ARMAGEDDON
PROGRAM LOADED
READY TO PROCEED
Push "record" button to record message.
COMPUTER,
RECOGNIZE
"END GAME"!

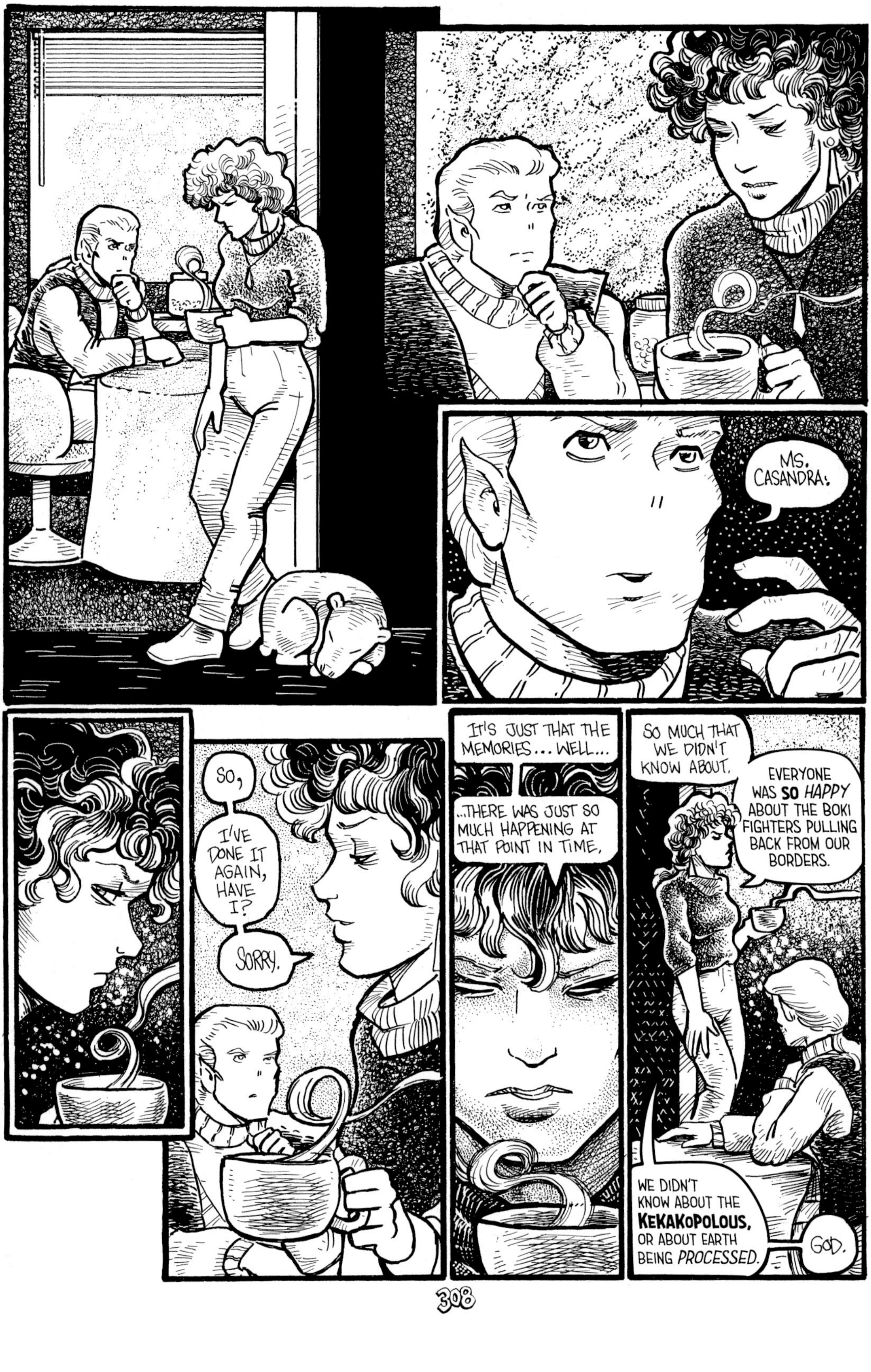
MS. CASANDRA:.
SO,
I'VE DONE IT AGAIN, HAVE I?
SORRY.
IT'S JUST THAT THE MEMORIES... WELL...
...THERE WAS JUST SO MUCH HAPPENING AT THAT POINT IN TIME,
SO MUCH THAT WE DIDN'T KNOW ABOUT.
EVERYONE WAS SO HAPPY ABOUT THE BOKI FIGHTERS PULLING BACK FROM OUR BORDERS.
WE DIDN'T KNOW ABOUT THE KEKAKOPOLOUS, OR ABOUT EARTH BEING PROCESSED.
GOD.

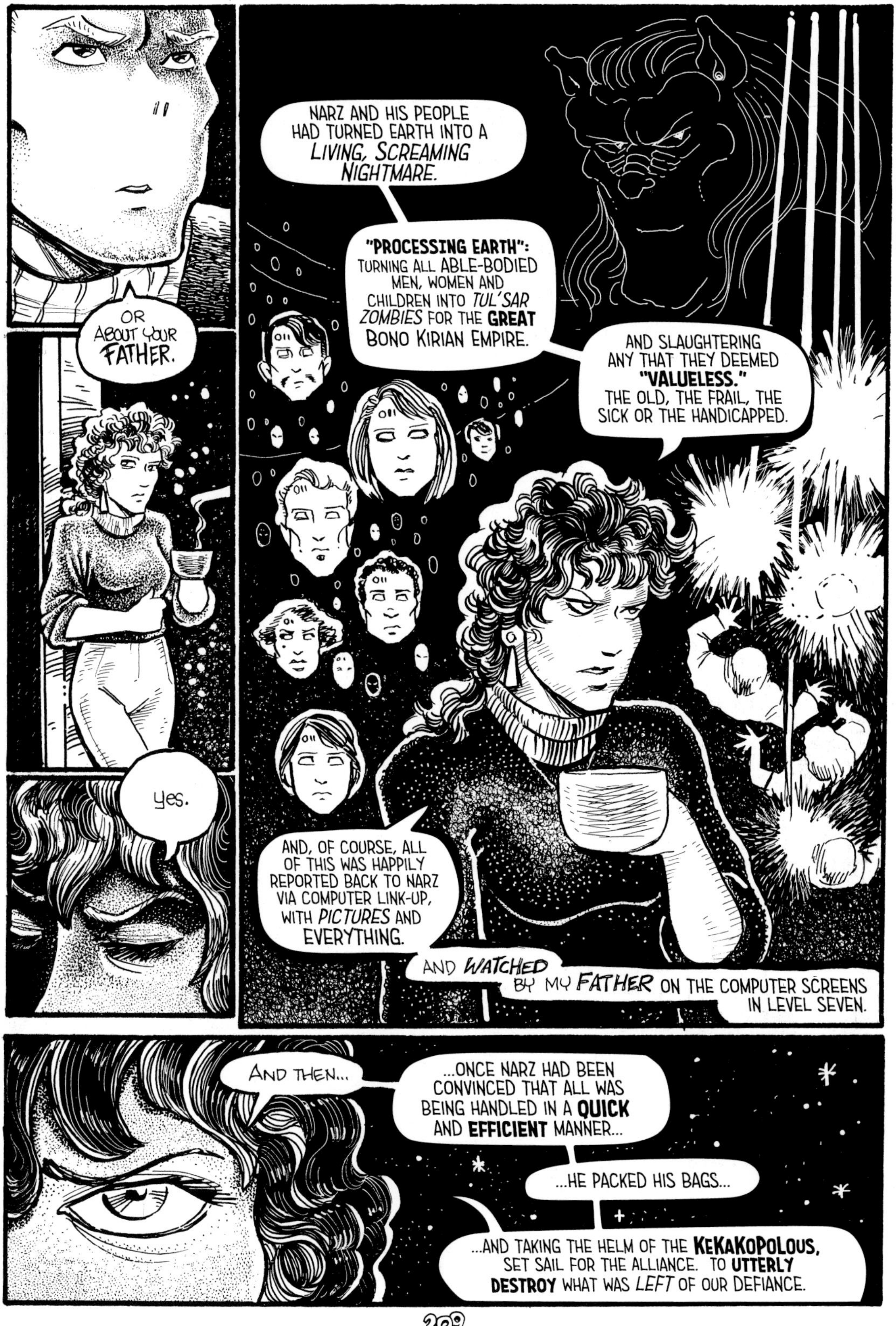

OR ABOUT YOUR FATHER.
yes.
NARZ AND HIS PEOPLE HAD TURNED EARTH INTO A LIVING, SCREAMING NIGHTMARE.
"PROCESSING EARTH": TURNING ALL ABLE-BODIED MEN, WOMEN AND CHILDREN INTO TUL'SAR ZOMBIES FOR THE GREAT BONO KIRIAN EMPIRE.
AND SLAUGHTERING ANY THAT THEY DEEMED "VALUELESS." THE OLD, THE FRAIL, THE SICK OR THE HANDICAPPED.
AND, OF COURSE, ALL OF THIS WAS HAPPILY REPORTED BACK TO NARZ VIA COMPUTER LINK-UP, WITH PICTURES AND EVERYTHING.
AND WATCHED BY MY FATHER ON THE COMPUTER SCREENS IN LEVEL SEVEN.
AND THEN...
...ONCE NARZ HAD BEEN CONVINCED THAT ALL WAS BEING HANDLED IN A QUICK AND EFFICIENT MANNER...
...HE PACKED HIS BAGS...
...AND TAKING THE HELM OF THE KEKAKOPOLOUS, SET SAIL FOR THE ALLIANCE. TO UTTERLY DESTROY WHAT WAS LEFT OF OUR DEFIANCE.

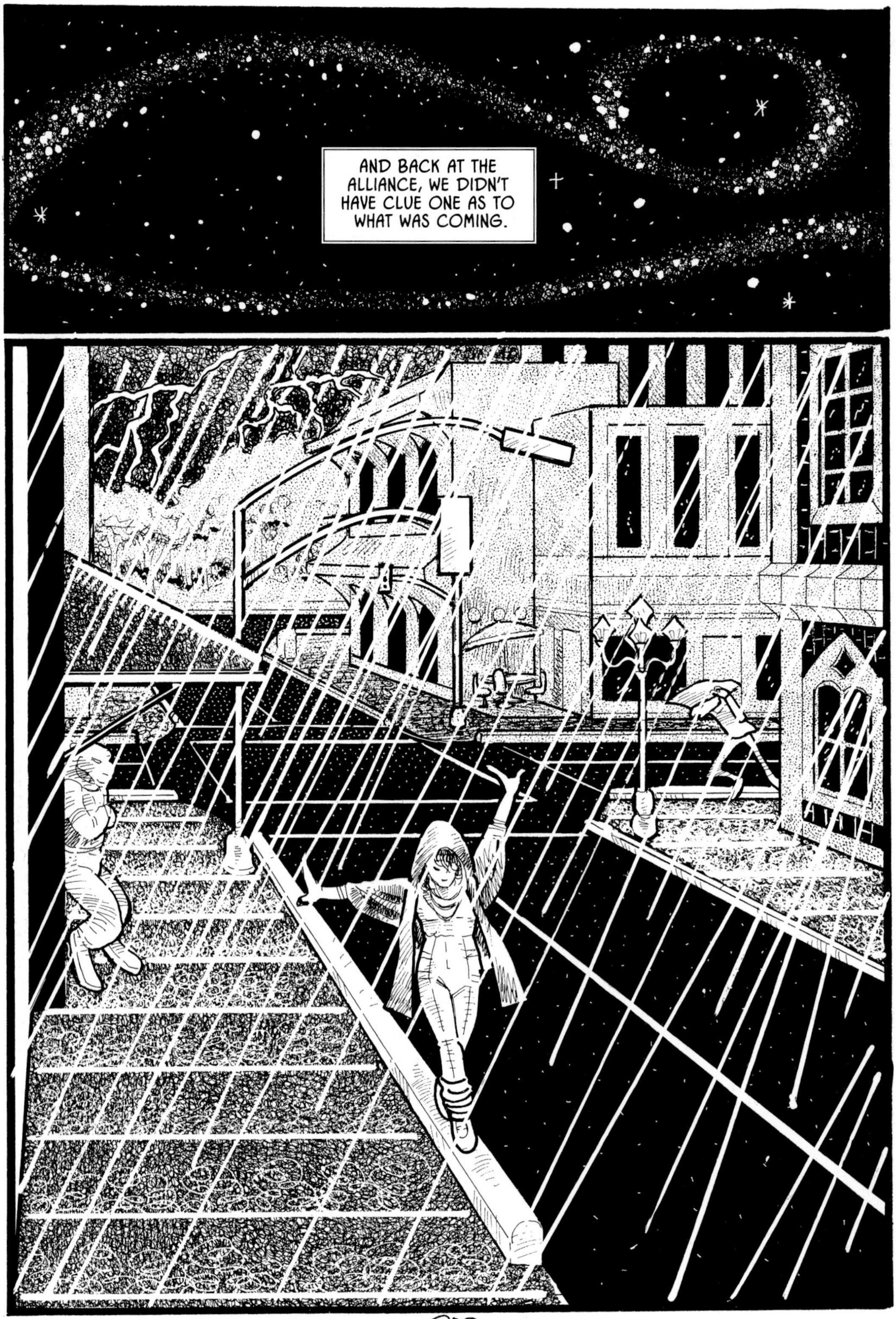
AND BACK AT THE ALLIANCE, WE DIDN'T HAVE CLUE ONE AS TO WHAT WAS COMING.

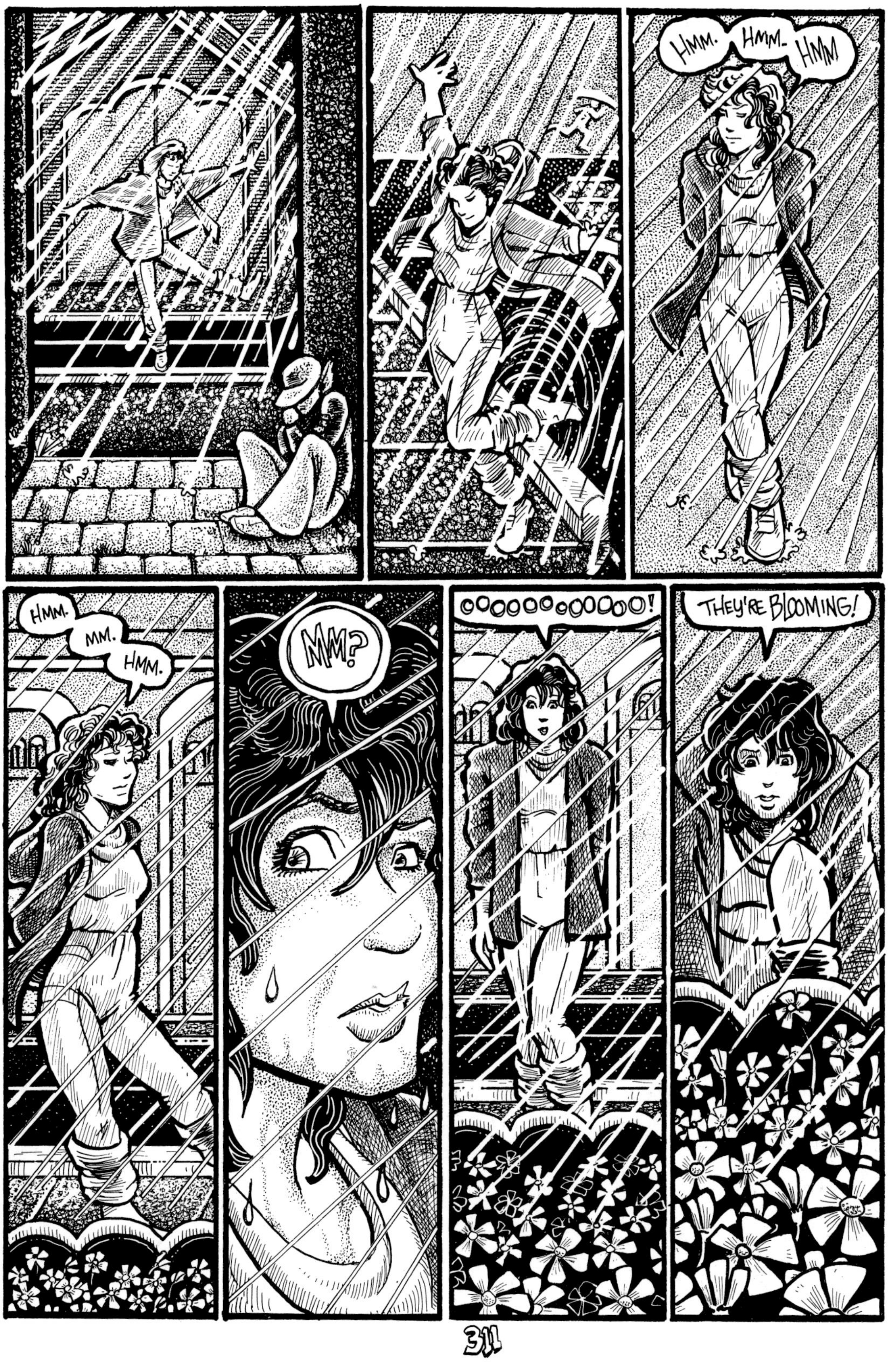
HMM. HMM- HMM
HMM.
MM.
HMM.
MM?
OOOOOOOOOOOOO!
THEY'RE BLOOMING!

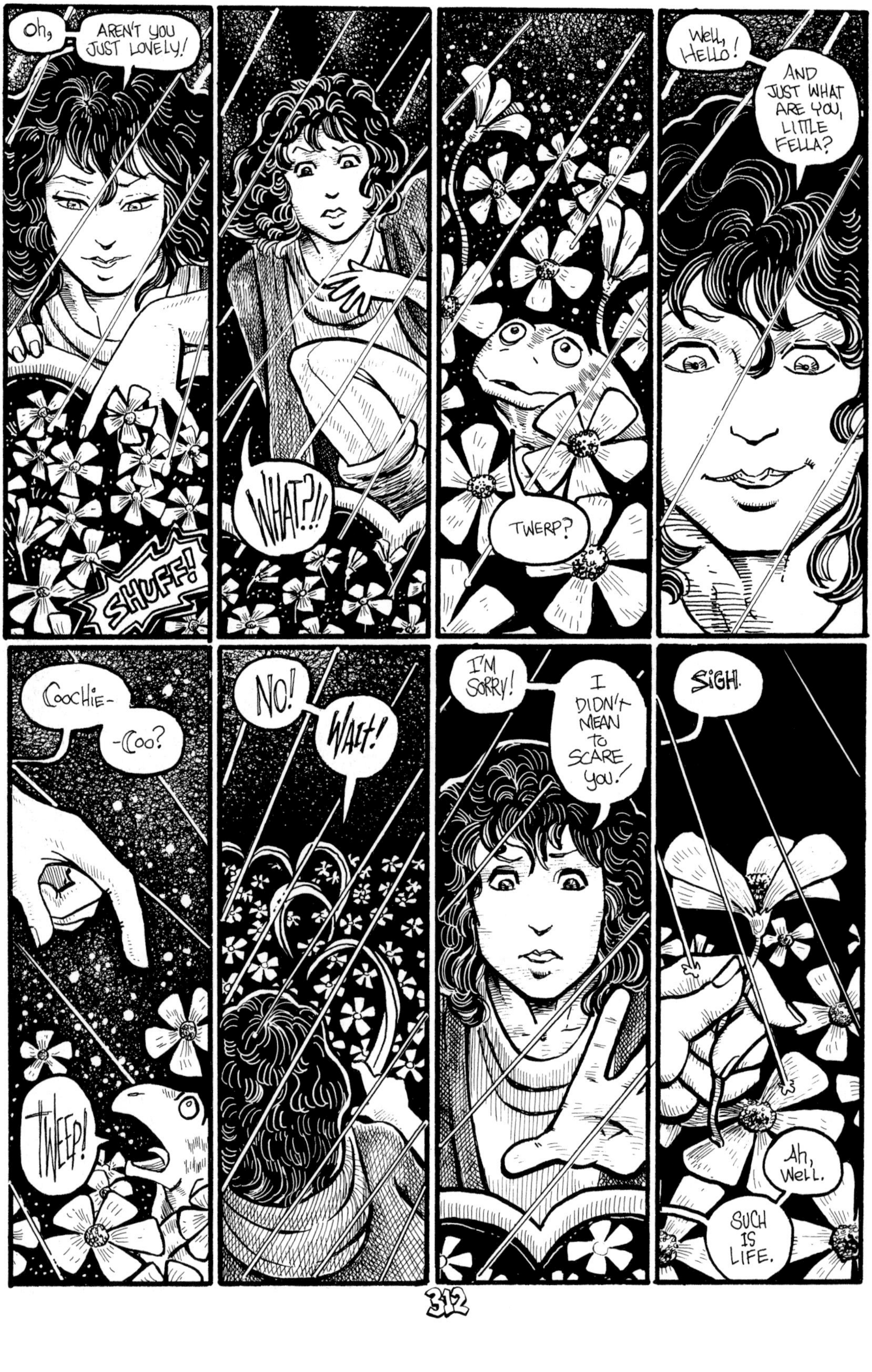
Oh,
AREN'T YOU JUST LOVELY!
SHUFF!
WHAT?!!
TWERP?
Well, HELLO!
AND JUST WHAT ARE YOU, LITTLE FELLA?
COOCHIE-
-COO?
TWEEP!
NO!
WAIT!
I'M SORRY!
I DIDN'T MEAN TO SCARE YOU.
SIGH.
Ah, Well.
SUCH IS LIFE.

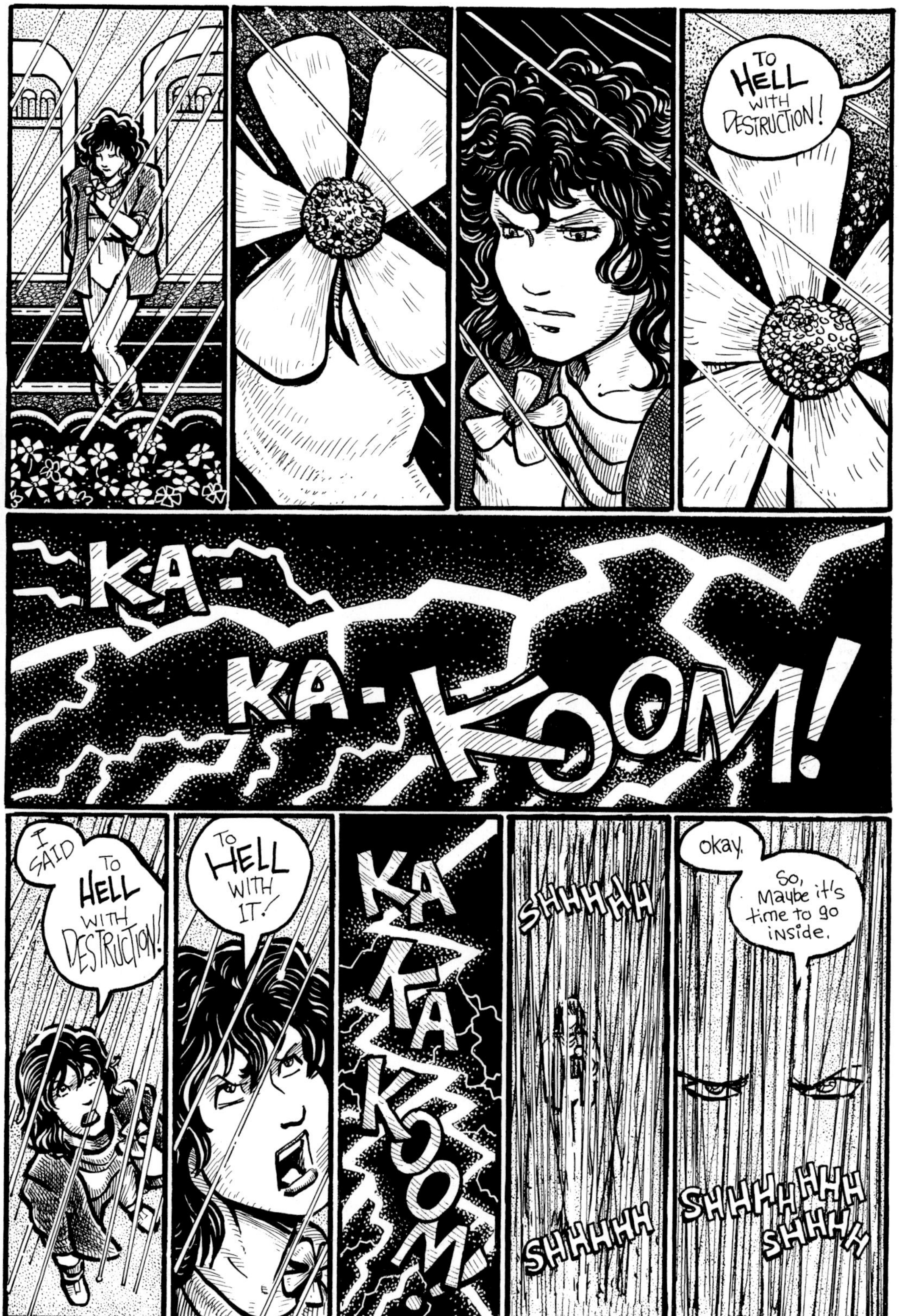
To HELL with DESTRUCTION!
KA- KA- KOOM!
I SAID To HELL with DESTRUCTION!
To HELL with IT!
KA KA KA KOOM!
SHHHHH
SHHHHH
okay.
So, Maybe it's time to go inside.
SHHHHHHH SHHHHH

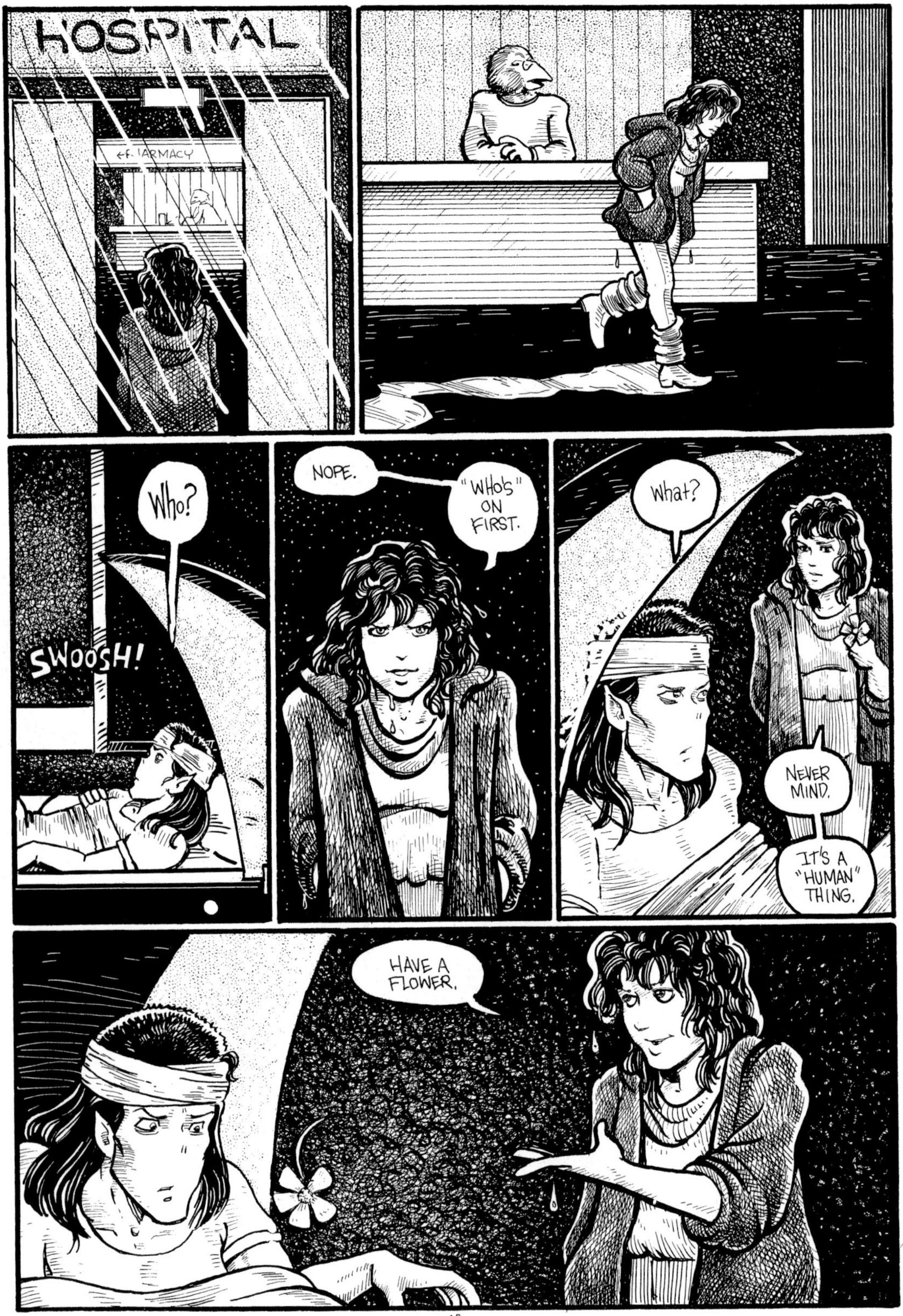
HOSPITAL
←PHARMACY
Who?
SWOOSH!
NOPE.
"WHO'S" ON FIRST.
What?
NEVER MIND.
IT'S A "HUMAN" THING.
HAVE A FLOWER.

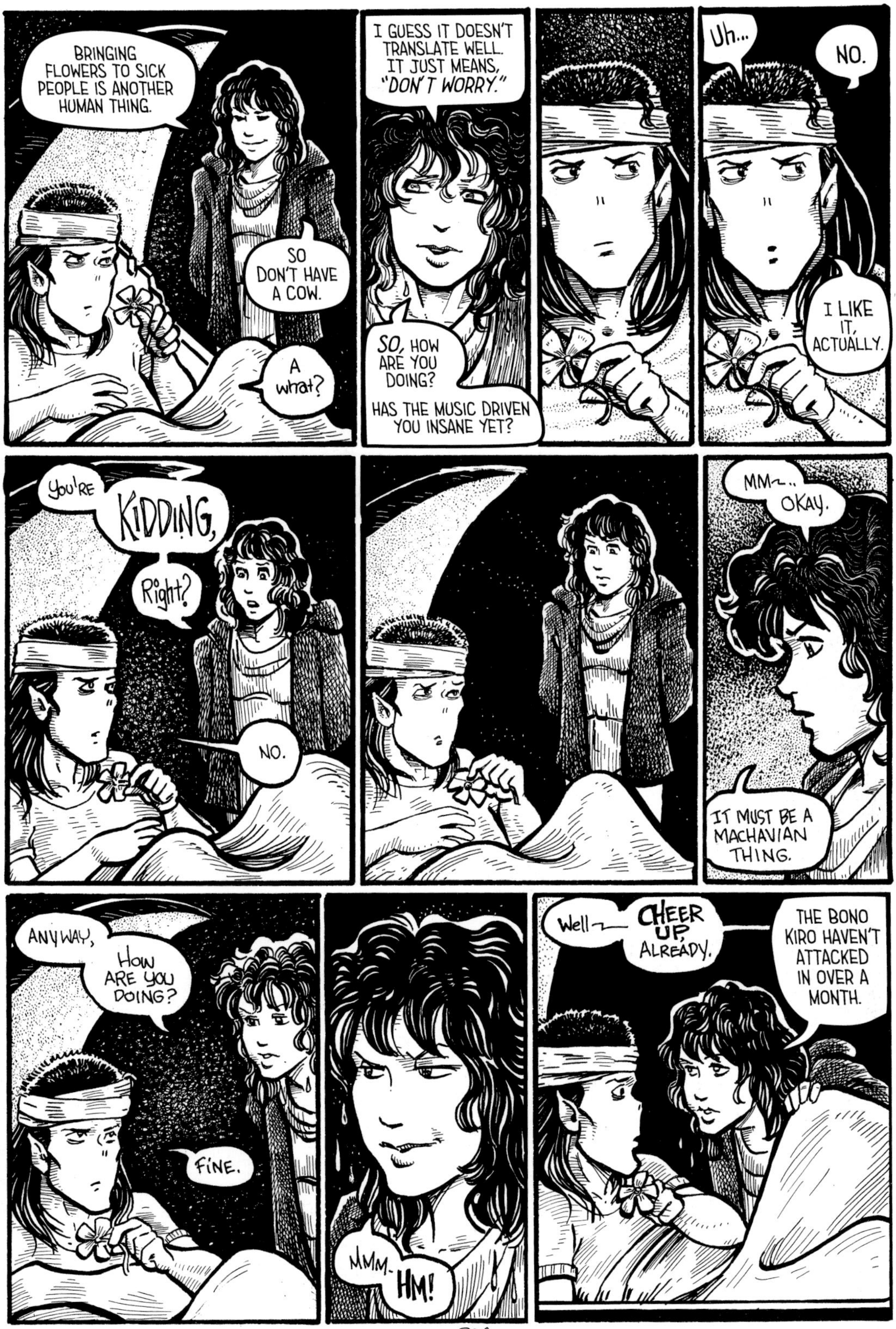
BRINGING FLOWERS TO SICK PEOPLE IS ANOTHER HUMAN THING.
SO DON'T HAVE A COW.
A what?
I GUESS IT DOESN'T TRANSLATE WELL. IT JUST MEANS, "DON'T WORRY."
SO, HOW ARE YOU DOING?
HAS THE MUSIC DRIVEN YOU INSANE YET?
Uh...
NO.
I LIKE IT, ACTUALLY.
You're KIDDING,
Right?
NO.
MM~.. OKAY.
IT MUST BE A MACHAVIAN THING.
ANYWAY,
How ARE you DOING?
FINE.
MMM-HM!
Well~ CHEER UP ALREADY.
THE BONO KIRO HAVEN'T ATTACKED IN OVER A MONTH.

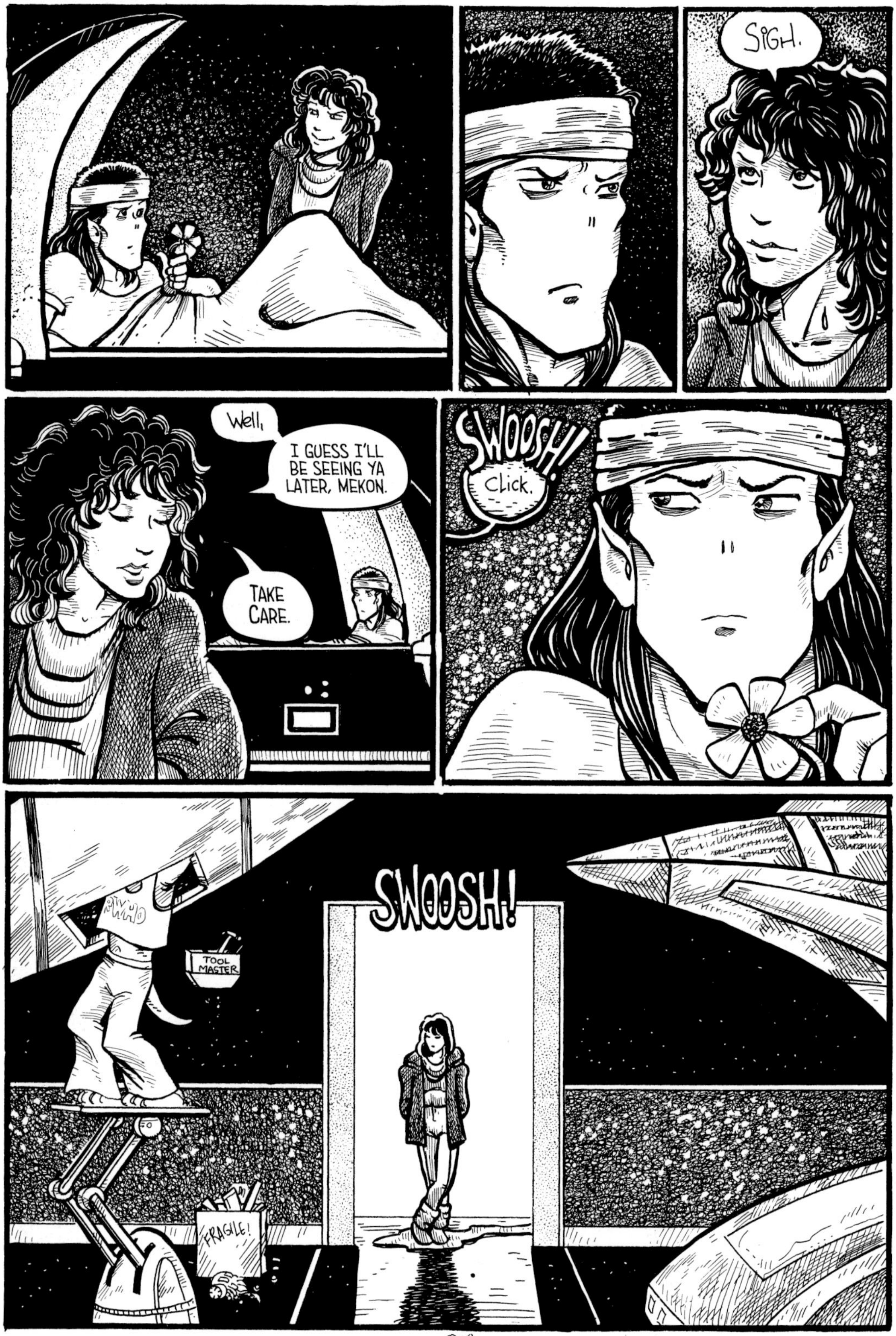
SIGH.
Well,
I GUESS I'LL BE SEEING YA LATER, MEKON.
TAKE CARE.
SWOOSH!
Click.
TOOL MASTER
SWOOSH!
FRAGILE!

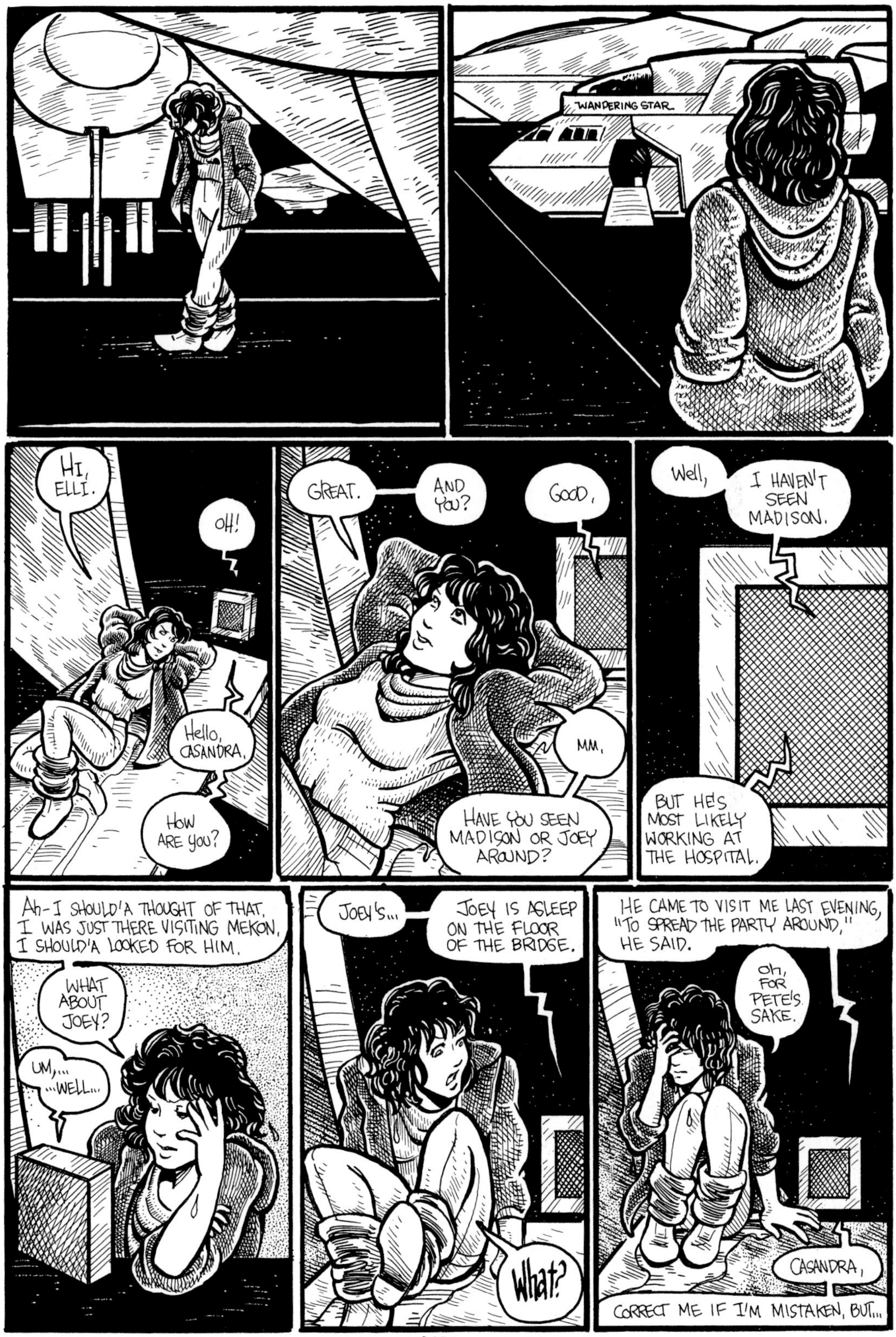
"WANDERING STAR"
HI, ELLI.
OH!
Hello, CASANDRA.
HOW ARE YOU?
GREAT.
AND YOU?
GOOD,
MM,
HAVE YOU SEEN MADISON OR JOEY AROUND?
Well,
I HAVEN'T SEEN MADISON.
BUT HE'S MOST LIKELY WORKING AT THE HOSPITAL.
Ah- I SHOULD'A THOUGHT OF THAT. I WAS JUST THERE VISITING MEKON. I SHOULD'A LOOKED FOR HIM.
WHAT ABOUT JOEY?
UM,... ...WELL...
JOEY'S...
JOEY IS ASLEEP ON THE FLOOR OF THE BRIDGE.
What?
HE CAME TO VISIT ME LAST EVENING, "TO SPREAD THE PARTY AROUND," HE SAID.
Oh, FOR PETE'S SAKE.
CASANDRA,
CORRECT ME IF I'M MISTAKEN, BUT...

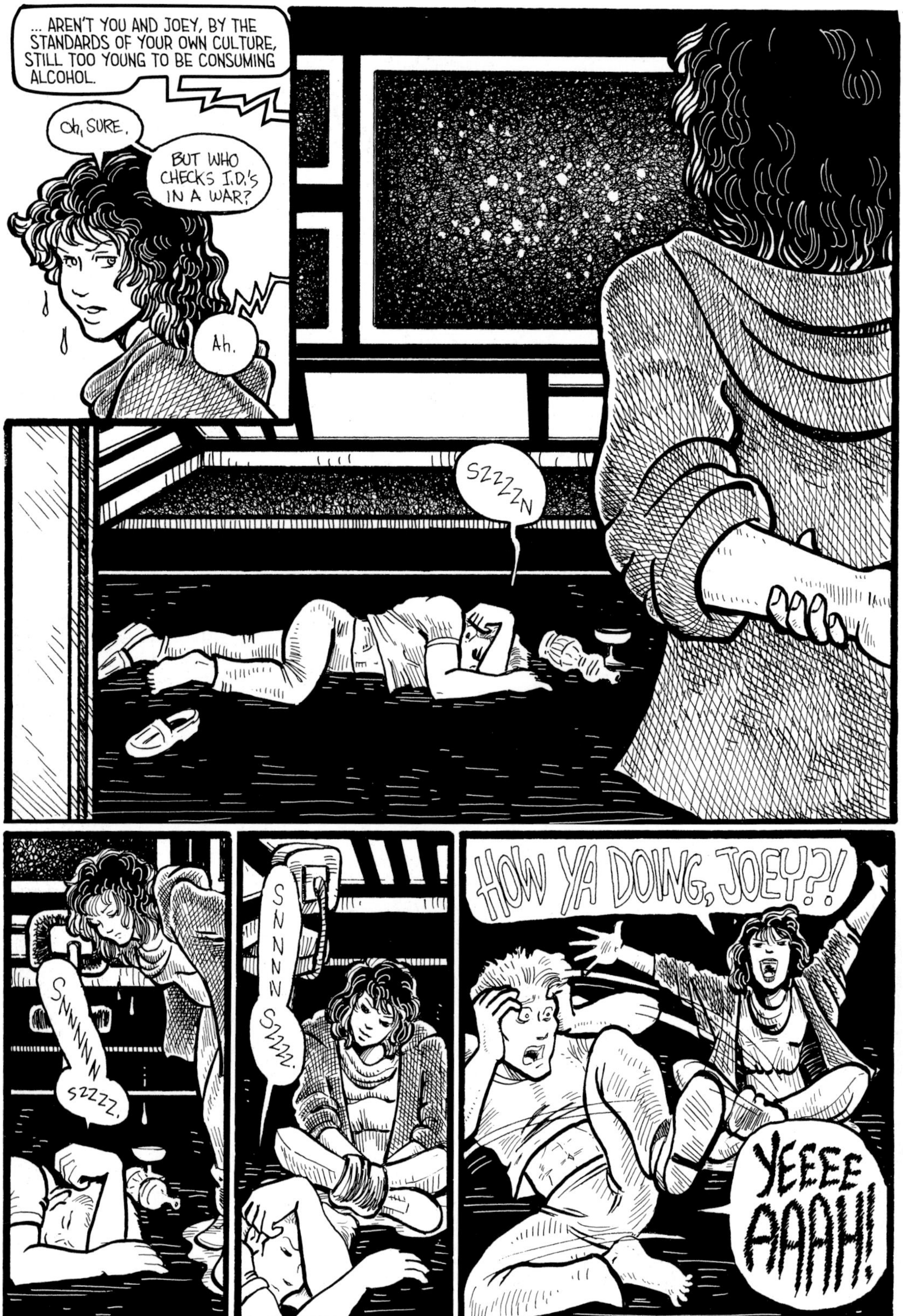
... AREN'T YOU AND JOEY, BY THE STANDARDS OF YOUR OWN CULTURE, STILL TOO YOUNG TO BE CONSUMING ALCOHOL.
Oh, SURE.
BUT WHO CHECKS I.D.'s IN A WAR?
Ah.
SZZZZN
SNNNNNN SZZZZ.
SNNNN SZZZZ.
HOW YA DOING, JOEY?!
YEEEE AAAH!

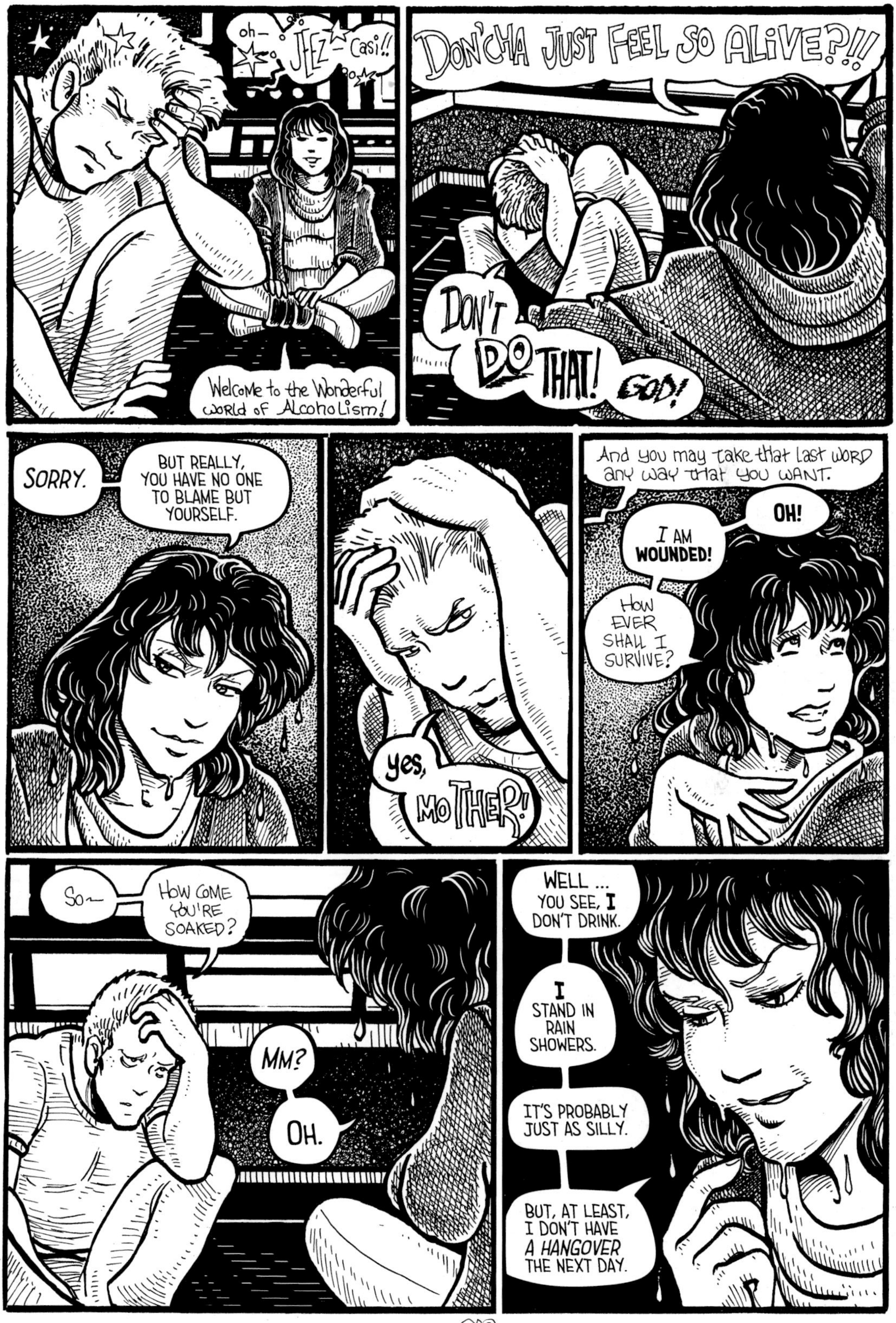
oh— JEEZ— Casi!!
Welcome to the Wonderful world of Alcoholism!
DON'CHA JUST FEEL SO ALIVE?!!
DON'T DO THAT! GOD!
SORRY.
BUT REALLY, YOU HAVE NO ONE TO BLAME BUT YOURSELF.
yes, MOTHER!
And you may take that last word any way that you WANT.
OH!
I AM WOUNDED!
HOW EVER SHALL I SURVIVE?
So—
HOW COME YOU'RE SOAKED?
MM?
OH.
WELL ... YOU SEE, I DON'T DRINK.
I STAND IN RAIN SHOWERS.
IT'S PROBABLY JUST AS SILLY.
BUT, AT LEAST, I DON'T HAVE A HANGOVER THE NEXT DAY.

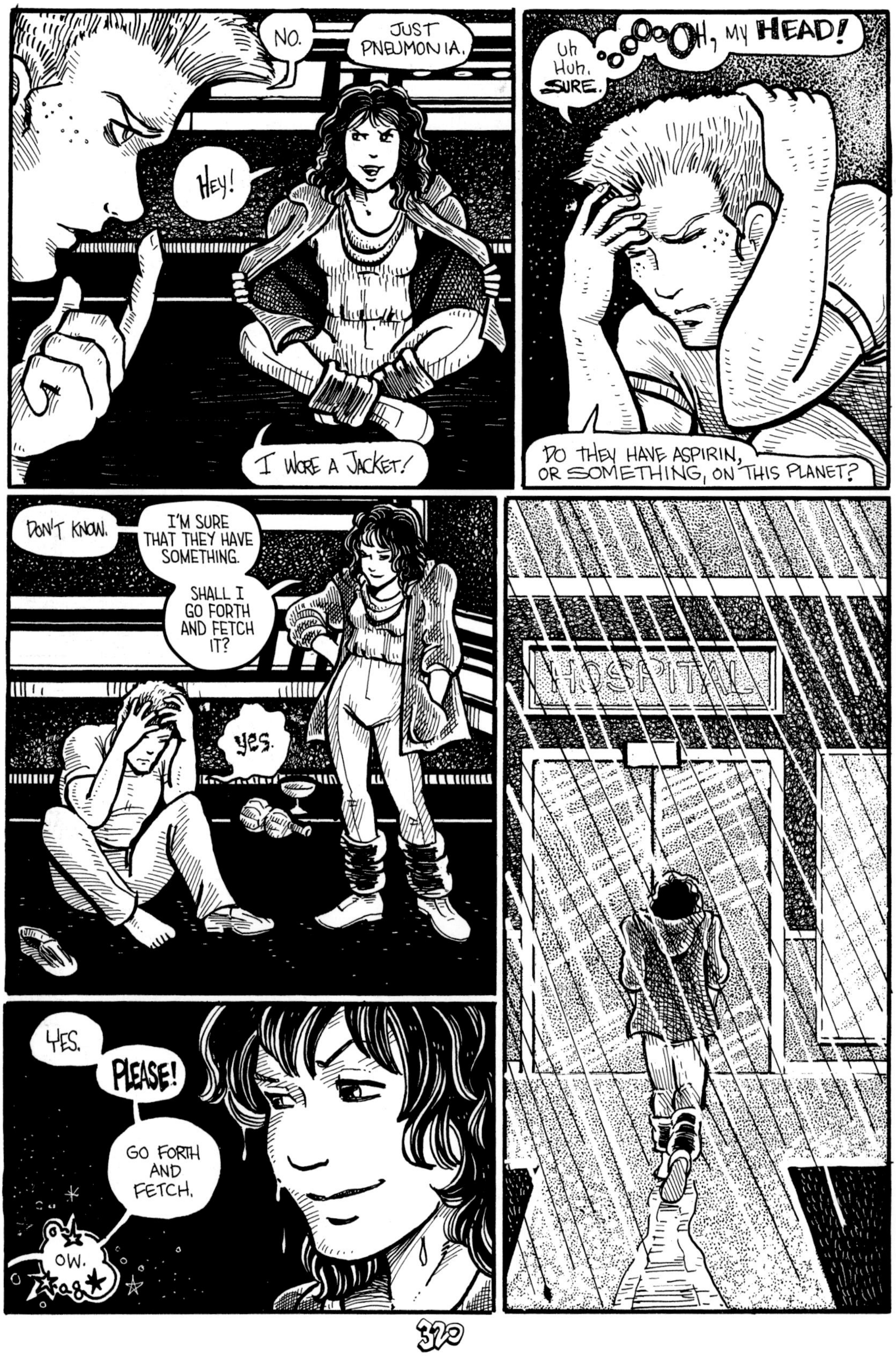
NO.
JUST PNEUMONIA.
HEY!
I WORE A JACKET!
Uh Huh. SURE.
OOOOOH, MY HEAD!
DO THEY HAVE ASPIRIN, OR SOMETHING, ON THIS PLANET?
DON'T KNOW.
I'M SURE THAT THEY HAVE SOMETHING.
SHALL I GO FORTH AND FETCH IT?
YES.
HOSPITAL
YES.
PLEASE!
GO FORTH AND FETCH.
OW.

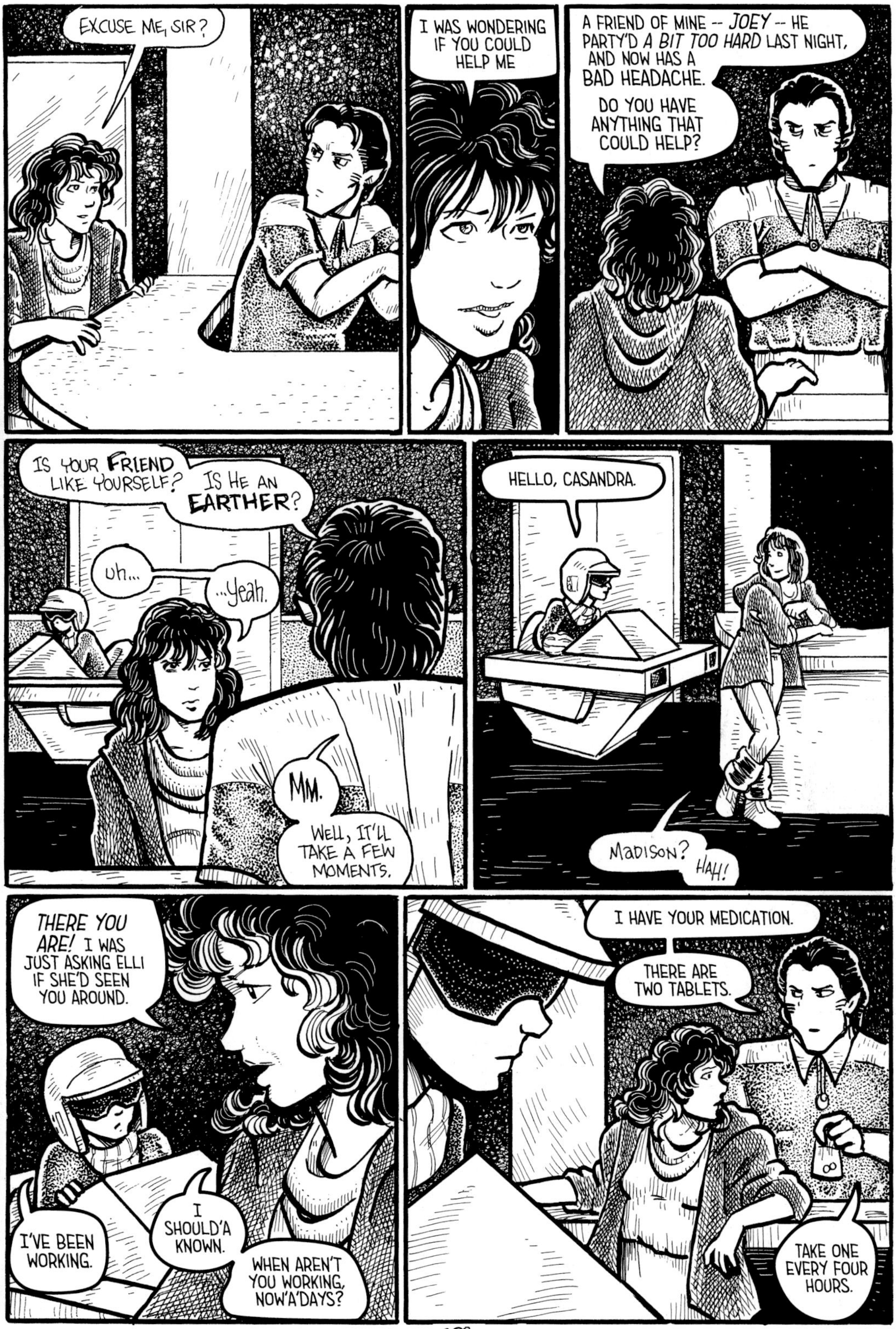
EXCUSE ME, SIR?
I WAS WONDERING IF YOU COULD HELP ME
A FRIEND OF MINE -- JOEY -- HE PARTY'D A BIT TOO HARD LAST NIGHT, AND NOW HAS A BAD HEADACHE.
DO YOU HAVE ANYTHING THAT COULD HELP?
IS YOUR FRIEND LIKE YOURSELF?
IS HE AN EARTHER?
uh...
...Yeah.
MM.
WELL, IT'LL TAKE A FEW MOMENTS.
HELLO, CASANDRA.
MADISON? HAH!
THERE YOU ARE! I WAS JUST ASKING ELLI IF SHE'D SEEN YOU AROUND.
I'VE BEEN WORKING.
I SHOULD'A KNOWN.
WHEN AREN'T YOU WORKING, NOW'A'DAYS?
I HAVE YOUR MEDICATION.
THERE ARE TWO TABLETS.
TAKE ONE EVERY FOUR HOURS.

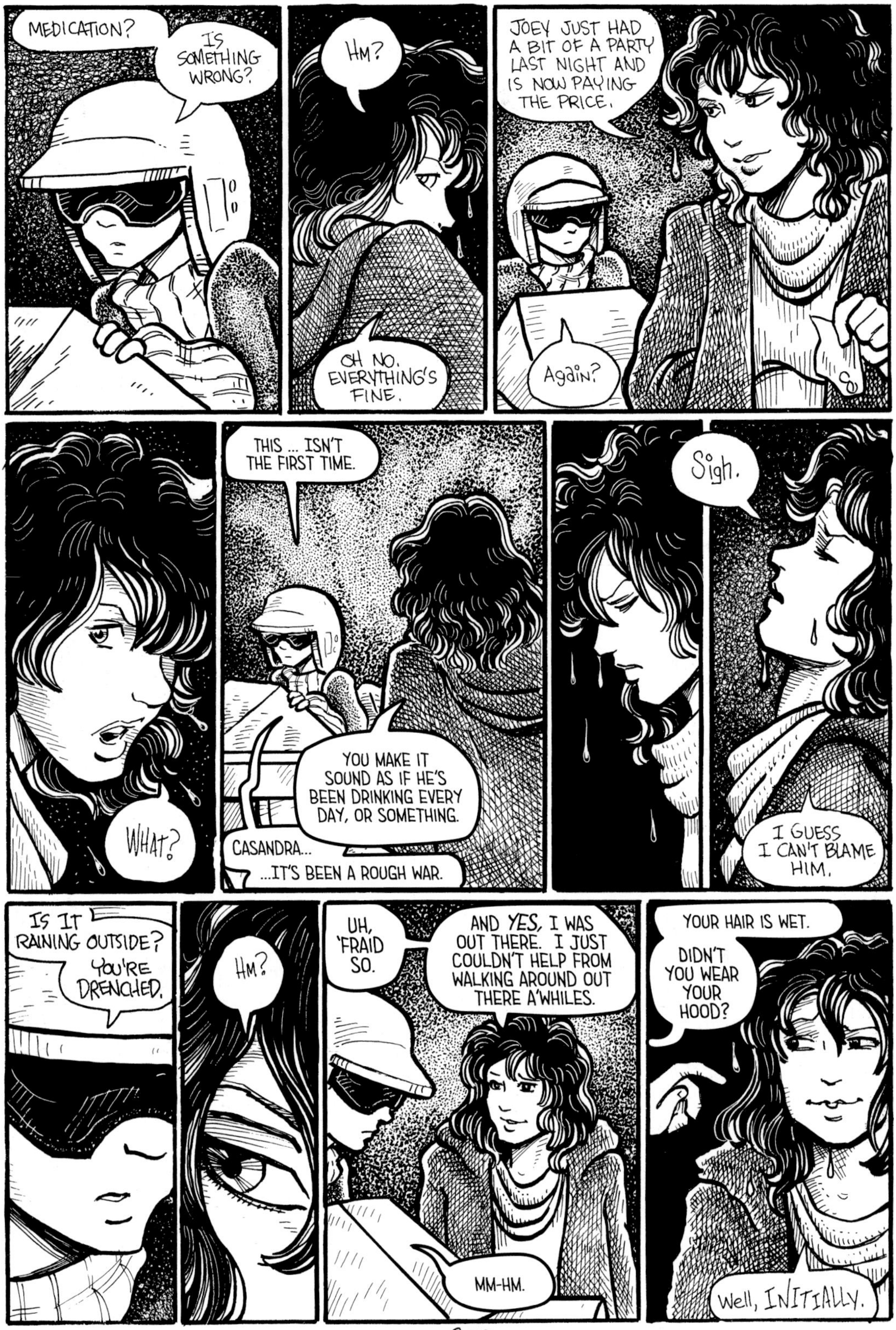
MEDICATION?
IS SOMETHING WRONG?
HM?
OH NO. EVERYTHING'S FINE.
JOEY JUST HAD A BIT OF A PARTY LAST NIGHT AND IS NOW PAYING THE PRICE.
Again?
THIS ... ISN'T THE FIRST TIME.
WHAT?
YOU MAKE IT SOUND AS IF HE'S BEEN DRINKING EVERY DAY, OR SOMETHING.
CASANDRA...
...IT'S BEEN A ROUGH WAR.
Sigh.
I GUESS I CAN'T BLAME HIM.
IS IT RAINING OUTSIDE?
YOU'RE DRENCHED.
HM?
UH, 'FRAID SO.
AND YES, I WAS OUT THERE. I JUST COULDN'T HELP FROM WALKING AROUND OUT THERE A'WHILES.
MM-HM.
YOUR HAIR IS WET.
DIDN'T YOU WEAR YOUR HOOD?
Well, INITIALLY.

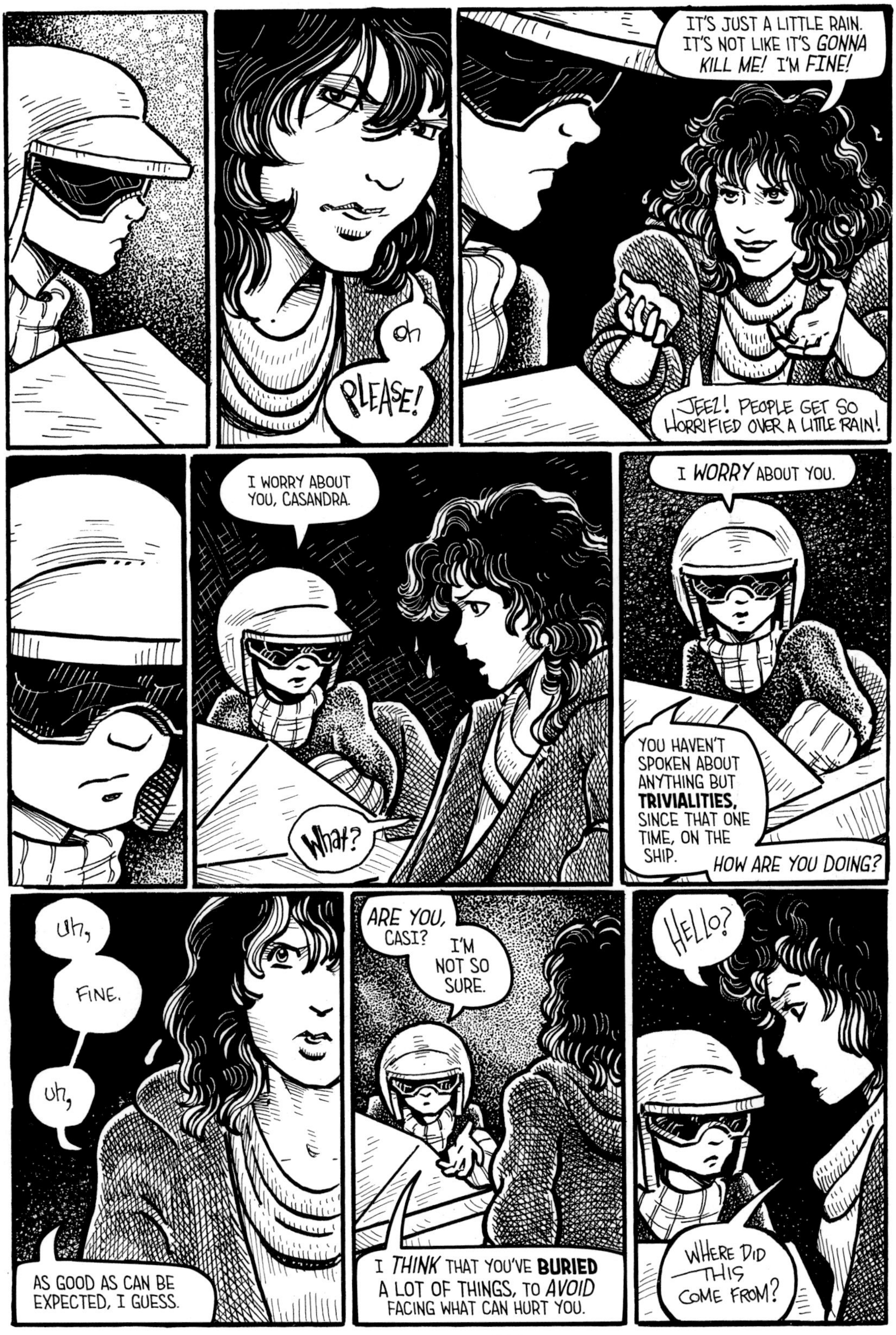
IT'S JUST A LITTLE RAIN. IT'S NOT LIKE IT'S GONNA KILL ME! I'M FINE!
oh
PLEASE!
JEEZ! PEOPLE GET SO HORRIFIED OVER A LITTLE RAIN!
I WORRY ABOUT YOU, CASANDRA.
What?
I WORRY ABOUT YOU.
YOU HAVEN'T SPOKEN ABOUT ANYTHING BUT TRIVIALITIES, SINCE THAT ONE TIME, ON THE SHIP.
HOW ARE YOU DOING?
uh,
FINE.
uh,
AS GOOD AS CAN BE EXPECTED, I GUESS.
ARE YOU, CASI?
I'M NOT SO SURE.
I THINK THAT YOU'VE BURIED A LOT OF THINGS, TO AVOID FACING WHAT CAN HURT YOU.
HELLO?
WHERE DID THIS COME FROM?

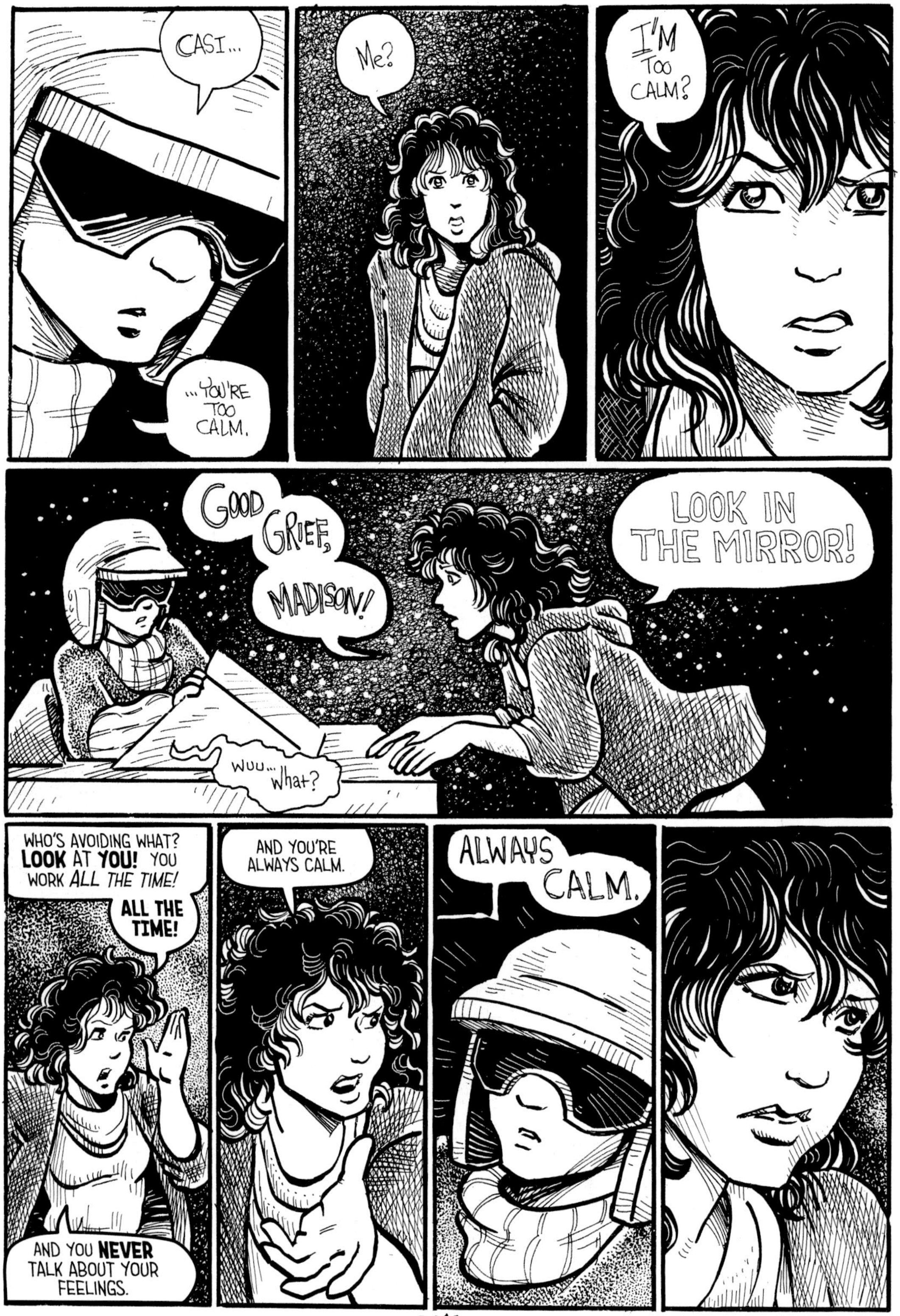
CASI...
...YOU'RE TOO CALM.
Me?
I'M TOO CALM?
GOOD GRIEF, MADISON!
LOOK IN THE MIRROR!
WUU... What?
WHO'S AVOIDING WHAT? **LOOK** AT **YOU!** YOU WORK *ALL THE TIME!*
ALL THE TIME!
AND YOU **NEVER** TALK ABOUT YOUR FEELINGS.
AND YOU'RE ALWAYS CALM.
ALWAYS CALM.

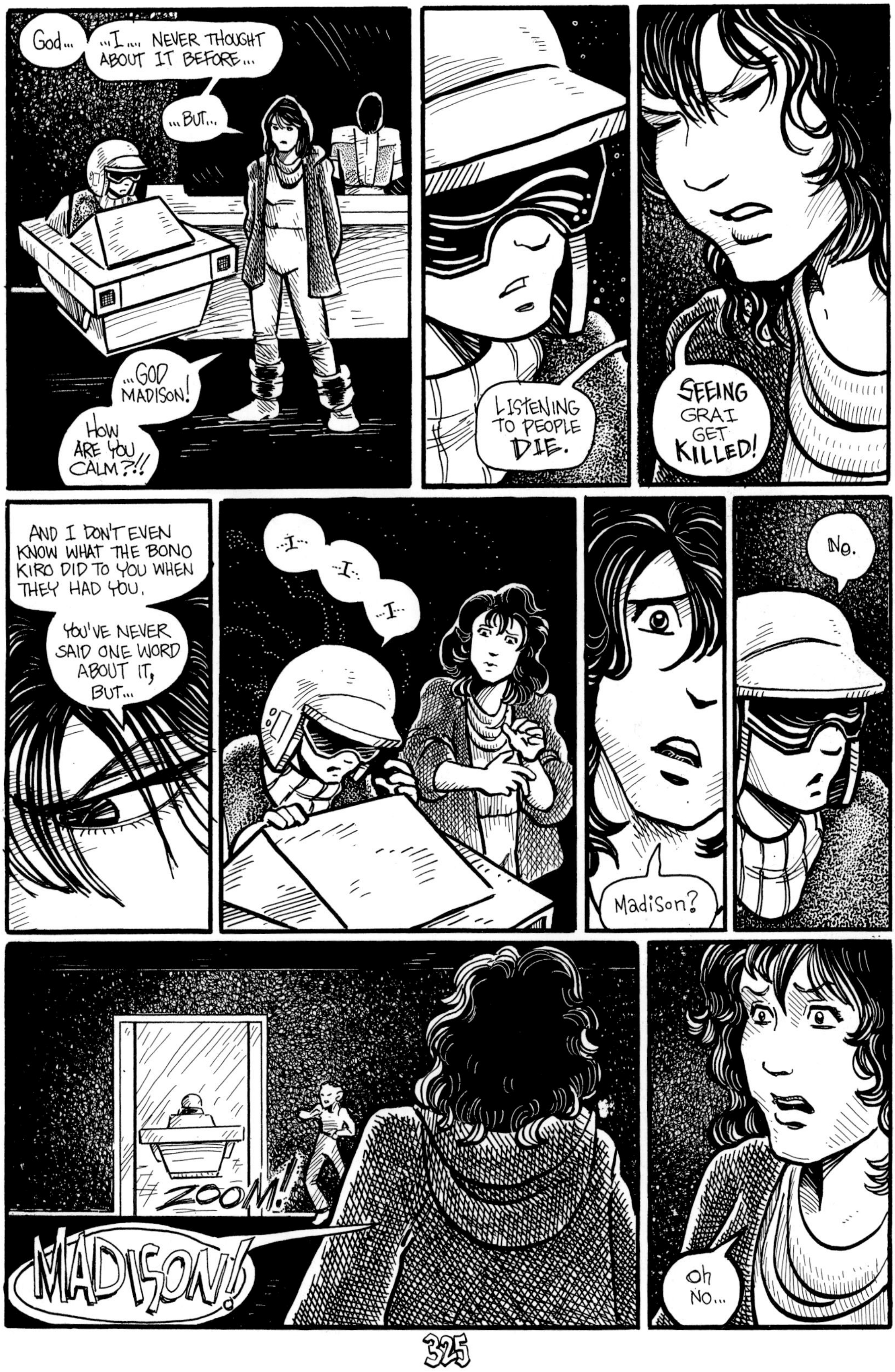
God...
...I.... NEVER THOUGHT ABOUT IT BEFORE...
...BUT...
...GOD MADISON!
HOW ARE YOU CALM?!!
LISTENING TO PEOPLE DIE.
SEEING GRAI GET KILLED!
AND I DON'T EVEN KNOW WHAT THE BONO KIRO DID TO YOU WHEN THEY HAD YOU.
YOU'VE NEVER SAID ONE WORD ABOUT IT, BUT...
...I...
...I...
...I...
Madison?
No.
ZOOM!
MADISON!
Oh No...

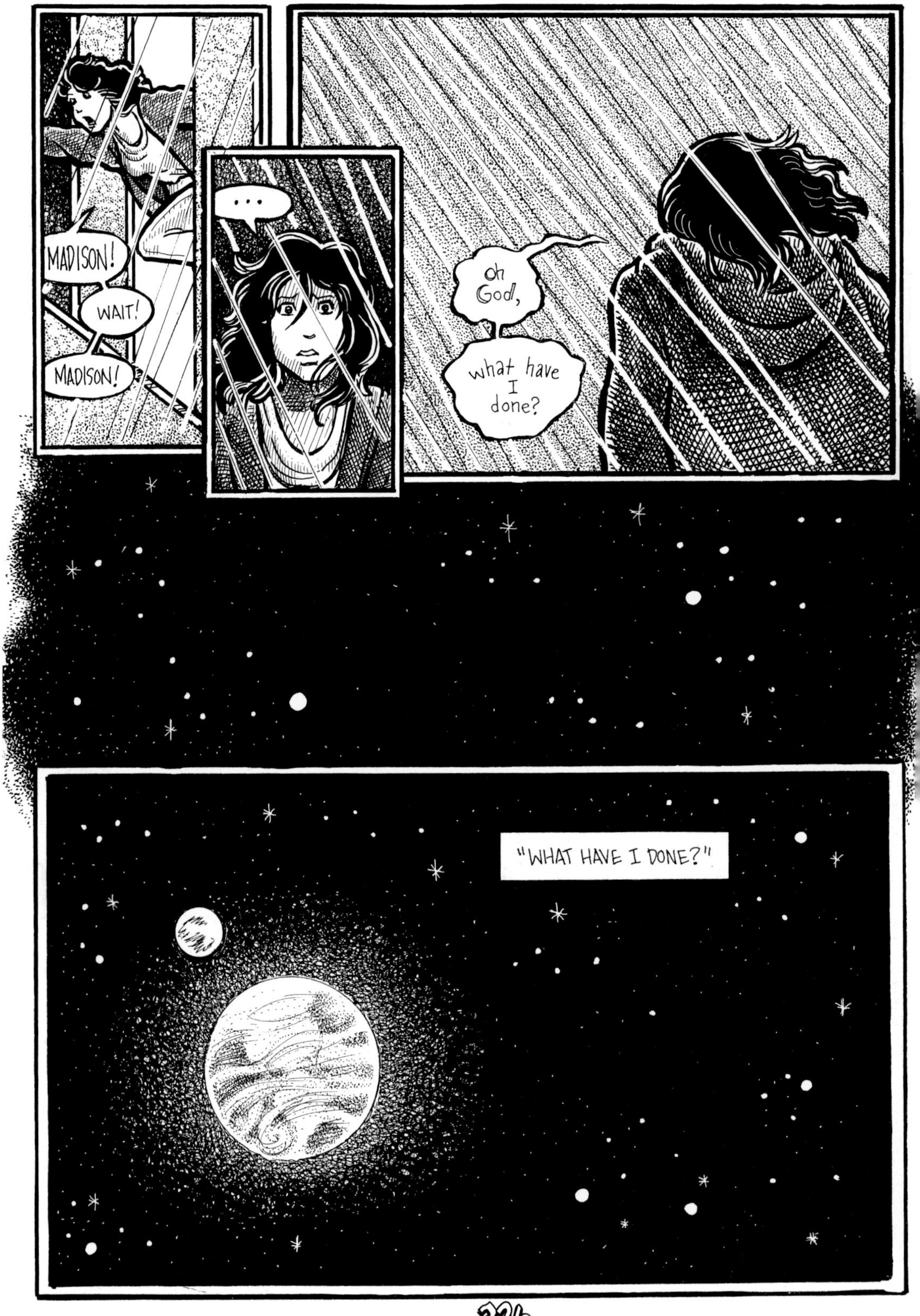
MADISON!
WAIT!
MADISON!
...
oh God,
what have I done?
"WHAT HAVE I DONE?"

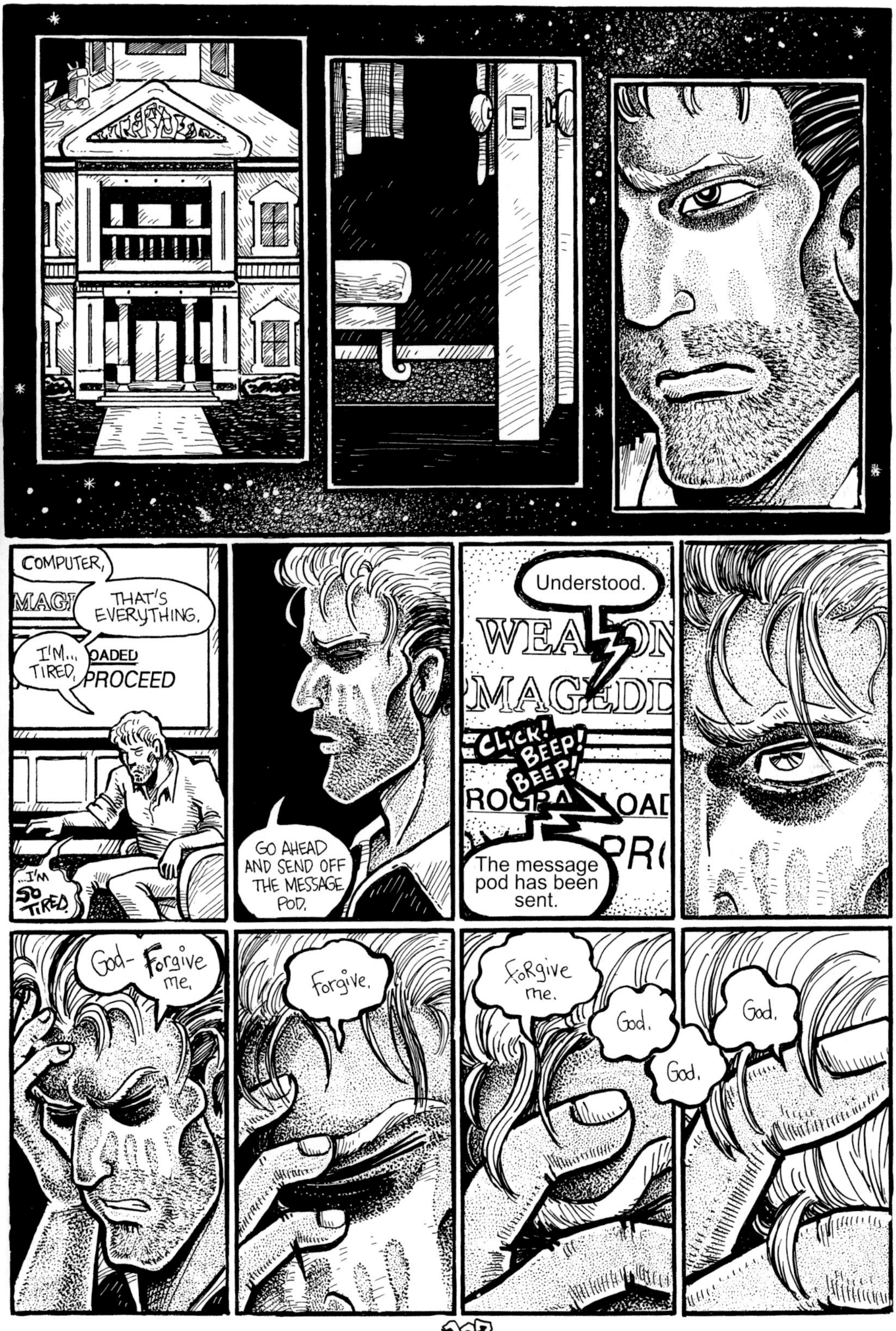
COMPUTER,
THAT'S EVERYTHING.
I'M... TIRED.
...I'M SO TIRED.
GO AHEAD AND SEND OFF THE MESSAGE POD.
Understood.
CLICK! BEEP! BEEP!
The message pod has been sent.
God- Forgive me.
Forgive.
Forgive me.
God.
God.
God.

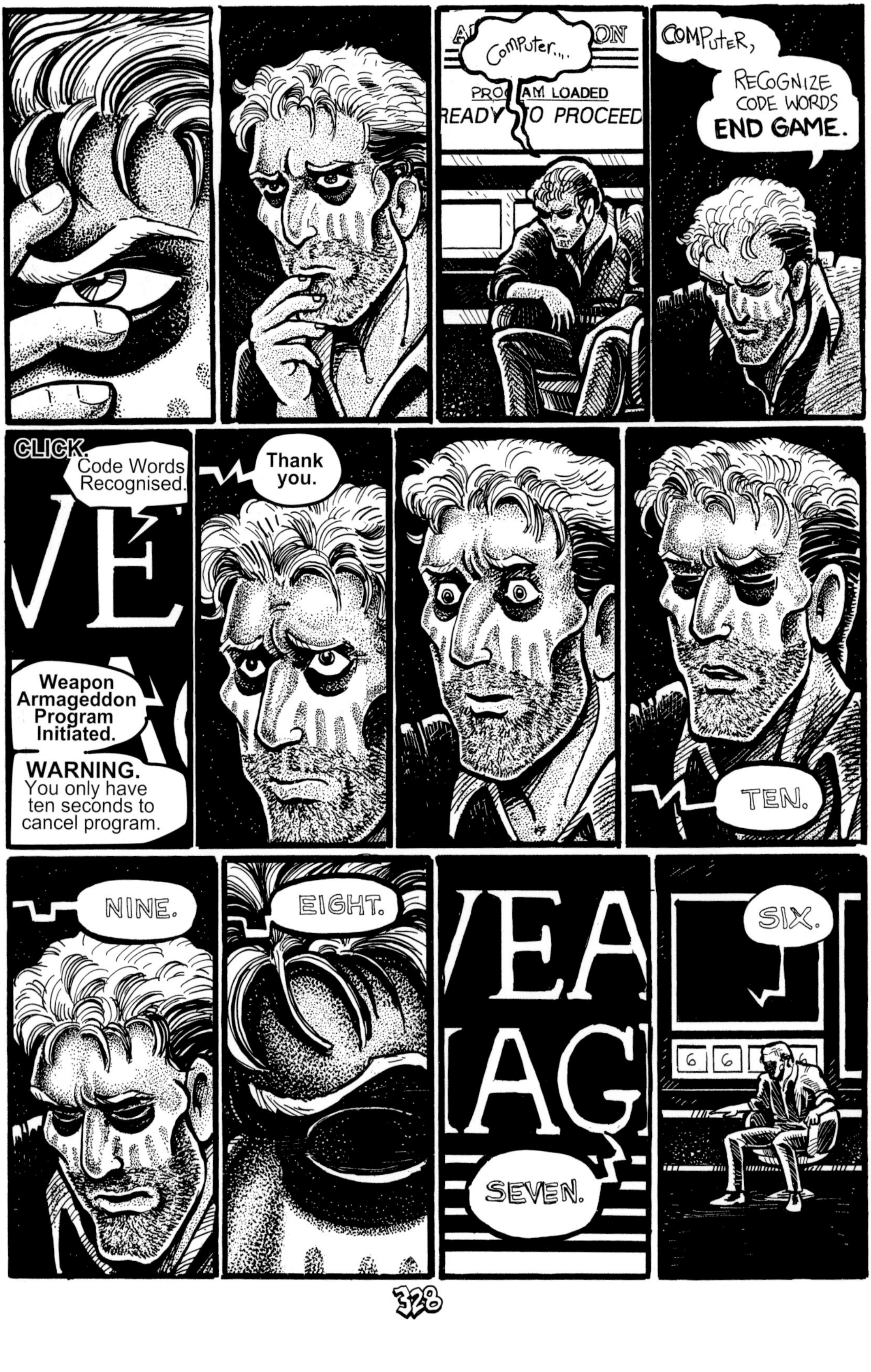
Computer....
COMPUTER,
RECOGNIZE CODE WORDS END GAME.
CLICK.
Code Words Recognised.
Weapon Armageddon Program Initiated.
WARNING. You only have ten seconds to cancel program.
Thank you.
TEN.
NINE.
EIGHT.
SEVEN.
SIX.

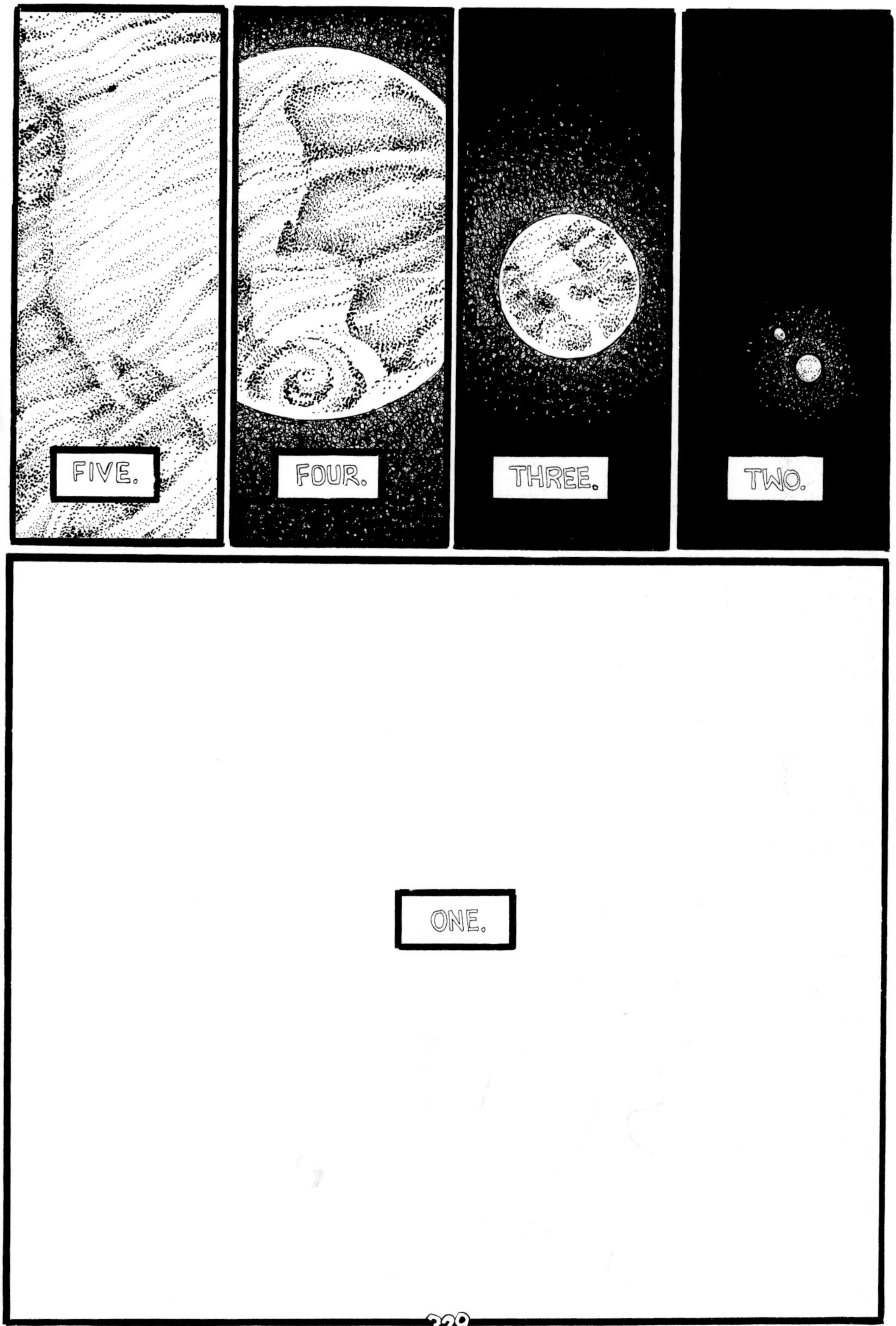
FIVE.
FOUR.
THREE.
TWO.
ONE.

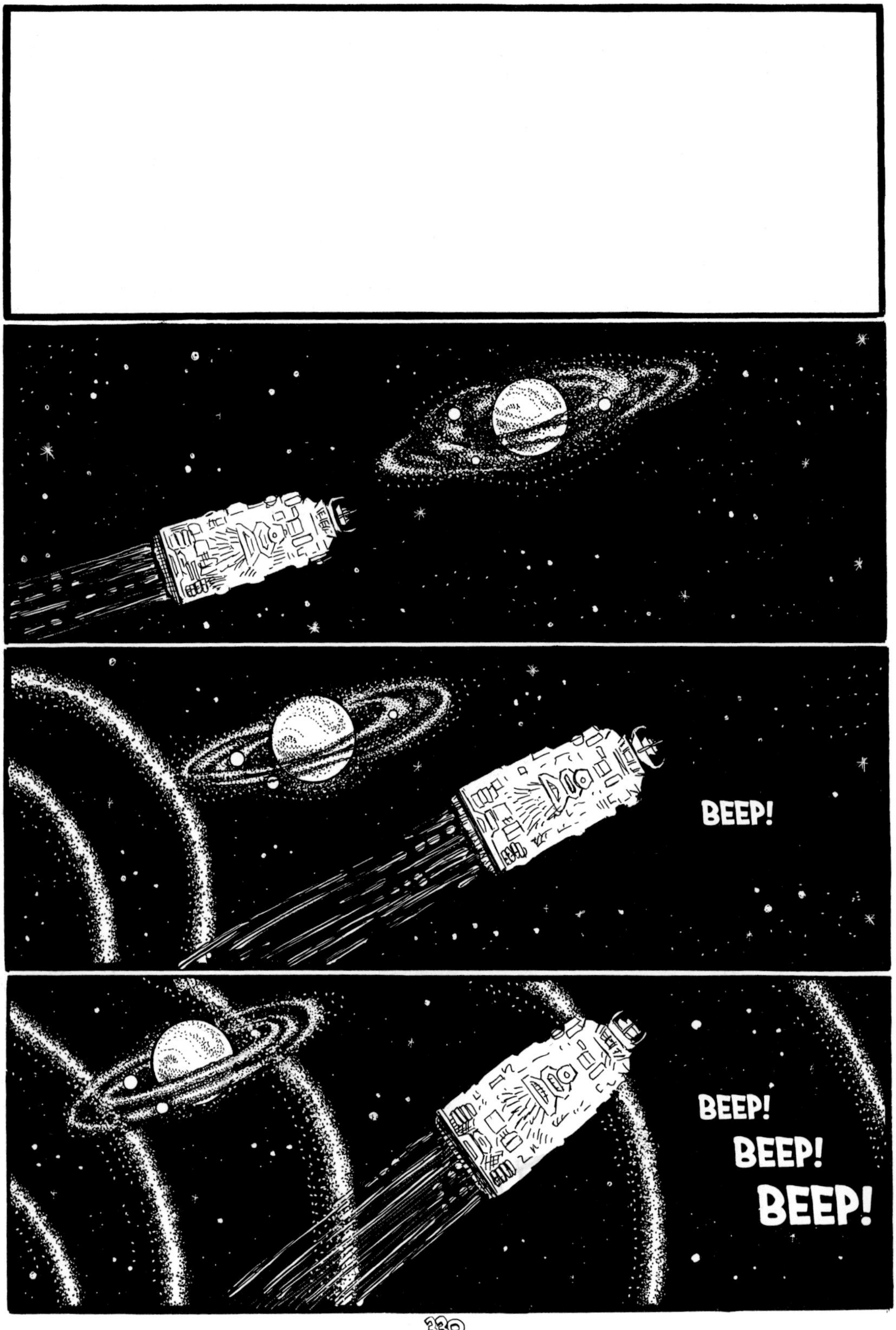
BEEP!
BEEP!
BEEP!
BEEP!

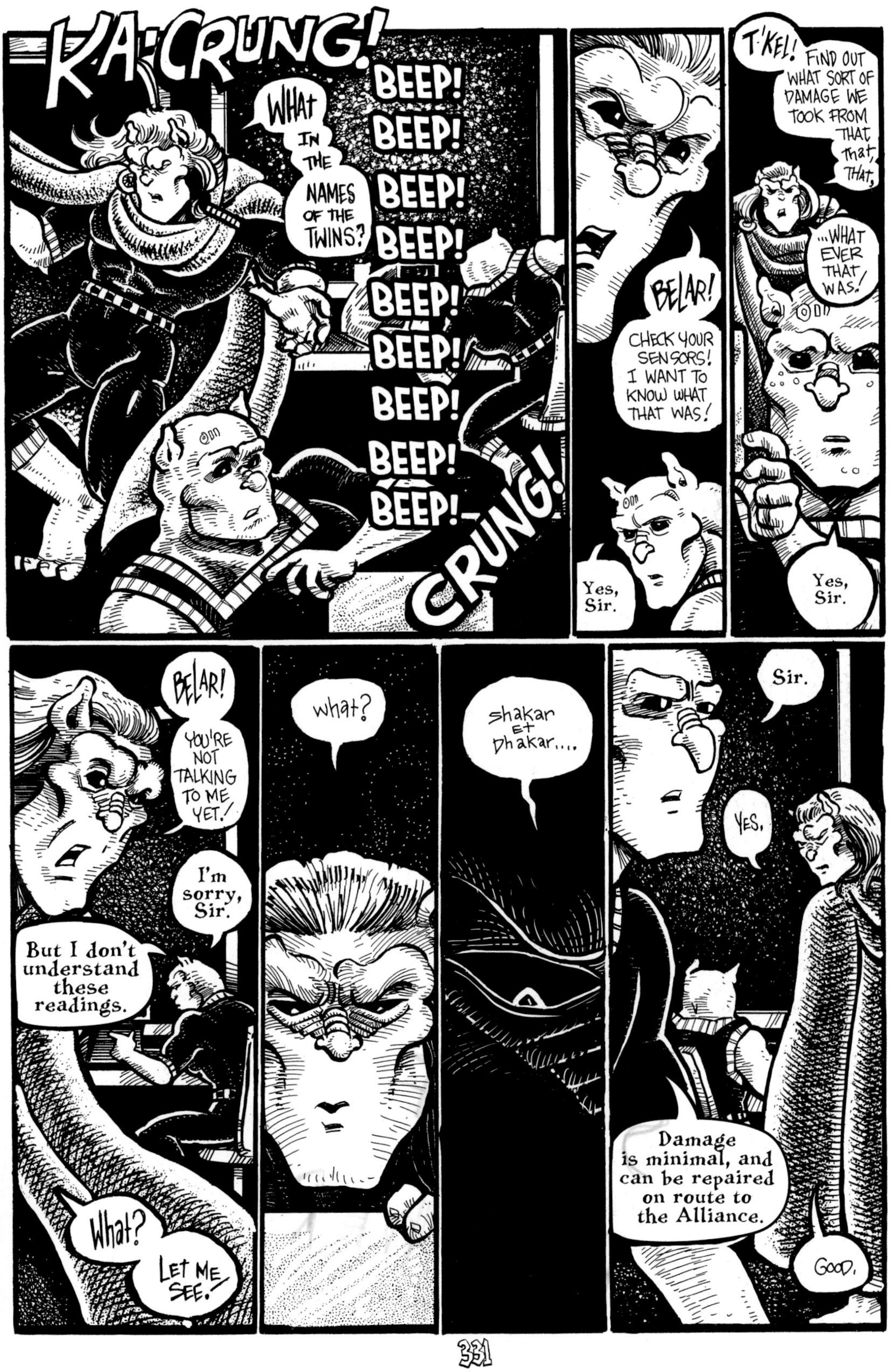
KA-CRUNG!
WHAT IN THE NAMES OF THE TWINS?
BEEP! BEEP! BEEP! BEEP! BEEP! BEEP! BEEP! BEEP! BEEP!
CRUNG!
BELAR! CHECK YOUR SENSORS! I WANT TO KNOW WHAT THAT WAS!
Yes, Sir.
T'KEL! FIND OUT WHAT SORT OF DAMAGE WE TOOK FROM THAT that, THAT,
...WHAT EVER THAT WAS!
Yes, Sir.
BELAR! YOU'RE NOT TALKING TO ME YET!
I'm sorry, Sir.
But I don't understand these readings.
What? LET ME SEE.
what?
shakar et Dhakar....
Sir.
YES.
Damage is minimal, and can be repaired on route to the Alliance.
GOOD.

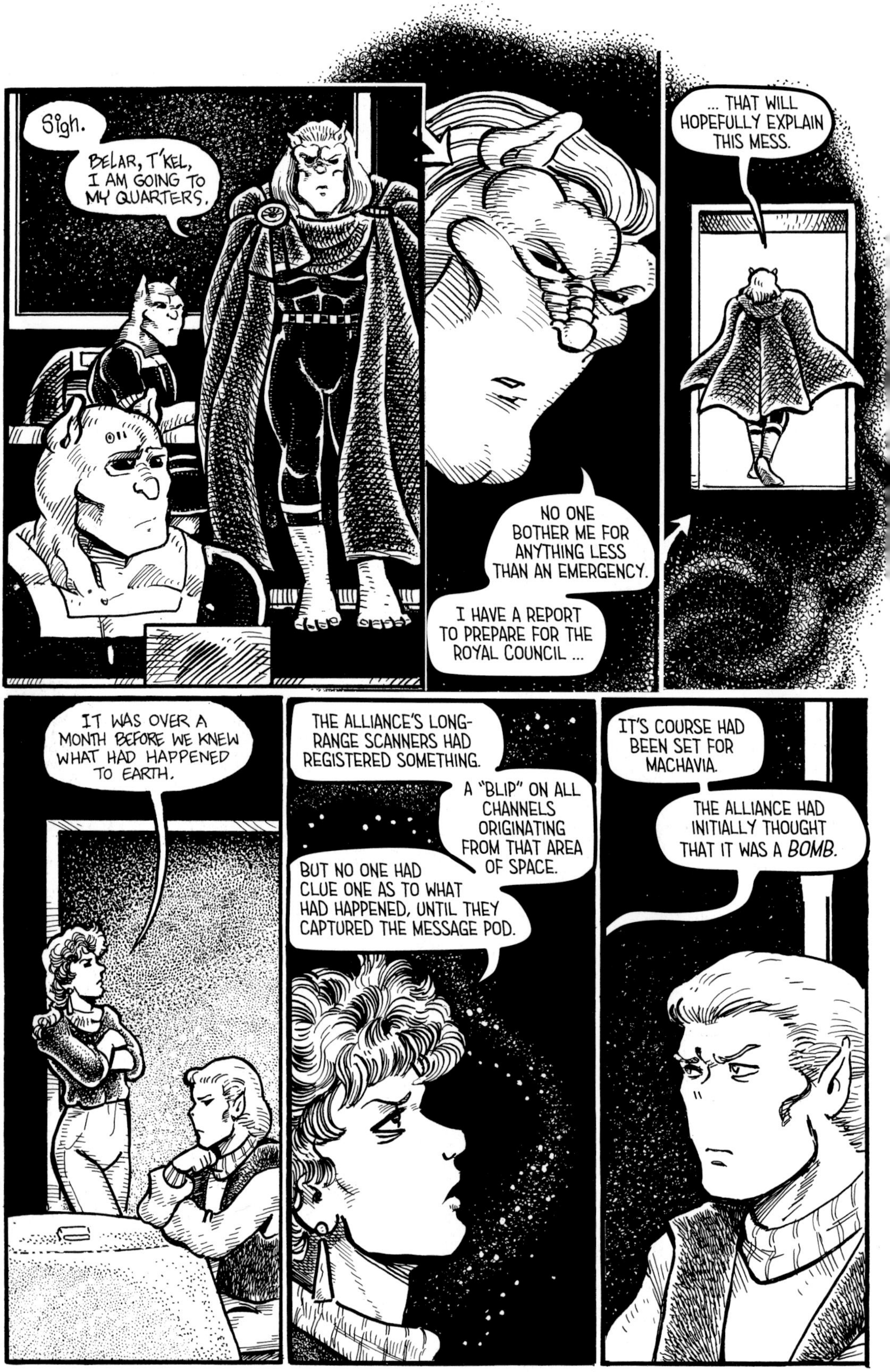
Sigh.
BELAR, T'KEL, I AM GOING TO MY QUARTERS.
NO ONE BOTHER ME FOR ANYTHING LESS THAN AN EMERGENCY.
I HAVE A REPORT TO PREPARE FOR THE ROYAL COUNCIL ...
... THAT WILL HOPEFULLY EXPLAIN THIS MESS.
IT WAS OVER A MONTH BEFORE WE KNEW WHAT HAD HAPPENED TO EARTH.
THE ALLIANCE'S LONG-RANGE SCANNERS HAD REGISTERED SOMETHING.
A "BLIP" ON ALL CHANNELS ORIGINATING FROM THAT AREA OF SPACE.
BUT NO ONE HAD CLUE ONE AS TO WHAT HAD HAPPENED, UNTIL THEY CAPTURED THE MESSAGE POD.
IT'S COURSE HAD BEEN SET FOR MACHAVIA.
THE ALLIANCE HAD INITIALLY THOUGHT THAT IT WAS A *BOMB*.

THERE HAD BEEN A LOT OF THEORIES IN 2104, ABOUT WHAT
EXACTLY WEAPON ARMAGEDDON WOULD DO, IF IT WAS EVER USED.

IT HAD AN EXPLOSIVE POWER FAR IN EXCESS OF ANY BOMB PREVIOUSLY CREATED
BY MAN. AND IT HAD BEEN BURIED ONE-FOURTH OF THE WAY DOWN, INTO OUR PLANET.

THEY SAID THAT IT WOULD
PROBABLY FRACTURE THE EARTH.

OR MAYBE, KNOCK IT SLIGHTLY OUT OF IT'S ORBIT AROUND THE
SUN, SHIFTING THE EARTH'S CRUST, AND SETTING OFF VOLCANOES AND TSUNAMIS.

OR, PERHAPS,

... IT WOULD EVEN MOMENTARILY HALT THE EARTH'S ROTATION, DISRUPTING GRAVITY,
AND SENDING EVERYTHING ON THE PLANET, INCLUDING THE ATMOSPHERE, SHOOTING OUT INTO SPACE.

BUT IN THE END, I SUPPOSE, ONLY ONE THING REALLY MATTERED...

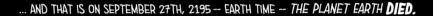

... AND THAT IS ON SEPTEMBER 27TH, 2195 -- EARTH TIME -- *THE PLANET EARTH* **DIED.**

PLANET TEKEL OF THE ALLIANCE.

THERE'S NOT A CLOUD IN THE SKY.

IT'S A *BEAUTIFUL* DAY, MADISON!

OPEN YOUR DOOR!

HE'S *SHUT OFF* HIS DOOR INTERCOM. *TISK!* MINE IS STILL ON. LET ME TRY, CASANDRA.

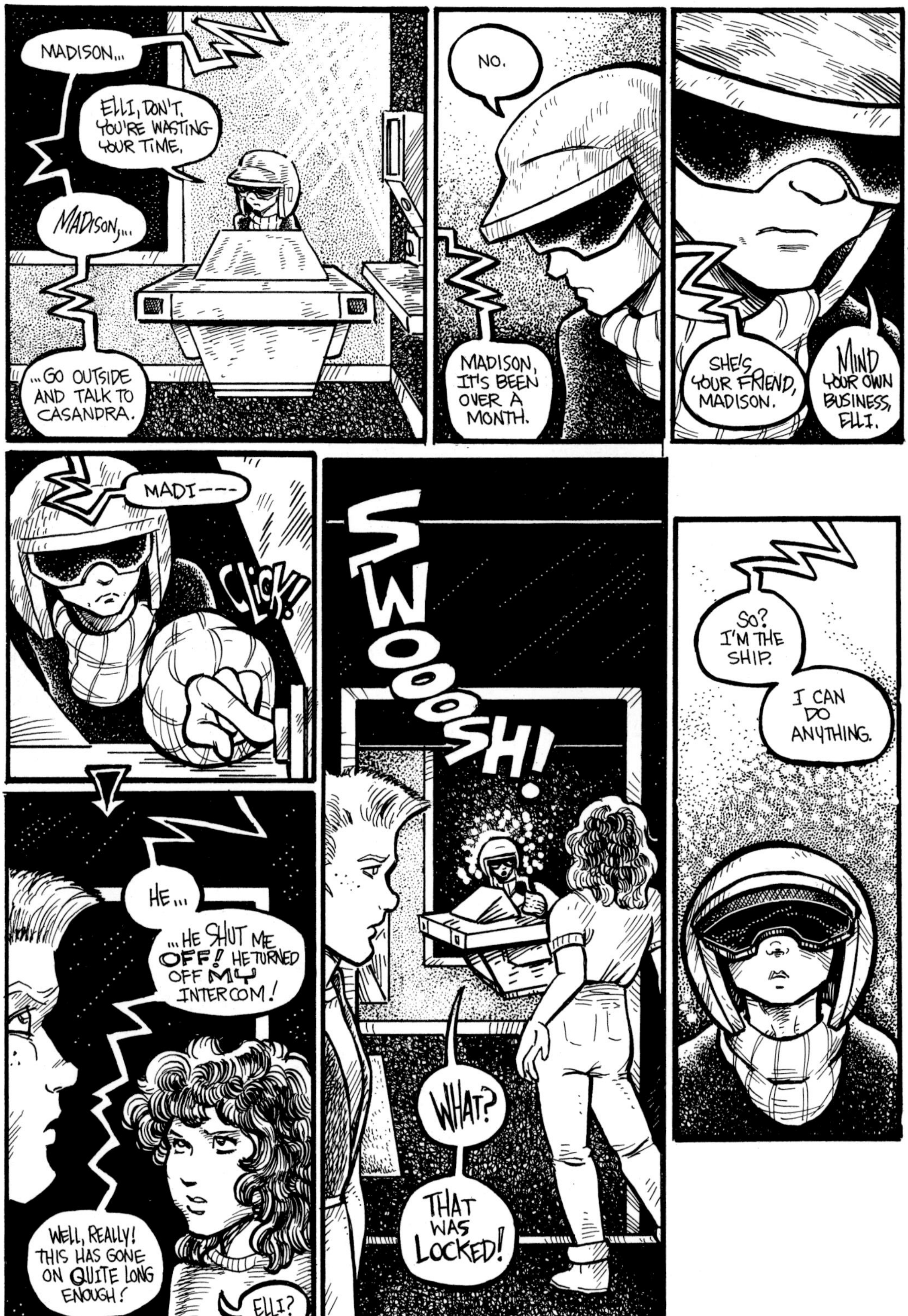
MADISON...
ELLI, DON'T. YOU'RE WASTING YOUR TIME.
MADISON,...
...GO OUTSIDE AND TALK TO CASANDRA.
NO.
MADISON, IT'S BEEN OVER A MONTH.
SHE'S YOUR FRIEND, MADISON.
MIND YOUR OWN BUSINESS, ELLI.
MADI---
CLICK!
HE...
...HE SHUT ME OFF! HE TURNED OFF MY INTERCOM!
WELL, REALLY! THIS HAS GONE ON QUITE LONG ENOUGH!
ELLI?
SWOOOSH!
WHAT?
THAT WAS LOCKED!
SO? I'M THE SHIP.
I CAN DO ANYTHING.

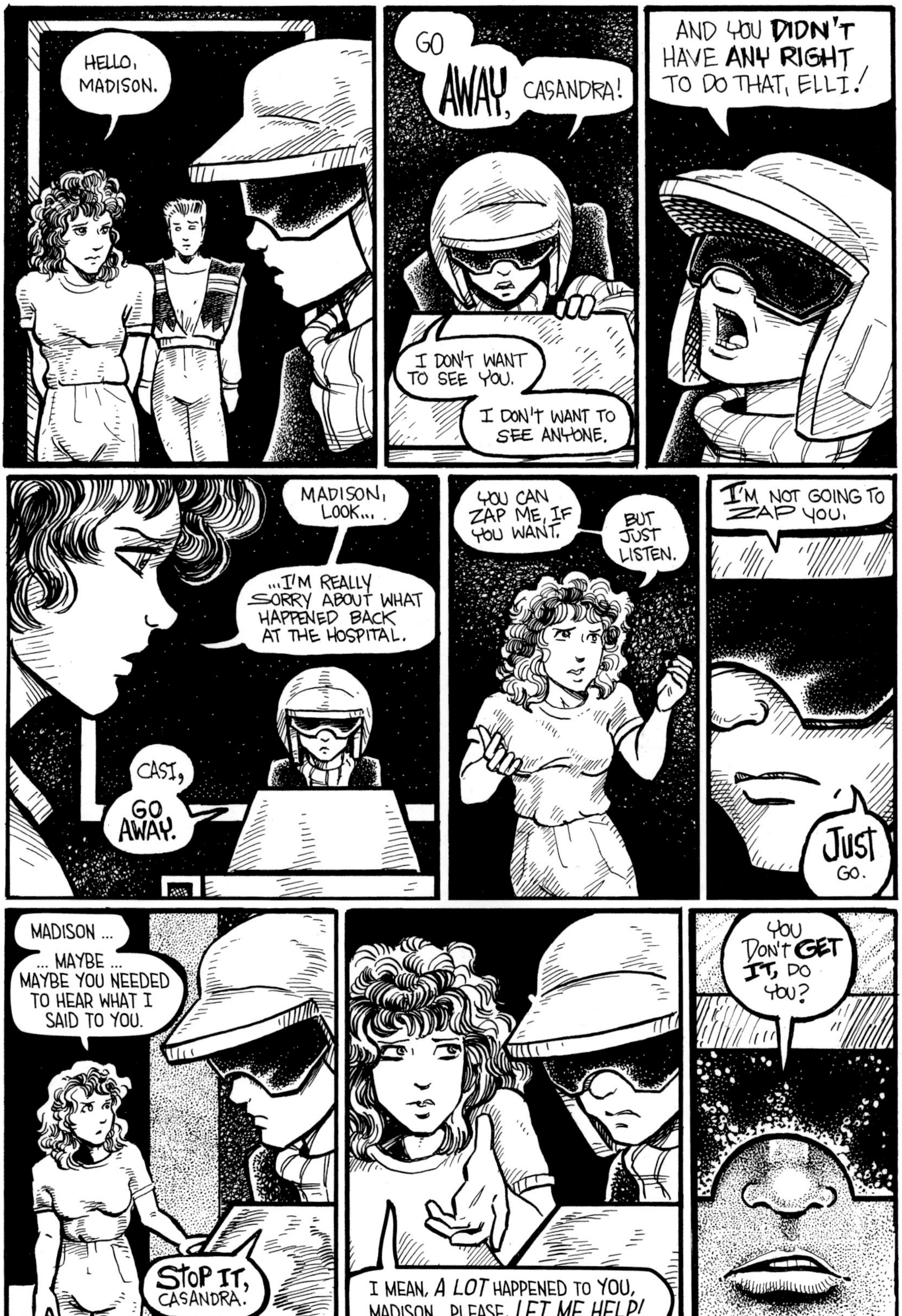
HELLO, MADISON.
GO AWAY, CASANDRA!
I DON'T WANT TO SEE YOU.
I DON'T WANT TO SEE ANYONE.
AND YOU DIDN'T HAVE ANY RIGHT TO DO THAT, ELLI!
MADISON, LOOK...
...I'M REALLY SORRY ABOUT WHAT HAPPENED BACK AT THE HOSPITAL.
CASI, GO AWAY.
YOU CAN ZAP ME, IF YOU WANT.
BUT JUST LISTEN.
I'M NOT GOING TO ZAP YOU.
JUST GO.
MADISON ...
... MAYBE ... MAYBE YOU NEEDED TO HEAR WHAT I SAID TO YOU.
STOP IT, CASANDRA.
I MEAN, A LOT HAPPENED TO YOU, MADISON. PLEASE, LET ME HELP!
YOU DON'T GET IT, DO YOU?

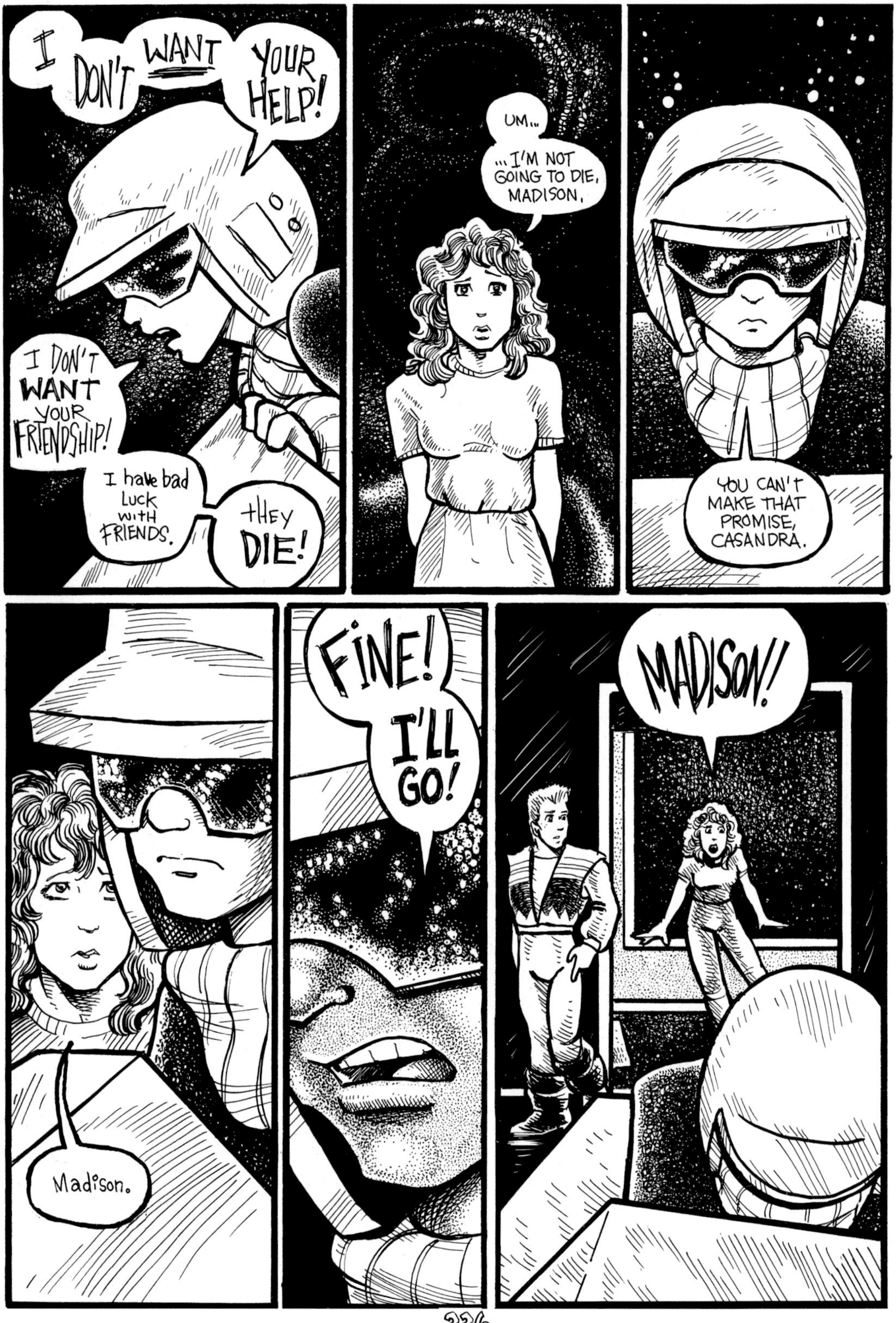
I DON'T WANT YOUR HELP!
I DON'T WANT YOUR FRIENDSHIP!
I have bad luck with FRIENDS.
tHEY DIE!
UM...
...I'M NOT GOING TO DIE, MADISON.
YOU CAN'T MAKE THAT PROMISE, CASANDRA.
Madison.
FINE!
I'LL GO!
MADISON!!

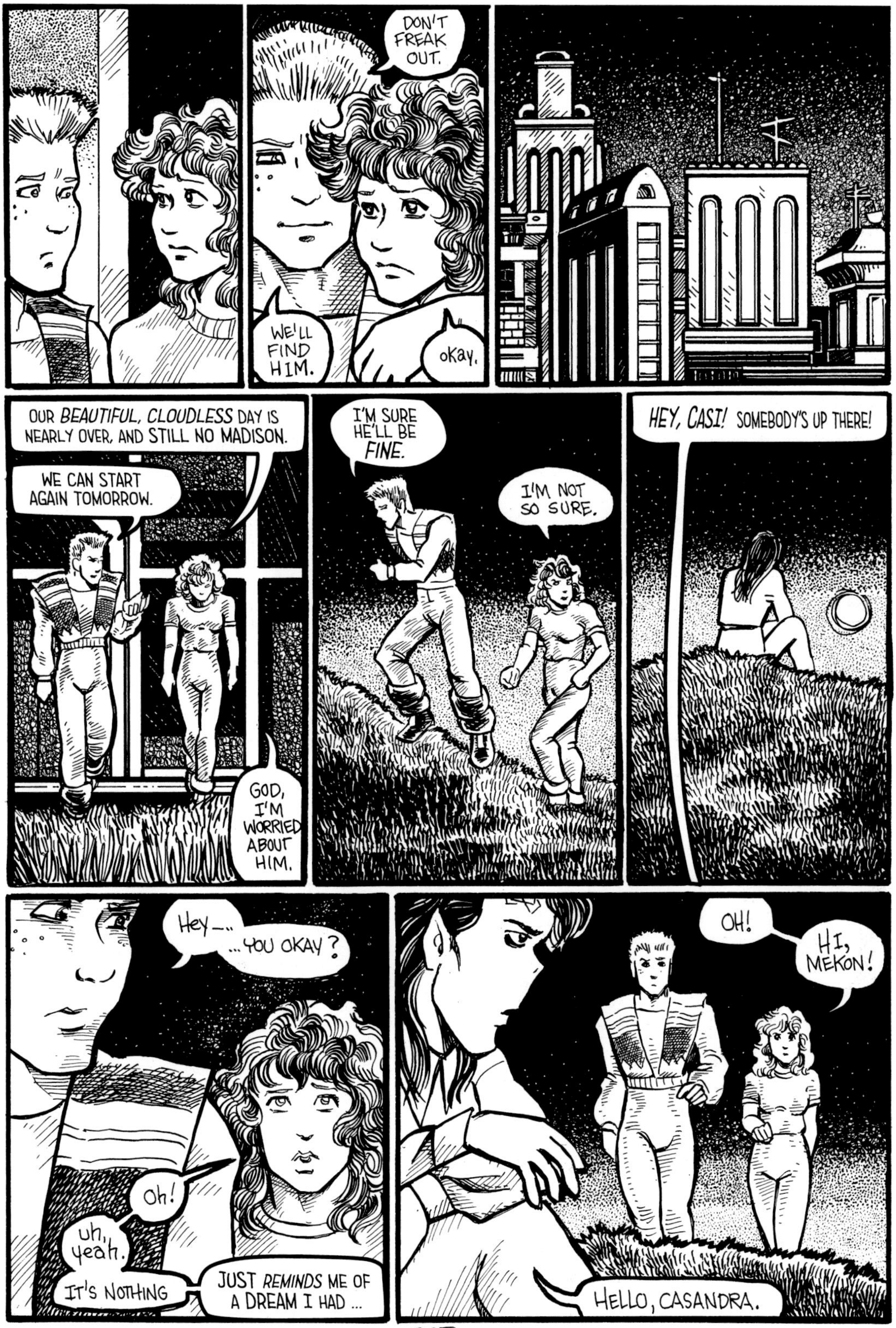
DON'T FREAK OUT.
WE'LL FIND HIM.
okay.
OUR BEAUTIFUL, CLOUDLESS DAY IS NEARLY OVER, AND STILL NO MADISON.
WE CAN START AGAIN TOMORROW.
GOD, I'M WORRIED ABOUT HIM.
I'M SURE HE'LL BE FINE.
I'M NOT SO SURE.
HEY, CASI! SOMEBODY'S UP THERE!
Hey— ...YOU OKAY?
Oh!
uh, yeah.
IT'S NOTHING
JUST REMINDS ME OF A DREAM I HAD ...
OH!
HI, MEKON!
HELLO, CASANDRA.

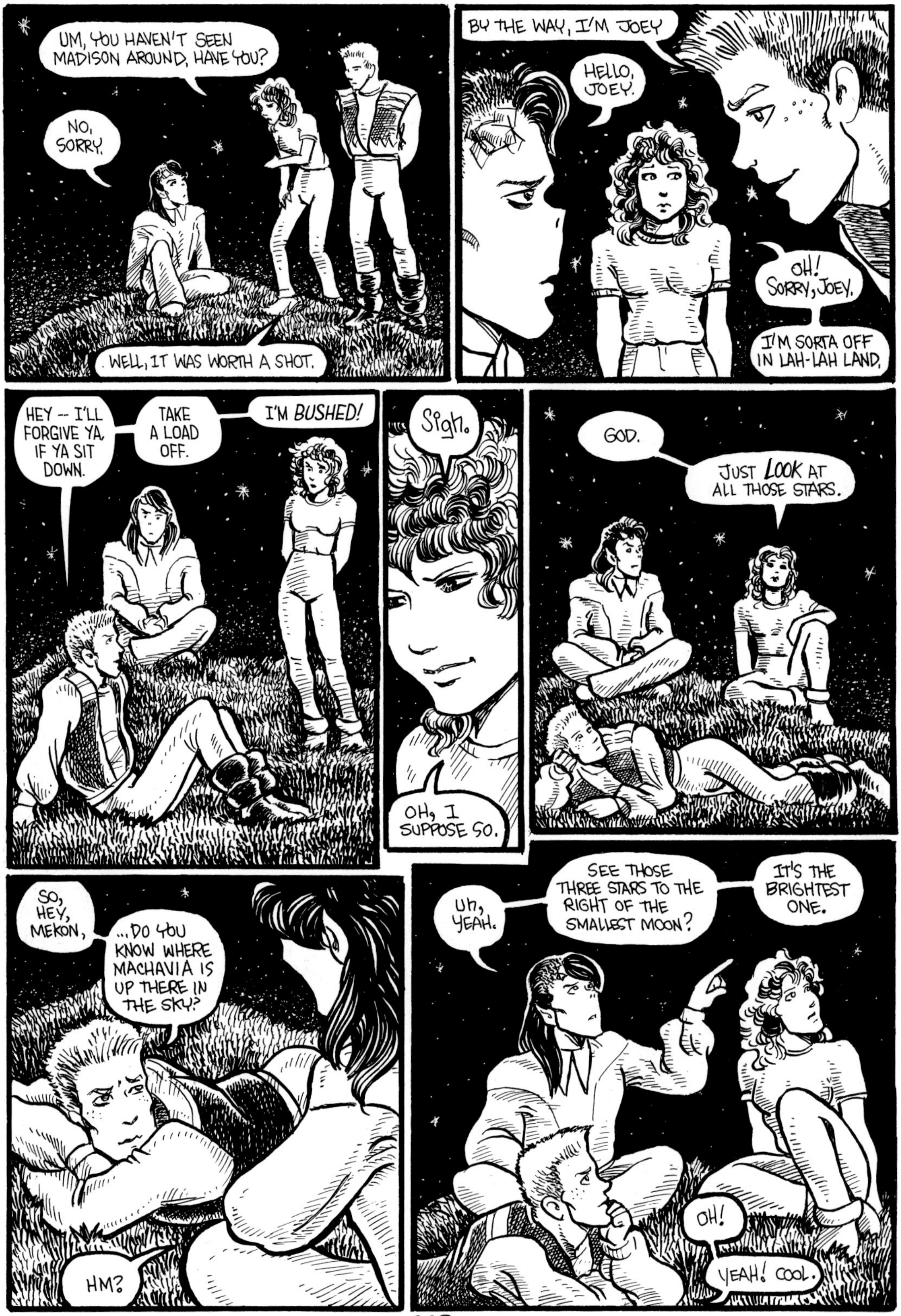
UM, YOU HAVEN'T SEEN MADISON AROUND, HAVE YOU?
NO, SORRY.
WELL, IT WAS WORTH A SHOT.
BY THE WAY, I'M JOEY
HELLO, JOEY.
OH! SORRY, JOEY.
I'M SORTA OFF IN LAH-LAH LAND.
HEY -- I'LL FORGIVE YA, IF YA SIT DOWN.
TAKE A LOAD OFF.
I'M BUSHED!
Sigh.
OH, I SUPPOSE SO.
GOD.
JUST LOOK AT ALL THOSE STARS.
SO, HEY, MEKON,
...DO YOU KNOW WHERE MACHAVIA IS UP THERE IN THE SKY?
HM?
Uh, YEAH.
SEE THOSE THREE STARS TO THE RIGHT OF THE SMALLEST MOON?
IT'S THE BRIGHTEST ONE.
OH!
YEAH! COOL.

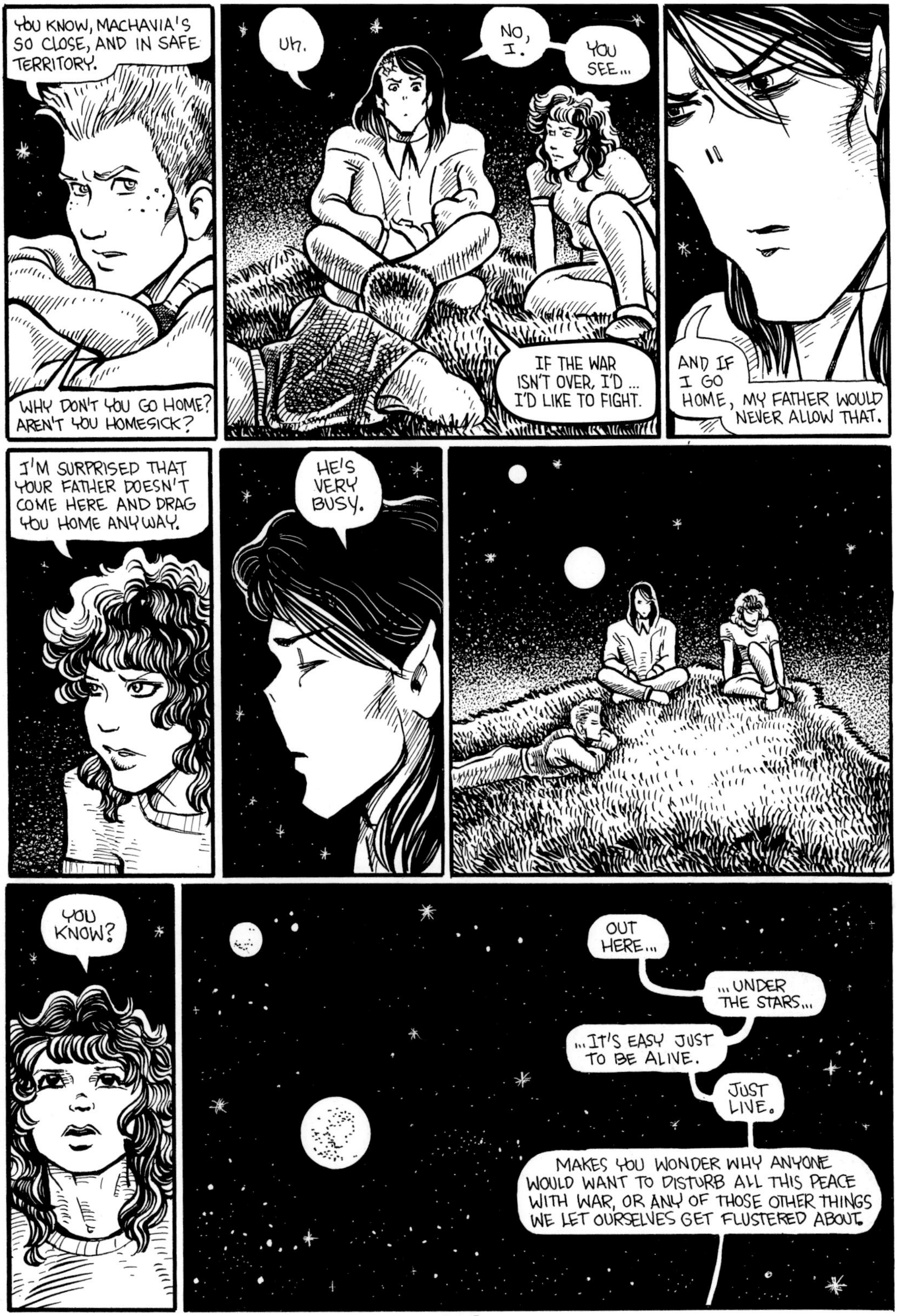
YOU KNOW, MACHAVIA'S SO CLOSE, AND IN SAFE TERRITORY.
WHY DON'T YOU GO HOME? AREN'T YOU HOMESICK?
Uh.
NO, I.
YOU SEE...
IF THE WAR ISN'T OVER, I'D ... I'D LIKE TO FIGHT.
AND IF I GO HOME, MY FATHER WOULD NEVER ALLOW THAT.
I'M SURPRISED THAT YOUR FATHER DOESN'T COME HERE AND DRAG YOU HOME ANYWAY.
HE'S VERY BUSY.
YOU KNOW?
OUT HERE...
...UNDER THE STARS...
...IT'S EASY JUST TO BE ALIVE.
JUST LIVE.
MAKES YOU WONDER WHY ANYONE WOULD WANT TO DISTURB ALL THIS PEACE WITH WAR, OR ANY OF THOSE OTHER THINGS WE LET OURSELVES GET FLUSTERED ABOUT.

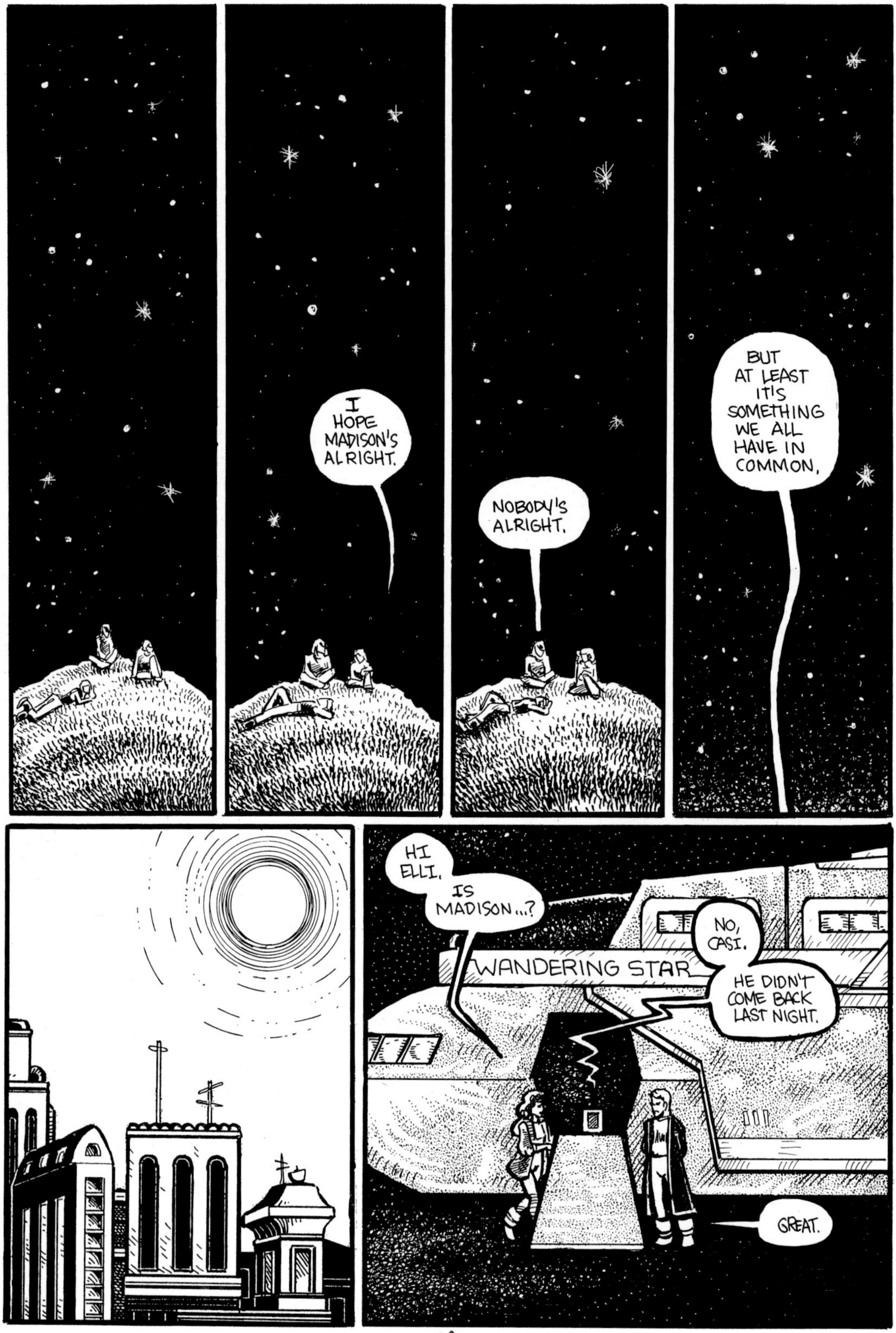
I HOPE MADISON'S ALRIGHT.
NOBODY'S ALRIGHT.
BUT AT LEAST IT'S SOMETHING WE ALL HAVE IN COMMON.
HI ELLI.
IS MADISON...?
NO, CASI.
WANDERING STAR
HE DIDN'T COME BACK LAST NIGHT.
GREAT.

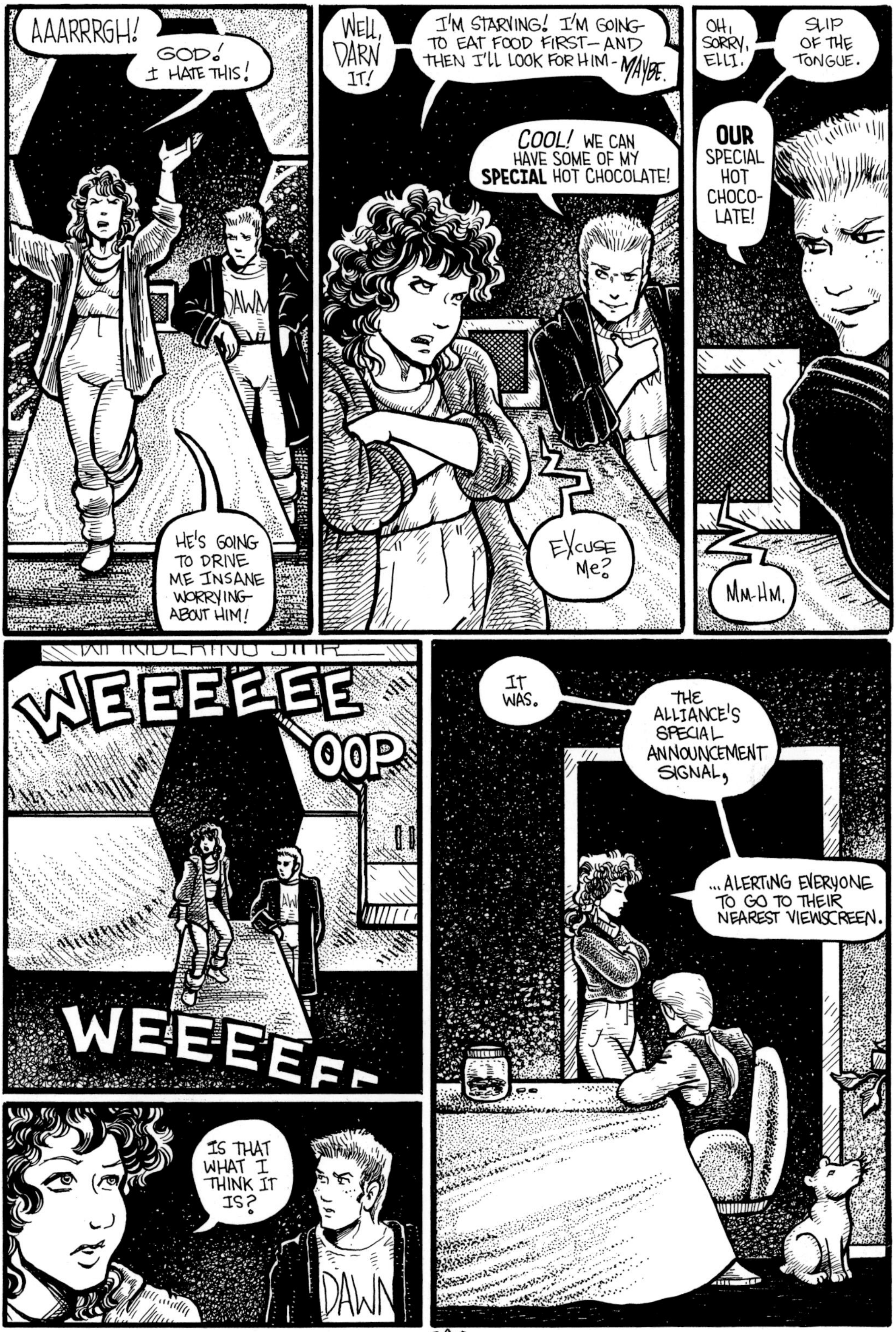
AAARRRGH!
GOD! I HATE THIS!
HE'S GOING TO DRIVE ME INSANE WORRYING ABOUT HIM!
WELL, DARN IT!
I'M STARVING! I'M GOING TO EAT FOOD FIRST— AND THEN I'LL LOOK FOR HIM - MAYBE.
COOL! WE CAN HAVE SOME OF MY SPECIAL HOT CHOCOLATE!
EXCUSE ME?
OUR SPECIAL HOT CHOCOLATE!
MM-HM.
OH, SORRY, ELLI.
SLIP OF THE TONGUE.
WEEEEEE
OOP
WEEEEEE
IS THAT WHAT I THINK IT IS?
IT WAS.
THE ALLIANCE'S SPECIAL ANNOUNCEMENT SIGNAL,
...ALERTING EVERYONE TO GO TO THEIR NEAREST VIEWSCREEN.

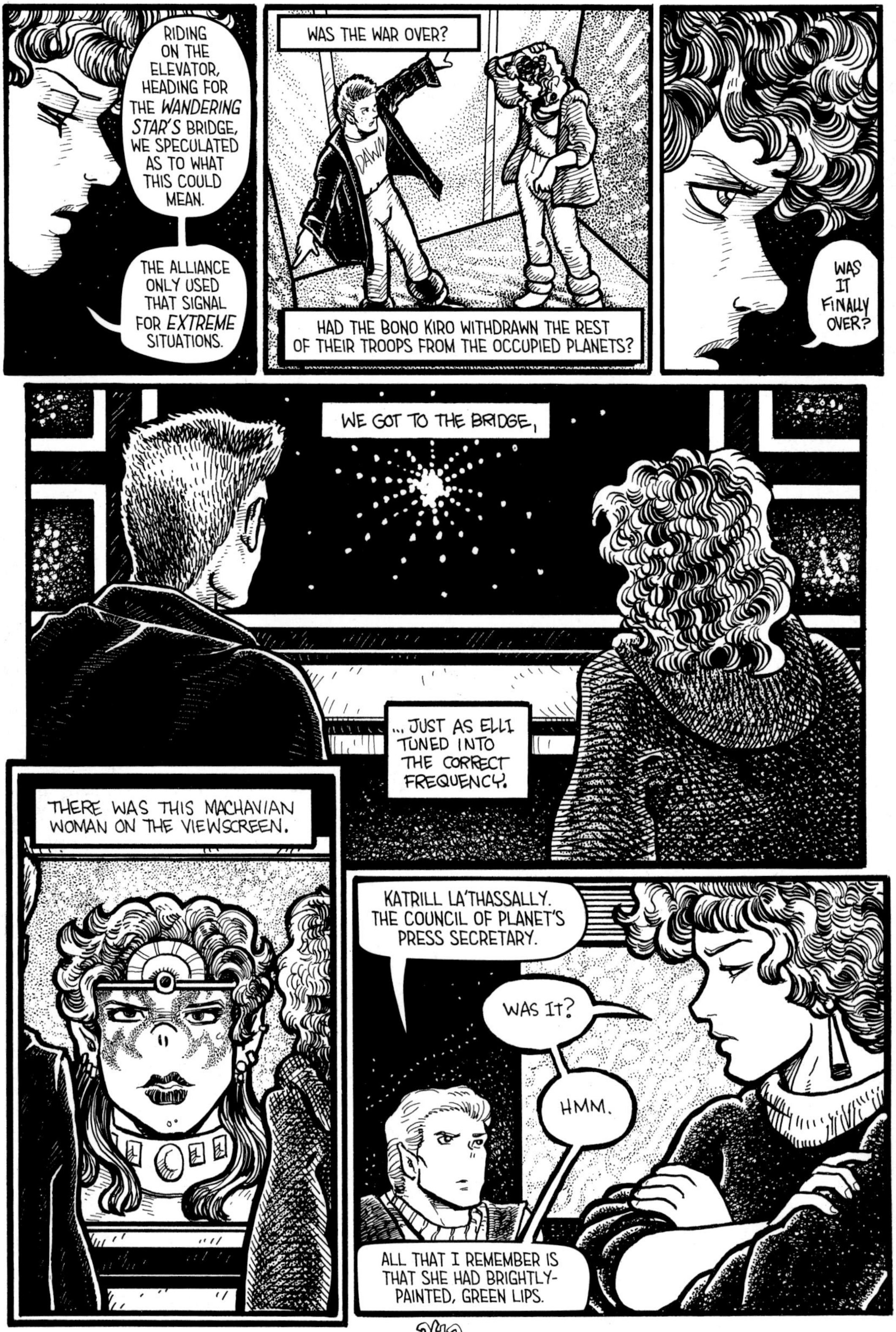

RIDING ON THE ELEVATOR, HEADING FOR THE WANDERING STAR'S BRIDGE, WE SPECULATED AS TO WHAT THIS COULD MEAN.
THE ALLIANCE ONLY USED THAT SIGNAL FOR EXTREME SITUATIONS.
WAS THE WAR OVER?
DAWN
HAD THE BONO KIRO WITHDRAWN THE REST OF THEIR TROOPS FROM THE OCCUPIED PLANETS?
WAS IT FINALLY OVER?
WE GOT TO THE BRIDGE,
...JUST AS ELLI TUNED INTO THE CORRECT FREQUENCY.
THERE WAS THIS MACHAVIAN WOMAN ON THE VIEWSCREEN.
KATRILL LA'THASSALLY. THE COUNCIL OF PLANET'S PRESS SECRETARY.
WAS IT?
HMM.
ALL THAT I REMEMBER IS THAT SHE HAD BRIGHTLY-PAINTED, GREEN LIPS.

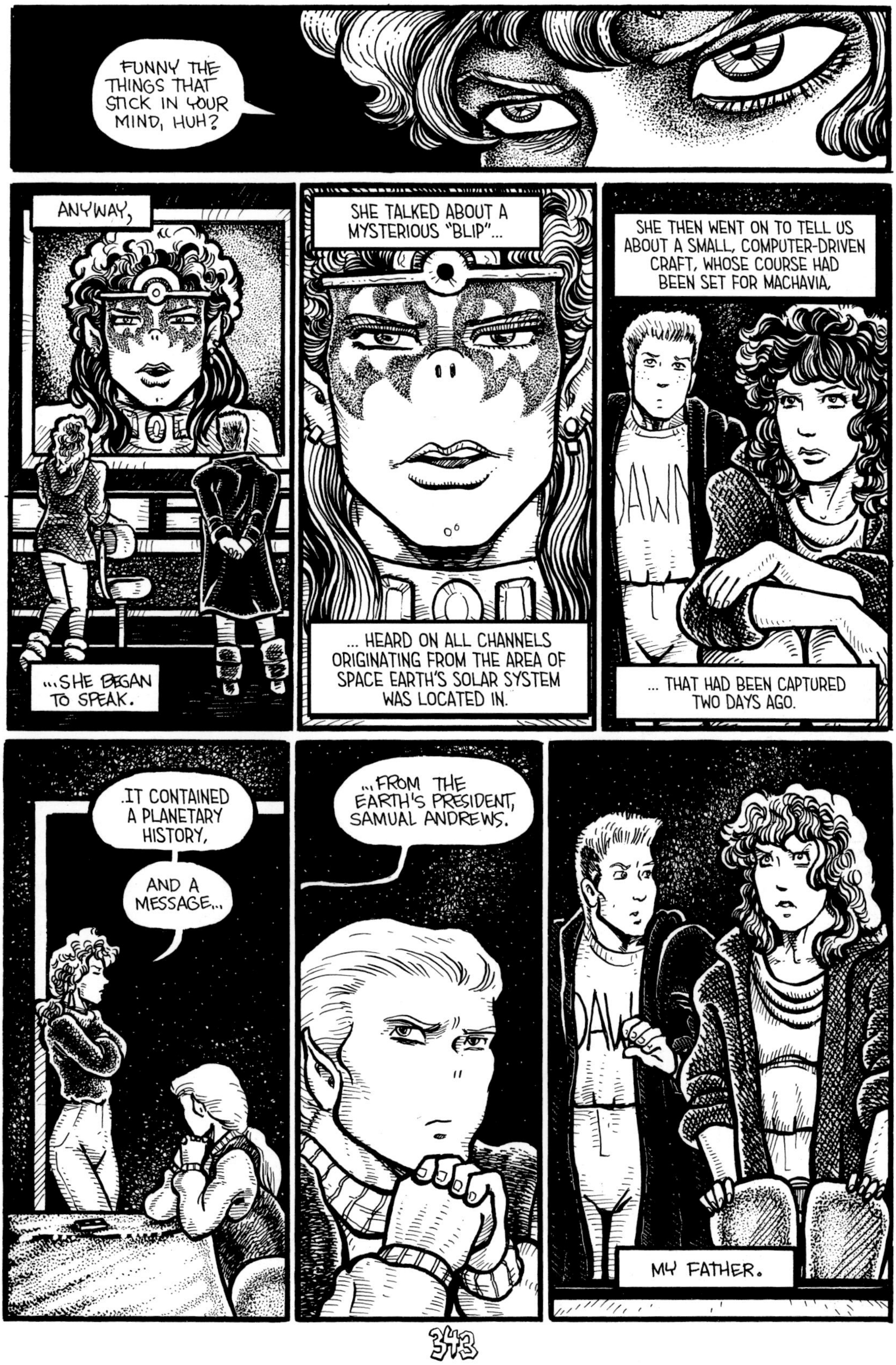
FUNNY THE THINGS THAT STICK IN YOUR MIND, HUH?
ANYWAY,
...SHE BEGAN TO SPEAK.
SHE TALKED ABOUT A MYSTERIOUS "BLIP"...
... HEARD ON ALL CHANNELS ORIGINATING FROM THE AREA OF SPACE EARTH'S SOLAR SYSTEM WAS LOCATED IN.
SHE THEN WENT ON TO TELL US ABOUT A SMALL, COMPUTER-DRIVEN CRAFT, WHOSE COURSE HAD BEEN SET FOR MACHAVIA,
... THAT HAD BEEN CAPTURED TWO DAYS AGO.
.IT CONTAINED A PLANETARY HISTORY,
AND A MESSAGE...
...FROM THE EARTH'S PRESIDENT, SAMUAL ANDREWS.
MY FATHER.

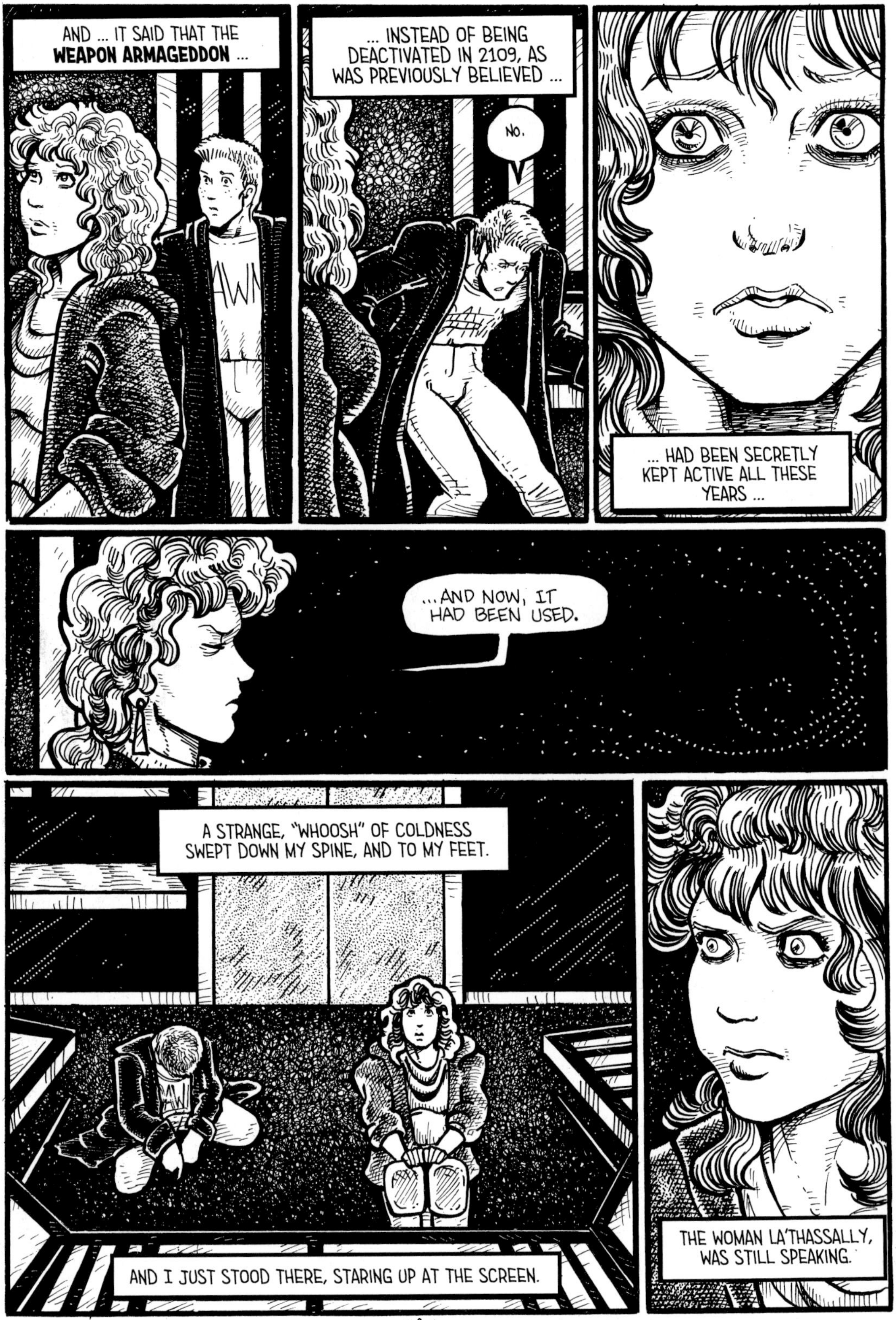
AND ... IT SAID THAT THE **WEAPON ARMAGEDDON** ...
... INSTEAD OF BEING DEACTIVATED IN 2109, AS WAS PREVIOUSLY BELIEVED ...
NO.
... HAD BEEN SECRETLY KEPT ACTIVE ALL THESE YEARS ...
...AND NOW, IT HAD BEEN USED.
A STRANGE, "WHOOSH" OF COLDNESS SWEPT DOWN MY SPINE, AND TO MY FEET.
AND I JUST STOOD THERE, STARING UP AT THE SCREEN.
THE WOMAN LA'THASSALLY, WAS STILL SPEAKING.

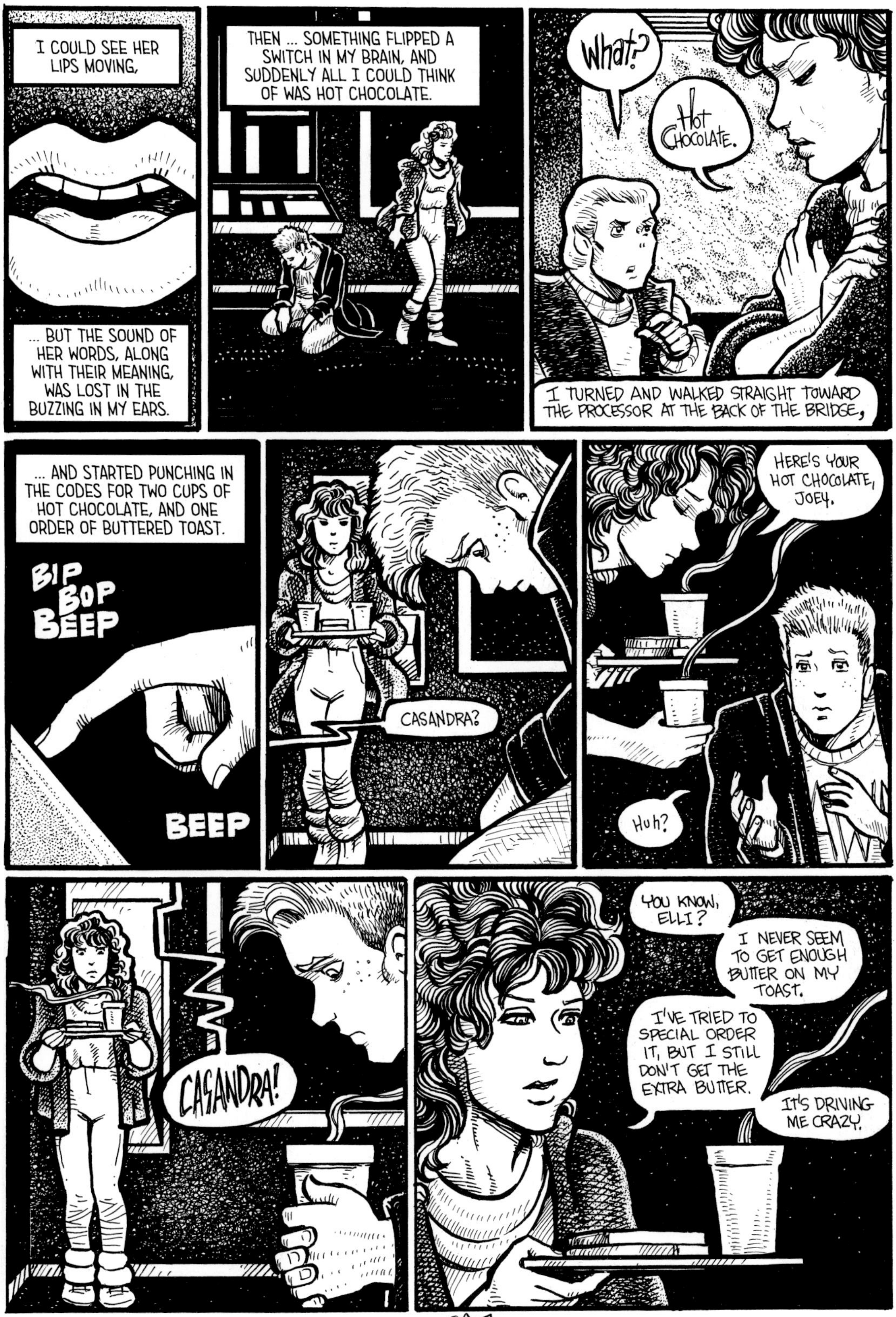
I COULD SEE HER LIPS MOVING,
... BUT THE SOUND OF HER WORDS, ALONG WITH THEIR MEANING, WAS LOST IN THE BUZZING IN MY EARS.
THEN ... SOMETHING FLIPPED A SWITCH IN MY BRAIN, AND SUDDENLY ALL I COULD THINK OF WAS HOT CHOCOLATE.
What?
Hot Chocolate.
I TURNED AND WALKED STRAIGHT TOWARD THE PROCESSOR AT THE BACK OF THE BRIDGE,
... AND STARTED PUNCHING IN THE CODES FOR TWO CUPS OF HOT CHOCOLATE, AND ONE ORDER OF BUTTERED TOAST.
BIP BOP BEEP
BEEP
CASANDRA?
HERE'S YOUR HOT CHOCOLATE, JOEY.
Huh?
CASANDRA!
YOU KNOW, ELLI?
I NEVER SEEM TO GET ENOUGH BUTTER ON MY TOAST.
I'VE TRIED TO SPECIAL ORDER IT, BUT I STILL DON'T GET THE EXTRA BUTTER.
IT'S DRIVING ME CRAZY.

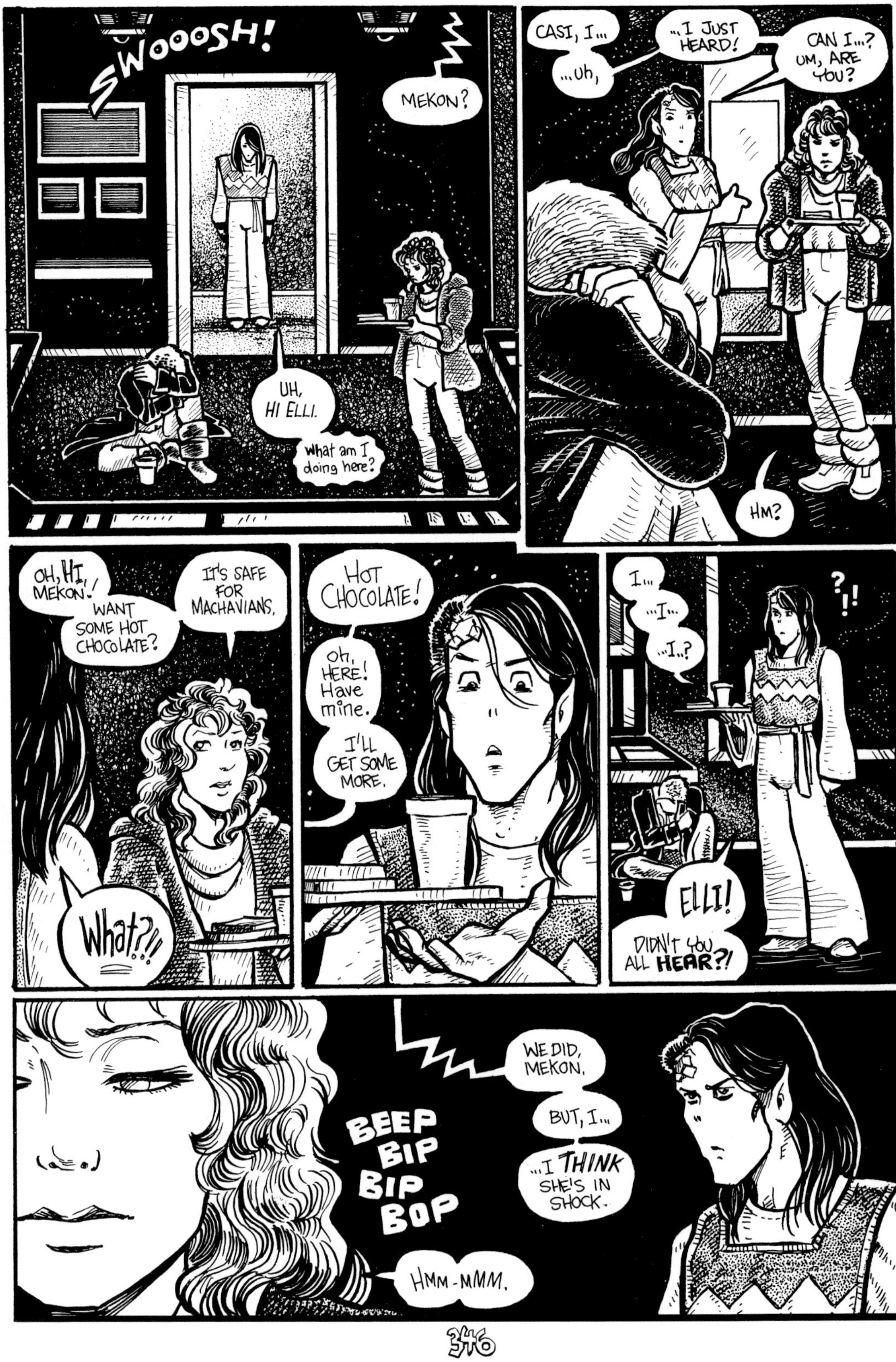
SWOOOSH!
MEKON?
UH, HI ELLI.
What am I doing here?
CASI, I...
...Uh,
...I JUST HEARD!
CAN I...? UM, ARE YOU?
HM?
OH, HI, MEKON!
WANT SOME HOT CHOCOLATE?
IT'S SAFE FOR MACHAVIANS.
What?!!
HOT CHOCOLATE!
Oh, HERE! Have mine.
I'LL GET SOME MORE.
I...
...I...
...I..?
?!!
ELLI!
DIDN'T YOU ALL HEAR?!
WE DID, MEKON.
BUT, I...
...I THINK SHE'S IN SHOCK.
BEEP BIP BIP BOP
HMM-MMM.

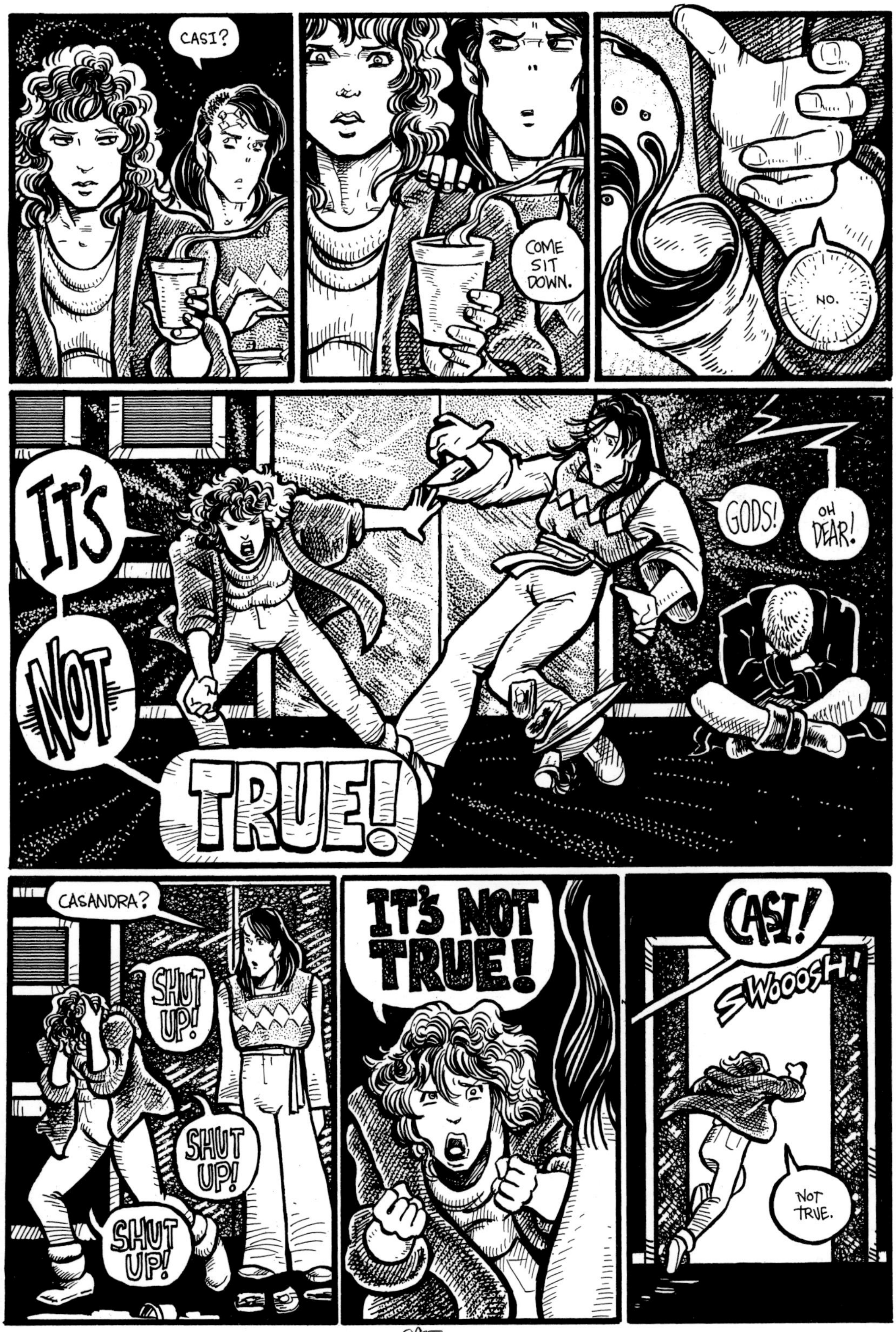
CASI?
COME SIT DOWN.
NO.
IT'S NOT TRUE!
GODS!
OH DEAR!
CASANDRA?
SHUT UP!
SHUT UP!
SHUT UP!
IT'S NOT TRUE!
CASI!
SWOOOSH!
NOT TRUE.

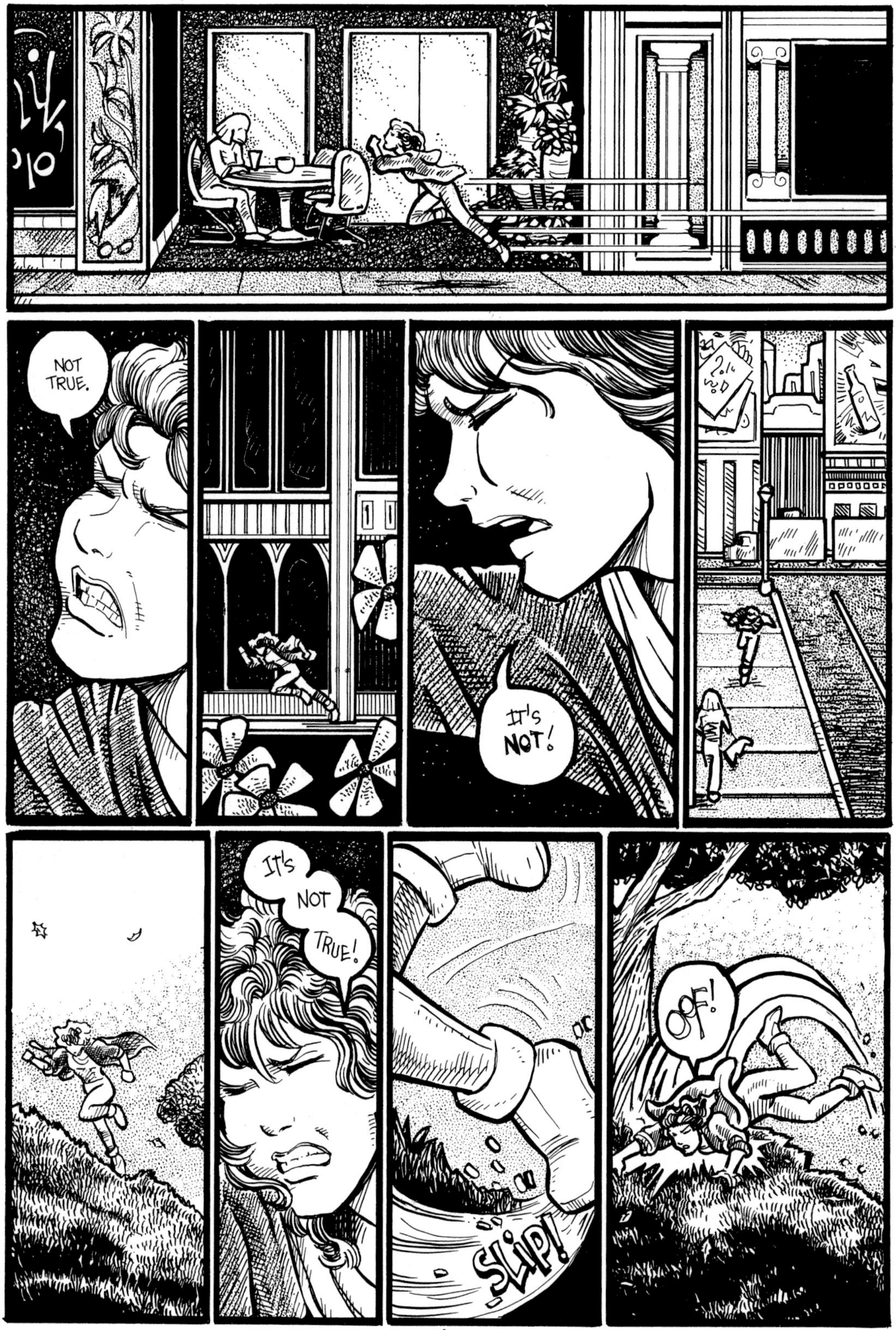
NOT TRUE.
IT'S NOT!
IT'S NOT TRUE!
SLIP!
OOF!

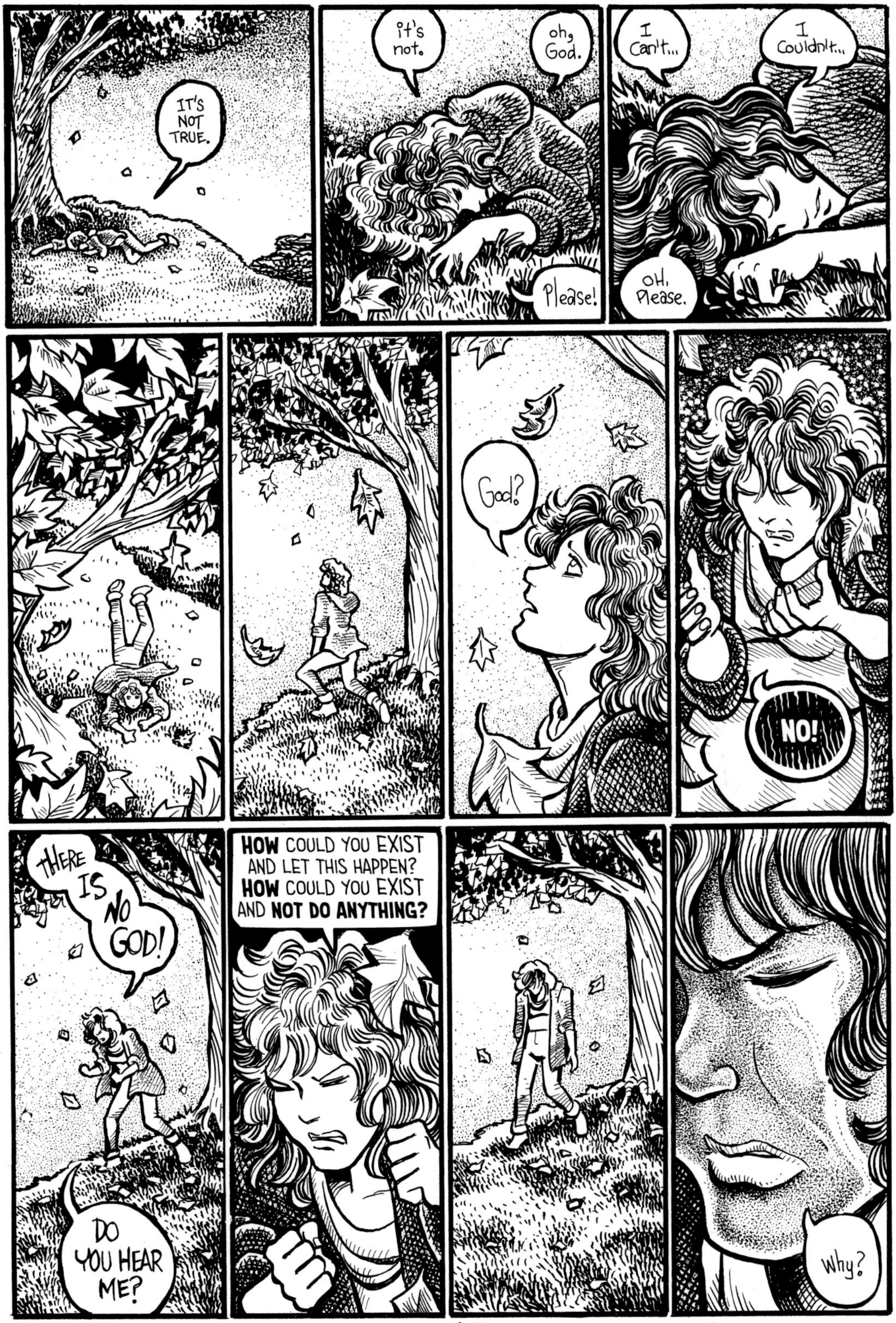
IT'S NOT TRUE.
it's not.
oh, God.
Please!
I can't...
I couldn't...
OH, Please.
God?
NO!
THERE IS NO GOD!
DO YOU HEAR ME?
HOW COULD YOU EXIST AND LET THIS HAPPEN? **HOW** COULD YOU EXIST AND **NOT DO ANYTHING?**
Why?

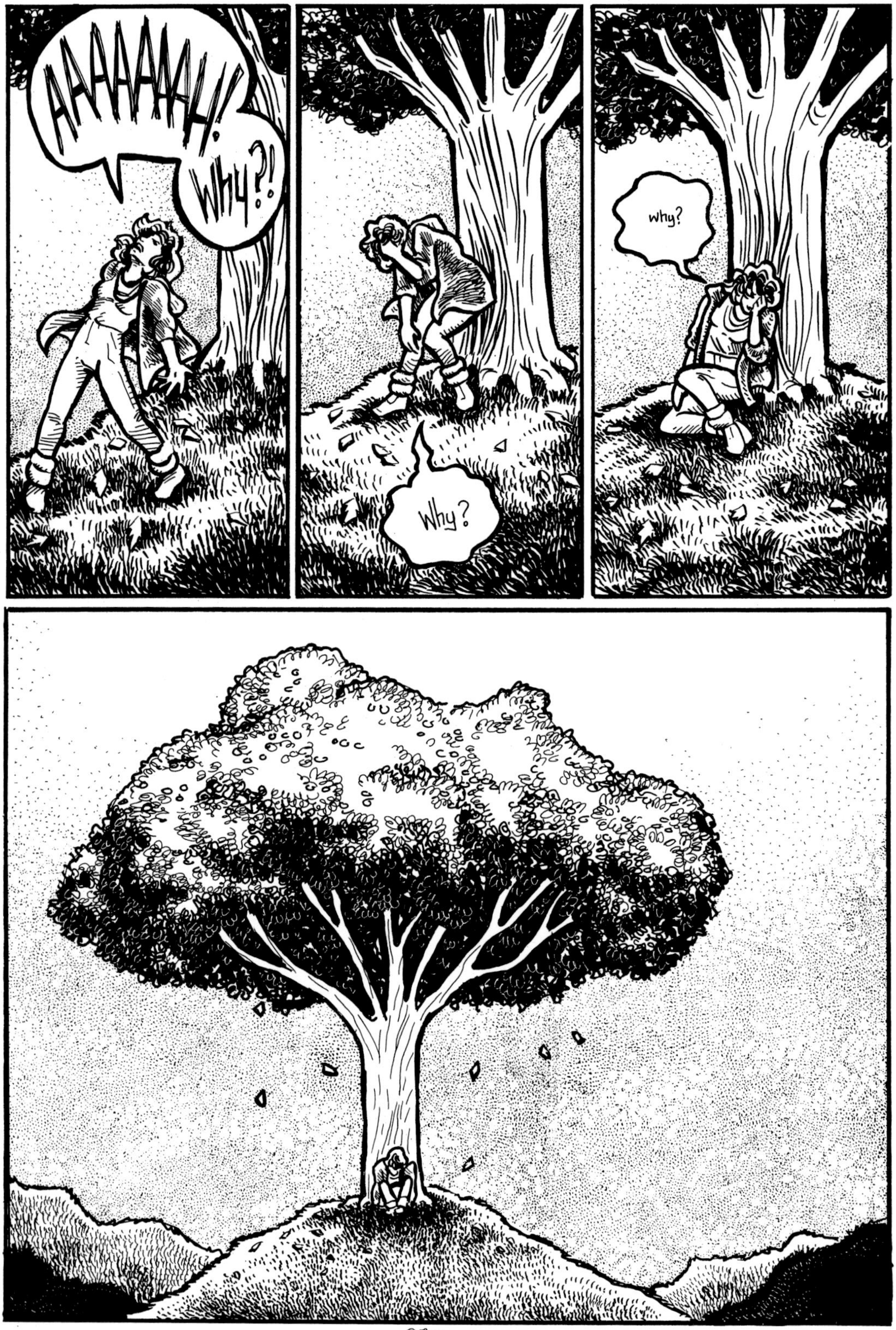
AAAAAAH!
Why?!
Why?
why?

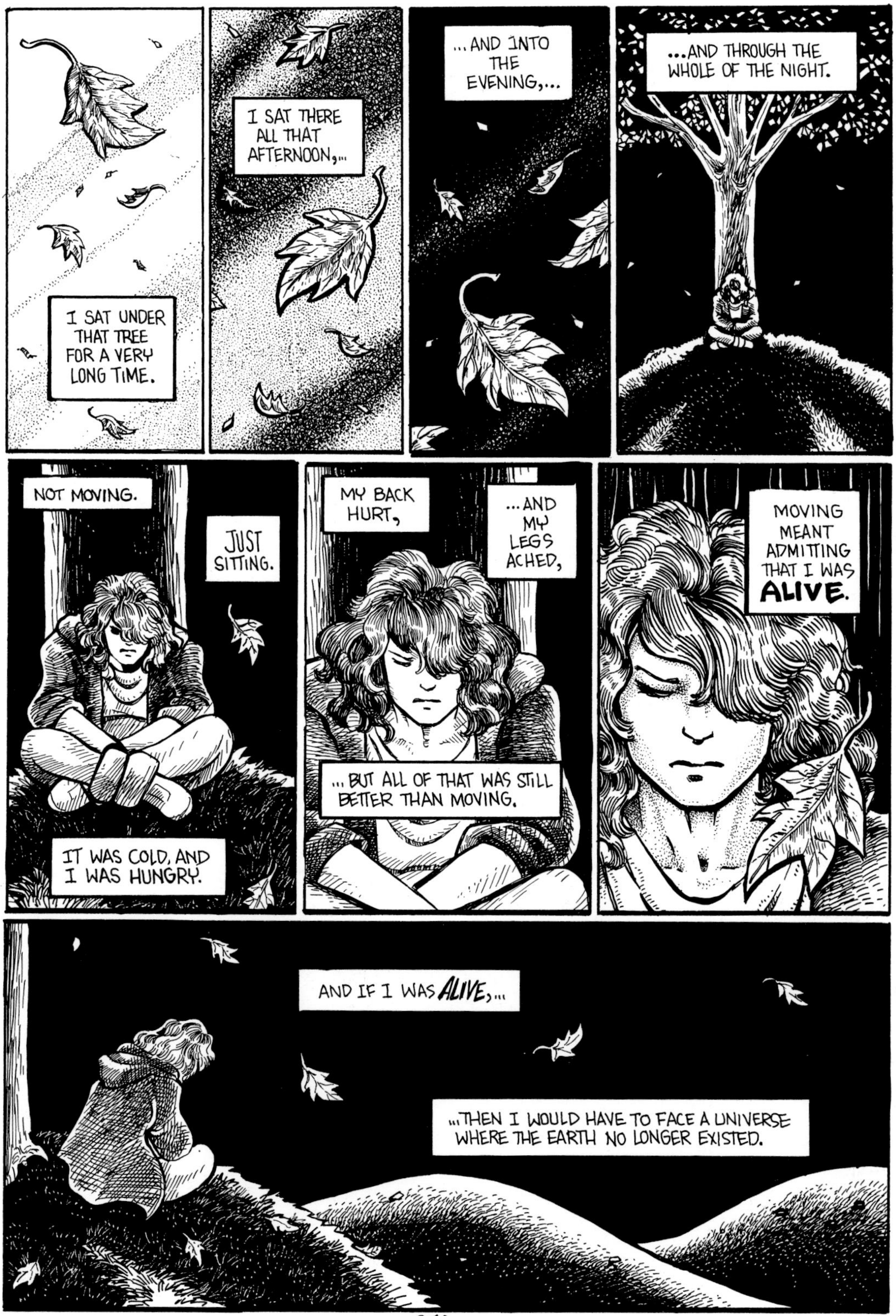
I SAT UNDER THAT TREE FOR A VERY LONG TIME.
I SAT THERE ALL THAT AFTERNOON,...
...AND INTO THE EVENING,...
...AND THROUGH THE WHOLE OF THE NIGHT.
NOT MOVING.
JUST SITTING.
IT WAS COLD, AND I WAS HUNGRY.
MY BACK HURT,
...AND MY LEGS ACHED,
...BUT ALL OF THAT WAS STILL BETTER THAN MOVING.
MOVING MEANT ADMITTING THAT I WAS ALIVE.
AND IF I WAS ALIVE,...
...THEN I WOULD HAVE TO FACE A UNIVERSE WHERE THE EARTH NO LONGER EXISTED.

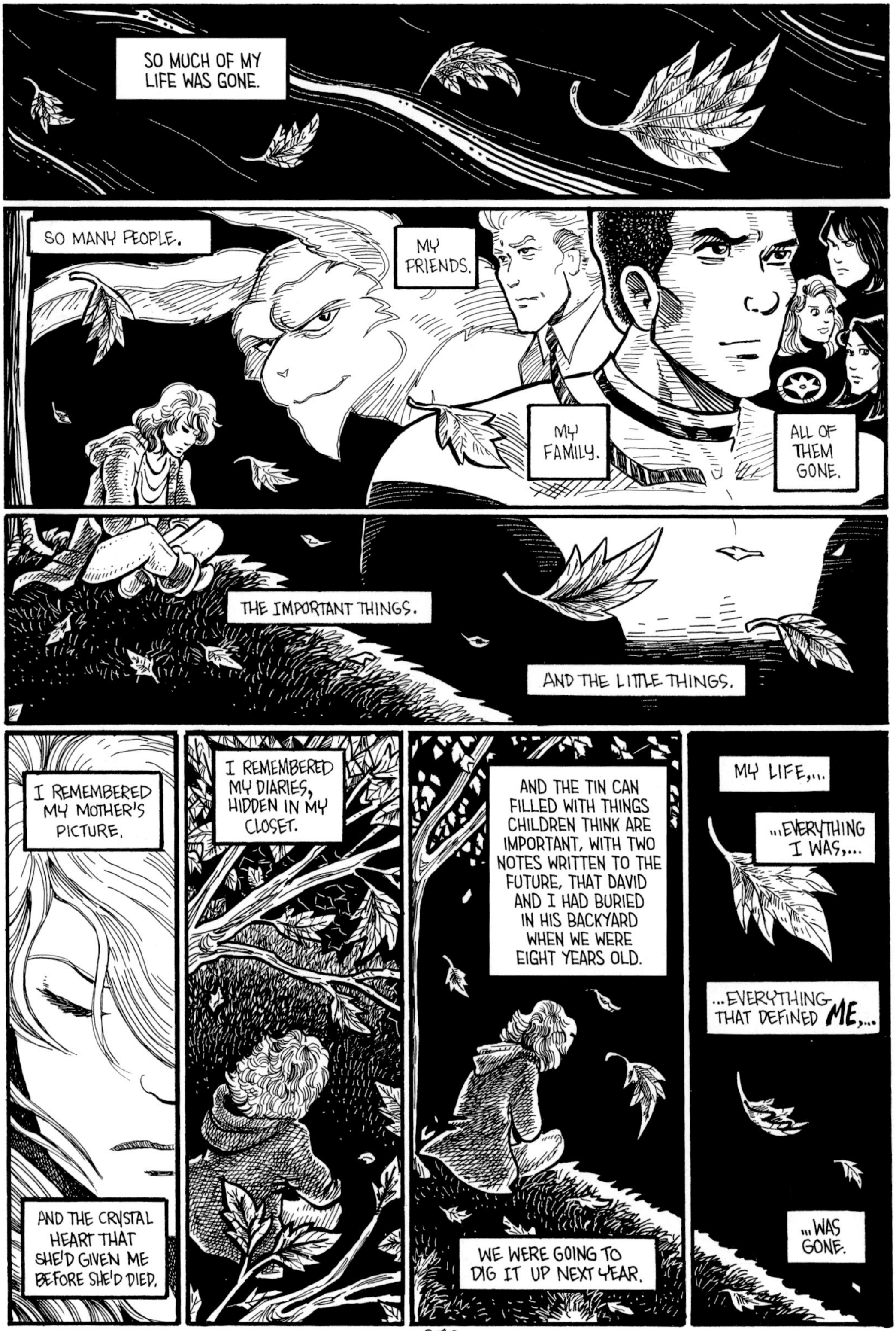
SO MUCH OF MY LIFE WAS GONE.
SO MANY PEOPLE.
MY FRIENDS.
MY FAMILY.
ALL OF THEM GONE.
THE IMPORTANT THINGS.
AND THE LITTLE THINGS.
I REMEMBERED MY MOTHER'S PICTURE.
AND THE CRYSTAL HEART THAT SHE'D GIVEN ME BEFORE SHE'D DIED.
I REMEMBERED MY DIARIES, HIDDEN IN MY CLOSET.
AND THE TIN CAN FILLED WITH THINGS CHILDREN THINK ARE IMPORTANT, WITH TWO NOTES WRITTEN TO THE FUTURE, THAT DAVID AND I HAD BURIED IN HIS BACKYARD WHEN WE WERE EIGHT YEARS OLD.
WE WERE GOING TO DIG IT UP NEXT YEAR.
MY LIFE,...
...EVERYTHING I WAS,...
...EVERYTHING THAT DEFINED ME,...
...WAS GONE.

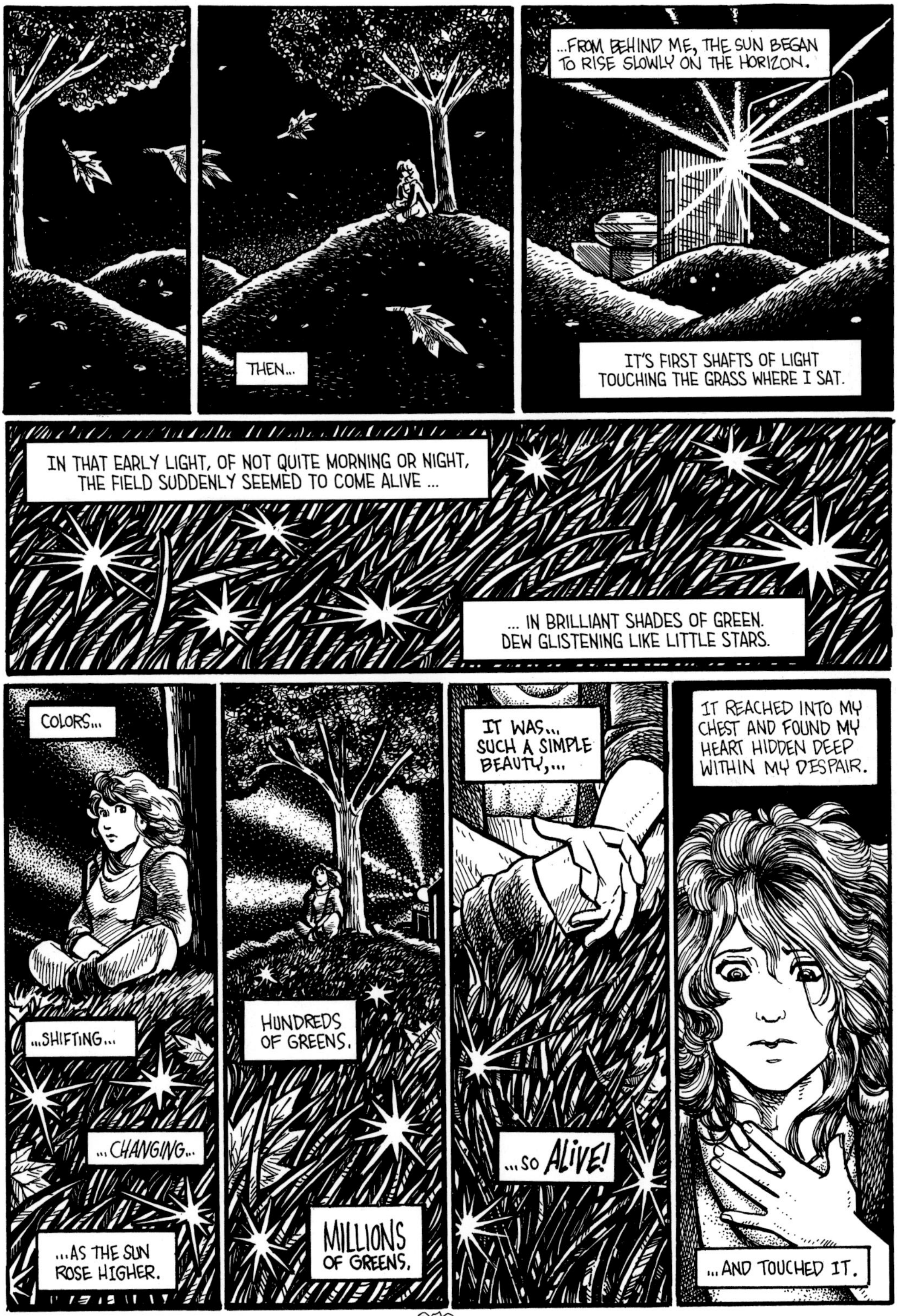
THEN...
...FROM BEHIND ME, THE SUN BEGAN TO RISE SLOWLY ON THE HORIZON.
IT'S FIRST SHAFTS OF LIGHT TOUCHING THE GRASS WHERE I SAT.
IN THAT EARLY LIGHT, OF NOT QUITE MORNING OR NIGHT, THE FIELD SUDDENLY SEEMED TO COME ALIVE ...
... IN BRILLIANT SHADES OF GREEN. DEW GLISTENING LIKE LITTLE STARS.
COLORS...
...SHIFTING...
...CHANGING...
...AS THE SUN ROSE HIGHER.
HUNDREDS OF GREENS.
MILLIONS OF GREENS.
IT WAS... SUCH A SIMPLE BEAUTY,...
...SO ALIVE!
IT REACHED INTO MY CHEST AND FOUND MY HEART HIDDEN DEEP WITHIN MY DESPAIR.
...AND TOUCHED IT.

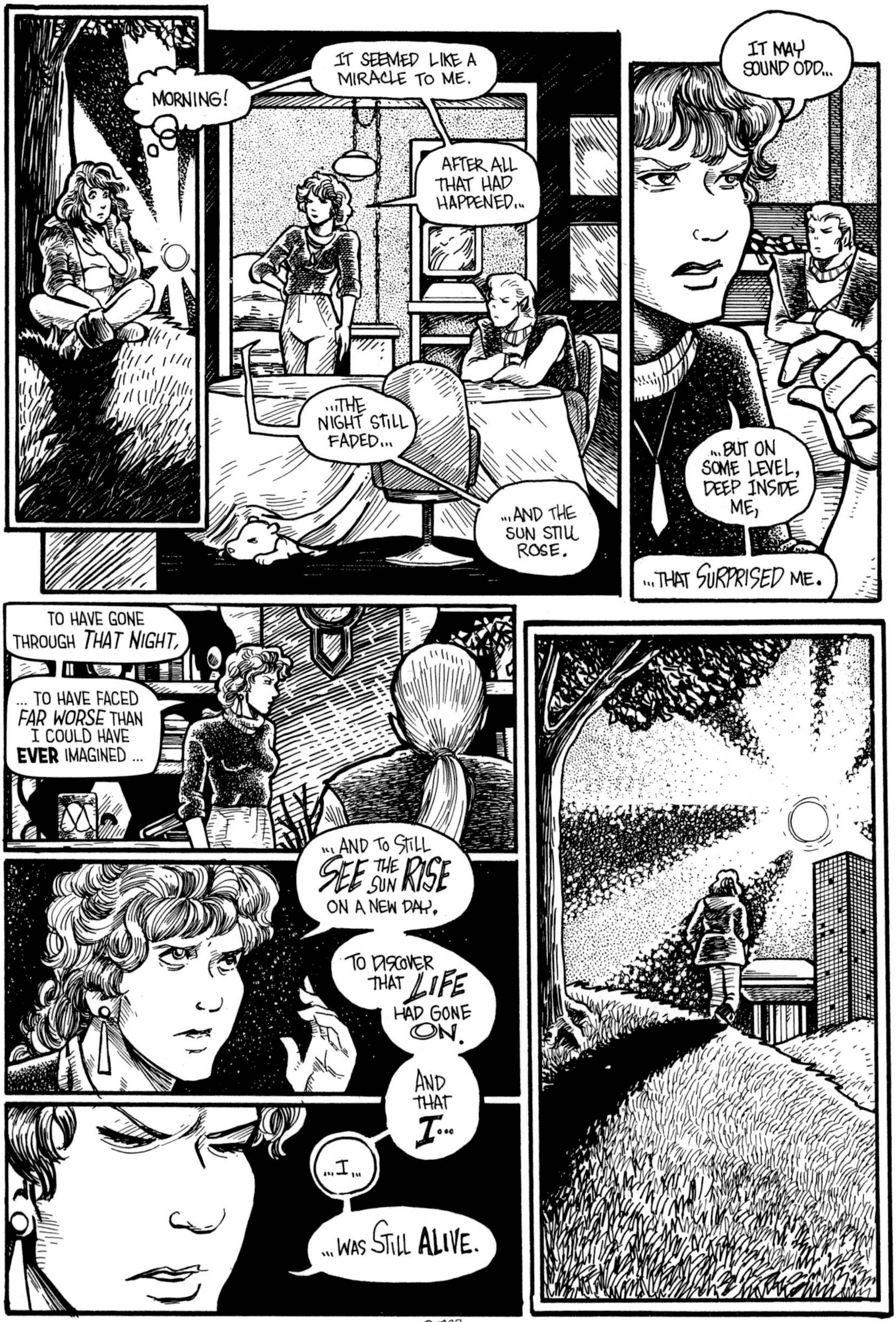
MORNING!
IT SEEMED LIKE A MIRACLE TO ME.
AFTER ALL THAT HAD HAPPENED...
...THE NIGHT STILL FADED...
...AND THE SUN STILL ROSE.
IT MAY SOUND ODD...
...BUT ON SOME LEVEL, DEEP INSIDE ME,
...THAT SURPRISED ME.
TO HAVE GONE THROUGH THAT NIGHT,
... TO HAVE FACED FAR WORSE THAN I COULD HAVE EVER IMAGINED ...
...AND TO STILL SEE THE SUN RISE ON A NEW DAY,
TO DISCOVER THAT LIFE HAD GONE ON.
AND THAT I...
...I...
...WAS STILL ALIVE.

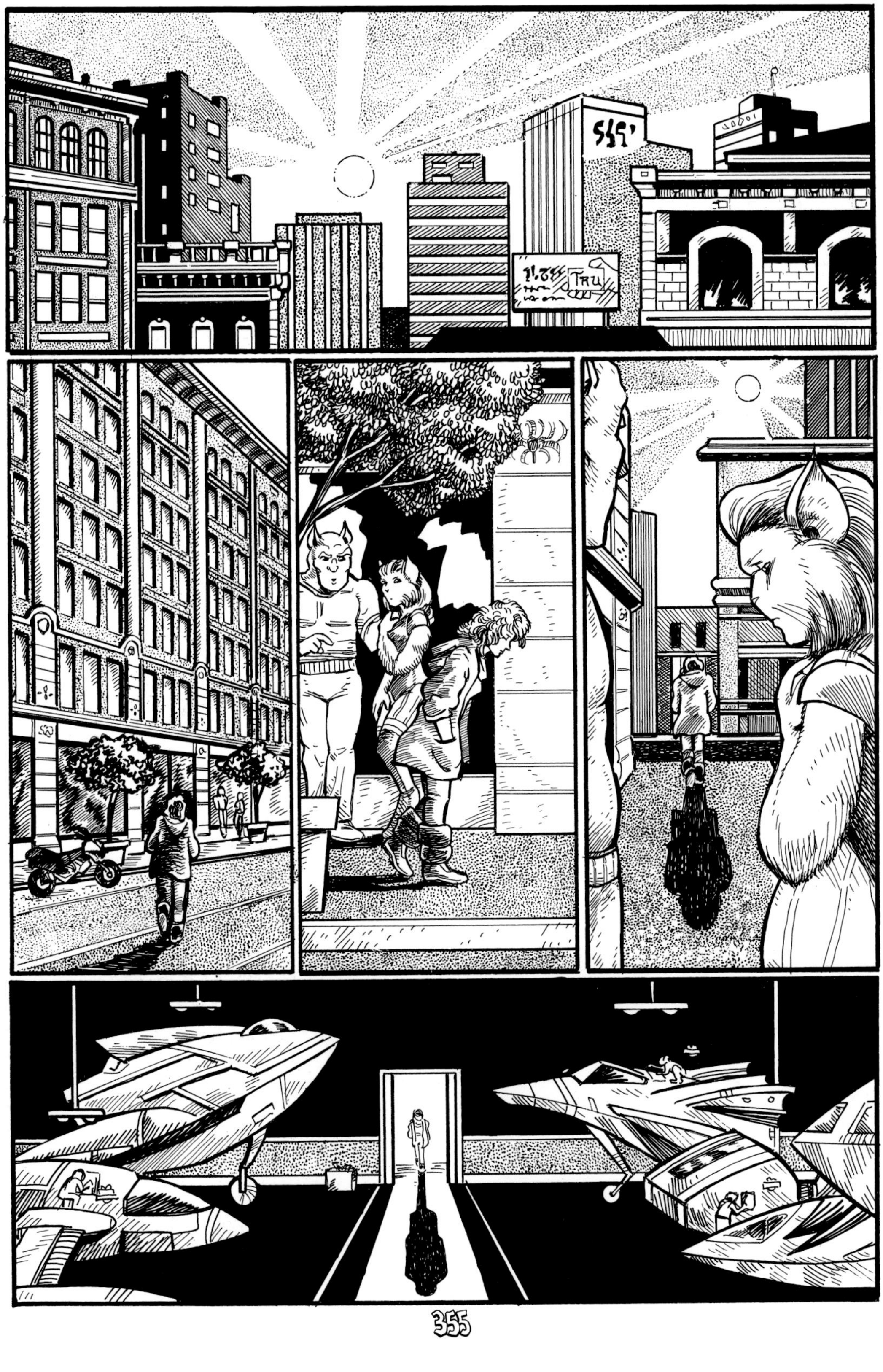
TRU

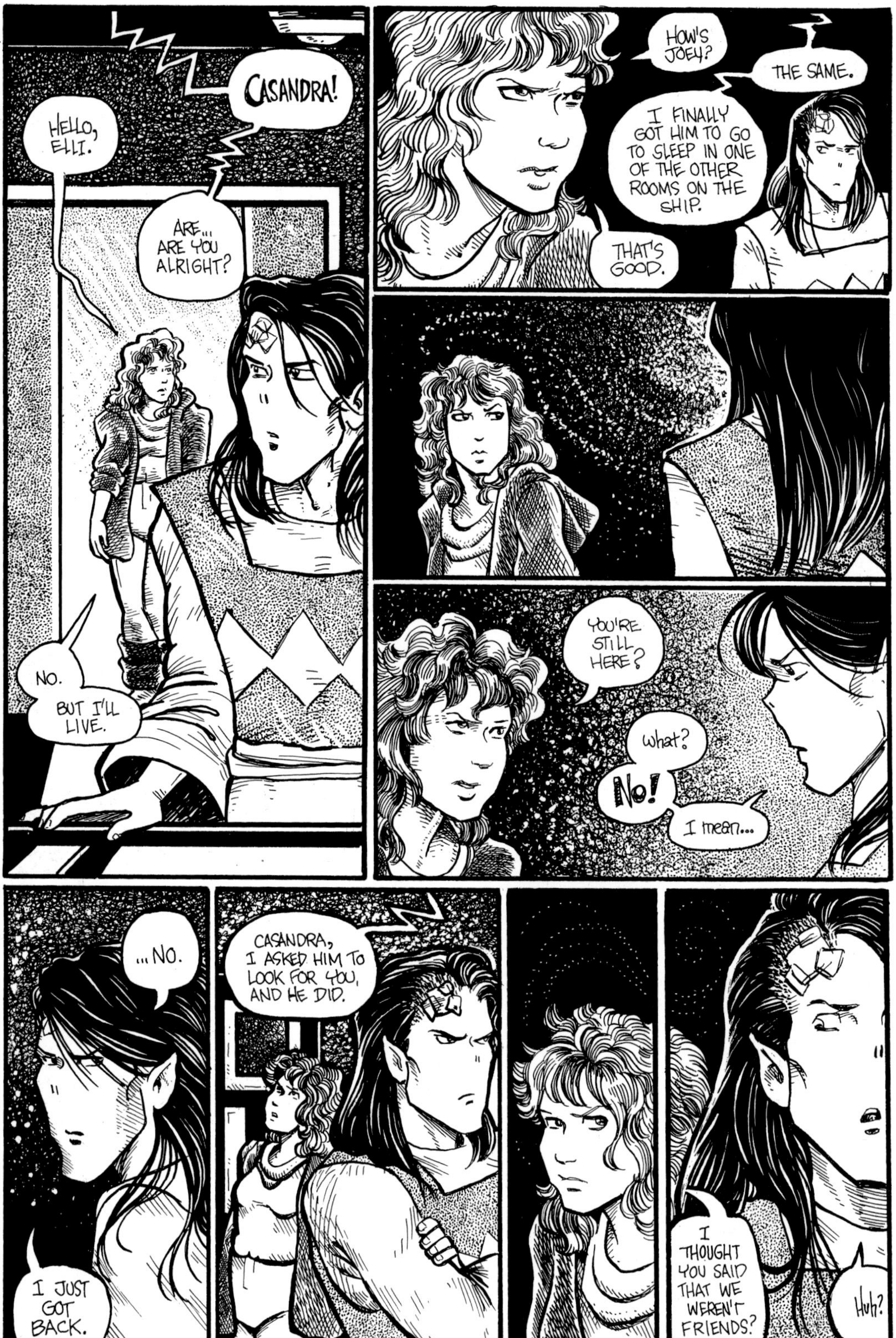

CASANDRA!
HELLO, ELLI.
ARE... ARE YOU ALRIGHT?
NO.
BUT I'LL LIVE.
HOW'S JOEY?
THE SAME.
I FINALLY GOT HIM TO GO TO SLEEP IN ONE OF THE OTHER ROOMS ON THE SHIP.
THAT'S GOOD.
YOU'RE STILL HERE?
what?
No!
I mean...
...NO.
I JUST GOT BACK.
CASANDRA, I ASKED HIM TO LOOK FOR YOU, AND HE DID.
I THOUGHT YOU SAID THAT WE WEREN'T FRIENDS?
Huh?

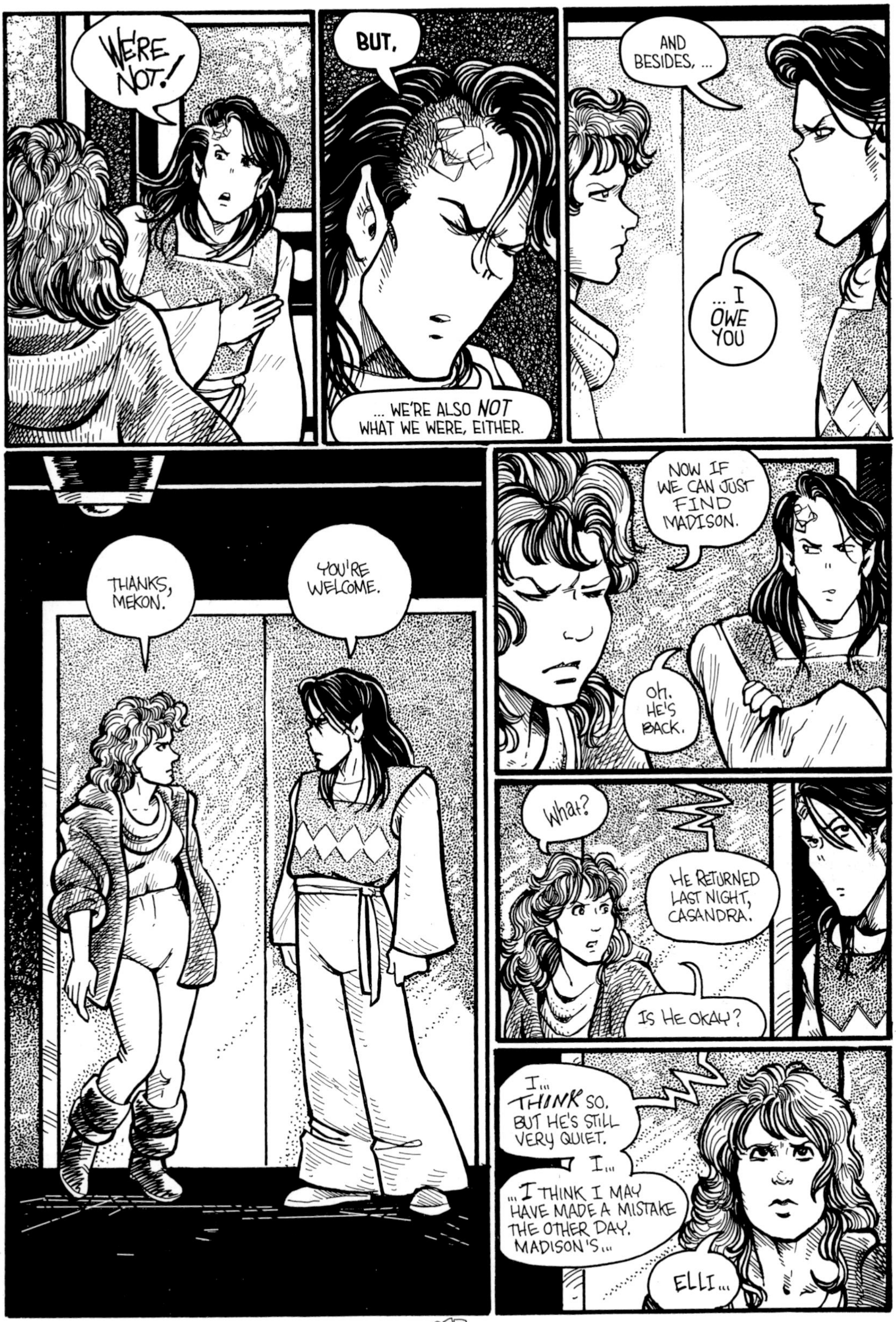
WE'RE NOT!
BUT,
... WE'RE ALSO NOT WHAT WE WERE, EITHER.
AND BESIDES, ...
... I OWE YOU
THANKS, MEKON.
YOU'RE WELCOME.
NOW IF WE CAN JUST FIND MADISON.
oh. HE'S BACK.
What?
HE RETURNED LAST NIGHT, CASANDRA.
IS HE OKAY?
I... THINK SO. BUT HE'S STILL VERY QUIET.
I...
...I THINK I MAY HAVE MADE A MISTAKE THE OTHER DAY. MADISON'S...
ELLI...

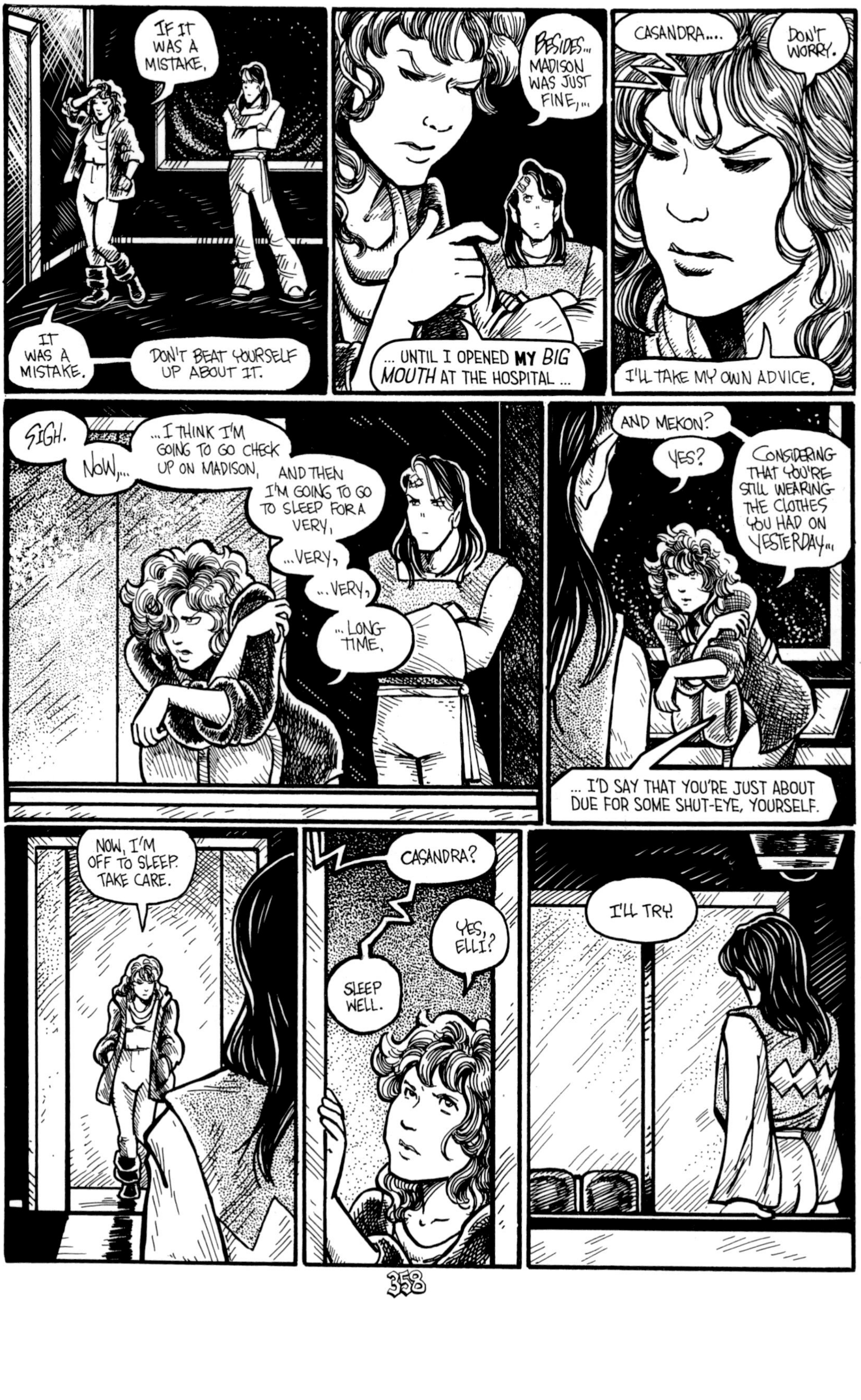
IF IT WAS A MISTAKE,
IT WAS A MISTAKE.
DON'T BEAT YOURSELF UP ABOUT IT.
BESIDES... MADISON WAS JUST FINE,...
... UNTIL I OPENED MY BIG MOUTH AT THE HOSPITAL ...
CASANDRA....
DON'T WORRY.
I'LL TAKE MY OWN ADVICE.
SIGH.
NOW,...
...I THINK I'M GOING TO GO CHECK UP ON MADISON,
AND THEN I'M GOING TO GO TO SLEEP FOR A VERY,
...VERY,
...VERY,
...LONG TIME.
AND MEKON?
YES?
CONSIDERING THAT YOU'RE STILL WEARING THE CLOTHES YOU HAD ON YESTERDAY...
... I'D SAY THAT YOU'RE JUST ABOUT DUE FOR SOME SHUT-EYE, YOURSELF.
NOW, I'M OFF TO SLEEP. TAKE CARE.
CASANDRA?
YES, ELLI?
SLEEP WELL.
I'LL TRY.

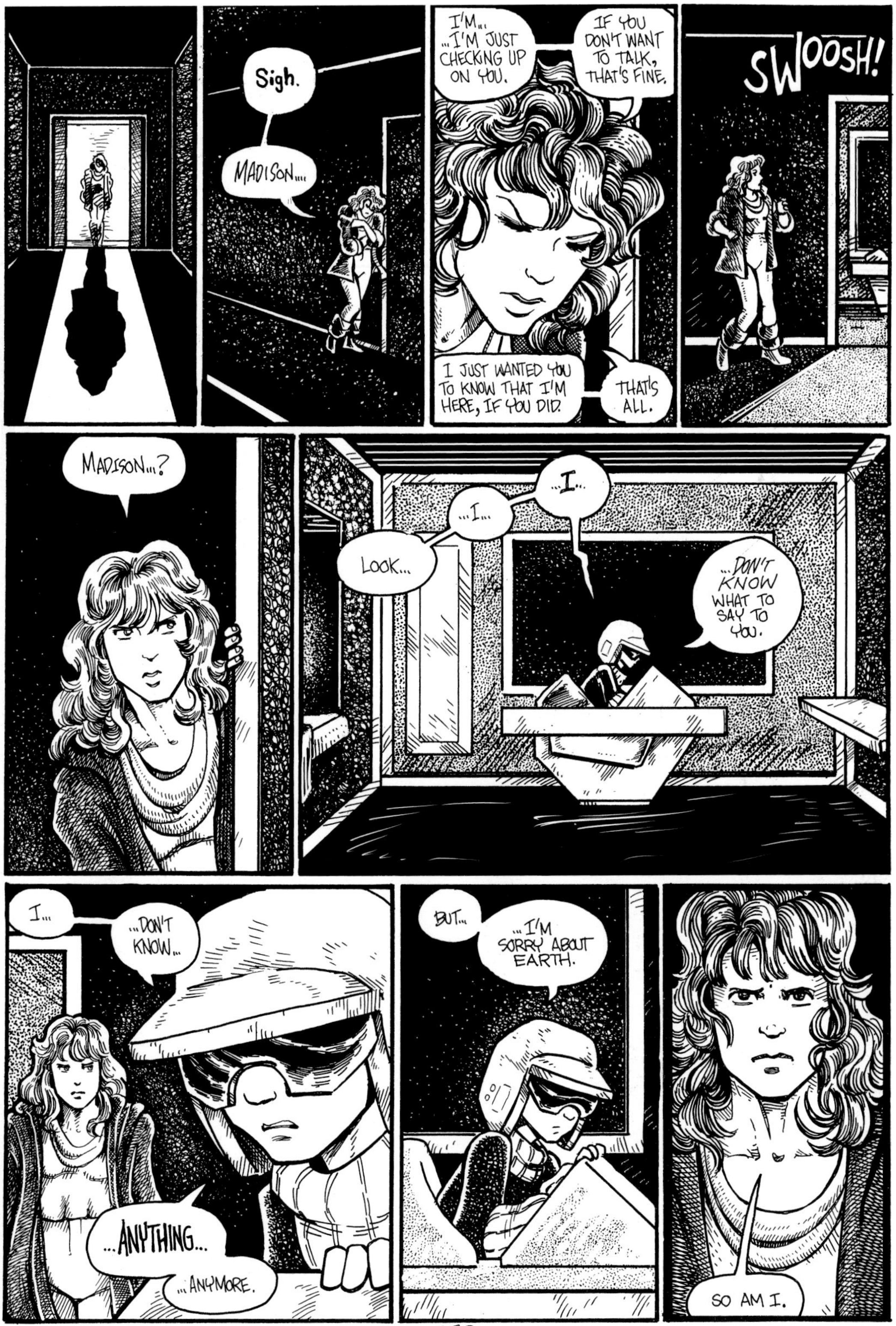
Sigh.
MADISON....
I'M... ...I'M JUST CHECKING UP ON YOU.
IF YOU DON'T WANT TO TALK, THAT'S FINE.
I JUST WANTED YOU TO KNOW THAT I'M HERE, IF YOU DID.
THAT'S ALL.
SWOOSH!
MADISON...?
LOOK...
...I...
...I...
...DON'T KNOW WHAT TO SAY TO YOU.
I...
...DON'T KNOW...
...ANYTHING...
...ANYMORE.
BUT...
...I'M SORRY ABOUT EARTH.
SO AM I.

MADISON, ARE WE STILL FRIENDS?

CASANDRA, PLEASE DON'T ASK ME THAT.

I...

...DON'T...

I DON'T KNOW.

I... WANT TO BE,

BUT,

... I DON'T *WANT* TO CARE ABOUT YOU.

OR ABOUT ELLI.

OR JOEY.

OR...

Madison...

NO!

LISTEN TO ME!

JUST LISTEN!

I'VE BEEN *THINKING,*

... A **LOT** LATELY,

... ABOUT LIFE, OR FATE, OR WHATEVER.

AND *HOW* IT CAN'T BE CONTROLLED, OR PREDICTED.

THAT YOU **CAN'T EVER** KNOW WHAT'S GOING TO HAPPEN TOMORROW, AND ...

"I *THINK*"

"... IT'S NOT **SAFE** TO CARE ABOUT ANYONE.

AND I REALLY, REALLY *HATE* LOSING PEOPLE I CARE ABOUT.

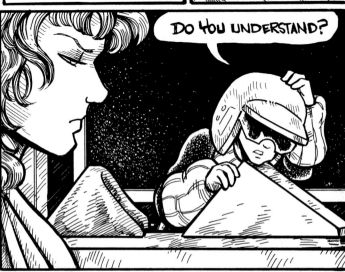

DO YOU UNDERSTAND?

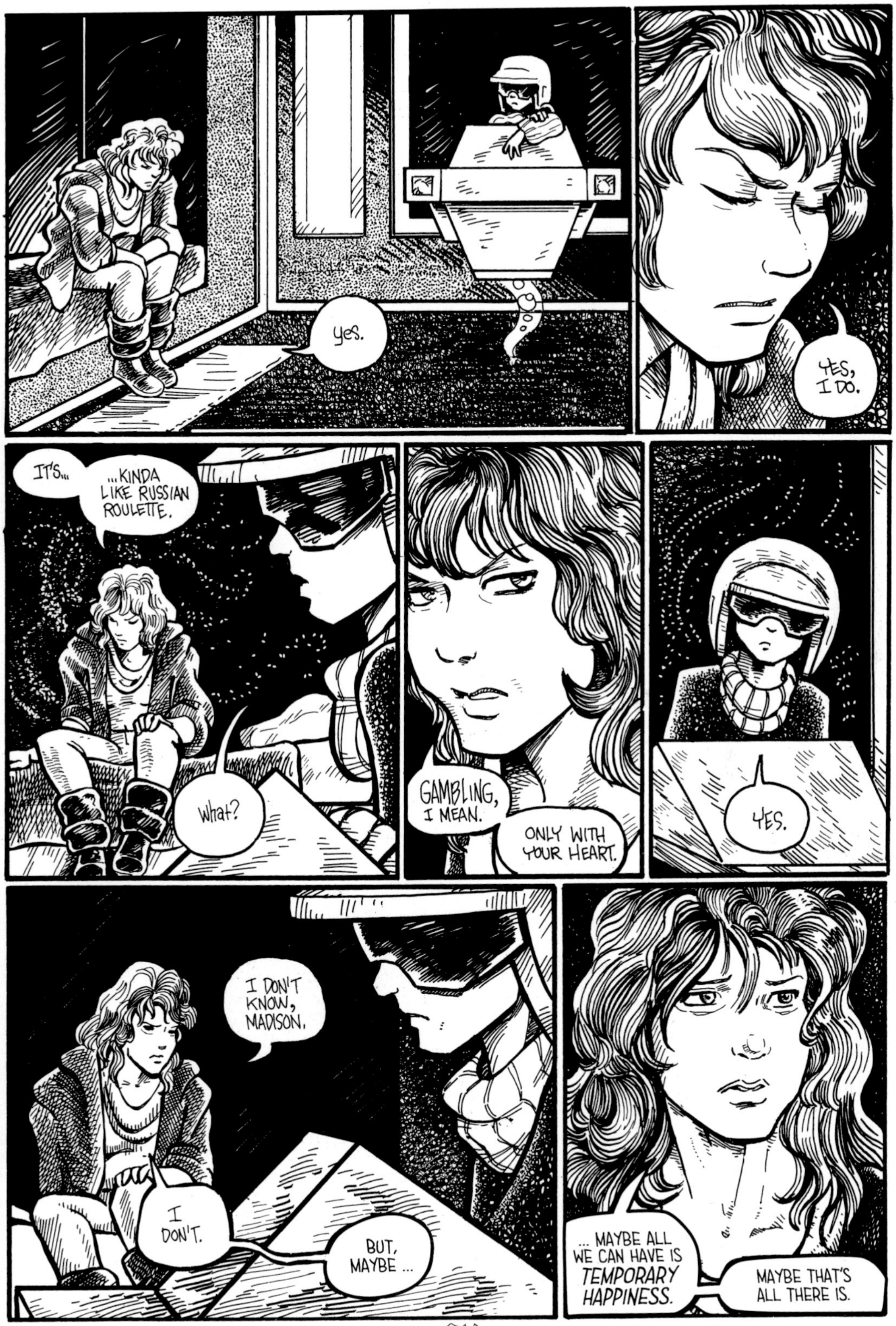
yes.
YES, I DO.
IT'S...
...KINDA LIKE RUSSIAN ROULETTE.
What?
GAMBLING, I MEAN.
ONLY WITH YOUR HEART.
YES.
I DON'T KNOW, MADISON.
I DON'T.
BUT, MAYBE ...
... MAYBE ALL WE CAN HAVE IS *TEMPORARY HAPPINESS.*
MAYBE THAT'S ALL THERE IS.

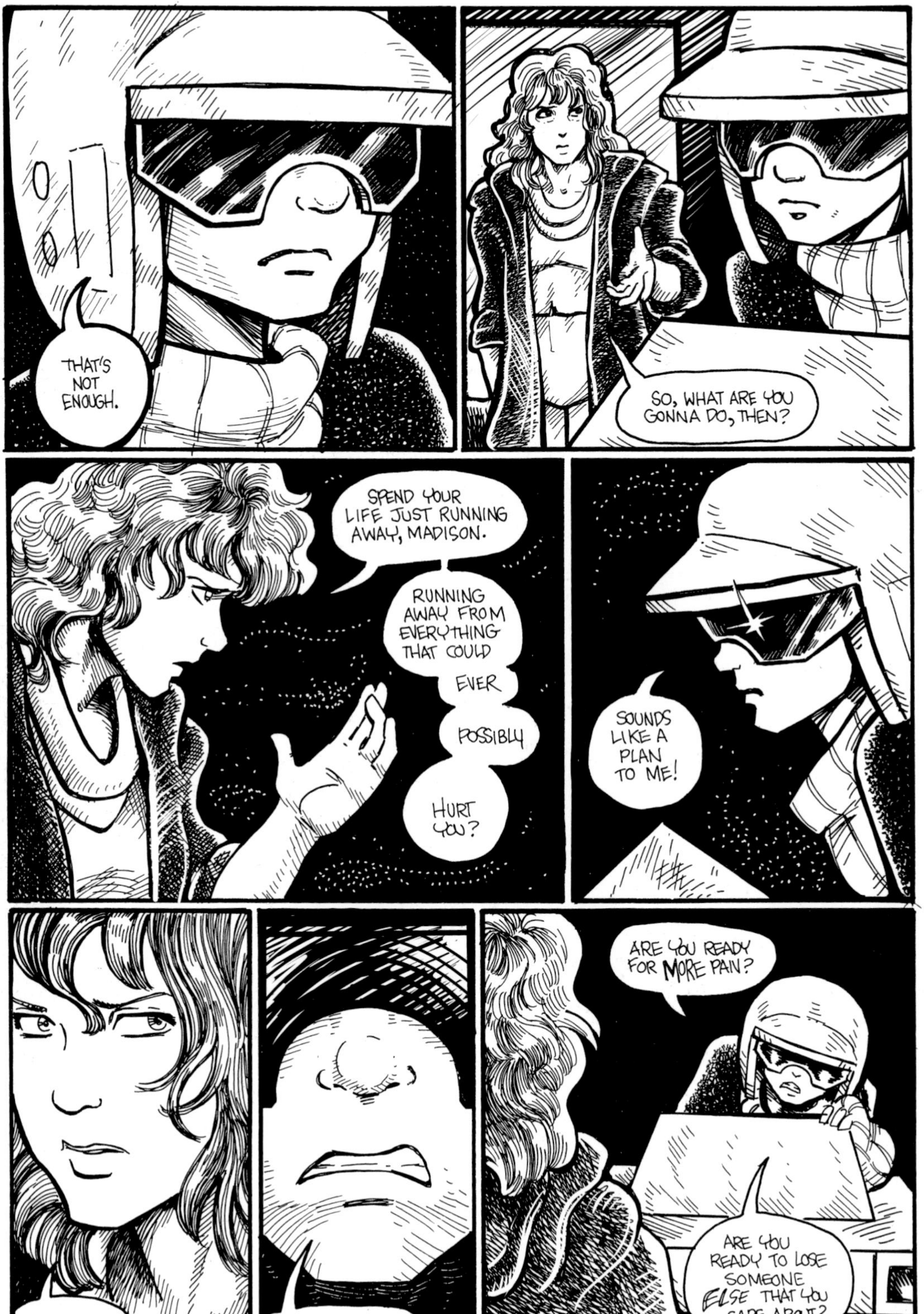
THAT'S NOT ENOUGH.
SO, WHAT ARE YOU GONNA DO, THEN?
SPEND YOUR LIFE JUST RUNNING AWAY, MADISON.
RUNNING AWAY FROM EVERYTHING THAT COULD
EVER
POSSIBLY
HURT YOU?
SOUNDS LIKE A PLAN TO ME!
Madison...
CASANDRA!
ARE YOU READY FOR MORE PAIN?
ARE YOU READY TO LOSE SOMEONE ELSE THAT YOU CARE ABOUT?

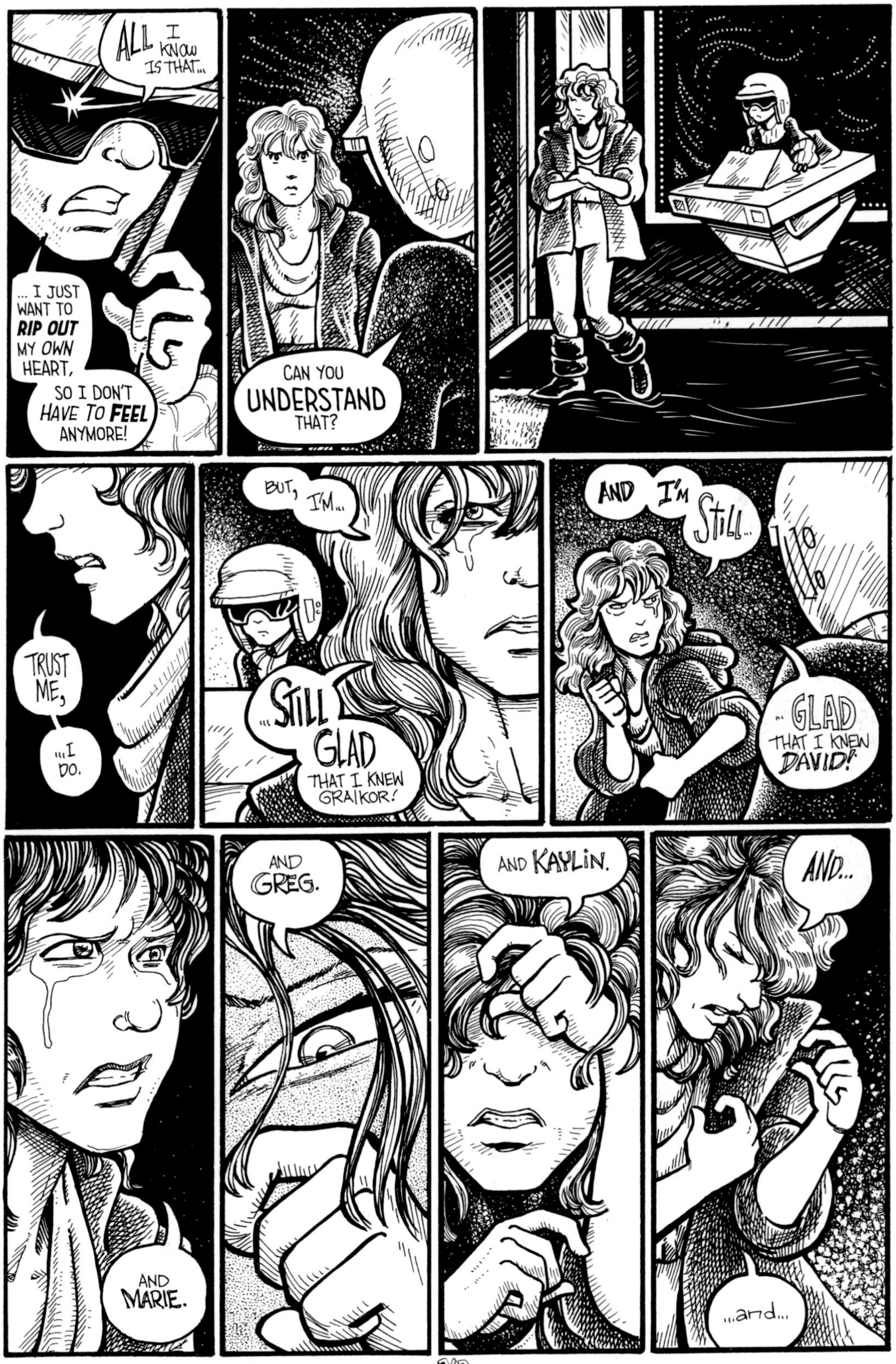
ALL I KNOW IS THAT...
... I JUST WANT TO RIP OUT MY OWN HEART,
SO I DON'T HAVE TO FEEL ANYMORE!
CAN YOU UNDERSTAND THAT?
TRUST ME,
...I DO.
BUT, I'M...
...STILL GLAD THAT I KNEW GRAIKOR!
AND I'M STILL...
...GLAD THAT I KNEW DAVID!
AND MARIE.
AND GREG.
AND KAYLIN.
AND...
...and...

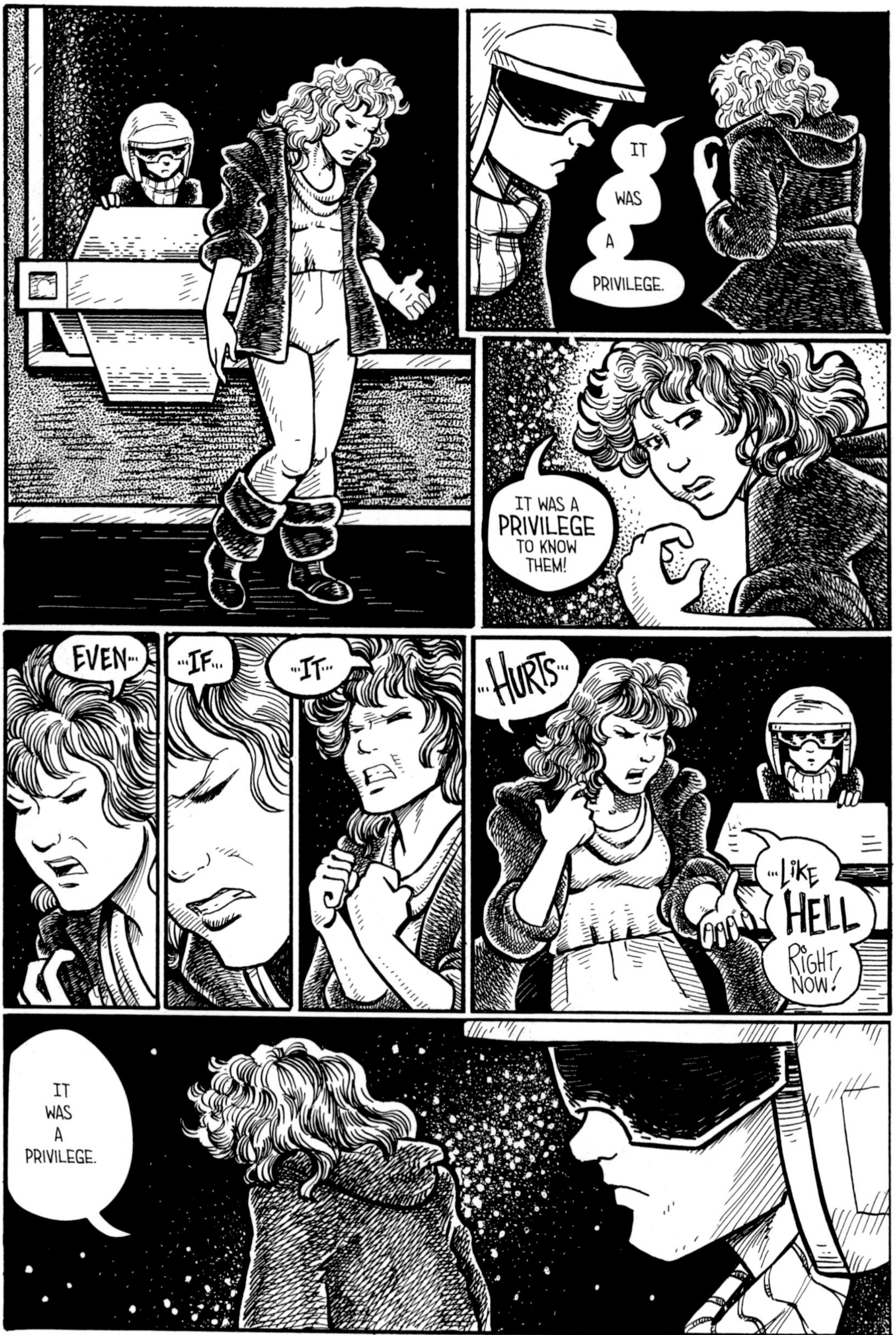
IT WAS A PRIVILEGE.
IT WAS A PRIVILEGE TO KNOW THEM!
EVEN...
...IF...
...IT...
...HURTS...
...LIKE HELL RIGHT NOW!
IT WAS A PRIVILEGE.

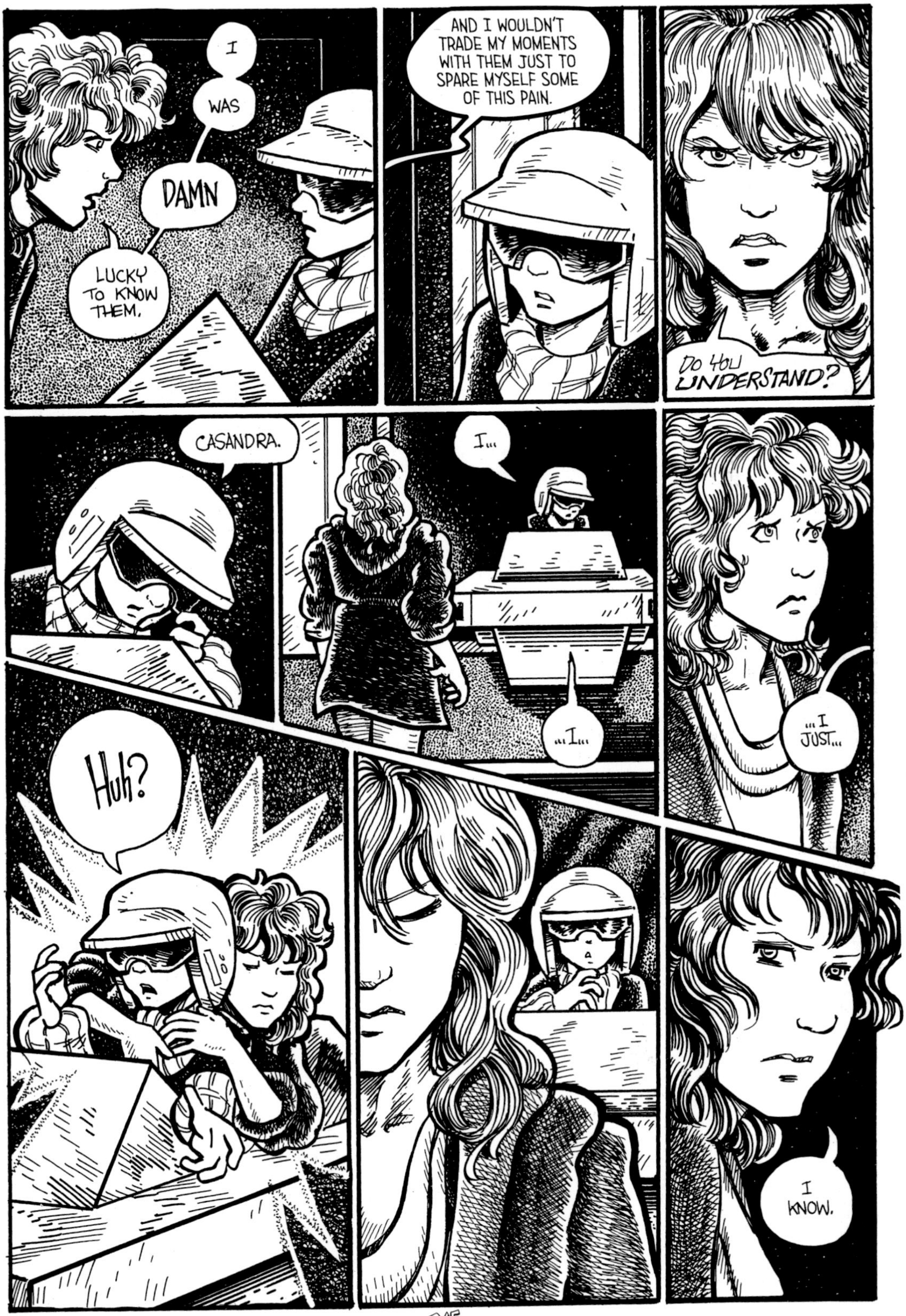
I
WAS
DAMN
LUCKY TO KNOW THEM.
AND I WOULDN'T TRADE MY MOMENTS WITH THEM JUST TO SPARE MYSELF SOME OF THIS PAIN.
DO YOU UNDERSTAND?
CASANDRA.
I...
...I...
...I JUST...
Huh?
I KNOW.

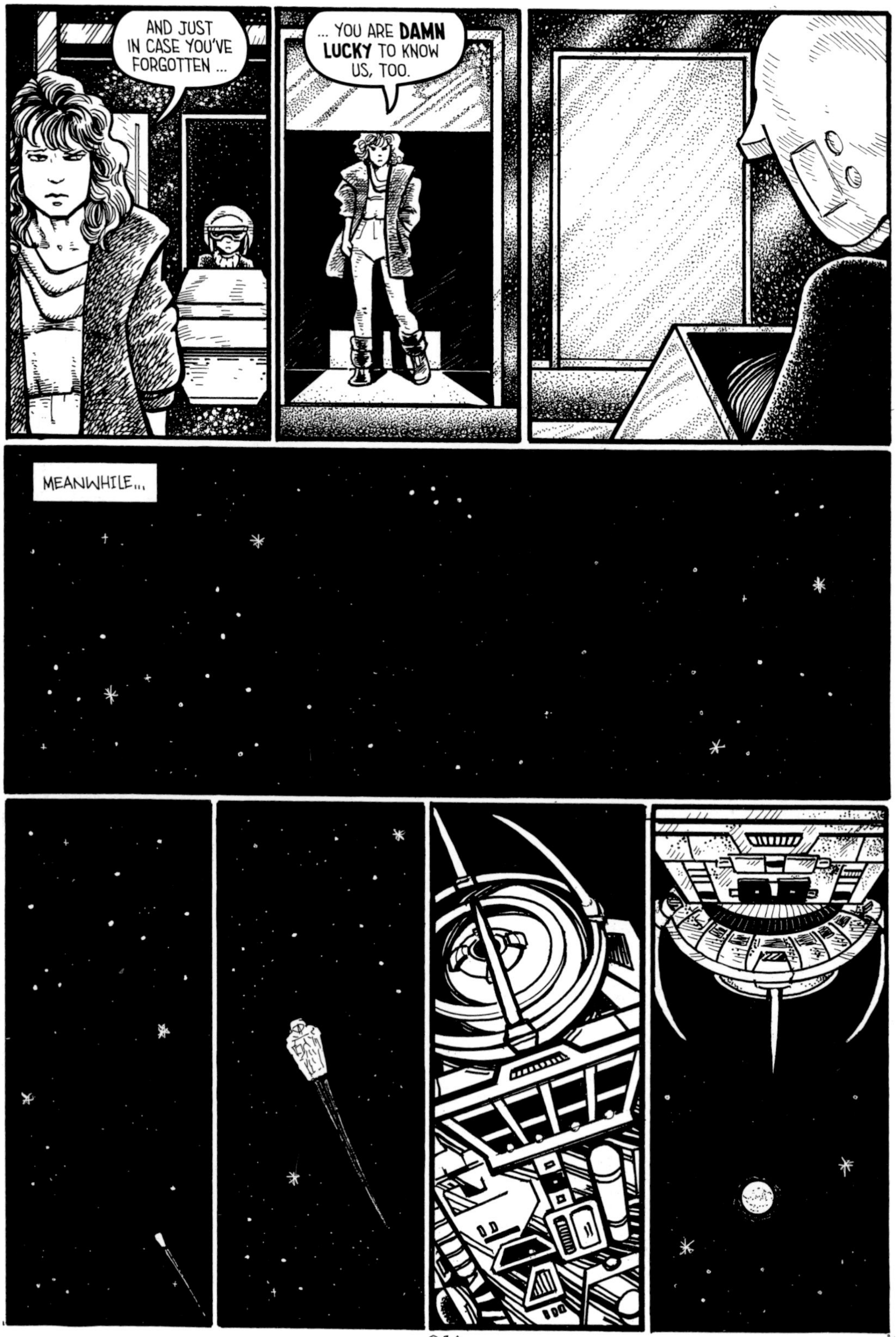
AND JUST
IN CASE YOU'VE
FORGOTTEN ...
... YOU ARE **DAMN LUCKY** TO KNOW
US, TOO.
MEANWHILE...

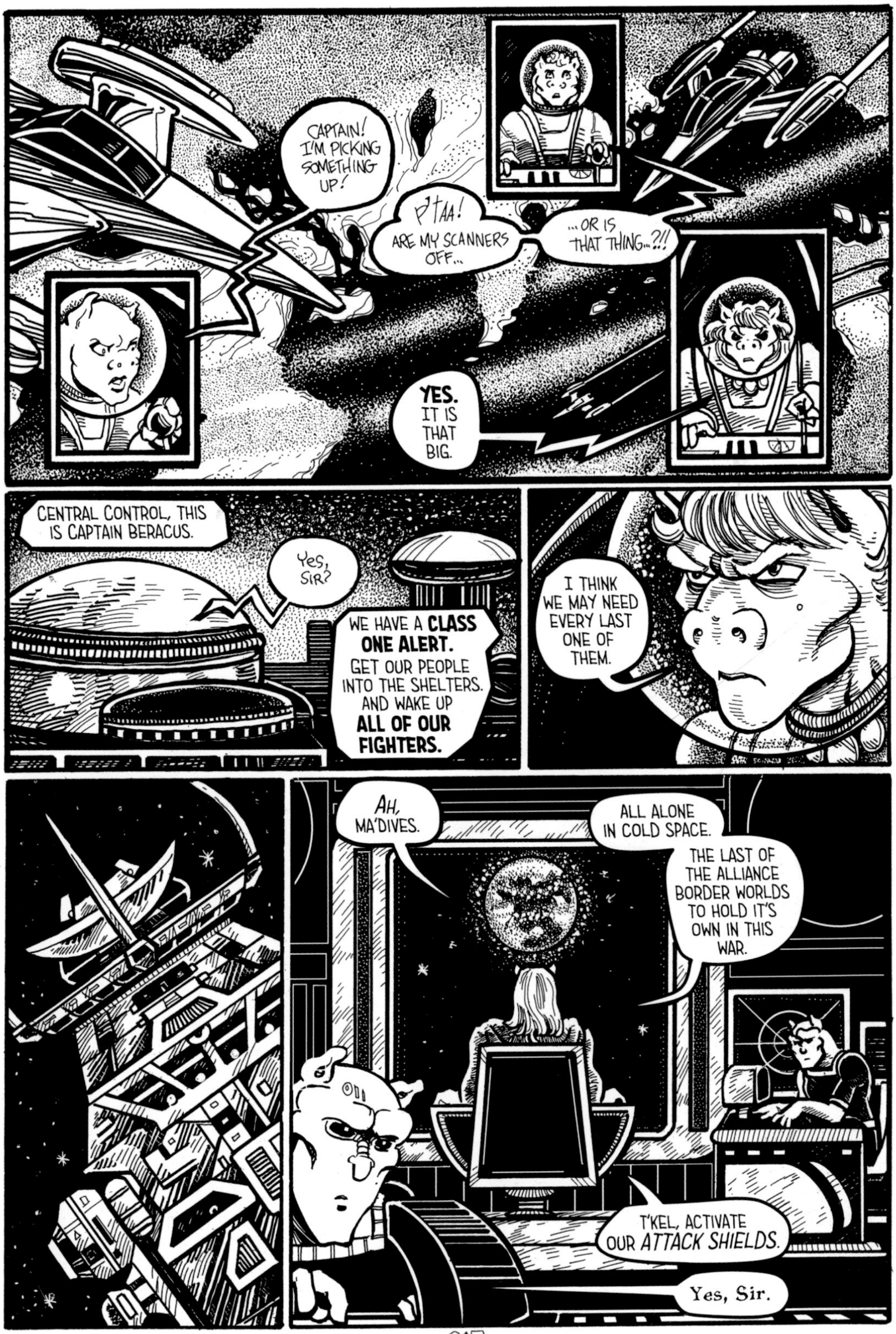

CAPTAIN! I'M PICKING SOMETHING UP!
P'TAA! ARE MY SCANNERS OFF...
...OR IS THAT THING...?!!
YES. IT IS THAT BIG.
CENTRAL CONTROL, THIS IS CAPTAIN BERACUS.
Yes, Sir?
WE HAVE A CLASS ONE ALERT. GET OUR PEOPLE INTO THE SHELTERS. AND WAKE UP ALL OF OUR FIGHTERS.
I THINK WE MAY NEED EVERY LAST ONE OF THEM.
AH, MA'DIVES.
ALL ALONE IN COLD SPACE.
THE LAST OF THE ALLIANCE BORDER WORLDS TO HOLD IT'S OWN IN THIS WAR.
T'KEL, ACTIVATE OUR ATTACK SHIELDS.
Yes, Sir.

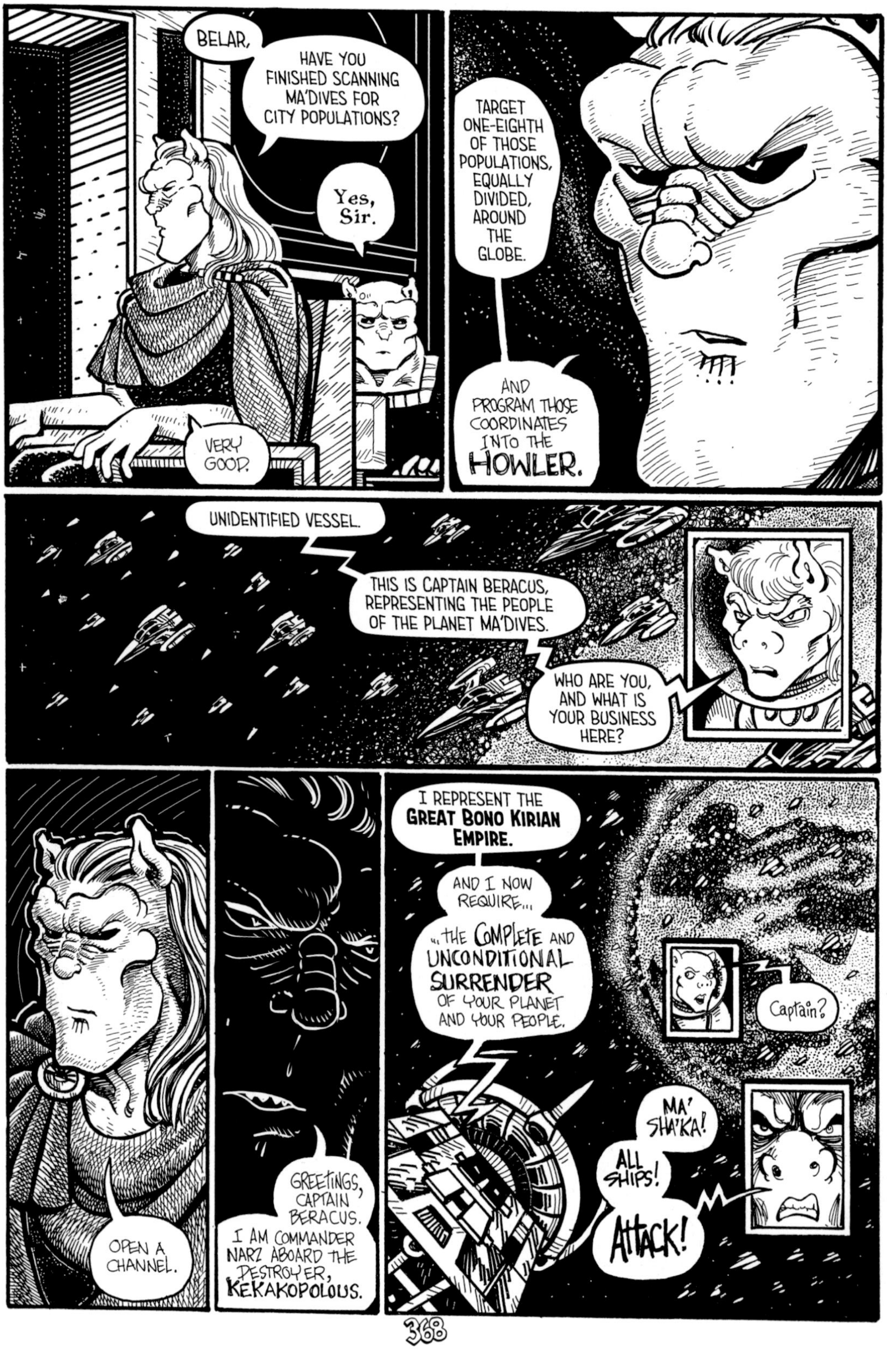
BELAR,
HAVE YOU FINISHED SCANNING MA'DIVES FOR CITY POPULATIONS?
Yes, Sir.
VERY GOOD.
TARGET ONE-EIGHTH OF THOSE POPULATIONS, EQUALLY DIVIDED, AROUND THE GLOBE.
AND PROGRAM THOSE COORDINATES INTO THE HOWLER.
UNIDENTIFIED VESSEL.
THIS IS CAPTAIN BERACUS, REPRESENTING THE PEOPLE OF THE PLANET MA'DIVES.
WHO ARE YOU, AND WHAT IS YOUR BUSINESS HERE?
OPEN A CHANNEL.
GREETINGS, CAPTAIN BERACUS.
I AM COMMANDER NARZ ABOARD THE DESTROYER, KEKAKOPOLOUS.
I REPRESENT THE GREAT BONO KIRIAN EMPIRE.
AND I NOW REQUIRE...
...THE COMPLETE AND UNCONDITIONAL SURRENDER OF YOUR PLANET AND YOUR PEOPLE.
Captain?
MA' SHA'KA!
ALL SHIPS!
ATTACK!

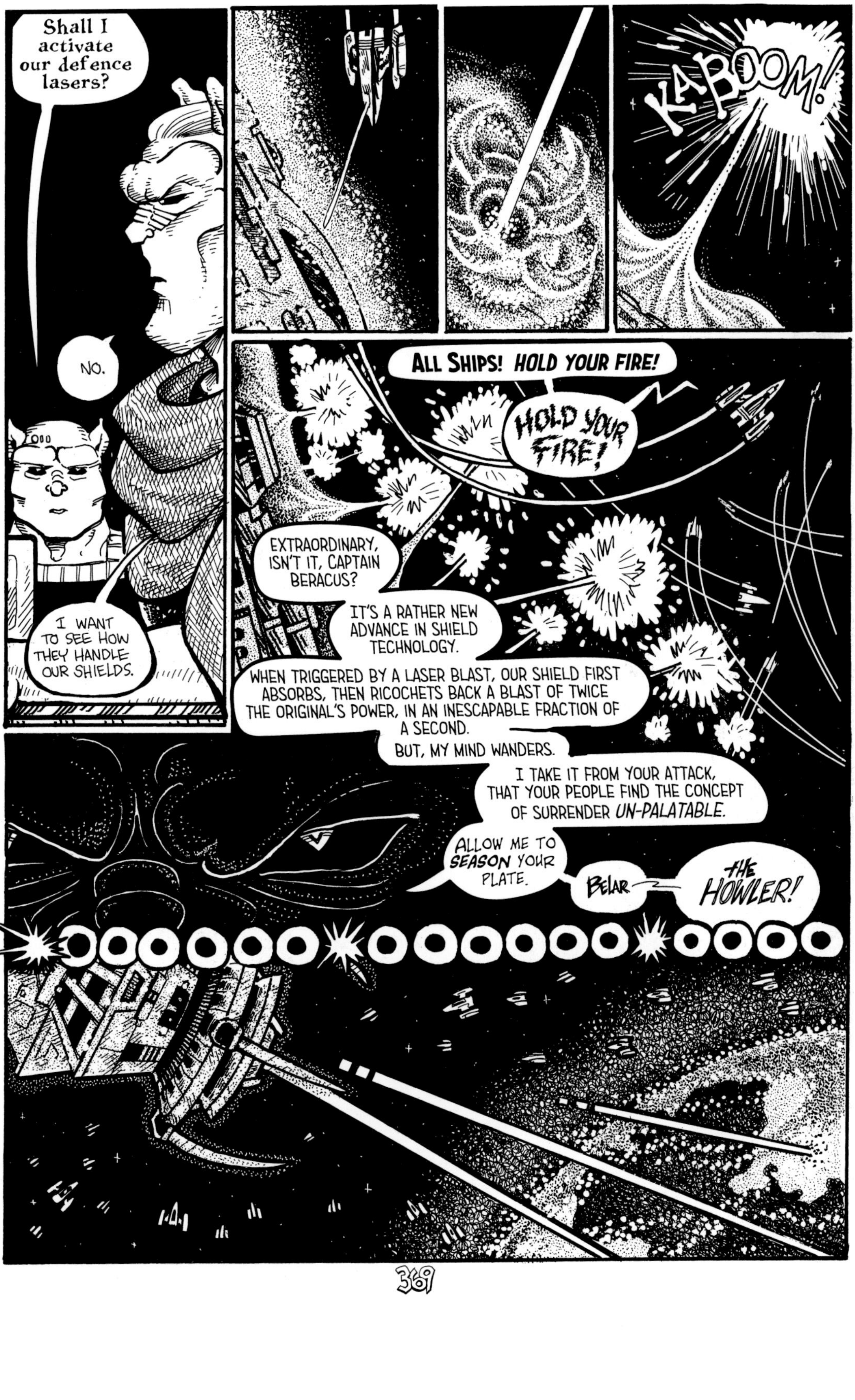
Shall I activate our defence lasers?
NO.
I WANT TO SEE HOW THEY HANDLE OUR SHIELDS.
KABOOM!
ALL SHIPS! HOLD YOUR FIRE!
HOLD YOUR FIRE!
EXTRAORDINARY, ISN'T IT, CAPTAIN BERACUS?
IT'S A RATHER NEW ADVANCE IN SHIELD TECHNOLOGY.
WHEN TRIGGERED BY A LASER BLAST, OUR SHIELD FIRST ABSORBS, THEN RICOCHETS BACK A BLAST OF TWICE THE ORIGINAL'S POWER, IN AN INESCAPABLE FRACTION OF A SECOND.
BUT, MY MIND WANDERS.
I TAKE IT FROM YOUR ATTACK, THAT YOUR PEOPLE FIND THE CONCEPT OF SURRENDER UN-PALATABLE.
ALLOW ME TO SEASON YOUR PLATE.
BELAR
THE HOWLER!

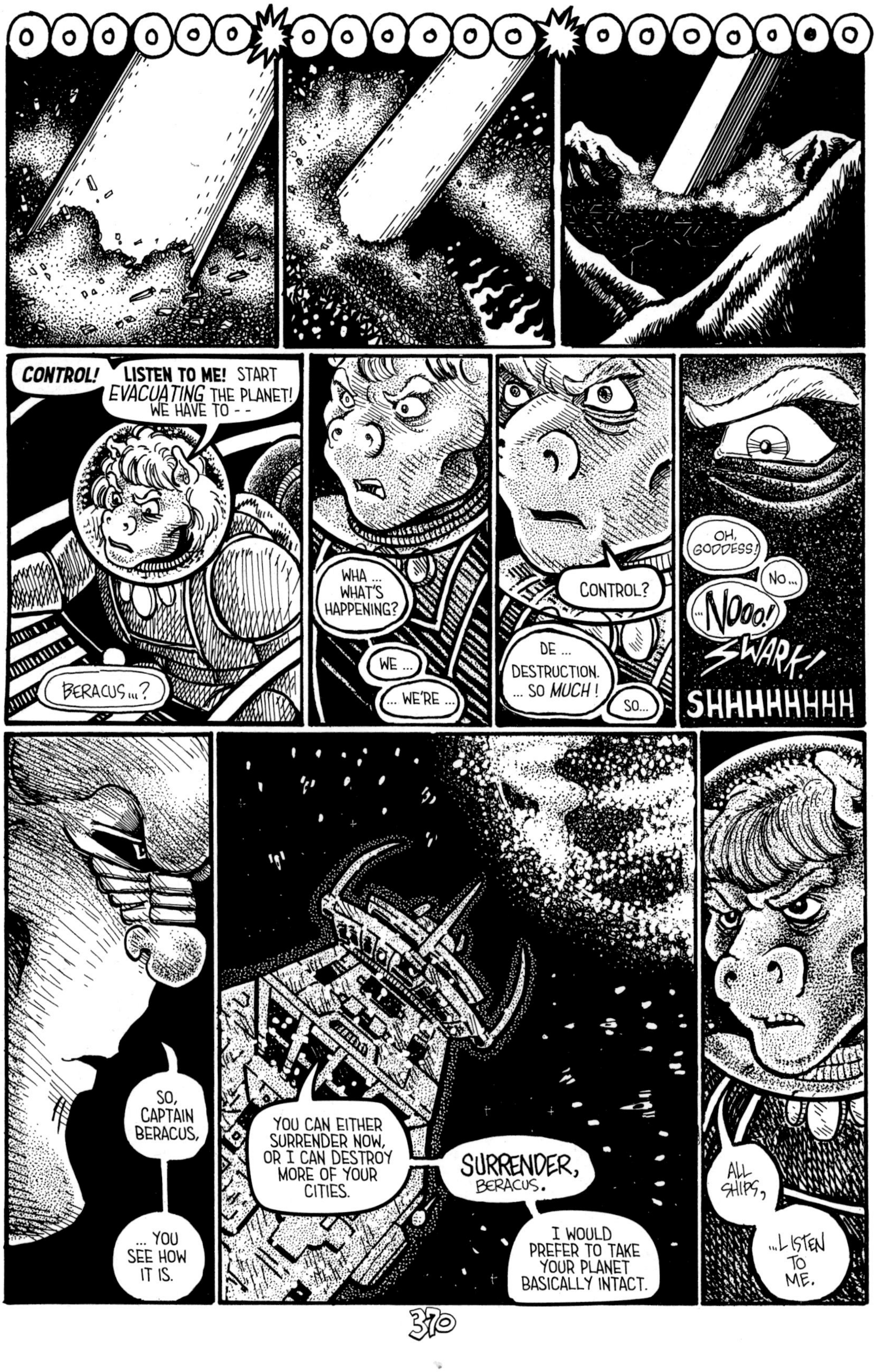

CONTROL!
LISTEN TO ME! START EVACUATING THE PLANET! WE HAVE TO - -
BERACUS...?
WHA ... WHAT'S HAPPENING?
WE ...
... WE'RE ...
CONTROL?
DE ... DESTRUCTION. ... SO MUCH!
SO...
OH, GODDESS!
NO...
...NOOO!
SWARK!
SHHHHHHHH
SO, CAPTAIN BERACUS,
... YOU SEE HOW IT IS.
YOU CAN EITHER SURRENDER NOW, OR I CAN DESTROY MORE OF YOUR CITIES.
SURRENDER, BERACUS.
I WOULD PREFER TO TAKE YOUR PLANET BASICALLY INTACT.
ALL SHIPS,
...LISTEN TO ME.

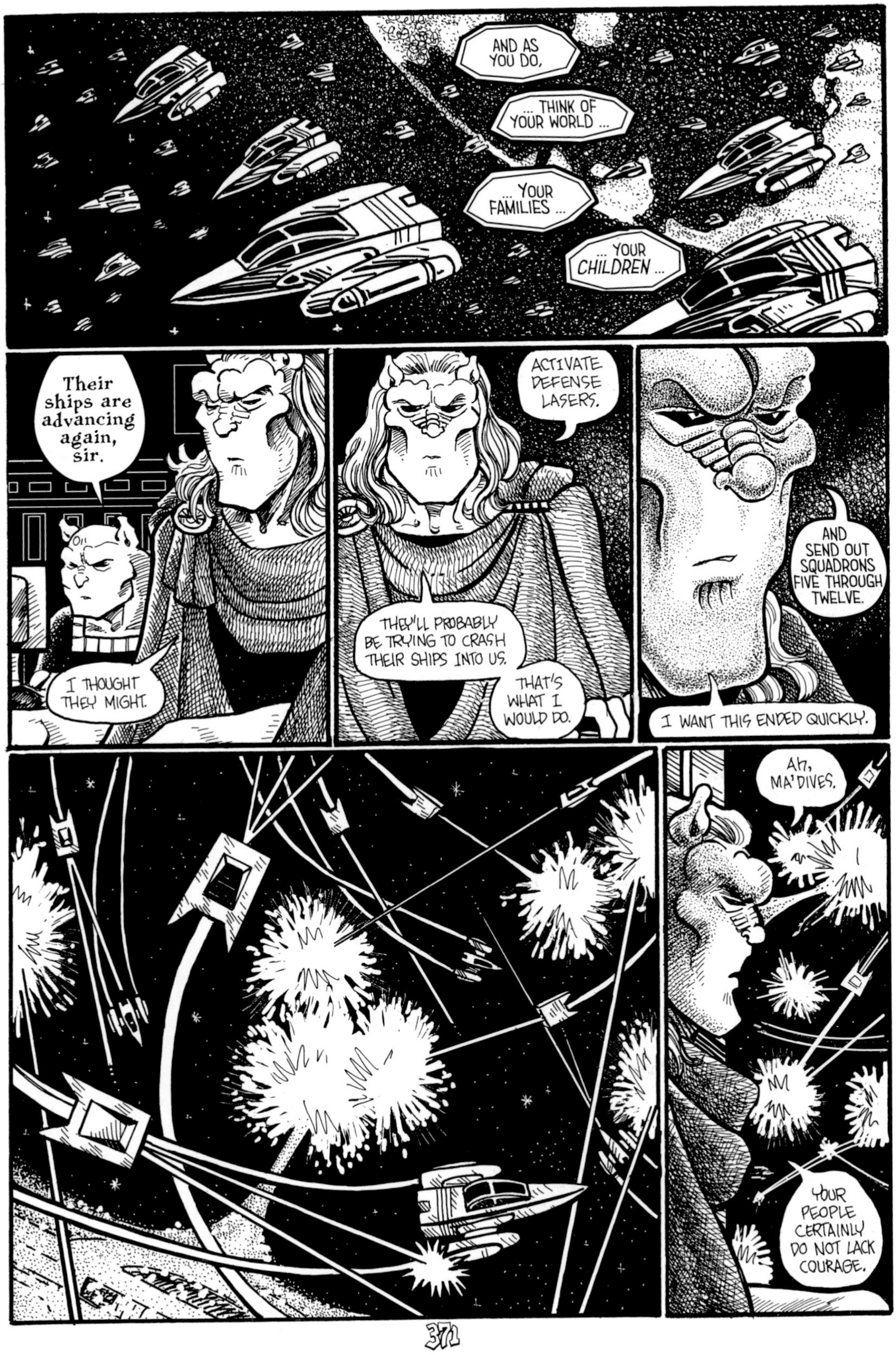
AND AS YOU DO,
... THINK OF YOUR WORLD ...
... YOUR FAMILIES ...
... YOUR CHILDREN ...
Their ships are advancing again, sir.
I THOUGHT THEY MIGHT.
ACTIVATE DEFENSE LASERS.
THEY'LL PROBABLY BE TRYING TO CRASH THEIR SHIPS INTO US.
THAT'S WHAT I WOULD DO.
AND SEND OUT SQUADRONS FIVE THROUGH TWELVE.
I WANT THIS ENDED QUICKLY.
Ah, MA'DIVES.
YOUR PEOPLE CERTAINLY DO NOT LACK COURAGE.

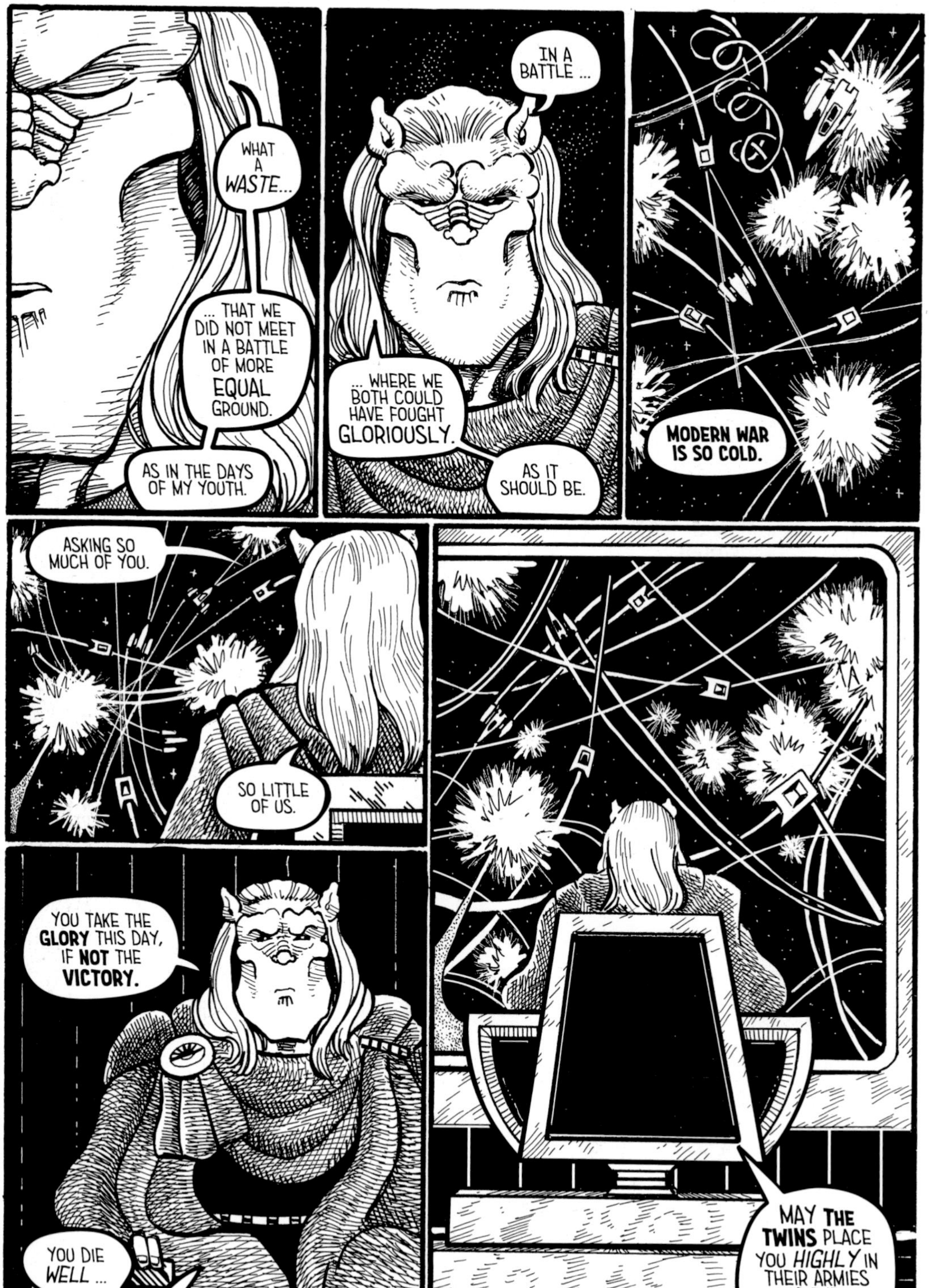
WHAT A WASTE...
... THAT WE DID NOT MEET IN A BATTLE OF MORE EQUAL GROUND.
AS IN THE DAYS OF MY YOUTH.
IN A BATTLE ...
... WHERE WE BOTH COULD HAVE FOUGHT GLORIOUSLY.
AS IT SHOULD BE.
MODERN WAR IS SO COLD.
ASKING SO MUCH OF YOU.
SO LITTLE OF US.
YOU TAKE THE GLORY THIS DAY, IF NOT THE VICTORY.
YOU DIE WELL ...
... WITH COURAGE.
MAY THE TWINS PLACE YOU HIGHLY IN THEIR ARMIES OF THE DARKLANDS.

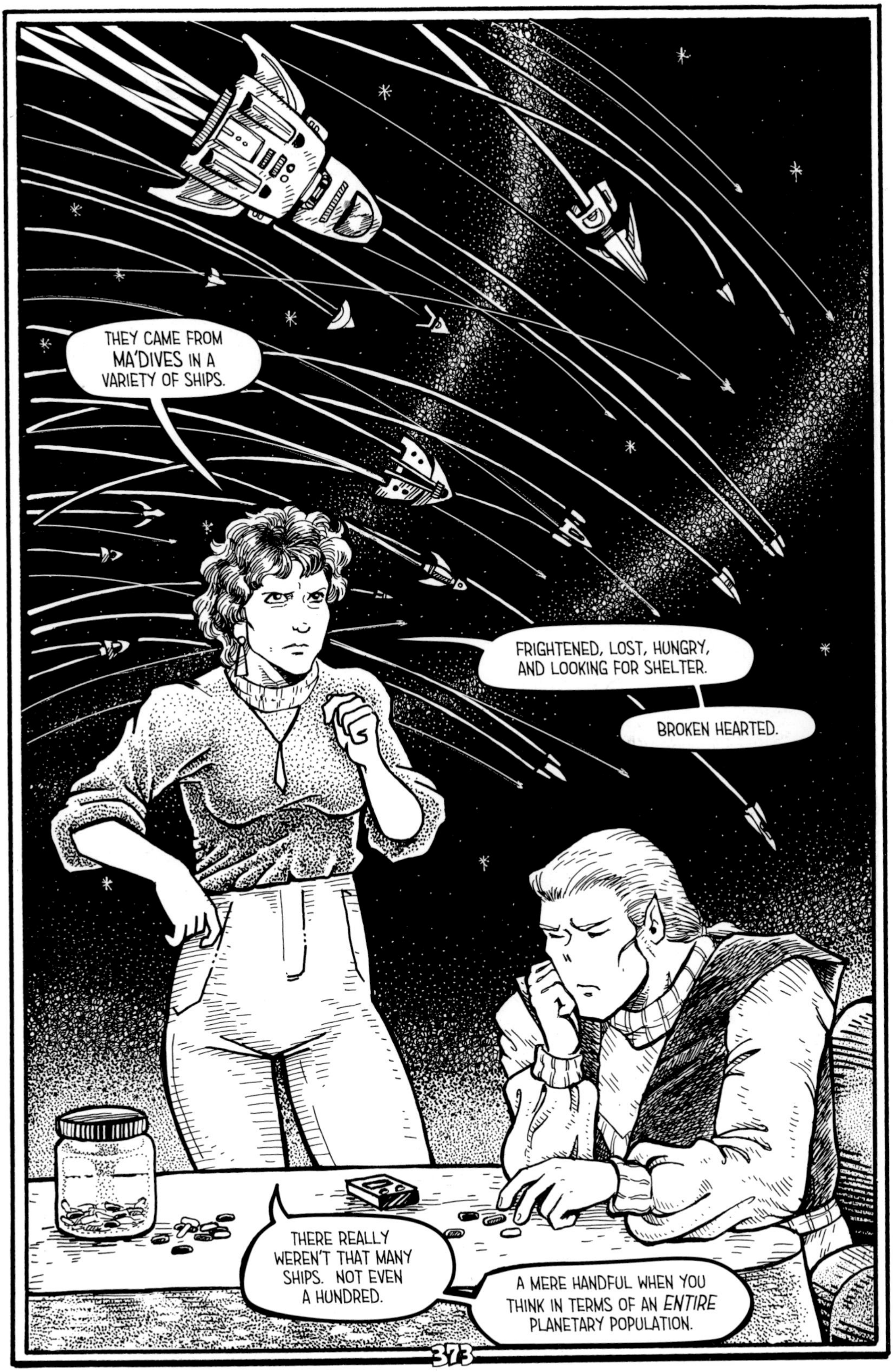
THEY CAME FROM MA'DIVES IN A VARIETY OF SHIPS.
FRIGHTENED, LOST, HUNGRY, AND LOOKING FOR SHELTER.
BROKEN HEARTED.
THERE REALLY WEREN'T THAT MANY SHIPS. NOT EVEN A HUNDRED.
A MERE HANDFUL WHEN YOU THINK IN TERMS OF AN *ENTIRE* PLANETARY POPULATION.

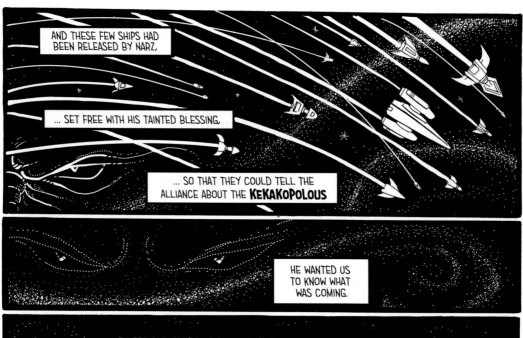

AND THESE FEW SHIPS HAD BEEN RELEASED BY NARZ,

... SET FREE WITH HIS TAINTED BLESSING,

... SO THAT THEY COULD TELL THE ALLIANCE ABOUT THE **KEKAKOPOLOUS**

HE WANTED US TO KNOW WHAT WAS COMING.

TO SET THE SEEDS OF FEAR. AND GIVE THEM TIME TO GERMINATE.

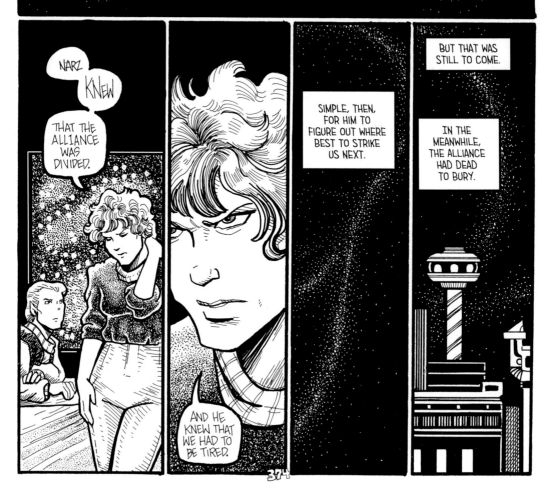

NARZ KNEW THAT THE ALLIANCE WAS DIVIDED.

AND HE KNEW THAT WE HAD TO BE TIRED.

SIMPLE, THEN, FOR HIM TO FIGURE OUT WHERE BEST TO STRIKE US NEXT.

BUT THAT WAS STILL TO COME.

IN THE MEANWHILE, THE ALLIANCE HAD DEAD TO BURY.

374

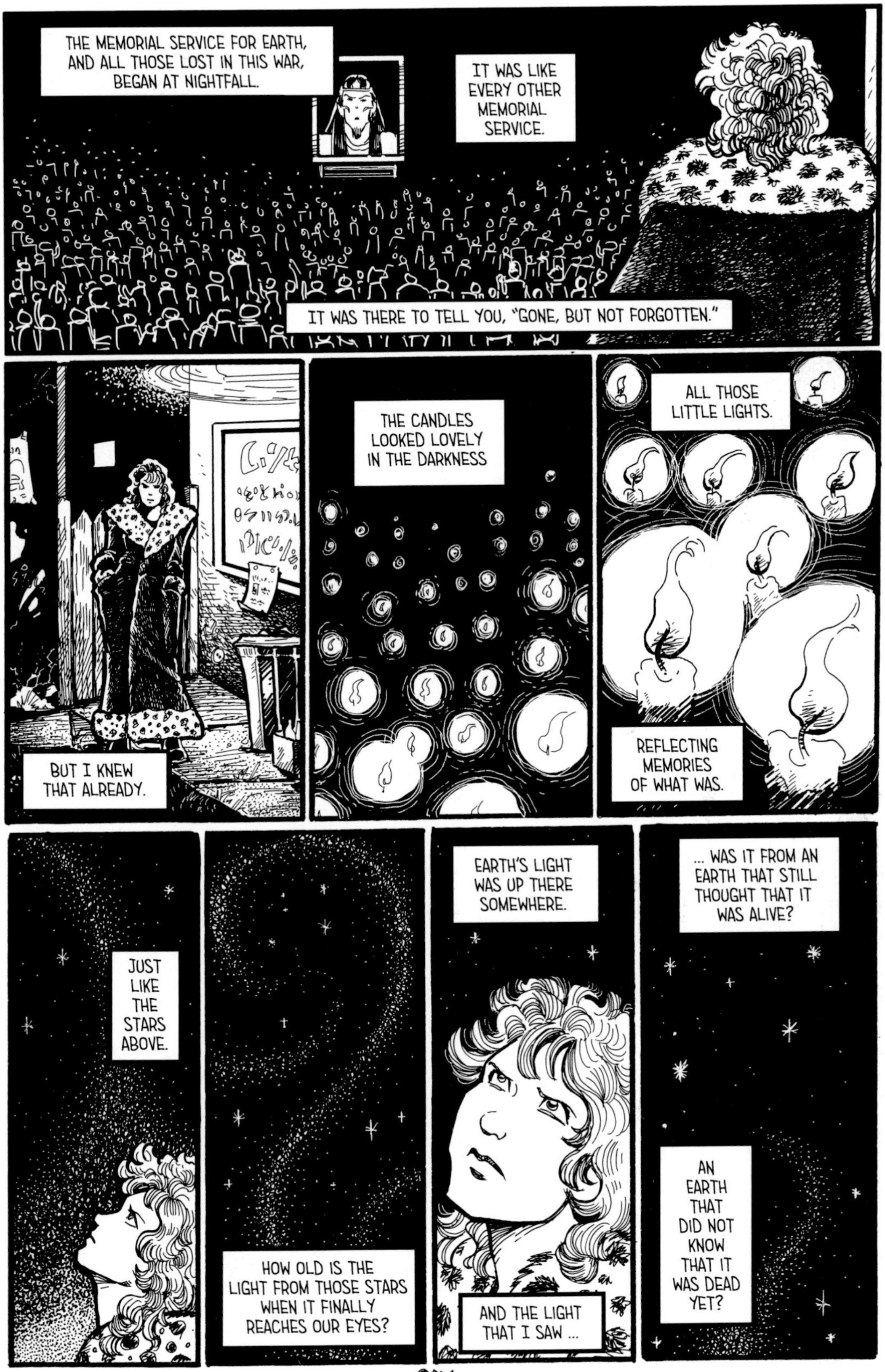
THE MEMORIAL SERVICE FOR EARTH, AND ALL THOSE LOST IN THIS WAR, BEGAN AT NIGHTFALL.
IT WAS LIKE EVERY OTHER MEMORIAL SERVICE.
IT WAS THERE TO TELL YOU, "GONE, BUT NOT FORGOTTEN."
BUT I KNEW THAT ALREADY.
THE CANDLES LOOKED LOVELY IN THE DARKNESS
ALL THOSE LITTLE LIGHTS.
REFLECTING MEMORIES OF WHAT WAS.
JUST LIKE THE STARS ABOVE.
HOW OLD IS THE LIGHT FROM THOSE STARS WHEN IT FINALLY REACHES OUR EYES?
EARTH'S LIGHT WAS UP THERE SOMEWHERE.
AND THE LIGHT THAT I SAW ...
... WAS IT FROM AN EARTH THAT STILL THOUGHT THAT IT WAS ALIVE?
AN EARTH THAT DID NOT KNOW THAT IT WAS DEAD YET?

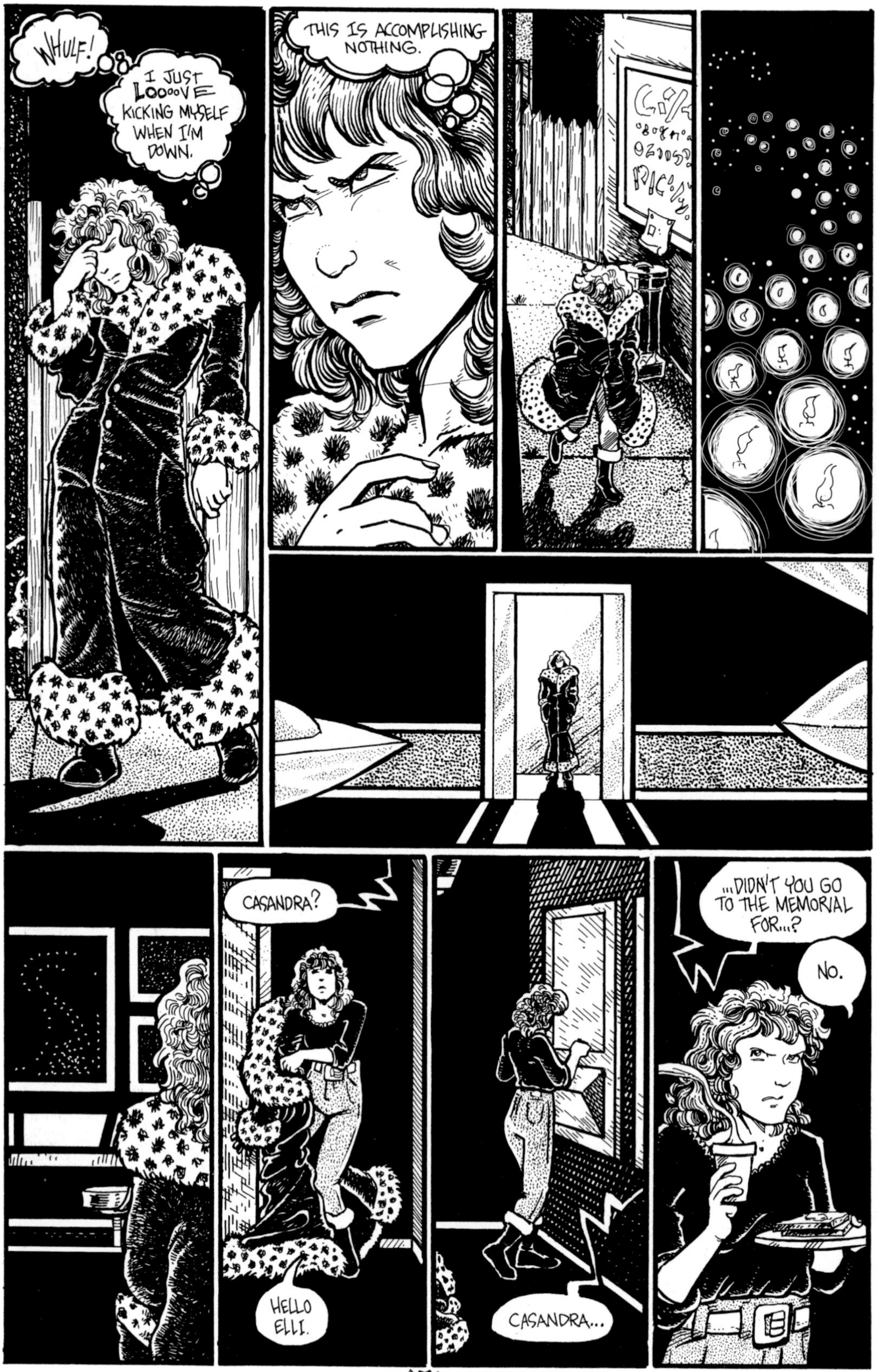
WHULF!
I JUST LOOOOVE KICKING MYSELF WHEN I'M DOWN.
THIS IS ACCOMPLISHING NOTHING.
CASANDRA?
HELLO ELLI.
CASANDRA...
...DIDN'T YOU GO TO THE MEMORIAL FOR...?
NO.

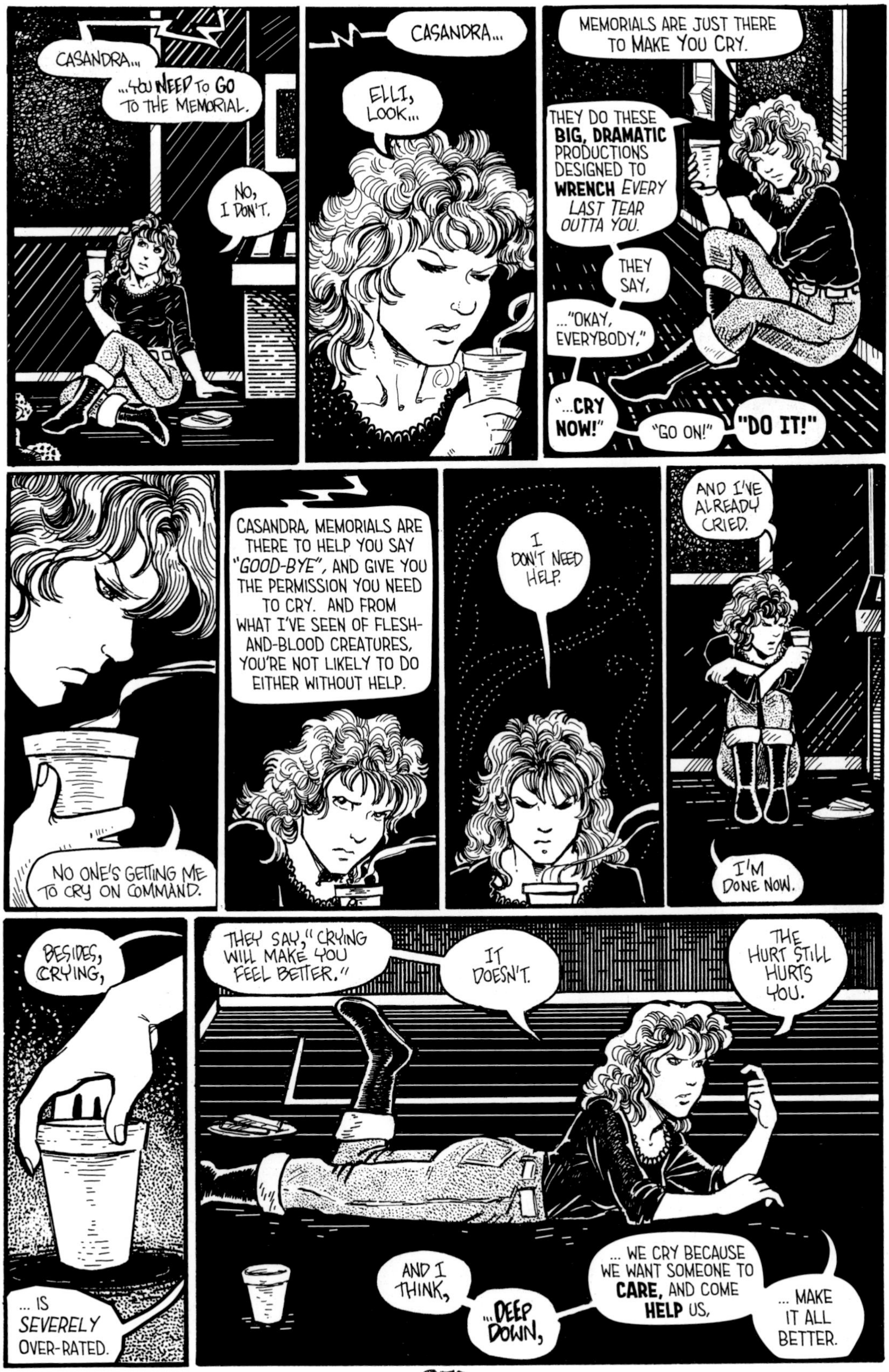
CASANDRA...
...YOU NEED TO GO TO THE MEMORIAL.
NO, I DON'T.
CASANDRA...
ELLI, LOOK...
MEMORIALS ARE JUST THERE TO MAKE YOU CRY.
THEY DO THESE BIG, DRAMATIC PRODUCTIONS DESIGNED TO WRENCH EVERY LAST TEAR OUTTA YOU.
THEY SAY,
..."OKAY, EVERYBODY,"
"...CRY NOW!"
"GO ON!"
"DO IT!"
NO ONE'S GETTING ME TO CRY ON COMMAND.
CASANDRA, MEMORIALS ARE THERE TO HELP YOU SAY "GOOD-BYE", AND GIVE YOU THE PERMISSION YOU NEED TO CRY. AND FROM WHAT I'VE SEEN OF FLESH-AND-BLOOD CREATURES, YOU'RE NOT LIKELY TO DO EITHER WITHOUT HELP.
I DON'T NEED HELP.
AND I'VE ALREADY CRIED.
I'M DONE NOW.
BESIDES, CRYING,
... IS SEVERELY OVER-RATED.
THEY SAY, "CRYING WILL MAKE YOU FEEL BETTER."
IT DOESN'T.
THE HURT STILL HURTS YOU.
AND I THINK,
...DEEP DOWN,
... WE CRY BECAUSE WE WANT SOMEONE TO CARE, AND COME HELP US,
... MAKE IT ALL BETTER.

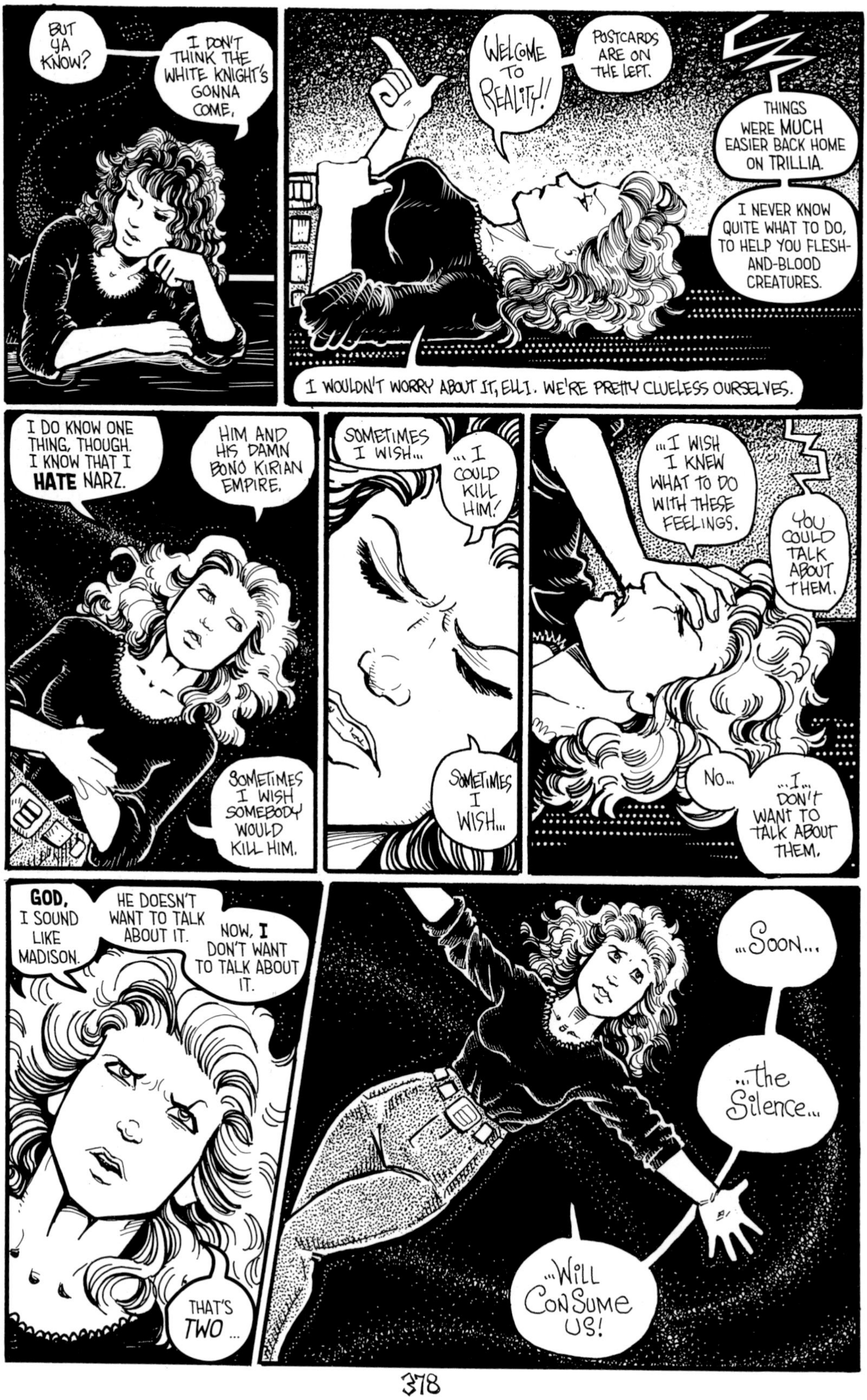
BUT YA KNOW?
I DON'T THINK THE WHITE KNIGHT'S GONNA COME.
WELCOME TO REALITY!!
POSTCARDS ARE ON THE LEFT.
THINGS WERE MUCH EASIER BACK HOME ON TRILLIA.
I NEVER KNOW QUITE WHAT TO DO, TO HELP YOU FLESH-AND-BLOOD CREATURES.
I WOULDN'T WORRY ABOUT IT, ELLI. WE'RE PRETTY CLUELESS OURSELVES.
I DO KNOW ONE THING, THOUGH. I KNOW THAT I HATE NARZ.
HIM AND HIS DAMN BONO KIRIAN EMPIRE.
SOMETIMES I WISH SOMEBODY WOULD KILL HIM.
SOMETIMES I WISH...
...I COULD KILL HIM!
SOMETIMES I WISH...
...I WISH I KNEW WHAT TO DO WITH THESE FEELINGS.
YOU COULD TALK ABOUT THEM.
NO...
...I... DON'T WANT TO TALK ABOUT THEM.
GOD, I SOUND LIKE MADISON.
HE DOESN'T WANT TO TALK ABOUT IT.
NOW, I DON'T WANT TO TALK ABOUT IT.
THAT'S TWO...
...SOON...
...THE SILENCE...
...WILL CONSUME US!

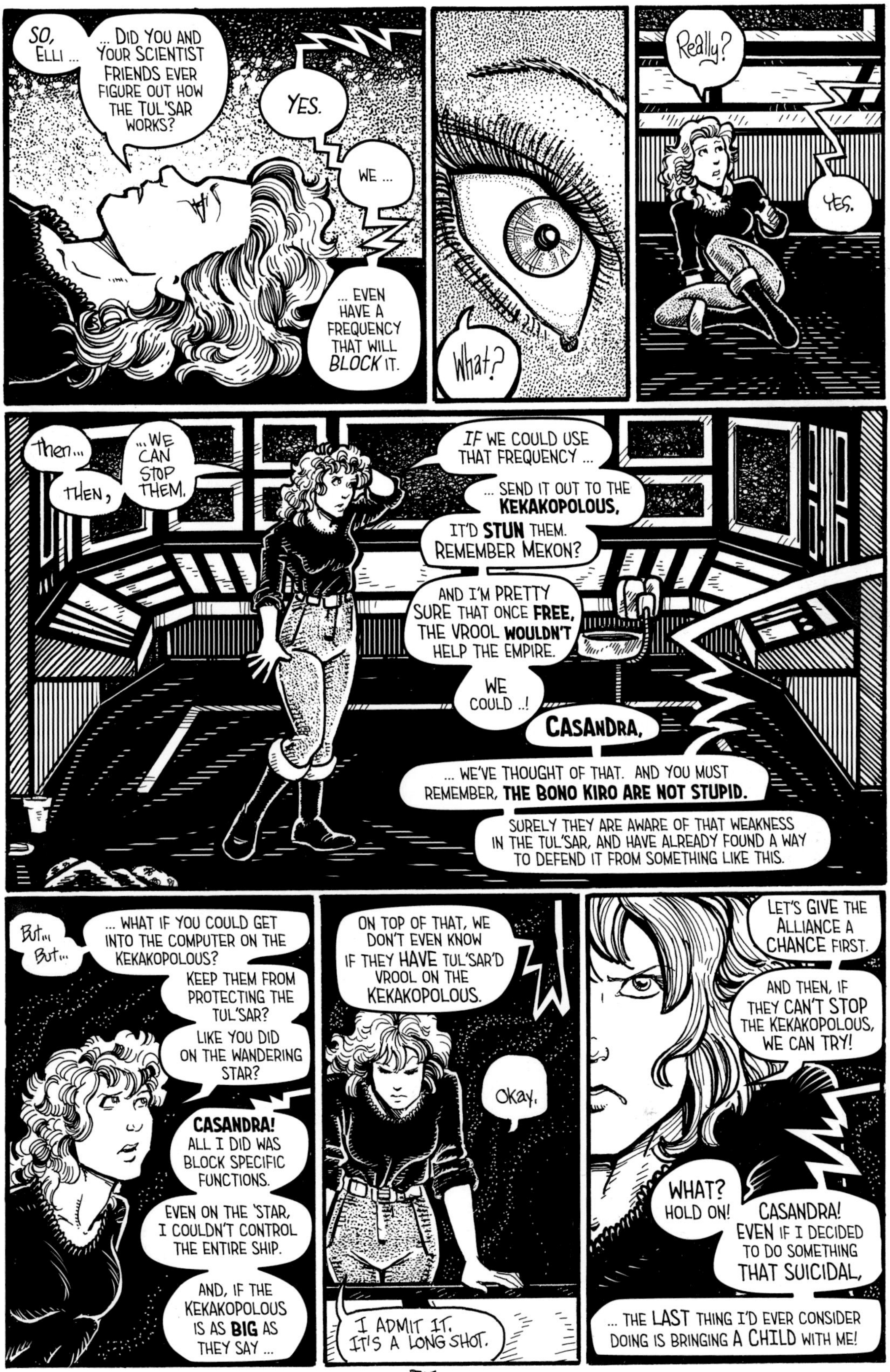
SO, ELLI ...
... DID YOU AND YOUR SCIENTIST FRIENDS EVER FIGURE OUT HOW THE TUL'SAR WORKS?
YES.
WE ...
... EVEN HAVE A FREQUENCY THAT WILL BLOCK IT.
What?
Really?
YES.
Then...
THEN,
...WE CAN STOP THEM.
IF WE COULD USE THAT FREQUENCY ...
... SEND IT OUT TO THE KEKAKOPOLOUS,
IT'D STUN THEM. REMEMBER MEKON?
AND I'M PRETTY SURE THAT ONCE FREE, THE VROOL WOULDN'T HELP THE EMPIRE.
WE COULD ..!
CASANDRA,
... WE'VE THOUGHT OF THAT. AND YOU MUST REMEMBER, THE BONO KIRO ARE NOT STUPID.
SURELY THEY ARE AWARE OF THAT WEAKNESS IN THE TUL'SAR, AND HAVE ALREADY FOUND A WAY TO DEFEND IT FROM SOMETHING LIKE THIS.
But... But...
... WHAT IF YOU COULD GET INTO THE COMPUTER ON THE KEKAKOPOLOUS?
KEEP THEM FROM PROTECTING THE TUL'SAR?
LIKE YOU DID ON THE WANDERING STAR?
CASANDRA! ALL I DID WAS BLOCK SPECIFIC FUNCTIONS.
EVEN ON THE 'STAR, I COULDN'T CONTROL THE ENTIRE SHIP.
AND, IF THE KEKAKOPOLOUS IS AS BIG AS THEY SAY ...
ON TOP OF THAT, WE DON'T EVEN KNOW IF THEY HAVE TUL'SAR'D VROOL ON THE KEKAKOPOLOUS.
Okay.
I ADMIT IT. IT'S A LONG SHOT.
LET'S GIVE THE ALLIANCE A CHANCE FIRST.
AND THEN, IF THEY CAN'T STOP THE KEKAKOPOLOUS, WE CAN TRY!
WHAT? HOLD ON!
CASANDRA! EVEN IF I DECIDED TO DO SOMETHING THAT SUICIDAL,
... THE LAST THING I'D EVER CONSIDER DOING IS BRINGING A CHILD WITH ME!

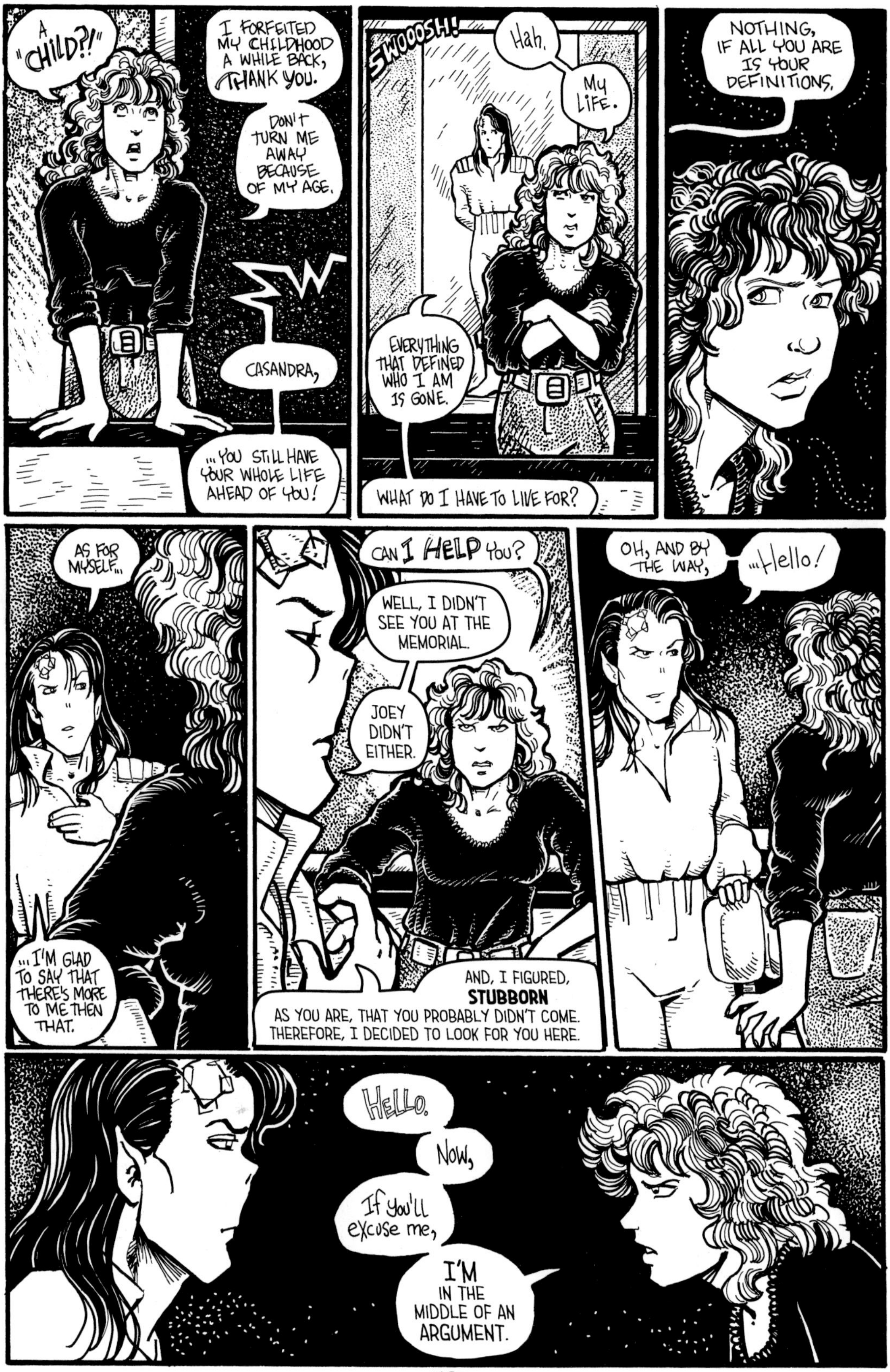
A "CHILD?!"
I FORFEITED MY CHILDHOOD A WHILE BACK, THANK YOU.
DON'T TURN ME AWAY BECAUSE OF MY AGE.
CASANDRA,
...YOU STILL HAVE YOUR WHOLE LIFE AHEAD OF YOU!
SWOOOSH!
Hah.
My Life.
EVERYTHING THAT DEFINED WHO I AM IS GONE.
WHAT DO I HAVE TO LIVE FOR?
NOTHING, IF ALL YOU ARE IS YOUR DEFINITIONS.
AS FOR MYSELF...
...I'M GLAD TO SAY THAT THERE'S MORE TO ME THEN THAT.
CAN I HELP YOU?
WELL, I DIDN'T SEE YOU AT THE MEMORIAL.
JOEY DIDN'T EITHER.
AND, I FIGURED, STUBBORN AS YOU ARE, THAT YOU PROBABLY DIDN'T COME. THEREFORE, I DECIDED TO LOOK FOR YOU HERE.
OH, AND BY THE WAY,
...Hello!
HELLO.
Now,
If you'll excuse me,
I'M IN THE MIDDLE OF AN ARGUMENT.

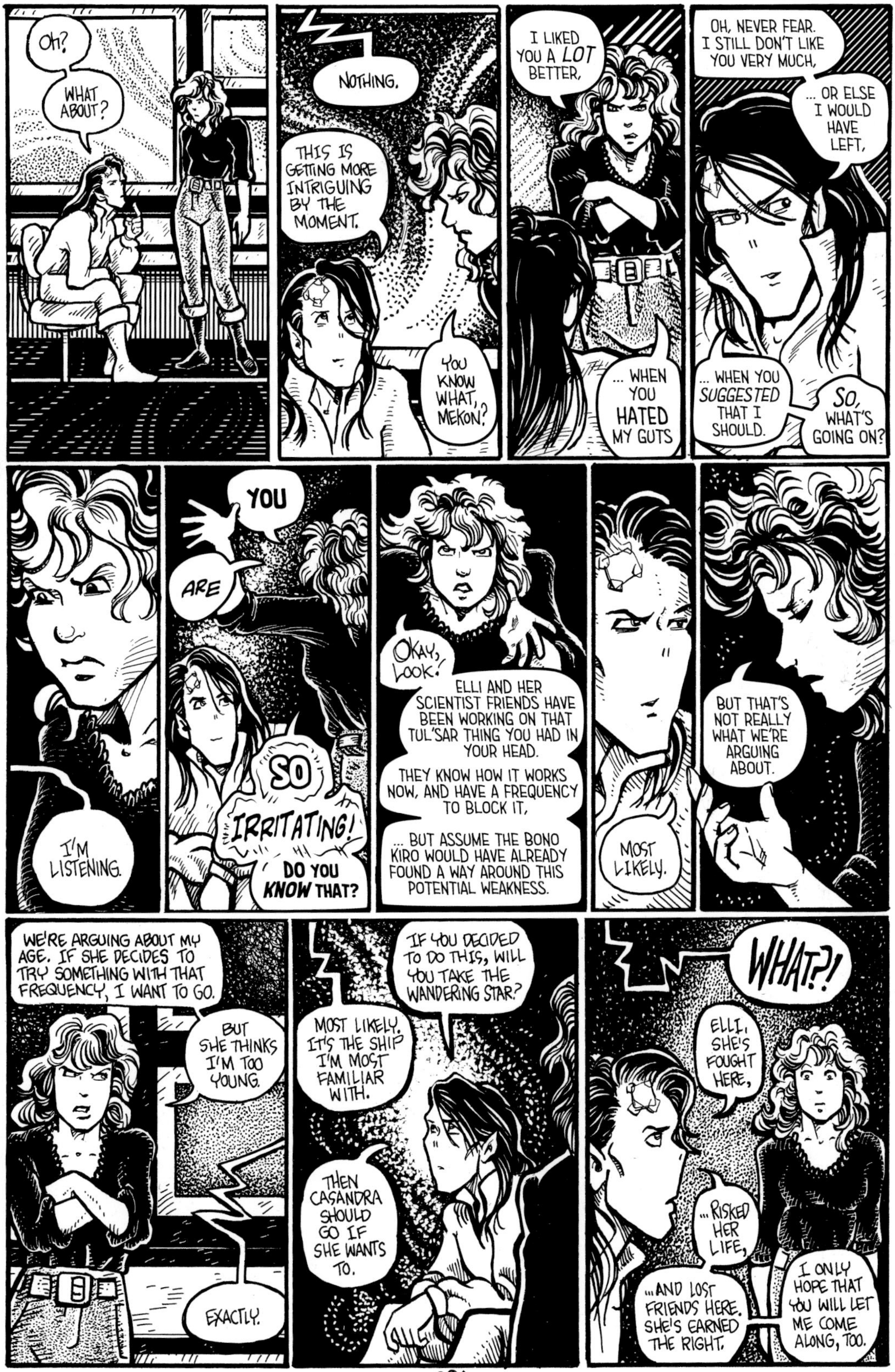
Oh?
WHAT ABOUT?
NOTHING.
THIS IS GETTING MORE INTRIGUING BY THE MOMENT.
YOU KNOW WHAT, MEKON?
I LIKED YOU A LOT BETTER,
... WHEN YOU HATED MY GUTS
OH, NEVER FEAR. I STILL DON'T LIKE YOU VERY MUCH,
... OR ELSE I WOULD HAVE LEFT,
... WHEN YOU SUGGESTED THAT I SHOULD.
SO, WHAT'S GOING ON?
I'M LISTENING.
YOU
ARE
SO
IRRITATING!
DO YOU KNOW THAT?
OKAY, LOOK!
ELLI AND HER SCIENTIST FRIENDS HAVE BEEN WORKING ON THAT TUL'SAR THING YOU HAD IN YOUR HEAD.
THEY KNOW HOW IT WORKS NOW, AND HAVE A FREQUENCY TO BLOCK IT,
... BUT ASSUME THE BONO KIRO WOULD HAVE ALREADY FOUND A WAY AROUND THIS POTENTIAL WEAKNESS.
MOST LIKELY.
BUT THAT'S NOT REALLY WHAT WE'RE ARGUING ABOUT.
WE'RE ARGUING ABOUT MY AGE. IF SHE DECIDES TO TRY SOMETHING WITH THAT FREQUENCY, I WANT TO GO.
BUT SHE THINKS I'M TOO YOUNG.
EXACTLY.
IF YOU DECIDED TO DO THIS, WILL YOU TAKE THE WANDERING STAR?
MOST LIKELY. IT'S THE SHIP I'M MOST FAMILIAR WITH.
THEN CASANDRA SHOULD GO IF SHE WANTS TO.
WHAT?!
ELLI, SHE'S FOUGHT HERE,
... RISKED HER LIFE,
... AND LOST FRIENDS HERE. SHE'S EARNED THE RIGHT.
I ONLY HOPE THAT YOU WILL LET ME COME ALONG, TOO.

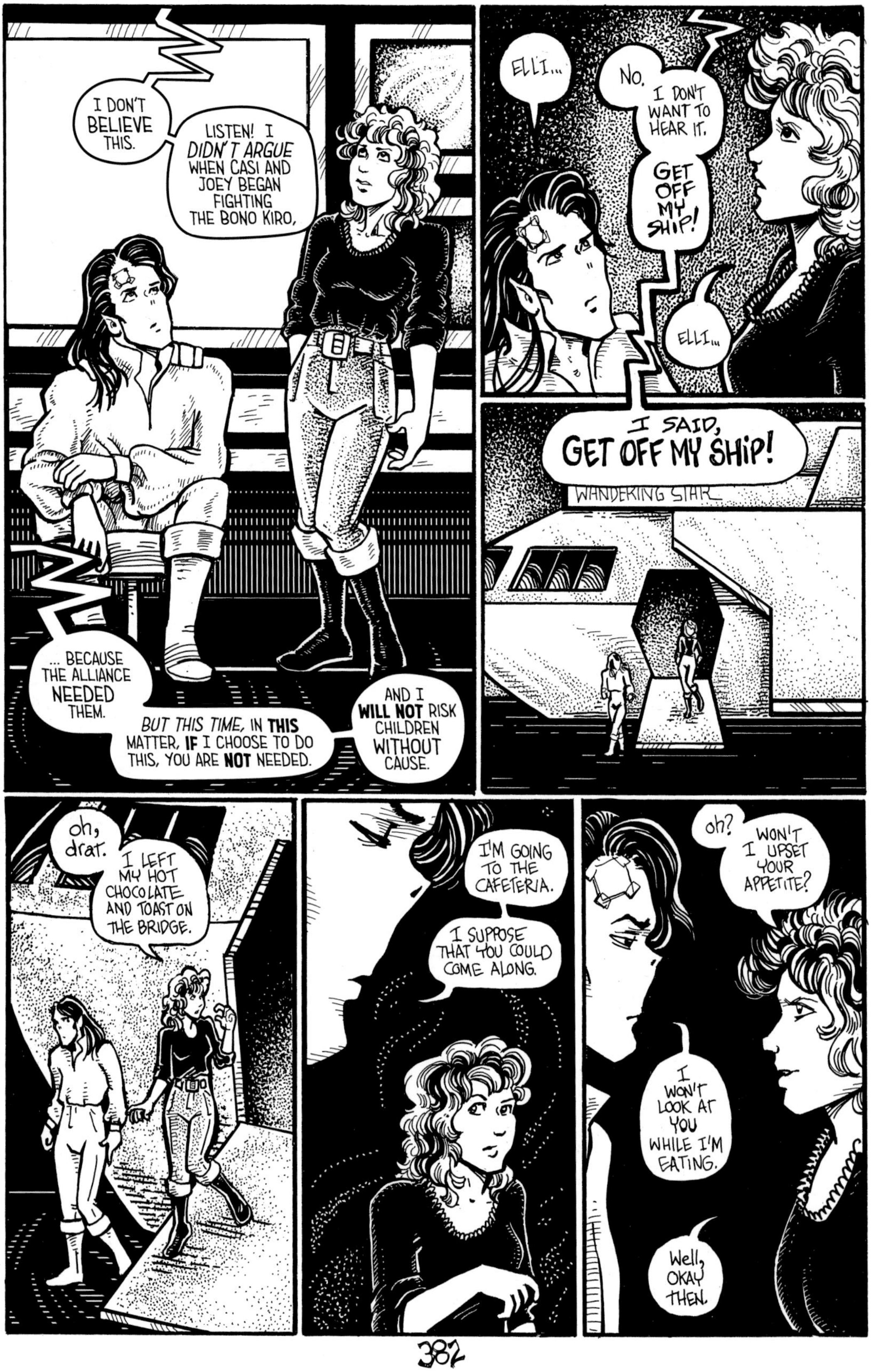
I DON'T BELIEVE THIS.
LISTEN! I DIDN'T ARGUE WHEN CASI AND JOEY BEGAN FIGHTING THE BONO KIRO,
... BECAUSE THE ALLIANCE NEEDED THEM.
BUT THIS TIME, IN THIS MATTER, IF I CHOOSE TO DO THIS, YOU ARE NOT NEEDED.
AND I WILL NOT RISK CHILDREN WITHOUT CAUSE.
ELLI...
No.
I DON'T WANT TO HEAR IT.
GET OFF MY SHIP!
ELLI...
I SAID, GET OFF MY SHIP!
WANDERING STAR
oh, drat.
I LEFT MY HOT CHOCOLATE AND TOAST ON THE BRIDGE.
I'M GOING TO THE CAFETERIA.
I SUPPOSE THAT YOU COULD COME ALONG.
oh?
WON'T I UPSET YOUR APPETITE?
I WON'T LOOK AT YOU WHILE I'M EATING.
Well, OKAY THEN.

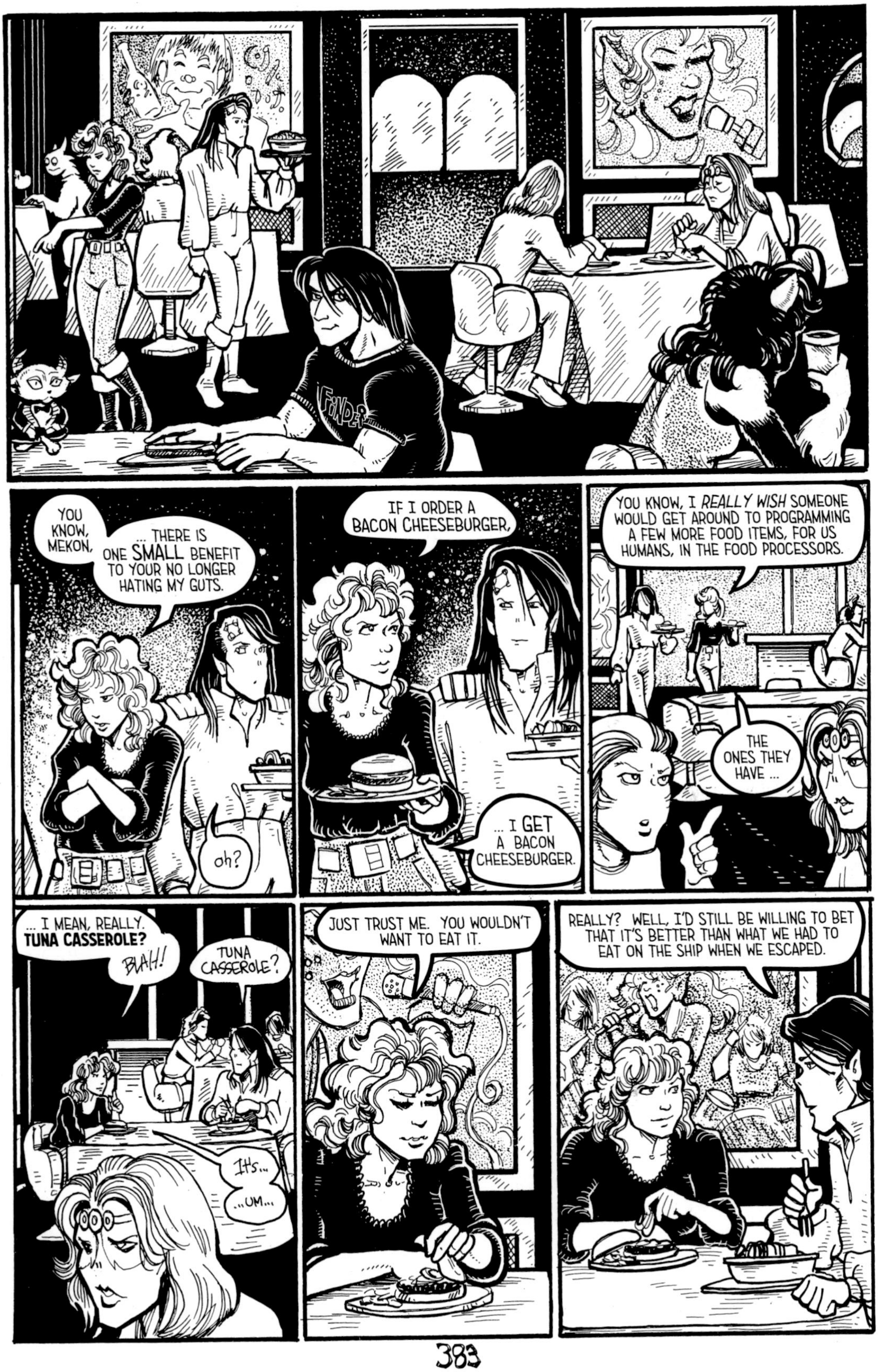
FINDER
YOU KNOW, MEKON,
... THERE IS ONE SMALL BENEFIT TO YOUR NO LONGER HATING MY GUTS.
oh?
IF I ORDER A BACON CHEESEBURGER,
... I GET A BACON CHEESEBURGER.
YOU KNOW, I *REALLY WISH* SOMEONE WOULD GET AROUND TO PROGRAMMING A FEW MORE FOOD ITEMS, FOR US HUMANS, IN THE FOOD PROCESSORS.
THE ONES THEY HAVE ...
... I MEAN, REALLY. **TUNA CASSEROLE?**
BLAH!!
TUNA CASSEROLE?
It's...
...UM...
JUST TRUST ME. YOU WOULDN'T WANT TO EAT IT.
REALLY? WELL, I'D STILL BE WILLING TO BET THAT IT'S BETTER THAN WHAT WE HAD TO EAT ON THE SHIP WHEN WE ESCAPED.

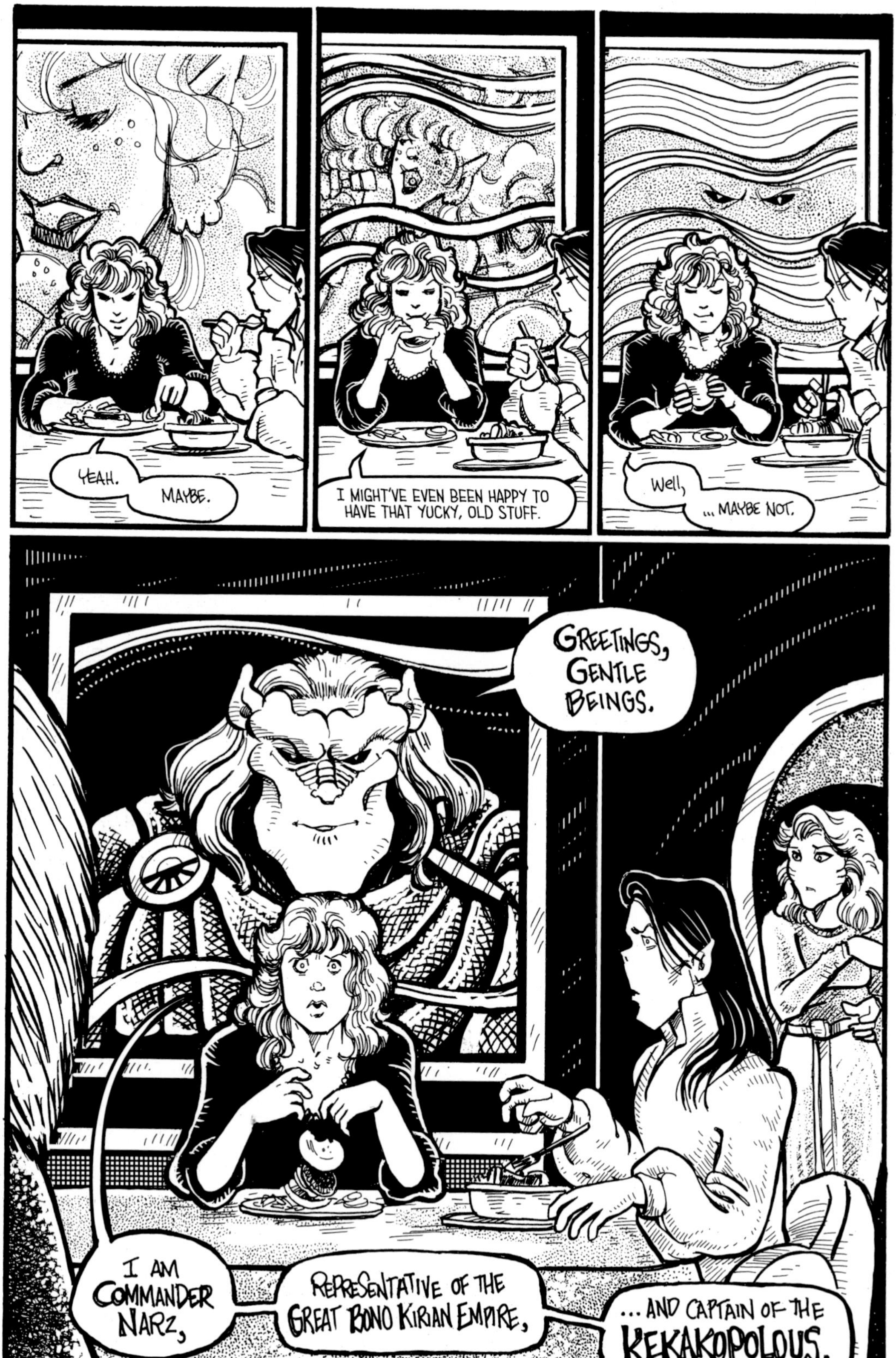
YEAH.
MAYBE.
I MIGHT'VE EVEN BEEN HAPPY TO HAVE THAT YUCKY, OLD STUFF.
Well,
... MAYBE NOT.
GREETINGS, GENTLE BEINGS.
I AM COMMANDER NARZ,
REPRESENTATIVE OF THE GREAT BONO KIRIAN EMPIRE,
... AND CAPTAIN OF THE KEKAKOPOLOUS.

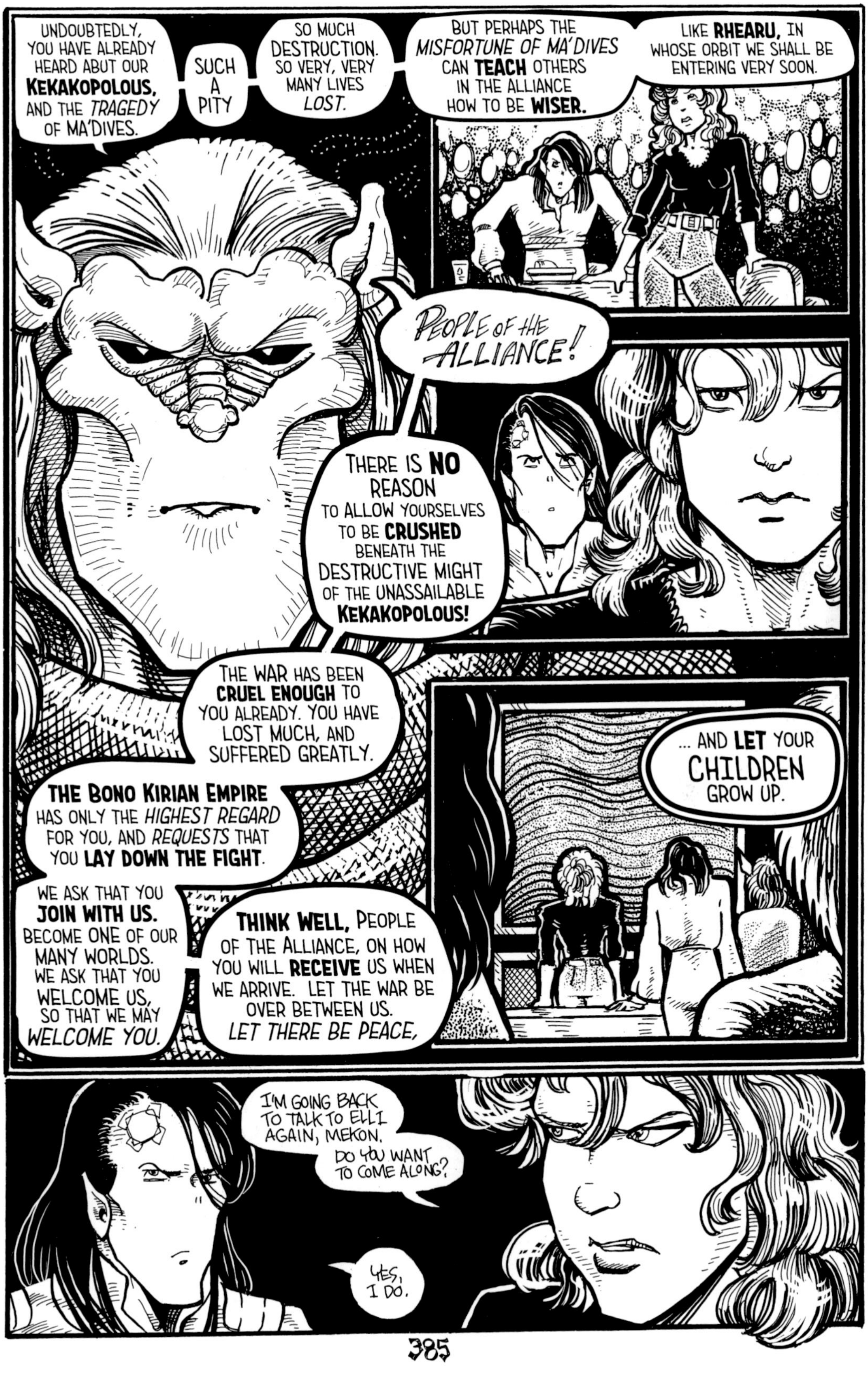
UNDOUBTEDLY, YOU HAVE ALREADY HEARD ABUT OUR **KEKAKOPOLOUS**, AND THE *TRAGEDY* OF MA'DIVES.
SUCH A PITY
SO MUCH DESTRUCTION. SO VERY, VERY MANY LIVES *LOST*.
BUT PERHAPS THE *MISFORTUNE OF MA'DIVES* CAN **TEACH** OTHERS IN THE ALLIANCE HOW TO BE **WISER**.
LIKE **RHEARU**, IN WHOSE ORBIT WE SHALL BE ENTERING VERY SOON.
PEOPLE OF THE ALLIANCE!
THERE IS **NO** REASON TO ALLOW YOURSELVES TO BE **CRUSHED** BENEATH THE DESTRUCTIVE MIGHT OF THE UNASSAILABLE **KEKAKOPOLOUS!**
THE WAR HAS BEEN **CRUEL ENOUGH** TO YOU ALREADY. YOU HAVE LOST MUCH, AND SUFFERED GREATLY.
THE BONO KIRIAN EMPIRE HAS ONLY THE *HIGHEST REGARD* FOR YOU, AND *REQUESTS* THAT YOU **LAY DOWN THE FIGHT**.
WE ASK THAT YOU **JOIN WITH US.** BECOME ONE OF OUR MANY WORLDS. WE ASK THAT YOU WELCOME US, SO THAT WE MAY *WELCOME YOU.*
THINK WELL, PEOPLE OF THE ALLIANCE, ON HOW YOU WILL **RECEIVE** US WHEN WE ARRIVE. LET THE WAR BE OVER BETWEEN US. *LET THERE BE PEACE,*
... AND **LET** YOUR CHILDREN GROW UP.
I'M GOING BACK TO TALK TO ELLI AGAIN, MEKON.
DO YOU WANT TO COME ALONG?
YES, I DO.

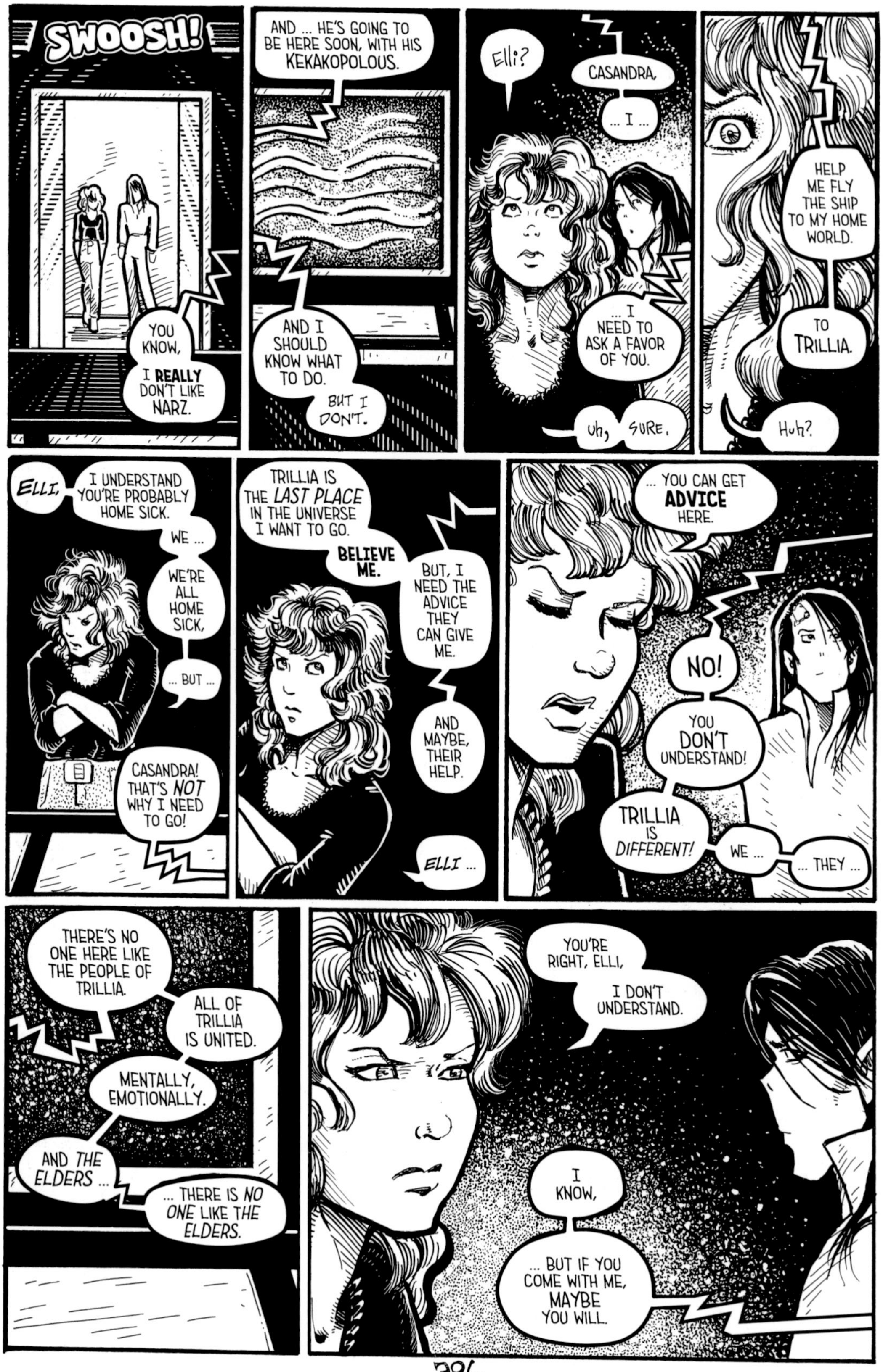
SWOOSH!
YOU KNOW,
I REALLY DON'T LIKE NARZ.
AND ... HE'S GOING TO BE HERE SOON, WITH HIS KEKAKOPOLOUS.
AND I SHOULD KNOW WHAT TO DO.
BUT I DON'T.
Elli?
CASANDRA,
... I ...
... I NEED TO ASK A FAVOR OF YOU.
Uh, SURE.
HELP ME FLY THE SHIP TO MY HOME WORLD.
TO TRILLIA.
Huh?
ELLI,
I UNDERSTAND YOU'RE PROBABLY HOME SICK.
WE ...
WE'RE ALL HOME SICK,
... BUT ...
CASANDRA! THAT'S NOT WHY I NEED TO GO!
TRILLIA IS THE LAST PLACE IN THE UNIVERSE I WANT TO GO.
BELIEVE ME.
BUT, I NEED THE ADVICE THEY CAN GIVE ME.
AND MAYBE, THEIR HELP.
ELLI ...
... YOU CAN GET ADVICE HERE.
NO!
YOU DON'T UNDERSTAND!
TRILLIA IS DIFFERENT!
WE ...
... THEY ...
THERE'S NO ONE HERE LIKE THE PEOPLE OF TRILLIA.
ALL OF TRILLIA IS UNITED.
MENTALLY, EMOTIONALLY.
AND THE ELDERS ...
... THERE IS NO ONE LIKE THE ELDERS.
YOU'RE RIGHT, ELLI,
I DON'T UNDERSTAND.
I KNOW,
... BUT IF YOU COME WITH ME, MAYBE YOU WILL.

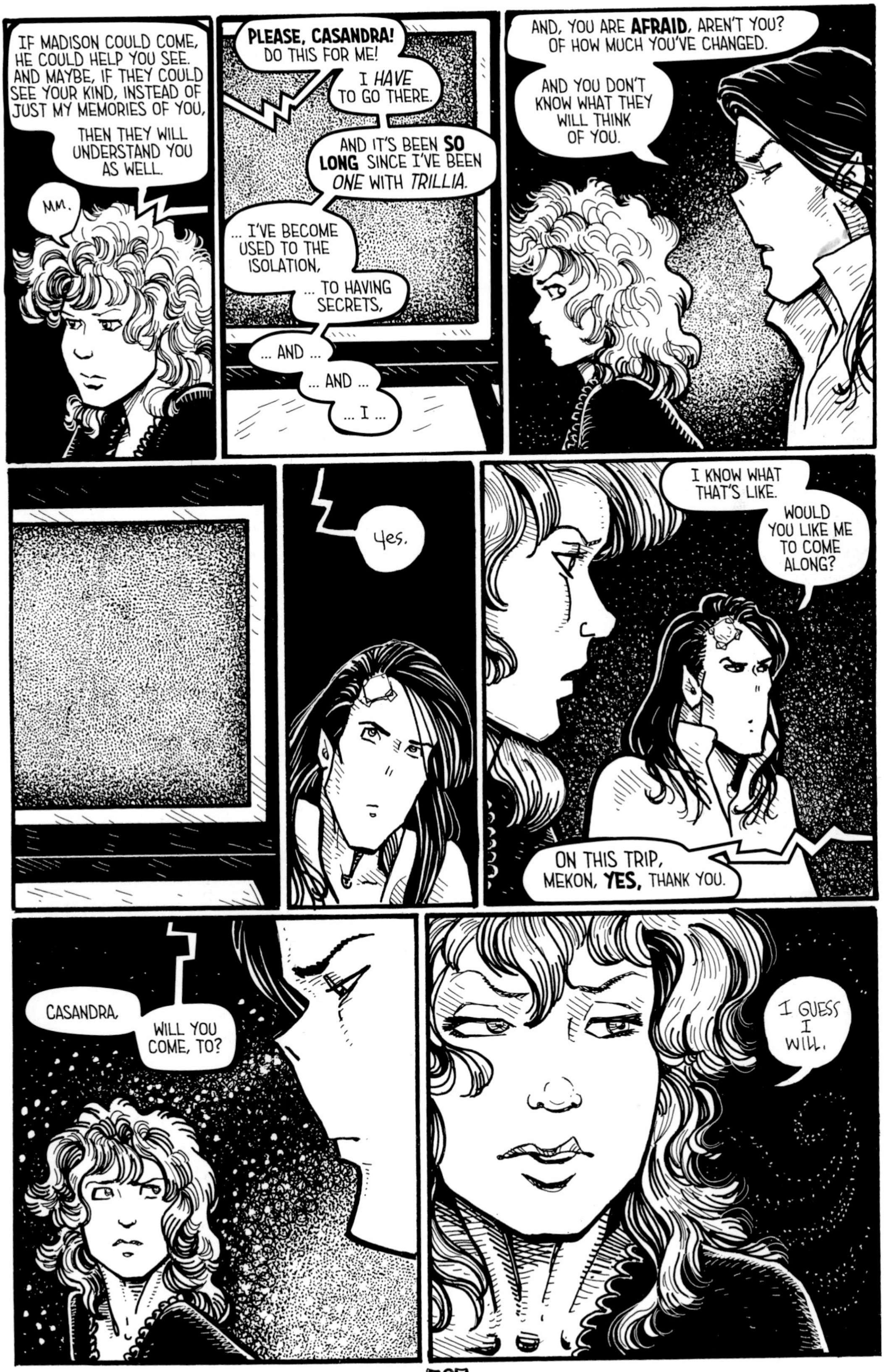

IF MADISON COULD COME, HE COULD HELP YOU SEE. AND MAYBE, IF THEY COULD SEE YOUR KIND, INSTEAD OF JUST MY MEMORIES OF YOU,
THEN THEY WILL UNDERSTAND YOU AS WELL.
MM.
PLEASE, CASANDRA! DO THIS FOR ME!
I HAVE TO GO THERE.
AND IT'S BEEN SO LONG SINCE I'VE BEEN ONE WITH TRILLIA.
... I'VE BECOME USED TO THE ISOLATION,
... TO HAVING SECRETS,
... AND ...
... AND ...
... I ...
AND, YOU ARE AFRAID, AREN'T YOU? OF HOW MUCH YOU'VE CHANGED.
AND YOU DON'T KNOW WHAT THEY WILL THINK OF YOU.
Yes.
I KNOW WHAT THAT'S LIKE.
WOULD YOU LIKE ME TO COME ALONG?
ON THIS TRIP, MEKON, YES, THANK YOU.
CASANDRA,
WILL YOU COME, TO?
I GUESS I WILL.

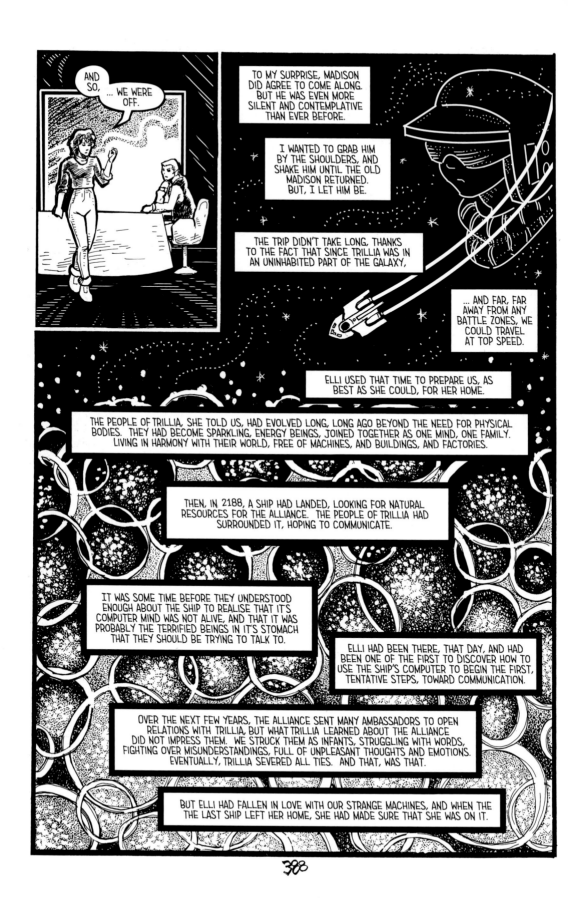

AND SO, ... WE WERE OFF.

TO MY SURPRISE, MADISON DID AGREE TO COME ALONG. BUT HE WAS EVEN MORE SILENT AND CONTEMPLATIVE THAN EVER BEFORE.

I WANTED TO GRAB HIM BY THE SHOULDERS, AND SHAKE HIM UNTIL THE OLD MADISON RETURNED. BUT, I LET HIM BE.

THE TRIP DIDN'T TAKE LONG, THANKS TO THE FACT THAT SINCE TRILLIA WAS IN AN UNINHABITED PART OF THE GALAXY,

... AND FAR, FAR AWAY FROM ANY BATTLE ZONES, WE COULD TRAVEL AT TOP SPEED.

ELLI USED THAT TIME TO PREPARE US, AS BEST AS SHE COULD, FOR HER HOME.

THE PEOPLE OF TRILLIA, SHE TOLD US, HAD EVOLVED LONG, LONG AGO BEYOND THE NEED FOR PHYSICAL BODIES. THEY HAD BECOME SPARKLING, ENERGY BEINGS, JOINED TOGETHER AS ONE MIND, ONE FAMILY. LIVING IN HARMONY WITH THEIR WORLD, FREE OF MACHINES, AND BUILDINGS, AND FACTORIES.

THEN, IN 2188, A SHIP HAD LANDED, LOOKING FOR NATURAL RESOURCES FOR THE ALLIANCE. THE PEOPLE OF TRILLIA HAD SURROUNDED IT, HOPING TO COMMUNICATE.

IT WAS SOME TIME BEFORE THEY UNDERSTOOD ENOUGH ABOUT THE SHIP TO REALISE THAT IT'S COMPUTER MIND WAS NOT ALIVE, AND THAT IT WAS PROBABLY THE TERRIFIED BEINGS IN IT'S STOMACH THAT THEY SHOULD BE TRYING TO TALK TO.

ELLI HAD BEEN THERE, THAT DAY, AND HAD BEEN ONE OF THE FIRST TO DISCOVER HOW TO USE THE SHIP'S COMPUTER TO BEGIN THE FIRST, TENTATIVE STEPS, TOWARD COMMUNICATION.

OVER THE NEXT FEW YEARS, THE ALLIANCE SENT MANY AMBASSADORS TO OPEN RELATIONS WITH TRILLIA, BUT WHAT TRILLIA LEARNED ABOUT THE ALLIANCE DID NOT IMPRESS THEM. WE STRUCK THEM AS INFANTS, STRUGGLING WITH WORDS, FIGHTING OVER MISUNDERSTANDINGS, FULL OF UNPLEASANT THOUGHTS AND EMOTIONS. EVENTUALLY, TRILLIA SEVERED ALL TIES. AND THAT, WAS THAT.

BUT ELLI HAD FALLEN IN LOVE WITH OUR STRANGE MACHINES, AND WHEN THE THE LAST SHIP LEFT HER HOME, SHE HAD MADE SURE THAT SHE WAS ON IT.

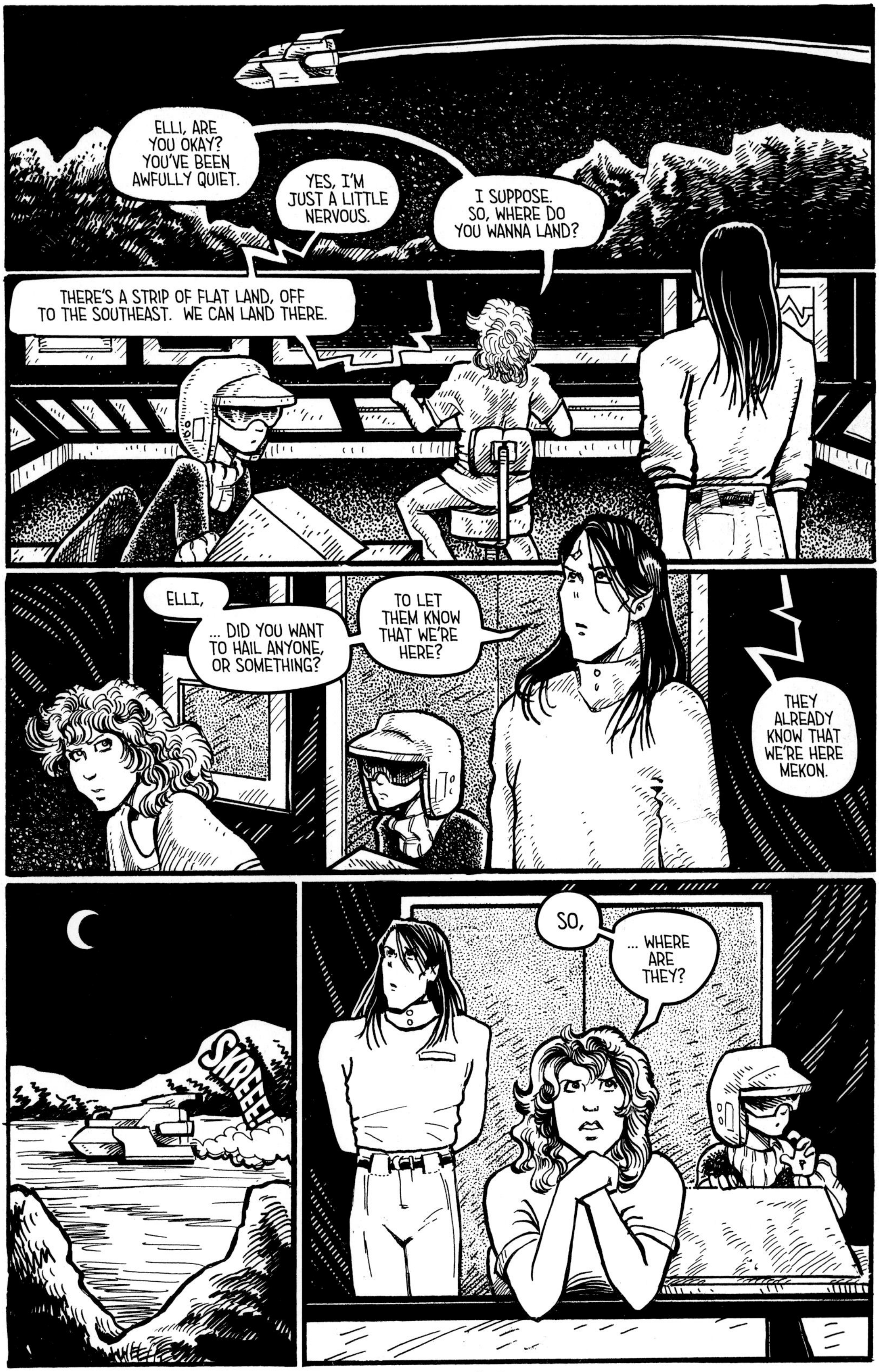
ELLI, ARE YOU OKAY? YOU'VE BEEN AWFULLY QUIET.
YES, I'M JUST A LITTLE NERVOUS.
I SUPPOSE. SO, WHERE DO YOU WANNA LAND?
THERE'S A STRIP OF FLAT LAND, OFF TO THE SOUTHEAST. WE CAN LAND THERE.
ELLI,
... DID YOU WANT TO HAIL ANYONE, OR SOMETHING?
TO LET THEM KNOW THAT WE'RE HERE?
THEY ALREADY KNOW THAT WE'RE HERE MEKON.
SKREEE!
SO,
... WHERE ARE THEY?

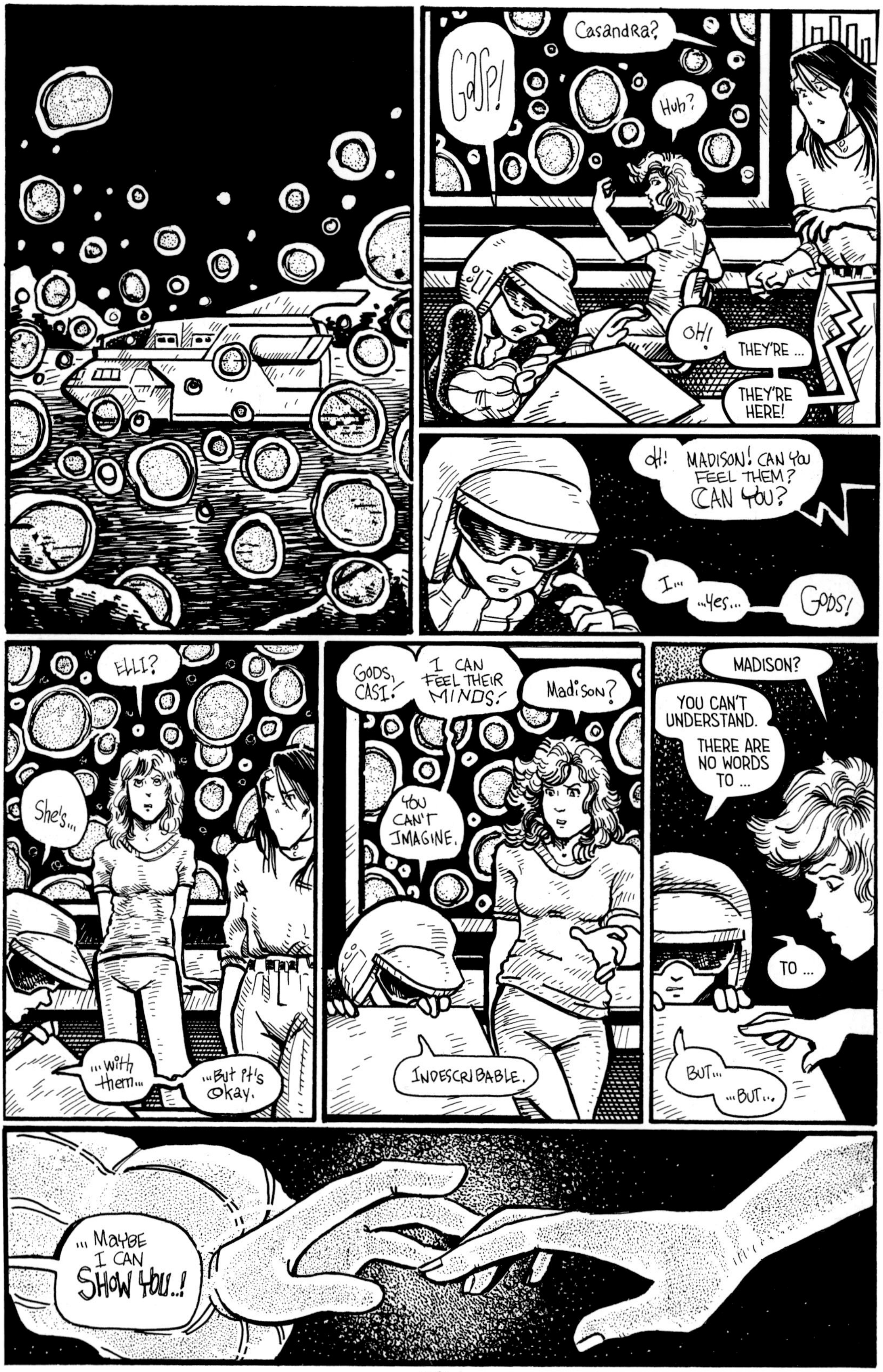
Gasp!
Casandra?
Huh?
OH!
THEY'RE ...
THEY'RE HERE!
oH! MADISON! CAN YOU FEEL THEM? CAN YOU?
I...
...yes...
GODS!
ELLI?
She's...
...with them...
...But it's okay.
GODS, CASI!
I CAN FEEL THEIR MINDS!
Madison?
YOU CAN'T IMAGINE.
INDESCRIBABLE.
MADISON?
YOU CAN'T UNDERSTAND.
THERE ARE NO WORDS TO ...
TO ...
BUT...
...BUT...
... MAYBE I CAN SHOW YOU..!

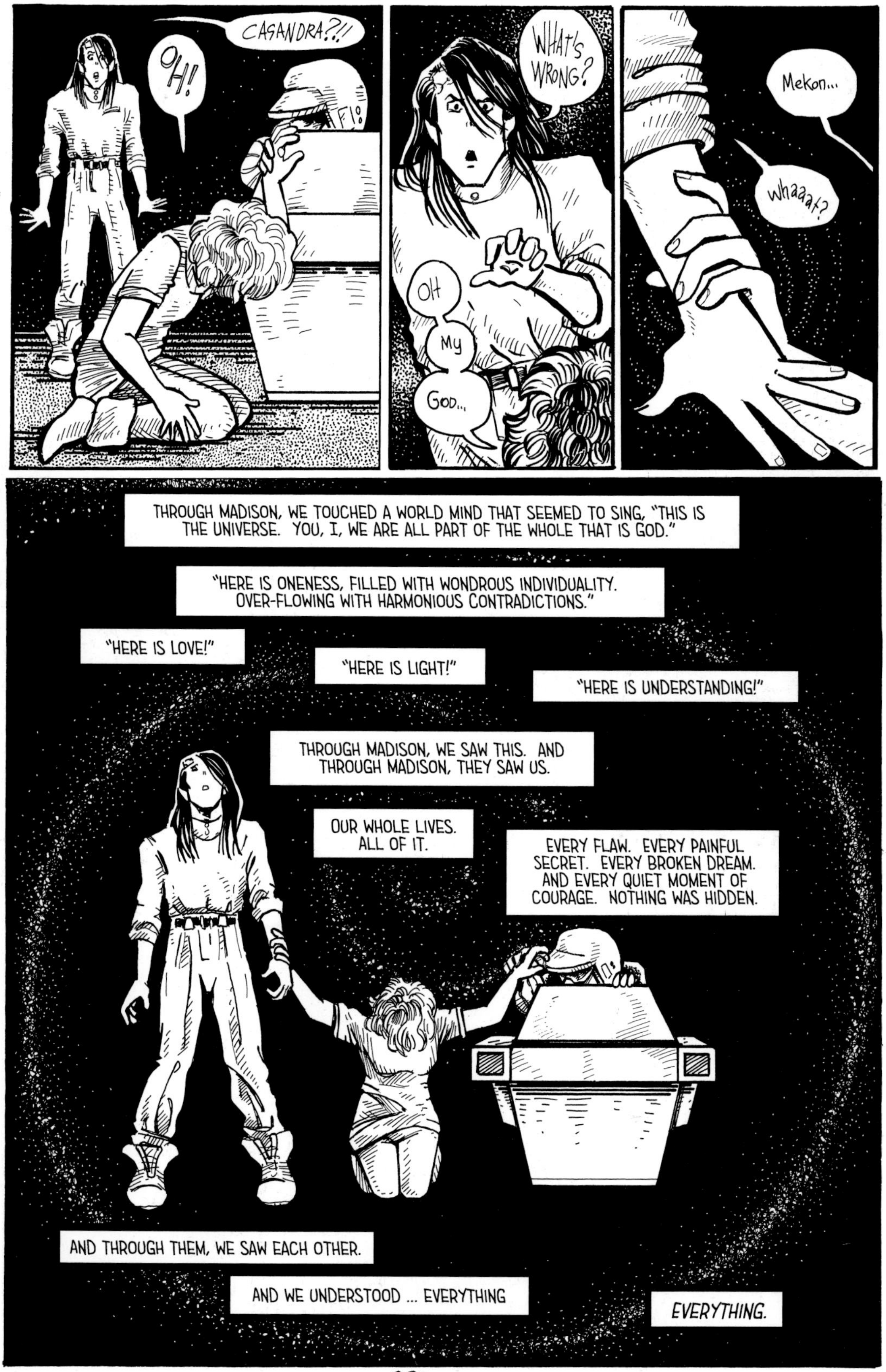
CASANDRA?!!
OH!
WHAT'S WRONG?
OH
MY
GOD...
Mekon...
whaaat?
THROUGH MADISON, WE TOUCHED A WORLD MIND THAT SEEMED TO SING, "THIS IS THE UNIVERSE. YOU, I, WE ARE ALL PART OF THE WHOLE THAT IS GOD."
"HERE IS ONENESS, FILLED WITH WONDROUS INDIVIDUALITY. OVER-FLOWING WITH HARMONIOUS CONTRADICTIONS."
"HERE IS LOVE!"
"HERE IS LIGHT!"
"HERE IS UNDERSTANDING!"
THROUGH MADISON, WE SAW THIS. AND THROUGH MADISON, THEY SAW US.
OUR WHOLE LIVES. ALL OF IT.
EVERY FLAW. EVERY PAINFUL SECRET. EVERY BROKEN DREAM. AND EVERY QUIET MOMENT OF COURAGE. NOTHING WAS HIDDEN.
AND THROUGH THEM, WE SAW EACH OTHER.
AND WE UNDERSTOOD ... EVERYTHING
EVERYTHING.

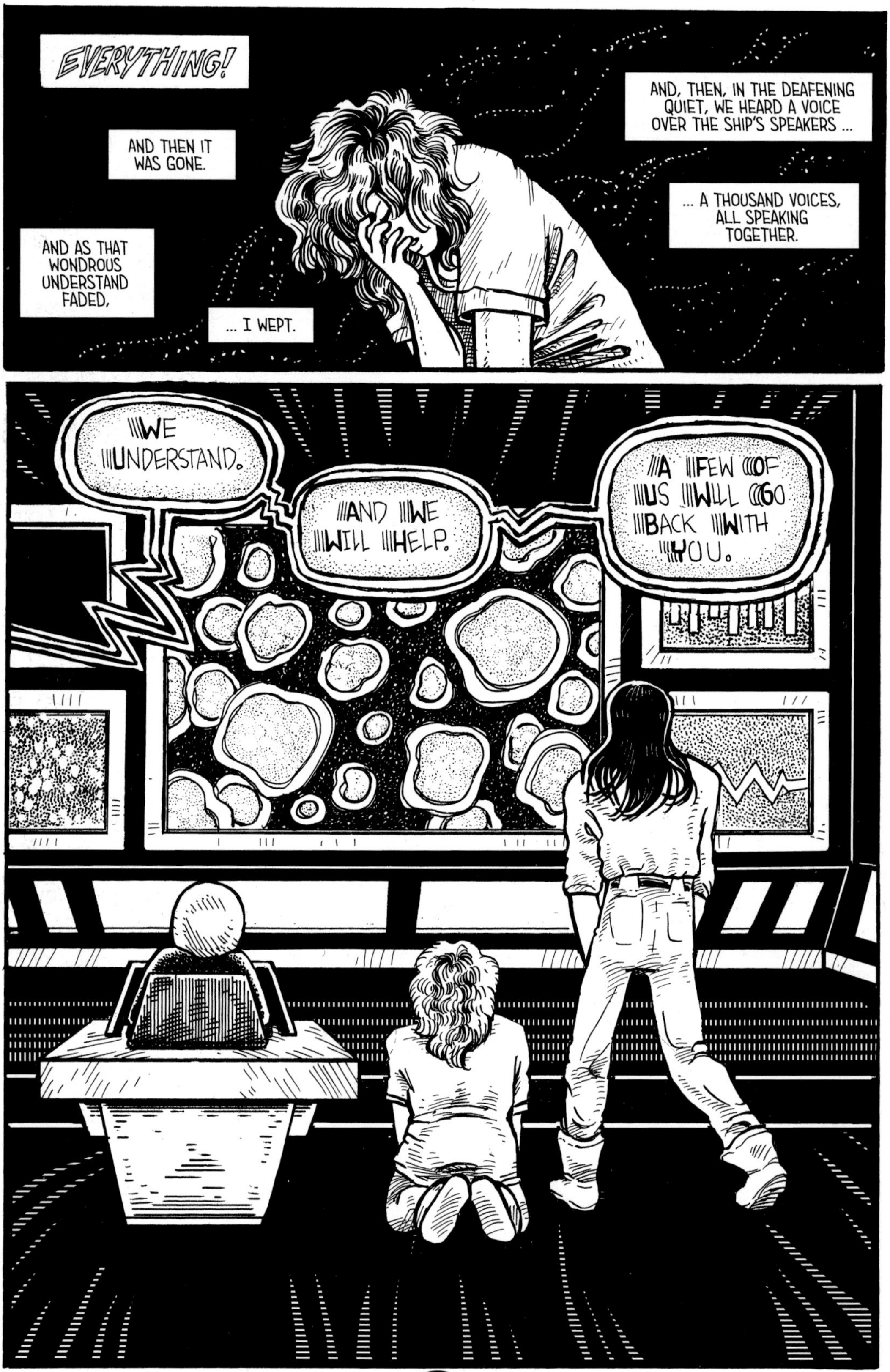
EVERYTHING!
AND THEN IT WAS GONE.
AND AS THAT WONDROUS UNDERSTAND FADED,
... I WEPT.
AND, THEN, IN THE DEAFENING QUIET, WE HEARD A VOICE OVER THE SHIP'S SPEAKERS ...
... A THOUSAND VOICES, ALL SPEAKING TOGETHER.
WE UNDERSTAND.
AND WE WILL HELP.
A FEW OF US WILL GO BACK WITH YOU.

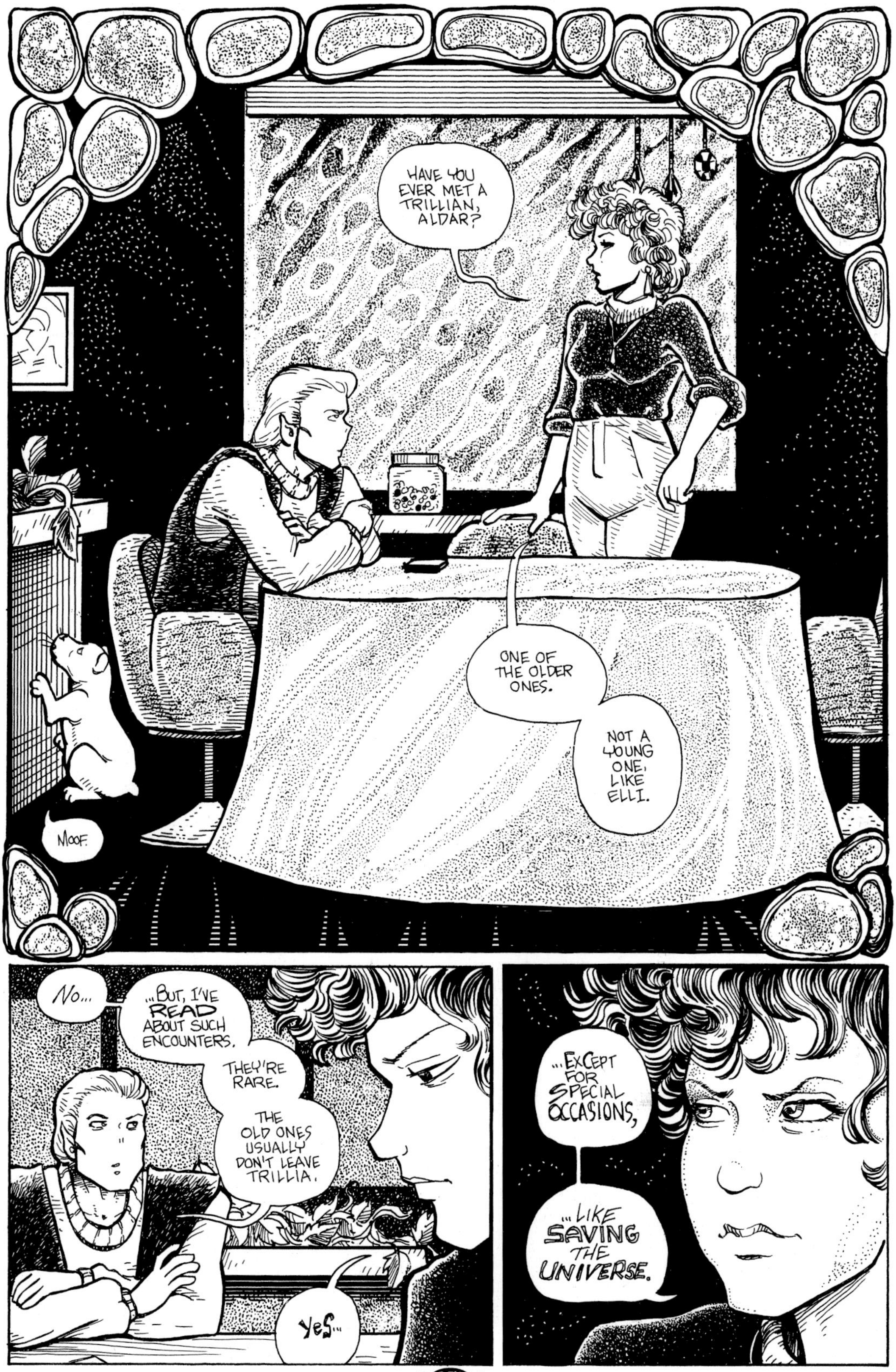
HAVE YOU EVER MET A TRILLIAN, ALDAR?
ONE OF THE OLDER ONES.
NOT A YOUNG ONE, LIKE ELLI.
MOOF.
No...
...BUT, I'VE READ ABOUT SUCH ENCOUNTERS.
THEY'RE RARE.
THE OLD ONES USUALLY DON'T LEAVE TRILLIA.
YES...
...EXCEPT FOR SPECIAL OCCASIONS,
...LIKE SAVING THE UNIVERSE.

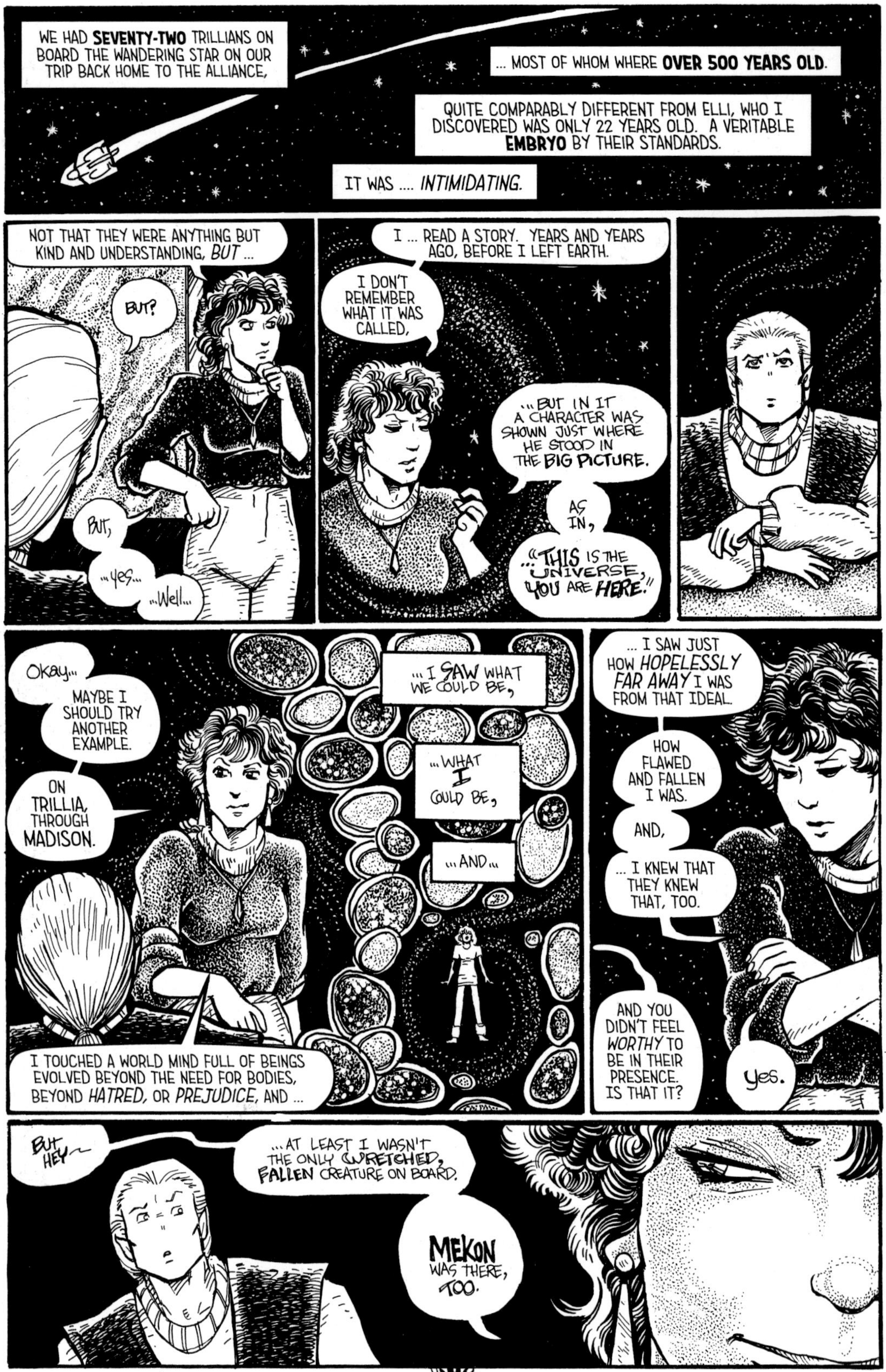
WE HAD SEVENTY-TWO TRILLIANS ON BOARD THE WANDERING STAR ON OUR TRIP BACK HOME TO THE ALLIANCE,
... MOST OF WHOM WHERE OVER 500 YEARS OLD.
QUITE COMPARABLY DIFFERENT FROM ELLI, WHO I DISCOVERED WAS ONLY 22 YEARS OLD. A VERITABLE EMBRYO BY THEIR STANDARDS.
IT WAS .... INTIMIDATING.
NOT THAT THEY WERE ANYTHING BUT KIND AND UNDERSTANDING, BUT ...
BUT?
BUT,
...YES...
...WELL...
I ... READ A STORY. YEARS AND YEARS AGO, BEFORE I LEFT EARTH.
I DON'T REMEMBER WHAT IT WAS CALLED,
...BUT IN IT A CHARACTER WAS SHOWN JUST WHERE HE STOOD IN THE BIG PICTURE.
AS IN,
..."THIS IS THE UNIVERSE, YOU ARE HERE."
OKAY...
MAYBE I SHOULD TRY ANOTHER EXAMPLE.
ON TRILLIA, THROUGH MADISON.
I TOUCHED A WORLD MIND FULL OF BEINGS EVOLVED BEYOND THE NEED FOR BODIES, BEYOND HATRED, OR PREJUDICE, AND ...
...I SAW WHAT WE COULD BE,
...WHAT I COULD BE,
...AND...
... I SAW JUST HOW HOPELESSLY FAR AWAY I WAS FROM THAT IDEAL.
HOW FLAWED AND FALLEN I WAS.
AND,
... I KNEW THAT THEY KNEW THAT, TOO.
AND YOU DIDN'T FEEL WORTHY TO BE IN THEIR PRESENCE. IS THAT IT?
YES.
BUT HEY~
...AT LEAST I WASN'T THE ONLY WRETCHED, FALLEN CREATURE ON BOARD.
MEKON WAS THERE, TOO.

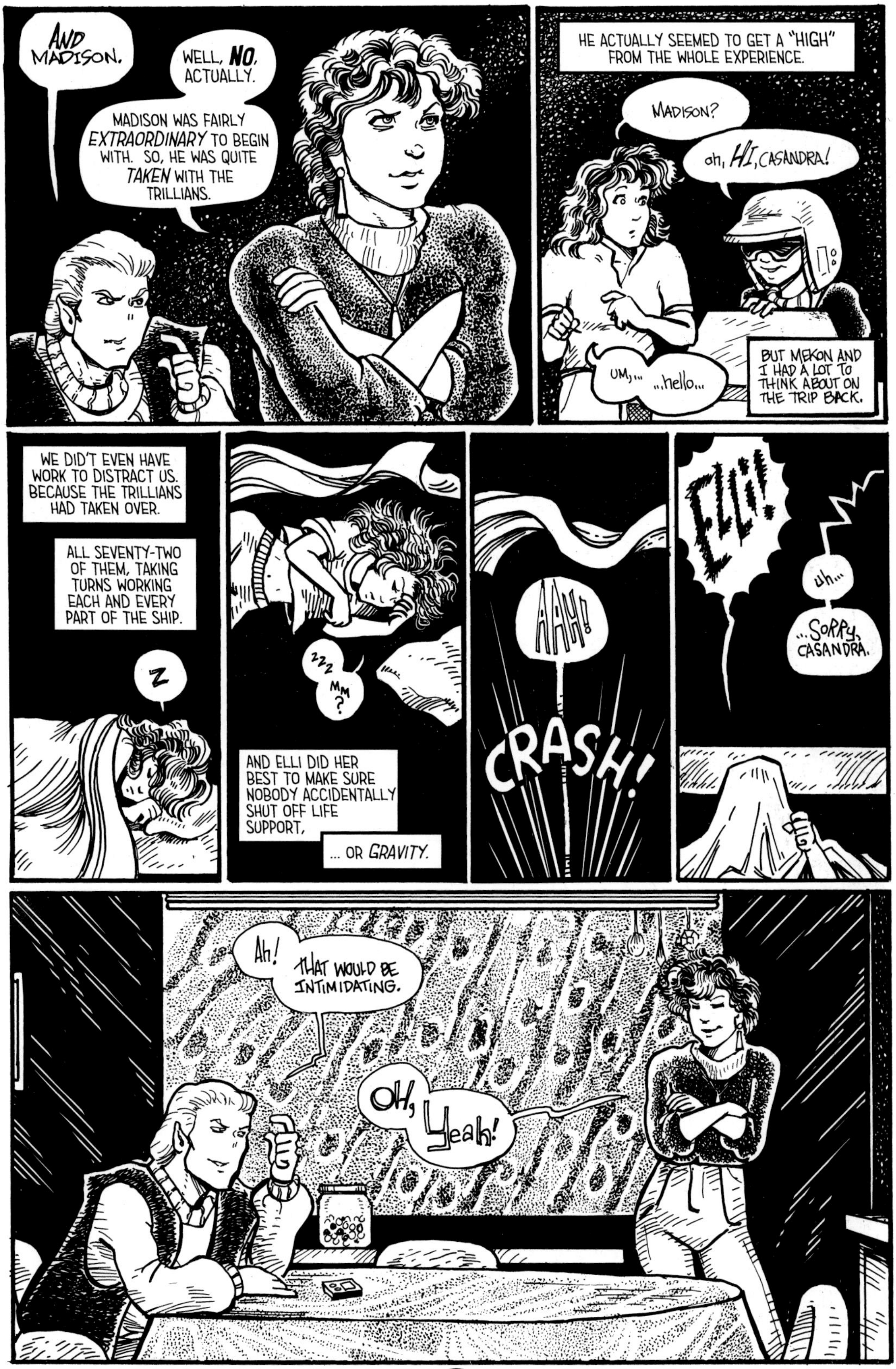

AND MADISON.
WELL, NO, ACTUALLY.
MADISON WAS FAIRLY EXTRAORDINARY TO BEGIN WITH. SO, HE WAS QUITE TAKEN WITH THE TRILLIANS.
HE ACTUALLY SEEMED TO GET A "HIGH" FROM THE WHOLE EXPERIENCE.
MADISON?
oh, HI, CASANDRA!
UM,...
...hello...
BUT MEKON AND I HAD A LOT TO THINK ABOUT ON THE TRIP BACK.
WE DID'T EVEN HAVE WORK TO DISTRACT US. BECAUSE THE TRILLIANS HAD TAKEN OVER.
ALL SEVENTY-TWO OF THEM, TAKING TURNS WORKING EACH AND EVERY PART OF THE SHIP.
Z
ZZZ MM ?
AND ELLI DID HER BEST TO MAKE SURE NOBODY ACCIDENTALLY SHUT OFF LIFE SUPPORT,
... OR GRAVITY.
AAAH!
CRASH!
ELLI!
uh...
...SORRY, CASANDRA.
Ah! THAT WOULD BE INTIMIDATING.
OH, Yeah!

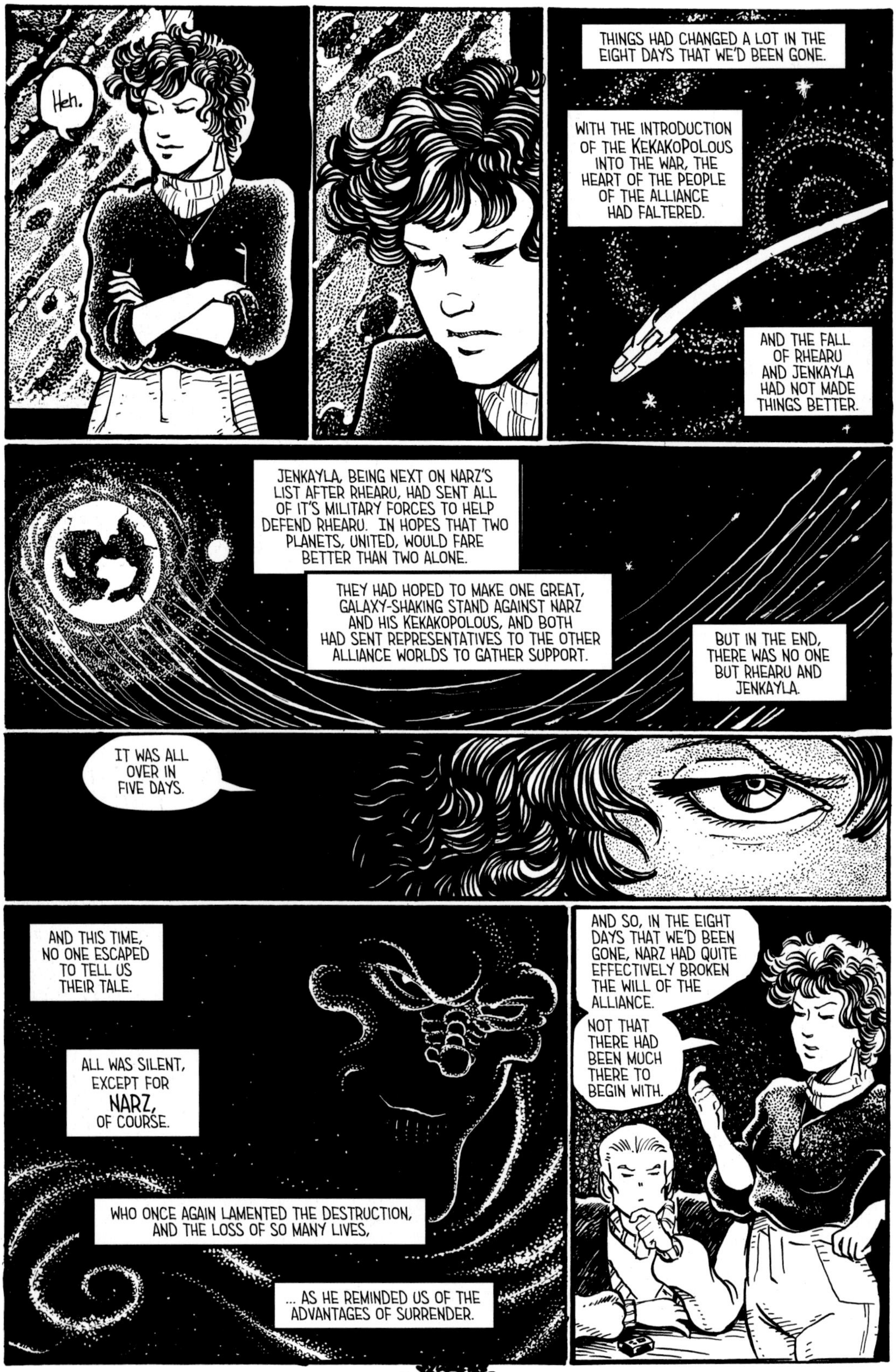
Heh.
THINGS HAD CHANGED A LOT IN THE EIGHT DAYS THAT WE'D BEEN GONE.
WITH THE INTRODUCTION OF THE KEKAKOPOLOUS INTO THE WAR, THE HEART OF THE PEOPLE OF THE ALLIANCE HAD FALTERED.
AND THE FALL OF RHEARU AND JENKAYLA HAD NOT MADE THINGS BETTER.
JENKAYLA, BEING NEXT ON NARZ'S LIST AFTER RHEARU, HAD SENT ALL OF IT'S MILITARY FORCES TO HELP DEFEND RHEARU. IN HOPES THAT TWO PLANETS, UNITED, WOULD FARE BETTER THAN TWO ALONE.
THEY HAD HOPED TO MAKE ONE GREAT, GALAXY-SHAKING STAND AGAINST NARZ AND HIS KEKAKOPOLOUS, AND BOTH HAD SENT REPRESENTATIVES TO THE OTHER ALLIANCE WORLDS TO GATHER SUPPORT.
BUT IN THE END, THERE WAS NO ONE BUT RHEARU AND JENKAYLA.
IT WAS ALL OVER IN FIVE DAYS.
AND THIS TIME, NO ONE ESCAPED TO TELL US THEIR TALE.
ALL WAS SILENT, EXCEPT FOR NARZ, OF COURSE.
WHO ONCE AGAIN LAMENTED THE DESTRUCTION, AND THE LOSS OF SO MANY LIVES,
... AS HE REMINDED US OF THE ADVANTAGES OF SURRENDER.
AND SO, IN THE EIGHT DAYS THAT WE'D BEEN GONE, NARZ HAD QUITE EFFECTIVELY BROKEN THE WILL OF THE ALLIANCE.
NOT THAT THERE HAD BEEN MUCH THERE TO BEGIN WITH.

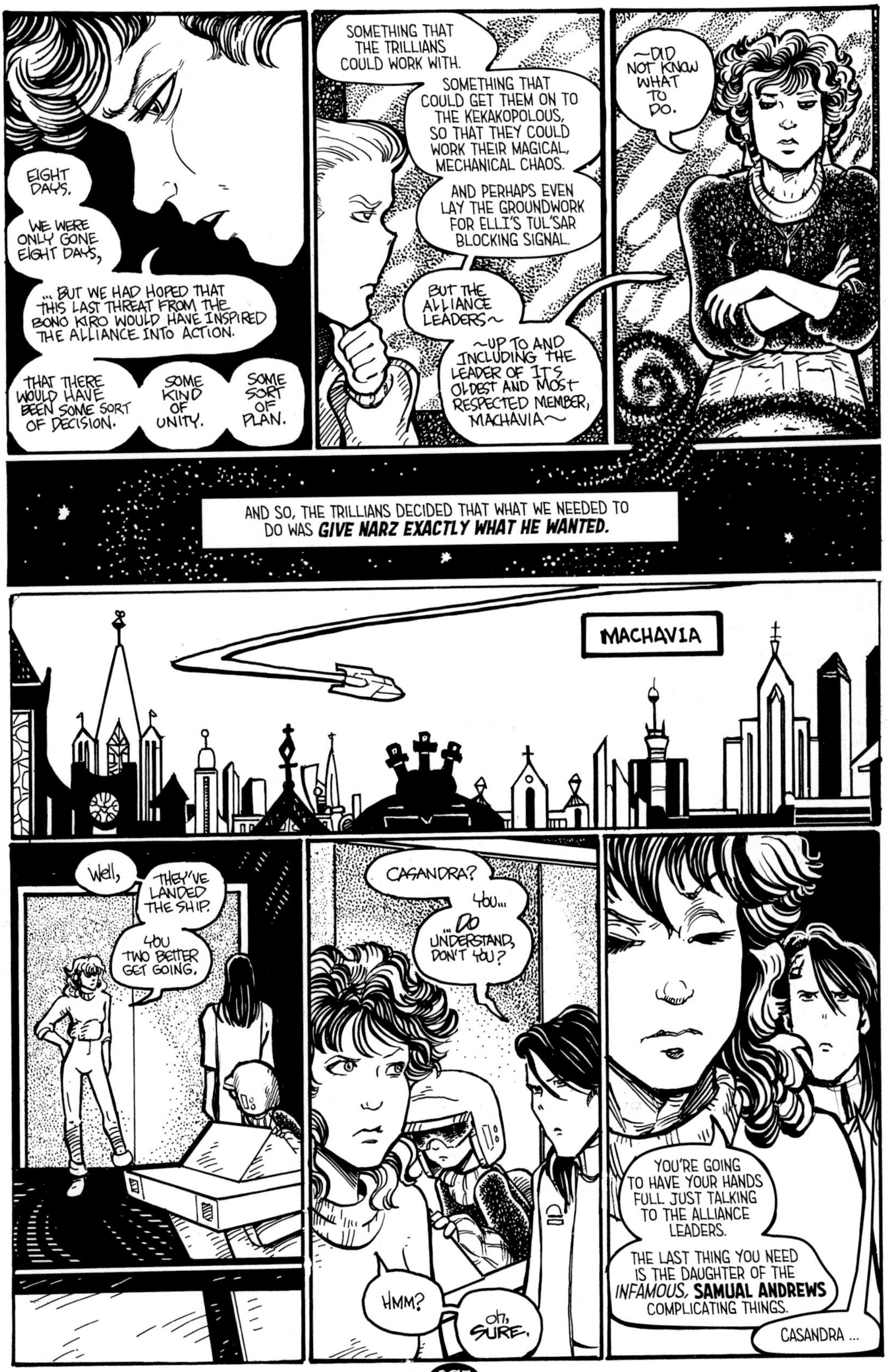
EIGHT DAYS.
WE WERE ONLY GONE EIGHT DAYS,
... BUT WE HAD HOPED THAT THIS LAST THREAT FROM THE BONO KIRO WOULD HAVE INSPIRED THE ALLIANCE INTO ACTION.
THAT THERE WOULD HAVE BEEN SOME SORT OF DECISION.
SOME KIND OF UNITY.
SOME SORT OF PLAN.
SOMETHING THAT THE TRILLIANS COULD WORK WITH.
SOMETHING THAT COULD GET THEM ON TO THE KEKAKOPOLOUS, SO THAT THEY COULD WORK THEIR MAGICAL, MECHANICAL CHAOS.
AND PERHAPS EVEN LAY THE GROUNDWORK FOR ELLI'S TUL'SAR BLOCKING SIGNAL.
BUT THE ALLIANCE LEADERS~
~UP TO AND INCLUDING THE LEADER OF IT'S OLDEST AND MOST RESPECTED MEMBER, MACHAVIA~
~DID NOT KNOW WHAT TO DO.
AND SO, THE TRILLIANS DECIDED THAT WHAT WE NEEDED TO DO WAS ***GIVE NARZ EXACTLY WHAT HE WANTED.***
MACHAVIA
Well,
THEY'VE LANDED THE SHIP.
YOU TWO BETTER GET GOING.
CASANDRA?
YOU...
...DO UNDERSTAND, DON'T YOU?
HMM?
Oh, SURE.
YOU'RE GOING TO HAVE YOUR HANDS FULL JUST TALKING TO THE ALLIANCE LEADERS.
THE LAST THING YOU NEED IS THE DAUGHTER OF THE *INFAMOUS*, **SAMUAL ANDREWS** COMPLICATING THINGS.
CASANDRA ...

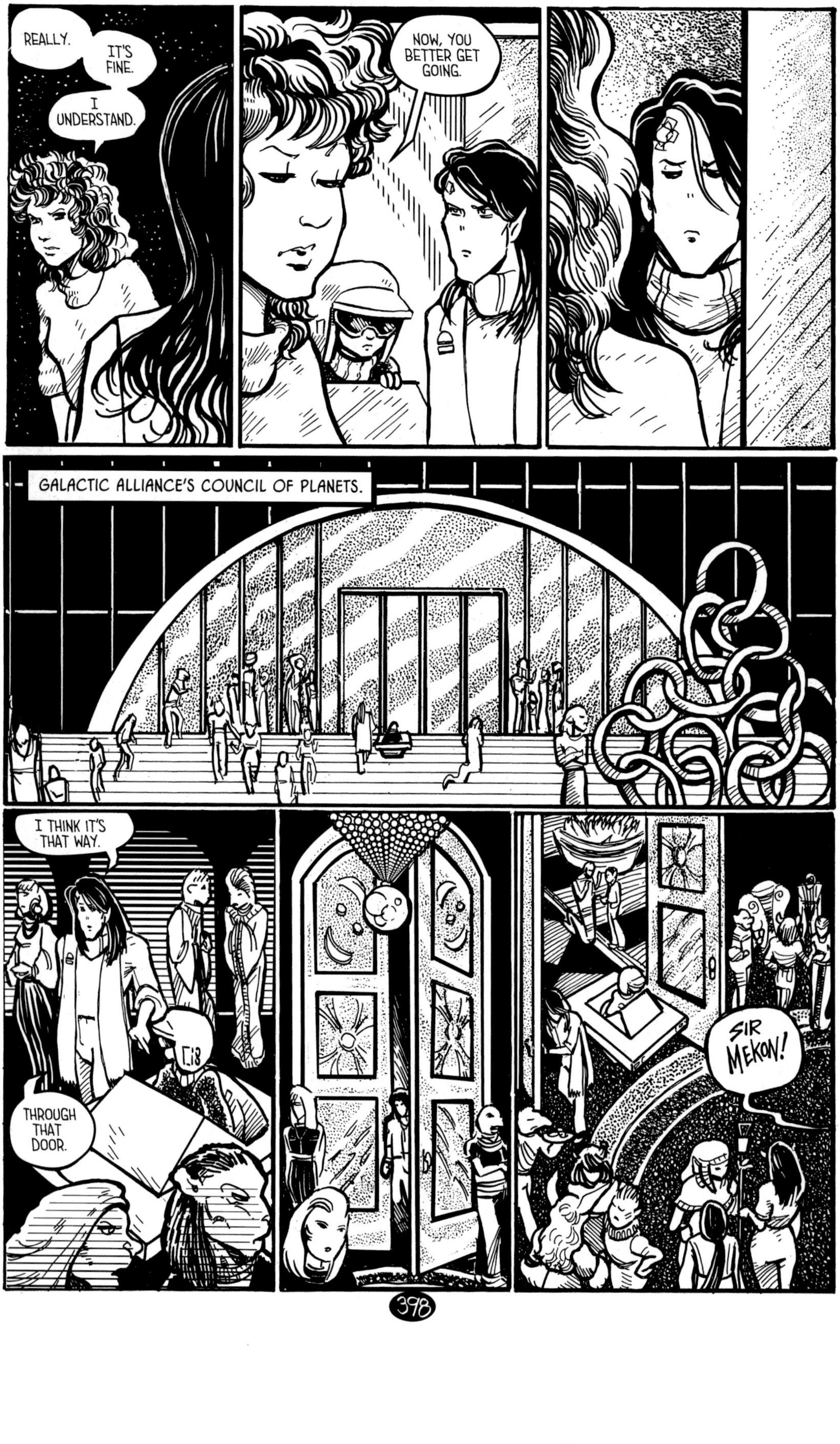
REALLY.
IT'S FINE.
I UNDERSTAND.
NOW, YOU BETTER GET GOING.
GALACTIC ALLIANCE'S COUNCIL OF PLANETS.
I THINK IT'S THAT WAY.
THROUGH THAT DOOR.
SIR MEKON!

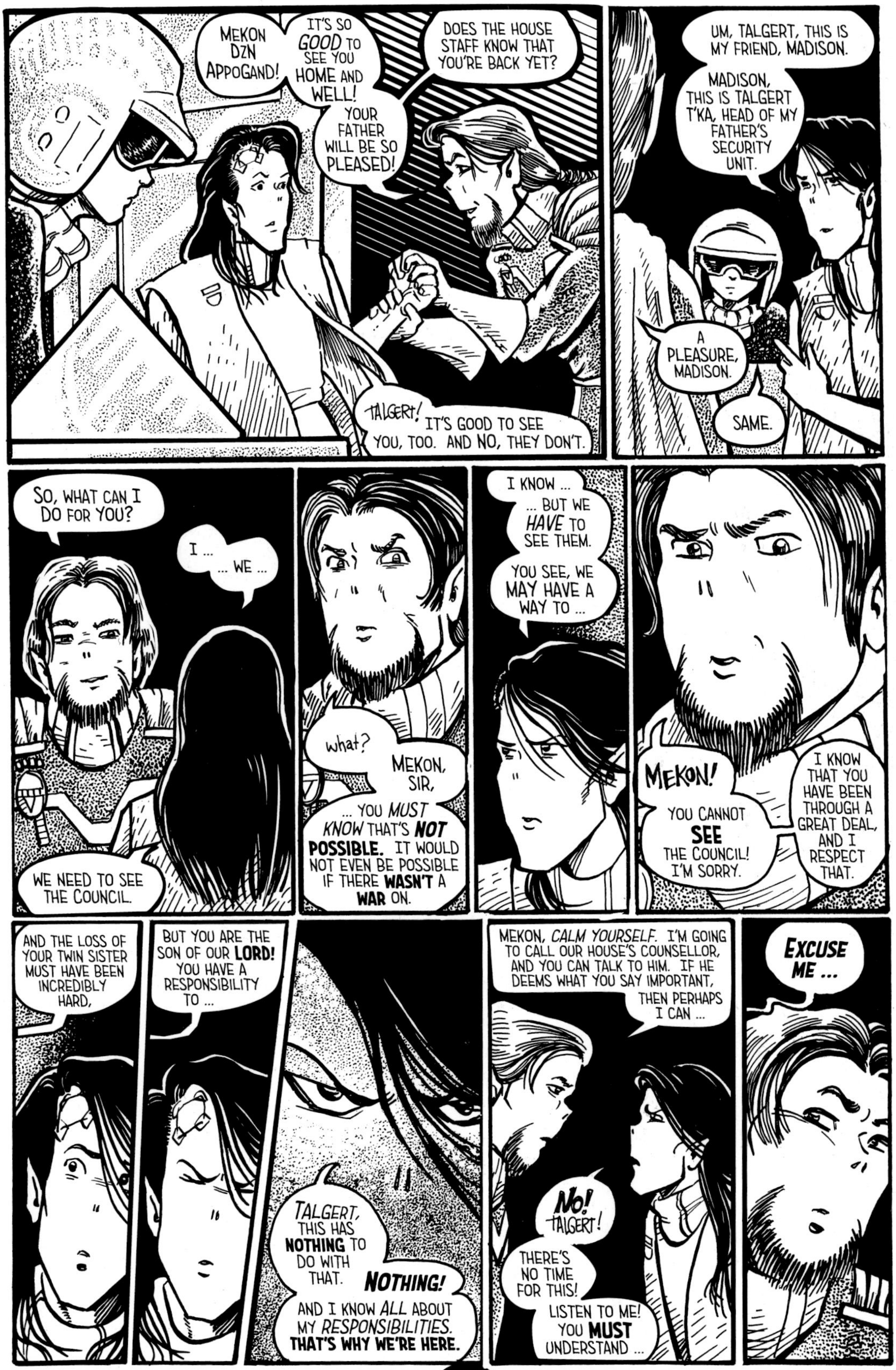
MEKON DZN APPOGAND!
IT'S SO *GOOD* TO SEE YOU HOME AND WELL!
YOUR FATHER WILL BE SO PLEASED!
DOES THE HOUSE STAFF KNOW THAT YOU'RE BACK YET?
TALGERT! IT'S GOOD TO SEE YOU, TOO. AND NO, THEY DON'T.
UM, TALGERT, THIS IS MY FRIEND, MADISON.
MADISON, THIS IS TALGERT T'KA, HEAD OF MY FATHER'S SECURITY UNIT.
A PLEASURE, MADISON.
SAME.
SO, WHAT CAN I DO FOR YOU?
I ... ... WE ...
WE NEED TO SEE THE COUNCIL.
what?
MEKON, SIR,
... YOU *MUST KNOW* THAT'S **NOT POSSIBLE.** IT WOULD NOT EVEN BE POSSIBLE IF THERE **WASN'T** A **WAR** ON.
I KNOW ...
... BUT WE *HAVE* TO SEE THEM.
YOU SEE, WE MAY HAVE A WAY TO ...
MEKON!
YOU CANNOT **SEE** THE COUNCIL! I'M SORRY.
I KNOW THAT YOU HAVE BEEN THROUGH A GREAT DEAL, AND I RESPECT THAT.
AND THE LOSS OF YOUR TWIN SISTER MUST HAVE BEEN INCREDIBLY HARD,
BUT YOU ARE THE SON OF OUR **LORD!** YOU HAVE A RESPONSIBILITY TO ...
TALGERT, THIS HAS **NOTHING** TO DO WITH THAT. **NOTHING!**
AND I KNOW *ALL* ABOUT MY *RESPONSIBILITIES.* **THAT'S WHY WE'RE HERE.**
MEKON, *CALM YOURSELF.* I'M GOING TO CALL OUR HOUSE'S COUNSELLOR, AND YOU CAN TALK TO HIM. IF HE DEEMS WHAT YOU SAY IMPORTANT, THEN PERHAPS I CAN ...
No! TALGERT!
THERE'S NO TIME FOR THIS!
LISTEN TO ME! YOU **MUST** UNDERSTAND ...
EXCUSE ME ...

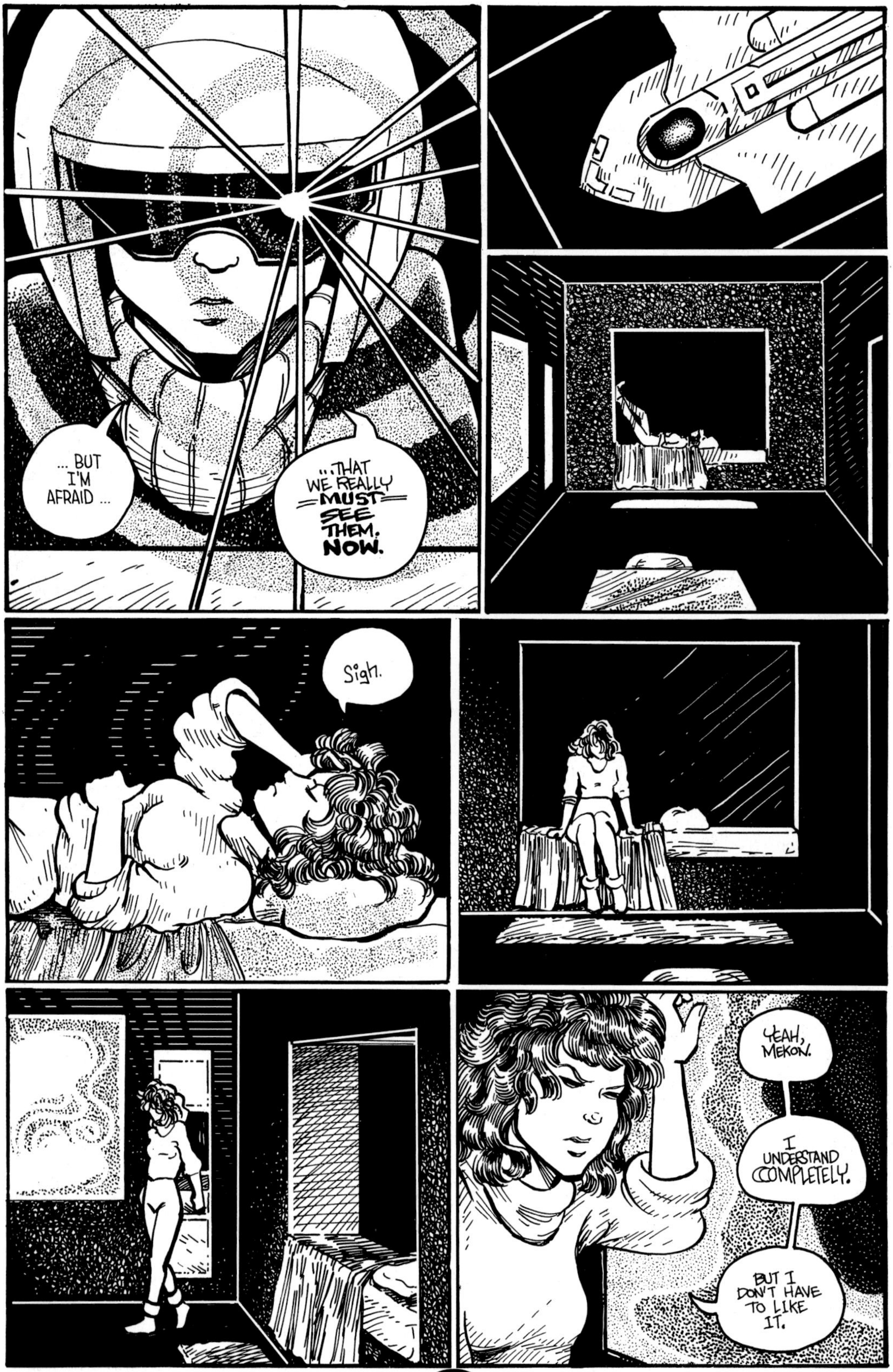
... BUT I'M AFRAID ...
...THAT WE REALLY MUST SEE THEM. NOW.
Sigh.
YEAH, MEKON.
I UNDERSTAND COMPLETELY.
BUT I DON'T HAVE TO LIKE IT.

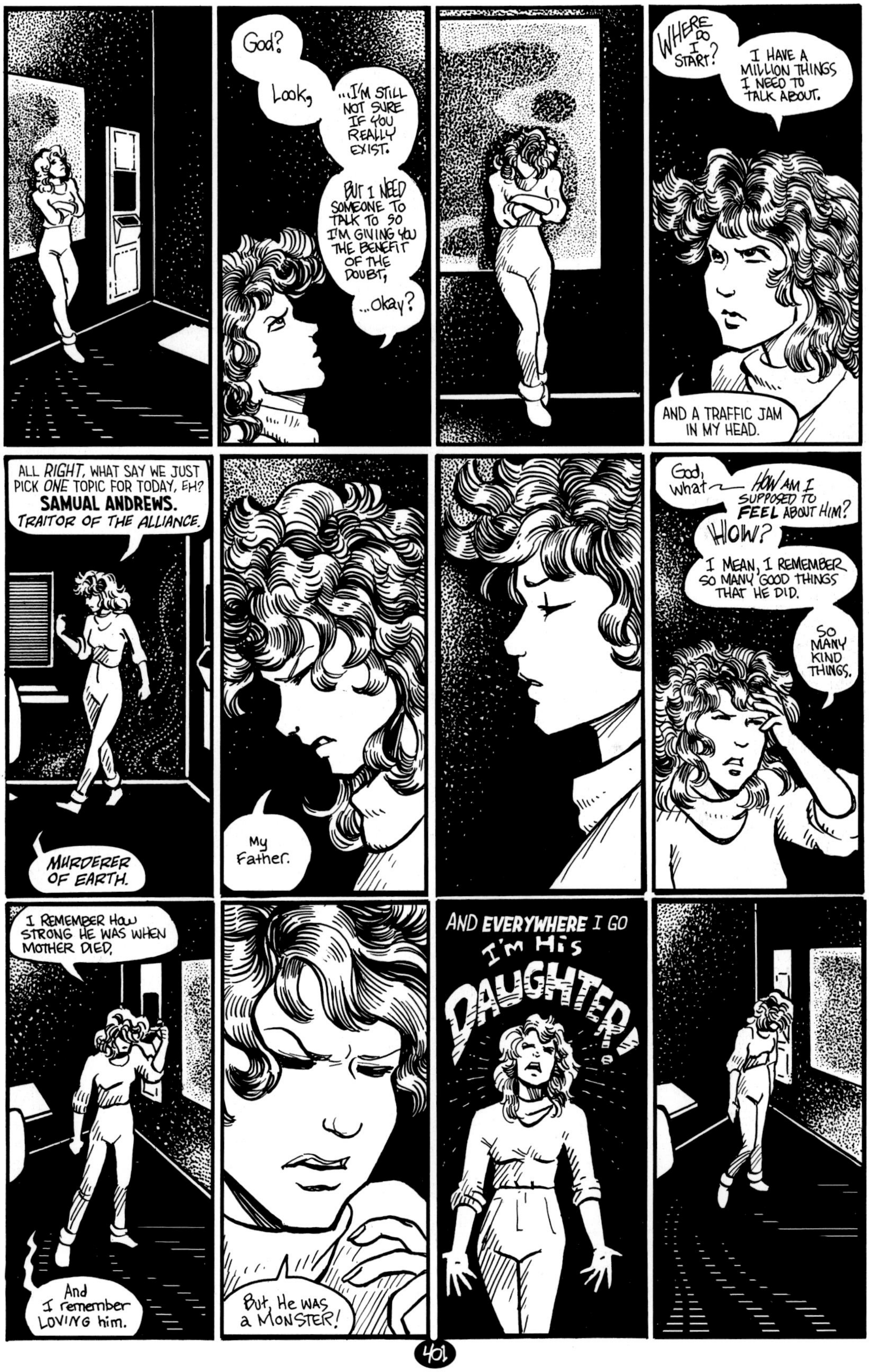
God?
Look,
...I'M STILL NOT SURE IF YOU REALLY EXIST.
BUT I NEED SOMEONE TO TALK TO SO I'M GIVING YOU THE BENEFIT OF THE DOUBT,
...Okay?
WHERE DO I START?
I HAVE A MILLION THINGS I NEED TO TALK ABOUT.
AND A TRAFFIC JAM IN MY HEAD.
ALL RIGHT, WHAT SAY WE JUST PICK ONE TOPIC FOR TODAY, EH? SAMUAL ANDREWS. TRAITOR OF THE ALLIANCE.
MURDERER OF EARTH.
My Father.
God, what—
HOW AM I SUPPOSED TO FEEL ABOUT HIM?
HOW?
I MEAN, I REMEMBER SO MANY GOOD THINGS THAT HE DID.
SO MANY KIND THINGS.
I REMEMBER HOW STRONG HE WAS WHEN MOTHER DIED,
And I remember LOVING him.
But, He WAS a MONSTER!
AND EVERYWHERE I GO I'm His DAUGHTER!

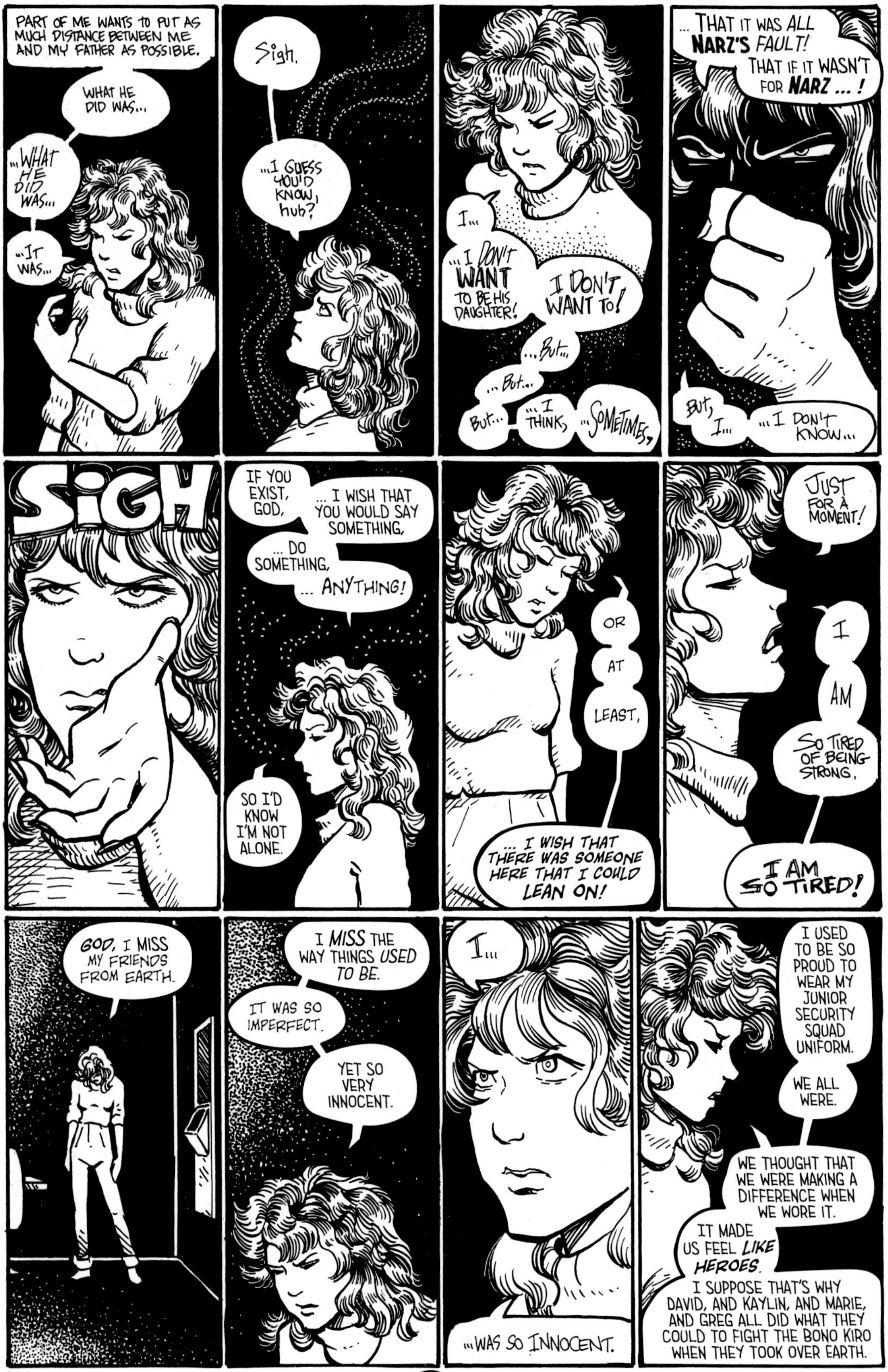
PART OF ME WANTS TO PUT AS MUCH DISTANCE BETWEEN ME AND MY FATHER AS POSSIBLE.
WHAT HE DID WAS...
...WHAT HE DID WAS...
...IT WAS...
Sigh.
...I GUESS YOU'D KNOW, huh?
I...
...I DON'T WANT TO BE HIS DAUGHTER!
I DON'T WANT TO!
...But...
...But...
But...
...I THINK,
...SOMETIMES,
...THAT IT WAS ALL NARZ'S FAULT!
THAT IF IT WASN'T FOR NARZ ...!
BUT, I...
...I DON'T KNOW...
SIGH
IF YOU EXIST, GOD,
... I WISH THAT YOU WOULD SAY SOMETHING,
... DO SOMETHING,
... ANYTHING!
SO I'D KNOW I'M NOT ALONE.
OR
AT
LEAST,
... I WISH THAT THERE WAS SOMEONE HERE THAT I COULD LEAN ON!
JUST FOR A MOMENT!
I
AM
SO TIRED OF BEING STRONG,
I AM SO TIRED!
GOD, I MISS MY FRIENDS FROM EARTH.
I MISS THE WAY THINGS USED TO BE.
IT WAS SO IMPERFECT.
YET SO VERY INNOCENT.
I...
...WAS SO INNOCENT.
I USED TO BE SO PROUD TO WEAR MY JUNIOR SECURITY SQUAD UNIFORM.
WE ALL WERE.
WE THOUGHT THAT WE WERE MAKING A DIFFERENCE WHEN WE WORE IT.
IT MADE US FEEL LIKE HEROES.
I SUPPOSE THAT'S WHY DAVID, AND KAYLIN, AND MARIE, AND GREG ALL DID WHAT THEY COULD TO FIGHT THE BONO KIRO WHEN THEY TOOK OVER EARTH.

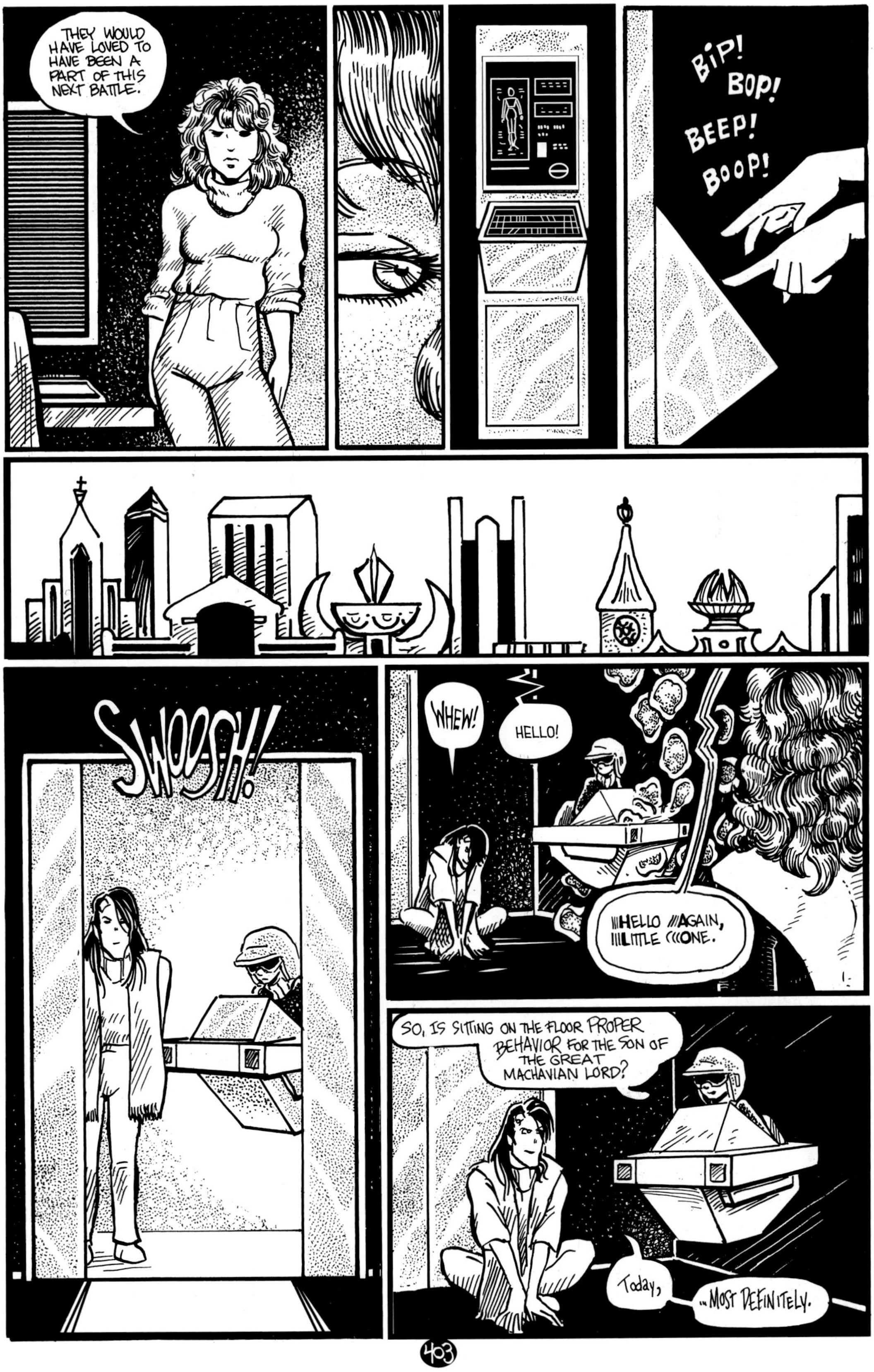
THEY WOULD HAVE LOVED TO HAVE BEEN A PART OF THIS NEXT BATTLE.
BIP! BOP! BEEP! BOOP!
SWOOSH!
WHEW!
HELLO!
HELLO AGAIN, LITTLE ONE.
SO, IS SITTING ON THE FLOOR PROPER BEHAVIOR FOR THE SON OF THE GREAT MACHAVIAN LORD?
Today,
...MOST DEFINITELY.

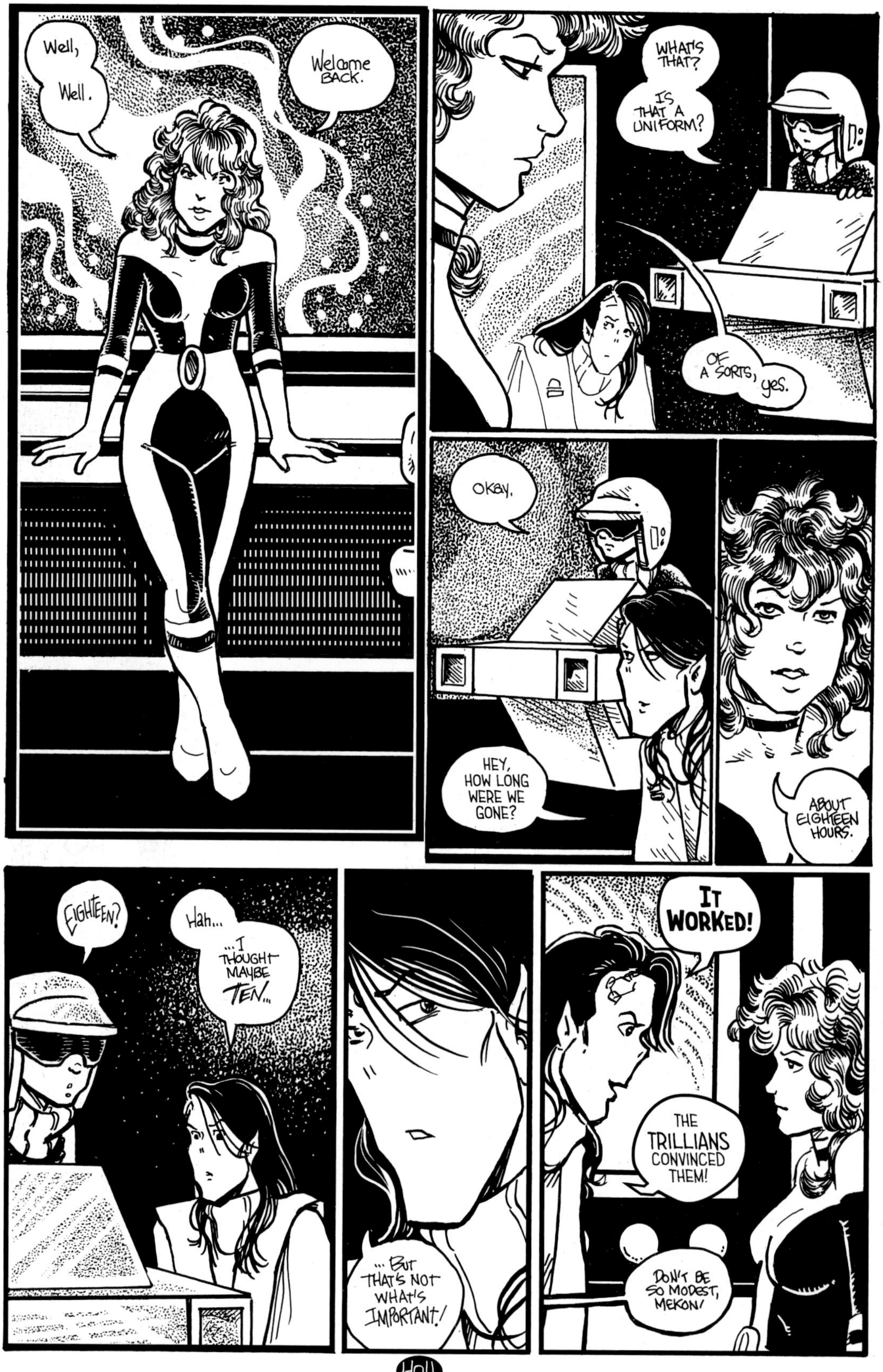
Well,
Well.
Welcome BACK.
WHAT'S THAT?
IS THAT A UNIFORM?
OF A SORTS, yes.
Okay.
HEY, HOW LONG WERE WE GONE?
ABOUT EIGHTEEN HOURS.
EIGHTEEN?
Hah...
...I THOUGHT MAYBE TEN...
...But THAT'S NOT WHAT'S IMPORTANT!
IT WORKED!
THE TRILLIANS CONVINCED THEM!
DON'T BE SO MODEST, MEKON!

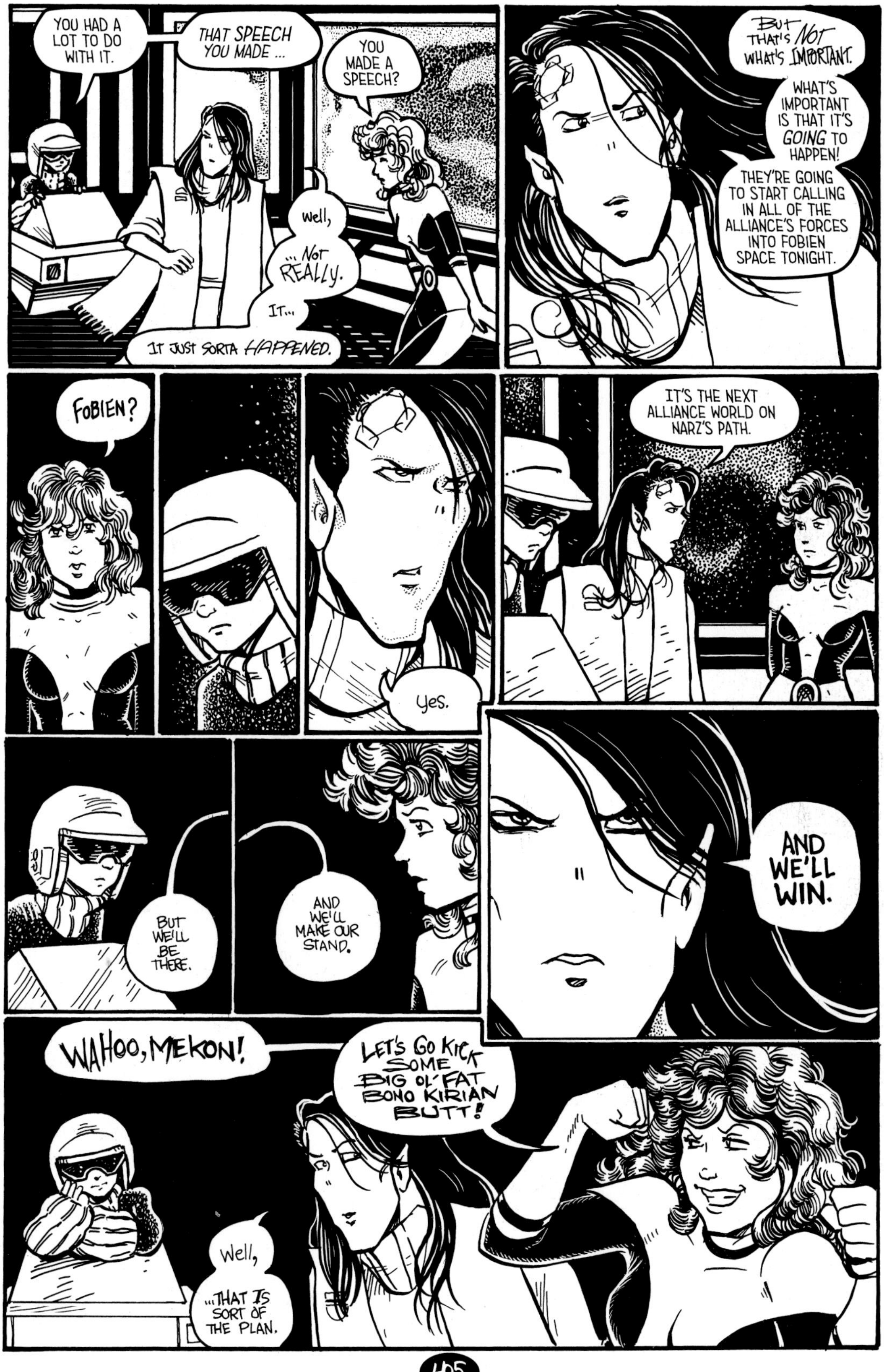

YOU HAD A LOT TO DO WITH IT.
THAT SPEECH YOU MADE ...
YOU MADE A SPEECH?
Well,
... Not REALLY.
It...
It just sorta HAPPENED.
But that's NOT what's IMPORTANT.
WHAT'S IMPORTANT IS THAT IT'S GOING TO HAPPEN!
THEY'RE GOING TO START CALLING IN ALL OF THE ALLIANCE'S FORCES INTO FOBIEN SPACE TONIGHT.
FOBIEN?
Yes.
IT'S THE NEXT ALLIANCE WORLD ON NARZ'S PATH.
BUT WE'LL BE THERE.
AND WE'LL MAKE OUR STAND.
AND WE'LL WIN.
WAHOO, MEKON!
LET'S GO KICK SOME BIG OL' FAT BONO KIRIAN BUTT!
Well,
...THAT IS SORT OF THE PLAN.

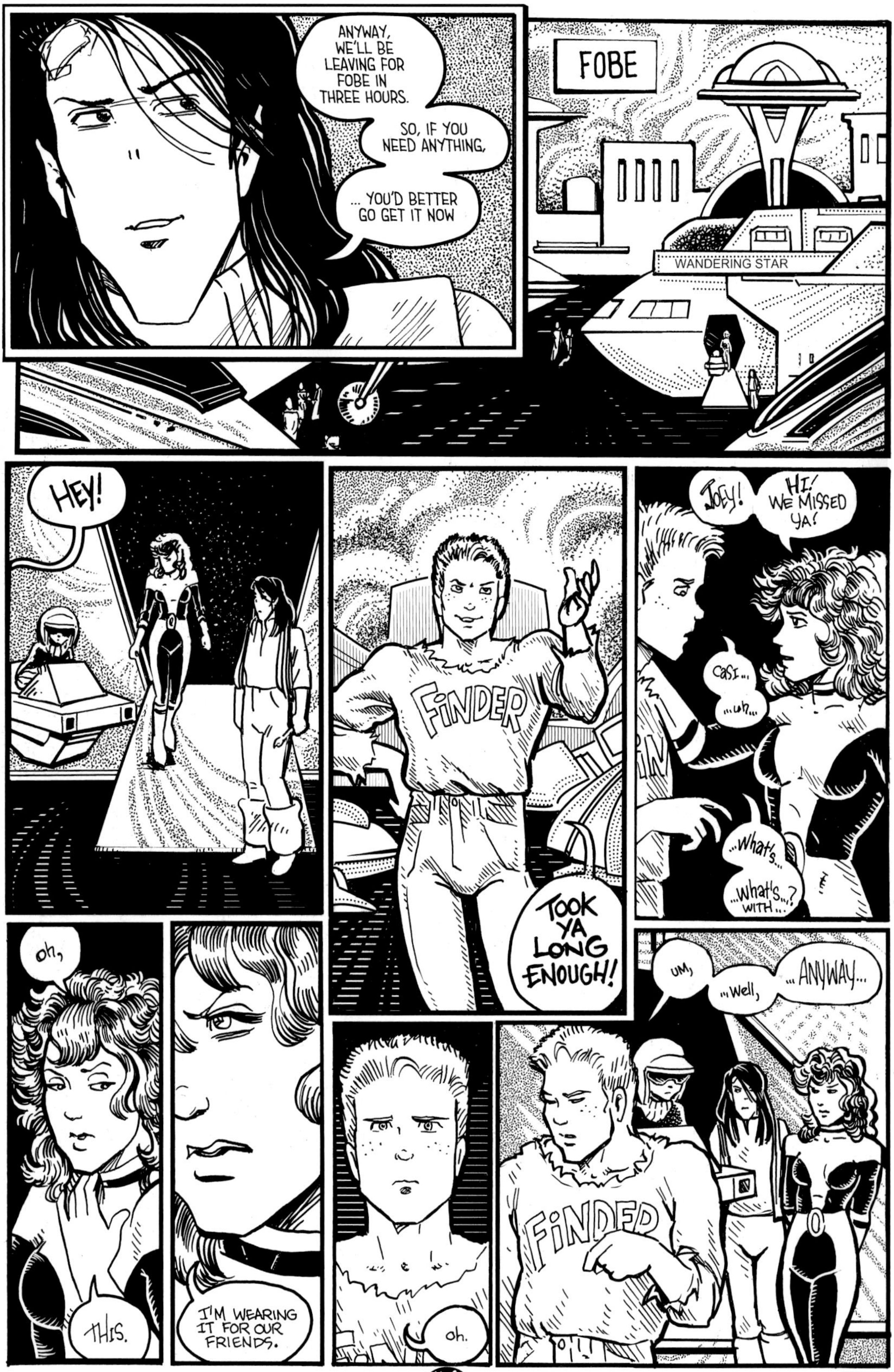
ANYWAY, WE'LL BE LEAVING FOR FOBE IN THREE HOURS.
SO, IF YOU NEED ANYTHING,
... YOU'D BETTER GO GET IT NOW
FOBE
WANDERING STAR
HEY!
TOOK YA LONG ENOUGH!
JOEY!
HI! WE MISSED YA!
CASI...
...uh...
...what's...
...what's...? WITH...
oh,
THIS.
I'M WEARING IT FOR OUR FRIENDS.
oh.
UM,
...Well,
...ANYWAY...
FINDER

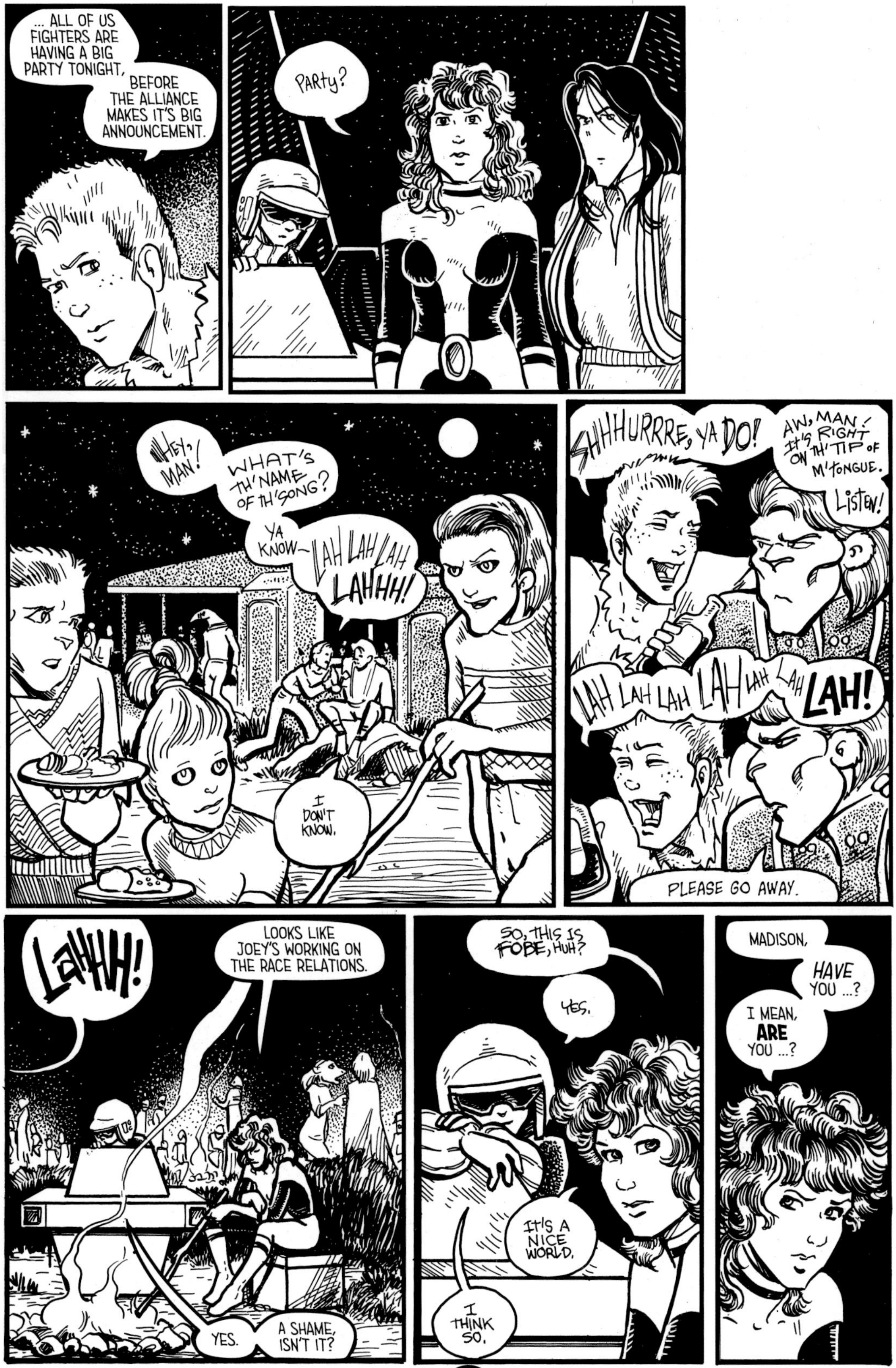

... ALL OF US FIGHTERS ARE HAVING A BIG PARTY TONIGHT,
BEFORE THE ALLIANCE MAKES IT'S BIG ANNOUNCEMENT.
Party?
HEY, MAN!
WHAT'S TH' NAME OF TH' SONG?
YA KNOW—
LAH LAH LAH LAHHH!
I DON'T KNOW.
SHHHURRRE, YA DO!
AW, MAN! IT'S RIGHT ON TH' TIP OF M'TONGUE.
LISTEN!
LAH LAH LAH LAH LAH LAH LAH!
PLEASE GO AWAY.
LAHHH!
LOOKS LIKE JOEY'S WORKING ON THE RACE RELATIONS.
YES.
A SHAME, ISN'T IT?
SO, THIS IS FOBE, HUH?
YES.
IT'S A NICE WORLD.
I THINK SO.
MADISON,
HAVE YOU ...?
I MEAN, ARE YOU ...?

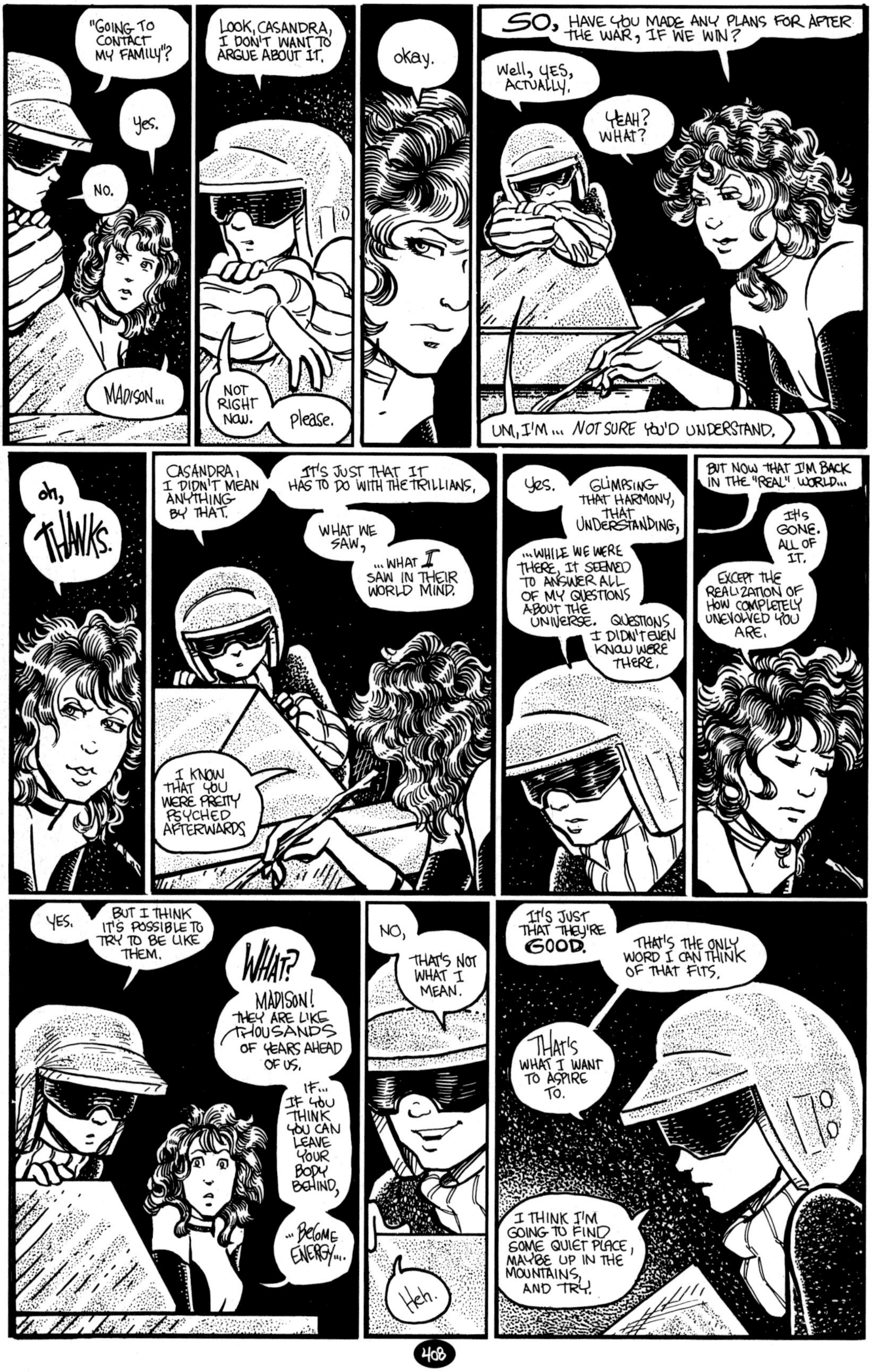
"GOING TO CONTACT MY FAMILY"?
YES.
NO.
MADISON...
LOOK, CASANDRA, I DON'T WANT TO ARGUE ABOUT IT.
NOT RIGHT NOW.
Please.
okay.
SO, HAVE YOU MADE ANY PLANS FOR AFTER THE WAR, IF WE WIN?
Well, YES, ACTUALLY.
YEAH? WHAT?
UM, I'M... NOT SURE YOU'D UNDERSTAND.
oh, THANKS.
CASANDRA, I DIDN'T MEAN ANYTHING BY THAT.
IT'S JUST THAT IT HAS TO DO WITH THE TRILLIANS,
WHAT WE SAW,
...WHAT I SAW IN THEIR WORLD MIND.
I KNOW THAT YOU WERE PRETTY PSYCHED AFTERWARDS.
Yes.
GLIMPSING THAT HARMONY, THAT UNDERSTANDING,
...WHILE WE WERE THERE, IT SEEMED TO ANSWER ALL OF MY QUESTIONS ABOUT THE UNIVERSE.
QUESTIONS I DIDN'T EVEN KNOW WERE THERE.
BUT NOW THAT I'M BACK IN THE "REAL" WORLD...
IT'S GONE. ALL OF IT.
EXCEPT THE REALIZATION OF HOW COMPLETELY UNEVOLVED YOU ARE.
YES.
BUT I THINK IT'S POSSIBLE TO TRY TO BE LIKE THEM.
WHAT?
MADISON! THEY ARE LIKE THOUSANDS OF YEARS AHEAD OF US.
IF... IF YOU THINK YOU CAN LEAVE YOUR BODY BEHIND,
...BECOME ENERGY...
NO,
THAT'S NOT WHAT I MEAN.
Heh.
IT'S JUST THAT THEY'RE GOOD.
THAT'S THE ONLY WORD I CAN THINK OF THAT FITS.
THAT'S WHAT I WANT TO ASPIRE TO.
I THINK I'M GOING TO FIND SOME QUIET PLACE, MAYBE UP IN THE MOUNTAINS, AND TRY.

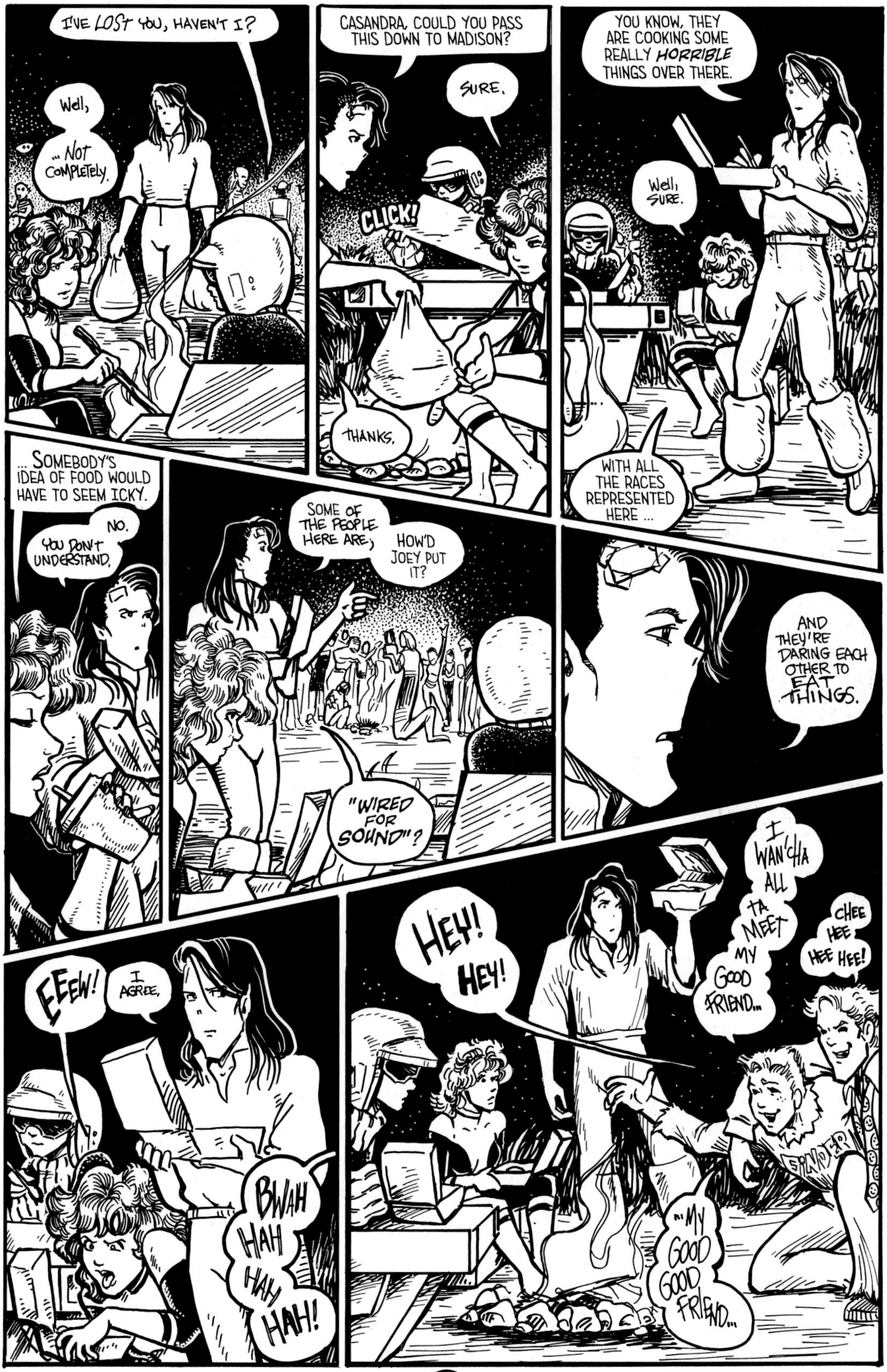
I'VE LOST YOU, HAVEN'T I?
Well,
... NOT COMPLETELY.
CASANDRA, COULD YOU PASS THIS DOWN TO MADISON?
SURE.
CLICK!
THANKS.
YOU KNOW, THEY ARE COOKING SOME REALLY HORRIBLE THINGS OVER THERE.
Well, SURE.
WITH ALL THE RACES REPRESENTED HERE ...
... SOMEBODY'S IDEA OF FOOD WOULD HAVE TO SEEM ICKY.
NO.
YOU DON'T UNDERSTAND.
SOME OF THE PEOPLE HERE ARE,
HOW'D JOEY PUT IT?
"WIRED FOR SOUND"?
AND THEY'RE DARING EACH OTHER TO EAT THINGS.
EEEW!
I AGREE.
BWAH HAH HAH HAH!
HEY! HEY!
I WAN'CHA ALL TA MEET MY GOOD FRIEND...
CHEE HEE HEE HEE!
...MY GOOD GOOD FRIEND...

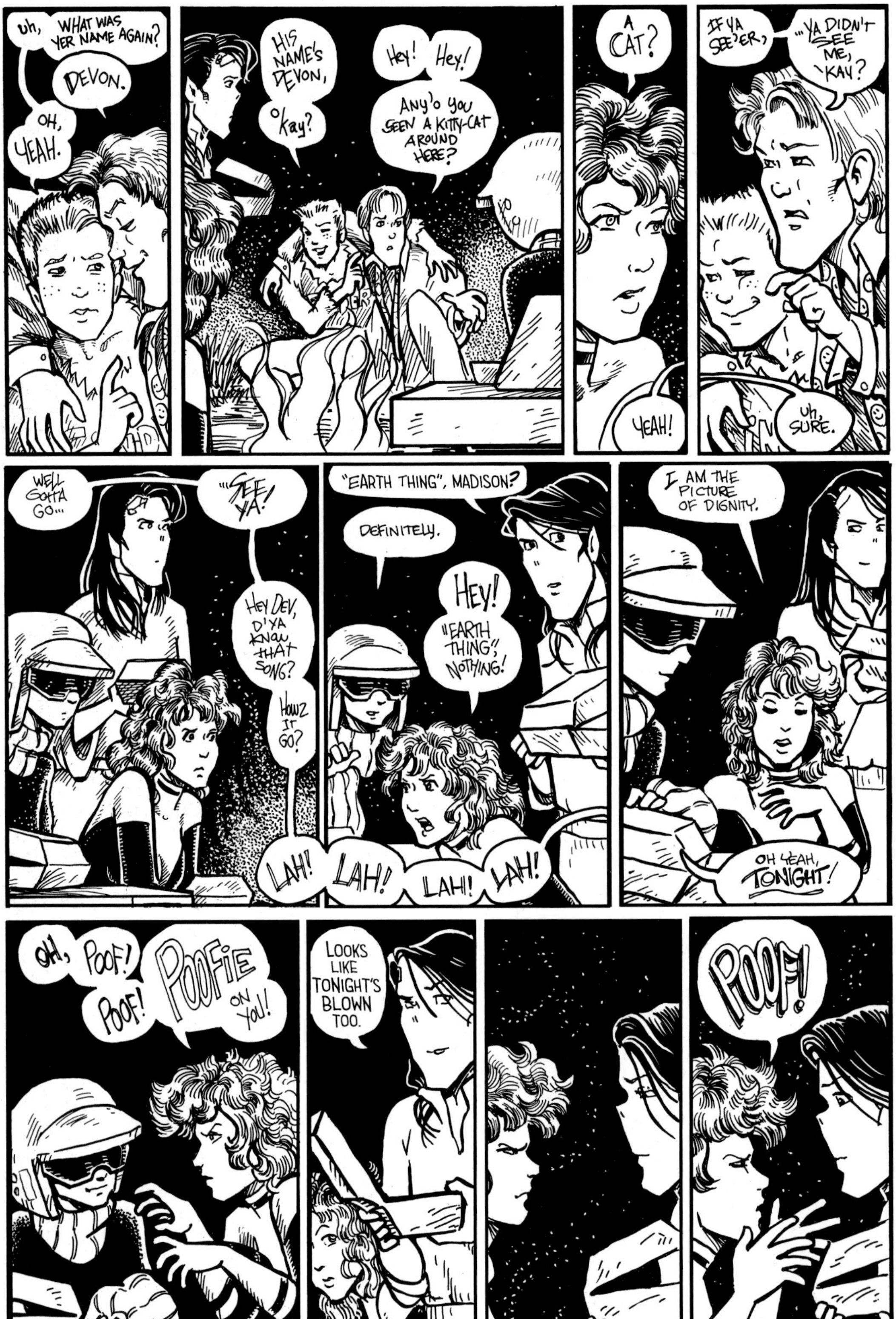
uh,
WHAT WAS YER NAME AGAIN?
DEVON.
OH, YEAH.
HIS NAME'S DEVON, 'kay?
Hey! Hey!
Any'o you seen a kitty-cat around here?
A CAT?
YEAH!
IF YA SEE 'ER,
...YA DIDN'T SEE ME, 'KAY?
uh, SURE.
WELL GOTTA GO...
...SEE YA!
Hey Dev, d'ya know that song?
Howz it go?
"EARTH THING", MADISON?
DEFINITELY.
HEY! "EARTH THING," NOTHING!
LAH! LAH! LAH! LAH!
I AM THE PICTURE OF DIGNITY.
OH YEAH, TONIGHT!
OH, POOF! POOF! POOFIE ON YOU!
LOOKS LIKE TONIGHT'S BLOWN TOO.
POOF!

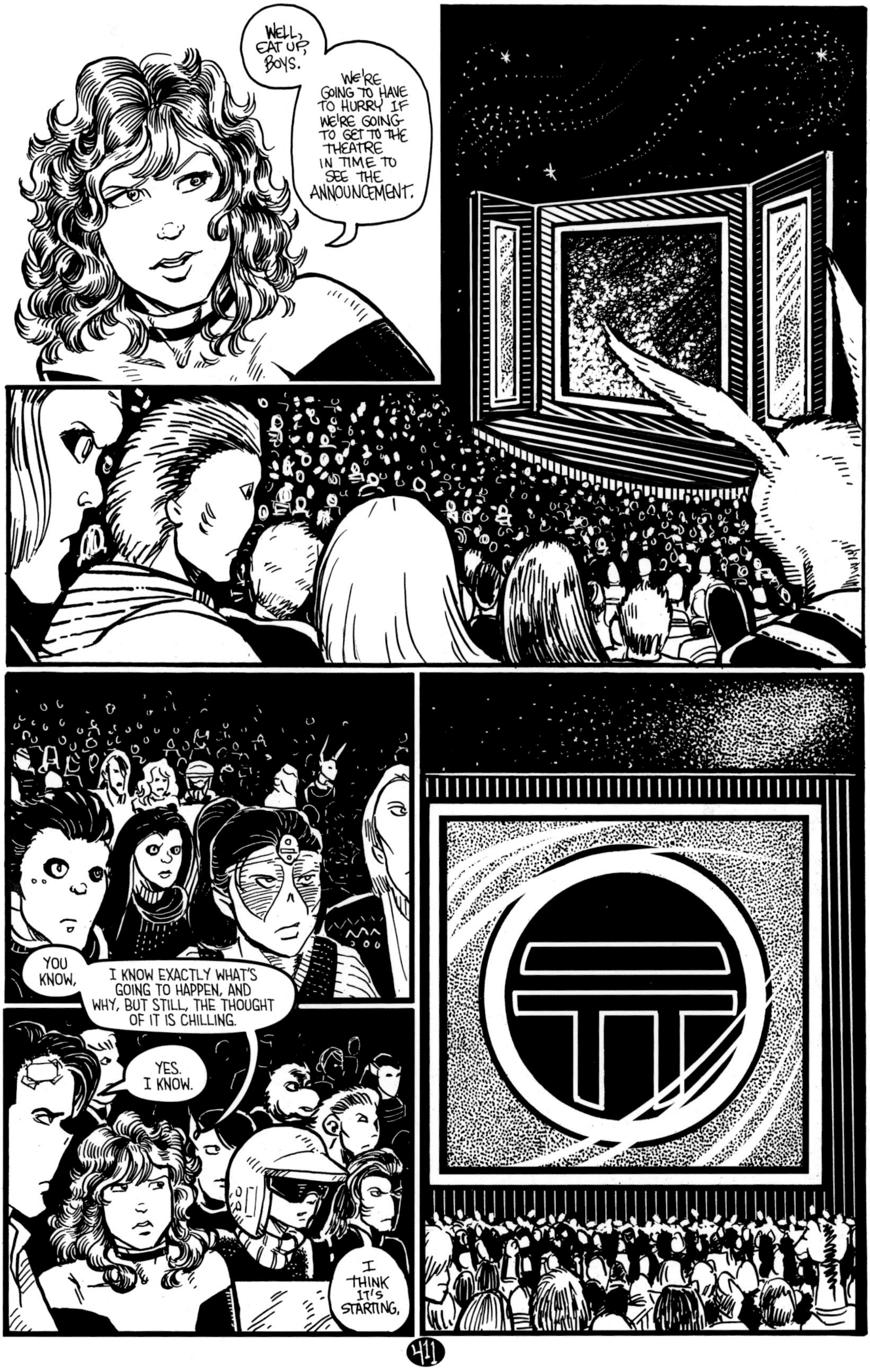
WELL, EAT UP, BOYS.
WE'RE GOING TO HAVE TO HURRY IF WE'RE GOING TO GET TO THE THEATRE IN TIME TO SEE THE ANNOUNCEMENT.
YOU KNOW,
I KNOW EXACTLY WHAT'S GOING TO HAPPEN, AND WHY, BUT STILL, THE THOUGHT OF IT IS CHILLING.
YES. I KNOW.
I THINK IT'S STARTING.

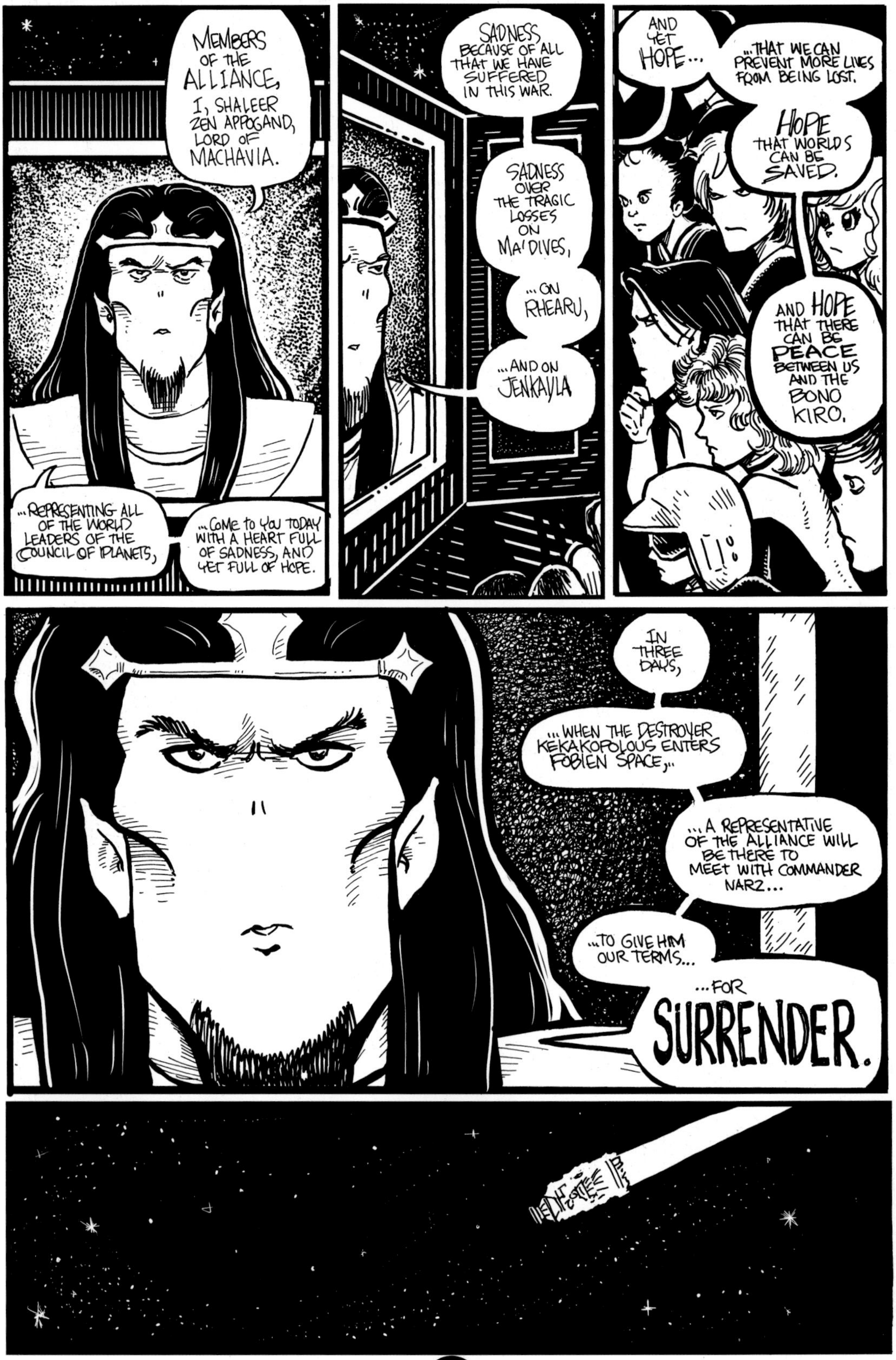
MEMBERS OF THE ALLIANCE, I, SHALEER ZEN APPOGAND, LORD OF MACHAVIA.
...REPRESENTING ALL OF THE WORLD LEADERS OF THE COUNCIL OF PLANETS,
...COME TO YOU TODAY WITH A HEART FULL OF SADNESS, AND YET FULL OF HOPE.
SADNESS BECAUSE OF ALL THAT WE HAVE SUFFERED IN THIS WAR.
SADNESS OVER THE TRAGIC LOSSES ON MA'DIVES,
...ON RHEARU,
...AND ON JENKAYLA
AND YET HOPE...
...THAT WE CAN PREVENT MORE LIVES FROM BEING LOST.
HOPE THAT WORLDS CAN BE SAVED.
AND HOPE THAT THERE CAN BE PEACE BETWEEN US AND THE BONO KIRO.
IN THREE DAYS,
...WHEN THE DESTROYER KEKAKOPOLOUS ENTERS FOBIEN SPACE,..
...A REPRESENTATIVE OF THE ALLIANCE WILL BE THERE TO MEET WITH COMMANDER NARZ...
...TO GIVE HIM OUR TERMS...
...FOR SURRENDER.

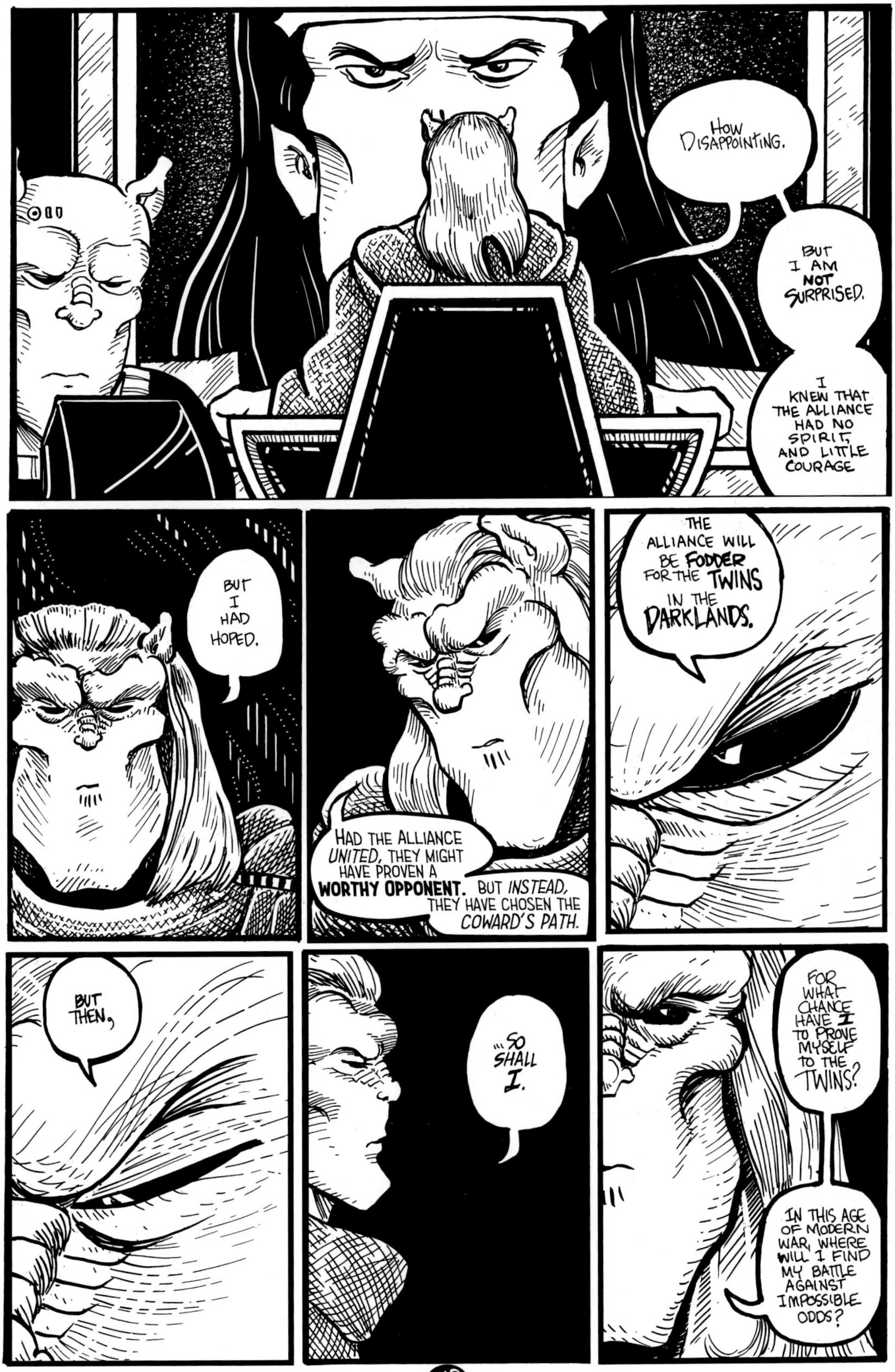

HOW DISAPPOINTING.
BUT I AM NOT SURPRISED.
I KNEW THAT THE ALLIANCE HAD NO SPIRIT, AND LITTLE COURAGE
BUT I HAD HOPED.
HAD THE ALLIANCE UNITED, THEY MIGHT HAVE PROVEN A WORTHY OPPONENT. BUT INSTEAD, THEY HAVE CHOSEN THE COWARD'S PATH.
THE ALLIANCE WILL BE FODDER FOR THE TWINS IN THE DARKLANDS.
BUT THEN,
...SO SHALL I.
FOR WHAT CHANCE HAVE I TO PROVE MYSELF TO THE TWINS?
IN THIS AGE OF MODERN WAR, WHERE WILL I FIND MY BATTLE AGAINST IMPOSSIBLE ODDS?

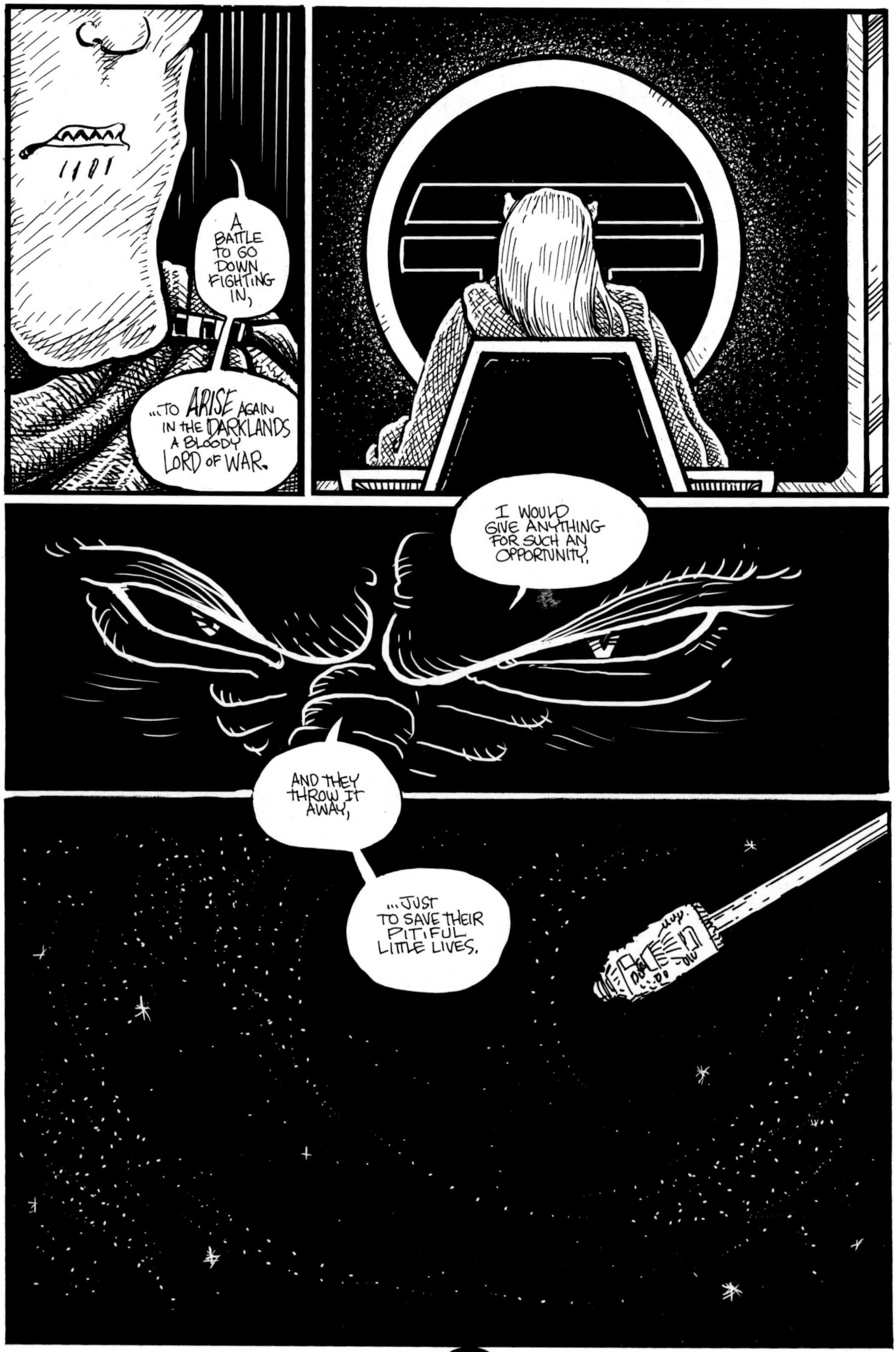
A BATTLE TO GO DOWN FIGHTING IN,
...TO ARISE AGAIN IN THE DARKLANDS A BLOODY LORD OF WAR.
I WOULD GIVE ANYTHING FOR SUCH AN OPPORTUNITY,
AND THEY THROW IT AWAY,
...JUST TO SAVE THEIR PITIFUL LITTLE LIVES.

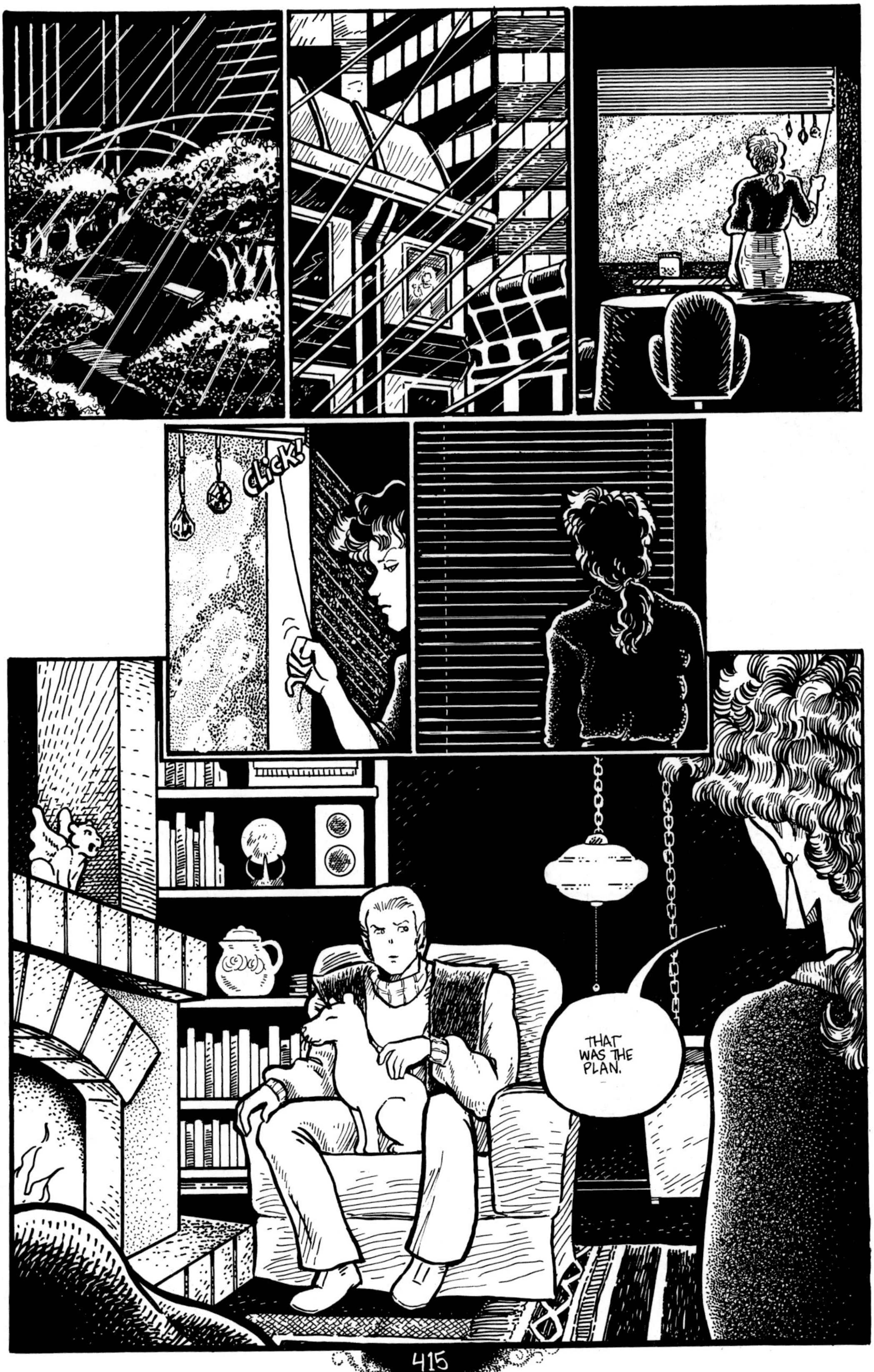
CLICK!
THAT WAS THE PLAN.

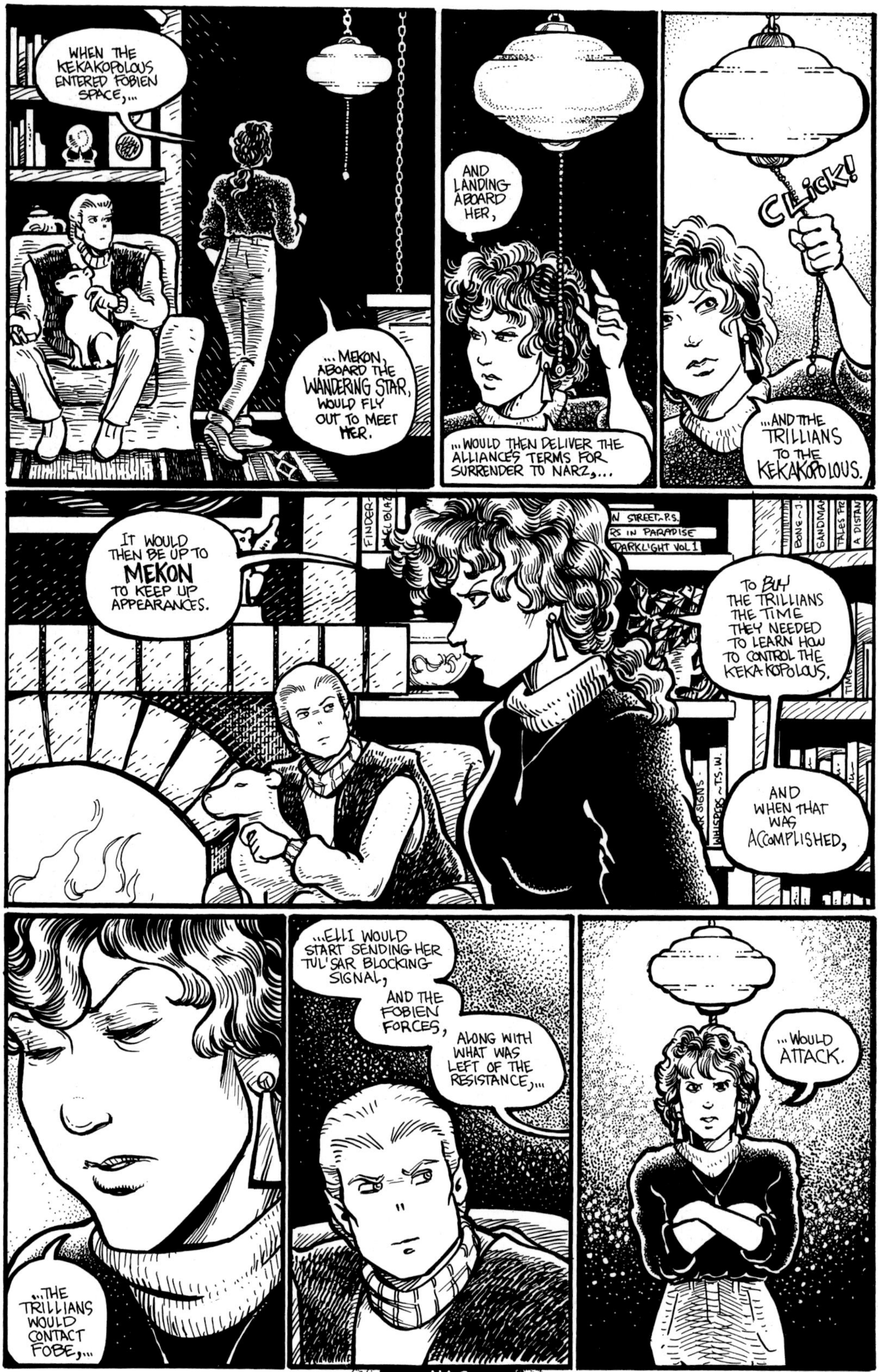
WHEN THE KEKAKOPOLOUS ENTERED FOBIEN SPACE,...
...MEKON, ABOARD THE WANDERING STAR, WOULD FLY OUT TO MEET HER.
AND LANDING ABOARD HER,
...WOULD THEN DELIVER THE ALLIANCE'S TERMS FOR SURRENDER TO NARZ,...
CLICK!
...AND THE TRILLIANS TO THE KEKAKOPOLOUS.
IT WOULD THEN BE UP TO MEKON TO KEEP UP APPEARANCES.
TO BUY THE TRILLIANS THE TIME THEY NEEDED TO LEARN HOW TO CONTROL THE KEKA-KOPOLOUS.
AND WHEN THAT WAS ACCOMPLISHED,
...THE TRILLIANS WOULD CONTACT FOBE,...
...ELLI WOULD START SENDING HER TUL'SAR BLOCKING SIGNAL,
AND THE FOBIEN FORCES,
ALONG WITH WHAT WAS LEFT OF THE RESISTANCE,...
...WOULD ATTACK.

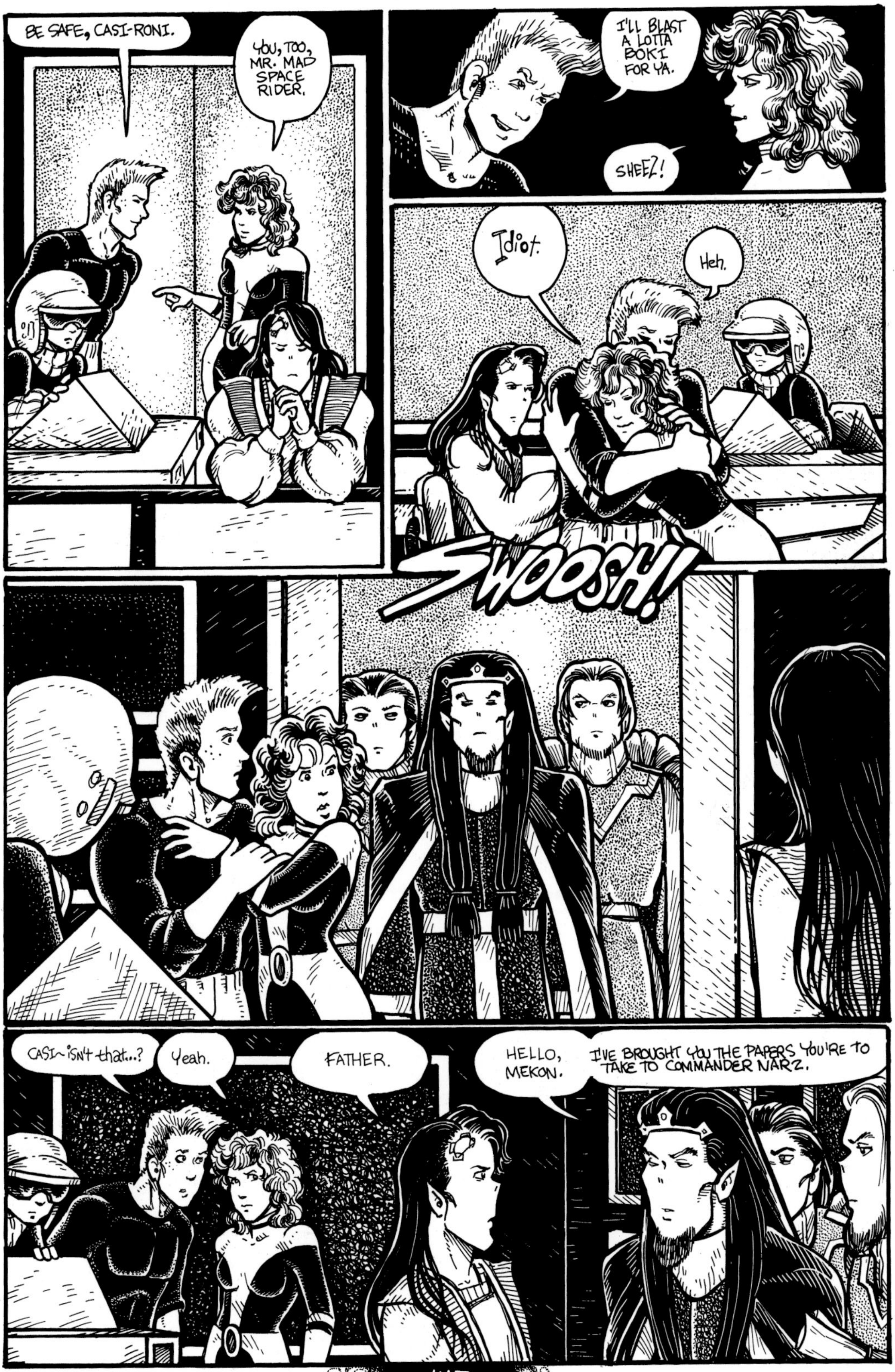
BE SAFE, CASI-RONI.
YOU, TOO, MR. MAD SPACE RIDER.
I'LL BLAST A LOTTA BOKI FOR YA.
SHEEZ!
Idiot.
Heh.
SWOOSH!
CASI~ isn't that...?
Yeah.
FATHER.
HELLO, MEKON.
I'VE BROUGHT YOU THE PAPERS YOU'RE TO TAKE TO COMMANDER NARZ.

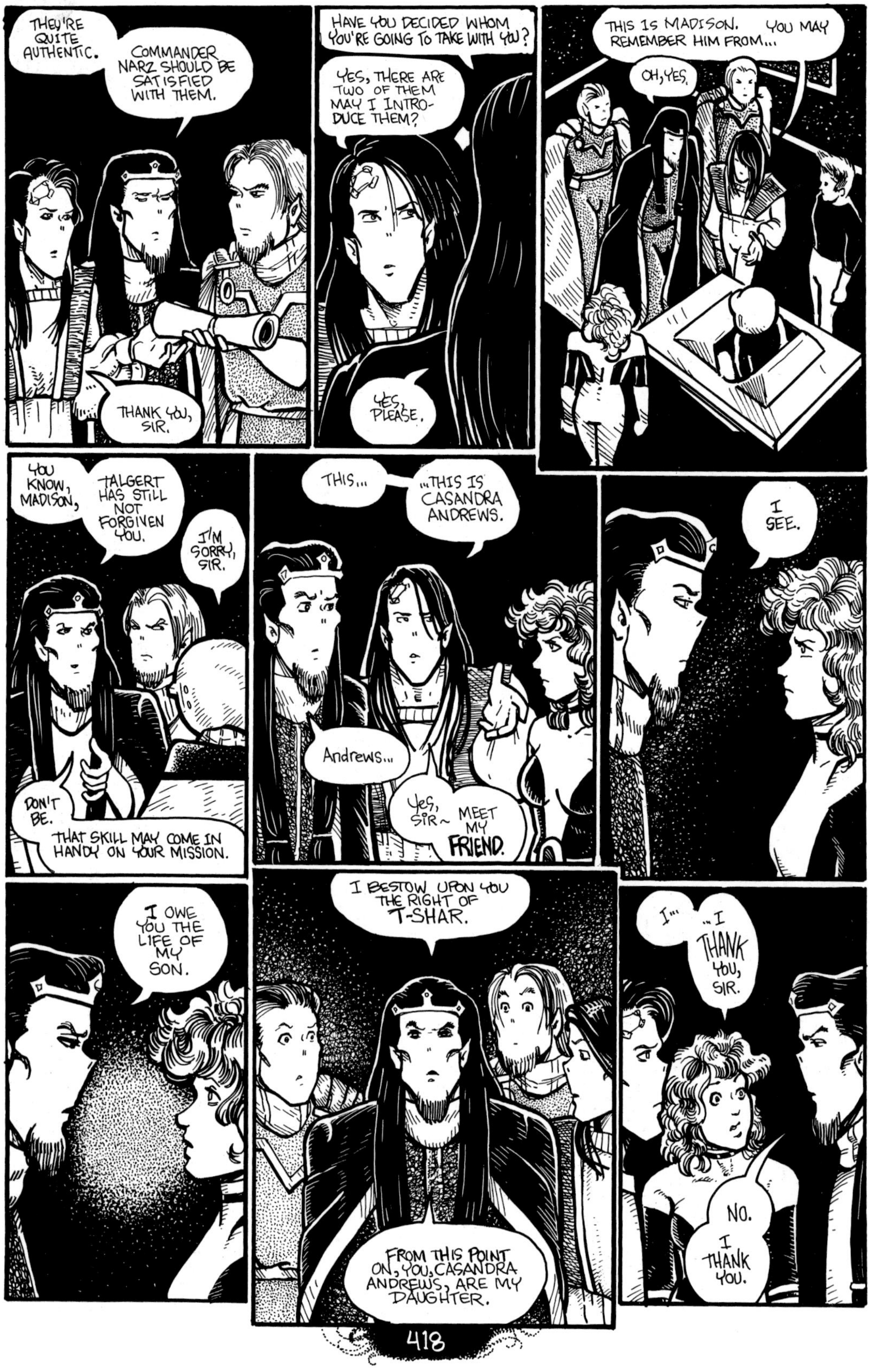
THEY'RE QUITE AUTHENTIC.
COMMANDER NARZ SHOULD BE SATISFIED WITH THEM.
THANK YOU, SIR.
HAVE YOU DECIDED WHOM YOU'RE GOING TO TAKE WITH YOU?
YES, THERE ARE TWO OF THEM MAY I INTRODUCE THEM?
YES, PLEASE.
THIS IS MADISON.
YOU MAY REMEMBER HIM FROM...
OH, YES.
YOU KNOW, MADISON,
TALGERT HAS STILL NOT FORGIVEN YOU.
I'M SORRY, SIR.
DON'T BE.
THAT SKILL MAY COME IN HANDY ON YOUR MISSION.
THIS...
...THIS IS CASANDRA ANDREWS.
Andrews...
Yes, SIR~
MEET MY FRIEND.
I SEE.
I OWE YOU THE LIFE OF MY SON.
I BESTOW UPON YOU THE RIGHT OF T-SHAR.
FROM THIS POINT ON, YOU, CASANDRA ANDREWS, ARE MY DAUGHTER.
I...
...I THANK YOU, SIR.
NO.
I THANK YOU.

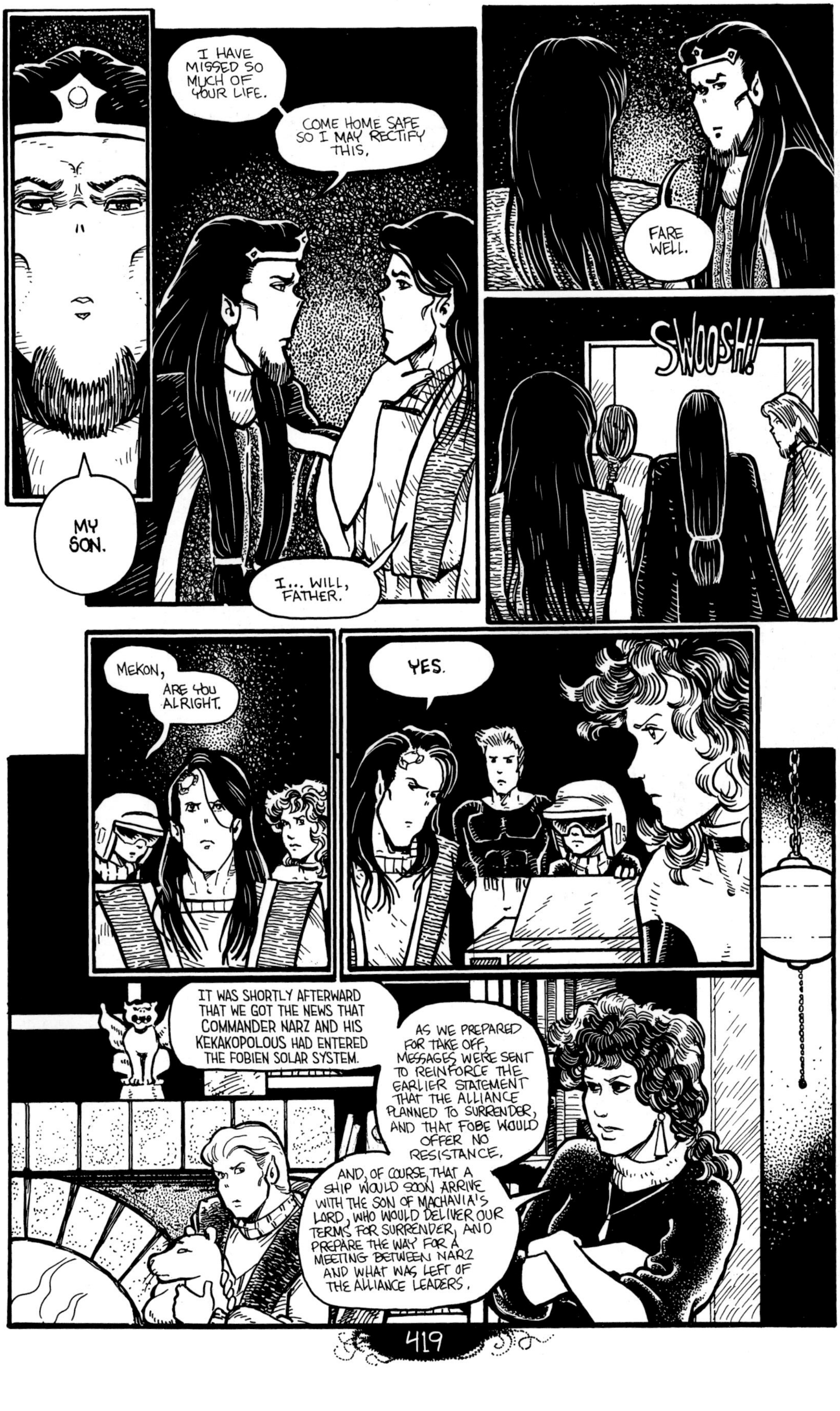
MY SON.
I HAVE MISSED SO MUCH OF YOUR LIFE.
COME HOME SAFE SO I MAY RECTIFY THIS.
I... WILL, FATHER.
FARE WELL.
SWOOSH!
MEKON, ARE YOU ALRIGHT.
YES.
IT WAS SHORTLY AFTERWARD THAT WE GOT THE NEWS THAT COMMANDER NARZ AND HIS KEKAKOPOLOUS HAD ENTERED THE FOBIEN SOLAR SYSTEM.
AS WE PREPARED FOR TAKE OFF, MESSAGES WERE SENT TO REINFORCE THE EARLIER STATEMENT THAT THE ALLIANCE PLANNED TO SURRENDER, AND THAT FOBE WOULD OFFER NO RESISTANCE,
AND, OF COURSE, THAT A SHIP WOULD SOON ARRIVE WITH THE SON OF MACHAVIA'S LORD, WHO WOULD DELIVER OUR TERMS FOR SURRENDER, AND PREPARE THE WAY FOR A MEETING BETWEEN NARZ AND WHAT WAS LEFT OF THE ALLIANCE LEADERS.

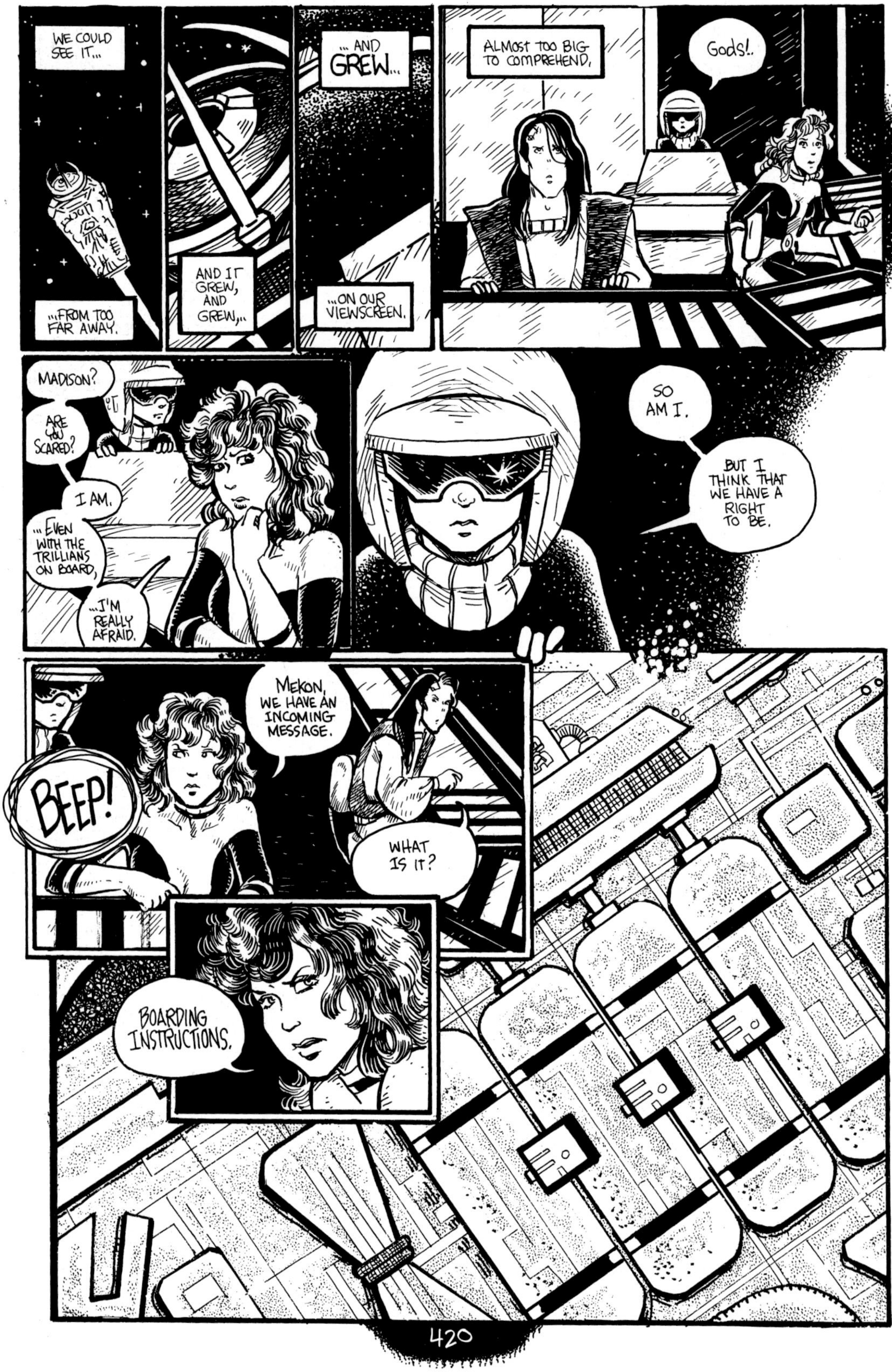
WE COULD SEE IT...
...FROM TOO FAR AWAY.
AND IT GREW, AND GREW,..
... AND GREW...
...ON OUR VIEWSCREEN.
ALMOST TOO BIG TO COMPREHEND,
Gods!.
MADISON?
ARE YOU SCARED?
I AM.
...EVEN WITH THE TRILLIANS ON BOARD,
...I'M REALLY AFRAID.
SO AM I.
BUT I THINK THAT WE HAVE A RIGHT TO BE.
BEEP!
MEKON, WE HAVE AN INCOMING MESSAGE.
WHAT IS IT?
BOARDING INSTRUCTIONS.

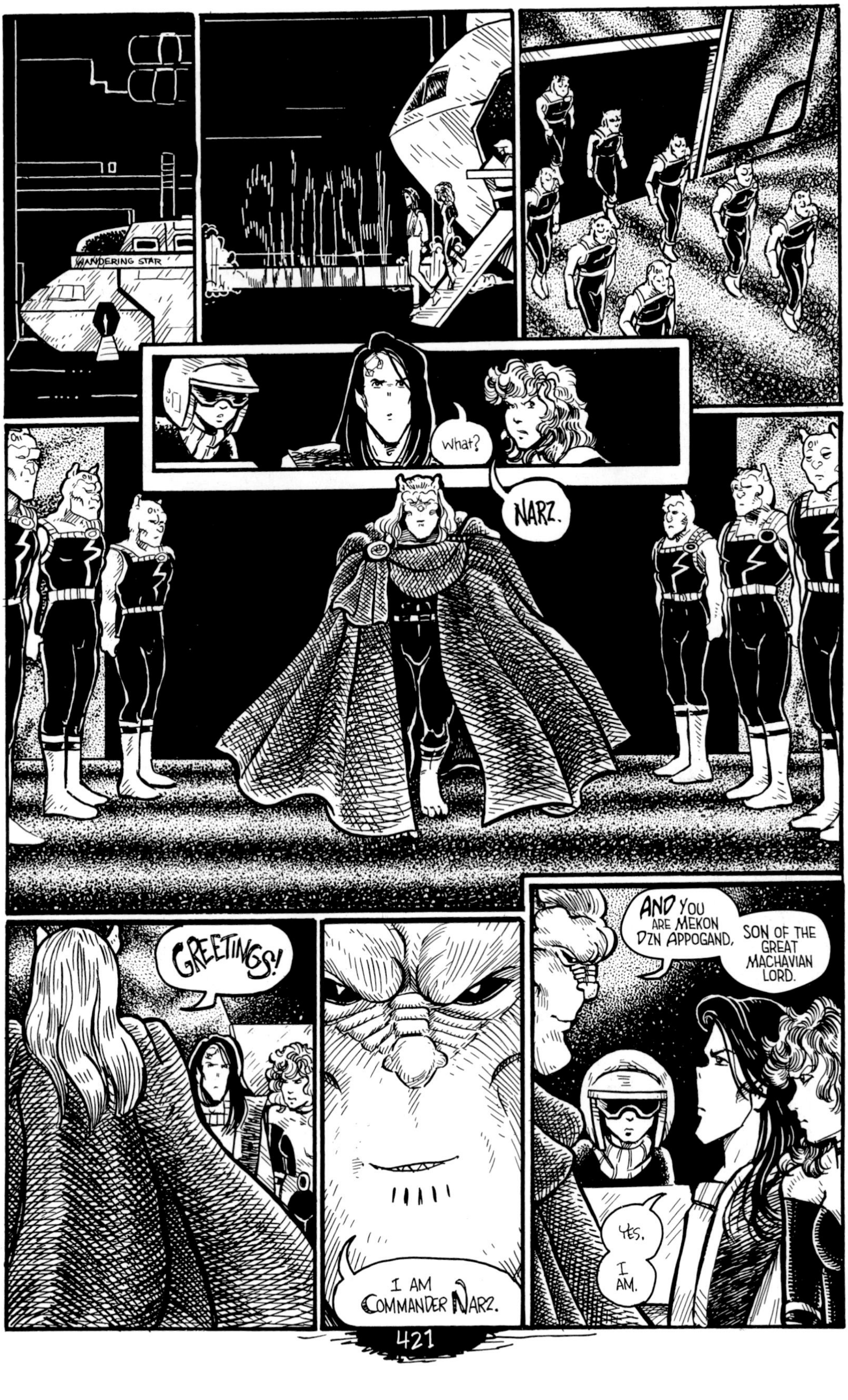
WANDERING STAR
SHOOSH
What?
NARZ.
GREETINGS!
I AM COMMANDER NARZ.
AND YOU ARE MEKON DZN APPOGAND,
SON OF THE GREAT MACHAVIAN LORD.
YES.
I AM.

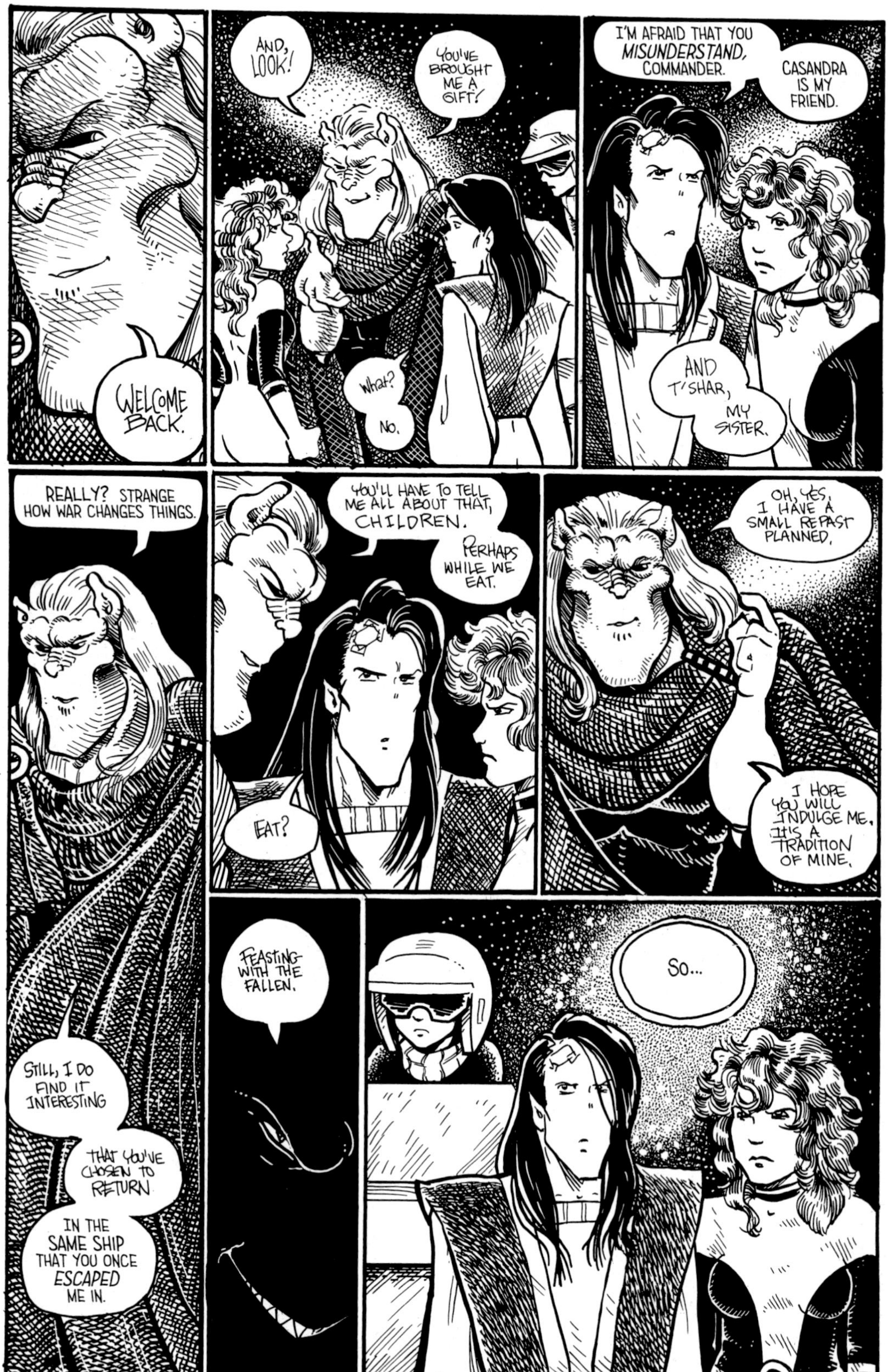
WELCOME BACK.
AND, LOOK!
YOU'VE BROUGHT ME A GIFT!
What?
No.
I'M AFRAID THAT YOU MISUNDERSTAND, COMMANDER.
CASANDRA IS MY FRIEND.
AND T'SHAR, MY SISTER.
REALLY? STRANGE HOW WAR CHANGES THINGS.
YOU'LL HAVE TO TELL ME ALL ABOUT THAT, CHILDREN.
PERHAPS WHILE WE EAT.
EAT?
OH, YES, I HAVE A SMALL REPAST PLANNED,
I HOPE YOU WILL INDULGE ME. IT'S A TRADITION OF MINE,
STILL, I DO FIND IT INTERESTING
THAT YOU'VE CHOSEN TO RETURN
IN THE SAME SHIP THAT YOU ONCE ESCAPED ME IN.
FEASTING WITH THE FALLEN.
SO...

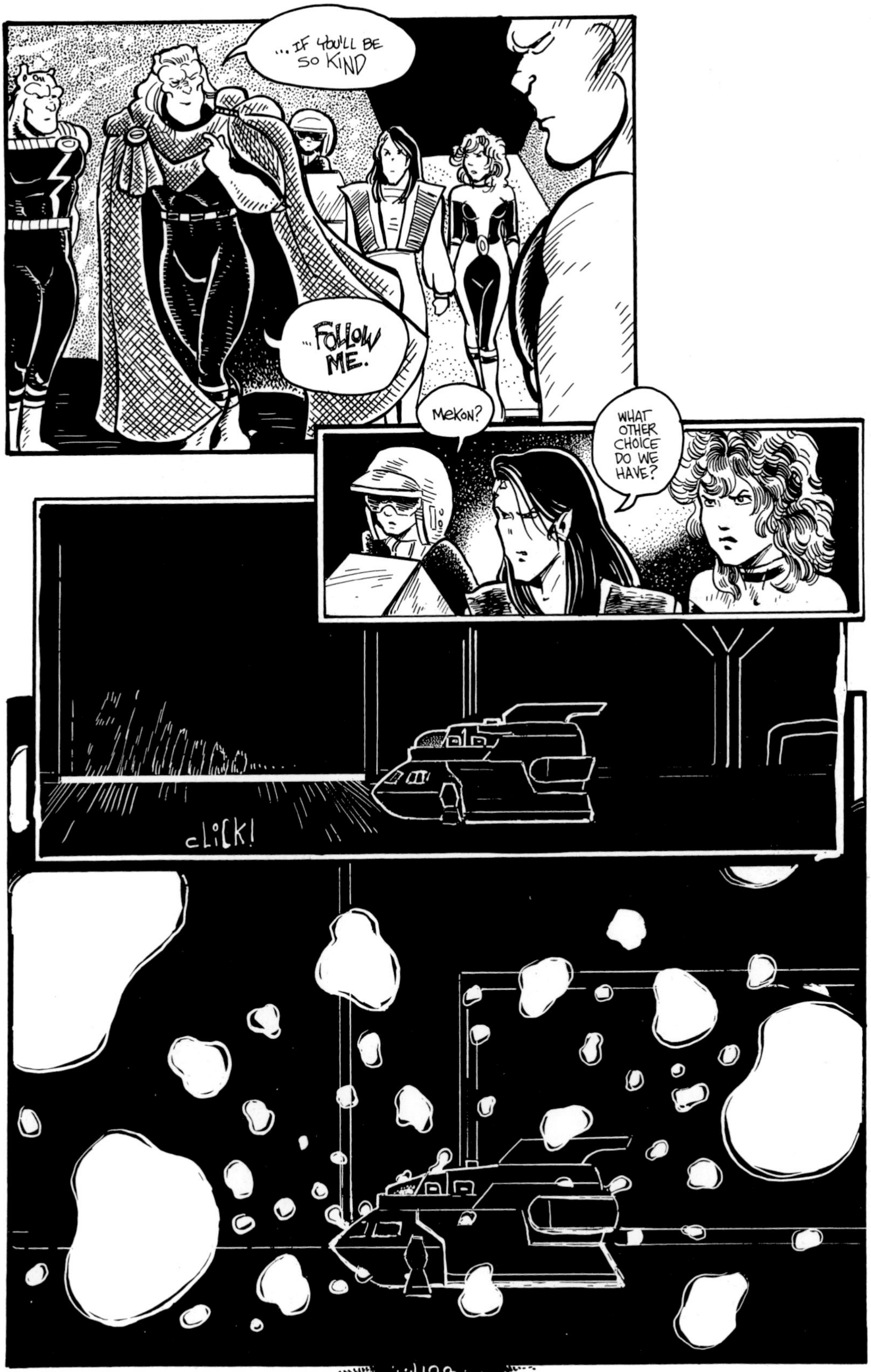
...IF YOU'LL BE SO KIND
...FOLLOW ME.
MEKON?
WHAT OTHER CHOICE DO WE HAVE?
SHHHHOO.....
CLICK!

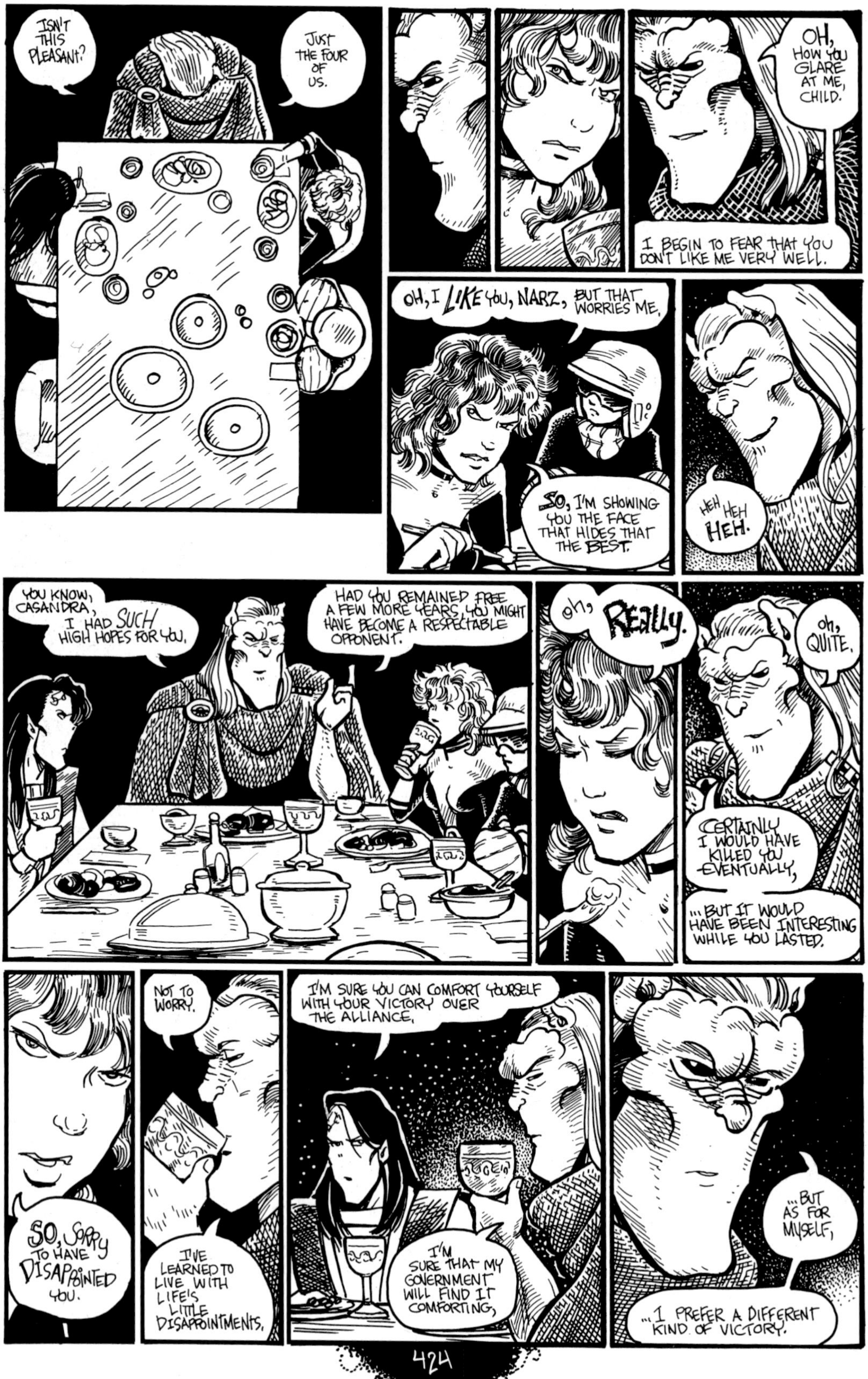
ISN'T THIS PLEASANT?
JUST THE FOUR OF US.
OH, HOW YOU GLARE AT ME, CHILD.
I BEGIN TO FEAR THAT YOU DON'T LIKE ME VERY WELL.
OH, I LIKE YOU, NARZ, BUT THAT WORRIES ME.
SO, I'M SHOWING YOU THE FACE THAT HIDES THAT THE BEST.
HEH HEH HEH.
YOU KNOW, CASANDRA, I HAD SUCH HIGH HOPES FOR YOU.
HAD YOU REMAINED FREE A FEW MORE YEARS, YOU MIGHT HAVE BECOME A RESPECTABLE OPPONENT.
oh, Really.
oh, QUITE.
CERTAINLY I WOULD HAVE KILLED YOU EVENTUALLY,
...BUT IT WOULD HAVE BEEN INTERESTING WHILE YOU LASTED.
SO, SORRY TO HAVE DISAPPOINTED YOU.
NOT TO WORRY.
I'VE LEARNED TO LIVE WITH LIFE'S LITTLE DISAPPOINTMENTS.
I'M SURE YOU CAN COMFORT YOURSELF WITH YOUR VICTORY OVER THE ALLIANCE,
I'M SURE THAT MY GOVERNMENT WILL FIND IT COMFORTING,
...BUT AS FOR MYSELF,
...I PREFER A DIFFERENT KIND OF VICTORY.

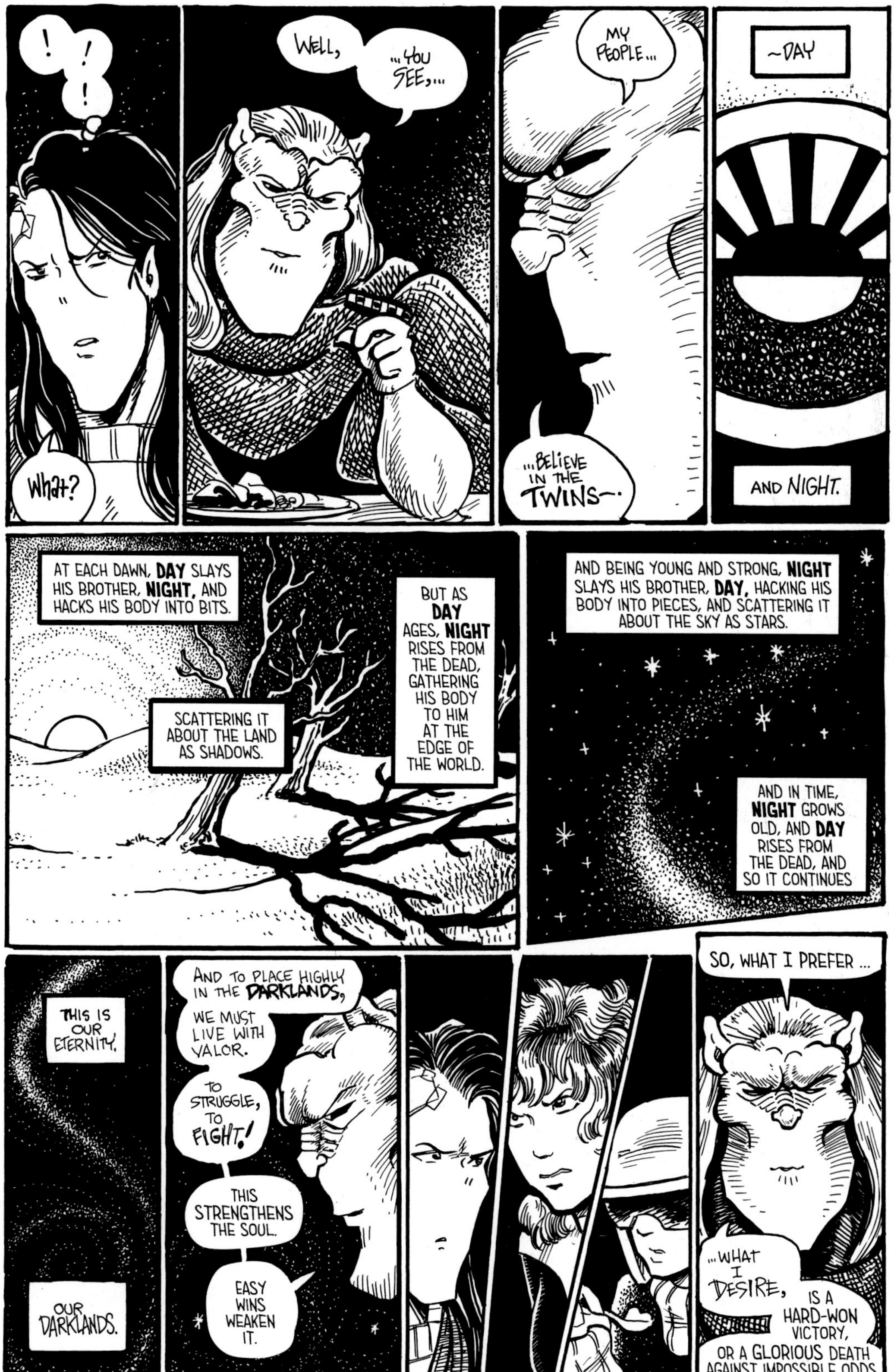
!
!
!
What?
WELL,
...YOU SEE,...
MY PEOPLE...
...BELIEVE IN THE TWINS~.
~DAY
AND NIGHT.
AT EACH DAWN, DAY SLAYS HIS BROTHER, NIGHT, AND HACKS HIS BODY INTO BITS.
SCATTERING IT ABOUT THE LAND AS SHADOWS.
BUT AS DAY AGES, NIGHT RISES FROM THE DEAD, GATHERING HIS BODY TO HIM AT THE EDGE OF THE WORLD.
AND BEING YOUNG AND STRONG, NIGHT SLAYS HIS BROTHER, DAY, HACKING HIS BODY INTO PIECES, AND SCATTERING IT ABOUT THE SKY AS STARS.
AND IN TIME, NIGHT GROWS OLD, AND DAY RISES FROM THE DEAD, AND SO IT CONTINUES
THIS IS OUR ETERNITY,
OUR DARKLANDS.
AND TO PLACE HIGHLY IN THE DARKLANDS,
WE MUST LIVE WITH VALOR.
TO STRUGGLE, TO FIGHT!
THIS STRENGTHENS THE SOUL.
EASY WINS WEAKEN IT.
SO, WHAT I PREFER ...
...WHAT I DESIRE,
IS A HARD-WON VICTORY, OR A GLORIOUS DEATH AGAINST IMPOSSIBLE ODDS.

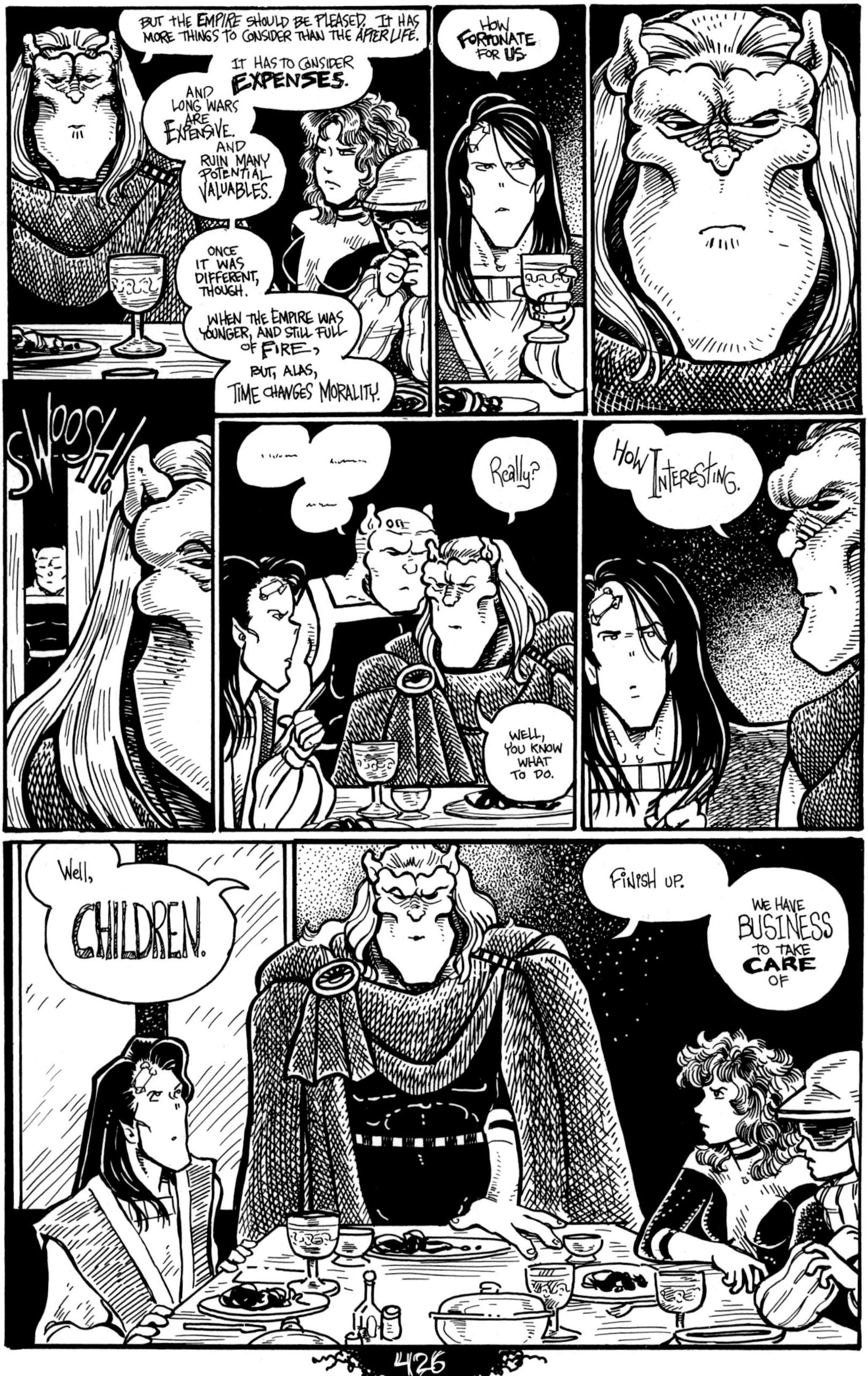
BUT THE EMPIRE SHOULD BE PLEASED. IT HAS MORE THINGS TO CONSIDER THAN THE AFTERLIFE.
IT HAS TO CONSIDER EXPENSES.
AND LONG WARS ARE EXPENSIVE.
AND RUIN MANY POTENTIAL VALUABLES.
ONCE IT WAS DIFFERENT, THOUGH.
WHEN THE EMPIRE WAS YOUNGER, AND STILL FULL OF FIRE,
BUT, ALAS, TIME CHANGES MORALITY.
HOW FORTUNATE FOR US.
SWOOSH!
Really?
HOW INTERESTING.
WELL, YOU KNOW WHAT TO DO.
Well, CHILDREN.
FINISH UP.
WE HAVE BUSINESS TO TAKE CARE OF

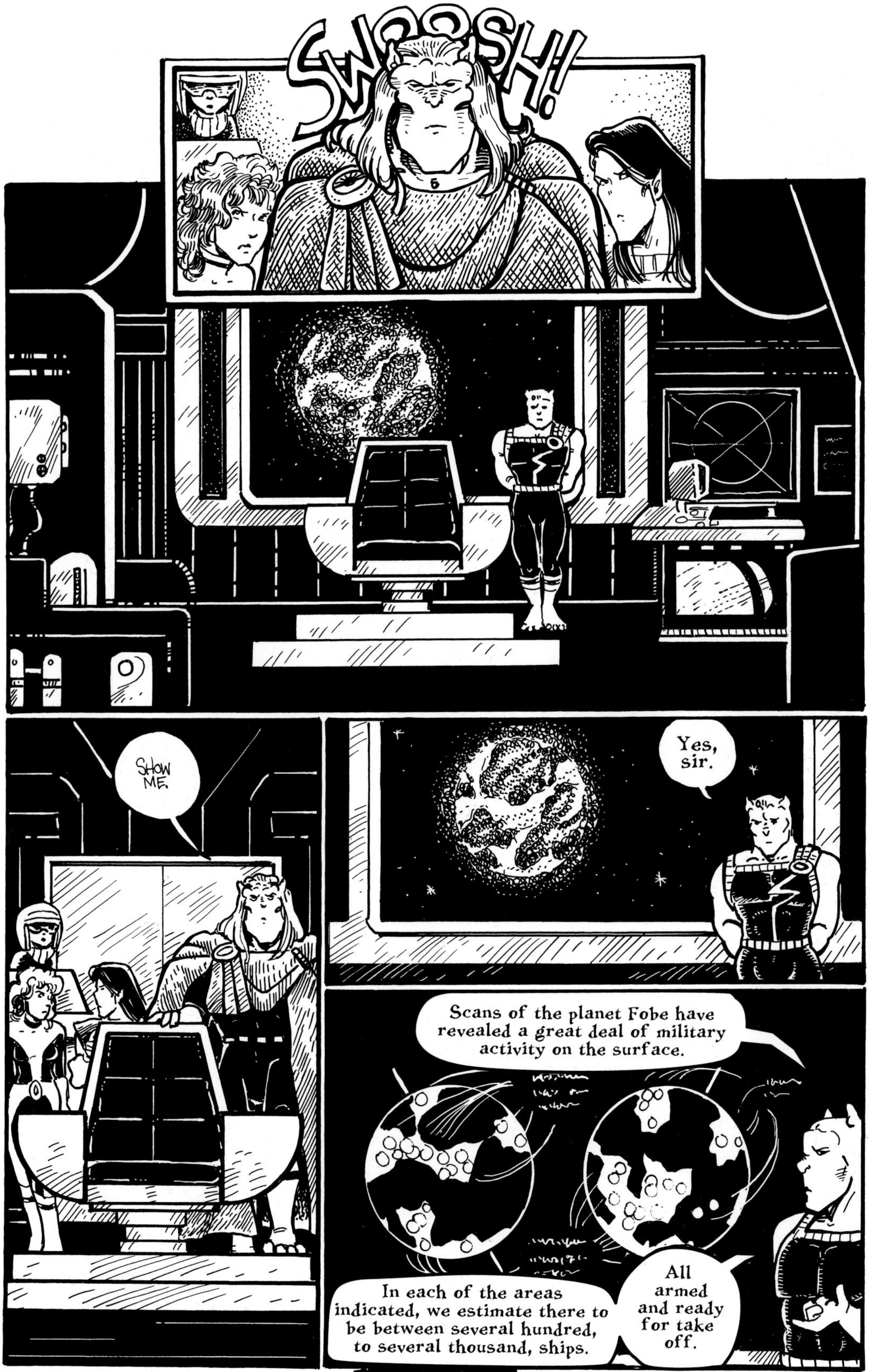
SWOOSH!
SHOW ME.
Yes, sir.
Scans of the planet Fobe have revealed a great deal of military activity on the surface.
In each of the areas indicated, we estimate there to be between several hundred, to several thousand, ships.
All armed and ready for take off.

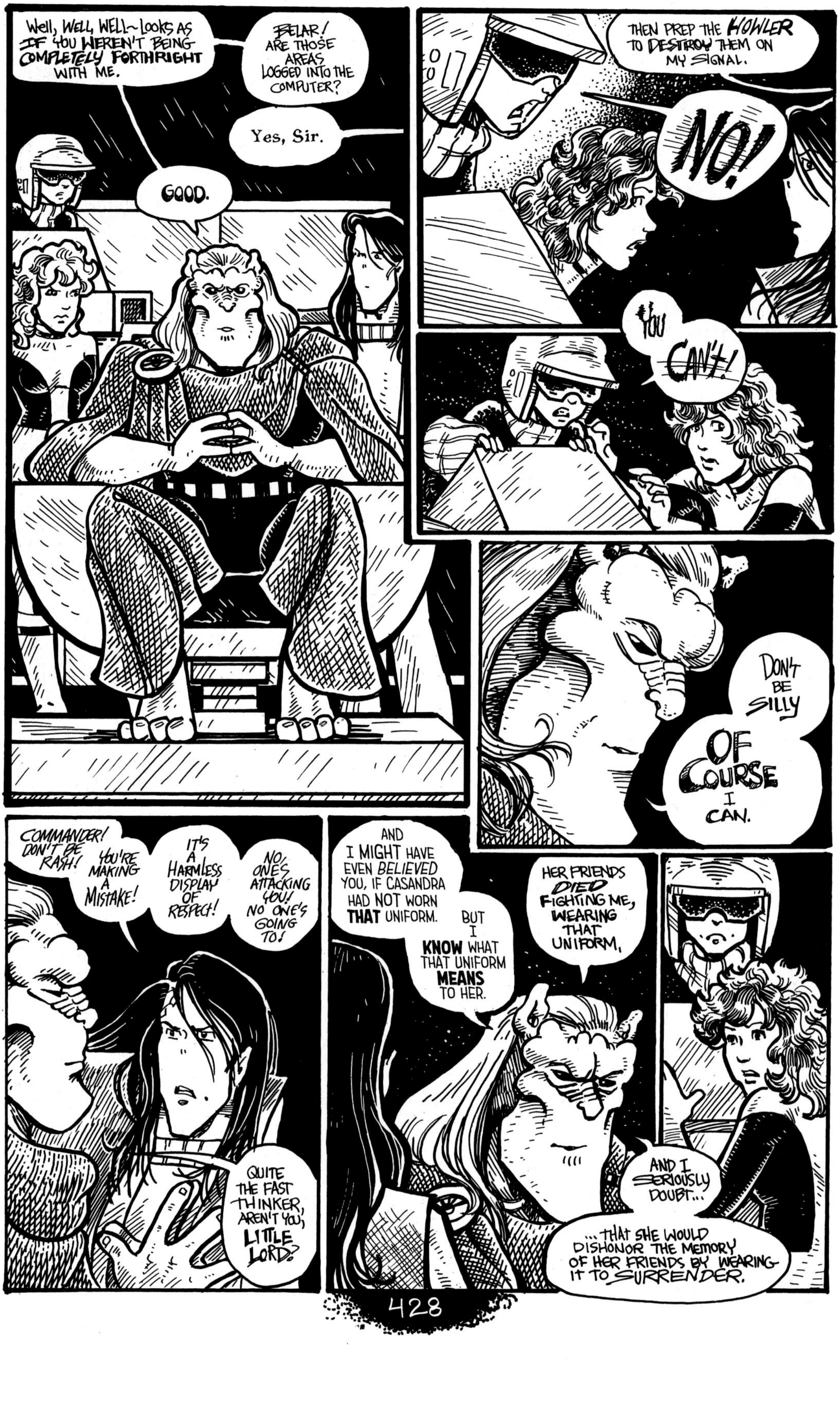

Well, WELL, WELL~ LOOKS AS IF YOU WEREN'T BEING COMPLETELY FORTHRIGHT WITH ME.
BELAR! ARE THOSE AREAS LOGGED INTO THE COMPUTER?
Yes, Sir.
GOOD.
THEN PREP THE HOWLER TO DESTROY THEM ON MY SIGNAL.
NO!
YOU CAN'T!
DON'T BE SILLY
OF COURSE I CAN.
COMMANDER! DON'T BE RASH!
YOU'RE MAKING A MISTAKE!
IT'S A HARMLESS DISPLAY OF RESPECT!
NO ONE'S ATTACKING YOU! NO ONE'S GOING TO!
QUITE THE FAST THINKER, AREN'T YOU, LITTLE LORD?
AND I MIGHT HAVE EVEN BELIEVED YOU, IF CASANDRA HAD NOT WORN THAT UNIFORM.
BUT I KNOW WHAT THAT UNIFORM MEANS TO HER.
HER FRIENDS DIED FIGHTING ME, WEARING THAT UNIFORM,
AND I SERIOUSLY DOUBT...
...THAT SHE WOULD DISHONOR THE MEMORY OF HER FRIENDS BY WEARING IT TO SURRENDER.

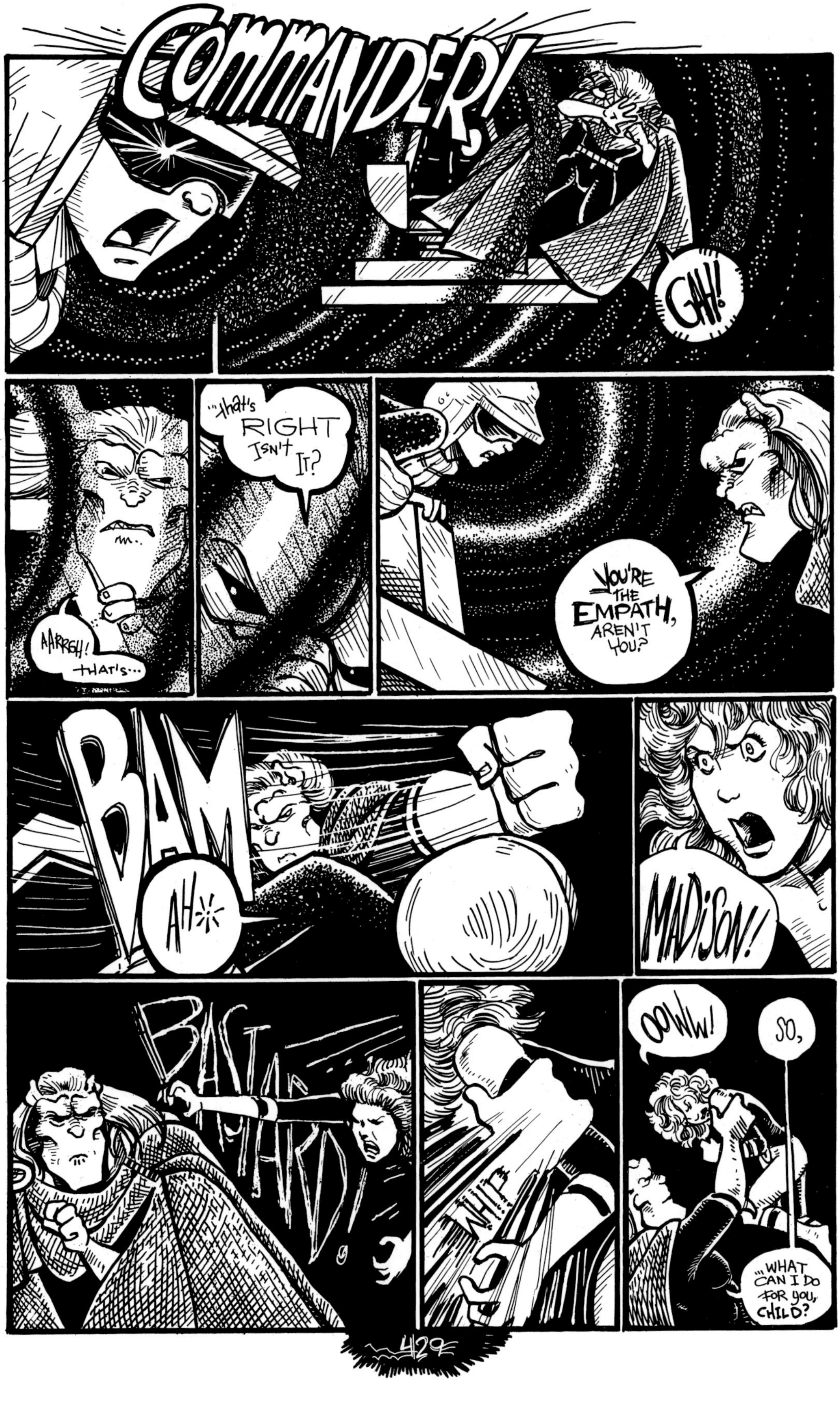
COMMANDER!
GAH!
AARRGH! THAT'S...
...THAT'S RIGHT ISN'T IT?
YOU'RE THE EMPATH, AREN'T YOU?
BAM
AH
MADISON!
BASTARD!
OOWW!
SO,
...WHAT CAN I DO FOR YOU, CHILD?

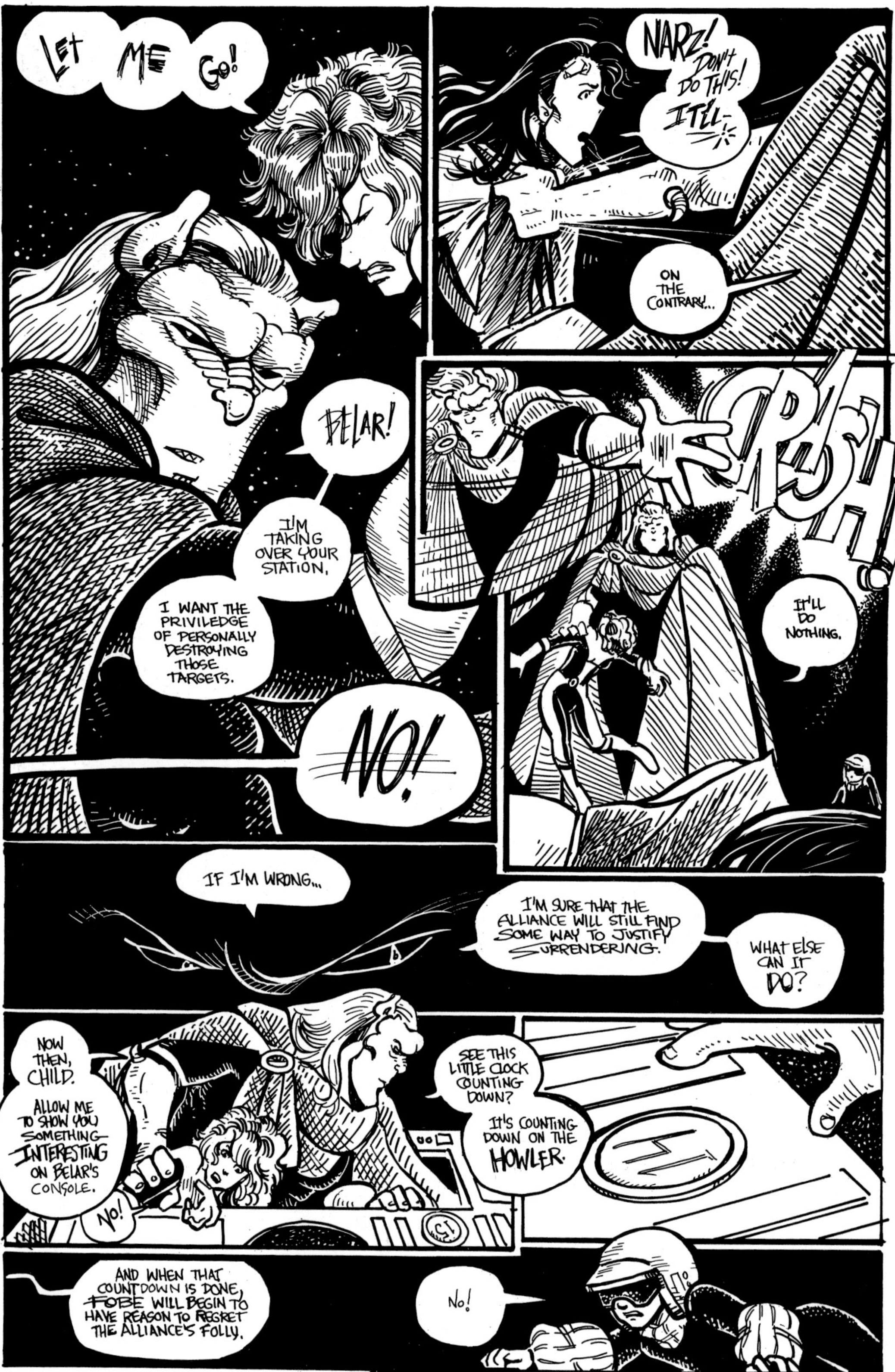
LET ME GO!
NARZ! DON'T DO THIS! IT'LL-
ON THE CONTRARY...
BELAR!
I'M TAKING OVER YOUR STATION,
I WANT THE PRIVILEDGE OF PERSONALLY DESTROYING THOSE TARGETS.
NO!
CRASH!
IT'LL DO NOTHING.
IF I'M WRONG...
I'M SURE THAT THE ALLIANCE WILL STILL FIND SOME WAY TO JUSTIFY SURRENDERING.
WHAT ELSE CAN IT DO?
NOW THEN, CHILD.
ALLOW ME TO SHOW YOU SOMETHING INTERESTING ON BELAR'S CONSOLE.
NO!
SEE THIS LITTLE CLOCK COUNTING DOWN?
IT'S COUNTING DOWN ON THE HOWLER.
AND WHEN THAT COUNTDOWN IS DONE, FOBE WILL BEGIN TO HAVE REASON TO REGRET THE ALLIANCE'S FOLLY.
No!

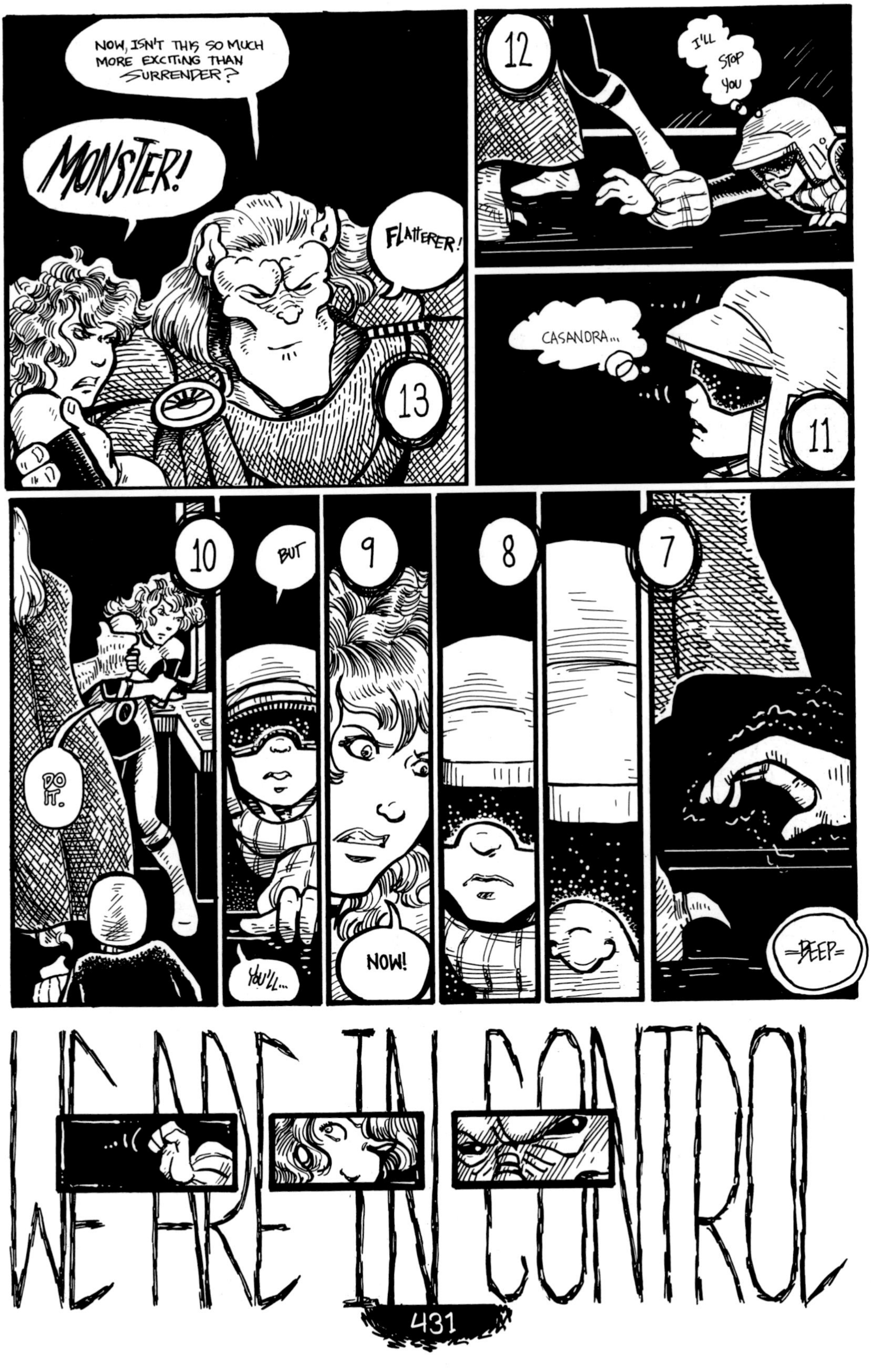
NOW, ISN'T THIS SO MUCH MORE EXCITING THAN SURRENDER?
MONSTER!
FLATTERER!
13
12
I'LL STOP YOU
CASANDRA...
11
10
DO IT.
BUT
YOU'LL...
9
NOW!
8
7
=BEEP=
WE ARE IN CONTROL

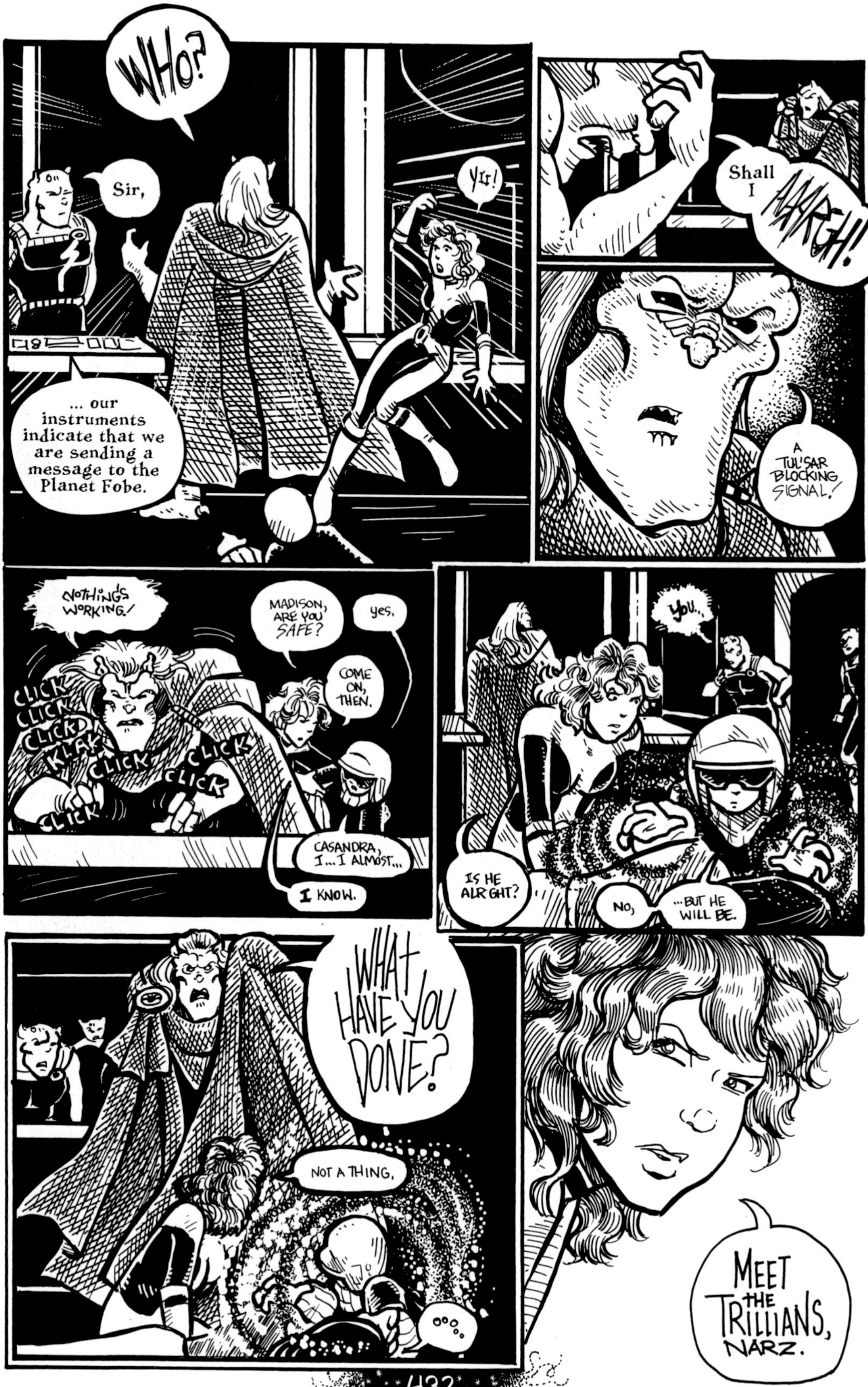
WHO?
Sir,
YI!
... our instruments indicate that we are sending a message to the Planet Fobe.
Shall I
AAARGH!
A TUL'SAR BLOCKING SIGNAL!
NOTHING'S WORKING!
CLICK CLICK CLICK KLAK CLICK CLICK CLICK CLICK
MADISON, ARE YOU SAFE?
yes.
COME ON, THEN.
CASANDRA, I...I ALMOST...
I KNOW.
YOU...
IS HE ALRIGHT?
NO,
...BUT HE WILL BE.
WHAT HAVE YOU DONE?
NOT A THING.
MEET THE TRILLIANS, NARZ.

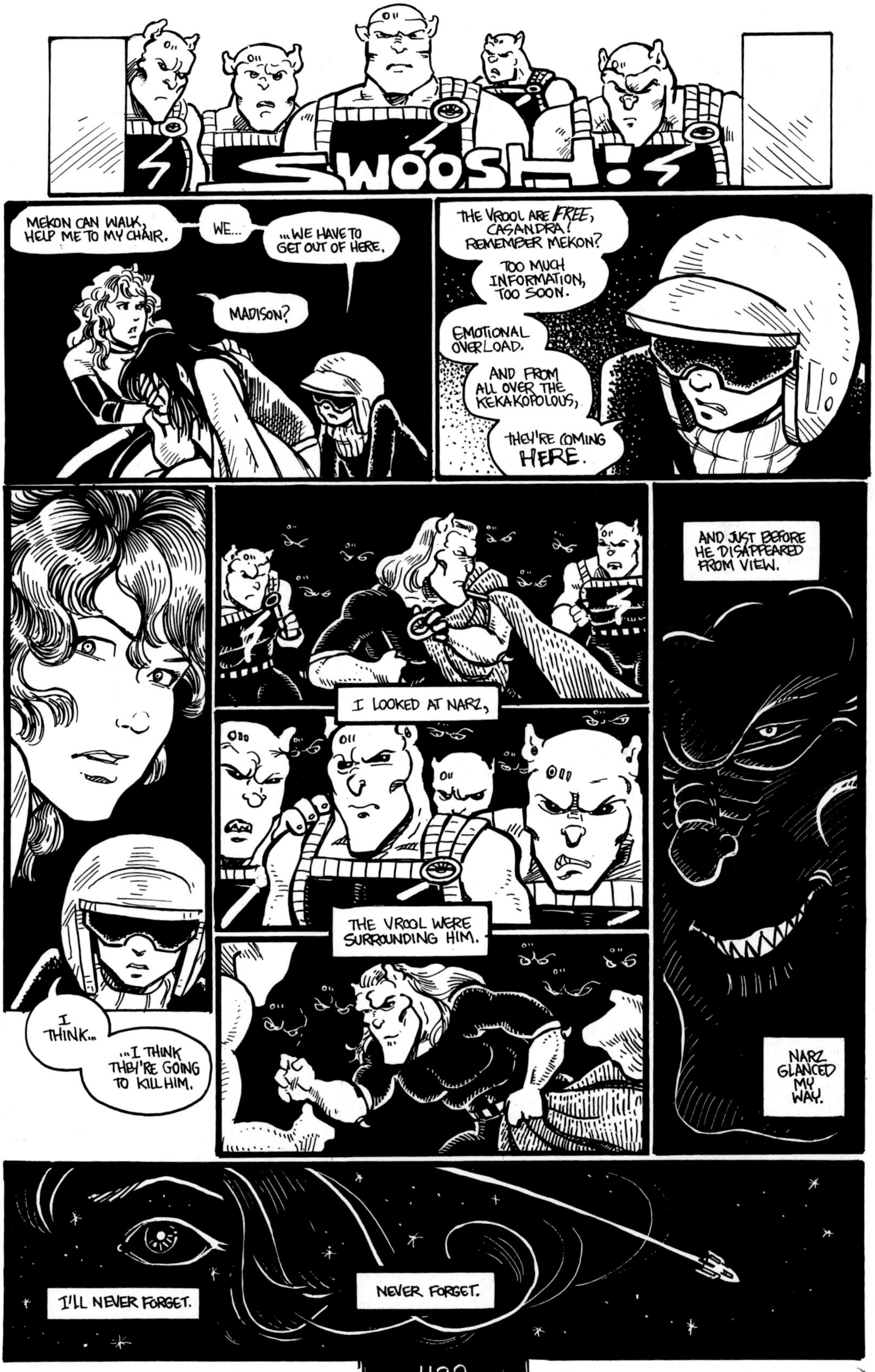
SWOOSH!
MEKON CAN WALK, HELP ME TO MY CHAIR.
WE...
...WE HAVE TO GET OUT OF HERE.
MADISON?
THE VROOL ARE FREE, CASANDRA! REMEMBER MEKON?
TOO MUCH INFORMATION, TOO SOON.
EMOTIONAL OVERLOAD.
AND FROM ALL OVER THE KEKAKOPOLOUS,
THEY'RE COMING HERE.
I THINK...
...I THINK THEY'RE GOING TO KILL HIM.
I LOOKED AT NARZ,
THE VROOL WERE SURROUNDING HIM.
AND JUST BEFORE HE DISAPPEARED FROM VIEW.
NARZ GLANCED MY WAY.
I'LL NEVER FORGET.
NEVER FORGET.

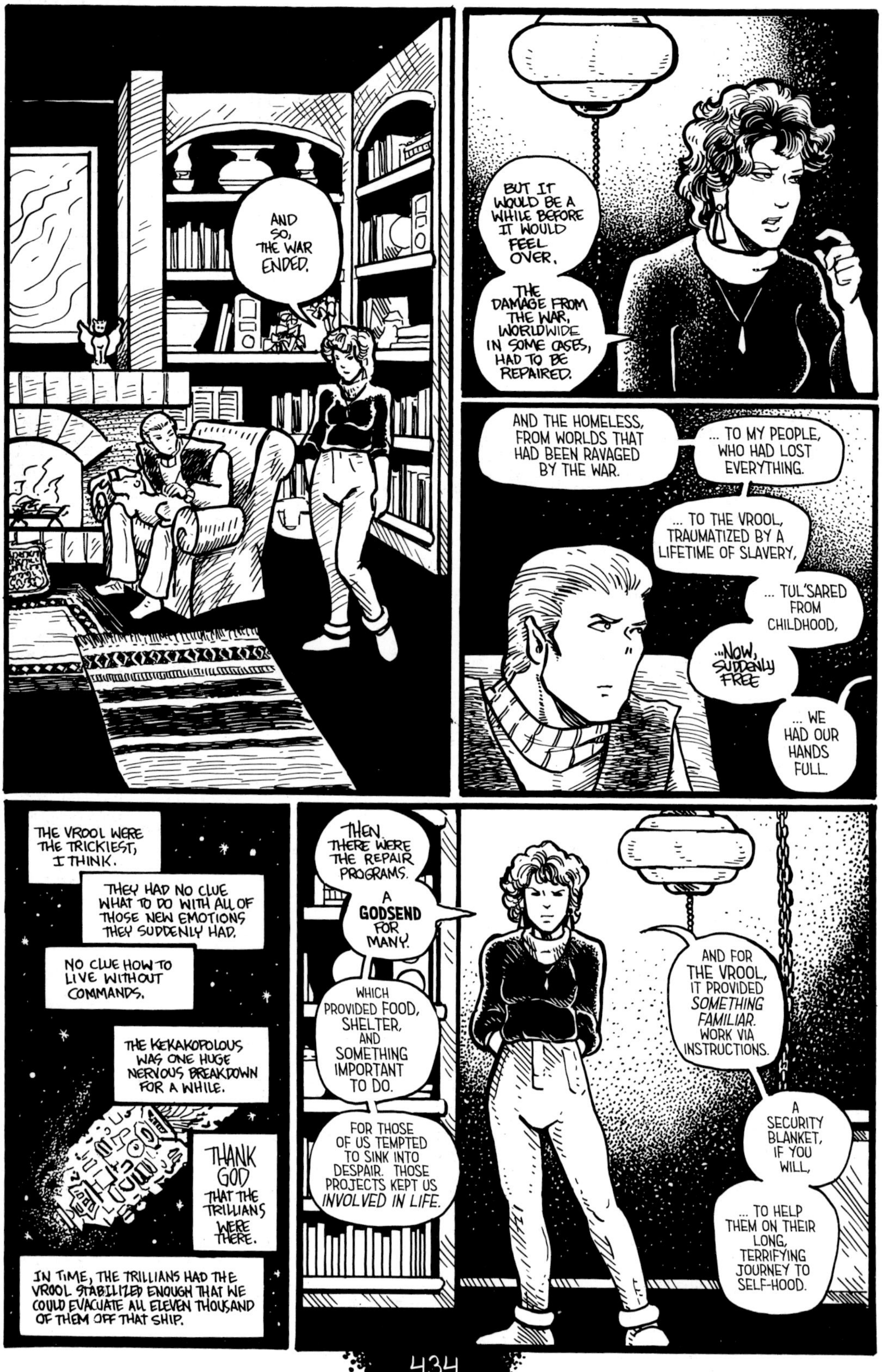
AND SO, THE WAR ENDED.
BUT IT WOULD BE A WHILE BEFORE IT WOULD FEEL OVER.
THE DAMAGE FROM THE WAR, WORLDWIDE IN SOME CASES, HAD TO BE REPAIRED.
AND THE HOMELESS, FROM WORLDS THAT HAD BEEN RAVAGED BY THE WAR.
... TO MY PEOPLE, WHO HAD LOST EVERYTHING.
... TO THE VROOL, TRAUMATIZED BY A LIFETIME OF SLAVERY,
... TUL'SARED FROM CHILDHOOD,
...NOW, SUDDENLY FREE
... WE HAD OUR HANDS FULL.
THE VROOL WERE THE TRICKIEST, I THINK.
THEY HAD NO CLUE WHAT TO DO WITH ALL OF THOSE NEW EMOTIONS THEY SUDDENLY HAD.
NO CLUE HOW TO LIVE WITHOUT COMMANDS.
THE KEKAKOPOLOUS WAS ONE HUGE NERVOUS BREAKDOWN FOR A WHILE.
THANK GOD THAT THE TRILLIANS WERE THERE.
IN TIME, THE TRILLIANS HAD THE VROOL STABILIZED ENOUGH THAT WE COULD EVACUATE ALL ELEVEN THOUSAND OF THEM OFF THAT SHIP.
THEN THERE WERE THE REPAIR PROGRAMS.
A **GODSEND** FOR MANY.
WHICH PROVIDED FOOD, SHELTER, AND SOMETHING IMPORTANT TO DO.
FOR THOSE OF US TEMPTED TO SINK INTO DESPAIR. THOSE PROJECTS KEPT US *INVOLVED IN LIFE*.
AND FOR THE VROOL, IT PROVIDED *SOMETHING FAMILIAR*. WORK VIA INSTRUCTIONS.
A SECURITY BLANKET, IF YOU WILL,
... TO HELP THEM ON THEIR LONG, TERRIFYING JOURNEY TO SELF-HOOD.

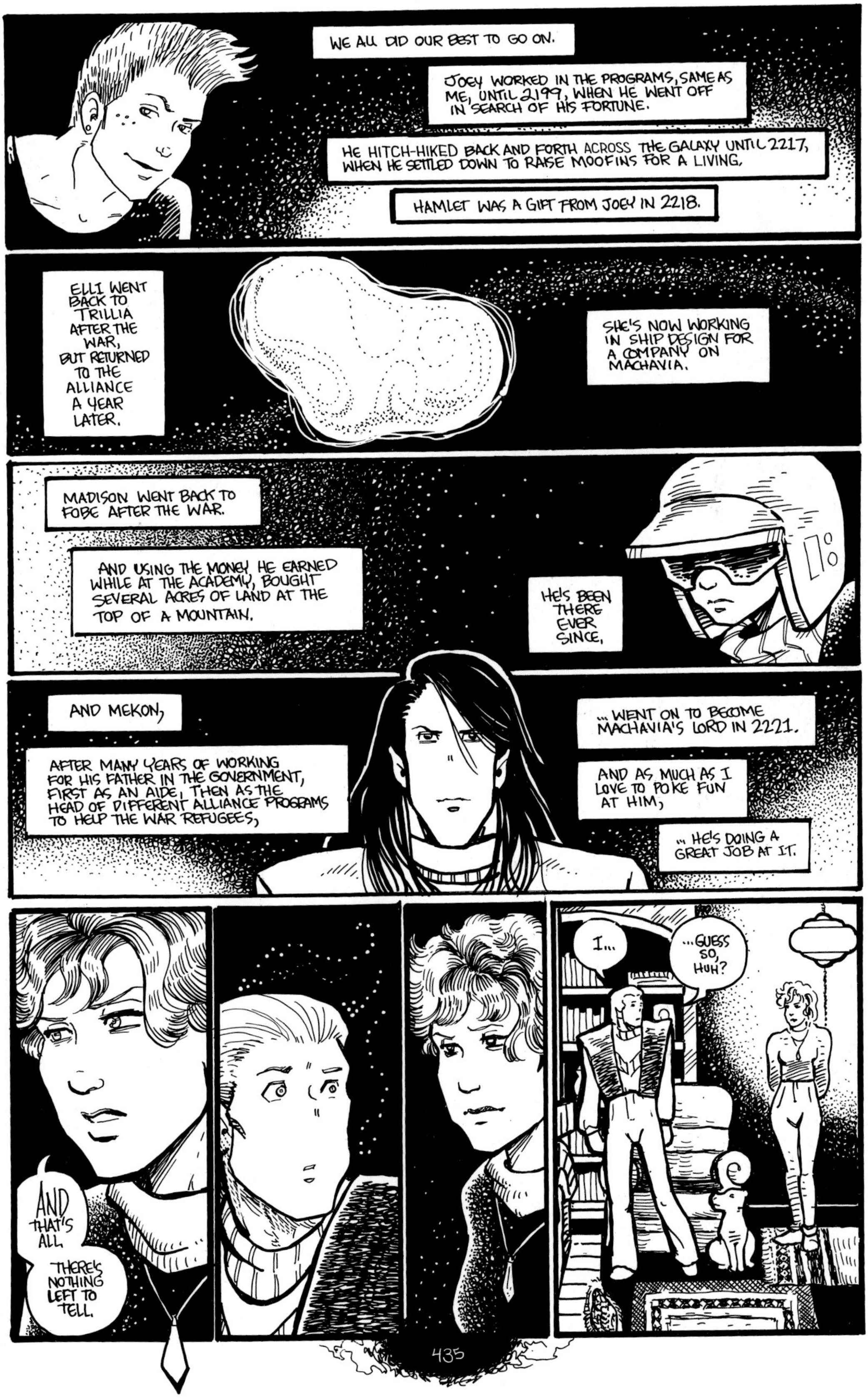

WE ALL DID OUR BEST TO GO ON.
JOEY WORKED IN THE PROGRAMS, SAME AS ME, UNTIL 2199, WHEN HE WENT OFF IN SEARCH OF HIS FORTUNE.
HE HITCH-HIKED BACK AND FORTH ACROSS THE GALAXY UNTIL 2217, WHEN HE SETTLED DOWN TO RAISE MOOFINS FOR A LIVING.
HAMLET WAS A GIFT FROM JOEY IN 2218.
ELLI WENT BACK TO TRILLIA AFTER THE WAR, BUT RETURNED TO THE ALLIANCE A YEAR LATER.
SHE'S NOW WORKING IN SHIP DESIGN FOR A COMPANY ON MACHAVIA.
MADISON WENT BACK TO FOBE AFTER THE WAR.
AND USING THE MONEY HE EARNED WHILE AT THE ACADEMY, BOUGHT SEVERAL ACRES OF LAND AT THE TOP OF A MOUNTAIN.
HE'S BEEN THERE EVER SINCE.
AND MEKON,
AFTER MANY YEARS OF WORKING FOR HIS FATHER IN THE GOVERNMENT, FIRST AS AN AIDE, THEN AS THE HEAD OF DIFFERENT ALLIANCE PROGRAMS TO HELP THE WAR REFUGEES,
... WENT ON TO BECOME MACHAVIA'S LORD IN 2221.
AND AS MUCH AS I LOVE TO POKE FUN AT HIM,
... HE'S DOING A GREAT JOB AT IT.
AND THAT'S ALL.
THERE'S NOTHING LEFT TO TELL.
I...
...GUESS SO, HUH?

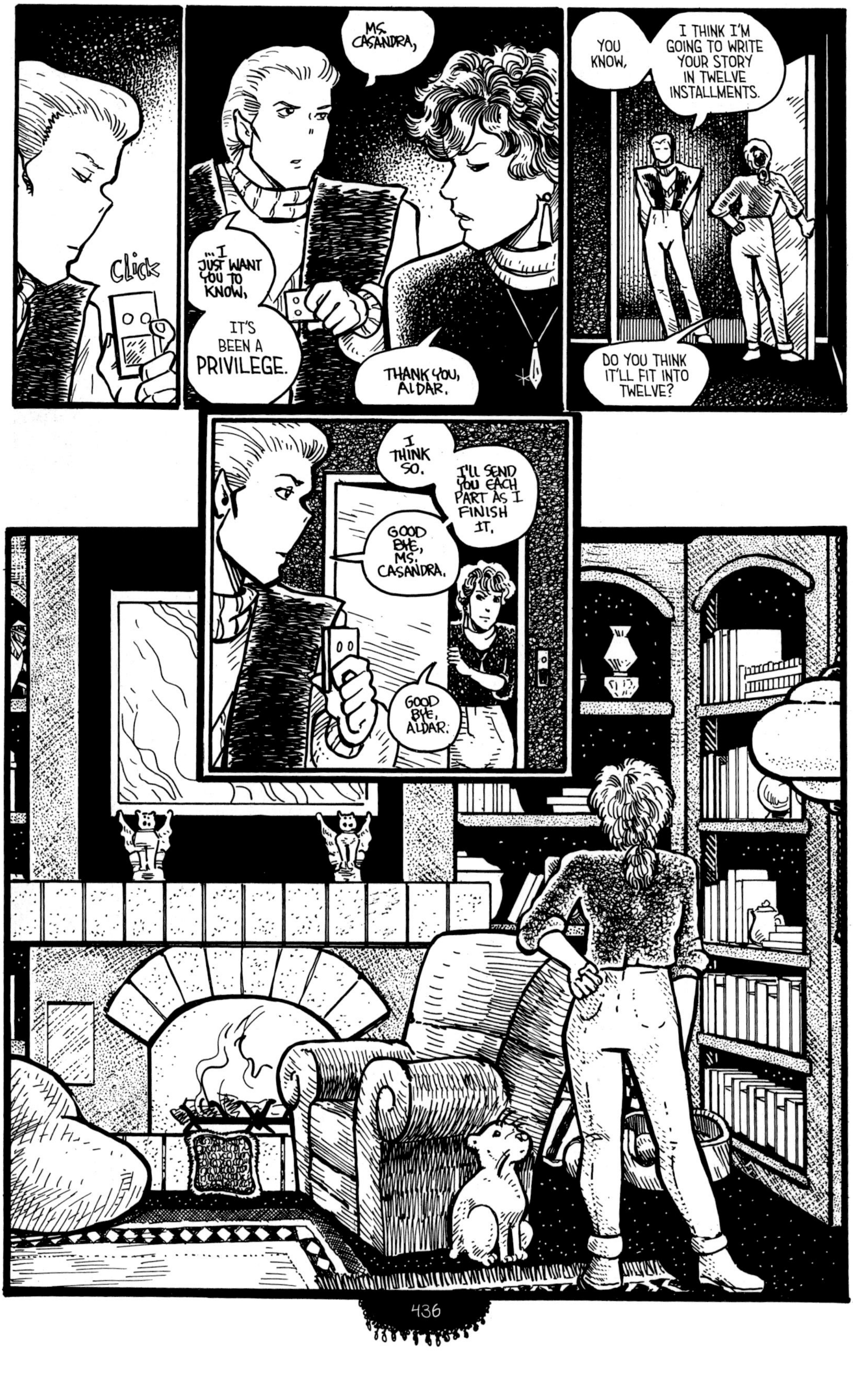
CLICK
MS. CASANDRA,
...I JUST WANT YOU TO KNOW,
IT'S BEEN A PRIVILEGE.
THANK YOU, ALDAR.
YOU KNOW,
I THINK I'M GOING TO WRITE YOUR STORY IN TWELVE INSTALLMENTS.
DO YOU THINK IT'LL FIT INTO TWELVE?
I THINK SO.
I'LL SEND YOU EACH PART AS I FINISH IT.
GOOD BYE, MS. CASANDRA.
GOOD BYE, ALDAR.

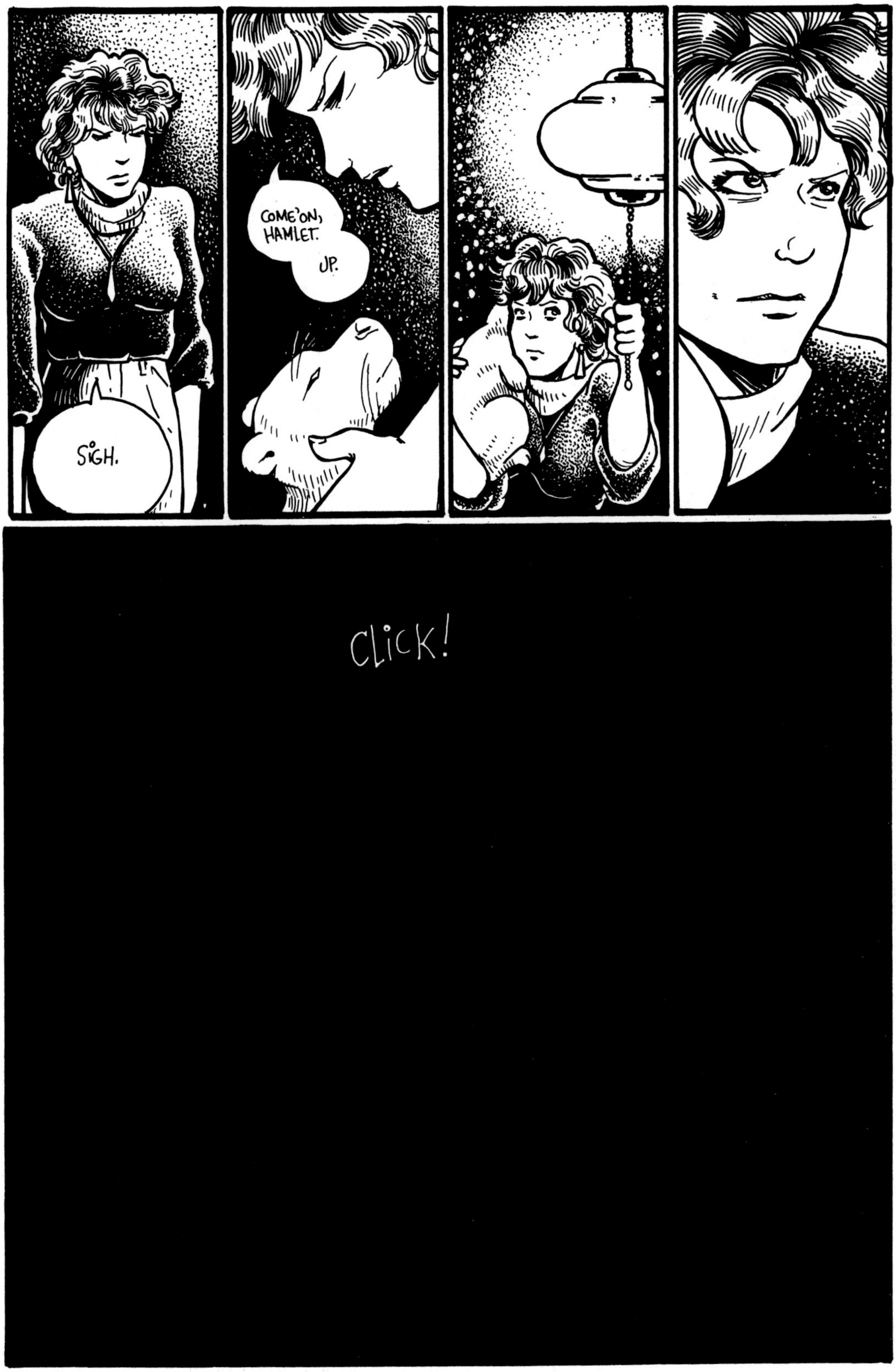
SIGH.
COME'ON, HAMLET.
UP.
CLICK!

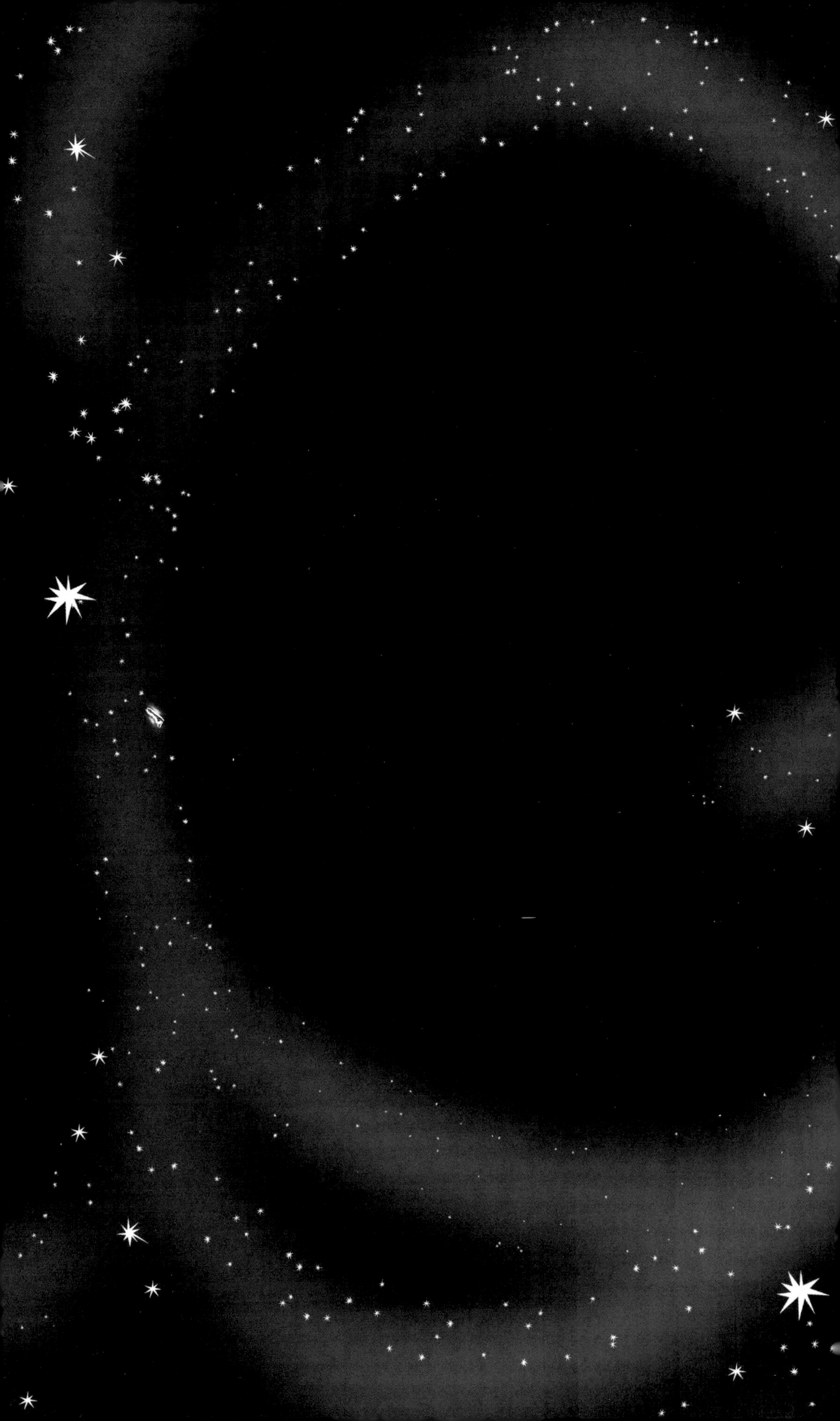

The following sixteen pages shows *Wandering Star* in its original incarnation—
as an underground, small press comic, before it became the professional comic book
collected in this omnibus edition.

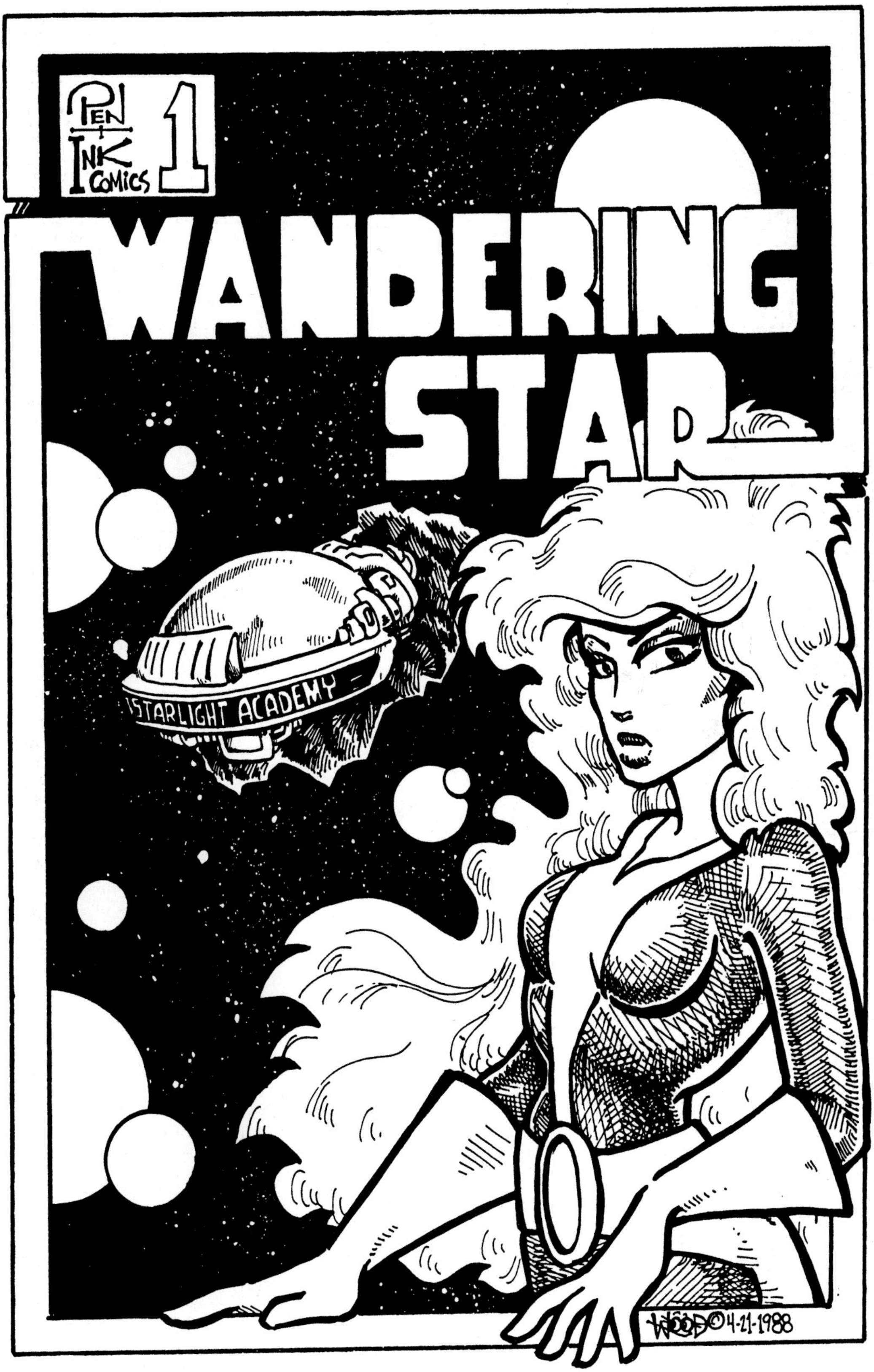
PEN & INK COMICS
1
WANDERING STAR
STARLIGHT ACADEMY
WOOD © 4-21-1988

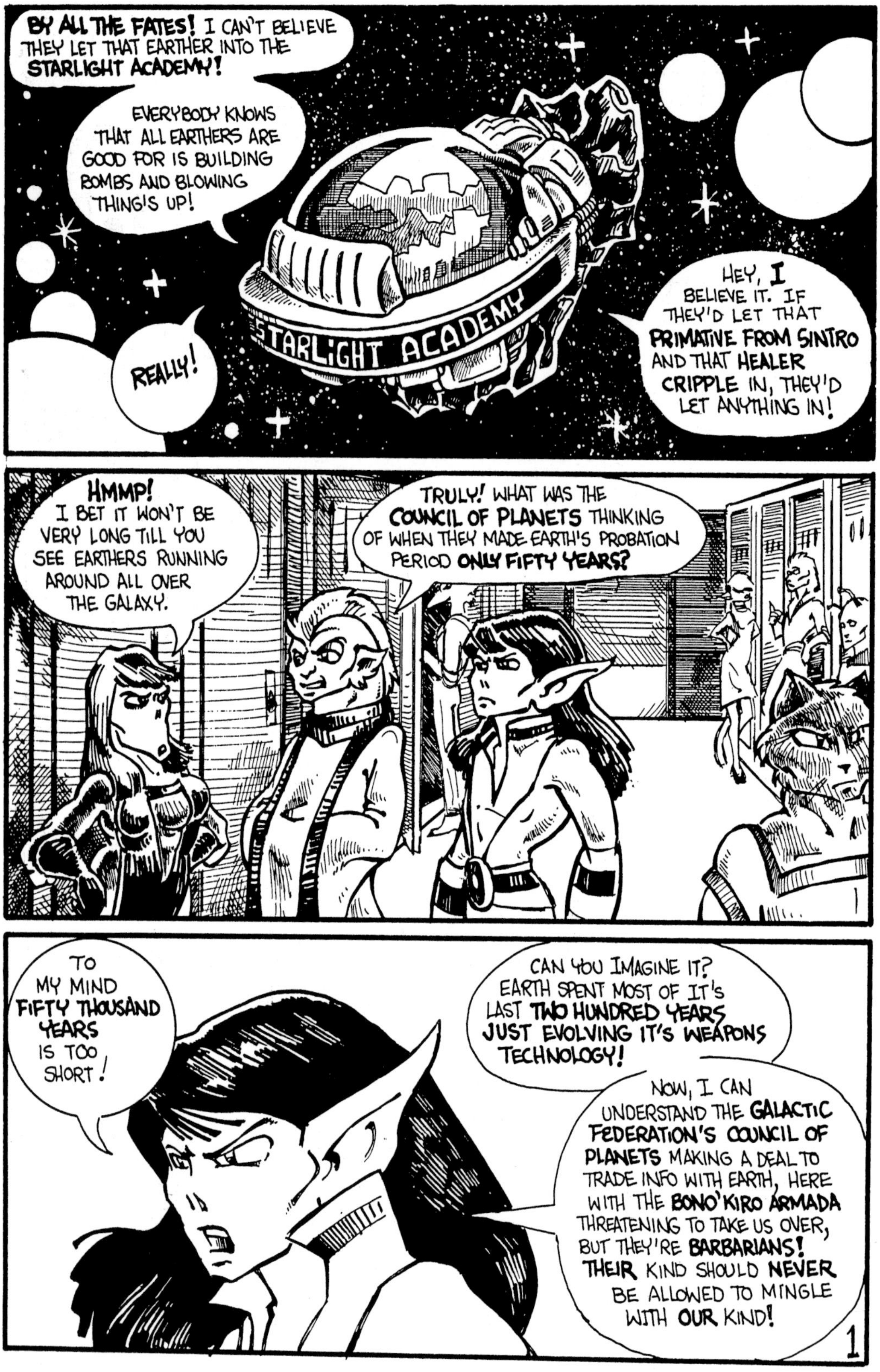
BY ALL THE FATES! I CAN'T BELIEVE THEY LET THAT EARTHER INTO THE STARLIGHT ACADEMY!
EVERYBODY KNOWS THAT ALL EARTHERS ARE GOOD FOR IS BUILDING BOMBS AND BLOWING THING'S UP!
STARLIGHT ACADEMY
REALLY!
HEY, I BELIEVE IT. IF THEY'D LET THAT PRIMATIVE FROM SINTRO AND THAT HEALER CRIPPLE IN, THEY'D LET ANYTHING IN!
HMMP! I BET IT WON'T BE VERY LONG TILL YOU SEE EARTHERS RUNNING AROUND ALL OVER THE GALAXY.
TRULY! WHAT WAS THE COUNCIL OF PLANETS THINKING OF WHEN THEY MADE EARTH'S PROBATION PERIOD ONLY FIFTY YEARS?
TO MY MIND FIFTY THOUSAND YEARS IS TOO SHORT!
CAN YOU IMAGINE IT? EARTH SPENT MOST OF IT'S LAST TWO HUNDRED YEARS JUST EVOLVING IT'S WEAPONS TECHNOLOGY!
NOW, I CAN UNDERSTAND THE GALACTIC FEDERATION'S COUNCIL OF PLANETS MAKING A DEAL TO TRADE INFO WITH EARTH, HERE WITH THE BONO'KIRO ARMADA THREATENING TO TAKE US OVER, BUT THEY'RE BARBARIANS! THEIR KIND SHOULD NEVER BE ALLOWED TO MINGLE WITH OUR KIND!

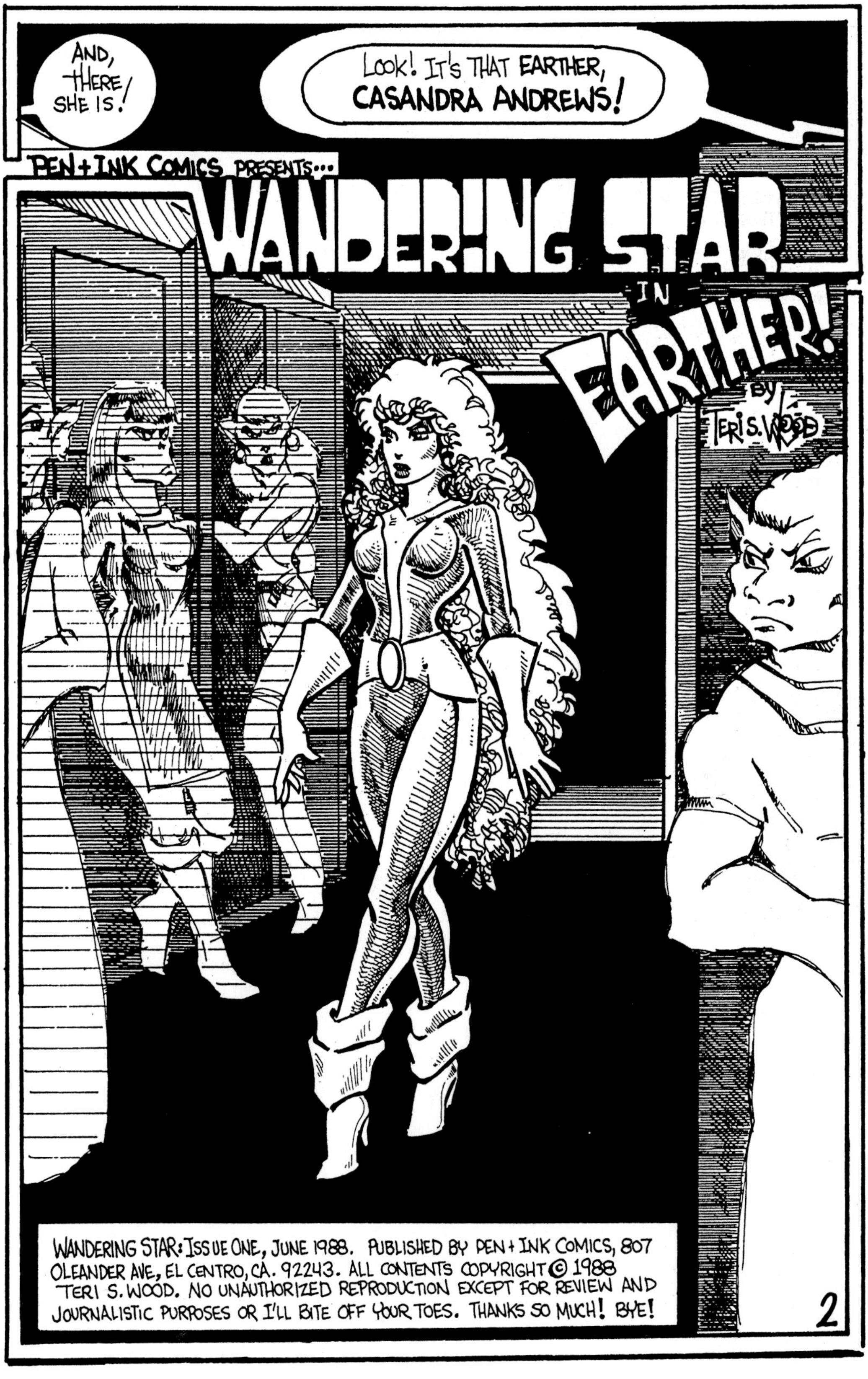

AND, THERE SHE IS!
LOOK! IT'S THAT EARTHER, CASANDRA ANDREWS!
PEN+INK COMICS PRESENTS...
WANDERING STAR
IN
EARTHER!
BY TERI S. WOOD

...BARBARIAN... HUMAN!

...SHOULDN'T BE HERE...

HMMP!

...EARTHER... ...WHAT'S THIS SCHOOL COMING TO?

...LETTING EVERYTHING IN...

...SHOULD KNOW HER PLACE...

...RIGHT...

...WHERE'S SHE GOING?

GYM ROOM A-21

THE GYM.

...ALWAYS THE GYM...

...PRIMATIVE PLACE FOR A PRIMATIVE...

FIGURES! IT'S SO OUTDATED ONLY SHE'D GO THERE.

...BUT IT'S SO UNADVANCED. THERE ARE SO MANY BETTER GYMS, WHY DOES SHE GO THERE?

WHO CARES?

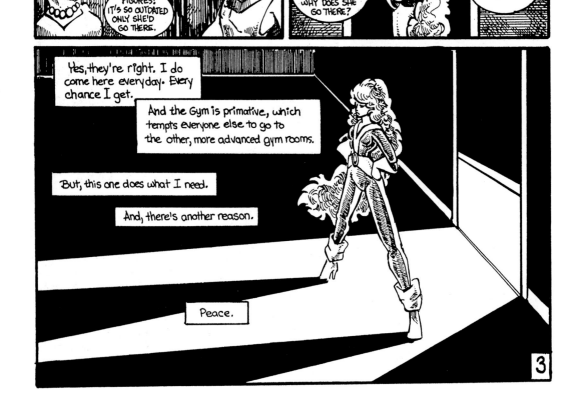

Yes, they're right. I do come here everyday. Every chance I get.

And the Gym is primative, which tempts everyone else to go to the other, more advanced gym rooms.

But, this one does what I need.

And, there's another reason.

Peace.

3

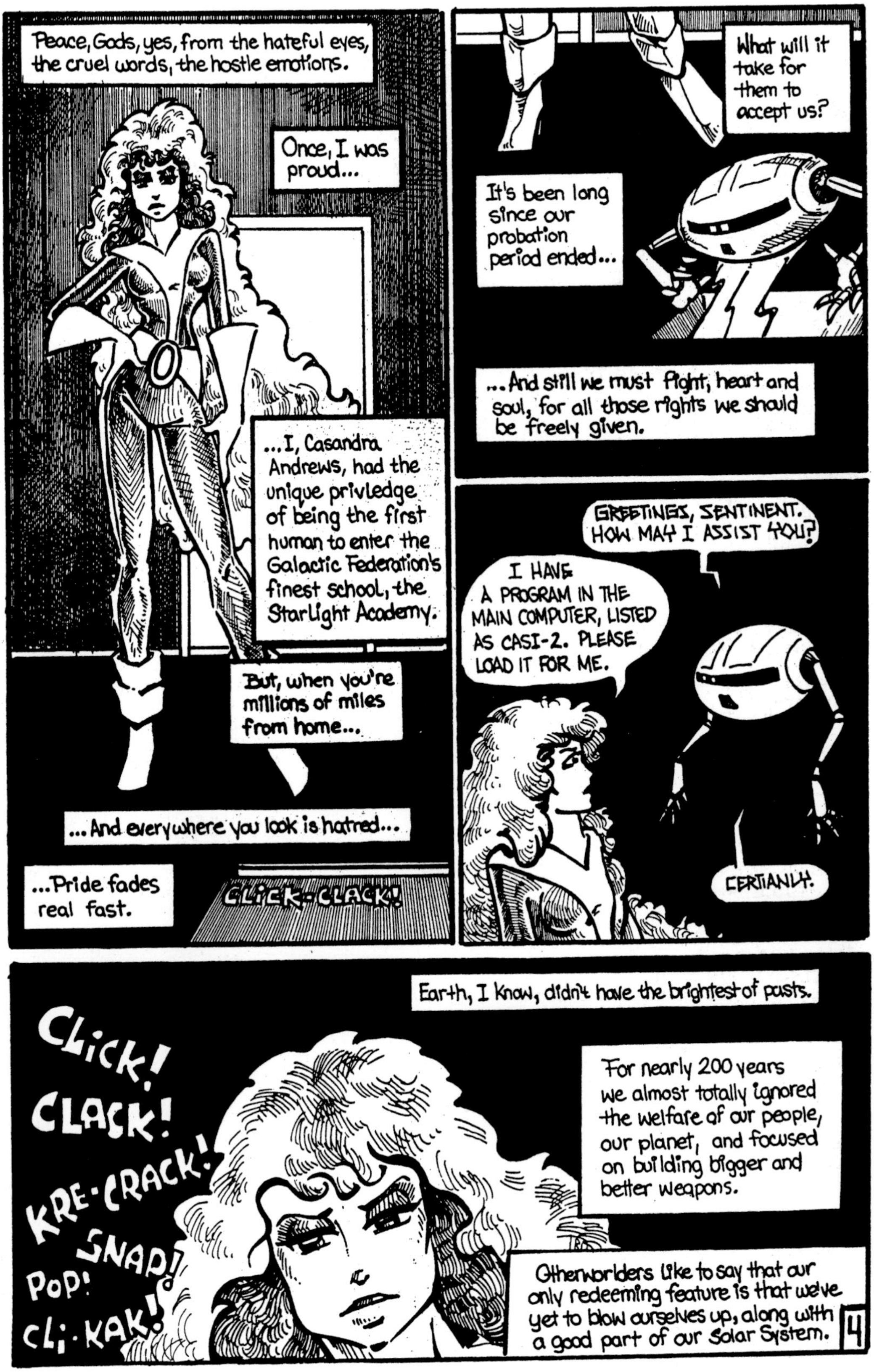
Peace, Gods, yes, from the hateful eyes, the cruel words, the hostle emotions.
Once, I was proud...
...I, Casandra Andrews, had the unique privledge of being the first human to enter the Galactic Federation's finest school, the Starlight Academy.
But, when you're millions of miles from home...
...And everywhere you look is hatred...
...Pride fades real fast.
CLICK-CLACK!
What will it take for them to accept us?
It's been long since our probation period ended...
...And still we must fight, heart and soul, for all those rights we should be freely given.
GREETINGS, SENTINENT. HOW MAY I ASSIST YOU?
I HAVE A PROGRAM IN THE MAIN COMPUTER, LISTED AS CASI-2. PLEASE LOAD IT FOR ME.
CERTIANLY.
Earth, I know, didn't have the brightest of pasts.
CLICK! CLACK! KRE-CRACK! SNAP! POP! CLI-KAK!
For nearly 200 years we almost totally ignored the welfare of our people, our planet, and focused on building bigger and better weapons.
Otherworlders like to say that our only redeeming feature is that we've yet to blow ourselves up, along with a good part of our Solar System.
4

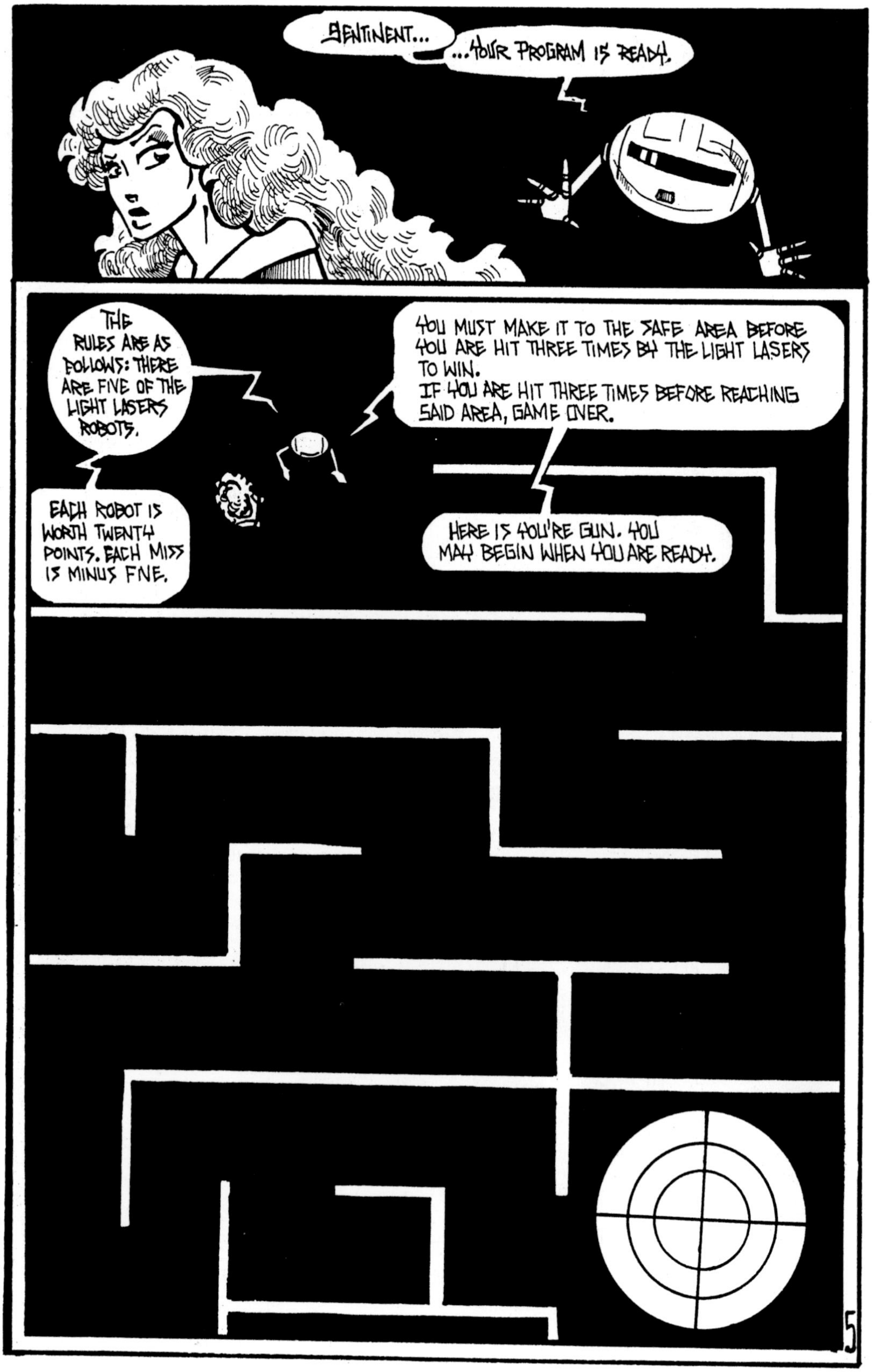
SENTINENT...
...YOUR PROGRAM IS READY.
THE RULES ARE AS FOLLOWS: THERE ARE FIVE OF THE LIGHT LASERS ROBOTS.
EACH ROBOT IS WORTH TWENTY POINTS. EACH MISS IS MINUS FIVE.
YOU MUST MAKE IT TO THE SAFE AREA BEFORE YOU ARE HIT THREE TIMES BY THE LIGHT LASERS TO WIN.
IF YOU ARE HIT THREE TIMES BEFORE REACHING SAID AREA, GAME OVER.
HERE IS YOU'RE GUN. YOU MAY BEGIN WHEN YOU ARE READY.

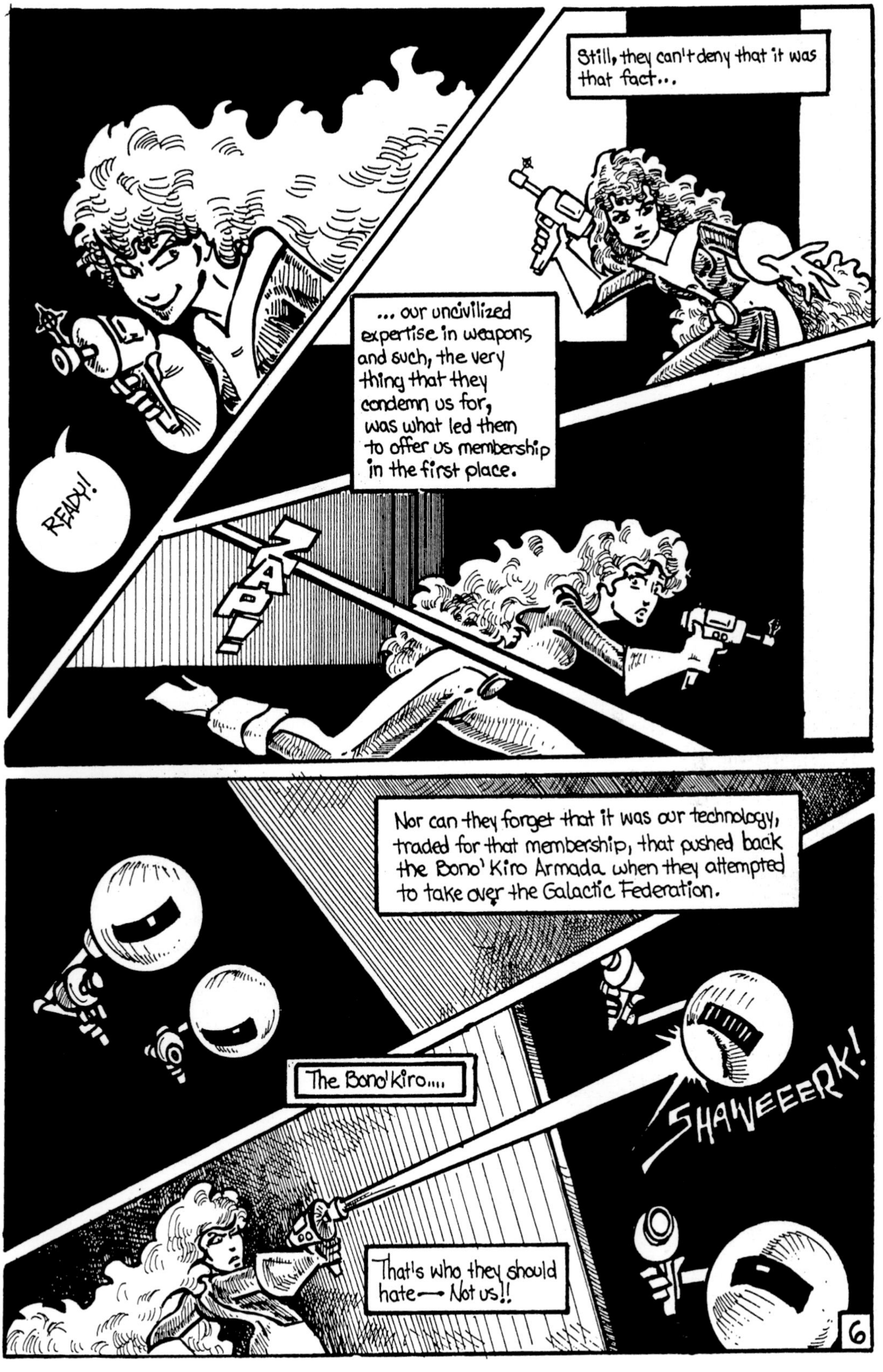
READY!
Still, they can't deny that it was that fact...
... our uncivilized expertise in weapons and such, the very thing that they condemn us for, was what led them to offer us membership in the first place.
ZAP!
Nor can they forget that it was our technology, traded for that membership, that pushed back the Bono' Kiro Armada when they attempted to take over the Galactic Federation.
The Bono'kiro....
SHAWEEERK!
That's who they should hate— Not us!!
6

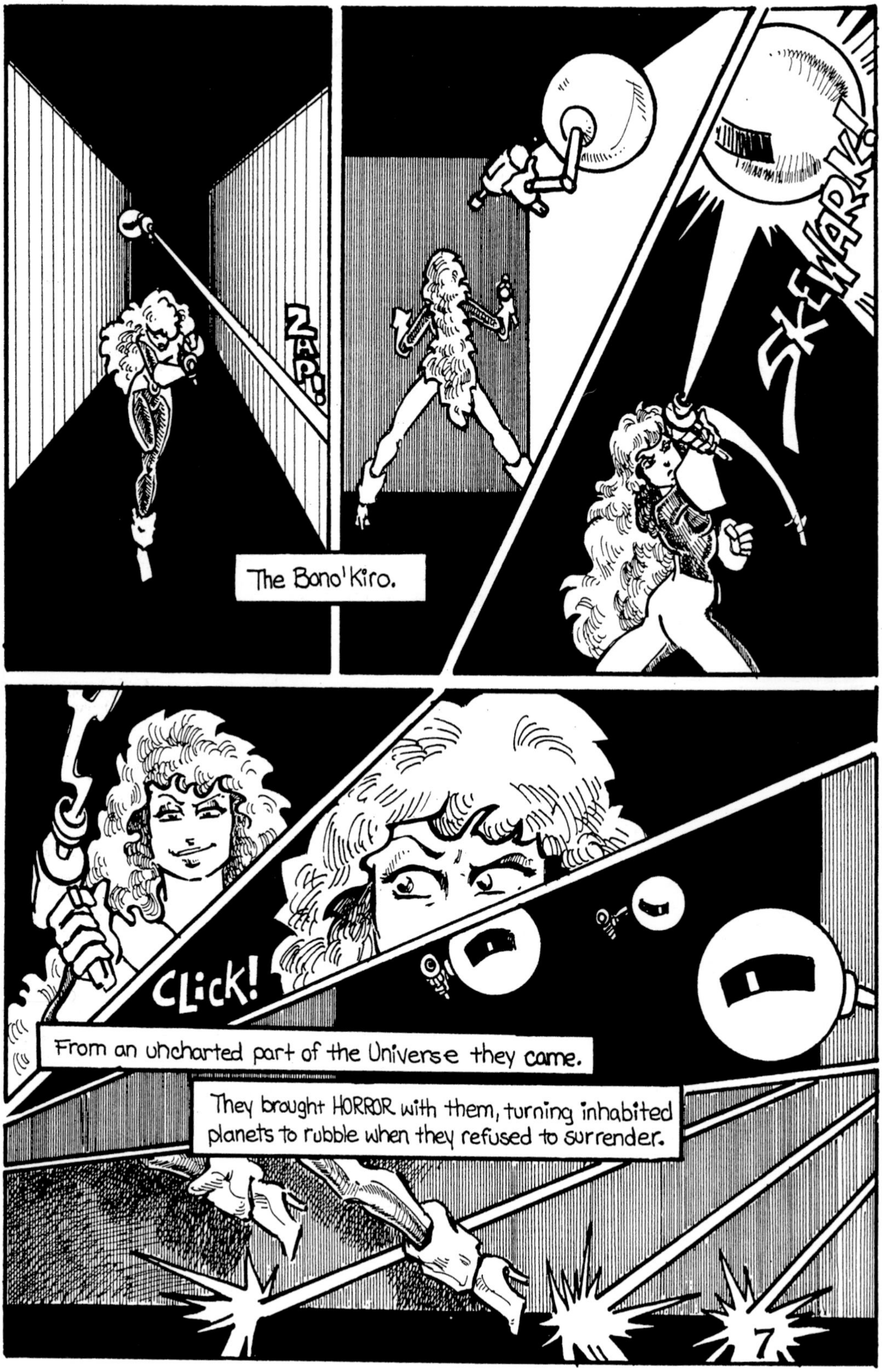

ZAP!
The Bono'Kiro.
SKEWARK!
CLICK!
From an uncharted part of the Universe they came.
They brought HORROR with them, turning inhabited planets to rubble when they refused to surrender.

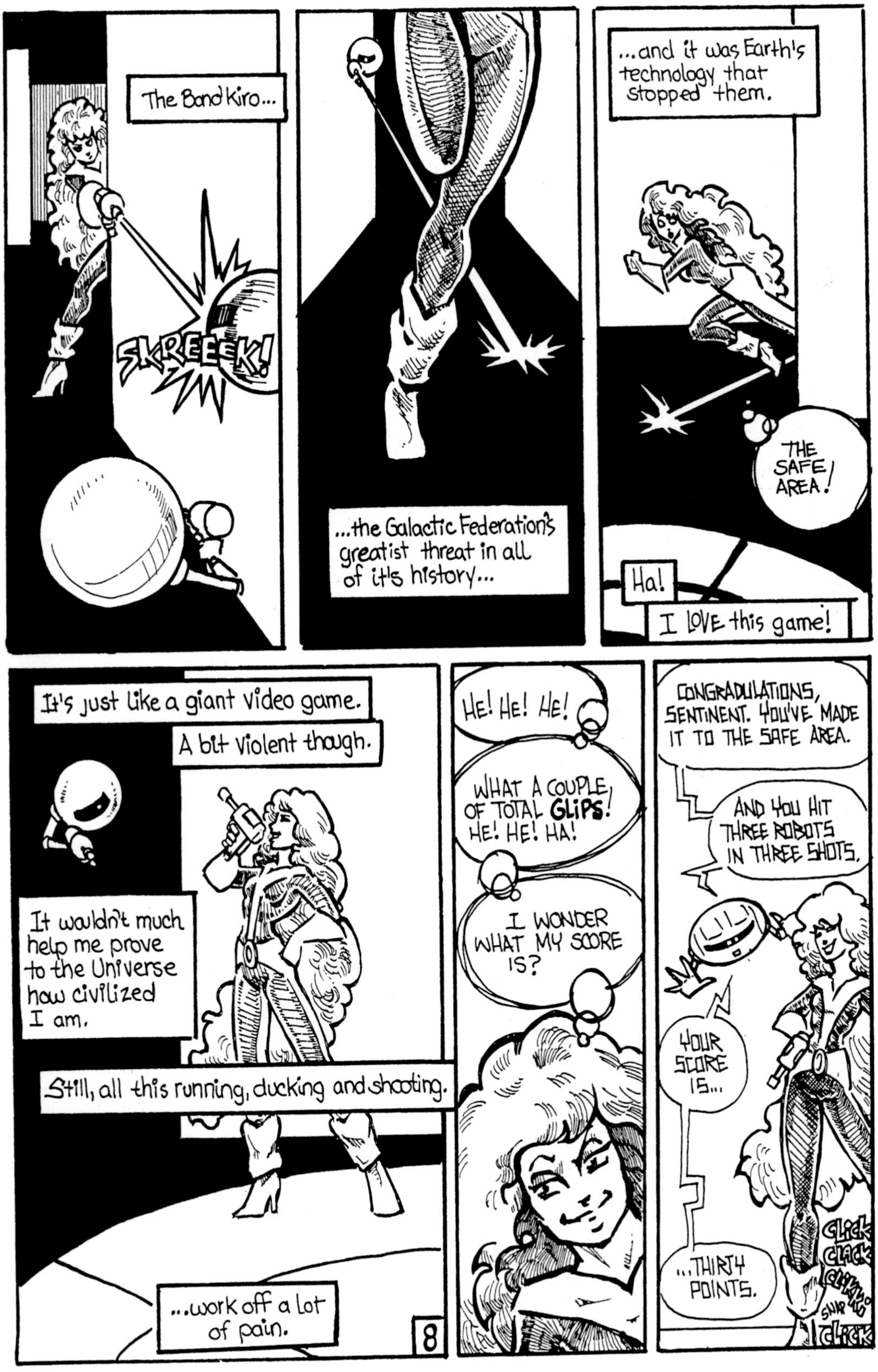

The Band Kiro...
SKREEEK!
...the Galactic Federation's greatest threat in all of it's history...
...and it was Earth's technology that stopped them.
THE SAFE AREA!
Ha!
I LOVE this game!
It's just like a giant video game.
A bit violent though.
It wouldn't much help me prove to the Universe how civilized I am.
Still, all this running, ducking and shooting.
...work off a lot of pain.
8
HE! HE! HE!
WHAT A COUPLE OF TOTAL GLIPS! HE! HE! HA!
I WONDER WHAT MY SCORE IS?
CONGRADULATIONS, SENTINENT. YOU'VE MADE IT TO THE SAFE AREA.
AND YOU HIT THREE ROBOTS IN THREE SHOTS.
YOUR SCORE IS...
...THIRTY POINTS.
CLICK CLACK

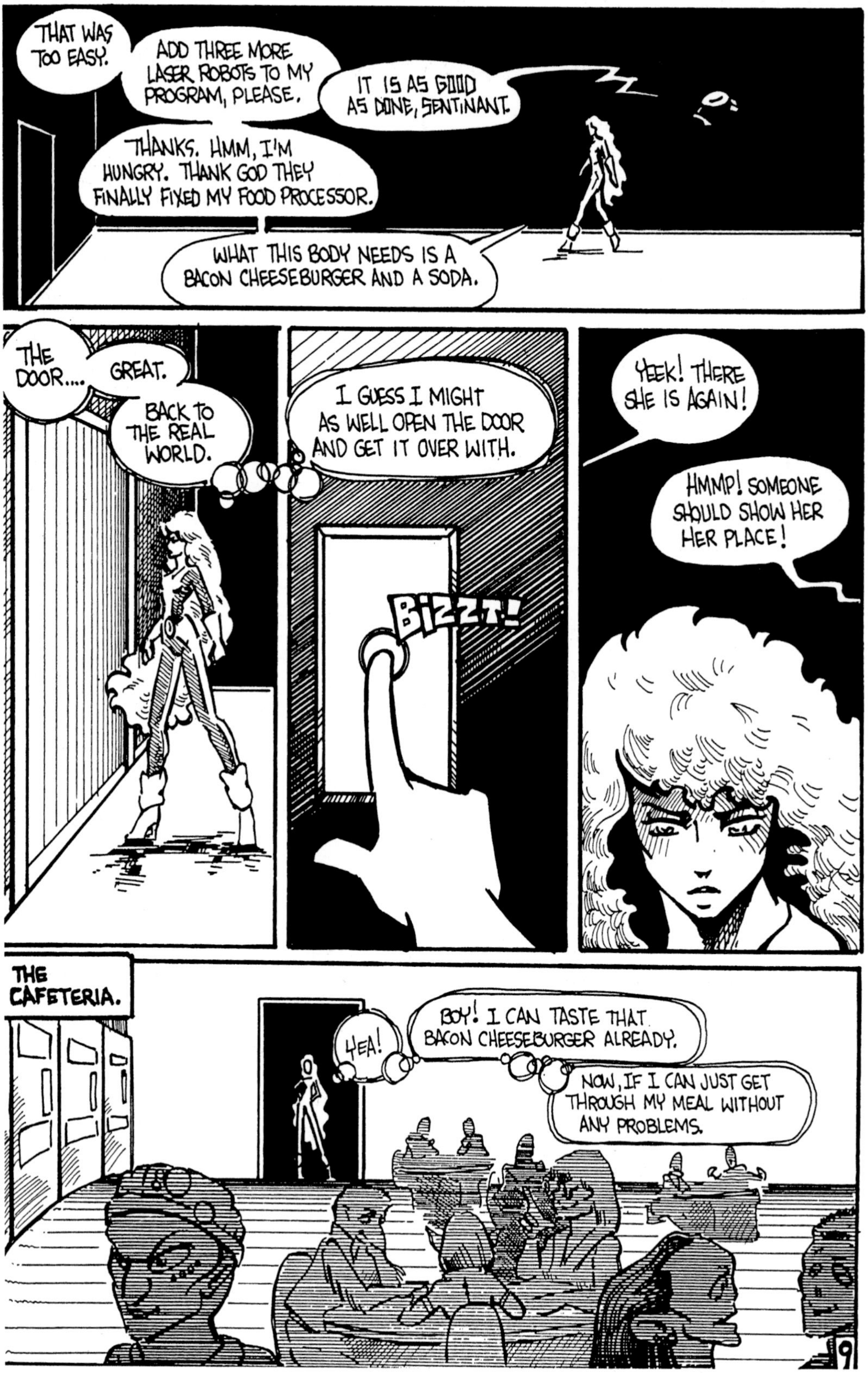
THAT WAS TOO EASY.
ADD THREE MORE LASER ROBOTS TO MY PROGRAM, PLEASE.
IT IS AS GOOD AS DONE, SENTINANT.
THANKS. HMM, I'M HUNGRY. THANK GOD THEY FINALLY FIXED MY FOOD PROCESSOR.
WHAT THIS BODY NEEDS IS A BACON CHEESEBURGER AND A SODA.
THE DOOR....
GREAT.
BACK TO THE REAL WORLD.
I GUESS I MIGHT AS WELL OPEN THE DOOR AND GET IT OVER WITH.
BIZZT!
YEEK! THERE SHE IS AGAIN!
HMMP! SOMEONE SHOULD SHOW HER HER PLACE!
THE CAFETERIA.
YEA!
BOY! I CAN TASTE THAT BACON CHEESEBURGER ALREADY.
NOW, IF I CAN JUST GET THROUGH MY MEAL WITHOUT ANY PROBLEMS.
9

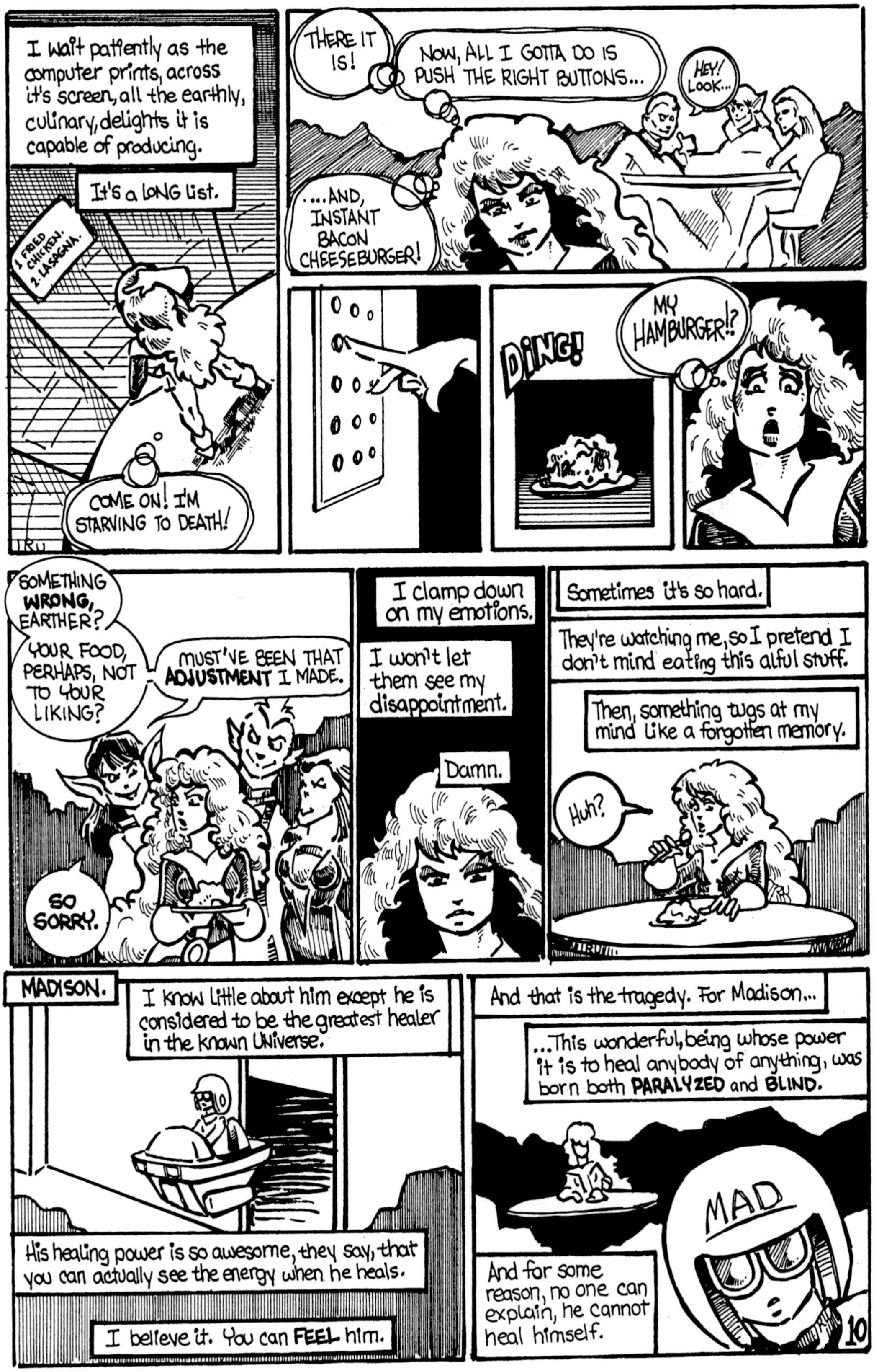

I wait patiently as the computer prints, across it's screen, all the earthly, culinary, delights it is capable of producing.
It's a LONG list.
1. FRIED CHICKEN. 2. LASAGNA.
COME ON! I'M STARVING TO DEATH!
THERE IT IS!
NOW, ALL I GOTTA DO IS PUSH THE RIGHT BUTTONS...
...AND, INSTANT BACON CHEESEBURGER!
HEY! LOOK...
DING!
MY HAMBURGER!?
SOMETHING WRONG, EARTHER?
YOUR FOOD, PERHAPS, NOT TO YOUR LIKING?
MUST'VE BEEN THAT ADJUSTMENT I MADE.
SO SORRY.
I clamp down on my emotions.
I won't let them see my disappointment.
Damn.
Sometimes it's so hard.
They're watching me, so I pretend I don't mind eating this alful stuff.
Then, something tugs at my mind like a forgotten memory.
Huh?
MADISON.
I know little about him except he is considered to be the greatest healer in the known Universe.
His healing power is so awesome, they say, that you can actually see the energy when he heals.
I believe it. You can FEEL him.
And that is the tragedy. For Madison...
...This wonderful, being whose power it is to heal anybody of anything, was born both PARALYZED and BLIND.
MAD
And for some reason, no one can explain, he cannot heal himself.
10

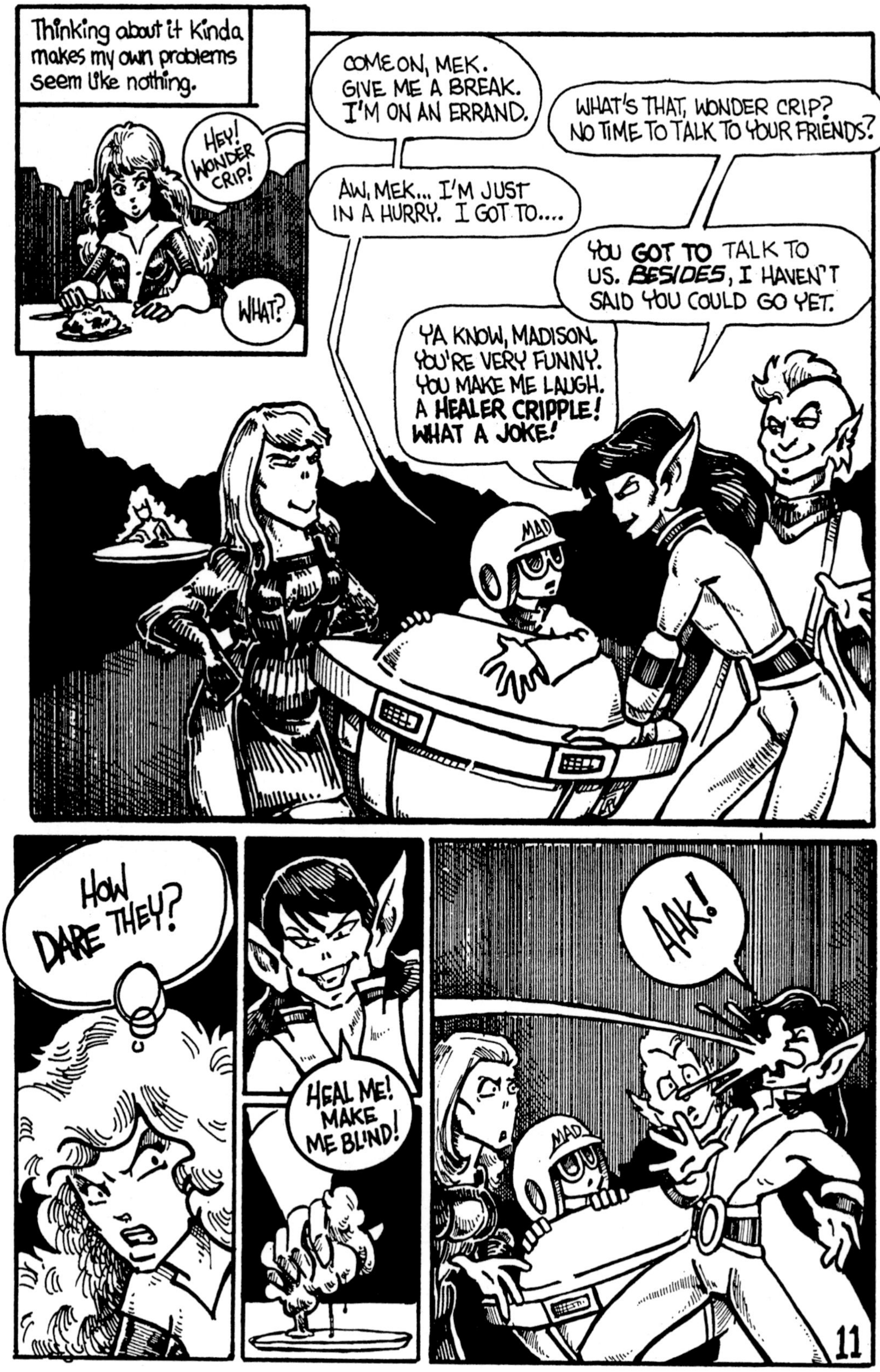
Thinking about it Kinda makes my own problems seem like nothing.
HEY! WONDER CRIP!
WHAT?
COME ON, MEK. GIVE ME A BREAK. I'M ON AN ERRAND.
WHAT'S THAT, WONDER CRIP? NO TIME TO TALK TO YOUR FRIENDS?
AW, MEK... I'M JUST IN A HURRY. I GOT TO....
YOU GOT TO TALK TO US. BESIDES, I HAVEN'T SAID YOU COULD GO YET.
YA KNOW, MADISON. YOU'RE VERY FUNNY. YOU MAKE ME LAUGH. A HEALER CRIPPLE! WHAT A JOKE!
MAD
HOW DARE THEY?
HEAL ME! MAKE ME BLIND!
AAK!
MAD

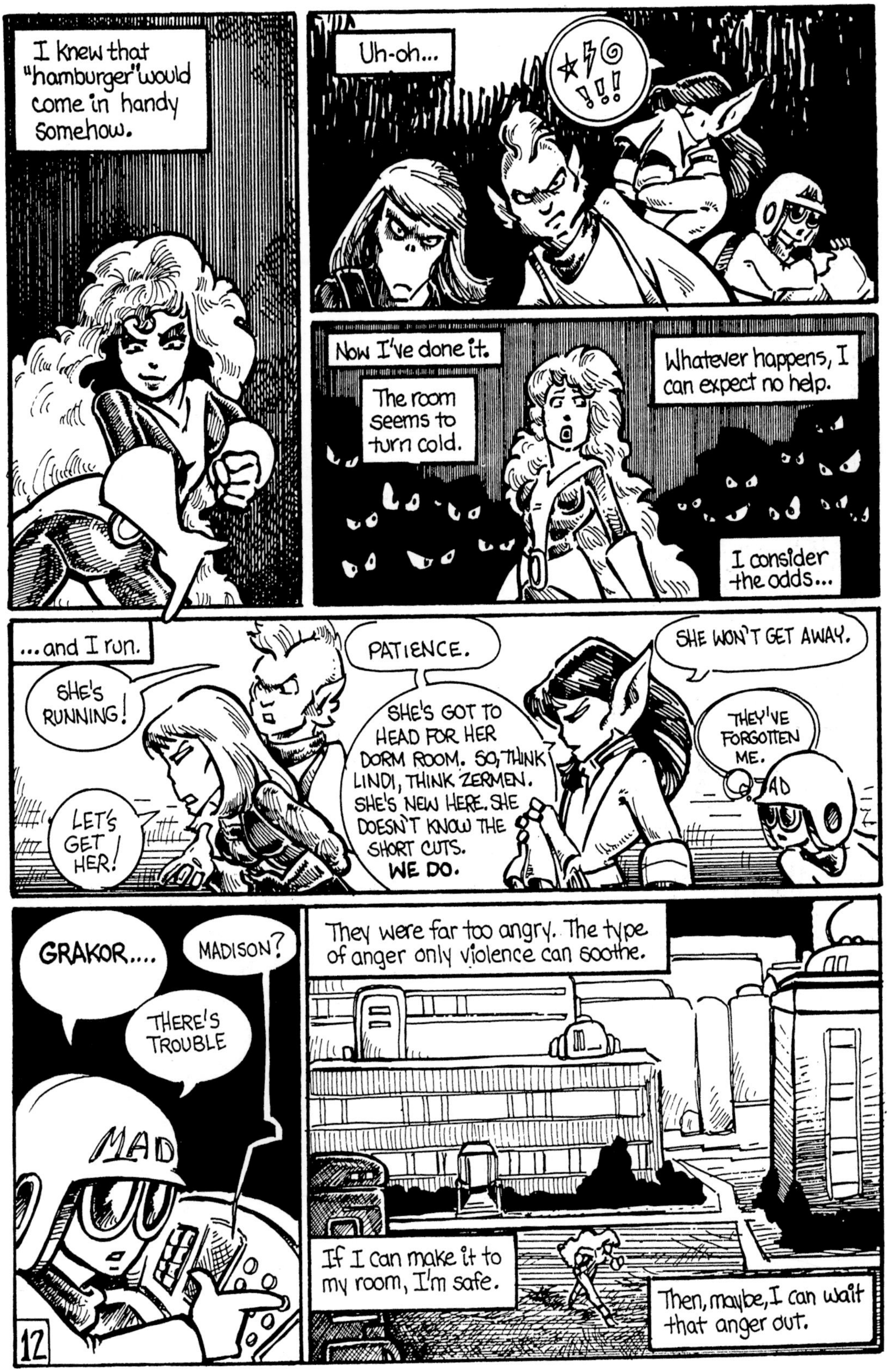
I knew that "hamburger" would come in handy somehow.
Uh-oh...
☆ϟ@ !!!
Now I've done it.
The room seems to turn cold.
Whatever happens, I can expect no help.
I consider the odds...
...and I run.
SHE'S RUNNING!
LET'S GET HER!
PATIENCE.
SHE'S GOT TO HEAD FOR HER DORM ROOM. SO, THINK LINDI, THINK ZERMEN. SHE'S NEW HERE. SHE DOESN'T KNOW THE SHORT CUTS. WE DO.
SHE WON'T GET AWAY.
THEY'VE FORGOTTEN ME.
GRAKOR....
MADISON?
THERE'S TROUBLE
They were far too angry. The type of anger only violence can soothe.
If I can make it to my room, I'm safe.
Then, maybe, I can wait that anger out.

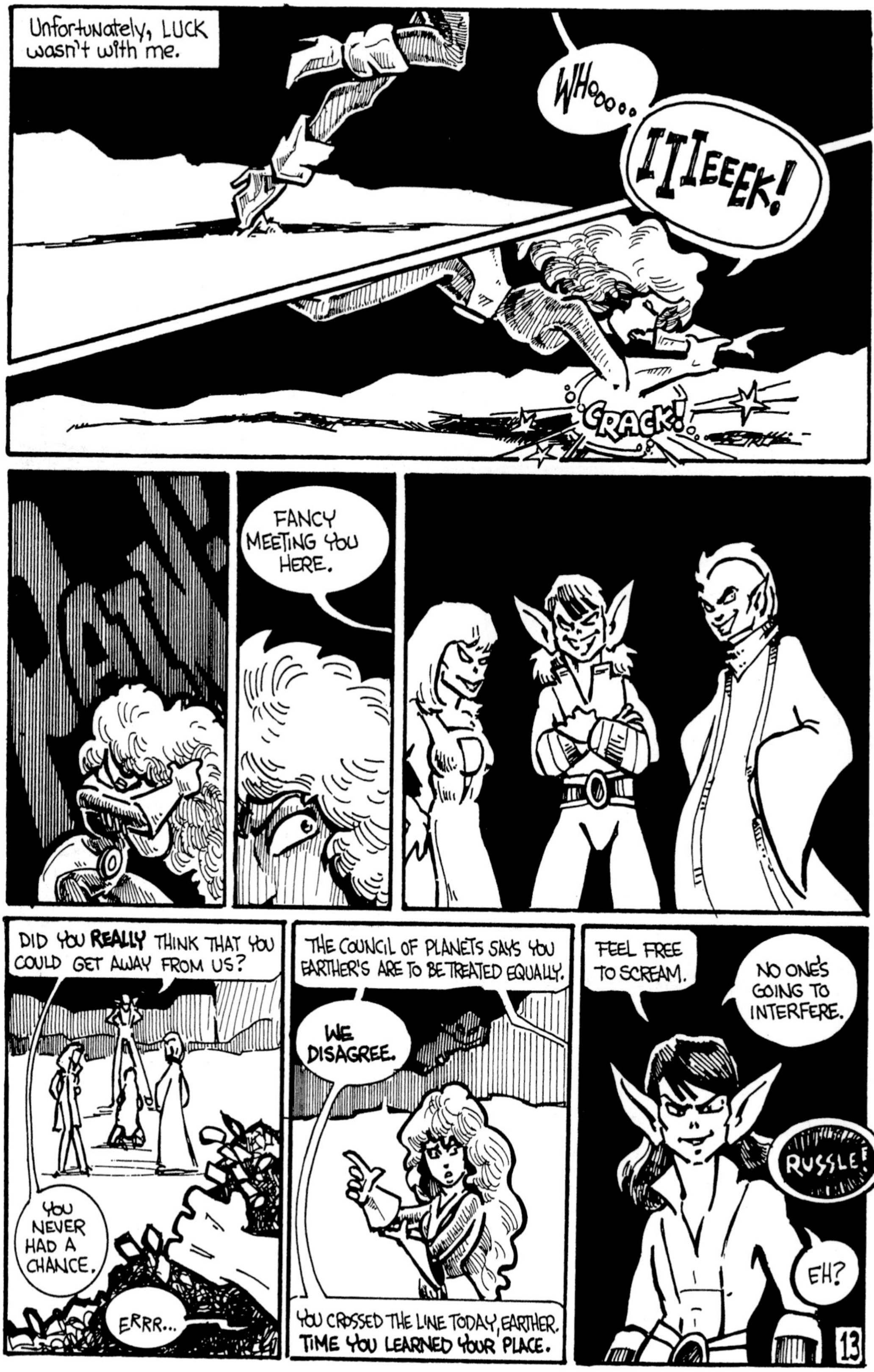

Unfortunately, LUCK wasn't with me.
WHooo...
IIIEEEK!
CRACK!
FANCY MEETING YOU HERE.
DID YOU REALLY THINK THAT YOU COULD GET AWAY FROM US?
YOU NEVER HAD A CHANCE.
ERRR...
THE COUNCIL OF PLANETS SAYS YOU EARTHER'S ARE TO BE TREATED EQUALLY.
WE DISAGREE.
YOU CROSSED THE LINE TODAY, EARTHER. TIME YOU LEARNED YOUR PLACE.
FEEL FREE TO SCREAM.
NO ONE'S GOING TO INTERFERE.
RUSSLE!
EH?

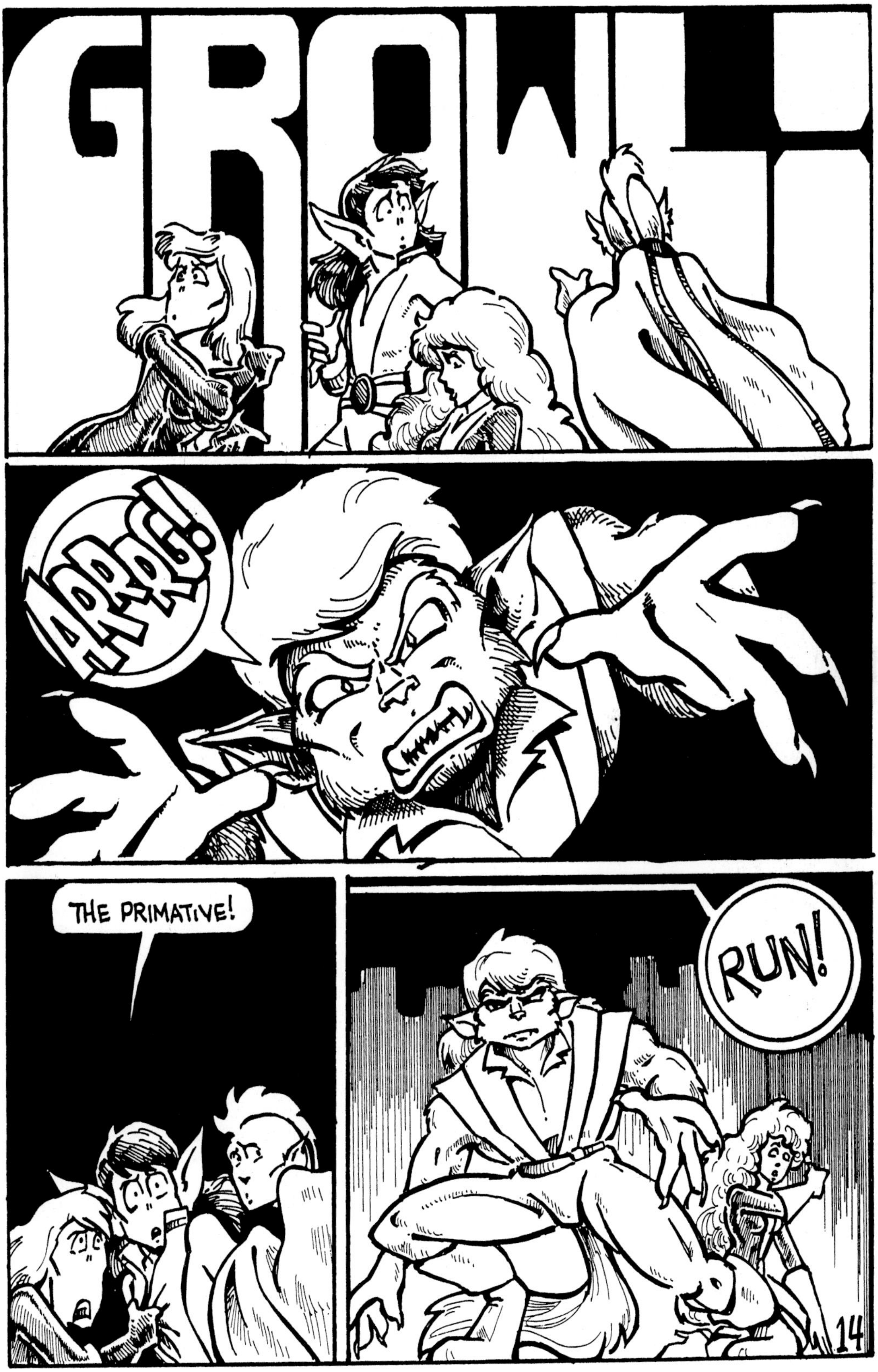
GROWL!
ARRGG!
THE PRIMATIVE!
RUN!
14

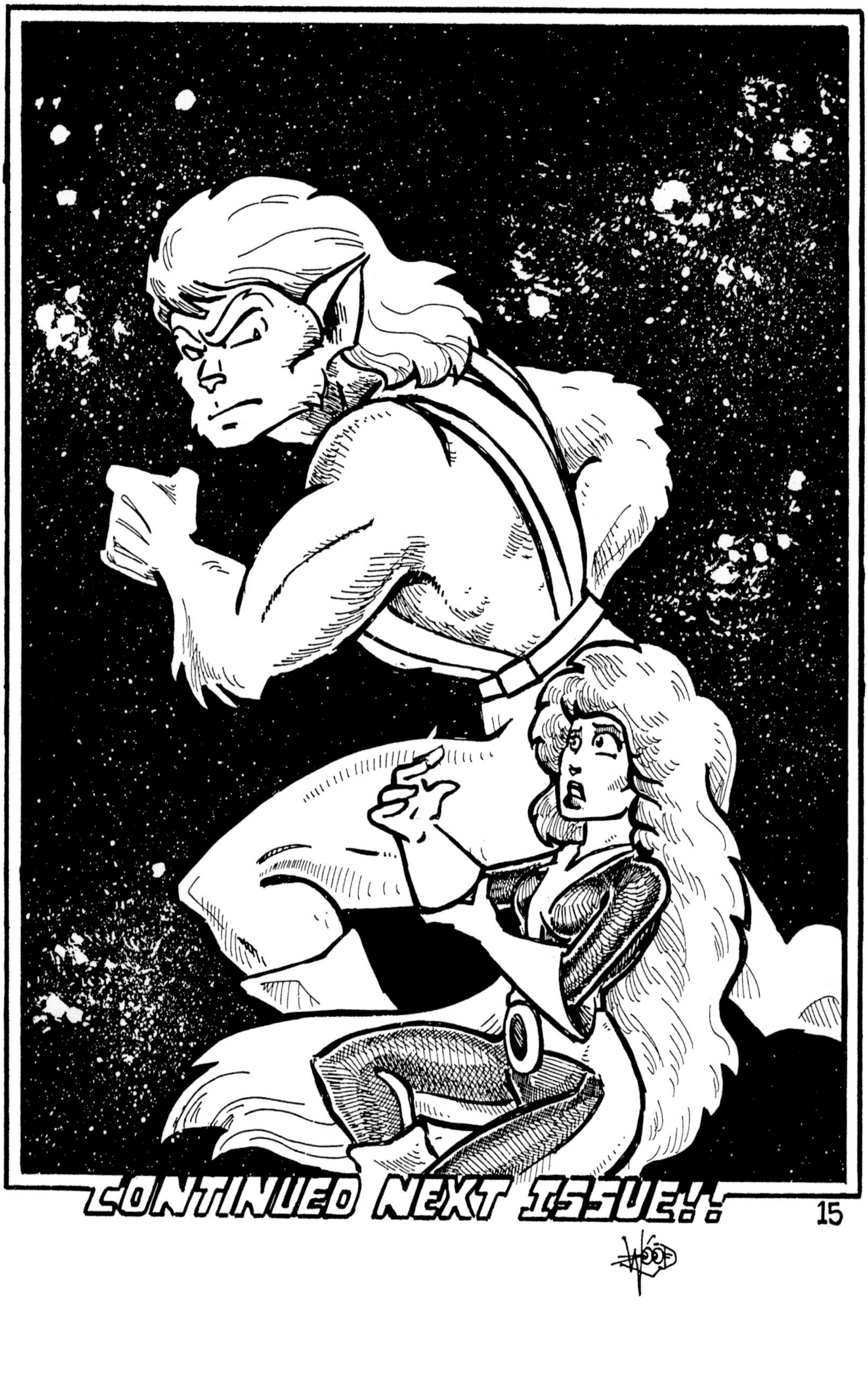
CONTINUED NEXT ISSUE!!

Wandering Star

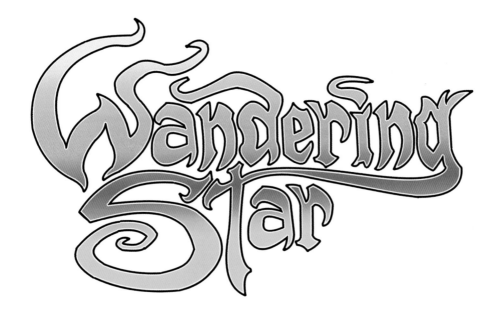

COVER GALLERY

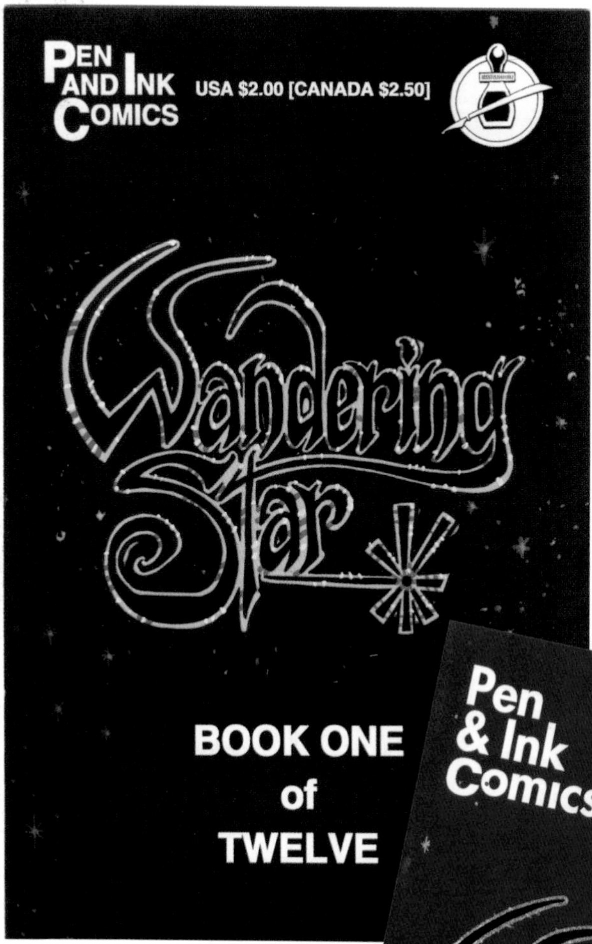
PEN AND INK COMICS
USA $2.00 [CANADA $2.50]
BOOK ONE
of
TWELVE

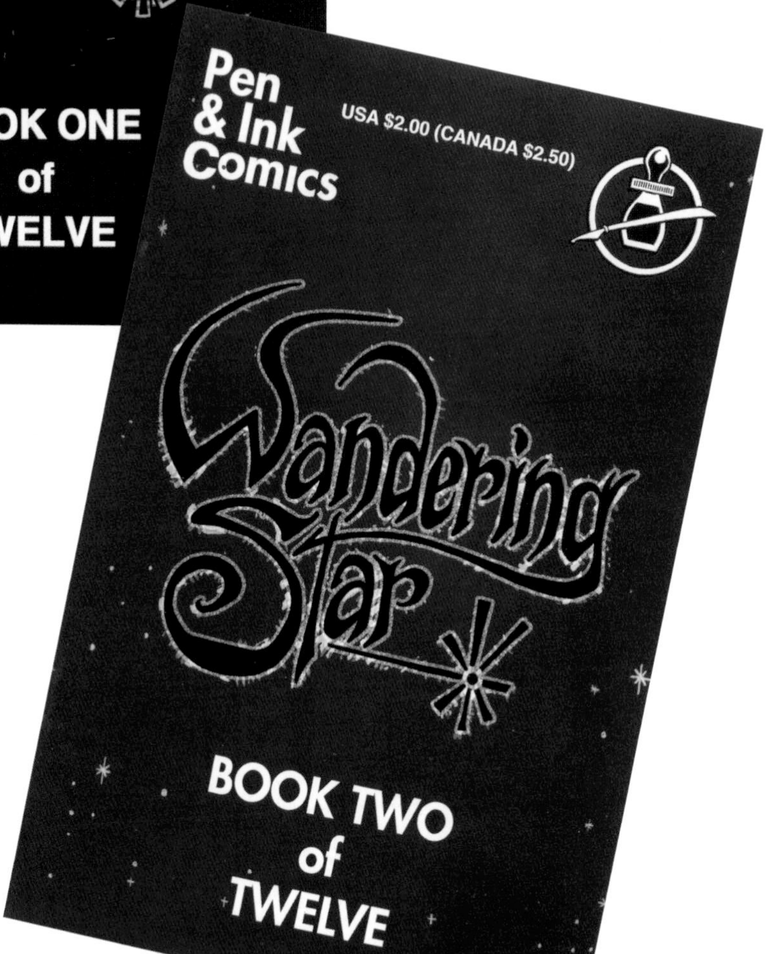
Pen & Ink Comics
USA $2.00 (CANADA $2.50)
BOOK TWO
of
TWELVE

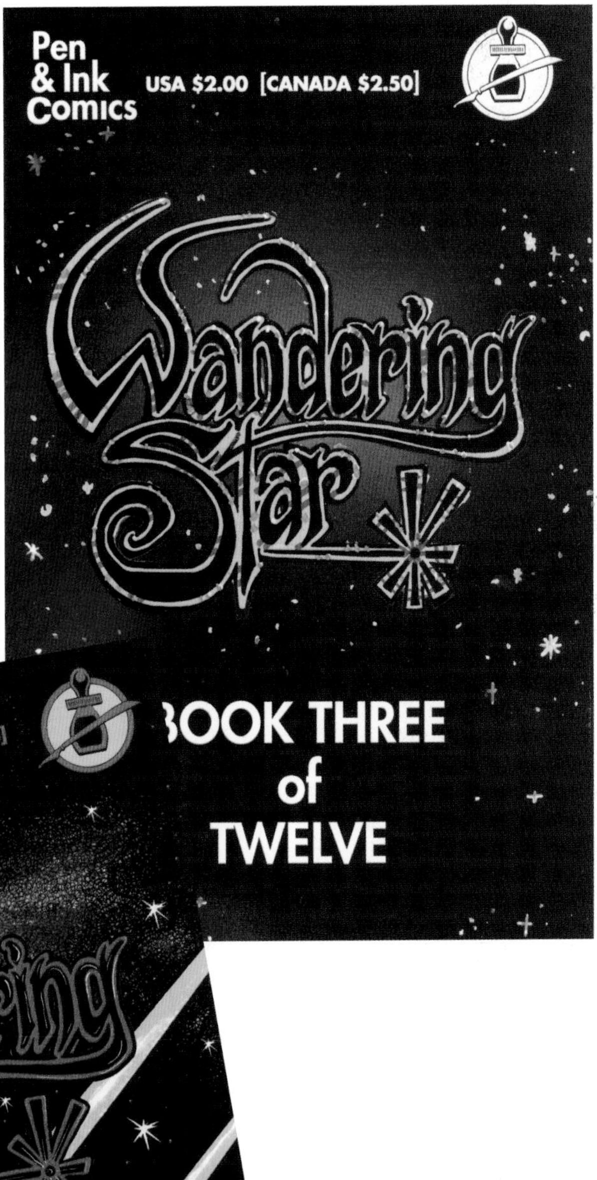
Pen & Ink Comics
USA $2.00 [CANADA $2.50]
Wandering Star
BOOK THREE of TWELVE

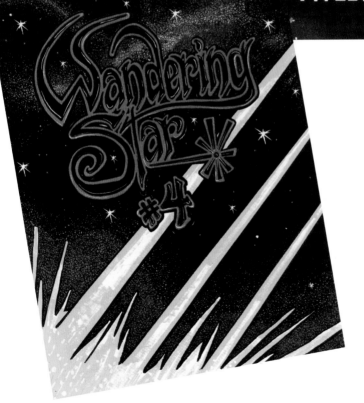

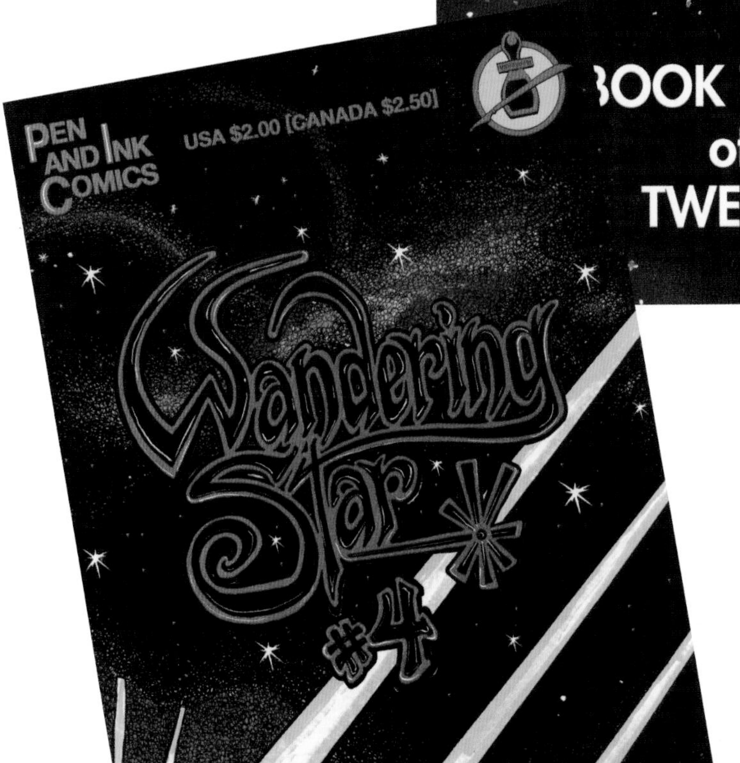
PEN AND INK COMICS
USA $2.00 [CANADA $2.50]
Wandering Star
#4

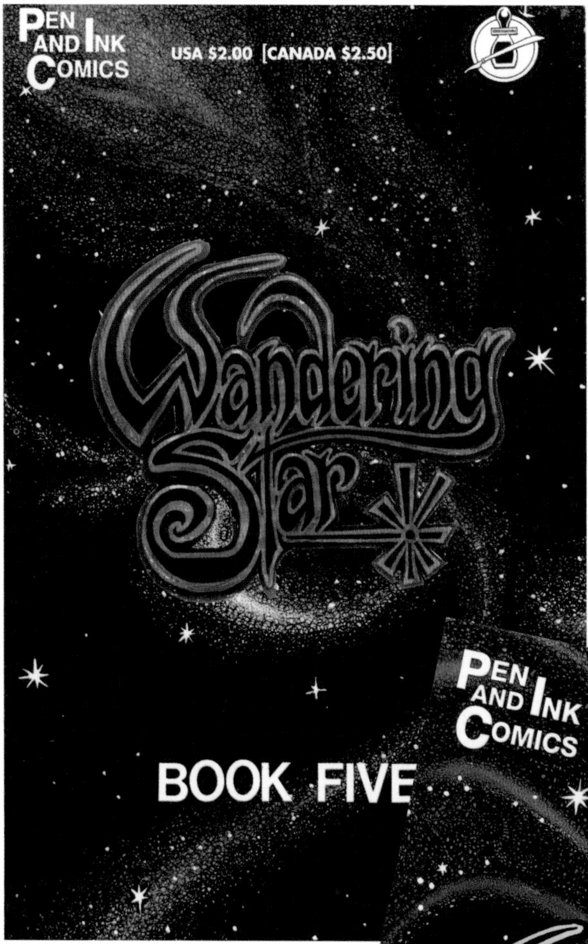
PEN AND INK COMICS
USA $2.00 [CANADA $2.50]
Wandering Star
BOOK FIVE

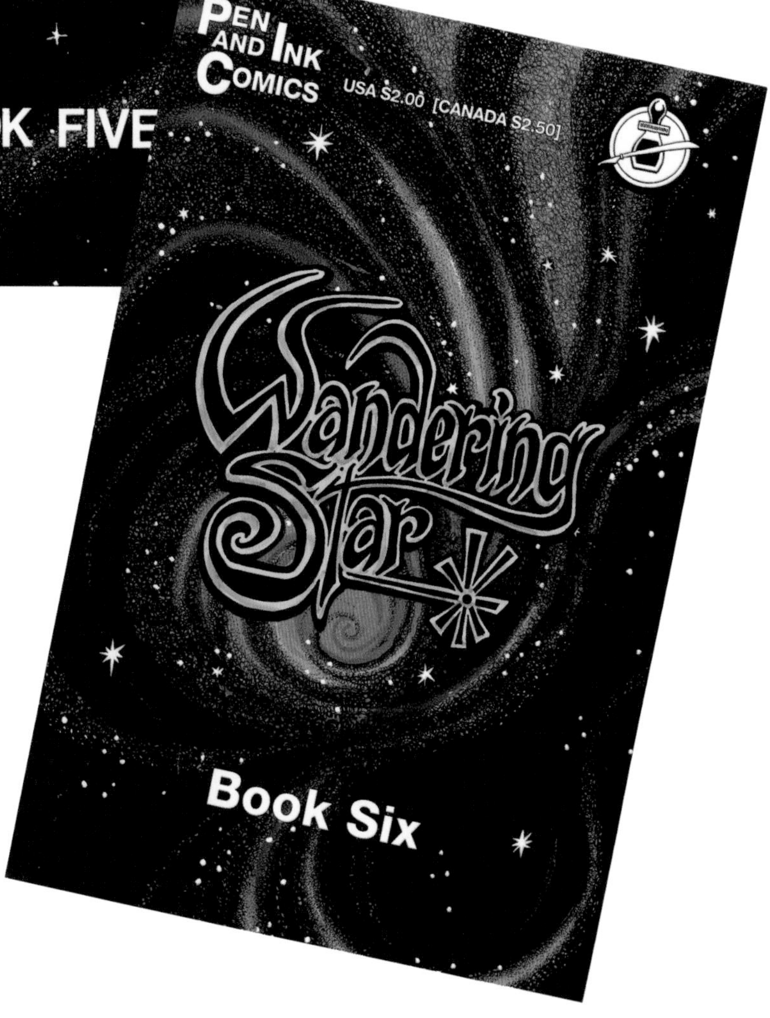
PEN AND INK COMICS
USA $2.00 [CANADA $2.50]
Wandering Star
Book Six

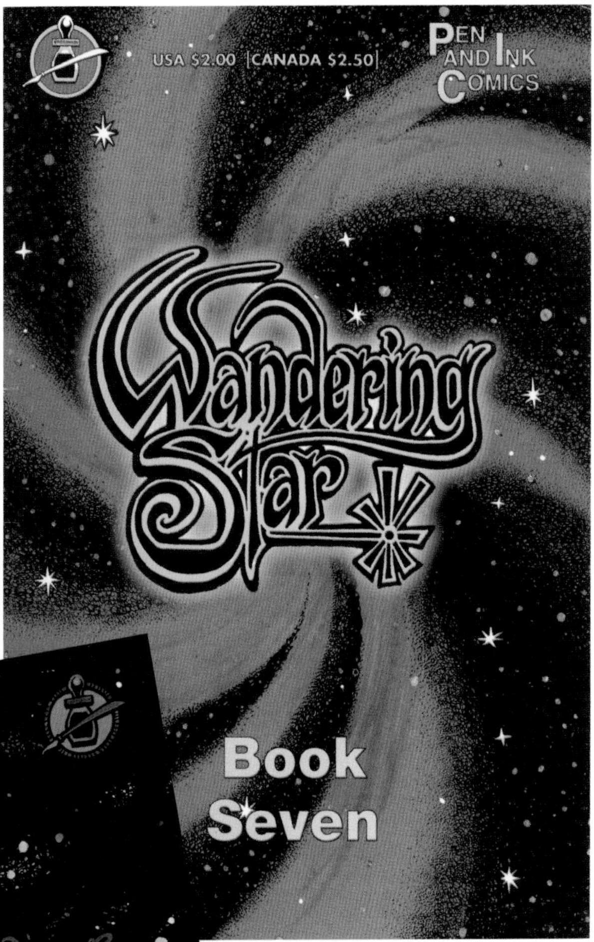
USA $2.00 [CANADA $2.50]
PEN AND INK COMICS
Wandering Star
Book Seven

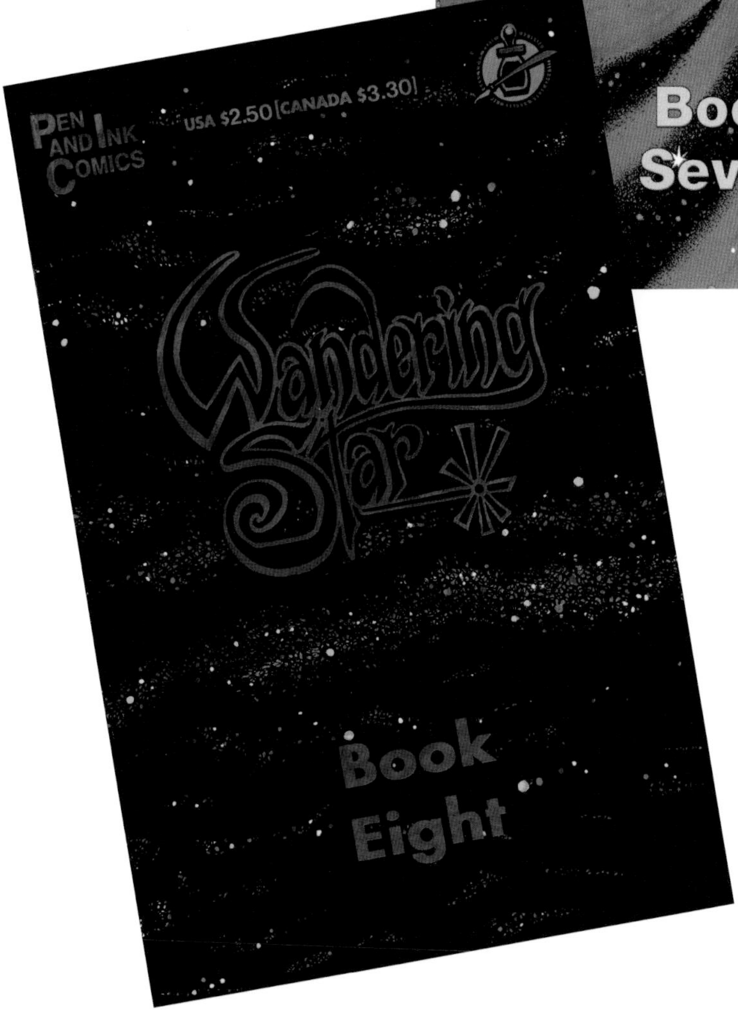
PEN AND INK COMICS
USA $2.50 [CANADA $3.30]
Wandering Star
Book Eight

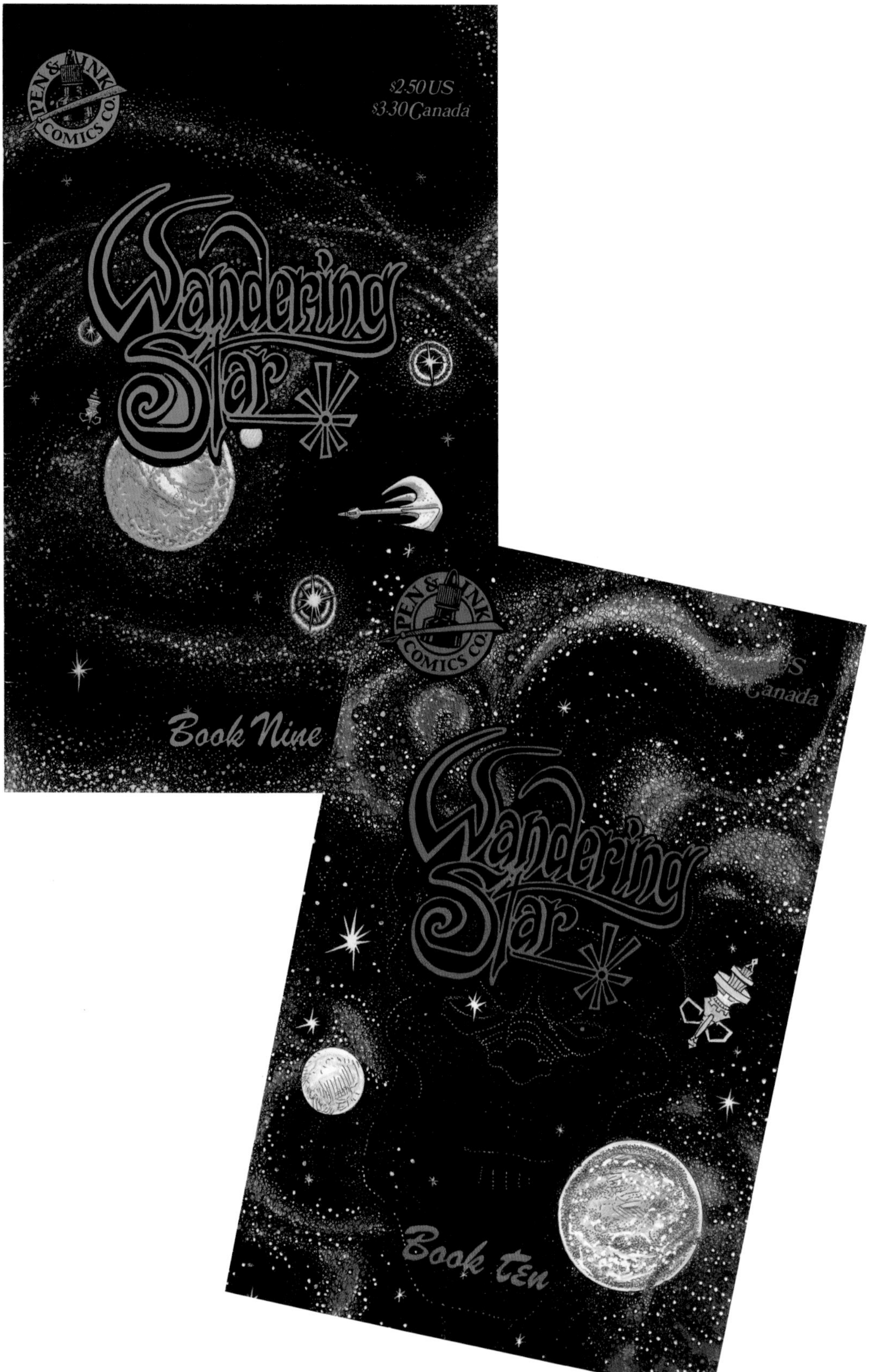
PEN & INK COMICS CO.
$2.50 US
$3.30 Canada
Wandering Star
Book Nine
PEN & INK COMICS CO.
Wandering Star
Book Ten

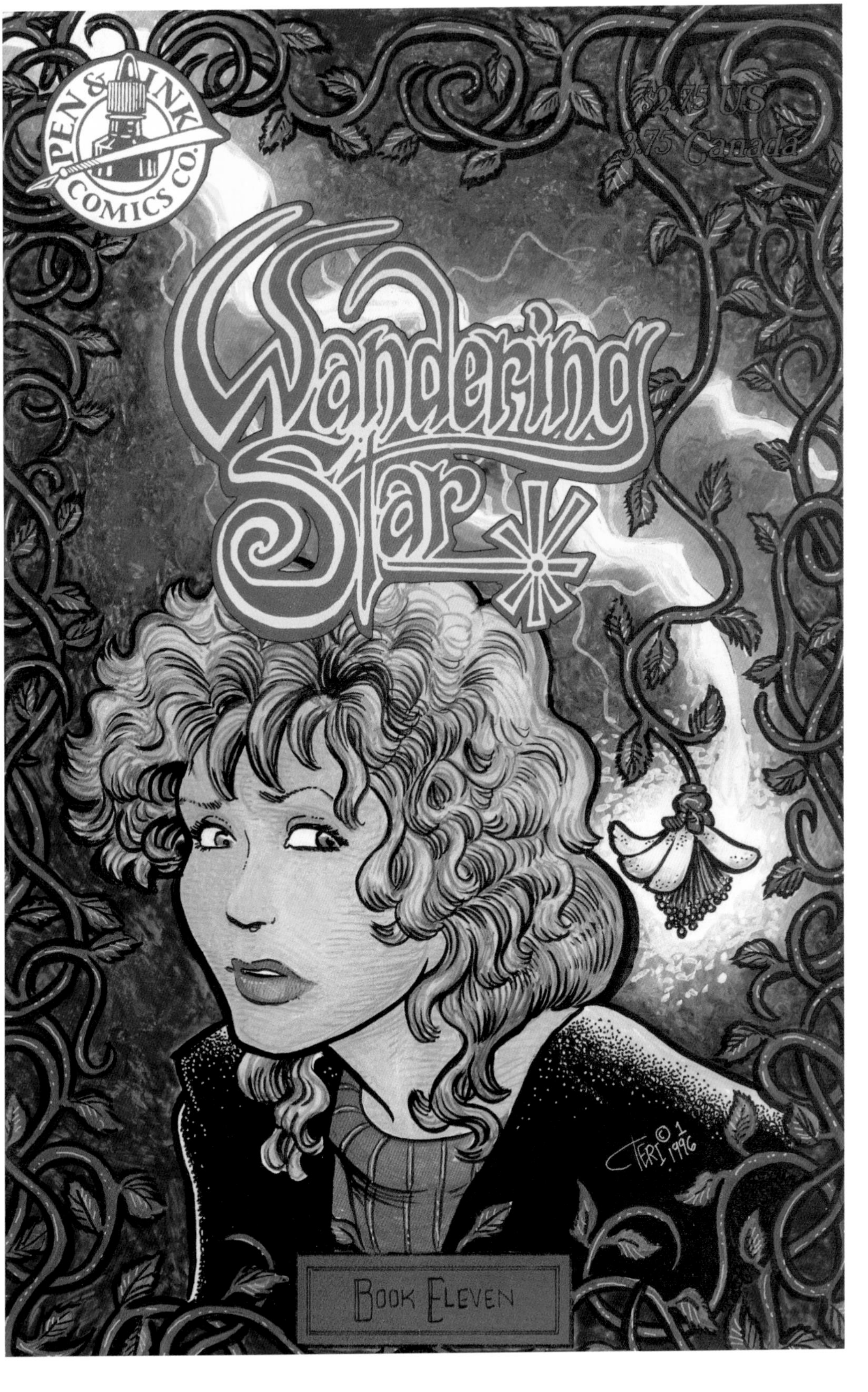
PEN & INK COMICS CO.
$2.75 US
3.75 Canada
Wandering Star
BOOK ELEVEN

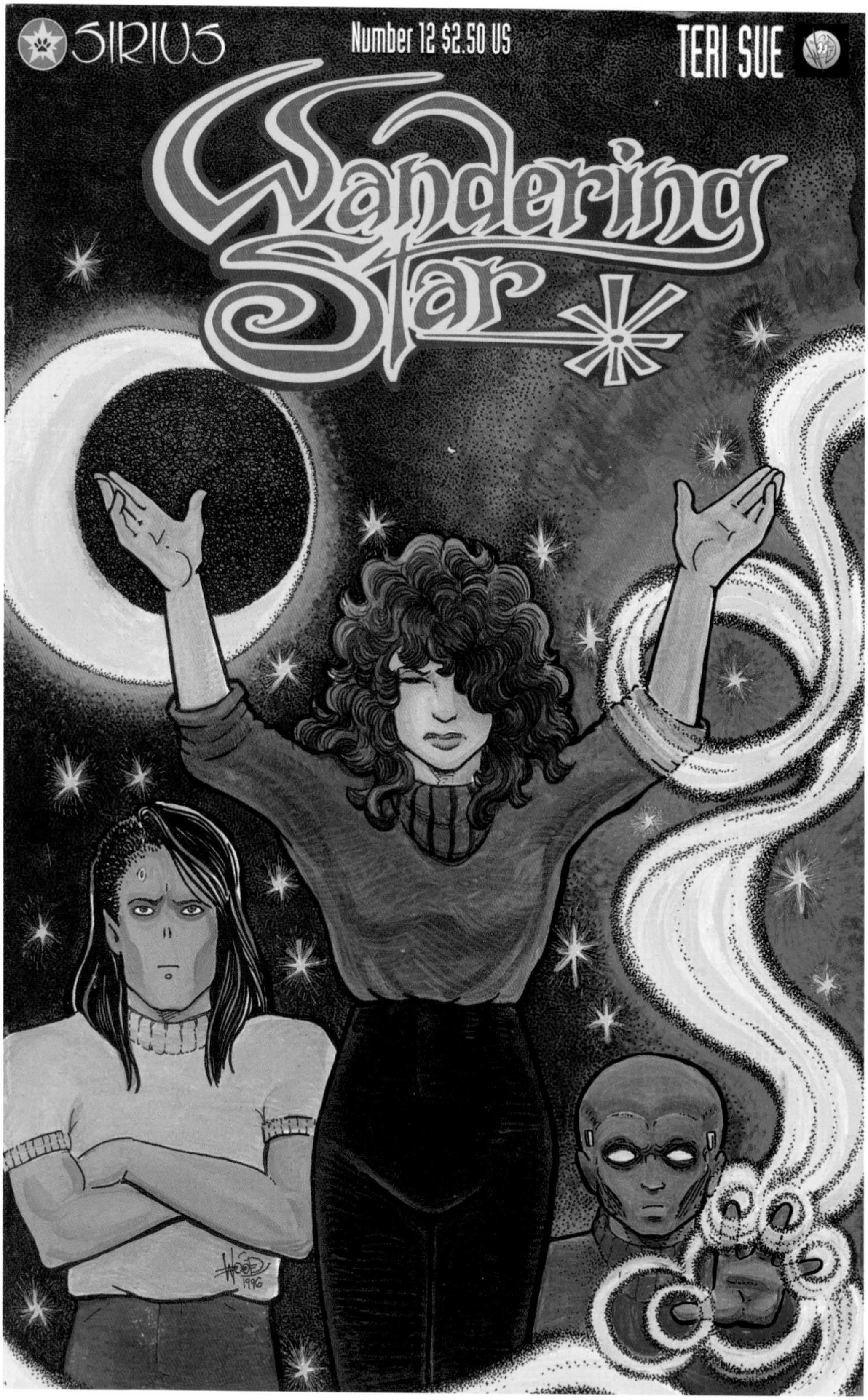
SIRIUS
Number 12 $2.50 US
TERI SUE
Wandering Star
WOOD 1996

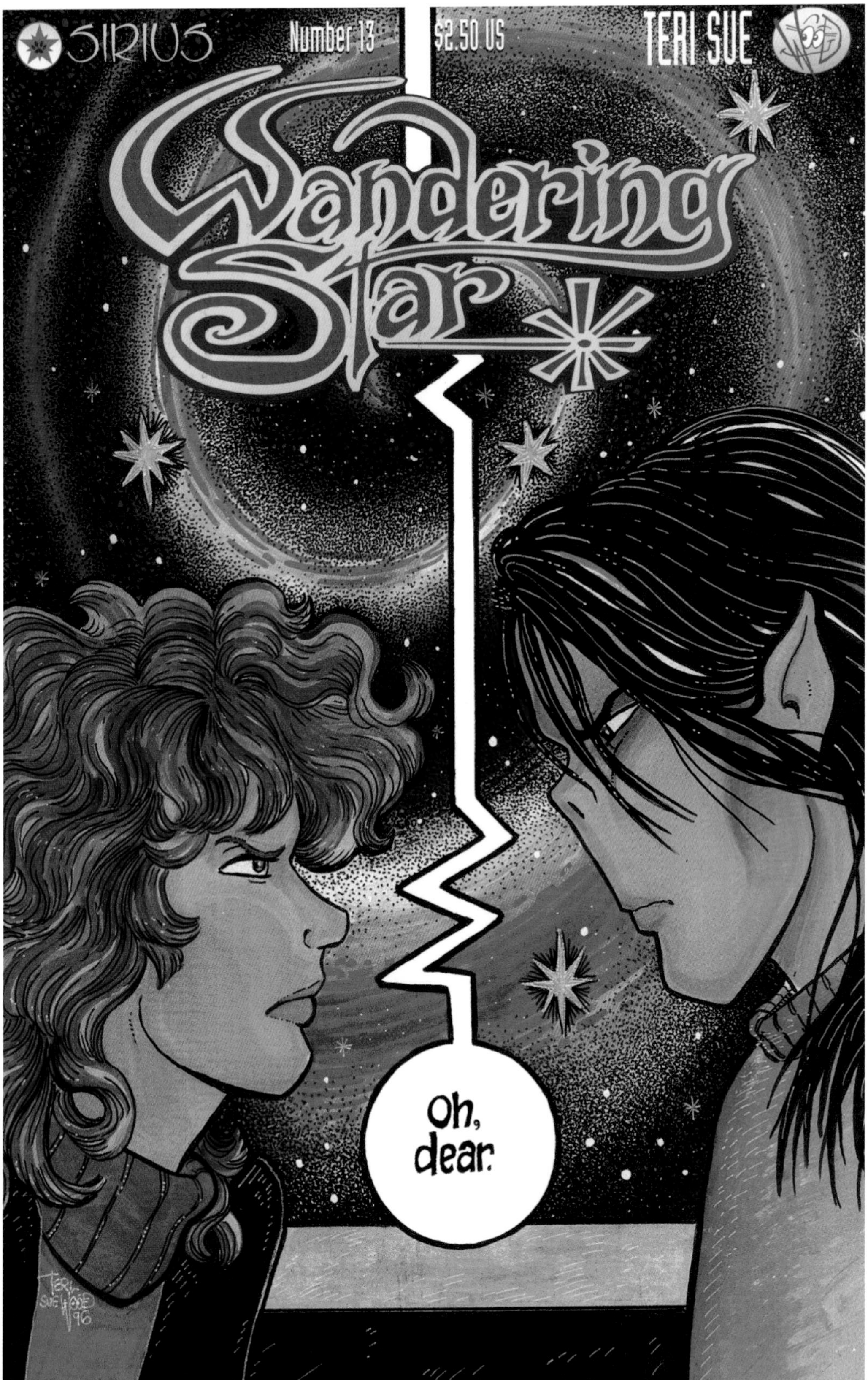
SIRIUS
Number 13
$2.50 US
TERI SUE
Wandering Star
Oh, dear.
TERI SUE HOOD '96

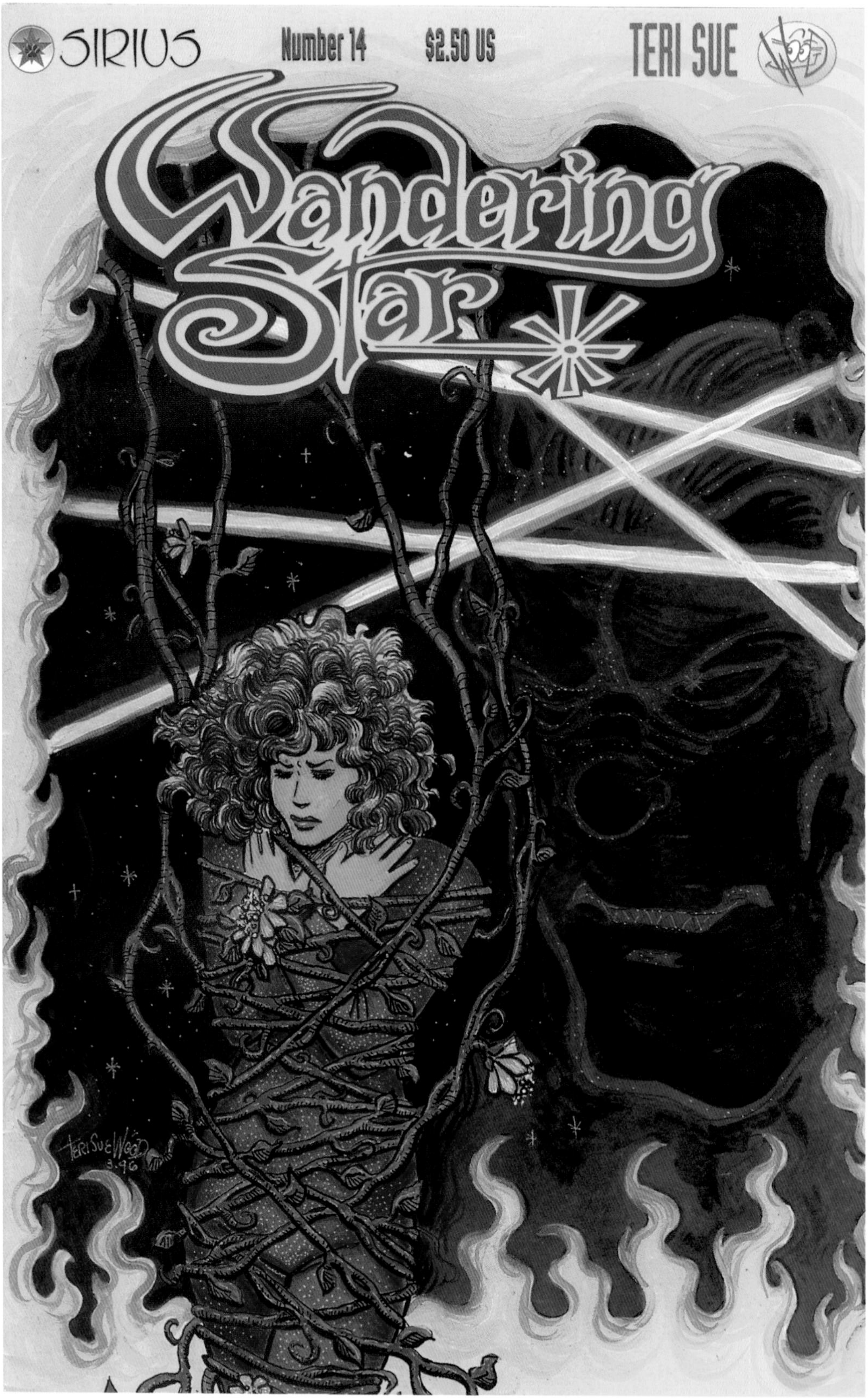
SIRIUS
Number 14
$2.50 US
TERI SUE
Wandering Star
TERI SUE WOOD 3.96

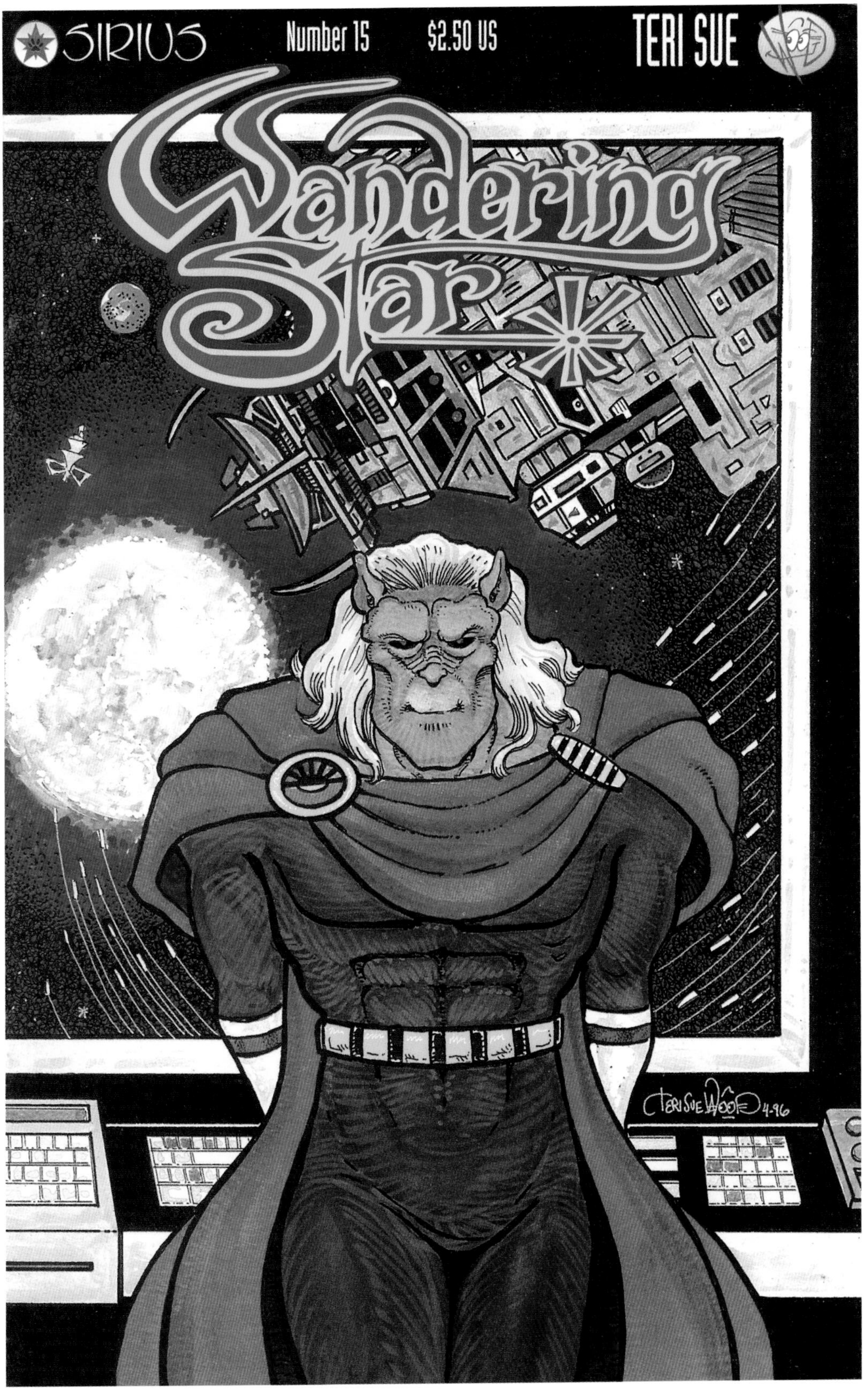
SIRIUS
Number 15
$2.50 US
TERI SUE
Wandering Star
TERI SUE WOOD 4-96

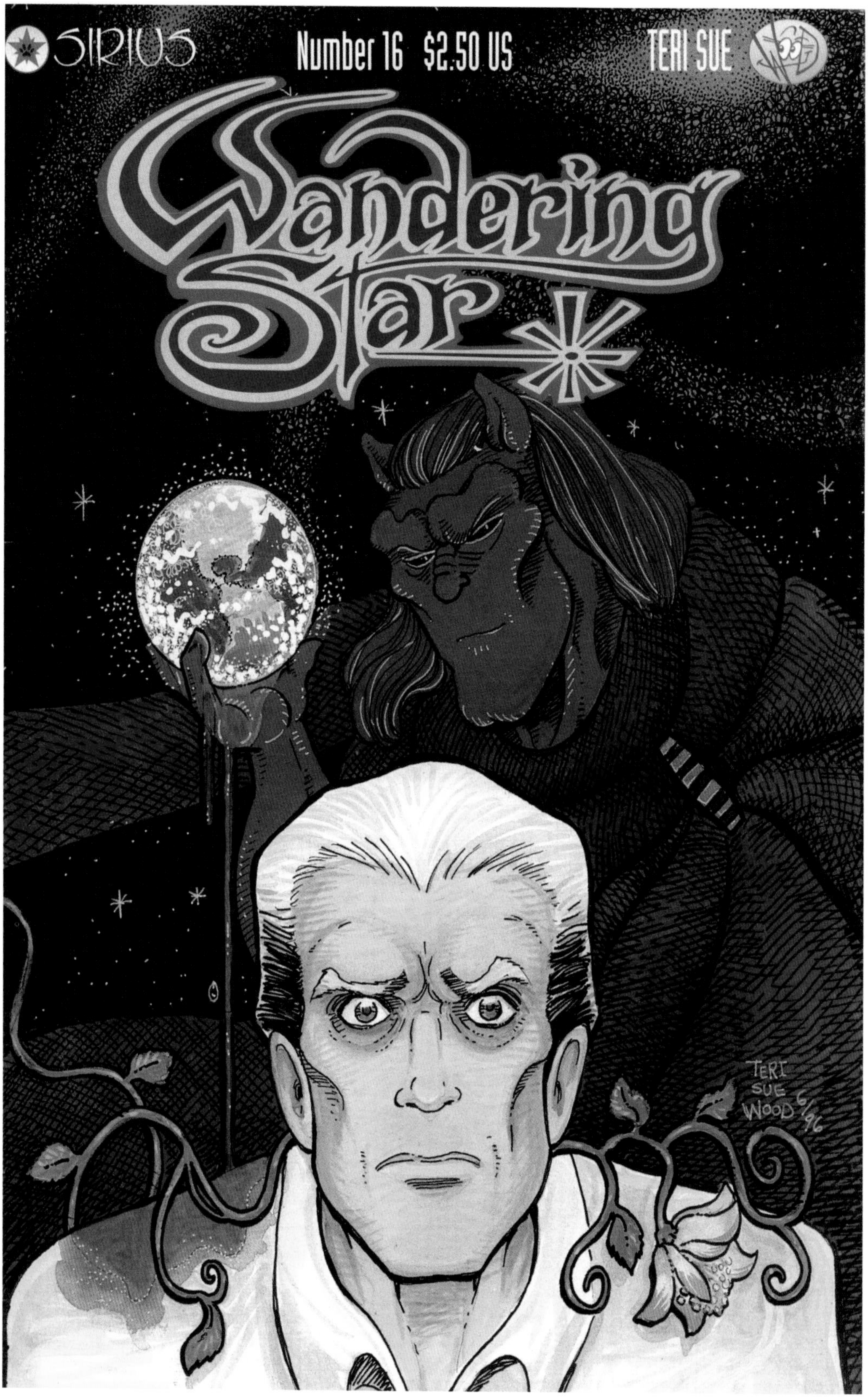
SIRIUS
Number 16 $2.50 US
TERI SUE
Wandering Star
TERI SUE WOOD 6/96

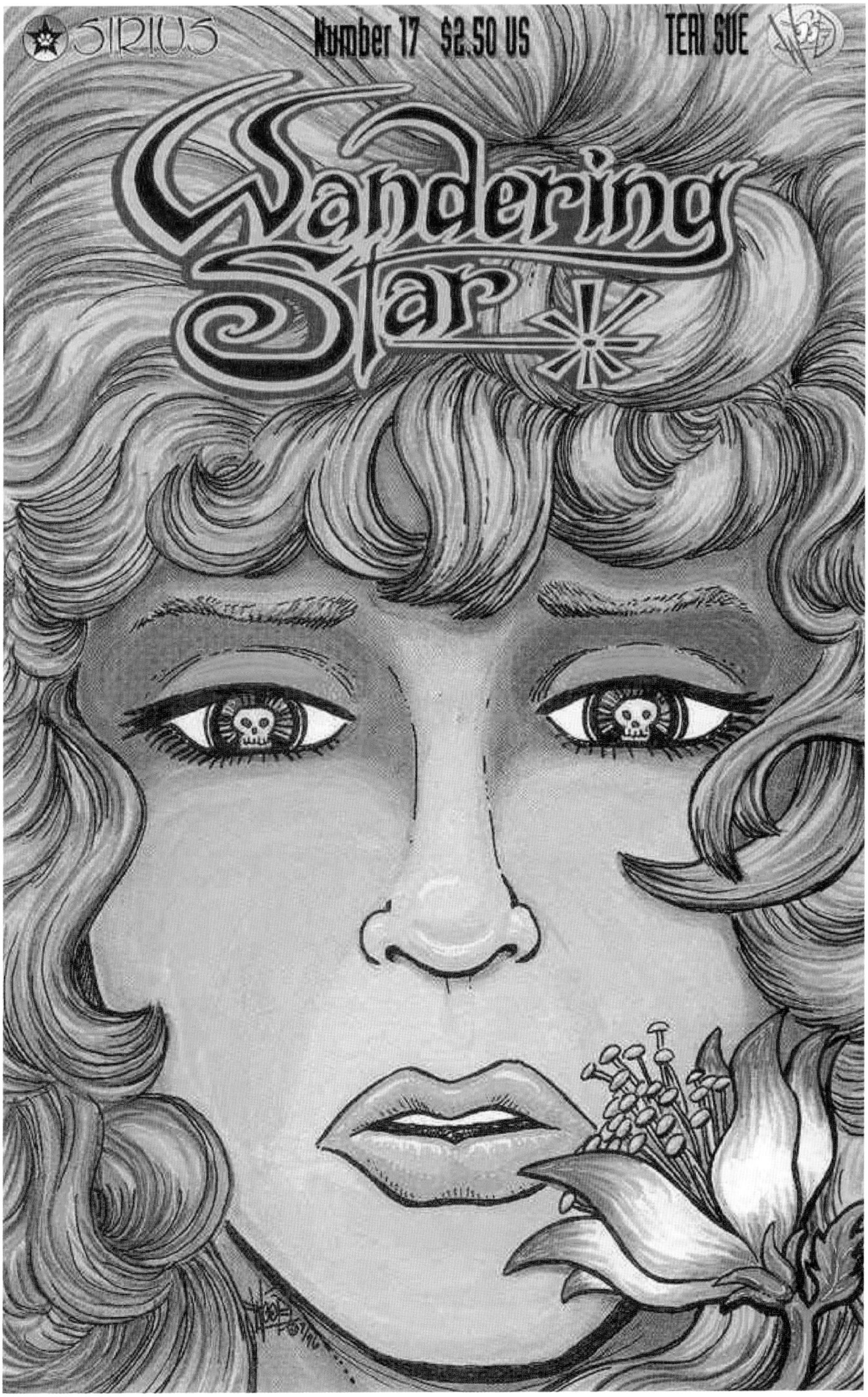
SIRIUS
Number 17 $2.50 US
TERI SUE
Wandering Star

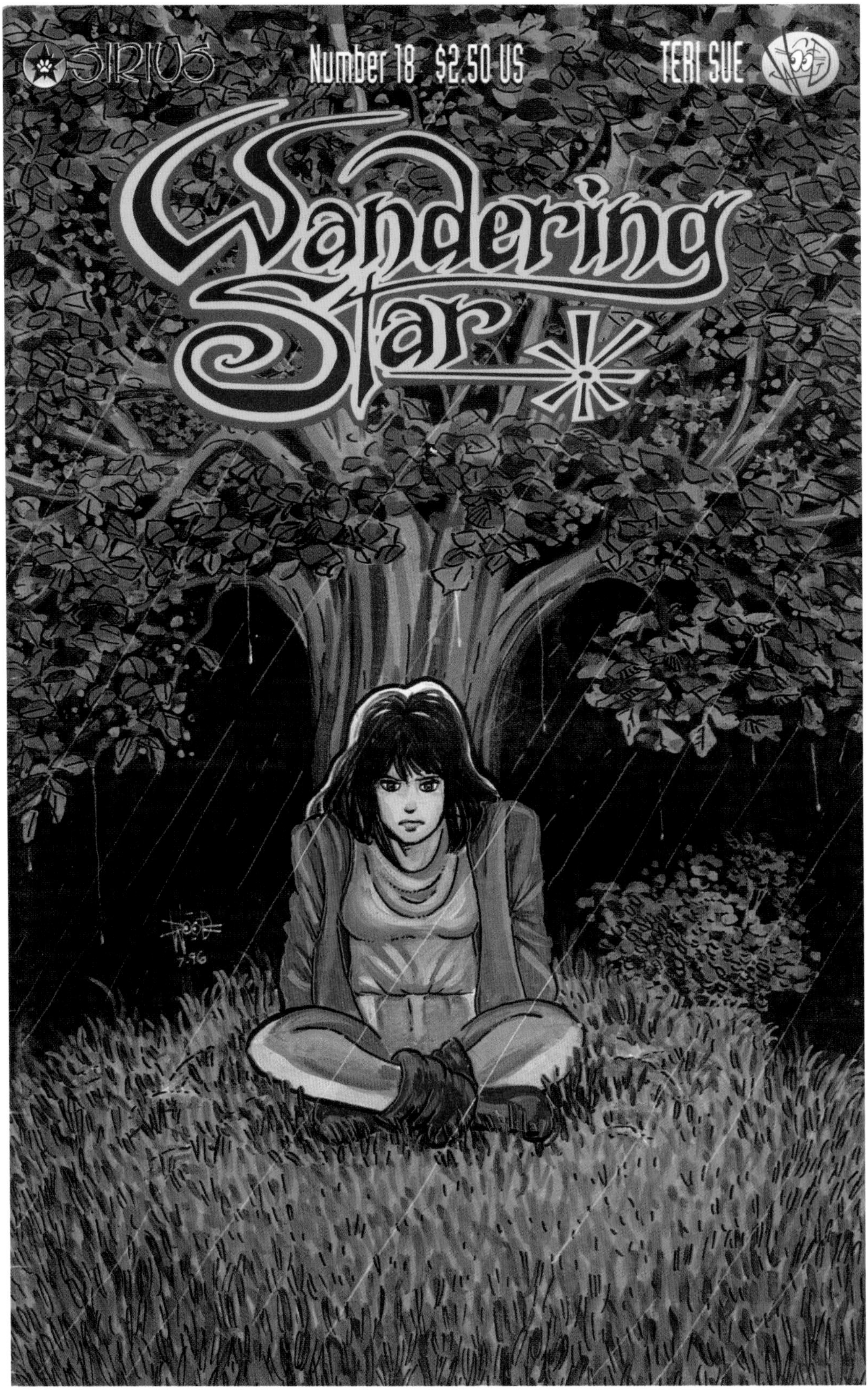
SIRIUS
Number 18 $2.50 US
TERI SUE
Wandering Star
7.96

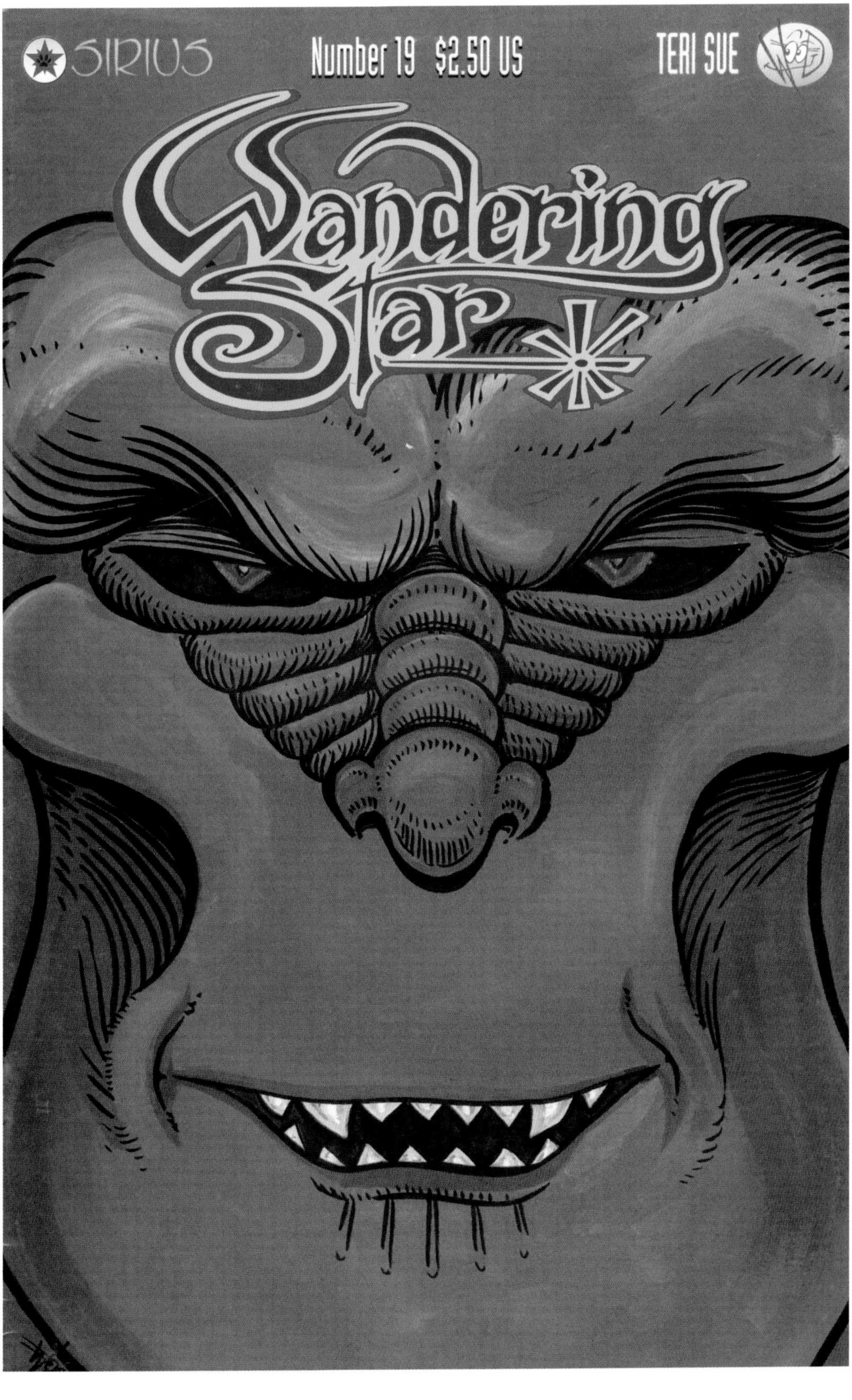
SIRIUS
Number 19 $2.50 US
TERI SUE
Wandering Star

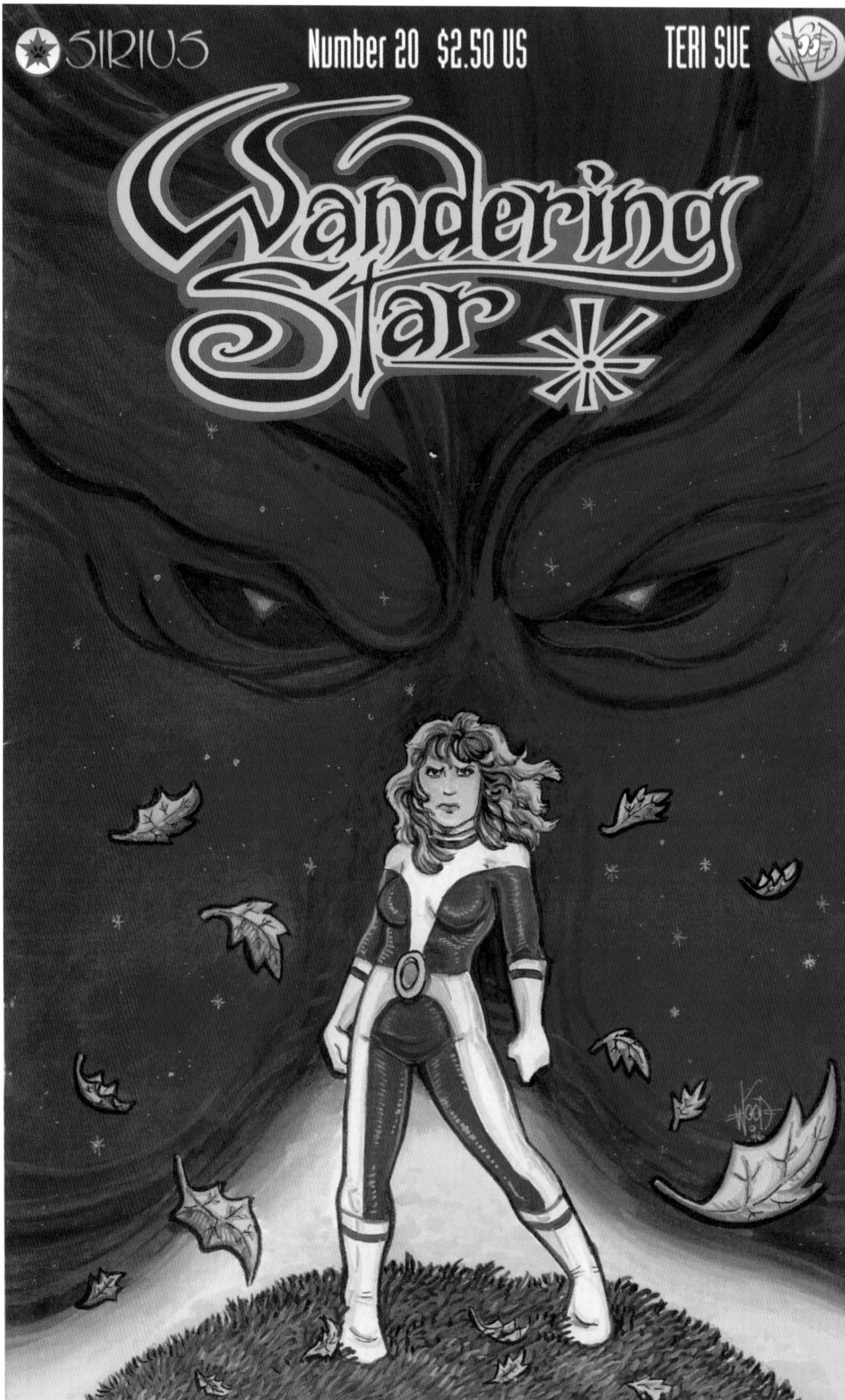

SIRIUS
Number 20 $2.50 US
TERI SUE
Wandering Star

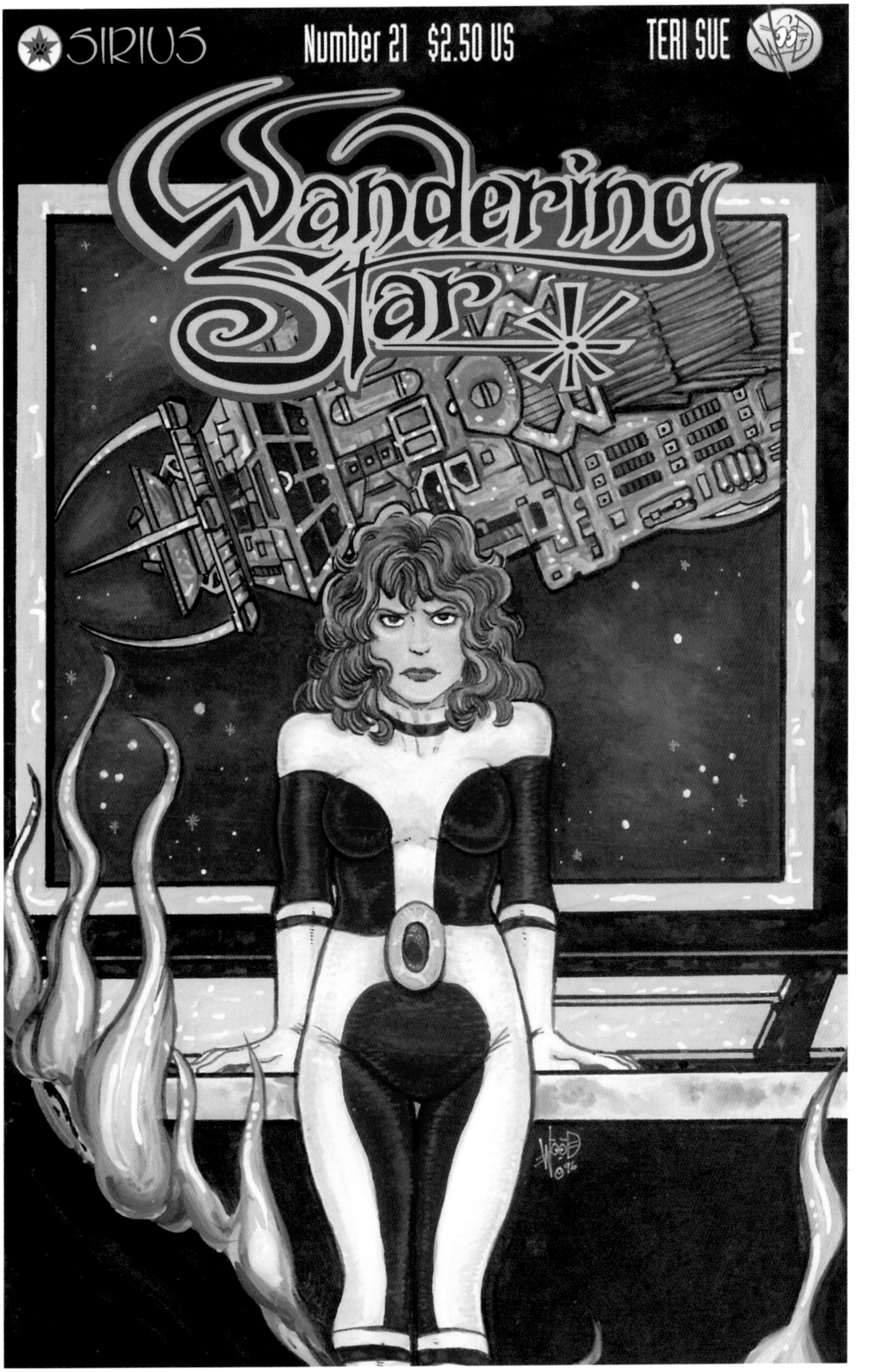
SIRIUS
Number 21 $2.50 US
TERI SUE
Wandering Star

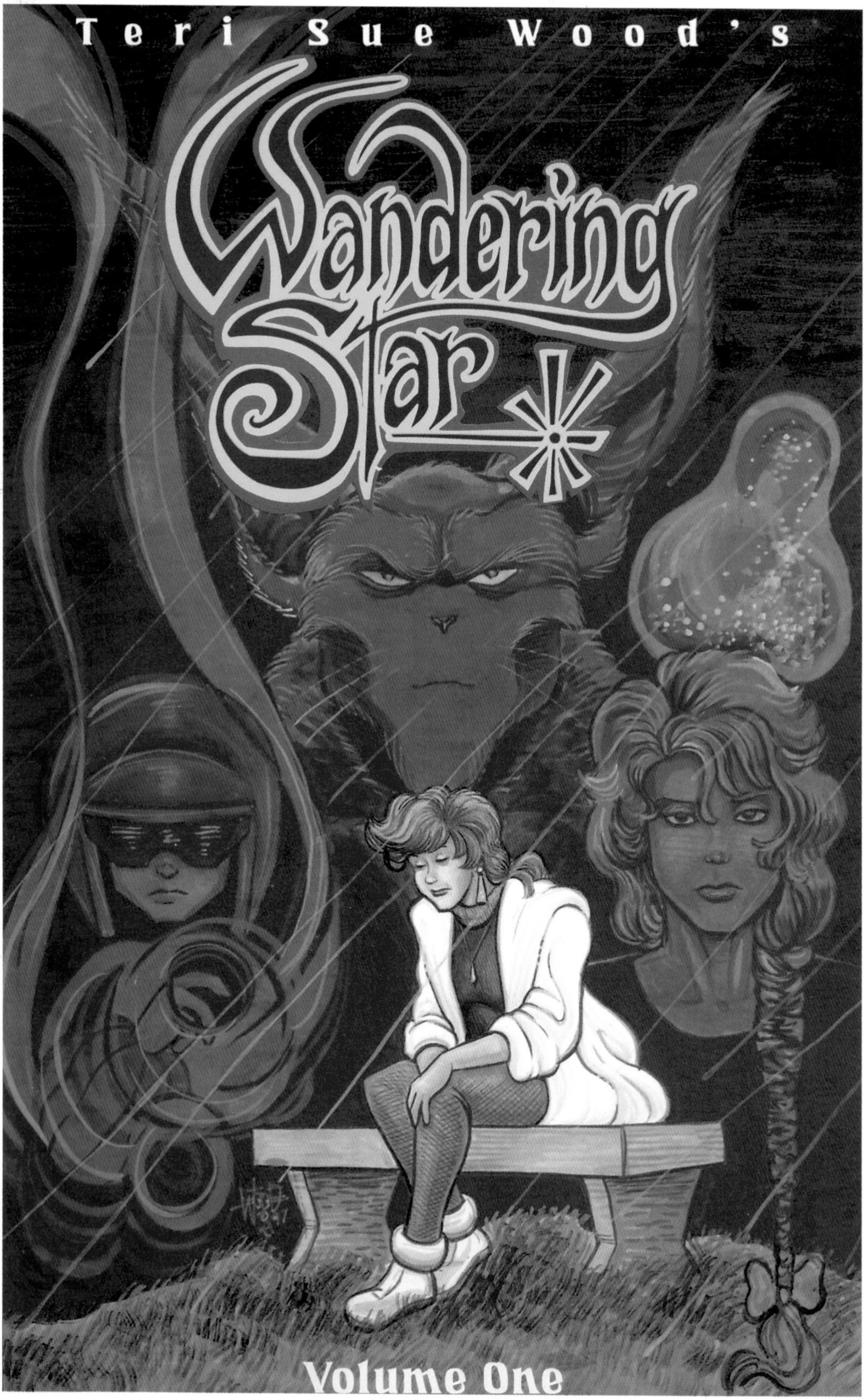
Teri Sue Wood's
Wandering Star
Volume One

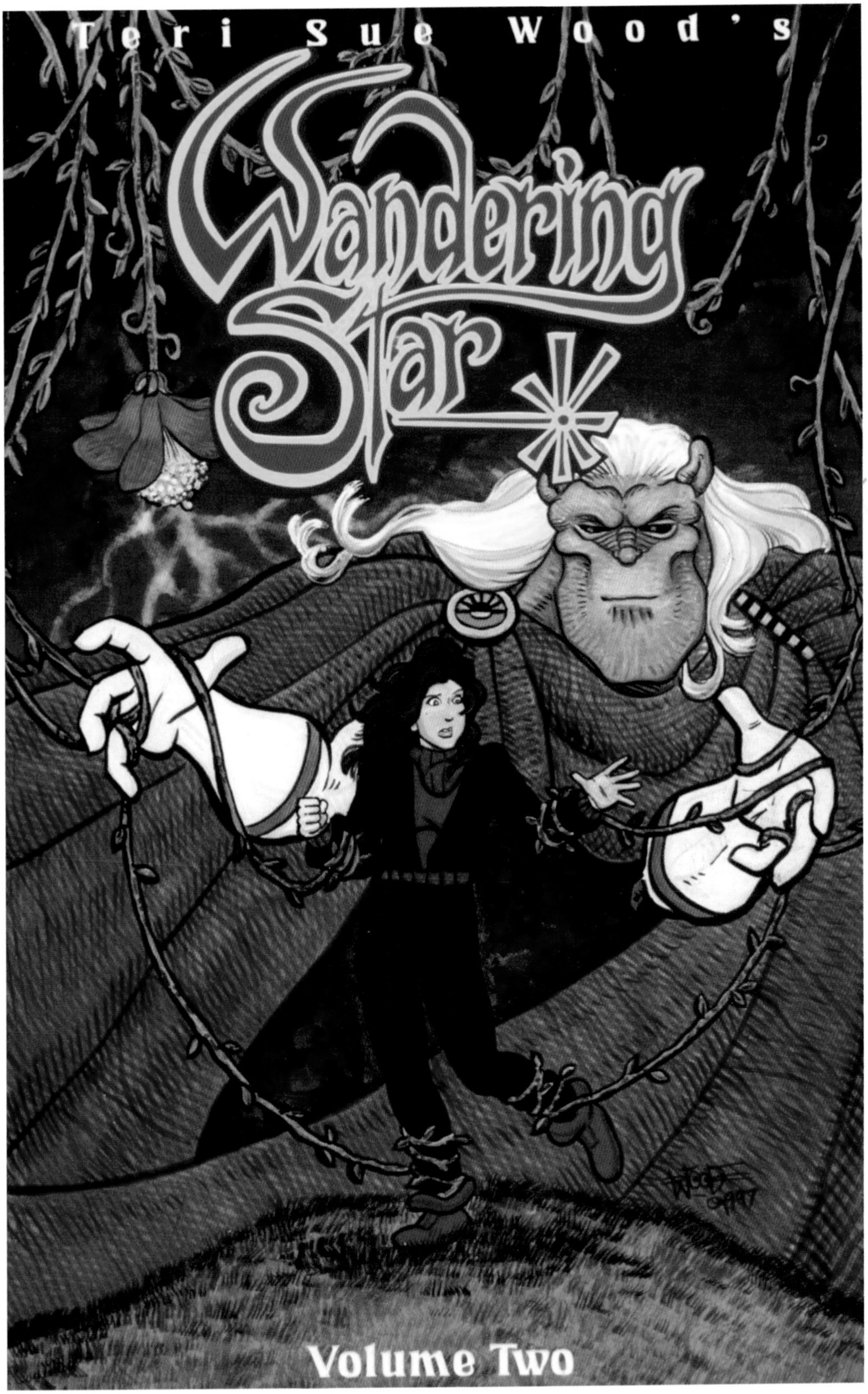
Teri Sue Wood's
Wandering Star
Volume Two

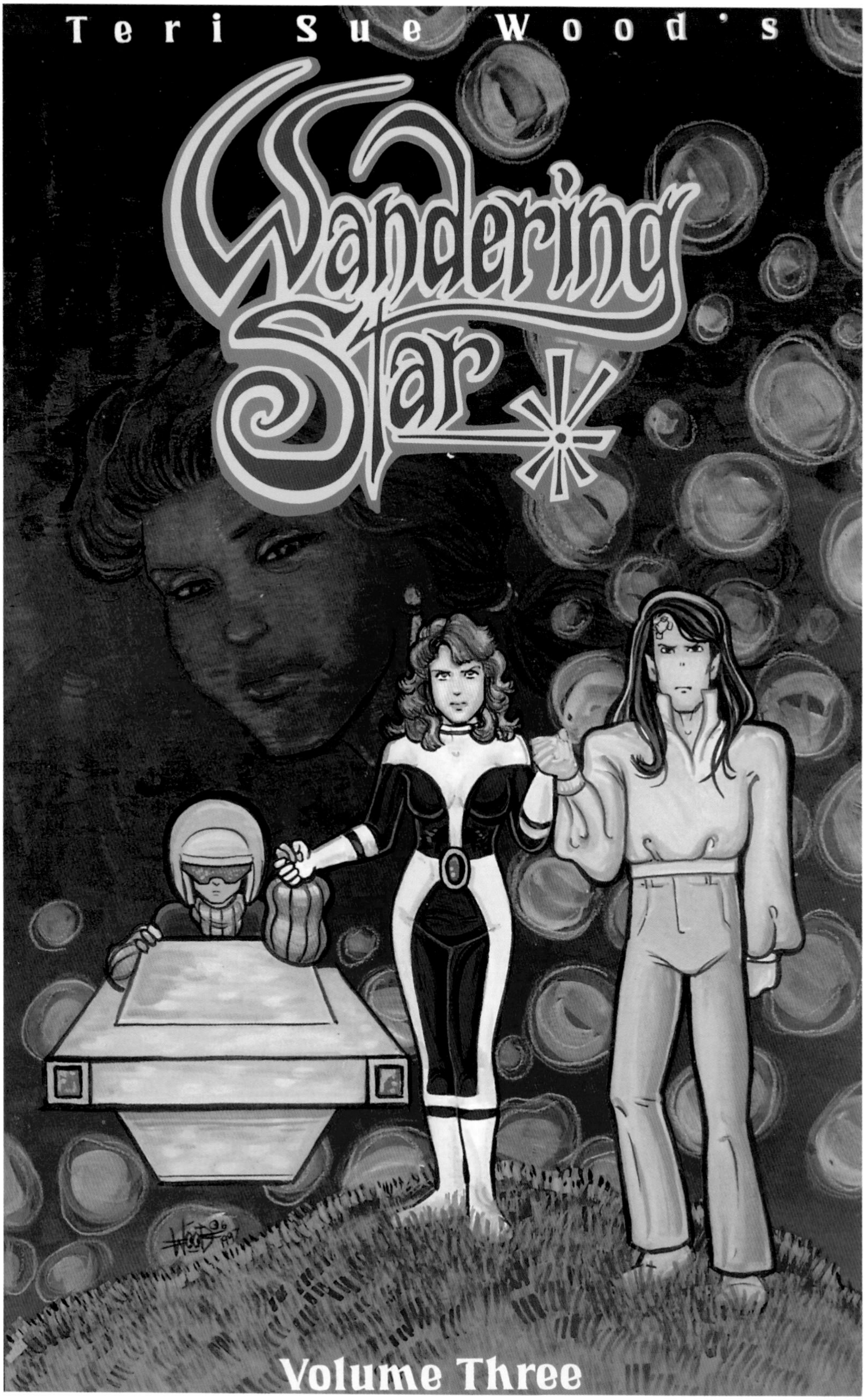
Teri Sue Wood's
Wandering Star
Volume Three

Wandering Star

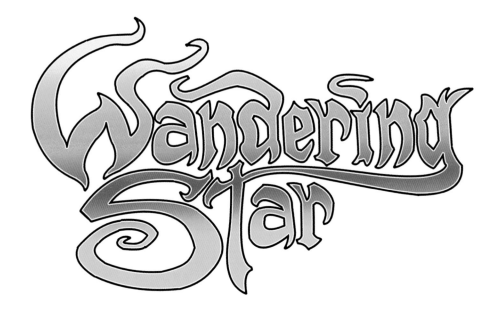

PRINT GALLERY

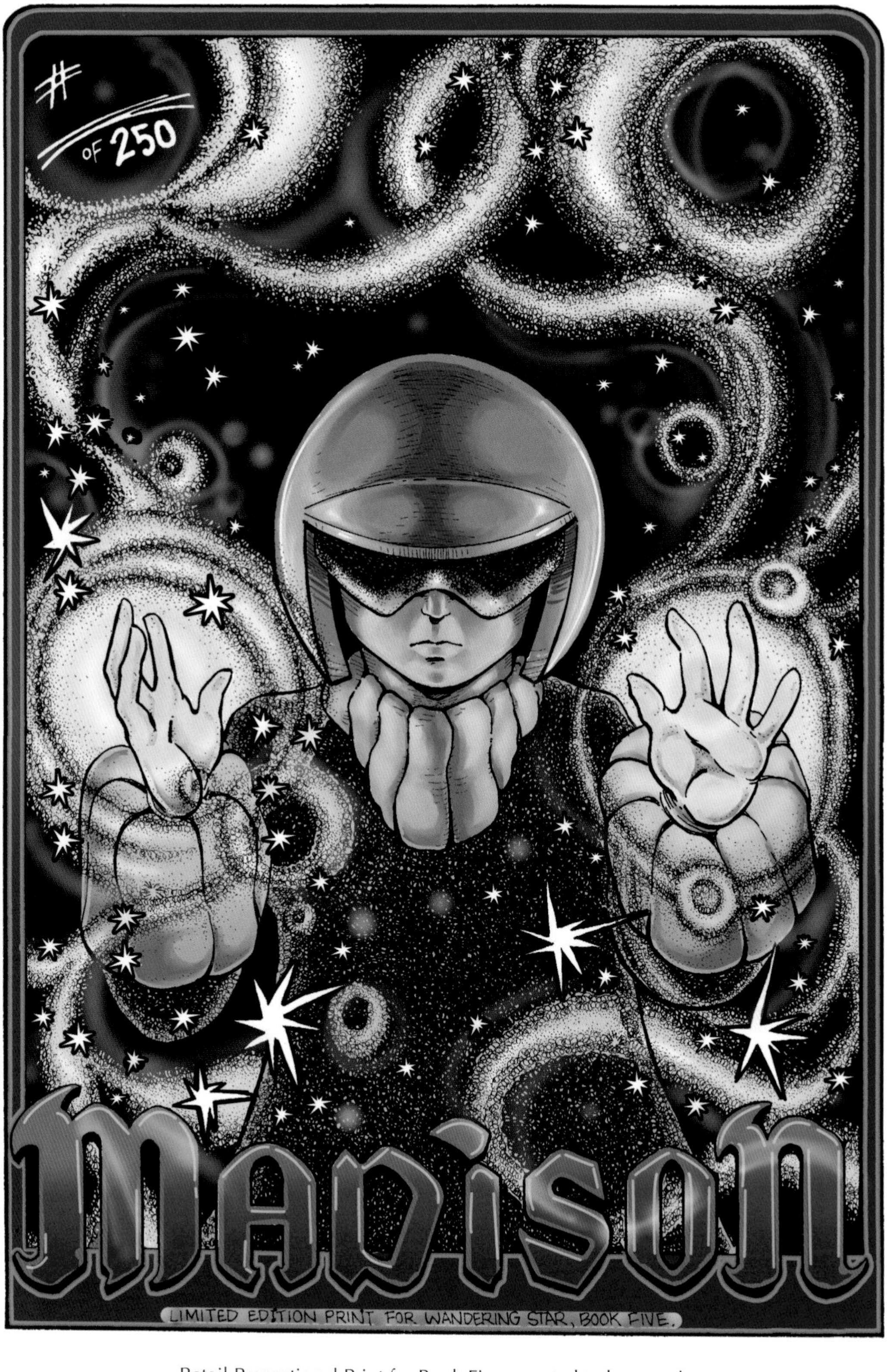
#
of 250
Madison
LIMITED EDITION PRINT FOR WANDERING STAR, BOOK FIVE.

Retail Promotional Print for Book Five, created to boost sales.
Basically I said, "buy a few extra copies of the book and get this nifty free 11 x 17 print."
Originally in black and white, but colored for the Dover Omnibus.

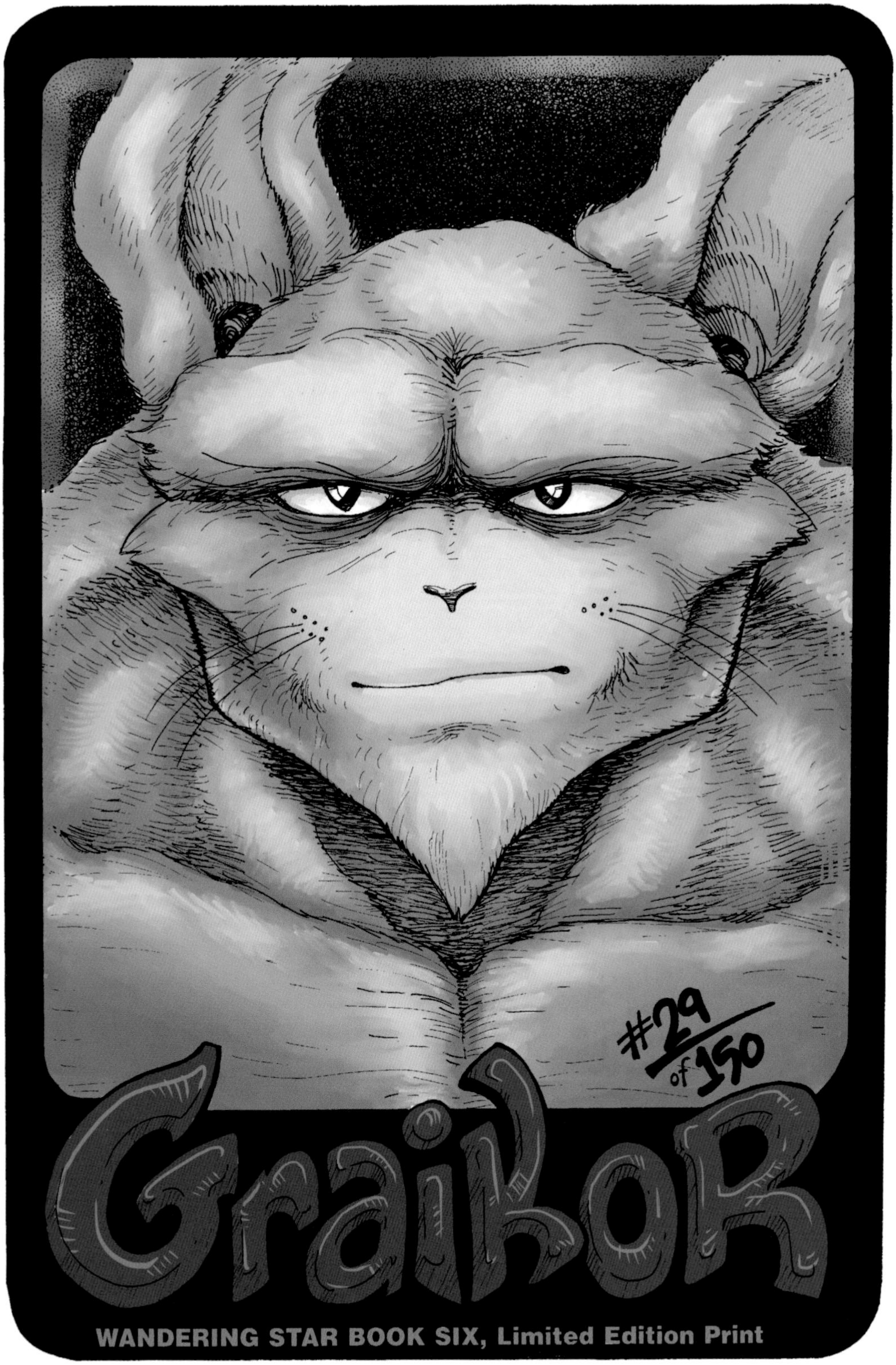
#29 of 150
Graikor
WANDERING STAR BOOK SIX, Limited Edition Print

Another Retail Print for Book Six. I really liked prints.
Originally 11 x 17 and in black and white, but colored for the Dover Omnibus.

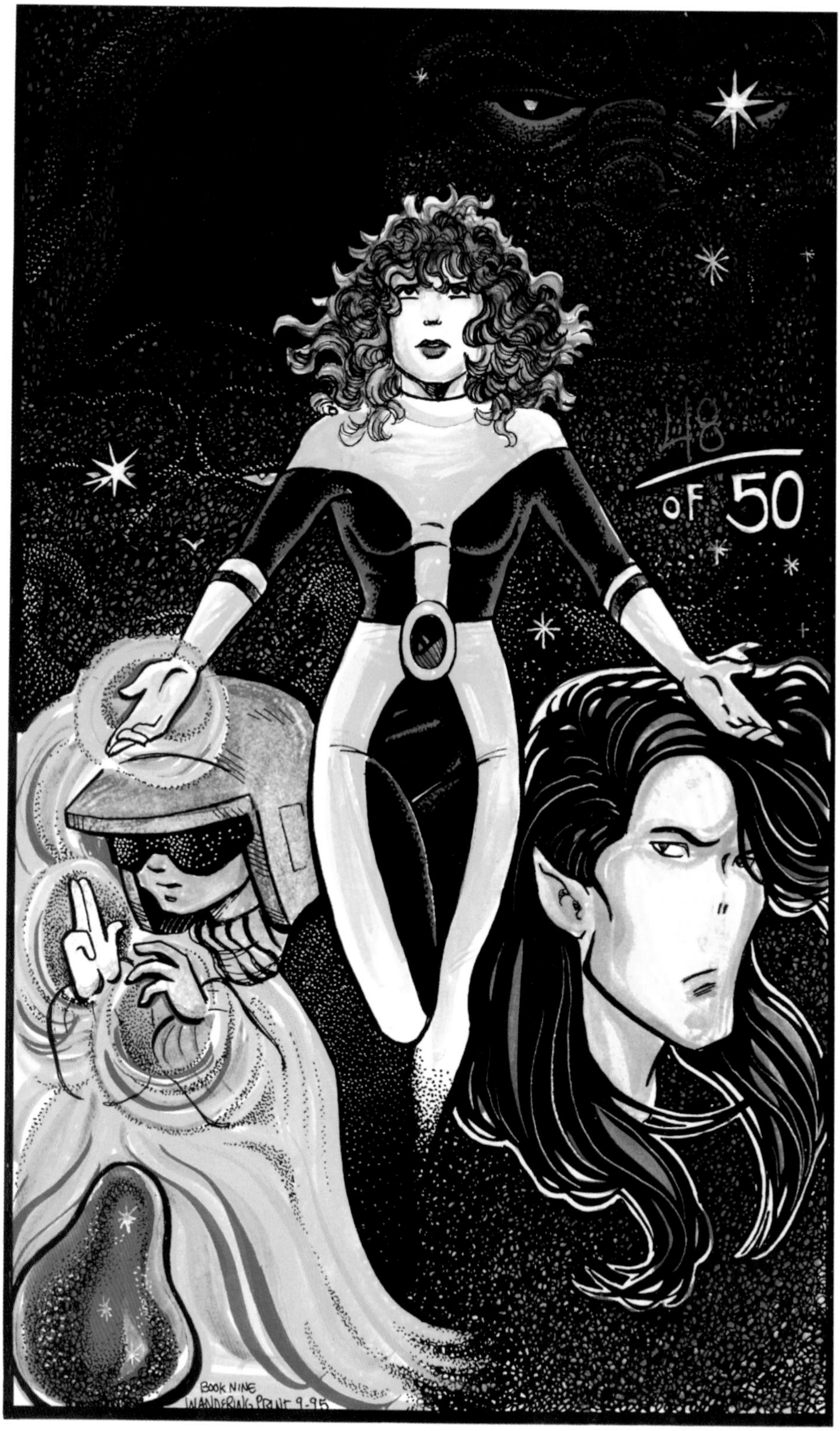
48
OF 50
BOOK NINE
WANDERING PRINT 9-95

In 1994, there was a crash in the industry that took down a great many comic shops, and all but a couple of distributors. This meant I did not get most of the money I was owed on Book Seven, or my first self-published trade paperback. Ouch! To raise money for Book Eight, I offered up a special retail package—with this print and an original art page. It saved the day!

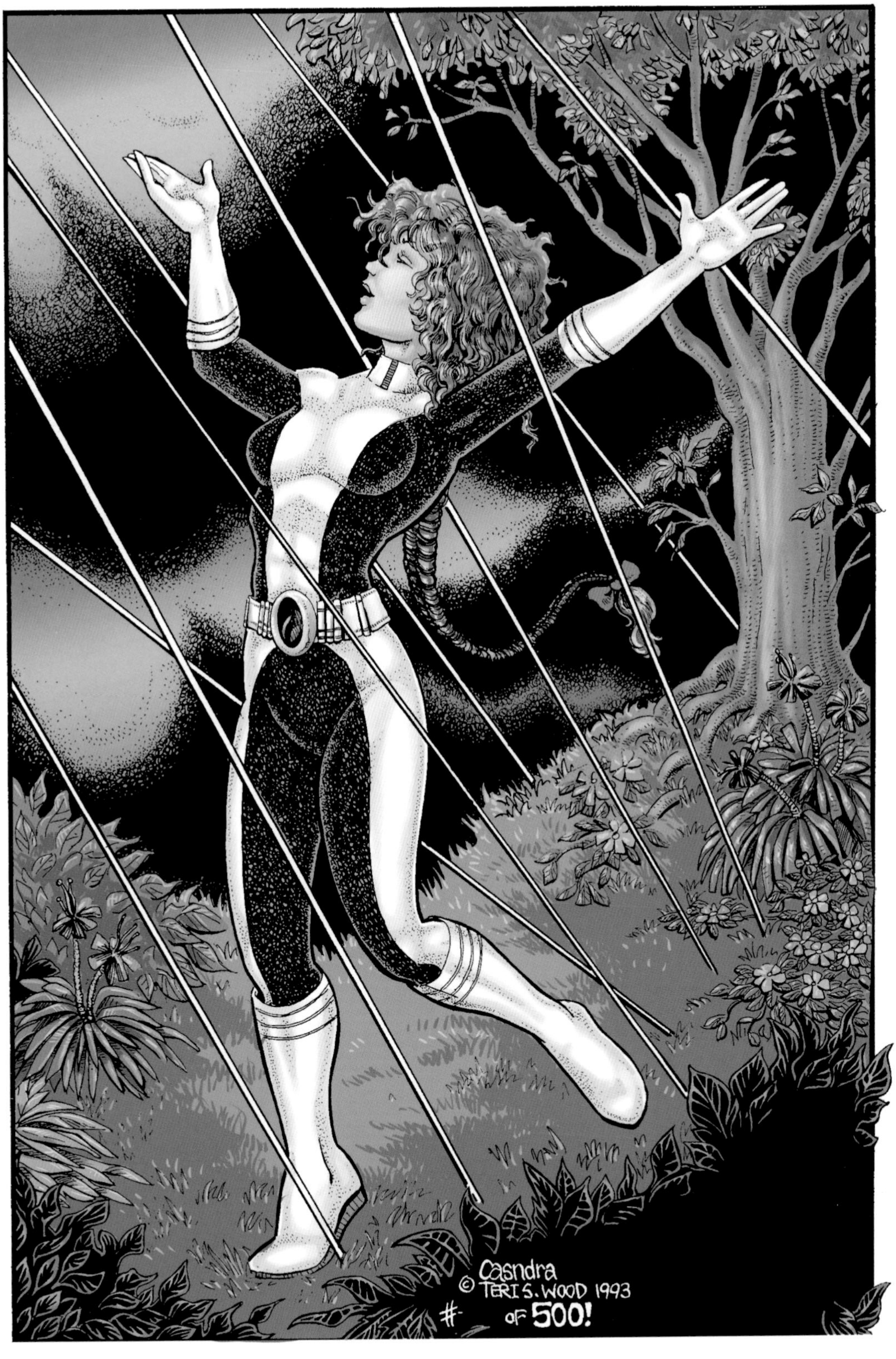
Casndra
© TERI S. WOOD 1993
#- of 500!

I created this print for the fans and also to raise publishing funds during the 1994 crash.
Here it is, now in color, for the Dover Omnibus.

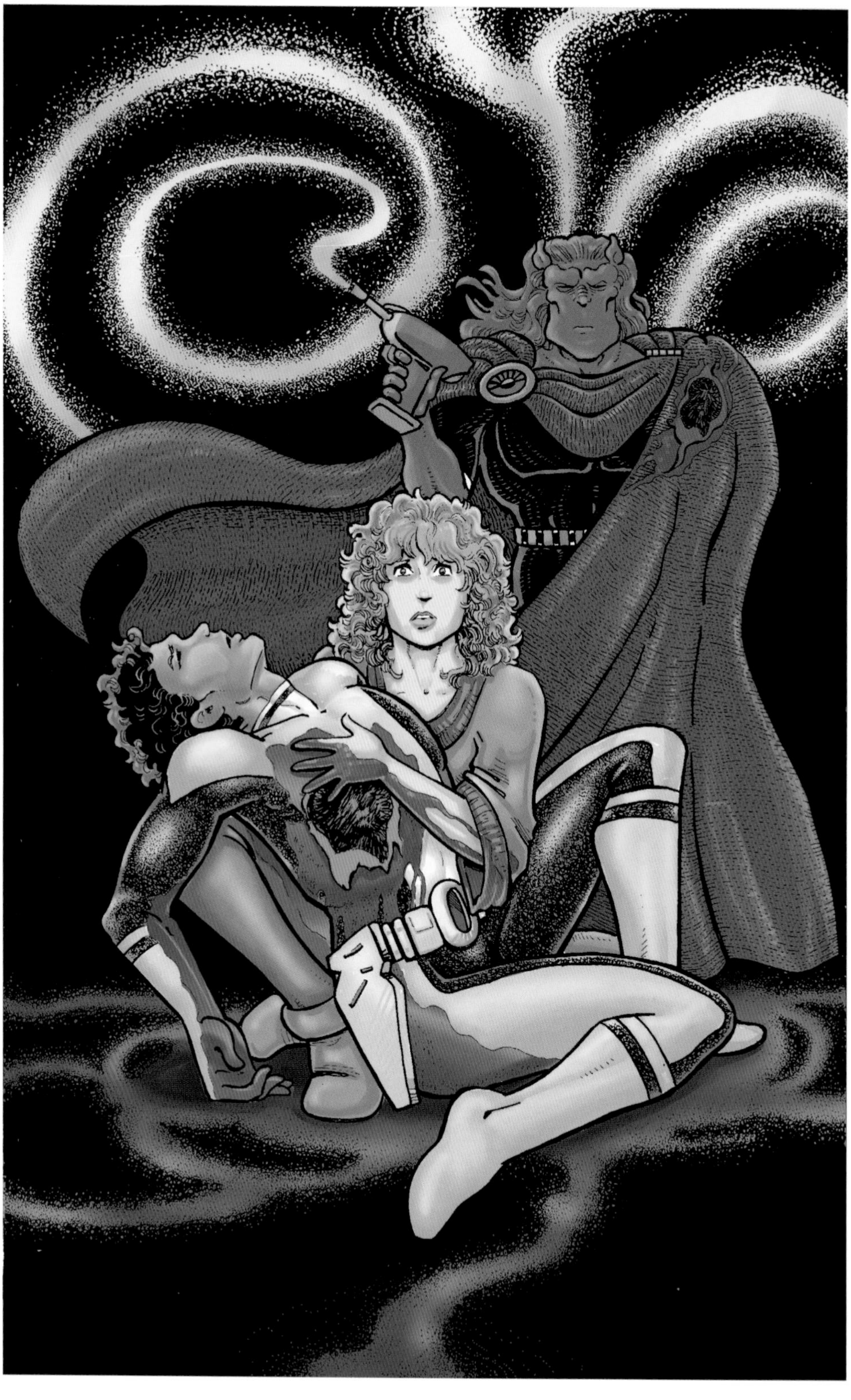

Sometimes around 1994-95, several independent comic creators, like myself, put out a trading card set through Topps. This was one of the designs that didn't make the cut. It was a shame, as it was my favorite. Here it is, in all its glory, colored and everything, for the Dover Omnibus.

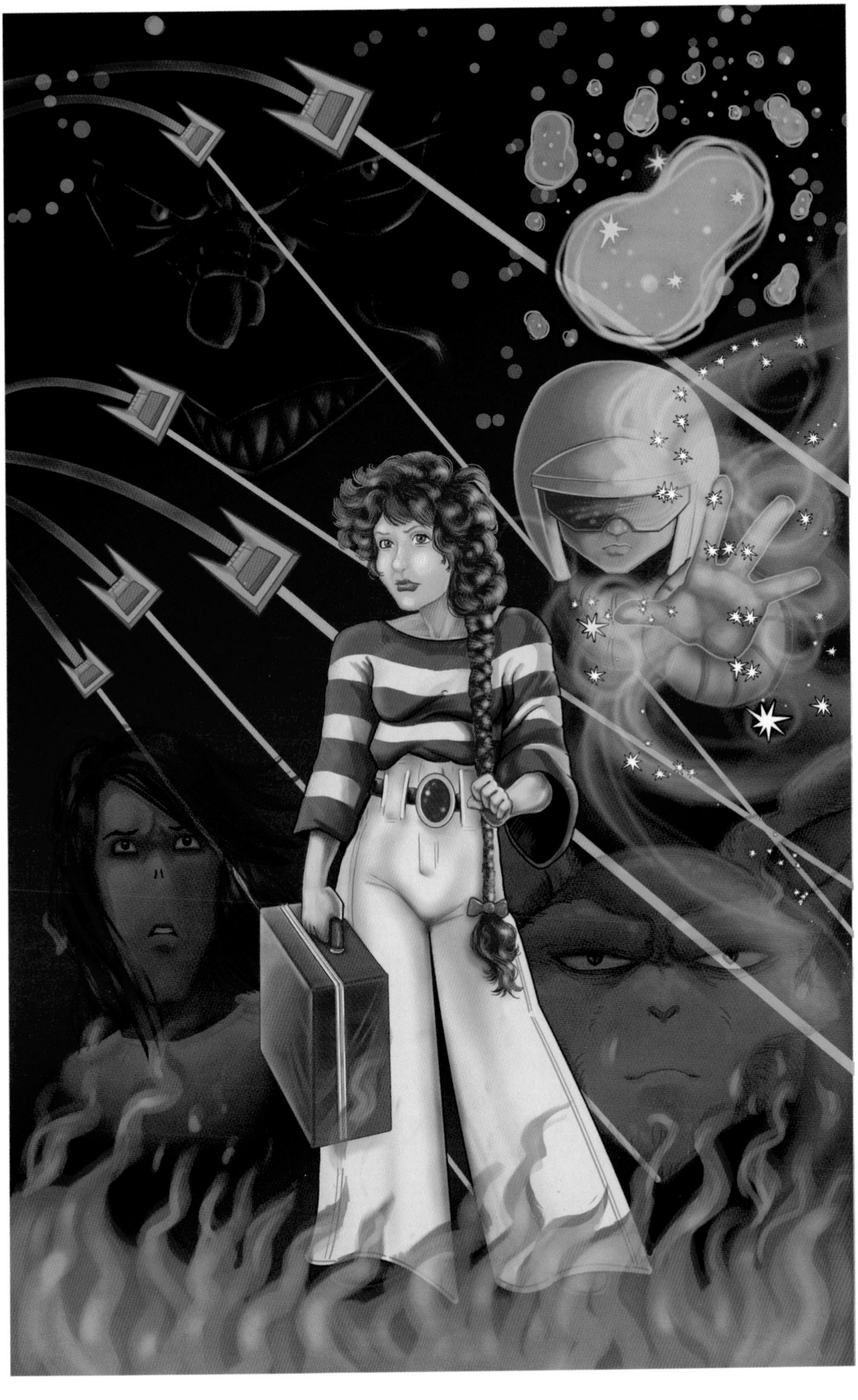

Sometimes around 1977, Sirius Entertainment, who had published the last ten issues of *Wandering Star*, put out a gallery book featuring art by many of its creators. This is my version of it today, repainted and redesigned.

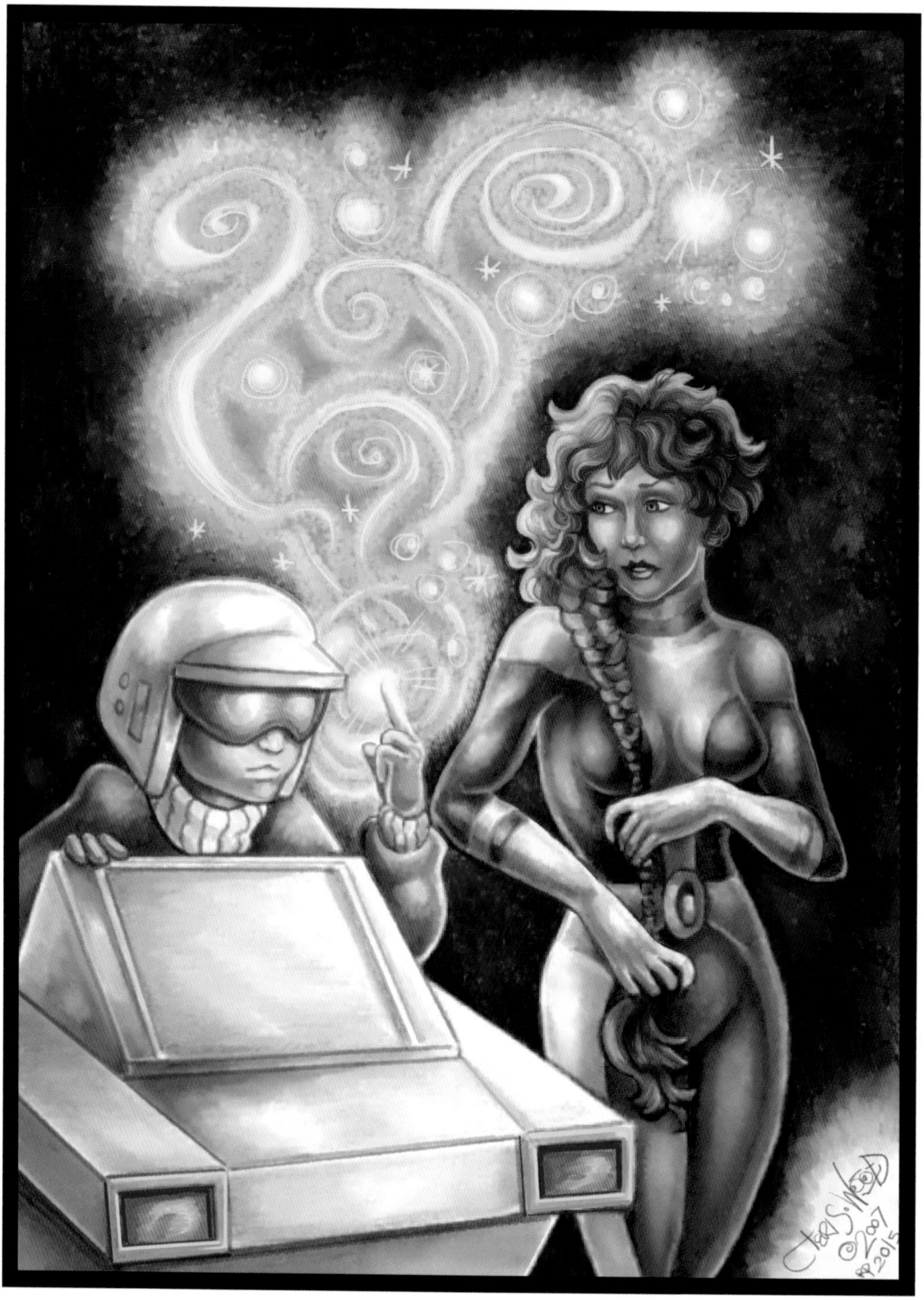

This … I did for a friend. I can't remember who, or why I did it.
But I loved it, so I spruced it up a bit for the Dover Omnibus. I hope you like it.

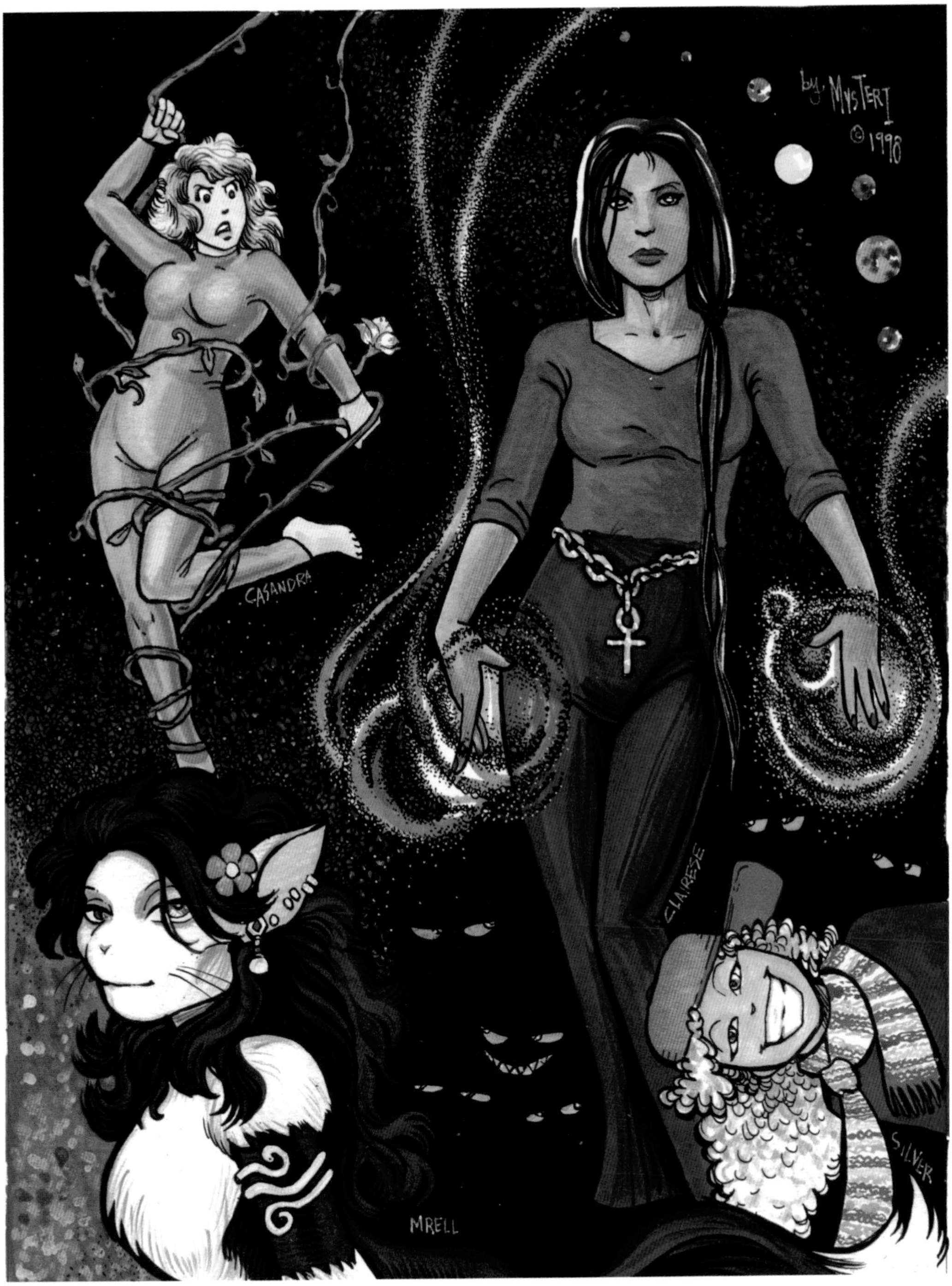
by, MysTERI
© 1998
CASANDRA
CLAIRESE
MRELL
SILVER

"Teri's Girls." This is a painting I did for David Morris in 1998. It features all "my girls"—Casandra (*Wandering Star*), Clairese (*Darklight*), Mrrell (*Rhudiprrt*) and Silver (*The Cartoonist*).

AFTERWORD

Back In the Old Neighborhood: *WANDERING STAR* did it before I did.

The early 90's in comics were a pretty different place. A lot of great makers were already on the scene: Alan Moore was doing *SWAMP THING*. Jaime and Gilbert Hernandez were doing *LOVE & ROCKETS*. Stan Sakai was doing *USAGI YOJIMBO*, Scott McCloud was doing *ZOT!* ... there were a lot of good comics. And an awful lot of horrible ones, and the horrible ones were all more or less alike, because they all existed for one reason: For a little while there, doing your own black-and-white book was like printing your own money.

The Internet didn't really exist back then, not like it does now. It's like looking back to a time before the flying saucers came. If you wanted to keep up with comics, you had to leg it around to whatever shops you could reach. The comparatively tiny trade shows helped, and creators who already had their own books often plugged or previewed books they liked. People doing their own books formed a neighborhood. Creators would draw pin-ups of each other's characters, and the back pages of Indy comics often served as a showcase and creative exchange.

The black-and-white boom had blown up and burst already, setting the scene for further collapse. Neighborhoods age and die and sometimes rebuild. The 90's had a lot of good neighbors, and one of these was *WANDERING STAR*.

WANDERING STAR wasn't a knockoff meant to capitalize on the trends of its times. It was a book meant to be a place for its creator to do her own thing. It was a webcomic before you could do webcomics. *WANDERING STAR* and its creator were part of what led to where we are now: a brilliant flourishing of the scene, comics galore, beautiful stuff everywhere, lots of new voices.

WANDERING STAR is a space opera. What's a space opera? *STAR WARS* is one, *STAR TREK* is another. *SPACE: 1999* is one also, and *BUCK ROGERS* and *FLASH GORDON*. They deal with war, and people out of place, and people who are alien. The stakes are usually high and the consequences dire. The person you get to know best in *WANDERING STAR* is the only human character in it. Casandra Andrews is the child of a prominent politician, and has grown up in wealth and privilege, and is going off to Starfleet Academy (I mean, the Galactic Academy. Space College.) She's the first human to be accepted into an educational conclave of the young people of the universe. Most college-bound young people are in for some shocks. Casi's are underlined a bit more deeply than others, because she is literally the only one of her kind. She can't insulate herself in the Human Sector, because she IS the Human Sector. She can't protect herself from the disregard and disapproval of her fellow students. She didn't know how generally despised humans are.

There's a lot she doesn't know. Space operas are about war. Even in telling her story later in life, Casandra Andrews is not living comfortably in the Human Sector. She can't even get the little things of her culture that would speak about home. She is displaced, a refugee. She's had to build her life from the unfamiliar materials available to her.

But nonetheless, she's done it. She's still around to tell her story to the next generation--of historians, at least. Her book has its place in the history of comics, in the neighborhood of storytelling, and on your shelf.

—Speed
www.lightspeedpress.com

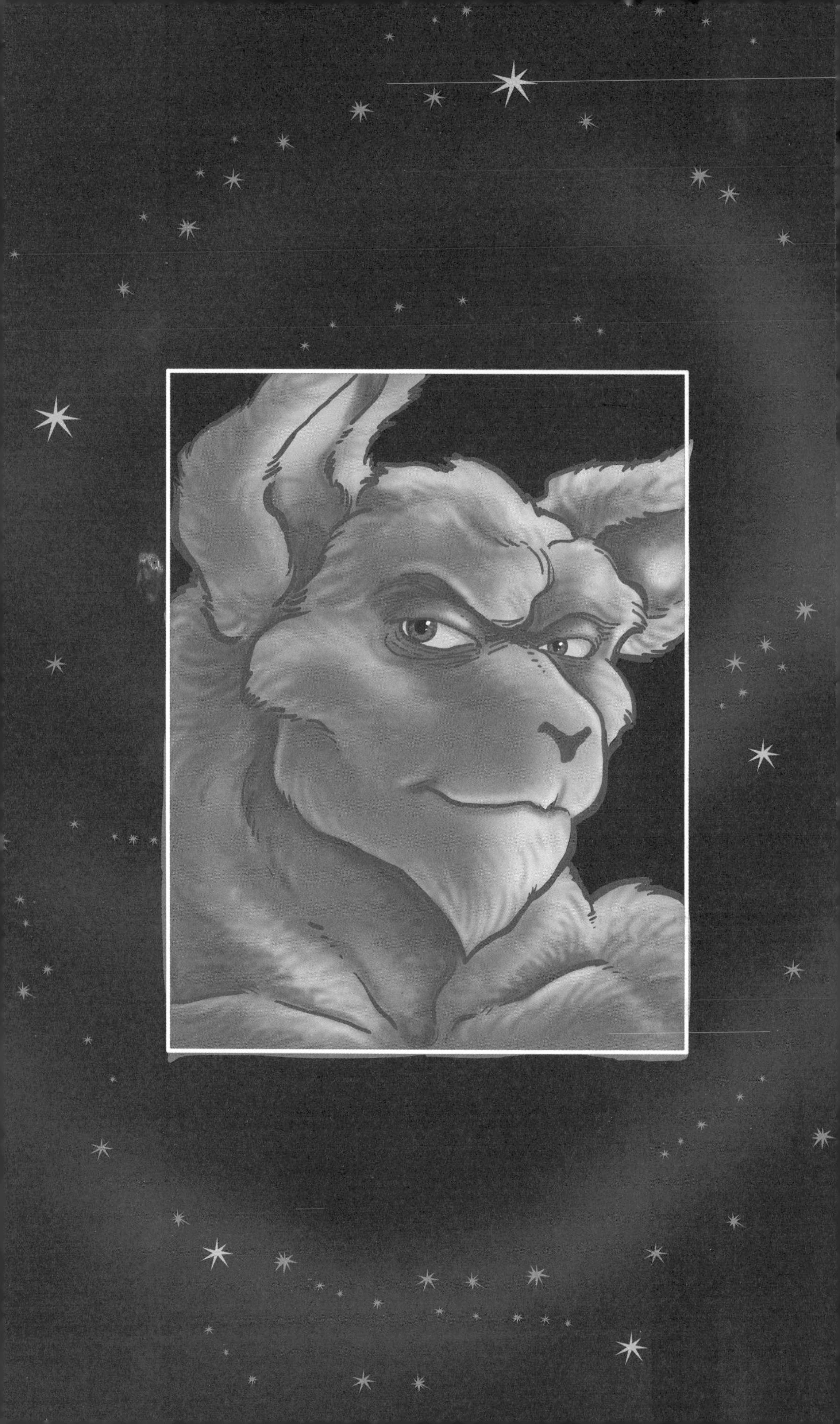